D0947072

WITHDRAWN
SAN ANTONIO PUBLIC LIBRARY

SAN ANTONIO PUBLIC LIBRARY

PEOPLE IN HISTORY

PEOPLE IN HISTORY

Volume 1: A-M

An Index to U.S. and Canadian Biographies in History Journals and Dissertations

Susan K. Kinnell
Editor

ABC-CLIO
Santa Barbara, California
Oxford, England

ISBN 0-87436-494-9 (v. 1)
ISBN 0-87436-493-0 (set)
ISSN 0894-0916

10 9 8 7 6 5 4 3 2 1

ABC-Clio, Inc.
2040 Alameda Padre Serra, Box 4397
Santa Barbara, California 93103

Clio Press Ltd.
55 St. Thomas' Street
Oxford, OX1 1JG, England

This book is printed on acid free paper ♾.
Manufactured in the United States of America.

TABLE OF CONTENTS

Volume I

Volume 2

INTRODUCTION

The rich store of biographical information in history journals and dissertations represents an important resource for the student, scholar, or compiler of family history. Here, for example, are in-depth analyses of the lives of famous people, extracts from letters or diaries of pioneer women, and facts from the daily lives of the relatively obscure men and women that give texture to the study of the history of a region or period.

Up to now access to much of this vast body of material has been scattered and difficult to identify by a subject name search. The purpose of this publication is to make this material readily available not only by name of the individual, but also by field of work, ethnic group, region, or contribution. In addition, the abstracts included for each article will give readers considerable biographical information without consulting the original articles.

Scope

For this index to biographical material the editors consulted ABC-CLIO's *America: History and Life* database, scanning entries from 1976 to the present to find dissertation citations and article abstracts in which the focus was primarily biographical. Of these, they chose only those articles that covered a significant portion of a person's life—usually at least four years unless a shorter time represented a period of great interest or importance, e.g., time in high public office. In the end, material was selected from 737 journals, resulting in more than 7600 citations to biographical articles and dissertations on over 6000 men and women in U.S. and Canadian history from colonial times to the present.

The subjects of these articles range from the prominent to the obscure—folk singers, football coaches, and fur traders; slaves, labor organizers, lawyers, and rabbis; theologians, traitors, and lumberjacks—men and women in all walks of life, from varying backgrounds, who are a part of the diversity of American history and culture. Kit Carson, Raymond Chandler, Cesar Chavez, Dianne Feinstein, Chief Joseph, Dred Scott, Mary Chesnut, Duncan Hines, Ida Tarbell, Sojourner Truth, and Charles Yeager are but a few of the people represented in this two-volume set. They range from Attakullakulla, an influential Cherokee diplomat in the 1700's; Oscar Edmund Berninghaus, a painter who recorded the West's history and contemporary life; and John C. Davis who joined the mercantile firm of J. W. Hugus in 1879 and helped make it the largest chain store and distributor of general merchandise in the Rocky Mountain area to the more familiar names of Dwight Eisenhower, J. Edgar Hoover, Jerome Kern, Alfred Steiglitz, and many more.

People born outside the U.S. or Canada are included if they immigrated or if they contributed significantly to American history or culture, e.g., Lafayette and Alexis de Tocqueville.

The dissertation citations are among those previously selected from *Dissertation Abstracts International* for inclusion in *America: History and Life* and indexed by the editors.

Arrangement

The names of the biographical subjects are listed alphabetically throughout the two volumes; multiple citations for each name are arranged alphabetically by author following the name. Cross references within the text lead the searcher from pseudonyms, nicknames, or other alternate names to the name used.

For works that treat the lives of two or more persons, a complete citation occurs under each name; however, the abstract of the article is given only under the name of the main subject with a "see" reference from all other citations. If all persons receive equal treatment in the article, the abstract is found with the citation under the person whose name is first alphabetically.

Dates following the abstract identify the time period covered in the article.

Indexes

The rotated subject index at the end of Volume 2 provides access by occupation, ethnic group, religion, interests, national origin, etc. "See" and "see also" references within the index aid in locating all relevant material. For more information on the subject profile index, see the note at the head of the index.

An index to authors of all articles and dissertations follows the subject index.

Future Plans

A companion publication indexing biographical material on people in other parts of the world is in progress. Future plans include regular supplements to both titles to maintain currency.

Biography as a Field of Study

Because the study of writing of life histories is receiving increasing attention, the editors compiled a selective bibliography of articles on the topic from the history journals of the last ten years. The resulting citations, given with abstracts, discuss the diversity of approaches to the study of people in U.S. and Canadian history as recorded in books, articles, and film. That bibliography, which follows, offers a beginning to research in this area.

LIFE WRITING: SELECTED REFERENCES

Anderson, David D. ANOTHER BIOGRAPHY? FOR GOD'S SAKE, WHY? *Georgia Rev. 1981 35(2): 401-406.* Discusses reasons for writing biographies, the demands and dangers of the art, and its contribution to knowledge. The biographer touches and reveals another life in a unique way. Biography demands respect for the subject, integrity to the times, the facts, and the person, accuracy in interpreting the significance of the facts, and selectivity in presenting the facts. Although prisoner of his own personality and reputation, the biographer must avoid recreating the subject in his own image. Critical biography defines and clarifies the subject's work, providing a depth and breadth of knowledge not exhibited through merely factual account of his life and work.

Barker, Steven Philip. "Fame: A Content Analysis Study of the American Film Biography." Ohio State U. 1983. 252 pp. *DAI 1984 44(9): 2609-A.* DA8400163

Barnard, Harry. BIOGRAPHY IN ERUPTION. *Hayes Hist. J. 1982 3(6): 6-8.* Discusses stylistic changes in biographical writing. While Lytton Strachey's work provides a model, the best modern biographies surpass Strachey in their dependence on psychological insights. Sexual matters thus receive greater emphasis currently than in older biographies, and must be handled with decency and balance.

Brackman, Harold. "BIOGRAPHY YANKED DOWN OUT OF OLYMPUS": BEARD, WOODWARD, AND DEBUNKING BIOGRAPHY. *Pacific Hist. Rev. 1983 52(4): 403-427.* William E. Woodward attempted to create biography that would fulfill the premises of the progressive New History. He maintained the connection between the subject's life and times, but he was influenced by Charles A. Beard's economic determinism. His debunking biographies published in the 1920's were favorably received because most historians were progressive, but some professional historians attacked them as amateurish and Beardianist. After 1930, Woodward sought to live down his debunking reputation, but his later biographies and his *A New American History* (1936) were unfavorably reviewed by professional historians, who now considered Woodward an amateur historian and biographer. Based on Woodward's works and critical reviews in contemporary periodicals; 91 notes.

Brown, Robert Craig. BIOGRAPHY IN CANADIAN HISTORY. *Hist. Papers [Canada] 1980: 1-8.* Since World War II, the search for a redefinition of the role of the individual in history, and the changing relationship between biography and history, has been very clear in French-Canadian writing. The change from a decidedly hagiographic tone has been more gradual in English-Canadian works. Biography, by definition, in recent years, should inform and enrich the study of social history. This aspect must balance with a sophisticated portraiture of character. Presented at the Annual Meeting of the Canadian Historical Association, 1980; 25 notes.

Conger, Lucinda D. BIOGRAPHICAL INFORMATION AND OTHER GOVERNMENT SECRETS. *RQ 1981 20(3): 282-290.* Government librarians use a variety of sources to locate biographical information on US and foreign diplomats, international figures, and American government officials. These sources include on-line services, monographs and back files, the card catalog, State Department and CIA publications, other government documents, and trade publications.

Culbert, David H. THE INFINITE VARIETY OF MASS EXPERIENCE: THE GREAT DEPRESSION, W.P.A. INTERVIEWS, AND STUDENT FAMILY HISTORY PROJECTS. *Louisiana Hist. 1978 19(1): 43-63.* Both the Works Progress Administration life histories and the 240 family histories written by the author's Louisiana State University students are excellent sources for the history of the common people during the Depression. Analyzes these sources, comparing them on the basis of area of coverage, persons interviewed, interviewers, documentation, attitudes of interviewers, focus, language, and historical value. Concludes that the "life histories offer an extraordinary record of those who survived the 1930s outside, for the most part, conventional society," while "the family histories provide a rich account of entire families during the 1930s." 10 photos, 48 notes.

Epstein, William H. MILFORD'S ZELDA AND THE POETICS OF THE NEW FEMINIST BIOGRAPHY. *Georgia Rev. 1982 36(2): 335-350.* Developing along with the most recent feminist movement is a new form of historical writing: the feminist biography. Using Nancy Milford's life of Zelda Fitzgerald as an example, the author shows that the feminist biography of the past 10 to 12 years has a unique grammar and structure that has grown to affect readers' and critics' expectations and responses to nonfiction works about women. 19 notes.

Farrell, Charlotte Ann Underwood. "Ethnobiography: Culture, Myth, and Personal History." U. of Texas, Dallas 1980. 371 pp. *DAI 1980 41(3): 1050-1051-A.* 8018862

Folsom, Burton W., II. THE COLLECTIVE BIOGRAPHY AS A RESEARCH TOOL. *Mid-Am. 1972 54(2): 108-122.* A bibliographical essay that analyzes the application of collective-biography techniques to the Jacksonian era, the Populist movement, and in status revolution theory. Democratic and Whig leadership stemmed from similar socioeconomic backgrounds; a high correlation exists between Whiggery and Unionism. Ethnicity, occupation, and age are among significant variables recently applied to Populist characteristics. Status revolution theory has been utilized to explain Progressivism, abolitionism, and the Mugwump persuasion during the Gilded Age. Collective biography has been most successful with Jacksonianism, least so in support of status revolution theory which so far lacks an essential psychological dimension. Based on recent studies utilizing collective biography. 52 notes.

Freeman, James M. and Krantz, David L. THE UNFULFILLED PROMISE OF LIFE HISTORIES. *Biography 1980 3(1): 1-13.* Most investigators of life histories have omitted detailed descriptions of their relationships with the narrators. Such data are indispensable for complete life histories, and they are not amenable to traditional social science analyses. The analysis of life histories requires reversal of the law of parsimony, an expansion rather than a contraction of complexity to explain the phenomena adequately, since the investigator's role in the creation of a life history is not an interference with but rather an integral part of the data.

Gustafson, Richard. THE VOGUE OF THE SCREEN BIOGRAPHY. *Film and Hist. 1977 7(3): 49-58.* Discusses films, 1929-49, which concentrated on serious biographies of famous and historical figures.

Haerle, Rudolf K., Jr. THE ATHLETE AS "MORAL" LEADER: HEROES, SUCCESS THEMES AND BASIC CULTURAL VALUES IN SELECTED BASEBALL AUTOBIOGRAPHIES, 1900-1970. *J. of Popular Culture 1974 8(2): 392-401.* Focuses attention on professional baseball during 1900-70 through the medium of biographies and autobiographies of baseball players to reveal basic cultural themes which pervade the world of professional sports.

Halpern, Jeanne W. BIOGRAPHICAL IMAGES: EFFECTS OF FORMAL FEATURES ON THE WAY WE SEE A LIFE. *Biography 1978 1(4): 1-15.* When biography is examined as a literary genre, then the selection of materials, the structure of the text, and the style of the prose are singularly important components of the image-making process. Such formal features not only reflect the biographer's vision of a life but also influence the impression the reader receives. [Based on contemporary texts from the documentary to the fictionalized].

Heilman, Robert B. TY COBB: THE HERO AND HIS WARTS. *Am. Scholar 1984 53(4): 541-546.* Reviews Charles C. Alexander's *Ty Cobb* (1984). Compares the printed biography with personal narratives about the baseball player. Reflects on the methodology of biography of heroes of popular culture.

Hoffman, Louise E. EARLY PSYCHOBIOGRAPHY, 1900-1930: SOME RECONSIDERATIONS. *Biography 1984 7(4): 341-351.* Many features of early psychobiographical interpretations were inherited from previous biographical traditions, especially pathography. Freudian concepts sometimes reinforced these qualities, but also provided novel concepts and methods which evolved along with psychoanalytic thought and which potentially allowed for more critical accounts of prominent individuals and their relationship to their societies.

Hoover, Thomas O.; McPherson, Marion White; and Popplestone, John A. DOCUMENTATION, A DIFFERENCE BETWEEN GOSSIP AND HISTORY. *Manuscripts 1974 26(3): 184-189.* Using the discipline of psychology as an example, the authors survey sources for personal data in writing biography and assessing historical movements. Biblio.

Hutch, Richard A. EXPLORATIONS IN CHARACTER: GAMALIEL BRADFORD AND HENRY MURRAY AS PSYCHOBIOGRAPHERS. *Biography 1981 4(4): 312-325.* Biography during the 19th century was a harbinger of modern psychological science. This is demonstrated by a comparison of the style of biographic inquiry of the obscure US biographer, Gamaliel Bradford (1863-1932), with the psychological methods of the famous US psychologist, Henry A. Murray. Thus, Murray's "explorations in personality" can be understood as a modern elaboration of Bradford's "psychography." Parallels between this tradition of life-writing and the work of other 19th-century biographers, like Thomas Carlyle, and other 20th-century psychologists, like Erik Erikson, are indicated.

Jacobs, Roberta Tansman. A WOMAN'S PLACE: ELIZABETH AMBLER OF VIRGINIA, 1780-1823. *J. of Popular Culture 1977 11(1): 211-218.* Historians, using quantitative methods and models from other social sciences, have extended their sources significantly in recent years. This has not been the case in women's history in spite of calls to break away from traditional approaches. This case study, which uses a traditional source (the Elizabeth Ambler papers of 1780-1823), illustrates the understanding of the female experience that may accrue through a biographical analysis. Primary and secondary sources; 25 notes.

Kenney, Alice P. AMERICA DISCOVERS COLUMBUS: BIOGRAPHY AS EPIC, DRAMA, HISTORY. *Biography 1981 4(1): 45-65.* Joel Barlow's epic *The Columbiad* first depicted Christopher Columbus's discovery as the starting point of American history. Washington Irving and William Hickling Prescott presented the discoverer as a dramatic hero like those of Shakespeare and Scott. Samuel Eliot Morrison's biography uses exhaustive historical research to support a narrative of epic sweep and dramatic power. The Columbian quincentennial can promote study and celebration of Hispanic-American traditions.

Kizer, George A. PROBLEMS OF BIOGRAPHY: THE LIVING LEGEND. *Vitae Scholasticae 1983 2(1): 303-314.* Discusses the problem of finding an objective methodology for researching the lives of famous and influential living persons, such as American progressive educator Ralph W. Tyler. German summary.

McMurry, Linda O. GEORGE WASHINGTON CARVER AND THE CHALLENGES OF BIOGRAPHY. *Vitae Scholasticae 1983 2(1): 1-17.* Explores the methodology of biography, using the example of research sources available and not available about the life of black American educator George Washington Carver. Reflects on the process of writing *George Washington Carver: Scientist and Symbol* (1981). Keynote address at conference of the Society for Educational Biography, Iowa State University, 29 April 1983.

Messenger, Christian K. SEMIOTICS AND ALCHEMY: BIOGRAPHY UNDER ATTACK. *American Quarterly 1985 37(1): 150-155.* Reviews David Nye's *The Invented Self: An Anti-Biography, from Documents of Thomas A. Edison* (1983). Criticizes biography as a narrative form through an analysis of the various interpretations and symbolic systems that appear in the many biographies of Edison. 2 notes.

Miller, Patricia McClelland. THE INDIVIDUAL LIFE. *Frontiers 1979 4(3): 70-74.* Presents a lesbian feminist interpretation of biography as a genre, with reference to several syndromes affecting the lives of all women, lesbians in particular: the "Deafening Silence Syndrome," the "Great Woman Syndrome," the "Freak of Nature Syndrome," "Patriarchal Old Chestnuts," and the "Is This a Kaffe Klatch or a Subversive Plot? Syndrome," and suggests new feminist strategies for writing women's biographies.

Miller, Robert Milton. "Show Business Biographical Drama in Film and Television: A Generic Analysis." Northwestern U. 1982. 403 pp. *DAI 1982 43(6): 1727-A.* DA8225979

Morse, Jonathan. MEMORY, DESIRE, AND THE NEED FOR BIOGRAPHY: THE CASE OF EMILY DICKINSON. *Georgia Rev. 1981 35(2): 259-272.* Traces the changing focus of biographical reality and reader self-perception through biographies of Emily Dickinson. At first biographers included only data which illuminated their text. After the 1920's, disillusionment made biography on the heroic model untenable. Biography requires more than memory mixed with desire. It is a convergent art, a pluralist thing. Through its presentation of historical form, context, and subject, it serves as a vehicle for reader participation in aesthetically fulfilled history. 18 notes.

Noland, Richard W. PSYCHOBIOGRAPHY: CASE HISTORY OR LIFE HISTORY? *Midwest Q. 1978 20(1): 7-17.* Discusses the controversy surrounding the new field of psychohistory, specifically psychobiography; also examines the work of Freud, Hans Meyerhoff, Erik Erikson, and others during the 20th century.

O'Brien, Michael. BIOGRAPHY AND THE OLD SOUTH: A REVIEW ESSAY. *Virginia Magazine of History and Biography 1985 93(4): 375-388.* Referring to 22 recent biographies of antebellum Southerners, reviews the status of the discipline of biography. Contemporary biography reflects recent interests sweeping the larger field of historiography, often to its detriment. Where historians today are concerned with social and ideological issues, the biographer's purpose must be dramatic reenactment of an individual's life and the realistic portrayal of that individual's character, without retreating into mechanistic psychobiographical or sociological explanations. Recent biography has produced bloated, monumental life histories rather than the more useful collections of papers and documents organizing these resources for future biographers. 13 notes.

Rogers, Lindsay. REFLECTIONS ON WRITING BIOGRAPHY OF PUBLIC MEN. *Pol. Sci. Q. 1973 88(4): 725-733.* "Reflects on the different styles that have been used and the problems encountered in writing biographies of public figures." Foreword prepared for the late author's projected biography of Nicholas Murray Butler.

Scharnhorst, Gary. BIOGRAPHICAL BLINDSPOTS: THE CASE OF THE COUSINS ALGER. *Biography 1983 6(2): 136-147.* Biographical blindspots exist when original sources about the lives of significant historical figures do not exist. A minor figure who retires long before death (e.g., W. R. Alger) or who becomes the subject of intense public interest only long after death (e.g., Horatio Alger, Jr.) may be lost entirely in such a blindspot.

Schrieber, Roy. BIOGRAPHY AS HISTORY. *Pro. of the Michiana Area Historians 1972 1(1): 1-4.* Advantages and disadvantages in using contemporarily written biographies to study history.

Schwalm, David E. LOCATING BELIEF IN BIOGRAPHY. *Biography 1980 3(1): 14-27.* All biographers *invent* their subjects. The mind of the biographer, not the objective reality of the subject's life, gives form and meaning to the information available about the subject. A biography is most likely to induce belief in the reader who shares to a great extent the conceptual paradigm of human nature that informs the biographer's invented reality.

Shloss, Carol. THE LIVES OF HART CRANE: REVISION OF BIOGRAPHY. *Biography 1980 3(2): 132-146.* In the act of composing a continuous prose narrative out of discrete data, biographers reveal the cultural presuppositions that condition their own interpretive categories. John Unterecker, whose *Voyager: A Life of Hart Crane* superseded Philip Horton's biography of Crane, rewrote Crane's life history in the interest of increased accuracy; but his book also reveals his changed attitudes about the nature of personality and the conventions of biography. 2 notes.

Shor, Francis. BIOGRAPHICAL MOMENTS IN THE WRITTEN AND CINEMATIC TEXT: DECONSTRUCTING THE LEGENDS OF JOE HILL AND BUFFALO BILL. *Film & History 1984 14(3): 61-68.* A comparison of literary and film biographies of both William F. "Buffalo Bill" Cody and early 20th-century labor activist Joe Hill demonstrate that cinematic biographies sacrifice historical fact and the complexities of cause-and-effect relationships in favor of simplicity and narrative drama, though they surpass their literary counterparts in capturing the various cultural factors that shape the individual.

Smith, Joan K. AUTOBIOGRAPHY AS SOURCE: SOME METHODOLOGICAL CAUTIONS. *Vitae Scholasticae 1983 2(1): 167-182.* Reflects on the methodology of biography using autobiographical sources, focusing on the memoirs of Margaret A. Haley, American feminist and teachers-union leader. Autobiography is seldom unbiased, either in its view of its subject or in its portrayal of others or of social conditions. 24 notes.

Styer, Sandra. A SELECTED LIST OF WOMEN'S BIOGRAPHIES FOR THE SOCIAL STUDIES. *Social Educ. 1984 48(7): 554, 556, 563-564.* Suggests criteria for evaluating the biographies of women to be used in social studies and presents an annotated bibliography of suitable works.

Swainson, Donald. TRENDS IN CANADIAN BIOGRAPHY. *Queen's Q. [Canada] 1980 87(3): 413-429.* Canadians are wedded to biography, and biography has become a crucial component of historical and humanist studies in Canada, so Canadian biography is big business. In one- or two-paragraph summaries, 24 Canadian biographies are discussed: three from the preconfederation period, six past politicians, three contemporary political leaders, two "biographies for the sake of biography," two business leaders, two cultural leaders, three biographies popularized for the general public, and three marked by an "innovative and critical use of evidence."

VanderMeer, Philip. COLLECTIVE BIOGRAPHY AND THE NEW POLITICAL HISTORY. *Indiana Social Studies Q. 1980-81 33(3): 5-20.* Discusses the limitations of the traditional narrative and chronological way of studying political history and the responses to it over the past two decades, focusing on collective biography in which information about many individuals in a particular group is collected, rather than focusing on a few "unusual characters."

Wachter, Phyllis E. CURRENT BIBLIOGRAPHY OF LIFE-WRITING *Biography 1986 9(4): 347-357.* Annotated lists of books and articles about biography, autobiography, and related aspects of life writing in British and American publications. Based on journals and publishers' lists, these bibliographies appear annually in the fourth issue of this journal.

Wagner, Sally Roesch. ORAL HISTORY AS A BIOGRAPHICAL TOOL. *Frontiers 1977 2(2): 87-92.* Interviews with family members provide an important tool for the biographer, as demonstrated by the reminiscences of the granddaughter of 19th-century feminist Matilda Joslyn Gage; part of a special issue on women's oral history.

Walker, Ronald W. THE CHALLENGE AND CRAFT OF MORMON BIOGRAPHY. *Brigham Young U. Studies 1982 22(2): 179-192.* A discussion of the problems encountered in writing Mormon biography. There are many Mormon journals and diaries, indeed, the keeping of a daily journal is a Mormon "tenet of faith." These writings cannot, however, be classed as good literature. They are usually piles of facts. To history's thoroughness, candor, and accuracy, the biographer adds the grace of literary art. Mormon biography is overwhelmed with emotions, such as reverence, affection, and religious belief and therefore, is prevented from being good biography if not tempered with openness and scholarly detachment. The Mormon biographer must analyze himself as to his motives in subject and fact selection, thus avoiding many distortions in interpretation. Only recently has the Mormon biographer begun to bring together the three essentials of good biography: investigation, technique, and openness, using social science tools together with the craft of literary writing to achieve laudable work. Lists some Mormon biographies. Based on a diary, letters, and an autobiography; 33 notes.

Woods, Joseph M. SOME CONSIDERATIONS ON PSYCHO-HISTORY. *Historian 1974 36(4): 722-735.* The increasing use by historians of psychoanalytic concepts in an effort to explain individual and group behavior, termed psychohistory, has aroused discussion about the nature of the discipline. The varied arguments which have arisen, especially concerning psychobiography, and the numerous problems involved are examined from the point of view of both analyst and historian. 48 notes.

Yeazell, Stephen C. PROFESSIONAL LIVES AND THE LIFE OF A PROFESSION. *Rev. in Am. Hist. 1976 4(4): 483-489.* Review article prompted by Maxwell Bloomfield's *American Lawyers in a Changing Society, 1776-1876* (Cambridge, Massachusetts: Harvard U. Pr., 1976); discusses the use of biography in writing social and intellectual history.

SAMPLE ENTRIES

ACCESS BY ENTRY:

Frémont, John C. ← Primary Biographical Subject

2374. ← Entry Number
Allin, Lawrence C. ← Article Author

2374. Allin, Lawrence C. FOUR ENGINEERS ON THE MISSOURI: LONG, FREMONT, HUMPHREYS, AND WARREN. *Nebraska Hist. 1984 65(1): 58-83.* ← Article Citation

Recounts the efforts of explorers Stephen H. Long, John C. Frémont, Andrew A. Humphreys, and Gouverneur K. Warren in mapping and describing the Missouri River basin. 2 illus., 86 notes. ← Article Abstract

1817-57 ← Dates Covered by Article

Long, Stephen H. ← Secondary Biographical Subject

4264. ← Entry Number
Allin, Lawrence C. ← Article Author

4264. Allin, Lawrence C. FOUR ENGINEERS ON THE MISSOURI: LONG, FREMONT, HUMPHREYS, AND WARREN. *Nebraska Hist. 1984 65(1): 58-83.* ← Article Citation

1817-57 ← Dates Covered by Article

For abstract see ***Frémont, John C.*** ← Cross Reference to Primary Biographical Subject

Gruenberg, Louis ← Primary Biographical Subject

2753. ← Entry Number
Nisbett, Robert Franklin. ← Dissertation Author

2753. Nisbett, Robert Franklin. "Louis Gruenberg: His Life and Work." Ohio State U. 1979. 441 pp. *DAI 1980* ← Dissertation Citation

40(10): 5243-A. ← *DAI* Order Number

1920's-50's ← Dates Covered by Dissertation

Little Carpenter ← Variant Name of Primary Biographical Subject

See Attakullakulla ← Cross Reference to Primary Biographical Subject

ACCESS THROUGH SUBJECT AND AUTHOR INDEXES:

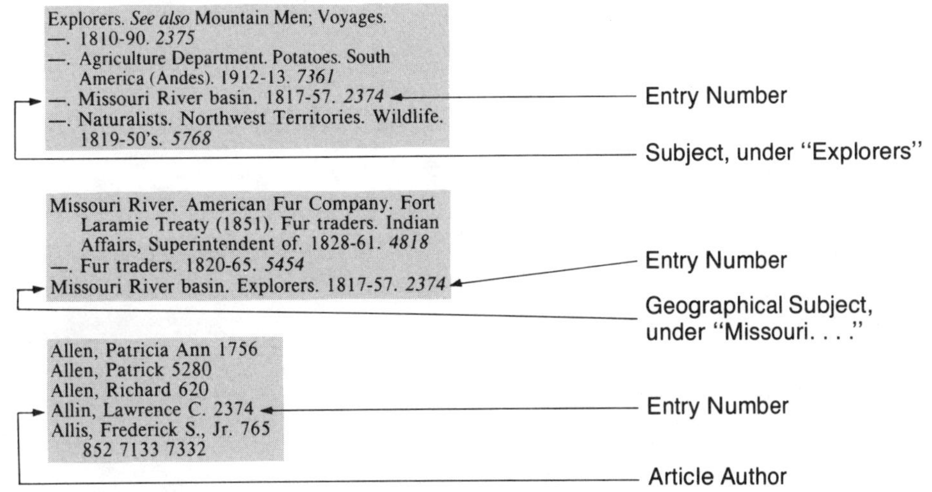

Explorers. *See also* Mountain Men; Voyages.
—. 1810-90. *2375*
—. Agriculture Department. Potatoes. South America (Andes). 1912-13. *7361*
—. Missouri River basin. 1817-57. *2374*
—. Naturalists. Northwest Territories. Wildlife. 1819-50's. *5768*
Entry Number
Subject, under "Explorers"
Missouri River. American Fur Company. Fort Laramie Treaty (1851). Fur traders. Indian Affairs, Superintendent of. 1828-61. *4818*
—. Fur traders. 1820-65. *5454*
Missouri River basin. Explorers. 1817-57. *2374*
Entry Number
Geographical Subject, under "Missouri. . . ."
Allen, Patricia Ann 1756
Allen, Patrick 5280
Allen, Richard 620
Allin, Lawrence C. 2374
Allis, Frederick S., Jr. 765 852 7133 7332
Entry Number
Article Author

LIST OF ABBREVIATIONS

A. . . . . Author-prepared Abstract
Acad. . . . . Academy, Academie, Academia
Agric. . . . . Agriculture, Agricultural
AIA . . . . Abstracts in Anthropology
Akad. . . . . Akademie
Am. . . . . America, American
Ann. . . . . Annals, Annales, Annual, Annali
Anthrop. . . . . Anthropology, Anthropological
Arch. . . . . Archives
Archaeol. . . . . Archaeology, Archaeological
Art. . . . . Article
Assoc. . . . . Association, Associate
Biblio. . . . . Bibliography, Bibliographical
Biog. . . . . Biography, Biographical
Bol. . . . . Boletim, Boletin
Bull. . . . . Bulletin
c. . . . . century (in index)
ca. . . . . circa
Can. . . . . Canada, Canadian, Canadien
Cent. . . . . Century
Coll. . . . . College
Com. . . . . Committee
Comm. . . . . Commission
Comp. . . . . Compiler
DAI . . . . Dissertation Abstracts International
Dept. . . . . Department
Dir. . . . . Director, Direktor
Econ. . . . . Economy, Econom-.
Ed. . . . . Editor, Edition
Educ. . . . . Education, Educational
Geneal. . . . . Genealogy, Genealogical, Genealogique
Grad. . . . . Graduate
Hist. . . . . History, Hist-.
IHE . . . . Indice Historico Espanol
Illus. . . . . Illustrated, Illustration
Inst. . . . . Institute, Institut-.
Int. . . . . International, Internacional, Internationaal, Internationaux, Internazionale
J. . . . . Journal, Journal-prepared Abstract
Lib. . . . . Library, Libraries
Mag. . . . . Magazine
Mus. . . . . Museum, Musee, Museo
Nac. . . . . Nacional
Natl. . . . . National, Nationale
Naz. . . . . Nazionale
Phil. . . . . Philosophy, Philosophical
Photo. . . . . Photograph
Pol. . . . . Politics, Political, Politique, Politico
Pr. . . . . Press
Pres. . . . . President
Pro. . . . . Proceedings
Publ. . . . . Publishing, Publication
Q. . . . . Quarterly
Rev. . . . . Review, Revue, Revista, Revised
Riv. . . . . Rivista
Res. . . . . Research
RSA . . . . Romanian Scientific Abstracts
S. . . . . Staff-prepared Abstract
Sci. . . . . Science, Scientific
Secy. . . . . Secretary
Soc. . . . . Society, Societe, Sociedad, Societa
Sociol. . . . . Sociology, Sociological
Tr. . . . . Transactions
Transl. . . . . Translator, Translation
U. . . . . University, Universi-.
US . . . . United States
Vol. . . . . Volume
Y. . . . . Yearbook

Abbreviations also apply to feminine and plural forms.
Abbreviations not noted above are based on *Webster's Third New International Dictionary* and the *United States Government Printing Office Style Manual.*

PEOPLE IN HISTORY

A

Abbot, John

1. Rogers-Price, Vivian and Griffin, William W. JOHN ABBOT: PIONEER ARTIST-NATURALIST OF GEORGIA. *Mag. Antiques 1983 124(4): 768-775.* Supporting his family by selling his exquisite graphite and watercolor illustrations, English-born John Abbot studied and depicted Savannah Valley natural history. 1776-1840

Abbott, Jacob

2. Nenstiel, Gregory Andrew. "Jacob Abbott: Mentor to a Rising Generation." U. of Maryland 1979. 247 pp. *DAI 1980 40(9): 4928-A.* 1825-75

Abel, Elijah

3. Bringhurst, Newell G. ELIJAH ABEL AND THE CHANGING STATUS OF BLACKS WITHIN MORMONISM. *Dialogue 1979 12(2): 22-36.* Discusses Elijah Abel, black member of the Mormon priesthood, in relation to the recent decision to abandon denial of the priesthood to blacks. No evidence of priesthood denial is evident prior to 1843; blacks were few, but enjoyed rights and duties equal to those of white members. The policy vacillated thereafter, with Abel usually at the very center of each controversy. The story remains vague and the evidence conflicting, but available data suggests that Brigham Young, rather than Joseph Smith, was finally responsible for the policy of black exclusion. Covers 1830's-70's. Photo, 89 notes. ca 1830-79

Abel, Mary Hinman

4. Levenstein, Harvey. THE NEW ENGLAND KITCHEN AND THE ORIGINS OF MODERN AMERICAN EATING HABITS. *Am. Q. 1980 32(4): 369-386.* Edward Atkinson (1827-1905), manufacturer of the slow-cooking Aladdin Oven, joined with nutritionists Mary Hinman Abel and Ellen H. Richards (1842-1911) to open the New England Kitchen in Boston in 1889. This public kitchen, which stimulated similar experiments in other cities, sought to change working-class menus and demonstrate slow-cooking. These reformers believed that working-class people needed cheaper diets which incorporated alternative sources of protein and carbohydrates. Immigrants and the working class generally ignored the message and retained their traditional eating habits. Atkinson, Abel, and Richards began catering to a middle-class clientele in 1897. Based on the Edward Atkinson Papers, the Mary H. Abel Papers, the Ellen H. Richards Papers, and other primary sources; 66 notes. 1889-97

Aberdeen and Temair, John Campbell Gordon, 1st Marquis of

5. Shackleton, Doris. LORD AND LADY ABERDEEN: THEIR OKANAGAN RANCHES. *Beaver [Canada] 1981 312(2): 10-18.* "Few occupants of Rideau Hall invested much time or fortune in Canada beyond their brief five-year official round." Such was not the case with the Aberdeens, who owned well over 14,000 acres in the Okanagan Valley. Their experiments failed financially. Always an innovator, Aberdeen experimented with a jam factory, which was one of his failures. However, by 1900 the area generally, and Coldstream Ranch in particular, began to grow fruit for export. In 1920, the Aberdeens sold their last interest in Coldstream Ranch. Considerable detail is provided on the topography as well as the leading individuals in western Canada. 8 photos. 1890-1920

Aberhart, William

6. Elliot, David R. and Miller, Iris. ABERHART AND THE CALGARY PROPHETIC BIBLE INSTITUTE. *Prairie Forum [Canada] 1984 9(1): 61-77.* Traces the career of fundamentalist minister William Aberhart, who founded an independent church in Calgary, Alberta, which became extremely large as a result of his personal popularity but which collapsed within six years of his death. 1927-49

Abraham, Raymond

7. —. KOOTENAI. *Idaho Heritage 1977 (10): 33-35.*

—. AN INTERVIEW WITH JOE MATHIAS, *pp. 33-34.* Joe Mathias, director of the Kootenai Indians' Outreach program, discusses progress in promoting community planning and participation and in improving educational and living environments for Idaho's Kootenai, 1970's.

Shottanana, Josephine. DIXIE COOPER AND RAYMOND ABRAHAM, *pp. 34-35.* Biographical sketches of two Kootenai tribal council members.

Friedlander, Margaret. KOOTENAI EDUCATION, *pp. 35.* Author recounts her experiences as a teacher among the Kootenai Indians, 1975-77. 1970's

Acheson, Dean

8. Acheson, Dean. "DEAR BOSS": UNPUBLISHED LETTERS FROM DEAN ACHESON TO EX-PRESIDENT HARRY TRUMAN. *Am. Heritage 1980 31(2): 44-48.* The author, who served as Secretary of State under Harry S. Truman from 1949 to 1953, kept up a lively and unusual correspondence with the former president after both men left office; 1953-65. 1953-65

Ackland, William Hayes

9. Kiser, John. SCION OF BELMONT. B. *Tennessee Hist. Q. 1979 38(2): 188-203.* Continued from a previous article. Part II. William Hayes Ackland's (1856-1940) edited memoirs offer interesting anecdotes of Nashville, New Orleans, Chicago, New York, and White Sulphur Springs, Virginia, in the 1870's. Belmont, the Ackland family estate in Nashville, Tennessee, was host to the visiting elite, and Ackland recalls many celebrated figures. 7 notes. 1871-78

10. Kiser, John. SCION OF BELMONT. A. *Tennessee Hist. Q. 1979 38(1): 34-61.* William Hayes Ackland was born at the stately mansion at Belmont, two miles from Nashville, Tennessee, in September 1855. He was well-educated, traveled widely in Europe after the Civil War, and was highly respected. Covers 1855-67. Excerpted from Ackland's proposed autobiography which is now part of the Southern Historical Collection of the University of North Carolina. Secondary sources; illus., 22 notes. Article to be continued. 1855-67

Acock, Robert Eaton

11. Goodrich, James W. ROBERT EATON ACOCK: THE GENTLEMAN FROM POLK. *Missouri Hist. Rev. 1979 73(3): 281-306.* Robert Eaton Acock, an early settler of Missouri, rose to public prominence during 1830's-60's. Acock was a successful farmer, landholder, and moneylender. His involvement in Democratic politics led to his election to the Missouri state legislature for four two-year terms and to

the state senate for one four-year term. The political career of Acock is discussed by focusing on the issue of establishing loan interest rates, debate regarding the legislative representation of counties, and controversy concerning bills for the construction of railroads in Missouri. 85 notes. 1830-60

Acree, Howard

12. Martin, Charles E. HOWARD ACREE'S CHIMNEY: THE DILEMMA OF INNOVATION. *Pioneer Am. 1983 15(1): 35-49.* Presents a brief biography of Howard Acree and describes the design and construction of the fireplace he built in his four-room frame house in eastern Kentucky in 1934. 1935-46

Adair family

13. Uhler, Margaret Anderson. "FLORIDA WHITE," SOUTHERN BELLE. *Florida Hist. Q. 1977 55(3): 299-309.* 1801-84

*For abstract see **Beatty, Ellen Adair White***

Adams, Abigail

14. Cole, Adelaide M. ABIGAIL ADAMS: A VIGNETTE. *Daughters of the Am. Revolution Mag. 1979 113(5): 494-499.* Biography of Abigail Adams (1744-1818), wife of John Adams and mother of John Quincy Adams. 1744-1818

15. Gelles, Edith B. ABIGAIL ADAMS: DOMESTICITY AND THE AMERICAN REVOLUTION. *New England Q. 1979 52(4): 500-521.* Describes Abigail Adams's (1744-1818) management of the family farm and finances in Massachusetts. John Adams sent her tea, handkerchiefs, and other items from Europe. She sold or traded these to meet her needs and, during his absences, she invested in land. She fulfilled a man's role but was no feminist. "She believed that women were domestic, that their primary functions were within the home as wife and mother." Based on family correspondence; 89 notes. 1774-82

16. Gelles, Edith B. "Abigail Adams: Domesticity and the American Revolution." U. of California, Irvine 1978. 206 pp. *DAI 1978 39(3): 1784-A.* 1770's-80's

17. Illick, Joseph E. JOHN QUINCY ADAMS: THE MATERNAL INFLUENCE. *J. of Psychohist. 1976 4(2): 185-195.* The role of Abigail Adams in forming the character of her son, John Quincy Adams, has been neglected, while the parallels between his career and philosophy and that of his father, John Adams, are noted. An examination of John Quincy Adams' childhood and adolescence shows that his mother, rather than his father, set his emotional tone. Primary sources; 23 notes. 1767-1800

18. Keller, Rosemary Skinner. "Abigail Adams and the American Revolution: A Personal History." U. of Illinois, Chicago Circle 1977. 350 pp. *DAI 1977 38(4): 2202-2203-A.* 1762-84

19. Palmer, Beverly Wilson. ABIGAIL ADAMS AND THE APPLE OF EUROPE. *New England Hist. and Geneal. Register 1981 135(Apr): 109-120.* Abigail Adams's residence in England and France during 1784-88 is fully documented in her many letters to family and friends. They reveal how the experience changed her thinking about both the old world and the new. She recognized that she had idealized the new nation and that her hopes for a more virtuous government were probably unachievable. 25 notes. 18c

Adams, Andy

20. Johnson, Carole M. A DEDICATION TO THE MEMORY OF ANDY ADAMS, 1859-1935. *Arizona and the West 1977 19(3): 202-206.* Indiana-born Andy Adams (1859-1935) spent the 1880's and 1890's in the cattle industry and mining in the Great Plains and Southwest. When an 1898 play's portrayal of Texans outraged him, he started writing plays, short stories, and novels drawn from his own experiences. His *The Log of a Cowboy* became a classic novel about the cattle business, especially the cattle drive. No other production from this inveterate writer could match it, and his later efforts were increasingly rejected by publishers. His works are acclaimed and criticized for their fidelity to truth and their lack of literary qualities. Illus., biblio. 19c-1935

Adams, Ansel

21. Wood, Jim. THE GENTLE CRUSADER: ANSEL ADAMS. *Hist. Preservation 1981 33(1): 32-39.* Biography of American photographer Ansel Adams (b. 1902), focusing on his 50-year fight to save the environment and his more recent struggle to insure that his Carmel Highlands, California, home will be saved as a center for creative photography. 1902-81

Adams, Brooks

22. Nagel, Paul C. BROOKS ADAMS AFTER HALF A CENTURY. *Massachusetts Hist. Soc. Pro. 1978 90: 38-57.* One of six children, Brooks Adams (1848-1927) was a complex figure whose life and character are only now beginning to be reassessed and understood. An irascible and pessimistic figure, he came into constant conflict with his brother Charles Francis II, particularly over the handling of the family finances in the 1890's. Brooks increasingly became the steward and spokesman for the family, attempting to preserve the family home and papers in Quincy, Massachusetts. He attempted to establish and explicate the family's role and importance in biographies of his grandfather John Quincy Adams, his father Charles Francis, and in a memorial of his brother Henry. Based on the Adams Family Papers at the Massachusetts Historical Society; 25 notes. 1860's-1927

Adams, Charles Francis

23. Perkins, Elliott; Abbott, John A.; and Adams, Thomas B. THREE VIEWS ON CHARLES FRANCIS ADAMS, II. *Massachusetts Hist. Soc. Pro. 1957-60 72: 212-237.* Provides accounts of the life of Charles Francis Adams, II (1835-1915) based on the memories of his three grandsons. 1835-1915

24. Riley, Stephen T. CHARLES FRANCIS ADAMS (1835-1915): CONSERVATIONIST. *Massachusetts Hist. Soc. Pro. 1978 90: 22-37.* Charles Francis Adams (1835-1915), well-known as a financier and railroad man, also had an important career as a conservationist in the late 19th century. Adams was influential in establishing parks and open spaces in his hometown of Quincy, Massachusetts, in the 1880's. Later, at the urging of Charles Eliot (1859-97) and others, he was the leader of the important committee established by the Metropolitan Park Commission Act of 1893. In the space of a few years, this commission gave Boston and its surrounding suburbs one of the most sophisticated systems of parks in the world. Based on the published autobiography of

Adams, the Adams Papers at the Massachusetts Historical Society, and other primary and secondary sources; 35 notes. 1880's-90's

Adams, Eleanor Burnham

25. Greenleaf, Richard E. ELEANOR BURNHAM ADAMS: HISTORIAN AND EDITOR. *New Mexico Hist. Rev. 1985 60(1): 5-9.* Reviews the career of historian Eleanor Burnham Adams, stressing her studies of northern New Spain, and her editorship of the *New Mexico Historical Review.* Photo, 2 notes. 1931-84

Adams, George G.

26. Pfaff, Christine E. GEORGE G. ADAMS: A NOTED LAWRENCE ARCHITECT REDISCOVERED. *Essex Inst. Hist. Collections 1980 116(3): 176-195.* Although not a great architect, George G. Adams (1850-1932) deserves to be recognized for his achievements. With no more than a local public school education, he became one of New England's most prominent architects. During 60 years of activity, he produced designs for at least 70 buildings in Lawrence, Massachusetts and throughout New England. His work's diversity and stylistic range is both impressive and remarkable. He was able to successfully adapt to changes in architectural tastes and styles. "As examples of the social and cultural attitudes and values of their time, as well as for their quality," the buildings Adams designed "deserve preservation and should be brought to the attention of a larger public." Appends an incomplete list of known Adams buildings. Primary sources; 10 photos, 29 notes. 1872-1932

Adams, George Jones

27. Holmes, Reed M. G. J. ADAMS AND THE FORERUNNERS. *Maine Hist. Soc. Q. 1981 21(1): 19-53.* Relates the life of George Jones Adams (1811-80) focusing on his role in organizing in Maine the Palestine Emigration Society and leading 157 of its members to Jaffa, Palestine, in 1866. The main purpose of the society was to prepare the way for Jewish emigration to Palestine. Adams's personality and goals created strong opinions for and against. The settlement failed within two years because of external opposition, internal bickering, lack of enough financial backing, and flaws in the personality of Adams. The settlers were, however, forerunners, and they paved the way for the modern state of Israel. Based on local newspapers, including Adams's, and State Department archives; photo, 50 notes. 1840-68

Adams, Henry Brooks

28. Diggins, John Patrick. "WHO BORE THE FAILURE OF THE LIGHT": HENRY ADAMS AND THE CRISIS OF AUTHORITY. *New England Quarterly 1985 58(2): 165-192.* Throughout his life Henry Adams was preoccupied with the question of authority. In examining the authority of women Adams developed a strange perception of the relationship of both religion to women and of faith to love. Adams recognized that women expressed their power by demanding and receiving men's love and adoration, which depended on the male's surrender of mind and will. Adams feared the irrationality and destructivness of feminine power and tried to discover the moment in history when power became alienated from authority. He found the key in religion, especially the Virgin Mary of medieval tradition. Rather than as a displaced patrician seeking lost status and influence, Adams is is better understood as an anguished humanist coming to grips with three realities of the 20th century: "knowledge without truth, society without spirit, and power without authority." 38 notes. 1870's-1918

29. Eppard, Philip Blair. "The Correspondence of Henry Adams and John Hay, 1881-1892." Brown U. 1979. 715 pp. *DAI 1980 40(11): 5913-A.* 8007004 1881-92

30. Friedrich, Otto. CLOVER AND HENRY ADAMS. *Smithsonian 1977 8(1): 58-67.* 1872-85
For abstract see ***Adams, Marian Hooper***

31. Hamill, Paul J. SCIENCE AS IDEOLOGY: THE CASE OF THE AMATEUR, HENRY ADAMS. *Can. Rev. of Am. Studies [Canada] 1981 12(1): 21-35.* In his autobiography, *The Education of Henry Adams* (1906), historian Henry Brooks Adams claimed that he accepted Darwinism from 1868 until 1901, sometimes conducting his own scientific experiments, for literary and political reasons. Eventually Adams concluded that Darwinism supplied no guide to understanding history, only to then devise a "Dynamic Theory of History" rooted in the principles of physics. Adams's inconsistency proves him a representative intellectual adrift in the "hazy borderline where scientific thought and the imaginative values of an era interfuse." Based on writings of Henry Adams and secondary sources; 22 notes. 1868-1901

32. Howell, Alan William. "Henry Adams and the Higher Life: History, Art, and Moral Philosophy." U. California, Santa Barbara 1976. 193 pp. *DAI 1977 38(4): 2126-2127-A.* 1869-1918

33. Schwehn, Mark Richard. "The Making of Modern Consciousness in America: The Works and Careers of Henry Adams and William James." Stanford U. 1978. 234 pp. *DAI 1978 38(12): 7517-A.* 1870's-1910's

34. Waterston, Elizabeth. THE GAP IN HENRY ADAMS' EDUCATION. *Can. Rev. of Am. Studies 1976 7(2): 132-138.* Reconstructs the professional and literary activities, personal problems and conflicts, and the evolution of the thinking of Henry Adams (1838-1918) between 1871 and 1891. These matters so troubled him that largely he omitted them from his *The Education of Henry Adams* (1906, 1918) and from his personal papers. Eventually he decided that sex was a primary historical determinant, but his writings contradict that view. 15 notes. 1871-91

Adams, Henry Carter

35. DeBrizzi, John. IDEOLOGY AND EARLY AMERICAN THEORY: THE CONTRIBUTIONS OF HENRY CARTER ADAMS. *J. of the Hist. of Sociol. 1979 1(2): 63-75.* Analyzes the sociological theories of Henry Carter Adams and his views concerning capitalism and the labor movement between 1880 and 1925. 1880-1925

Adams, Herbert Baxter

36. Higham, John. HERBERT BAXTER ADAMS AND THE STUDY OF LOCAL HISTORY. *Am. Hist. Rev. 1984 89(5): 1225-1239.* Following his appointment to a fellowship at Johns Hopkins University in 1876, Herbert Baxter Adams began his research and teaching on local history. Much of his energy was spent forging an alliance between the teachers of history he was training and the amateur local historians he met. His efforts were not successful because most professional historians in the 19th century regarded local history as the equivalent of antiquarianism. Based on the Adams Papers in the Milton E. Eisenhower Library, Johns Hopkins University, and on secondary sources; 44 notes. 1876-1900

Adams, John

37. Ferling, John E. "OH THAT I WAS A SOLDIER": JOHN ADAMS AND THE ANGUISH OF WAR. *Am. Q. 1984 36(2): 258-275.* Examines the actions and feelings of John Adams during the French and Indian War, the American Revolution and the Quasi-War with France. Adams never served in the military and he was emotionally distressed at these times, feeling that he should do more for his country. 47 notes. 1756-99

38. Rowen, Herbert H. JOHN ADAMS' VISION OF THE DUTCH REPUBLIC. *Consortium on Revolutionary Europe 1750-1850: Pro. 1979: 3-14.* During much of 1780-82 John Adams lived in the Dutch Republic. He worked to win official Dutch recognition of the United States and to obtain loans for the new American republic. In some ways an acute observer of Dutch politics and society, Adams realized that the Dutch had lost their economic supremacy in Europe, though he did not know why this had occurred. He failed to understand the division of power among the provinces and the various political bodies, and did not fully appreciate the composition and aims of the Dutch regents. Adams saw, however, that the Dutch and American republics had at least as many differences as similarities. His experiences in the Dutch Republic thus helped him to clarify his ideas about American government. 1780-82

39. Shaw, Peter. JOHN ADAMS' CRISIS OF CONSCIENCE. *J. of the Rutgers U. Lib. 1980 42(1): 1-25.* Uncertainty and wavering marked John Adams's (1735-1826) mind during 1761-76. The mystery of his state of mind was not cleared up in his voluminous reminiscences but does throw light on the vicissitudes of patriotism in the years before Independence. In an effort to penetrate the mystery the author examines Adams's relationships with leading patriot James Otis, Jr. (1725-83), and Thomas Hutchinson (1711-80), who served as representative of the British ministry in Massachusetts throughout the prerevolutionary disturbances. 48 notes. 1761-76

40. Thompson, Harry C. THE SECOND PLACE IN ROME: JOHN ADAMS AS VICE PRESIDENT. *Presidential Studies Q. 1980 10(2): 171-178.* Examines the experience of John Adams as this country's first vice-president. The vice-presidency had few designated powers, and in many ways was relegated to an inferior position. Adams grew frustrated with the position, but recognized its importance when, as vice-president, he stated: "In esse [in actuality] I am nothing—but in posse [in potentiality] I am everything." 28 notes.
1789-97

Adams, John (b.1875)

41. Adams, John. MEMORIES OF AN OLD MAN. *Massachusetts Hist. Soc. Pro. 1957-60 72: 294-299.* Reprints a paper delivered by John Adams (b. 1875) in 1958 covering 1875-97. 1875-97

42. Adams, John. RANDOM SKETCHES OVER EIGHTY YEARS. *Massachusetts Hist. Soc. Pro. 1957-60 72: 300-308.* This paper covering 1880-97 of John Adams's (b. 1875) life was read at a 1959 meeting of the Massachusetts Historical Society and adds to a previous paper presented to the Society in 1958. 1880-97

Adams, John Quincy

43. Baron, Stephen Mark. "John Quincy Adams and the American Party System." Northern Illinois U. 1978. 142 pp. *DAI 1979 39(12): 7493-A.* 1790's-1820's

44. Illick, Joseph E. JOHN QUINCY ADAMS: THE MATERNAL INFLUENCE. *J. of Psychohist. 1976 4(2): 185-195.* 1767-1800
For abstract see ***Adams, Abigail***

45. Jones, Maldwyn A. JOHN QUINCY ADAMS. *Hist. Today [Great Britain] 1980 30(Nov): 5-8.* Traces John Quincy Adams's political career, stressing his failure as a president and his more successful service in the House of Representatives; 1783-1848. 1783-1848

46. Kaye, Jacqueline. JOHN QUINCY ADAMS AND *THE CONQUEST OF IRELAND. Éire-Ireland 1981 16(1): 34-54.* After losing to Andrew Jackson in the presidential election of 1828, John Quincy Adams broke off all personal dealings with him even though they had been friends of long standing. The reason for this severance is revealed in Adams's *The Conquest of Ireland,* a poem written in 1831 in four Byronic cantos that condemned Dermot MacMurrogh, the 12th-century king of Leinster who bargained away Ireland to the English and helped them conquer it after he had been expelled from Ireland by another king angered by his adultery. Adams was genuinely sympathetic to Irish independence, but he also wished to compare MacMurrogh and Jackson, whose marriage to Mrs. Rachel Robards before she had been legally divorced was a prominent issue in the campaign of 1828. Adams believed that respect for the family unit affected respect for public morality. 48 notes.
1828-31

47. Klingelhofer, Herbert E. JOHN QUINCY ADAMS, LITERARY EDITOR. *Manuscripts 1983 35(4): 265-272.*
1831
For abstract see ***McKinney, Thomas L.***

Adams, Louisa Catherine Johnson

48. Challinor, Joan Ridder. "Louisa Catherine Johnson Adams: The Price of Ambition." Am. U. 1982. 639 pp. *DAI 1982 43(5): 1651-A.* DA8224007 1775-1852

49. Corbett, Katharine T. LOUISA CATHERINE ADAMS: THE ANGUISHED "ADVENTURES OF A NOBODY." Kelley, Mary, ed. *Woman's Being, Woman's Place: Female Identity and Vocation in American History* (Boston: G. K. Hall, 1979): 67-84. Studies Louisa Catherine Adams, daughter-in-law of Abigail Adams. While Abigail personified Republican motherhood, Louisa, though fully committed to wifehood and motherhood, was unsuccessful in fulfilling the role. She considered herself an alien, possessing qualities of an upper-middle-class-English woman, which were inappropriate for the United States. Her relationship with her husband was strained, as was her relationship with her children. The interest in Louisa Adams lies not so much in the experience of failure as in her ability to articulate that experience. Her memoirs and letters for 1797-1812 shed light upon the role played by large numbers of women, the inherent strains in the role, and its effect upon the conception of self. Based on memoirs and letters of Louisa Adams; 64 notes.
1797-1812

Adams, Lytle S.

50. Kerfoot, Glenn. ALL AMERICAN AVIATION: "THE AIRWAY TO EVERYWHERE." *Aviation Q. 1980 6(2): 192-203.* Discusses Dr. Lytle S. Adams's invention of the airmail system and the pilots who flew the mail from the 1920's until 1949. 1920-49

Adams, Marian Hooper

51. Friedrich, Otto. CLOVER AND HENRY ADAMS. *Smithsonian 1977 8(1): 58-67.* Relates details of the marriage of Marian "Clover" Hooper Adams and Henry Brooks Adams from 1872 until her suicide in 1885, after which Adams commissioned a memorial statue to her by Augustus Saint-Gaudens. 1872-85

Adams, Mary Newbury

52. Lex, Louise Moede. MARY NEWBURY ADAMS: FEMINIST FORERUNNER FROM IOWA. *Ann. of Iowa 1976 43(5): 323-341.* Through her writing, speaking, and organizational abilities, Iowan Mary Newbury Adams (1837-1901) tried to change the attitudes of 19th-century women toward themselves. Women, she believed, needed to know much more about their own history because knowledge of what women in the past had achieved would encourage succeeding generations. A forerunner in the struggle for female equality, Adams helped prepare the way for eventual improvement in the social status of women. Primary and secondary sources; 47 notes. 1850-1900

Adams, Maude

53. Kuehnl, Eileen Karen. "Maude Adams, an American Idol: True Womanhood Triumphant in the Late-Nineteenth and Early-Twentieth Century Theatre." U. of Wisconsin, Madison 1984. 448 pp. *DAI 1985 45(10): 3030-A.* DA8415568 1897-1918

Adams, Robert McCormick

54. Jacobs, Madeleine. A NEW SECRETARY TAKES CHARGE AT THE SMITHSONIAN. *Smithsonian 1984 15(7): 118-127.* Gives biographical data on Robert McCormick Adams, an archaeologist and anthropologist who has worked extensively in Iraq since 1950, who authored *Heartland of Cities: Surveys of Ancient Settlement and Land Use on the Euphrates* (1981), and who became, on 17 September 1984, the ninth secretary of the Smithsonian Institution. 1926-84

Adams, Roger

55. Tarbell, D. S.; Tarbell, Ann T.; and Joyce, R. M. THE STUDENTS OF IRA REMSEN AND ROGER ADAMS. *Isis 1980 71(259): 620-626.* Summarizes the careers of doctoral students of two leading American organic chemists, Ira Remsen, who directed the Johns Hopkins University chemistry department from 1876 to 1913, and Roger Adams, head of the department at the University of Illinois from 1926 to 1954. Both were excellent teachers, and each led an outstanding department in his generation. It is a reflection of their somewhat different interests that most of Remsen's students went into college teaching, while the largest number of Adams's students went into industry. Based on university archives and secondary works in the history of chemistry; 6 tables, 7 notes. 1876-1954

Adams, Samuel

56. O'Toole, James M. THE HISTORICAL INTERPRETATIONS OF SAMUEL ADAMS. *New England Q. 1976 49(1): 82-96.* Traces Samuel Adams' (1722-1803) historiographical image through two centuries. Contemporaries and 19th-century historians viewed him in dichotomous moral terms, either as totally corrupt or as an enlightened democrat. Progressive historians of the early 20th century focused on Adams' goals rather than his actions and stressed his radical ideology. Consensus historians of midcentury rejected this view and pictured him as a conservative pragmatist. They were followed by New Left historians who combined both views, saying that Adams sought revolutionary goals in a pragmatic way. Alongside these recent interpretations, another image of Adams as a propagandist developed. All of these interpretations suffer from their attempt at "relevance" for their times, and only the last decade has brought a dispassionate assessment of Adams. This process is not yet complete but promises the possibility of a final interpretation of Adams' true significance. Based on secondary sources; 40 notes. 1770-1976

57. Sogrin, V. V. BIOGRAFII OTTSOV-OSNOVATELEI SSHA V AMERIKANSKOI ISTORIOGRAFII 1970-KH GODOV [Biographies of the Founding Fathers of the United States in American historiography during the 1970's]. *Novaia i Noveishaia Istoriia [USSR] 1980 (1): 154-163.* Reviews recent biographies of Thomas Paine, Thomas Jefferson, Alexander Hamilton, George Washington, Samuel Adams, and Benjamin Franklin. The author characterizes each biography briefly, mentioning over 25 works. All of them are imbued with the current official American line: consensus is stressed while social conflict is neglected. 39 notes. 1760-1800

Adams family

58. Dumas, David W., ed. BACON-ADAMS-WHITNEY-KINGSBURY FAMILY RECORDS. *New England Hist. and Geneal. Register 1984 138(Jan): 32-38.* 17c-19c
For abstract see ***Bacon family***

Adamson, Sarah Browne Armstrong

59. Riley, Glenda and Benning, Carol. THE 1836-1845 DIARY OF SARAH BROWNE ARMSTRONG ADAMSON OF FAYETTE COUNTY, OHIO. *Old Northwest 1984 10(3): 285-306.* Discusses the life of Sarah Browne Armstrong Adamson (1783-1851) and her diary, which gives a detailed account of her family's economic, social, and personal activities on their Fayette County, Ohio, farm. Selections from the diary, including poetry, offer insights into the primary interests and concerns of a farm woman and her family on the farm frontier in the mid-19th century. Based on the diary of Sarah Browne Armstrong Adamson, in the possession of Dr. Cecil T. Adamson, Cedar Falls, Iowa. 1836-45

Addams, Jane

60. Barker-Benfield, G. J. MOTHER EMANCIPATOR: THE MEANING OF JANE ADDAMS' SICKNESS AND CURE. *J. of Family Hist. 1979 4(4): 395-420.* Describes settlement house founder and social reformer Jane Addams's life as a struggle between "the values represented by her father and those she associated with her mother." Addams overtly rejected traditional maternal and wifely roles but found close psychological substitutes in her marriage to social reform and mothering of Hull House. Covers 1880-1920. 13 notes, biblio. 1880-1920

61. Cavallo, Dominick. SEXUAL POLITICS AND SOCIAL REFORM: JANE ADDAMS, FROM CHILDHOOD TO HULL HOUSE. Albin, Mel, ed. *New Directions in Psychohistory: The Adelphi Papers in Honor of Erik H. Erikson* (Lexington, Mass.: Heath, 1980): 161-182. Studies social settlement worker Jane Addams's (1860-1935) childhood and adolescence, focusing on the cultural interfaces where individual life history meets social history and where biography and collective behavior interact. The problems and successes of Addams's early years were related to culturally prescribed paradigms of moral valuation and social behavior, especially the ways in which late-19th-century Americans perceived female and male social roles. The links between cultural paradigms and Addams's personal experiences, when placed in the context of late-19th-century urban and industrial changes, throw light on the relationship between her resolution of private conflicts and her decision to become a social reformer and thereby to help resolve society's public conflicts. She did this by opening Hull House, a social settlement institution, in Chicago in 1889. Secondary sources; 83 notes. 1860-89

62. James, Janet Wilson. ISABEL HAMPTON AND THE PROFESSIONALIZATION OF NURSING IN THE 1890'S. Vogel, Morris J. and Rosenberg, Charles E., ed. *The Therapeutic Revolution: Essays in the Social History of American Medicine* (Philadelphia: U. of Pennsylvania Pr., 1979): 201-244. 1889-1910
For abstract see ***Hampton, Isabel***

63. Knawa, Anne Marie. JANE ADDAMS AND JOSEPHINE DUDZIK: SOCIAL SERVICE PIONEERS. *Polish Am. Studies 1978 35(1-2): 13-22.* 1860-1918
For abstract see ***Dudzik, Mary Theresa***

64. Lammers, A. JANE ADDAMS [Jane Addams]. *Spiegel Hist. [Netherlands] 1980 15(5): 259-265.* Jane Addams, born in Illinois in 1860, achieved fame by founding Hull House in Chicago in 1889. Described by W. T. Stead in *If Christ Came to Chicago* (1894), this was a sanctuary for poor immigrants in a city teeming with slums and rife with poverty. It was modelled on Toynbee Hall in East London, England. In 1912 Addams's political activities reached their height when she joined the Progressive Party under Theodore Roosevelt. She died in 1935 and, despite her social achievements, faded into obscurity until the 1960's when her reputation was revived by the feminist movement. 8 photos, plate, table. 1889-1920

Addems, Walt

65. Perlitch, Julie. WALT ADDEMS: A PLANE AND PROPPER MAN. *Aviation Q. 1980 6(4): 342-355.* Pilot Walt Addems, now 81, began flying in 1916 in a homemade glider and may be the oldest continuously active pilot. 1916-80

Addison, Joseph

66. Lewis, Janette Seaton. "A TURN OF THINKING": THE LONG SHADOW OF THE *SPECTATOR* IN FRANKLIN'S *AUTOBIOGRAPHY. Early Am. Literature 1978-79 13(3): 268-277.* 18c
For abstract see ***Franklin, Benjamin***

Adee, Alvey A.

67. Calkin, Homer L. ALVEY A. ADEE COMMENTS ON STATE DEPARTMENT BUREAUCRACY. *Soc. for Hist. of Am. Foreign Relations. Newsletter 1979 10(4): 10-13.* Alvey A. Adee, with the State Department from 1870 to 1924, complained, as much as any modern bureaucrat, about the volume of paperwork. 1870-1924

68. DeNovo, John A. THE ENIGMATIC ALVEY A. ADEE AND AMERICAN FOREIGN RELATIONS, 1870-1924. *Prologue 1975 7(2): 69-80.* Alvey Augustus Adee (1842-1924) was the administrative support of the State Department, 1870-1924. He provided six presidents and their secretaries of state with continuity in foreign policy and insights to a rich diplomatic tradition. His functions included counseling on substantive problems of diplomacy and international law, overseeing the mechanics of the State Department, and drafting and censoring diplomatic messages. As second assistant of state, he epitomized the public administrator, executing rather than originating policies and basing his conservative policy recommendations on historical precedent and the political attitudes of those he served. 66 notes. 1870-1924

Adler, Cyrus

69. Coolick, Gayle Meyer. "The Public Career of Cyrus Adler." Georgia State U. 1981. 271 pp. *DAI 1982 42(8): 3717-3718-A.* 8202096 1890's-1941

Adler, Samuel

70. Greenberg, Gershon. THE DIMENSIONS OF SAMUEL ADLER'S RELIGIOUS VIEW OF THE WORLD. *Hebrew Union Coll. Ann. 1975 46: 377-412.* Samuel Adler (1809-91) was a German-born reform-rabbi who spent the last 35 years of his life as rabbi of Temple Emanuel of New York. For him Judaism is a significant level in the growth of moral consciousness where morality is amplified into an ontological realm, identical to the idealized world of creation. *Wissenschaft* becomes the God-given methodology for achieving insights into the moral possibilities of all literature and history. 100 notes. ca 1829-91

Adler, Selig

71. Adler, Joseph G. SELIG ADLER (1909-1984). *American Jewish History 1985 74(4): 404-405.* Presents a tribute to the academic career of Selig Adler, professor of American History at the State University of New York, Buffalo, who lectured frequently on Judaism and modern Zionism, and who died in 1984. 1930-84

72. —. RECOLLECTIONS AND REMINISCENCES. Plesur, Milton, ed. *An American Historian: Essays to Honor Selig Adler* (Buffalo: State U. of N.Y., 1980): 3-33.

Plesur, Milton. SELIG ADLER: AN APPRECIATION, pp. 3-21.

Ketter, Robert L. SELIG ADLER AND THE UNIVERSITY, p. 22.

Pratt, Julius W. A LETTER TO SELIG ADLER, pp. 23-25.

Horton, John T. "THE GOOD OF THE ORDER," pp. 26-30.

Yearley, Clifton K. A LETTER TO SELIG ADLER, p. 31.

Loubere, Leo. A BRIEF RECOLLECTION, p. 32.

Adler, Joseph F. A TRIBUTE TO DAD, p. 33.

Tributes to and reminiscences of writer, scholar, and professor Selig Adler (b. 1909) on his retirement from the State University of New York in 1980. 1920's-80

Affleck, Isaac Dunbar

73. Wooster, Ralph A. WITH THE CONFEDERATE CAVALRY IN THE WEST: THE CIVIL WAR EXPERIENCES OF ISAAC DUNBAR AFFLECK. *Southwestern Hist. Q. 1979 83(1): 1-28.* Isaac Dunbar Affleck, son of Texas planter Thomas Affleck, served with the Confederate Eighth Texas Cavalry Regiment in Kentucky, Louisiana, and Arkansas. His letters home, 1861-1865, show the Civil War through a private's eyes. He is more concerned with personal comfort than with the enemy and constantly demands supplies from home. He has a low opinion of officers, is confident of Confederate superiority, and grows in character through his years of service. Based on the Affleck papers and other primary sources; 13 illus., 60 notes. 1861-65

Agassiz, Louis

74. Bell, Ian F. A. DIVINE PATTERNS: LOUIS AGASSIZ AND AMERICAN MEN OF LETTERS. SOME PRELIMINARY EXPLORATIONS. *J. of Am. Studies [Great Britain] 1976 10(3): 349-381.* Discusses Louis Agassiz (1807-1873) and his contributions to the history of ideas. Agassiz's ideas were discussed widely in the 19th century and he was regarded as an outstanding thinker. In the 20th century, commentators on the history of ideas have mostly ignored him. However, a few—notably Ezra Pound (1885-1972)—attempted to revive Agassiz's reputation. Based on writings by and about Agassiz; 38 notes. 19c-20c

Agee, James

75. Newton, Scott. DAVID MCDOWELL ON JAMES AGEE. *Western Humanities Rev. 1980 34(2): 117-130.* Discusses the friendship between publisher David McDowell and author James Agee from 1936 until Agee's death in 1955, and reproduces McDowell's account of that friendship and of Agee's work. 1936-55

Ager, Waldemar Theodore

76. Kilde, Clarence. DARK DECADE: THE DECLINING YEARS OF WALDEMAR AGER. *Norwegian-American Studies 1979 28: 157-191.* Waldemar Theodore Ager (1868-1941) was a Norwegian immigrant steadfastly committed to three goals: total abstinence from alcohol, retention of the Norwegian language and culture by Norwegian Americans, and the creation of a genre of literature by and about Norwegian Americans in their immigrant experience. These three ideals ruled his life. For 38 years he edited *Reform,* a Norwegian-language temperance newspaper published in Eau Claire, Wisconsin. His ideals were also expressed in several novels, all written in Norwegian and all about the immigrant experience. Ager's last decade moved from twilight to darkness: depression eroded *Reform*'s subscriber list, Prohibition was repealed, and Norwegian-Americans increasingly used English. Waldemar Ager Papers, Norwegian-American Historical Association, Northfield, Minnesota; 39 notes. 1893-1941

Aggrey, James E. K.

77. Yancey, Dorothy Cowser. PROFESSOR JAMES EMMAN KWEGYIR AGGREY'S PERSONALITY. *Negro Hist. Bull. 1977 40(4): 722-724.* Discusses the career and thought of black educator James E. K. Aggrey (1875-1927), who was born on the Gold Coast, educated at missionary schools and at Livingstone College, North Carolina, and Columbia University. Aggrey taught at Cape Coast, at Livingstone College, and finally at Prince of Wales College in Achimoto where he influenced Kwame Nkrumah. He served for a time as pastor of two rural churches in the South where he fostered agricultural and community organizations. In 1919, the Phelps-Stokes Commission sent him to Africa to survey educational work. A follower of Booker T. Washington's philosophy, he at the same time stressed the values of African culture and the Africanization of education on that continent. Based on secondary material; 22 notes. 1898-1927

Aguirre, José Antonio

78. Haggland, Mary H. DON JOSE ANTONIO AGUIRRE: SPANISH MERCHANT AND RANCHERO. *J. of San Diego Hist. 1983 29(1): 54-68.* Describes the career as an importer, merchant, and landowner of José Antonio Aguirre, a prominent figure in San Diego and Santa Barbara, California. 1833-60

Aguirre, Martin

79. Hoffman, Abraham. THE CONTROVERSIAL CAREER OF MARTIN AGUIRRE: THE RISE AND FALL OF A CHICANO LAWMAN. *California History 1984 63(4): 293-304, 339-341.* Traces the law enforcement career of Martin Aguirre. A native Californio, Aguirre acquired early fame when he rescued 19 people from the Los Angeles River in a January 1886 rainstorm. He served as sheriff of Los Angeles County, 1888-90, losing a reelection bid in a hotly contested election. His loyalty to the Republican Party won him an appointment as warden of San Quentin Prison in 1899, but his term was marred by accusations of political favoritism and graft. Thereafter he served as a deputy sheriff and bailiff in Los Angeles County until his death in 1929. Illus., 5 photos, 48 notes. 1880's-1929

Aiken, George D.

80. Sanford, Dudley Gregory. YOU CAN'T GET THERE FROM HERE: THE PRESIDENTIAL BOOMLET FOR GOVERNOR GEORGE D. AIKEN, 1937-1939. *Vermont Hist. 1981 49(4): 197-208.* Six years after the Putney nurseryman entered politics, Aiken won national attention as a Republican who could be elected governor in the 1936 Democratic landslide. Aiken's "new Republicanism," formulated in *Speaking from Vermont* (1939), sought to win the votes of youth, labor, and small business by accepting more federal welfare without deficit spending and by fostering local "cooperation." The 1936 New England flood dramatized the need for regional flood control, and Aiken became the New England spokesman for one-purpose dams, leaving power and other rights to the states and private business. He campaigned outside Vermont, with the aid of Leo Casey, retiring publicity director of the Republican National Committee, less to win the 1940 presidential nomination than to rejuvenate the Republican Party as a bulwark against the New Deal flood control program. Based mainly on the Aiken Papers, University of Vermont; 30 notes. 1937-39

Aiken, Howard Hathaway

81. Welch, Gregory W. HOWARD HATHAWAY AIKEN: THE LIFE OF A COMPUTER PIONEER. *Computer Museum Report 1985 (12): 3-11.* Chronicles the life of Harvard physicist Howard Hathaway Aiken, whose influential 1937 paper "Proposed Automatic Calculating Machine" led to his collaboration with IBM from 1937 to 1944 in the construction of the first electromechanical digital computer, the Mark I. 1920's-73

Ailey, Alvin

82. Mazo, Joseph H. AILEY AND COMPANY. *Horizon 1984 27(6): 18-24.* Describes the 25-year history of the Alvin Ailey Dance Theatre, a black modern-dance company based in New York City's Harlem, and the life of its founder, Alvin Ailey. 1960-85

Airola, Manuel

83. Burrows, Jack. THE GREATEST BRONC BUSTER WHO EVER LIVED. *Am. West 1983 20(3): 54-58.* Manuel Airola (1888-1925) was "the archetypal cowboy whose Homeric exploits on bucking broncs" is a legend still remembered in the hill country of northern California. "Manny" or "Mandy" defied danger, sustained repeated broken bones and injuries, won numerous prizes, and earned the awe and respect of rodeo audiences. 5 illus. 1910's-25

Aitken, Robert

84. Spawn, William. EXTRA-GILT BINDINGS OF ROBERT AITKEN, 1787-88. *Pro. of the Am. Antiquarian Soc. 1983 93(2): 415-417.* Examines the Chinoiserie-style gilt bookbindings on an edition of Hugh Blair's *Lectures on Rhetoric and Belles Lettres,* originally owned by Charles Thomson, secretary of the Continental Congress. The career of Robert Aitken, the publisher, is briefly surveyed. 2 illus. 1784-88

Aitken, Roger

85. Dunlop, A. C. A HOUSE IS NOT A HOME—REV. ROGER AITKEN AND THE STRUGGLE FOR A LUNENBURG RECTORY. *Collections of the Royal Nova Scotia Hist. Soc. [Canada] 1982 41: 47-63.* Reverend Roger Aitken spent the last years of his life as an Episcopal clergyman in Lunenburg, one of eight missions in Nova Scotia sponsored by the Society for the Propagation of the Gospel in Foreign Parts. His sojourn as rector of St. John's Anglican Church, Lunenburg, was one of the most tumultous in the history of the congregation, with the congregation splitting over the issue of the rectory in the Wentzell House. Aitken showed "determination and dedication" not only in the rectory issue, but in his very active involvement in such community affairs as schools and road-building. 69 notes. 1814-25

Akroff, George

86. Ursenbach, Charles. THE GREAT CROWSNEST PASS TRAIN HOLDUP. *Alberta Hist. [Canada] 1984 32(2): 1-8.* Three men from Great Falls, Montana, George Akroff, Tom Bassoff, and Alex Areloff (or Auloff), held up a train at Crowsnest Pass, Alberta, 7 August 1920. Five days later a gun battle resulted in the death of Areloff while Akroff and Bassoff, though wounded, escaped. Two policemen were also killed. An extensive manhunt ensued that on 11 August resulted in the arrest of Bassoff, then 31 years of age. He received a two-day trial in October, and death by hanging on 22 December 1920. Akroff was eventually tracked down in Portland, Washington, and was returned to Canada where he died after serving only three years of his seven-year prison sentence. 22 notes, 4 photos. 1920-24

Albright, Jacob

87. Warman, John B. FRANCIS ASBURY AND JACOB ALBRIGHT. *Methodist Hist. 1978 16(2): 75-81.* Compares Francis Asbury (1745-1816), Bishop of the Methodist Episcopal Church, and Jacob Albright (1759-1808), founder of the Evangelical Association, and their work in the early years of their respective churches in America. 8 notes. 1765-1816

Alcott, Amos Bronson

88. Charles, Don C. BRONSON ALCOTT: EDUCATIONAL-CHILD PSYCHOLOGIST. *Vitae Scholasticae 1984 4[i.e., 3](2): 421-432.* Explores Bronson Alcott's impact on psychological and educational thinking about children. Alcott has been passed over in the history of education. He was an influential educator whose pedagogical theories grew out of his firm convictions about the nature of the child and the importance of childhood. Alcott's studies later influenced the works of G. S. Hall, John Dewey, and Jean Piaget. In Boston, Alcott opened the Temple School, an "infant school" that exercised his ideas on the importance of activity and children's built-in capability to understand. The school closed due to Alcott's teaching of unorthodox views of Christianity. 42 notes. 1799-1888

89. Dahlstrand, Frederick Charles. "Amos Bronson Alcott: An Intellectual Biography." U. of Kansas 1977. 609 pp. *DAI 1978 38(12): 7509-7510-A.* 19c

90. Ledbetter, Patsy S. and Ledbetter, Billy. THE AGITATOR AND THE INTELLECTUALS: WILLIAM LLOYD GARRISON AND THE NEW ENGLAND TRANSCENDENTALISTS. *Mid-America 1980 62(3): 173-183.* 1830-60

For abstract see ***Garrison, William Lloyd***

Alcott, Louisa May

91. Crompton, Margaret. *LITTLE WOMEN:* THE MAKING OF A CLASSIC. *Contemporary Rev. [Great Britain] 1971 218(1261): 99-104.* Describes the family background of Louisa May Alcott (1832-88) and how she came to write *Little Women* in 1868. 1832-88

92. Halttunen, Karen. THE DOMESTIC DRAMA OF LOUISA MAY ALCOTT. *Feminist Studies 1984 10(2): 233-254.* The life and fiction of Louisa May Alcott are explored in the context of the influence of Bronson Alcott, Louisa's father, and changing Victorian society. Bronson Alcott, a transcendentalist, introduced theater to his young daughters in an effort to teach them purity of mind and body, and to establish a harmonious family and domestic bliss. Louisa May Alcott used theater to represent her personal struggle, as evidenced in the plays presented in *Little Women,* in which the March girls act out *Pilgrim's Progress* and "The Witch's Curse." In a larger context, Alcott's "domestic dramas" provide a mechanism by which the American Victorian family is preserved against the forces of Jacksonian individualism. Paper presented at the National Women's Studies Association Conference, Bloomington, Indiana, May 1980; secondary sources. 1832-88

93. Stern, Madeleine B. LOUISA M. ALCOTT IN PERIODICALS. *Studies in the Am. Renaissance 1977: 369-386.* A great deal of the literary work of Louisa M. Alcott (1832-88) lies neglected in magazines, work which is significant for bibliographers, biographers, and literary historians. A judicious use of this material would reveal many interesting aspects of Alcott's personality, writing styles, and business ability which have previously gone unnoticed. Based on magazine stories by Alcott; 60 notes, appendix. 1851-87

94. Stern, Madeleine B. LOUISA ALCOTT'S FEMINIST LETTERS. *Studies in the Am. Renaissance 1978: 429-452.* Louisa May Alcott (1833-88) engaged in a variety of reform movements from abolitionism to temperance, but woman

suffrage was her primary concern. In her correspondence, we can perceive her forceful commitment to feminism. Her activity was neither strident nor aggressive but rather "reflected the traditional values of her family.... Louisa Alcott's feminism of a human being impatient with indifference, apathy, and intolerance." Based on the writings and correspondence of Louisa May Alcott; 41 notes. 1853-85

95. Van Buren, Jane. LOUISA MAY ALCOTT: A STUDY IN PERSONA AND IDEALIZATION. *Psychohistory Rev. 1981 9(4): 282-299.* Psychoanalysis offers insights into the life and career of Louisa May Alcott. Alcott symbolizes the role strain typified in the lives of many 19th-century American women. Offers explanation of Alcott's conflicts based on penis envy and narcissism. Examines the Mary/Eve symbol and its importance for understanding conflicts in the life of Alcott. Alcott's numerous physical illnesses are seen as psychosomatic in origin. Alcott's life was one of torment and confusion. 46 notes. 1832-85

Alcott, William

96. Van Buren, Martin Cornelius. "The Indispensable God of Health: A Study of Republican Hygiene and the Ideology of William Alcott." U. of California, Los Angeles 1977. 410 pp. *DAI 1977 38(5): 3003-A.* 1829-60

Alderman, Alonza Elvis "Tony"

97. Green, Archie. GRAPHICS NUMBER 64: FAREWELL TONY. *JEMF Q. 1983 19(72): 231-240.* Presents anecdotes from the life of Alonza Elvis "Tony" Alderman, a member of an early country-western music band, the Hill Billies, and reprints some illustrations of the band. 1920's-70's

Aldington, Richard

98. Fraser, Keath. THE CANONIZATION OF T. S. ELIOT. *U. of Windsor Rev. [Canada] 1977 13(1): 5-17.* 1914-50's

For abstract see ***Eliot, T. S.***

Aldrich, Bess Streeter

99. Keating, William Patrick. "Fulfilled Visions: The Life and Work of Bess Streeter Aldrich." Indiana U. of Pennsylvania 1985. 224 pp. *DAI 1985 46(4): 982-983-A.* DA8513091 1900's-54

Aleshire, Mary

100. Lady, Claudia Lynn. FIVE TRI-STATE WOMEN DURING THE CIVIL WAR. *West Virginia Hist. 1982 43(3): 189-226, (4): 303-321.* Part 1. DAY TO DAY LIFE. Examines the lives of five women—Frances Dallam Peter, Mary Wilson Gilchrist, Mary Aleshire, Henrietta Fitzhugh Barr, and Eugenia Miller Thackston—who lived in the border area of West Virginia, Kentucky, and Ohio, and discussed the Civil War in their letters and diaries. Covers personal relationships, education, daily life, and social activities during the Civil War. Part 2. VIEWS ON THE WAR. Discusses their differing feelings about the military and political aspects of the Civil War. Based on published diaries and papers and other primary and secondary sources; 8 illus., 247 notes. 1859-65

Alexander, Archie Alphonso

101. Smith, Raymond A., Jr. "HE OPENED HOLES LIKE MOUNTAIN TUNNELS." *Palimpsest 1985 66(3): 87-92, 97-100.* Discusses the college football career of Archie Alphonso Alexander and the context in which he became the first black player at the State University of Iowa. 1909-11

102. Wynes, Charles E. "ALEXANDER THE GREAT," BRIDGE BUILDER. *Palimpsest 1985 66(3): 78-86.* Presents a biography of Archie Alphonso Alexander, the first black football player at the State University of Iowa and owner of a successful civil engineering company. 1888-1958

Alexander, Charles

103. Corning, Howard M. ALL THE WORDS ON THE PAGES.

I: H. L. DAVIS. *Oregon Hist. Q. 1972 73(4): 293-331.* Discusses the literary activities and achievements of Harold Lenoir Davis (1894-1960). Davis won the Levinson Award in *Poetry* in 1919. He also wrote extensively in prose, especially for the *American Mercury.* His articles described life in the Oregon range country. Provides much autobiographical material and observations regarding other literati of the time. Based largely on personal reminiscence and first-hand experience; 10 photos.

II: CHARLES ALEXANDER: YOUTH OF THE OREGON MOOD. *Oregon Hist. Q. 1973 74(1): 34-70.* Discusses the fiction of Charles Alexander (1897-1962) of Albany, focusing on his description of life in the Willamette Valley. The author met Charles Alexander, editor of a Sunday section of the *Albany Democrat* that featured poetry and prose by Oregon writers. Sketches Alexander's literary career, way of life, and outdoor interests. Discusses other writers of the period.

III: A. R. WETJEN: BRITISH SEAMAN IN THE WESTERN SUNRISE. *Oregon Hist. Q. 1973 74(2): 145-178.* Discusses the literature of British author Albert Richard Wetjen (1900-48), focusing on his stories of Oregon and the sea. He had a meteoric career after publishing his first sea adventure in 1922. The author discusses his relationships with various writers including Carl Sandburg, who resided in Salem, Albany, and Portland. 8 photos.

IV: THE PROSE AND THE POETRY OF IT. *Oregon Hist. Q. 1973 74(3): 244-267.* Evaluates the work of Harold Davis, Charles Alexander, and Albert Richard Wetjen. Indicates their major literary achievements. All were in some sense poets, though their poetry was expressed in their prose. All were largely self-educated; only Davis graduated from high school. ca 1915-70

Alexander, David George

104. Neary, Peter. DAVID GEORGE ALEXANDER. *J. of Can. Studies [Canada] 1980 15(2): 128.* David George Alexander, one of Canada's foremost economic historians, died on 25 July 1980. He had taught at the Memorial University of Newfoundland since 1960 and had written *Retailing in England during the Industrial Revolution* (1970) and *The Decay of Trade: An Economic History of the Newfoundland Saltfish Trade, 1935-1965* (1977). 1939-80

Alexander, E. Porter

105. Hoover, John E. THE CSRA AND EARLY SIGNAL CORPS HISTORY. *Richmond County History 1984 16(2): 5-10.* Traces the career of E. Porter Alexander, who assisted in the founding of the US Army's Signal Corps in 1860, and who later became the first signal officer in the Confederate Army. 1856-65

Alexander, Henry

106. Karlstrom, Paul J. THE SHORT, HARD, AND TRAGIC LIFE OF HENRY ALEXANDER. *Smithsonian 1982 12(12): 108-117.* The artist committed suicide in 1894 at the age of 35; now his enigmatic realistic paintings are being rediscovered by critics and historians; his unhappy life reflects the problem of the late 19th-century American artist trained in Europe, who returned with great expectations that his country was not prepared to fulfill, leading to his isolation and individuality. 1880-94

Alexander, John Hanks

107. Gatewood, Willard B., Jr. JOHN HANKS ALEXANDER OF ARKANSAS: SECOND BLACK GRADUATE OF WEST POINT. *Arkansas Hist. Q. 1982 41(2): 103-128.* Discusses the family background and career of John Hanks Alexander, who graduated from West Point in 1887 and served as a lieutenant with the 9th Cavalry. Based on the Alexander Papers, other correspondence, and newspapers; photo, 91 notes. 1840's-94

Alexander, John White

108. Leff, Sandra. MASTER OF SENSUOUS LINE. *American Heritage 1985 36(6): 82-89.* John White Alexander became one of America's preeminent painters of the early 20th century. After a short career as an office boy at *Harper's Weekly,* he studied art in Europe in 1877. Four years later he returned to New York and his paintings exhibited the influence of Munich realism. In Paris during 1890-1901, he began to develop his own distinctive style that emphasized mood and emotion, color and line. His last 14 years were spent in New York. 8 illus. 1877-1915

Alexander, Moses

109. Weyne, Arthur. THE FIRST JEWISH GOVERNOR: MOSES ALEXANDER OF IDAHO. *Western States Jewish Hist. Q. 1976 9(1): 21-42.* Moses Alexander (1853-1932), a Bavarian immigrant to the United States, first entered politics in Chillicothe, Missouri, where he was elected as city councilman and mayor. Stagnant business conditions prompted him to move his dry goods business to Boise, Idaho. After two terms as Boise's mayor, the Democratic Party persuaded him to run for governor in 1914. As a two-term governor (1915-18) Alexander's chief accomplishment was to cut back expenditures. He was also credited with passage of a prohibition law, enactment of a workman's compensation act, creation of a state highway system, and construction of the Arrowrock Dam and the Dalles-Celilo Canal. Critics charged that he used his veto power too frequently against the legislature. After his second term of office Alexander became an informal elder statesman while remaining active in his merchandizing business. Based on family records and published material; 3 photos, 27 notes. 1914-32

Alexander, Sydenham B.

110. Steelman, Lala Carr. THE ROLE OF ELIAS CARR IN THE NORTH CAROLINA FARMERS' ALLIANCE. *North Carolina Hist. Rev. 1980 57(2): 133-158.* 1887-95
For abstract see ***Carr, Elias***

Alexander, Walter G.

111. Dickerson, Dennis C. WALTER G. ALEXANDER: A PHYSICIAN IN CIVIL RIGHTS AND PUBLIC SERVICE. *New Jersey History 1983 101(3-4): 36-59.* Walter G. Alexander graduated from Lincoln University and received his medical training at the Boston College of Physicians and Surgeons. He settled in Orange, New Jersey, where he remained for the rest of his professional career. Active as a medical reformer and in politics, Alexander's social activism was generally undertaken in an effort to better the lives of black New Jerseyans. He was elected to the state legislature as a Republican in 1920, but changed his allegiance to the Democrats 10 years later. Alexander advocated integration but was still able to work within a segregated society for the benefit of blacks. Based on interviews, newspaper stories, New Jersey Assembly documents, and secondary sources; 3 illus., 57 notes. 1900's-53

Alger, Horatio

112. Blackbeard, Bill. NOVELS THAT BOYS OF A CENTURY AGO COULDN'T PUT DOWN. *Smithsonian 1977 8(8): 122-136.* Describes the life, work, and myth of Horatio Alger (1832-99) from his early writing, concentrating on his first real commercial success, *Ragged Dick* (1867), a series based on the life of New York street boys, to the scores of books published over the rest of the 19th century. Virtually all of Alger's heroes succeeded through the "wildest of coincidences or lucky happenstances," but the reader's Victorian parents made the "one-to-one connection between hard work, study, and perseverance on the one hand, and certain rise to success on the other," creating the myth which may survive as "long as the nation itself," while the books are scarcely remembered. 12 illus. 1860's-90's

113. Scharnhorst, Gary. "Good Fortune in America: The Life and Works of Horatio Alger, Jr. and the Fate of the Alger Hero from the Civil War to World War II." Purdue U. 1978. 389 pp. *DAI 1978 39(5): 2911-A.* 1860-1947

Algren, Nelson

114. Raymer, John D. NELSON ALGREN AND SIMONE DE BEAUVOIR: THE END OF THEIR AFFAIR AT MILLER, INDIANA. *Old Northwest 1979-80 5(4): 401-407.* The love affair between Nelson Algren and Simone de Beauvoir, during which he introduced her to postwar life in America's Midwest, including Chicago's skid row, lasted from 1947 to 1951 and terminated in Miller, Indiana. Beauvoir recreated the affair in three of her later works—*The Mandarin, America Day by Day,* and "American Rendezvous"—causing Algren to retaliate rather unfairly in a 1965 *Harper's* review. 8 notes. 1947-65

Allaire, Peter

115. Lopez, Claude-Anne. THE MAN WHO FRIGHTENED FRANKLIN. *Pennsylvania Mag. of Hist. and Biog. 1982 106(4): 515-526.* Traces the career of Peter Allaire, an American-born double agent living in England and France. Benjamin Franklin had him imprisoned, suspecting that the

spy had poisoned his Madeira. Based on the Franklin and Bache papers, American Philosophical Society; published sources, and secondary works; 24 notes. 1774-91

Allee, Warder Clyde

116. Banks, Edwin M. WARDER CLYDE ALLEE AND THE CHICAGO SCHOOL OF ANIMAL BEHAVIOR. *Journal of the History of the Behavioral Sciences 1985 21(4): 345-353.* Warder Clyde Allee was a pioneer American scientist in the fields of ecology and animal behavior. Discusses his contributions to the development of a general animal sociology, with particular attention to his concept of animal cooperation and his research in the area of dominance hierarchies. 1910's-55

Allen, Bob

117. Thévenet, André. LE VERITABLE EXPLOIT DU SIECLE: IL A SAUTE SANS PARACHUTE [The real feat of the century: he jumped without a parachute]. *Historama [France] 1984 (1): 54-56.* 1965
*For abstract see **Pack, Rod***

Allen, Carey H.

118. Daniel, Harry. CAREY H. ALLEN. *Filson Club Hist. Q. 1983 57(3): 315-318.* Relates the sparse details of the brief ministry of Carey H. Allen. Allen was ordained as Presbyterian minister in 1790. A very effective public speaker, he proved to be a popular preacher in rural Virginia and Kentucky. He died in 1795. 1767-95

Allen, Eric W.

119. Gilbert, David A. ERIC W. ALLEN: JOURNALISM EDUCATOR AND HISTORIAN. *Journalism Hist. 1975 2(2): 50-53.* An appreciation of the life and work of Eric W. Allen (1879-1944), especially his courage and originality as a journalist and as a teacher when he was Dean of the Oregon School of Journalism. 1900-44

Allen, Ethan

120. Linscott, Elizabeth. ETHAN ALLEN: SOLDIER, ORATOR, AUTHOR. *New-England Galaxy 1977 19(2): 49-56.* Describes the roles played by Ethan Allen in the settlement of Vermont, in its development as an independent republic, and in the American Revolution. Highlights his capture of Fort Ticonderoga, his capture by the British at Montreal, and his captivity in England. Illus. 1738-89

121. McWilliams, John. THE FACES OF ETHAN ALLEN: 1760-1860. *New England Q. 1976 49(2): 257-282.* Sketches Allen's life (1738-89) and major writings, analyses the work of the five antebellum historians who wrote of Allen, and examines Allen's image in the romantic literature of the era, concluding that the public's view of the highly controversial Allen became by the Civil War that of a typical American hero and had little touch with reality. Based on secondary works; 22 notes. 1760-1860

122. Sabine, David B. ETHAN ALLEN AND THE GREEN MOUNTAIN BOYS. *Am. Hist. Illus. 1977 11(9): 8-15.* Gives an account of the life of Ethan Allen and the establishment of the Green Mountain Boys, and their part in the American Revolution, especially the capture of Fort Ticonderoga in 1775. 1775-77

Allen, Florence Ellinwood

123. Cook, Beverly B. THE FIRST WOMAN CANDIDATE FOR THE SUPREME COURT—FLORENCE E. ALLEN. *Supreme Court Hist. Soc. Y. 1981: 19-35.* Discusses the legal career of Florence Ellinwood Allen from 1914, when she received her law degree, to her death in 1966. During her career, Allen served most importantly as a member of the Ohio Supreme Court and as judge of the US Court of Appeals for the 6th Circuit. In the 1930's and 1940's, under Roosevelt and Truman, she was the first woman candidate for the US Supreme Court, largely due to the impetus supplied by the women's suffrage and reform movements. Explains the role of public opinion, politics, and the wishes of the sitting justices in her failure to be nominated. Relies on the papers of Allen, Roosevelt, and Truman, and Gallup polls; 4 photos, 122 notes. 1914-40's

Allen, Fred

124. Havig, Alan. FRED ALLEN AND HOLLYWOOD. *J. of Popular Film and Television 1979 7(3): 273-291.* Discusses Fred Allen's acting career in Hollywood as an example of the complements and competition between radio and films, 1920's-50's. 1920's-50's

Allen, Macon B.

125. Contee, Clarence G. MACON B. ALLEN: "FIRST" BLACK IN THE LEGAL PROFESSION. *Crisis 1976 83(2): 67-69.* Macon B. Allen is believed to have been the first black lawyer in the United States. Born in 1816 in Indiana as a non-slave, he studied law in Maine under an antislavery leader, Samuel Fessenden. He was passed into the Maine bar in 1844, and was later admitted to the Massachusetts bar. After the Civil War Allen moved to Charleston, South Carolina, where he became a judge. He died in 1894. 1844-94

Allen, Nathaniel Topliff

126. Cadwallader, Lynn J. "Nathaniel Topliff Allen, 1823-72, A Case Study in the Professionalization of Nineteenth Century Teaching." U. of Massachusetts 1983. 191 pp. *DAI 1983 44(1): 88-A.* DA8310270 1842-72

Allen, Thomas

127. Potter, Gail M. PITTSFIELD'S FIGHTING PARSON: THOMAS ALLEN. *New-England Galaxy 1976 18(1): 33-38.* Rev. Thomas Allen was chairman of the Pittsfield, Massachusetts, Committe of Correspondence from 1774 to 1777, and chaplain to three Berkshire regiments. He participated in the battle of Bennington, Vermont. Illus. 1774-77

Allen, Viola

128. Plotnicki, Rita Mary. "The Evolution of a Star: The Career of Viola Allen, 1882-1918." City U. of New York 1979. 249 pp. *DAI 1979 39(12): 7056-A.* 1882-1918

Allen, William G.

129. Blackett, R. J. M. WILLIAM G. ALLEN: THE FORGOTTEN PROFESSOR. *Civil War Hist. 1980 26(1): 39-52.* Discusses William G. Allen, who was an abolitionist and defender of human rights. In ca. 1838, his education was sponsored by Gerrit Smith in Oneida (New York) Institute. As a Boston law clerk in 1847, he opposed colonization by advocating national amalgamation. First black-American professor at a white college, New York Central College at McGrawville, he married a white student, Mary King, in

1853. Fleeing to Great Britain, Allen never won the usual black popularity; his literary-philosophical approach to lecturing and his opening the first black-led school there left him strangely destitute. The Allens remained frustrated exiles. Based on personal and society papers and secondary sources; 44 notes. 1820-78

Alline, Henry

130. Scott, Jamie S. "TRAVELS OF MY SOUL": HENRY ALLINE'S AUTOBIOGRAPHY. *J. of Can. Studies [Canada] 1983 18(2): 70-90. The Life and Journal of the Rev. Mr. Henry Alline* expresses Alline's personal encounter with the sacred. The Nova Scotian's work is both a historical record and a symbolic expression of his efforts to transform alienation and despair into confidence and hope. Based on *The Life and Journal of the Rev. Mr. Henry Alline;* 66 notes. 1776-84

Allison, Susan Moir

131. Shields, Carol. THREE CANADIAN WOMEN: FICTION OR AUTOBIOGRAPHY. *Atlantis [Canada] 1978 4(1): 49-54.* Examines the writing of Susanna Moodie, Jane Ellice, and Susan Moir Allison, who incorporated fiction and autobiography in books about their Canadian experiences during the 19th century. 19c

Allport, Floyd H.

132. Post, David L. FLOYD H. ALLPORT AND THE LAUNCHING OF MODERN SOCIAL PSYCHOLOGY. *J. of the Hist. of the Behavioral Sci. 1980 16(4): 369-376.* Floyd H. Allport's contributions to the development of modern experimental social psychology are discussed. His work is viewed both as a protest against "group mind" and "instinct" theories popular in the early years of the 20th century and as an outgrowth of specific positive influences at Harvard during his graduate training. Allport's social psychology brought theoretical rigor and experimental precision to an area that had been a loose amalgamation of sociology, instinct psychology, and evolutionary theory. Its impact on contemporary developments in the field has been decisive. [Covers ca. 1915-39]. 1915-39

Allred, James V.

133. Atkinson, William Eugene. "James V. Allred: A Political Biography, 1899-1935." Texas Christian U. 1978. 397 pp. *DAI 1978 39(5): 3098-A.* 1899-1935

Allston, Washington

134. Ratcliff, Carter. ALLSTON AND THE HISTORICAL LANDSCAPE. *Art in Am. 1980 68(8): 96-104.* Washington Allston (1780-1843) sought to incorporate landscape painting with historical themes under the guise of Romanticism, but failed, so he is regarded as a contributor to the subsequent inwardness and reductivism of modernism; 1810's-43. ca 1810-43

135. Strazdes, Diana J. "Washington Allston's Early Career, 1796-1811." Yale U. 1982. 292 pp. *DAI 1982 43(5): 1329-A.* DA8222327 1796-1811

136. Wolf, Bryan J. WASHINGTON ALLSTON AND THE AESTHETICS OF PARODY. *Georgia Rev. 1980 34(2): 333-356.* Washington Allston (1779-1843), America's first major Romantic painter, used artistic parody as a means for transcending the boundaries of prevailing aesthetic theory. Allston's style in "Portrait of Samuel Williams" is contrasted with techniques used by Henri Magritte in "The Field Glass" and by Caspar David Friedrich in "Woman at the Window." 4 photos, 20 notes. ca 1800-43

Alrich, John (family)

137. Krick, Robert I. THE ALRICHES OF SPOTSYLVANIA. *Lincoln Herald 1980 82(1): 311-318.* Discusses the Alrich family of Spotsylvania County, Virginia, and focuses on their participation in the Civil War, beginning with John Alrich's enrollment in Company E of the Ninth Virginia Cavalry; covers 1830-1979. 1830-1979

Alston, Mary Niven

138. Chitty, Arthur Ben. WOMEN AND BLACK EDUCATION: THREE PROFILES. *Hist. Mag. of the Protestant Episcopal Church 1983 52(2): 153-165.* Brief vignettes of three women who made significant contributions to black higher education in the Protestant Episcopal Church. Anna Haywood Cooper (ca. 1858-1965) was only the fourth Negro woman to earn a doctorate from the Sorbonne—and at the age of 65. She became second president of Frelinghuysen University in Raleigh, North Carolina. While her forte was adult education, she never neglected the social and educational needs of children and youth. Isabella Gibson Robertson (1892-1976) was a financially comfortable white woman who was vitally concerned with supporting Saint Augustine College in Raleigh, North Carolina, a school she never saw but to which she contributed large sums. Mary Niven Alston (1918-81) was another white Episcopal woman who befriended black Episcopal schools. In her will she left $50,000 to Vorhees College in Denmark, South Carolina, a school she had never visited, but one of the numerous institutions she assisted in higher education. 3 photos. 1875-1981

Alter, J. Cecil

139. Murphy, Miriam B. J. CECIL ALTER, FOUNDING EDITOR OF *UTAH HISTORICAL QUARTERLY. Utah Hist. Q. 1978 46(1): 37-44.* J. Cecil Alter (1879-1964), founding editor of the *Utah Historical Quarterly,* is credited with the journal's success during its formative years. As editor from 1927-45, his involvement in the total publication process was remarkable. He wrote material himself, revised and polished contributions of others, corresponded with authors, annotated and wrote introductions for primary materials, consulted printers, and promoted and sold the final product. Scientist, historian, writer, inventor, administrator, and conservationist, his standard of excellence and intelligence gave the journal an invaluable legacy. Primary and secondary sources; illus., 19 notes. 1927-45

Alther, Lisa

140. Feinberg, Andrew. VERMONT'S AMBIVALENT SOUTHERNER. *Horizon 1981 24(5): 56-60.* Brief introductory biography of novelist Lisa Alther, born in Kingsport, Tennessee, who now lives in Hinesburg, Vermont, focusing on the success of her first novel, *Kinflicks* (1976), and discusses her second novel, *Original Sins* (1981), about the transition of the South in the past 25 years. 1950's-81

Ames, Edward Scribner

141. Pope, Richard M. EDWARD SCRIBNER AMES AND THE AMERICAN DEMOCRATIC FAITH. *Encounter 1978 39(4): 395-404.* Outlines the work of Edward Scribner Ames (1870-1958), as it applies to the evolution of liberalism among the Disciples of Christ, during the early 20th century. 1900's-30's

Ames, Mary Clemmer

142. Beasley, Maurine. MARY CLEMMER AMES: A VICTORIAN WOMAN JOURNALIST. *Hayes Hist. J. 1978 2(1): 57-63.* Mary Clemmer Ames (1831-84) gained a national reputation as a Washington correspondent through her column, "A Woman's Letter From Washington," in the New York *Independent* (1866-84). Her career illustrated how a woman could manipulate the cultural framework of the Victorian period, and achieve success without sacrificing her femininity. Though promoting the Victorian ideology that women possessed purer morals than men, Ames did not lead the kind of life her column advocated; she was divorced and self-sufficient. It was Ames' womanly duty, through her column, to campaign for an elevation of public life. Primary and secondary sources; 4 illus., 38 notes. 1866-84

Ames, Nathaniel

143. Stowell, Marion Barber. THE INFLUENCE OF NATHANIEL AMES ON THE LITERARY TASTE OF HIS TIME. *Early Am. Lit. 1983 18(2): 127-145.* Nathaniel Ames, who published the almanac *Astronomical Diary,* had a significant influence as a literary figure on the colonial American public. He not only appealed to the farmers of Massachusetts, but he also promulgated Copernican astronomy. Ames was a versatile writer; he excelled in the art of writing essays, especially on health and astronomy, and possessed a distinct talent for poetry, humor, and satire. Ames also excelled in the specialized genre of writing proverbs. Because Ames introduced his readers to important English writers of his time and also to his original literary work, he was one of the most influential figures in shaping American literary tastes in the 18th century. 29 notes. 1726-64

Amlie, Thomas

144. Weiss, Stuart L. THOMAS AMLIE AND THE NEW DEAL. *Mid-Am. 1977 59(1): 19-38.* Sketches the political career of Thomas Amlie, US Representative from Wisconsin's First District. In 1931, Amlie began as a Republican; but he soon founded the Wisconsin Progressive Party and ended his career as a Democrat. During the 1930's he was an ardent New Dealer and proposed radical economic programs based on "production for use" and preserving "democratic values." His nomination to the Interstate Commerce Commission in 1939 was withdrawn at his own request because of conservative criticism from his home state. Amlie was a realistic liberal. Primary and secondary sources; 125 notes. 1931-39

Ammann, Othmar Hermann

145. Durrer, Margot Ammann. MEMORIES OF MY FATHER. *Swiss Am. Hist. Soc. Newsletter 1979 15(2): 26-35.* Personal portraits of Othmar Hermann Ammann (1879-1965) by his daughter. 1900-65

146. Widmer, Urs C. OTHMAR HERMANN AMMANN, 1879-1965: HIS WAY TO GREAT BRIDGES. *Swiss Am. Hist. Soc. Newsletter 1979 15(2): 4-25.* A biography of Othmar Hermann Ammann (1879-1965), including notes, diagrams, and photographs of all the major bridges he built through 1954. 1893-1954

147. Widmer, Urs C. BIBLIOGRAPHY: PUBLICATIONS BY AND ABOUT O. H. AMMANN. *Swiss Am. Hist. Soc. Newsletter 1979 15(2): 34-41.* A bibliography of publications by and about Othmar Hermann Ammann (1879-1965). 1915-77

Anaya, Toney

148. Vigil, Maurilio E. THE ELECTION OF TONEY ANAYA AS GOVERNOR OF NEW MEXICO: ITS IMPLICATIONS FOR HISPANICS. *J. of Ethnic Studies 1984 12(2): 81-98.* Toney Anaya's election as New Mexico's fourth Hispanic governor on November 2, 1982 was due to his combination of charisma and his record of public service as a reformist-activist attorney general, as contrasted with the "good ole boy" demeanor of his opponents. Most importantly, his liberal positions on jobs, education, and social programs, along with union support, enabled him to carry the Hispanic counties in the north and center of the state. Evaluation of past elections shows that Anaya fulfilled the major conditions for a Hispanic candidate to win: he was a Democrat, running in a crowded primary race; he appealed not only to the Hispanic north but to metropolitan Bernalillo County; and he had an Anglo running mate. Based on newspapers and other sources; 2 tables, 20 notes. 1968-82

Ancker, Albert

149. Fogelson, George J. AN ODE TO ALBERT ANCKER OF TEHACHAPI. *Western States Jewish History 1985 17(4): 347-351.* Presents a biographical sketch of Albert Ancker (1860-1952), a Prussian-born Jew who moved to Tehachapi, California, in 1892 and eventually became president of the Bank of Tehachapi; and prints an ode to Ancker, first published in the *Tehachapi News* in 1938. 11 notes, illus. 1870's-1952

Ancker, Henrietta

150. Stern, Norton B. THE CHARITABLE JEWISH LADIES OF SAN BERNARDINO AND THEIR WOMAN OF VALOR, HENRIETTA ANCKER. *Western States Jewish Hist. Q. 1981 13(4): 369-376.* Henrietta Ancker (1835-90) came to San Bernardino, California, with her husband Louis in 1870. She was very active in social and charitable activities, and in 1886 she helped organize the Ladies' Hebrew Benevolent Society. In tribute to her energetic leadership, the members changed the name to the Henrietta Hebrew Benevolent Society in 1891. Based on interviews and newspaper accounts; 2 photos, 34 notes. 1870-91

Anderson, Chandler

151. Harrison, Benjamin T. CHANDLER ANDERSON AND BUSINESS INTERESTS IN MEXICO: 1913-1920: WHEN ECONOMIC INTERESTS FAILED TO ALTER U.S. FOREIGN POLICY. *Inter-American Econ. Affairs 1979 33(3): 3-23.* Chandler Anderson was an international attorney who represented business interests in Mexico during Woodrow Wilson's presidency; Chandler failed to win Wilson's support in protecting American commercial interests, 1913-20. 1913-20

Anderson, Clinton P.

152. Baker, Richard Allan. "Senator Clinton P. Anderson and the Politics of Conservation, 1949-1964." U. of Maryland 1982. 466 pp. *DAI 1983 44(4): 1177-1178-A.* DA8318868 1949-64

Anderson, David

153. Peake, F. A. DAVID ANDERSON: THE FIRST LORD BISHOP OF RUPERT'S LAND. *J. of the Can. Church Hist. Soc. [Canada] 1982 24(1): 3-46.* David Anderson became the first lord bishop of the bishopric of Rupert's Land in 1849. According to the Church Missionary Society in England, his episcopal duties were to train the Indians to be ministers and to translate the Bible into their tongues. His relations with the Hudson's Bay Company, upon whom he depended for all his material needs, were strained. While he encouraged an agricultural life for the Indians, the company's profits demanded that they remain nomadic hunters and fishermen. Anderson also experienced strained relations with his poorly selected and undertrained clergy and with Presbyterians. He returned to England in 1865. Primary sources; 56 notes. 1839-85

Anderson, George Edward

154. Francis, Rell G. VIEWS OF MORMON COUNTRY: THE LIFE AND PHOTOGRAPHS OF GEORGE EDWARD ANDERSON. *Am. West 1978 15(6): 14-29.* At the age of 17, after serving as an apprentice where he mastered the principles and techniques of photography, Mormon George Edward (George Ed) Anderson (1860-1928) set up business for himself. He was quick to adopt new ideas and to devise such things as portable studios. He traveled throughout southern Utah to remote villages, mining camps, or wherever opportunity for people-centered civic activities, rural industry, and community celebrations beckoned. About two-thirds of his some 40,000 photographs were studio portraits. He was also motivated by an insatiable quest to document Mormon Church history and subjects. Anderson's work has been featured in several publications and in recent exhibits. Based on a forthcoming book; 18 illus. 1877-1928

Anderson, Gilbert M.

155. Parkhurst, Donald B. BRONCHO BILLY AND NILES, CALIFORNIA: A ROMANCE OF THE EARLY MOVIES. *Pacific Hist. 1982 26(4): 1-22.* Reviews the career of Gilbert M. Anderson (Broncho Billy, 1883-1971), moving picture director, writer and actor. He chose Niles, California for the location of his company and produced 375 one-reel films during 1912-16; Charlie Chaplin, Ben Turpin and Chester Conklin were featured. Sources include 21 interviews with Niles residents; 14 illus. 1912-16

Anderson, James Patton

156. Rayburn, Larry. "WHEREVER THE FIGHT IS THICKEST": GENERAL JAMES PATTON ANDERSON OF FLORIDA. *Florida Hist. Q. 1982 60(3): 313-336.* James Patton Anderson (1822-72) rose steadily in the Confederate Army. He saw action in Shiloh, Muphreesboro, Chattanooga, and Atlanta. After the war he refused to sign a presidential pardon, maintaining that his wartime actions were honorable. His death was hastened by the wounds of war. Based on James Patton Anderson Papers, University of Florida, and other sources; 92 notes. 1860-72

Anderson, James Wallace (family)

157. Anderson, George M. AN EARLY COMMUTER: THE LETTERS OF JAMES AND MARY ANDERSON. *Maryland Hist. Mag. 1980 75(3): 217-232.* James Wallace Anderson (1797-1881) and Mary, his wife, owned a farm called Vallombrosa in Montgomery County, two miles north of Rockville, Maryland. Working as an auditor in the US Post Office in Washington, D.C., 1854-61, James was able to go home only twice a month or so, and thus carried on a frequent correspondence with his wife. Their 400 or so letters, here discussed and quoted by their great-grandson, provide an unusually full picture of urban boarding house life in the capital and rural farm existence in the mid-19th century. Brief biographical details of the couple's eight children are also included, along with the history of the farm to 1960. 96 notes. 1854-1960

Anderson, James (1782-1858)

158. McFarland, K. T. H., ed. DR. ANDERSON'S TRAVELS. *Western Pennsylvania Historical Magazine 1985 68(3): 291-298.* Presents a biography of Dr. James Anderson, a respected physician in 19th-century Montgomery County, Pennsylvania, and excerpts original documents describing a journey he took in 1836 to what is now Clarion County, Pennsylvania. 1782-1858

Anderson, James (1831-1920)

159. Anderson, George M. A CAPTURED CONFEDERATE OFFICER: NINE LETTERS FROM CAPTAIN JAMES ANDERSON TO HIS FAMILY. *Maryland Hist. Mag. 1981 76(1): 62-69.* Captain James Anderson (1831-1920), of Montgomery County near Rockville, Maryland, enlisted in 1861 in the 35th Battalion of Virginia Cavalry and was captured by Union forces during a skirmish at Harpers Ferry in October 1862. In letters from federal prison camps at Johnson's Island, Point Lookout, and Fort Delaware, he gives a picture of his generally good treatment, his physical needs, and some of his attitudes as a southerner, especially his antipathy toward northern views on slavery. After the war he lived in Rockville and served as clerk of the circuit court until 1897. 28 notes. 1861-65

Anderson, Jane

160. Edwards, John C. ATLANTA'S PRODIGAL DAUGHTER: THE TURBULENT LIFE OF JANE ANDERSON AS EXPATRIATE AND NAZI PROPAGANDIST. *Atlanta Hist. J. 1984 28(2): 23-41.* Highlights the colorful but tragic career of Atlanta-born Jane Anderson, including her early years as a newspaper correspondent, her international love affairs, and her capture and imprisonment by anti-Franco forces during the Spanish Civil War; during 1940-41, she was recruited by the German Reichrundfunk for Nazi radio propaganda during World War II. 1900's-42

Anderson, John A.

161. Roosa, Alma Carlson and Hamilton, Henry W. HOMESTEADING IN THE 1880'S: THE ANDERSON-CARLSON FAMILIES OF CHERRY COUNTY. *Nebraska Hist. 1977 58(3): 371-394.* Alma Carlson Roosa was five years old when her parents and grandparents homesteaded in Cherry County, Nebraska, in the 1880's. Her uncle, photographer John A. Anderson (1869-1948), lived in 1879 in the home of a married sister, Amanda Anderson Carlson. Her daughter, Alma Carlson Roosa, contributed valuable reminiscences to the editor and his wife as they prepared their biography of Anderson. 1880's

Anderson, Joseph Richard "Skookum Joe"

162. Mueller, George D. REAL AND FANCIED CLAIMS: JOSEPH RICHARD "SKOOKUM JOE" ANDERSON, MINER IN CENTRAL MONTANA, 1880-1897. *Montana 1985 35(2): 50-59.* Joseph Richard "Skookum Joe" Anderson was a legendary prospector in central Montana. Stories abound of his exploits in the Northwest, Utah, and California before he settled in Montana, where he discovered several rich veins of gold. Between 1886 and 1895 "Skookum Joe" recorded his activities in diaries by which we can measure the legendary prospector against the real life miner. Joe was a hard-working prospector who knew his business, made valuable gold discoveries, and organized their exploitation. He was not the isolated prospector of legend; rather, he was a friendly man with great curiosity about the outside world. Based on the Joseph Richard Anderson Diaries, Montana Historical Society Archives, Helena, and on secondary sources; illus., 5 photos, 32 notes. 1860-97

Anderson, Margaret

163. Johnson, Abby Ann Arthur. THE PERSONAL MAGAZINE: MARGARET C. ANDERSON AND THE *LITTLE REVIEW,* 1914-1929. *South Atlantic Q. 1976 75(3): 351-363.* Margaret Anderson edited and controlled all the articles appearing in the *Little Review.* The magazine reflected her interests in feminism, world peace, literary censorship, and Dada art. Ezra Pound spent several years as foreign editor of the journal, getting the early works of Ford Madox Ford, T. S. Eliot, W. B. Yeats, and others, published for the first time in the United States. James Joyce's *Ulysses* appeared in serial form in 1918 and provoked a tremendous legal struggle. In 1923 Anderson turned control over to her lifelong companion Jane Heap, who kept the *Little Review* fitfully alive for only a few years. Primary and secondary sources; 32 notes. 1914-29

Anderson, Mary

164. Conn, Sandra. THREE TALENTS: ROBINS, NESTOR, AND ANDERSON OF THE CHICAGO WOMEN'S TRADE UNION LEAGUE. *Chicago Hist. 1980-81 9(4): 234-247.* 1903-20

For abstract see ***Robins, Margaret Dreier***

Anderson, Maxwell

165. Luckett, Perry Downington. "The Mind and Matter of Maxwell Anderson." U. of North Carolina, Chapel Hill 1979. 283 pp. *DAI 1980 40(7): 4041-A.* 1924-50's

166. Tees, Arthur T. MAXWELL ANDERSON'S CHANGING ATTITUDE TOWARD WAR. *North Dakota Q. 1980 48(3): 5-11.* Traces American playwright Maxwell Anderson's attitude toward war through his writings from his 1924 antiwar play *What Price Glory?* to his 1948 letter to the *New York Times,* in which he advocated defeat of the USSR at any price. 1924-48

Anderson, May

167. Oman, Susan Staker. NURTURING LDS PRIMARIES: LOUIE FELT AND MAY ANDERSON, 1880-1940. *Utah Hist. Q. 1981 49(3): 262-275.* Louie Felt and May Anderson cooperated in the Primary Association to improve the religious education of Mormon children. Brought together by friendship between the two families, these two ladies worked closely for the remainder of their lives. From their efforts, the magazine *Children's Friend* was begun. Today, the *Friend* continues with international subscriptions. In 1921 and 1922, the Children's Convalescent Home and Day Nursery was begun as a result of their efforts to improve facilities for children. 3 photos, 47 notes. 1880-1940

Anderson, Nels

168. Anderson, Nels. SOCIOLOGY HAS MANY FACES: PART I. *J. of the Hist. of Sociol. 1980-81 3(1): 1-26.* The author recounts his experiences from 1910 to 1917, emphasizing the time he spent as a hobo working in mining and ranching. 1910-17

Anderson, Oscar Edward, Jr.

169. Hewlett, Richard G. and Dupree, A. Hunter. [OSCAR EDWARD ANDERSON, JR., 1918-1976]. *Am. Hist. Rev. 1978 83(3): 860-861.* Oscar Edward Anderson, Jr. (1918-76), specialist in the history of American technology, was director of the international program policy division of the National Aeronautics and Space Administration in Washington, D.C. ca 1940-76

Anderson, Paul Y.

170. Lambeth, Edmund B. THE LOST CAREER OF PAUL Y. ANDERSON. *Journalism Q. 1983 60(3): 401-406.* Examines the career highlights of journalist Paul Y. Anderson as a case study of the intricate relationship between investigative reporting and journalistic ethics. This Pulitzer Prize winner used both muckraking tactics and literary talent in exposing public scandals, including the Teapot Dome affair during the Warren G. Harding administration. 1914-38

Anderson, Robert Ball

171. Wax, Darold D. ROBERT BALL ANDERSON, EX-SLAVE, A PIONEER IN WESTERN NEBRASKA, 1884-1930. *Nebraska Hist. 1983 64(2): 163-192.* Robert Ball Anderson, a slave born in Kentucky on 1 March 1843, joined the Union army in the fall of 1864 and served in the 125th Colored Infantry. After the Civil War, Anderson worked as a farmer and farmhand in Nebraska and Kansas. In 1884, he filed a claim under the Timber Culture Act near Hemingford in the Nebraska Sandhills. Anderson's small farm prospered and grew, and by 1910 he was a widely respected citizen and the largest black landowner in Nebraska. His autobiography, published in 1927, relates primarily Anderson's experiences as a slave in Kentucky. Based on Robert Anderson's autobiography and other primary sources; 4 photos, 102 notes. 1884-1930

172. Wax, Darold D. THE ODYSSEY OF AN EX-SLAVE: ROBERT BALL ANDERSON'S PURSUIT OF THE AMERICAN DREAM. *Phylon 1984 45(1): 67-79.* Discusses the life of Robert Ball Anderson from the time he escaped slavery to join the Union Army in 1864, until his decision to settle in Nebraska in 1884. This decision took many years to materialize, but at his death in 1930, Anderson was the largest black landowner in Nebraska. Primary sources; 52 notes. 1864-84

173. Wax, Darold D. ROBERT BALL ANDERSON, A KENTUCKY SLAVE, 1843-1864. *Register of the Kentucky Hist. Soc. 1983 81(3): 255-273.* Born to a slave woman on 1 March 1843, Robert Ball Anderson lived to the age of 87 and achieved a substantial fortune in land and livestock in western Nebraska. Anderson's Greene County Kentucky owner considered him a favorite and recognized his qualities, but conflicts with the owner's wife led to his transfer to field work in 1859. In late 1864, Anderson left the plantation and

joined the Union army. In 1870, he acquired 80 acres of land in Nebraska through the Homestead Act, and, after some initial difficulties, success and wealth came to him in the Nebraska panhandle. 4 photos, 37 notes. 1843-64

Anderson, Sherwood

174. Anderson, David D. SHERWOOD ANDERSON'S OHIO. *Old Northwest 1979 5(2): 181-189.* The works of Sherwood Anderson, from his first published book, *Windy McPherson's Son* (1916), through his posthumously published *Memoirs* (1942), are based on his Ohio background, his boyhood in Clyde during the 1880's and 1890's, and his later career as a businessman in Elyria. Although his novels are set in small-town Ohio, the characters are drawn from life everywhere and deal with the universal rather than the particular. Although his works look back with nostalgia to preindustrial small towns, his last works express his conviction that man will survive industrialism. ca 1880-1942

175. Baker, William. SHERWOOD ANDERSON IN SPRINGFIELD. *Am. Lit. Realism 1870-1910 1982 15(1): 47-61.* Describes the life of American writer Sherwood Anderson at a boarding house named "The Oaks" in Springfield, Illinois, in 1899; where he made lifelong friends and gained the material for his unpublished story, "Talbot, the Actor." 1899

176. Harvey, Cathy. DEAR LYLE/SHERWOOD ANDERSON. *Southern Studies 1979 18(3): 320-338.* Sherwood Anderson (1876-1941), famous American author, sponsored and supported many young American writers, some of whom became very famous. One minor writer, Lyle Saxon (1891-1946), exemplifies how Anderson's encouragement and connections greatly aided young writers. Consists of letters between Saxon and Anderson during 1924-27 covering literary ideas, publishing problems, personal problems of illness and moving, and gossip. Based on the Lyle Saxon Collection in Tulane University Library and Sherwood Anderson Papers at Newberry Library in Chicago; 86 notes. 1924-27

Anderson, Walter

177. Burton, Marda Kaiser. PORTRAITIST OF NATURE. *Horizon 1982 25(2): 41-49.* Biography of US artist Walter Anderson (1903-65), recluse and mystic, an unknown genius who painted and wrote prodigiously, a schizophrenic influenced by impressionist Henry McCarter. 1923-65

Anderson, William Wright

178. Williams, F. Michael. "The Diary and Memoirs of William Wright Anderson, Oregon Pioneer and Forty-Niner." Ball State U. 1984. 292 pp. *DAI 1985 45(7): 2236-A.* DA8423042 1848-49

Anderson-Kent, Margaret E.

179. Kent-Paxton, Laura Belle. "A Linguistic Analysis of the Diaries of M. E. Anderson-Kent, Pioneer Woman." East Texas State U. 1983. 393 pp. *DAI 1983 44(6): 1777-A.* DA8323502 1896-1928

Andrade, Flores de

180. Gamio, Manuel. SEÑORA FLORES DE ANDRADE. Mora, Magdalena and DelCastillo, Adelaida R., ed. *Mexican Women in the United States: Struggles Past and Present* (Los Angeles: U. of California Chicano Studies Res. Center, 1980): 189-192. Provides a personal account of the life of Flores de Andrade, a Mexican immigrant who came to El Paso, Texas, in 1906. In 1909 she founded the Daughters of Cuauhtemoc, a women's secret organization allied with the Liberal Party in opposition to the dictatorship of Porfirio Diaz in Mexico. In 1911 she was nearly executed for her activities, but escaped. Reprinted from Manuel Gamio's *The Mexican Immigrant: His Life Story* (1931). 1890-1911

Andreas, Alfred Theodore

181. Conzen, Michael P. MAPS FOR THE MASSES: ALFRED T. ANDREAS AND THE MIDWESTERN COUNTY ATLAS TRADE. *Chicago History 1984 13(1): 46-63.* Alfred Theodore Andreas, Chicago mapmaker, created atlases that appealed to a broad range of the population, especially his popular county landownership maps. 1860's-1900

Andrew, Abram Pratt

182. Gray, Andrew, ed. THE CARPETBAGGER LETTERS. *Louisiana Hist. 1979 20(4): 431-451.* Abram Pratt Andrew (1843-1935), like many other Union veterans, moved to the South after the Civil War with high hopes of making a fortune by growing cotton. He and his brother-in-law entered into a one-year partnership with the Carson family of Airlie Plantation in Carroll Parish, Louisiana. This series of 21 letters to his family in Indiana during 1866 details his expenses and his ebbing enthusiasm in the face of sickness and army worms. 1866

Andrews, Christopher C.

183. Gower, Calvin W. CHRISTOPHER C. ANDREWS AND AMERICAN BLACKS: FROM APOLOGIST FOR SLAVERY TO CHAMPION OF FREEDOM. *Midwest Rev. 1981 3: 11-18.* Christopher C. Andrews (1829-1922) in the early 1850's argued that slavery was justified in the South where it had a long history, but soon after the start of the Civil War he began to speak out against slavery and continued to do so until his death. 1850-1922

Andrews, John N.

184. Copiz, Pietro E. JOHN N. ANDREWS: THE PRINCE OF SCHOLARS. *Adventist Heritage 1984 9(1): 57-64.* In order to further his European missionary duties for the Seventh-day Adventist Church, John N. Andrews mastered French and, to a lesser degree, German and Italian. 1874-83

185. Graybill, Ronald. JOHN N. ANDREWS: THE FAMILY MAN. *Adventist Heritage 1984 9(1): 10-23.* Describes the personal life of Seventh-day Adventist John N. Andrews as he pursued his career as a writer and a missionary for the church. 1843-83

186. Smoot, Joseph G. JOHN N. ANDREWS: HUMBLEST MAN IN ALL OUR RANKS. *Adventist Heritage 1984 9(1): 24-33.* Describes John N. Andrews's career as one of the early leaders of the Seventh-day Adventist Church. 1850-83

187. Smoot, Joseph G. JOHN N. ANDREWS: FAITHFUL TO HIS SERVICE. *Adventist Heritage 1984 9(1): 3-8.* John N. Andrews was prominent in the early history of the Seventh-day Adventist Church, both as an expounder of Adventist theological thought and as a missionary in Europe. 1850-83

Angel, Jimmie

188. Holl, John R. ANGEL ON SILVER WINGS. *Américas (Organization of Am. States) 1980 32(8): 53-57.* Account of the discovery of the world's highest waterfall in Venezuela in 1933 by American pilot Jimmie Angel, for whom the falls were named; discusses Angel (1899-1956) and his many flights in the United States and Latin America. 1899-1956

Angell, Robert Cooley

189. Angell, Robert Cooley. THE JOYS OF MODEST SUCCESS. *Society 1980 18(1): 72-81.* Sketches the author's years as student and professor of sociology at Ann Arbor, his development as a sociologist, his research and writings and eventual involvement in international affairs. 1920-80

Angelou, Maya

190. Kent, George E. MAYA ANGELOU'S *I KNOW WHY THE CAGED BIRD SINGS* AND BLACK AUTOBIOGRAPHICAL TRADITION. *Kansas Q. 1975 7(3): 72-78.* Examines Maya Angelou's autobiography, *I Know Why the Caged Bird Sings* (1969) as it fits into the tradition of black autobiography, 1920's-60's. 1920's-69

Angers, François-Albert

191. Grube, John. LES HÉROS DE LA PAIX [The heroes of peace]. *Action Natl. [Canada] 1980 69(7): 549-561.* François-Albert Angers was a heroic Quebec pacifist whose writings opposed 1) conscription during World War II, 2) European conflicts and the Cold War, and 3) war itself. His opposition to participation in World War II partially derived from the defensive neutrality of the French Canadian minority who saw conscription as a force for their assimilation into English Canada. He argued that Canada, as a small power, was in a position to preserve civilized values during a brutal era. As an ardent Catholic, he constantly recalled the traditional and contemporary teachings of the Church which stressed the ideal of Christian pacifism. 42 notes. 1940-79

Angius, Ivo Vasov

192. Hart, Mary Nicklanovich. MERCHANT AND MINER: TWO SERBS IN EARLY BISBEE. *J. of Arizona Hist. 1980 21(3): 313-334.* Contrasts the lives of Ivo Vasov Angius and Vido Markov Milutinovich as immigrants to Bisbee, Arizona. Both were from the same Serbian clan but Angius grew rich as an entrepreneur while Milutinovich failed as a union organizer and retired as a poor man. Both belonged to the Serbian assistance organization and each derived help from it. Based on interviews, periodicals, and secondary sources; 6 photos, 85 notes. 1874-1942

Anglin, Timothy Warren

193. Baker, William M. AN IRISH-CANADIAN JOURNALIST-POLITICIAN AND CATHOLICISM: TIMOTHY ANGLIN OF THE SAINT JOHN FREEMAN. *Study Sessions: Can. Catholic Hist. Assoc. [Canada] 1977 44: 5-24.* Timothy Warren Anglin during 1849-83 supported Catholicism while acting as editor of the *Freeman,* a newspaper in Saint John, New Brunswick. 1849-83

Angus, Samuel

194. Langley, Harold D. RESPECT FOR CIVILIAN AUTHORITY: THE TRAGIC CAREER OF CAPTAIN ANGUS. *Am. Neptune 1980 40(1): 23-37.* Traces Samuel Angus's (1784-1840) career, during which he suffered several wounds, in the Quasi and Barbary Wars and the War of 1812. After the last war Angus was assigned to recruiting duty. In 1823 he wrote a series of letters to Secretary of the Navy Samuel L. Southard (1787-1842) seeking a change of duty. In the last letter Angus threatened to appeal over Southard's head to the President should he not receive an answer to his request. For doing so he was summarily dismissed from the Navy without consideration for his 24 years of service or the possibility that various blows to the head received in the line of duty could have led him to act irrationally in writing the letter. Angus's appeals to Presidents John Quincy Adams (1767-1848) and Andrew Jackson (1767-1845) and to Congress for reinstatement were rejected. Angus and his widow did receive small pensions, but his life shows how little tolerance and few options there were for dealing with temporary insanity at the time. Based on records in the National Archives; 44 notes. 1800-40

Anhalt, Istvan

195. Anhalt, Istvan. WHAT TACK TO TAKE? AN AUTOBIOGRAPHICAL SKETCH (LIFE IN PROGRESS . . .). *Queen's Quarterly [Canada] 1985 92(1): 96-107.* Hungarian-Canadian composer, conductor, and pianist Istvan Anhalt reviews his thinking as he outlines the major parts of his autobiography. 1940's-84

Anker, Rudolph

196. Fogelson, George J. RUDOLPH ANKER: SAN BERNARDINO PIONEER. *Western States Jewish Hist. 1985 17(2): 129-136.* Rudolph Anker immigrated from Europe to America in 1882 and became a pioneering Jewish businessman in San Bernardino. Based on correspondence and newspaper accounts; 24 notes. 1856-1925

Anson, Adrian "Cap"

197. Porter, David L. CAP ANSON OF MARSHALLTOWN: BASEBALL'S FIRST SUPERSTAR. *Palimpsest 1980 61(4): 98-107.* Adrian "Cap" Anson's (1852-1922) baseball career included amateur, semipro, and professional ball, most notably during 1876-97 as firstbaseman, captain, and manager of the Chicago White Stockings. 1876-97

Anthony, Susan B.

198. Beeton, Beverly and Edwards, G. Thomas. SUSAN B. ANTHONY'S WOMAN SUFFRAGE CRUSADE IN THE AMERICAN WEST. *J. of the West 1982 21(2): 5-15.* In 1871 Susan B. Anthony and Elizabeth Cady Stanton visited several western states. They were especially interested in Wyoming and Utah where women had equal suffrage, but spoke everywhere they traveled on issues important in the women's movement. While Mrs. Stanton's talks had some favorable press reviews, their feminist causes were denounced by the opinion makers—the politicians, ministers, and editors. Anthony returned to the West in 1877, 1895, and 1896. By the time of her last trip, at age 76, Anthony's views had gained popularity and respect. Women's rights leaders concentrated on the single issue of suffrage and went directly to the opinion makers to educate them and to persuade them to support the goal of suffrage. 5 photos. 1871-96

Antin, Mary

199. Warner, Sam Bass, Jr. LISTENING FOR THE DEAD. *Public Hist. 1983 5(4): 63-70.* Reflects on the worldview of immigrant Mary Antin, a Russian Jew, and her life in Chelsea, Massachusetts. 1890's-1901

Antisarlook, Mary

200. Brooks, Maria. REMEMBERING THE REINDEER QUEEN. *Frontiers 1981 6(3): 59-61.* Recalls the life of Eskimo Mary Antisarlook, owner of one of the largest reindeer herds in Alaska, 1870-1949. 1870-1949

201. Ray, Dorothy Jean. SINROCK MARY: FROM ESKIMO WIFE TO REINDEER QUEEN. *Pacific Northwest Quarterly 1984 75(3): 98-107.* Sheldon Jackson, Presbyterian missionary and first general agent of education for Alaska, imported a domesticated reindeer herd from Russia to Alaska in 1892 to provide a new industry for Eskimos. He initiated the experiment on the Sinuk River and placed the herd under the supervision of Charlie and Mary Antisarlook. Under their careful management the herd increased, but Charlie's death in 1900 sparked a legal battle with his relatives who wished to take control of the herd from Mary. Her courtroom victory was expensive, but Mary emerged with full control of the reindeer. Prior to her death in 1948, Mary had become a legend because of her generosity toward other Eskimos and her adoption of eleven Eskimo children. Based on government documents and the W. T. Lopp Papers at the University of Oregon Library; illus., 5 photos, 31 notes. 1890-1907

Antony, Milton

203. Moores, Russell R. "EXEGIT MOMENTUM AERE PERENNIUS": MILTON ANTONY, M.D. *Richmond County Hist. 1977 9(1): 10-17.* Biography (1800-39) of Milton Antony, an Augusta doctor responsible for establishing the Medical College of Georgia. 1800-39

Apes, William

204. McQuaid, Kim. WILLIAM APES, PEQUOT: AN INDIAN REFORMER IN THE JACKSON ERA. *New England Q. 1977 50(4): 605-625.* Sketches William Apes's (b. 1798) troubled youth and shows that his religious approach to Indian-white relations and his belief in racial equality was nonconformist during the era of Indian removal. Focuses on his leadership of the Wampanoag Indians of Mashpee, Massachusetts, in their partially successful struggle for control of their own political, economic and religious affairs. Based on Apes' writings and secondary sources; 29 notes. 1830-40

Apolonio Tuliyahuit

205. Warren, Claude N. and Hodge, Donna J. APOLONIO, THE CANOE BUILDER, AND THE USE OF MISSION RECORDS. *J. of California and Great Basin Anthrop. 1980 2(2): 298-304.* Discusses the genealogy of the Chumash Indian Apolonio Tuliyahuit as recorded in the records of Mission Santa Barbara, to rectify the methodological errors in identifying the canoe builder discussed by Travis Hudson, Janis Timbrook, and Melissa Rempe in *Tomol: Chumash Watercraft as Described in the Ethnographic Notes of John P. Harrington* (1978). 1978-80

Appel, Nathan Benjamin

206. Lamb, Blaine P. FIFTY-FOUR YEARS ON THE SOUTHWEST FRONTIER: NATHAN BENJAMIN APPEL IN NEW MEXICO, ARIZONA AND SOUTHERN CALIFORNIA. *Western States Jewish Hist. 1984 16(2): 125-133.* Briefly traces the career of German immigrant Nathan Benjamin Appel, who arrived in New Mexico from St. Louis, Missouri, in 1847. His business interests in merchandising and wagon freighting took him to Arizona and Sonora, Mexico. In later years, he moved to Los Angeles, California, where he served on the police force until his death. Primary sources; 2 photos, 16 notes. 1847-1901

Applegate, Jesse

207. Baker, Abner S., III. EXPERIENCE, PERSONALITY AND MEMORY: JESSE APPLEGATE AND JOHN MINTO RECALL PIONEER DAYS. *Oregon Hist. Q. 1980 81(3): 228-259.* Discusses the experiences of Oregon pioneers Jesse Applegate (d. 1888), who came in 1843, and John Minto (ca. 1822-1914), who arrived in 1844. By examining personality characteristics as evidenced in their writings, the author explains why Applegate disliked recalling the past while Minto enjoyed recounting his participation. Based on letters, family papers, and secondary sources; 2 illus., 8 photos, 83 notes. 1840-88

Appleseed, Johnny

See Chapman, John

Appleton, John

208. Gold, David M. CHIEF JUSTICE JOHN APPLETON. *Maine Hist. Soc. Q. 1979 18(4): 192-216.* John Appleton (1804-91) was born and brought up in New Ipswich, New Hampshire, attended Bowdoin College, studied law and settled in Maine, and became a prominent lawyer in Bangor. He was appointed to the Maine Supreme Court in 1852, became Chief Justice in 1862, and retired in 1883. His legal scholarship and opinions indicate that he was a 19th-century liberal, concerned about injustice and a believer in the principle of laissez faire. He was influenced by utilitarianism, rationalism, and Unitarianism. Based on legal records and the Appleton papers; illus., 71 notes. 1820's-83

209. Gold, David M. "John Appleton and Responsible Individualism in Nineteeth-Century Law." Ohio State U. 1982. 465 pp. *DAI 1982 43(5): 1652-A.* DA8222085 1804-91

Appleton, William Sumner, Jr.

210. Rich, Katharine H. BEACON. *Old-Time New England 1976 66(3-4): 42-60.* Tells of William Sumner Appleton, Jr., founder of the Society for the Preservation of New England Antiquities, and his ancestors on Beacon Hill, Boston, whose cultural activities, especially collecting, from the early 19th century provided the familial background to his interest in historic preservation. 5 illus., 45 notes. 1806-1947

Arbenz, Henry J.

211. Wolf, Edward C. HENRY J. ARBENZ: WHEELING MUSIC MASTER. *Upper Ohio Valley Hist. Rev. 1984 14(1): 2-22.* Details the musical career of renowned pianist, organist, conductor, and composer Henry J. Arbenz from his birth in 1860 into a culturally versatile family in Wheeling, West Virginia, to his education at the Royal Conservatory of

Music in Stuttgart, Germany, during 1877-83, to his directorship of the Maennerchor and his numerous contributions to Wheeling's musical life until his death in 1928. 1870's-1928

Arbuckle, John

212. Fugate, Francis L. ARBUCKLES'—THE COFFEE THAT WON THE WEST. *Am. West 1984 21(1): 61-68.* Reviews both the success of Arbuckle Bros. pre-roasted coffee, whose brand name came to be synonymous with the word "coffee," and the success of John Arbuckle, who provided such additional consumer benefits as coupons for his mail-order business, coffee cards, and multi-purpose shipping boxes. 1860-1912

Archambault, Joseph-Papin

213. Arès, Richard. LE PERE JOSEPH-PAPIN ARCHAMBAULT, S.J., ET L'ECOLE SOCIALE POPULAIRE—TEMOIGNAGE [Father Joseph-Papin Archambault, S.J., and the École Sociale Populaire—remembrance]. *Rev. d'Hist. de l'Amérique Française [Canada] 1982 35(4): 563-587.* Reviews the life and work of Archambault, a Jesuit who was director of the École Sociale Populaire in Montreal, editor of various Catholic journals, and founder of a corporatist organization in the 1930's. 48 notes. 1911-59

214. Arès, Richard. UN DEFENSEUR DU FRANÇAIS: LE PERE JOSEPH-PAPIN ARCHAMBAULT, S.J. [A defender of the French: Reverend Joseph-Papin Archambault, S.J.]. *Action Natl. [Canada] 1981 70(9): 757-764, (10): 843-858.* Part I. Archambault attended St. Mary's College in Montreal, a bilingual Jesuit institution from 1891 to 1897. Joining the Jesuit order, he returned to teach at that college in 1904. He soon became active in both the Association Catholique de la Jeunesse Canadienne-Française and the École Sociale Populaire. After having published, in *Devoir,* a series of articles laying the foundation for the Ligue des Droits du Français, he was ordained a priest on 28 July 1912. A year of spiritual reflection in France introduced him to social Catholicism and inspired him to lead a movement based on its principles in Quebec. Part II. In 1912, while completing his theological studies, Archambault published, under a pseudonym, a series of articles in *Devoir* concerning the revival of the French language among Quebec and Montreal businesses. He was especially critical of French businesses that had adopted the exclusive use of English. In 1913, he participated in the foundation of the Ligue des Droits du Français and, in 1917, its successor Ligue d'Action Français. He was also an ardent supporter of the Ligue d'Action Nationale after 1929. Although committed to Quebec nationalism, Archambault was also instrumental in the establishment of religious closed retreats. An apostle of Catholic social action, he founded the Semaines Sociales du Canada in 1921 and served as a director of the École Sociale Populaire from 1929 to 1959. 1891-1959

215. Arès, Richard. LE PÈRE JOSEPH-PAPIN ARCHAMBAULT, S. J. [Father Joseph-Papin Archambault, S. J.]. *Action Natl. [Canada] 1981 70(8): 637-644.* Joseph-Papin Archambault (1880-1966) devoted his career to the defense and promotion of the French language, the expansion of religious closed retreats, and the development of Quebec social Catholicism. Descended from two influential Quebec families, the Jesuit priest collaborated with Lionel Groulx in the creation of the *Ligue des Droits du Français,* which later became the *Ligue de l'Action Française.* 1910-66

Ardrey, Robert

216. Rodney, Peter Marc. "Robert Ardrey: A Biography and Critical Analysis." Case Western Reserve U. 1980. 317 pp. *DAI 1981 41(10): 4121-A.* 8108318 1936-80

Areloff, Alex

217. Ursenbach, Charles. THE GREAT CROWSNEST PASS TRAIN HOLDUP. *Alberta Hist. [Canada] 1984 32(2): 1-8.* 1920-24
For abstract see ***Akroff, George***

Arendt, Hannah

218. Cranston, Maurice. HANNAH ARENDT, PERSONALLY: LIGHT ON THE LIFE OF A PHILOSOPHER. *Encounter [Great Britain] 1982 59(6): 54-60.* Presents a biography of Hannah Arendt, demonstrating the development of her political and personal philosophies, as well as her aesthetic. 20c

219. Eslin, Jean-Claude. UNE LOI QUI VAILLE POUR L'HUMANITÉ [A law which is of value to humanity]. *Esprit [France] 1980 (6): 41-45.* Examines the philosophy of American university professor Hannah Arendt (1906-75) found in *Eichmann in Jerusalem* (1963), which combined Greek, Jewish, and Christian traditions, and discusses accusations by Jews that the book lacked a spirit of solidarity with the Jewish people. 1963

220. Eslin, Jean-Claude. L'ÉVÉNEMENT DE PENSER [The event of thinking]. *Esprit [France] 1980 (6): 7-18.* Studies the philosophy of Hannah Arendt (1906-75), a German Jew, who became an American citizen in 1950 and taught philosophy and political science. 1950-75

221. Hinchman, Lewis P. and Hinchman, Sandra K. IN HEIDEGGER'S SHADOW: HANNAH ARENDT'S PHENOMENOLOGICAL HUMANISM. *Rev. of Pol. 1984 46(2): 183-211.* Examines Hannah Arendt's political theory in light of Martin Heidegger's philosophy and of the phenomenology and existentialism prevalent in Germany. Like Heidegger, she based her humanism on antimetaphysical thought. However, she believed, contrary to Heidegger, that human rights depend on recognition by the state that human beings are individuals. 64 notes. 1920's-50's

222. McCarthy, Mary. HANNAH ARENDT AND POLITICS. *Partisan Rev. 1984-85 51-52(4-1): 729-738.* Politics consumed Hannah Arendt's life and thought at the level of political theory, civic virtue, and history. She was a republican in sentiment, fearful of mindless bureaucracy and ideological conformity. As a Jew, a refugee, and as an intellectual, her politics drew on Kantian presuppositions as applied in a century of ideological extremes. 1933-70

Argall, Samuel (family)

223. Alsop, James D. SIR SAMUEL ARGALL'S FAMILY, 1560-1620. *Virginia Mag. of Hist. and Biog. 1982 90(4): 472-484.* A genealogical study of the ancestry of Sir Samuel Argall, an important figure in the 17th-century English colonizing movement and the Virginia Company. Based on British Public Records, manuscripts in the British Library, biographical and other secondary sources; 78 notes. 1560-1620

Arlen, Harold

224. Rimler, Walter. GREAT SONGWRITERS. *Midstream 1984 30(1): 31-34.* Presents biographical sketches of five Jewish songwriters from New York City: Jerome Kern, Irving Berlin, George Gershwin, Richard Rodgers, and Harold Arlen. 1885-1979

Armas, Joaquin

225. Frost, Rossie and Frost, Locky. THE KING'S BULLOCK CATCHER. *Hawaiian J. of Hist. 1977 11: 175-187.* A Mexican, Joaquin Armas (1809-50), developed a beef industry for King Kamehameha III of Hawaii, 1831-48. 33 notes. 1831-48

Armer, Laura Adams

226. Dicker, Laverne Mau. LAURA ADAMS ARMER, CALIFORNIA PHOTOGRAPHER. *California Hist. Q. 1977 56(2): 128-139.* Laura Adams Armer (1874-1963), a native Californian, achieved fame as a portrait photographer, artist, author, film producer, and historian. After studying painting and drawing she took up photography in 1899, favoring the new concept of naturalistic photography. Her photographs were notable for the use of light and shadow and lack of contrivance. In 1902 she married Sidney Armer and gave up her career for the next 20 years. She recommenced her career at age 50 and developed an interest in Indians' folklore, particularly Navajo and Hopi sandpainting. She produced an Indian-language motion picture in 1928 and went on to write and illustrate children's books and essays on Indian culture. Based on contemporary and secondary published works; illus., photos, 24 notes. 1899-1963

Arms, John Taylor

227. Pelletier, S. William. JOHN TAYLOR ARMS: AN AMERICAN MEDIAEVALIST. *Georgia Rev. 1976 30(4): 908-935.* John Taylor Arms's illustrious career as an etcher spanned nearly five decades of the 20th century. His superb style and detail resulted from his use of regular sewing needles as etching instruments and his remarkable eyesight which allowed him to observe even the finest detail. Arms's greatest etchings were *Lace in Stone* and *In Memoriam.* 1915-53

Armstrong, David Maitland

228. Husch, Gail E. DAVID MAITLAND ARMSTRONG. *Mag. Antiques 1984 126(5): 1175-1185.* David Maitland Armstrong, like many other artists active during the "American Renaissance," abandoned painting to work in the decorative arts; examines Armstrong's career and illustrates examples of his paintings, stained glass, and mosaics. 1850's-90's

Armstrong, Samuel Chapman

229. Hunter, Wilma King. "Coming of Age: Hollis B. Frissell and the Emergence of Hampton Institute, 1893-1917." Indiana U. 1982. 357 pp. *DAI 1983 43(11): 3677-A.* DA8307980 1893-1917

Arndt, Philip and Elizabeth

230. Kendig, John D. THE PHILIP ARNDTS OF MANHEIM (1797-1888). *Pennsylvania Folklife 1985 35(1): 27-34.* Chronicles the lives and achievements of Philip and Elizabeth Arndt, who were leading citizens of Manheim, Pennsylvania. 1830's-88

Arnold, Benedict

231. Martin, James Kirby. BENEDICT ARNOLD'S TREASON AS POLITICAL PROTEST. *Parameters 1981 11(3): 63-74.* Instead of ascribing Benedict Arnold's betrayal of the American Revolution to evil intentions or a flaw in his character, it can be argued that he acted out of frustration with the civilian population. His act might then be described as an extreme individual protest against the failure of the country to support the army and the war effort with volunteers, provisions, and encouragement as well as a protest against his own treatment with regard to being overlooked for promotions. All these factors gave him just cause for concluding that he had been betrayed in his devotion to the revolution. Based on the papers of Arnold and secondary sources. 1775-80

232. Murdoch, Richard K. BENEDICT ARNOLD AND THE OWNERS OF THE CHARMING NANCY. *Pennsylvania Mag. of Hist. and Biog. 1960 84(1): 22-55.* Portrays Benedict Arnold as a hardheaded businessman who, with others, was attempting to avoid the loss of valuable property in permitting a small schooner, the *Charming Nancy,* to leave enemy-occupied Philadelphia in 1778 to avoid seizure by the British. 1778

Arnold, Mae

233. Henning, Charles. SHE HAD SOME TIMES. *Pacific Hist. 1980 24(2): 196-206.* Oral history account of the life of Mae Arnold (née Rose Crawford), colorful pioneer lady of Delonegha Springs on the Kern River in California. Covers ca. 1891-1919. Photo, note. 1891-1919

Arnold, Richard James

234. Hoffman, Charles and Hoffman, Tess. NORTH BY SOUTH: THE TWO LIVES OF RICHARD JAMES ARNOLD. *Rhode Island Hist. 1984 43(1): 19-33.* Richard James Arnold, a member of a prominent Rhode Island family, married into a prominent Georgia family in 1823 and divided his time between managing and expanding his wife's rice plantation, and his business and other interests in the North. When the Civil War broke out, he sold the plantation and slaves to his son and returned to Rhode Island, but in 1865 he bought back the land and invested heavily in restoring the property to its former productivity. Based on unpublished diaries, manuscripts, and plantation records; published diaries and papers; and newspapers; 4 illus., 52 notes. 1820's-73

Arnold, Welcome

235. Coyle, Franklin Stuart. "Welcome Arnold (1745-1798), Providence Merchant: The Founding of an Enterprise." Brown U. 1972. 232 pp. *DAI 1979 39(11): 6911-6912-A.* 1772-98

Arrington, Leonard James

236. Arrington, Leonard J. HISTORIAN AS ENTREPRENEUR: A PERSONAL ESSAY. *Brigham Young U. Studies 1977 17(2): 193-209.* Author traces his own academic development and career. He provides candid insights into the Historical Department of the Mormon Church; the developing historiography of Mormonism, and the Church's attitude toward its vast primary source holdings on western Americana. 20c

237. Whittaker, David J. [LEONARD J. ARRINGTON: HIS LIFE AND WORK AND A BIBLIOGRAPHY]. *Dialogue 1978 11(4): 23-47.*

LEONARD JAMES ARRINGTON: HIS LIFE AND WORK, *pp. 23-32.* Uses the 20-year anniversary of the 1958 publication of Arrington's *Great Basin Kingdom* as opportunity to celebrate the personal and professional accomplishments of the church historian of the Church of the Latter Day Saints (Mormons). A Mormon by faith, and a historian trained at the University of North Carolina, Arrington personifies the new generation of Mormon historians who have integrated into Mormon studies a larger understanding of institutional, social, and economic developments in western history. Illus., list of six sources.

BIBLIOGRAPHY OF LEONARD JAMES ARRINGTON, *pp. 33-47.* Lists chronologically all work published by Arrington between the beginning of his career in 1935 and the present. For each year, writings are divided into the following categories: articles in professional publications, articles in nonprofessional publications, reviews, books, addresses and duplicated papers, and monographs. 1917-79

Arrott, James W.

238. Wallace, W. S. JAMES W. ARROTT, 1895-1959. *New Mexico Hist. Rev. 1959 34(4): 305-307.* Obituary of James W. Arrott of New Mexico, historian of the American West with a special interest in old Fort Union on the Santa Fe Trail. 1910-59

Arthur, Chester A.

239. Reeves, Thomas C. THE IRONY OF THE PENDLETON ACT. *Hayes Historical Journal 1984 4(3): 38-43.* Discusses the political background of the man who signed the civil service reform bill into law, President Chester A. Arthur. An attorney by trade, Arthur's political career was forged in the company of the most noted spoilsmen of the day, culminating in appointment to the prize of the spoils hierarchy, and the particular target of civil service reformers, the office of collector of the New York Custom House. Arthur signed the reform bill partly because of the furor that would have occurred had he not signed it, and partly because he wished to bury his own past. 1870's-83

Arthur, George

240. Murison, Barbara C. "ENLIGHTENED GOVERNMENT": SIR GEORGE ARTHUR AND THE UPPER CANADIAN ADMINISTRATION. *J. of Imperial and Commonwealth Hist. [Great Britain] 1980 8(3): 161-180.* Discusses the role of Sir George Arthur (1784-1854) as Lieutenant Governor of Upper Canada from the Rebellion to the Union (1837-41). Coming to the post with considerable experience and a record of being a reformer, Arthur soon found that his hands were tied by the Colonial Office, but he managed to make important contributions and initiated almost every reform that was carried out by his successor. Based on the Arthur Papers and materials in the Ottawa Archives and the Colonial Office Papers at the Public Record Office, London; 87 notes. 1837-41

Arthurs, Robert

241. Arthurs, Robert. THE MAN WHO PLAYED DOCTOR. *Civil War Times Illus. 1980 19(5): 36-38.* In August 1886, Robert Arthurs wrote a long letter describing his adventures as the impersonator of a surgeon with the Union Army in Virginia in 1864-65. 1864-65

Asbury, Francis

242. Warman, John B. FRANCIS ASBURY AND JACOB ALBRIGHT. *Methodist Hist. 1978 16(2): 75-81.* 1765-1816

*For abstract see **Albright, Jacob***

Ashe, Samuel A'Court

243. Faulkner, Ronnie. "Samuel A'Court Ashe: North Carolina Redeemer and Historian, 1840-1938." U. of South Carolina 1983. 395 pp. *DAI 1984 45(3): 918-A.* DA8409306 1860's-1938

Ashley, John

244. Hardy, Evelyn. JOHN ASHLEY AND A FORERUNNER OF THE DECLARATION OF INDEPENDENCE. *Contemporary Rev. [Great Britain] 1976 228(1322): 139-143.* Outlines the life of Colonel and Judge John Ashley (1709-1802) of Sheffield, Massachusetts, and reproduces his "Sheffield Declaration of Independence" of 1773. 1730's-1802

Ashley, Jonathan

245. Coughlin, Robert C. JONATHAN ASHLEY: TORY MINISTER. *Hist. J. of Western Massachusetts 1979 7(2): 35-40.* Jonathan Ashley, minister of Deerfield, was one of a number of Massachusetts ministers whose support for the King caused serious conflicts for them with their congregations. As the dispute between the colonies and the mother country intensified, he found himself cut off from his flock. The town expressed its displeasure with his views by cutting off his supply of firewood during the winter as an alternative to removing him. When Ashley died in 1780 the conflict had not been resolved. Based on town records, manuscript sermons, and other material in the Historic Deerfield collection; 23 notes. 1766-80

Aslin, Neil C.

246. King, Jim Lane. "Neil C. Aslin: Educator." U. of Missouri, Columbia 1979. 388 pp. *DAI 1980 41(5): 2049-A.* DA8024368 1929-72

Astor, John Jacob

247. Humins, John H. FURS, ASTOR AND INDIANS. *Michigan History 1985 69(2): 24-31.* John Jacob Astor founded a fur empire, aided by friendly politicians and the federal government. The end result was that both white and Indian traders became indebted to Astor. Subsequently, these debts helped convince the Indians to accept the treaties offered by the US government, bringing great quantities of land into the public domain and making Astor an extemely wealthy man. Based on US government reports and documents and secondary sources; 3 photos, 3 illus., 28 notes. 1808-47

Atanasoff, John Vincent

248. Silag, William. THE INVENTION OF THE ELECTRONIC DIGITAL COMPUTER AT IOWA STATE COLLEGE, 1930-42. *Palimpsest 1984 65(5): 150-164, 173-177.* John Vincent Atanasoff and his assistant, Clifford E. Berry, developed the basic engineering concepts underlying the modern digital computer and built a working prototype, the Atanasoff Berry Computer. 1930-42

Athearn, Robert G.

249. West, Elliot et al. A TRIBUTE TO ROBERT G. ATHEARN. *Montana 1984 34(1): 62-64.* Friends and colleagues wrote these personal tributes to Robert G. Athearn (1914-1983) following his death in November 1983. Athearn, professor of Western history at the University of Colorado, was a prolific writer, teacher, and book review editor for *Montana.* In these capacities he was well-known to students of the American West. 2 photos. 1949-83

Atherton, Gertrude

250. Forrey, Carolyn. GERTRUDE ATHERTON AND THE NEW WOMAN. *California Hist. Q. 1976 55(3): 194-209.* Describes the career of Gertrude Atherton (1857-1948), author of 56 novels and numerous stories. Strongwilled and rebellious in her youth, Atherton found an intellectual outlet in writing fiction. Following the early death of her husband in a loveless marriage, Atherton set out to pursue a literary career. After initial unfavorable reviews she went to Europe and became a huge success there, particularly in England. A favorable reception to her novels then followed in the United States. The heroines in Atherton's novels fit the pattern of the "New Woman"—intellectually superior, athletic, independent, and sexually attractive. Such heroines greatly resembled Atherton's self-image. She had no patience with men who stereotyped women as submissive home-bound objects lacking intellectual capacity. Moreover, her heroines, in combining intellect with sexuality, represented a definition of feminism that Atherton herself attempted to fulfill throughout her long life. Based on primary and secondary sources; photos, 41 notes. 1890's-1910's

Atkins, Harmon Albro

251. Baker, Rollin H. A WATCHER OF BIRDS. *Michigan Hist. 1982 66(5): 40-45.* From 1842 to 1885, Dr. Harmon Albro Atkins served as a country doctor in Locke Township, Ingham County, while at the same time engaging in a "serious study of the bird life of his immediate area." Presents a selection of annotated excerpts from letters exchanged between Atkins and Edgar Alexander Mearns, a New York physician and ornithologist. 4 pictures, 5 notes. 1842-85

Atkinson, Edward

252. Levenstein, Harvey. THE NEW ENGLAND KITCHEN AND THE ORIGINS OF MODERN AMERICAN EATING HABITS. *Am. Q. 1980 32(4): 369-386.* 1889-97
For abstract see ***Abel, Mary Hinman***

Attakullakulla

253. Kelly, James C. NOTABLE PERSONS IN CHEROKEE HISTORY: ATTAKULLAKULLA. *J. of Cherokee Studies 1978 3(1): 2-34.* Attakullakulla, also known as Little Carpenter, was born between 1700 and 1712. From 1730 to his death ca. 1780 he was an influential Cherokee diplomat. He was pro-British, except for an interlude in the 1750's when he sided with the French. During the American Revolution he remained loyal to the British, but accommodated himself to the Americans when no other alternative was available. An early highlight of his carrer was a trip to England in 1730. 7 illus., 190 notes. 1730-80

Atwood, Henry Stiles

254. Brooks, Daniel Fate. HENRY STILES ATWOOD: ANTEBELLUM ECCENTRIC OF WILCOX COUNTY. *Alabama Rev. 1981 34(1): 20-30.* Examines the migration of both Northerners and Southerners, and, in particular, that of Henry Stiles Atwood to Wilcox County, Alabama, during the first quarter of the 19th century. Atwood, who purchased land in the county in 1821, established himself as a very energetic merchant. His business success provided him with the revenue to buy vast landholdings and a large number of slaves. His eccentric ways, secretiveness, reputation as a "rainmaker," and devotion to the anti-masonic movement were culminated in his "strange will," which charged his executors with providing educational opportunities and monetary support for his seven mulatto children. Based on documents found in the James B. Sellers Collection, Auburn University, and records in the Wilcox County Courthouse; 65 notes. 1817-68

Atwood, Margaret

255. Atwood, Margaret. AN END TO AN AUDIENCE. *Dalhousie Rev. [Canada] 1980 60(3): 415-433.* Autobiographical discussion of Atwood's role as a storyteller in Canada, as well as other storytellers and their roles. Note. 1950-80

256. Lilienfeld, Jane. SILENCE AND SCORN IN A LYRIC OF INTIMACY: THE PROGRESS OF MARGARET ATWOOD'S POETRY. *Women's Studies 1980 7(1-2): 185-194.* Traces the successive stages of the Canadian writer Margaret Atwood's poetic development toward artistic maturity, 1966-74. 1966-74

Atzeroth, Joseph (family)

257. Slusser, Cathy Bayless. THE JOSEPH ATZEROTH FAMILY: MANATEE COUNTY PIONEERS. *Tampa Bay Hist. 1982 4(2): 20-44.* Joseph Atzeroth and his wife, Julia, German-American immigrants, homesteaded 160 acres on Terra Ceia Island in Manatee County, Florida in 1843; their descendants were involved in county life until ca. 1910. 1840's-1910

Audubon, John James

258. Rosta, Paul. JOHN JAMES AUDUBON. *American History Illustrated 1985 20(6): 22-31.* Recounts the life of John James Audubon, master artist of American birds, honoring the 200th anniversary of his birth on 26 April 1785. 1785-1851

Audubon, John James (and sons)

259. Reynolds, Gary. AN AMERICAN FAMILY OF PAINTERS: JOHN JAMES AUDUBON AND HIS SONS. *Art & Antiques 1982 5(1): 48-57.* Biographies of John James Audubon (1785-1851) and his two sons, Victor Gifford Audubon (1809-60) and John Woodhouse Audubon (1812-62), focusing on the paintings of animals and birds John did in collaboration with his two sons; he also painted portraits and gave painting lessons during 1820-26 in order to support his family. 1785-1862

Audubon, Lucy Bakewell

260. Delatte, Carolyn Elizabeth. "An American Odyssey: A Biography of Lucy Bakewell Audubon." Louisiana State U. and Agric. and Mechanical Coll. 1979. 358 pp. *DAI 1979 40(6): 3487-A.* 1802-74

Auld, Alexander

261. Miller, Terry E. ALEXANDER AULD, 1816-1898: EARLY OHIO MUSICIAN. *Cincinnati Hist. Soc. Bull. 1975 33(4): 244-260.* Auld was Ohio's first musician to gain national prominence. 1816-98

Aultman, Otis

262. Beezley, William H. SHOOTING THE MEXICAN REVOLUTION. *Américas (Organization of Am. States) 1976 28(11/12): 17-19.* Texas photographer Otis Aultman traveled with revolutionaries in Mexico in order to photograph the events of the Mexican revolution, 1910-16, which later earned him a job in Hollywood as a cameraman during the 1920's. 1910-16

Aurand, Henry S.

263. Reese, John Russell. "Supply Man: The Army Life of Lieutenant General Henry S. Aurand, 1915-52." Kansas State U. 1984. 206 pp. *DAI 1985 45(11): 3436-A.* DA8426335 1915-52

Avery, Milton

264. Wernick, Robert. A QUIET AMERICAN PAINTER WHOSE ART IS NOW BEING HEARD. *Smithsonian 1982 13(7): 110-117.* Biography of American modern artist Milton Avery, whose fame as a painter came posthumously. 1905-65

Avery, William Waightstill

265. Gass, W. Conard. THE MISFORTUNE OF A HIGH MINDED AND HONORABLE GENTLEMAN: W. W. AVERY AND THE SOUTHERN CODE OF HONOR. *North Carolina Hist. Rev. 1979 56(3): 278-297.* On Tuesday, 11 November 1851, William Waightstill Avery (1816-64), a lawyer, shot and killed Samuel Flemming (b. 1812), a businessman and politician, in the Burke County courthouse at Morganton, North Carolina. Three weeks earlier Flemming had cowhided and beaten an unarmed and surprised Avery on the main street of Marion, North Carolina, culminating their several years of political, legal, and personal disputes. Avery, of an upper class North Carolina family, felt he had to kill Flemming to retain his standing according to the southern gentleman's code of honor. Tried immediately after the killing, Avery was acquitted by a jury which believed so firmly in that code that it was willing to overlook outright murder to uphold it. Based on newspaper accounts, published and unpublished family papers, and court minutes; 9 illus., 65 notes. 1851

Aycock, Charles Brantley

266. Roper, John Herbert. CHARLES BRANTLEY AYCOCK: A STUDY IN LIMITATION AND POSSIBILITY. *Southern Studies 1977 16(3): 277-291.* Charles Brantley Aycock (1859-1912), the "Education Governor" of North Carolina 1901-05, was known for building schools, establishing libraries, and supporting summer teacher improvement. Yet he campaigned in 1898 and 1900 on a strongly racist platform, supported disenfranchisement of most blacks in the state, and spent less on education for blacks than the previous administration. Aycock claimed he was taking a moderate stance, preserving peace, and preparing blacks for future, fuller participation in the intellectual and political life of the country. Primary and secondary sources; 39 notes. 1895-1912

B

Babb, Max W.

267. Babb, Irving T. ROBERT TODD LINCOLN'S MILWAUKEE FRIEND: MAX BABB OF ALLIS-CHALMERS. *Milwaukee History 1984 7(2): 62-68.* In 1904, Robert Todd Lincoln recommended that the Allis-Chalmers Company offer Max W. Babb the position of legal counsel—a position which Babb accepted on his way to becoming president of the Milwaukee company. 1904-43

Babbidge, Homer Daniels, Jr.

268. Greene, John C. HOMER DANIELS BABBIDGE, JR. *Pro. of the Am. Antiquarian Soc. 1984 94(1): 23-27.* Babbidge received an American Studies Ph.D. from Yale, and spent most of his career in various educational agencies of the federal government, administering the National Defense Education Act and supporting federal advancement of higher education. He later became president of the University of Connecticut, and edited selected writings of Noah Webster. After resigning the presidency in 1972, he spent the remainder of his life in higher education and edited two books on corkscrews. 1925-84

Babel, Isaac

269. Schwartz, Musia Miriam. "Prophets for a Cold Age: Isaac Babel and Nathanael West." McGill U. [Canada] 1980. *DAI 1980 41(3): 1051-A.* 1921-40

Baca, Felipe

270. Baca, Luis and Baca, Facundo. HISPANIC PIONEER: DON FELIPE BACA BRINGS HIS FAMILY NORTH TO TRINIDAD. *Colorado Heritage 1982 (1): 26-35.* Don Felipe Baca (1829-74) and 12 other Hispano families moved from New Mexico in 1862 to the area of Trinidad, Colorado. He was active in Colorado territorial politics and was a large sheep producer. Two of his sons, Luis (an engineer) and Facundo (a physician) left personal narratives of their father, excerpts from which are included. Also included is a comment in Spanish made "in an Albuquerque Spanish-language newspaper" on Felipe's wife, Maria Gonzales Baca. The Baca adobe house is now a regional museum operated by the Colorado Historical Society. 10 photos. 1862-74

Bachelle, Werner Von

271. Beaudot, William J. K. A MILWAUKEE IMMIGRANT IN THE CIVIL WAR. *Milwaukee History 1984 7(1): 18-28.* Examines the life of Werner Von Bachelle, a German-born Milwaukee resident who became a captain in the Union Army during the Civil War and was killed at Antietam. 1824-62

Bachman, John Baptist (family)

272. Bauckman, Frank A. JOHN BAPTIST BACHMAN OF LUNENBURG TOWNSHIP, NOVA SCOTIA. *Nova Scotia Hist. Q. [Canada] 1975 5(3): 297-306.* A genealogy of John Baptist Bachman (1720-94), who arrived in Halifax in 1752 among a company of German immigrants. Mentions his descendants down to 1952. 1752-1952

Bachman, J. A. (family)

273. Bachmann-Dick, Fritz. THE BACHMAN FAMILY IN SWITZERLAND AND THE UNITED STATES. *Swiss American Historical Society Newsletter 1984 20(2): 21-47.*

Bachmann-Dick, Fritz. THE RELATIONSHIP BETWEEN THE FAMILY OF JOHANN JAKOB KAPPELER AND THE BACHMANN FAMILIES AT THUNDORF AND STETTFURT, *pp. 21-38.* Gives a history and genealogy of the Kappeler and Bachmann families of Canton Thurgau, Switzerland, during the 14th-19th centuries.

Bachman, Joachim Arnold. AUTOBIOGRAPHICAL SKETCH, *pp. 39-41.* Recounts events in the life of J. A. Bachman, including his immigration to America in 1852, his service in the Civil War, and his founding of a tobacco company in 1889.

—. TWO *KANSAS CITY JOURNAL* ARTICLES ON THE BACHMANS DURING THE 1870'S AND 1880'S, *pp. 42-44.* Prints two newspaper articles that describe J. A. Bachman's tobacco business in Kansas City and the wedding of Bachman's daughter Emma.

Bachman, Gustave Bryant. AUTOBIOGRAPHICAL SKETCH, *pp. 45-47.* Recounts events in the life of G. B. Bachman, professor of chemistry at Purdue University from 1941 to 1971. 14c-1982

Backus, Isaac

274. Grenz, Stanley J. ISAAC BACKUS AND THE ENGLISH BAPTIST TRADITION. *Baptist Q. [Great Britain] 1984 30(5): 221-231.* Gives an account of Isaac Backus's involvement with the Separate Baptists of New England, emphasizing his encouragement of close ties between English and American Baptists; organizer and pastor of the Baptist church in Middleborough, Massachusetts, Backus has been called the "Father of American Baptists." 1745-65

275. Grenz, Stanley J. ISAAC BACKUS AND RELIGIOUS LIBERTY. *Foundations 1979 22(4): 352-360.* Sees a need to review New England Baptist clergyman Isaac Backus's (1724-1806) contribution to religious liberty. Recent historians have argued that his contribution was not as important as once thought. Concludes that his contributions were large, but that some of his views were not on the mark, in that truths he held were more complex than he thought. Based mostly on *Isaac Backus on Church, State, and Calvinism & Pamphlets, 1754-1789* and other sources; 35 notes. 1754-89

Bacon, Albion Fellows

276. Barrows, Robert G. "THE HOMES OF INDIANA": ALBION FELLOWS BACON AND HOUSING REFORM LEGISLATION, 1907-1917. *Indiana Magazine of History 1985 81(4): 309-350.* After six years of intense effort, Albion Fellows Bacon was able to convince the Indiana legislature to enact the state's first laws regulating the construction of multi-dwelling housing and empowering state health officers to order corrective action in any dwelling deemed unfit for human habitation. She accomplished this by winning support from women's clubs, civic improvement associations, and health officials, and by lobbying through the newspapers to legislative committees. Her work was a prototype of the reforms called for by later Progressive politicians and social critics. Based on newspaper accounts, personal memoirs, letters of A. F. Bacon, and Indiana legislative records; 8 illus., 112 notes. 1907-17

Bacon, Henry

277. Richman, Michael. DANIEL CHESTER FRENCH AND HENRY BACON: PUBLIC SCULPTURE IN COLLABORATION, 1897-1908. *Am. Art J. 1980 12(3): 46-64.* Sculptor Daniel Chester French (1850-1931) and architect Henry Bacon (1886-1924) collaborated successfully on a series of great public sculptures; the George Hamilton Perkins Memorial (1899-1902), the James Anderson Memorial (1902-04), the Francis Parkman Memorial (1904-07), and the Melvin Memorial (1907). Although French worked with other architects as well, the collaborations were neither as congenial, creative, nor successful as that with Bacon. Based on Daniel Chester French Family Papers in the Library of Congress and other primary sources; 23 plates, 40 notes. 1897-1908

Bacon, Julian Smith

278. Tuggle, Troy S. "SMITTY": THE LIVING LEGACY OF JEDEDIAH AND PETER SMITH. *Pacific Hist. 1981 25(3): 62-71.* 19c-20c

For abstract see ***Smith, Jedediah Strong and Peter (family)***

Bacon, Thomas

279. Deibert, William E. THOMAS BACON, COLONIAL CLERGYMAN. *Maryland Hist. Mag. 1978 73(1): 79-86.* Surveys the American career of the Anglican priest Thomas Bacon (1700-68), rector of St. Peter's Parish, Talbot County, Maryland, and after 1758 of All Saints Church in Frederick. Though he was fundamentalist and conservative in religious and political beliefs, Bacon's ministry had a progressive social content, and he not only preached that slaves should be taught Christianity but also founded perhaps the first charity working school in Maryland. His project of publishing the laws of Maryland flung him into a four-year political battle (centered on inclusion or omission of the 1661 Tonnage Act) between the proprietary and antiproprietary parties in the General Assembly. Minister, musician, physician, educator, gardener, and student of law, he exemplified the 18th-century Renaissance man and achieved a prominence matched by few Maryland clergymen. Primary and secondary sources; illus., 65 notes. ca 1745-68

Bacon family

280. Dumas, David W., ed. BACON-ADAMS-WHITNEY-KINGSBURY FAMILY RECORDS. *New England Hist. and Geneal. Register 1984 138(Jan): 32-38.* Presents a genealogical record by John Bacon that goes beyond the usual genealogical information to include several families related by marriage. It corrects and adds to some previously published family histories. 17c-19c

Badger, Alfred G.

281. Simpson, Mary Jean. "Alfred G. Badger (1815-1892), Nineteenth-Century Flutemaker: His Art, Innovations, and Influence on Flute Construction, Performance and Composition, 1845-1895." U. of Maryland 1982. 384 pp. *DAI 1983 43(7): 2151-2152-A.* DA8227993 1830's-92

Badger, Robert and Roderick

282. Robinson, Henry S. ROBERT AND RODERICK BADGER, PIONEER GEORGIA DENTISTS. *Negro Hist. Bull. 1961 24(4): 77-80* Provides biographies of Robert (1829-?) and Roderick (1834-90) Badger, half-brothers, and two of the first black dentists in the United States; also provides their respective families' genealogies until 1958. 1829-1958

Badgley, David

283. Yeager, Lyn Allison. DAVID BADGLEY, PIONEER MINISTER IN THE ILLINOIS TERRITORY. *Foundations 1977 20(3): 263-278.* Virginia Baptists under David Badgley (5 November 1749-16 December 1824) moved to southwest Illinois. Focuses on Badgley's life in connection with the Baptist Church he pastored in New Design, Illinois. Discusses all the major problems facing a pioneer. 71 notes. 1769-1824

Badt, J. Selby

284. Sheerin, Chris H. THREE WHO DARED: J. SELBY BADT, "VAN" AND ULA VANDIVER. *Northeastern Nevada Hist. Soc. Q. 1980 (4): 98-113.* J. Selby Badt (1881-1971), James Louis Vandiver (1883-1967), and Ula Vandiver (b. 1896) in 1938 began a lifelong partnership with the purchase of the rundown Agee Ranch south of Wells, Nevada, made it a successful working ranch, and sold it in 1945. 1938-80

Badt, Milton B.

285. Badt, Gertrude N. MILTON BENJAMIN BADT. *Northeastern Nevada Hist. Soc. Q. 1978 (3): 91-112.* A biography of Nevada state supreme court Justice Milton B. Badt (1884-1966), written by his wife and including family portraits. 20c

Baer, George F.

286. Shirk, Annadora V. "The Rhetoric of George F. Baer during the Anthracite Strike of 1902." Temple U. 1977. 178 pp. *DAI 1977 38(4): 1738-1739-A.* 1902

Baer, John M.

287. Reid, Bill G. JOHN MILLER BAER: NONPARTISAN LEAGUE CARTOONIST AND CONGRESSMAN. *North Dakota Hist. 1977 44(1): 4-13.* John M. Baer became a fulltime cartoonist for the *Nonpartisan Leader* in 1916. He graphically depicted the struggle of the North Dakota Nonpartisan League's reform movement against the opposition of the Democratic and Republican Parties. Baer's cartoons provided simplistic images of the honest, stalwart, democratic farmer in battle with "Big Biz" and "Crafty" in the fight to control state government and make it truly responsive to the needs of the people. Baer served a term and a half in Congress, under the League's banner, during and immediately after World War I. During his tenure, he was unfairly accused of pro-German sentiments. He later became a cartoonist for *Labor,* a publication of the railroad unions. 1886-1970

Bagley, Edward E.

288. Soule, William Harris. VERMONT'S "MARCH KING." *Vermont Hist. 1981 49(3): 154-158.* Edward E. Bagley (1857-1922), born into a musical family in Craftsbury, Vermont, started at nine as a boy soprano with Leavitt's Bellringers, became solo cornetist for the Swiss Bellringers and then the Boston Symphony and the Germania Band. In the 1880's at Randolph, Vermont, he wrote the popular *National Emblem March.* From 1893, he toured the vaudeville circuit, composed, taught and directed music from a Keene, New Hampshire, base. 13 notes. 1866-1922

Bagley, Sarah G.

289. Wright, Helena. SARAH G. BAGLEY: A BIOGRAPHICAL NOTE. *Labor Hist. 1979 20(3): 398-413.* Provides biographical details about New Hampshire born Sarah G. Bagley (b. 1806), the founder and first president of the Female Labor Reform Association of Lowell, Massachusetts. After 1848, there is no record available. Based on company records, tax lists, and probate records; 34 notes. 1806-48

Bagnall, Benjamin (family)

290. Roesler, Robert B. BAGNALL'S FORTUNE. *Milwaukee History 1984 7(1): 2-17.* Traces the life of Ben Bagnall, a 19th-century businessman who amassed his fortune in lumber and real estate, as well as the conflicts in his family over his legacy after his death in 1926. 1817-1980

Bailey, Anne Hennis

291. Cole, Adelaide M. ANNE BAILEY: WOMAN OF COURAGE. *Daughters of the Am. Revolution Mag. 1980 114(3): 322-325.* English-born Anne Hennis Bailey (1742-1825) came to America at 19 after her parents died and lived in the Shenandoah Valley, Virginia, with relatives where she married and became famous as a messenger and a scout for the Continental Army. 1761-1825

Bailey, Margaret Jewett

292. Nelson, Herbert B. RUTH ROVER'S CUP OF SORROW. *Pacific Northwest Q. 1959 50(3): 91-98.* An account of the life of Margaret Jewett Bailey, a missionary of the Methodist Church, who during 1837-50 was involved in various romantic scandals and an unsuccessful marriage in Oregon, described in her novel *The Grains, or Passages in the Life of Ruth Rover, with Occasional Pictures of Oregon, Natural and Moral* (1854). 1837-50

Bailey, Vernon

293. Sterling, Keir. NATURALISTS OF THE SOUTHWEST AT THE TURN OF THE CENTURY. *Environmental Rev. 1978 3(1): 20-33.* American naturalists Clinton Hart Merriam, Vernon Bailey, E. W. Nelson, Edward Alphonso Goldman, and T. S. Palmer were prominent scientists who spent much of their careers, 1880's-1910's, exploring and recording facts on the indigenous floral, faunal, and human populations of the Southwest. 1880's-1910's

Bailly de Messein, François-Augustin

294. Michel, Louis. UN MARCHAND RURAL EN NOUVELLE-FRANCE: FRANÇOIS-AUGUSTIN BAILLY DE MESSEIN, 1709-1771 [A rural merchant in New France: François-Augustin Bailly de Messein, 1709-71]. *Rev. d'Hist. de l'Amérique Française [Canada] 1979 33(2): 215-262.* Bailly, the son of a soldier in Quebec, set up as a shopkeeper in Varennes in the early 1730's; in 40 years, he amassed one of the largest fortunes in the province through commerce in local products (although not furs), sales of foodstuffs, investments in land, and, most importantly, the extension of credit to local borrowers. Focuses on the debts owed to Bailly, the method of repayment, and a statistical analysis of his fortune. Based on notarial records in the National Archives of Quebec; 17 tables, 118 notes. 1730-71

Baird, A. Craig

295. Peterson, Owen. A. CRAIG BAIRD (1883-1979). *Southern Speech Communication J. 1982 47(2): 130-134.* Biographical sketch of A. Craig Baird, professor of speech at Ohio Wesleyan, Dartmouth, and Bates colleges. 1900-79

Baird, Absalom

296. Baird, John A., Jr. "FOR GALLANT AND MERITORIOUS SERVICE": MAJOR GENERAL ABSALOM BAIRD. *Civil War Times Illus. 1976 15(3): 4-9, 45-48.* Discusses the military career of Absalom Baird, a Union general. 1861-65

Baird, Spencer Fullerton

297. Bonta, Marcia. BAIRD OF THE SMITHSONIAN. *Pennsylvania Heritage 1980 6(3): 19-23.* Recounts the life and career of Spencer Fullerton Baird (1823-89), Pennsylvania naturalist, professor, and second secretary of the Smithsonian Institution in Washington, D.C. 1823-89

298. Deiss, William A. SPENCER F. BAIRD AND HIS COLLECTORS. *J. of the Soc. for the Biblio. of Natural Hist. [Great Britain] 1980 9(4): 635-645.* Spencer F. Baird (1823-87), successively Assistant Secretary and Second Secretary to the Smithsonian Institution in Washington, D.C., employed some and encouraged other collectors to send him natural history specimens for the Natural History Museum's collections. Paper presented at the International Conference on the History of Museums and Collections in Natural History, London, 3-6 April 1979; ref. 1823-87

Baker, Edgar Crow

299. Brooks, G. W. S. EDGAR CROW BAKER: AN ENTREPRENEUR IN EARLY BRITISH COLUMBIA. *BC Studies [Canada] 1976 (31): 23-43.* Edgar Crow Baker (d. 1920) was a representative entrepreneur in Victoria when that city was the social, business, and political center of British Columbia. Although he came to Victoria as an employee, he had ideas and ambitions, a valuable family connection, and fraternal affiliations that allowed him into the business life of the city. Baker was involved in almost every major economic activity in the province: land, lumber, railroads, coal, shipping, public utilities. He was also active in municipal, provincial, and federal politics. 51 notes. 1872-98

Baker, Edward

300. Hill, Helen M. THE BAKER JOURNALS: GLIMPSES OF DANIEL WEBSTER. *Manuscripts 1985 37(3): 195-208.* 1830-52
*For abstract see **Webster, Daniel***

301. Hill, Helen M. THE BAKER JOURNAL: BOYHOOD IN CROOKED LANE. *Manuscripts 1984 36(3): 173-186.* Extracts of a journal kept by Edward Baker of Crooked Lane in the northeast corner of Duxbury, Massachusetts, illustrate village life in 19th-century New England. 3 illus. 1845-95

Baker, Edward Dickinson

302. Vandenhoff, Anne. EDWARD DICKINSON BAKER. *Pacific Hist. 1979 23(4): 1-8.* Edward Dickinson Baker (1811-61) was a close personal friend of Abraham Lincoln. English-born, he migrated to the United States, settling in Illinois. He later moved to California, where he became active in politics while he continued his law practice. Shortly after Oregon entered the Union in 1859 he moved to the Willamette Valley. As the clouds of secession began to rise, his powerful oratory contributed greatly toward keeping the two states in the union. Oregon sent him to the Senate in 1860, and Lincoln relied heavily on his old friend in matters relative to the Far West. He died in 1861, having spent just a little over a year in the Senate. 3 illus. 1840-61

Baker, George

303. Lincoln, C. Eric and Mamiya, Lawrence H. DADDY JONES AND FATHER DIVINE: THE CULT AS POLITICAL RELIGION. *Religion in Life 1980 49(1): 6-23.* 1920-79
*For abstract see **Jones, Jim***

Baker, George (Father Divine)

304. Pearson, Fred Lamar, Jr. and Tomberlin, Joseph Aaron. JOHN DOE, ALIAS GOD: A NOTE ON FATHER DIVINE'S GEORGIA CAREER. *Georgia Hist. Q. 1976 60(1): 43-48.* George Baker (later, "Father Divine") was born in Savannah and grew up in the South. He became involved with Samuel Morris, "Father Jehovia," in Baltimore and assumed the title "The Messenger." The trinity was completed with the addition of St. John the Vine Hickerson. There was soon to be conflict over divinity, and Hickerson and "The Messenger" moved in independent directions. Baker went to Valdosta where he began to develop a following, mainly of black females. Eventually (1914) he was taken to court, and after a series of court battles, he was acquitted and left Valdosta with some of his followers. Primary and secondary sources; 29 notes. 1899-1914

Baker, George L.

305. Waters, W. Kenneth, Jr. THE BAKER STOCK COMPANY AND THE COMMUNITY. *Oregon Hist. Q. 1981 82(3): 229-270.* Discusses George L. Baker (1868-1941) and his theater stock company, which performed from headquarters in Portland, Oregon, during ca. 1903-15. The company continued but declined under other management until 1922. Focuses on the company's relationship to its audience, the Portland press, and local clergymen. Based on interviews and newspapers; 20 illus., 74 notes. ca 1902-15

Baker, James C.

306. Tom, James Leroy. "Through Such Men: The Life and Ministry of James C. Baker." Claremont Grad. School 1984. 331 pp. *DAI 1984 45(4): 1139-A.* DA8416465 1920's-69

Baker, John W. B.

307. Baker, John W. B. INTO THE NORTH. *Alberta History [Canada] 1985 33(2): 19-27.* As a pioneer resident of the Peace River area in Alberta during the last great days of fur trading, John W. B. Baker addressed the opening of the Fort St. John Museum in February 1984 by recounting his life in the Canadian North during 1928-48. He describes the topography, Eskimo life, animal life, trade under the jurisdiction of the Hudson's Bay Company, and key individuals—bush pilots, missionaries—in this geographical area, and discusses his careers as a radio operator at Watson Lake, and later as a chief dispatcher for Canadian Pacific Air Lines. 5 photos. 1928-48

Baker, Lorenzo Dow

308. Bartlett, Wilson Randolph, Jr. "Lorenzo Dow Baker and the Development of the Banana Trade Between Jamaica and the United States, 1881-1890." Am. U. 1977. 276 pp. *DAI 1978 38(11): 6887-A.* 1881-90

Baker, Nelson Henry

309. Fish, Lydia. FATHER BAKER: LEGENDS OF A SAINT IN BUFFALO. *New York Folklore 1984 10(3-4): 23-33.* Gives a brief biography of Catholic priest Nelson Henry Baker and discusses the popular legends surrounding the priest in Buffalo, New York, where he performed many charitable deeds. 1860's-20c

Balance, Alice

310. Poliakoff, Phaye. "THOUGHT WE WERE JUST SOME POOR OLD COUNTRY PEOPLE": AN INTERVIEW WITH ALICE BALANCE. *Southern Exposure 1983 11(6): 30-32.* Alice Balance recalls her youth on a farm in Bertie County, North Carolina, her sharecropping days, and being forced off the land by mechanized farming. 1920-83

Baldassarre, Raffaele

311. Baldassarre, Raffaele; Troy, Ferdinand M., ed., transl.; Steele, Thomas J., transl. FATHER BALDASSARRE WRITES HOME. *Colorado Coll. Studies 1982 (19): 187-191.* Raffaele Baldassarre wrote a letter in Italian to friends in Italy describing daily life and religious customs in the Jesuit parish in Conejos, Colorado, which was published in *Lettere Edificanti dei Padri della Compagnia di Gesu della Provincia Napoletana* [Edifying letters of the fathers of the Naples Province of the Society of Jesus], vol. 1 (1874), pp. 82-84. Ferdinand M. Troy [Trojanek] translated it into Latin and added comments in his undated typescript, "Historica Societatis Jesu in Novo Mexico et Colorado" [History of the Society of Jesus in New Mexico and Colorado], Regis Jesuit History Library, Denver. Prints an English translation of Troy's Latin compared with the Italian original. 1874-80

Baldwin, Alice Mary

312. Brandstadter, Dianne Puthoff. "Developing the Coordinate College for Women at Duke University: The Career of Alice Mary Baldwin, 1924-1947." Duke U. 1977. 174 pp. *DAI 1977 38(4): 2297-A.* 1924-47

Baldwin, Nathaniel

313. Singer, Merrill. NATHANIEL BALDWIN, UTAH INVENTOR AND PATRON OF THE FUNDAMENTALIST MOVEMENT. *Utah Hist. Q. 1979 47(1): 42-53.* Nathaniel Baldwin (1878-1961), inventor, writer, and philanthropist, helped Utah become a leading manufacturer of radio loudspeakers and headsets. His products were marketed worldwide and especially were sought by the US Navy in World War I. A Mormon Fundamentalist, he advocated plural marriage. This led to his disfellowship by the LDS Church. Apparently a poor businessman and poor judge of character, he lost his multimillion dollar business, was sent to prison for fraudulent use of the mails for advertising, and died impoverished. 4 illus., 31 notes. 1900's-61

Baldwin, Robert

314. Cross, Michael S. and Fraser, Robert L. "THE WASTE THAT LIES BEFORE ME": THE PUBLIC AND PRIVATE WORLDS OF ROBERT BALDWIN. *Hist. Papers [Canada] 1983 164-183.* Short biography and psychohistory of Canadian political reformer Robert Baldwin, whose apparent success in public life masked inner torment unknown even to his family. 105 notes. French summary. 1819-59

Baldwin, Tom

315. Raymond, Arthur E. EARLY NON-RIGID DIRIGIBLES 1898-1915: ROY KNABENSHUE AND HIS ERA. *American Aviation Historical Society 1985 30(1): 58-67.* 1898-1915

For abstract see ***Knabenshue, Roy***

Baldwin, William G.

316. Hadsell, Richard M. and Coffey, William E. FROM LAW AND ORDER TO CLASS WARFARE: BALDWIN-FELTS DETECTIVES IN THE SOUTHERN WEST VIRGINIA COAL FIELDS. *West Virginia Hist. 1979 40(3): 268-286.* William G. Baldwin and Thomas L. Felts formed Baldwin-Felts Detectives in the 1890's and for 30 years provided a private police and guard service for West Virginia coal mines. Their agents infiltrated unions, evicted undesirables, guarded nonstrikers, and kept order on mine property. Their antiunion activities became paramount and many were killed in gun battles or ambushes. By the 1930's they were outmoded and even illegal. Based on Justus Collins papers and other primary sources; 72 notes. 1890's-1935

Ballengee, Joseph Harmon

317. Wortman, Ruth Ballengee, ed. A BURLINGTON RAILROAD TELEGRAPHER, JOSEPH HARMON BALLENGEE. *Nebraska Hist. 1984 65(2): 221-244.* A personal narrative by Joseph Harmon Ballengee covering his years as a railroad telegrapher. His service was with two companies, the Chicago, Burlington and Quincy Railroad and the Chicago and Northwestern Railroad, chiefly in northwest Nebraska and southwest South Dakota. His most interesting service occurred during the 1890's and early 1900's at Crawford and nearby Fort Robinson in Nebraska. 5 illus., 36 notes. 1880's-1932

Ballenger, Tom Lee

318. Agnew, Brad. AROUND TAHLEQUAH COUNCIL FIRES: THE LIFE OF OKLAHOMA HISTORIAN T. L. BALLENGER. *Chronicles of Oklahoma 1982 60(3): 310-321.* After graduating from Ouachita Baptist College in 1905, Tom Lee Ballenger accepted a number of short-term teaching assignments that he alternated with work on a graduate degree. He completed the doctorate at the University of Oklahoma in 1939 and returned to Northeastern State Teachers College in Tahlequah, where he had been teaching since 1914. Ballenger has received praise as a superb teacher, but his main contribution to scholarship is his collecting of Cherokee archival materials and writing about local history topics. Based on interviews and Ballenger's unpublished manuscripts; 4 photos, 26 notes. 1905-82

Ballinger, Richard A.

319. Tanner, Thomas. THE BOONESBORO CONNECTION: RICHARD A. BALLINGER AND RAY LYMAN WILBUR. *Palimpsest 1985 66(1): 30-40.* Presents biographical sketches of Boonesboro, Iowa, natives Richard A. Ballinger and Ray Lyman and describes the years each man spent as secretary of the interior. 1900's-30's

Ballou, Sylvester Allen

320. Apostol, Jane. SYLVESTER ALLEN BALLOU: ARGONAUT IN THE STATEHOUSE. *Pacific Hist. 1983 27(2): 52-63.* Sylvester Allen Ballou moved from Ohio to California in 1849. At various times he was a miner, a trader, assemblyman, and teacher. He served four terms in the legislature and is remembered for his eloquence and wit; he won special acclaim as a spokesman for popular sovereignty in 1858. Sources include manuscripts from the Ballou Collection at the Huntington Library. 1848-99

Bancroft, George

321. Johnson, Edgar Hutchinson, III. "George Bancroft, Slavery, and the American Union." Auburn U. 1983. 227 pp. *DAI 1984 44(11): 3466-A.* DA8404091 17c-1789

322. Shulsinger, Stephanie. THE WIDE WORLD OF GEORGE BANCROFT. *New-England Galaxy 1976 18(1): 15-21.* Traces the career of George Bancroft (1800-91), historian, teacher, government official, and ambassador. 3 illus. 1800-91

Bancroft, Wilder D.

323. Servos, John W. A DISCIPLINARY PROGRAM THAT FAILED: WILDER D. BANCROFT AND THE *JOURNAL OF PHYSICAL CHEMISTRY,* 1896-1933. *Isis 1982 73(267): 207-232.* Traces the career and influence of Wilder D. Bancroft, a somewhat contentious secondary figure in American chemistry during the early 20th century. Bancroft was a member of the Cornell faculty and founded and edited the *Journal of Physical Chemistry* during 1896-1932. Based on the papers of Bancroft and contemporaries and secondary works; 84 notes. 1896-1933

Banks, Moses and Joshua

324. Marshall, J. Furber. A BANKS FAMILY OF NOVA SCOTIA. *Nova Scotia Hist. Q. [Canada] 1977 7(2): 175-188.* Traces the genealogy of Moses Banks (1739-1833) and Joshua Banks (1749-1843), of Granville, Nova Scotia. Primary sources; biblio. 1739-1843

Banting, Frederick Grant

325. Quinn, Kevin F. BANTING AND HIS BIOGRAPHERS: MAKER OF MIRACLES, MAKERS OF MYTH. *Queen's Q. [Canada] 1982 89(2): 243-259.* Frederick Grant Banting's winning of the Nobel Prize (1923) for his discovery of insulin, followed by his untimely death while on active duty in World War II, caused him to become for Canadians a cultural hero of mythic proportions. The biographies of Banting that attempt to explain why he was great by focusing on what he did are doomed to failure, for it was not what he did but what he meant to Canadian nationalism that was important. Secondary sources; 15 notes. 1902-72

Banvard, John

326. Hanners, John. "IT WAS PLAY OR STARVE": JOHN BANVARD'S ACCOUNT OF EARLY SHOWBOATS. *Theatre Res. Int. [Great Britain] 1983 8(1): 53-64.* Reproduces excerpts from an unpublished autobiography by John Banvard (1815-91), the American adventurer, painter, poet, and theater owner, in which he describes his experiences with the Chapman Family as a scenic artist on America's first showboat, 1833-34, and during two seasons when he operated his own showboats, 1834-36. 1833-36

327. Hanners, John. "The Adventures of an Artist: John Banvard (1815-1891) and his Mississippi Panorama." Michigan State U. 1979. 183 pp. *DAI 1980 40(9): 4805-A.* 1815-91

328. Hanners, John. "VICISSITUDE AND WOE": THE THEATRICAL MISADVENTURES OF JOHN BANVARD. *Theatre Survey 1982 23(2): 177-187.* Recounts the career of painter, playwright, theatrical entrepreneur, and museum director John Banvard during 1842-91, focusing on the establishment and subsequent financial failure of his Broadway Theatre in New York City during 1867-79. 1867-79

329. —. [JOHN BANVARD'S MISSISSIPPI]. *Am. Hist. Illus. 1982 17(7): 30-39.*

Hanners, John. JOHN BANVARD'S MISSISSIPPI PANORAMA, *pp. 30-31, 36-39.* Describes the career of 19th-century American painter John Banvard, focusing on his monumental work, "Mississippi Panorama," which he exhibited in London during 1849-50.

—. PORTFOLIO: BANVARD'S RIVER SCENES, *pp. 32-35.* Additional Mississippi River scenes by Banvard as they looked in the 19th century. 1815-91

Bara, Theda

330. Lockwood, Charles. PRIESTESS OF SIN. *Horizon 1981 24(1): 64-69.* Theda Bara, who acted the vamp both on and off screen from 1915 to 1919, served as an ideal sex symbol in that she offered sexual allure without seriously threatening the morality of the time. 1915-19

Baraga, Frederic

331. Jezernik, Maksimilijan. FRIDERIK BARAGA: ZBIRKA RIMSKIH DOKUMENTOV [Friderik Baraga: collection of documents in Rome]. *Acta Ecclesiastica Sloveniae [Yugoslavia] 1980 2: 13-195.* Describes and categorizes documents located primarily in the Vatican archives relating to the career of Catholic missionary Frederic Baraga, who became the bishop of the Diocese of Sault Ste. Marie and Marquette in the western Great Lakes region. 1800-68

Barbeau, Victor

332. Trépanier, Pierre. VICTOR BARBEAU ET ALBINY PAQUETTE [Victor Barbeau and Albiny Paquette]. *Action Natl. [Canada] 1978 68(4): 324-330.* Although best known as a writer, linguist, and critic, Victor Barbeau was a prophet of the Quebec consumer cooperative movement. He urged its extension throughout the world as a model for a new society based on rationality of service rather than profit. Albiny Paquette was a medical doctor, mayor, prefect, deputy, provincial secretary, minister of health under Maurice Duplessis, and legislative councillor. He launched crusades against tuberculosis and infant mortality, and was both a political conservative and a staunch Catholic. Covers ca. 1900-45. Review of "Victor Barbeau, hommages et tributes," *Cahiers de*

l'Académie canadienne-française, No. 15 (Montreal, Fides, 1978), and Paquette, *33 années à la législature de Québec, Soldat—médecin—maire—député—ministre, Souvenirs d'une vie de travail et de bonheur* (1977). 11 notes. 1900-45

Barber, Theodore Moses

333. Rudoff, Andrew E. A HUMBLE AND ASSIDUOUS STUDENT: THE LIFE OF THEODORE BARBER, 1846-1915. *Western Pennsylvania Hist. Mag. 1980 63(2): 171-183.* Biography of Theodore Moses Barber who was a professor of Latin, rhetoric, and English at the Western University of Pennsylvania from 1870 to 1889. 1846-1915

Barbiere, Francis Joseph, Jr.

334. Purcell, Douglas Clare. JOSEPH BARBIERE: TENNESSEE CONFEDERATE IN ALABAMA. *Alabama Rev. 1982 35(4): 243-259.* Follows the career of journalist, lawyer, statesman, soldier, and orator Francis Joseph Barbiere, Jr. (1831-92), who served for two years during the Civil War in Talladega, Alabama, as chief enrolling officer of conscripts for the 4th Congressional District. Based on Civil War records, correspondence, and other primary and secondary sources; 51 notes. 1831-92

Barker, Albert Winslow

335. Simmons, Barbara T. ALBERT WINSLOW BARKER, PHOTOGRAPHER. *Pennsylvania Mag. of Hist. and Biog. 1982 106(1): 99-110.* Albert Winslow Barker, known for his lithographs, also recorded Pennsylvania's countryside in little-known photographs. Based on Albert Winslow Barker Collection of Glass Plate Negatives, Historical Society of Pennsylvania, and Barker Papers, Bryn Mawr College; 11 plates, 8 notes. 1874-1947

Barker, Elliott S.

336. Barker, Elliott S. WILDERNESS IN MY LIFE. *Palacio 1981-82 87(4): 33-38.* Autobiographical account of the New Mexican naturalist's camping trip to the Pecos wilderness in 1897 as a child of ten; it led him to pursue his lifelong career. 1897

Barker, James

337. Morrow, Phyllis. PHOTOGRAPHER OF THE NORTH: JAMES BARKER. *Alaska J. 1978 8(4): 296-309.* Briefly describes James Barker's life (to date) and techniques, and provides 16 of his photographs of Eskimos in the Yukon Territory and the Kuskokwim River area in Alaska, 1973-78. 1970-78

Barkley, Alben W.

338. Davis, Polly Ann. ALBEN W. BARKLEY: VICE PRESIDENT. *Register of the Kentucky Hist. Soc. 1978 76(2): 112-132.* After 36 years as a senator, Alben W. Barkley became vice president in 1949. Barkley was an intelligent statesman, a model patriot, an effective public speaker, one of the greatest senators of the 20th century, and a popular vice president. He returned to the Senate in 1955 and died in 1956. Primary and secondary sources; 86 notes. 1949-56

339. Libbey, James K. ALBEN BARKLEY'S CLINTON DAYS. *Register of the Kentucky Hist. Soc. 1980 78(4): 343-361.* Alben W. Barkley moved to Clinton, Kentucky, in 1891 at the age of 14. It was in Clinton that Barkley gained the formal education vital to his later political career. He attended Marvin College in Clinton, graduating in 1897. Family poverty forced him to work hard while in college, and, although his grades were not outstanding, his work in speech and debate were noteworthy. Barkley left Clinton in 1898 and his Clinton experience receded as he became known as the "Paducah politician." Based on newspapers and secondary sources; 3 illus., 35 notes. 1877-98

Barlow, Joel

340. Mulford, Carla Jean. "Joel Barlow's Letters, 1775-1788." U. of Delaware 1983. 422 pp. *DAI 1984 45(6): 1753-A.* DA8420980 1775-88

Barnard, Frederick A. P.

341. Mellown, Robert O. EARLY PHOTOGRAPHY, F. A. P. BARNARD, AND THE UNIVERSITY OF ALABAMA. *Alabama Rev. 1984 37(1):25-33.* Discusses the brief photographic career of University of Alabama science professor Frederick Augustus Porter Barnard, who operated a daguerreotype gallery in Tuscaloosa with Dr. William H. Harrington during 1841-42. Barnard invented a chemical process that shortened the exposure time of daguerreotypes and continued his photographic research until he left Alabama in 1854. 17 notes. 1841-54

342. Segal, Howard P. AMERICAN COLLEGE AND UNIVERSITY PRESIDENTS: FOUR BIOGRAPHICAL STUDIES. *Hist. of Educ. Q. 1982 22(1): 99-102.* Reviews Glenn C. Altschuler's *Andrew D. White—Educator, Historian, Diplomat* (1979), William J. Chute's *Damn Yankee! The First Career of Frederick A. P. Barnard—Educator, Scientist, Idealist* (1978), Marvin E. Gettleman's *An Elusive Presence: The Discovery of John H. Finley and His America* (1979), and Albert Marrin's *Nicholas Murray Butler* (1976), four traditional biographies of prominent American educators. Note. 1850's-1945

Barnard, George

343. Willingham, John. GEORGE BARNARD: TRADER AND MERCHANT ON THE TEXAS FRONTIER. *Texana 1973 12(4): 305-334.* In the late 1830's George Barnard came to the Waco, Texas region from Hartford, Connecticut. Only 19 years of age at the time, he was the first white settler in the region. Becoming resident agent there at a post established by the firm of John F. Torrey and Brothers of Houston, he traded with the area Indians and invested heavily in land. By 1857 he was financially secure and went into semi-retirement, dying in 1883. Based on primary and secondary sources; 85 notes. 1830-83

Barnard, George Grey

344. Adams, Leland B. GEORGE GREY BARNARD, SCULPTOR OF LINCOLN. *Lincoln Herald 1979 81(1): 5-9.* A biography of George Grey Barnard, sculptor of the busts of Abraham Lincoln. 1863-1938

345. Comminges, Elie de. GEORGE G. BARNARD ET L'ACHAT DES CHAPITEAUX DE SAINT-MICHEL-DE-CUXA [George G. Barnard and the purchase of the capitals of Saint-Michel-de-Cuxa]. *Ann. du Midi [France] 1981 93(151): 71-82.* The American sculptor, G. G. Barnard (1863-1938), having had financial difficulties in finishing the groups which were to decorate the front of the Pennsylvania Statehouse at Harrisburg, became an antique dealer in order to make a living. The author recounts here, from the artist's documents, how Barnard acquired the capitals and other

fragments of the Romanesque cloister of Saint-Michel-de-Cuxa between 1907 and 1913, and how he sought in vain to resell this collection until 1925, when it was bought by John D. Rockefeller who gave it to the Metropolitan Museum of New York for the Cloisters. 1907-25

Barnes, Charles W.

346. Anderson, Kelly Dennis. "The Contributions of Charles W. Barnes to the Development of the Baptist Student Union Work at the University of Alabama during 1940-74." Southwestern Baptist Theological Seminary 1983. *DAI 1984 45(1): 141-A.* 1940-74

Barnes, Clyde Teancum

347. Bitton, Davis. CLAUDE T. BARNES, UTAH NATURALIST. *Utah Hist. Q. 1981 49(4): 317-339.* Clyde Teancum Barnes grew up in Utah, undertook a law degree at the University of Michigan with his wife Anne, returned to Utah to write for the *Deseret News* articles on ornithology. Combining a law practice, he continued to extol the virtues of nature for the balance of his life. 8 photos, lithograph, 62 notes. 1884-1968

Barnes, Ernie

348. MacTavish, Merry. ERNIE BARNES: FROM ATHLETE TO ARTIST. *Westways 1983 75(2): 36-39, 79.* Presents a biography of North Carolina artist and former National Football League defensive guard, Ernie Barnes, discussing the aesthetic philosophy and messages of his paintings. 1938-82

Barnes, Harry Elmer

349. Turnbaugh, Roy. THE FBI AND HARRY ELMER BARNES: 1936-1944. *Historian 1980 42(3): 385-398.* The Federal Bureau of Investigation's investigation of historian, reformer, and political commentator Harry Elmer Barnes from 1936 to 1944 reveals much about the motives and priorities of that organization. Initially, Barnes was branded by the FBI as an enemy for his criticism of that agency's failure to pursue organized crime. His opposition to America's entry into World War II before Pearl Harbor and his growing alienation from the Roosevelt administration kept alive the agency's interest in his activities. An ill-considered speech in October 1942 before the Rotary Club in Utica, New York, allowed the FBI to take its revenge by trying to brand him as a seditionist; yet he was not prosecuted in the Sedition Trial of 1944. The entire Barnes affair was more than simply FBI chief J. Edgar Hoover's animosity toward Barnes. In essence, Hoover's attitudes toward hostile criticism had so pervaded the Bureau by 1936 that relatively obscure speeches drew tremendous attention. Primary sources; 44 notes. 1936-44

350. Turnbaugh, Roy. "Harry Elmer Barnes: The Quest for Truth and Justice." U. of Illinois, Urbana-Champaign 1977. 358 pp. *DAI 1977 38(1): 442-443-A.* 1918-41

Barnet, Robert Ayres

351. Zukerman, Robert Samuel. "Robert Ayres Barnet: American Playwright and Lyricist." City U. of New York 1981. 544 pp. *DAI 1982 42(9): 3811-A.* DA8203345 1890-1906

Barnett, George

352. Bartlett, Merrill L. OUSTER OF A COMMANDANT. *US Naval Inst. Pro. 1980 106(11): 60-65.* Major General George Barnett (1859-1930), Commandant of the US Marines from 1914 to 1920, was suddenly relieved of his duties by Secretary of the Navy Josephus Daniels. During his tour, the Marine Corps grew from fewer than 10,000 men to more than 75,000 men, and Marine units were committed to battle in France during World War I. Though Barnett had managed to alienate Daniels on several counts, he did receive renewal of his appointment in February 1918; but Daniels did not want him to serve longer than necessary. In June 1920, Daniels relieved Barnett and John A. Lejeune became the new commandant. Barnett remained on active duty until 1923, but remained bitter. He retired because of age in 1923. Primary sources, with a short accompanying essay on the source materials; 3 photos. 1914-23

Barney, Joshua

353. Levin, Alexandra Lee. HOW COMMODORE JOSHUA BARNEY OUTWITTED THE BRITISH AT NORFOLK. *Maryland Hist. Mag. 1978 73(2): 163-167.* Summarizes the colorful career of the "Prince of privateers and adventurers," Commodore Joshua Barney (1759-1818), ardent Francophile, who in August, 1797 was blockaded in Norfolk by a British squadron seeking to intercept the two French frigates commanded by Barney with supplies for St. Domingo. Executing "one of his most brilliant feats of seamanship," Barney gave the British the slip by hiding behind a point on the Eastern Shore and making Vice-Admiral Vandeput think he'd gone to sea the previous night. Barney's service to the nation during the war of 1812 while commanding the *Rossie,* and his fight at Bladensburg caused the citizenry of the Chesapeake region to cease holding his service in the French navy against him. Based on Daniel Bedinger's correspondence and standard biographies; 15 notes. 1771-1818

Barney, Natalie Clifford

354. Orenstein, Gloria Feman. THE SALON OF NATALIE CLIFFORD BARNEY: AN INTERVIEW WITH BERTHE CLEYRERGUE. *Signs 1979 4(3): 484-496.* Describes the activities and life-style of American writer Natalie Clifford Barney, through an interview with her French companion and servant of 45 years, Berthe Cleyrergue. Barney maintained a legendary salon in Paris from 1909 until her death in 1972, where frequent visitors included Gertrude Stein, Alice B. Toklas, Romaine Brooks, and Dolly Wilde. Suggests the need for further research on the history of female support networks like the one fostered by Barney. 3 notes. 1909-72

Barnhouse, Donald Grey

355. Russell, C. Allyn. DONALD GREY BARNHOUSE: FUNDAMENTALIST WHO CHANGED. *J. of Presbyterian Hist. 1981 59(1): 33-57.* For 33 years Donald Grey Barnhouse consistently drew the largest Bible study congregations on the fundamentalist-evangelical circuit in the United States and abroad. Based at Philadelphia's Tenth Presbyterian Church, he spent most of his time elsewhere. In addition to extensive publishing ventures, he conducted a coast-to-coast radio broadcast. His social and theological beliefs are discussed, as are the famous case before the Presbytery of Philadelphia (1929-1935), and Barnhouse's New Year's Resolution of 1953, in which he apologized for previous attitudes and conduct toward colleagues, and stated his resolve to work

more closely with them. Reasons for Barnhouse's change are posited, and his strengths and weaknesses are evaluated. Illus., 72 notes. 1927-60

Barnum, P. T.

356. Couser, G. Thomas. PROSE AND CONS: THE AUTOBIOGRAPHIES OF P. T. BARNUM. *Southwest Review 1985 70(4): 451-469.* Describes P. T. Barnum's preoccupation with practical jokes, which began in boyhood and carried over into his business, his American Museum, and his autobiographies. 1855-89

357. Green, Gregory. SHOW-MAN. *J. of Popular Culture 1980 14(3): 385-393.* Credits the flamboyant P. T. Barnum (1810-1891) with almost single-handedly assaulting the restrictive nature of 19th-century Protestantism. His weapons were entirely visual, and he possessed an uncanny knack for knowing how far he could push his visual deceptions in loosening the hold of Puritan morality on American entertainment. Emphasizes the period 1830-69. 18 notes. 1830-69

358. Stephens, Lester D. THE MERMAID HOAX: INDICATIONS OF SCIENTIFIC THOUGHT OF CHARLESTON, SOUTH CAROLINA, IN THE 1840S. *Pro. of the South Carolina Hist. Assoc. 1983: 45-55.* In 1842, P. T. Barnum exhibited a small "mermaid" that he claimed had been discovered in the Fiji Islands. In reality, he had glued together the head and torso of a monkey and the tail of a fish. It was brought to Charleston in 1843 and caused a controversy. Although the exhibit was a success, it was denounced as a fraud by the scientific community and leading newspapers. Based on newspapers and secondary sources; 27 notes. 1842-43

Baron, Salo Wittmayer

359. —. [SALO W. BARON: A TRIBUTE AND REPLY]. *Am. Jewish Hist. 1982 71(4): 493-500.*

Karp, Abraham J. PROF. SALO WITTMAYER BARON: A TRIBUTE, *pp. 493-496.* Appreciation and acclaim on behalf of the American Jewish Historical Society to historian Salo Wittmayer Baron for his monumental contributions to American Jews.

Baron, Salo W. REPLY TO PROFESSOR ABRAHAM KARP'S ADDRESS, *pp. 497-500.* Recalls events during Baron's 1953-55 presidency of the American Jewish Historical Society, contrasting the heightened status and activities of the society today with the same during the 1950's. Reprints the addresses of the Annual Meeting of the American Jewish Historical Society, New York City, 16 May 1981. 1937-81

Barr, D. Eglinton

360. Fowler, Arlen L. CHAPLAIN D. EGLINTON BARR: A LINCOLN YANKEE. *Hist. Mag. of the Protestant Episcopal Church 1976 45(4): 435-438.* When the Civil War began, Northern-born D. Eglinton Barr was rector of St. John's Episcopal Church, Baton Rouge, Louisiana. Because of his Northern heritage, he was suspect in the eyes of the Confederates. He went to the Federal lines in New Orleans, volunteered as a Chaplain, and was assigned to the 81st Regiment of US Colored Troops. Later he was apprehended and imprisoned by Confederates, but escaped and returned to New Orleans. At the end of the war, with former Confederates returning to power he was not allowed employment. He thus returned to the Army chaplaincy, was again assigned to a black regiment, and conducted school for his troops until he retired in 1872. The Department of Education of Texas presented him with a letter of appreciation for his work in the field of public education. His story provides an insight into the human side of times and events that are often forgotten. Material for the article was found in Selected Appointment, Commission and Personal Branch Records, D. E. Barr file, Record Group 94, National Archives, Washington, D.C. 1851-72

Barr, Henrietta Fitzhugh

361. Lady, Claudia Lynn. FIVE TRI-STATE WOMEN DURING THE CIVIL WAR. *West Virginia Hist. 1982 43(3): 189-226, (4): 303-321.* 1859-65

For abstract see ***Aleshire, Mary***

Barr, John Gorman

362. Hubbs, G. Ward. LETTERS FROM JOHN GORMAN BARR. *Alabama Rev. 1983 36(4): 271-284.* Details events during the last 18 months of Alabama humorist John Gorman Barr's life, especially his reactions to London and Paris, which he visited on his way to become US consul in Melbourne, Australia. He died en route. Reprints a letter written by Barr during the Mexican War, when he was captain of Company A, 1st Alabama Battalion. Based on Barr's collected correspondence at the University of Alabama; 34 notes. 1848-58

Barr, Lucien Francis

363. Cole, Dermot. THE WORST WAY TO FLY: THE STORY OF BUSH PILOT FRANK BARR. *Alaska J. 1984 14(1): 91-102.* Prints a biography of airplane pilot Lucien Francis Barr, emphasizing his one-man, one-plane Alaska airline. His company's motto was, "If you feel you must get there the worst way, fly with Barr." Tells of his disappearance en route in 1938, the massive search conducted for him, and his rescue. 7 photos. 1928-39

Barrows, Henry D.

364. Konig, Michael F. HENRY D. BARROWS: CALIFORNIA RENAISSANCE MAN. Dodd, Horace L. and Long, Robert W., ed. *People of the Far West* (Brand Book no. 6; San Diego: Corral of the Westerners, 1979): 131-137. Recounts the career of Henry D. Barrows of Los Angeles, California, historian, US marshal, school superintendent, agriculturalist, and Republican Party leader, 1854-77. 1854-77

Barry, John Waller

365. Conover, Cheryl, ed. KENTUCKIAN IN "KING ANDREW'S" COURT: THE LETTERS OF JOHN WALLER BARRY, WASHINGTON, D.C., 1831-1835. *Register of the Kentucky Hist. Soc. 1983 81(2): 168-198.* Continued from a previous article. After his graduation from West Point, Barry's letters displayed a greater awareness of what was happening in and around Washington. Barry supported his father, the postmaster-general, despite political attacks against him and his boss, Andrew Jackson. 5 illus., 38 notes. 1831-35

Barry, Kate

366. Miller, Mary Montgomery. KATE BARRY. *Daughters of the American Revolution Magazine 1984 118(9): 644-646.* Recounts the life of Kate Barry and her exploits as a volunteer scout for the Patriot forces in South Carolina during the American Revolution. 1776-83

Barry, Robertine

367. Boivin, Aurélien and Landry, Kenneth. FRANÇOISE ET MADELEINE: PIONNIÈRES DU JOURNALISME FÉMININ AU QUÉBEC [Françoise and Madeleine: pioneers of feminine journalism in Quebec]. *Atlantis [Canada] 1978 4(1): 63-74.* At the beginning of the 20th century, Françoise and Madeleine, pseudonyms of Robertine Barry and Anne-Marie Gleason respectively, through their articles worked at improving the condition of women and reminded their readers of the importance of the role of women. 1900-19

Barry, William Sullivan Taylor

368. Wyatt, Lee T., III. WILLIAM S. BARRY, ADVOCATE OF SECESSION, 1821-1868. *J. of Mississippi Hist. 1977 39(4): 339-355.* Describes the public career of William Sullivan Taylor Barry (1821-68), a Yale graduate, lawyer, state legislator, and congressman (1853-55). A superb orator, a militant secessionist, and "one of the most prominent Mississippians" in the 1850's, Barry was elected president of the 1861 Mississippi secession convention and served as an officer in the Confederate Army. Based upon newspapers and various unpublished manuscripts; 50 notes. 1845-68

Bartels, Irma Louise

369. Wetzel, David N. CHILDHOOD IN COLORADO: A GIRL'S LIFE AT THE TURN OF THE CENTURY. *Colorado Heritage 1983 (1-2): 74-79.* Irma Louise Bartels was born in Denver in 1888. The family moved often within Denver, causing Irma and her younger sister, Elsa, to change schools frequently. The girls developed friendships both with adults and contemporaries. Irma was an avid reader and took a special interest in famous women of her day, such as Queen Wilhelmina of the Netherlands and actress Blanche Walsh. She was active in her church and in the Christian Endeavor Movement. Irma died of pneumonia in January 1901. Based on material in the Colorado Historical Society, Denver; 4 illus. 1888-1901

Barthelme, Donald

370. Brans, Jo. EMBRACING THE WORLD: AN INTERVIEW WITH DONALD BARTHELME. *Southwest Rev. 1982 67(2): 121-137.* A November 1981 interview with author Donald Barthelme, discussing the influence of his father, a modern architect, on his work; his major themes; his use of language; and his thoughts on other writers, among them Ernest Hemingway. 1981

Bartholomew, Harland

371. Johnston, Norman J. HARLAND BARTHOLOMEW: PRECEDENT FOR THE PROFESSION. *J. of the Am. Inst. of Planners 1973 39(2): 115-124.* Biographical sketch of Harland Bartholomew (b. 1889) includes discussion of his achievements in city planning, urban renewal, rural land use policy, and housing policy formation, 1910's-20's. 1910's-20's

Bartlett, John Russell

372. Haskell, John Duncan, Jr. "John Russell Bartlett (1805-1886): Bookman." George Washington U. 1977. 336 pp. *DAI 1977 38(6): 3119-3120-A.* 1840-86

Bartlett, Robert Abram

373. Horwood, Harold. BOB BARTLETT, MASTER OF THE ARCTIC SEAS. *Can. Geographic [Canada] 1979 98(2): 44-49.* Robert Abram Bartlett (d. 1946), a native of Newfoundland, was instrumental in Arctic and polar exploration, 1900's-45. 1900's-45

Bartol, Cyrus

374. Heath, William G., Jr. CYRUS BARTOL'S TRANSCENDENTAL CAPITALISM. *Studies in the Am. Renaissance 1979: 399-408.* Cyrus Bartol, minister of the Unitarian West Church in Boston, was a familiar figure in the religious, intellectual, and literary life of New England during the 19th century. He was, however, besides a religious figure, also a shrewd businessman, and had no rival "in combining the dual roles of seer and doer." Bartol became acquainted with Manchester-by-the-Sea in Massachusetts in the 1850's, and made his first important real estate purchase in 1871. Over the next quarter century Bartol bought, improved, and sold additional properties in Manchester. His business investments were to him for spiritual benefit. He used his investments as a means of putting into practice some of his strongest religious beliefs. He conceived nature as chaotic and in need of improvement by man. It is not hard to see a connection between this idea and his tremendous effect on the development of Manchester. Based on archives in the Manchester Historical Society and other primary sources; 29 notes. 1850-96

Barton, Benjamin Smith

375. Graustein, Jeannette E. THE EMINENT BENJAMIN SMITH BARTON. *Pennsylvania Mag. of Hist. and Biog. 1961 85(4): 423-438.* Traces the life and varied career of Benjamin Smith Barton (1766-1815), a leading US intellectual, who served in various positions in the American Philosophical Society (1802), the Linnaean Society, and the Philadelphia Medical Society (1808-12); discusses his books and his influence on students, particularly Thomas Nuttall, a major scholar of American natural history. 1786-1815

Barton, Clara

376. Gilbo, Patrick F. CANDID, "CRANKY" CLARA BARTON GAVE US THE RED CROSS. *Smithsonian 1981 12(2): 126-142.* Recounts the sometimes stormy career of Clara Barton, the founder of the American Red Cross, who led the organization from its founding in 1881 to 1904 and who conducted 19 major relief operations. 1881-1904

377. Henle, Ellen Langenheim. "Against the Fearful Odds: Clara Barton and American Philanthropy." Case Western Reserve U. 1977. 292 pp. *DAI 1978 38(8): 5005-A.* 1860's-1912

378. Henle, Ellen Langenheim. CLARA BARTON, SOLDIER OR PACIFIST? *Civil War Hist. 1978 24(2): 152-160.* The study of Clara Barton, founder of the American Red Cross and active in three major wars, contributes new perspectives on women's future military roles. She viewed war as a fact of life and wanted women to take part in it, including military education and combat service. She believed that women's secondary citizen status was directly related to exclusion from war. A complex person, Clara Barton was attracted and repelled by war. She viewed herself as a soldier, appreciating the adventure; in a real sense, her humanitarianism provided an alternative to a military career. Yet she

genuinely longed for and worked for peace, particularly through her Red Cross movement. Based on the Barton Papers and secondary sources; 31 notes. 1860's-90's

379. Stewart, Sally. SHARING MORE THAN MARBLE PALACES. *Daughters of the Am. Revolution Mag. 1981 115(3): 188-191.* Clara Barton, Mabel Boardman, and Jane Delano were all both Daughters of the American Revolution and American Red Cross pioneers: Clara Barton served as a Civil War nurse and founded the American Red Cross in 1881; Mabel Boardman served as a Red Cross administrator for four decades until 1944; and Jane Delano, as head of the National Committee on Red Cross Nursing Service, administered the Red Cross nursing operation during World War I. ca 1881-1944

Barton, Larry

380. Robertson, Pat. DIMENSION WITH LIGHT. *Sporting Classics 1985 4(3): 36-45.* Examines the art and life of Larry Barton, who in 1979 quit his award-winning career as a political cartoonist and began to paint wildlife. 1964-85

Barton, Roy Franklin

381. Staniukovich, M. V. NEOBYCHNAIA BIOGRAFIIA (ROI FRENKLIN BARTON, 1883-1947) [An unusual biography (Roy Franklin Barton, 1883-1947)]. *Sovetskaia Etnografiia [USSR] 1979 (1): 76-83.* The paper deals with the life and research work of Roy Franklin Barton, an American ethnographer and folklore student who may by right be regarded as an outstanding 20th century specialist in Philippine studies. Barton had for many years observed the life of hitherto little-known peoples of the Philippine Archipelago and had collected invaluable material. He is the author of about 40 works on the social relations, economy, religion and folklore of the Philippine peoples. However, his name does not hold the place due to him in the history of research. The only works dedicated to R. F. Barton are a few reviews of his books and two obituaries. The scholar spent the years from 1930 to 1940 in the USSR, where he worked as research fellow in the Institute of Ethnography, USSR Acadmey of Sciences. Some of his manuscripts are preserved in the archives of the Museum of Anthropolgoy and Ethnography. The author of the present paper aims at a fuller description of R. F. Barton's research work and the correction of certain errors in former publications. The paper is based mainly upon archive materials comprising the researcher's correspondence, his autobiography etc. 1883-1947

Barton, Thomas

382. Jeffries, Theodore W. THOMAS BARTON (1730-1780): VICTIM OF THE REVOLUTION. *J. of the Lancaster County Hist. Soc. 1977 81(1): 39-64.* Discusses the turmoil endured by Thomas Barton, an intellectual and member of the American Philosophical Society, during the American Revolution when he was forced to choose between his religion and patriotism to America, 1770-76. 1770-76

Barton, William

383. Mazet, Horace S. FROM REVOLUTIONARY WAR HERO TO VERMONT PRISONER. *Am. Hist. Illus. 1982 16(10): 10-11, 46-47.* Discusses the heroism of William Barton during the American Revolution, when he captured British General Richard Prescott in order to exchange him for the release of General Charles Lee of the Continental Army in 1777, and Barton's subsequent imprisonment from 1812 to 1825 for refusing to pay damages to Jonathan Allyn in a civil suit over some land; Barton died in 1831. 1775-1831

Bartram, John and William

384. Callahan, Nancy. THE BARTRAMS: PLANTMEN EXTRAORDINAIRE. *Daughters of the Am. Revolution Mag. 1980 114(5): 638-643.* Discusses John Bartram (1699-1777), a Pennsylvania farmer, his son William Bartram (1739-1823), a Philadelphia Quaker, and their interest in botany and natural history; John is known as the father of American botany, and William, the first naturalist-artist in the colonies, wrote extensively about his travels and discoveries. 1699-1823

385. Kastner, Joseph. COLONIAL BOTANIST, SELF-TAUGHT, FILLED EUROPEAN GARDENS. *Smithsonian 1977 8(7): 122-129.* John Bartram (1699-1777), American farmer and self-taught botanist working out of Philadelphia, systematically collected and shipped plant specimens through his primary contact Peter Collinson in London, to the highest levels of European society avid for new plants. During four decades he introduced nearly one-third of the 600 American plants then known in Europe. Appointed King's botanist in 1765, he explored the Carolinas, Georgia, and Florida, opening untouched regions to the study of natural history. 8 illus. 1699-1777

386. Merritt, J. I., III. WILLIAM BARTRAM IN AMERICA'S EDEN. *Hist. Today (Great Britain) 1978 28(11): 712-721.* Brief biography of American botanist and explorer William Bartram (1739-1823), detailing his explorations in the American South. 1760's-70's

Baruch, Bernard

387. Krueger, Thomas A. THE PUBLIC LIFE AND TIMES OF BERNARD BARUCH. *Rev. in Am. Hist. 1982 10(1): 115-119.* Reviews Jordan A. Schwarz's *The Speculator: Bernard M. Baruch in Washington, 1917-1965* (1981), a biography of the multimillionaire, political benefactor and presidential counselor, focusing on his public career. 1917-65

388. Schwarz, Jordan A. "THE LEADING JEW IN AMERICA." *Commentary 1980 70(6): 55-61.* Describes to what extent the economic and political activities of Bernard Baruch (1870-1965) were affected by his Jewish origin. ca 1900-50

Barzun, Jacques

389. Holton, John Thomas. "The Educational Thought of Jacques Barzun: Its Historical Foundation and Significance for Teacher Education." Ohio State U. 1980. 227 pp. *DAI 1981 41(7): 3162-A.* DA8100168 1920-79

Bascom, John

390. Jorgensen, Stan William. "A Passage of Faith: The Thought of John Bascom (1827-1911) and His Intellectual Successors." U. of North Carolina, Chapel Hill 1976. 413 pp. *DAI 1977 38(2): 975-A.* 1855-1911

Basilone, John

391. Dieckmann, Edward A., Sr. MANILA JOHN BASILONE. *Marine Corps Gazette 1963 47(10): 28-32.* Recounts the exploits of Sgt. John Basilone of the Marines, fatally wounded on Guadalcanal, Solomon Islands, in 1942. 1942

Bass, Sam

392. Robbins, Peggy. SAM BASS: THE TEXAS ROBIN HOOD. *Am. Hist. Illus. 1982 17(4): 37.* Brief biography of the short-lived cowboy and bandit, Sam Bass, who became known as "the Texas Robin Hood" because he paid poor folks for various services and friendly gestures with gold pieces he had stolen. 1851-78

Bassett, Ebenezer Don Carlos

393. Wynes, Charles E. EBENEZER DON CARLOS BASSETT, AMERICA'S FIRST BLACK DIPLOMAT. *Pennsylvania Hist. 1984 51(3): 232-240.* Ebenezer Don Carlos Bassett served as minister resident and consul general to Haiti from 1869 to 1877. Born in Litchfield, Connecticut, he made his home in Philadelphia, where he was principal of the Institute for Colored Youth for 14 years. From 1879 to 1888 and again briefly in the early 1900's, he was Haitian consul general in the United States, and also served briefly as Haitian chargé in Washington. Bassett wrote *Handbook for Haiti,* which was published by the Bureau of American Republics in four languages in 1892. 20 notes. 1869-1908

Bassoff, Tom

394. Ursenbach, Charles. THE GREAT CROWSNEST PASS TRAIN HOLDUP. *Alberta Hist. [Canada] 1984 32(2): 1-8.* 1920-24

*For abstract see **Akroff, George***

Batchelder, Mildred L.

395. Anderson, Dorothy Jean. "Mildred L. Batchelder: A Study in Leadership." Texas Woman's U. 1981. 404 pp. *DAI 1982 42(8): 3332-3333-A.* 8201703 1936-80

Bateman, F. O. (Red)

396. Wakeley, Philip C. F. O. (RED) BATEMAN, PIONEER SILVICULTURALIST. *J. of Forest Hist. 1976 20(2): 91-99.* F. O. Bateman (d. 1941), chief ranger of the Great Southern Lumber Company in Louisiana, was a pioneer in the South's forestry practice. His outstanding contributions were in prevention and suppression of fires and in techniques of forest planting. In 1924 he developed planting techniques still in general use for southern pines. 5 illus., 12 notes. 20c

Bates, Daisy

397. Trescott, Jacqueline. DAISY BATES: BEFORE AND AFTER LITTLE ROCK. *Crisis 1981 88(5): 232-235.* Daisy Bates, a journalist and civil rights leader, was an important worker behind the scene during the armed crisis surrounding the integration of Central High School in Little Rock, Arkansas, in 1957. As founder and editor of the *Arkansas State Press* and leader of the state's NAACP, she had been a crusader against discrimination from the 1940's. Bates prepared the children and community for the 1957 struggle. She built bridges between both sides as the conflict raged. Her home became the target of fire bombs, rocks, gun fire, and burning crosses. Quietly, she negotiated a solution. 1945-57

Bates, Elisha

398. Good, Donald G. ELISHA BATES AND THE BEACONITE CONTROVERSY. *Quaker Hist. 1984 73(1): 34-47.* In their evangelical publications against what they took to be the doctrines of Elias Hicks, Quakers Elisha Bates, of Mount Pleasant, Ohio, and Isaac Crewdson, of Manchester, England, based their arguments on the authority of the Bible. Crewdson's *A Beacon to the Society of Friends* (1835) led to controversy among English Quakers and the separation of the "Beaconites." Bates associated with Anna and Isaac Braithwaite, Beaconite sympathizers, on his two trips to England, 1833-36. His belief in the primacy of Scripture convinced him to be baptized with water, for which he was disowned by the Society of Friends in 1837. 49 notes. 1833-37

399. Good, Donald G. ELISHA BATES AND THE HICKSITE CONTROVERSY. *Quaker Hist. 1981 70(2): 104-117.* According to Elisha Bates, an evangelical Quaker in Mount Pleasant, Ohio, Christianity was divided into denominations, differing in sacraments, ritual, and polity, but united on a creed including the divinity of Christ, His atonement to save sinners, and the authority of the Bible. In 1825 he had published extracts from the writings of early Friends and an exposition of Quaker doctrine. In 1827 he founded the *Miscellaneous Repository* to defend orthodoxy against such Hicksites as William Gibbon, editor of the Wilmington, Delaware, *Berean.* Bates was prominent in the schism of Ohio Yearly Meeting precipitated by Elias Hicks's 1828 visit. Bates seemed to enjoy controversy and exaggerated his opponents' views. 49 notes. 1825-28

Bates, Lucious Christopher

400. Smith, C. Calvin. FROM "SEPARATE BUT EQUAL TO DESEGREGATION": THE CHANGING PHILOSOPHY OF L. C. BATES. *Arkansas Hist. Q. 1983 42(3): 254-270.* Analyzes the career of black journalist Lucious Christopher Bates, focusing on his years as the crusading editor of the *Arkansas State Press* (1941-59), in which he argued for blacks' right to vote in primary elections and for desegregated public education. Based on newspapers and interviews; 56 notes. 1941-59

Bateson, Gregory

401. Pogliano, Claudio. GREGORY BATESON [Gregory Bateson]. *Belfagor [Italy] 1984 39(5): 545-564.* Traces Gregory Bateson's education, intellectual influences, work in New Guinea and Bali, as well as his academic experience, as an introduction to his innovative ethnographies. 1904-80

Bathe, Greville

402. Maass, Eleanor A. GREVILLE BATHE'S THEATRE OF MACHINES": THE EVOLUTION OF A SCHOLAR AND HIS COLLECTION. *Technology and Culture 1978 19(4): 713-723.* Describes the career of Greville Bathe (1883-?1950) as a historian of technology. His collection of rare books is housed at the Swarthmore College Library. 4 illus., 7 notes. ca 1900-55

Batt, Joseph

403. Batt, Ronald E. JOSEPH BATT AND THE CHAPEL: A BIOGRAPHICAL SKETCH OF AN ALSATIAN IMMIGRANT. *Niagara Frontier 1976 23(2): 49-55.* Discusses the role of Alsatian immigrant, Joseph Batt, in the building of the Chapel of Our Lady Help of Christians in Cheektowaga, in the Buffalo area, 1789-1872. 1789-1872

Bauer, Adolphus Gustavus

404. Prioli, Carmine Andrew. THE INDIAN "PRINCESS" AND THE ARCHITECT: ORIGIN OF A NORTH CAROLINA LEGEND. *North Carolina Hist. Rev. 1983 60(3): 283-303.* Examines the accuracy of a popular North Carolina story that Adolphus Gustavus Bauer, a successful Raleigh architect and building contractor, married Rachel Blythe, a full-blooded Cherokee Indian princess, in 1895, in Washington, D.C., because North Carolina law prohibited interracial marriage and that Raleigh society immediately rejected Rachel and refused to patronize Adolphus. Undaunted, the couple bought a house in town and eventually won legitimization of their marriage in the General Assembly. Rachel died in childbirth and Adolphus committed suicide in grief a year after building Rachel's elaborate graveside monument. Actually Rachel was half Indian and not a princess, the couple married secretly in Raleigh eight months earlier than their Washington public wedding, Rachel isolated herself upon returning to Raleigh because she was six months pregnant though only four weeks married, Rachel died of bowel problems, and Adolphus killed himself after suffering repeated head pain and depression from a train-carriage collision and from its unsatisfactory financial settlement. Based primarily on the Bauer papers, North Carolina Division of Archives and History, and newspaper accounts; 12 illus., 82 notes. 1858-98

Baughman, Willis J.

405. Brindley, Syble Hazelrig. THE LIFE OF WILLIS J. BAUGHMAN AND HIS CONTRIBUTIONS TO HEALTH, PHYSICAL EDUCATION, AND RECREATION. *Vitae Scholasticae 1983 2(1): 113-122.* Gives a professional biography of Willis J. Baughman, the father of school health education of the state of Alabama. Chronicles his achievements as a master teacher and his uphill battle to make physical education part of the curriculum. 13 notes. Spanish summary. 1950's-70's

406. Brindley, Syble Hazelrig. "The Life of Willis J. Baughman and His Contributions to the Area of Health, Physical Education, and Recreation." U. of Alabama 1981. 334 pp. *DAI 1982 42(9): 3627-B.* DA8204834 1950's-70's

Baum, L. Frank

407. Luehrs, Robert B. L. FRANK BAUM AND THE LAND OF OZ: A CHILDREN'S AUTHOR AS SOCIAL CRITIC. *Nineteenth Cent. 1980 6(3): 55-57.* Recounts the life history of L. Frank Baum (1856-1919) and provides a descriptive analysis of the children's literature he created in partnership with some of the most talented illustrators of his day, a literature which on a social-critical level "dealt with the fate of agrarian assumptions and the viability of the Jeffersonian concept of state and society as they grated against the hard demands of industrialism." 1880-1919

408. McFall, Russell P. THE BAUM EXPLOSION. *Chicago Hist. 1978 7(1): 59-62.* Review article covering recent works on the life of Chicago-based L. Frank Baum (1856-1919), particularly focusing on the Oz series and the 1939 film, The *Wizard of Oz.* 1897-1970's

409. Billman, Carol. L. FRANK BAUM: THE WIZARD BEHIND OZ. *American History Illustrated 1985 20(5): 42-48.* Relates the life story of Lyman Frank Baum, who was a journalist, playwright, and merchant in addition to being the author of the *Wizard of Oz* and 13 subsequent *Oz* books. 1882-1914

Baumann, Gustave

410. Currie, Juliet. GUSTAVE BAUMANN: A CENTURY OF DELIGHT. *Palacio 1981 87(1): 25-32.* Gustave Baumann (b. 1881), a German immigrant, began his career in commercial art but turned to color woodcuts early in his career; focuses on his years in Santa Fe, New Mexico, from 1918, in light of a centennial retrospective of his work in June 1981 in Santa Fe. 1881-1981

Baxter, Annette Kar

411. Kerber, Linda K. and Levy, Darline Gay. ANNETTE KAR BAXTER (1926-1983). *American Quarterly 1983 35(5): 455-457.* Annette Kar Baxter was a pioneer in the teaching of women's history, a cultural historian, and a strong advocate of women's colleges. Baxter spent her entire professional career at Barnard College, and was Adolph S. and Effie Ochs Professor of History and chairman of the Department of History from 1974 until her untimely death. 1926-83

Baxter, James Phinney, III

412. Sawyer, John Edward. OBITUARY: JAMES PHINNEY BAXTER, 3RD. *Pro. of the Am. Antiquarian Soc. 1975 85(2): 357-360.* James Phinney Baxter III (1893-1975) was born in Portland, Maine, and educated at Williams College and at Harvard University (where he joined the faculty after graduation). He was always interested in national defense; he served in several civilian military capacities during World War II. A fine historian, he was a charter member of the American Antiquarian Society. Among his publications were *Scientists Against Time,* which chronicled the efforts of scientists and technologists in the war effort and won the Pulitzer Prize in 1947. His presence, fine mind, and unfailing good humor will be sorely missed. 1893-1975

Baxter, Percival Proctor

413. —. [PERCIVAL P. BAXTER.] *Maine Hist. Soc. Q. 1981 20(4): 227-260.*

Hakola, John W. PERCIVAL P. BAXTER: THE WILDERNESS CONCEPT, *pp. 227-256.* Traces the concept of wilderness that Percival Proctor Baxter (1876-1969) had in mind when he donated land to create Baxter State Park. From about 1917 he was concerned with conservation and the idea of creating a wilderness area in the state of Maine. He began to donate land toward that goal in 1931, continuing to make additional grants over the next 30 years. The stipulations and restrictions made by Baxter on the use of that land varied over the years, and at times later stipulations conflicted with earlier ones. Overall, it seems that he modified his positions when convinced it would be in the best interests of the park and its use. Based on papers in the Maine State Library, the Bowdoin College Library, and the records of the Baxter State Park Authority; 62 notes.

Schriver, Edward O. PERCIVAL P. BAXTER: A COMMENT, *pp. 257-260.* Places Baxter's efforts in Maine and national contexts. He was a pioneer in conservation, and a variety of pressures and changing attitudes toward the environment led him to change his position on conserving a wilderness area and allowing public use of it. 1917-69

Baylen, Joseph O.

414. Baylen, Joseph O. REMINISCENCES OF AN ACADEMIC NOBODY. *Pro. and Papers of the Georgia Assoc. of Hist. 1981: 51-63.* Prints an autobiography of historian Joseph O. Baylen of Georgia State University. The child of Ukrainian immigrants, he grew up in Chicago during the Depression. He was drafted and served in the army during World War II. After the war, he combined an academic career with further military service. 20c

Bayless, John Clark

415. Jobson, Robert C. JOHN CLARK BAYLESS, A KENTUCKY PRESBYTERIAN MINISTER, 1841-1875. *Filson Club Hist. Q. 1983 57(2): 188-206.* John Clark Bayless was educated at Centre College and Princeton Theological Seminary and entered the ministry. He served as pastor for Presbyterian churches in West Virginia, Indiana, and Kentucky. Despite poor health, Bayless proved to be an effective preacher and attracted many members to his congregations. Based on an unpublished family history and papers; 65 notes. 1841-75

Beach, Amy Marcy

416. Eden, Myrna Garvey. "Anna Hyatt Huntington, Sculptor, and Mrs. H. H. A. Beach, Composer: A Comparative Study of Two Women Representatives of the American Cultivated Tradition in the Arts." Syracuse U. 1977. 362 pp. *DAI 1978 38(8): 4415-A.* 1865-1920

Beach, John

417. Mappen, Marc. ANGLICAN HERESY IN EIGHTEENTH CENTURY CONNECTICUT: THE DISCIPLINING OF JOHN BEACH. *Hist. Mag. of the Protestant Episcopal Church 1979 48(4): 465-472.* The only colonial Connecticut Anglican clergyman ever charged with heresy, John Beach (1700-82), was a convert from Congregationalism. He rejected much of the theology of his former colleagues, and even wrote devastating pamphlets against them. In 1755, he published a book asserting that at the moment of death each individual comes into the presence of Christ and is judged then, rather than on Judgment Day. The Connecticut Congregational clergy, spotting this potential heresy, sent a copy of the work to Beach's ecclesiastical superiors in England. Reprimand followed. Beach backed down and went on to serve the Church, being the last Anglican parson in Connecticut to pray for the King's health. Based on the author's doctoral dissertation, records of the Society for the Propagation of the Gospel, Beach's writings, and secondary sources; 28 notes. 1720-82

Beach, Rex

418. Buske, Frank E. REX BEACH. *Alaska J. 1980 10(4): 37-42.* Rex Beach (1877-1949) in many novels and short stories about Alaska strongly preached for its greater development and the danger of conservation. Most of what Beach knew of Alaska came from personal experience, and his works were sufficiently popular to have been made into movies. His major influence in Alaska affairs was his successful lobbying in 1936 for a bill that allowed mining in Glacier Bay National Monument. ca 1897-1939

Beal, William James

419. Thomas, David. "KEEP ON SQUINTIN": THE LIFE OF WILLIAM JAMES BEAL. *Michigan Hist. 1984 68(4): 16-23.* Born in 1833 to pioneer parents in Adrian, Michigan, William James Beal attended the University of Michigan and Harvard University, specializing in zoology and botany. After teaching at the University of Chicago and other institutions, Beal was hired by Michigan Agricultural College in 1871 as a professor of botany and horticulture. Beal remained on the college's staff for 39 years, making a profound contribution in his field and leaving a permanent legacy in Beal Gardens, a living botanical laboratory and a major attraction for campus visitors. 13 photos, 25 notes. 1850's-1924

Beale, Edward Fitzgerald

420. Thompson, Gerald. "The Public Career of Edward Fitzgerald Beale, 1845-1893." U. of Arizona 1978. 523 pp. *DAI 1978 39(2): 1065-A.* 1845-93

421. Thompson, Gerald. EDWARD FITZGERALD BEALE AND THE CALIFORNIA GOLD RUSH, 1848-1850. *Southern California Q. 1981 63(3): 198-225.* Traces the movement and activities of Edward Fitzgerald Beale (1822-1903). Having served as an acting naval lieutenant with distinction in the Mexican War, Beale traveled across Mexico with official reports on the discovery of gold in California. He won fame in Washington, D. C., as word spread of his perilous trip and the news he brought. Beale traveled back and forth between California and the East several times between 1848 and 1850. He found time to marry, shared the excitement of the gold rush with his friend John C. Frémont, and guided journalist Bayard Taylor around the gold fields. Beale also brought east a copy of California's new state Constitution. Not yet 30 years old, by 1850 Beale had become a well-known figure on the verge of a long and successful career. 57 notes. 1848-50

Beals, Carleton

422. Britton, John. CARLETON BEALS AND CENTRAL AMERICA AFTER SANDINO: STRUGGLE TO PUBLISH. *Journalism Q. 1983 60(2): 240-245, 310.* Traces the career of leftist US journalist Carleton Beals who vigorously opposed US intervention in Nicaragua in 1928. He was an outspoken supporter of Augusto César Sandino's guerrilla revolutionary movements. He opposed the US-backed regimes of Anastasio Somoza García and his son, Anastasio Somoza Deboyle. Chronicles Beals's difficulty getting his reports published between World War II and the era of the Vietnam War. 27 notes. 1928-70's

Beals, Jessie Tarbox

423. Moenster, Kathleen. JESSIE BEALS: OFFICIAL PHOTOGRAPHER OF THE 1904 WORLD'S FAIR. *Gateway Heritage 1982 3(2): 22-29.* Jessie Tarbox Beals (1870-1942) defied tradition to become the first woman photographer officially accredited to photograph the 1904 Louisiana Purchase Exposition at St. Louis, Missouri. Her success in 1904 led to a professional career in photography. She ventured abroad, performing overseas assignments in Latin America, Africa, and Asia. Beals published extensively in American newspapers and magazines, and her fame ensured her a place on the public lecture circuit. Biblio., 16 photos. 1904-42

Beamish, Thomas (family)

424. Punch, Terrence M. BEAMISH OF KILVURRA AND HALIFAX. *Nova Scotia Hist. Q. [Canada] 1979 9(3): 269-278.* Traces the genealogy of the Beamish family through five generations. Thomas Beamish (ca. 1743-ca. 1792), second son of John Beamish emigrated from Ireland to Halifax in

1765. He was the first Port Warden appointed in Halifax. His descendants include teachers, lawyers, farmers, ministers, and merchants. 1765-1970's

Beanes, William

425. Conner, Eugene H. WILLIAM BEANES, M.D. (1749-1829) AND THE *STAR-SPANGLED BANNER*. *J. of the Hist. of Medicine and Allied Sci. 1979 34(2): 224-229.* Dr. William Beanes, a physician of Upper Marlboro, Maryland, offered British General Robert Ross (1766-1814) the use of his home for headquarters during the War of 1812. Then, angered at British stragglers who pillaged the countryside on the way back to their ships from the burning of Washington, D.C., Beanes and former governor Robert Bowie (1750-1818) recruited men to capture and confine the stragglers. General Ross, angered at his former host, ordered him arrested and held as hostage for the release of the British soldiers. Beanes's friends went to lawyer Francis Scott Key for advice, and Key requested permission to negotiate for the physician's release. That brought Key to witness the bombardment of Fort McHenry. After the battle, Key and Dr. Beanes went to the Indian Queen Hotel in Baltimore, where Key wrote the poem that would become the *Star Spangled Banner.* 13 notes. 1814

Bear family

426. Best, Jane E. THREE BEARS OF EARL TOWNSHIP, LANCASTER COUNTY, PENNSYLVANIA, AND OTHER EARLY BEARS. *Pennsylvania Mennonite Heritage 1981 4(4): 12-27.* Traces the ancestry of the Baer, Bair, Bare, Barr, and Bear families in Lancaster County, Pennsylvania, from 1716 to the mid-1800's. 1716-1850

427. Best, Jane E. EUROPEAN ROOTS OF THE BEAR FAMILIES OF LANCASTER COUNTY, PENNSYLVANIA: AN UPDATE. *Pennsylvania Mennonite Heritage 1984 7(1): 21-36.* Traces Bear family genealogy from Lancaster County, Pennsylvania, to Rifferswil, in the canton of Zurich, Switzerland. ca 1630-1910

Beard, Charles A.

428. Braeman, John. THE HISTORIAN AS ACTIVIST: CHARLES A. BEARD AND THE NEW DEAL. *South Atlantic Q. 1980 79(4): 364-374.* American historian Charles A. Beard supported the first two administrations of Franklin D. Roosevelt, despite occasional trepidation. But when Roosevelt geared up for the 1940 campaign, Beard scathingly denounced the New Deal's failures. Long before Pearl Harbor he predicted that Roosevelt was determined to bring the United States into war with Hitler, either directly or by provoking a war with Japan. Beard's growing disillusionment with the New Deal roughly paralleled that of many liberal intellectuals. Even his commitment to isolationism was typical. What distinguished Beard was the depth and intensity of his bitterness. Based on the Beard File (microfilm), DePauw University Archives; the Roosevelt Papers, Franklin D. Roosevelt Library; Beard's letters and writings, and secondary materials; 26 notes. 1932-48

429. Braeman, John. CHARLES A. BEARD: THE ENGLISH EXPERIENCE. *J. of Am. Studies [Great Britain] 1981 15(2): 165-189.* American historian Charles A. Beard (1874-1948) began "noncollegiate" postgraduate studies at Oxford University in 1898. However, he devoted most of his energies from 1898 to 1902 to the founding of Ruskin Hall labor college in Oxford and to establishing educational extension programs for workingmen. Beard undertook the difficult but essential organizational work which Ruskin Hall movement leader Walter Vrooman generally avoided. 109 notes. 1898-1902

430. Nore, Ellen. CHARLES A. BEARD'S ACT OF FAITH: CONTEXT AND CONTENT. *J. of Am. Hist. 1980 66(4): 850-866.* Charles A. Beard's defense in the early 1930's of the relativistic or subjective approach to the writing of history did not constitute a sharp or sudden break with his earlier career. During the 1920's and 1930's, Beard was merely following the theoretical science of his time into new and uncertain areas. For Beard the act of writing history was similar to the quantum jumps taken by physicists such as Niels Bohr and Albert Einstein in their efforts to escape the determinism of Newtonian physics. Beard's flight from historical determinism led him toward relativism, but he never became an absolute relativist. Several factors influenced Beard's relativism regarding historical knowledge, including the New History, the writings of Benedetto Croce, and the social theory of Karl Mannheim. 48 notes. 1920's-33

Beard, Mary Ritter

431. Smith, Bonnie G. SEEING MARY BEARD. *Feminist Studies 1984 10(3): 399-416.* Reviews Mary Beard's historiography, using the viewpoint she herself applied to history. Just as she noted that women are invisible to historians, her work has been largely ignored or misunderstood by others. She rejected the accumulation of facts as a tool for understanding history. Crucial to understanding Mary Beard's "weirdness and asymmetry" is a recognition of her belief in history as viewpoint, and that the absence or presence of women in history depends entirely on the perspective of the historian. The fact that she did not receive full recognition for her work, whereas her husband Charles Beard was given both blame and credit for it, reinforces her own observations about history and historians. 27 notes. 1930-58

432. Turoff, Barbara Kivel. MARY BEARD: FEMINIST EDUCATOR. *Antioch Rev. 1979 37(3): 277-292.* Mary Ritter Beard (1876-1958) strove during 1934-54 to establish an international women's archives and a university which would educate with a feminist perspective; she did not achieve her original goals, but did establish the Schlesinger Library at Radcliffe College and the Sophia Smith Collection at Smith College. 1934-54

Bearden, Romare

433. Ellison, Ralph. THE ART OF ROMARE BEARDEN. *Massachusetts Rev. 1977 18(4): 673-680.* Romare Bearden, born in Charlotte, North Carolina, in 1914, studied at New York University, the Art Student's League, and the Sorbonne. In 1971 he was honored by a retrospective showing at New York's Museum of Modern Art. The series of collages and projections represented a special triumph. Painters have projected the "prose" of Harlem; Bearden has released its poetry. By painting familiar scenes he exposes their humanity and makes social commentary thereon. Bearden is a light-skinned Negro who resembles a Slavic Caucasian. Bearden's art is an affirmation of race as a limiting force in the arts. 1914-77

434. Hooton, Bruce Duff. ODYSSEY OF AN ARTIST. *Horizon 1979 22(8): 16-25.* Traces the career of black American artist Romare Bearden who paints "in the tradition of American artist-reporters," such as Andrew Wyeth, Jack Levine, Andy Warhol, James Rosenquist, and George Segal, since his first exhibition at Caresse Crosby's Gallery in Wash-

ington, D.C., in 1943, and discusses Bearden's childhood in Charlotte, North Carolina, based on a 1979 interview. 1914-79

Beardy, Jackson

435. Hughes, Kenneth James. THE LIFE. *Can. Dimension [Canada] 1979 14(2): 4-17.* Recounts the life and career of Cree artist Jackson Beardy (1944-78), and his struggle for identity. 1944-78

Beasley, Charles

436. Weitze, Karen J. CHARLES BEASLEY, ARCHITECT (1827-1913): ISSUES AND IMAGES. *J. of the Soc. of Architectural Hist. 1980 39(3): 187-207.* Outlines moral influences on the life of Charles Beasley, especially slavery during 1850-65 and Chinese immigration of the 19th century. Beasley was a self-made architect with a special penchant for developing Chinese-style building patterns in central California. He designed the Agricultural Pavilion of 1887 in Stockton, the earliest known date of a "Chinese" design in the United States. Based on newspaper archives, photograph collections, the Pioneer Museum, Haggin Galleries, and other sources; 32 illus., 84 notes, list of Beasley's works. ca 1850-1913

Beattie, Ann

437. Parini, Jay. A WRITER COMES OF AGE. *Horizon 1982 25(8): 22-24.* Chronicles the career of American novelist and short-story writer Ann Beattie, author of *Distortions* (1976), *Chilly Scenes of Winter* (1976), *The Burning Bush* (1982), and other works. 1975-82

Beatty, Ellen Adair White

438. Uhler, Margaret Anderson. "FLORIDA WHITE," SOUTHERN BELLE. *Florida Hist. Q. 1977 55(3): 299-309.* Ellen Adair White Beatty (1801-84), wife of Florida congressman Joseph M. White, enjoyed popularity and admiration in prominent social circles both here and abroad. She also figured in the Adair family genealogy. Based mainly on MS. and newspaper sources; 2 illus., 37 notes. 1801-84

Beaumont, William

439. Numbers, Ronald L. WILLIAM BEAUMONT AND THE ETHICS OF HUMAN EXPERIMENTATION. *J. of the Hist. of Biology [Netherlands] 1979 12(1): 113-135.* Discusses the relationship between Dr. William Beaumont (d. 1853) and Alexis St. Martin (d. 1880), the patient with the hole in his side. Because Beaumont could watch St. Martin's gastric process after St. Martin suffered a gunshot wound and subsequent fistula in 1822, the doctor conducted many experiments in the name of advancing science during 1823-25 and 1829-33. While not unaware of the bioethical question, Beaumont, influenced by class considerations, took a paternalistic attitude toward St. Martin, a French Canadian. In brief, Beaumont was neither a hero nor a villain in the history of bioethics. 1823-33

Beaux, Cecilia

440. Bailey, Elizabeth Graham. CECILIA BEAUX: BACKGROUND WITH A FIGURE. *Art and Antiques 1980 3(2): 54-61.* Despite her conservative and conventional upbringing, and the prejudice against women in professional art during the 19th century, American painter, Cecilia Beaux (1855-1942), achieved an international reputation for her 300 portraits, 1870's-1920's. 1870's-1920's

Beck, Adam

441. Beckman, Thomas. THE BECK & PAULI LITHOGRAPHING COMPANY. *Imprint 1984 9(1): 1-6.* Traces the careers of Clemens J. Pauli and Adam Beck, both German-born illustrators who founded the Beck & Pauli Lithographing Company in Milwaukee in 1878, which specialized in printing aerial perspective lithographs of Midwestern cities. 1866-1922

Beck, Joe

442. Beck, Joe. PIONEERING IN TELEVISION IN THE TWIN CITIES. *Minnesota Hist. 1979 46(7): 274-285.* A personal account of the author's part in getting television started in Minneapolis-St. Paul, and promoting its development in the last half of the 1940's. Beginning as director of television for WTCN in Minneapolis when radio broadcasters had little enthusiasm for TV's potential, he soon formed his own company, Beck Studios, Inc. By 1947 the company opened its Twin City Television Lab to train people in the use of this new medium. Students came from all parts of the country, and eventually supplied a large percentage of the TV personnel over the whole nation. Several experiments in public service proved the worth of television despite the slowness with which funding was available for development. 15 photos, 26 notes. 1945-50

Beck, Mary Menessier

443. Whitley, Edna Talbot. MARY BECK AND THE FEMALE MIND. *Register of the Kentucky Hist. Soc. 1979 77(1): 15-24.* Mary Menessier Beck was born in France and came to the United States with her husband, artist George Beck, sometime during 1792-99. In 1805, Beck opened an academy for girls in Lexington, Kentucky. With a full curriculum, Beck broke with the tradition that suggested less education for women. Among her students during her nearly 35 years of educating young women was Mary Todd. Primary and secondary sources; 27 notes. 1790's-1833

Becker, Christian C.

444. Iseminger, Gordon L. C. C. BECKER: MCINTOSH COUNTY GERMAN-RUSSIAN PIONEER. *North Dakota Hist. 1983 50(3): 4-13.* Describes the experiences on the Dakota frontier of Christian C. Becker, one of the German-Russian pioneers who settled the area in the late 1800's. Settling soon after McIntosh County was opened in 1884, Becker and his family faced the hardships of droughts, prairie fires, and blizzards common for frontier farmers. Establishing himself as a farmer, Becker was a leader in forming a school for the immigrant children, in establishing the Zion Lutheran Church, and in establishing the new political structure of the community. 11 photos, 17 notes. 1885-1910

Becker, Thomas Andrew

445. Peterman, Thomas Joseph. "Thomas Andrew Becker, the First Catholic Bishop of Wilmington, Delaware, and Sixth Bishop of Savannah, Georgia, 1831-1899." Catholic U. of Am. 1982. 619 pp. *DAI 1982 43(4): 1254-A.* DA8221443 1860's-99

Beckley, Delia Engel

446. Luthy, Dorothy Beckley. MEMOIRS OF DELIA BECKLEY. *Oregon Hist. Q. 1982 83(1): 5-23.* Narrates the experiences during 1888-98 of Delia Engel Beckley who came to the Oregon country with her husband, John, and seven children. At first a farmer, John became a Methodist min-

ister, and they lived in a number of places including Milwaukie, Portland, and Salem, Oregon. 8 illus., 1 map, 5 notes. 1888-98

Bedinger, Henry

447. Levin, Alexandra Lee. HENRY BEDINGER OF VIRGINIA: FIRST UNITED STATES MINISTER TO DENMARK. *Virginia Cavalcade 1980 29(4): 184-191.* Biography of Henry Bedinger (1812-58), the first United States minister to Denmark, focusing on his American political career as a Democrat in the House of Representatives, his law career, and his appointment as minister to Denmark from 1854-58. 1854-58

Beebe, Lucius

448. Jenks, George M. A BIBLIOGRAPHY OF BOOKS AND ARTICLES BY AND ABOUT LUCIUS BEEBE. *Bull. of Biblio. 1980 37(3): 132-141, 155.* Brief introductory biography of author and journalist, Lucius Beebe (1902-66), followed by a bibliography of books and articles by and about the railroad enthusiast, written from 1921 to 1979. 1921-79

Beecher, Catherine

449. Lambert, Pierre D. WOMEN IN EDUCATION: THE KNOWN, THE FORGOTTEN, THE UNKNOWN. *Vitae Scholasticae 1983 2(1): 93-112.* Presents biographical sketches of seven American women educators: Emma Willard, who supported women's education in New England and New York; Mary Lyon, who founded Mount Holyoke Seminary in 1837; Catherine Beecher, who started women's schools in Hartford and Cincinnati; Helen Parkhurst, who studied under Maria Montessori in Italy and promoted her system of education in the United States, devising the Dalton Plan of individualized contracts for students; Caroline Pratt, who founded the City and Country School in Greenwich Village in 1914; and Lucy Sprague Mitchell and Marietta Johnson, both of whom were progressive educators. 28 notes. French summary. 19c-20c

Beecher, Edward

450. Arkin, Marc Maxine. "Edward Beecher: The Development of an Ecclesiastical Career, 1803-1844." Yale U. 1983. 489 pp. *DAI 1984 45(5): 1356-A.* DA8411506 1803-44

Beecher, Henry Ward

451. Duduit, James Michael. "Henry Ward Beecher and the Political Pulpit." Florida State U. 1983. 194 pp. *DAI 1983 44(3): 783-A.* DA8317369 1847-87

Beef, Joe

452. DeLottinville, Peter. JOE BEEF OF MONTREAL: WORKING-CLASS CULTURE AND THE TAVERN, 1869-1889. *Labour [Canada] 1981-82 8-9(Aut-Spr): 9-40.* The tavern is one of the most overlooked features of the 19th-century urban landscape. This article examines the career of one Montreal tavern keeper to illustrate the intricate connections between drink and working-class culture along the Montreal waterfront. Recreation, social services, and labour activities all relied upon the tavern as a working-class stronghold. By the late 1880's, however, the role of the tavern diminished with changes in the harbour's casual labour market and with the successes of the temperance and urban reform movements. This decline influenced the nature of working-class response to industrial capitalism. 1869-89

Beeson, Desdemona Stott

453. James, Laurence P. and Taylor, Sandra C. "STRONG MINDED WOMEN": DESDEMONA STOTT BEESON AND OTHER HARD ROCK MINING ENTREPRENEURS. *Utah Hist. Q. 1978 46(2): 136-150.* Desdemona Stott Beeson (1897-1976), trailblazer for women in mining, grew up in a Utah mining camp. She married geologist Joseph J. Beeson, took courses in mining engineering and geology, and was her husband's partner as an independent mining entrepreneur. Other women in the early 20th century whose knowledge of mining engineering or ability to handle financial operations gained them status as "female mining men" were Leatha Millard Arnott, Lena Larsen, Mrs. Mary J. Stewart, Elizabeth Pollet, and Josie Pearl. Primary and secondary sources; 7 illus., 36 notes. 20c

Beeson, Duane

454. Fry, Garry L. "BOISE BEE": THE DUANE BEESON STORY. *Am. Aviation Hist. Soc. J. 1978 23(4): 242-259.* Duane Beeson (1921-47) of Boise, Idaho, joined the Royal Canadian Air Force in June 1941 and in 1942 was transferred with his outfit to the US Army Air Force; in P-47's and P-51's he scored 24 victories, was shot down by antiaircraft fire, and spent 1944-April 1945 as a POW in Germany. 1941-45

Beeson, John

455. Norwood, Frederick A. TWO CONTRASTING VIEWS OF THE INDIANS: METHODIST INVOLVEMENT IN THE INDIAN TROUBLES IN OREGON AND WASHINGTON. *Church Hist. 1980 49(2): 178-187.* Contrasts the attitudes of David E. Blaine, John Beeson, and their families, toward the Indians in Oregon and Washington during the 1850's. Both were Methodists: Blaine was a minister and Beeson a layman. Whereas the Blaines grew disillusioned about the native inhabitants, Beeson became an advocate of the Indian cause, and wrote *A Plea For The Indians.* 27 notes. 1850-59

Begbie, Matthew Baillie

456. Williams, David R. SIR MATTHEW BAILLIE BEGBIE. *Pacific Northwest Q. 1980 71(3): 101-106.* Matthew Baillie Begbie (1819-94) came to British Columbia in 1858 to serve as the first judge of the newly opened gold frontier. In addition to presiding over a demanding circuit court, he prepared the most important legislation in this British colony, acted as attorney general, and served as an ex officio member of the legislative council. In 1871, after Confederation, Begbie became chief justice of the province and served ably for 23 years. Though always a representative of the establishment, he took unpopular stances in defense of Indians, the Chinese, and common citizens. Begbie's energy and devotion to duty made British Columbia's mining frontier more orderly than that found in the United States. 5 photos. 1858-94

Beilhardt, Jacob

457. Fogarty, Robert S. and Grant, H. Roger. FREE LOVE IN OHIO: JACOB BEILHARDT AND THE SPIRIT FRUIT COLONY. *Ohio Hist. 1980 89(2): 206-221.* Discusses the life of Jacob Beilhardt (1846-1908), and the community he founded near Lisbon, Ohio, named the Spirit Fruit

Society. Under his charismatic leadership, the utopian community attracted much publicity, mostly for its sexual philosophy. Primary sources; 49 notes. 1865-1908

458. Grant, H. Roger. PRAIRIE STATE UTOPIA: THE SPIRIT FRUIT SOCIETY OF CHICAGO AND INGLESIDE. *Chicago Hist. 1983 12(1): 28-35.* Details the life of Jacob Beilhart, founder of the Spirit Fruit Society, the philosophy of the group he led, and its short-lived existence in Ohio and Illinois; covers 1887-1908. 1887-1908

Belaney, Archibald Stansfeld

See Grey Owl

Belasco, David

459. Harper, Charles Harold. "Mrs. Leslie Carter: Her Life and Acting Career." U. of Nebraska, Lincoln 1978. 219 pp. *DAI 1979 39(7): 3925-A.* 1895-1906

Belknap, Jeremy

460. Kirsch, George B. JEREMY BELKNAP AND THE PROBLEM OF BLACKS AND INDIANS IN EARLY AMERICA. *Hist. New Hampshire 1979 34(3-4): 202-222.* Historian and Congregational minister Jeremy Belknap (1744-98) was one of the first analysts to think critically about a multiracial society in America. Although his upbringing often led him to judge nonwhites harshly if they deviated from his idea of proper personal conduct, he was more sympathetic to them than were most Americans. In his *History of New Hampshire* (1784, 1791-92), Belknap tried to be objective about Indians and their experiences with Europeans, although he became pessimistic about their future. Belknap wrote less about blacks than about Indians, but was an active opponent of slavery, and was hopeful about their future. 40 notes. 17c-1792

Belknap, Waldron Phoenix, Jr.

461. Weeks, Edward A. WALDRON PHOENIX BELKNAP, JR.: A PROFILE. *Massachusetts Historical Society Proceedings 1983 95: 126-131.* Waldron Phoenix Belknap, Jr. enjoyed a varied career as banker, architect, and art historian. Forced into retirement due to poor health, Belknap privately pursued research into the history of American portraiture and confirmed that there was a definite link between English mezzotints and American portraits painted between 1700 and 1750. Death cut short his writing of a definitive study of American portraiture. He is also known for his bequest to the Harvard University Press to establish the Belknap Press, a publishing arm similar to Oxford's Clarendon Press. 1899-1949

Bell, Alexander Graham

462. Brannan, Beverly W. and Thompson, Patricia T. ALEXANDER GRAHAM BELL: A PHOTOGRAPHIC ALBUM. *Q. J. of the Lib. of Congress 1977 34(2): 72-96.* Photographs from the Gilbert J. Grosvenor Collection, recently donated to the Library by the National Geographic Society, present professional and personal facets of the life of Alexander Graham Bell. In 1870 he moved with his parents from Scotland to Canada, and then to Boston. There he was absorbed by his work with the deaf. He developed a respiratory device which was the forerunner of the iron lung. His wife helped finance his work with tetrahedral kites and the Aerial Experiment Association. He continued his work with the deaf, and helped Helen Keller's father locate Annie Sullivan, "who became Helen's miracle worker." Illus., 12 notes. 1870-1922

Bell, Goodloe Harper

463. Lindsay, Allan Gibson. "Goodloe Harper Bell: Pioneer Seventh-day Adventist Christian Educator." Andrews U. 1982. 472 pp. *DAI 1983 44(5): 1357-1358-A.* DA8320337 1850's-99

Bell, J. Franklin

464. Raines, Edgar Frank, Jr. "Major General J. Franklin Bell and Military Reform: The Chief of Staff Years, 1906-1910." U. of Wisconsin, Madison 1976. 709 pp. *DAI 1977 38(1): 442-A.* 1906-10

Bell, Joseph

465. Bell, Joseph and Lawther, Dennis E., ed. REMINISCENCES OF HIS SCHOOLBOY DAYS: AN OCTOGENARIAN TELLS OF PLACES, CONDITIONS, AND EVENTS IN EARLY WHEELING, 1905. *Upper Ohio Valley Hist. Rev. 1980 9(2): 14-22.* Reminiscences by Joseph Bell (1819-1908). 1905

Bell, Montgomery

466. Dalton, Robert E. MONTGOMERY BELL AND THE NARROWS OF HARPETH. *Tennessee Hist. Q. 1976 35(1): 3-28.* Outlines the career of Dickson County ironmaker Montgomery Bell (1769-1855). Called Tennessee's first industrialist, Bell practiced his art from its beginnings to its emergence as a major industry. The tunnel that he completed at the Narrows of Harpeth before 1820, now listed in the *National Register of Historic Places*, is an engineering masterpiece and possibly the oldest extant tunnel in the United States. Bell built his Patterson Forge ironworks at the narrows after attempting for a decade to sell his land to the federal government for an armory. Based on primary and secondary sources; map, illus., 2 photos, 70 notes. ca 1790-1855

Bell, Thomas

467. Berko, John F. THOMAS BELL: SLOVAK-AMERICAN NOVELIST. *Jednota Ann. Furdek 1977 16: 147-162.* Discusses the novels and labor organizing of Thomas Bell (Belejčák), a Slovak American, 1920's-63. 1920's-63

Bell, Walter D.

468. Bell, Iris. WALTER D. BELL: LAWYER, JURIST AND LEGISLATOR. *Tampa Bay History 1985 7(1): 61-75.* Describes the career of Walter D. Bell as a lawyer and judge in De Soto County, Florida. 1901-30's

Bell, William J.

469. Chambees, Clarke A. WILLIAM J. BELL, DISCIPLE OF THE SOCIAL GOSPEL. *Minnesota History 1985 49(6): 241-251.* Though William J. Bell set out to be a Presbyterian missionary to lumberjacks, changing times dictated that he serve the immigrant miners of Minnesota. Between 1913 and 1931 his ministry staff grew, as it served 19 ethnic groups. Bell's vision of mingled democracy, social progress, and Christianity also included an element less common to his peers, an appreciation of the backgrounds of his flock. From 1932 until his retirement in 1967, he worked in other capacit-

ies, including head of a Presbyterian mission for Minnesota, Wisconsin, and the Dakotas. 8 illus., 40 notes. 1888-1984

Bellamy, Edward

470. McHugh, Christine. "Edward Bellamy and the Populists: The Agrarian Response to Utopia, 1888-1898." U. of Illinois, Urbana-Champaign 1977. 431 pp. *DAI 1977 38(1): 439-A.* 1888-98

Bellamy, Joseph

471. Anderson, Michael Patrick. "The Pope of Litchfield County: An Intellectual Biography of Joseph Bellamy, 1719-1790." Claremont Graduate School 1980. 315 pp. *DAI 1981 42(3): 1280-1281-A.* 8119916 1736-90

472. Conforti, Joseph. JOSEPH BELLAMY AND THE NEW DIVINITY MOVEMENT. *New England Hist. and Geneal. Register 1983 137(Apr): 126-138.* Joseph Bellamy graduated from Yale in 1735 and studied theology under Jonathan Edwards at Northampton, Massachusetts. Bellamy returned to Connecticut where, as a minister and writer, he became an influential proponent of Edwards's New Divinity movement. 42 notes. 1735-90

Bellamy, Marjory

473. Bellamy, Marjory. BEYOND THE CALL OF DUTY. *Manitoba Pageant [Canada] 1975 20(4): 13-17.* Recounts the author's experiences as the wife of Royal Canadian Mounted Policeman, Joe Bellamy, in western Canada during the 1920's and 1930's. 1920's-30's

Bellanca, Dorothy Jacobs

474. Asher, Nina Lynn. "Dorothy Jacobs Bellanca: Feminist Trade Unionist, 1894-1946." State U. of New York, Binghamton 1982. 335 pp. *DAI 1982 43(5): 1650-A.* DA8223493 1894-1946

Bellini, Carlo

475. Evans, Frank B. CARLO BELLINI AND HIS RUSSIAN FRIEND FEDOR KARZHAVIN. *Virginia Mag. of Hist. and Biog. 1980 88(3): 338-354.* Traces through meager sources the career of Carlo Bellini (d. 1805) of the College of William and Mary, who was the first professor of modern languages in North America. Patronized by Phillip Mazzini, who sheltered him when he came to Virginia in 1773, and by Thomas Jefferson, who apparently secured him a clerkship as Virginia legislature translator, and his academic post, Bellini served in the latter capacity to 1803. Given to exaggerated statements and perhaps not well grounded in any foreign language other than Italian, Bellini did not prosper financially or academically. Fedor Karzhavin, a Russian adventurer and Bellini's acquaintance, had similar unfulfilled hopes to use his linguistic skills. 65 notes. 1773-1805

Belter, John Henry

476. Franco, Barbara. JOHN HENRY BELTER: A ROCOCO REVIVAL CABINETMAKER IN THE LIMELIGHT. *Nineteenth Cent. 1980 6(2): 30-33.* German-born John Henry Belter (ca. 1806-63), of New York City, was a famous cabinetmaker whose parlor furniture was made of rosewood, mahogany, and oak, 1844-63. 1844-63

Benchley, Robert

477. Herrman, Dorothy. ROBERT BENCHLEY: BOTHERED, BEWILDERED BUT A BRILLIANT WIT. *Smithsonian 1982 12(11): 122-142.* Discusses the life and career of American actor and drama critic Robert Benchley (1889-1945), who was editor of *Vanity Fair,* drama critic for *Life* and *The New Yorker* and character actor in many movies. 1914-45

Benedict, Kirby

478. Kubicek, Earl C. LINCOLN'S FRIEND: KIRBY BENEDICT. *Lincoln Herald 1979 81(1): 9-20.* A biography of Kirby Benedict, close friend of Abraham Lincoln for 30 years. 1835-74

Benedict, Ruth Fulton

479. Briscoe, Virginia Wolf. RUTH BENEDICT: ANTHROPOLOGICAL FOLKLORIST. *J. of Am. Folklore 1979 92(366): 445-476.* Ruth Benedict's (1887-1948) work as an anthropological folklorist centered on the themes of cultural configuration and cultural relativism. She encouraged great activity by women in the American Folklore Society during the 1920's and 1930's, and became recognized as a founder of the Culture and Personality school of anthropology. Based on Benedict's unpublished papers, Vassar College Special Collections, Poughkeepsie, New York; 82 notes. 1920's-30's

480. Modell, Judith. "A Biographical Study of Ruth Fulton Benedict." U. of Minnesota 1978. 588 pp. *DAI 1978 39(2): 964-A.* 1914-48

Benezet, Anthony

481. Bruns, Roger A. A QUAKER'S ANTISLAVERY CRUSADE: ANTHONY BENEZET. *Quaker Hist. 1976 65(2): 81-92.* The voices of a few antislavery Friends before 1756 were smothered by the comfortable, respectable weight of American Quakerism. Anthony Benezet believed that Friends were indifferent to the evils of slavery because they did not know them. From the 1759 publication of his first major pamphlet until his death in 1784, he was an "old white-haired busybody of good works scurrying around" to individual Friends and their meetings with letters and tracts, speaking against slave trading and holding. Discrimination continued. Although the Philadelphia Yearly Meeting (comprising Delaware, Pennsylvania, and much of New Jersey) excommmunicated slaveholding members in 1776, it did not abolish the color bar to membership until 1796. 56 notes. 1759-84

Benge, Bob

482. Evans, E. Raymond. NOTABLE PERSONS IN CHEROKEE HISTORY: BOB BENGE. *J. of Cherokee Studies 1976 1(2): 98-106.* Bob Benge, a mixed-blood Cherokee leader, was born about 1760. He was extremely anti-American and led many forays against the Americans after the Revolution. He gained a considerable reputation among both Indians and whites for his exploits. Most of his career was military, and in Tennessee and Virginia. Benge, a relative of Sequoyah, was killed in ambush by a Virginia militia officer named Hobbs on 9 April 1794. Primary and secondary sources; map, 33 notes. 1770's-94

Bengough, John Wilson

483. Kutcher, Stan. J. W. BENGOUGH AND THE MILLENNIUM IN HOGTOWN: A STUDY OF MOTIVATION IN URBAN REFORM. *Urban Hist. Rev. [Canada] 1976 76(2): 30-49.* The career of John Wilson Bengough (1851-1923), cartoonist and author, illustrates the idealism of certain aspects of the urban reform movement. Religiously motivated, he believed in worshiping God by serving mankind. Concerned with the social conditions of Toronto, he used his weekly satirical magazine, *Grip,* to promote morality in city government. He became involved in politics by serving as an alderman for three years. Frustrated by the necessity of political compromise, he retired from office in 1909, preferring the freedom of an outside critic. Based on the Bengough Papers, secondary sources, and newspapers; 76 notes. 1873-1910

Benjamin, Asher

484. Quinan, Jack. ASHER BENJAMIN AND AMERICAN ARCHITECTURE: INTRODUCTION. *J. of the Soc. of Architectural Hist. 1979 38(3): 244-252.* As an influential popularizer of architectural style, Asher Benjamin dominated the field of architectural writing in the United States for more than 50 years. Benjamin recognized the distinctiveness of US architecture and attempted to give that distinction a consistent form in his handbooks. His *Practical House Carpenter* became the most popular architectural handbook of the 19th century. Between 1810 and 1828 Benjamin operated a paint store and worked as a mill agent. Before then he used Federal style, and after, Greek Revival. He is better known for his Federalist work. In his buildings, as distinct from his writings, Benjamin emulated Charles Bulfinch for more than 30 years. His later Greek Revival architecture has been generally ignored. Recent findings promise more study in this Greek Revival area. 11 fig., 41 notes. 1797-1856

Benjamin, Samuel

485. Goode, James F. A GOOD START: THE FIRST AMERICAN MISSION TO IRAN, 1883-1885. *Muslim World 1984 74(2): 100-118.* Diplomatic relations with Iran, established largely through the efforts of Samuel Benjamin, were brought about by the need to protect Christians threatened by the Kurdish violence in 1880. Although Benjamin was successful in protecting missionary interests, he was not wholly in sympathy with their activities, as he respected Islam and its culture. He was unsuccessful in improving US-Iran trade links largely because of the great distances involved, poor transportation facilities, and a lack of American interest. Benjamin retired from Tehran in 1885 following the election of Grover Cleveland, and the post was of minor importance to the new administration and to subsequent administrations until the mid 20th century. Based on State Department records, the Margaret Y. Halliday Papers, and secondary sources; 47 notes. 1883-85

Benjamin, Sarah Mary

486. Eldred, Richard O. THE HEROINE OF YORKTOWN. *Daughters of the American Revolution Magazine 1984 118(9): 634-636, 698.* Sarah Mary Benjamin followed her second husband, Aaron Osborn, as he served in Washington's army in the American Revolution and witnessed the British surrender at Yorktown; she later moved to Mount Pleasant Township, Wayne County, Pennsylvania, where she lived to be over 100 and became famous as one of the last survivors of the war. 1780-1858

Bennard, George

487. Pies, Frank John, Sr. and Pies, Timothy Mark. THE OLD RUGGED CROSS. *Michigan Hist. 1984 68(5): 36-39.* Methodist minister George Bennard authored over 350 religious songs, of which the most prominent was "The Old Rugged Cross." Bennard was born in Youngstown, Ohio, in 1873, but moved to Michigan in his adult life. The song brought fame and notoriety to Bennard, who traveled to 46 states to give lectures on the song's origin and to preach the gospel message. Through it all, Bennard retained a humble perspective and died quietly in Reed City, Michigan, in 1958. Based on Bennard's unpublished memoir, oral interviews, and secondary sources; 5 illus., 14 notes. 1890's-1958

Bennett, Gwendolyn

488. Govan, Sandra Yvonne. "Gwendolyn Bennett: Portrait of an Artist Lost." Emory U. 1980. 248 pp. *DAI 1981 41(7): 3106-A.* 8101931 1900-45

Bennett, Isabel Harris

489. Stapleton, Carolyn L. BELLE HARRIS BENNETT: MODEL OF HOLISTIC CHRISTIANITY. *Methodist Hist. 1983 21(3): 131-142.* Gives a biography of religious and ecumenical leader Isabel Harris Bennett of the Methodist Episcopal Church, South. Bennett felt compelled by her faith to advocate social change. She repudiated racism, fought for women's suffrage, and especially worked for the advancement of black women. 27 notes. 1875-1922

Bennett, James Gordon, Jr.

490. Lamb, Julia. "THE COMMODORE" ENJOYED LIFE: BUT N.Y. SOCIETY WINCED. *Smithsonian 1978 9(8): 132-140.* Describes the life, career, exploits, and eccentric behavior of James Gordon Bennett, Jr. (1841-1918), Commodore of the New York Yacht Club, publisher of the *New York Herald,* and leading American sportsman. Bennett sent Henry Stanley to Africa to find Dr. David Livingstone, sponsored expeditions to find the North Pole and explore Alaska and the Congo, introduced weather forecasts to newspapers, and put sports on the front page. His other interests included yachting, polo, tennis, cycling, and walking. He also established trophies for car racing and prizes for air balloon and biplane races. 17 illus. 1841-1918

Bennett, W. A. C.

491. —. [USES OF ORAL HISTORY IN BIOGRAPHY]. *Canadian Oral History Association Journal [Canada] 1983 6: 33-37.*

Mitchell, David. ORAL HISTORY AND THE BIOGRAPHY OF PUBLIC FIGURES, *pp. 33-36.* Relates the early development of the biography of W. A. C. Bennett, former premier of British Columbia, in which the recording of oral history lent a color and life to the biography.

Fisher, Robin. CONCLUDING REMARKS, *pp. 36-37.* Expresses the desirability of being able to converse with the person about whom one is writing as it affords an opportunity for immediate correction. 1976-83

Bennett, William H.

492. Grant, H. Roger. THE NEW COMMUNITARIANISM: WILLIAM H. BENNETT AND THE HOME EMPLOYMENT CO-OPERATIVE COMPANY, 1894-1905. *Missouri Hist. Soc. Bull. 1976 33(1): 18-26.* Describes utopian experiments by William H. Bennett in Dallas County, Missouri. His last undertaking, the Home

Employment Co-operative Company, briefly served hundreds of Ozark farm families beginning in 1895, only to be disbanded when post-Spanish American War prosperity reduced the need for cooperative utopias. Based on primary and newspaper sources; map, 2 photos, 34 notes. 1894-1905

Benning, Henry Lewis

493. Cobb, James C. THE MAKING OF A SECESSIONIST: HENRY L. BENNING AND THE COMING OF THE CIVIL WAR. *Georgia Hist. Q. 1976 60(4): 313-323.* Describes the career of the radical Georgian Henry Lewis Benning, a noted jurist and frustrated politician, who advocated secession as early as 1849. Primary and secondary sources; 34 notes. 1832-75

Bennitt, James

494. Menius, Arthur C., III. JAMES BENNITT: PORTRAIT OF AN ANTEBELLUM YEOMAN. *North Carolina Hist. Rev. 1981 58(4): 305-326.* James Bennitt, whose home on the Hillsborough-Durham road served as the place of General Joseph E. Johnston's surrender to Union General William T. Sherman in 1865, represents the typical antebellum Southern yeoman farmer. In debt and frequently sued for nonpayment as he attempted to establish a farm and family in the 1830's, Bennitt was able to purchase his own land in 1846. His account book for 1839-49 describes his sales, including excess food crops (little cotton), and expenditures, including labor at specific times of the year, new farm implements and repair of worn ones, magazines, newspapers, and books. Further study of "plain folks" records is needed to change long held misconceptions. Based primarily on the Bennitt Papers at Duke University, manuscript county records at the North Carolina Archives, and numerous secondary sources; 11 illus., 113 notes. 1830-70

Bense, Johann

495. Bense, Johann; Doblin, Helga B., transl.; Lynn, Mary C., intro. A BRUNSWICK GRENADIER WITH BURGOYNE: THE JOURNAL OF JOHANN BENSE, 1776-1783. *New York History 1985 66(4): 420-444.* Although most of the German troops hired by England during the Revolutionary War were Hessians, some 4,000 were from Brunswick. One of the latter, an enlisted man named Johann Bense, kept a journal covering his service from his departure from home early in 1776 to his return in May of 1783. During that time he fought in Burgoyne's army, was captured in late 1777, and spent the remainder of the war as a prisoner. The journal, on microfilm in the Library of Congress for over a half-century, was recently translated and is reprinted here. It is sketchy but reveals a great deal about the life of a hired enlisted soldier during those years. 40 notes, 7 illus. 1776-83

Benson, Berry Greenwood

496. Bradberry, David. THE MAN ON THE MONUMENT. *Richmond County History 1985 17(2): 15-22.* Presents a biography of Berry Greenwood Benson, a South Carolinian who fought for the Confederacy in the Civil War, escaped from a Union prison, became a popular writer after the war, and was the model for a war memorial erected in 1878 in Augusta, Georgia. 1843-1923

Benson, Charles

497. Richardson, Katherine W. THE TRAVELS AND TRIBULATIONS OF CHARLES BENSON, STEWARD ON THE *GLIDE,* 1861-1881. *Essex Inst. Hist. Collections 1984 120(2): 73-109.* Reprints extracts from four journals kept by Charles Benson, a black resident of Salem, Massachusetts, while a steward on the bark *Glide* during 1861-81. The journals provide the source material to reconstruct voyages made by the *Glide* in 1862, 1864, 1878, 1879, and 1880. In addition to the journal extracts, examines the trading history between the United States and Zanzibar, especially the role of Salem in it, and gives a biography of Charles Benson. Based on Charles Benson's logbooks in the Essex Institute, Salem, Massachusetts; 7 photos, 18 notes. 1830-80

Benson, Eugene

498. Scholnick, Robert J. BETWEEN REALISM AND ROMANTICISM: THE CURIOUS CAREER OF EUGENE BENSON. *Am. Lit. Realism, 1870-1910 1981 14(2): 242-261.* Discusses American writer Eugene Benson, especially his essays for *Galaxy* denouncing the corruption of the post-Civil War years and his inability to secure a stable literary position. 1864-1908

Benson, Ezra Taft

499. Schapsmeier, Edward L. and Schapsmeier, Frederick H. RELIGION AND REFORM: A CASE STUDY OF HENRY A. WALLACE AND EZRA TAFT BENSON. *J. of Church and State 1979 21(3): 525-535.* Henry A. Wallace and Ezra Taft Benson typify moralists of both left and right who functioned fairly well when controlled by moderates, but on their own, adopted extreme moral views, consequently losing what influence they had. Considers their careers, independent of the moderating influences of presidents Roosevelt and Eisenhower. Based on the writeups and papers of Henry A. Wallace and Ezra Taft Benson; 28 notes. 1933-60

Bentley, Arthur F.

500. Hale, Dennis. ARTHUR F. BENTLEY: POLITICS AND THE MYSTERY OF SOCIETY. *Pol. Sci. Reviewer 1983 13: 1-42.* Examines seven books by Arthur F. Bentley, originally published 1908-69. Arthur Bentley may be credited with the formulation of early group theory. His interdisciplinary research became the foundation for the scientific study of politics and group processes. 47 notes. 1890's-1957

Bentley, Charles Edwin

501. Dummett, Clifton O. CHARLES EDWIN BENTLEY: A GENUINE EMANCIPATOR. *Crisis 1979 86(4): 133-135.* Charles Edwin Bentley was born on 21 February 1859 in Cincinnati, Ohio. In 1885 he entered the Chicago College of Dental Surgery. After earning his degree he established one of the largest practices in Chicago. He was also professor of oral surgery at Rush and at Harvey Medical Centers. Bentley organized the Odontographic Society in 1888, the largest local dental society in the world. His fame grew out of being an innovator, filling professional voids. He became the "father of public school oral hygiene" programs. Bentley was among prominent black Americans who formed the Niaraga Movement in 1905, and he served on the Board of Directors of the NAACP from its incorporation in 1910 until his death in 1929. He was a leader in American dentistry during a period of intense racial discord. 1885-1929

Bentley, William

502. Farnam, Anne. DR. BENTLEY'S ACCOUNT BOOKS: DOCUMENTATION FOR THE CREATION OF A HISTORICAL SETTING. *Essex Inst. Hist. Collections 1980 116(4): 206-222.* The ignored account books of the Reverend William Bentley of Salem, 1783-1819, juxtaposed with his

diary, provide new insights into Bentley's daily life. While a boarder from 1791 to 1819 at Hannah Crowninshield's house, now a part of the Essex Institute, Bentley participated in the remodeling of the house in 1794. His account books detail his involvement. They also contain a 1794 inventory in which he categorized all his possessions, clothing, and books. This allows us to archaeologically reconstruct his living quarters. Includes a well-indexed and annotated copy of this inventory. Based on Bentley's Account Books; 4 photos, 74 notes. 1791-1819

Benton, Thomas Hart

503. Berman, Avis. THOMAS HART BENTON: AMERICAN IMAGES. *Art & Antiques 1981 4(5): 52-59.* Biography of American artist Thomas Hart Benton (1899-1975), focusing on his artistic career, which spanned the Cubist, Pop, Op, and Minimalist movements. 1899-1975

504. Herr, Pamela. THE LIFE OF JESSIE BENTON FRÉMONT. *Am. West 1979 16(2): 4-13, 59-63.* 1841-1902

*For abstract see **Frémont, Jessie Benton***

505. —. THOMAS HART BENTON'S ORIGINAL ILLUSTRATIONS FOR MARK TWAIN CLASSICS. *Missouri Hist. Rev. 1981 75(4): 385-395.* A brief biography of Thomas Hart Benton (1889-1975) and 18 examples of his watercolor, tempera, pen, brush and ink illustrations included in *The Adventures of Tom Sawyer, Adventures of Huckleberry Finn* and *Life on the Mississippi,* published by The Limited Edition Club of New York City in 1939, 1942 and 1944. The illustrations are part of an exhibition at the State Historical Society of Missouri's Art Gallery, drawn from the 203 works given to the Society by the Neosho-born artist. 1939-44

Berelson, Bernard

506. Asheim, Lester. BERNARD BERELSON (1912-1979). *Lib. Q. 1980 50(4): 407-409.* Bernard Berelson was dean of the University of Chicago Graduate Library School and held such diverse posts in his life as director of the Behavioral Sciences Division of the Ford Foundation and president of the Population Council. His interests ranged from the social sciences to Chaucer. His reputation for almost constant research and publishing was well-earned. He was far from the stereotypical scientist, for his learning covered a great range of subjects. ca 1930-79

Berger, Samuel

507. Fiske, Jack. THE 1904 OLYMPIC GAMES HEAVYWEIGHT BOXING CHAMPION. *Western States Jewish Hist. 1984 16(4): 348-352.* Chronicles the life and career of Samuel Berger, a San Francisco Jewish boxer who became world amateur heavyweight champion at the 1904 Olympic Games in St. Louis. Berger was part of a trio of San Francisco Jewish boxers, along with Joe Choynski and Abe Attell. Based on newspaper sources; 13 notes. 1904-24

Berger, Vilhelm

508. Beijbom, Ulf. VILHELM BERGER, EN SKILDRARE AV EMIGRANTERNAS HUNDÅR [Vilhelm Berger, a delineator of the emigrants' hard times]. *Personhistorisk Tidskrift [Sweden] 1981 77(2-3): 64-81.* Summarizes some of the data on the characteristics of the Swedish-American emigrant literature, its authors, and research in this field. Vilhelm Berger (1867-1938), who immigrated to the United States in 1898, is a prototype for the Swedish-American author. He became an important novelist and his main contribution is the analysis of the intellectual immigrant's confrontation with the big city milieu and manual labor. He was an articulate exponent of the American competitive society. This study examines the different areas and topics covered by Berger's works and their contributions as social documents. 1867-1938

509. Lindquist, Emory. VILHELM BERGER: SWEDISH-AMERICAN JOURNALIST AND AUTHOR. *Swedish Pioneer Hist. Q. 1981 32(4): 248-264.* Vilhelm Berger was the youngest of 10 children born to the Berger family in Nysund, Sweden, in 1867. Two of his brothers were prominent in Swedish life, but Vilhelm became the "black sheep." He came to the United States in 1896 and settled in Chicago. Life was difficult and jobs were scarce, and he survived only through the generosity of friends. A year later he traveled to New York on foot and another year of privation followed. He traveled throughout New England selling subscriptions to a Swedish language newspaper. He settled in Boston. In 1902 he began to write and draw and continued until 1936. He was well-known for his promotion of Swedish-American relations. He died in 1938. Based in part on Berger's writings; photo, 49 notes. 1867-1938

Bergman, Ray

510. Casada, Jim. RAY BERGMAN: EVERY MAN'S FISHERMAN. *Sporting Classics 1985 4(2): 18-24.* Biography of Ray Bergman, a popular writer and authority on fishing, who popularized sport fishing in the 20th century. 1891-1967

Bergner, Peter

511. Whyman, Henry C. PETER BERGNER, PIONEER MISSIONARY TO SWEDISH SEAMEN AND IMMIGRANTS. *Swedish Pioneer Hist. Q. 1979 30(2): 103-116.* Peter Bergner (1797-1866) and his family arrived in New York City in 1832 to settle there after Peter had led the sailor's life. He was converted to active Christianity in 1844 and began to preach to immigrant Swedes and Swedish sailors in their own language. These services were held on ships, or floating Bethels, under the auspices of the Methodist Church. This article is the story of Peter Bergner and also of these Bethel Ships. Peter Bergner died in 1866, having worked for the Lord for 17 years. Based on records of the *New York City Tract Society* and several autobiographs and articles in Methodist journals; 3 photos, 25 notes. 1832-66

Bergsagel, Endre

512. Arestad, Sverre, ed. PIONEERING IN MONTANA. *Norwegian-American Studies 1965 22: 104-143.* Reprints a personal narrative by Endre Bergsagel, a homesteader in Montana during 1913-41. Bergsagel came from Norway in 1910 and went straight to San Francisco to an aunt's home; after searching for work he eventually went to Eureka and found work in the lumber mills. In 1913, at the instigation of a cousin, he moved to Malta, Montana, to homestead. Discusses daily life as a homesteader, including accounts of planting, harvesting, and keeping livestock. In 1926, he was able to finance the purchase of a car as well as a pleasure trip to Sweden. 1910-41

Berlin, Irving

513. Rimler, Walter. GREAT SONGWRITERS. *Midstream 1984 30(1): 31-34.* 1885-1979

*For abstract see **Arlen, Harold***

Bernal, Juan Pablo

514. Delgado, James P. JUAN PABLO BERNAL: CALIFORNIA PIONEER. *Pacific Hist. 1979 23(3): 50-62.* Discusses Juan Pablo Bernal (1810-78), whose family had come to California in the early period of Spanish rule. Born in San José de Guadalupe, he saw the territory pass to Mexican rule in 1822, his father obtaining a Mexican land grant. Increase in wealth through cattle breeding on his ranch and successful business transactions in Pueblo de San José in addition to his original El Rancho de Santa Teresa made possible his gaining title to El Valle de San José in partnership with others of his family. In 1846 the area fell to its American conquerors. After legal battles to maintain titles with American authorities, and bad business deals, he lost much of his wealth. In 1877, one year before his death, he was interviewed at the request of Hubert Howe Bancroft to get material for his *History of California.* Primary sources; 7 photos, 1 map, 13 notes, biblio. 1822-78

Bernard, Simon

515. Planchot, Françoise. LE GENERAL SIMON BERNARD, INGENIEUR MILITAIRE AUX ETATS-UNIS (1816-1831) [General Simon Bernard, military engineer in the United States, 1816-31]. *Rev. Française d'Etudes Américaines [France] 1982 7(13): 87-98.* In 1816, French General Simon Bernard, after having served as aide-de-camp to Napoleon, left for the United States where, for 15 years, he planned the defense system of the maritime borders and then took part in the development of networks of internal communication including the Chesapeake & Delaware Canal and the Washington to New Orleans road. 1816-31

Bernath, Stuart Loren

516. Bernath, Gerald J. and Bernath, Myrna F. STUART LOREN BERNATH, PH.D. *Soc. for Hist. of Am. Foreign Relations. Newsletter 1979 10(3): 35-39.* Outlines the career of Stuart Loren Bernath (1939-1970), US history scholar whose death from bone cancer in 1970 caused his parents to set up the annual Stuart L. Bernath Book Prize, the Bernath Young Speaker Award, and the Bernath Article Grant through the Society for Historians of American Foreign Relations in his memory. 1939-75

Bernays, Karl Ludwig

517. Hirsch, Helmut. KARL LUDWIG BERNAYS: EIN EMIGRIERTER SCHRIFTSTELLER ALS US-KONSUL IN DER SCHWEIZ [Karl Ludwig Bernays: An emigrant writer as US Consul in Switzerland]. *Jahrbuch des Instituts für Deutsche Geschichte [Israel] 1975 4: 147-165.* Karl Ludwig Bernays was born in Mainz, Germany, on 16 November 1815 as Lazarus Bernays; he died in St. Louis, Missouri, in 1879. His family's conversion to Christianity caused him to change his name to Karl Ludwig. His journalistic jibes at the Bavarian nobles and even King Ludwig forced him to flee Germany for France. In France he received several diplomatic posts before finally immigrating to the United States where he continued his occupation as a journalist, especially for German-language newspapers. His writings against slavery in the St. Louis papers and his involvement with the Republican Party and Abraham Lincoln brought him into political prominence. After organizing 60 companies for the Union Army, he was appointed in 1861 as US Consul to Switzerland. His appointment was opposed by hundreds of Swiss Americans in Highland, Illinois, where he had once lived, and by the *Züricher Zeitung.* He was officially accepted by the Swiss government in September 1861. As consul he was instrumental in informing Swiss and German exiles in Switzerland of the Union cause. He wrote in newspapers throughout Switzerland and Germany about the US position in the Civil War. He developed lists of the capabilities of Swiss manufacturing. At his own request he was given a financially more lucrative post as Consul to Denmark in January 1862. Based on newspaper articles, published primary and secondary sources; 63 notes. 1815-79

Bernhisel, John M.

518. Barrett, Glen. DELEGATE JOHN M. BERNHISEL, SALT LAKE PHYSICIAN FOLLOWING THE CIVIL WAR. *Utah Hist. Q. 1982 50(4): 354-360.* John M. Bernhisel, born in Loysville, Pennsylvania, received his medical degree from the University of Pennsylvania in 1827, became a Mormon, and joined as personal physician to Joseph Smith in Nauvoo, Illinois. After the Mormon exodus to Salt Lake Valley, Bernhisel was elected first delegate to Congress, returned and established in Salt Lake City. Believing in bleeding, he wrote pamphlets, administered to many patients, and remained a strong friend to Brigham Young. Bernhisel was an early believer in the restriction of salt to maintain a healthy life. He died peacefully after completing house calls. 2 photos, 5 notes. 1865-81

Berninghaus, Oscar Edmund

519. Kodner, Martin. OSCAR EDMUND BERNINGHAUS, 1874-1952: ST. LOUIS-BORN PAINTER OF WESTERN SCENES. *Gateway Heritage 1983-84 4(3): 38-48.* Oscar Edmund Berninghaus began his successful career as an artist in 1899, first painting significant watercolor sketches of the Southwest for the Denver and Rio Grande Railroad. He recorded the West's geographical and natural splendor and captured the epic qualities of its history and contemporary life in watercolors, murals, and oil paintings. 16 photos. 1899-1952

Bernstein, Aline

520. Stutman, Suzanne T. "The Complete Correspondence of Thomas Wolfe and Aline Bernstein." Temple U. 1980. 859 pp. *DAI 1980 41(5): 2113-2114-A.* DA8025163 1925-36

Berry, Albert Gleaves

521. Brearly, Margaret M. REAR-ADMIRAL ALBERT GLEAVES BERRY, 1848-1938. *Tennessee Hist. Q. 1981 40(1): 85-94.* Soon after Andrew Johnson assumed the presidency, he appointed his fellow Tennessean, 16-year-old Albert Gleaves Berry, to the US Naval Academy. A native of Nashville, and the son of a bookstore owner, Berry graduated in 1869. For the next 40 years he served, often at sea, retiring in 1910. His service included action in the Spanish-American War and command of the cruiser *Tennessee,* which was launched in 1906. Following his retirement, Admiral Berry lived for 28 years in California until his death at 90 in 1938. Based mainly on letters and contemporary newspapers; 14 notes. 1865-1938

Berry, Brian J. L.

522. Halvorson, Peter and Stave, Bruce M. A CONVERSATION WITH BRIAN J. L. BERRY. *J. of Urban Hist. 1978 4(2): 209-238.* Interviews Brian J. L. Berry, a leading urban geographer. Describes his family background and education in England and his academic career in America. Of special interest are the discussions of how difficult it was to get colleagues to accept his early quantitative methods as geography and his comments on Marxist geographers. 54 notes, biblio. 1950-78

Berry, Clifford E.

523. Silag, William. THE INVENTION OF THE ELECTRONIC DIGITAL COMPUTER AT IOWA STATE COLLEGE, 1930-42. *Palimpsest 1984 65(5): 150-164, 173-177.* 1930-42

*For abstract see **Atanasoff, John Vincent***

Berry, Ellis Yarnell

524. Schulte, Steven C. REMOVING THE YOKE OF GOVERNMENT: E. Y. BERRY AND THE ORIGINS OF INDIAN TERMINATION POLICY. *South Dakota Hist. 1984 14(1): 48-67.* During his congressional career, South Dakota congressman Ellis Yarnell Berry was instrumental in the formulation of the federal government's policy of termination of special status for Indians. Berry, and other conservative terminationists, maintained that governmental interference in the lives of Indians was the greatest impediment to Indian progress. Berry's goals of withdrawal of federal protection and forced assimilation indicated an ethnocentric attitude of the superiority of Anglo-Saxon values over those of cultural pluralism. Based on the E. Y. Berry Papers, Black Hills State College, Spearfish, South Dakota, and other primary sources; 2 photos, 65 notes. 1951-71

Berry, Martha

525. Henry, Inez. FAMOUS GEORGIA WOMEN: MARTHA BERRY. *Georgia Life 1979 6(2): 30-32.* Martha Berry (1866-1942) of Oak Hill, Georgia, founded four Sunday schools, four day schools, the Boy's Industrial School (changed in 1909 to the Berry Schools, with the addition of a girl's school), and a Junior College. 1866-1942

Berry, Thelma

526. Aston, B. W. and Jacobs, Ken. MRS. JOHN (THELMA) BERRY. *West Texas Historical Association Year Book 1983 59: 156-160.* Relates the contributions of rancher Thelma Berry to the preservation of West Texas history through her civic work in Abilene and Clyde, publications in local history, and as an officer in the West Texas Historical Association. 1926-83

Berry, Vern (family)

527. Berry, Vern. CARAVAN WEST: FAMILY SURVIVAL DURING HARD TIMES ON THE COLORADO PLAINS. *Am. West 1984 21(4): 47-50.* In 1927, the author and her family moved from Iowa to eastern Colorado; describes their life in Colorado during the Great Depression, when hailstorms, duststorms, and unemployment left them nearly destitute and forced them to abandon their dream of living in the West. 1927-33

Berry, Walter

528. Edel, Leon. WALTER BERRY AND THE NOVELISTS: PROUST, JAMES, AND EDITH WHARTON. *Nineteenth-Century Fiction 1984 38(4): 514-529.* Describes the career of author Walter Berry, who became an expatriate living in Paris, the nature of his friendship with Edith Wharton, and his contacts with Marcel Proust and Henry James. 1914-27

Berryman, John

529. Jones, Sonya L. "A Mile to Avalon: The Role of Alcoholism in the Life and Work of John Berryman." Emory U. 1983. 159 pp. *DAI 1983 44(3): 753-A.* DA8316284 1926-72

Bertalanffy, Ludwig von

530. Royce, Joseph R. A PERSONAL PORTRAYAL OF LUDWIG VON BERTALANFFY (1901-1972): SYSTEM THEORIST AND INTERDISCIPLINARY SCHOLAR AT THE UNIVERSITY OF ALBERTA. *J. of the Hist. of the Behavioral Sci. 1981 17(3): 340-342.* Bertalanffy is generally regarded as the founder of general system theory, a conceptual framework which has the potential of being *the* scientific paradigm of the nonphysical sciences. The distinctive aim of this approach is to understand the properties and principles of any organized complexity, regardless of content. Thus, a system is any organized complex of interacting parts. Bertalanffy's scholarly interests included both the humanities and the sciences, but his major contributions were in the biological and the behavioral sciences. A eulogy presented at a conference at the University of Alberta in May 1979. 1926-72

Bertinatti, Eugenia Bate Bass

531. Durham, Walter T. TENNESSEE COUNTESS. *Tennessee Hist. Q. 1980 39(3): 323-340.* Tennessee-born Eugenia Bate Bass (1826-1906), widow of a wealthy Mississippi planter, dazzled Washington society in 1865 by marrying Count Giuseppe Bertinatti, the Italian envoy. She traveled between the United States and Italy, visiting frequently her family in Tennessee, while watching over her estates, especially Riverside Plantation in Mississippi. She eventually settled in Nashville, where she died. Based on the Bate Family Papers of the Tennessee State Library and Archives; 2 illus., 20 notes. 1826-1906

Berzins, Elfrida K.

532. Gregory, C. Jane. ELFRIDA K. BERZINS: WORLD RECORD HOLDER, OLYMPIC ATHLETE, CONCERT SOLOIST, AUTHOR, AND PIONEER PHYSICAL EDUCATOR. *Canadian J. of Hist. of Sport and Physical Educ. [Canada] 1979 10(2): 1-14.* Biography of Latvian Olympic athlete, ballet dancer, and lyric soprano Elfrida K. Berzins (b. 1904), who became a pioneer in physical education in Canada beginning in 1948, where she is still active in music and drama. 1904-79

Best, Bessie Kidd

533. Kyte, Elinor C. A TOUGH JOB FOR A GENTLE LADY. *Journal of Arizona History 1984 25(4): 385-398.* Summarizes Bessie Kidd Best's 43 years as Coconino County, Arizona's school superintendent, and describes Best's efforts to meet the educational needs of children attending isolated rural schools. Based on interviews, school records, and secondary sources; 3 photos, 27 notes. 1929-83

Bethune, Angus

534. Russell, Hilary. ANGUS BETHUNE. Judd, Carol M. and Ray, Arthur J., ed. *Old Trails and New Directions: Papers of the Third North American Fur Trade Conference* (Toronto: U. of Toronto Pr., 1980): 177-190. Investigates the career of Angus Bethune (1783-1858) one of the members of the North West Company of Canada who joined the Hudson's Bay Company in 1821. As a Nor'Wester, he was involved in the takeover of Astoria, the company's adventure to China between 1814 and 1816, the "rebellion" of the wintering partners, and the negotiations which led to the coalition of 1821. His career in the Hudson's Bay Company was less dramatic. As a chief factor in the southern department, he clashed with Governor William Williams and other governmental and company officials. His career was not crowned by

many personal successes despite his rank. Nevertheless, his failures influenced the course of the fur trade. 57 notes. 1808-58

Bethune, Donald

535. Baskerville, Peter. DONALD BETHUNE'S STEAMBOAT BUSINESS: A STUDY OF UPPER CANADIAN COMMERCIAL AND FINANCIAL PRACTICE. *Ontario Hist. [Canada] 1975 67(3): 135-149.* Discusses the financial fortunes of the mid-19th-century Canadian steamboat proprietor, Donald Bethune, for the purpose of illuminating the changing and increasingly reckless commercial and financial environment in which he operated. 19c

Bethune, Joanna Graham

536. Miller, Page Putnam. WOMEN IN THE VANGUARD OF THE SUNDAY SCHOOL MOVEMENT. *J. of Presbyterian Hist. 1980 58(4): 311-325.* Examines the leadership of three Presbyterian women in the Sunday school movement: Joanna Graham Bethune (1770-1860), who organized a school in New York's Brick Presbyterian Church, which ultimately led to a full-grown Sunday school; Margaretta Mason Brown (1772-1838), who organized the first Sunday school in Kentucky, out of which was formed the First Presbyterian Church of Frankfort; and Anne Clay (1796-1844), who organized a Sabbath School on her brother's plantation in Georgia for the instruction of slave children. The Sunday school movement opened up a whole array of opportunities for women, not only providing them the opportunity for classroom teaching, but also the potential for social work, theological study, preparation of curriculum materials, establishment of libraries, innovation of teaching methods, organization of local schools, and experience in a national institutional network. Based on author's Ph.D. dissertation, biographical studies, and other materials; 2 photos, 37 notes. 1800-50

Bethune, Mary McLeod

537. Blackwell, Barbara Grant. "The Advocacies and Ideological Commitments of a Black Educator: Mary McLeod Bethune, 1875-1955." U. of Connecticut 1979. 272 pp. *DAI 1979 39(12): 7148-7149-A.* 1904-55

538. Leffall, Doris C. and Sims, Janet L. MARY MC LEOD BETHUNE—THE EDUCATOR; ALSO INCLUDING A SELECTED ANNOTATED BIBLIOGRAPHY. *J. of Negro Educ. 1976 45(3): 342-359.* Presents a brief biography of Mary McLeod Bethune, the daughter of former slaves and founder of the school in Daytona Beach, Florida which became Bethune-Cookman College. Includes a 15 page annotated bibliography of related materials. 2 notes. 1875-1955

539. Newsome, Clarence Genu. "Mary McLeod Bethune in Religious Perspective: A Seminal Essay." Duke U. 1982. 281 pp. *DAI 1982 43(4): 1194-1195-A.* DA8221151 ca 1900-55

Bevan, Allan

540. Waite, P. B. ALLAN BEVAN'S DALHOUSIE. *Dalhousie Rev. [Canada] 1983 63(1): 7-12.* A Canadian historian reminisces about former colleague and editor of the *Dalhousie Review*, Allan Bevan. 1949-83

Beverley, Robert, II

541. Schell, Ernest H. VIRGINIA'S PATRIOT HISTORIAN: ROBERT BEVERLEY II. *Early Am. Life 1982 13(1): 42, 44, 46.* Beverley, son of one of the richest Virginians, was a "keen-eyed naturalist, a sympathetic anthropologist, a disarming politician, . . . a valient patriot," a wealthy politician, and the author of *The History and Present State of Virginia* (1705). 1673-1722

Bevier, Isabel

542. Bartow, Beverly. ISABEL BEVIER AT THE UNIVERSITY OF ILLINOIS AND THE HOME ECONOMICS MOVEMENT. *J. of the Illinois State Hist. Soc. 1979 72(1): 21-38.* Reviews the life and works of Isabel Bevier (1860-1942), especially in relation to her pioneer work in home economics at the University of Illinois during 1900-21. Covers briefly the first halting steps in the field, beginning with the acceptance of women in universities. Bevier came to the University of Illinois from a solid educational background, determined to place home management on the level of a science. Relates the steps she took to do so, the victories, and the trials and tribulations. Closes with a few notes about her later works. 10 illus., 87 notes. 1900-21

Bickel, Alexander M.

543. Polsby, Nelson W. IN PRAISE OF ALEXANDER M. BICKEL. *Commentary 1976 61(1): 50-54.* Alexander M. Bickel (1924-74) was a lawyer with many talents. He taught, was a legal historian, wrote political philosophy, and entered the public arena as a political activist to educate the American people on current political questions, which turned more and more on legal and constitutional interpretation. Bickel believed in a government of institutions, both stable and flexible, relying on a balance between order and liberty to preserve society. He approved of civil disobedience, which was for him a quite different form of political behavior from revolutionary activity. He brought his views to the public on the pages of *Commentary* and the *New Republic*, as well as in legal journals and works such as *The Morality of Consent.* Personal recollection. 1924-74

Bickley, George Washington Lafayette

544. Hall, James O. A MAGNIFICENT CHARLATAN. *Civil War Times Illus. 1980 18(10): 40-42.* A native Virginian turned professional con man, George Washington Lafayette Bickley (1823-64) made a career of deceit and is perhaps best known for his leadership in the Knights of the Golden Circle, a secret order originally committed to American expansion in Mexico but later tied to prosouthern attitudes and the Copperheads in the midwest during the Civil War. 1850-64

Bidamon, Emma Hale Smith

545. Avery, Valeen Tippetts and Newell, Linda King. THE LION AND THE LADY: BRIGHAM YOUNG AND EMMA SMITH. *Utah Hist. Q. 1980 48(1): 81-97.* After Joseph Smith's death in 1844, Emma Hale Smith (later Bidamon) and Brigham Young conflicted over the succession to the Mormons' presidency, and the settling of Joseph's estate. Young felt that Emma had taken property belonging to the Mormons. Emma's legacy of debt left her feeling that Young had swindled her out of wealth. Neither understood that there had been no wealth. Nauvoo, Illinois, was built on speculative economy. Their conflict led to later institutionalized rancor between two churches (the Latter-day Saints and the Reorganized Latter-day Saints) claiming the same founder.

Based on Brigham Young Papers, LDS Archives, Emma Smith Bidamon Papers, RLDS Library-Archives, and other primary sources; 6 illus., 42 notes. 1832-79

546. Avery, Valeen Tippetts. EMMA SMITH THROUGH HER WRITINGS. *Dialogue 1984 17(3): 101-106.* Surveys the letters of Emma Hale Smith Bidamon (1804-79) for evidence of the woman as she understood herself. She was Joseph Smith's faithful and loving wife, as can be seen from his letters to her, including one written on the day he was murdered, 27 June 1844. Many Mormons resented her subsequent marriage to Lewis Bidamon and her refusal to follow Brigham Young to Utah. While members of the (Utah) Church of Jesus Christ of Latter-Day Saints came to see her as an example of faithless perfidy, the (Missouri) Reorganized Church of Jesus Christ of Latter Day Saints regarded her as the embodiment of righteousness and the mother of their hereditary patriarchs. Paper presented in the Charles Redd Center Lecture Series, 6 December 1983, Provo, Utah, and at the Mormon History Association, 11 May 1984, Provo, Utah. Primary sources; 18 notes. 1837-69

547. Newell, Linda King. THE EMMA SMITH LORE RECONSIDERED. *Dialogue 1984 17(3): 86-100.* Controversy among Mormons about the wife of Joseph Smith, Emma Hale Smith Bidamon (1804-79), including semilegendary accounts that she burned his revelation on plural marriage, attempted to poison him, and was partly responsible for his death, arises from bitterness about her refusal to follow Brigham Young to Utah and her endorsement of her children's Reorganized Church of Jesus Christ of Latter Day Saints. Paper presented at the Charles Redd Center Lecture Series, 6 December 1983, Provo, Utah, and at the Mormon History Association, 11 May 1984, Provo, Utah. Primary sources; photo, 64 notes. 1840-50

Bidamon, Lewis C.

548. Avery, Valeen Tippetts and Newell, Linda King. LEWIS C. BIDAMON: STEPCHILD OF MORMONDOM. *Brigham Young U. Studies 1979 19(3): 375-388.* Lewis C. Bidamon, unaffiliated with any church, married Emma Smith, widow of Joseph Smith, in 1847, in Nauvoo, Illinois. In 1849, he joined the gold rush to California; he returned in 1850 to Nauvoo and Emma. Despite his love of liquor, lack of religion, and extramarital affairs, Emma continued to love him. Based on Church and Reorganized Church of Latter Day Saints archives; 55 notes. 1842-80

Biddle, Anthony J. Drexel

549. Asprey, Robert B. THE KING OF KILL. *Marine Corps Gazette 1967 51(5): 31-35.* A biography of Colonel Anthony J. Drexel Biddle (1874-1948), millionaire, socialite, philanthropist, and marine. 1874-1948

Biddle, Thomas

550. Wainwright, Nicholas B. THE LIFE AND DEATH OF MAJOR THOMAS BIDDLE. *Pennsylvania Mag. of Hist. and Biog. 1980 104(3): 308-325.* Congressman Spencer Pettis, goaded on by Jacksonian and anti-Bank friends, and anti-Jacksonian Major Thomas Biddle both died as a result of their duel on 26 August 1831. The death of Biddle, brother of Nicholas Biddle, cut short the career of a man deeply respected by family and society in his adopted St. Louis. Based on the Andalusia Papers at the Historical Society of Pennsylvania, and the Nicholas Biddle Papers at the Library of Congress; 57 notes. 1831

Bidwell, Annie Ellicott Kennedy

551. Mathes, Valerie Sherer. INDIAN PHILANTHROPY IN CALIFORNIA: ANNIE BIDWELL AND THE MECHOOPDA INDIANS. *Arizona and the West 1983 25(2): 153-166.* Using her own family resources and acting on her own initiative, Annie Ellicott Kennedy Bidwell worked with a small band of California Mechoopda Indians to "civilize" them. Encouragd by her wealthy California rancher and congressman husband, she worked closely with the Mechoopda, provided them a school and a church, and supported them financially almost from her marriage in 1868 to her death. 5 illus., 34 notes. 1868-1918

Bieber, Ralph Paul

552. Loos, John L. A DEDICATION TO THE MEMORY OF RALPH P. BIEBER, 1894-1981. *Arizona and the West 1983 25(2): 104-108.* Ralph Paul Bieber (1894-1981) earned his graduate degrees in American institutional history at the University of Pennsylvania. Except for summer visiting appointments, his academic career, 1919-67, was spent at Washngton University. His research and publications concerned the Southwestern frontier; he contributed eight volumes to the Southwest Historical Series. An active professional, Bieber served as president of the Mississippi Valley Historical Association. Illus., biblio. 1919-67

Bien, Herman M.

553. Clar, Reva and Kramer, William M. JULIUS ECKMAN AND HERMAN BIEN: THE BATTLING RABBIS OF SAN FRANCISCO. PART 3. *Western States Jewish Hist. Q. 1983 15(4): 341-359.* Continued from a previous article. In 1860-61, Herman Bien's weekly Jewish newspaper, *The Pacific Messenger,* failed. He then had a varied career for several years, running a general merchandise store in New York, and working on newspapers in Nevada Territory and New York City. In 1879, he went to Dallas as a rabbi; from 1881 to 1885 he was rabbi of Chicago's Congregation Beth Shalom. His final post was that of rabbi of Congregation Anshe Chesed in Vicksburg, Mississippi. Bien died by his own hand in 1895 after losing his Vicksburg rabbinate. Julius Eckman changed the name of his San Francisco paper to the *Hebrew Observer* in 1865, but resigned as editor several months later to resume religious duties. Based on newspaper articles; 67 notes. 1860-95

554. Clar, Reva and Kramer, William M. JULIUS ECKMAN AND HERMAN BIEN: THE BATTLING RABBIS OF SAN FRANCISCO. *Western States Jewish Hist. Q. 1983 15(2): 107-130, (3): 232-253.* Part 1. Julius Eckman and Herman M. Bien were San Francisco's first two elected rabbis, and founders of the first two Jewish newspapers in the West. Eckman's mild nature was not suited for the contentious career of a rabbi, but his erudition served him well as publisher of the *Weekly Gleaner,* founded in January 1857. Bien's competing paper, *Voice of Israel,* founded three months earlier than the *Gleaner,* reflected the radical outlook of its publisher, and failed in April 1857. The bitter feud between the two rabbis was based in part on Bien's youth and his efforts to reform the services of Congregation Emanu-El, and on Eckman's attacks on Bien's qualifications. Part 2. In 1859, Eckman was joined by a young reporter, Isidor N. Choynski, who was later to become the leading Jewish journalist on the West Coast. The next year, Israel Joseph Benjamin, an international Jewish correspondent, toured the West, and his travels were fully reported in Eckman's *Weekly Gleaner.* The feud between Eckman and Bien cooled down

while Bien successfully wrote and produced a play based on the story of Samson and Delilah. Based on newspaper accounts; 162 notes. Article to be continued. 1854-61

Bierce, Ambrose

555. Bates, Lincoln. TO WIT: AMBROSE BIERCE. *Westways 1977 69(1): 22-26, 66.* Chronicles the many-faceted California career of author Ambrose Bierce, as journalist, author, wit, and bandit, 1866-87; includes a compilation of Bierce witticisms. 1866-87

556. Francendese, Janet Malverti. "Ambrose Bierce as Journalist." New York U. 1977. 235 pp. *DAI 1977 38(4): 2125-2126-A.* 1868-1909

Bierstadt, Albert

557. Pringle, Allan. ALBERT BIERSTADT IN CANADA. *American Art Journal 1985 17(1): 2-27.* Beginning in 1874, the popular and prominent American landscape painter Albert Bierstadt traveled throughout Canada sketching and painting. His work was supported particularly by the directors of the new Canadian Pacific Railway for the specific purpose of popularizing and promoting the western lands that the railroad would serve. Bierstadt's work greatly influenced the first generation of Canadian landscape painters, and he was highly regarded in Canada. 5 photos, 19 plates, map, 58 notes. 1874-90

Bilbo, Theodore G.

558. Giroux, Vincent Arthur, Jr. "Theodore G. Bilbo: Progressive to Public Racist." Indiana U. 1984. 333 pp. *DAI 1985 46(1): 245-A.* DA8506105 1930's-40's

559. Smith, Charles Pope. "Theodore G. Bilbo's Senatorial Career: The Final Years, 1941-1947." U. of Southern Mississippi 1983. 268 pp. *DAI 1983 44(5): 1551-1552-A.* DA8321500 1941-47

Billings, Hammatt

560. O'Gorman, James F. WAR, SLAVERY, AND INTEMPERANCE IN THE BOOK ILLUSTRATIONS OF HAMMATT BILLINGS. *Imprint 1985 10(1): 2-10.* Details the life and career of Hammatt Billings, who illustrated the first edition of Harriet Beecher Stowe's *Uncle Tom's Cabin* (1852), and who became a major figure in the world of Boston book illustrating in the 1850's-60's. 1850-70

Billings, John Shaw

561. Blake, John B. BILLINGS AND BEFORE: NINETEENTH CENTURY MEDICAL BIBLIOGRAPHY. Blake, John B., ed. *Centenary of Index Medicus, 1879-1979* (Bethesda, Md.: U.S. Dept. of Health and Human Services, Public Health Service, Natl. Inst. of Health, Natl. Lib. of Medicine, 1980): 31-52. Traces John Shaw Billings's career during 1838-79, the events leading up to the appearance of the *Index Medicus* in 1879, and Billings's motives for introducing it to the medical world; mentions other useful bibliographic tools which preceded the *Index Medicus* and which are discussed in *The Development of Medical Bibliography* (1954) by Dr. Estelle Brodman; and discusses Frederick Leypoldt's role in publishing the *Index Medicus.* 19c

Billings, K. LeMoyne

562. Michaelis, David. THE PRESIDENT'S BEST FRIEND. *Am. Heritage 1983 34(4): 12-27.* K. LeMoyne Billings was John F. Kennedy's best friend from prep school days in the 1930's. When Kennedy became president, Billings turned down several job offers in order to remain a friend, not an employee, of the president. He was one in whom the president confided and upon whom he often played practical jokes. 8 photos. 1930's-63

Billings, William

563. DeJong, Mary Gosselink. "BOTH PLEASURE AND PROFIT": WILLIAM BILLINGS AND THE USES OF MUSIC. *William and Mary Q. 1985 42(1): 104-116.* William Billings published the first tune book containing only American music, *The New-England Psalm-Singer* (1770). Some 300 tunes by Billings have survived. Discusses Billings's contributions, including his music theory. Billings's works are compared with other early music publications. A growing taste for more decorous music caused a decline of interest in Billings's music, although in rural areas his music remained popular. Comments on the revival of interest in Billings's music. Based on Billings's works and other primary sources; 50 notes. 17c-18c

564. Thomas, Ruth Colby. MUSIC OF THE REVOLUTIONARY TIMES. *Daughters of the Am. Revolution Mag. 1984 118(10): 720-721, 773, 790.* Biographical vignettes of three early American composers: Francis Hopkinson, James Lyon, and William Billings. 1746-1800

Billington, Ray Allen

565. Lamar, Howard R. RAY ALLEN BILLINGTON. *Pro. of the Am. Antiquarian Soc. 1982 92(1): 19-23.* Surveys the range of Billington's career as a historian of the American frontier and the westward movement. Briefly reviews his major writings on the frontier and surveys his effort to give the frontier idea an intellectual and psychological context. 1903-81

566. Leopold, Richard W. RAY ALLEN BILLINGTON. *Massachusetts Hist. Soc. Pro. 1981 93: 119-122.* Ray Allen Billington (1903-81) will be remembered as a great historian of the American West, foremost expositor of the Turner thesis, and an active force in the Organization of American Historians. Taking degrees from Wisconsin, Michigan, and Harvard, Billington studied social and intellectual history under Arthur M. Schlesinger. His teaching career included appointments at Clark University, Smith College, and Northwestern before he settled into the senior research associate position at the Huntington Library. His major writings include *The Protestant Crusade, 1800-1860: A Study of the Origins of American Nativism* (1938), *Westward Expansion* (1949), *The Far Western Frontier, 1830-1860* (1956), *Frederick Jackson Turner: Historian, Scholar, Teacher* (1973), and *Land of Savagery, Land of Promise: The European Image of the American Frontier in the Nineteenth Century* (1980). 1903-81

567. Ridge, Martin. RAY ALLEN BILLINGTON, 1903-1981: HISTORIAN OF THE AMERICAN FRONTIER. *Am. West 1981 18(3): 22-23.* Ray Allen Billington (1903-81) did more than any other contemporary scholar to explain the American West. He was a thoroughgoing follower of the Frederick Jackson Turner school of Western historians, but he clearly set out the limitations of Turner's perceptions. He persistently believed that the westering experience shaped the

character of the American people and their institutions. He advocated comparing the American experience with that of people in other countries. Billington's professional life included teaching, lecturing, professional service, high honors, and publications ranging from textbooks to monographs to biography. Photo. 1949-81

568. Ridge, Martin. RAY ALLEN BILLINGTON, 1903-1981. *Am. Studies Int. 1980 19(1): 63-64.* Obituary of the dean of western historians, past president of the American Studies Association, and the Western History Association, and the Organization of American Historians, who taught at Clark University, Smith College, and Northwestern University before joining the senior research staff of the Huntington Library. Always ready to assist other researchers, a strong supporter of freedom of expression, he "completely embodied the generous and enlightened scholar." 1924-81

569. Ridge, Martin. RAY ALLEN BILLINGTON (1903-1981). *Western Hist. Q. 1981 12(3): 244-250.* In high school and college, Ray Allen Billington was an active journalist with career ambitions in that field. He decided on an academic career instead and earned graduate degrees in history. After teaching for 30 years in eastern and midwestern universities, he spent his remaining years as a senior research associate in the Huntington Library in California. Billington was active in professional organizations; he served four as their president. He had "phenomenal skill as a platform speaker." He wrote "at an astonishing rate," publishing nearly 200 essays and more than 50 books and pamphlets; and he edited or wrote introductions for many other books. His reputation has a broad base, but it rests principally on his becoming "a leading exponent of both western history and the Turnerian view of the American past." Illus., 3 notes. 1933-81

Billy the Kid

See Bonney, William

Binder, Erwin

570. Kinsey, Ron R. A NEW VISION OF SEQUOYAH. *Masterkey 1979 53(1): 4-9.* 1809-21
For abstract see ***Sequoyah***

Binga, Jesse

571. Binga, Anthony J., Sr. JESSE BINGA: FOUNDER AND PRESIDENT, BINGA STATE BANK, CHICAGO, ILLINOIS. *J. of the Afro-American Hist. and Geneal. Soc. 1981 2(4): 146-152.* Biography of Jesse Binga (1865-1950), founder and president of the Binga State Bank from the bank's founding in 1908 to its closure in 1932. 1865-1950

Bingham, George Caleb

572. Ehrlich, George. GEORGE CALEB BINGHAM: A VARIANT VIEW OF HIS GENRE WORKS. *Am. Studies Int. 1978 19(2): 41-55.* A look at George Caleb Bingham as ethnographer, through his Western-theme paintings completed between 1845 and 1855. Examines why Bingham dropped a successful career as a portraitist to paint frontier scenes and personalities. Bingham began to emphasize ethnographic documentation, although he was also giving his subjects a romantic aura of exoticism. But this twist in his career, which was short-lived, came largely at the urging of the American Art-Union, and these paintings were designed to fill a gap in the Western record. 10 illus., 27 notes. 1845-65

Bingham, Hiram

573. Miller, Char. THE MAKING OF A MISSIONARY: HIRAM BINGHAM'S ODYSSEY. *Hawaiian J. of Hist. 1979 13: 36-45.* Examines Hiram Bingham's early life in Vermont before he sailed for Hawaii in 1819. Age 21 was a turning point for Bingham (1789-1869), because at that time he was to become his parents' caretaker. Instead, he publicly took the vows of the Lord. His conversion to Congregationalism gave him an excuse to break his commitment to his parents. This decision was due largely but not solely to his ambition. Bingham was raised in a religion that demanded intense commitment that went beyond family ties. The demands of his forceful and uncompromising personality fit the requirements of his missionary vocation. Notes. 1789-1819

574. Miller, Char, ed. "TEACH ME O MY GOD": THE JOURNAL OF HIRAM BINGHAM (1815-1816). *Vermont Hist. 1980 48(4): 225-235.* At Middlebury College, 1813-16, Hiram Bingham groped toward a missionary career in the Sandwich Islands (Hawaii), 1819-39. At Andover Theological Seminary, 1816-18, he was active in the Tract Society. Bingham learned Hawaiian, opened Hawaiian schools, became influential with the royal family, and incurred the enmity of merchants and sailors for his Moral Wars on alcohol, prostitution, and gambling. 1815-39

Bingham, Hiram (family)

575. Bingham, Afred M. SYBIL'S BONES, A CHRONICLE OF THE THREE HIRAM BINGHAMS. *Hawaiian J. of Hist. 1975 9: 3-36.* Traces the lives of two generations of Binghams. The first Hiram Bingham and his wife Sybil were the models for James Michener's missionary sequence in his novel *Hawaii.* He made free use of the first Hiram Bingham's *A Residence of Twenty-one Years in the Sandwich Islands.* In later years the Binghams returned to New England, and were dismissed by the American Board of Commissioners for Foreign Missions. The second Hiram Bingham spent his missionary years in the Gilbert Islands until ill health forced his return to Hawaii. The third Hiram Bingham, the author's father, was responsible for moving the bones of Sybil, the first Hiram's first wife, into a grave next to her husband. 1820-1975

Bingham, Hiram, III

576. Miller, Char. "THE WORLD CREEPS IN": HIRAM BINGHAM III AND THE DECLINE OF MISSIONARY FERVOR. *Hawaiian J. of Hist. 1981 15: 80-99.* In choosing a secular over a religious career, Hiram Bingham III broke a long-standing family tradition of dedication to missionary life. In his youth, Bingham found his invalid parents' preoccupation with death, their rigid adherence to Congregational morality, and the idiosyncratic rituals repulsive. Changing values in the islands and a decline in missionary influence and power in the late 19th century influenced Bingham away from a religious career. Bingham's education at Phillips Academy and Yale finalized the break with his religious roots. Upon graduation, Bingham returned to Hawaii and briefly taught Bible school; however, he declined his parents' wish to pursue a missionary career in China. In 1899, Hiram, at age 24, sailed to San Francisco and began graduate work in history at the University of California at Berkeley. Primary sources; fig., 64 notes. 1875-1900

Bingham, Robert Worth

577. Ellis, William E. ROBERT WORTH BINGHAM AND LOUISVILLE PROGRESSIVISM, 1905-1910. *Filson Club Hist. Q. 1980 54(2): 169-195.* Robert Worth Bingham, a well-educated lawyer, was a leader in the effort to reform city government in Louisville, Kentucky. After the Kentucky Court of Appeals voided the corrupt 1905 city elections, Governor J. C. W. Beckham appointed Bingham acting mayor of Louisville in June 1907. In his four-month tenure as mayor, Bingham depoliticized the police and fire departments, exposed official corruption, and closed saloons on Sundays. While Bingham's reforms weakened the Democratic machine—the Republicans won the November 1907 election—they did not lead to permanent Progressive leadership or reforms. Based on the Bingham Papers at the Filson Club, Louisville, Kentucky, and contemporary newspapers; photo, 63 notes. 1905-10

Binkley, William Campbell

578. Nance, Joseph Milton. A DEDICATION TO THE MEMORY OF WILLIAM CAMPBELL BINKLEY, 1889-1970. *Arizona and the West 1981 23(4): 312-316.* William Campbell Binkley (1889-1970) was a student of Herbert E. Bolton at the University of California. His doctoral dissertation subject became his lifelong research interest. He became one of the most outstanding historians of the revolutionary and republic periods of Texas history. These were essentially years of racial and cultural conflict. He spent most of his academic career at Vanderbilt and Tulane universities. He was founding editor of the *Tennessee Historical Quarterly,* managing editor of the *Journal of Southern History,* and editor of the *Mississippi Valley Historical Review.* He served as president of the Southern Historical Association and the Mississippi Valley Historical Association. Illus., biblio. 1930-70

Bird, Francis William

579. Marti, Donald B. FRANCIS WILLIAM BIRD: A RADICAL'S PROGRESS THROUGH THE REPUBLICAN PARTY. *Hist. J. of Massachusetts 1983 11(2): 82-93.* A survey of the political odyssey of Bird who, as a radical reformer, was active in the Free Soil Party, the Republican Party from its inception, and then bolted it for the Liberal Republican Party when he felt the Republicans had become too conservative. 2 illus., 30 notes. 1848-72

Bird, R. A.

580. —. R. A. BIRD, PHOTOGRAPHER. *Alberta Hist. [Canada] 1983 31(4): 20-27.* R. A. Bird was a commercial photographer in Calgary, who drew his subjects primarily from southern Alberta. In 1925, he opened the Central Photo Studio in Calgary and ran it until his retirement in the early 1960's. He photographed architectural subjects, rodeos, Indians, landscapes, and many general views of the Calgary area. Many of his negatives were sold to the Glenbow Museum in 1962 and form the basis of their photographic collection. 13 photos. 1916-66

Bird, Robert Montgomery

581. Kilman, John Collins. "Robert Montgomery Bird: Physician and Man of Letters." U. of Delaware 1978. 265 pp. *DAI 1978 39(3): 1571-A.* 1820's-40's

Birkbeck, Samuel Bradford

582. Macmillan, David S. and Plomley, Brian. AN AMERICAN SURVEYOR IN MEXICO, 1827-1860. *New Mexico Hist. Rev. 1959 34(1): 1-8.* Account of Illinois surveyor Samuel Bradford Birkbeck's years in Mexico as surveyor, manager, and director for several British companies in the silver mining industry and as a surveyor on his own; based on his diary and travel accounts. 1827-60

Bishop, Elizabeth

583. Brown, Ashley. ELIZABETH BISHOP: IN MEMORIAM. *Southern Rev. 1980 16(2): 257-259.* Memorial to American poet Elizabeth Bishop from 1964 when the author met her in Rio de Janeiro, Brazil, until her death in 1979. 1964-79

584. Keller, Lynn. WORDS WORTH A THOUSAND POSTCARDS: THE BISHOP/MOORE CORRESPONDENCE. *Am. Lit. 1983 55(3): 405-429.* Analyzes the artistic development of Elizabeth Bishop and her friendship with poet Marianne Moore through their correspondence during the 1930's-40's. The 1930's were an apprenticeship period for Bishop, and her letters served as literary exercise and development. She also gained needed self-confidence and reinforcement from Moore's letters. During the 1940's Bishop established her aesthetic independence from her mentor, and their relationship stabilized as one between equals. Based on letters in the Elizabeth Bishop Collection, Vassar College Library; 16 notes. 1930's-40's

585. Travisano, Thomas Joseph. "Elizabeth Bishop: Introspective Traveler." U. of Virginia 1981. 239 pp. *DAI 1983 43(10): 3320-A.* DA8300081 20c

Bishop, Harriet E.

586. Bolin, Winifred D. Wandersee. HARRIET E. BISHOP: MORALIST AND REFORMER. Stuhler, Barbara and Kreuter, Gretchen, ed. *Women of Minnesota: Selected Biographical Essays* (St. Paul: Minnesota Historical Society Press, 1977): 7-19. In 1847, Harriet E. Bishop arrived in the frontier community of St. Paul, Minnesota. Trained by Catharine Beecher, Bishop brought with her the missionary zeal of the social reformer and a belief in the moral superiority of women. A Baptist, she established the first public school and the first Sunday School in St. Paul. Discusses her activities as a temperance advocate, largely negative attitudes toward the local Indians, efforts to help the destitute, prose and poetry, and two matrimonial opportunities. Bishop died in 1883. By then she was largely unknown in the growing metropolis, but her life "personified a whole generation of women" who tried to fulfill their destinies within the boundaries of convention and who labored to meet the responsibilities imposed by their presumed innate superiority. Primary and secondary sources; illus., 34 notes. 1847-83

Bishop, John Peale

587. Young, Thomas Daniel and Hindle, John, ed. ALLEN TATE AND JOHN PEALE BISHOP: AN EXCHANGE OF LETTERS, 1931. *Southern Rev. 1980 16(4): 879-906.* Brief background to the friendship between Allen Tate and John Peale Bishop from their first meeting in 1925 until Bishop's death in 1944, focusing on a series of letters to each other in 1931 offering encouragement and critiques of their respective writing. 1931

Bissell, Samuel

588. Hettinger, George B. "Samuel Bissell: Humanitarian and Educator, 1797-1895." U. of Akron 1981. 303 pp. *DAI 1981 42(3): 1030-1031-A.* DA8117713 1817-95

Biven, Rasey

589. Methmann, Alicia Compton. RASEY BIVEN, THE DUELLING EDITOR, AND THE DE ANZA CONNECTION. *Pacific Hist. 1977 21(4): 327-332.* Presents a biographical sketch of Rasey Biven, early Stockton, California, newspaper editor. Focuses on 1849-68. 1849-68

Bixler, David

590. Bixler, Miriam E. DAVID BIXLER, FOLK ARTIST. *J. of the Lancaster County Hist. Soc. 1977 81(1): 31-38.* Discusses the family, genealogy, and folkart of Lancaster County resident, David Bixler, 1800-48. 1800-48

Bjork, Kenneth O.

591. Lovoll, Odd S. KENNETH O. BJORK: TEACHER, SCHOLAR, AND EDITOR. Lovoll, Odd S., ed. *Makers of an American Immigrant Legacy: Essays in Honor of Kenneth O. Bjork* (Northfield, Minn.: Norwegian-American Hist. Assoc., 1980): 3-14. Honors Kenneth O. Bjork (b. 1909), teacher, scholar, and since 1960, managing editor of the Norwegian-American Historical Association's publications, both for his service and his contributions to Norwegian-American historical scholarship. 1909-80

Black, John

592. Robbins, Rebecca. COLONEL JOHN BLACK OF ELLSWORTH (1781-1856). *Maine Hist. Soc. Q. 1978 17(3): 121-156.* Traces the business career of John Black from 1798 until his death in 1856. Describes his role as agent for the "Bingham Lands" at Gouldsboro and Ellsworth, his activities as a lumberman, and his involvement in building "Woodlawn." His marriage to Mary Cobb in 1802 and his problems with his son, Henry, are also noted. 67 notes. 1798-1856

Black, William Leslie

593. Carlson, Paul. WILLIAM L. BLACK AND THE BEGINNING OF THE WEST TEXAS ANGORA GOAT INDUSTRY. *West Texas Hist. Assoc. Year Book 1980 56: 3-13.* Discusses William Leslie Black's contributions, beginning in the 1880's. ca 1880-1979

Black Hawk

594. Krupt, Arnold. THE INDIAN AUTOBIOGRAPHY: ORIGINS, TYPE AND FUNCTION. *Am. Literature 1981 53(1): 22-42.* The Indian autobiography flourished as a genre only in the 20th century, but the early model for a great many books of this type was J. B. Patterson's *Life of Ma-Ka-tai-me-she-kia-kiak or Black Hawk* published in 1833. The work was a collaborative effort for which Black Hawk acted as "subject-author" and Patterson as "editor-author." Patterson's book featured the basic principle of Indian autobiography, that of "bicultural composite authorship." Based on Patterson's *Life of Black Hawk* and several Indian biographies; 31 notes. 1833

Blackadar, Hugh (family)

595. Stayner, Charles St. Clair. THE BLACKADAR FAMILY OF HALIFAX. *Nova Scotia Hist. Rev. [Canada] 1981 1(1): 67-72.* Traces the genealogy of the Blackadar family through Hugh Blackadar (1773-1818), a shipwright, and his four children. Hugh William Blackadar (1908-63) learned the printing trade and assumed management of the *Acadian Recorder* in 1937. Charles Coleman Blackadar (1847-1930) became publisher of the paper in 1901 and continued until his death. Archives' Manuscripts MG100, vol. 111, No. 36C. 1773-1980

Blackburn, Joseph

596. Aykroyd, Elizabeth A. R. JOSEPH BLACKBURN, LIMNER, IN PORTSMOUTH. *Hist. New Hampshire 1975 30(4): 231-243.* Joseph Blackburn, portrait painter, arrived in Boston in 1754. He subsequently lived in Portsmouth for several years before departing for England in 1763. He executed more than 130 portraits while in America. Although he was a minor artist who relied on a few formulae of pose and background and had "difficulty in characterizing his subjects," Blackburn left "a valuable record of the merchant aristocracy of New England, particularly Portsmouth. . . ." 6 illus., 8 notes. 1754-63

Blackburn, Joseph Clay Stiles

597. Schlup, Leonard. JOSEPH BLACKBURN OF KENTUCKY AND THE PANAMA QUESTION. *Filson Club Hist. Q. 1977 51(4): 350-362.* Describes the later public career of Senator Joseph Clay Stiles Blackburn of Kentucky. Blackburn was concerned about the aggressive foreign policy followed by President Theodore Roosevelt in Panama. As a result, Blackburn voted against the final treaty which granted the United States the Canal Zone. Despite Blackburn's opposition to the treaty, Roosevelt appointed the Kentuckian to the Isthmian Commission in 1907. He served as civilian governor for two years, working closely with Secretary of War and President William Howard Taft. Based on the Taft Papers, Library of Congress; 43 notes. 1901-09

Blackburne, Anna

598. Wystrach, V. P. ANNA BLACKBURNE (1726-1793): A NEGLECTED PATRONESS OF NATURAL HISTORY. *J. of the Soc. for the Biblio. of Natural Hist. [Great Britain] 1977 8(2): 148-168.* Anna Blackburne, an amateur botanist, gave her name to the Blackburnian warbler of the Northeastern United States. 1726-93

Blackden, Samuel

599. Case, James R. COLONEL SAMUEL BLACKDEN: AT DEATH-BED OF JOHN PAUL JONES. *Daughters of the Am. Revolution Mag. 1980 114(4): 506-507.* Briefly discusses the military career (1775-79) of Colonel Samuel Blackden of Connecticut; he was the last person to see John Paul Jones alive (in Paris, in 1792); in Paris as a trader, he later mysteriously disappeared with his wife. 1775-90's

Blackmur, Richard Palmer

600. Fraser, Russell. R. P. BLACKMUR: AMERICA'S BEST CRITIC. *Virginia Q. Rev. 1981 57(4): 569-593.* Richard Palmer Blackmur, (1904-65) who considered his life a failure, was called "our best American critic" by Allen Tate. A New Englander whose formal education ended in high school, he spent his last 25 years at Princeton University where he became a great teacher and, in 1951, a full professor. While his "personal life ended in disaster," he was a

specialist in diction and did his homework extremely well. His permanent reputation depends upon *Language as Gesture* (1952). 1904-65

Blackwell, Elizabeth

601. Henderson, Janet Karen. "Four Nineteenth Century Professional Women." Rutgers U., New Brunswick 1982. 315 pp. *DAI 1982 43(3): 698-A.* DA8218323 19c

602. Morantz, Regina Markell. FEMINISM, PROFESSIONALISM, AND GERMS: THE THOUGHT OF MARY PUTNAM JACOBI AND ELIZABETH BLACKWELL. *Am. Q. 1982 34(5): 459-478.* 1849-90
*For abstract see **Jacobi, Mary Putnam***

603. Smith, Dean. A PERSISTENT REBEL. *Am. Hist. Illus. 1981 15(9): 28-35.* Biography of English-born Elizabeth Blackwell (1821-1910), who became America's first female physician, after studies at Geneva College in New York state during 1847-49; after that she studied in Paris and London, practiced in the United States, and encouraged many women to become physicians. 1847-1910

Blackwell, Samuel (family)

604. Horn, Margo E. "SISTERS WORTHY OF RESPECT": FAMILY DYNAMICS AND WOMEN'S ROLES IN THE BLACKWELL FAMILY. *J. of Family Hist. 1983 8(4): 367-382.* Discusses the five daughters of Hannah and Samuel Blackwell. Born between 1816 and 1826, the sisters never married. Four went on to make major achievements in the arts and sciences; their similar careers reflect family values and practices. Biblio. 1820-80

Blackwood, James

605. Tucker, Stephen R. PENTECOSTALISM AND POPULAR CULTURE IN THE SOUTH: A STUDY OF FOUR MUSICIANS. *J. of Popular Culture 1982 16(3): 68-80.* Brief biographical sketches of James Blackwood, Johnny Cash, Jerry Lee Lewis, and Tammy Wynette illustrate the important influence of pentecostalism on Southern popular music from gospel to rockabilly. Based on interviews; 55 notes. 1950's-70's

Blaettermann, George W.

606. Head, Ronald B. THE DECLENSION OF GEORGE W. BLAETTERMANN: FIRST PROFESSOR OF MODERN LANGUAGES AT THE UNIVERSITY OF VIRGINIA. *Virginia Cavalcade 1982 31(4): 182-191.* Saxony-born George W. Blaettermann (1782-1850) immigrated to the United States in 1824, began teaching at the University of Virginia, and quickly established a reputation as a poor teacher and a "rude, cantankerous, arrogant, and spiteful" person who whipped his wife (Elizabeth) twice in public and was terminated from the university in 1840 because of it. 1782-1850

Blaine, Anita McCormick

607. Antler, Joyce. FEMALE PHILANTHROPY AND PROGRESSIVISM IN CHICAGO. *Hist. of Educ. Q. 1981 21(4): 461-469.* Reviews Gilbert Harrison's *A Timeless Affair: The Life of Anita McCormick Blaine.* Blaine, born in 1876 to a wealthy Chicago family, was more than heiress to the McCormick reaper fortune. Impressed by the ideas of John Dewey and desirous of a good education for her son, she played an important part in developing progressive educational programs during the early 1900's. She also participated in world peace movements from World War I to the 1950's. Although not formally a feminist, she was peripherally engaged in the suffrage struggle through work with such groups as Hull House, the Women's Trade Union League, and the Consumer's League. Her life exemplified the influence of women on philanthropic and progressive trends, but also revealed conflicts faced by career-oriented women. 4 notes. ca 1900-54

Blaine, David E.

608. Norwood, Frederick A. TWO CONTRASTING VIEWS OF THE INDIANS: METHODIST INVOLVEMENT IN THE INDIAN TROUBLES IN OREGON AND WASHINGTON. *Church Hist. 1980 49(2): 178-187.* 1850-59
*For abstract see **Beeson, John***

Blaine, John J.

609. O'Brien, Patrick G. SENATOR JOHN J. BLAINE: AN INDEPENDENT PROGRESSIVE DURING "NORMALCY." *Wisconsin Mag. of Hist. 1976 60(1): 25-41.* Analyzes John J. Blaine's record as Senator 1927-33 and concludes that he was an insurgent Republican whose progressivism, as reflected in key Congressional votes, was exceeded only by a few Republicans during his single term in office. Some of the major issues which reflected Blaine's stand included his repudiation of Hoover for President, his opposition to the Republican party's choice for president pro tempore of the Senate and for committee assignments, his defense of civil liberties and opposition to the Ku Klux Klan, his support for an excess-profits tax to end privilege and redistribute income, and his opposition to "dollar diplomacy" which he saw as the policy of imperialism and colonialism. 10 illus., 78 notes. 1927-33

Blair, Duncan B.

610. Sinclair, D. M. REV. DUNCAN BLACK BLAIR, D.D. (1815-1893): PIONEER PREACHER IN PICTOU COUNTY, GAELIC SCHOLAR AND POET. *Nova Scotia Hist. Soc. Collections [Canada] 1977 39: 155-168.* Duncan Black Blair's poem "Eas Niagara" is regarded as one of the "two most celebrated Gaelic poems composed on Canadian soil." His Gaelic *Diary* provides not only interesting information on society but also on the youthful author's education, including 1834-38, when he was enrolled at the University of Edinburgh. In 1846 he came to Nova Scotia as a Free Church [Presbyterian] missionary, remained slightly more than one year, only to return in 1848 to accept the call of the congregation at Barney's River-Blue Mountain where he remained until his death in 1893. Regarded as "the best Gaelic scholar in America, in his time" Blair wrote *Rudiments of Gaelic Grammar,* "a most complete Gaelic dictionary," as well as some poetry, examples of which are provided in this article. 1846-93

Blair, Elizabeth

611. Laas, Virginia J. THE COURTSHIP AND MARRIAGE OF ELIZABETH BLAIR AND SAMUEL PHILLIPS LEE: A PROBLEM IN HISTORICAL DETECTION. *Midwest Quarterly 1985 27(1): 13-29.* The four-year courtship of Elizabeth Blair and Samuel Phillips Lee illustrates the complexities of social customs among antebellum America's middle and upper classes. Blair, part of a powerful Washington political family, and Lee, a career navy officer and grandson of Richard Henry Lee, had to deal with the separations caused by navy life and the disapproval of Elizabeth's father, partly due to Samuel's position in society. The two left a trail

of correspondence that enables historians to piece together their tumultuous courtship and wedding and thus understand the formation of an important political and military couple. Based on personal letters and official records and correspondence. 1839-43

Blair, John

612. Frank, Perry. BICENTENNIAL GAZETTE: THE FRAMERS OF THE CONSTITUTION: VIRGINIA. *This Constitution 1985 (7): 38-40.* Capsule biographies of Virginia's delegation to the constitutional convention of 1787 are provided; profiles George Washington, James Madison, Edmund Randolph, George Mason, George Wythe, John Blair, and James McClurg. 1787

Blake, Alice

613. Foote, Cheryl J. ALICE BLAKE OF TREMENTINA: MISSION TEACHER OF THE SOUTHWEST. *J. of Presbyterian Hist. 1982 60(3): 228-242.* Alice Blake was typical of devout American Presbyterian women who felt the call to take the civilizing aspects of the Protestant gospel to those who were under the iron hand of Romanism in the Southwest. Chronicles her labors, which culminated in the village of Trementina, New Mexico, where she labored for 30 years. In addition to being a teacher, she took the necessary courses that qualified her as a public health nurse, while at the same time she filled in from time to time as leader in worship when no minister was present. Protestant mission teachers like Blake came to the area laden with the same attitudes of ethnic and cultural superiority that characterized their countrymen. But they also brought a firm and sincere commitment to the Christian faith and a loving desire to serve. Based on articles by Alice Blake, studies in Presbyterian home missions in the Southwest, and oral interviews; photo, 53 notes. 1910-50

Blake, Clarence John

614. Viets, Henry R. THE RESIDENT HOUSE STAFF AT THE OPENING OF THE BOSTON CITY HOSPITAL IN 1864. *J. of the Hist. of Medicine and Allied Sci. 1959 14(2): 179-190.* Biographical data on the first house officers of the Boston City Hospital, all of whom later distinguished themselves in medicine: John Dole (1838-72), Michael Freebern Gavin (1844-1915), David Francis Lincoln (1841-1916), Edward Greely Loring (1837-1888), and Clarence John Blake (1843-1919). 1864-1919

Blake, Eubie

615. Morath, Max. THE 93 YEARS OF EUBIE BLAKE. *Am. Heritage 1976 27(6): 56-65.* Discusses a 1976 interview with 93-year-old pianist and composer Eubie Blake, by Max Morath, also an entertainer. Subjects covered include the difficulties facing a black entertainer, Blake's acquaintance with other entertainers, and his predictions for trends in music. 7 illus. ca 1890-1976

Blalock, Alice Grundy

616. Carter, Doris Dorcas. ALICE GRUNDY BLALOCK: A PORTRAIT OF LOVE. *North Louisiana Hist. Assoc. J. 1982 13(4): 131-138.* Alice Grundy Blalock was a leader in the struggle to eliminate illiteracy in the black communities of Louisiana. Prior to beginning her long career as a teacher-trainer at Louisiana Normal and Industrial Institute (now Grambling State University) in 1929, she taught successfully in several public schools. She worked hard to make Grambling a reputable institution of higher learning and earned a reputation as a "master teacher." 40 notes. ca 1920-70

Blanchard, Jonathan

617. Taylor, Richard S. BEYOND IMMEDIATE EMANCIPATION: JONATHAN BLANCHARD, ABOLITIONISM, AND THE EMERGENCE OF AMERICAN FUNDAMENTALISM. *Civil War Hist. 1981 27(3): 260-274.* Details the career of Jonathan Blanchard (1811-92), Congregationalist pastor, president of Knox College, and founder of Wheaton College. Blanchard's involvement in the temperance, antislavery and antisecret society crusades stemmed from his idea of the "moral autonomy of the individual" and demonstrated his relationship with the development of Christian evangelicalism rather than with the Social Gospel. Covers the 1830's-80's. 66 notes. 1830's-80's

Blanchard, Rufus

618. Selmer, Marsha L. RUFUS BLANCHARD: EARLY CHICAGO MAP PUBLISHER. *Chicago History 1984 13(1): 23-31.* Outlines the contribution of Rufus Blanchard to Chicago mapmaking during the second half of the 19th century, noting his cartographic and publishing innovations. 1854-1904

Blanchet, François

619. Bernier, Jacques. FRANÇOIS BLANCHET ET LE MOUVEMENT RÉFORMISTE EN MÉDECINE AU DÉBUT DU XIXe SIÈCLE [François Blanchet and the medical reform movement of the early 19th century]. *Rev. d'Hist. de l'Amérique Française [Canada] 1980 34(2): 223-244.* In the late 18th century, the practice of medicine in Canada was monopolized by British military doctors and suffered from a lack of professional standards. François Blanchet (b. 1776), a Columbia University-trained physician, was a founder of the first professional medical society in Quebec, and one of the few doctors in the Canadian Parliament. His group worked for changes in the examination system for doctors and for the establishment of a medical school in Montreal, fought charlatans, and set up new facilities to treat contagious diseases. His efforts were a major step in the professionalization of medicine in Canada. Based on materials from archives in Quebec and the National Library of Medicine in Bethesda, Maryland; 70 notes. 1776-1824

Bland, Salem

620. Allen, Richard. SALEM BLAND: THE YOUNG PREACHER. *J. of the Can. Church Hist. Soc. [Canada] 1977 19(1-2): 75-93.* After World War I, Salem Bland became recognized as a leader in the social gospel and liberal theology movements. The formative period for Bland was his early years as a Methodist minister in Canada. Though successful as a preacher, he held some suspect views and disliked the numerous theological controversies going on around him. Using his various talents, Bland sought to show that there was no important difference between science and religion and that Christian perfection meant not freedom from mistakes, but the constant desire to do what was right. Seeking at all times to combine the good from his own culture and fundamental Christian ideas, Bland rejected the evangelistic approach of both the Methodists and the Salvation Army because he felt that they could not help combine the old and the new. Primary and secondary sources; 69 notes. This issue is *J. of the Can. Church Hist. Soc.* 1977 19(1-2) and *Bull. of the United Church of Can.* 1977 26. 1880-86

Blankenhorn, Heber

621. Gall, Gilbert J. HEBER BLANKENHORN: THE PUBLICIST AS REFORMER. *Historian 1983 45(4): 513-528.* Historians have failed to explore the role played by labor publicists and public relations practitioners in creating a hospitable social environment for the labor movement during 1919-50. The career of Heber Blankenhorn illustrates the manner in which intellectuals outside of labor's formal structure contributed their time and energy in efforts to aid the Congress of Industrial Organizations. A journalist and labor researcher, Blankenhorn secured employment with the National Labor Relations Board in 1935 and later, as a strategist for the La Follette Committee, helped to shape the interplay of events that gave the industrial union its first key victories. 28 notes. 1919-50

Blaugdone, Barbara

622. Scheffler, Judith. PRISON WRITINGS OF EARLY QUAKER WOMEN. *Quaker Hist. 1984 73(2): 25-37.* Considers the writings of six traveling Quaker women ministers who were less concerned with self-justification than with the exposition of their religious missions and sympathy for prisoners' sufferings: Elizabeth Hooton, first converted by George Fox in 1647; Barbara Blaugdone, an enthusiast in England and Ireland, reporting many hair-breadth deliverances; Mary Dyer, hanged on Boston Common; Katharine Evans and Sarah Cheevers, imprisoned by the Inquisition at Malta in 1659; and Elizabeth Stirredge of Gloucestershire. Couched in the standard Quaker prose of the period, usually biblical, they reveal individual missionaries and brutal prison conditions. 42 notes. 1651-83

Blease, Coleman Livingston

623. Hollis, Daniel W. COLE L. BLEASE AND THE SENATORIAL CAMPAIGN OF 1924. *Pro. of the South Carolina Hist. Assoc. 1978: 53-68.* Examines the political career of Democrat Coleman L. Blease and his victory in the South Carolina senatorial elections of 1924. Unlike his previous campaigns, Blease did not take a stand on any significant issue. Reflecting the sterility of South Carolina politics during the 1920's, Blease's victory indicated the rise of isolation in South Carolina. This was Blease's last political victory, but he continued to be a force in South Carolina politics until 1938. Based primarily on newspapers; 92 notes. 1924

624. Hollis, Daniel W. COLE BLEASE: THE YEARS BETWEEN THE GOVERNORSHIP AND THE SENATE, 1915-1924. *South Carolina Hist. Mag. 1979 80(1): 1-17.* Traces the legal career and political dealings of South Carolinian Coleman Livingston Blease between his terms as governor and senator, 1915-24. 1915-24

Blegen, Theodore Christian

625. Flanagan, John T. A DEDICATION TO THE MEMORY OF THEODORE C. BLEGEN, 1891-1969. *Arizona and the West 1984 26(3): 204-208.* Theodore Christian Blegen devoted most of his professional career as a historian to the study of his Norwegian-American heritage and his native Minnesota. Besides years of public school, college, and university teaching, he headed his state's historical society, was dean of the state university's graduate school, was a founder of national professional archival and historical societies, and held presidencies of national historical societies. His writings in Norwegian-American studies were models of excellence for other students of ethnic and immigrant history. Illus., biblio. 1915-69

626. Qualey, Carlton C. THEODORE C. BLEGEN. *Norwegian-American Studies 1962 21: 3-13.* Theodore C. Blegen served as the editor of the publications of the Norwegian-American Society, 1925-60, but beyond his interest in Norwegians in America, he also served as the dean of the graduate school at the University of Minnesota. His main interests in terms of historiography included immigrant studies and local history, the latter of which he spent a great deal of his spare time pursuing, and in many cases, defending. While his writings on immigrant history covered a diversity of ethnic groups, his main area of interest was with the Norwegian Americans. Secondary sources; 9 notes, biblio. 1925-60

Blenk, James Hubert

627. O'Brien, Miriam Therese. PUERTO RICO'S FIRST AMERICAN BISHOP. *Records of the Am. Catholic Hist. Soc. of Philadelphia 1980 91(1-4): 3-37.* Traces the life of James Hubert Blenk, emphasizing hs work as Roman Catholic Bishop of Puerto Rico from 1898 to 1905, especially his efforts to resist division of the island into two dioceses. Based on archives, correspondence, interviews and official records; drawing, 98 notes, biblio. 1898-1905

Blennerhassett, Harman

628. Auvergne, Caroline. EARLY AMERICAN DESTINATIONS: BLENNERHASSETT. *Early American Life 1985 16(4): 49-51, 75-76.* Discusses the lives of Harman and Margaret Blennerhassett on an Ohio River island, which is now Blennerhassett Island, West Virginia, and their flight from the island after Harman was indicted for treason for becoming involved in Aaron Burr's plot to begin his own empire. 1794-1842

Blériot, André

629. Baird, Betty. ALBERTA FERRY AND ITS BLERIOT CONNECTION. *Can. Geog. [Canada] 1983-84 103(6): 36-38.* Brief biographical sketch of André Blériot, who homesteaded in Alberta and operated a small ferry at Red Deer River. ca 1897-1925

Blewett, George John

630. Paterson, Morton. THE MIND OF A METHODIST: THE PERSONALIST THEOLOGY OF GEORGE JOHN BLEWETT IN ITS HISTORICAL CONTEXT. *Bulletin of the Com. on Arch. of the United Church of Can. [Canada] 1978 (27): 4-41.* Biography of Canadian Methodist George John Blewett (1873-1912) focusing on his work as minister and professor, and his personalism. 1873-1912

Bliemel, Emmeran

631. Meaney, Peter J. VALIANT CHAPLAIN OF THE BLOODY TENTH. *Tennessee Hist. Q. 1982 41(1): 37-47.* Traces the career of Benedictine Father Emmeran Bliemel (1831-64), chaplain of the 10th Confederate Infantry and friend of the 4th Kentucky Regiment. The German-born Bliemel went from ordination in Pennsylvania to the diocese of Nashville, where he became attached to the Confederate cause. He died during the Battle of Jonesborough, Georgia, thus becoming the first Catholic chaplain to die in action serving his men. Primary sources; 36 notes. 1851-64

Bliss, Philip P.

632. Neil, Bobby Joe. "Philip P. Bliss (1838-1876): Gospel Hymn Composer and Compiler." New Orleans Baptist Theological Seminary 1977. 235 pp. *DAI 1977 38(4): 1731-1732-A.* 1850-76

Bliss family

633. McInerny, Paul M. CHARLES WESLEY BLISS AND THE *MONTGOMERY NEWS*. *J. of the Illinois State Hist. Soc. 1977 70(3): 201-207.* Gives an account of four generations of the Bliss family of central Illinois, who have published the weekly *Montgomery News* since 1892. C. W. Bliss (1846-1913) served as president of the Illinois Press Association and was inducted into the Editor's Hall of Fame. 4 illus., 24 notes. 1892-1977

Bloch, Felix

634. Chodorow, M.; Hofstadter, R.; Rorschach, H.; and Schalow, A. FELIX BLOCH. *Rice U. Studies 1980 66(3): v-x.* Biographical introduction to a special issue dedicated to the Nobel-Prize-winning Swiss American physicist Felix Bloch (b. 1905) on his 75th birthday. 1926-71

Blochman, Lazar E.

635. Hoexter, David F. and Hoexter, Mary R. LAZAR E. BLOCHMAN OF SAN FRANCISCO, SANTA MARIA AND BERKELEY. *Western States Jewish Hist. Q. 1980 13(1): 53-62.* Lazar E. Blochman (1856-1946) was born and raised in San Francisco, but moved to Santa Maria as a young man. In 1888 he married Ida Twitchell, a teacher with a lifelong interest in botany, who shared his reformer's views of temperance and women's suffrage. In 1906, oil was discovered on the Blochman property, enabling the couple to retire and move to Berkeley. Lazar enrolled at the University of California as a 59-year-old freshman, majoring in meteorology. After Ida's death in 1931, Lazar bicycled and walked long distances, continuing his activities until age 89, when killed by a car in San Francisco. Based on Blochman's "Bibliographical Memoirs," unpublished manuscripts in the Bancroft Library, University of California, Berkeley, and interviews with family members; photo, 35 notes. 1880-1946

Block, Eleazer

636. Rosenwaike, Ira. ELEAZER BLOCK: HIS FAMILY AND CAREER. *Am. Jewish Arch. 1979 31(2): 142-149.* Eleazer Block (1797-1886) was an atypical member of his generation of American Jews. A highly educated lawyer and businessman, Block pursued the dream of opening an academy of education for the Jews of New York. 1813-85

Blodgett, Bill

637. Spooner, Fred. PACIFIC PORTRAIT: BILL BLODGETT, STEAMBOAT MAN. *Pacific Hist. 1981 25(1): 8-12.* A personal account of Vermonter Bill Blodgett, who moved to California ca. 1910. He was 20 years of age when he took a job as a hotel clerk. Later he found work as a purser on steamboats in the Sacramento-San Joaquin Delta where he worked for 50 years. 1910-81

Blood, Benjamin Paul

638. Marks, Robert Walker. "The Philosophic Faith of Benjamin Paul Blood: A Study of the Thought and Times of an American Mystic." New School of Soc. Res. 1953. 178 pp. *DAI 1982 43(1): 186-A.* DA8213591 ca 1870-1919

Bloomer, Amelia Jenks

639. Noun, Louise. AMELIA BLOOMER, A BIOGRAPHY: PART I, THE LILY OF SENECA FALLS. *Annals of Iowa 1985 47(7): 575-617.* Born and reared in New York, Amelia Jenks Bloomer worked during most of her early life as a temperance leader. Married to Dexter Bloomer, she continued her temperance activities, writing newspaper articles. During this time she joined the suffragette movement, and her newspaper, the *Lily*, became the principal outlet for her views after 1850. Bloomer pioneered a change in women's clothing, although she was mocked for wearing the infamous pants named for her. With Elizabeth Cady Stanton she campaigned for women's suffrage, and in 1854, she moved to Council Bluffs, Iowa, continuing publication of the *Lily* there. 4 illus., 77 notes. Article to be continued. 1818-56

640. Schmidt, Cheryl. MANUSCRIPT COLLECTIONS: THE PAPERS OF AMELIA JENKS BLOOMER AND DEXTER BLOOMER. *Ann. of Iowa 1979 45(2): 135-146.* Contains a brief biography of Amelia Jenks Bloomer (1818-94), women's rights and temperance advocate. Largely through the efforts of her husband, Dexter Bloomer, many of her manuscripts and publications have been preserved. Various collections of Bloomer manuscripts are noted, with a lengthy bibliography of published material relating to Bloomer's life. Photo. 1818-1900

Blow, George

641. Williams, Gary M. COLONEL GEORGE BLOW: PLANTER AND POLITICAL PROPHET OF ANTEBELLUM SUSSEX. *Virginia Mag. of Hist. and Biog. 1982 90(4): 432-455.* A biography of Edmund Ruffin's friend and distant cousin, George Blow, Virginia gentleman, progressive agriculturalist, and social commentator. Blow's correspondence and diaries provide a unique view of antebellum Virginia, as their articulate author was a visionary and incisive thinker. Among the many topics he addressed were prison reform, new agricultural techniques, slave insurrections, North-South tensions over tariffs and slavery, and states rights. Blow predicted the Civil War and the severing of West Virginia from Virginia almost 30 years before those events took place. Based on the Blow Family Collection at the College of William and Mary, genealogical notes in the possession of R. H. Kitchen, Sussex and Norfolk County records, contemporary newspapers, and secondary sources; portrait, 91 notes. 1800-65

Bluemner, Oscar

642. Hayes, Jeffrey Russell. "Oscar Bluemner: Life, Art, and Theory." (Vol. 1-4) U. of Maryland 1982. 584 pp. *DAI 1983 44(2): 309-A.* DA8227983 1892-1938

Blum, Abraham

643. Kramer, William M. and Clar, Reva. RABBI ABRAHAM BLUM: FROM ALSACE TO NEW YORK BY WAY OF TEXAS AND CALIFORNIA: PART I. *Western States Jewish Hist. Q. 1979 12(1): 73-88; 1980 12(2): 170-184, (3): 266-281.* Part I. Abraham Blum was born and educated in Alsace under the liberal, tolerant rule of France. After emigrating to America in 1866, he served at synagogues in Dayton (Ohio), Augusta (Georgia), and Galveston (Texas), where he distinguished himself in the field of religious education and earned an M.D. degree from the Medical College of Galveston in 1872. His failing health prompted him to seek a position in the mild climate of Los Angeles, California. Based on newspapers and interviews; 2 photos, 66 notes. Part II.

Rabbi Blum became superintendant, and his wife principal, of the religious school of Los Angeles Congregation B'nai B'rith. Enrollment grew during 1889-94. His relationship with the congregation declined because he did not seem to be an active fund raiser for a new temple. Photo, 63 notes. Part III. Rabbi Blum resigned as rabbi in 1895, but Leopold Loeb, the synagogue's organist, then accused him of improprieties with Mrs. Loeb. Blum denied the charge, but moved to New York City, where he was appointed chaplain for various city and state institutions, apparently was happy and successful, and was active in religious and civic events until his death in 1921. 50 notes. 1866-1921

Blumer, Abraham

644. Parsons, William T. "DER GLARNER": ABRAHAM BLUMER OF ZION REFORMED CHURCH, ALLENTOWN. *Swiss Am. Hist. Soc. Newsletter 1977 13(2): 7-22.* Chronicles the ministerial career of Abraham Blumer (1736-1822), a pastor ordained in Switzerland in the German Reformed Church, highlighting his tenure with Pennsylvania parishes, 1771-1801, especially Zion Reformed Church in Allentown. 1771-1822

Blyden, Edward Wilmot

645. Blake, Cecil A. EDWARD WILMOT BLYDEN: A PRODIGY OF THE VIRGIN ISLANDS AND NEW YORK. *Afro-Americans in New York Life and Hist. 1977 1(1): 67-80.* Discusses Edward Wilmot Blyden, a black who dedicated his life to establishing an African past for American blacks, 1850-1912; Blyden lived much of his life in Liberia and Sierra Leone. 1850-1912

Blyth, Alfred

646. —. ALFRED BLYTH, EDMONTON PHOTOGRAPHER. *Alberta Hist. [Canada] 1982 30(4): 17-24.* Born in Scotland in 1901, Alfred Blyth came to Canada in 1913 and by 1928 was becoming "one of Edmonton's leading photographers." He recorded many aspects of the changing Edmonton scene "along with portraiture and group pictures." He was also the official photographer for the royal visits of 1939 and 1951, and he also "filmed the opening of the first session of the Alberta Legislature under the Aberhart administration." He "brought to all his photographs the hallmark of a craftsman." 12 photos. 1901-74

Blythe, Rachel

647. Prioli, Carmine Andrew. THE INDIAN "PRINCESS" AND THE ARCHITECT: ORIGIN OF A NORTH CAROLINA LEGEND. *North Carolina Hist. Rev. 1983 60(3): 283-303.* 1858-98
For abstract see ***Bauer, Adolphus Gustavus***

Boardman, Mabel

648. Stewart, Sally. SHARING MORE THAN MARBLE PALACES. *Daughters of the Am. Revolution Mag. 1981 115(3): 188-191.* ca 1881-1944
For abstract see ***Barton, Clara***

Boas, George

649. Gombrich, E. G. IN MEMORY OF GEORGE BOAS. *J. of the Hist. of Ideas 1981 42(2): 335-354.* A tribute by a personal friend with a selected bibliography of George Boas's works, listing his contributions to the *Journal of the History of Ideas* and to the *Journal of Aesthetics and Art Criticism;* 1891-1980. Based on Boas's works and the author's recollections; 26 notes. 1891-1980

Boatright, Mody C.

650. Speck, Ernest B. MODY BOATRIGHT'S COWBOY AS HERO. *Southwest Rev. 1981 66(3): 268-276.* The works of American writer and ranch hand Mody C. Boatright glorified the cowboy from his first book, *Tall Tales from Texas Cow Camps* (1934), to his "Cowboy as Hero," which he was working on when he died in 1970. 1934-70

Bock, Anna

651. Bronner, Simon J. "WE LIVE WHAT I PAINT AND I PAINT WHAT I SEE": A MENNONITE ARTIST IN NORTHERN INDIANA. *Indiana Folklore 1979 12(1): 5-17.* Discusses Mennonites in the United States from the 1830's and the life and work of ceramic, wood, and canvas painter, Anna Bock (b. 1924) of Elkhart County, Indiana, in the context of the cultural and religious practices of the Old Order Mennonite groups of which she is a member. 1830's-1970's

Bock, Richard W.

652. Hallmark, Donald Parker. "Chicago Sculptor Richard W. Bock: Social and Artistic Demands at the Turn of the Twentieth Century." St. Louis U. 1980. 455 pp. *DAI 1981 41(7): 2806-A.* 8101257 1890-1949

Bodmer, Karl

653. Hunt, David C. KARL BODMER AND THE AMERICAN FRONTIER. *Imprint 1985 10(1): 11-19.* Both a romantic painter and a documentary artist, Karl Bodmer is best known for his paintings of American Indians from his expedition into the trans-Mississippi West with Prince Maximilian in 1832-34. 1832-34

654. Mann, Maybelle. KARL BODMER: FROM FRONTIER AMERICA TO THE BARBIZON WOODS. *Art & Antiques 1982 5(2): 52-61.* Biography of Swiss painter, Karl Bodmer, noted for the drawings and watercolors he did while on an expedition led by Alexander Philip Maximilian, Prince of Wied-Neuwied in Rhenish Prussia, resulting in *Travels in the Interior of North America, 1832-1834* and an accompanying *Atlas,* most famous for his paintings of US Indians. 1822-93

Boeckmann, Carl Ludwig

655. Anderson, Marilyn Boeckmann. CARL L. BOECKMANN: NORWEGIAN ARTIST IN THE NEW WORLD. *Norwegian-American Studies 1979 28: 309-323.* Carl Ludwig Boeckmann (1867-1923) briefly studied art in Norway at Knut Bergslein's school and with Christian Krogh and his associates. After migrating to America in 1886, he wandered among the larger cities of the Midwest, settling in Minneapolis in 1905. Famous for portraits of Norwegian seamen called Norse Pilot Heads, he excelled in portraiture generally. Many prominent Norwegian Americans and other Americans posed for him. Boeckmann also painted seascapes, landscapes, historical scenes, and a number of altar paintings. 4 illus., 32 notes. 1886-1920

Boehm, John Philip

656. Frantz, John B. JOHN PHILIP BOEHM: PIONEER PENNSYLVANIA PASTOR. *Pennsylvania Folklife 1982 31(3): 128-134.* John Philip Boehm (1683-1749), born at Hochstadt, Germany, settled in southeastern Pennsylvania in 1720, served as a minister in the Reformed German Church, and was responsible for preserving the church in America. 1720-49

Boellner, Louis B.

657. Fleming, Elvis E. "LUTHER BURBANK OF NEW MEXICO": DR. LOUIS B. BOELLNER, 1872-1951. *New Mexico Hist. Rev. 1983 58(3): 271-290.* In 1903 Louis B. Boellner and his family moved to Roswell, New Mexico, where he started a jewelry and optometry business. The business prospered and Boellner began to devote himself to horticulture studies. Among his many successes in hybridization were his Kwik-Krop Black Walnut and perfumed dahlia. 2 photos, 73 notes. 1903-51

Boggs, Dock

658. O'Connell, Barry. DOCK BOGGS, MUSICIAN AND COAL MINER. *Appalachian J. 1983-84 11(1-2): 44-57.* Profiles the financial and emotional turmoil in the life of Appalachian banjo player Dock Boggs, of West Norton, Virginia; discusses his brief recording career in 1927, which seemed to offer an escape from a life of coal mining, and describes his rediscovery during the folk revival of the 1960's. 1920's-60's

Bohnen, Eli A.

659. Bohnen, Eli A. OUR RABBI WITH THE RAINBOW DIVISION: A WORLD WAR II REMINISCENCE. *Rhode Island Jewish Hist. Notes 1980 8(2): 81-90.* Recalls some of the incidents and people the author encountered while he was a Jewish chaplain in the US Army with the 42d Infantry (Rainbow) Division during World War II. 1941-45

Bok, Edward

660. Schell, Ernest H. EDWARD BOK AND THE *LADIES' HOME JOURNAL. Am. Hist. Illus. 1982 16(10): 16-23.* Traces the success of the *Ladies' Home Journal,* founded in 1883 by Cyrus Curtis and edited by Edward Bok from 1889 to 1919, focusing on Bok's complete control of the magazine and his ideas and activities in promoting domestic and social reforms; his interest in reform continued after he left the magazine, for he participated in Philadelphia's civic affairs until his death in 1930. 1883-1930

661. Shi, David. EDWARD BOK & THE SIMPLE LIFE. *Am. Heritage 1984 36(1): 100-109.* Edward Bok's influence over American women was strong because of the messages he directed to them as editor of the *Ladies' Home Journal,* 1889-1919. A moral reformer, Bok advocated simplicity as the way to the good life. Thrift, conservation, and volunteerism were all advocated. Women's place was in the home, and Bok urged them to make the most of it. 5 illus., photo. 1889-1919

Bolin, E. H.

662. Cawthon, John Ardis. E. H. BOLIN, SCHOOL MAN OF WEBSTER PARISH (1870-1947). *North Louisiana Hist. Assoc. J. 1984 15(1): 40-48.* E. H. Bolin, teacher, principal, school board member, and long-time member of the Louisiana State Board of Education, was one of the most influential persons in Louisiana education in the first half of the 20th century. Includes a letter Bolin wrote to Ardis Cawthon in 1939, in which he described some of his early experiences. Based on Bolin family records and primary and secondary sources; 2 photos, 31 notes. ca 1890-1940

Bolles, Lucius

663. Johnson, Parkes R. LUCIUS BOLLES: PASTOR AND FRIEND OF MISSIONS. *Foundations 1979 22(4): 306-312.* Lucius Bolles (1779-1844) was for 22 years pastor of the Salem, Massachusetts, Baptist Church, and for 16 years senior correspondent for the American Baptist Board of Foreign Missions. Describes his life, especially his work with and interest in missions. Based on Bolles's journal; 22 notes. ca 1800-44

Bolton, Henry Carrington

664. Roemer, Danielle M. HENRY CARRINGTON BOLTON, AMERICAN CHEMIST AND FOLKLORIST. *Kentucky Folklore Record 1982 28(3-4): 61-70.* Traces the life and manifold interests of Henry Carrington Bolton as a chemist, folklorist, and world-traveler who believed in the quest for social and cultural progress through the efforts of rational people; among his most important works are *The Counting-Out Rhymes of Children* (1888) and his *Select Bibliography of Chemistry, 1492-1892,* in addition to studies on the history of chemistry, and publications on such varied topics as alchemy, astrology, fortune-telling, musical sand, and the camera obscura. 1868-1903

Bolton, William Jay

665. Clark, Willene B. GOTHIC REVIVAL STAINED GLASS OF WILLIAM JAY BOLTON: A PRESERVATION PROJECT AND CENSUS. *Nineteenth Cent. 1981 7(2): 30-34.* Gives a biography and describes the work of English-American stained-glass architect William Jay Bolton, who decorated several Episcopal churches in the United States and later served as a parish priest in the Church of England. 1839-48

Bonacci, Frank

666. Notarianni, Philip F. RISE TO LEGITIMACY: FRANK BONACCI AS UNION ORGANIZER IN CARBON COUNTY, UTAH. *Rendezvous 1983 19(1): 67-74.* Outlines the career of Italian immigrant Frank Bonacci and his role as a union organizer and activist in Carbon County, Utah, from 1919 until his election to the Utah state legislature in 1936. Bonacci's patience and relentless struggle in a state where labor relations in the coal mining industry had been marked by an anti-union bias were rewarded with success and legitimacy within the system he had once battled. Based on the Frank Bonacci Papers, Utah State Historical Society, Salt Lake City, Utah, and other primary sources; 34 notes. 1919-36

Bonch-Bruevich, Vladimir

667. Klymasz, Robert B. V. D. BONCH-BRUEVICH AND THE LENIN CONNECTION IN NEW WORLD FOLKLORISTICS. *J. of Am. Folklore 1980 93(369): 317-324.* Vladimir Dmitrievich Bonch-Bruevich (1873-1955) was both folklorist of Canada's Russian Dukhobor sect and Party faithful in the USSR under V. I. Lenin. Bruevich canvassed every Dukhobor household to obtain a complete collection of Dukhobor psalms. 22 notes. 1899-1955

Bond, Frank

668. Grubbs, Frank H. FRANK BOND: GENTLEMAN SHEEPHERDER OF NORTHERN NEW MEXICO, 1883-1915. *New Mexico Hist. Rev. 1960 35(3): 169-199, (4): 292-308; 1961 36(2): 138-158, (3): 230-243, (4): 274-345; 1962 37(1): 43-71.* A multi-part series on sheepherder Frank Bond of northern New Mexico from his arrival in 1883, when he and his brother George bought out a mercantile store in Espanola which became the G. W. Bond & Bro. Company; focuses on the business activities and interests of the Bond brothers until 1915 and provides a background to trade in New Mexico, beginning in the mid-19th century. 1883-1915

Bond, Horace Mann

669. Fultz, Michael. A "QUINTESSENTIAL AMERICAN": HORACE MANN BOND, 1924-1939. *Harvard Educational Review 1985 55(4): 416-442.* Discusses Horace Mann Bond, noted black historian who brought attention to the inferior education and environmental conditions suffered by blacks in the United States. 1924-39

Bonderman, David

670. Greve, Frank. DAVID BONDERMAN, ESQ.: PRESERVATION'S UNSENTIMENTAL HERO. *Hist. Preservation 1983 35(1): 24-27.* Presents a profile of David Bonderman, noted preservationist lawyer, and his success in formulating preservationist law. 1970-82

Bonenfant, Jean-Charles

671. Hamelin, Jean. NÉCROLOGIE: JEAN-CHARLES BONENFANT 1912-1977 [Obituary: Jean-Charles Bonenfant; 1912-77]. *Hist. Papers 1978 [Canada] 243-245.* Jean-Charles Bonenfant (1912-77) taught at Laval University, Quebec, Quebec. Highlights his career as an educator and pays tribute to his accessibility, intellectual curiosity, loyalty to his craft, and respect for others. Reprinted from Laval University's *Au fil des événements,* 13 October 1977. 1930's-77

Bonfanti, Maria

672. Barker, Barbara Mackin. "The American Careers of Rita Sangalli, Giuseppina Morlacchi and Maria Bonfanti: Nineteenth Century Ballerinas." New York U. 1981. 308 pp. *DAI 1982 42(7): 2935-A.* 8127890 1866-90

Bonney, William

673. Simmons, Marc. BILLY THE KID AND THE LINCOLN COUNTY WAR. *Am. Hist. Illus. 1982 17(4): 40-44.* Provides a brief biography of Billy the Kid, and discusses his participation in the Lincoln County War—a vigilante-like operation—in the southeastern corner of Texas, which was fought over the control of the territory's economy and politics, and which culminated in the Five Days Battle during 15-19 July 1878. 1859-81

Bonnin, Gertrude Simmons (Zitkala Sa)

674. Fisher, Dexter. ZITKALA SA: THE EVOLUTION OF A WRITER. *Am. Indian Q. 1979 5(3): 229-238.* Gertrude Simmons Bonnin (Zitkala Sa), a Yankton Sioux, left home at eight to study in boarding school and later attended Earlham College. Adopting the name Zitkala Sa, she won writing honors before marrying and beginning work for Indian citizenship, employment, and land claims. She founded the National Council of American Indians in 1926 and served as president until her death in 1938. She had found a way to use her white-taught communication skills on behalf of Indians. Based on Bureau of Indian Affairs records and writings of Zitkala Sa; 12 notes. 1900-38

Boodin, John Elof

675. Nelson, Charles H. JOHN ELOF BOODIN, PHILOSOPHER-POET. *Swedish-American Hist. Q. 1984 35(2): 124-150.* John Elof Boodin immigrated to the United States in 1887 from Pjätteryd, Småland, Sweden, intent on assimilation and an education. He became a prominent philosopher and teacher, with a metaphysical, idealistic approach balanced by pragmatism and realism. Boodin completed normal school in 1890 in Macomb, Illinois, then spent six years teaching, working with Swedish-Episcopal congregations, and studying at the universities of Colorado and Minnesota and at Brown University. Working under Josiah Royce and William James at Harvard, he received a Ph.D. in 1899. After positions at Iowa College and the University of Kansas, he ended his distinguished career at the University of California, Los Angeles. Based primarily on Boodin's papers at the University of California, Los Angeles, Research Library, Boodin's works, and interviews with students; illus., 3 photos, 94 notes. 1887-1950

Boone, Daniel

676. Bloom, Jo Tice. DANIEL BOONE: TRAILBLAZER TO A NATION. *Gateway Heritage 1985 5(4): 28-39.* Long before his death, Daniel Boone was the subject of American frontier legends that, whatever their exaggerations, contributed to building national unity and pride in America. Furthermore, Boone's real achievements, such as his leadership in western trailblazing, remain historical legacies that Boone mythologies can never obscure. Secondary sources; map, 20 photos, 35 notes. 1756-1820

Boone, Daniel (family)

677. McCarthy, Koren P. DANIEL BOONE: THE FORMATIVE YEARS. *Pennsylvania Heritage 1985 11(1): 34-37.* Traces the history of the Boone family from their immigration to Pennsylvania in 1717 until 1773, when the young Daniel Boone left the colony to settle in the Kentucky wilderness. 1717-73

Boone, Nathan

678. Walker, Wayne T. NATHAN BOONE: THE FORGOTTEN HERO OF MISSOURI. *J. of the West 1979 18(2): 85-94.* Nathan Boone (1781-1856), youngest son of Kentucky pioneer Daniel Boone, settled on his father's Spanish land grant within the Louisiana Territory in 1799. The Boone family's holdings were located in what is now Missouri, near Femme Osage Creek. After the United States purchased the Louisiana Territory, Nathan Boone became a surveyor, guide, and captain of the Missouri Mounted Rangers. Boone served on many military expeditions in several western states between 1812 and 1853; then he retired from the Army as a Lieutenant Colonel. 8 photos, map, biblio. 1799-1853

Boorne, W. Hanson

679. —. W. HANSON BOORNE: PHOTOGRAPHIC ARTIST. *Alberta Hist. [Canada] 1977 25(2): 15-22.* The firm of Boorne and May was prominent in the west 1886-93. W. Hanson Boorne opened a studio in Calgary in 1886 and one in Edmonton in 1891. In 1893 he returned to England. Most of his negatives are in the Provincial Archives, Edmon-

ton. Boorne is noted for his outstanding scenic views and for his views of the Blood Indian self-torture ritual. 13 illus. 1886-93

Booth, Edwin

680. Commeret, Lorraine Marion. "Edwin Booth's German Tour, 1883." U. of Illinois, Urbana-Champaign 1980. 327 pp. *DAI 1980 41(6): 2356-2357-A.* 8026472 1883

681. LaCasse, Donald Emile, Jr. "Edwin Booth: Theatre Manager." Michigan State U. 1979. 190 pp. *DAI 1980 40(12): 6072-6073-A.* DA8013765 1863-73

Booth, James Curtis

682. Rafert, Stewart. JAMES CURTIS BOOTH: DELAWARE'S FIRST GEOLOGIST. *Delaware Hist. 1976 17(2): 139-146.* Describes the life and career of James Curtis Booth, 1810-88, who studied medicine, chemistry, mineralogy, and geology in the United States and Europe. In 1836 he established what may be the first teaching chemistry laboratory in America and throughout his life was a dogged advocate of practical chemistry. In 1837 he started the Delaware geological survey and concluded that the main features of Maryland and New Jersey geology continued in Delaware. He located mineral resources in Delaware, educated farmers in the use of minerals, and wrote a durable report, *Memoir of the Geological Survey of Delaware* (1841). 34 notes. 1810-88

Booth, John Wilkes

683. Head, Constance. INSIGHTS ON JOHN WILKES BOOTH FROM HIS SISTER ASIA'S CORRESPONDENCE. *Lincoln Herald 1980 82(4): 540-544.* 1852-74
For abstract see ***Clarke, Asia Booth***

684. Head, Constance. JOHN WILKES BOOTH, 1864: PROLOGUE TO ASSASSINATION. *Lincoln Herald 1983 85(4): 254-262.* Examines events, including persistent illness and psychological factors, motivating John Wilkes Booth's plots against Abraham Lincoln. 1864

685. Kubicek, Earl C. THE CASE OF THE MAD HATTER. *Lincoln Herald 1981 83(3): 708-719.* 1832-1908
For abstract see ***Corbett, Thomas H.***

686. Loux, Arthur F. THE ACCIDENT-PRONE JOHN WILKES BOOTH. *Lincoln Herald 1983 85(4): 263-268.* Describes John Wilkes Booth's history of injury to himself and others. 1860-65

687. Miller, Ernest C. JOHN WILKES BOOTH AND THE LAND OF OIL. *Pennsylvania Heritage 1981 7(3): 9-12.* Biography of Abraham Lincoln's assassin John Wilkes Booth (1838-65), focusing on his interest in the oil region of northwestern Pennsylvania, particularly his investments in land there that he eventually sold because of a low volume of oil. ca 1858-65

688. Withers, Nan Wyatt. "The Acting Style and Career of John Wilkes Booth." U. of Wisconsin, Madison 1979. 224 pp. *DAI 1980 41(1): 27-A.* 8007581 1855-65

Booth, Rosalie

689. Head, Constance. THE BOOTH SISTERS OF BEL AIR. *Lincoln Herald 1981 84[i.e., 83](3[i.e., 4]): 759-764.* Biographies of the two sisters of John Wilkes and Edwin Booth, Rosalie Booth (1823-89) and Asia Booth Clarke (1835-88) who grew up in Bel Air and Baltimore. 1823-89

Borden, Frederick W.

690. Miller, Carman. FAMILY, BUSINESS AND POLITICS IN KING'S COUNTY, N.S.: THE CASE OF F. W. BORDEN, 1874-1896. *Acadiensis [Canada] 1978 7(2): 60-75.* First elected to Parliament in 1874, Frederick W. Borden survived 37 years with only one defeat, despite an initial narrow victory and lack of high-level Liberal Party support. He achieved wealth by exploiting the existing economic system based on family alliances. Borden invested first in small lots and coastal shipping, then in lumbering, farming, and wholesaling. Borden's political hold was shaky initially with his support coming from stagnating coastal areas. After 1882 he supported growing Kentville and the County's railway interests. 62 notes. 1874-96

Boreman, Arthur I.

691. Effland, Anne Wallace. RECENT ADDITIONS TO THE ARTHUR I. BOREMAN PAPERS IN THE WEST VIRGINIA REGIONAL HISTORY COLLECTION. *West Virginia Hist. 1982 44(1): 54-61.* Discusses the career of Arthur I. Boreman as the first governor of West Virginia and as a senator. Recent additions to Boreman's papers include correspondence for 1861-95. 1859-75

Borg, Carl Oscar

692. Tomlinson, Tommy. GALLERY: EXHIBITING ARTIST: CARL OSCAR BORG. *Westways 1981 73(4): 33-38.* Carl Oscar Borg, who grew up in Sweden during the 1890's, emigrated to California in 1901; there he settled in Santa Barbara and became a well-known painter of scenes from California and southwestern history. ca 1890-1947

Borg, Selma Josefina

693. Myhrman, Anders. SELMA JOSEFINA BORG: FINLAND: SWEDISH MUSICIAN, LECTURER, AND CHAMPION OF WOMEN'S RIGHTS. *Swedish Pioneer Hist. Q. 1979 30(1): 25-34.* Selma Josefina Borg was born in Gamlarkarleby, Finland, in 1838, the youngest of nine children in an apparently well-to-do middle-class family. She studied music in Finland, Sweden, and Switzerland. She taught music in Helsinki for some years before coming in 1864 to Philadelphia, where she established herself as a private music and language teacher. In collaboration with Marie A. Brown, she began translating current Swedish works into English. Borg joined a women's committee formed to promote the Centennial Exposition of 1876 in Philadelphia and returned to Finland in 1875 to arouse interest and possibly participation in the celebration. She had, by this time, become a champion of the rights of women and most of her lectures dealt with developments and conditions in America. Describes her lecture tour. Returning to America, she became well known as a musician and speaker on women's rights. 1858-90

Borofsky, Jonathan

694. Simon, Joan. AN INTERVIEW WITH JONATHAN BOROFSKY. *Art in Am. 1981 69(9): 156-167.* Discusses the life and work of Jonathan Borofsky, an artist, whose work is a combination of paintings, sculptures and multi-medium pieces utilizing free association, stream of consciousness, and Jungian archetypes; 1960-80. 1960's-81

Borrero Echevarría, Esteban

695. Toledo, Arnaldo. ESTEBAN BORRERO Y "EL CIERVO ENCANTADO" [Esteban Borrero and "The Enchanted Deer"]. *Islas [Cuba] 1984 (79): 51-70.* Recounts the life of Cuban writer Esteban Borrero Echevarría, and discusses his short story "The Enchanted Deer," in which he articulates his nationalistic sentiments and his fears of North American intervention in his country. 1870's-1906

Borsodi, Ralph

696. Schubart, Richard Douglas. "Ralph Borsodi: The Political Biography of a Utopian Decentralist, 1886-1977." State U. of New York, Binghamton 1984. 395 pp. *DAI 1984 44(11): 3469-3470-A.* DA8404639 1900's-77

Bosak, Michael

697. Krajsa, Joseph C. MICHAEL BOSAK: A MOST FORCEFUL SLOVAK AND FRATERNAL PERSONALITY. *Jednota Ann. Furdek 1982 21: 139-143.* Discusses the career of Michael Bosak, honorary president of the First Catholic Slovak Union, banker, and publisher, who contributed to Slovak fraternal, cultural, educational, and civic life, especially in Pennsylvania, from 1900 to 1937. 1900-37

Bosque y Fanqui, Cayetana Susana

698. DeGrummond, Jane Lucas. CAYETANA SUSANA BOSQUE Y FANQUI, "A NOTABLE WOMAN". *Louisiana Hist. 1982 23(3): 277-294.* Life of a noted New Orleans beauty, the second wife of the provisional governor of Louisiana and later US Senator William Charles Cole Claiborne and, after his death, wife of John R. Grymes, lawyer and former US district attorney for the Louisiana district. Includes information on the careers of her husbands and the marital adventures of her numerous offspring. Based on church and family records, letters, and newspapers; 51 notes. 1790-1890

Bossier, Pierre

699. Thomas, Lajeane Gentry. GENERAL PIERRE EVARISTE JEAN BAPTISTE BOSSIER. *North Louisiana Hist. Assoc. J. 1980 11(1): 22-26.* Pierre Bossier was a Creole aristocrat who served as a military leader, planter, member of the Louisiana legislature and the US Congress, but he is best remembered for a tragic duel in which he shot a Whig opponent, General Francois Gainnie, in 1839. Bossier died a few years later at age 47, perhaps a suicide. Based on primary sources including the *Congressional Globe, Niles Weekly Register* and secondary items; 29 notes. 1838-45

Boston Tarbaby

See Langford, Sam

Bostwick, William

700. Lavin, Marilyn Anne. "William Bostwick: Connecticut Yankee in Antebellum Georgia." Columbia U. 1977. 378 pp. *DAI 1978 38(10): 6272-6273-A.* 1819-45

Boswell, Ben D. and Emma

701. Munford, Kenneth and Moore, Harriet. THE BOSWELLS OF BOSWELL SPRINGS. *Oregon Hist. Q. 1982 83(4): 340-370.* Narrates the lives of Captain Ben D. Boswell and his wife, Emma, who were owners of Boswell Springs, a health resort, in Douglas County, Oregon, at the turn of the century. Enlisting as a private at the start of the Civil War, Boswell rose to the rank of major by 1864. He was wounded and disabled during the seige of Vicksburg, and this injury, plus several misdiagnosed maladies, plagued him during his eccentric military career. Following his retirement from the service in 1878, the Boswells spent 10 years in California and then returned to Oregon to settle and manage the resort. Based on the Boswell papers, National Archives; letters in the files of Bureau of Pensions, National Archives, and numerous Oregon newspaper articles; 5 photos, map, 158 notes. 1860-1908

Botkin, Benjamin A.

702. Jackson, Bruce. BENJAMIN A. BOTKIN (1901-1975). *J. of Am. Folklore 1976 89(351): 1-6.* An obituary of Benjamin A. Botkin, a leading American folklorist concerned with American folklore in its broadest and most social sense. Illus. 1901-75

Bottoms, Lawrence W.

703. Brackenridge, R. Douglas. LAWRENCE W. BOTTOMS: THE CHURCH, BLACK PRESBYTERIANS AND PERSONHOOD. *J. of Presbyterian Hist. 1978 56(1): 47-60.* Interviews Lawrence Bottoms, first black Moderator of the Southern Presbyterian Church, and first black to head any major white Protestant denomination's black work. Traces Bottoms's life through his educational and pastoral career, giving insights into prejudice which confronted him. Out of such experiences his religious philosophy of personhood emerged. Bottoms strongly urged the Presbyterian Church in the South to reach out to the growing black middle class. Illus., 2 notes. 1930-75

Botts, Earlie

704. Marshall, John. EARLIE BOTTS. *Kentucky Folklore Record 1978 24(3-4): 81-88.* Describes the career (1946-77) of Earlie Botts (of Monroe County, Kentucky), "one of the few traditional 'standing hand' banjo players left in an area where that method of playing was once prevalent." 1946-77

Boucher, Jonathan

705. Clark, Michael D. JONATHAN BOUCHER AND THE TOLERATION OF ROMAN CATHOLICS IN MARYLAND. *Maryland Hist. Mag. 1976 71(2): 194-204.* An Anglican minister of Queen Anne's Parish, Jonathan Boucher has been cited "as an exception to the almost universal anti-Catholicism of colonial Protestants, especially for his 1774 sermon 'On the Toleration of Papists.'" Others have noted his hypocrisy in holding out sympathy for Catholics only to enlist them in the Loyalist cause during the Revolution. Actually the more just verdict of him is "opportunism". A devotee of 18th-century paternalistic conservatism, with a "melioristic position," Boucher had an ecumenical disposition which urged the reunion of Catholic, Protestant Englishman, and Presbyterian, with the Anglican confession being the most fit "centre of union." Moreover, the collapse of Jacobitism after 1746 had removed much of the political rationale for Catholic-baiting. Though he urged freedom of religious conviction, Boucher remained fixed in his period's belief that such toleration did not extend to granting equality

of political status to dissenters. Primarily extracted from Boucher's own writings and secondary sources; 39 notes. 1774-97

Boucicault, Dion

706. Ó haodha, Michéal. SOME IRISH AMERICAN THEATRE LINKS. Doyle, David Noel and Edwards, Owen Dudley, ed. *America and Ireland, 1776-1976: The American Identity and the Irish Connection* (Westport, Conn.: Greenwood Pr., 1980): 295-306. Discusses the careers of playwrights Dionysius Lardner Boucicault and Eugene O'Neill. Boucicault was a flamboyant 19th-century figure who changed his name several times. He is famous for his dictum, "plays are not written, they are rewritten." His greatest success in New York was *The Shaughraun.* O'Neill's plays reflect only the darker side of his Irishness. 19c-20c

Boudinot, Elias Cornelius

707. Colbert, Thomas Burnell. "Prophet of Progress: The Life and Times of Elias Cornelius Boudinot." Oklahoma State U. 1982. 448 pp. *DAI 1983 43(8): 2764-A.* DA8300146 ca

708. Luebke, Barbara Francine. "Elias Boudinot, Cherokee Editor: The Father of American Indian Journalism." U. of Missouri, Columbia 1981. 403 pp. *DAI 1982 42(9): 3796-A.* DA8205400 ca

Boudinot, Harriet Gold

709. —. THE DEATH OF HARRIET GOLD BOUDINOT. *J. of Cherokee Studies 1979 4(2): 102-107.* Harriet Gold Boudinot was a native of Cornwall, Connecticut, who became the wife of Elias Boudinot, a leader of the Treaty Party of Cherokees. Almost all of her married life, apparently about 10 years, was spent with the Cherokee Indians of northern Georgia. Her last days, and her death on 15 August 1836, were described in a letter to her parents from her husband. Reproduced from *The New York Observer,* 26 November 1836. Fig. 1820's-36

Bouquet, Henry

710. Waddell, Louis M. THE AMERICAN CAREER OF HENRY BOUQUET, 1755-1765. *Swiss Am. Hist. Soc. Newsletter 1981 17(1): 13-38.* Sketches the bibliography of the Swiss mercenary soldier Henry Bouquet (1719-65) and describes his military service as an officer for the British during the French and Indian War. 1755-65

Bourassa, Henri

711. Levitt, Joseph. IMAGES OF BOURASSA. *J. of Can. Studies [Canada] 1978 13(1): 100-113.* The attitudes of Canadian historians, both Anglophone and Francophone, toward Henri Bourassa (1868-1952) consistently have been colored by the position of each on the major issues Bourassa addressed during his more than 40 years in public life (1890's-1930's). Goldwin Smith, a fellow anti-imperialist, introduced him into historical literature in 1902. The isolationism of the 30's and the biculturalism of the 60's (Bourassa, while a champion of Francophone rights, always opposed separatism) occasioned favorable treatment of Bourassa among Anglophones, while Lionel Groulx, his onetime foe, described him in 1971 as "l'incomparable Èveilleur." Bourassa's position on social issues—Catholic, moderately reformist, emphasizing the family and agricultural values—likewise has called forth praise and blame. Calls for a view of Bourassa that is truer to the man himself. Primary sources; 120 notes. 1902-71

Bourgeois, Louise

712. Storr, Robert. LOUISE BOURGEOIS: GENDER & POSSESSION. *Art in America 1983 71(4): 130-137.* Although American artist Louise Bourgeois produced major paintings and sculptures during the 1940's-80's, her work was largely ignored until the 1970's with the emergence of feminism. 1938-83

Bourget, Ignace

713. Perin, Roberto. ST-BOURGET, ÉVÊQUE ET MARTYR [St. Bourget, bishop and martyr]. *J. of Can. Studies [Canada] 1980-81 15(4): 43-55.* Sketches the strange personality of Ignace Bourget (1799-1885), focusing on the second bishop of Montreal's private political interventions. The received opinion that the prelate's acts prejudiced both Conservatives and Liberals is unfounded. Bourget kept himself above political parties to better control them, but acted only when politicians or officials hampered the vested interests of the Catholic Church. Archival documents; 84 notes. ca 1860-75

Bourke, John Gregory

714. Porter, Joseph Charles. "John Gregory Bourke, Victorian Soldier Scientist: The Western Apprenticeship, 1869-1886." U. of Texas, Austin 1980. 685 pp. *DAI 1982 43(6): 2066-A.* DA8217955 1869-86

715. Turchesneske, John A., Jr. JOHN G. BOURKE: TROUBLED SCIENTIST. *J. of Arizona Hist. 1979 20(3): 323-344.* A study of the career of Captain John G. Bourke, US Army (1846-96). Following service in the Union Army during the Civil War and graduation from the US Military Academy he served the remainder of his life in the Southwest. His very carefully prepared ethnological studies of Apache Indians and Hispanic people of the area were a major contribution to the field. Yet during this whole period he was never able to achieve an acceptable inner adjustment to what he saw as a conflict in duty as an army officer and as a scientist, despite every encouragement to do so by those above him. Primary sources; 62 notes. ca 1865-96

Bourne, Lizzie

716. Reid, Robert L. ON THE TRAIL OF LIZZIE BOURNE. *New-England Galaxy 1978 19(4): 21-29.* Emphasizes the author's research into the life of Lizzie Bourne triggered by his discovery of a monument on the slopes of Mount Washington which noted her tragic death there in a terrible windstorm on 14 September 1855. She was born in Kennebunk, Maine, 20 June 1832 or 1833, the daughter of Edward Emerson Bourne, noted lawyer, legislator, and judge. Lizzie was taught to love outdoor life, personal independence, and freedom by her father. 6 illus. 1832-55

Bourne, Randolph

717. Fuchsman, Kenneth Alan. "Desire and Intelligence: Randolph Bourne and the Cycle of Progressivism." Rutgers U., New Brunswick 1982. 582 pp. *DAI 1982 43(3): 900-A.* DA8218320 ca 1900-20

718. Roosevelt, Jinx. RANDOLPH BOURNE: THE EDUCATION OF A CRITIC: AN INTERPRETATION. *Hist. of Educ. Q. 1977 17(3): 257-274.* In his brief life, Randolph Bourne (1886-1918) attacked most established American institutions and dealt with such subjects as socialism, feminism, and progressive education. A hunchback, Bourne, feeling society's scorn for deformity, was psychologically well-suited to the role of critic, and his brilliance made him an effective one. Born into what he considered a rather cold, Calvinistic family with little discipline or attention for the children, Bourne educated himself. He was close to his younger sister, Natalie, who had defended him from the ridicule of other children when they were young. Decline in family fortunes necessitated a postponement of university education and work in factories, but during 1909-13, Bourne was a student at Columbia and thereafter wrote for *The New Republic.* He found inspiration in the Greek and Latin classics and in the philosophy of John Dewey. Despite his not living long, Bourne's restless spirit epitomized the *Zeitgeist* of his generation. 55 notes. 1886-1918

719. Sandeen, Eric John. "The Letters of Randolph Bourne: A Comprehensive Edition." U. of Iowa 1977. 855 pp. *DAI 1978 38(7): 4235-A.* ca 1914-20

Bourne, Robin

720. Hawthorn, Tom. A BOURNE-AGAIN SPOOK. *Can. Dimension [Canada] 1981 15(8)-16(1): 7-9.* Examines the past and current activities of former chief of Canadian civilian intelligence gathering, Robin Bourne, and several of his former associates and questions the ethics of his intelligence gathering and dissemination of data on Canadian citizens. 1977-81

Boutelle, Frazier A.

721. Johnson, Charles, Jr. FRAZIER A. BOUTELLE: MILITARY CAREER OF A BLACK SOLDIER. *J. of the Afro-American Hist. and Geneal. Soc. 1982 3(3): 99-104.* Sketches the military career of Frazier A. Boutelle from 1861 to 1897; he fought in the Civil War, served on the western frontier, and was responsible for various duties from recruitment to command assignments. 1861-95

Boutwell, George Sewall

722. Brown, Thomas H. "George Sewall Boutwell: Public Servant (1818-1905)." New York U. 1979. 285 pp. *DAI 1979 40(5): 3485-A.* 1818-1905

Bouvier, Émile

723. Genest, Jean. LE PERE EMILE BOUVIER, S.J. (1906-1985) [Father Émile Bouvier, S.J. (1906-85)]. *Action Nationale [Canada] 1984 74(10): 967-975.* Traces the life of Émile Bouvier, considered to be the first economist of Quebec, focusing on his understanding of the importance of universities in the 20th century, his intellectual achievements and prolific writings, and his religious beliefs concerning incarnation and redemption. 1930's-84

Bowditch, Henry Pickering

724. Fye, W. Bruce. WHY A PHYSIOLOGIST? THE CASE OF HENRY P. BOWDITCH. *Bull. of the Hist. of Medicine 1982 56(1): 19-29.* Henry Pickering Bowditch, teacher and researcher, was a pivotal figure in the professionalization of American physiology, not just a physician pursuing scientific interests as an avocation. At the Lawrence Scientific School he came under the influence of Jeffries Wyman, who also devoted himself to teaching and research in natural history and comparative anatomy. At Harvard Medical School, Bowditch was impressed with the scientific approach of Eduard Brown-Sequard, and, after graduation, Bowditch studied with Carl Ludwig in Germany. In the 1870's, Bowditch became professor of physiology at Harvard University. Based on the Eliot and Bowditch papers; 51 notes, 3 illus. 1860-80

Bowditch, Nathaniel

725. Ocko, Stephanie. NATHANIEL BOWDITCH. *Early Am. Life 1979 10(6): 38-39, 70-74.* Recounts the life of Nathaniel Bowditch (1773-1838), navigator, mathematician, and astronomer, whose *New American Practical Navigator* (1802) became the standard text for mariners. 1780's-1838

Bowen, Dana Thomas

726. Sykora, T. A. DANA THOMAS BOWEN. *Inland Seas 1980 36(1): 53-54.* Dana Thomas Bowen (1896-1980) was "one of the best known, authoritative and readable Great Lakes historians." He concentrated on the history and lore of the vessels and men who sailed the lakes. He amassed a large collection of photographs and artifacts. He published his first book, *Lore of the Lakes,* in 1940 and his last in 1967. He was a charter member of the Great Lakes Historical Society and was an avid boater on the lakes and in Florida. 1896-1980

Bower, Bertha Muzzy

727. Bloodworth, William A., Jr. MULFORD AND BOWER: MYTH AND HISTORY IN THE EARLY WESTERN. *Great Plains Q. 1981 1(2): 95-104.* Discusses the western novels of Clarence Edward Mulford, who created Hopalong Cassidy, and Bertha Muzzy Bower, the only woman to become an important writer of westerns, comparing their westerns as sources of comedy and their emphasis on themes of community rather than individualism as reflective of the optimism of the Progressive Era; 1904-16. 1904-16

Bowers, Claude

728. Little, Douglas. CLAUDE BOWERS AND HIS MISSION TO SPAIN: THE DIPLOMACY OF A JEFFERSONIAN DEMOCRAT. Jones, Kenneth Paul, ed. *U.S. Diplomats in Europe, 1919-1941* (Santa Barbara, Calif.: ABC-Clio, 1981): 129-146. Discusses the career of American diplomat Claude Bowers (1878-1958), especially as ambassador to Spain, 1933-39. Bowers prophesied that Washington's unwillingness to take action during the Spanish Civil War would make wider war inevitable. His influence was minimal, however, because 1) he was a political appointee rather than a career diplomat, and many experienced policymakers in the recently professionalized US Foreign Service were bound to discount him as an amateur; 2) in his first three years in Madrid he had come down on the wrong side of political and economic disputes between the United States and Spain; and 3) once the civil war erupted in 1936, he was stranded in France. His superiors tended to rely more heavily on reports from American officials who were actually in the war zone. Primary sources; 75 notes. 1933-39

Bowers, J. Milton

729. Stern, Norton B. and Kramer, William M. THE PHOSPHORESCENT JEWISH BRIDE: SAN FRANCISCO'S FAMOUS MURDER CASE. *Western States Jewish Hist. Q. 1980 13(1): 63-72.* Cecilia Benhayon Levy, wife of Dr. J.

Milton Bowers, died at the age of 29 in 1885. As she was the third of Dr. Bowers's young wives to sicken and die, and her life insurance was considerable, an autopsy was performed. Evidence of phosphorous poisoning convicted Bowers of murder. After lengthy appeals, the charges were dropped and Bowers returned to medical practice. The case is significant because the victims and witnesses were Jews; the accused had converted to Judaism. Based on newspaper articles and other primary sources; 33 notes. 1885-89

Bowers, Stephen

730. Smith, Wallace E. THE REVEREND STEPHEN BOWERS: "CURIOSITY HUNTER OF THE SANTA BARBARA CHANNEL ISLANDS." *California History 1983 62(1): 26-37.* Traces the controversial career of Reverend Stephen Bowers, an amateur archaeologist who excavated Indian burial grounds on the Santa Barbara Channel Islands. Born in Indiana and ordained as a Methodist minister, Bowers came to California in 1874. He spent three years excavating sites on the islands and sent thousands of artifacts to the Smithsonian Institution and the Peabody Museum. He also sold large numbers of artifacts to private collectors. Bowers has been criticized for the crude methods he employed in digging up skeletons and artifacts, thereby ruining the sites for later generations of professionally trained archaeologists. In later years, Bowers became a controversial newspaper publisher, eventually alienating former friends through his editorial intemperance. Illus., 5 photos, 44 notes. 1874-1907

Bowles, Chester

731. Wofford, Harris. YOU'RE RIGHT, CHET. YOU'RE RIGHT. AND YOU'RE FIRED. *Washington Monthly 1980 12(5-6): 46-54, 56.* Surveys the career of Chester Bowles—former governor, ambassador, congressman, and Office of Price Administration chief—as advisor in the John F. Kennedy administration (1961-63) and concludes that his consistent correctness was largely ignored because of his diffident personality, indicating that aggressive personalities dominate even presidential decisionmaking sessions, with implications for the country's political leadership. 1953-78

Bowman, Bill

732. Casada, Jim. THE SEARCH FOR BILL BOWMAN. *Sporting Classics 1986 5(1): 18-24.* Reviews the life and work of acclaimed 19th-century duck and shorebird carver and painter Bill Bowman, whose decoys sell for as much as $10,000 today. 1875-1900

Boyce, Hawley Meeks

733. McMacken, David. CAPT. HAWLEY MEEKS BOYCE. *Inland Seas 1982 38(2): 107-110.* Hawley Meeks Boyce was born near Watertown, New York in 1852 into a family of sailors. In 1869 he went to work as a deckhand. He became a mate in 1878 and a master in 1884. During 1904-24 he commanded the steamer *John Oakes* in the salt trade out of Manistee, Ludington, and Buffalo. Boyce married Bertha Brooks Weller in 1890, retired in 1924, and died in 1944. 1852-1944

Boyce, William Waters

734. Leemhuis, Roger P. WILLIAM W. BOYCE: A LEADER OF THE SOUTHERN PEACE MOVEMENT. *Pro. of the South Carolina Hist. Assoc. 1978: 21-30.* William Waters Boyce (1818-90), a South Carolina Democrat, is known primarily for his efforts as a Confederate congressman who promoted the idea of a negotiated peace with the North between 1863 and 1865. Although his efforts attracted some support in the South, the peace initiative died in February 1865 when the Hampton Roads Conference failed. After the war, Boyce moved to Washington, D.C., and developed a successful law practice. Based on government documents and published works; 40 notes. 1861-65

Boyd, Belle

735. Davis, Curtis Carroll. "THE PET OF THE CONFEDERACY" STILL? FRESH FINDINGS ABOUT BELLE BOYD. *Maryland Hist. Mag. 1983 78(1): 35-53.* Recounts the life of Belle Boyd, who during the Civil War achieved notoriety as a spy for the Confederacy. Boyd suffered two failed marriages and bouts with insanity after the war. She eventually formed a theatrical group with her third husband and travelled through the country presenting reenactments of wartime events. Mostly primary sources; 2 illus., 80 notes. 1861-1900

Boyd, Ed

736. Kendall, Charles P. PLANKS ACROSS THE DUNES. *J. of Arizona Hist. 1980 21(4): 391-410.* Summarizs the promethean effort of Ed Fletcher and Ed Boyd in constructing a plank road to facilitate travel between Yuma, Arizona, and San Diego, California. 13 photos, map, 33 notes. 1901-20

Boyd, Helen

737. Boyd, Helen; Crawley, T. A., ed. GROWING UP PRIVILEGED IN EDMONTON. *Alberta Hist. [Canada] 1982 30(1): 1-10.* Daughter of a prominent Albertan politician, Helen Boyd (1905-80) reminisces about her early childhood in Edmonton. Notes such matters as tent-dwellers, family attempts at gardening, impact of the outbreak of World War I, her early schooling, fear of diseases, and summer vacations in the country. Refers to such leading politicians as Clifford Sifton, especially with reference to social events. 4 photos. 1905-30

Boyd, Julian Parks

738. Mason, Alpheus Thomas. JULIAN PARKS BOYD 1903-1980. *Princeton U. Lib. Chronicle 1980 42(1): 53-54.* Obituary of Julian Parks Boyd, editor, librarian, historian, and author, who was associated with Princeton University as University Librarian from 1940 to 1952, and as a member of the Department of History beginning in 1952. 1940-80

739. Wiggins, James Russell. JULIAN PARKS BOYD. *Pro. of the Am. Antiquarian Soc. 1980 90(2): 291-299.* Boyd's (1903-80) most notable contribution to the historical profession is his work on the Jefferson Papers, but he had a long and notable career in addition to this work. A leader in the preservation of the nation's archives, he climaxed his career with his presidency of the American Philosophical Society. Provides an annotated survey of his writings. 1903-80

740. Wiggins, James Russell. JULIAN PARKS BOYD. *Massachusetts Hist. Soc. Pro. 1980 92: 160-163.* Julian Boyd, who had a distinguished career as a scholar, librarian, and historian at Princeton University, died on 28 May 1980. In 1944, Boyd began the massive task of editing the Jefferson papers. With accuracy the paramount object, Boyd meticulously mined the papers and managed to complete 20 volumes before his death. It was his firm determination to produce the definitive edition so that scholars of the future

would never need to duplicate the effort. More importantly, it was Boyd's desire to have Thomas Jefferson understood as clearly as possible. 1943-80

Boyer, Carl B.

741. Gillispie, Charles C. ÉLOGE: CARL B. BOYER, 1906-1976. *Isis 1976 67(239): 610-614.* Carl B. Boyer, a professor of mathematics at Brooklyn College in the City University of New York, was more widely known as a historian of mathematics and physics, an officer in the History of Science Society, and a member of the board of the *Dictionary of Scientific Biography.* A full bibliography of his writings appears in the autumn 1976 issue of *Historia Mathematica.* 1906-76

Boyle, John R.

742. Boyd, Helen; Crowley, T. A., ed. EARLY ALBERTA POLITICS: MEMORIES OF J. R. BOYLE. *Alberta Hist. [Canada] 1982 30(3): 9-18.* Lawyer, Edmonton city councilman (1904), member of parliament (1905-36), deputy speaker, minister of education, attorney general, and then leader of the Opposition, John R. Boyle (1870-1936) lived in Edmonton during a period of its remarkable growth. His influence was marked. Problems such as the establishment of a provincial system of education, the outbreak of World War I, the impact of the Union government in Ottawa, and the enforcement of prohibition are all dealt with, some in considerable detail. 3 photos, 14 notes. 1870-1936

Bracher, Frederick

743. Bracher, Frederick. HOW IT WAS THEN: THE PACIFIC NORTHWEST IN THE TWENTIES. *Oregon Hist. Q. 1983 84(4): 340-363.* Narrates work experiences of Frederick Bracher of Portland, Oregon, who spent the summer of 1922 on a farm in the wheat country of eastern Oregon, near Pendleton, and the summers of 1924-25 working at Tilton Spur, a small sawmill camp located about 40 miles southeast of Tacoma, near Mt. Rainier. Among other things, he observed the generally unsuccessful attempts of the Industrial Workers of the World to organize the sawmill workers. Based on portions of the author's autobiography; 9 photos. Article to be continued. 1922-25

Brackenridge, Hugh Henry

744. Galvin, Martin George. "Hugh Henry Brackenridge and the Popular Press." U. of Maryland 1977. 176 pp. *DAI 1978 38(7): 4166-A.* 1779-1815

745. Grant, Barry K. LITERARY STYLE AS POLITICAL METAPHOR IN *MODERN CHIVALRY. Can. Rev. of Am. Studies [Canada] 1980 11(1): 1-11.* Generally historians and literary analysts have concluded that Hugh Henry Brackenridge's four-volume *Modern Chivalry* (1792-1815) was essentially "genial satire upon democratic excesses" in America. But that interpretation ignored much of the author's political thinking, which became more complex as his thought changed during the 23 years over which his volumes were published. Furthermore, closer linguistic analysis of *Modern Chivalry* reveals that Brackenridge, in seeking new standards for American literature, joined postrevolutionary Americans attempting to liberate themselves from their British political, literary, and linguistic heritage. Based on writings of Brackenridge and his literary contemporaries and secondary sources; 34 notes. 1792-1815

Brackett, George A.

746. Driscoll, Cynthia B. BRACKETT'S ROAD TO GOLD. *Alaska Journal 1982 12(4): 32-37.* George A. Brackett, pioneer and former mayor of Minneapolis, was forced by financial reverses to leave for Alaska at the age of 61 to seek his fortune. In 1897, he headed for the Klondike and became involved in a scheme to build a wagon road over White Pass in southeastern Alaska to facilitate the movement of men and supplies to the gold fields. Although his road did not bring him the financial returns he sought, his continual promotion of the promise of Alaska helped open up the territory to many. Based on the George Augustus Brackett Papers, Minnesota Historical Society; 12 photos. 1893-1905

Braden, Anne

747. Braden, Anne. A VIEW FROM THE FRINGES. *Southern Exposure 1981 9(1): 68-74.* Anne Braden, wife of liberal activist and journalist Carl Braden reminisces about segregationist attempts to discredit civil rights organizations and activists by calling them subversive, and relating them to Communism; 1950's-1960's. ca 1954-69

748. Thrasher, Sue and Wigginton, Eliot. AN INTERVIEW WITH ANNE BRADEN: YOU CAN'T BE NEUTRAL. *Southern Exposure 1984 12(6): 79-85.* Sketches the life of Anne Braden, who worked for civil rights in Kentucky and Alabama, and prints portions of an interview with her about her childhood, her years in Stratford College in Virginia, and her work as a reporter for the *Anniston Star* and the *Birmingham News* in Alabama. 1924-82

Braden, Spruille

749. Rawls, Shirley Nelson. "Spruille Braden: A Political Biography." U. of New Mexico 1976. 588 pp. *DAI 1978 38(7): 4319-4320-A.* 1933-47

Bradford, Alexander Blackburn

750. Bradford, Ronald W. ALEXANDER BLACKBURN BRADFORD: A KNIGHT OF THE SOUTH (1799-1873). *J. of Mississippi Hist. 1981 43(1): 59-64.* A biographical sketch of Alexander Blackburn Bradford, reflecting the aristocratic nature of the Old South. The chivalric traits of this "southern gentleman" are described in the areas of law, leadership, politics, and the military. The author discusses Bradford's service in the Second Seminole War against Osceola, his contributions in recruiting Tennesseeans to fight in the Texas Revolution, and his valor and leadership as third-in-command of the Mississippi regiment during the Mexican War. 23 notes. ca 1820-73

Bradford, Cornelia

751. Handen, Ella. IN LIBERTY'S SHADOW: CORNELIA BRADFORD AND WHITTIER HOUSE. *New Jersey History 1982 100(3-4): 48-69.* During the 1890's, Cornelia Bradford, the fairly well-to-do daughter of a Congregationalist minister, established Whittier House as the first settlement house in Jersey City, New Jersey. Influenced by activities of English settlement houses, Bradford hoped to provide services to city residents that their government could not. A kindergarten, dispensary, and summer youth camp were three of her programs. In addition to reform interests locally, Bradford involved herself in statewide efforts. She retired in 1926 and by the time of her death had witnessed her settlement house change into a boy's club. Based on the Whittier House

archives at the New Jersey Historical Society, newspaper stories, and secondary sources; 2 illus., 109 notes. 1890-1935

Bradford, Gamaliel

752. Hutch, Richard A. EXPLORATIONS IN CHARACTER: GAMALIEL BRADFORD AND HENRY MURRAY AS PSYCHOBIOGRAPHERS. *Biography 1981 4(4): 312-325.* Biography during the 19th century was a harbinger of modern psychological science. This is demonstrated by a comparison of the style of biographic inquiry of the obscure US biographer, Gamaliel Bradford (1863-1932), with the psychological methods of the famous US psychologist, Henry A. Murray. Thus, Murray's "explorations in personality" can be understood as a modern elaboration of Bradford's "psychography." Parallels between this tradition of life-writing and the work of other 19th-century biographers, like Thomas Carlyle, and other 20th-century psychologists, like Erik Erikson, are indicated. 1890-1981

Bradford, George Partridge

753. Mathews, James W. GEORGE PARTRIDGE BRADFORD: FRIEND OF TRANSCENDENTALISTS. *Studies in the Am. Renaissance 1981: 133-156.* Traces the life and career of George Partridge Bradford, focusing on his quiet contributions to the transcendentalist movement, his friendships with Emerson, Bronson Alcott, Hawthorne, and Thoreau, and his career as educator at the Brook Farm experimental school in Massachusetts up to 1842. Throughout his life, Bradford's intellectual potential, which many deemed considerable, was often thwarted by indecision and self-deprecation. His role in 19th-century US thought, then, was more that of confidant to the era's more vocal thinkers. Draws on the letters and papers of Hawthorne, Emerson, and Alcott and the published reminiscences of former students of Bradford; 125 notes. 1820's-50's

Bradley, Anne Maddison

754. Thatcher, Linda. THE "GENTILE POLYGAMIST": ARTHUR BROWN, EX-SENATOR FROM UTAH. *Utah Hist. Q. 1984 52(3): 231-245.* 1899-1907
*For abstract see **Brown, Arthur***

Bradley, Mary

755. Bradley, Mary. MARY BRADLEY'S REMINISCENCES: A DOMESTIC LIFE IN COLONIAL NEW BRUNSWICK. *Atlantis [Canada] 1981 7(1): 92-101.* Born in Gagetown, New Brunswick, in 1771, Mary Bradley (neé Coy) "experienced religion" at age 16. Kept from public speaking by conventions of the time Bradley married in 1793 and sought fulfillment through marriage. Unsuccessful in this attempt she eventually joined the Methodist Church whose "doctrines best reflected her own well-thought-out religious views and which offered an expanding sphere for female energy." Based on Bradley's *A Narrative of the Life and Christian Experience of Mrs. Mary Bradley* (1849). 1787-1803

Bradley, Phillips

756. Dilliard, Irving. THREE TO REMEMBER: ARCHIBALD MACLEISH, STANLEY KIMMEL, PHILLIPS BRADLEY. *J. of the Illinois State Hist. Soc. 1984 77(1): 45-59.* Combined obituaries of poet-dramatist-Librarian of Congress Archibald MacLeish, scholar of the assassination of Abraham Lincoln and historian of the Civil War Stanley Kimmel, and student of Alexis de Tocqueville and educator-administrator in the field of labor relations Phillips Bradley. MacLeish opposed Marxism in the 1930's, the Fascists in World War II, and McCarthyism in the 1950's. Kimmel's most significant volume was *The Mad Booths of Maryland* (1940) as well as *Mr. Lincoln's Washington* and *Mr. Davis's Richmond.* Bradley served on the faculties of several prominent universities. 7 illus. 1910's-82

Bradley, William J.

757. Clark, Dennis. *ÉIREANNACH ÉIGIN:* WILLIAM J. BRADLEY (1892-1981), SINN FÉIN ADVOCATE. *Éire-Ireland 1983 18(2): 116-126.* William J. Bradley, a Philadelphia businessman, for many years was a very active and successful organizer and propagandist for the Irish republican movement. Between 1913 and 1921, especially, Bradley worked with Clan-na-Gael, wrote for the Irish-American press under the pen name Éireannach Éigin ["Exile Irishman"], conducted letter-writing campaigns directed at Philadelphia newspapers, and collected funds for the Irish Volunteers and Sinn Féin. As late as 1969 Bradley articulately protested against British policies in Northern Ireland. Based on the Bradley Papers, interviews with Bradley's relatives, and material by and about him in the press; 19 notes. 1913-21

Bradstreet, Anne

758. King, Anne. ANNE HUTCHINSON AND ANNE BRADSTREET: LITERATURE AND EXPERIENCE, FAITH AND WORKS IN MASSACHUSETTS BAY COLONY. *Int. J. of Women's Studies [Canada] 1978 1(5): 445-467.* Examines the lives and political, religious, and social attitudes of Anne Hutchinson (1591-1643) and Anne Bradstreet (1612-72) who, through polarizing the question of faith versus works and through questioning the position of women, introduced tensions in American life and ideology which led to eventual social change. 1630's-70's

Brady, Dorothy Stahl

759. Easterlin, Richard A. DOROTHY STAHL BRADY, 1903-1977. *J. of Econ. Hist. 1978 38(1): 301-303.* Tribute to the late Dorothy Stahl Brady, professor of economics and economic history at the University of Pennsylvania. Professor Stahl broke new ground in economic measurement, particularly in the consumption of goods and services by different social classes in the United States. 1903-77

Brady, John Green

760. Hinckley, Ted C. THE INFLUENCE OF AN 1860'S INDIANA BOYHOOD IN THE REGENERATION OF A MANHATTAN STREET ARAB. *Old Northwest 1981 7(1): 3-21.* John Green Brady (1848-1918), later a prominent minister, businessman, and governor of Alaska, was sent to Indiana for adoption after being taken off the streets of New York City as a runaway boy of eight. Brady's experiences in Indiana between 1859 and 1870, when he went to Yale University to study for the ministry, included receiving a good education, farming, and teaching. Though Brady's later successes cannot all be attributed to his Indiana upbringing, the envigorating environment he experienced there contributed greatly to his becoming a productive citizen. Based on the John G. Brady Papers in the Beinecke Library at Yale University, and other primary sources; 38 notes. 1859-70

761. Hinckley, Ted C. "WE ARE MORE TRULY HEATHEN THAN THE NATIVES": JOHN G. BRADY AND THE ASSIMILATION OF ALASKA'S TLINGIT INDIANS. *Western Hist. Q. 1980 11(1): 37-55.* John Green Brady's Alaska career, 1878-1906, gradually shifted from missionary

to secular leader. His relations with the Tlingit Indians variously included his roles as missionary-teacher, farmer-settler, businessman, judge, and governor. Brady and other like-minded allies labored to protect and civilize Alaska's natives. As a consequence of their efforts, those Indians "may well enjoy the strongest socioeconomic power base of any Amerindian group." 46 notes. 1878-1906

Brady, Mathew B.

762. Kunhardt, Philip B., Jr. [MATHEW BRADY].

IMAGES OF WHICH HISTORY WAS MADE BORE THE MATHEW BRADY LABEL. *Smithsonian 1977 8(4): 24-35.* Soon after Mathew Brady came to New York City in the early 1840's, he opened his own Daguerrean Miniature Gallery which was an instant success. The following year he sought such giants as Webster, Jackson, and Calhoun, to make a "museum of their faces for posterity." Sitting for Brady became a Presidential tradition. In 1860 he took his first picture of Abraham Lincoln, and proceeded to make an unparalled collection of portraits of the people who surrounded Lincoln. Illus.

HOLD STILL: DON'T MOVE A MUSCLE: YOU'RE ON BRADY'S CAMERA! *Smithsonian 1977 8(5): 58-67.* "With studio aids such as neck clamps, and a weighty volume for resting a hand on, the famous photographer worked his magic." From the 1840's into the 1870's Mathew B. Brady photographed many of the outstanding men of the period. He specialized in Abraham Lincoln and the Civil War. Describes the advances he made in photography during his long career. Illus. 1840's-70's

Brady, Mathew E.

763. Gollin, Rita K. THE MATTHEW BRADY PHOTOGRAPHS OF NATHANIEL HAWTHORNE. *Studies in the Am. Renaissance 1981: 379-391.* Traces the career of photographer Matthew Brady from the 1840's to the 1860's, focusing on his dealings and those of his employee Alexander Gardner with Nathaniel Hawthorne in early 1862. Hawthorne had four photographs taken of himself in Brady's Washington studio that year. His reaction to Brady's work and the events leading up to the photographic session are described. Draws on the letters of Hawthorne and secondary sources; 4 photos, 17 notes. 1862

Bragdon, Claude

764. Siegfried, David Allen. "Claude Bragdon, Artist-in-the-Theatre." U. of Illinois, Urbana-Champaign 1979. 191 pp. *DAI 1980 40(10): 5251-A.* 1890's-1930's

Bragdon, Henry Wilkinson.

765. Allis, Frederick S., Jr. HENRY WILKINSON BRAGDON. *Massachusetts Hist. Soc. Pro. 1980 92: 146-150.* Henry W. Bragdon (1906-80) will be remembered as an excellent history teacher and administrator whose unperturbable optimism coaxed the best effort from his students. While teaching at Phillips Exeter Academy, Bragdon wrote the high school history text, *History of a Free People* (1954), which is in its 9th edition. An admiration for President Wilson and the field of education led to his writing of *Woodrow Wilson: The Academic Years* (1967), a volume which received much praise. His service in teaching, athletic and administrative roles at Brooks School and Phillips Exeter Academy spanned almost 40 years. Secondary sources; 5 notes. 1906-80

Brainerd, David

766. Conforti, Joseph. DAVID BRAINERD AND THE NINETEENTH CENTURY MISSIONARY MOVEMENT. *Journal of the Early Republic 1985 5(3): 309-329.* Despite a tragically short life marked by illness, personal loss, and repeated disappointment, the Connecticut evangelical minister David Brainerd became a revered figure among early 19th-century evangelical missionaries. Thanks to Jonathan Edwards's extremely popular and highly romanticized *Life of Brainerd* (1748), Brainerd's meager missionary achievements took on heroic proportions. Missionary groups looking for a new role model found inspiration in Brainerd's work among Eastern Indian tribes and discovered the revivalist-pietist impact of the First Great Awakening. An outgrowth of Brainerd's popular appeal was the emphasis Edwards placed on disinterested benevolence and regeneration. Although disinterested benevolence fired missionary zeal, it could not overcome ethnocentrism and selfish attention to personal conversion. In Edwards's hands, Brainerd's life resembled a Puritan devotional work, and it provided a model for 19th-century missionary memoirs. Based on biographies of Brainerd, including Jonathan Edwards's and Brainerd's journal; 46 notes. 1742-1850's

767. Conforti, Joseph. JONATHAN EDWARDS'S MOST POPULAR WORK: *THE LIFE OF DAVID BRAINERD* AND NINETEENTH-CENTURY EVANGELICAL CULTURE. *Church History 1985 54(2): 188-201.* The life of David Brainerd (1718-47), notable for his missionary work among the Indians and for his expulsion from Yale because of his radical religious enthusiasm, was the subject of a 1749 work by Jonathan Edwards that became an evangelical classic. Edwards's *An Account of the Life of the Late Reverend Mr. David Brainerd* became so influential in 19th-century evangelical culture because of its succinct presentation of a life representing true holiness and benevolence. It is through this work that Edwards most influenced 19th-century evangelical religious reform. 45 notes. 1739-1842

Braithwaite, William Stanley Beaumont

768. Warren, Joseph Wyrick. "The Life and Works of William Stanley Beaumont Braithwaite." Ohio State U. 1982. 271 pp. *DAI 1983 43(10): 3321-A.* DA8305409 1906-29

Brandeis, Louis D.

769. Friesel, Evyatar. BRANDEIS' ROLE IN AMERICAN ZIONISM HISTORICALLY RECONSIDERED. *Am. Jewish Hist. 1979 69(1): 34-59.* Zionism in America was a developed and organized movement before the advent of Louis D. Brandeis. Advances during Brandeis's ascendancy were part of a general flowering of American Jewry. The appearance of Brandeis and his group upset the development of American Zionism and reduced it to a modest position. Covers 1898-1921. 40 notes. 1898-1921

770. Halpern, Ben. THE AMERICANIZATION OF ZIONISM, 1880-1930. *Am. Jewish Hist. 1979 69(1): 15-33.* Reinterprets the Louis D. Brandeis-Chaim Weizmann quarrel of 1920-21 as well as its background, the personalities of Justice Brandeis and other American Zionist leaders, and the issues separating American and European Zionists during 1880-1930. 38 notes. 1880-1930

771. Murphy, Bruce Allen. "Supreme Court Justices as Politicians: The Extrajudicial Activities of Justices Louis D. Brandeis and Felix Frankfurter." U. of Virginia 1978. 477 pp. *DAI 1983 43(10): 3408-A.* DA8300066 20c

772. Popkova, L. N. SOTSIAL'NO POLITICHESKI VZGLIADY LUISA D. BRANDEISA [The social and political views of Louis D. Brandeis]. *Amerikanskii Ezhegodnik [USSR] 1983: 254-270.* Louis D. Brandeis was among the leaders of bourgeois reformism. He became popular as the people's lawyer and defender of the interests of Americans against monopolies. He played a significant role in Wilson's administration. This brief biographical sketch of Brandeis is also an analysis of the works about him. Based on Brandeis's letters and secondary sources; 58 notes. 1856-1941

773. Wigdor, David. LAW, REFORM, AND THE MODERN ADMINISTRATIVE STATE. *Rev. in Am. Hist. 1982 10(2): 234-240.* Review article on Donald A. Ritchie's *James M. Landis: Dean of the Regulators* (1980), a biography of the New Deal administrator, and Nelson L. Dawson's *Louis D. Brandeis, Felix Frankfurter, and the New Deal* (1980), about the intellectuals involved in the New Deal. 1930's

Brandenstein, Henry U.

774. Dalin, David G. and Rothman, John F. HENRY U. BRANDENSTEIN OF SAN FRANCISCO. *Western States Jewish History 1985 18(1): 3-21.* Presents a biographical study of Henry U. Brandenstein, a respected lawyer, a leading figure in the San Francisco Jewish community, and a devoted scholar of the classics. Based on correspondence and other sources; 69 notes. 1890's-1940

Brangwyn, Frank

775. Davis, Angela. FORGOTTEN ARTIST: SIR FRANK BRANGWYN, 1867-1956. *Manitoba History [Canada] 1984 (7): 10-13.* Frank Brangwyn, a native of Belgium, was an early student of the political and artistic ideas of William Morris. In 1885 he moved to the Kent coast and, in subsequent years, traveled to Algeria, Morocco, Asia Minor, Russia, Spain, Romania, South Africa, Malaya, and Japan. Influenced by Jules Bastien-Lepage and by Millet, he was more highly esteemed in North America and continental Europe than in England. His works included oils, water colors, wood, prints, furniture, stained glass, and architectural and interior design. He executed the mural at the entrance to Manitoba's Legislative Chamber and influenced two of the province's foremost artists, Lionel LeMoine Fitzgerald and Walter J. Phillips. Illus., 31 notes. 1867-1956

Branscombe, Gena

776. Marlow, Laurine Annette Elkins. "Gena Branscombe (1891-1977): American Composer and Conductor." U. of Texas, Austin 1980. 522 pp. *DAI 1981 41(11): 6536-A.* 8109201 1907-77

Branson, Lindley Clark

777. Byrkit, James W. LINDLEY C. BRANSON AND THE JEROME *SUN*. *J. of the West 1980 19(2): 51-63.* Lindley Clark Branson (1865-1943) arrived in the copper boomtown of Jerome in December 1916. At first, Branson's paper, the Jerome *Sun*, avoided controversy, but by mid-1917, labor tensions and strong arm tactics of the United Verde Copper Company drew Branson to the side of labor. Advertisers and subscribers abandoned the *Sun* as it took on the town's establishment. United Verde Company agents succeeded in having the press machinery repossesed for debts, ending the paper's publication on 9 April 1918. Based on articles in the Jerome *Sun* and material in the James W. Byrkit collection; 4 photos, 50 notes. 1916-18

Bransten, Florine Haas

778. Dalin, David G. FLORINE AND ALICE HAAS AND THEIR FAMILIES. *Western States Jewish Hist. Q. 1981 13(2): 135-141.* Florine Haas Bransten (1881-1973) and Alice Haas Lilienthal (1885-1972), daughters of San Francisco merchant William Haas, were leaders of the city's social and cultural community as their husbands were prominent in business. The Haas-Lilienthal House on Franklin Street, commissioned by William Haas in 1886, and inherited by Alice, is a San Francisco historical landmark. Based on published sources; 4 photos, 5 notes. ca 1900-81

Brant, Joseph

779. O'Donnell, James. JOSEPH BRANT. Edmunds, R. David, ed. *American Indian Leaders: Studies in Diversity* (Lincoln: U. of Nebraska Pr., 1980): 21-40. The Mohawk leader Thayendenegea, or Joseph Brant, allied himself and his people with the British during the American Revolution. The British were unable to protect their allies, and the Mohawk lands were overrun and occupied by the colonists. The British, however, provided a refuge for him and his people, establishing the Grand River Reserve in 1784 in Ontario. This success was partly due to Brant's formal European education and familiarity with European ideas. Mainly secondary sources; map, 39 notes. 1767-1807

Brass, William

780. Teatero, William. THE CROWN V. WILLIAM BRASS. *Ontario Hist. [Canada] 1979 71(3): 139-158.* William Brass was convicted of rape in 1837. He had a record of financial problems stemming from his fur-trading and merchandising business. The defense argued that the charge was false, the result of a conspiracy by, among others, a lawyer he had hired, who intended to swindle Brass. The evidence and arguments are presented, as is the aftermath, with its political overtones. The defense was valid. Evidence showing this was not brought out at the trial is presented here. The subsequent careers of the conspirators are briefly outlined; the lawyer became a successful politician while the others involved were initially associated with peculiar land dealings touching Brass's property before they disappeared. Based on documents and contemporary newspapers; 4 illus., 98 notes. 1835-40

Braude William G.

781. Braude, William G. RECOLLECTIONS OF A SEPTUAGENARIAN: PART II, ATTEMPTS TO LEAD A CONGREGATION, TO FIGHT FOR CAUSES, AND STUDY TORAH. *Rhode Island Jewish Hist. Notes 1982 8(4): 401-441.* Continued from a previous article. Autobiography of Rabbi William G. Braude of Providence, Rhode Island, recalling his involvement in community affairs and the black civil rights movement, his travels, and the studies he has pursued since retiring in 1974. 1932-82

Brauer, Ernst August

782. Bogenschneider, Ronald. E. A. BRAUER: CHAMPION OF CONFESSIONAL LUTHERANISM. *Concordia Hist. Inst. Q. 1982 55(3): 121-127.* Chronicles the career of Lutheran minister Ernst August Brauer during 1847-96; Brauer was a leader of the confessionalist movement and an

influential Lutheran educator in the Midwest, where he served mainly in Illinois churches and taught at Concordia Seminary in St. Louis. 1847-96

Breck, Samuel

783. Wainwright, Nicholas B. THE DIARY OF SAMUEL BRECK. *Pennsylvania Mag. of Hist. and Biog. 1978 102(4): 469-508; 1979 103(1): 85-113, (2): 222-251.* Part I. Covers 1814-22. Respected, socially prominent, Federalist, Philadelphian, Episcopalian, musician, artist, scholar, historian, and a civic promoter, Breck was elected to the Pennsylvania and national legislatures. Some of the diary was published in 1877. 94 notes. Part II. Covers 1823-27. Breck mentions his dinner for Lafayette. 61 notes. Part III. Covers 1827-33. Breck discusses public as well as personal business, including his angry reaction to Jackson's anti-Bank proposal. 71 notes. Article to be continued. 1814-33

Breckinridge, Madeline McDowell

784. Hay, Melba Porter. "Madeline McDowell Breckinridge: Kentucky Suffragist and Progressive Reformer." U. of Kentucky 1980. 307 pp. *DAI 1980 41(6): 2736-A.* 8027980 1898-1920

Breckinridge, Mary

785. Campbell, Anne G. MARY BRECKINRIDGE AND THE AMERICAN COMMITTEE FOR DEVASTATED FRANCE: THE FOUNDATIONS OF THE FRONTIER NURSING SERVICE. *Register of the Kentucky Hist. Soc. 1984 82(3): 257-276.* Mary Breckinridge established the Frontier Nursing Service in Leslie County, Kentucky, in 1925. Building on her two years of experience with a relief agency in post-World War I France, she established a headquarters and centers around outlying areas, bringing medical treatment to remote areas. World War I thus contributed to improved medical services in rural Appalachia. Based on the Mary Breckinridge Papers, University of Kentucky Library, personal interviews, and secondary sources; 4 photos, 49 notes. 1919-25

786. Crowe-Carraco, Carol. MARY BRECKINRIDGE AND THE FRONTIER NURSING SERVICE. *Register of the Kentucky Hist. Soc. 1978 76(3): 179-191.* Personal tragedies led Mary Breckinridge to work for a family centered health care system in frontier Kentucky areas. From the mid-1920's until her death 40 years later, Breckinridge and the Frontier Nursing Service provided assistance in midwifery, general family care, and disease prevention. From small beginnings, the FNS network grew to cover an area of almost 700 square miles. Primary and secondary sources; 2 illus., 51 notes. 1925-65

787. Dye, Nancy Schrom. MARY BRECKINRIDGE, THE FRONTIER NURSING SERVICE AND THE INTRODUCTION OF NURSE-MIDWIFERY IN THE UNITED STATES. *Bull. of the Hist. of Medicine 1983 57(4): 485-507.* In 1925, Mary Breckinridge, a trained nurse, established the Frontier Nursing Service (FNS) in an attempt to transplant the European tradition of professional midwifery to the United States. She not only reduced infant and maternal mortality in a rural county in the heart of Appalachia, but she pioneered in developing an autonomous professional role for nurses and established the profession of nurse-midwifery in the United States. Her work spread to other counties in Kentucky, but she was unable to secure funding to expand into other areas, a situation exacerbated by the Depression. Breckinridge never intended that the FNS should challenge the medical system directly, but envisioned a program for impoverished rural areas lacking physicians. Based largely on manuscripts at the University of Kentucky; 84 notes. 1925-37

788. Matthies, Katharine. MARY BRECKINRIDGE AND THE FRONTIER NURSING SERVICE. *Daughters of the Am. Revolution Mag. 1980 114(5): 692-694.* Mary Breckinridge (1889-1965) served in Washington, D.C., during the influenza epidemic in 1918, was a volunteer for the American Committee for Devastated France during 1918-20, became a certified midwife serving rural Kentucky mountaineers, and established the Frontier Nursing Service. 1889-1965

Breckinridge, Robert J.

789. Howard, Victor B. ROBERT J. BRECKINRIDGE AND THE SLAVERY CONTROVERSY IN KENTUCKY IN 1849. *Filson Club Hist. Q. 1979 53(4): 328-343.* Robert J. Breckinridge was a consistent champion of the gradual emancipation of Kentucky's slaves. He found that his beliefs barred him from a political career in 1830, but he was a leader in the movement that persuaded the state legislature to end the importation of slaves in 1833. In 1849, he was an unsuccessful candidate for delegate to the state constitutional convention. His platform included a gradual, compensated emancipation combined with the colonization of the freed blacks in Africa. Based on the Breckinridge Family Papers at the Library of Congress and contemporary newspapers; 60 notes. 1830-49

Breckinridge, Sophonisba P.

790. Travis, Anthony R. SOPHINISBA BRECKINRIDGE, MILITANT FEMINIST. *Mid-America 1976 58(2): 111-118.* Sophinisba Breckinridge, 1866-1948, was a militant suffragette, progressive reformer, women's rights advocate, the first woman-appointee to the Kentucky bar, trade-union advocate, author of numerous works on urban-industrial problems, and professor of public welfare at the University of Chicago. Concerned for professional and working-class women as well as for prostitutes, she opposed the Equal Rights Amendment because of its possible effect on protective legislation for working women. She was influenced by Hull House and devoted her life to generous and public-spirited effort. Based on Breckinridge manuscripts, Library of Congress; 23 notes. 1880's-1948

791. Cook, Beverly B. SOPHONISBA P. BRECKINRIDGE (1866-1948). *Women & Pol. 1983 3(1): 95-102.* Frustrated in founding a legal or teaching career, Sophonisba P. Breckinridge entered settlement work in Chicago, then moved to academe where her publications on women and social work contributed to the nation's social conscience. 1901-48

Breckinridge, W. C. P.

792. Klotter, James C. SEX, SCANDAL, AND SUFFRAGE IN THE GILDED AGE. *Historian 1980 42(2): 225-243.* W. C. P. Breckinridge's affair with student Madeline Pollard began in 1884 and ended in a political scandal during 1893-94. Breckinridge, a Democrat in the House of Representatives since 1881, was known nationally as the "silver tongued orator of Kentucky." His scandal is indicative of the views of sex, morality, and politics during this period. The Gilded Age's morality has traditionally incorporated two images—that of a low state of public morals and strict Victorian outlook. In retrospect, "if sexual transgression could be quan-

tified, the known examples of public officials would very probably fall beneath the general public's Gilded Age average." Primary sources; 61 notes. 1884-1904

Breeden, Jane Rooker Smith

793. Otto, Kathryn. DAKOTA RESOURCES: THE JANE BREEDEN PAPERS AT THE SOUTH DAKOTA HISTORICAL RESOURCE CENTER. *South Dakota Hist. 1980 10(3): 241-244.* Jane Rooker Smith Breeden (1853-1955) was a leader of the woman suffrage and temperance movements in South Dakota. Along with material on the suffrage and temperance activities, the papers include items about other social organizations with which Breeden was involved, and information on World War I anti-German propaganda. Based on the Breeden Papers at the South Dakota Historical Resource Center in Pierre, South Dakota; photo. 1874-1932

Brennan, John R.

794. Borst, John C. DAKOTA RESOURCES: THE JOHN R. BRENNAN FAMILY PAPERS AT THE SOUTH DAKOTA HISTORICAL RESOURCE CENTER. *South Dakota Hist. 1984 14(1): 68-72.* Discusses the life of John R. Brennan, his career in South Dakota from 1876 to 1919, and his family papers in the South Dakota Historical Resource Center in Pierre. Brennan was a hotel manager, a prospector, a co-founder of Rapid City, South Dakota, a postmaster, a railroad agent, a politician, a businessman, and an Indian agent for the Pine Ridge Indian Reservation. Brennan's papers consist primarily of material concerned with the Pine Ridge Indian agency along with some business and financial records. Based on the John R. Brennan Family Papers at the South Dakota Historical Resource Center, Pierre, South Dakota; 2 photos, note. 1876-1919

Brent, Charles Henry

795. Reilly, Michael C. CHARLES HENRY BRENT: PHILIPPINE MISSIONARY AND ECUMENIST. *Philippine Studies 1976 24(3): 303-325.* Provides a biographical article on Charles Henry Brent, first Protestant Episcopal Bishop of the Philippines, 1901-18. Examines Brent's mission and Christian philosophy through his speeches and later writings. He was an advocate of American paternalism, though with liberal positions on most controversial subjects. Based mostly on Brent's publications. 70 notes. 1901-18

Breton, William L.

796. Snyder, Martin P. WILLIAM L. BRETON, NINETEENTH-CENTURY PHILADELPHIA ARTIST. *Pennsylvania Mag. of Hist. and Biog. 1961 85(2): 178-209.* Discusses the life and artistic career of William L. Breton from 1824 until his death in 1855, during which period he created paintings and lithographs of many Philadelphia buildings; and includes six reproductions of his works. 1824-55

Breuning family

797. Adams, Robert G. THE SEARCH FOR OUR GERMAN ANCESTORS CONTINUED: THE BREUNINGS OF MÖHRINGEN. *Pennsylvania Folklife 1984 33(3): 125-128.* Presents information about the Breuning family of Möhringen, now a suburb of Stuttgart, some of whose descendants settled in Blooming Grove, now Cogan Station, in Pennsylvania. 1470-1897

Brewer, Edward

798. Johnston, Patricia Condon. EDWARD BREWER: ILLUSTRATOR AND PAINTER. *Minnesota Hist. 1980 47(1): 2-15.* Edward Brewer may have been best-known for his Cream of Wheat paintings, which appeared nationally from 1911 to 1926. His career, however, spanned six decades, as a portrait painter, as a muralist, and as a commercial artist. The author discusses Brewer's work, home, love of artifacts, family, and financial success and provides a brief history of the Cream of Wheat Company. 19 illus., 39 notes. 1911-71

Brewer, Jim

799. Riley, Joe. AN INTERVIEW WITH JIM BREWER. *JEMF Q. 1981 17(64): 215-218.* An interview of acoustic blues guitarist, Jim Brewer, by Joe Riley, preceded by a brief biography of Brewer, who by the late 1940's was playing on Maxwell Street in Chicago, where he stayed for 25 years, and whose style is based on the Mississippi Delta blues. 1920-80

Brewer, Lucy

800. Kittle, Laurie L. A FEMALE MARINE ABOARD THE *CONSTITUTION. Marine Corps Gazette 1980 64(2): 53-56.* Details the active duty, 1812-15, during the War of 1812, of Lucy Brewer, the first woman to serve in the US Marines; she was disguised as a man. 1812-15

Brewer, Thomas M.

801. Trotzig, E. G. THURE KUMLIEN, PIONEER NATURALIST. *Swedish Pioneer Hist. Q. 1979 30(3): 196-204.* 1843-88

For abstract see ***Kumlien, Thure***

Brewington, Marion Vernon

802. Dodge, Ernest S. MARION VERNON BREWINGTON. *Massachusetts Hist. Soc. Pro. 1974 86: 95-98.* Marion Vernon Brewington (1902-74) was elected a member of the Massachusetts Historical Society in 1958. Although he was a banker rather than a historian by training, Brewington made a tremendous contribution to the field of maritime history. His early publications concerned the maritime history of the Chesapeake Bay region, and from 1956-66 he was curator of maritime history at the Peabody Museum in Salem, Massachusetts. His major works include *Ship Carvers of North America* (1962), *The Peabody Museum Collection of Navigating Instruments* (1963), and *The Marine Paintings and Drawings in the Peabody Museum* (1968), written with his wife Dorothy. During 1966-74, Brewington was director of the Kendall Whaling Museum in Sharon, Massachusetts. He was at work on a catalog of the collections at Mystic Seaport at the time of his death. Index. 1902-74

Brewster, Charles

803. Pilcher, John E. CHARLES BREWSTER OF FORT MADISON: A PROFILE IN ENTERPRISE, 1845-1875. *Ann. of Iowa 1979 44(8): 602-626.* Analyzes the economic activities of "merchant capitalist" Charles Brewster (1813-93), a prominent Fort Madison, Iowa, dry goods merchant and banker. Describes the operation of Brewster's dry goods store, his growing involvement with land dealings and mortgages, and his eventual emergence as a leading banker. 1845-75

Bridges, Charles

804. Hood, Graham. A NEW LOOK AT CHARLES BRIDGES, COLONIAL VIRGINIA PAINTER, 1735-45. *Am. Art J. 1977 9(2): 57-67.* Discusses Virginia artist, Charles Bridges, and gives examples of his paintings during 1735-45. 1735-45

Bridges, Harry

805. Schwartz, Harvey. HARRY BRIDGES AND THE SCHOLARS: LOOKING AT HISTORY'S VERDICT. *California Hist. 1980 59(1): 66-79.* Appraises Harry Bridges and his controversial career as leader of the International Longshoreman's and Warehouseman's Union. Retired since 1977, Bridges first gained national attention with his leadership of the international longshoremen's strike and the San Francisco general strike of 1934. For 19 years afterward, the federal government tried to deport Bridges, a native of Australia, but failed to prove his Communist connections. The charge of Communist sympathizer-member has long been attached to Bridges, whose outspoken views have included consistent pro-Soviet statements, approval of Communist unionists, cooperation with Communists, endorsement of the general strike, opposition to American entry in the Korean War, and support of Henry Wallace in 1948. Scholars have varied widely in their assessment of Bridges, from supporting his union activities to condemning his pro-Communist views. Recent scholarly efforts have shown more moderation, and recognize that his view of labor unity was practical, traditional in method, and international in outlook. Calls the question of his relationship to the Communist Party beside the point. Photos, 43 notes. 1934-79

Briggs, Cyril V.

806. Samuels, Wilfred David. "Five Afro-Caribbean Voices in American Culture, 1917-1929: Hubert H. Harrison, Wilfred A. Domingo, Richard B. Moore, Cyril V. Briggs, and Claude McKay." U. of Iowa 1977. 181 pp. *DAI 1978 38(7): 4234-A.* 1917-29

Brin, Fanny Fligelman

807. Stuhler, Barbara. FANNY BRIN: WOMAN OF PEACE. Stuhler, Barbara and Kreuter, Gretchen, ed. *Women of Minnesota: Selected Biographical Essays* (St. Paul: Minnesota Historical Society Press, 1977): 284-300. In 1884, three-month-old Fanny Fligelman came to Minneapolis with her Romanian Jewish parents. A serious student in high school and at the University of Minnesota, Fanny was active in the Minerva Literature Society and was elected to Phi Beta Kappa. She became a teacher, and in 1913 wed Arthur Brin, a successful businessman. Fanny raised a family, became a prominent volunteer activist, and worked for woman suffrage, world peace, democracy, and Jewish heritage. During the 1920's and 30's, she was especially active in the National Council of Jewish Women and served as director of the Minneapolis Woman's Committee for World Disarmament. Stimulated by the Nazi attack on Jews, Fanny became a strong Zionist. As the alternate delegate for the Women's Action Committee for Lasting Peace, Fanny attended the 1945 San Francisco meetings which gave birth to the United Nations. An excellent speaker, Fanny served in many organizations, promoted many causes, took civic responsibilities as serious duties, and worked to better use women and their contributions to improve world affairs. Primary and secondary sources; photo, 44 notes. 1913-60's

Brindley, Ethel Mae

808. Brindley, Esther E. ETHEL MAE BRINDLEY, BIOGRAPHICAL SKETCH. *Chronicles of Oklahoma 1981 59(2): 237-240.* Life on a turn of the century farm near Mustang, Oklahoma, proved hard but adventurous for Ethel Mae Brindley. The death of her husband in 1921 left Brindley without an income and she moved to Edmond, Oklahoma, to open a rooming house. During the 1920's she undertook several business ventures, including a very successful role as one of Oklahoma's first women oil brokers. Always civic-minded and progressive, she still remains active in Mustang's community affairs. 1889-1981

Brink, Nicholas (family)

809. Brink, Andrew. THE BRINK FAMILY IN ONTARIO. *Halve Maen 1982 57(1): 6-9, 13, 17.* Traces the history of the Brink family in Ontario from 1797, when Nicholas Brink (1770-1834) was granted a tract of land in what is now Oxford County, until 1857. 1797-1857

Brinton, Ada Mae Brown

810. Riley, Glenda, ed. EIGHTY-SIX YEARS IN IOWA: THE MEMOIR OF ADA MAE BROWN BRINTON. *Ann. of Iowa 1981 45(7): 551-567.* Written in 1977, the memoirs of Ada Mae Brown Brinton (b. 1891) contain descriptions of life on an Iowa farm, school and church activities, and social events in the town of Stuart; 1868-1974. 3 photos, 7 notes. 1868-1974

Brisbane, Albert

811. Pettitt, Richard Norman, Jr. "Albert Brisbane: Apostle of Fourierism in the United States, 1834-1890." Miami U. 1982. 357 pp. *DAI 1983 44(1): 265-266-A.* DA8311269 1834-90

812. Rohler, Lloyd Earl, Jr. "The Utopian Persuasion of Albert Brisbane, First Apostle of Fourierism." Indiana U. 1977. 197 pp. *DAI 1977 37(4): 1738-A.* 1840-44

Briscoe, Anne M.

813. Briscoe, Anne M. DIARY OF A MAD FEMINIST CHEMIST. *Int. J. of Women's Studies [Canada] 1981 4(4): 420-430.* Although faced with sex discrimination in her career in academe, this biochemist has achieved some measure of success and recognition, but more of it is due to her involvement in the women's movement, her leadership in the Association for Women in Science, and the altered climate of the 1970's with the feminist movement, than to her hard work and commitment to the sciences in the 50's and 60's. 1950-81

Brodhead, John Romeyn

814. Howard, Ronald. JOHN ROMEYN BRODHEAD. *Halve Maen 1985 59(1): 7-10, 27.* Biography of John Romeyn Brodhead, a 19th-century American historian who wrote what was considered at the time to be the definitive history of New York in the 17th century. 1658-1873

Brodie, Bernard

815. Wildrick, Craig D. BERNARD BRODIE: PIONEER OF THE STRATEGY OF DETERRENCE. *Military Rev. 1983 63(10): 39-45.* Bernard Brodie authored significant works dealing with the political and military consequences of nuclear strategy, particularly nuclear deterrence. His insights

influenced US nuclear posture for more than two decades. Describes some of Brodie's publications, focusing on their key points and impact on policy. Brodie's thoughts on national military strategy are significant for today's military leaders, who must also understand the political consequences of all military actions. Secondary sources; photo, 24 notes. 1940-78

Brodie, Fawn M.

816. Cooley, Everett L. IN MEMORIAM: FAWN MCKAY BRODIE 1915-81. *Utah Hist. Q. 1981 49(2): 204-208.* Fawn McKay Brodie taught at the University of Chicago, University of California, Los Angeles, and Princeton University. She was a noted historical author who received many awards. Her acceptance remarks at the Utah State Historical Society's Annual Meeting, 23 September 1967, when she received the society's highest honor—the Fellow Award, acknowledged the academic freedom granted by Society. 1915-81

817. Loewenberg, Peter. FAWN MCKAY BRODIE. *Pacific Hist. Rev. 1981 50(3): 383-384.* Sketches the life, work, and character of Fawn McKay Brodie (1915-81), American historian and biographer. She authored important biographies on Joseph Smith, Thaddeus Stevens, Richard Burton, Thomas Jefferson, and Richard Nixon and taught a popular course in American political biography. 1915-81

818. McMurrin, Sterling M. A NEW CLIMATE OF LIBERATION: A TRIBUTE TO FAWN MCKAY BRODIE, 1915-1981. *Dialogue 1981 14(1): 73-76.* Fawn McKay Brodie authored numerous historical biographies, employing the methodology of psychohistory. In this method, the historian attempts to achieve empathetic understanding of the subject of historical events, to grasp the circumstances, interests, and motives which produced them. The Mormon church excommunicated Professor Brodie for her biography of Joseph Smith. As a result of her work, however, Mormon historical work has moved toward more openness and objectivity. Based on an interview with Brodie, her writings, and book reviews; 4 notes. 1945-81

Brogan, Denis W.

819. Nicholas, H. G. DENIS WILLIAM BROGAN, 1900-1974. *Pro. of the British Acad. [Great Britain] 1976 62: 399-410.* Obituary of author of *The American Political System* and *The Development of Modern France,* whose work sparked an interest in things American and French among the British. 5 notes. 1900-74

Brombaugh, John

820. Morris Kienzle, Marga Jeanne. "The Life and Work of John Brombaugh, Organ Builder." U. of Cincinnati 1984. 102 pp. *DAI 1985 46(3): 551-A.* DA8509487 1968-84

Bromfield, Louis

821. Anderson, David D. LOUIS BROMFIELD'S MYTH OF THE OHIO FRONTIER. *Old Northwest 1980 6(1): 63-74.* Discusses the life and literary career of US novelist and expatriate Louis Bromfield, author of *The Green Bay Tree* (1924) and *The Farm* (1933). Both novels were inspired by his first 20 years spent in Mansfield, Ohio. Bromfield's themes included the clash between agricultural self-sufficiency and industrialism, the values of post-agricultural towns, and, especially, the dehumanizing effect of industrialization. 6 notes. 1920-48

Bronson, Flora Adelaide Holcomb

822. Leiber, Justin; Pickering, James; and White, Flora Bronson, ed. "MOTHER BY THE TENS": FLORA ADELAIDE HOLCOMB BRONSON'S ACCOUNT OF HER LIFE AS AN ILLINOIS SCHOOLTEACHER, POET, AND FARM WIFE, 1851-1927. *J. of the Illinois State Hist. Soc. 1983 76(4): 283-307.* Memoirs of Flora Adelaide Holcomb Bronson, a native of Pennsylvania who lived and taught in Owosso, Michigan; Chicago; and central Illinois. After the death of her husband, Allen Walter Bronson, in 1918, she moved to Chicago and later to Lake Worth, Florida. Topics include farm life, poetry, rural religion, early sexuality, inadequate salaries for teachers, and death and illness. 12 illus., 12 notes. 1851-1927

Bronson, Isaac

823. Morrison, Grant. A NEW YORK CITY CREDITOR AND HIS UPSTATE DEBTORS: ISAAC BRONSON'S MONEYLENDING, 1819-1836. *New York Hist. 1980 61(3): 255-276.* Isaac Bronson, a New York City financier, exemplifies the role of the individual moneylender in providing capital for economic development in the rural districts of northern and western New York. His extensive long-term loans to rural settlers after 1819 were concentrated in counties prospering from the Erie Canal. Increased competition in the New York City money market caused other city capitalists to make loans to upstate rural entrepreneurs. Bronson as moneylender acted through agents located in upstate communities. Most borrowers were men of substance and reputation in the market towns of heavily agricultural areas. Based on the Bronson Papers in the New York Public Library, mortgage books in county clerks' offices, Phelps-Gorham Papers in the New York State Library; 8 illus., map, 2 tables, 40 notes. 1819-36

Brooke, John Mercer

824. Brooke, George M., Jr. "A HIGH OLD CRUISE": JOHN MERCER BROOKE AND THE AMERICAN VOYAGE OF THE *KANRIN MARU. Virginia Cavalcade 1980 29(4): 174-183.* Discusses American naval officer John Mercer Brooke (1826-1906), focusing on his trip as a naval advisor on the Japanese steamer *Kanrin Maru,* which sailed from Japan to the United States in February 1860 to exchange ratifications of the 1858 Harris Treaty opening new trade ports in Japan, and his voyage as an escort to the Japanese mission that sailed to the United States in an American man-of-war. 1860

Brookhart, Smith Wildman

825. McDaniel, George W. PROHIBITION DEBATE IN WASHINGTON COUNTY, 1890-1894: SMITH WILDMAN BROOKHART'S INTRODUCTION TO POLITICS. *Ann. of Iowa 1981 45(7): 519-536.* Contrary to widely held historical opinion, Smith Wildman Brookhart did not begin his political career as an antirailroad politician. Rather his introduction to politics came in 1894 when the dry faction of the Washington County, Iowa, Republican Party succeeded in gaining Brookhart's nomination for the office of county attorney. Brookhart easily won the office and thus began a career in politics that would eventually lead to the US Senate. Based on local newspapers; 3 photos, 38 notes. 1890-94

826. McDaniel, George W. SMITH WILDMAN BROOKHART. *Palimpsest 1982 63(6): 174-183.* Describes the politically turbulent life of Smith Wildman Brookhart (1869-1944), Republican Senator from Iowa, who fought for progressive reforms, particularly for the Iowan farmer and

against railroad abuses; later Brookhart served under Franklin D. Roosevelt in the Agricultural Adjustment Administration; focuses on the 1920's and 30's. 1869-1944

Brooking, William T.

827. Rezab, Gordana. THE MEMOIR OF WILLIAM T. BROOKING, MCDONOUGH COUNTY PIONEER, PART 2. *Western Illinois Regional Studies 1981 4(2): 136-151.* Continued from the previous article. Memoir of William T. Brooking of Macomb, Illinois, covering 1844-54, detailing his participation in the Mormon War, his marriage, and his love for hunting. 1844-54

828. Rezab, Gordana. THE MEMOIR OF WILLIAM T. BROOKING, MCDONOUGH COUNTY PIONEER (PART 1). *Western Illinois Regional Studies 1981 4(1): 5-24.* Memoir of William T. Brooking of Macomb, McDonough County, Illinois, dictated to his son in 1906, from 1834 when he arrived in Macomb as a boy. Article to be continued. 1834-1906

Brookings, Robert S.

829. Critchlow, Donald T. ROBERT S. BROOKINGS: THE MAN, THE VISION AND THE INSTITUTION. *Review of Politics 1984 46(4): 561-581.* St. Louis businessman Robert S. Brookings, founder of the Brookings Institution, retired wealthy to devote himself to philanthropy in 1895. He served in government advisory positions and with private foundations. Combining his experience in these two areas, in 1916 he became a founding trustee of the private Institute for Government Research. He supported government intervention in the economy, agricultural cooperation, federal unemployment insurance, and a European trading union. In 1927, he reorganized the institution into his namesake Brookings Institution to focus on government economic policy. The social scientists supported by his institution were less interested in reform, hostile to the liberal state of Franklin Delano Roosevelt, and opposed to Keynesian economics. 42 notes. 1890's-1930's

Brooks, Ebenezer

830. Hagy, James William. WITHOUT A PROPER THEATRE: THE MANY CAREERS OF EBENEZER BROOKS. *Register of the Kentucky Hist. Soc. 1982 80(3): 267-280.* Ebenezer Brooks, preacher, doctor, author, teacher, and politician, was in the center of controversy in each of his careers. He was involved in the movement for statehood for Kentucky, although not as significantly as has been claimed. In fact, at the 4th Kentucky statehood convention in 1786, he opposed separation from Virginia. He was no more successful in preventing statehood than he had been in obtaining it earlier. Primary sources; 3 illus., 45 notes. 1775-1800

Brooks, Gwendolyn

831. Lynch, Charles Henry. "Robert Hayden and Gwendolyn Brooks: A Critical Study." New York U. 1977. 257 pp. *DAI 1977 38(4): 2128-A.* 1940's-70's

Brooks, Sara

832. Brooks, Sara and Simonsen, Thordis. YOU MAY PLOW HERE. *Southern Exposure 1980 8(3): 50-61.* Personal narrative tracing the life of Alabama-born Sara Brooks (b. 1911) on a 53-acre farm owned by her father even though blacks of her father's generation did not usually own land; ca. 1918-23. ca 1918-23

Brooks, William Keith

833. Benson, Keith Rodney. "William Keith Brooks (1848-1908): A Case Study in Morphology and the Development of American Biology." Oregon State U. 1979. 363 pp. *DAI 1979 40(4): 2233-A.* 1890's-1908

Brophy, Lawrence William

834. Geary, Helen Brophy. AFTER THE LAST PICTURE SHOW. *Chronicles of Oklahoma 1983 61(1): 4-27.* Lawrence William Brophy arrived in Oklahoma during November 1907 and soon opened his first movie theater in Chandler. During the following two decades, he operated 21 theaters across Oklahoma, Arkansas, and Missouri. Presenting both motion pictures and vaudeville acts, Brophy offered the most recent movies in the most comfortable of buildings. Along with other theater managers he resisted church opposition to Sunday showings and excessive censorship. In 1915 he was elected first vice-president of the Motion Picture Theatre Exhibitors' League, but 11 years later he sold all of his buildings and turned to other successful business ventures. Based on newspapers; 8 photos, 41 notes. 1907-26

Brough, Charles Hillman

835. Cook, Charles Orson. "Arkansas's Charles Hillman Brough, 1876-1935: An Interpretation." U. of Houston 1980. 207 pp. *DAI 1981 42(1): 344-345-A.* 8115452 1890-1935

836. Cook, Charles Orson. *BOOSTERISM AND BABBITTRY:* CHARLES HILLMAN BROUGH AND THE "SELLING" OF ARKANSAS. *Arkansas Hist. Q. 1978 37(1): 74-83.* Charles Hillman Brough (1876-1935), college professor, Arkansas governor (1917-21), and orator, was well known as a propagandist for Arkansas during the 1920's and early 1930's. Although he spouted "facts" which pictured Arkansas as a veritable Garden of Eden, few nonresidents were influenced by his boosting. Primary and secondary sources; 35 notes. 1920's-35

Broun, Heywood

837. Wilder, Robin Gibbs. "The Mind of Heywood Broun: 1921-1934." U. of Wisconsin, Madison 1984. 426 pp. *DAI 1984 45(2): 613-A.* DA8405458 1920's-39

Browder, Earl Russell

838. Rosenberg, Roger Elliot. "Guardian of the Fortress: A Biography of Earl Russell Browder, U.S. Communist Party General-Secretary from 1930-1944." U. of California, Santa Barbara 1982. 453 pp. *DAI 1984 44(9): 2861-2862-A.* DA8400047 1930-44

Brower, David

839. Devall, Bill. DAVID BROWER. *Environmental Review 1985 9(3): 238-253.* Discusses the life work and philosophy of reform environmentalist David Brower, past executive director of the Sierra Club and the founder of Friends of the Earth, and assesses Brower's position within the leadership of the environmental movement. 1930's-85

Brown, Arthur

840. Thatcher, Linda. THE "GENTILE POLYGAMIST": ARTHUR BROWN, EX-SENATOR FROM UTAH. *Utah Hist. Q. 1984 52(3): 231-245.* Arthur Brown, a lawyer and former senator from Utah, was shot to death by his mistress, Anne Maddison Bradley, in Washington, D.C., in December

1906. Bradley, enraged that Brown would not acknowledge their sons and frustrated by his broken promises of marriage, pleaded not guilty by reason of temporary insanity to the murder charge. Public opinion turned against the prosecution case as Brown's injustices to Bradley and details of his notorious philandering came to light, and the jury found for the defense. Illus., 3 photos, 51 notes. 1899-1907

Brown, Charles Brockden

841. Berthold, Dennis. CHARLES BROCKDEN BROWN, *EDGAR HUNTLY,* AND THE ORIGINS OF THE AMERICAN PICTURESQUE. *William and Mary Q. 1984 41(1): 62-84.* Charles Brockden Brown's writings reflected contemporary taste for picturesque landscape. Traces the development of the picturesque style and related books and painting, focusing on Brown's *Edgar Huntly;* evaluates Brown's significance as a major innovator in American fiction. 55 notes. 1790-1810

842. Bingham, Deborah Marie. "The Identity Crisis of Charles Brockden Brown." Bowling Green State U. 1977. 225 pp. *DAI 1978 38(9): 5661-A.* 1789-1810

843. Fussell, Edwin Sill. *WIELAND:* A LITERARY AND HISTORICAL READING. *Early Am. Lit. 1983 18(2): 171-186.* More than a Gothic tale, Charles Brockden Brown's *Wieland* (1798) may be the most significant piece of American writing between Jefferson's Declaration of Independence in 1776 and Cooper's *The Pioneers* in 1823. In *Wieland,* Brown helped to create a national literature for the new republic, but the creation of such a literature depended on a political revolution, an event caused in part by writers. To create a literary work that reflected the nation's transformation, Brown himself had to be transformed. 9 notes. 1771-98

Brown, Charles Oliver

844. Wallace, Dewey D., Jr. CHARLES OLIVER BROWN AT DUBUQUE: A STUDY IN THE IDEALS OF MIDWESTERN CONGREGATIONALISTS IN THE LATE NINETEENTH CENTURY. *Church Hist. 1984 53(1): 46-60.* Charles Oliver Brown represented a combination of Finneyite revivalism, patriotic and reformist idealism about a Christian America, pride in distinctive Congregationalist characteristics, and a commitment to an eloquent oratorical style as a means of communication. No period in Brown's varied career illustrated these characteristics better than his tenure as a Congregational minister in Dubuque, Iowa. 72 notes. 1868-1941

Brown, Charlotte Hawkins

845. Hunter, Tera. THE CORRECT THING: CHARLOTTE HAWKINS BROWN AND THE PALMER INSTITUTE. *Southern Exposure 1983 11(5): 37-43.* After only one year of college training, Charlotte Hawkins Brown founded the Alice Freeman Palmer Memorial Institute in Sedalia, North Carolina, in 1902 and raised this young black women's school to national prominence despite the social barriers that faced all black women. 1902-71

846. Smith, Sandra N. and West, Earle H. CHARLOTTE HAWKINS BROWN. *J. of Negro Educ. 1982 51(3): 191-206.* Charlotte Hawkins Brown (1883-1961) was founder and president of Palmer Memorial Institute in Greensboro, North Carolina, during 1902-52. Brown's varying groups of primary financial supporters caused her to shift the school's primary focus from vocational training to being an elite finishing school. By the 1940's, Brown shifted from accommodating to condemning discrimination. A self-conscious race leader working through women's clubs, Brown urged white women to support equal education and to respect black women and black class lines. She also encouraged black women to become cultured and to support black organizations. Based on publications of Charlotte Hawkins Brown, manuscripts and newspaper accounts; 53 notes. 1902-61

Brown, Cleyson L.

847. McCoy, Sondra Van Meter. THE PATRIARCH OF ABILENE: CLEYSON L. BROWN AND THE UNITED EMPIRE, 1898-1935. *Kansas Hist. 1982 5(2): 107-119.* The Abilene *Reflector* once said that Cleyson L. Brown had done more for Abilene than any other man. Converting his father's mill to an electric plant in 1898, Brown then built an industrial empire that included some 85 industries. Enduring contributions are United Telecommunications, the third largest telephone holding company in America and now part of Kansas Power and Light Company and the Brown Memorial Foundation. The thrifty Brown forced all of his workers to save for their future and to invest in his enterprises. He even established a welfare program to help workers in need. Based on newspapers, tax and corporate records, Kansas State Historical Society, Museum of Independent Telephony, Abilene; illus., 30 notes. 1898-1935

Brown, Dee

848. Courtemanche-Ellis, Anne. MEET DEE BROWN: AUTHOR, TEACHER, LIBRARIAN. *Wilson Lib. Bull. 1978 52(7): 552-561.* A biography and interview with Dee Brown (1908-), describing his research methods and experiences with source material for such best-sellers as *Bury My Heart At Wounded Knee.* 1929-77

Brown, Edmund G. "Pat"

849. Rapoport, Roger. THE POLITICAL ODYSSEY OF PAT BROWN. *California History 1985 64(1): 2-9.* Profiles the political career of Edmund G. "Pat" Brown, governor of California from 1958 to 1966. A native of California, Brown began his career by winning an election as San Francisco district attorney in 1943. In 1950, he became attorney general, the only Democrat to hold a statewide office. Brown capitalized on Republican political blunders in 1958 to capture the governorship. As governor he backed the state's development of water projects, freeways, and higher education. Although a believer in law and order, Brown was defeated in his bid for reelection in 1966 after the Watts riots and the Berkeley student demonstrations. Brown is remembered as an old-style politician whose vision for California brought important advances in the state's growth and development. Based on interviews, newspapers, secondary sources; illus., 7 photos, 23 notes. 1943-85

Brown, Ernest

850. Holmgren, Eric J. ERNEST BROWN, PHOTOGRAPHER. *Alberta Hist. [Canada] 1980 28(4): 16-27.* Ernest Brown emigrated from Yorkshire, England to Canada in 1902. Employed by photographer C. W. Mathers in Edmonton, he soon bought out the business. He trained one assistant, Gladys Reeves, with whom he worked to document on film the development of a city. Financially overextended by 1914, he suffered during World War I. Bitter, Brown left photography in 1929. He wrote histories of the West and of photography. Neither was published. He also cataloged his approximately 50,000 negatives, founded a Pioneer Days Museum (1933), and strove to create a museum, either civic or

provincial, to house, among other artifacts, his own photography collection. A character of sorts, he "recognized the need to record pictorially the development of Edmonton." 17 photos, 7 notes. 1902-51

Brown, Hallie Quinn

851. McFarlin, Annjennette S. HALLIE QUINN BROWN: BLACK WOMAN ELOCUTIONIST. *Southern Speech Communication J. 1980 46(1): 72-82.* Neglected by scholars until 1975, Hallie Quinn Brown (1849-1945) was an internationally famous elocutionist, a prominent educator, and a tireless worker for sexual and racial equality. 1873-1945

Brown, Herbert Ross

852. Allis, Frederick S., Jr. HERBERT ROSS BROWN. *New England Q. 1981 54(1): 3-13.* From March 1945 to March 1981, Herbert Ross Brown edited over 140 issues of The *New England Quarterly.* Joining Bowdoin College as an English instructor in 1925, he became a full professor in 1939, retiring in 1972. Besides his editorial accomplishments, his career included significant achievements in other pursuits, such as public speaking, authorship, and civic accomplishments in his town, state, and country. His editorship was noteable for the practice Brown adopted of writing "pastoral letters" to his board of editors. 1945-81

Brown, Homer Sylvester

853. Cunningham, Constance A. HOMER S. BROWN: FIRST BLACK POLITICAL LEADER IN PITTSBURGH. *J. of Negro Hist. 1981-82 66(4): 304-317.* After graduating from law school in 1923, Homer Sylvester Brown became a community leader, civil rights activist, state legislator, and judge. He was a central figure in the Pittsburgh Renaissance of the 1940's. Brown spoke for the black minority in Pittsburgh. He was highly respected as a state constitutional scholar. Interviews, family, and state archives; 66 notes. 1923-80

Brown, Jerry.

854. Leapman, Michael. THE AMERICAN MOOD: 1979: PRESIDENT CARTER'S FIRST 30 MONTHS PROVE A DISAPPOINTMENT. *Round Table [Great Britain] 1979 (276): 343-346.* 1977-79
For abstract see ***Carter, Jimmy***

Brown, Jesse L.

855. Weems, John E. BLACK WINGS OF GOLD. *US Naval Inst. Pro. 1983 109(7): 35-39.* Ensign Jesse L. Brown was the first black designated an aviator in the US Navy. In October 1950 he was shot down over North Korea and died as a result of his injuries while rescuers attempted to free him from his plane. Based on reminiscences and newspaper accounts; 12 notes. 1948-50

Brown, Jock

856. Reilly, Nolan; Ralston, Keith; and Friesen, Gerald. AN INTERVIEW WITH JOCK BROWN. *Manitoba Hist. [Canada] 1982 (3): 21-25.* Brown emigrated to Manitoba in 1913, joining cooperatives and serving as the first president of the farm branch of the provincial Cooperative Commonwealth Federation (CCF) in the mid-1930's. In 1940, he resigned because the CCF had betrayed truly socialist principles and was oriented toward pacifism. He served as general manager and president of Canadian Co-operative Implements from 1941 to 1969, founded the Winnipeg *Citizen,* and organized several group tours to China. Brown had a low opinion of both John Bracken and T. A. Crerar. Major influences in his political education included Stewart Chase's *Tragedy of Waste,* R. H. Tawney's *Sickness of this Acquisitive Society,* and the *American Guardian* of Oscar Armoringer. 2 illus. 1913-81

Brown, John

857. Oates, Stephen B. GOD'S ANGRY MAN. *American History Illustrated 1986 20(9): 10-21.* Discusses the life of abolitionist John Brown whose actions against the slavery system of the South resulted in his own execution and helped to usher in the Civil War. 1800-59

858. Oates, Stephen B. YEARS OF TRIAL: JOHN BROWN IN OHIO. *Timeline 1985 2(1): 2-13.* Details abolitionist John Brown's attempts to acquire a fortune in the speculative land boom of the 1830's in Ohio's Portage County, an effort that ended in failure in the financial panic of 1837. 1835-46

Brown, John L.

859. Horton, Loren N. A STRUGGLE FOR OFFICE: THE SHERMAN-BROWN IMBROGLIO. *Palimpsest 1984 65(1): 33-40.* Describes the dispute between Iowa governor Buren R. Sherman and the state auditor, John L. Brown, over alleged auditing irregularities, for which Sherman removed Brown from office; the ensuing trial exonerated Brown but effectively ended the political careers of both men. 1885-86

Brown, John Nicholas

860. Brown, Anne S. K. JOHN NICHOLAS BROWN: TRIBUTES FROM THE YOUNG. *Rhode Island Hist. 1981 40(1): 3-15.* Memoir of her husband (1900-79) celebrates John Nicholas Brown's relationship with young people, including god-children, cousins, and others in whom he took an interest in Providence, Rhode Island. Based on the author's recollections and letters in her possession; 26 illus. 1920-79

861. Hammond, Mason. JOHN NICHOLAS BROWN. *Massachusetts Hist. Soc. Pro. 1979 91: 232-234.* Brief memoir of John Nicholas Brown (1900-79) of Rhode Island. Born to great wealth, Brown was educated at Harvard College (Class of 1922) and pursued a life-long career in the "service of scholarship, education, the arts, his church, and public affairs at the local, state, and national levels." Among the institutions supported by Mr. Brown were Harvard, Brown, the Boston Symphony, the Medieval Academy of America, and the Episcopal Church. He married Anna Seddon Kinsolving in 1930. Mr. Brown was a widely admired figure. ca 1918-79

Brown, John Y., Jr.

862. —. JOHN Y. BROWN, JR. *Register of the Kentucky Hist. Soc. 1980 78(2): 95-97.* A biographical sketch of Kentucky's 51st governor, John Y. Brown, Jr. (b. 1933). Brown, a Democrat, was elected to the office in 1979. His prior career included business, civic, and political positions. Illus. ca 1955-80

Brown, M. E. D.

863. Courtney, Rosemary. M. E. D. BROWN (1810-1896): AMERICAN LITHOGRAPHER AND PAINTER. *Am. Art J. 1980 12(4): 66-77.* Mannevillette Elihu Dearing Brown (1810-96) was born in New Hampshire and learned lithography in the William and John Pendleton Shop in Boston in the 1820's. Brown opened a lithography shop in Philadelphia and during 1831-34 produced a number of very fine lithographs of birds, animals, flora, and portraits. After traveling in Europe 1839-49, he settled in Utica, New York, and painted portraits until his death. Primary sources; 15 plates, 29 notes. ca 1828-96

Brown, Margaret Tobin

864. McGinty, Brian. THE IRREPRESSIBLE MOLLY. *Westways 1983 75(2): 48-51.* Brief biography of Margaret Tobin Brown, whose life and actions in Missouri and in the gold mining towns of Colorado formed the basis of the successful Broadway musical, *The Unsinkable Molly Brown.* 1867-1930

Brown, Margaretta Mason

865. Miller, Page Putnam. WOMEN IN THE VANGUARD OF THE SUNDAY SCHOOL MOVEMENT. *J. of Presbyterian Hist. 1980 58(4): 311-325.* 1800-50
*For abstract see **Bethune, Joanna Graham***

Brown, Oliver L.

866. Masters, Isabell. "The Life and Legacy of Oliver Brown, the First Listed Plaintiff of *Brown* vs. *Board of Education,* Topeka, Kansas." U. of Oklahoma 1980. 195 pp. *DAI 1981 42(1): 112-A.* 8113243 1940-61

Brown, Peter

867. Vaudry, Richard W. PETER BROWN, THE TORONTO *BANNER,* AND THE EVANGELICAL MIND IN VICTORIAN CANADA. *Ontario History [Canada] 1985 77(1): 3-18.* Peter Brown was perhaps the most controversial editor in Upper Canada in the 1840's. This was due to his very pronounced religious views, which did not fit into any recognized dogmatic system. Briefly sketches his early life in Scotland and New York, before he went to Toronto, at the invitation of supporters of the Free Church of Scotland and edited the *Banner.* Comments on his more controversial views and the reactions they provoked, and briefly summarizes the rest of his career. Based on files of the Toronto *Banner;* 95 notes. 1840-50

Brown, Philip King

868. Downey, Lynn Alison. PHILIP KING BROWN AND THE AREQUIPA SANATORIUM. *Pacific Historian 1985 29(1): 46-55.* Describes the work of San Francisco physician Philip King Brown, who sought a cure for tuberculosis in a city plagued by poor living conditions following the earthquake and fire of 1906. Brown, who ran the Tuberculosis Polyclinic, was most interested in prevention and treatment of the first stage of tuberculosis. Borrowing many ideas from Edward L. Trudeau of New York, Brown was instrumental in establishing the Arequipa Sanatorium for women near Fairfax, California. From 1911 to 1957, the sanatorium provided bed rest, wholesome food, and exposure to fresh air to the tubercular women. To prevent the degenerating influences of long continued idleness, a variety of occupational therapy programs were instituted over the years. Based on an interview and annual reports of the institution; 7 photos, 10 notes. 1909-40

Brown, Ralph Hall

869. Miles, Linda Jeanne. "Ralph Hall Brown: Gentlescholar of Historical Geography." U. of Oklahoma 1982. 180 pp. *DAI 1982 43(2): 547-548-A.* DA8215913 1920's-48

Brown, Violet Goldsmith

870. Brown, Violet. OVER THE RED DEER: LIFE OF A HOMESTEAD MISSIONARY. *Alberta History [Canada] 1985 33(3): 9-18.* Prints the memoirs of Violet Goldsmith Brown, who arrived in Saskatchewan in 1905, married the Reverend John Brown, who became a Presbyterian minister the next year, and spent the rest of her life as a homesteading missionary. Follows the family's travels and settlement in Saskatchewan, and finally near the Red Deer River in Alberta. Illness and debt plagued the Browns, but farming and hunting in the area provided a fresh food supply. 4 photos. 1905-64

Brown, Wilburt S. "Bigfoot"

871. Simmons, Edwin H. BIGFOOT BROWN. *Marine Corps Gazette 1973 57(9): 18-27.* A biographical account of the military career of the late Major General Wilburt S. Brown (1900-68) of the US Marines. ca 1920-68

Brown, William Carey

872. Mitterling, Doris, comp. and Brennan, John A., ed. GUIDE TO THE WILLIAM CAREY BROWN PAPERS, 1854-1939. *Western Hist. Collections, U. of Colorado Lib. 1978: 1-141.* General William Carey Brown served a long military career, particularly in the Indian wars, in which he specialized in the research and writing of. 1854-1939

Brown, William Wells

873. Falk, Leslie A. BLACK ABOLITIONIST DOCTORS AND HEALERS, 1810-1885. *Bull. of the Hist. of Medicine 1980 54(2): 258-272.* A number of black abolitionist doctors and healers practiced in America during 1810-85. These include James McCune Smith (1811-65), the first American black to obtain a medical degree, David Ruggles (1810-49), an early advocate of hydrotherapy, and William Wells Brown (1816-84), who lectured in England and later practiced medicine in Boston. Others were Harriet Tubman (1820-1913), a nurse and healer, and Sarah Parker Remond (b. 1826), who moved to Rome and practiced medicine there. 61 notes. 1810-85

Brown, Willis

874. Schlossman, Steven L. and Cohen, Ronald D. THE MUSIC MAN IN GARY: WILLIS BROWN AND CHILD-SAVING IN THE PROGRESSIVE ERA. *Societas 1977 7(1): 1-17.* Traces the checkered career of the juvenile reformer Willis Brown, concentrating on 1910-12 in the growing industrial city of Gary, Indiana. Immigration and technological advances created concern about juvenile delinquency. Brown's controversial, and not very successful, solutions "highlighted dangers implict in Progressive child-saving ideology in general... " Based on collections at the Library of Congress, Indiana University, and Cornell University. Primary and secondary sources; 43 notes. 1910-12

Browning, John Moses

875. Golino, Lorenzo. LE ARMI E LE MUNIZIONI DI JOHN MOSES BROWNING [The firearms and munitions of John Moses Browning]. *Riv. Militare [Italy] 1976 99(2): 97-107.* Study in historical and biographical context of firearms invented by John Moses Browning (1855-1926). 1855-1926

Brownlee, John Edward

876. Foster, Franklin Lloyd. "John Edward Brownlee: A Biography." Queen's U. [Canada] 1981. *DAI 1981 42(2): 815-A.* 20c

Brownlow, William Gannaway

877. Conklin, Forrest. PARSON BROWNLOW JOINS THE SONS OF TEMPERANCE (PART II). *Tennessee Hist. Q. 1980 39(3): 292-309.* Continued from the previous article. William Gannaway Brownlow's leadership in the Sons of Temperance during the 1850's gave him a base of public recognition for his east Tennessee political career. He opportunistically advocated liquor control during lulls in the political issues. For its part, the temperance movement benefited from his fine organization and oratory. Based on material in the Knoxville *Whig* and other sources; 34 notes. 1851-67

878. Conklin, Forrest. PARSON BROWNLOW JOINS THE SONS OF TEMPERANCE (PART I). *Tennessee Hist. Q. 1980 39(2): 178-194.* William Gannaway "Parson" Brownlow (1805-77) was a Methodist minister who became editor of *The Whig* (Knoxville) in 1838, and forsook his traveling ministry. At this time, efforts for greater liquor control were developing. One of the sources for temperance reform was the temperance societies. Brownlow carried on the fight for reform in the columns of his paper and in 1851 engaged in verbal debate over the issue. Largely material from the Knoxville and the Jonesboro *Whig;* 50 notes. Article to be continued. 1838-51

879. Kelly, James C. WILLIAM GANNAWAY BROWNLOW. *Tennessee Historical Quarterly 1984 43(1): 25-43, (2): 155-172.* Part 1. William Gannaway Brownlow was born in Virginia in 1805 and became a preacher after being deeply affected by a camp meeting in 1825. Brownlow proved "to have an unexcelled talent for ridicule and invective," and acquired "a reputation for pugnacity, eloquence, and ugliness." He became the first editor of the *Tennessee Whig* newspaper in 1839 and later moved his paper to Knoxville, where it became the *Knoxville Whig* and achieved a circulation that equalled all other East Tennessee newspapers combined. Brownlow became involved in state politics and engaged in "wholesale abuse of individuals in language of unparalleled severity." Although he was proslavery, he opposed secession. Part 2. Brownlow's *Whig* was the only newspaper in the Confederacy in June 1861 that opposed the existence of a Confederate government, and it met with broad support in East Tennessee, where most residents were opposed to the Confederacy. Making his way to federally controlled Nashville and later to Ohio, Brownlow became a celebrity and something of a hero. His 1862 book *Sketches of the Rise, Progress, and Decline of Secession,* later to become known simply as *Parson Brownlow's Book,* became a best-seller, and Brownlow toured the North making speeches of a patriotic nature. After the Civil War, Brownlow became governor of Tennessee, which embroiled him in Reconstruction politics, and later a United States senator. 4 illus., 137 notes. 1825-77

Brownson, Henry Francis

880. Ryan, Thomas R. A MEMOIR OF HENRY FRANCIS BROWNSON. *Records of the Am. Catholic Hist. Soc. of Philadelphia 1976 87(1-4): 51-63.* Relatively little is known of Henry Francis Brownson (1835-1900), one of Orestes A. Brownson's sons, editor of his works, and one of the outstanding Catholic laymen of his day. Supplements the account in the *National Cyclopedia of American Biography.* 29 notes. 1835-1900

Brownson, Orestes A.

881. Barcus, James E. STRUCTURING THE RAGE WITHIN: THE SPIRITUAL AUTOBIOGRAPHIES OF NEWMAN AND ORESTES BROWNSON. *Cithara 1975 15(1): 45-57.* John Henry Newman and Orestes A. Brownson were noted 19th-century Protestants who converted to Roman Catholicism. Each wrote an autobiography which defended his change of religion. Newman's *Apologia pro Vita Sua* (1864) and Brownson's *The Convert* (1857) show many parallels, including a sense of inner rage. 1857-64

882. McDaniel, Isaac. ORESTES A. BROWNSON ON IRISH IMMIGRANTS AND AMERICAN NATIVISM. *Am. Benedictine Rev. 1981 32(2): 122-139.* Analyzes how Orestes A. Brownson, who converted to Catholicism in October 1844, attempted to resolve the issue of ethnicity and pluralism in mid-19th-century America. He had to defend his right to be Catholic against native Americans, and his right to be American against Irish Catholic immigrants. 31 notes. 1844-76

Bruce, John Edward

883. Crowder, Ralph L. JOHN EDWARD BRUCE: PIONEER BLACK NATIONALIST. *Afro-Americans in New York Life and Hist. 1978 2(2): 47-66.* In many newspaper and scholarly articles, 1874-1924, black activist John Edward Bruce (1856-1924) advocated black nationalism (which entailed rejection of Americanism), economic independence, self-help, and racial solidarity. 1874-1924

Brumder, George (family)

884. Mallman, Sharon M. THE BRUMDERS OF MILWAUKEE. *Milwaukee Hist. 1980 3(3): 66-79.* Traces the history of the Brumder family of Milwaukee, particularly of George and Henriette Brumder, who founded a bookstore and publishing business which became the country's largest and most influential German-language publishing business, and whose legacy has remained in Milwaukee and Wisconsin; 1839-1980. 1839-1980

Bruml, Moses

885. Bruml, Moses. FROM A POLISH TOWN TO GOLD RUSH CALIFORNIA. *Western States Jewish Hist. 1984 17(1): 91-94.* Presents the memoirs of Moses Bruml, a merchant in Lockeford, California. Deals primarily with Bruml's immigration to America and early years in the country, 1849-57. The essay was written in 1900, one year before Bruml's death. 7 notes. 1823-69

Brundage, Avery

886. Guttmann, Allen. THE GAMES MUST GO ON: ON THE ORIGINS OF AVERY BRUNDAGE'S LIFE CREDO. *Stadion [West Germany] 1979 5(2): 253-262.* Avery Brundage's career in business disposed him to see amateur sports as a model of fair play and objective achievement. His own participation in the 1912 Olympics left him persuaded that

Olympism was a secular religion, a moral alternative to the sordidly materialistic world of business and politics. Based on documents from the Brundage Archives and secondary material, 25 notes. 1912-73

Brunet, Michel

887. Brunet, Michel. MES ANNEES DE FORMATION, LE REVISIONNISME DE LA DECENNIE DE 1950 ET MES ENGAGEMENTS [My educational years, revisionism of the 1950's, and my responsibilities]. *Action Nationale [Canada] 1985 74(10): 989-995.* Prints personal reflections of Michel Brunet on his career as a historian, his activities concerning the 1950's conflict between British and French Canadians, his administrative responsibilities as head of the history department at the University of Montreal, the end of his administrative career in 1967, and his career as a researcher and speaker since 1968. 1952-78

Brunk, Henry L.

888. Martin, Jerry Lavern. "Henry L. Brunk and Brunk's Comedians: Tent Repertoire Empire of the Southwest." Texas Tech U. 1981. 340 pp. *DAI 1981 42(4): 1355-A.* 8121894 1921-60

Brünnow, Franz F. E.

889. Plotkin, Howard. HENRY TAPPAN, FRANZ BRÜNNOW, AND THE FOUNDING OF THE ANN ARBOR SCHOOL OF ASTRONOMERS, 1852-1863. *Ann. of Sci. [Great Britain] 1980 37(3): 287-302.* Through the combined efforts of Henry P. Tappan (1805-1881) and Franz F. E. Brünnow (1821-91), the University of Michigan played a major role in the training of professional astronomers in the United States during the second half of the nineteenth century. Tappan, the university's first president, was a firm adherent of the Prussian system of education, and endeavored to transform Michigan into a distinguished institution modeled on the German university ideal. One of the keys to his success was Brünnow, who was lured to Ann Arbor from Berlin. Brünnow became the first director of the university's new observatory, and taught advanced classes in practical and theoretical astronomy based on the mathematically rigorous German method. He strongly believed that the training of future professional astronomers was as important as his own research. As a result, he forged the first link in a continuous chain of astronomers trained in the German method at Michigan, a group now known as the Ann Arbor school of astronomers. 63 notes, appendix. 1852-63

Brunson, Alfred

890. Schulte, Steven C. ALFRED BRUNSON AND THE WISCONSIN MISSIONARY FRONTIER. *Methodist Hist. 1981 19(4): 231-237.* Alfred Brunson became a Methodist preacher in 1810. After serving in the War of 1812, he started to ride a circuit in western Pennylvania and Ohio. In 1835 he proposed that the church found an Indian mission in Wisconsin. Brunson accepted the invitation to become one of the missionaries. He helped in many ways to help build the American Methodist Church and to carry civilization into the wildernesses of the United States. Based upon the writings of Brunson and his papers in the State Historical Society of Wisconsin; 32 notes. 1793-1883

Bryan, Daniel

891. Studer, Wayne Malcolm. "The Frustrated Muse: The Life and Works of Daniel Bryan, c. 1790-1866." U. of Minnesota 1984. 353 pp. *DAI 1985 45(12): 3641-A.* DA8503104 1790-1866

Bryan, Hugh

892. Jackson, Harvey. THE CAROLINA CONNECTION: JONATHAN BRYAN, HIS BROTHERS, AND THE FOUNDING OF GEORGIA, 1733-1752. *Georgia Hist. Q. 1984 68(2): 147-172.* 1733-52
For abstract see ***Bryan, Jonathan***

Bryan, Jonathan

893. Jackson, Harvey. THE CAROLINA CONNECTION: JONATHAN BRYAN, HIS BROTHERS, AND THE FOUNDING OF GEORGIA, 1733-1752. *Georgia Hist. Q. 1984 68(2): 147-172.* Discusses the role of South Carolinians Jonathan Bryan and his older brothers Joseph and Hugh in the founding and early days of the Georgia colony. 46 notes. 1733-52

Bryan, Joseph

894. Jackson, Harvey. THE CAROLINA CONNECTION: JONATHAN BRYAN, HIS BROTHERS, AND THE FOUNDING OF GEORGIA, 1733-1752. *Georgia Hist. Q. 1984 68(2): 147-172.* 1733-52
For abstract see ***Bryan, Jonathan***

Bryan, William Jennings

895. Coletta, Paolo E. WILL THE REAL PROGRESSIVE STAND UP? WILLIAM JENNINGS BRYAN AND THEODORE ROOSEVELT TO 1909. *Nebraska Hist. 1984 65(1): 15-57.* Examines how Progressive principles influenced the careers of Bryan and Roosevelt. Based on the William Jennings Bryan and Theodore Roosevelt papers; 6 illus., 116 notes. 1890-1909

Bryant, Abraham (family)

896. Lainhart, Ann S. THE DESCENDANTS OF ABRAHAM BRYANT OF READING. *New England Hist. and Geneal. Register 1983 137(July): 235-259, (Oct): 317-339.* Part 1. Little information beyond the third generation has been published to date about the descendants of Abraham Bryant. He was probably born in England and died on 6 July 1720 in Reading, Massachusetts. Considerable material on the life and activities of Abraham, his three wives, five children, many grandchildren and beyond is included in this genealogy. Part 2. Traces nine third-generation sons. All presumably born in Reading, Massachusetts, none moved far afield, although one died in Jaffrey, New Hampshire. The records are extensive and reflective of the life of the period. 17c-19c

Bryant, John Howard

897. Berfield, Karen. THREE ANTISLAVERY LEADERS OF BUREAU COUNTY. *Western Illinois Regional Studies 1980 3(1): 46-65.* Discusses the abolitionist activities of Owen Lovejoy, from 1837 to his death in 1864, John Howard Bryant, active from the 1840's to his death in 1862, and his nephew, Julian Bryant (1836-65), a commander of black soldiers in the Civil War, all of Bureau County, Illinois. 1831-65

Bryant, Julian

898. Berfield, Karen. JULIAN BRYANT: MARTYR FOR EQUALITY. *Civil War Times Illus. 1983 22(2): 36-41.* Chronicles the Civil War career of Julian Bryant, nephew of abolitionist William Cullen Bryant, and a distinguished officer of black troops in the Union army during 1863-65. 1863-65

899. Berfield, Karen. THREE ANTISLAVERY LEADERS OF BUREAU COUNTY. *Western Illinois Regional Studies 1980 3(1): 46-65.* 1831-65
*For abstract see **Bryant, John Howard***

Bryant, William Cullen

900. Baxter, David J. WILLIAM CULLEN BRYANT: ILLINOIS LANDOWNER. *Western Illinois Regional Studies 1978 1(1): 1-14.* William Cullen Bryant, editor of the *New York Review and Atheneum Magazine* (1825-26) and editor of the *New York Evening Post* (1829-78), was interested in settlement of the West, particularly Illinois, where he invested in land and made periodic visits in the mid-19th century. 19c

901. Ferguson, Robert A. WILLIAM CULLEN BRYANT: THE CREATIVE CONTEXT OF THE POET. *New England Q. 1980 53(4): 431-463.* American poet William Cullen Bryant wrote his most creative verse during 1811-25, when he was a student and a lawyer. He felt it his duty to society to be actively engaged in a worldly profession rather than being a man of letters exclusively. The petty quarrels he engaged in daily in his profession gave him a distaste for law. His poetry, which borrows from the English Romantics, contrasts nature with the ceaseless activity of city life. The conflicts Bryant faced in his years as a lawyer instilled his poetry with creative tension which was missing in his poetry written after 1825, when he assumed the comparably serene position of editor of New York's *Evening Post.* 68 notes. 1811-25

Brzezinski, Zbigniew

902. Colard, Daniel. ZBIGNIEW BRZEZINSKI, LE CONSIELLER SPECIAL "VENU DU FROID" [Zbigniew Brzezinski, the adviser "who came in from the cold"]. *Défense Natl. [France] 1978 34(3): 77-87.* Biographical sketch of President Jimmy Carter's national security adviser; focuses on the "Brzezinski doctrine," which seeks world peace through the institutionalization of American alliances. 1966-78

Buck, Alfred Eliab

903. Bhurtel, Shyam Krishan. "Alfred Eliab Buck: Carpetbagger in Alabama and Georgia." Auburn U. 1981. 283 pp. *DAI 1982 42(10): 4552-A.* DA8205642 1867-1902

Buck, Paul Herman

904. Schlesinger, Arthur M., Jr. PAUL HERMAN BUCK. *Massachusetts Hist. Soc. Pro. 1979 91: 217-220.* Memoir of Paul Herman Buck (1899-1978), historian. Born in Ohio, Buck was educated at Ohio State University and Harvard (PhD 1935). His long career at Harvard began in 1938 and continued until his death. His publications included *The Road to Reunion, 1865-1900* (1937), and the history of the Old South remained his teaching speciality. Buck served an extremely important role as provost of Harvard from 1945 to 1953, and was Director of the University Library from 1955 to 1964. His book on *Libraries and Universities* (1964) remains a standard work. ca 1920-78

Buckingham, Joseph Tinker

905. Tawa, Nicholas. BUCKINGHAM'S MUSICAL COMMENTARIES IN BOSTON. *New England Q. 1978 51(3): 333-347.* Sketches the life of Joseph Tinker Buckingham (1779-1861) and analyzes his writings on current musical events, particularly writings which appeared in *The Polyanthos* (1806-07, 1812-14), *The New-England Galaxy* (1817-28), and *The New England Magazine* (1831-34), all of which he controlled. Buckingham believed music "to be a recreative necessity for all humanity and a conduit to morality and civilized pleasure." It has, he believed, a power to move the listener and any artist aiming only to entertain was criticized. His music criticism on this and other grounds led to many arguments with musicians but his ideas influenced music in Boston for the entire century. Based on Buckingham's memoirs and other writings; 34 notes. 1806-34

Buckner, Lewis S.

906. Rabun, Josette Hensley and Blakemore, Robbie G. LEWIS S. BUCKNER, BLACK ARTISAN (C. 1856-1924) OF SEVIERVILLE, TENNESSEE. *Tennessee Folklore Soc. Bull. 1982 48(1): 1-10.* Biography of cabinetmaker and carpenter Lewis S. Buckner (ca. 1856-1924), with photographs of some of his work. ca 1856-1924

Buckner, Simon Bolivar

907. Graybar, Lloyd J. THE BUCKNERS OF KENTUCKY. *Filson Club Hist. Q. 1984 58(2): 202-218.* Describes the military careers of Simon Bolivar Buckner, Sr., and Simon Bolivar Buckner, Jr. The elder Buckner was a West Point graduate, served in the Mexican War, was a Confederate general, and was elected governor of Kentucky in 1887. His son, also a West Point graduate and a general in World War II, was killed on Okinawa in 1945. Secondary sources; 2 photos, 35 notes. 1844-1945

908. Harrison, Lowell. SIMON BOLIVAR BUCKNER: A PROFILE. *Civil War Times Illus. 1978 16(10): 37-45.* Simon Buckner (1823-1914) attended West Point, taught there, fought in the Mexican War, and had a business career. Discusses his command in Kentucky; also the surrender of Fort Donelson. Buckner was a prisoner of war, and again upon exchange, commanded in Kentucky and the District of the Gulf. He was with Bragg at Chickamauga and became second in command for the Trans-Mississippi theater. Discusses Buckner's postwar career, including his term as governor of Kentucky. 1861-63

Buell, Charles

909. Whitley, Patricia Rice. "Dr. Charles Buell: Leader in Physical Education for the Visually Impaired." U. of North Carolina, Greensboro 1980. 227 pp. *DAI 1981 42(2): 602-603.* 8114887 1938-74

Buenger, Theodore Arthur

910. Buenger, Theodore Arthur; Buenger, Richard E., transl. AUTOBIOGRAPHY OF THEODORE ARTHUR BUENGER 1886-1957. *Concordia Hist. Inst. Q. 1980 53(3): 98-116.* Autobiography of Theodore Arthur Buenger, son of a German Lutheran minister in Illinois; he was a student at

Concordia Seminary in St. Louis, and later a minister himself, preaching in German to his largely German-speaking congregations; covers 1886-1909. 1886-1909

Buffalo Bill

See Cody, William F.

Bufford, John Henry

911. Tatham, David. JOHN HENRY BUFFORD: AMERICAN LITHOGRAPHER. *Pro. of the Am. Antiquarian Soc. 1976 86(1): 47-74.* John Henry Bufford was a successful lithograph artist, a major printer and publisher of prints, and a teacher of notable American artists (including Winslow Homer). Only one other person, Nathaniel Currier, had a longer association with lithography. After the Civil War, with the introduction of new processes of pictorial reproduction, Bufford and other lithographers struggled to survive. Unlike Currier and Ives, Bufford was unable to create lasting myths through his prints. Based on primary and secondary sources; 12 illus., 39 notes. 1810-70

Buhler, Augustus Waldeck

912. Butler, Joyce. AUGUSTUS WALDECK BUHLER: THE ARTIST AS HISTORIAN. *Log of Mystic Seaport 1985 37(2): 62-69.* Surveys the career of Augustus Waldeck Buhler, who painted the coast, the sea, and the local fishermen around his summer home on the Cape Ann peninsula in Massachusetts with an insistence on accuracy and authenticity. 1885-1920

Bulkley, Robert J.

913. Jenkins, William D. ROBERT BULKELY: PROGRESSIVE PROFILE. *Ohio Hist. 1979 88(1): 57-72.* Within the broad mainstream of progressivism stood Democratic Congressman Robert J. Bulkley. During his two terms in the House he became a recognized authority on banking and helped frame two important pieces of legislation; The Federal Reserve Act, (US, 1913) and the Federal Farm Loan Act (US, 1916). Influenced by courses studied at Harvard, Bulkley was interested in problems of the inner city. He was in sympathy with using the state as a protector of the poor, the laborer and the child. However, he was a moderate in matters of government and held a liberal stance toward social welfare, antitrust, and tariff legislation. Photo, 54 notes, ref. 1906-30

Bull, Ole

914. Bull, Inez Stewart. "Ole Bull's Activities in the United States between 1843 and 1880." New York U. 1979. 186 pp. *DAI 1979 40(3): 1139-A.* 1843-80

Bull, Willie

915. Blaine, Charles G. WILLIE BULL AT HARVARD. *Newport Hist. 1981 54(3): 64-79.* Discusses the adventures and ensuing disciplinary action over the antics of Newport resident Willie Bull (William Tillinghast Bull, M.D., 1849-1909) while a student at Harvard College, based on correspondence between Willie's parents, Thomas Hill, President of Harvard College, and Willie, and newspaper articles describing his troublemaking, 1865-68. 1865-68

Bullard, Arthur

916. Vaughn, Stephen. ARTHUR BULLARD AND THE CREATION OF THE COMMITTEE ON PUBLIC INFORMATION. *New Jersey Hist. 1979 97(1): 45-53.* Arthur Bullard, a journalist and novelist in the muckraking tradition, was probably more instrumental in creating the Committee on Public Information (CPI), the major US propaganda organ during World War I, than either President Wilson's cabinet or George Creel, another journalist and the CPI's first chairman. Bullard's general writings reflected the philosophy of the CPI. His book, *Mobilizing America,* was scrutinized closely by Colonel Edward Mandell House before the war. It is almost certain that House passed on Bullard's thoughts to Wilson. In effect, Bullard argued that the United States should make the world safe for democracy. In the zeal of trying to accomplish this ideal, American liberties may have been jeopardized. Based on Bullard's papers, CPI records, and secondary sources; 27 notes. 1917-18

Bullins, Ed

917. Andrews, W. D. E. THEATER OF BLACK REALITY: THE BLUES DRAMA OF ED BULLINS. *Southwest Rev. 1980 65(2): 178-190.* Discusses the work of Ed Bullins, one of the major black playwrights of the 1960's, and his concern as a dramatist with the tensions in a life-pattern seen as uniquely black. 1960-70

918. Mayo, Sandra. ED BULLINS, NEW YORK'S RESIDENT BLACK DRAMATIST. *Afro-Americans in New York Life and Hist. 1981 5(2): 51-57.* Discusses the accomplishments of Ed Bullins, "the most prolific Black playwright of the sixties and seventies," 1967-80. 1967-80

Bullitt, William C.

919. Stam, A. WILLIAM C. BULLITT, EEN AMERIKAANSE DIPLOMAAT [William C. Bullitt, an American diplomat]. *Spiegel Hist. [Netherlands] 1981 16(2): 77-82.* The career of William C. Bullitt spanned two world wars and diplomatic service under Woodrow Wilson and Franklin D. Roosevelt, 1917-43. Bullitt's strong views, particularly with regard to the USSR, brought him into sharp conflict with both presidents. Primary sources; 6 illus. 1917-43

Bullock, Wynn

920. Dilley, Clyde Hobson. "The Photography and Philosophy of Wynn Bullock." U. of New Mexico 1980. 168 pp. *DAI 1980 41(5): 1815-A.* 8025026 1921-73

Bulosan, Aurelio

921. Chow, Christopher. A BROTHER REFLECTS: AN INTERVIEW WITH AURELIO BULOSAN. *Amerasia J. 1979 6(1): 155-166.* Transcript of an interview with Aurelio Bulosan conducted on 25 May 1978. Provides an insight into the life of a Filipino immigrant in the United States and to his relationship with his brother Carlos Bulosan. 1904-78

Bulosan, Carlos

922. Bulosan, Carlos. SELECTED LETTERS OF CARLOS BULOSAN 1937-1955. *Amerasia J. 1979 6(1): 143-154.* Segments of 27 letters written by author Carlos Bulosan provide insight into Bulosan's thinking and the difficulty of being a Filipino in America. The letters were selected from

Dolores S. Feria, ed., *Sound of Falling Light: Letters in Exile* (1960) and from the Carlos Bulosan Papers, University of Washington Archives, Seattle, Washington. 1937-55

923. Evangelista, Susan P. CARLOS BULOSAN AND THIRD WORLD CONSCIOUSNESS. *Philippine Studies [Philippines] 1982 30(1): 44-58.* Examines the life and literary works of Carlos Bulosan. Bulosan's experiences as a migrant worker in California, after emigrating from the Philippines, were articulated in his writings. They help illuminate a critical period (1929-54) in Filipino-American history, during which the new immigrants were relegated to the lowest rung on the socioeconomic ladder and were vulnerable to severe exploitation until their social status improved after World War II. Bulosan's prose and poetry are distinguished by a bitter social realism and an identification with colonized and oppressed people, an attitude today commonly called a third world consciousness. 15 notes. 1929-54

924. SanJuan, E., Jr. CARLOS BULOSAN: AN INTRODUCTION. *Asian & Pacific Q. of Cultural and Social Affairs [South Korea] 1978 10(2): 43-48.* Carlos Bulosan (1913-56) emigrated from the Philippines to the United States in 1931. His dreams of a better life under American democracy soon crumbled before the presence of repressive monopoly capitalism and the Great Depression years. Moving progressively to the left, Bulosan actively contributed to the expanding labor movement in the 1930's. His literary works embody the twin Marxist goals of criticizing bourgeois culture and creating a proletarian literary tradition. Secondary sources; 2 notes. 1931-56

Burbank, Luther

925. Glass, Bentley. THE STRANGE ENCOUNTER OF LUTHER BURBANK AND GEORGE HARRISON SHULL. *Pro. of the Am. Phil. Soc. 1980 124(2): 133-153.* Although he received several grants from the Carnegie Institute of Washington, Luther Burbank's status as a scientist was questioned by many of his contemporaries. George Harrison Shull, delegated by the Institute to examine the substance and methods of Burbank's work, reported on them in 1906. The previously unpublished, lengthy report gives a recently trained PhD's sympathetic but honest reaction to Burbank's unprofessional scientific methodology. Based on the Shull Papers and the C. B. Davenport Papers (Library, American Philosophical Society), annual *Yearbook* of the Carnegie Institution and numerous secondary articles on Burbank; 58 notes. 1887-1914

Burch, Selina

926. Devereux, Sean. THE REBEL IN ME. *Southern Exposure 1976 4(1-2): 4-15.* Interviews Selina Burch on her labor organizing with the Communications Workers of America, 1945-73. 1945-73

Burdette, Clara

927. Miller, Dorothy Grace. "Within the Bounds of Propriety: Clara Burdette and the Women's Movement." U. of California, Riverside 1984. 243 pp. *DAI 1985 45(12): 3729-A.* DA8504785 1893-1920's

Burger, Warren E.

928. Buckner, Kermit George. "An Analysis of Chief Justice Burger's Influence in Supreme Court Cases Affecting Public Education." U. of North Carolina, Greensboro 1980. 256 pp. *DAI 1980 41(4): 1292-A.* 8021768 1969-78

Burgess, William Hubert

929. Kurutz, Gary. "CALIFORNIA IS QUITE A DIFFERENT PLACE NOW": THE GOLD RUSH LETTERS AND SKETCHES OF WILLIAM HUBERT BURGESS. *California Hist. Q. 1977 56(3): 210-229.* Describes the career of William Hubert Burgess (1825-93), artist, jeweler, sportsman, inventor, and Gold Rush prospector. Burgess emigrated from England with his brothers during the Gold Rush era. He arrived in California in 1850 and, until 1858, made repeated trips to the gold fields. Besides prospecting, which achieved little result, Burgess wrote letters home and made sketches of his experiences. Burgess found little romanticism in the Gold Rush; he noted the gambling, brutality, and environmental destruction. He carried firearms as self-protection. An avid sportsman, he condemned the felling of the big trees and polluting of the streams. After 1858, he embarked on a career as an art teacher, author, and inventor in the San Francisco Bay area. Based on the letters and sketches of Burgess, whose papers were recently donated to the California Historical Society Library; illus. 1850-93

Burgesser, William Slater

930. Vining, James W. SLATER BURGESSER AND HIS FAMOUS SPRING. *Western Illinois Regional Studies 1982 5(2): 184-195.* Discusses the life and career of William Slater Burgesser, 1853-1927, proprietor of the Burgesser Mineral Springs Farm of Brown County, Illinois. 1853-1927

Burgwyn, Anna Greenough

931. Davis, Archibald Kimbrough. THE LADY FROM BOSTON. *Massachusetts Hist. Soc. Pro. 1979 91: 67-85.* Anna Greenough of Boston married Henry King Burgwyn of New Bern, North Carolina, in 1838 and had to adjust to slavery and other aspects of the antebellum South. Burgwyn Family Papers at the University of North Carolina Library, and other sources; 46 notes. 1838-65

Burk, Martha Jane Cannary

932. Bachs, Agustí. CALAMITY JANE. [Calamity Jane]. *Hist. y Vida [Spain] 1984 17(190): 64-78.* Presents a brief biography of Martha Jane Cannary "Calamity Jane" Burk, with reference to purportedly autobiographical materials. 1852-ca 1900

Burke, Edward A.

933. Vivian, James F. MAJOR E. A. BURKE: THE HONDURAS EXILE, 1889-1928. *Louisiana Hist. 1974 15(2): 175-194.* Describes the largely fruitless investment in money and time in gold mining operations in the Honduras made by Louisiana-born Edward A. Burke, 1889-1928. 1889-1928

Burke, Thomas

934. Watterson, John S. THOMAS BURKE, PARADOXICAL PATRIOT. *Historian 1979 41(4): 664-681.* Thomas Burke, delegate to the Continental Congress (1777-81) and later governor of North Carolina (1781-82), has been a puzzling figure in Revolutionary historiography. Traces Burke's ideological transformation, matched by a complex personal background, from an idealist in 1776 with a commitment to republican ideology, to a pragmatic nationalist in 1783 with a distrust of popular government. Primary sources; 66 notes. 1776-83

Burke, Yvonne Brathwaite

935. Elliot, Jeffrey M. THE CONGRESSIONAL BLACK CAUCUS: AN INTERVIEW WITH YVONNE BRATHWAITE BURKE. *Negro Hist. Bull. 1977 40(1): 650-652.* Outlines the legal and political career of Burke since 1956 and the functions of the Congressional Black Caucus since its formation in 1971. 1956-77

Burkhart, Emerson

936. Barsotti, John. "PICTURE PAINTER, COLUMBUS, OHIO": A REMINISCENCE OF EMERSON BURKHART. *Timeline 1984-85 1(2): 20-28.* Profiles artist Emerson Burkhart and illustrates examples of his paintings. 1930's-69

Burlingame, Anson

937. Anderson, David L. ANSON BURLINGAME: REFORMER AND DIPLOMAT. *Civil War Hist. 1979 25(4): 293-308.* Anson Burlingame skyrocketed from Michigan frontiersman to Massachusetts Free-Soil stalwart and state senator. As US Representative from 1854, he wielded wide, effective Republican leadership. For that support, President Lincoln appointed him minister to China. Burlingame's personality, oratory, optimism, sensitivity, and boldness in furthering democracy helped him accomplish more than his more gifted rivals. These talents also caused him to grasp China's need for cooperative support in internal and external (diplomatic) reform and to carry through soundly and brilliantly. Proof was his appointment as first imperial envoy to the West, 1867-69. Based on family papers, State Department China Dispatches, and other sources; 56 notes. 1854-69

Burnett, Henry Cornelius

938. Craig, Berry F. HENRY CORNELIUS BURNETT: CHAMPION OF SOUTHERN RIGHTS. *Register of the Kentucky Hist. Soc. 1979 77(4): 266-274.* Henry Cornelius Burnett, representative from Kentucky's first District, worked hard to get Kentucky to secede. Failing ultimately, he did all he could to aid the South, raising troops, leading efforts to block war legislation, and helping in other ways. Expelled from Congress in 1861, he joined the Confederate Army briefly before becoming a member of the Confederate Senate. Later he was charged with treason, but he was never tried. 49 notes. 1860-66

Burnett, Leander

939. Thomas, David and Thomas, Marc. LEANDER BURNETT. *Michigan History 1986 70(1): 12-15.* Leander Burnett, an American Indian from Harbor Springs, Michigan, earned nine varsity letters at Michigan State College during 1888-92 and has been called Michigan State College's "first bona fide athletic hero." Unlike many college athletic heroes of today, Burnett did not reap financial rewards after college and died of pneumonia at the age of 38. Based on interviews and secondary sources; 6 illus., 14 notes. 1868-1906

Burnham, Daniel Hudson

940. Wolner, Edward Wallace. "Daniel Burnham and the Tradition of the City Builder in Chicago: Technique, Ambition and City Planning." New York U. 1977. 343 pp. *DAI 1977 38(4): 2215-A.* 1835-1909

Burns, Bill

941. Kuyek, Joan and Burns, Bill. WORKING FOR MA BELL. *Can. Dimension [Canada] 1979 14(3): 29-31.* Bill Burns recounts his work for Bell Canada, 1963-79, emphasizing the deterioration of the quality of telephone system components and of repair and installation service. 1963-79

Burns, Lucy

942. Bland, Sidney R. "NEVER QUITE AS COMMITTED AS WE'D LIKE": THE SUFFRAGE MILITANCY OF LUCY BURNS. *J. of Long Island Hist. 1981 17(2): 4-23.* Describes the suffrage career of Lucy Burns of Brooklyn, who served as "chief organizer, lobby head, newspaper editor, suffrage educator and teacher, orator, architect of the banner campaign, [and] rallying force and symbol" for the Congressional Union and its successor, the National Woman's Party, during 1913-19. Based on correspondence, newspapers, and other primary and secondary sources; 2 photos, 81 notes. 1908-19

Burns, Milton J.

943. Falk, Peter Hastings. MILTON J. BURNS, MARINE ARTIST. *Log of Mystic Seaport 1984 36(1): 15-30.* Describes the career of Milton J. Burns, an artist and magazine illustrator who specialized in marine subjects. 1869-1930's

Burns, Thomas D.

944. Torrez, Robert J. "EL BORNES": LA TIERRA AMARILLA AND T. D. BURNS. *New Mexico Hist. Rev. 1981 56(2): 161-175.* The development and direction of the area of northern New Mexico known as la Tierra Amarilla between 1865 and 1916 was influenced by Thomas D. Burns (1844-1916), a successful businessman and politician, more than any other individual. Burns, who became wealthy through his mercantile business and land holdings, was also a powerful political figure in New Mexico. Burns made significant contributions to the development of the railroad, banking, lumber, and ranching industries of the state. Despite these achievements, many people in northern New Mexico have a negative view of Burns because of his involvement in the loss of the Tierra Amarilla Land Grant. Primary sources; photo, 53 notes. 1865-1916

Burnside, Ambrose E.

945. Cullen, Joseph P. "THE VERY *BEAU IDEAL* OF A SOLDIER": A PERSONALITY PROFILE OF AMBROSE E. BURNSIDE. *Civil War Times Illus. 1977 16(5): 4-10, 38-44.* Reviews the Civil War career of Union General Ambrose E. Burnside. Burnside was a civilian graduate of West Point when the war began. His unfailing honesty, dislike of intrigue, and unwillingness to blame subordinates for his own mistakes made him popular. He was rapidly promoted to commander of the Army of the Potomac, a position he neither sought nor wanted. He lacked confidence; his battles were uniformly disastrous; and President Lincoln finally had to remove him from command. 12 photos. 1861-65

946. Tenney, Craig Davidson. "Major General A. E. Burnside and the First Amendment: A Case Study of Civil War Freedom of Expression." Indiana U. 1977. 288 pp. *DAI 1977 38(4): 2311-2312-A.* 1863

947. Thomas, Donna. AMBROSE E. BURNSIDE AND ARMY REFORM, 1850-1881. *Rhode Island Hist. 1978 37(1): 3-13.* Ambrose E. Burnside, a West Point graduate (1847), showed an early interest in reform. As a Senator (1875-81) he was a leading figure in the unsuccessful struggle for military reform. Based on manuscripts in the Rhode Island Historical Society, Providence, published documents, and secondary accounts; 6 illus., 47 notes. 1850-81

Burr, Aaron

948. Geissler, Suzanne B. AARON BURR, JR.: DARLING OF THE PRESBYTERIANS. *J. of Presbyterian Hist. 1978 56(2): 134-147.* Although both his maternal grandfather (Jonathan Edwards) and his father (Aaron Burr, Sr.) had been presidents of the College of New Jersey (Princeton), and thus much was anticipated and expected of him, Aaron Burr, Jr. (1756-1836) never lived up to the hopes which his family and friends held out for him. His prestigious background made him "that darling of the Presbyterians." He was never able to be himself. His ancestry provided him with fame, connections, and a good many votes in the political arena and he ran for President in 1800; however it also provided him with a reputation impossible to live up to, dooming him to a lifetime of comparisons to his illustrious forebears. Secondary sources; illus., 64 notes. 1772-1805

949. Harrison, Lowell H. THE AARON BURR CONSPIRACY. *Am. Hist. Illus. 1978 13(3): 16-25.* Aaron Burr (1756-1836) was born in Newark, New Jersey, graduated from Princeton, and was state attorney-general and US Senator before becoming Vice-President in 1800. He challenged Alexander Hamilton for the top legal position in New York City in 1783; that rivalry ended in an infamous duel years later. Faced by indictments in New York and New Jersey, Burr purchased 350,000 acres on the Washita River and organized an expedition to settle it. Covertly, he considered taking Spanish-held Baton Rouge and New Orleans, possibly to use the latter as a base for a sea invasion of Mexico. Betrayed by a coconspirator, James Wilkinson, Burr was arrested and taken to Richmond for trial. Thomas Jefferson pushed the prosecution, but Wilkinson proved a poor witness as his involvement with Burr became apparent. Presiding Judge John Marshall's interpretation of treason as requiring an overt act (rather than just advising treason) made possible the exclusion of most collateral testimony, and Burr's acquittal followed. Primary and secondary sources; 12 illus. 1783-1836

950. Shneidman, J. Lee and Levine-Shneidman, Conalee. SUICIDE OR MURDER? THE BURR-HAMILTON DUEL. *J. of Psychohistory 1980 8(2): 159-181.* The traditional interpretation of the duel between Alexander Hamilton and Aaron Burr in July 1804 is that Burr was angry with Hamilton because of the latter's role in his defeat in the New York gubernatorial election of 1801. This paper provides a psychohistory of the two, suggesting that Hamilton's own lack of self-esteem led to the duel, which can then be seen as an act of suicide. Presented at the International Psychohistorical Association Convention, New York City, 1980. Primary sources; 86 notes. 1750-1804

951. Swindler, William F. VICTIM OR VILLAIN?: THE TRIALS OF AARON BURR. *Supreme Court Hist. Soc. Y. 1978: 18-24.* Briefly traces the life of Aaron Burr, focusing on his schemes in the Old Southwest and the resulting treason trial. 1782-1836

Burr, Esther

952. Crumpacker, Laurie. "Esther Burr's Journal 1754-1757: A Document of Evangelical Sisterhood." Boston U. Grad. School 1978. 444 pp. *DAI 1978 38(12): 7331-A.* 1754-57

Burrough, William

953. Moes, Robert J. THE ELUSIVE DR. BURROUGH: ALTA CALIFORNIA'S FIRST PHYSICIAN. *Southern California Q. 1982 64(4): 265-280.* Provides information on William Burrough, the first civilian physician to take up residence in Alta California. Little is known about Burrough beyond the scanty information found in a contract for services with the Santa Barbara Presidio, a baptismal record, a marriage record, and other scattered documents. The available records reveal he was probably born in New York. He may have had some medical training but not a full education. He arrived in California around 1823, was baptized the following year into the Catholic faith, married in 1825, and had two children. He appears in the 1850 and 1852 censuses, but other information is sketchy. 15 notes. 1823-52

Burroughs, John

954. Leverette, William E., Jr. NATURE AND NOSTALGIA: JOHN BURROUGHS'S ALTERNATIVE TO MODERN AMERICA. *Proceedings of the South Carolina Historical Association 1984: 32-42.* Discusses the influence and some of the writings of John Burroughs, who led the back-to-nature movement in the late 19th and early 20th centuries. Burroughs was popular because his writings "met the need of many Americans for a kind of folk hero, a gentle sage of enduring values," who offered a new approach to life which did not reject accepted norms. Based on Burroughs's writings and secondary works; 19 notes. 1860's-1921

Burrow, Reuben Huston

955. Rogers, William Warren. RUBE BURROW, "KING OF OUTLAWS," AND HIS FLORIDA ADVENTURES. *Florida Hist. Q. 1980 59(2): 182-198.* Reuben Huston Burrow gained fame as a train robber. The Southern Express Company hired detective Thomas Jackson to track Burrow. For two years Jackson trailed Burrow in and out of Florida. He was killed in a shoot-out in October 1890. Based on newspaper accounts; 2 fig., 39 notes. 1885-90

Burt, Olive Woolley

956. Schindler, Harold. IN MEMORIAM: OLIVE WOOLLEY BURT, 1894-1981. *Utah Hist. Q. 1981 49(4): 388-390.* Born in Ann Arbor, Michigan, Olive Woolley Burt came to Salt Lake City, Utah, in 1897 and from that time spent her lifetime in literary pursuits—school reporter, *Deseret News* librarian, teacher, and author of over 50 books. Many of her works were popular histories. Winner of the Mystery Writers of America Edgar award, her works have been translated into many languages. Widowed from Clinton Ray Burt in 1967, she received the University of Utah's Distinguished Alumni Award in 1978. Note. 1917-81

Burt, William A.

957. Brown, Alan S. WILLIAM A. BURT AND THE UPPER PENINSULA. *Michigan Hist. 1980 64(3): 14-17.* A brief account of William A. Burt, the man who first surveyed most of the Upper Peninsula. He also discovered Michigan's iron ore riches. 2 maps. 1824-58

Burton, María Amparo Ruiz

958. Crawford, Kathleen. MARIA AMPARO RUIZ BURTON: THE GENERAL'S LADY. *Journal of San Diego History 30(3): 198-211.* María Amparo Ruiz Burton met Harry Stanton Burton, later a Civil War general, during the American takeover of La Paz, Baja California, in 1848 and married him the next year in Monterey, California; her adult life in San Diego paralleled the transition period from Mexican to US rule in California. 1848-95

Burton, Robert Wilton

959. Hitchcock, Bert. REDISCOVERING ALABAMA LITERATURE: THREE WRITERS OF LAFAYETTE. *Alabama Rev. 1983 36(3): 175-194.* Brief biographies and discussions of the work of Catharine Towles, Robert Wilton Burton, and George W. Hooper. Secondary sources; 13 notes. ca 1850-1900

Burton, Sarah Fenn

960. Bracken, James K. SARAH FENN BURTON'S DIARY OF A JOURNEY TO ILLINOIS. *Western Illinois Regional Studies 1981 4(2): 115-135.* Reprints the 1835 diary kept by Sarah Fenn Burton during her and her family's migration from Connecticut to Illinois along the Main Line route, a 2,200-mile route utilizing steamboats and railroads to Philadelphia, canals and railroads to Pittsburgh, and steamboats to St. Louis and Quincy, which describes the route's pitfalls; provides background on the route for 1834-42 and presents a brief follow-up of the Burton family once they settled until 1873. 1835

Burton, William L.

961. Harrington, Drew. WILLIAM L. BURTON: CYPRESS MILLIONAIRE AND PHILANTHROPIST. *Louisiana Hist. 1983 24(2): 155-164.* Career of the cypress lumberman, who, alone or with various partners, developed lumber interests in the area of Vicksburg, Mississippi, in Louisiana, and in Florida, and engaged in real estate developments on the North Shore of Long Island. His philanthropic interests included a home for orphan boys, the Young Men's Christian Association, and various churches. Based on city and company records, newspapers, interviews; 43 notes. 1870-1927

Bush, Olivia Ward

962. Guillaume, Bernice Forrest. "The Life and Work of Olivia Ward Bush (Banks), 1869-1944." Tulane U. 1983. 243 pp. *DAI 1984 44(9): 2861-A.* DA8400797 1900's-44

Bush, Vannevar

963. Meigs, Montgomery Cunningham. "Managing Uncertainty: Vannevar Bush, James B. Conant and the Development of the Atomic Bomb, 1940-1945." U. of Wisconsin, Madison 1982. 296 pp. *DAI 1983 43(7): 2426-A.* DA8215951 1940-45

Bushyhead, Dennis

964. Miner, H. Craig. DENNIS BUSHYHEAD. Edmunds, R. David, ed. *American Indian Leaders: Studies in Diversity* (Lincoln: U. of Nebraska Pr., 1980): 192-205. Dennis Bushyhead (1826-1898), an acculturated, mixed-blood leader who attempted to unify the Cherokee Indians, was determined to defend the sovereignty of his tribe from state and federal encroachment. He appreciated the great political influence held by large corporations during the 1880's and decided that the Cherokees' only chance for survival lay in developing a partnership with the business community. If major railroad or mining companies were granted special privileges by the Cherokee Nation, perhaps they would use their political influence to help the tribe defend its status against the US government. This was the line of diplomacy he used during his years of tenure, 1879-87, as principal chief of the Cherokees. Map, 18 notes. 1879-98

Buslett, Ole Amundsen

965. Hustvedt, Lloyd. OLE AMUNDSEN BUSLETT, 1855-1924. Lovoll, Odd S., ed. *Makers of an American Immigrant Legacy: Essays in Honor of Kenneth O. Bjork* (Northfield, Minn.: Norwegian-American Hist. Assoc., 1980): 131-158. Biography of poet, novelist, newspaper journalist, and Wisconsin Assemblyman (1908-10), Ole Amundsen Buslett (1855-1924), a Norwegian American, focusing on his literature. 1855-1924

Butcher, Solomon D.

966. Carter, John E. PRAIRIE PHOTOGRAPHER SOLOMON D. BUTCHER. *American History Illustrated 1986 20(9): 26-37.* Reviews the life and work of photographer Solomon D. Butcher, who photographed the homesteading era on the plains of Nebraska. 1880-1927

Butler, Benjamin F.

967. Ekirch, Arthur A., Jr. BENJAMIN F. BUTLER OF NEW YORK: A PERSONAL PORTRAIT. *New York Hist. 1977 58(1): 47-68.* Sketches the career of Benjamin F. Butler, a New York jurist, law partner of Martin Van Buren, member of the Albany Regency, and cabinet officer in the Andrew Jackson administration. Although a secondary figure in American history, he was influential during his own time, 1795-1858. 4 illus., 47 notes. 1795-1858

968. Horowitz, Murray M. BEN BUTLER AND THE NEGRO: "MIRACLES ARE OCCURRING." *Louisiana Hist. 1976 17(2): 159-186.* Details the career of Democratic General Benjamin F. Butler 1861-64 and analyzes his complete reversal of positions in such a brief time. The former "pro-slavery Democrat of the worst school" had become the darling of the Radicals. The actual experiences of war in the deep South, especially his contact with Negroes, caused the reversal. Illus., 43 notes. 1861-64

Butler, Marion

969. Hunt, James L. THE MAKING OF A POPULIST: MARION BUTLER, 1863-1895. *North Carolina Historical Review 1985 62(1): 53-77.* Populist leader Marion Butler was president of the Farmer's Alliance, a supporter of the Democratic Party, and a "Fusionist." In Sampson County, Butler's early life was comfortable and religious as he worked on the family farm. He presented orations at the University of North Carolina (1881-85) on racist and Southern themes later important to the Populist movement. After graduation, Butler taught school, purchased a local newspaper, *The Caucasian,* and soon became a leader in the newly formed Southern Alliance. Based primarily on Butler's papers and college records at the University of North Carolina; 9 illus., 67 notes. Article to be continued. 1863-90

Butler, Nat

970. Watts, Heather M. NAT BUTLER AND BURNS PIERCE: NOVA SCOTIAN HEROES OF THE CYCLE TRACKS. *Nova Scotia Hist. Rev. [Canada] 1982 2(2): 4-8.* Nat Butler, a native of Halifax, began bicycle racing in 1893 and continued racing until a serious injury forced him to quit in 1906. During his career he broke several indoor track records. Burns Pierce, East Sable River, set the world's record for a 25-mile race in 1896 and the world distance championship in 1898. He retired from racing in 1905 and lived quietly in Nova Scotia until his death. Based on personal interviews and Public Archives of Nova Scotia MG9 v.111-114, 116; 6 notes. 1893-1906

Butler, Nicholas Murray

971. Howlett, Charles F. NICHOLAS MURRAY BUTLER'S CRUSADE FOR A WARLESS WORLD. *Wisconsin Mag. of Hist. 1983-84 67(2): 99-120.* Examines the philosophy and practice of peace activist Nicholas M. Butler, who was Columbia University president and president of the Carnegie Endowment for International Peace. Butler's approach to peace, reflected in his *The International Mind,* emphasized the use of legal machinery for the peaceful resolution of disputes between nations, but he nevertheless supported American military involvement in both world wars. 9 illus., 64 notes. 1900-45

972. Howlett, Charles F. NICHOLAS MURRAY BUTLER AND THE AMERICAN PEACE MOVEMENT. *Teachers Coll. Record 1983 85(2): 291-313.* Nicholas Murray Butler was a leader of several antiwar movements in the first half of the 20th century. Although both world wars engendered in him a patriotism at odds with his professed pacifism, he nevertheless remained committed to a judicialist, peace-through-internationalism approach to ending conflict. Between the wars he opposed the League of Nations for its overemphasis on diplomacy and supported the Kellogg-Briand Pact. While consistently advocating disarmament, he was forced to support reluctantly the military buildup prior to World War II. Some of his apparent inconsistency can be attributed to his efforts to reunite a fragmented peace movement. Based on the Nicholas Murray Butler Papers, the Carnegie Endowment for International Peace Papers, and secondary sources; 71 notes. 1900-47

973. Segal, Howard P. AMERICAN COLLEGE AND UNIVERSITY PRESIDENTS: FOUR BIOGRAPHICAL STUDIES. *Hist. of Educ. Q. 1982 22(1): 99-102.* 1850's-1945

For abstract see ***Barnard, Frederick A. P.***

Butler, Pierce

974. Coghlan, Francis. PIERCE BUTLER, 1744-1822, FIRST SENATOR FROM SOUTH CAROLINA. *South Carolina Hist. Mag. 1977 78(2): 104-119.* Pierce Butler fought in the American Revolution and then was South Carolina's first senator. 1761-1822

975. Noonan, John T., Jr. THE CATHOLIC JUSTICES OF THE UNITED STATES SUPREME COURT. *Catholic Hist. Rev. 1981 67(3): 369-385.* Discusses five Catholic justices of the United States Supreme Court: Roger Brooke Taney (1777-1864), Edward Douglas White (1845-1921), Joseph McKenna (1843-1926), Pierce Butler (1866-1939), and Frank Murphy (1890-1949). The article looks at the points where their Catholicism had an impact upon their careers in terms of their appointments or their judicial actions and the points where, conversely, their careers had an impact on the Catholic Church. Based on correspondence and other primary sources; 70 notes. 19c-20c

Butler, Smedley Darlington

976. Carr, Stephen M. SMEDLEY BUTLER: HERO OR DEMAGOGUE? *Am. Hist. Illus. 1980 15(1): 30-38.* Smedley Butler (1881-1940), raised a Hicksite Quaker in West Chester, Pennsylvania, became a major general in the Marine Corps and was presented with two Congressional Medals of Honor; he was also court-martialed in 1931 for conduct unbecoming an officer after he denounced war and spoke in public against questionable State Department activities in Nicaragua in 1912; Butler continued to speak out until his death. 1881-1940

977. Cochran, Robert T. SMEDLEY BUTLER: A PINT-SIZE MARINE FOR ALL SEASONS. *Smithsonian 1984 15(3): 137-156.* Smedley Butler served in the Spanish-American War, the Boxer Rebellion, World War I, and various military expeditions in Central America, the Caribbean, and elsewhere, and was twice awarded the Medal of Honor for bravery; after leaving the Marines in 1931, Butler became an outspoken isolationist. 1898-1940

978. Venzon, Anne Cipriano. "The Papers of General Smedley Darlington Butler, USMC, 1915-1918." Princeton U. 1982. 465 pp. *DAI 1982 42(11): 4909-A.* DA8208552 1915-18

Butterfield, Lyman Henry

979. Bell, Whitfield J., Jr. LYMAN HENRY BUTTERFIELD. *Pro. of the Am. Antiquarian Soc. 1983 93(1): 47-51.* Butterfield was a historian, biographer, and the first editor-in-chief of *The Adams Papers.* He began his editorial career in 1944 at Franklin and Marshall College with the discovery of a hitherto unknown letter describing the beginning of that institution. This led him to work on the *Letters of Benjamin Rush, The Papers of Thomas Jefferson,* and finally to the directorship of the Institute of Early American History and Culture. He joined *The Adams Papers* staff in 1954. Twenty volumes later he retired, in 1975. 1944-82

Buttersworth, James E.

980. Carr, J. Revell. J. E. BUTTERSWORTH: PAINTER OF SAIL AND STEAM. *Nautical Res. J. 1976 22(3): 111-117.* Provides information on the relatively obscure 19th-century artist James E. Buttersworth, who was known by contemporaries for his drawings of clipper ships and who thus preserved the history of ships in America for almost 60 years. 1813-70's

Button Chief

981. Nix, J. Ernest. BUTTON CHIEF: A NATIVE HERO. *Alberta Hist. [Canada] 1981 29(1): 10-14.* Also known as Medicine Calf (Natose Onista), Button Chief, a minor chief of the Blood tribe of the Blackfoot confederacy in Alberta, was renowned in his earlier years and celebrated in the folkore of his tribe. He was responsible for negotiating, in part, the Treaty Seven in September 1877 with the Canadian officials. Reprints letters from Methodist missionary John Maclean that reveal Button Chief's consistent philosophy that the destiny of the West and of his people lay with the arriving whites. 2 sketches, 17 notes. ca 1855-84

Byington, Cyrus

982. Coleman, Louis. CYRUS BYINGTON: MISSIONARY TO THE CHOCTAWS. *Chronicles of Oklahoma 1984-85 62(4): 360-387.* Despite his training as a lawyer, Cyrus Byington became a fervent missionary for the American Board of Commissioners for Foreign Missions during 1820. He first served the Choctaw Indians at Mayhew Mission in central Mississippi, and then accompanied them to their new home in southeastern Oklahoma in 1835. In addition to ministering to the Indians, Byington wrote a Choctaw hymnal, grammar, and dictionary, all noted for their accuracy and comprehensiveness. His poor health and Choctaw factionalism during the Civil War troubled Byington's later years, but he remained at his post almost to the time of his death. Based on the *Missionary Herald* and Byington's manuscripts at the Oklahoma Historical Society; 2 maps, 4 photos, 100 notes. 1820-68

Byrd, Richard E.

983. Harrison, Richard A. PALADIN AND PAWN: ADMIRAL RICHARD E. BYRD AND THE QUAGMIRE OF PEACE POLITICS IN THE 1930S. *Peace and Change 1984 9(4): 29-48.* An account of Richard E. Byrd's involvement in a peace crusade between his second and third Antarctic expeditions. 1935-38

Byrd, William

984. Greenberg, Michael. WILLIAM BYRD II AND THE WORLD OF THE MARKET. *Southern Studies 1977 16(4): 429-456.* Presents the values, experiences, and aspirations of one of the dominant personalities in colonial Virginia, William Byrd II (1674-1744). He spent most of his time in Virginia directing his economic activities, but closely corresponded with friends in England concerning economic, political, and special conditions there. He had a high opinion of himself and the American aristocracy. He envisaged the establishment of a fully developed market society in America, which would make possible a truly civilized existence and sustain social subordination and consequently slavery, about which he was otherwise uneasy. Primary and secondary sources; 52 notes. 1694-1744

985. Rosenwald, Lawrence Alan. "Three Early American Diarists." Columbia U. 1979. 182 pp. *DAI 1980 40(10): 5444-A.* 17c-18c

Byrne, Edwin V.

986. Miriam Thérèse, Sister. RAINBOWS WITH RAGGED EDGES: ARCHBISHOP EDWIN V. BYRNE. *Records of the American Catholic Historical Society of Philadelphia 1983 94(1-4): 61-79.* Reviews the life of Edwin V. Byrne (1891-1963), who began his career in the priesthood in Philadelphia but whose assignments included the Philippines, Puerto Rico, and New Mexico, due to his interest in missionary work. Studies his work as a bishop in Puerto Rico and the effects of this appointment on the nationalist movement there. Based on correspondence and personal narratives; illus., 39 notes. 1915-63

Byrne, John

987. Sarbaugh, Timothy. JOHN BYRNE: THE LIFE AND TIMES OF THE FORGOTTEN IRISH REPUBLICAN OF LOS ANGELES. *Southern California Q. 1981 63(4): 374-391.* A profile of John Byrne (1866-1962), supporter of an independent Ireland, who led the movement in Los Angeles, California. Born in Dublin, Byrne came to America in 1890; after living in Philadelphia, he arrived in Los Angeles in 1906, found employment, and joined the Ancient Order of Hibernians and the Gaelic League. With the unsuccessful 1916 Easter rising, Byrne joined the Friends of Irish Freedom and helped raise funds for Irish relief. After World War I, Sinn Fein leader Eamon De Valera came to the United States on a controversial tour. Byrne became a life-long supporter of De Valera, serving as secretary-treasurer of the American Association for the Recognition of the Irish Republic for 16 years. When De Valera outlawed the Irish Republican Army, Byrne backed him despite extremist local opposition. Byrne then retired from active support in 1936. In 1954 he visited Ireland and met President De Valera again. His last years were spent in Los Angeles. 51 notes. 1890-1962

Byrnes, James F.

988. Moore, Winfred B., Jr. "SOUL OF THE SOUTH": JAMES F. BYRNES AND THE RACIAL ISSUE IN AMERICAN POLITICS, 1911-1941. *Pro. of the South Carolina Hist. Assoc. 1978: 42-52.* Examines how South Carolina's James F. Byrnes handled racial issues as a US Congressman from 1911 to 1925 and a US Senator from 1931 to 1941. "For Byrnes . . . white paternalism and black subordination within a clearly defined, unchallenged framework of white supremacy constituted the ideal state of race relations. Accordingly, Byrnes dedicated himself to defending this ideal state from what he felt were the disruptive attacks of unscrupulous southern race-baiters on his right as well as misguided national reformers on his left." Based on the Byrnes papers and on newspapers; 24 notes. 1911-41

989. Moore, Winfred B., Jr. JAMES F. BYRNES: THE ROAD TO POLITICS, 1882-1910. *South Carolina Historical Magazine 1983 84(2): 72-88.* Writers have incorrectly described James F. Byrnes's background as one of grinding poverty, when his family, in fact, enjoyed at least an average standard of living. His mother and Benjamin Rutledge, a lawyer Byrnes worked for in Charleston, had the greatest impact on developing his talents and molding his values. His driving ambition led him into law, journalism, and politics. In 1910 he won a seat in Congress as a representative of a new generation desiring to bring South Carolina into the mainstream of national life. Later he served as a US senator, Supreme Court justice, secretary of state, and governor of South Carolina. Based primarily on the James F. Byrnes Manuscripts, Clemson University, and newspaper reports; 45 notes. 1882-1910

990. Partin, John William. "'Assistant President' for the Home Front: James F. Byrnes and World War II." U. of Florida 1977. 386 pp. *DAI 1978 38(11): 6896-A.* 1942-44

C

Cabet, Etienne

991. Chicoineau, Jacques C. ETIENNE CABET AND THE ICARIANS. *Western Illinois Regional Studies 1979 2(1): 5-19.* Etienne Cabet (1788-1858), born in France, was one of several founders of utopian societies in the United States as a response to the rapid rise of technology and industrialization; Cabet's Icaria, named after his book, *Voyage en Icarie (Voyage in Icaria)* (1840), first was located in

Nauvoo, Illinois, later in Corning, Iowa, and finally in Sonoma County, California, where it was dissolved in 1895. 1840-95

992. Tumminelli, Roberto. ETIENNE CABET E IL MODELLO POLITICO-SOCIALE DI ICARIA [Etienne Cabet and the socio-political model of Icaria]. *Politico [Italy] 1979 44(1): 92-112.* Discusses Etienne Cabet's (1788-1856) communist political and social theories, his utopian experiment at Icaria in Illinois, and his newspaper career. Cabet belongs to the totalitarian democratic schools, and he represents an important conceptual connection between Gracchus Babeuf and Karl Marx. 1820's-56

Cable, George Washington

993. Bendixen, Alfred. GEORGE W. CABLE AND THE GARDEN. *Louisiana Studies 1976 15(3): 310-315.* George Washington Cable (1844-1925) left New Orleans for Massachusetts in 1886 but continued his civic reforms as well as writing of fiction. One of his minor but typical interests is reflected in his book *The Amateur Garden* (1914), consisting of several previously published articles. Cable believed that maintaining a garden helped to improve its owner by giving an understanding of leisure, a sense of home and community, a respect for nature, and spiritual uplift. He recommended an annual garden contest to pursue these goals. 1886-1925

994. Farley, Benjamin W. GEORGE W. CABLE: PRESBYTERIAN ROMANCER, REFORMER, BIBLE TEACHER. *J. of Presbyterian Hist. 1980 58(2): 166-181.* In the last 25 years there have been three biographies of George Washington Cable (1844-1925), Southern Presbyterian, ex-Confederate soldier, and author of Creole stories. All three acknowledge his Presbyterian roots, and examine the influence of his church and home on his life and work. Concentrates attention on Cable as a Presbyterian, and explores his life, stories, and reforming activities in light of his Calvinistic heritage. Emphasizes the influence of his early home and training on his work and habits, the role of New Orleans Presbyterianism in his development, and, as his career advanced and his vision matured, how he drew upon and reacted against his Presbyterian heritage. Based on Cable's writings and studies about him, particularly the biography by Lucy Leffingwell Cable Biklè, *George W. Cable, His Life and Letters* (1928); illus., 65 notes. ca 1870-1925

995. Hill, Cason Louis. "A Bibliographical Study of George Washington Cable and a Check List of Criticism, 1870-1970." U. of Georgia 1977. 259 pp. *DAI 1978 38(8): 4816-A.* 1870-1970

996. Trotman, C. James. GEORGE W. CABLE AND TRADITION. *Texas Q. 1976 19(3): 51-58.* In 1879 the publication of *Old Creole Days* made George Washington Cable famous, though today few people read his work. Cable fit into the local color tradition, but he fit the romantic mold, too. In later years he dropped social criticism from his work, a price he paid for success. Based on primary and secondary sources; 8 notes. 1879-1925

Cabot, James Elliot

997. Simmons, Nancy Craig. "Man Without a Shadow: The Life and Work of James Elliot Cabot, Emerson's Biographer and Literary Executor." Princeton U. 1980. 591 pp. *DAI 1980 41(6): 2608-A.* 8028661 1835-1903

998. Simmons, Nancy Craig. THE "AUTOBIOGRAPHICAL SKETCH" OF JAMES ELLIOT CABOT. *Harvard Lib. Bull. 1982 30(2): 117-152.* James Elliot Cabot, the authorized biographer of Ralph Waldo Emerson, died in 1903. Shortly before his death he wrote a brief sketch of his life, which reveals much about the man who was called "the serene idealist." The original of the sketch has disappeared but two copies are available, one a typescript in the Schlesinger Library, Radcliffe College, and the other a privately printed version. The sketch reproduced here is based largely on the Schlesinger version. In simple, straightforward style, Cabot traced his life and revealed much about his attitudes and the optimistic outlook that characterized his life. Primary sources; 45 notes, 1 illus. 1821-1903

999. Simmons, Nancy Craig. ARRANGING THE SIBYLLINE LEAVES: JAMES ELLIOT CABOT'S WORK AS EMERSON'S LITERARY EXECUTOR. *Studies in the American Renaissance 1983: 335-389.* Discusses the editorial work of James Elliot Cabot on the unpublished manuscripts of Ralph Waldo Emerson. Toward the end of his life, Emerson began to lose his memory and his ability to concentrate. The philosopher's daughter was unable to provide sufficient editorial help for him to complete all the obligations to publishing houses with which he had contracted. Cabot proved able to select various writings and synthesize them into essays. As an editor, Cabot lived up to Victorian ideals of editorship by presenting a finished image of Emerson as a "committed conscience." It is, however, vain to look for modern editorial standards of accuracy in his work. Based on the works of Cabot and Emerson and secondary sources; 152 notes. 1875-93

Cabus, Joseph

1000. Hanks, David. KIMBEL & CABUS: 19TH-CENTURY NEW YORK CABINETMAKERS. *Art & Antiques 1980 3(5): 44-53.* Describes the furniture made by Anthony Kimbel and Joseph Cabus, during the 1870's, particularly the modern Gothic style, and discusses the background of the two men and the influence of various designers, cabinetmakers, and European styles on their pieces. 1850-99

Čačić, Tomo

1001. Rasporich, Anthony. TOMO ČAČIĆ: REBEL WITHOUT A COUNTRY. *Can. Ethnic Studies [Canada] 1978 10(2): 86-94.* Surveys the career of Tomo Čačić (1896-1969), Croatia-born radical Communist labor organizer in the western United States and western Canada. In Ontario he was a Communist Party organizer and newspaperman until his arrest and imprisonment. In 1934, he was deported to England; soon he escaped to Moscow. After three years he enlisted in the Spanish Civil War. He returned to Yugoslavia in 1941 and fought there with the Partisans throughout the war. After the war he continued his interest in the Canadian radical cause. Primary sources; 50 notes. ca 1913-69

Cadet, Joseph

1002. Mimeault, Mario. LES ENTREPRISES DE PECHE A LA MORUE DE JOSEPH CADET 1751-1758 [The fishing businesses of Joseph Cadet, 1751-58]. *Rev. d'Hist. de l'Amérique Française [Canada] 1984 37(4): 557-572.* Born in 1719, Cadet began his early business activities by provisioning the army and engaging in trade between New France, the West Indies, and France. He also became a major landowner and established a cod-fishing company. Cadet hired fishermen and equipped their vessels in return for a share of their catch. In the late 1750's, his company closed because of the declining interest of his partner and the war between France and

England. Yet he had amassed a fortune far in excess of his fishing profits, and in 1763 was convicted of illicit business activities. Primary sources; table, 47 notes. 1751-58

Cadieux, Lorenzo

1003. Gervais, Gaetan. LORENZO CADIEUX, S.J., 1903-1976. *Ontario Hist. [Canada] 1977 69(4): 214-218.* Father Cadieux was born in Granby, Quebec, educated in Montreal and Edmonton, and closely associated with the study of northern Ontario. Outlines his career as a teacher, and mentions organizations he was associated with. Gives examples of his work, and lists some titles of his publications. The obituary is in English and French. 1903-76

Cadish family

1004. —. THE LOS ANGELES BRODERS: A PICTURE STORY. *Western States Jewish Hist. Q. 1981 13(3): 225-229.* 1922-70

For abstract see ***Broder family***

Cadman, Charles Wakefield

1005. Perison, Harry D. "Charles Wakefield Cadman: His Life and Works." U. of Rochester 1978. 491 pp. *DAI 1978 39(4): 1919-1920-A.* 1881-1946

Cadmus, Paul

1006. Eliasoph, Philip I. "Paul Cadmus: Life and Work." State U. of New York, Binghamton 1979. 552 pp. *DAI 1979 39(9): 5188-A.* 1930's-40's

Caffery, Jefferson

1007. Dur, Philip F. JEFFERSON CAFFERY OF LOUISIANA: HIGHLIGHTS OF HIS CAREER. *Louisiana Hist. 1974 15(1): 5-34, 15(4): 367-402.* Part I. Describes Caffery's early diplomatic career, 1911-33, in many foreign nations. Part II. Examines the diplomatic career of Jefferson Caffery, highlighting his terms of office in Cuba (1933-37) and Brazil (1937-44). 1911-44

Caffin, Charles H.

1008. Underwood, Sandra Lee. "Charles H. Caffin: A Voice for Modernism 1897-1918." Indiana U. 1981. 468 pp. *DAI 1981 42(3): 899-900-A.* DA8119087 1897-1918

Cage, John

1009. Bither, David. JOHN CAGE: A GRAND OLD RADICAL. *Horizon 1980 23(12): 48-55.* Composer John Cage (b. 1912) grew up in Los Angeles, studied with Arnold Schoenberg at the University of Southern California, and during the same period was influenced by the work of Henry Cowell, Edgard Varèse, and George Antheil; during the 1930's Cage invented his famous prepared piano, experimented with electronic music, and then, under the influence of Oriental culture, began to write music in imitation of nature, a course he is still pursuing. 1930-80

Cain, Richard Harvey

1010. Lewis, Ronald L. CULTURAL PLURALISM AND BLACK RECONSTRUCTION: THE PUBLIC CAREER OF RICHARD CAIN. *Crisis 1978 85(2): 57-60, 64-65.* Richard Harvey Cain (1825-87) was a South Carolina State Senator, a US Congressman, a newspaper editor, an African Methodist Episcopal Bishop, and a college president. Born in 1825, he lived through slavery and the Civil War and worked to improve economic, political, and social conditions for blacks during Reconstruction. He died in 1887, having left a legacy of tireles effort and significant progressive change. 1850's-87

Calder, Alexander

1011. Goldin, Amy. ALEXANDER CALDER, 1898-1977. *Art in Am. 1977 65(2): 70-73.* Discusses the work of Alexander Calder, inventor of the mobile and the stabile; a retrospective exhibition of his work coincided with his death in 1977. 1940-77

Caldwell, Billy

1012. Clifton, James A. MERCHANT, SOLDIER, BROKER, CHIEF: A CORRECTED OBITUARY OF CAPTAIN BILLY CALDWELL. *J. of the Illinois State Hist. Soc. 1978 71(3): 185-210.* Challenges the prevailing characterization of Billy Caldwell (1780-1841) as a successful half-Indian trader and Potawatomi chief on the Great Lakes frontier. Applying ethnohistorical methods, the author concludes that Caldwell was an alien in his tribal Mohawk society, in his childhood in Canada, in his early adulthood in the British Indian Department, and especially in his later years in post-revolutionary America. Far from being a power broker, Caldwell was usually an instrument of others; nor did he think of himself as an Indian. Based on Caldwell papers in Canada, Michigan, Wisconsin, Missouri, and Illinois; Illus., 4 maps, 83 notes. 1797-1841

Caldwell, Charles

1013. Erickson, Paul. THE ANTHROPOLOGY OF CHARLES CALDWELL, M.D. *Isis 1981 72(262): 252-256.* American physician Charles Caldwell (1772-1853) practiced in Philadelphia and taught at Transylvania College and the Medical Institute of Louisville. By avocation he was also an anthropologist who held that the human races are fundamentally different because they were of different origins. His arguments about monogenism and polygenism were based largely on what he knew of physiology, blended with the pseudosciences phrenology and animal magnetism. 15 notes. ca 1800-53

Caldwell, Clifton Mott

1014. Beckham, John L. CLIFTON MOTT CALDWELL: CITIZEN OF TEXAS. *West Texas Hist. Assoc. Year Book 1980 56: 68-79.* Biography of leading citizen and developer of west Texas, Clifton Mott Caldwell (1880-1968). ca 1900-68

Caldwell, David

1015. Miller, Mark Francis. "David Caldwell: The Forming of a Southern Educator." U. of North Carolina, Chapel Hill 1979. 264 pp. *DAI 1980 41(1): 370-A.* 8013971 1730-1824

Caldwell, Erskine

1016. Broadwell, Elizabeth Pell and Hoag, Ronald Wesley. "A WRITER FIRST": AN INTERVIEW WITH ERSKINE CALDWELL. *Georgia Rev. 1982 36(1): 82-101.* Erskine Caldwell, author of *Tobacco Road, God's Little Acre, Journeyman,* and other works, discusses his life, his career as a writer, and his view of the American South. 1932-80

1017. Caldwell, Erskine; Kelly, Richard and Pankake, Marcia, interviewers. FIFTY YEARS SINCE TOBACCO ROAD: AN INTERVIEW WITH ERSKINE CALDWELL. *Southwest Rev. 1984 69(1): 33-47.* Interview with author Erskine Caldwell about humor, screenwriting, his early life in the South, and his becoming a writer. 1920's-82

1018. Caldwell, Erskine; Staats, Marilyn Dorn, interviewer. ERSKINE CALDWELL AT EIGHTY-ONE: AN INTERVIEW. *Arizona Quarterly 1985 41(3): 247-257.* In an interview, Erskine Caldwell reflects on his 50 years as a writer of novels and short fiction, discussing his social, political, and religious views, and commenting on his writing and its critical reception. 1930-85

Calf Shirt

1019. Dempsey, Hugh A. THE SNAKE MAN. *Alberta Hist. [Canada] 1981 29(4): 1-5.* Calf Shirt (1844-1901), of the Many Tumors band of Blackfoot Indians (Blood), had a strange power that permitted him to talk to rattlesnakes. He presented himself as a paradox in his roles as informer and tribal leader, as well as police scout and criminal. In 1888 he formed a new band called the Crooked Backs, which settled near Lethbridge, Alberta. His exploits with snakes resulted in him being featured in numerous shows, including the Territorial Exhibition in Regina in 1895. 8 notes, 3 photos. 1844-1901

Calhoun, John C.

1020. Spiller, Roger J. CALHOUN'S EXPANSIBLE ARMY: THE HISTORY OF A MILITARY IDEA. *South Atlantic Q. 1980 79(2): 189-203.* John C. Calhoun served as Secretary of War in James Monroe's cabinet, 1817-25. He inherited the problem of an American suspicion toward a large standing army, something with which George Washington himself had grappled. Washington had proposed a skeleton army, a stage higher than militia. Winfield Scott had envisioned a reduced army into which recruits could be assimilated in the event of war. Calhoun proposed an expansible army based on that of the French under Napoleon, whereby a basic cadre of 6,000 officers and men could be expanded into 11,000 without adding additional officers or companies. His task was to convince Congress that political and military expediency were not always mutually exclusive in a democratic republic. Congress pretty well scuttled Calhoun's proposal, but he is best known because of this idea. Stillborn though it was, the concept of the expansible army survived the Civil War. Based on published *Papers of John C. Calhoun;* Letters Received by the Secretary of War relating to Military Affairs, National Archives Record Group 107, microcopy 221; Vandeventer Papers, William L. Clements Library, University of Michigan; Swift Papers, Library of U.S. Military Academy; 37 notes. 1817-25

Calkins, Mary Whiton

1021. Furumuto, Laurel. MARY WHITON CALKINS (1863-1930): FOURTEENTH PRESIDENT OF THE AMERICAN PSYCHOLOGICAL ASSOCIATION. *J. of the Hist. of the Behavioural Sci. 1979 15(4): 346-356.* Relatively little has been published about the life and contributions of Mary Whiton Calkins (1863-1930), 14th president of the American Psychological Association. A student of William James, Josiah Royce, and Hugo Münsterberg at Harvard in the 1890's, Calkins completed all the requirements for the Ph.D. but was not granted the degree because she was a woman. Calkins's contributions to psychology include the invention of the paired-associate technique, the founding of one of the early psychological laboratories, and the development of a system of self-psychology. She published prolifically in both psychology and philosophy but was always more interested in theoretical and philosophical issues than in laboratory psychology. Although in the latter half of her career Calkins moved away from psychology into philosophy, her work contained a unifying theme: the emphasis on the importance of the self. 1890's-1930

Call, Harry

1022. Mace, Kenneth D. PIONEER AIRMEN OF KANSAS. *Aviation Q. 1979 5(2): 152-163.* Discusses Kansas aviators and builders Harry Call, William Purvis, Charles Wilson, and Albin K. Longren, 1908-29. 1908-29

Callaghan, Morley

1023. Conron, Brandon. MORLEY CALLAGHAN AND HIS AUDIENCE. *J. of Can. Studies [Canada] 1980 15(1): 3-7.* Morley Callaghan has written for more than 50 years with consistent artistic vision and integrity. His insight into private emotion and thought, and his belief in a meaningful universe, have appealed to an audience which has been both intrigued and baffled by his work. Readers may have difficulty with Callaghan's novels because he makes them judge, rejudge, and misjudge his characters, and because the novels end in annihilating violence or "blank unfulfillment," or arouse expectations of happy endings which do not occur. There can be no final assessment of Callaghan's place in Canadian or world literature as yet. 1930-80

1024. Latham, David. A CALLAGHAN LOG. *J. of Can. Studies [Canada] 1980 15(1): 18-29.* A chronological list of selected events in Morley Callaghan's life, 1903-79. The list includes Callaghan's books, periodical publications and plays (except his 1940's monthly column for *New World Illustrated),* and theses, books, and articles about him and his work. 1903-79

Callahan, Patrick Henry

1025. Ellis, William E. KENTUCKY CATHOLIC AND MARYLAND SKEPTIC: THE CORRESPONDENCE OF COLONEL PATRICK HENRY CALLAHAN AND H. L. MENCKEN. *Filson Club Hist. Q. 1984 58(3): 336-348.* Examines the relationship between H. L. Mencken and Patrick Henry Callahan. The two met at the Scopes trial in 1925 and kept up a lively correspondence until Callahan's death in 1940. Although they disagreed on Prohibition and the New Deal, they enjoyed each other's humor and were in broad agreement on issues of individual liberties. Based on the Mencken Papers at the New York Public Library and Callahan letters; 21 notes, 2 photos. 1925-40

1026. Ellis, William E. CATHOLICISM AND THE SOUTHERN ETHOS: THE ROLE OF PATRICK HENRY CALLAHAN. *Catholic Hist. Rev. 1983 69(1): 41-50.* Patrick Henry Callahan, son of Irish Catholic immigrants, endeavored to accommodate Catholicism to the Southern ethos, but also sought to uplift that character in crusades against religious and racial prejudices. He blended roles as manufacturer, profit-sharing pioneer, leader in the fight for tolerance, and prohibitionist into a busy life. During World War I, he directed a Knights of Columbus campaign against anti-Catholicism. In the interwar period he often stepped outside official Catholic circles and developed his own distinctive antiprejudice programs. Prior to World War II, Callahan served as a valuable independent critic of the Southern ethos. 1910's-40

1027. Ellis, William E. PATRICK HENRY CALLAHAN: A KENTUCKY DEMOCRAT IN NATIONAL POLITICS. *Filson Club Hist. Q. 1977 51(1): 17-30.* Patrick Henry Callahan of Louisville, Kentucky, was an innovative businessman and a major spokesman for Catholics in the national Democratic Party. Callahan achieved fame by introducing a highly successful profit sharing plan in his Louisville Varnish Company. His strong commitment to prohibition was strengthened by his friendship with William Jennings Bryan and led Callahan to oppose Al Smith's presidential nomination in 1928. Callahan was an early supporter of Franklin D. Roosevelt and the New Deal. He defended the Roosevelt administration against attacks on its Mexican policy and from the challenge of Father Charles Coughlin. Based on the Callahan Papers at Catholic University and the Roosevelt, Bryan, and Woodrow Wilson Papers; 50 notes. 1866-1940

Callaway, Fuller E.

1028. Whitley, Donna Jean. "Fuller E. Callaway and Textile Mill Development in LaGrange, 1895-1920." Emory U. 1984. 344 pp. *DAI 1984 45(6): 1847-1848-A.* DA8420302 1895-1920

Callender, James Thomson

1029. Fair, Charles A. "James Thomson Callender: A Political Journalist in the Beginning of National Politics." Ohio U. 1978. 251 pp. *DAI 1979 39(11): 6377-A.* 1793-1803

1030. Jellison, Charles A. JAMES THOMSON CALLENDER: "HUMAN NATURE IN A HIDEOUS FORM." *Virginia Cavalcade 1979 29(2): 62-69.* James Thomas Callender was a political writer and opponent of both the Federalists and Republicans in the 1790's when factionalism was violent and widespread; it was Callender who initiated the rumors about Thomas Jefferson and his slave Sally Hemings. 1790's

Calverton, V. F.

1032. Wilcox, Leonard I. "V. F. Calverton: A Critical Biography." U. of California, Irvine 1977. 515 pp. *DAI 1978 38(9): 5485-5486-A.* 1920's-30's

Calvin, Ross Randall

1033. Moses, L. G. "IF THERE BE SERMONS IN STONES, I HAVE NOT HEARD THEM": A BIOGRAPHY OF ROSS RANDALL CALVIN (1889-1970). *Hist. Mag. of the Protestant Episcopal Church 1977 46(3): 333-347.* Sketches the life of Episcopal priest, Ross Randall Calvin (1889-1970), who wrote several valuable books. *Sky Determines: An Interpretation of the Southwest* (U. of New Mexico Pr., 1965) was a popular essay on nature in New Mexico. He contributed to the lore of the Southwest by conveying scientific knowledge in a pleasing and articulate manner. He never equated the beauty of nature with the revelation of God. He served in Silver City and Clovis, New Mexico. Based largely on the Calvin Papers, University of New Mexico, Albuquerque, New Mexico; 66 notes. 1889-1970

Camacho, Jesús

1034. Hall, Dick. JESÚS CAMACHO: THE MAYOR OF MEYER STREET. *J. of Arizona Hist. 1979 20(4): 445-465.* When Jesús Camacho (1883-1949) was 27, he was recommended for the police force in Tucson. He became the most respected and feared policeman in the toughest part of Tucson, and was called the "Mayor of Meyer Street." He officially retired in 1945. 7 photos, 2 maps, notes. 1910-49

Cameron, Alexander W.

1035. Orrell, John. EDMONTON THEATRES OF ALEXANDER W. CAMERON. *Alberta Hist. [Canada] 1978 26(2): 1-10.* In 1906, Alexander W. Cameron brought vaudeville to Edmonton at the Empire Theater. Until 1913, Cameron was the driving force in this aspect of Edmonton's cultural life. He was either the main investor, or planner, of the Edmonton Opera House, the Kevin, Orpheum, and Lyric Theaters. Cameron was innovative. When attendance dropped at the opera house, he converted the building into a roller skating rink during the weekdays. Cameron left the Edmonton area around 1913. Based on newspaper accounts and government documents. 4 illus., 16 notes. 1906-13

Cameron, Donaldina

1036. McClain, Laurene Wu. DONALDINA CAMERON: A REAPPRAISAL. *Pacific Hist. 1983 27(3): 24-35.* Reviews Donaldina Cameron's career with the Presbyterian Mission Home in San Francisco and her efforts to save illegally imported Chinese women from the slave trade. Her attitude toward the women exhibited little tolerance or sympathy and hampered her attempts to rehabilitate them. Although she spent 40 years in Chinatown she did not speak Chinese and referred to the Chinese as heathens. 7 illus., 18 notes. 1869-1920

Cameron, Ralph Henry

1037. Lamb, Blaine P. "A MANY CHECKERED TOGA": ARIZONA SENATOR RALPH H. CAMERON, 1921-1927. *Arizona and the West 1977 19(1): 47-64.* Ralph Henry Cameron (1863-1953) was the first Republican Senator from Arizona. His single term, 1921-27, was controversial. He did not hesitate to castigate the federal bureaucracy and to seek federal aid at the same time. He was charged with personal impropriety and political corruption. He alienated many of his colleagues and constitutuents and lost his bid for reelection. 2 illus.; 43 notes. 1920-27

Cameron, William Andrew

1038. Harrop, G. Gerald. THE ERA OF THE "GREAT PREACHER" AMONG CANADIAN BAPTISTS. *Foundations 1980 23(1): 57-70.* Compares Canadian Baptist preachers William Andrew Cameron (1881-1956), John J. MacNeill (1874-1937), and Englishman Thomas Todhunter Shields (1873-1955), as preachers and church leaders. Covers 1910-41. Based on published sermons and other materials; 23 notes. 1910-41

Camp, Walter Chauncey

1039. Borkowski, Richard Patrick. "The Life and Contributions of Walter Camp to Football." Temple U. 1979. 365 pp. *DAI 1979 40(5): 2539-2540-A.* 1880's-1925

Campbell, Alexander

1040. Miethe, Terry Lee. "The Philosophy and Ethics of Alexander Campbell: From the Context of American Religious Thought, 1800-1866." U. of Southern California 1984. *DAI 1985 45(11): 3316-3317-A.* 1800-66

Campbell, Angus

1041. Katz, Daniel. IN MEMORIAM: ANGUS CAMPBELL, 1910-1980. *Public Opinion Q. 1981 45(1): 124-125.* Behavioral and social scientist Angus Campbell died on 21 December 1980. In 1948 he helped form the Institute for Social Research at the University of Michigan. He held a post there until 1977. An active research director and productive scholar, he collaborated in the writing of *The American Voter* (1960), which formed a methodological breakthrough in the study of national politics, and authored two works that assessed, using national surveys, people's well-being and satisfaction: *The Quality of American Life: Perceptions, Evaluations and Satisfactions* (1976) and *The Sense of Well-Being in America: Recent Trends and Patterns* (1980). 1936-80

Campbell, Arthur

1042. Hagy, James William. ARTHUR CAMPBELL AND THE WEST, 1743-1811. *Virginia Mag. of Hist. and Biog. 1982 90(4): 456-471.* Traces the career of Arthur Campbell of Washington County. An ambitious man, he helped shape the military and political policies of the state of Virginia, but his stubborn personality prevented his achieving the power and fame he desired. During the 1770's and 1780's, Campbell, as county lieutenant, was instrumental in ridding the western frontier of both Indians and Tories, but he was unwilling to send his militia east to fight the British. Later, Campbell was active in unsuccessful separatist movements that would have made new states from portions of southwestern and western Virginia, North Carolina, and Kentucky. Based on correspondence in the Lyman C. Draper manuscript collection, State Historical Society of Wisconsin, Papers of the Continental Congress, Virginia statutes and county court records, Colonial Office records, other manuscripts, and secondary sources; 51 notes. 1770-1800

Campbell, Doak S.

1043. Oliver, William Lewis, Jr. "Doak S. Campbell, Educator." Florida State U. 1978. 282 pp. *DAI 1978 39(3): 1384-A.* 1888-1973

Campbell, George

1044. Campbell, Colin. LIEUTENANT COLONEL GEORGE CAMPBELL, KING'S AMERICAN REGIMENT. *New England Hist. and Geneal. Register 1983 137(Oct): 306-316.* Covers the life of George Campbell, whose family came to New York from Scotland in the late 1730's. Presents Campbell's record of service with the Tory King's American Regiment in the American Revolution. 59 notes. 1776-99

Campbell, John

1045. Hartlen, John. JOHN CAMPBELL: A TRUE PROSPECTOR AND A GOOD GEOLOGIST. *Nova Scotia Hist. Q. [Canada] 1979 9(4): 319-334.* John Campbell, a placer prospector, reported to the legislature that he found gold at Fort Clarence at Halifax Harbour, Nova Scotia, in 1857. In 1861, he extended his efforts to the Sable Island area and discovered gold in the sand and gravel near the island; he also prospected in eastern Nova Scotia. His discoveries had a heavy impact on Nova Scotia's early gold mining industry. 30 notes, biblio. 1857-63

Campbell, John Archibald

1046. Jordan, Christine. LAST OF THE JACKSONIANS. *Supreme Court Hist. Soc. Y. 1980: 78-88.* John Archibald Campbell, a native of Georgia, was educated at the University of Georgia and at West Point before being admitted to the Georgia bar in 1829. He developed a very successful private law practice in Alabama and was appointed to the Supreme Court in 1853. He resigned his seat in 1861 and the following year became Assistant Secretary of War for the Confederacy. After the war Campbell returned to private practice with great success and at the time of his death was considered one of the nation's leading lawyers. Campbell was a Jacksonian Democrat whose juridical career on both sides of the bench was marked by strong adherence to state sovereignty, strict construction of federal power, opposition to the power of corporations, and judicial guardianship of individual rights. Based on court records and other primary and secondary sources; illus., 53 notes. 1829-89

Campbell, Richard

1047. Goodrich, James W. RICHARD CAMPBELL: THE MISSOURI YEARS. *Missouri Hist. Rev. 1977 72(1): 25-37.* Focuses primarily on Richard Campbell's economic ventures in Missouri and Louisiana during 1819-25. Involved in land speculation and the Indian trade, Campbell's financial situation fluctuated with the conditions of the frontier economy. After three bad years in Missouri, he made his first trip to Santa Fe in 1825. From then until his death in 1860 he was a trapper and trader of note throughout the Southwest. 1819-60

Campbell, Thomas D.

1048. —. [FARMING THE GREAT PLAINS AND THE CANADIAN PRAIRIES]. *Agric. Hist. 1977 51(1): 78-91.*

Drache, Hiram. THOMAS D. CAMPBELL—THE PLOWER OF THE PLAINS. Thomas D. Campbell was one of the first successful large-scale farmers. With capital from Eastern bankers he established a huge wheat farm in Montana using big machines. Assuming ownership of the farm in 1921, Campbell proved the economies of scale in large, mechanized farming by succeeding in a decade of low wheat prices. Campbell pioneered in the use of windrow harvesting, motorized wagon trains, soil conservation, and enlightened labor practices. 18 notes. 1915-1940

Campbell, Tom

1049. Campbell, Allen. REPUBLICAN POLITICS IN DEMOCRATIC ARIZONA: TOM CAMPBELL'S CAREER. *J. of Arizona Hist. 1981 22(2): 177-196.* The author's father, Tom Campbell, achieved prominence in Arizona and national political events despite being a Republican in a Democratic state. Besides the governorship, Tom Campbell played a leading role in state labor laws, tax laws, US relations with Mexico, the Bureau of Reclamation, and the US Civil Service Commission from 1901-32. Based on unpublished memoirs and secondary sources; 2 photos, 39 notes. 1875-1944

Campos, Albizu

1050. Poiarkova, N. T. ALBISU CAMPOS: NATSIONALNII GEROI PUERTO RICO [Albizu Campos: national hero of Puerto Rico]. *Novaia i Noveishaia Istoriia [USSR] 1972 (6): 130-141.* Discusses the life of Albizu Campos (1891-1965), the leader of Puerto Rico's struggle for independence. Considers his childhood, the influence the American occupation and colonization had on him, his education at the University of Vermont, his national service, his studies at the university after the war, the formation of the Nationalist Party in 1922, the development of his political ideas, and his return to his native land in 1921. Also examines his entry into the Nationalist Party in 1924, the development of the nationalist movement in the 1930's, the demonstration of March 1937, Campos's imprisonment, his release in 1947, his continued activity and imprisonment, and his influence on his fellow countrymen. Spanish and American secondary sources; 17 notes. 1910-65

Canby, Henry Seidel

1051. Harvey, LeRoy. "Days of Confidence: The Early Life of Henry Seidel Canby." U. of Michigan 1984. 464 pp. *DAI 1984 45(2): 561-A.* DA8412153 1920's-30's

Canevin, John F. Regis

1052. Schmandt, Raymond H. THE FRIENDSHIP BETWEEN BISHOP REGIS CANEVIN OF PITTSBURGH AND DR. LAWRENCE FLICK OF PHILADELPHIA. *Western Pennsylvania Hist. Mag. 1978 61(4): 283-300.* Describes the 40 year relationship between two prominent Pennsylvania Catholics, Bishop Regis Canevin (1853-1927) and Dr. Lawrence Flick (1856-1938). 1870's-1927

1053. Schmandt, Raymond H. SOME NOTES ON BISHOP J. F. REGIS CANEVIN OF PITTSBURGH (1904-1921). *Records of the American Catholic Historical Society of Philadelphia 1984 95(1-4): 91-107.* During John F. Regis Canevin's career as bishop of St. Paul's Cathedral in Pittsburgh, the diocese saw spectacular development, both physically and spiritually. Historians call the bishop "an astonishing man" because of his accomplishments, but since he avoided publicity, his personality has remained elusive. The warm, personal tone of a group of 96 extant letters between Canevin and his friend Lawrence Flick, collected at the Archives of the Catholic University of America, may help dispel Canevin's reputation as a cool, detached man. Reprints 16 Canevin-Flick letters, dated 1885 to 1921, with commentary. Based on letters in the Flick Collection of the Archives of the Catholic University of America, Washington, D.C. 1885-1921

Canfield, Martin (family)

1054. Ball, Lynn. THE VISITABLE PAST OF LAVINIA HARTWELL EGAN. *North Louisiana Hist. Assoc. J. 1978 9(1): 1-11.* Discusses Lavinia Hartwell Egan and her forebears who settled at Mount Lebanon, Louisiana, from 1835, when Martin Canfield was the first to settle in the area, to 1945, when Egan died. 1835-1945

Caniff, William

1055. MacDougall, Heather. PUBLIC HEALTH IN TORONTO'S MUNICIPAL POLITICS: THE CANIFF YEARS, 1883-1890. *Bull. of the Hist. of Medicine 1981 55(2): 186-202.* In March 1883, the Toronto city council named Dr. William Caniff as the first permanent medical health officer. Under his direction, the city's Medical Health Department increased its size and budget, developed a framework for dealing with various complaints, and made the initial efforts to strengthen public support for the idea of preventive medicine. Drawing upon British and American precedents, he successfully institutionalized public health work as an integral part of Toronto's municipal government. Based on contemporary newspapers and municipal reports; 65 notes. 1883-90

Cannon, Clarence

1056. Lilley, Stephen Ray. A MINUTEMAN FOR YEARS: CLARENCE CANNON AND THE SPIRIT OF VOLUNTEERISM. *Missouri Hist. Rev. 1980 75(1): 33-50.* Representative Clarence Cannon of Missouri achieved some fame during World War II when, as chairman of the House Appropriations Committee, he fought to secure funds for the Manhattan Project that was revolutionizing warfare. A believer in activism, Cannon fought for 20 years to gain a military commission during the Spanish-American War, the US punitive expedition against Mexico, and during World War I. Cannon's motives for making this long campaign are explored. Based on books, newspapers, interviews, the Cannon papers at the University of Missouri, Columbia; illus., 44 notes. 1898-1945

Cannon, Joseph Gurney

1057. Parshall, Gerald. "CZAR CANNON." *Am. Hist. Illus. 1976 11(3): 34-41.* Joseph Gurney Cannon (1836-1926), a Republican, was Speaker of the House 1901-11 but lost much of his power in the "Revolution of 1910" engineered by Democrats and rebellious Republicans. 1901-11

1058. Petterchak, Janice A. CONFLICT OF IDEALS, SAMUEL GOMPERS *V.* "UNCLE JOE" CANNON. *J. of the Illinois State Hist. Soc. 1981 74(1): 31-40.* Joseph Gurney Cannon, a conservative Republican from Danville, Illinois, served as Speaker of the US House of Representatives from 1903 to 1911. He did not share the good relationship with labor leader Samuel Gompers enjoyed by his predecessor Thomas B. Reed. Cannon's obstruction of labor legislation led Gompers to merge unionism with politics and issue, in 1906, a labor blacklist. Cannon was reelected in that year despite strong labor support in his district for Socialist John H. Walker. In the 1908 campaign, the American Federation of Labor endorsed the Democratic ticket. Cannon shared in the Republican victory of that year and was reelected in every campaign but one until his retirement in 1923. 6 illus., 38 notes. 1906-08

Cannon, Martha Hughes

1059. Lieber, Constance L. "THE GOOSE HANGS HIGH": EXCERPTS FROM THE LETTERS OF MARTHA HUGHES CANNON. *Utah Hist. Q. 1980 48(1): 37-48.* Martha Hughes Cannon (1857-1932) was the fourth polygamous wife of Angus Munn Cannon, president of the Salt Lake Stake of the Mormon Church. To prevent Angus Cannon's arrest for polygamy, Martha exiled herself to England during 1885-87. Her letters reveal loneliness, constant fear of exposure, fear of Cannon's arrest, and jealousy of other wives. The 1890 Manifesto allowed her to live openly in Salt Lake City and continue her medical career. In 1896 she became the first woman state senator in the United States. Based on letters and diaries in the Angus Munn Cannon collection, LDS Archives; 6 illus., 23 notes. 1885-96

Cannon, Mary

1060. Kernaghan, Lois. A MAN AND HIS MISTRESS: J. F. W. DES BARRES AND MARY CANNON. *Acadiensis [Canada] 1981 11(1): 23-42.* 1751-1827
*For abstract see **DesBarres, Joseph Frederic Wallet***

Cannon, Walter Bradford

1061. Fleming, Donald. WALTER B. CANNON AND HOMEOSTASIS. *Social Research 1984 51(3): 609-640.* Physiologist Walter Bradford Cannon contributed to the modern understanding of the physiology of digestion, the emotions, and neurotransmission, particularly the regulatory function of the sympathetic nervous system and its chemical neurotransmitters. 1897-1975

Capehart, Homer E.

1062. Taylor, John Raymond. "Homer E. Capehart: United States Senator, 1944-1962." Ball State U. 1977. 502 pp. *DAI 1977 38(3): 1607-A.* 1944-62

Capper, Arthur

1063. Partin, John W. THE DILEMMA OF "A GOOD, VERY GOOD MAN": CAPPER AND NONINTERVENTIONISM, 1936-1941. *Kansas Hist. 1979 2(2): 86-95.* Arthur Capper was a Republican senator from Kansas during 1919-49. Always a pacifist, he became a prominent noninterventionist. He made speeches advocating nationalization of the arms industry, reduction of armed forces, strict neutrality legislation, and a constitutional amendment for a popular referendum on war. When war came in 1941, however, Capper gave it his full support. Based on newspapers and manuscripts in the Library of Congress and Kansas State Historical Society; illus., 33 notes. 1936-41

Cappon, Lester Jesse

1064. Smith, James Morton. LESTER JESSE CAPPON. *Am. Arch. 1982 45(1): 105-108.* Lester J. Cappon enjoyed a distinguished career as history professor and archivist at the University of Virginia, first archivist of Colonial Williamsburg, director of the Institute of Early American History and Culture, and editor of the *William and Mary Quarterly.* Cappon also initiated the Papers of John Marshall Project and was the author or compiler of numerous bibliographical, historical, and archival works. In 1969, Cappon moved to the Newberry Library, where he became editor-in-chief of the Atlas of American History Project. Photo. 1940-81

1065. Tate, Thad W. LESTER JESSE CAPPON. *Pro. of the Am. Antiquarian Soc. 1982 92(1): 23-25.* Reviews the course of Cappon's career and the thrust of his research. His strengths as an editor and archivist reached their zenith with his editing of the *Atlas of Early American History: The Revolutionary Era, 1760-1776* (1976). 1900-81

Capps, Edwin M.

1066. Brownlee, John C. "BULL STRONG, HORSE HIGH, AND HOG TIGHT": THE WORK AND CHARACTER OF EDWIN M. CAPPS. *Journal of San Diego History 1984 30(3): 181-197.* A native of Tennessee, Edwin M. Capps began his career as a civil engineer in San Diego, California, in 1886. He served as the city's mayor in 1899-1902 and 1915-17, and as city engineer during 1911-15, directing several public works projects that helped control San Diego's booming growth. 1886-1923

Carden, Allen D.

1067. Crouse, David L. ALLEN D. CARDEN: EARLY TENNESSEE MUSICIAN. *Tennessee Hist. Q. 1980 39(1): 11-15.* A brief biography of Allen D. Carden (1796-1859), who conducted singing schools in Nashville. He also published three tunebooks for frontier churches, to maintain "a uniform system of music—that there may be a little more harmony of the different churches": *The Missouri Harmony* (1820), *The Western Harmony* (1824), and *United States Harmony* (1829). The first went through 22 editions during 1820-59. 14 notes. 1820-59

Cárdenas, Benigno

1068. Chavez, Angelico. A NINETEENTH-CENTURY NEW MEXICO SCHISM. *New Mexico Hist. Rev. 1983 58(1): 35-54.* Although suspended by the Catholic Church, Padre Nicholás Valencia and Fray Benigno Cárdenas administered the sacraments in the Belen-Tomé area of New Mexico during 1848-51. They performed invalid marriages and illegal baptisms, but the Church's efforts to end their schismatic behavior was complicated by the new US civil government. Bishop Lamy's arrival in 1851 ended Valencia's and Cárdenas's schism, although both continued to act as clergymen. Cárdenas later sought clerical posts in Europe, became a Methodist minister, and eventually reentered the Catholic Church. He spent his last days in Cuba. Valencia, under Bishop Lamy's supervision, became a recognized priest in Socorro and later served the Jémez Indian mission. Photo, 54 notes. 1845-85

Cardozo, Benjamin Nathan

1069. Brubaker, Stanley Charles. "Benjamin Nathan Cardozo: An Intellectual Biography." U. of Virginia 1979. 369 pp. *DAI 1980 40(9): 5165-A.* 1890's-1938

Cardozo, Francis L.

1070. Richardson, Joe M. FRANCIS L. CARDOZO: BLACK EDUCATOR DURING RECONSTRUCTION. *J. of Negro Educ. 1979 48(1): 73-83.* Cardozo was a freeborn South Carolina mulatto who obtained a European education before the Civil War. In 1865 he returned to Charleston, South Carolina, to direct a school under the auspices of the American Missionary Association for the newly freed blacks. His school quickly became the premier freedmen's school of South Carolina. His strong leadership abilities led him toward politics; he left his school in 1868 to serve in the state constitutional convention, and subsequently was elected to two major state offices. 37 notes. 1865-70

Careless, George

1071. Maxwell, Bruce David. GEORGE CARELESS, PIONEER MUSICIAN. *Utah Historical Quarterly 1985 53(2): 131-143.* Shortly after his arrival in Salt Lake City, Englishman George Careless, at Brigham Young's request, organized a series of professional classical-music concerts. Careless later conducted the Mormon Tabernacle Choir, coedited, with David O. Calder, the *Utah Musical Times,* and rewrote the *Latter-Day Saints' Psalmody.* 7 photos, 40 notes. 1865-1932

Carles, Arthur B.

1072. Wolanin, Barbara Ann Boese. "Arthur B. Carles, 1882-1952: Philadelphia Modernist." U. of Wisconsin, Madison 1981. 566 pp. *DAI 1981 42(2): 434-435-A.* 8112575 1900-52

Carless, Ray

1073. Roberts, Wayne. CARLESS: ROWDYMAN CARTOONIST. *Can. Dimension [Canada] 1981 15(8)-16(1): 47-49.* Surveys the career of Ray Carless, Canada's leading labor-oriented political cartoonist. 1932-81

Carleton, Guy

1074. Gorn, Michael Herman. "To Preserve Good Humor and Perfect Harmony: Guy Carleton and the Governing of Quebec, 1766-1774." U. of Southern California 1978. *DAI 1978 39(5): 3093-3094-A.* 1766-74

Carleton, Will

1075. Fallon, Jerome A. WILL CARLETON. *Michigan Hist. 1981 65(6): 33-39.* Will Carleton was once Michigan's premier poet. After the *Toledo Blade* published one of his poems in 1871, his fortune and reputation were made. *Harper's Weekly* began to publish his poems, both singly and in book form. The key to Carleton's success was his "homely philosophy, embracing love of country, integrity, and concern for the poor and aged" which "was understood by most Americans." 6 illus., 15 notes. 1871-1912

Carlin, George

1076. Carlin, George. LIFE ON THE ST. JOHNS DITCH. *J. of Arizona Hist. 1981 22(2): 159-176.* Author reminisces about his adolescence as a farm boy in Arizona, 1914-16. Based on personal experiences; 5 photos. 1914-16

Carlo, Kathleen

1077. Bauman, Margaret. SCULPTOR KATHLEEN CARLO. *Alaska Journal 1982 12(1): 4-9.* Reviews the career of Kathleen Carlo, an Alaskan sculptor and mask-maker whose work incorporates contemporary Western and traditional Athabascan influences. Carlo has held supervisory, instructional, and artist-in-residence posts in the Alaska interior and has gained prominence for her work in teak, birch, walnut, cedar, and other woods. Based on an interview with the artist; 13 photos. 1971-82

Carlos

1079. Reilly, Stephen Edward. A MARRIAGE OF EXPEDIENCE: THE CALUSA INDIANS AND THEIR RELATIONS WITH PEDRO MENÉNDEZ DE AVILÉS IN SOUTHWEST FLORIDA, 1566-1569. *Florida Hist. Q. 1981 59(4): 395-421.* Carlos, Calusa Indian chief, manipulated Pedro Menéndez de Avilés, the adelantado of Florida, into marrying Doña Antonia, a sister and wife of the chief. The marriage was to centralize political power for Carlos. The event provides a glimpse into the world of a little known but advanced Indian culture. Based on Spanish memoirs and records and other sources; 87 notes. 1566-69

Carlsen, Emil

1080. Sill, Gertrude. EMIL CARLSEN: LYRICAL IMPRESSIONIST. *Art and Antiques 1980 3(2): 88-95.* Examines the little-known work and career of Danish-born impressionist painter Emil Carlsen (1853-1933), who emigrated to the United States in 1872. Despite several visits to Europe for further study, Carlsen lived most of his life in the United States. Provides examples of his landscapes and still lifes. 1872-1933

Carlson, Ken

1081. Sasser, Ray. KEN CARLSON: STROKES OF INTENSITY. *Sporting Classics 1985 4(2): 29-37.* Discusses the lifestyle and artworks of Minnesotan Ken Carlson, whose wildlife paintings emphasize mood over detail. 1950's-84

Carmichael, William

1082. Segger, Martin. "WILLIAM MAURICE CARMICHAEL, SILVERSMITH", BRITISH COLUMBIA PROVINCIAL MUSEUM. *Material Hist. Bull. [Canada] 1981 (12): 70-77.* An exhibit in the British Columbia Provincial Museum of the work of Victoria-born and -educated silversmith William Carmichael illustrates his career spanning 1920-54. 1920-54

Carmines, Al

1083. Cioffi, Robert Joseph. "Al Carmines and the Judson Poets' Theater Musicals." New York U. 1979. 336 pp. *DAI 1980 40(11): 5649-A.* 8010330 1961-69

1084. Helm, Robert Boynton. "The Rev. Al Carmines and the Development of the Judson Poets' Theater." West Virginia U. 1979. 207 pp. *DAI 1980 40(12): 6259-A.* DA8012924 1960-79

Carmony, Donald F.

1085. Moss, Edward J. DONALD F. CARMONY. *Indiana Mag. of Hist. 1976 72(3): 256-260.* A portrait of the many faceted personality of Professor Donald F. Carmony, editor of the *Indiana Magazine of History* for 21 years. 1955-76

Carnegie, Andrew

1086. Deitch, Joseph. BENEVOLENT BUILDER: APPRAISING ANDREW CARNEGIE. *Wilson Library Bulletin 1984 59(1): 16-22.* Reviews philanthropic efforts of Andrew Carnegie, who had a tremendous impact on mass culture and education. 20c

1087. Farrah, Margaret Ann. "Andrew Carnegie: A Psychohistorical Sketch." Carnegie-Mellon U. 1982. 193 pp. *DAI 1982 42(11): 4906-A.* DA8209384 1865-1919

Carnes, Peter

1088. Hill, Raymond D. THE SEARCH FOR PETER CARNES. *Richmond County Hist. 1978 10(2): 5-10.* Peter Carnes (1749-94) lived in New Jersey, Maryland, and Georgia, and owned the Indian Queen Tavern in Bladensburg, Maryland, 1774-84, where he staged the first authenticated balloon launching in the United States in 1784. 1774-84

Carnevale, Emanuel

1089. Holte, James Craig. PRIVATE LIVES AND PUBLIC FACES: ETHNIC AMERICAN AUTOBIOGRAPHY. *Ethnic Groups 1982 4(1-2): 61-83.* Italian American autobiographies reveal a complex history and document diverse experiences. While no selection would be fully representative, the autobiographies of Constantine Panunzio, Leonard Covello, and Emanuel Carnevale provide firsthand accounts of the experiences of three Italian immigrants who responded to the pressures of a strange new land in three different ways. Panunzio argues for the adoption of American values as the path for success while Covello supports cultural pluralism. Carnevale tells the story of an immigrant who came to the United States and returned to Italy. 1880-1933

Carpenter, James F.

1090. Basham, Mickey L. THE CARPENTER FAMILY OF NORTHWEST TENNESSEE: "A FAMILY TOUCHED BY WAR" 1797-1966. *West Tennessee Hist. Soc. Papers 1978 (32): 20-31.* Centers around the life of Captain James F. Carpenter, CSA (1829-92). Cites several of his letters to his wife during the Civil War. Based largely on papers in the library of the author and on court records; 5 photos, 45 notes. 1797-1966

Carpenter, Ted

1091. Hilenski, Ferdinand Alexi. MOUNTAIN GUERRILLA: THE LIFE, DEATH, AND LEGACY OF BROADSIDE TV. *Kentucky Folklore Record 1980 26(1-2): 23-34.* Traces the background of Ted Carpenter, founder of Broadside TV of Johnson City, Tennessee, an alternative small format video station, noting Carpenter's interest in the people and communication in Tennessee; focuses on Broadside's programming from 1972 to 1974, the purpose of which was to provide community interaction and involvement. 1972-74

Carr, Elias

1092. Steelman, Lala Carr. THE ROLE OF ELIAS CARR IN THE NORTH CAROLINA FARMERS' ALLIANCE. *North Carolina Hist. Rev. 1980 57(2): 133-158.* Elias Carr (1839-1900), since 1859 master of Bracebridge Plantation, in eastern North Carolina entered state agricultural politics during the 1880's. By 1887 he was president of the newly formed North Carolina Farmers' State Association, which was absorbed the following year into the North Carolina Farmers' Alliance. Despite his upper class standing, Carr became a leader in the militant and powerful farm protest movement, first as executive committee chairman (1887-89) and then as Alliance president (1889-91). In these powerful positions, Carr, working with two other important Alliance leaders, Leonidas L. Polk (1837-92) and Sydenham B. Alexander (1840-1921), dealt with a number of tough and controversial problems, such as removing inept staff, establishing a viable business agency, boycotting the jute bagging trust, overseeing the educational programs, maintaining membership standards, and avoiding partisan politics while still supporting Senator Zebulon Vance. Though the Alliance under Carr sometimes faltered, it emerged from his presidency a stronger organization. Based primarily on Carr Papers at East Carolina University, and published proceedings of the Alliance; 14 illus., 112 notes. 1887-95

1093. Steelman, Lala Carr. THE LIFE-STYLE OF AN EASTERN NORTH CAROLINA PLANTER: ELIAS CARR OF BRACEBRIDGE HALL. *North Carolina Hist. Rev. 1980 57(1): 17-42.* Elias Carr (1839-1900), a wealthy planter, agricultural political leader, democrat, and North Carolina governor (1892-96), maintained a graceful, prosperous, satisfying lifestyle before and after the Civil War on his Edgecombe County estate, Bracebridge Hall. Unlike others of similar antebellum social and economic position, Carr managed to avoid the pitfalls of one-crop farming, sharecropping, labor unrest, and financial failure by diversifying his farming operations, employing workers at good wages, using fair labor practices, and using the latest scientific farming techniques. Based on recently discovered Elias Carr Papers at East Carolina University and published Carr genealogy records; 18 illus., 102 notes. 1839-1900

Carr, Emily

1094. Hirsch, Gilah Yelin. EMILY CARR. *Women's Studies 1978 6(1): 75-87.* Emily Carr, the Canadian painter, acquired her fame posthumously. Her success, while she was alive, was handicapped by her Victorian upbringing, economic distress, and insular lifestyle. Carr attended the San Francisco Art School, Westminster School of Art in London, St. Ives school in Cornwall, and the Academie Colorossi in Paris. In Paris she came under the influence of impressionism and fauvism. Her early paintings documented Indian history, life, and art. Her later works pursued expression of spirituality. Many of Carr's paintings are in the National Gallery in Ottawa. 7 fig., note. 1871-1945

Carr, Jeanne Caroline Smith

1095. Apostol, Jane. JEANNE CARR: ONE WOMAN AND SUNSHINE. *Am. West 1978 15(4): 28-33, 62-63.* Vermont-born Jeanne Caroline Smith Carr (1825-1903) was married to a medical scientist professor whose university assignments took them to California by way of Wisconsin. She became widely known as a feminist, author, botanist, officeholder, and educational reform activist. She met backwoods farmer John Muir while reporting on an exhibit of his inventions in Madison, Wisconsin. She became a close friend, correspondent, and mentor to Muir, whom she called "the Poet-Naturalist of our Coast." 4 illus., note, biblio. 1850's-1903

Carr, Mary Louise

1096. Smith, Catherine Parsons. A MUSICAL APPRENTICESHIP IN SAN FRANCISCO. *Halcyon 1985 7: 41-58.* Recounts the music education and early career of opera soprano Mary Louise Carr. 1889-95

Carroll, Charles

1097. McNamara, Robert F. CHARLES CARROLL OF BELLE VUE: CO-FOUNDER OF ROCHESTER. *Rochester Hist. 1980 42(4): 1-28.* Biography of Major Charles Carroll (1767-1823), who with Colonel Nathaniel Rochester and Colonel William Fitzhugh, founded Rochester. 1790-1823

Carroll, John

1098. Spalding, Thomas W. JOHN CARROLL: CORRIGENDA AND ADDENDA. *Catholic Historical Review 1985 71(4): 505-518.* Four problems in the life of John Carroll, the father of American Catholicism, have gone unremarked or unresolved. The first is that he was born in 1736, not 1735, as all of his American biographers have stated. The second is the date of his ordination was 1761 and not 1759 or 1769. The third is his relationship with Charles Henry Wharton, a literary antagonist, who was his first cousin once removed on his mother's side. The fourth is the large number of other "black sheep" relatives ignored by his biographers, most notably his Darnall uncles and cousin, and their impact on his attitude toward others. 71 notes. 1736-1815

Carson, Christopher (Kit)

1099. Jacquin, Philippe. KIT CARSON, LE "SELF-MADE MAN" DE L'OUEST [Kit Carson, the "self-made man" of the West]. *Histoire [France] 1982 (45): 84-87.* Kit Carson was an excellent marksman, brave adventurer, and defender of good causes, who served as a model for immigrants who ventured farther west than the Mississippi. 1809-68

1100. McKee, James Reese. "Kit Carson: Man of Fact and Fiction." Saint Louis U. 1977. 207 pp. *DAI 1978 38(9): 5553-A.* 1829-68

Carson, Will

1101. Horan, John F., Jr. WILL CARSON AND THE VIRGINIA CONSERVATION COMMISSION, 1926-1934. *Virginia Mag. of Hist. and Biog. 1984 92(4): 391-415.* A tribute to the career and contributions of Will Carson, founder of the Virginia Conservation and Development Commission during Harry F. Byrd's gubernatorial term. Carson emphasized development of the Old Dominion through conservation and promotion of the state as a tourist and vacation site. During his tenure as head of the commission, and with the support of presidents Hoover and Roosevelt, Carson created the Shenandoah National Park and its Blue Ridge Parkway. A falling out with the Byrd machine took Carson away from the commission after only seven years, but his efforts had a significant positive impact on the state's economy and growth. Based on 20th-century histories of Virginia and the South, the Henry D. Flood Papers and Claude A. Swanson's political correspondence (both at the Library of Congress), Virginia senate journals, and the Harry F. Byrd Papers (University of Virginia), the E. Griffith Dodson Papers (Virginia Historical Society), and contemporary newspapers; 79 notes. 1926-34

Carter, Brenda

1102. Walton, Carolyn. ARTIST BRENDA CARTER: A FASCINATION WITH THE ARCTIC'S VASTNESS AND THE ROLE OF MAN AND WILDLIFE IN IT. *Can. Geog. [Canada] 1984 104(5): 66-71.* Portrays the work of Canadian wilderness artist Brenda Carter, who specializes in depicting the wildlife of the Canadian Arctic. 1968-83

Carter, Charles W.

1103. Carter, Charles W. MEMORIES OF THE ALASKA GOLD RUSH. *Family Heritage 1978 1(4): 113-117.* Autobiography (recorded in 1941) of Charles W. Carter, who was born in 1870; describes his prospecting and jobs in Alaska during the Klondike Stampede, 1897-1906. 1897-1906

Carter, Fannie Cobb

1104. Frazier, Kitty and Simmons, Diana. FANNIE COBB CARTER (1872-1973). *J. of the West Virginia Hist. Assoc. 1983 6(1): 1-10.* Summarizes the career of black educator Fannie Cobb Carter and the education of black youth in West Virginia. 1891-1977

Carter, James Gordon

1105. Clark, Sylvia Marie. "James Gordon Carter: His Influence in Massachusetts Education, History, and Politics from 1820-1850." Boston Coll. 1982. 248 pp. *DAI 1982 43(2): 384-A.* DA8215460 1820-50

Carter, Jimmy

1105-A. Leapman, Michael. THE AMERICAN MOOD: 1979: PRESIDENT CARTER'S FIRST 30 MONTHS PROVE A DISAPPOINTMENT. *Round Table [Great Britain] 1979 (276): 343-346.* Outlines the personal characteristics and policies of President Jimmy Carter, 1977-79, and compares them with those of two of his rivals in his second-term campaign, Senator Edward M. Kennedy and Governor Jerry Brown. 1977-79

Carter, Leslie (Mrs.)

1106. Harper, Charles Harold. "Mrs. Leslie Carter: Her Life and Acting Career." U. of Nebraska, Lincoln 1978. 219 pp. *DAI 1979 39(7): 3925-A.* 1895-1906

Carter, Samuel Powatan

1107. Burns, Robert Carter. GENERAL AND ADMIRAL TOO. *East Tennessee Hist. Soc. Publ. 1976 48: 29-33.* Samuel Powatan Carter of Carter County, Tennessee, held the ranks of both general and admiral in the armed forces of the United States. After serving five years in the US Navy, he became one of the 60 men who formed the first class at Annapolis in 1845. When the Civil War broke out Carter was ordered from service aboard the steam sloop *Seminole* to temporary duty with the US Army. He performed meritorious duty during the war achieving the rank of Major General. At the conclusion of the war, he returned to duty with the Navy. Among his duty stations was a stint as Commandant of the Naval Academy. Illus., 9 notes. 1819-91

Carter, William Hodding, Jr.

1108. Garrison, Bruce M. WILLIAM HODDING CARTER JR: A DIFFERENT PERSPECTIVE OF THE CRUSADING EDITOR. *Journalism Hist. 1976 3(3): 90-93, 96.* Newspaperman Carter's campaign against political corruption and unfair government, and his work for racial justice from the 1930's to the 1950's, led to several clashes with the authorities in Mississippi. ca 1930-60

Cartier, George-Etienne

1109. Vigod, B. L. BIOGRAPHY AND POLITICAL CULTURE IN QUEBEC. *Acadiensis [Canada] 1977 7(1): 141-147.* Three recent biographies of Quebec political leaders during the 19th-20th centuries are discussed in this review article prompted by Alastair Sweeny's *George-Etienne Cartier* (Toronto: McClelland and Stewart, 1976), Robert Rumilly's *Maurice Duplessis et son temps* (2 vols., Montreal: Fides, 1973), and Conrad Black's *Duplessis* (Toronto: McClelland and Stewart, 1973), plus an analytical work by Jean-Louis Ray *La Marche des Québéçois: le temps des ruptures 1945-1960* (Montreal: Leméac, 1967). 19c-20c

Cartier, Jacques

1110. Jacquin, Philippe. JACQUES CARTIER ET LA DECOUVERTE DU CANADA [Jacques Cartier and the discovery of Canada]. *Histoire [France] 1984 (67): 38-46.* Describes the journeys of explorer Jacques Cartier to Canada and the beginnings of French colonization of the New World. 1530-50

1111. Koleneko, V. A. PUTESHESTVIIA ZHAKA KART'E (IZ ISTORII OTKRYTIIA KANADY) [Jacques Cartier's voyages (on the history of the discovery of Canada)]. *Amerikanskii Ezhegodnik [USSR] 1982: 272-294.* Describes three voyages to Canada during 1534-42 by Jacques Cartier, a French navigator and explorer. Initiated by the French king for the purpose of acquiring new territory and mineral wealth, the journals of the expeditions became one of the primary original sources on the cartography, flora and fauna, and Indian cultures of Canada. Based on Cartier's journals and secondary sources; 139 notes. 1534-42

1112. —. SPECIAL CANADA. 1: LA DECOUVERTE [Canada special. 1: the discovery]. *Historama [France] 1984 (3): 52-66.*

LaCroix, Robert de. LA FORMIDABLE AVENTURE DE JACQUES CARTIER [Jacques Cartier's great adventure]. *pp. 52-60.* Describes Jacques Cartier's voyages to Canada and French colonization of the New World.

Meyer, Jean. CHAMPLAIN FONDE LA NOUVELLE-FRANCE [Champlain founds New France]. *pp. 61-66.* Describes the French fur and mining industries in the New World, Samuel de Champlain's dealings with the Indians, the lives of early French colonists, and the founding of Quebec. 1534-43

Cartledge, Samuel

1113. Cartledge, Tony W. SAMUEL CARTLEDGE: COLONIAL "SAUL OF TARSUS." *Viewpoints 1982 8: 13-31.* Samuel Cartledge was a Baptist pastor in Georgia and South Carolina during 1790-1843; discusses his conversion and the style of his sermons. 1790-1843

Cartwright, Peter

1114. Bray, Robert. BEATING THE DEVIL: LIFE AND ART IN PETER CARTWRIGHT'S AUTOBIOGRAPHY. *Illinois Historical Journal 1985 78(3): 179-194.* The *Autobiography of Peter Cartwright, the Backwoods Preacher* (1856) sold over 30,000 copies in the United States and was equally successful when published in England three years later. It was the story of Peter Cartwright, a Methodist revivalist preacher. The autobiography was structured in terms of diametric oppositions: Cartwright as a Southern, Western, rural, masculine, and Methodist type versus the Yankee, Eastern, urban, feminine, and other religious types. 4 illus., 24 notes. 1810's-50's

Caruso, Enrico

1115. Kobler, John. BRAVO CARUSO! *Am. Heritage 1984 35(2): 104-110.* Enrico Caruso did much to stimulate opera in America. He preferred American audiences and spent much of his career in the United States. He came to the United States in 1903 and over the next 15 years gave an average of 40 performances per year at New York's Metropolitan Opera. His travels led him across the country. He survived the 1906 earthquake and a scandal in San Francisco. When his long-time female companion deserted him in 1908, Caruso turned to numerous amours until he met and married New Englander Dorothy Benjamin in 1918. A series of illnesses, including pneumonia and pleurisy, took his life just two months after he left the United States in 1921. 7 photos, 2 illus. 1903-21

Carver, Ada Jack

1116. Ford, Oliver. ADA JACK CARVER: THE BIOGRAPHY OF A SOUTHERN TRADITIONALIST. *Southern Studies 1979 18(2): 133-178.* Ada Jack Carver's (1890-1972) short stories, novels, and plays in the 1920's, set in her native region of Natchitoches, Louisiana, were awarded literary prizes and enthusiastic public acclaim. Her reputation has not remained high because she was unable to transcend her own circumstances. Her works are suffused with southern romanticism, stock characters, and plots in which characters are unable to break out of their isolation or niche in society. She was unable to accept the realism in the literature of her time. Her stories concerned, for the most part, alienated or socially disenfranchised and aging women. Her most successful short story was "Redbone" in 1924. Based on Melrose Collection at Northwestern State U., Louisiana, and other primary sources; 76 notes. 1920's

Carver, William Owen

1117. Dobbins, Gaines S. WILLIAM OWEN CARVER, MISSIONARY PATHFINDER. *Baptist Hist. and Heritage 1978 14(4): 2-6, 15.* William Owen Carver (1868-1954), a professor at the Southern Baptist Theological Seminary, taught a "Comparative Religion and Missions" course, which emphasized the Bible's missionary message, and that every Christian should be committed to being a missionary. Carver's ideas represented the turning point in Baptist thought after 50 years of the "great split" between the pro-missionaries and the anti-missionaries. 1859-1954

Cary, Samuel Fenton

1118. Dannenbaum, Jed. THE CRUSADER: SAMUEL CARY AND CINCINNATI TEMPERANCE. *Cincinnati Hist. Soc. Bull. 1975 33(2): 136-151.* Chronicles Samuel Fenton Cary's fight against alcohol in Cincinnati, Ohio, and his active membership in temperance movements both locally and nationally, 1845-1900. 1845-1900

Cash, Johnny

1119. Tucker, Stephen R. PENTECOSTALISM AND POPULAR CULTURE IN THE SOUTH: A STUDY OF FOUR MUSICIANS. *J. of Popular Culture 1982 16(3): 68-80.* 1950's-70's

For abstract see ***Blackwood, James***

Cass, Lewis

1120. Klunder, Willard Carl. "Lewis Cass, 1782-1866: A Political Biography." U. of Illinois, Urbana-Champaign 1981. 606 pp. *DAI 1982 42(9): 4119-4120-A.* DA8203503 1800-66

Cassedy, Charles

1121. Durham, Walter T. CHARLES CASSEDY, EARLY NINETEENTH CENTURY TENNESSEE WRITER. *Tennessee Hist. Q. 1977 36(3): 305-329, (4): 493-511.* Part I. Charles Cassedy produced his first article in Tennessee in 1810. He worked for various newspapers, was a friend of Andrew Jackson, and was a long-time defender of Brigadier General James Winchester, who was charged with misconduct at the Battle of the River Raisin in 1813. Cassedy published several notices of an intended history of Tennessee, but it never appeared. Primary and secondary sources; 96 notes. Part II. Charles Cassedy continued to produce articles and letters to newspapers, 1832-52. His choice of subjects knew no limits, but he wrote mostly about politics and politicians. He planned books on both history and language, though they were never published. His career was severely hampered by poverty aggravated by alcoholism. He died before 1858. Primary and secondary sources; 71 notes. 1810-50's

Cassidy, Butch

See Parker, Robert LeRoy

Cassidy, Harry

1122. Irving, John Allen. "A Canadian Fabian: The Life and Work of Harry Cassidy." U. of Toronto [Canada] 1983. *DAI 1984 44(9): 2855-A.* 1930's-40's

Casson, John

1123. Stanciu, Ion. JOHN CASSON, DIPLOMAŢIA AMERICANĂ ŞI INDEPENDENŢA ROMÂNIEI (1877-1880) [John Casson, American diplomacy and Romania's independence, 1877-80]. *Rev. de Istorie [Romania] 1977 30(6): 1035-1050.* Examines US diplomacy in Southeastern Europe, especially in Romania, during and after the Russo-Turkish War, 1877-78. Focuses on the role of John Casson, Ambassador in Vienna, in informing the US government of political developments and encouraging the establishment of consular representation in the newly independent countries. The consulate in Bucharest was the principal channel for the Romanian government to communicate its policies with Washington, but financial problems delayed the extension of diplomatic relations after the war. Casson pressed the US government to develop diplomatic representation in Bucharest and Belgrade to further diplomatic and commercial interests. As a direct result, the first US diplomatic representative in Bucharest was named in 1880 and became ambassador continuing Casson's work, and a Romanian ambassador to Washington was named, confirming US official recognition of Romania's independence. 73 notes. 1877-80

Castañeda, Carlos Eduardo

1124. Almaráz, Félix D., Jr. CARLOS E. CASTAÑEDA'S RENDEZVOUS WITH A LIBRARY: THE LATIN AMERICAN COLLECTION, 1920-27—THE FIRST PHASE. *J. of Lib. Hist. 1981 16(2): 315-328.* Discusses the career of Carlos Eduardo Castañeda. He was born in 1896 in Mexico, and then attended school in Texas. He was regional director of President Franklin D. Roosevelt's Committee on Fair Employment Practices, librarian of the Benson Latin American Collection at the University of Texas at Austin, and a first-rate historian of the Borderlands. This article discusses the first phase of Castañeda's involvement with the library, which began in 1920 and concluded in 1927, when he assumed responsibility for the Latin American Collection. Personal correspondence; 38 notes. 1920-27

Castañer, Juan

1125. Díaz, Luis E. ACTIVIDADES FINANCIERAS DE UN HACENDADO CAFETALERO EN PUERTO RICO EN EL SIGLO XIX [Financial activities of a 19th-century owner of a coffee hacienda in Puerto Rico]. *Horizontes [Puerto Rico] 1982 25(50): 69-77.* During the 19th century, the Balearic Islands supplied many immigrants to Puerto Rico, among whom was Juan Castañer, a young man from Majorca. He became owner of a coffee hacienda and a commercial house in Yauco. Among his activities were moneylending and the organization of the first credit and savings bank in Ponce. Based on primary sources in Puerto Rican archives; 30 notes. 1860-1912

Castex, Raoul

1126. Hunt, Barry D. THE OUTSTANDING NAVAL STRATEGIC WRITERS OF THE CENTURY. *Naval War Coll. Rev. 1984 37(5): 86-107.* 1880's-1984
For abstract see ***Corbett, Julian S.***

Cater, Harry William

1127. Clark, W. Leland. HARRY CATER: THE PERSONIFICATION OF THE SUCCESSFUL MUNICIPAL POLITICIAN? *Tr. of the Hist. and Sci. Soc. of Manitoba [Canada] 1977-79 (34-35): 163-176.* Harry William Cater, a small-businessman and self-proclaimed voice of the working man, dominated Brandon's mayoral politics during 1914-18, 1921-31, and 1933-37. Opposed by the supporters of growth and development, Cater emphasized civic economy and retrenchment. His theme of limited taxation was supported by retired farmers, small businessmen, and wage-earners. Although accused of dictatorial tendencies, Cater was ultimately defeated by two factors beyond his control: the passage of time and Brandon's financial collapse. 120 notes. 1914-37

Cather, Willa

1128. Bennett, Mildred R. THE CHILDHOOD WORLDS OF WILLA CATHER. *Great Plains Q. 1982 2(4): 204-209.* Briefly describes the childhood of Willa Cather and its influence on her fiction; born in Virginia, she moved with her family to Nebraska in 1883. 1873-1900

1129. Benson, Peter. WILLA CATHER AT THE *HOME MONTHLY*. *Biography 1981 4(3): 227-248.* Willa Cather's first full-fledged literary apprenticeship came as managing editor of a women's domestic magazine where her writing germinated within the strictly defined genres of 19th-century popular journalism. However, critical neglect of these early writings and a serious error of fact, perpetuated by generations of scholars, have obscured these important influences on her early development. 1896-1900

1130. Cherny, Robert W. WILLA CATHER AND THE POPULISTS. *Great Plains Q. 1983 3(4): 206-218.* Examples in the writing of Willa Cather reveal her negative opinion of Populists in Nebraska as lazy, radical complainers. 1890's-1948

1131. Klug, Michael A. WILLA CATHER: BETWEEN RED CLOUD AND BYZANTIUM. *Can. Rev. of Am. Studies [Canada] 1981 12(3): 287-299.* Writing early in the 20th century, American novelist Willa Cather (1876-1947) was troubled by the same spiritual and aesthetic contradictions that have frustrated 20th-century artists more recently. On the broadest level, Cather shares with her literary successors the conflicts inherent to the artistic desire for freedom and personal success and artists' opposite impulses to make social equality and human brotherhood paramount. Based on Cather's writings and secondary sources; 12 notes. 20c

1132. Knopf, Alfred A. RANDOM RECOLLECTIONS OF A PUBLISHER. *Massachusetts Hist. Soc. Pro. 1961 73: 92-103.* Publisher Alfred A. Knopf of New York shares anecdotes about authors Thomas Mann, Clarence Day, Willa Cather, Kahlil Gibran, and H. L. Mencken, whom he admired professionally, and, quite frankly, savored, from the days when literary relations were personal, before modernization and professional editing techniques; 1901-61. 1901-61

1133. Lovering, Joseph P. THE FRIENDSHIP OF WILLA CATHER AND DOROTHY CANFIELD. *Vermont Hist. 1980 48(3): 144-154.* From their collaboration in writing a prize short story in 1894 until Cather's death in 1947, the two authors corresponded with and visited each other, except for a decade of unexplained coolness between them from about 1905 to early 1916. The hiatus perhaps relates to the elder woman's direct rise from frontier Nebraska, with less social status or grace than Canfield, but earlier literary success. 1894-1947

1134. Parks, B. K. A DEDICATION TO THE MEMORY OF WILLA CATHER, 1873-1947. *Arizona and the West 1979 21(3): 210-214.* Throughout her years at the University of Nebraska, in journalism in Pennsylvania and publishing in New York, and in retirement, Willa Cather (1873-1947) wrote poetry, short stories, and novels. Her early writings reflected her bitterness toward the shallow crudeness of western (principally Nebraskan) and southwestern life. Later she came to view the West as a stage on which the fulfillment as well as the frustration of universal desires were played. She celebrated the "singular vitality" of European cultural contributions to the West. Illus., biblio. 1890's-1940's

1135. Rowse, A. L. ON THE TRACK OF WILLA CATHER IN NEBRASKA. *Blackwood's Mag. [Great Britain] 1980 328(1978): 84-92, (1979): 164-171.* Part I. Reminiscences about Willa Cather, whom the author met when he visited her sister Elsie and friend Louise Pound on occasional visits to Lincoln and Red Cloud, Nebraska, where Cather grew up and set some of her fiction; 1957-79. Part II. Continuing the description of Cather's life in Nebraska which inspired her novels, focuses on discussions with Cather's sister and Louise Pound, covering the early 20th century through 1979. 20c

1136. Slote, Bernice. AN EXPLORATION OF CATHER'S EARLY WRITING. *Great Plains Q. 1982 2(4): 210-217.* Describes the 20 years of Willa Cather's career as journalist and editor prior to her first novels, *Alexander's Bridge* (1912) and *O Pioneers!* (1913); finds influences and attitudes not usually ascribed to her later works. 1890's-1910

1137. Southwick, Helen C. WILLA CATHER'S EARLY CAREER: ORIGINS OF A LEGEND. *Western Pennsylvania Hist. Mag. 1982 65(2): 85-98.* Discusses the inaccuracies of many biographies about Willa Cather such as those by Elizabeth Moorhead, and by E. K. Brown and Leon Edel, focusing on Cather's years in Pittsburgh and her friendship with Isabelle McClung. 1896-1981

1138. Stineback, David. THE CASE OF WILLA CATHER. *Can. Rev. of Am. Studies [Canada] 1984 15(4): 385-395.* Although literary analysts have claimed that nostalgia for the past preoccupied novelist Willa Cather, references to the historical past did not pervade her writings to the exclusion of sensitivity and concern with her own times. Other analysts misjudged Cather's art by confusing her keen awareness of contemporary American culture and its values with her reputed alienation from American life in the 20th century. Based on Cather's writings and secondary sources; 14 notes. 1913-47

1139. Woodress, James. THE USES OF BIOGRAPHY: THE CASE OF WILLA CATHER. *Great Plains Q. 1982 2(4): 195-203.* Because most fiction is autobiographical in some sense, biographers of authors may be able to use the fictive work to draw out valuable data; study of the author's life in turn will supply information on the inspiration for the novel; utilizes the life and novels of Willa Cather to demonstrate the methodology. ca 1873-1920's

1140. Yongue, Patricia Lee. WILLA CATHER'S ARISTOCRATS. *Southern Humanities Rev. 1980 14(1): 43-56.* Part I. Discusses Willa Cather's desire to have a successful career, succeed in a world of men as an artist, and be a lady like her mother; based on information from her biographers and close friends, focuses on Cather's friendship with British aristocrat Stephen Tennant and her enjoyment of beauty, wealth, and expensive tastes, contrary to the female characters portrayed in her novels and short stories who lived honest, rugged pioneer lives; 1915-47. Article to be continued. 1915-47

Catlin, George

1141. Cohen, George M. GEORGE CATLIN: INDIAN PAINTER WITH A NOBLE MISSION. *Art & Antiques 1981 4(1): 50-57.* George Catlin (1796-1872) painted American Plains Indians from 1830 to 1836 and opened Catlin's Indian Gallery in New York City in 1837, but suffered disappointments during the rest of his life while arranging Indian exhibitions and other projects. ca 1830-72

1142. Hassrick, Royal B. GEORGE CATLIN'S INDIAN GALLERY. *Am. West 1978 15(1): 20-33.* George Catlin (1796-1872) was trained as a lawyer. He gave up practice after a few years to become a portrait painter. Self-trained, he met with "fair success," especially with miniatures, and was recognized and exhibited by leading art academies. Inspired by a costumed Indian delegation on its way to the national capital, Catlin dedicated his talents to a pictorial and written record of the Indians. He was a showman and lecturer as well and his Indian Gallery was exhibited widely throughout England, France, and the United States. He painted hundreds of portraits of 55 tribes in their home locations. Excerpted from a recently published book. 10 illus. 1830-60's

1143. Millichap, Joseph R. GEORGE CATLIN. *Am. Hist. Illus. 1977 12(5): 4-9, 43-48.* George Catlin, renowned for his paintings of Indian life, dedicated his life during 1832-48 to capturing the disappearing cultures on canvas and promoting their cause among the public in the eastern United States as well as Great Britain. 1832-48

Cattell, Jonas

1144. Cunningham, John T. FASTER THAN FOXES. *New Jersey Hist. 1979 97(1): 37-44.* During the American Revolution Jonas Cattell, a long distance runner, was scout and messenger. After the war he served as a guide and "whipper-in" for the Gloucester Fox Hunting Club. He met challenges from local runners. In his old age he satisfied himself with shorter runs, hearty walks, and the life of a woodsman. He gradually wore out, and died in his nineties. Based on Cattell's pamphlet, *Memoirs of the Gloucester Fox Hunting Club,* 1830; 7 illus. 1775-1830's

Catton, Bruce

1145. Jensen, Oliver. BRUCE CATTON. *Pro. of the Am. Antiquarian Soc. 1978 88(2): 169-173.* Bruce Catton's death in August 1978 removed a fascinating person and devoted historian from our midst. Surveys Catton's life (1899-1978) and his love affair with history. His major contribution was probably to treat history as literature, an approach ably reflected through his efforts with *American Heritage.* 1954-78

Causey, George (T. L.)

1146. Burroughs, Jean M. THE LAST OF THE BUFFALO HUNTERS, GEORGE CAUSEY: HUNTER, TRADER, RANCHER. *Palacio 1974 80(4): 15-21.* George (T. L.) Causey was first introduced to the Great Plains and the Texas-New Mexico Llano Estacado as a buffalo hunter and trader, 1865 ff.; but when slaughter of buffalo and settlement diminished herds, Causey settled near Ranger lake, New Mexico, to establish a cattle and mustang ranch, 1881-1903. 1865-1903

Cave, Daniel

1147. Kramer, William M. DANIEL CAVE: SOUTHERN CALIFORNIA PIONEER DENTIST, CIVIC LEADER AND MASONIC DIGNITARY. *Western States Jewish Hist. Q. 1977 9(2): 99-121.* Daniel Cave (1841-1936) had practiced dentistry in Vienna, Austria, before coming to America in 1873 to improve his skills. He established a practice in San Diego, California, later moving to Los Angeles. As founder of the Dental Society of San Diego he emphasized that dentistry was a scientific medical profession. He was named a special clinician at the University of Southern California Dental School in 1897, attended every conference in his profession, and had a special interest in new equipment and techniques. Active participation in San Diego civic and political organizations was an important responsibility to Cave, who was a library trustee, president of the San Diego Water Company, an officer of the Society for the Prevention of Cruelty to Animals, and Republican candidate for alderman in 1889. Cave was also a leader of Masonic lodges in San Diego and Los Angeles. Based on interviews, personal correspondence and published material; 3 photos, 68 notes. 1873-1936

Cave, Robert Catlett

1148. Pearson, Samuel C., Jr. THE CAVE AFFAIR: PROTESTANT THOUGHT IN THE GILDED AGE. *Encounter 1980 41(2): 179-203.* Recounts the life and theology of Robert Catlett Cave (1843-1924), whose sermon of 1889 in St. Louis, Missouri, which challenged the literal interpretation of the Bible, created a controversy among the Disciples of Christ. 1840's-90's

1149. Pearson, Samuel C., Jr. RATIONALIST IN AN AGE OF ENTHUSIASM: THE ANOMALOUS CAREER OF ROBERT CAVE. *Missouri Hist. Soc. Bull. 1979 35(2): 99-108.* A theological liberal, Robert Catlett Cave (1843-1923) became pastor of the Central Christian Church at St. Louis in 1888. From that pulpit he challenged many traditional Christian views and was, as a consequence, ousted from his pastorate. Case and his followers then formed their own congregation and, for more than a decade, Cave remained on Protestantism's most "liberal fringe." Eventually he became an advocate of universalist theology based on nature and reason. Archival sources and secondary works; photo, 54 notes. 1867-1923

Cazneau, William and Jane

1150. May, Robert E. LOBBYISTS FOR COMMERCIAL EMPIRE: JANE CAZNEAU, WILLIAM CAZNEAU, AND U.S. CARIBBEAN POLICY, 1846-1878. *Pacific Hist. Rev. 1979 48(3): 383-412.* The entrepreneurial, diplomatic, and lobbying activities of Jane and William Cazneau influenced the reorientation of US policy in the Caribbean area from territorial imperialism to commercial expansionism. They were interested in the annexation and commercial exploitation of Cuba, Texas colonization near the Mexican border, business investments in the Dominican Republic, and claims to guano deposits at Swan Island off the Central American coast. William Cazneau was twice a US diplomat in the Dominican Republic, and he and Jane Cazneau lobbied for development of a US naval base at Samana Bay. They were especially interested in US business penetration of the Dominican Republic. Most of their expansionist causes failed, but their writings and activities reflect changing US attitudes and policies toward the Caribbean area. Based on archival sources, personal papers, contemporary imprints, and secondary sources; 60 notes. 1846-78

Cervin, Emma

1151. Cervin, Olof Z. EMMA CERVIN, A PIONEER MOTHER. *Swedish-American Hist. Q. 1982 33(3): 207-213.* A biographical sketch of Olof Cervin's mother. Emma Cervin, born in 1833, was married in 1864 and emigrated from Sweden to Chicago with her Lutheran pastor husband and their adopted twin girls. Four more children were born to the family, and Emma spent her life mothering them and anyone else who needed help, until her death in 1915. Based on the papers of Olof Z. Cervin in the Swenson Swedish Immigration Research Center at Augustana College, Rock Island, Illinois; photo. 1833-1915

Chaban, Teklia

1152. Woywitka, Anne B. A PIONEER WOMAN IN THE LABOUR MOVEMENT. *Alberta Hist. [Canada] 1978 26(1): 10-16.* Teklia Chaban was born in the Ukraine. She moved to Alberta in 1914, the year of her marriage. Her husband worked in the Cardiff coal mines, 15 miles north of Edmonton. Follows the family for the next 10 years, with agitation for a labor organization, dealings with the United Mine Workers of America, and strikes and violence in the early 1920's. She was active in Ukrainian cultural movements that were part of the labor efforts. In the mid-1920's the family moved to Edmonton, and again was involved in agitation for labor recognition, spending some time in jail and suffering periodic unemployment for their efforts. 2 illus. 1914-20's

Chadwick, French Ensor

1153. Peake, Louis A. REAR ADMIRAL FRENCH ENSOR CHADWICK: SAILOR AND SCHOLAR. *West Virginia Hist. 1980-81 42(1-2): 75-87.* Describes the career of French Ensor Chadwick, a West Virginia native and graduate of the US Naval Academy who played an important role in the US navy in the latter part of the 19th century. After serving on the board of inquiry which investigated the sinking of the battleship *Maine* in Havana Harbor, Chadwick commanded the *New York* during the Spanish-American War, and participated in the Battle of Santiago. During 1900-03 he served as president of the Naval War College. He also wrote numerous scholarly works. Illus., 2 photos, 57 notes. 1855-1919

Chalfant, Jefferson David

1154. Gorman, Joan H. JEFFERSON DAVID CHALFANT: STILL LIFE AND GENRE PAINTER. *Am. Art & Antiques 1979 2(4): 104-109.* Jefferson David Chalfant (b. 1856) painted most of his trompe l'oeils from 1887 to 1890, and after 1890 painted genre paintings using photographs as a guide for the intricate detail. 1887-1927

Challe, Robert

1155. Runte, Roseann. ROBERT CHALLE: AN EARLY VISITOR TO ACADIA AND QUEBEC. *Nova Scotia Hist. Q. [Canada] 1979 9(3): 201-214.* Robert Challe (b. 1659) accompanied an expedition to the coast of Acadia in 1681. The company chose a site at Chedabucto at the head of the Bay of Canso to establish a settlement. Challe's journal (Journal de Voyage), written 25 years later, presents a history of the settlement and includes descriptions of the country, a plan for colonizing the area, criticisms of the French management of the colony, and his own personal experiences. 17 notes. 1681

Chaloult, René

1156. Chouinard, Denis and Jones, Richard. LA CARRIERE POLITIQUE DE RENE CHALOULT: L'ART DE PROMOUVOIR UNE POLITIQUE NATIONALISTE TOUT EN SAUVEGARDANT SON AVENIR POLITIQUE [The Political career of René Chaloult: the art of promoting a nationalist policy while safeguarding a political future]. *Revue d'Histoire de l'Amérique Française [Canada] 1985 39(1): 25-50.* René Chaloult was a member of the Quebec legislature from 1936 to 1952. A nationalist, he was an independent member and prolonged his career by shifting his political alliances several times. The domination of the Union Nationale after 1944 reduced his maneuverability and isolated him. Based on the Lionel Groulx archives and the René Chaloult papers, Archives Nationales, Quebec; 165 notes. 1936-52

Chamberlain, John

1157. Annunziata, Frank. THE POLITICAL THOUGHT OF JOHN CHAMBERLAIN: CONTINUITY AND CONVERSION. *South Atlantic Q. 1975 74(1): 74-85.* John Chamberlain is the classic example of a 1920's radical becoming a 1950's conservative. His 1932 *Farewell to Reform* issued a blistering condemnation of New Deal Liberalism for attempting to rescue a foundering capitalism. Disappointment with Soviet Russia led him in *The American Stakes* (1940) to reject any state-led attempt at social salvation. Worldwide postwar repression of personal liberty pushed him to the Right as he first joined Henry Hazlitt and Susan La Follette in publishing the conservative journal *Freeman* and then supported McCarthyism. Later ties with Henry Luce made him endorse policies similar to those he denounced in 1932. Based on primary and secondary sources; 58 notes. 1920's-65

Chamberlain, Mariam

1158. Glauberman, Susan. A CONVERSATION WITH MARIAM CHAMBERLAIN AND FRED CROSSLAND. *Change 1981 13(8): 32-37.* Focuses on the careers and accomplishments of Fred Crossland and Mariam Chamberlain, influential members of the Ford Foundation, during 1963-81, who left to pursue other interests in higher education. 1963-81

Chambers, Jordan

1159. Gillespie, J. David and Gillespie, Judi F. STRUGGLE FOR IDENTITY: THE LIFE OF JORDAN CHAMBERS. *Phylon 1979 40(2): 107-118.* Henry Jordan Clay Caldwell Chambers (1813-92) claimed that he was the child of white parents and was sold into slavery at age 11. He served until emancipation, frequently mentioning his white ancestry. Discusses independent corroboration of more than 60 names, dates, and events in Jordan's *Memoirs* and his youngest daughter's recollections, suggesting that Chambers' claim to be white was probably true. 33 notes. 1813-92

Chambers, Samuel D.

1160. —. SAINT WITHOUT PRIESTHOOD: THE COLLECTED TESTIMONIES OF EX-SLAVE SAMUEL D. CHAMBERS. *Dialogue 1979 12(2): 13-21.* Samuel D. Chambers, long-time black member of the Church of Jesus Christ of Latter Day Saints, converted to Mormonism in 1844 while a slave youth, and though illiterate and soon isolated from other members of the faith, remained true to its teachings for 25 years, until circumstances permitted him to emigrate to Salt Lake City. He soon became a Deacon, but being black prohibited advancement to the priesthood. Contains publication of minutes of his testimonies during 1873-76, primarily consisting of thanks to God and the church for the good life he enjoyed. 2 photos, 7 notes. 1844-76

Chambrun, Adolphe de

1161. Tissier, André. CES COUPLES QUI TRAVERSENT L'HISTOIRE [These couples who traverse history]. *Ecrits de Paris [France] 1979 (391): 83-88.* Biography of Adolphe de Chambrun (1831-91) and his wife Marthe de Corcelle, grandparents of René de Chambrun, and direct descendants of the Marquis de Lafayette. Describes the letters Marthe and Adolphe exchanged while Adolphe was on a diplomatic mission in the United States at the end of the Civil War, 1865. 1865

Champlain, Samuel de

1162. —. SPECIAL CANADA. 1: LA DECOUVERTE [Canada special. 1: the discovery]. *Historama [France] 1984 (3): 52-66.* Meyer, Jean. CHAMPLAIN FONDE LA NOUVELLE-FRANCE [Champlain founds New France]. 1534-43

For abstract see ***Cartier, Jacques***

Chandler, Elizabeth Margaret

1163. Jones, Mary Patricia. "Elizabeth Margaret Chandler: Poet, Essayist, Abolitionist." U. of Toledo 1981. 277 pp. *DAI 1983 43(8): 2668-A.* DA8229784 1807-34

1164. Yates, Dorothy Langdon. MICHIGAN'S FEMALE ABOLITIONIST. *Chronicle 1981 17(3): 28-31.* Recounts the life of Elizabeth Margaret Chandler (1807-34), a Quaker from Michigan, who was the "first female writer in America to make abolition her principal theme." 1807-36

Chandler, Joseph Ripley

1165. Gerrity, Frank. JOSEPH RIPLEY CHANDLER AND THE *CATHOLIC HERALD*: A NOTE. *Records of the Am. Catholic Hist. Soc. of Philadelphia 1982 93(1-4): 103-106.* Examines the career of Joseph Ripley Chandler, an editor of Philadelphia's first Catholic newspaper, the *Catholic Herald.* After he retired from politics, apparently because of adverse reaction to his conversion to Catholicism, he assumed editorship of the paper from August 1855 to May 1856. Describes reasons for his becoming editor as well as those for his resignation. 10 notes. 1855-56

Chandler, Raymond

1166. Smith, David. THE PUBLIC EYE OF RAYMOND CHANDLER. *J. of Am. Studies [Great Britain] 1980 14(3): 423-441.* Raymond Chandler (b. 1888) came to Los Angeles, California, in 1919, and there observed the rapid transformation of the area into a sprawling metropolis during the next several decades. An oil executive who became a writer of detective book fiction in the 1930's, Chandler interpreted this new westward movement, focusing on the frustrations of migrants who, expecting a western utopia, helped to fashion a society contrary to their ideals. Chandler's earliest novels included *The Big Sleep* (1939), *Farewell, My Lovely* (1940), and the *The High Window* (1943). Based on Chandler's writings; 65 notes. ca 1930-80

Channing, William Ellery

1167. McGuffie, Duncan S. WILLIAM ELLERY CHANNING'S RELIGION AND ITS INFLUENCE. *Tr. of the Unitarian Hist. Soc. [Great Britain] 1980 17(2): 45-53.* A note on William Ellery Channing on the bicentennial of his birth describes Channing's religious convictions, including his reaction against Calvinism, and his early attempts to bridge the gulf between Unitarians and Trinitarians. Although he resisted the idea, there was a transcendental element in Channing's religious outlook. It stemmed from the Puritan tradition and 18th-century rationalism, and produced a belief of human perfectibility expressed in rational vocabulary. 35 notes. 1780-1840

Chaplin, Millicent Mary

1168. Sparling, Mary. THE LIGHTER AUXILIARIES: WOMEN ARTISTS IN NOVA SCOTIA IN THE EARLY NINETEENTH CENTURY. *Atlantis [Canada] 1979 5(1): 83-106.* Focuses on painters Maria Morris (1813-75), Alicia Anne Jeffery (b. 1808), and Millicent Mary Chaplin (active 1838-44). 19c

Chapman, John

1169. Hoaglund, Edward. JOHNNY APPLESEED: THE QUIETLY COMPELLING LEGEND OF AMERICA'S GENTLEST PIONEER. *Am. Heritage 1979 31(1): 61-73.* Describes the life of John Chapman (1774-1845) as he disseminated apple tree seedlings and Swedenborgianism throughout the frontier west; 1795-1840. 1795-1840

Chapman, John Jay

1170. Mullen, John E. "The Enigma of John Jay Chapman." U. of Iowa 1980. 214 pp. *DAI 1980 41(4): 1598-A.* 8022052 1877-1933

Chapman, R. R.

1171. Chapman, R. R. CHEYENNE-ARAPAHO HOMESTEAD. *Chronicles of Oklahoma 1980 58(3): 343-346.* Relates the reminiscences of the author and his family who established a homestead near Arapaho, Oklahoma, in 1898. Though pioneering in a dugout was difficult, other farmers soon arrived and helped establish a school, church, and post office in the vicinity. The author discusses the shooting of a farmer by a cattleman, and the deaths of two people from typhoid fever. 1898-1910

Chargaff, Erwin

1172. Edsall, John T. [MEMOIRS OF ERWIN CHARGAFF]. *Isis 1979 70(252): 276-277.* A review article of Erwin Chargaff's *Heraclitean Fire: Sketches from a Life Before Nature* (New York: Rockefeller U. Pr., 1978). Chargaff, one of the distinguished biochemists of the 20th century, describes his youth in Austria, early work in Berlin, and career at Columbia University, 1935-75. His account of the development of biochemistry, especially the study of DNA, and the work of his professional colleagues, combines gratification for scientific progress with deep disappointment over the misapplication of science and technology and the excessive ambition within the profession. 20c

Charters, Werrett Wallace, Sr.

1173. Russell, John Charters. "Werrett Wallace Charters, Sr. (1875-1952): His Life, Career and Influence upon Pharmaceutical Education." Loyola U., Chicago 1981. 267 pp. *DAI 1981 41(11): 4624-A.* 8109965 1900-52

Chase, Henrietta Clay Curtis

1174. Armstrong, Ruth W. NETTIE CHASE'S WORLD: THE LIFE OF A NEW MEXICO RANCH WOMAN. *Palacio 1981 87(2): 33-37.* Biography of pioneer Henrietta Clay Curtis Chase (1880-1927). ca 1900-27

Chase, Josephine Streeper

1175. Dix, Fae Decker, ed. THE JOSEPHINE DIARIES: GLIMPSES OF THE LIFE OF JOSEPHINE STREEPER CHASE, 1881-94. *Utah Hist. Q. 1978 46(2): 167-183.* Josephine Streeper Chase (1835-94) was the polygamous second wife of George Ogden Chase in Centerville, Utah. She was the mother of 15 children and one foster daughter, sunday school teacher, successful manager of a large household, and faithful church member. Her diary, covering 1881-94, is a priceless journal of daily life in a busy Mormon home, describing with surprising detail housecleaning, outdoor chores, baking, preserving, churning, and hog killing. She voices the spirit and ordeal of her time. Primary and secondary sources; 3 illus., 16 notes. 1881-94

Chase, Philip Putnam

1176. Sutherland, Malcolm R. PHILIP PUTNAM CHASE. *Massachusetts Hist. Soc. Pro. 1978 90: 140-142.* A memoir of Philip Putnam Chase (1878-1978), a lawyer and member of the Massachusetts Historical Society. A graduate of Harvard College in 1900, Chase took his law degree at Harvard in 1903, and was associated with the University in various capacities for the next quarter century. A long-time resident of Milton, Massachusetts, Chase was involved in many civic, church, and charitable organizations. With his wife Anna Cornelia Wigglesworth, Chase shared a great love of sailing the New England coast. Based on the author's recollections of the deceased, Harvard Class Reports, and family reminiscences; note. 1878-1978

Chase, Salmon P.

1177. Blue, Frederick. CHASE AND THE GOVERNORSHIP: A STEPPING STONE TO THE PRESIDENCY. *Ohio Hist. 1981 90(3): 197-220.* Discusses the career of Salmon P. Chase during 1850-73, particularly his election as governor of Ohio in 1855 and his unrelenting bid to capture the Republican nomination for the presidency. As Ohio's governor, Chase managed to maintain a national prominence by subordinating state issues to national ones. Although he was a leader in the formation of the antislavery party, he ultimately failed to secure the presidential nomination because his stands on sectional issues, his obvious personal ambition, his past partisan record, and his inability to establish a smoothly functioning political machine alienated the moderates and conservatives within the Republican Party. Based on the Salmon P. Chase Papers at the Library of Congress, the Ohio Historical Society and the Historical Society of Pennsylvania, various archival collections of Harvard University and the Massachusetts Historical Society; photo, 74 notes. 1850-73

1178. Kazarian, Richard, Jr. "Working Radicals: The Early Careers of William Seward, Thaddeus Stevens, Henry Wilson, Charles Sumner, Salmon P. Chase and Hannibal Hamlin." Brown U. 1981. 518 pp. *DAI 1982 43(2): 526-A.* DA8209068 1840's-60

Chase, William Merritt

1179. Bryant, Keith L., Jr. GENTEEL BOHEMIAN FROM INDIANA: THE BOYHOOD OF WILLIAM MERRITT CHASE. *Indiana Magazine of History 1985 81(1): 14-47.* From very early in his childhood years in Indianapolis, William Merritt Chase showed artistic talent and desire. Despite his father's wish to have William enter business, the young boy finally prevailed on his family to support his artistic education. During his long career as a premier American artist, Chase's work reflected his devotion to family, a strong work ethic, a love of the outdoors, and a sense of Americanism. Based on newspapers, art catalogs, and secondary sources; 15 illus., 50 notes. 1849-1916

Chavez, Cesar

1180. Batzer, Arild. LA HUELGA, LANDARBEIDEREN OG CESAR CHAVEZ [The strike, farmworkers, and Cesar Chavez]. *Samtiden [Norway] 1970 79(10): 649-662.* Describes Cesar Chavez (founder of the United Farm Workers Union) and the strike by California grape pickers, 1965-70. 1965-70

1181. Hammerback, John C. and Jensen, Richard J. THE RHETORICAL WORLDS OF CÉSAR CHÁVEZ AND REIES TIJERINA. *Western J. of Speech Communication 1980 44(3): 166-176.* Reies Tijerina, a Chicano political and religious leader in Texas, and Cesar Chavez, a union organizer among California farm laborers, gained political aims for the groups they led through persistent public appearances and development of persuasive rhetorical styles; 1960's-70's. 1960's-70's

1182. Roberts, Donovan Orman. "Theory and Practice in the Life and Thought of Cesar E. Chavez: Implications for a Social Ethic." Boston U. Grad. School 1978. 643 pp. *DAI 1978 39(5): 2996-A.* 1960's-70's

Chavis, John

1183. Hudson, Gossie Harold. JOHN CHAVIS, 1763-1838: A SOCIAL-PSYCHOLOGICAL STUDY. *J. of Negro Hist. 1979 64(2): 142-156.* John Chavis (1763-1838), a North Carolina freedman, was an educator involved in state politics and closely allied with the Presbyterian Church; he eschewed emancipation for blacks and supported accommodationism and white patronization, 1800-38. 1800-38

Cheatham, Benjamin Franklin

1184. Johnson, Timothy D. BENJAMIN FRANKLIN CHEATHAM: THE EARLY YEARS. *Tennessee Hist. Q. 1983 42(3): 266-280.* Traces the early military career of Benjamin Franklin Cheatham from a volunteer captaincy in the Mexican War to a political appointment as brigadier general in the Confederate forces of the Army of Tennessee. In the Mexican War, Cheatham's 1st Tennessee Volunteer Infantry regiment fought bravely at Monterrey and later Vera Cruz before disbanding. Cheatham returned to Mexico in 1847 as a colonel of the 3d Tennessee Volunteer Infantry, which was assigned to protect Mexico City from guerrilla attack. From his Mexican War experiences, Cheatham learned the basics of military operations, administration, and discipline. Based on the Benjamin Franklin Cheatham Papers, Tennessee State Library and Archives, Nashville, and other primary sources; 2 illus., photo, 46 notes. 1846-61

Cheatham, Henry P.

1185. Reid, George W. FOUR IN BLACK: NORTH CAROLINA'S BLACK CONGRESSMEN, 1874-1901. *J. of Negro Hist. 1979 64(3): 229-243.* John A Hyman, James E. O'Hara, Henry P. Cheatham, and George H. White served in Congress from the Second Congressional District of North Carolina between 1874 and 1901. Hyman was the only Republican to win election to the House of Representatives in 1874. O'Hara, born in the West Indies, was elected to two successive terms in 1882-84. Cheatham, elected in 1890, was one of two Negroes in Congress with his colleague John M. Langston. White was elected as a Republican and was the only Afro-American member of Congress between 1897 and 1901. Based on public records; 67 notes. 1874-1901

Cheesborough, Esther B.

1186. Sutherland, Daniel E. THE RISE AND FALL OF ESTHER B. CHEESBOROUGH: THE BATTLES OF A LITERARY LADY. *South Carolina Historical Magazine 1983 84(1): 22-34.* Born in Charleston in 1826, Esther Cheesborough rose to prominence in Southern literary circles only to see her fame disappear and end her life in New York more than 20 years after the Civil War. Her literary style included intellectual honesty and a passion for naturalness. In her poems, short stories, and essays her characters survived lost or unfulfilled loves, which Cheesborough may have endured in her own life. During the Civil War her writing offered a view of Southern prisoners-of-war as well as deserters. Her social satire exposed "the absurdity of high society's values, taste, and conduct." 26 notes. 1826-87

Cheevers, Sarah

1187. Scheffler, Judith. PRISON WRITINGS OF EARLY QUAKER WOMEN. *Quaker Hist. 1984 73(2): 25-37.* 1651-83

For abstract see ***Blaugdone, Barbara***

Chelminski, Jan V.

1188. Daniec, Jadwiga I. IN THE FOOTSTEPS OF JAN CHELMINSKI [CHEŁMIŃSKI], 1851-1925 [FROM THE SERIES OF SILHOUETTES OF POLISH ARTISTS IN THE UNITED STATES]. *Polish Rev. 1979 24(4): 59-91.* A biography of Polish painter Jan V. Chelminski, who specialized in equestrian works but was also a sensitive portrayer of women. Sporting scenes dominated his early production, but the artist later developed a strong interest in historical scenes, especially the depiction of Polish horsemen serving in the armies of Napoleon I in the hope that their participation would lead to the restoration of Polish independence. Chelminski left Poland in his 20's and lived in the capitals of Europe for many years before settling permanently in the United States in 1915. 9 fig., 102 notes, 2 appendixes. 1870-1925

Cheney, Brainard

1189. Young, James Edwin, II. "The Search for a Hero: A Literary Biography of Brainard Cheney, Southern Novelist, Reporter, and Polemicist." George Peabody Coll. for Teachers 1979. 214 pp. *DAI 1980 41(1): 256-257-A.* 8016127 1920-70

Cheney, Moses (family)

1190. Highes, Charles W. THE CHENEYS: A VERMONT SINGING FAMILY. *Vermont Hist. 1977 45(3): 155-168.* The Cheney Family Singers consisted of Moses, four of his sons and a daughter. Moses was a Sanbornton, New Hampshire, farmer, Free Will Baptist preacher, versifier, and singer. Moses Ela taught at singing schools and common schools, directed church choirs, and pioneered musical conventions. Peripatetic as a young man, he settled in Barnard, Vermont. Simeon lived in Dorset, Vermont, was a spiritualist, and published *The American Singing Book* (Boston: White, Smith & Co., 1879). 55 notes. 1839-91

Cheshire, Johnathan Singleton

1191. Peyton, Rupert. A WEBSTER PARISH COUNTRY DOCTOR'S RECORD. *North Louisiana Hist. Assoc. J. 1979 10(3): 103-110.* Johnathan Singleton Cheshire, M.D. (1830-91), left a diary which omitted all references to his medical practice. Later, however, a secret record was found that detailed his experiences, his patients, and his trials and tribulations during 1882-88. The author, Cheshire's grandson, opened the record in spite of the doctor's earlier wishes. 1882-88

Cheslock, Louis

1192. Sprenkle, Elam Ray. "The Life and Works of Louis Cheslock." Johns Hopkins U. 1979. 233 pp. *DAI 1979 40(6): 2977-2978-A.* 1898-1979

Chesnut, Mary Boykin

1193. Faust, Drew Gilpin. IN SEARCH OF THE REAL MARY CHESNUT. *Rev. in Am. Hist. 1982 10(1): 54-59.* Reviews Elisabeth Muhlenfeld's *Mary Boykin Chesnut: A Biography* (1981) and C. Vann Woodward's *Mary Chesnut's Civil War* (1981), examinations of feminist and slavery critic Mary Chesnut's life and the journal she kept during 1830's-86. 1830's-86

1194. Hoffert, Sylvia D. MARY BOYKIN CHESNUT: PRIVATE FEMINIST IN THE CIVIL WAR SOUTH. *Southern Studies 1977 16(1): 81-89.* Mary Boykin Miller Chesnut (1823-1886) was from South Carolina and became a member of the Confederate social elite in Washington, Montgomery, Charleston, and Richmond. She kept a diary during 1860-65 in which she described Southern institutions in surprisingly blunt language. She never was a prominent public personality, nor did she express her ideas publicly. She is important as a private woman of the time who provides insights into how at least one woman felt about her life in the 19th century. Although she conformed outwardly to the accepted feminine roles of her day, she complained in her diary of male dominance, the humiliating position of married women, the personal limitations that motherhood imposed on women, and slavery. She disapproved of slavery and was totally against miscegenation. Based on Mary Chesnut diary and secondary sources; 30 notes. 19c

1195. Muhlenfeld, Elisabeth Showalter. "Mary Boykin Chesnut: The Writer and Her Work." U. of South Carolina 1978. 918 pp. *DAI 1979 39(11): 6765-A.* 1840's-86

1196. Wiley, Bell I. DIARIST FROM DIXIE: MARY BOYKIN CHESNUT. *Civil War Times Illus. 1977 16(1): 22-32.* Presents Mary Chesnut's memoirs, which are based on her recollections on a wartime journal. Her husband helped organize the Confederacy and elect president Jefferson Davis. The Chesnuts were close friends of the Davis's. Mary believed that the Confederacy's greatest weakness was the quarrelsomeness of its leaders due largely to the excessive individualism nurtured by the plantation. Little is known of her life after the war. She died in 1886. Illus. 1861-65

Chesterton, G. K.

1197. Ward, Leo R. THE INNOCENCE OF G. K. CHESTERTON. *Modern Age 1975 19(2): 146-156.* Discusses G. K. Chesterton's (1874-1936) biography and moral philosophy that "thrift is for property; property, for freedom; freedom, for man; and man, for God." Includes extensive passages on his life in the United States. 1874-1936

Chew, Benjamin

1198. Wainwright, Nicholas B. MASON AND DIXON'S MAP. *Princeton U. Lib. Chronicle 1983 45(1): 28-32.* Recounts the role of Benjamin Chew in the Pennsylvania-Maryland border dispute and the Mason-Dixon survey that resolved it; the Princeton University Library recently acquired some of the survey documents from the Chew family. 1731-68

Chickering, Jonas

1199. Kornblith, Gary J. THE CRAFTSMAN AS INDUSTRIALIST: JONAS CHICKERING AND THE TRANSFORMATION OF AMERICAN PIANO MAKING. *Business History Review 1985 59(3): 349-368.* Jonas Chickering was the premier American piano manufacturer in the early 19th century. A highly skilled craftsman in his own right, he also introduced into his production system many of the key techniques associated with factory organization in the emerging Industrial Revolution. In effect, he merged the new industrial capitalism with the older craft tradition and thereby made the former more palatable to both workers and the consuming public. Chickering's example also weakens the arguments of past economic historians, who saw only the merchant capitalist providing entrepreneurial leadership in the Industrial Revolution. 3 illus., 93 notes. 1823-53

Child, Henrietta Ellery

1200. Alvey, R. Gerard. THE STORY WOMAN. *Kentucky Folklore Record 1977 23(3-4): 66-71.* Henrietta Ellery Child, though originally from Boston, moved to the Appalachian Mountains in Kentucky and spent the majority of her life, (1912-68) teaching at Berea College and in the small backwoods schools where she gained her reputation in storytelling. 1922-68

Child, Lydia Maria

1201. Holland, Patricia G. LYDIA MARIA CHILD AS A NINETEENTH-CENTURY PROFESSIONAL AUTHOR. *Studies in the Am. Renaissance 1981: 157-167.* Traces the life and writing career of Lydia Maria Child, focusing on her involvement in the abolitionist and feminist movements. Throughout her life, Child directed her talents to the writing of books and articles that dealt with antislavery and women's issues, and with the special needs of children, as is evident in her role in the founding of *Juvenile Miscellany* in 1826, a periodical aimed at younger readers. Draws on the writings and letters of Child and on secondary sources; 35 notes. 1820-80

Childs, Clarence C.

1202. Klopfenstein, Carl G. CLARENCE C. CHILDS: MUSICIAN, SOLDIER, AND ATHLETE. *Hayes Historical Journal 1985 5(2): 6-12.* On 25 April 1898 a Fremont, Ohio, high school student, Clarence C. Childs, was mustered in Company K of the 16th Ohio regiment as a musician. Discharged after a year that included a four-month stint in Cuba with an Army occupation force, Childs resumed his education at Kenyon College and Yale University. Childs excelled in track and field and participated in the 1912 Olympic Games in Stockholm, placing third in the hammer throw. In 1916, Childs returned to military service, serving on the Mexican border and in Europe with the 147th Infantry regiment. In 1922, he succeeded in getting a short-lived patronage appointment as Supervisor of Collectors' offices in the Treasury Department in the Harding Administration. Mystery surrounds his later life and the record of Childs's government work is nonexistent. Childs died in Washington, D.C., in 1960 at the age of 79. 27 notes. 1881-1922

Childs, Richard Spencer

1203. Hirschhorn, Bernard. "In the Practice of Democracy: Richard Spencer Childs, Political Reformer, 1882-1978." Columbia U. 1981. 1139 pp. *DAI 1983 43(12): 4011-4012-A.* DA8307581 1900-20

Chin Gee-hee

1204. Jue, Willard G. CHIN GEE-HEE, CHINESE PIONEER ENTREPRENEUR IN SEATTLE AND TOISHAN. *Annals of the Chinese Historical Society of the Pacific Northwest 1983: 31-38.* Outlines the career of Chinese-born Seattle, Washington, labor contractor and Toishan, China, railway builder Chin Gee-hee. 1870's-1930

Chiniquy, Charles

1205. Brettell, Caroline B. FROM CATHOLICS TO PRESBYTERIANS: FRENCH-CANADIAN IMMIGRANTS IN CENTRAL ILLINOIS. *American Presbyterians 1985 63(3): 285-298.* Prints a narrative of the life of Charles Chiniquy, a French-Canadian priest who, in Canada during the 1830's-40's, preached total abstinence from alcohol, a position not popular among Catholics. Under pressure from his bishop, he ultimately left Canada and migrated to Illinois near Kankakee, in 1851. Soon afterward he and most of his congregation united with the Presbyterian Church. Based on materials in the Presbyterian Historical Society, Philadelphia; Archives of the Seminaire de Quebec; University Archives of McGill University; and McCormick Theological Seminary, Chicago; and on other primary and secondary sources; 3 illus., 53 notes. 1830-99

Chipman, George

1206. MacPherson, Ian. GEORGE CHIPMAN AND THE INSTITUTIONALIZATION OF A REFORM MOVEMENT. *Tr. of the Hist. and Sci. Soc. of Manitoba [Canada] 1975-76 32: 53-65.* George Chipman (1882-1935), a teacher who emigrated from the Maritimes to the prairies in 1903 and became a journalist in Winnipeg in 1905, for 26 years was editor of *The Grain Growers Guide.* He was an outspoken proponent of both the national agrarian and the cooperative movements. Into the 1920's, under his leadership, his periodical voiced western grievances and supported elements of Ontario Clear Grittism, British Fabianism, American Populism, the social gospel, prohibition, and European agrarian radicalism. Chipman supported the women's movement, educational reform, the single tax, and the initiative, recall, and referendum, and attacked tariffs, banks, farm implement manufacturers, and food trusts. An electoral defeat in 1922 increased the conservatism of both editor and journal. 36 notes. 1905-30

Chiu, Alfred Kaiming

1207. Wong, William Sheh. ALFRED KAIMING CHIU AND CHINESE AMERICAN LIBRARIANSHIP. *Coll. and Res. Lib. 1978 39(5): 384-388.* Discusses Alfred Kaiming Chiu (1898-1977). 1910's-77

Chol, Emmanuel

1208. Croom, John Robert. "I. Emmanuel Chol (1835-1916), His Life and a Catalogue of his Musical Compositions. II. Symphony for Brass and Percussion, an Original Composition." Louisiana State U. and Agric. and Mechanical Coll. 1979. 202 pp. *DAI 1980 40(10): 5239-A.* 1835-1916

Chorpenning, Charlotte B.

1209. Bedard, Roger Lee. "The Life and Work of Charlotte B. Chorpenning." U. of Kansas 1979. 185 pp. *DAI 1980 41(1): 23-A.* 8014368 20c

Chouteau, Marie Thérèse Bourgeois

1210. Foley, William E. THE LACLEDE-CHOUTEAU PUZZLE: JOHN FRANCIS MCDERMOTT SUPPLIES SOME MISSING PIECES. *Gateway Heritage 1983 4(2): 18-25.* Controversy persists regarding the identity of the father of the four youngest siblings of Marie Thérèse Bourgeois Chouteau, a prominent figure in St. Louis commerical and social circles during 1764-1814. Historian John Francis McDermott located three documents in the national archives of France and Spain that indicate Pierre Laclède was the father. 9 photos, 33 notes. 1755-78

Chouteau, Pierre

1211. Foley, William E. THE LEWIS AND CLARK EXPEDITION'S SILENT PARTNERS: THE CHOUTEAU BROTHERS OF ST. LOUIS. *Missouri Hist. Rev. 1983 77(2): 131-146.* Examines the career of Auguste and Pierre Chouteau as advisers, outfitters, and behind-the-scenes facilitators of the Lewis and Clark expedition. Pierre became the first Indian agent, and in this capacity he took two groups of Osage Indians to Washington to meet government officials. Based on the William Clark Papers and the Pierre Chouteau Letterbook, Missouri Historical Society, St. Louis; and the Thomas Jefferson Papers, Library of Congress; 7 illus., 47 notes. 1803-06

1212. Foley, William E. and Rice, Charles David. PIERRE CHOUTEAU: ENTREPRENEUR AS INDIAN AGENT. *Missouri Hist. Rev. 1978 72(4): 365-387.* Pierre Chouteau, a fur trader and first Indian agent in Upper Louisiana Territory during 1804-18, is portrayed as a man striving to handle complex Indian-White relations developing during the westward movement particularly among the Osage Indians. Primary and secondary sources; illus., 88 notes. 1804-18

Christenson, John (family)

1213. Hartley, William G. CHILDHOOD IN GUNNISON, UTAH. *Utah Hist. Q. 1983 51(2): 108-132.* The John Christenson family (John Christenson, Christena Christenson, and Johanna Christenson) plus 11 children lived in Gunnison for three decades, during which time they farmed their lots, cooperatively interacted, had some schooling at Sampete Academy, and attended Mormon functions. Most children in their later teens moved to other Utah locations. No hostilities were evident between the two wives, and children of each cooperatively farmed, did housework, and acted as one family. 8 photos, 67 notes. 1865-96

Christie, Emma Stratton

1214. Peavy, Linda and Smith, Ursula. WOMEN IN WAITING IN THE WESTWARD MOVEMENT: PAMELIA DILLIN FERGUS AND EMMA STRATTON CHRISTIE. *Montana 1985 35(2): 2-17.* The men who came to the Montana frontier frequently left their wives and families awaiting their return. With their husbands absent, these "women in waiting" assumed new responsibilities managing farms and businesses as well as households. The lives of these "widows" form a heretofore unexamined element of the frontier experience. The letters between Pamelia Dillin Fergus (1824-87) and James Fergus (1813-1902), and Emma Stratton Christie (1854-1921) and David Christie (1848-1920) portray the growth of self-reliance and independence among the "widows" as they endured their husbands' absences. These traits served them well when they rejoined their husbands on the frontier. Based on the James Fergus Papers, Mansfield Library Archives, Missoula, Montana; and the David B. Christie Collection, Minnesota Historical Society, St. Paul; 8 photos, 86 notes. 1860-85

Christie, Sarah

1215. Christie, Jean. "AN EARNEST ENTHUSIASM FOR EDUCATION": SARAH CHRISTIE STEVENS, SCHOOLWOMAN. *Minnesota Hist. 1983 48(6): 245-254.* Sarah Christie, seen as a school girl, young teacher, mature wife, middle-aged political aspirant, and county superintendent of education offers yet another entree into the expectations, fears, and societal limitations common to late 19th-century women, at least those living in middling circumstances in the upper Midwest. Active in Baptist, Women's Christian Temperance Union, and Farmers' Alliance work in the late 1880's, she was able to gain election in Minnesota's Blue Earth County (Mankato) as one of the state's dozen female superintendent's in 1890. She lost the next two elections, as alliance strength split, and in the face of continued somewhat sexist arguments. Based mainly on the Christie Family Papers (1823-1949) at the Minnesota Historical Society, 38 notes, 7 illus. 1870-1900

Christowe, Stoyan

1216. Dzhukeski, Alexander. STOYAN CHRISTOWE—A WORTHY REPRESENTATIVE OF THE MACEDONIAN PEOPLE IN THE USA. *Macedonian Review [Yugoslavia] 1985 15(2): 201-205.* Discusses the life and work of Stoyan Christowe (b. 1892), who immigrated to the United States in 1911 from Macedonia, and traces his contribution to Macedonian culture through his historical and literary works. 20c

Church, Alexander Hamilton

1217. Jelinek, Mariann. TOWARD SYSTEMATIC MANAGEMENT: ALEXANDER HAMILTON CHURCH. *Business Hist. Rev. 1980 54(1): 63-79.* Frederick W. Taylor traditionally has been regarded as the founding father of scientific management. Alexander Hamilton Church deserves, however, greater credit than he has thus far received for his own contributions to the field. Church began where Taylor left off, concentrating on the key areas of cost accounting and general management theory, and developing ideas that were more fundamental and inclusive than those of Taylor. Where Taylor focused on the tasks of the individual worker, Church centered upon the coordination systems that would enable managers to best control their organizations. Covers 1885-1915. Based on Chruch's writings; 39 notes. 1885-1915

Church, Benjamin

1218. Walker, Jeffrey. BENJAMIN CHURCH'S COMMONPLACE BOOK OF VERSE: EXEMPLUM FOR A POLITICAL SATIRIST. *Early Am. Lit. 1980-81 15(3): 222-236.* Benjamin Church, articulate and celebrated Whig political satirist on the eve of the American Revolution, developed his poetic skills as a student at Harvard University during the early 1750's. Writing satire allowed Church to compete for position and honor at Harvard; fellow classmates, tutors, and events became the subjects of his wit. Based on Church's unpublished commonplace book in the Houghton Library's American Manuscript Collection at Harvard (Ms. Am. 1369); 14 notes. ca 1750-54

Church, Frederic

1219. Rubin, Joan Gassisi. "Frederic Church, Jackson Pollock, and Christo: Three Visions of the American Landscape." New York U. 1983. 263 pp. *DAI 1984 44(7): 1958-A.* DA8325212 19c-20c

Church, Robert R., Jr.

1220. Biles, Roger. ROBERT R. CHURCH, JR. OF MEMPHIS: BLACK REPUBLICAN LEADER IN THE AGE OF DEMOCRATIC ASCENDANCY, 1928-1940. *Tennessee Historical Quarterly 1983 42(4): 362-382.* Independently wealthy Memphis businessman Robert R. Church, Jr., was the most influential of the black Republicans who were middlemen between the black electorate and the party's white bosses. Successful in keeping the Tennessee Republican Party leadership biracial, Church failed to dent the complacency of the national Republican leadership on issues affecting black voters. When Church lost his patronage during the New Deal era, the Shelby County Democratic machine launched a campaign of harassment that destroyed Church's local power and personal wealth. Based on the Church family papers; 2 photos, 39 notes. 1928-40

Church, Robert R., Sr.

1221. Miller, M. Sammy. LAST WILL AND TESTAMENT OF ROBERT REED CHURCH, SENIOR (1839-1912). *J. of Negro Hist. 1980 65(2): 156-163.* Robert Reed Church, Sr., was the most successful black businessman in Memphis, Tennessee, by the time of his death in 1912. He was one of the wealthiest Afro-Americans of his generation, and his children distinguished him as well. 8 notes. 1912

Churchill, Winston (1871-1947)

1222. Blodgett, Geoffrey. WINSTON CHURCHILL: THE NOVELIST AS REFORMER. *New England Q. 1974 47(4): 495-517.* Studies the career of novelist Winston Churchill (1871-1947) to understand the way in which he united a successful career as a novelist with his Progressive political and socioeconomic views and thereby played an important role in "catalyzing reform behavior in his adopted state of New Hampshire." Churchill's early progress toward reform and insurgency was gradual and uncharted. "Reform was what happened to him when he tried, as an affluent young outsider coming into New Hampshire at the turn of the century, to use politics as a means of fashioning his new surroundings to his taste." With some of his contemporaries he considered that the pursuit of particular personal and group goals might also advance the common welfare. 48 notes. ca 1900-47

Cilley, Jonathan

1223. Thayer, Shelly A. THE DELEGATE AND THE DUEL: THE EARLY POLITICAL CAREER OF GEORGE WALLACE JONES. *Palimpsest 1984 65(5): 178-188.* 1820's-96

*For abstract see **Jones, George Wallace***

Clafin, William H., Jr.

1224. Coolidge, Daniel J. WILLIAM HENRY CLAFIN, JR. *Massachusetts Hist. Soc. Pro. 1982 94: 85-87.* Clafin enjoyed a successful financial career as a partner in Tucker, Anthony and Company, president of the Soledad Sugar Company, treasurer of Harvard College (1938-48), and director of many banks and companies, including the United Fruit Company and State Street Bank and Trust Company. An avid student of archaeology and ethnology, Clafin amassed a large personal collection of American Indian artifacts. 1920's-82

Claflin, Tennie C.

1225. Ocko, Stephanie. VICTORIA WOODHULL'S SIEGE OF NEW YORK. *Am. Hist. Illus. 1981 16(1): 32-37.* 1870-1927

*For abstract see **Woodhull, Victoria Claflin***

Claiborne, William Charles Cole

1226. DeGrummond, Jane Lucas. CAYETANA SUSANA BOSQUE Y FANQUI, "A NOTABLE WOMAN". *Louisiana Hist. 1982 23(3): 277-294.* 1790-1890

*For abstract see **Bosque y Fanqui, Cayetana Susana***

Clanton, Willa

1227. Propst, Nell Brown. WILLA CLANTON: A REMARKABLE LINK WITH COLORADO'S PAST. *Colorado Mag. 1979 56(1-2): 45-55.* A biography of a 102-year-old Coloradoan, Willa Clanton (b. 1877). Her parents, from Alabama, settled near the future Sterling in 1874. The author first discusses many aspects of pioneer Colorado life as it was experienced by the Clantons, and by Willa in particular: farming, Indian relations, weather, hard times, and religion. Then she turns to Willa's education and her career as a teacher of music. Interviews, family letters, and biographical material; 6 photos, 8 notes. 1877-1979

Clapp, Hannah Keziah

1228. Totton, Kathryn Dunn. HANNAH KEZIAH CLAPP: THE LIFE AND CAREER OF A PIONEER NEVADA EDUCATOR, 1824-1908. *Nevada Hist. Soc. Q. 1977 20(3): 167-183.* Describes the professional and political reform activities of Hannah Keziah Clapp in Nevada. From 1881 to 1901, she was a staff member of the University of Nevada, making significant contributions to the institution by upgrading and enlarging to University's library. She also worked for kindergartens in Reno and was active in women suffrage movements, among them the Nevada Equal Suffrage Association in which she was an officer. Based on newspapers and manuscript collections at the Nevada Historical Society; 2 photos, 39 notes. 1824-1908

Clapp, Theodore

1229. Reilly, Timothy F. PARSON CLAPP OF NEW ORLEANS: ANTEBELLUM SOCIAL CRITIC, RELIGIOUS RADICAL, AND MEMBER OF THE ESTABLISHMENT. *Louisiana Hist. 1975 16(2): 167-191.* "Unitarianism in antebellum New Orleans was among the most distinctive religious forces in the Old South. The Church was founded and shepherded by Parson Theodore Clapp, a New England native and former Presbyterian who continually challenged sacred dictums of Christian orthodoxy." Arriving in New Orleans in 1822 and remaining until 1856, Clapp opposed revivalism and theological concepts involving the Trinity, everlasting punishment, and predestination. He defended slavery "because he recognized the supremacy of the large business class in New Orleans and the rest of the South. Such a compromise . . . entitled him to a position of social respectability. Clapp valued the propagation of his radical theology above everything else." Primary and secondary sources; 3 photos, 68 notes. 1822-56

Clar, Henry Jacob (family)

1230. —. COLORADO HOMESTEADER AND LOS ANGELES INVESTOR. *Western States Jewish Hist. Q. 1982 14(4): 302-307.* Henry Jacob Clar (1885-1970) was born in Russia, but grew up in Denver, Colorado. In 1906 he and his wife, Augusta (Kaminsky), homesteaded a 320-acre farm near Fort Morgan. The Clars raised corn and wheat until 1922, when they leased to tenant farmers and resettled in Los Angeles. Discovery of oil on the farm in 1953 financed a number of investments in both Los Angeles and Colorado. Based on an interview with daughter, Elizabeth Clar; 8 photos, 7 notes. 1905-50's

Clar, Max (family)

1231. —. THE CLARS OF COLORADO AND CALIFORNIA: A PICTURE STORY. *Western States Jewish Hist. Q. 1980 12(3): 209-214.* Max and Ida Clar, Russian emigrants, came to America in 1887. In the 1890's, they moved to Colorado as homesteaders; later, Max worked as a Hebrew teacher in Denver. They moved again in the late 1920's to Los Angeles, California, where Max continued his career as a teacher. The Clars' 11 children lived in Los Angeles, San Francisco, and Oakland, California. Based on interviews with family members; 8 photos, 5 notes. 1887-1940's

Clark, Charles Badger

1232. Lee, Shebby. DAKOTA RESOURCES: RESEARCHING THE WORKS OF BADGER CLARK. *South Dakota Hist. 1983 13(4): 388-394.* An attempt to locate and record all the poems, articles, and papers of Charles Badger Clark, the first poet laureate of South Dakota, that he wrote between 1906 and his death in 1957 has proven elusive. Clark's papers are not only located in several places, but some were destroyed, some were never published, and some different works appeared under nearly identical titles. The preparation of an annotated bibliography of Clark's works will assure that his literary legacy will survive. Photo. 1906-57

Clark, Dan Elbert

1233. Bingham, Edwin R. A DEDICATION TO THE MEMORY OF DAN ELBERT CLARK, 1884-1956. *Arizona and the West 1976 18(2): 106-110.* Dan Elbert Clark (1884-1956) was educated in history and political science at the State University of Iowa. For nearly a decade he taught Iowa history, served as editor of the historical society's publications, and published several books and articles on Iowa history. In 1921 he went to the University of Oregon and worked in Western history. He was a president of the Pacific Coast Branch of the American Historical Association and a cofounder of its *Pacific Historical Review.* His principal claim to prominence as a Western historian was established with a textbook which pioneered new approaches to the subject. Illus., biblio. 1910-50

Clark, Daniel

1234. Wohl, Michael Stephen. "A Man in Shadow: The Life of Daniel Clark." Tulane U. 1984. 221 pp. *DAI 1985 45(12): 3731-A.* DA8504840 1780's-1813

Clark, Frances

1235. Kern, Robert Fred. "Frances Clark: The Teacher and Her Contributions to Piano Pedagogy." U. of Northern Colorado 1984. 280 pp. *DAI 1984 45(5): 1327-A.* DA8418129 20c

Clark, Galen

1236. Sargent, Shirley. CLARK'S STATION. *Pacific Hist. 1980 24(4): 386-395.* For 50 years, Galen Clark lived in Yosemite and helped the area become world famous. Sketches his numerous contributions as an unofficial developer and later administrator of Yosemite Valley. Clark's Station was an early provisioning center in the valley which he operated at one time. 4 pictures, bibliographic essay. 1855-75

Clark, George Rogers

1237. Waller, George M. GEORGE ROGERS CLARK AND THE AMERICAN REVOLUTION IN THE WEST. *Indiana Mag. of Hist. 1976 72(1): 1-20.* Assesses the role played by George Rogers Clark (1752-1818) in the western campaigns of the American Revolution and the problems confronted by preservationists in their attempts to save the vanishing physical evidence of that conflict. Clark's success in the West, particularly against the British outposts at Kaskaskia and Vincennes, largely resulted from his knowledge of the region's topography and astute assessment of the strategic value of the various British positions. While a consistent military effort was impossible, Clark's adoption of Indian guerrilla tactics allowed him to protect American positions, pin down large numbers of British troops and their Indian allies, and thus enhance the bargaining position of American peace negotiators. 5 maps, 10 notes. 1750-85

Clark, George W.

1238. Hendrickson, Walter B. JACKSONVILLE ARTISTS OF THE 1870'S. *J. of the Illinois State Hist. Soc. 1977 70(4): 258-275.* Discusses the careers of Bohemian artist Ebenezer Mason, portraitist-turned-banker William S. Woodman, artist-photographer George W. Clark, and painter-sculptor Robert Campbell Smith. Considers their works and assesses the influence of Jacksonville, Illinois, a small town that is unusually rich in colleges, private academies, and cultural and literary associations. 17 illus., 82 notes. 1870's

Clark, Greg

1239. —. "IN FLANDERS FIELDS": RADIO SERIES AND ORAL HISTORY. *Can. Oral Hist. Assoc. J. [Canada] 1981-82 5(1): 1-5.* Prints parts of an interview with Greg Clark, recalling his military service with Canadian forces in World War I; the interview was conducted as part of the Canadian Broadcasting Corporation's radio series "In Flanders Fields," the records of which were transferred in 1980 to the Public Archives of Canada. 1914-18

Clark, Joseph

1240. Craven, W. Frank. JOSEPH CLARK AND THE REBUILDING OF NASSAU HALL. *Princeton U. Lib. Chronicle 1979 41(1): 54-68.* Discusses Presbyterian minister Joseph Clark's (1751-1813) manuscript account of his fund raising journey for the rebuilding of Princeton University's Nassau Hall, destroyed by fire in 1802. 1802-04

Clark, Kelly

1241. Hughes, Kenneth James. KELLY CLARK: THERE AND BACK AGAIN. *Can. Dimension [Canada] 1980 14(8): 23-46.* Discusses Canadian-born artist Kelly Clark, tracing the evolution of his art in four periods in addition to his student years and his work on layout and design for *Canadian Dimension;* his London period of 1960-64, his erotica of 1969-70, his drawings at the Plug-In, Winnipeg show in 1975, and his 1978-79 work at Lake Manitoba. 1960-79

Clark, Peter Humphries

1242. Foner, Philip S. PETER H. CLARK: PIONEER BLACK SOCIALIST. *J. of Ethnic Studies 1977 5(3): 17-35.* After reviewing the approach of American Utopian Socialists and early German American Marxists to the questions of wage and chattel slavery before the Civil War, chronicles the career of Peter Humphries Clark (1829-1926), outstanding Cincinnati educator, editor, abolitionist, and leader of the Colored Teachers' Co-operative Association, apparently the first trade union of teachers in American history. In 1877 Clark left the Republican Party for the Workingmen's Party, where he strongly supported the railroad strikers of the great conflagration of 1877. Long excerpts of Clark's speeches as reported in William Haller's *The Emancipator,* the *Cincinnati Commercial,* and the Socialist Labor Party's *The Socialist,* are given, along with details of Clark's founding of Gaines High School for Negroes during the 1860's. Contemporary papers, secondary writings; 50 notes. 1849-81

1243. Grossman, Lawrence. IN HIS VEINS COURSED NO BOOTLICKING BLOOD: THE CAREER OF PETER H. CLARK. *Ohio Hist. 1977 86(2): 79-95.* Nineteenth-century black history in Cincinnati, Ohio, is illuminated in this biographical sketch of one of Ohio's most prominent black men. Peter H. Clark, schoolteacher and champion of antebellum Cincinnati black rights, became a figure of national importance in racial matters by the 1880's. His childhood, education, jobs, and appointment as the first black member of the Board of Trustees of The Ohio State University are discussed. Emphasizes Clark's intense involvement in politics. Based on manuscript, newspaper, contemporary, and secondary sources; illus., 55 notes. 1880's-1925

Clark, Robert Lee

1244. Clark, Robert Lee. THE C-130. *Aerospace Hist. 1979 26(4): 233-237.* Personal account of the author who has logged over 2,500 flying hours in the C-130, in weather reconnaissance in the WC-130, 1968-72, and in missions in the AC-130 gunship, 1973. 4 photos. 1968-73

Clark, S. D.

1245. Harrison, Deborah Ann. "Canada and the Limits of Liberalism: A Study of S. D. Clark." York U. [Canada] 1979. *DAI 1980 40(9): 5192-A.* 1970's

1246. Hiller, Harry H. RESEARCH BIOGRAPHY AND DISCIPLINARY DEVELOPMENT: S. D. CLARK AND CANADIAN SOCIOLOGY. *J. of the Hist. of Sociol. 1980-81 3(1): 67-86.* Examines the work of Canadian sociologist S. D. Clark because the changes his work underwent through time demonstrate changes in the general discipline of sociology as it emerged from a dependent undifferentiated position to that of an autonomous, highly differentiated discipline; 1925-75. 1925-75

Clark, Tom

1247. West, Ellis M. JUSTICE TOM CLARK AND AMERICAN CHURCH-STATE LAW. *J. of Presbyterian Hist. 1976 54(4): 387-404.* Tom Clark (1899-) was an Associate Justice of the US Supreme Court, 1949-67. While on the Court he wrote major opinions in the areas of civil rights, separation of powers, antitrust, national security and church-state relations. His opinions in the cases of *US* v. *Seeger* and *Abington School District* v. *Schemp* were historic in church-state relations and of far reaching consequences. The latter struck down officially prescribed prayer and Bible-reading in the public schools. Points out that Clark, a very dedicated Presbyterian layman, was a constructive moderate who argued for the essential autonomy of religion and government but refused to support their complete separation. Based largely on Supreme Court decisions and Clark's writings; illus., 90 notes. 1949-67

Clark, William

1248. Holt, Glen E. AFTER THE JOURNEY WAS OVER: THE ST. LOUIS YEARS OF LEWIS AND CLARK. *Gateway Heritage 1981 2(2): 42-48.* Returning to St. Louis on 23 September 1806, explorers Meriwether Lewis and William Clark had completed their historic journey to the Pacific coast. Afterwards Lewis saw his repute sullied and suffered financial reverses before he died in 1809, either a victim of murder or suicide. Clark resided at St. Louis until his death in 1833, becoming one of the city's most prominent citizens. He held important federal posts including an Indian affairs superintendency and the office of surveyor general for Illinois, Missouri, and Arkansas. Based on the William Clark Papers at the Missouri Historical Society and secondary sources; 11 photos, 43 notes. 1806-33

Clark, William Andrews

1249. Malone, Michael P. MIDAS OF THE WEST: THE INCREDIBLE CAREER OF WILLIAM ANDREWS CLARK. *Montana 1983 33(4): 2-17.* William Andrews Clark was a classic example of Horatio Alger's "rags to riches" man as a frontier capitalist. He began his career in merchandising and banking in Montana, then invested in Butte's infant silver and copper mining industry. In time he added the United Verde cooper mine in Jerome, Arizona, a railroad linking Salt Lake City and Los Angeles, and other investments nationwide. He was one of the nation's wealthiest men at the time of his death in 1925, but his personal life and his political corruption as a US senator shadowed his social acceptability and he has subsequently been forgotten by all but regional historians. Based on contemporary newspapers and secondary sources; 8 illus., 40 notes. 1863-1925

Clark, William (family)

1250. Primm, James Neal. SEAL OF THE TERRITORY OF LOUISIANA: A DISCOVERY AMID A CLARK FAMILY COLLECTION. *Gateway Heritage 1984 4(4): 17-21.* In 1983, the Missouri Historical Society discovered a collection of documents and historical artifacts related to William Clark and other Clark family members, all of whom were descendants of William Clark, the celebrated explorer of the West. Besides significant letters documenting Clark family affairs and participation in Santa Fe Trail commerce before the Mexican War, the collection includes an official seal of the Territory of Louisiana. Territorial Governor William Clark retained the seal as a memento of his 1813-18 tenure in office. 8 photos. 1813-46

Clarke, Asia Booth

1251. Head, Constance. THE BOOTH SISTERS OF BEL AIR. *Lincoln Herald 1981 84[i.e., 83](3[i.e., 4]): 759-764.* 1823-89

*For abstract see **Booth, Rosalie***

1252. Head, Constance. INSIGHTS ON JOHN WILKES BOOTH FROM HIS SISTER ASIA'S CORRESPONDENCE. *Lincoln Herald 1980 82(4): 540-544.* Conveys a portrait of John Wilkes Booth, depicted by his sister Asia Booth Clarke in 45 letters written between 1852 and 1874 to her childhood friend Jean Anderson. 1852-74

Clarke, Thomas P.

1253. Marion, John L. THOMAS P. CLARKE: SOTHEBY'S EXPERT IN AMERICAN BOOKS AND MANUSCRIPTS. *Manuscripts 1984 36(2): 89-94.* While employed at Sotheby's North America for over 50 years, Thomas P. Clarke made significant contributions to the study and cataloging of American books and manuscripts. His most outstanding work was accomplished in three great auctions: the Lincoln collection of Oliver Barrett, 1952; the library of Thomas Winthrop Streeter, 1966-67; and the collection of Philip D. Sang, 1978-81. 3 illus. 1933-83

Clarkson brothers

1254. Staab, Rodney, ed. THE MATTHEW CLARKSON MANUSCRIPTS. *Kansas Hist. 1982 5(4): 256-278.* Matthew Flint Clarkson arrived at Hays City, Kansas, in 1868. He was joined by his brothers Charles Ross and George Bernard. They soon became buffalo hunters, during their career killing some 22,000 of the beasts. They were only three of many thousands of men who engaged in this bloody business, but Matthew was one of the few to leave a written record reflecting the viewpoint of actual participants. Most buffalo hunters passed from the scene quickly, but the Clarksons remained in Kansas. Matthew's records provide a sustained perspective on the successive occupations of teamster, woodcutter, hunter, rancher, and farmer. Based on the Matthew Clarkson manuscripts, Fort Hays Kansas State College; illus., map, 81 notes. 1868-80

Clay, Anne

1255. Miller, Page Putnam. WOMEN IN THE VANGUARD OF THE SUNDAY SCHOOL MOVEMENT. *J. of Presbyterian Hist. 1980 58(4): 311-325.* 1800-50

*For abstract see **Bethune, Joanna Graham***

Clay, Brutus J.

1256. Hood, James Larry. THE UNION AND SLAVERY: CONGRESSMAN BRUTUS J. CLAY OF THE BLUEGRASS. *Register of the Kentucky Hist. Soc. 1977 75(3): 214-221.* Brutus J. Clay, brother of Cassius M. Clay, was elected to Congress in 1863 as a Union Democrat. In Washington, he found himself supporting much of the Republican platform, although he was not in favor of ending slavery. He hoped that both slavery and the Union could be saved. His loyalty to the Union cost him his career in Congress. Primary and secondary sources; 29 notes. 1863-65

Clay, Clement and Virginia

1257. Bleser, Carol K. and Heath, Frederick M. THE IMPACT OF THE CIVIL WAR ON A SOUTHERN MARRIAGE: CLEMENT AND VIRGINIA TUNSTALL CLAY OF ALABAMA. *Civil War History 1984 30(3): 197-220.* Profiles the marriage of Clement Claiborne Clay and Virginia Tunstall Clay against the background of social and political events of the time. Although a senator from Alabama in both the US and Confederate congresses, Clement was a rather melancholy person who emerged from the Civil War with broken health and economic difficulties. Virginia, a vivacious, frivolous belle, became the stronger partner. Based on correspondence and other primary and secondary sources; 60 notes. 1843-82

Clay, Edward Williams

1258. Davison, Nancy Reynolds. "E. W. Clay: American Political Caricaturist of the Jacksonian Era." (Vol. 1 and 2) U. of Michigan 1980. 421 pp. *DAI 1980 41(3): 835-A.* 8017241 1819-52

Clay, Henry

1259. Holder, Ray. PARSON WINANS AND MR. CLAY: THE WHIG CONNECTION, 1843-1846. *Louisiana Hist. 1984 25(1): 57-75.* 1843-46
*For abstract see **Winans, William***

1260. Mathias, Frank F. HENRY CLAY AND HIS KENTUCKY POWER BASE. *Register of the Kentucky Hist. Soc. 1980 78(2): 123-139.* Analyzes Henry Clay's efforts to build a political power base in Kentucky during the 1820's and 1830's. Each of his successes at home, paradoxically, contributed to his failure to win the presidency. The economic struggle between the relief and antirelief factions caught Clay in the middle, and his maneuverings in Washington served to polarize Kentucky politics. Whig support for the antirelief forces worked in Kentucky but hurt the party (and Clay) nationally. 3 illus., 35 notes. 1820-44

1261. Teague, William Joseph. "An Appeal to Reason: Daniel Webster, Henry Clay, and Whig Presidential Politics, 1836-1848." North Texas State U. 1977. 384 pp. *DAI 1978 38(12): 7518-A.* 1836-48

Clayton, John M.

1262. Wire, Richard Arden. YOUNG SENATOR CLAYTON AND THE EARLY JACKSON YEARS. *Delaware Hist. 1976 17(2): 104-126.* Describes the Senatorial career of John M. Clayton during 1829-33. Clayton, who was the architect of anti-Jackson opposition in Delaware, sought a Union of order and stability. Clayton supported tariff and internal improvements legislation, orderly land disposal, Senate participation in removals from public office, recharter of the Bank, and a compromise tariff and attack on nullification. He tried to steer a middle course between states' rights and "unbridled presidential power." 61 notes. 1829-33

Clayton, Powell

1263. Burnside, William H. POWELL CLAYTON: AMBASSADOR TO MEXICO, 1897-1905. *Arkansas Hist. Q. 1979 38(4): 328-344.* Describes the service as minister to Mexico (1897-1905) of Powell Clayton (1833-1914), former general, Arkansas governor and Republican Party leader. Discusses his diplomacy and aspects of his character appropriate to his period and position. 28 notes. 1897-1905

Clayton, Susan Haines

1264. Hoar, Jay S. SUSAN HAINES CLAYTON, AMERICAN LADY, 1851-1948. *Oregon Hist. Q. 1983 84(2): 206-210.* Examines milestones in the life of Susan Haines Clayton, who nursed the sick and wounded during the Civil War. While her family was living in Indiana, she, at the age of 10, was allowed by her mother to help nurse men at Camp Carrington at Indianapolis. Following her marriage to a former soldier in 1869, she homesteaded in southern Kansas and Montana and later was instrumental in organizing the Women's Relief Corps in those states. Based on letters from relatives of Susan Clayton and newspaper accounts; 6 notes. 1851-1948

Cleary, Henry J.

1265. Rankin, Ernest H., Sr. CAPTAIN HENRY J. CLEARY: LIFESAVER-SHOWMAN. *Inland Seas 1977 33(1): 4-11, 44, (2): 128-130, 139-141.* Part I. Henry J. Cleary (1862-1916) joined the Life Saving Service in 1881. He had charge of the Deer Park (Michigan) Station, 1885-91, and that at Marquette, Michigan, 1891-1916. He commanded the crews of surfmen who performed at the Columbian and other expositions during 1893-1904 and trained the crew which performed at the Alaska-Yukon Pacific Exposition in 1909. Reprints a September 1895 account of the rescue of the crew of the steamer *Kershaw* by Cleary and his men from the Marquette Station and describes the drills conducted by the lifesaving crew at Marquette. Illus. Part II. Describes the surfboats and lifeboats in use during the late 19th century. In 1900 Cleary installed a Superior gasoline engine in a lifeboat, to produce the first powered life saving craft. Sixteen years later he died just as the Life Saving Service was being absorbed by the Coast Guard. 1881-1916

Clemens, Jeremiah

1266. Martin, John M. THE SENATORIAL CAREER OF JEREMIAH CLEMENS, 1849-1853. *Alabama Hist. Q. 1981 43(3): 186-235.* Narrates the activities of Jeremiah Clemens as a senator from Alabama, including some details on his election. Focuses on his votes and justifications for compromise measures, particularly as evident in his controversy with Robert Barnwell Rhett. Based on letters and newspaper articles; 71 notes. 1849-53

Clemens, Samuel

See Twain, Mark

Clements, James

1267. Maxwell, Margaret F. JAMES CLEMENTS OF ANN ARBOR: A NINETEENTH CENTURY ENTREPRENEUR. *Michigan Hist. 1978 62(1): 16-30.* Self-made man and entrepreneur James Clements (1829-95), born in England, began his business career as a gas engineer in Brooklyn, New York, in 1853, went to Ann Arbor in 1858 to contract the change from kerosene lamps with gas lamps on the city's streets, soon became interested in politics, and amassed a fortune with his investments in midwestern gas companies. 1853-95

Clemons, Alexander

1268. Wolcott, Merlin D. FRONTIER ADVENTURE: THE LIFE OF ALEXANDER CLEMONS. *Northwest Ohio Q. 1976/77 49(1): 19-33.* Biography of Alexander Clemons, an eventual resident of Ohio, his participation in the War of 1812 and the Civil War and major events of his life, 1794-1886. 1794-1886

Cleveland, H. W. S.

1269. Tishler, William H. and Luckhardt, Virginia S. H. W. S. CLEVELAND, PIONEER LANDSCAPE ARCHITECT TO THE UPPER MIDWEST. *Minnesota History 1985 49(7): 281-291.* After a noteworthy career as a landscape architect in New Jersey, New England, and then Chicago, H. W. S. Cleveland (1814-1900) moved to Minneapolis in 1886. There he worked to enlarge and complete a set of proposals dealing with an encircling park system, preservation of the Mississippi River bluffs, and a systematic development of certain major avenues he had first offered the Twin Cities in 1871. By the time he retired in 1895, much progress had been made toward a park system now recognized as one of the nation's finest. 37 notes, 11 illus. 1886-95

Clever, Charles P.

1270. Fierman, Floyd S. THE FRONTIER CAREER OF CHARLES CLEVER. *Palacio 1979-80 85(4): 2-6, 34-35.* Traces the careers in retailing, political office, and army service of Charles P. Clever, born in Prussia, who came to the United States in 1849 and was important in developing the frontier Southwest, particularly in New Mexico territory, until 1869. 1849-69

Clift, Montgomery

1271. Huddleston, Eugene L. REVIEW ESSAY: TWO BIOGRAPHIES OF MONTGOMERY CLIFT. *J. of Popular Film and Television 1979 7(2): 212-217.* Review article prompted by Robert LaGuardia's *Monty: A Biography of Montgomery Clift* (New York: Arbor House, 1977) and Patricia Bosworth's *Montgomery Clift: A Biography* (New York: Harcourt Brace Jovanovich, 1978). 1920-66

Clinton, DeWitt

1272. Lagana, Michael P. THE POLITICAL CAREER OF DE WITT CLINTON: A NEED FOR REINTERPRETATION. *Niagara Frontier 1974 21(3): 74-77.* Evaluates the influence which the political career of DeWitt Clinton had in the state of New York, 1800-22. 1800-22

Clinton, George

1273. Bradshaw, Serena Moody. "A Study in Incompetency: Governor George Clinton and the New York Opposition, 1743-1754." Ohio State U. 1977. 352 pp. *DAI 1978 38(8): 5001-5002-A.* 1743-54

Clonney, James Goodwyn

1274. Giese, Lucretia H. JAMES GOODWYN CLONNEY (1812-1867): AMERICAN GENRE PAINTER. *Am. Art J. 1979 11(4): 4-31.* James Goodwyn Clonney (1812-67) was born in England but by 1830 was producing lithographs in New York. His career was devoted to genre works primarily in outdoor settings. His style changed little over the years. His focus was on the relation of figures to each other and to a surface pattern. Adults are either mildly exaggerated in feature or idealized. Most of his works (6 paintings and 67 drawings) are in the Karolik Collection at the Museum of Fine Arts in Boston. His works are generally unsentimental with a noncommital directness. Clonney was among the first group of American genre painters. 32 illus., 43 notes. 1830-67

Clyman, James

1275. Rhodes, Richard. THE FARTHER CONTINENT OF JAMES CLYMAN. *Am. Heritage 1978 30(1): 50-59.* James Clyman (1792-1881), surveyor, soldier, businessman, explorer, and farmer, was born in Virginia. Traveling the American West, he kept diaries which were finally edited and published in 1928 and in 1960. Geographic discoveries, landscapes, and philosophic musings and observations fill his pages. 4 illus. 1800's-81

Clymer, John

1276. Reed, Walt. JOHN CLYMER: HISTORIAN WITH A PAINTBRUSH. *Am. West 1976 13(6): 18-29.* After several years as a commercial illustrator in the East, artist John Clymer decided to paint historical events of the West. He systematically explored the American and Canadian West and studied its history. His paintings are widely exhibited and have earned several awards. Adapted from a recent book; 6 illus. 1960's-70's

Coakley, Daniel

1277. Russell, Francis. THE KNAVE OF BOSTON. *Am. Heritage 1976 27(5): 73-80.* In an era controlled by ward bosses, one of Boston's worst was Daniel Coakley (1865-1952). A lawyer and friend of influential figures in state and local government, Coakley preferred dishonesty as the route to financial success. Fraudulent schemes and friendship with the right people (district attorneys, for example) led to great success, yet soon gained Coakley many enemies. Disbarred in 1922, he was acquitted of criminal charges; and in 1932 he was elected to the governor's council, where he worked hard getting easy pardons and the like until impeached from that office by the Massachusetts legislature in 1941. 4 illus. ca 1900-42

Coates, Eugene Butler

1278. Eaton, E. L. EUGENE BUTLER COATES, O. B. E.: SKIPPER UNUSUAL. *Nova Scotia Hist. Q. [Canada] 1979 9(3): 257-267.* Eugene Butler Coates (1891-1978) began his career at sea at the age of 15 and progressed from cabin boy to cook, able seaman, mate, and finally to Captain. He earned a certificate as Master in Sail in 1914 and another for passenger steamships in the coastal trade three years later; both from Yarmouth Navigation School. He won honors for his participation in World War II, and was employed by the Department of Transport of Canada (1950-1958) on various lightships. 20c

Coates, George M.

1279. Miller, George L. GEORGE M. COATES, POTTERY MERCHANT OF PHILADELPHIA, 1817-1831. *Winterthur Portfolio 1984 19(1): 37-49.* An analysis of the account books of George M. Coates, a Philadelphia merchant. The development of manufacturers' capital and the growth of the Staffordshire potteries explain the emergence of an auction market for ceramics. The account books explain the development of a rural trade for Coates. Based on the Coates Papers in the Winterthur Museum, price lists, and other sources; fig., 4 tables, 23 notes. 1817-31

Cobb, Hilda Smith

1280. Cobb, W. Montague. HILDA SMITH COBB, 1906-1976. *Crisis 1976 83(8): 292-294.* Hilda Smith Cobb was born in Washington, D.C. She graduated from Dunbar High School, and from Howard University in 1936. She and her husband were life members of the NAACP, to which she dedicated much of her energy. A teacher, she inspired her students and friends to emphasize the equality of persons and to maximize their achievement. 1906-76

Cobb, Ty

1281. Heilman, Robert B. TY COBB: THE HERO AND HIS WARTS. *Am. Scholar 1984 53(4): 541-546.* Reviews Charles C. Alexander's *Ty Cobb* (1984). Compares the printed biography with personal narratives about the baseball player. Reflects on the methodology of biography of heroes of popular culture. 1918-29

Cochran, Jacob

1282. —. THE COCHRAN FANATICISM IN YORK COUNTY. *Maine Hist. Soc. Q. 1980 20(1): 20-39.*

Gaffney, Thomas L. EDITOR'S NOTE, *pp. 20-22.* Summarizes Jacob Cochran's career and gives a bibliography on the subject.

—. THE COCHRAN FANATICISM IN YORK COUNTY, *pp. 23-39.* The unknown author, writing in 1867, gives a morally indignant account of the brief (1817-19) religious career of Jacob Cochran (b. 1785) in York County, Maine. Cochran used his charismatic personality to lead a religious movement known as Cochranism or the Society of Free Brethren and Sisters. He attacked organized Christianity and advocated "spiritual" marriage and free love. After he was convicted of adultery and served time in prison, his movement gradually disappeared. Based on interviews with eyewitnesses. 1817-19

Cochrane, Henry Clay

1283. Holden-Rhodes, J. F. THE ADVENTURES OF HENRY CLAY COCHRANE. *Marine Corps Gazette 1982 66(11): 69-70, (12): 14-15, 67(1): 32-33, (2): 46-47, (3): 50-51, (4): 54-55.* Part 1: "THE MARINES WOULD STAY." Includes a biographical sketch of Henry Clay Cochrane and describes his journey to Cuba in 1898 and his part in the siege of a hill. Part 2: LIFE AT SEA. Life for Cochrane on the USS *Jamestown* after the Civil War was miserable and boring. Part 3: ASSAULT ON THE CONSULATE. Cochrane lowered the flag at the American consulate in Hawaii under orders from his commander but against the wishes of the consul in tribute to deceased Queen Kalama. Part 4: THIS SMART AND FAITHFUL FORCE. Cochrane served on the USS *Lancaster* in the Mediterranean during the early 1880's. Part 5: PARIS EXPOSITION, 1889. Cochrane directed a US Marine detachment in a performance at the 1889 Paris Exposition. Part 6: COMMANDING MARINE BARRACKS. Details Cochrane's management of the Marine Corps barracks at Newport, Rhode Island, during 1897-98. 1860's-98

Cockburn, James

1284. Swainson, Donald. "FORGOTTEN MEN" REVISITED—SOME NOTES ON THE CAREER OF THE HON. JAMES COCKBURN, A DESERVEDLY "NEGLECTED" FATHER OF CONFEDERATION. *Ontario Hist. [Canada] 1980 72(4): 230-242.* Scottish-born James Cockburn (1819-83) was brought to Canada as a child, where he was educated, became a lawyer, and, when his practice failed, entered local politics. Shifts of allegiance facilitated his movement up the political ladder and into the provincial cabinet before Confederation, and to the Speakership of the House of Commons afterward. After 1873 he was only a minor figure. His defeat in the 1873 elections may be a factor here, even though he was reelected in 1878. 80 notes, mainly from public archives. 1855-83

Cocke, Louisa Maxwell Holmes

1285. Urbach, Jon Leonard. "God and Man in the Life of Louisa Maxwell Holmes Cocke: A Search for Piety and Place in the Old South." Florida State U. 1983. 641 pp. *DAI 1984 45(4): 1189-A.* DA8416730 1788-1843

Cockrell, Sarah Horton

1286. Enstam, Elizabeth York. OPPORTUNITY VERSUS PROPRIETY: THE LIFE AND CAREER OF FRONTIER MATRIARCH SARAH HORTON COCKRELL. *Frontiers 1981 6(3): 106-114.* Sarah Horton Cockrell was a founder of Dallas, Texas, and became one of its richest and most socially prominent citizens, 1819-92. 1819-92

Codman, Ernest Amory

1287. Reverby, Susan. STEALING THE GOLDEN EGGS: ERNEST AMORY CODMAN AND THE SCIENCE AND MANAGEMENT OF MEDICINE. *Bull. of the Hist. of Medicine 1981 55(2): 156-171.* Ernest Amory Codman (1869-1940) tried to make medicine more efficient by developing the end result system, following patients to determine whether the treatment has succeeded, and then to inquire, if not, why not. In 1910, Codman and Edward Martin, a clinical professor of surgery at the University of Pennsylvania, began to campaign for the implementation of the system nationwide. Codman opened a private hospital in Boston in 1911 and issued periodic studies on hospital efficiency, which he mailed to hospitals around the country. Although some hospitals did try the system, its most lasting results were achieved through the hospital standardization work of the American college of Surgeons beginning in 1916. Based on primary, including the Codman papers at the Countway Library, Boston, and secondary sources; illus., 71 notes. 1910-23

Codman, Ogden, Jr.

1288. Metcalf, Pauline C. OGDEN CODMAN, JR. AND "THE GRANGE." *Old-Time New England 1981 71(258): 68-83.* Biography of Ogden Codman, Jr., "the last member of the Codman family to carry out interior changes and alterations" to "The Grange" in Lincoln, Massachusetts, focusing on Codman's career as a reputable architect and interior decorator from 1891 until 1920, and his restoration and redesign of the Codman House. 1891-1920

1289. Metcalf, Pauline C. OGDEN CODMAN, JR.: A CLEVER YOUNG BOSTON ARCHITECT. *Nineteenth Cent. 1981 7(1): 45-47.* Prints a biography of Ogden Codman, Jr., an American architect who did most of his work in France. 1891-1931

Codman family

1290. Adams, Thomas Boylston. LINCOLN AND THE CODMANS. *Old-Time New England 1981 71(258): 1-14.* Personal narrative about the Codman family, upperclass members of Lincoln, Massachusetts, society; includes information on social customs; 1890-1920. 1890-1920

1291. Howie, Robert L., Jr. CODMAN CONNECTIONS: PORTRAIT OF A FAMILY AND ITS PAPERS. *Old-Time New England 1981 71(258): 150-157.* Provides a genealogy of the Codmans and describes the Codman Family Manuscripts Collection, 100,000 items that the Society for the Preservation of New England Antiquities acquired with the Codman House in 1969, covering the period 1715-1969, and describes the organization of the collection. 1715-1979

Cody, William F. (Buffalo Bill)

1292. Mitterling, Philip I. BUFFALO BILL AND CARRY NATION: SYMBOLS OF AN AGE. *North Dakota Q. 1982 50(1): 62-71.* Presents brief biographical sketches of Buffalo Bill Cody, western Indian fighter, and prohibitionist Carry Nation, who were "among the first personalities created by Americans to satisfy national anxieties and desires." 1840's-1900

Coffee, John Trousdale

1293. Hulston, John K. and Goodrich, James W. JOHN TROUSDALE COFFEE: LAWYER, POLITICIAN, CONFEDERATE. *Missouri Hist. Rev. 1983 77(3): 272-295.* John Trousdale Coffee, who had a distinguished career in Missouri law and politics, is usually remembered as a successful recruiter for the Confederate cause and as a rebel cavalry leader. His forces, operating in Missouri and Arkansas, caused Union sympathizers to fear for their lives and property. Coffee was not a Confederate guerrilla in the mold of William C. Quantrill, but his mission, if not his tactics, was similar: to keep a maximum number of Union troops engaged in protecting loyal Union citizens. 8 illus., 3 photos, 88 notes. 1840's-90

Cohen, Arthur A.

1294. Cole, Diane. PROFESSION: RENAISSANCE MAN: ARTHUR A. COHEN. *Present Tense 1981 9(1): 32-35.* Discusses the career of Jewish publisher, novelist, and editor Arthur A. Cohen, who wrote *In the Days of Simon Stern,* and worked for several of America's largest publishing houses during the 1960's. 1950-80

Cohen, Benjamin V.

1295. Louchheim, Katie. THE LITTLE RED HOUSE. *Virginia Q. Rev. 1980 56(1): 119-134.* This house in Washington, D.C., was where Thomas Gardiner Corcoran and Benjamin V. Cohen lived for three and a half years from June 1933. There they prepared and lobbied for many of the New Deal measures. Provides short biographies of these men and sidelights on tactics, personalities, and characteristics of many New Deal leaders. 1933-37

Cohen, Harry

1296. Kauffmann, Stanley. ALBUM OF MR. COHEN. *Am. Scholar 1982-83 52(1): 49-64.* Prints personal narratives about Stanley Kauffmann's father-in-law, Harry Cohen, the son of Jewish immigrants, a youthful socialist, and a lifelong atheist. He lived in East Orange, New Jersey, and Chicago, Illinois. Emphasizes his personal relationships and his political attitudes. 1938-68

Cohen, I. Bernard

1297. Cohen, I. Bernard. A HARVARD EDUCATION. *Isis 1984 75(276): 13-20.* Recollections of I. Bernard Cohen, a Harvard University professor of the history of science, of his student years in the 1930's-40's, with special reference to Professor George Sarton and the early development of the Harvard program in the history of science. 2 photos, 4 notes. 1930's-40's

Cohen, Mendes

1298. Gibb, Hugh R. MENDES COHEN: ENGINEER, SCHOLAR AND RAILROAD EXECUTIVE. *Maryland Hist. Mag. 1979 74(1): 1-10.* A testimonial to the life and career of Mendes Cohen (1831-1915) of Baltimore, whose engineering innovations were instrumental in the expansion of the early Baltimore & Ohio. As president of the Pittsburgh & Connellsville Railroad, he unsuccessfully fought the Pennsylvania Railroad for control of the Pittsburgh traffic in the 1870's. One of Baltimore's leading citizens, he served on commissions for everything from streetcar fenders to a sanitary sewage system, and was closely involved with the Maryland Historical Society—as secretary during 1882-1904 and as president during 1904-13. His home at 825 North Charles Street was a center of civic activity, philanthropy, and American railroad history. Primary sources; 27 notes. 1847-1915

Cohen, Morris Raphael

1299. Rosenfield, Leonora Cohen. THE JUDAIC VALUES OF A PHILOSOPHER: MORRIS RAPHAEL COHEN, 1880-1947. *Jewish Social Studies 1980 42(3-4): 189-214.* The Jewish philosopher Morris Raphael Cohen espoused a number of Jewish values according to which he lived his life, including: 1) the welfare of world Jewry depends upon the liberalism of society, 2) every Jew should know something about his roots and Judaic heritage, 3) Jews must venerate learning and constantly probe for knowledge, 4) the Hebrew prophets must inspire Jews to spiritual values, universal truth, and eternity of ideas, 5) a Jew must be a loyal defender of his people, and 6) Jews must be actively committed to social justice, righteousness, and compassion. Cohen demonstrated many of these values through his work on behalf of the Conference on Jewish Relations, which he helped to found. Based on Cohen's letters and writings; 29 notes, appendix. 1880-1947

1300. Slive, David Ira. "Morris Raphael Cohen as Educator." State U. of New York, Buffalo 1985. 505 pp. *DAI 1985 46(3): 645-A.* DA8510366 1890's-1947

Cohn, Annie

1301. Stern, Norton B. A NINETEENTH CENTURY CONVERSION IN LOS ANGELES. *Western States Jewish Hist. 1984 16(4): 360-367.* 1889-1921
*For abstract see **Kinney, Edward W.***

Cohn, Avern

1302. Kaufman, Ira G. MICHIGAN JUDICIARY OF JEWISH LINEAGE, PAST AND PRESENT: PART II. *Michigan Jewish History 1983 23(1): 15-19.* Continued from a previous article. Examines the careers of the following judges of the federal courts: Lawrence Gubow (1919-78), Avern Cohn (b. 1924), and Stewart A. Newblatt (b. 1927). 1919-83

Cohn, Bernard

1303. Stern, Norton B. THE FIRST JEW TO RUN FOR MAYOR OF LOS ANGELES. *Western States Jewish Hist. Q. 1980 12(3): 246-258.* Bernard Cohn (1835-89) had a general merchandise business in Los Angeles from 1857 to his partial retirement in 1877. In 1876, he was elected to the city council. While serving as council chairman, he was appointed Mayor *pro tem* to fill the vacancy left by the death of Mayor Frederick A. MacDougall in 1878. Shortly before this temporary appointment, Cohn was selected as nominee of the People's Party for the mayor's office. Despite his qualities of civic concern and leadership, Cohn was not personally popular. Anti-Semitism may have been a factor in his defeat by the Workingmen's Party candidate, James R. Toberman. Cohn was later elected to several more terms as city councilman. Based on newspaper accounts, and other published works; photo, 60 notes. 1857-89

Cohn, Mina Norton

1304. —. MINA NORTON: FIRST TEACHER AT SANTA MONICA CANYON SCHOOL, A PICTURE STORY. *Western States Jewish Hist. Q. 1981 14(1): 76-81.* Following graduation from the California State Normal School at Los Angeles in 1894, Mina Norton found a teaching position at the newly opened Santa Monica Canyon School. She stayed there only one year, then taught at the Ann Street School of Los Angeles from 1895 until 1903. Her marriage to Isidor Cohn in 1904 ended her professional career. Isidor Cohn later established the Cohn-Asher Hat Company, the largest manufacturer of hats in the West in the 1920's. Based on interviews and newspaper articles; 6 photos, 9 notes. 1895-1927

Coit, Dorothy

1305. Rodman, Ellen Rena. "Edith King and Dorothy Coit and the King-Coit School and Children's Theatre." New York U. 1980. 242 pp. *DAI 1980 41(2): 463-A.* 8017523 1923-58

Colby, Abby M.

1306. Taylor, Sandra C. ABBY M. COLBY: THE CHRISTIAN RESPONSE TO SEXIST SOCIETY. *New England Q. 1979 52(1): 68-79.* Women, who comprised two-thirds of the missionaries to Japan in the late 19th century, received lower pay than men and were only allowed to vote on matters of "women's work" within their organization. Abby M. Colby (1848-1917) was a feminist who served as a Congregational missionary in Japan between 1879 and 1914 and opposed these practices as much as she did Japanese practices of male-dominated marriages, concubinage, and prostitution. Based on Colby's letters in the papers of the American Board of Commissioners for Foreign Missions at Houghton Library, Harvard University; 29 notes. 1879-1914

Colcord, Lincoln

1307. Albee, Parker Bishop, Jr., ed. PORTRAIT OF A FRIENDSHIP: SELECTED CORRESPONDENCE OF SAMUEL ELIOT MORISON AND LINCOLN COLCORD, 1921-1947. *New England Q. 1983 56(2): 166-199.* Letters exchanged by Samuel Eliot Morison and Lincoln Colcord offer a poignant and charming insight into two friends joined by a common love of the sea. Colcord, who lived in Seasport, Maine, was a short-story writer, novelist, and journalist who published books of sea stories, compiled the *Record of Vessels Built on Penobscot River and Bay,* founded the Penobscot Marine Museum, and served as editor of the *American Neptune.* Over 300 letters remain; Morison's at Harvard University and Colcord's in the possession of his son. The sample reprinted here reveals the character of the two men, chronicles the major events of their lives, and conveys the quality of their friendship. 62 notes. Article to be continued. 1921-47

1308. Albee, Parker Bishop, Jr., ed. SELECTED CORRESPONDENCE OF SAMUEL ELIOT MORISON AND LINCOLN COLCORD, 1921-1947. PART 2. *New England Q. 1983 56(3): 398-424.* Continued from a previous article. Presents letters exchanged between historian Samuel Eliot Morison and author-mariner Lincoln Colcord. The 16 letters, written between 1938 and 1947, reveal the characters of the two men, chronicle the major events of their lives during this period, and convey the quality of their friendship. 66 notes. 1938-47

Colden, Cadwallader

1309. Hoermann, Alfred R. CADWALLADER COLDEN AND THE MIND-BODY PROBLEM. *Bull. of the Hist. of Medicine 1976 50(3): 392-404.* Ireland-born Cadwallader Colden (1688-1776), a graduate of the University of Edinburgh with medical training in London, migrated to the American colonies, and after a brief medical practice assumed a career in government in New York. His writings indicate an attempt to resolve the mind-body problem. His views were dominated by his natural philosophy. He insisted on two active and disparate substances, and that created dilemmas which prevented any satisfactory explanation or resolution. 62 notes. ca 1700-76

1310. Hoermann, Alfred R. A SAVANT IN THE WILDERNESS: CADWALLADER COLDEN OF NEW YORK. *New York Hist. Soc. Q. 1978 62(4): 270-288.* Scotch-born Cadwallader Colden came to the English colonies at the age of 22 and played a prominent role in American life, first in Philadelphia and then New York. In addition to a career in politics—he served as lieutenant-governor of New York—he was a physician, scientist, merchant, botanist, philosopher, and historian. In the latter capacity, he urged better treatment for the Indians in his two-part history of the Iroquois. Colden's writings as well as his correspondence with such men as Benjamin Franklin and Samuel Johnson reveal him to have been a man of the Enlightenment in America and one who had ties with the Old World as well as the New. Primary sources; 4 illus., 40 notes. 1688-1776

Cole, Louis

1311. Walker, Perry. REV. LOUIS COLE, BLACK BAPTIST CIRCUIT PREACHER, 1901-1981. *Southern Quarterly 1985 23(3): 48-69.* An autobiographical statement by Reverend Louis Cole as told by a man who knew him summarizes the life experiences of a black Baptist circuit preacher in northern Mississippi and southwestern Tennessee, focusing on his calling to the ministry and his theology. 1920's-81

Cole family

1312. Auman, Dorothy Cole and Zug, Charles G., III. NINE GENERATIONS OF POTTERS: THE COLE FAMILY. *Southern Exposure 1977 5(2-3): 166-174.* The Cole family has been involved in pottery manufacture in North Carolina for 200 years. The family's pottery making tradition has been traced back to 18th-century England, and some family members may have made pottery during the early 17th century in Jamestown. For most of the 19th and early 20th centuries, the Coles manufactured simply designed, utilitarian pottery for local and regional use and sale. During the 1920's-30's, a greater variety of designs was introduced along with pottery aimed at tourism, garden use, and artistic forms. Despite some modern innovations, pottery making still retains many ties to traditional modes of manufacture. Based on participant observation. 1700's-1977

Coleman, Benjamin

1313. Roeber, Anthony Gregg. "HER MERCHANDIZE... SHALL BE HOLINESS TO THE LORD": THE PROGRESS AND DECLINE OF PURITAN GENTILITY AT THE BRATTLE STREET CHURCH, BOSTON, 1715-1745. *New England Hist. and Geneal. Register 1977 131: 175-194.* Examines the life and thought of Benjamin Coleman, pastor of Boston's Brattle Street Church and minister to many of the town's wealthy merchants. The congregation was at the center of a number of controversies which shook Massachusetts during 1715-40, most notably the great credit debates. Coleman's special mission was to bring the "gentility" of 18th-century England to Boston and blend it with Puritan piety. The Puritan gentility had a distinct social dimension. Coleman advocated a social hierarchy with the clergy at the top assisted by a mercantile elite serving as guardians of church and society. However, Coleman never adequately defined his concept of gentility. In the end his ideas were overwhelmed by changes in Puritan thought and in America's attitude toward the mother country. Primary and secondary sources; 56 notes. 1715-45

Coles, Edward

1314. Leichtle, Kurt Edwin. "Edward Coles: An Agrarian on the Frontier." U. of Illinois, Chicago Circle 1982. 248 pp. *DAI 1982 43(1): 242-A.* DA8213926 1819-68

Collier, John

1315. Hauptman, Laurence M. ALICE JAMISON: SENECA POLITICAL ACTIVIST, 1901-1964. *Indian Hist. 1979 12(2): 15-22, 60-62.* 1930's-50's

*For abstract see **Jamison, Alice Lee***

Collins, John Andrew

1316. Logan, Kevin John. "No Permanent Remedy: The Public Life of John Andrew Collins." U. of Maine 1978. 231 pp. *DAI 1978 39(6): 3779-3780-A.* 1830's-50's

Collins, Mary Clementine

1317. Borst, John C. THE MARY C. COLLINS FAMILY PAPERS AT THE SOUTH DAKOTA HISTORICAL RESOURCE CENTER. *South Dakota History 1982 12(4): 248-253.* Traces the life and career of Mary Clementine Collins, a missionary to the Sioux in South Dakota during 1875-1910, and describes the contents of the Mary C. Collins Family Papers which are divided into two categories: those dealing with Mary C. Collins; and those concerning the family of Ethel Collins Jacobsen, her niece (who was also involved in mission work among the Sioux). Included in the Mary C. Collins material are correspondence dealing with various aspects of mission life and the problems involved in gaining fair treatment and legal rights for the Indians, a short autobiography, diaries, genealogical information, and photographs. The Ethel Jacobsen material contains diaries of Ethel and her husband Elias, correspondence, genealogical information, and miscellaneous folders. The material is valuable for the study of 19th- and early 20th-century missionary efforts among the Sioux Indians of South Dakota. Based on the Mary C. Collins Family Papers located at the South Dakota Historical Resource Center, Pierre, South Dakota; 2 photos. 1875-1920

1318. Clow, Richmond L., ed. AUTOBIOGRAPHY OF MARY C. COLLINS, MISSIONARY TO THE WESTERN SIOUX. *South Dakota Historical Collections 1982 41: 1-66.* Consists of the autobiography of Mary Clementine Collins, who describes her work as a missionary of the Congregational Church to the Western Sioux in South Dakota from 1875 to 1910. Collins discusses her religious upbringing, her assignment to the Oahe Mission, the condition of the Indians' lives near the mission, and her memories of friends and acquaintances, both white and Indian. Among the prominent figures she encountered were Sitting Bull and the many Indian agents assigned to the Sioux agencies in North and South Dakota. By 1900 Collins began to question government policies intended to lead to Indian self-sufficiency, and she aired her complaints in letters to the Indian commissioners and at the Lake Mohonk Conferences. Illus., 22 photos, 34 notes. 1875-1910

Collins, Thomas LeRoy

1319. Wagy, Thomas Ray. "A South to Save: The Administration of Governor Leroy Collins of Florida." Florida State U. 1980. 377 pp. *DAI 1980 41(3): 1192-A.* 8020364 1955-61

Collinson, Peter

1320. Kastner, Joseph. COLONIAL BOTANIST, SELF-TAUGHT, FILLED EUROPEAN GARDENS. *Smithsonian 1977 8(7): 122-129.* 1699-1777

*For abstract see **Bartram, John***

Colman, Samuel

1321. Craven, Wayne. SAMUEL COLMAN (1832-1920): REDISCOVERED PAINTER OF FAR-AWAY PLACES. *Am. Art J. 1976 8(1): 16-37.* Samuel Colman "in the latter half of the 19th century... was one of the most colorful, versatile, prolific, admired and successful of American artists." In his 60-year career he traveled widely, working at oil painting, water colors, etching, Oriental art collecting, interior design, and theoretical writing, and producing perhaps a thousand works. Based on primary and secondary sources; 28 illus., 49 notes. 1860-1920

Colquitt, Oscar Branch

1322. Taylor, Dencil R. "The Political Speaking of Oscar Branch Colquitt, 1906-1913." Louisiana State U. and Agric. and Mechanical Coll. 1979. 271 pp. *DAI 1979 40(4): 1748-A.* 1906-13

Colt, Samuel

1323. Hacker, Rick. COLONEL COLT'S PISTOLS: THE GUNS THAT WON THE WEST. *Sporting Classics 1985 4(5): 64-71.* Samuel Colt struggled for years to market the revolver he had invented in 1831, falling bankrupt several times until he finally achieved success in 1848; after his death in 1862, the company he founded continued to produce pistols that have become part of American folklore. 1814-1985

Colum, Mary

1324. Rimo, Patricia Ann. "Mary Colum: Woman of Letters." U. of Delaware 1982. 237 pp. *DAI 1983 43(7): 2345-2346-A.* DA8227530 1884-1957

Colum, Pádraic

1325. Murphy, Ann. PÁDRAIC COLUM (1881-1972), NATIONAL POET. *Éire-Ireland 1982 17(4): 128-147.* Presents a biographical appreciation of Pádraic Colum, for 70 years—in Ireland and the United States—a prolific poet, dramatist, novelist, essayist, critic, and folklorist. Colum saw himself as an authentic national poet because—unlike W. B. Yeats, Lady Gregory, George W. Russell (AE), and others—he came from the Catholic peasantry and sought to express realistically the peasant heritage. In his various literary forms, Colum celebrated the piety, quiet heroism, and natural poetic qualities of the Irish peasants, with their awareness of mythology and folklore and inherited knowledge of ballads, legends, and historical tales. Based on unpublished documents at the National Library of Ireland and the New York Public Library (Berg Collection), an interview with Colum, correspondence with Irish writers, and the published works of Colum; 58 notes. 1902-72

Comer, George

1326. Calabretta, Fred. CAPTAIN GEORGE COMER AND THE ARCTIC. *Log of Mystic Seaport 1984 35(4): 118-131.* Captain George Comer, a successful whaling master, was also an amateur anthropologist and scientist who collected museum specimens during his many voyages to the Arctic; he made extensive studies of the Hudson Bay Eskimos and the Arctic environment. 1875-1919

Comfort, Nicholas

1327. Cottrell, Bob. THE SOCIAL GOSPEL OF NICHOLAS COMFORT. *Chronicles of Oklahoma 1983-84 61(4): 386-413.* Nicholas Comfort embraced the concept that clergymen should engage directly in actions that will correct social ills. As a Presbyterian minister and dean of the Oklahoma School of Religion in Norman, he espoused many unpopular causes in the politically conservative state. Although a veteran of World War I, he preached a strident antimilitarism during the 1930's, attacking military training at the University of Oklahoma, as well as the inflated national military budgets. Comfort routinely criticized American business leaders for their greed, and championed the cause of black civil rights. Censured at various times by the American Legion, the Ku Klux Klan, and Governor Leon Phillips, Comfort weathered the attacks and remained committed to social change through the new Progressive Party of Henry Wallace. Based on Oklahoma newspapers and the Oklahoma School of Religion Collection at the University of Oklahoma; 4 photos, 65 notes. 1927-56

Compere, Ebenezer Lee

1328. Gardner, Robert G. EBENEZER LEE COMPERE, CHEROKEE GEORGIA BAPTIST MISSIONARY. *Viewpoints: Georgia Baptist Hist. 1976 5: 91-102.* Ebenezer Lee Compere, a missionary from the Baptist Church, ministered to the Cherokee Indians in northeast Oklahoma 1854-65. 1854-65

Compton, Henry

1329. O'Neill, Jean. HENRY COMPTON, BISHOP OF LONDON: GUARDIAN OF EDUCATION AND RELIGION IN COLONIAL VIRGINIA. *Virginia Cavalcade 1979 29(2): 88-98.* Henry Compton (1632-1713), Bishop of London, participated in the Glorious Revolution and was appointed to organize the Church of England in America. 1650's-1713

Conacher, Lionel Pretoria

1330. Morrow, Don. LIONEL PRETORIA CONACHER. *J. of Sport Hist. 1979 6(1): 5-37.* Lionel Pretoria Conacher (1900-54) was Canada's outstanding male athlete of the first half of the 20th century. From 1912 to 1937, he excelled in football, hockey, lacrosse, baseball, boxing, and wrestling, and at times even played three professional sports during the same year. Although football was his favorite sport, the increasing popularity of professional hockey in the 1920's provided him with a means of support. He was a one-man team who preferred team sports but who preferred to go it alone. Although he dominated a variety of sports for 25 years, he has been ignored as an outstanding Canadian, as an outstanding athlete, and as a subject worthy of serious academic study by historians. Table, 174 notes. 1912-37

Conaghan, B. F.

1331. Conaghan, B. F. THREE SANDS: EXPERIENCES IN AN EARLY OIL FIELD. *Chronicles of Oklahoma 1980 58(1): 65-76.* Presents the reminiscences of an oil field worker who participated in the development of the important Three Sands oil field of Kay and Noble Counties, Oklahoma, during the 1920's. In addition to describing the daily work and development of new technology, he relates the history of local law enforcement, educational facilities, business enterprises, and other social aspects. Map, 5 photos. 1920's

Condon, Eddie

1332. Kenney, William Howland, III. EDDIE CONDON IN ILLINOIS: THE ROOTS OF A "JAZZ PERSONALITY." *Illinois Historical Journal 1984 77(4): 255-268.* Eddie Condon, born in Goodland, Indiana, 16 November 1905, moved to Momence, Illinois, in 1908. He was introduced to many elements of jazz in the songs, band and choral music, and ragtime compositions he heard as a youth in Momence, which had close ties to Chicago. The son of an Irish pubkeeper, he experienced the repressive aspects of the prohibitionist movement. When prohibitionists forced his family to relocate in Chicago, Condon became familiar with the Afro-American blues tradition. For him, jazz remained associated with liberation from nonmusical restraints. 6 illus., 29 notes. 1908-20's

Condon, Thomas

1333. Gustafson, Eric Paul, ed. THOMAS CONDON'S PRIVATE LOG: AROUND THE HORN, 1852-53. *Oregon Hist. Q. 1983 84(3): 229-242.* Thomas Condon, pioneer geologist and Congregational missionary in Oregon for 55 years, kept a meticulous record of daily position readings during his 103-day voyage from New York to California on the clipper *Trade Wind.* A fire on the deck of the ship highlighted the voyage of 1852-53. 3 photos, map, 9 notes. 1852-53

Congdon, Bradford Sumner

1334. Carter, Joseph C., ed. THE PHILOSOPHER OF DANBY. *Vermont Hist. 1982 50(2): 95-98.* Annotates, with biographical introduction, an 1888 letter of Bradford Sumner Congdon of Danby Four Corners, Vermont, to his cousin, L. J. Grinnell of Spencer, Massachusetts, exemplifying the rural view that farming safeguards American values and preserves true moral and democratic power from the "luxurious dissipation" of the cities. 6 notes. 1888

Congdon, Herbert Wheaton

1335. Graffagnino, J. Kevin. HERBERT WHEATON CONGDON AND THE ARCHITECTURAL HERITAGE OF VERMONT. *Vermont Hist. 1982 50(1): 5-12.* A summer visitor until he moved to Arlington in 1923, Congdon hiked and mapped the Long Trail of the Green Mountain Club and engaged in the desultory practices of architecture and photography. For a quarter century, he had helped his father, Henry Martyn Congdon, design Episcopal churches in the Gothic style. As underpaid professional field worker for the University of Vermont's Old Buildings Project, Congdon photographed and researched the state's pre-1850 structures. He published *Old Vermont Houses* (1940) and *Covered Bridge* (1941), and he continued to record early Vermont architecture as long as he lived. Based on the Congdon Papers, University of Vermont; 5 photos, 25 notes. 1923-65

Conger, Omar D.

1336. Rubenstein, Bruce A. OMAR D. CONGER: MICHIGAN'S FORGOTTEN FAVORITE SON. *Michigan Hist. 1982 66(5): 32-39.* Omar D. Conger had a lengthy career as a Michigan politician in the 19th century. When elected to the state senate in 1855, he was a vital figure in Michigan Republican politics. During 1868-80 he served as congressman from the 5th District, and in 1880, with the aid of the "Port Huron Custom House Ring," secured election to the US Senate. A falling out with John Sanborn, collector of customs at Port Huron and dispenser of political patronage in the port area, ended Conger's chances for reelection. Conger died in obscurity, a once powerful man whom no one remembered. 8 pictures, 39 notes. 1818-98

Conklin, Edwin Grant

1337. Atkinson, J. W. E. G. CONKLIN ON EVOLUTION: THE POPULAR WRITINGS OF AN EMBRYOLOGIST. *Journal of the History of Biology 1985 18(1): 31-50.* The career of Edwin Grant Conklin is a good indication of how popular authors of science brought their craft to the public's attention and, in a limited sense, became cultural heroes. As a leading embryologist who taught in several schools, including the University of Pennsylvania and Princeton, Conklin wrote for a significant lay audience during 1920-40. He supported a thesis of teleology in his science in numerous writings on aspects of the theory of evolution. He believed that while the progressive intellectual and physical evolution of man had come to an end, social (or cultural) progress had just begun. In his theoretical evolutionary philosophy, Conklin anticipated the later popularity of Teilhard de Chardin and such writers as Roger Sperry. 89 notes. 1890's-1952

Conkling, Margaret

1338. Brockmoller, Janet Y. A MUSIC OF TWO SPHERES: THE STORY OF MARGARET CONKLING. *Password 1985 30(3): 143-147.* Discusses the El Paso years of accomplished musician and archaeological and historical researcher Margaret Conkling, who with her husband Roscoe Conkling authored the authoritative historical work *The Butterfield Overland Mail, 1857-1869.* 1920-47

Connell, James H.

1339. May, Irvin, Jr. J. H. CONNELL: AGGIE ADMINISTRATOR, THE TEXAS YEARS. *Red River Valley Hist. Rev. 1978 3(1): 93-108.* James H. Connell directed the Texas Agricultural Experiment Station, 1893-1902. 1893-1902

Conner, William

1340. Larson, John L. and Vanderstel, David G. AGENT OF EMPIRE: WILLIAM CONNER ON THE INDIANA FRONTIER, 1800-1855. *Indiana Mag. of Hist. 1984 80(4): 301-328.* William Conner lived two separate lives on the Indiana frontier. As Indian trader and agent he organized the exchange of commodities between Indians and fur-trading companies; he also helped in relocating the Delaware tribe from Indiana to Missouri. As a pioneer white settler he became a land speculator, town founder, and merchant banker who traded farm crops for supplies. His early presence in Indiana and his immersion in Delaware Indian culture made it possible for him simultaneously to represent Indians and white settlers. Based on newspapers and local histories of Indiana communities; map, 3 photos, 45 notes. 1800-55

Conroy, George

1341. Perin, Roberto. TROPPO ARDENTI SACERDOTI: THE CONROY MISSION REVISITED. *Can. Hist. Rev. [Canada] 1980 61(3): 283-304.* Reassesses the mission of George Conroy (1832-78), an Irish bishop and Apostolic Delegate to the province of Quebec in 1877-78. Worried about the French Canadian clergy's involvement in politics, the Holy See chose Cardinal Paul Cullen's protégé to impose a solution elaborated in Rome. Conroy did not study the roots of the crisis within the Quebec Church, but rather sought to appease the ruling Liberal Party in Ottawa. In so doing, he transformed the Catholic Church from a vital institution, relatively free from the partisan manipulation characterizing Canadian life since the advent of responsible government in 1848, into a tool of the politicians. Until 1878, the Church had been a rampart against an aggressive Anglo-Saxon nationalism which sought to mold Canada in its image. After this date, it was much less effective in resisting the "political compromises" which led to the triumph of this nationalism. Based on the Archives of the Propaganda Fide in Rome and other primary sources; 81 notes. 1877-78

Conway, Moncure Daniel

1342. D'Entremont, John Philip. "Moncure Conway: The American Years, 1832-1865." Johns Hopkins U. 1981. 565 pp. *DAI 1981 42(4): 1760-A.* 8120017 1832-65

1343. Pitman, Ursula Wall. "Moncure Daniel Conway: The Development and Career of a Southern Abolitionist." Boston Coll. 1978. 695 pp. *DAI 1978 38(12): 7516-7517-A.* 1850's-60's

Cook, George Hammell

1344. Sidar, Jean Wilson. "George Hammell Cook, A Life in Agriculture and Geology: 1818-1889." Rutgers U. 1979. *DAI 1979 40(3): 1657-A.* 1864-88

Cook, Guy and Crystal Lisle

1345. Frajola, Ruth Cook, ed. THEY WENT WEST. *South Dakota Hist. 1976 6(3): 281-306.* Biographies of the author's parents, with the use of reminiscences of family history written by her father, Guy Cook, and mother, Crystal Lisle Cook, homesteaders in the Dakotas, 1880's-1954. 1880's-1954

Cook, Joseph

1346. Pointer, Steven R. JOSEPH COOK—APOLOGETICS AND SCIENCE. *American Presbyterians 1985 63(3): 299-308.* Joseph Cook was an unordained 19th-century Congregationalist who determined to rescue science from its alleged support of infidel conclusions and to utilize its testimony for the defense and advancement of the Christian faith. Representative of popular Protestant thought, he was in a tradition that attempted to defend and verify the truth claims of Christianity by means of the accumulation of evidences capable of being evaluated by man's rational faculties. His "Monday Lectures" given weekly in Boston (and later published in 11 volumes) were more marked by his oratorical delivery than objective content. Based on Joseph Cook's published works and contemporary writings; 65 notes. 1870-1900

1347. Pointer, Steven R. "The Perils of History: The Meteoric Career of Joseph Cook (1838-1901)." Duke U. 1981. 234 pp. *DAI 1982 43(1): 189-A.* DA8212973 1870's-1901

Cook, Maria

1348. Semowich, Charles. THE LIFE AND MINISTRY OF MISS MARIA COOK. *New York Folklore 1979 5(3-4): 146-149.* Biography of Universalist preacher, Maria Cook (1779-1835), focusing on her ministry mainly in New York but also in northern Pennsylvania from 1811 until her retirement about five years later. 1811-16

Cook, Sherburne Friend

1349. Borah, Woodrow W. OBITUARY: SHERBURNE FRIEND COOK (1896-1974). *Hispanic Am. Hist. Rev. 1975 55(4): 749-759.* Sherburne F. Cook (1896-1974) was a social biologist who applied his biological training to the study of populations in California and Mexico. His life and his writings are reviewed in this obituary. 94 notes. 1896-1974

1350. Jacobs, Wilbur R. SHERBURNE FRIEND COOK: REBEL-REVISIONIST (1896-1974). *Pacific Historical Review 1985 54(2): 191-199.* Although trained academically as a physiologist, most of Sherburne Friend Cook's work was in the area of historical demography. From the beginning, his research and conclusions sparked controversy. His academic productivity was prodigious, rapidly promoting him through the rank of associate professor. But so unusual were his methodologies and conclusions that it took several years before he could be advanced to the rank of full professor. Among his more controversial contributions were his estimation of the pre-Columbian Indian population at 100 million, his questioning whether there was a tendency among Mexican Americans to seek civil rather than religious weddings, and his interpretation of the size of Indian potsherds—"the size would depend upon how far the oldest woman will walk to dump her garbage." His lifetime work totaled some 160 research publications. Based on the Library Key to the Sherburne F. Cook Papers, Bancroft Library, University of California, Berkeley, and interviews; 31 notes. 1920-74

Cooke, Grace MacGowan

1351. Gaston, Kay Baker. THE MACGOWAN GIRLS. *California Hist. 1980 59(2): 116-125.* Traces the careers of Grace MacGowan Cooke (1863-1944) and her sister Alice MacGowan (1858-1947), prolific authors of popular novels, short stories, and poems. Born in Ohio and raised in Tennessee, the sisters joined Upton Sinclair for a time at his literary colony in New Jersey before coming to Carmel-by-the-Sea, California, in December 1908. For more than three decades the sisters collaborated with each other, with other writers, and in single authorship to produce a body of literature which, while not profound, brought them financial success. As literary figures they were on intimate terms with Sinclair Lewis (who worked as their secretary for a time), Jack London, George Sterling, and other west coast luminaries. Photos, 38 notes. 1908-47

Cooke, Jay

1352. Popowski, Howard J. GRANDADDY OF THE GREENBACK: JAY COOKE. *Civil War Times Illus. 1982 21(8): 28-35.* Traces the career of Jay Cooke, who organized Union financing of the war effort by means of bond issues, helping to win the war and embroiling the federal government permanently in the nation's economy. 1835-65

Cooke, John Esten

1353. Bratton, Mary Jo. JOHN ESTEN COOKE AND HIS "CONFEDERATE LIES." *Southern Literary J. 1981 13(2): 72-91.* The writings of southerner John Esten Cooke are a mixture of biography, history, and fiction, and concern the antebellum South as well as the Civil War. ca 1840-70

Coolbrith, Ina

1354. Herr, Pamela. PORTRAIT FOR A WESTERN ALBUM. *Am. West 1978 15(3): 30-31.* The family of Josephine Donna Smith (1841-1928) fled from the violence and persecution the Mormons suffered in Nauvoo, Illinois. In her teen years in Los Angeles, California, she became a recognized poet and also experienced a disastrous marriage. She changed her name to Ina Coolbrith and hid the secrets of her Mormon background and unfortunate marriage. She relocated in San Francisco, and her fame spread. Her energies were soon consumed, however, when she accepted full-time employment to support four relatives and friends. Despite decreased literary production, she was honored by California as its poet laureate. Illus., biblio. 1850's-80's

Cooley, Charles Horton

1355. Dibble, Vernon K. THE YOUNG CHARLES HORTON COOLEY AND HIS FATHER: A SCEPTICAL NOTE ABOUT PSYCHOBIOGRAPHIES. *J. of the Hist. of Sociol. 1982 4(1): 1-26.* Criticizes the conclusions drawn by Edward Jandy in his psychobiography, *Charles Horton Cooley: His Life and His Social Theory* (1942), as limited because Jandy relied on Cooley's *Journals* alone and failed to recognize Cooley's admiration for Emerson and Thoreau; reading the letters of Cooley and his family would provide a more accurate picture of Cooley's life and thought. 19c

Cooley, Corydon Eliphalet

1356. Welsh, Michael E. CORYDON E. COOLEY: PIONEER IN TWO WORLDS. *J. of Arizona Hist. 1979 20(3): 283-296.* An account of the career of Corydon Eliphalet Cooley (1836-1917) New Mexico and Arizona trader, scout, soldier, miner, rancher, US Marshall and local politician. Having married the two daughters of a White Mountain Apache chief, and operating the largest ranch in the area he was a major influence in bridging the gap between the two cultures, promoting understanding, and stimulating settlement. Primary sources; 2 photos, 47 notes. ca 1850-1917

Coolidge, Calvin

1357. Kilmartin, Thomas W. THE LAST SHALL BE FIRST: THE AMHERST COLLEGE DAYS OF CALVIN COOLIDGE. *Hist. J. of Western Massachusetts 1977 5(2): 1-12.* Discusses President Calvin Coolidge's years at Amherst College based on his own writings and those of his classmates. Illus., 79 notes. 1891-95

1358. Perry, Phillip M. WITH CALVIN COOLIDGE IN NORTHAMPTON. *New-England Galaxy 1977 18(3): 37-43.* Discusses Calvin Coolidge's life in Northampton, Massachusetts from March 1929 after he left the presidency until his death on 5 January 1933. His reactions to visitors were described by his secretary, Herman Beaty, and by his chauffeur, John Bukoski. Illus. 1929-33

1359. Silver, Thomas B. COOLIDGE AND THE HISTORIANS. *Am. Scholar 1981 50(4): 501-517.* Calvin Coolidge was an educated, dignified, decent, moral, patriotic, and deeply democratic human being. He was enormously popular, elected by large majorities every time he ran except once. This is in sharp contrast to the popular images drawn by Samuel E. Morrison, Arthur Schleisinger, Jr., and others. 1900-30

Coolidge, Dane

1360. Ulph, Owen. A DEDICATION TO THE MEMORY OF DANE COOLIDGE, 1873-1940. *Arizona and the West 1981 23(1): 1-4.* Dane Coolidge spent his summers, while a student at Stanford University, collecting natural history specimens in the American Southwest and northern Mexico for the British Museum and for US institutions. He started graduate work in biology at Harvard University but soon found the experience too "stultifying." He and his wife, Mary Elizabeth Burroughs Roberts, a Mills College sociology professor, actively pursued field research and collaborated on two volumes of Navajo and Seri Indian cultural anthropology. Coolidge himself wrote three nonfiction works on cowboys and was preparing for another. The bulk of his efforts, however, are contained in over 40 works of fiction. He was a realist and a "scholarly romantic" whose insistence on authenticity and "uncompromising disregard for conventionality" hurt the marketability of his efforts as westerns. Illus., biblio. 1910-40

1361. Ulph, Owen. DANE COOLIDGE: WESTERN WRITER AND PHOTOGRAPHER. *Am. West 1977 14(6): 32-47.* Dane Coolidge (1873-1940) was a photographer and a prolific writer of western fiction (more than 40 works) and nonfiction. Despite his insistence on accuracy, his conviction that the West was romantic affected his writings. He failed to harmonize the mythical West with the historical. His photography of the range country, as the range cowboy was becoming virtually extinct, 1907-16, was more successful. In his "subterfugenous photography," Coolidge nearly combined these two conflicting elements. 2 illus. Appended with a portfolio of 20 Coolidge photographs of the Chiricahua Cattle Company. 1907-39

Cooper, Anna Haywood

1362. Chitty, Arthur Ben. WOMEN AND BLACK EDUCATION: THREE PROFILES. *Hist. Mag. of the Protestant Episcopal Church 1983 52(2): 153-165.* 1875-1981
For abstract see ***Alston, Mary Niven***

Cooper, Colin Campbell

1363. Goolsby, Tina. COLIN CAMPBELL COOPER: AN AMERICAN IMPRESSIONIST WITH A GLOBAL PERSPECTIVE. *Art & Antiques 1983 6(1): 56-63.* Biographical sketch of American impressionist painter Colin Campbell Cooper, with color reproductions of the artist's work. 1880's-1937

Cooper, Dixie

1364. —. KOOTENAI. *Idaho Heritage 1977 (10): 33-35.*
Shottanana, Josephine. DIXIE COOPER AND RAYMOND ABRAHAM, *pp. 34-35.* 1970's
For abstract see ***Abraham, Raymond***

Cooper, Edward E.

1365. Gatewood, Willard B., Jr. EDWARD E. COOPER & "10 GREATEST NEGROES" OF 1890. *Negro Hist. Bull. 1977 40(3): 708-710.* Describes a contest during 1890, launched by Edward E. Cooper, editor of the Indianapolis *Freeman,* to choose the "ten greatest Negroes" by ballot of *Freeman* readers. Among the judges was Cooper's closest associate on the *Freeman* staff. The contest aroused great interest but provoked widespread attack when Cooper's own name appeared among the winners. Traces Cooper's earlier career from slavery. Based on contemporary newspapers and secondary material; photo, 19 notes. 1890

1366. Gatewood, Willard B., Jr. EDWARD E. COOPER, BLACK JOURNALIST. *Journalism Q. 1978 55(2): 269-275.* As the editor and publisher of a series of journals, Edward E. Cooper (1859-1908) achieved prominence in the black press of the 1890's. His second journal, *Freeman,* published in Indianapolis, appealed to a national audience with articles on black social activities and political issues. The *Freeman*'s financial problems, induced by his lavish personal spending, led Cooper to leave for Washington, D.C., in 1893. There he launched the widely-read *Colored American,* which received strong financial support from Booker T. Washington (1856-1915). As a confidant of Washington, Cooper gained influence in black political and business organizations, but in 1902 he was defamed by charges of personal profiteering. 42 notes. 1882-1908

Cooper, Fannie Adams

1367. Whitlow, Leonard A. and Whitlow, Catherine Cooper, ed. MY LIFE AS A HOMESTEADER (PART 1). *Oregon Hist. Q. 1981 82(1): 65-84.* Memoirs by Fannie Adams Copper on the experiences and hardships of homesteading in various wild sections of Oregon in the 1890's. There were boundary problems, wild animals, lack of money and frequent moves for her growing family. 6 illus., photo. Article to be continued. 1889-99

1368. Whitlow, Leonard A. and Whitlow, Catherine Cooper, ed. MY LIFE AS A HOMESTEADER (PART 2). *Oregon Hist. Q. 1981 82(2): 152-168.* Continued from a previous article. Reminiscences of Fannie Adams Cooper (d. 1942) describe her occupations and relocations and those of her family members in various parts of Oregon from 1899 through the mid-1930's. Based on reminiscences; 2 illus., 5 photos, 5 notes. 1899-1935

Cooper, Frank B.

1369. Nelson, Bryce E. FRANK B. COOPER: SEATTLE'S PROGRESSIVE SCHOOL SUPERINTENDENT, 1901-22. *Pacific Northwest Q. 1983 74(4): 167-177.* Frank B. Cooper served as Seattle's school superintendent for two critical decades, during which he introduced experimentation and reform at all levels. He redesigned the curriculum for each grade to promote civic awareness, critical reasoning, and a broad liberal-arts education. He likewise promoted more classroom independence for teachers and a greater collective voice in overall policymaking. Physical education, health care, and special education programs were also devised to nurture other dimensions of human development. World War I brought military recruitment and textbook censorship crusades to Seattle, both of which Cooper resisted. Based on the Seattle Public Schools Archives and Annual Reports; 15 photos, 30 notes. 1901-22

Cooper, James Fenimore

1370. Palmer, Richard F. JAMES FENIMORE COOPER AND THE NAVY BRIG *ONEIDA*. *Inland Seas 1984 40(2): 90-99.* James Fenimore Cooper participated in the construction and outfitting of the naval brig *Oneida* at Oswego, New York, in 1808-09. He recounted the experience in *The Pathfinder* and in *Lives of Distinguished American Naval Officers.* The *Oneida* served in the navy until 1825, and as a lake trader until about 1837. Biblio. 1808-37

Cooper, James Graham

1371. Coan, Eugene. JAMES GRAHAM COOPER: PIONEER NATURALIST AND FOREST CONSERVATIONIST. *J. of Forest Hist. 1983 27(3): 126-129.* James Graham Cooper was a pioneer naturalist who published 145 books and papers, introduced 138 new zoological taxa, compiled an extensive catalog of North American forest trees, and created two extensive forest-distribution maps of the continent. Cooper also formulated significant ideas about the relationship between forests and climate, and promoted both the creation of forest reserves and the establishment of a national silviculture program. Photo, illus., map, 15 notes. 1850's-1902

Cooper, Job A.

1372. King, William M. THE END OF AN ERA: DENVER'S LAST LEGAL PUBLIC EXECUTION, JULY 27, 1886. *J. of Negro Hist. 1983 68(1): 37-53.* 1880-90
For abstract see ***Green, Andrew***

Cooper, John Sherman

1373. Franklin, Douglas A. THE POLITICIAN AS DIPLOMAT: KENTUCKY'S JOHN SHERMAN COOPER IN INDIA, 1955-1956. *Register of the Kentucky Hist. Soc. 1984 82(1): 28-59.* John Sherman Cooper served as US ambassador to India and Nepal during part of his long and distinguished public career. Accepting the position only after a personal appeal from President Eisenhower, Cooper's sensitivity to India's problems and his willingness to listen and learn earned him high praise from Indian Prime Minister Nehru. Based on interviews, manuscripts, and secondary sources; 11 photos, 98 notes. 1955-56

Cooper, Peter

1374. Alemanne, Nicholas. PETER COOPER, THE WORKINGMAN'S ADVOCATE. *Social Studies 1985 76(5): 212-215.* Peter Cooper dedicated the latter part of his life to advocating reform and improvement in the lives of working-class people. His philosophy called not for revolution but for education and enlightenment. 16 notes. 1851-83

Cooper, Thomas

1375. Cohen, Seymour S. TWO REFUGEE CHEMISTS IN THE UNITED STATES, 1794: HOW WE SEE THEM. *Pro. of the Am. Phil. Soc. 1982 126(4): 301-315.* Examines the lives of Thomas Cooper (1759-1839) and Joseph Priestley (1753-1804) and the results of entertwining events that brought them to the United States in 1794. While both men were chemists, it was their political involvements that cast shadows over their scientific accomplishments and made them suspect in England during the French Revolution. In addition, Priestley's Unitarian posture acerbated his accomplishments in chemistry and physics. Previous efforts to segregate the various aspects of their lives failed to appreciate the wholeness and consistency of their philosophies and actions, and the effects of the forces of their environment on their scholarly and practical work. Based on the published works of Cooper, Priestley's memoirs, and biographies; 62 notes. 1775-1800

Cooper, Washington Bogart

1376. O'Leary, Beth Lokey. WASHINGTON BOGART COOPER, 1802-1888: THE INFLUENCES ON HIS WORK. *Tennessee Hist. Q. 1978 37(1): 68-75.* Washington Bogart Cooper was the most popular portrait artist in 19th-century Nashville. Self-taught, he painted about 35 portraits a year. Secondary sources; 21 notes. 1830's-88

Cope, Edward Drinker

1377. Laurent, Goulven. UN NÉO-LAMARCKIEN AMÉRICAIN: EDWARD DRINKER COPE (1840-1896) [An American neo-Lamarckian: Edward Drinker Cope (1840-96)]. *Rev. de Synthèse [France] 1979 100(95-96): 297-309.* Edward Drinker Cope, noted American paleontologist, was convinced that the derivation of species was provoked by a process of modification transmitted through heredity. He was not content to accept that fact of evolution only, but also entered into research into the causes of evolution. He concluded that a living being did not remain passive during a change in the milieu in which it lived, but reacted in all its organs and parts. Cope was anti-Darwinian and pro-Lamarckian in his analysis of evolution. 24 notes. 1860's-96

Copeland, Lammot du Pont

1378. Achorn, Robert C. LAMMOT DU PONT COPELAND. *Pro. of the Am. Antiquarian Soc. 1983 93(2): 281-285.* Born into Delaware's du Pont family, Lammot du Pont Copeland became an influential business and banking leader. Copeland supported various educational and philanthropic organizations—particularly those active in the fields of Americana, historical technology, and horticulture—through Longwood Gardens, the Eleutherian Mills-Hagley Foundation, and the Henry Francis du Pont Winterthur Museum. 1905-83

Copley, John Singleton

1379. Klayman, Raymond. AN ARTIST'S FORMATIVE YEARS: COPLEY'S EDUCATION IN BOSTON. *Biography 1985 8(1): 68-82.* Explores the childhood education of colonial Boston's premier portrait painter, John Singleton Copley. Copley's family is credited with nurturing and supporting his artistic inclinations. In addition, the Boston public schools encouraged basic education for children such as Franklin, Revere, and Copley. And finally, Copley benefited from a private schoolmaster, his stepfather Peter Pelham. 1745-53

1380. Klayman, Richard. "The Education of an Artist: The American Years of John Singleton Copley, 1738-1774." U. of New Hampshire 1981. 166 pp. *DAI 1982 42(12): 5222-A.* DA8212788 1738-74

Coppin, Fanny Jackson

1381. Perkins, Linda M. HEED LIFE'S DEMANDS: THE EDUCATIONAL PHILOSOPHY OF FANNY JACKSON COPPIN. *J. of Negro Educ. 1982 51(3): 181-190.* Fanny Jackson Coppin was the principal of the Female Department during 1865-69 and then principal during 1869-1902 of the Institute for Colored Youth in Philadelphia, Pennsylvania. She abolished tuition to reach poor students and developed a normal school with a student teaching program without sacrificing liberal arts to vocational education. She also urged the wider black community to avoid elitism and to practice racial solidarity and service through self-help by establishing such homes as she helped start for elderly and young black women. Based on Fanny Jackson Coppin's autobiography, manuscripts and secondary sources; 35 notes. 1865-1913

1382. Perkins, Linda M. "Fanny Jackson Coppin and the Institute for Colored Youth: A Model of Nineteenth Century Black Female Educational and Community Leadership, 1837-1902." U. of Illinois, Urbana-Champaign 1978. 356 pp. *DAI 1978 39(5): 2786-2787-A.* 1865-1902

Coppinger, Jose

1383. Norris, L. David. "Jose Coppinger in East Florida, 1816-1821: A Man, a Province, and A Spanish Colonial Failure." Southern Illinois U., Carbondale 1981. 461 pp. *DAI 1982 43(5): 1649-1650-A.* DA8221949 1816-21

Corbett, Boston

1384. Swenson, Grace Stageberg. BOSTON CORBETT: A FINAL CHAPTER? *Lincoln Herald 1984 86(3): 150-156.* Boston Corbett, the sergeant who confessed to firing the shot that killed John Wilkes Booth, pursued diverse careers after 1865 and entered an insane asylum in Kansas in 1887, escaping in 1888. There is no definite record of Corbett's life after this point, but it is possible that he ended up in Minnesota in 1894, and died in the famous Hinckley fire in Pine County. 1865-94

Corbett, Julian S.

1385. Hunt, Barry D. THE OUTSTANDING NAVAL STRATEGIC WRITERS OF THE CENTURY. *Naval War Coll. Rev. 1984 37(5): 86-107.* Although Captain Alfred Thayer Mahan predominates in any review of the leading naval theorists or historians of the past century, others, like Julian S. Corbett in the United States, Admiral Raoul Castex in France, and Vice Admiral Wolfgang Wegener in Germany, made significant contributions to naval history and theory. Nonetheless, there have been too few naval professionals like Rear Admiral Henry Eccles and Admiral Stansfield Turner who have tried to bridge the gap between political-military theory and the actualities of naval operations. 36 notes. 1880's-1984

Corbett, Thomas H.

1386. Kubicek, Earl C. THE CASE OF THE MAD HATTER. *Lincoln Herald 1981 83(3): 708-719.* Biography of Thomas H. "Boston" Corbett, a hat finisher who claimed to have shot John Wilkes Booth while part of the detail that participated in the search for Booth after the assassination of President Abraham Lincoln; Corbett disappeared in 1908. 1832-1908

Corbin, Hannah Lee

1387. Dawe, Louise Belote and Treadway, Sandra Gioia. HANNAH LEE CORBIN: THE FORGOTTEN LEE. *Virginia Cavalcade 1979 29(2): 70-77.* Hannah Lee Corbin (1728-82), widowed at 32, looked after the affairs of the Pecktone estate in Virginia and bore her lover, Richard Lingen Hall, two children, because her husband had stipulated in his will that she could not retain the estate and remarry. 1740's-82

Corbit, William (family)

1388. Bushman, Claudia. THE WILSON FAMILY IN DELAWARE AND INDIANA. *Delaware Hist. 1982 20(1): 27-49.* 1768-1925
For abstract see ***Wilson, David (family)***

Corcelle, Marthe de

1389. Tissier, André. CES COUPLES QUI TRAVERSENT L'HISTOIRE [These couples who traverse history]. *Ecrits de Paris [France] 1979 (391): 83-88.* 1865
For abstract see ***Chambrun, Adolphe de***

Corcoran, Thomas Gardiner

1390. Louchheim, Katie. THE LITTLE RED HOUSE. *Virginia Q. Rev. 1980 56(1): 119-134.* 1933-37
For abstract see ***Cohen, Benjamin V.***

Corder, James

1391. —. JAMES CORDER: "RIGHT HERE ON EARTH." *Southern Exposure 1976 4(3): 39-40.* In this interview Corder, a black minister of four Primitive Baptist Churches in and around Aliceville, Alabama, discusses his religious and civil rights work, 1965-75. 1965-75

Corliss, George H.

1392. Kenny, Robert W. GEORGE H. CORLISS: ENGINEER, ARCHITECT, PHILANTHROPIST. *Rhode Island Hist. 1981 40(2): 48-61.* Traces the career of George H. Corliss as an inventor, designer, and manufacturer of steam engines. His fame is from increasing the efficiency of steam engines with an automatic cut-off mechanism. His manufacturing firm in Providence, Rhode Island, built the power plant for Machinery Hall at the Centennial Exposition of 1876 in Philadelphia. Corliss's Victorian mansion, built in 1882 was the first radiantly heated, thermostatically controlled house in the United States. Based on the Corliss Papers at Brown University and on an unpublished biography of Corliss written by Samuel J. Berard; 5 photos, plate. 1817-88

Cornelius, Elias

1393. Ackerman, Evelyn Bernette. THE ACTIVITIES OF A COUNTRY DOCTOR IN NEW YORK STATE: DR. ELIAS CORNELIUS OF SOMERS, 1794-1803. *Hist. Reflections [Canada] 1982 9(1-2): 181-193.* Elias Cornelius (1758-1823) was a typical country doctor in Westchester County, New York. Almost half his patients came from the towns of Somers and Carmel and most patients were farmers or artisans. Camphor, a common 18th-century stimulant, was the most common remedy prescribed by name. Cornelius was also a farmer, a role which made him more approachable. Based on Dr. Cornelius' account book ("Ledger D") and secondary sources; 3 tables, 42 notes. 1794-1803

Cornish, Samuel E.

1394. Wolseley, Roland E. SAMUEL E. CORNISH—PIONEER BLACK JOURNALIST AND PASTOR. *Crisis 1976 83(8): 288-289.* Samuel E. Cornish (1796-1859) was born in Delaware in a nonslave home, attended Princeton University, and became a Presbyterian minister in New York City. In 1827 he was editor and copublisher, with John B. Russwurm, of the first black newspaper in the United States, *Freedom's Journal.* Cornish wrote hard-hitting editorials on any issue that he felt retarded black progress. After Russwurm left for Liberia, financial difficulties resulted in the collapse of *Freedom's Journal.* Cornish made several more attempts at journalism, but his real impact was as a strong spokesman for abolition. 1820's-59

Cornwall, George M.

1395. McKinney, Gage. "A MAN AMONG YOU, TAKING NOTES": GEORGE M. CORNWALL AND THE *TIMBERMAN. J. of Forest Hist. 1982 26(2): 76-83.* Relates the life of a trade journalist on the West Coast and explains the role of a lumber-trade journal in promoting the industry. George M. Cornwall was born near Aberdeen, Scotland, immigrated to America at age 16, and founded the *Timberman* at age 32. His subsequent career was devoted to keeping lumbermen abreast of technical and marketing changes, defending the industry against outside criticism, and promoting cooperative efforts in politics and forest conservation. Based on the *Timberman* and secondary sources; 10 illus., biblio. 1899-1962

Cornwall, J. Spencer

1396. Gregory, Fern Denise. "J. Spencer Cornwall: The Salt Lake Mormon Tabernacle Choir Years, 1935-1957." U. of Missouri, Kansas City 1984. 109 pp. *DAI 1984 45(3): 678-A.* DA8414821 1935-57

Cornwall, James Kennedy

1397. Inkster, Tom H. I REMEMBER PEACE RIVER JIM. *Alberta Hist. [Canada] 1983 31(3): 9-13.* James Kennedy Cornwall (Peace River Jim) played a leading role in the development of Canada's northland. As the owner of trading posts and a river transportation company "he opened the door for entry to the fabulous Peace River country and left his mark from Waterways and Fort McMurray to Aklavik and Coppermine" in the Northwest Territories. 3 photos. ca 1885-1955

Corona, Bert

1398. Hammerback, John C. AN INTERVIEW WITH BERT CORONA. *Western J. of Speech Communication 1980 44(3): 214-220.* Interview with Chicano political activist and social reformer Bert Corona (b. 1918) centers on his role in political activism within the Chicano movement in California, during the 1960's-70's and the importance of rhetoric and public speaking in creating a cohesive political movement. 1960's-70's

Coronel, Antonio F.

1399. Sanchez, Federico Alberto. "Antonio F. Coronel, a Californio and a Ranchero: His Life and Times in Mexican Alta California, 1834-1850." U. of Southern California 1983. *DAI 1984 45(2): 607-A.* 1834-50

Corrigan, Michael Augustine

1400. Browne, J. A. "'Egregius Archiepiscopus': A Life of Michael Augustine Corrigan, 1839-1902, Archbishop of New York." National U. of Ireland [Ireland] 1981. 586 pp. *DAI-C 1985 46(2): 338; 10/1646c.* 1839-1902

Corson, Hiram

1401. Welden, Linda Frances. "Hiram Corson: Interpretative Reader, English Teacher, Literary Scholar." Louisiana State U. and Agric. and Mechanical Coll. 1977. 376 pp. *DAI 1978 38(7): 3807-A.* 1850's-1911

Cory, Fanny Y.

1402. Cooney, Bob and Dodgson, Sayre Cooney. FANNY CORY COONEY: MONTANA MOTHER AND ARTIST. *Montana 1980 30(3): 2-17.* Fanny Young Cory Cooney (1877-1972) was an illustrator, artist, and cartoonist, 1896-1956. Under the name Fanny Y. Cory, her works appeared in such periodicals as *Life, Century, Harper's Bazaar,* and *Saturday Evening Post,* plus dozens of children's books. She interrupted her artistic career when she married Fred Cooney in 1904. They raised four children on a ranch near Canyon Ferry, Montana, and she was a devoted mother. To help finance education for her children, she returned to art and began two nationally syndicated cartoon strips, *Sonnysayings* and *Little Miss Muffet,* which ran in newspapers from 1926 to 1956. Based on authors' reminiscences; 32 illus. 1896-1972

Cosley, Joseph Clarence

1403. DeSanto, Jerome S. THE LEGENDARY JOE COSLEY. *Montana 1980 30(1): 12-27.* Joseph Clarence Cosley (1870-1944) trapped in the Glacier National Park region and in northern Alberta and Saskatchewan from the mid-1890's until his death in 1944. An admirer of John G. (Kootenai) Brown, Cosley also wrote prose and poetry and became well known for his exotic dress, flowery speech, and fanciful story telling: creating his own legend which survives in Glacier Park today. During 1910-14, Cosley was one of the Park's first rangers. He left to join the Canadian Army during World War I, then returned to trapping (illegally) in the Park until 1929, and then in Canada. In the Belly River region of the Park, Cosley Lake and Cosley Ridge bear his name and several trees survive with his name carved on them. Based on materials in the Historical Collections, Glacier National Park, items in the Glenbow-Alberta Institute, Calgary, and secondary sources; 12 illus, map, 75 notes. 1890's-1944

Cossitt, Ranna

1404. Wade, Mason. ODYSSEY OF A LOYALIST RECTOR. *Vermont Hist. 1980 48(2): 96-113.* Ranna Cossitt, missionary of the Society for the Propagation of the Gospel, served in Claremont, New Hampshire, and adjacent Vermont and New Hampshire settlements, and was confined to the limits of Claremont, December 1775-January 1779, when he appeared in New York. Intrigue aiming to win the Connecticut and Champlain Valleys for the Empire, or settle Tories in Canada across the Vermont border, had failed by 1785. He served as rector in Sydney on Cape Breton Island, 1786-1805, and died at Yarmouth, Nova Scotia, in 1815. 58 notes. 1773-1815

Costigan, Edward P.

1405. Mitterling, Doris, comp. and Brennan, John A., ed. GUIDE TO THE EDWARD P. COSTIGAN PAPERS 1874-1939. *Western Historical Collections, U. of Colorado Lib. 1980 (Jan): 1-100.* Entire issue devoted to the biography of Progressive and later Democratic politician Edward P. Costigan (1874-1939) of Colorado, and an inventory of his papers and personal files. 1874-1939

Côté, Jean L.

1406. Côté, J. G. J. L. COTE, SURVEYOR. *Alberta Hist. [Canada] 1983 31(4): 28-32.* Born in Les Eboulements, Quebec, Jean L. Côté was educated in Montmagny and then worked in Ottawa prior to becoming a qualified land surveyor and joining the Department of the Interior. His work included the Alaska Boundary Commission Survey and railroad surveys. Entering politics in 1909, Côté later served as provincial secretary and as minister of mines and of railways. Interest in the natural resources of the province led him to form the Scientific and Industrial Research Council of Alberta in 1919 and four years later he was made a senator. Côté died in 1924. 3 photos. 1893-1924

Cotner, Robert Crawford

1407. Nance, Joseph Milton. ROBERT CRAWFORD COTNER. *West Texas Hist. Assoc. Year Book 1981 57: 99-106.* Dr. Robert Crawford Cotner, long-time member of the West Texas Historical Association, was Professor Emeritus of History at the University of Texas at Austin when he retired in 1977; he had received many scholarly honors and awards. 1906-80

Cottam, Clarence

1408. Thorup, H. Christian. "Clarence Cottam: Conservationist. The Welder Years." Brigham Young U. 1983. 284 pp. *DAI 1984 45(1): 280-A.* DA8406980 1954-74

Cotten, Sallie Southall

1409. Stephenson, William. HOW SALLIE SOUTHALL COTTEN BROUGHT NORTH CAROLINA TO THE CHICAGO WORLD'S FAIR OF 1893. *North Carolina Hist. Rev. 1981 58(4): 364-383.* Sallie Southall Cotten (1846-1929), wife of a planter and rural store owner in Pitt County, North Carolina, rose to statewide prominence between 1890 and 1893 as alternate lady manager for North Carolina to the World's Columbian Exposition (Chicago, 1893). A moderate feminist with no experience in public affairs, Cotten successfully took charge of several important matters including fund raising for a North Carolina building at the fair and locating and designing exhibit materials. She also served as unofficial North Carolina hostess during the fair. Her work on the fair launched Cotten's national career in public service, especially in the National Congress of Mothers and the General Federation of Women's Clubs. Based on family manuscript collections at the University of North Carolina, newspaper clippings, and published primary materials on the World's Fair; 12 illus., 47 notes. 1890-95

Cotton, Clinton Neal

1410. Fellin, John Kevin. THE ROLE OF C. N. COTTON IN THE DEVELOPMENT OF NORTHWESTERN NEW MEXICO. *New Mexico Hist. Rev. 1980 55(2): 151-156.* Portrays the life of Clinton Neal Cotton (1859-1936), one of the early traders in the Southwest, during the period of his trading business from 1884 to 1932. Cotton's main trading establishment in Gallup, New Mexico, was the first large-scale wholesale business in that town. The main sources of income for Cotton were the sale of Navajo blankets and filling railroad and government contracts, especially those for supplying Indian reservations. Cotton, who was involved in other civic and business activities such as politics and banking, played an important role in the settlement of northwestern New Mexico. Photo, 27 notes. 1884-1932

Couch, Bill

1411. Hubler, David M. IOWA'S EARLY BIRDS. *Palimpsest 1981 62(6): 162-169.* 1886-1919
*For abstract see **Duede, Carl***

Coughlin, Charles Edward

1412. Brinkley, Alan. COMPARATIVE BIOGRAPHY AS POLITICAL HISTORY: HUEY LONG AND FATHER COUGHLIN. *Hist. Teacher 1984 18(1): 9-16.* 1930-40
*For abstract see **Long, Huey P.***

1413. Athans, Mary Christine. "The Fahey-Coughlin Connection: Father Denis Fahey, C.S.Sp., Father Charles E. Coughlin, and Religious Anti-Semitism in the United States, 1938-1954." Grad. Theological Union 1982. 304 pp. *DAI 1983 43(9): 3030-A.* DA8302428 1938-54

1414. Bouton, Michael Wickham. "Depression Era Extremists: A Study of Three Demagogues and Their Tactics." Illinois State U. 1978. 212 pp. *DAI 1979 39(12): 7480-A.* 1930's

Coulon, George David

1415. Bonner, Judith Hopkins. GEORGE DAVID COULON: A NINETEENTH CENTURY FRENCH LOUISIANA PAINTER. *Southern Q. 1982 20(2): 41-61.* French-born George David Coulon was New Orleans's best-known, most prolific painter of the 19th century. In an age when art provided no certain sustenance for its creators, Coulon was able to live comfortably by painting scores of landscapes and portraits, and by accepting commissions to decorate buildings and stage settings. Other members of his immediate family were also successful, though less renowned, artists. Coulon taught art during most of his adult life. 5 illus. ca 1850-1904

Coulter, Ellis Merton

1416. Coleman, Kenneth. ELLIS MERTON COULTER. *Pro. and Papers of the Georgia Assoc. of Hist. 1981: 46-50.* Prints a bibliographical biography as a tribute to Georgia historian Ellis Merton Coulter. 19c

1417. Lerda, Valeria Gennaro. ELLIS MERTON COULTER: A PERSONAL TRIBUTE. *Georgia Hist. Q. 1981 65(4): 307-315.* Personal recollections of Ellis Merton Coulter (1890-1981), Georgia history professor and author, by an Italian friend and colleague. 1974-81

1418. Saye, Albert B. A TRIBUTE TO ELLIS MERTON COULTER. *Georgia Hist. Q. 1981 65(3): 183-188.* Biographical information on and tribute to Dr. Ellis Merton Coulter (1890-1981), professor of Georgian and Southern history at the University of Georgia for many years. Photo. ca 1930's-81

1419. Spalding, Phinizy. ELLIS MERTON COULTER. *Georgia Hist. Q. 1981 65(1): npp.* Obituary of Ellis Merton Coulter (1890-1981), Georgia and Southern historian, professor at the University of Georgia at Athens for almost 40 years, and editor of the *Georgia Historical Quarterly* for 50 years. Photo. 1890-1981

1420. Woodward, Michael Vaughan. E. MERTON COULTER AND THE ART OF BIOGRAPHY. *Georgia Hist. Q. 1980 64(2): 159-171.* Historian Ellis Merton Coulter has written many articles and books, including 10 biographies of Georgians and other southern personalities: William G. Brownlow, Thomas Spalding, John Jacobus Flournoy, the Jones family of Wormsloe, James Barrow, James Monroe Smith, Joseph Vallence Bevan, William Montague Browne, Daniel Lee, and George Walton Williams. 32 notes. 1940-76

1421. Woodward, Michael Vaughan. ELLIS MERTON COULTER: A CASE STUDY IN THE DEVELOPMENT OF CONSERVATIVE RACISM IN THE NEW SOUTH. *Midwest Q. 1979 20(3): 269-280.* Gives the biography of southerner Ellis Merton Coulter (b. 1890), and discusses his attitudes in the present-day South to understand paternalistic racism in southern history. 1890-1979

Coulter, William Alexander

1422. White, Raymond D. MARINE ART: AN APPRECIATION OF WILLIAM ALEXANDER COULTER. *Sea Hist. 1981 (22): 29-31.* Provides a biographical sketch of William Alexander Coulter, an Irish sailor who settled in San Francisco in the late 19th century, leaving a legacy of maritime history in his paintings of ocean-going ships. 1875-1936

Coulthard, Stan

1423. Lane, Tony. A MERSEYSIDER IN DETROIT. *Hist. Workshop J. [Great Britain] 1981 (11): 138-153.* Stan Coulthard (b. 1898) describes his emigration from Birkenhead, near Liverpool, to the United States in 1922, his dreams of going to college to become a dentist, his experiences in the Detroit car plants and dairies, his activities as a union organizer, his return to Merseyside in 1935, and his activities in the British Communist Party, 1935-50. The author's introduction examines Coulthard's life and career, the background to emigration from Liverpool, 1820-1950, the links between Liverpool and labor organizations in the United States, and other British union organizers in Detroit, 1930's-40's. Secondary sources; 41 notes. 1922-35

Countryman, Gratia Alta

1424. Rohde, Nancy Freeman. GRATIA ALTA COUNTRYMAN: LIBRARIAN AND REFORMER. Stuhler, Barbara and Kreuter, Gretchen, ed. *Women of Minnesota: Selected Biographical Essays* (St. Paul: Minnesota Historical Society Press, 1977): 173-189. Gratia Alta Countryman (1866-1953) attended the University of Minnesota where she was an active student leader and member of Phi Beta Kappa. After graduating, she became one of six assistants hired to open and operate the new Minneapolis Public Library. Gratia soon became head of the catalog department. During 1904-36 she was the head librarian, the first woman to direct a major library in the United States. Countryman especially encouraged extended library services to meet the needs of all sectors of society. She also agitated for state library laws, promoted the Minnesota Library Association, served on the State Library Commission, and was nationally renowned for her work. She served on the council, executive board, and as president of the American Library Association. A popular speaker, Countryman lectured not only on library subjects but also on woman's suffrage, social reform, and international peace. She helped organize the Minneapolis Women's Welfare League and the Business Women's Club. In 1936, she chaired the national convention of the Women's International League for Peace and Freedom. A dedicated, efficient, and decisive librarian, social reformer, and civic leader, Countryman remained active after her retirement. She died on 26 July 1953. Primary sources; photo, 54 notes. 1890's-1953

Counts, George S.

1425. Romanish, Bruce A. "An Historical Analysis of the Educational Ideas and Career of George S. Counts." Pennsylvania State U. 1980. 228 pp. *DAI 1981 41(8): 3916-A.* 8105800 20c

Couper, James Hamilton

1426. Bagwell, James Emmett. "James Hamilton Couper, Georgia Rice Planter." U. of Southern Mississippi 1978. 355 pp. *DAI 1979 39(9): 5677-5678-A.* 1816-50

Couts, Cave Johnson

1427. Starr, Raymond, ed. EMIGRANTS AND INDIANS: SELECTIONS FROM C. J. COUTS' MILITARY CORRESPONDENCE, 1849. *Journal of San Diego History 1983 29(3): 165-184.* Outlines the career of Cave Johnson Couts and reproduces extracts from his military correspondence held in the San Diego Historical Society's Couts Collection. The letters pertain to Couts's service as escort to the boundary survey in the Yuma crossing area. 1849

Cove, John William

1428. Campbell, Bertha J. SPRINGHILL'S FIRST DOCTOR. *Nova Scotia Hist. Q. [Canada] 1979 9(4): 297-312.* John William Cove (1838-1901) was born in Claremont, received his medical training at the University of Pennsylvania, and settled in Springhill in 1873 as the first doctor for the Springhill Mining Co. He bought land, established the Acadia Drug Store (the first in the area), and was an active member of the community. For 10 years he was the only doctor in the growing coal mining community. He also acted as coroner for Cumberland County. His medical register listed 3,200 births. He treated many mine injuries in addition to ministering to the general public. 10 notes. 1873-1901

Covello, Leonard

1429. Holte, James Craig. PRIVATE LIVES AND PUBLIC FACES: ETHNIC AMERICAN AUTOBIOGRAPHY. *Ethnic Groups 1982 4(1-2): 61-83.* 1880-1933
*For abstract see **Carnevale, Emanuel***

Covici, Pascal

1430. Fensch, Thomas Charles. "Between Author and Editor: The Selected Correspondence of John Steinbeck and Pascal Covici, 1945-1952." Syracuse U. 1977. 408 pp. *DAI 1978 38(8): 4427-A.* 1945-52

Cowan, Margery Jacoby

1431. Coleman, Alice Cowan. MISS JACOBY: 19TH CENTURY EDUCATOR, 20TH CENTURY GUARDIAN OF EXCELLENCE. *Montana 1978 28(2): 36-49.* Margery Jacoby Cowan came to Montana in 1883. She grew up in the Highwood Mountains near Fort Benton, and eventually became a school teacher in the vicinity. In 1894 she was elected Superintendent of Schools for Chouteau County. She worked vigorously to improve schools and teacher training during her four years in office. In 1899 Margery Jacoby married William T. Cowan, a Box Elder merchant and political leader. She abandoned her career, devoting full time to her responsibilities as wife and mother of four children. She supported her husband's career as postmaster, US Land Commissioner, joint founder of Northern Montana College, and "father of the Marias River Irrigation Project." Largely through Cowan's persistent efforts, Congress passed legislation financing construction of the Tiber Dam in 1952. William Cowan died the year before, but Margery Cowan attended ground-breaking ceremonies for Tiber Dam to indicate her long-standing support for her husband's work and for the prosperity of north-central Montana. Based on family records in the author's collection; 16 illus. 1883-1952

Cowles, Betsy Mix

1432. DeBlasio, Donna Marie. "Her Own Society: The Life and Times of Betsy Mix Cowles, 1810-1876." Kent State U. 1980. 252 pp. *DAI 1981 41(11): 4811-A.* 8108310 1830-76

Cowley, Josephine Hutmacher

1433. Cowley, Malcolm. MOTHER AND SON. *Am. Heritage 1983 34(2): 28-35.* Writer Malcolm Cowley tells of his mother's life, trials, and tribulations. From her birth in 1864 until her death in 1937, Josephine Hutmacher Cowley led a life of compassion and generosity, yet a life filled with sorrow and deprivations. 6 photos. ca 1890-1940

Cowley, W. H.

1434. Caldwell, Brenda Sue. "W. H. Cowley: A Life in Higher Education." U. of Oklahoma 1983. 323 pp. *DAI 1983 44(3): 680-681-A.* DA8314759 1920-78

Cox, Lewis

1435. Peters, Norman R., ed. THE CIVIL WAR PENSION FILE OF LEWIS COX AND HIS WIFE LUCRETIA EVANS. *Journal of the Afro-American Historical and Genealogical Society 1985 6(1): 31-33.* Prints Civil War pension file abstracts of former Alabama slave Lewis Cox and his wife Lucretia Evans, with whom he lived in Oklahoma, and points out the usefulness of such files to the genealogist. 1846-1927

Cox, Oliver C.

1436. Hunter, Herbert M. OLIVER C. COX: A BIOGRAPHICAL SKETCH OF HIS LIFE AND WORK. *Phylon 1983 46(4): 249-261.* Despite a crippling experience with poliomyelitis, Trinidad-born sociologist Oliver C. Cox was also trained in law and economics before embarking on his career as a teacher and author. His teaching career was spent at Wiley College in Texas, Tuskegee Institute in Alabama, Lincoln College in Missouri, and as a visiting professor at Wayne State University in Michigan. Some of his publications, including *Caste, Class, and Race* (1948) and articles in such foreign journals as the East Indian *The Aryan Path* brought Cox a reputation as a radical; he was, in fact, an impartial critic of social systems who believed in the integration of black and white society rather than pluralism. Based on interviews, Cox's correspondence, and secondary sources, 53 notes. 1938-74

1437. Hunter, Herbert M. "The Life and Work of Oliver C. Cox." Boston U. 1981. 361 pp. *DAI 1981 41(12): 5256-5257-A.* DA8112205 20c

Cox, Samuel Hanson

1438. Mounger, Dwyn Mecklin. SAMUEL HANSON COX: ANTI-CATHOLIC, ANTI-ANGLICAN, ANTI-CONGREGATIONAL ECUMENIST. *J. of Presbyterian Hist. 1977 55(4): 347-361.* Samuel Hanson Cox (1813-80) was a typical New School Presbyterian in his ecumenical aspirations: he worked energetically to promote interdenominational cooperation through numerous benevolence and mission societies to produce a wholly Protestant America. Thus his ecumenism was more limited than that of similar positions today, for it embraced only denominations which he regarded as "evangelical," which included only those practicing revivalism. He viewed Catholicism, Anglicanism, and the resurgent denominationalism of the 1840's as major threats to a triumphantly Protestant America. To counterbalance such movements, he labored hard for the Evangelical Alliance and the American Alliance and to prevent a North-South schism in the New School Presbyterian Church. Yet all these efforts were doomed to fail because of the slavery issue. As Moderator of the New School in 1846 he was successful in preventing abolitionism from dividing the Church that year; yet division came 11 years later. In his zeal for ecumenism he had been prepared to sacrifice the slave upon the altar of evangelical unity. Based largely on the author's doctoral dissertation on Cox (Union Theological Seminary, New York), writings of Cox, and other biographical data; illus., 58 notes. 1840's

Crabtree, A.

1439. Faibisy, John D. THE GREENING OF A. CRABTREE: THE DOWNEAST ADVENTURES OF A REVOLUTIONARY PRIVATEERSMAN. *Am. Neptune 1982 42(1): 5-24.* Describes Crabtree's (1739-1804) career as a privateer. In his use of a small schooner for coastal raids on Nova Scotia, his year-around pursuit of the profession, and his almost total disregard for admiralty law, he was representative of Maine privateersmen, who differed from the typical American privateersmen of the era. Based on newspapers, manuscripts in Nova Scotia, Massachusetts, and the Public Record Office; 65 notes. 1775-83

Craft, Robert

1440. Peyser, Joan. STRAVINSKY-CRAFT, INC. *Am. Scholar 1983 52(4): 513-518.* 1948-82
*For abstract see **Stravinsky, Igor (family)***

Craft, William and Ellen

1441. Blackett, R. J. M. FUGITIVE SLAVES IN BRITAIN: THE ODYSSEY OF WILLIAM AND ELLEN CRAFT. *J. of Am. Studies [Great Britain] 1978 12(1): 41-62.* In 1848, William Craft (d. 1900) and Ellen Craft (d. 1890), slaves on a Georgia plantation, escaped to Philadelphia and later moved to Boston where they remained until Congress passed the Fugitive Slave Act of 1850. Their owners then demanded extradition of the Crafts to Georgia. Despite aid from antislavery groups, extradition appeared inevitable, forcing the Crafts to flee to Great Britain where they remained until the American Civil War ended. In England, the Crafts played prominent roles in helping British abolitionist groups oppose slavery. Based on archival, newspaper, and secondary sources; 54 notes. 1848-65

Crafton, Allen

1442. Gaffney, Paul J. "Allen Crafton: American Theatre Pioneer." U. of Kansas 1979. 539 pp. *DAI 1980 41(1): 24-A.* 8014380 1913-66

Craig, Margaret

1443. Allen, Marney. PRAIRIE LIFE: AN ORAL HISTORY OF GRETA CRAIG. *Atlantis [Canada] 1982 7(2): 89-102.* Transcript of an oral history interview with Margaret (Greta) Craig, born 1893. Craig recounts her parents and her own life in Western Canada from 1831 to the 1940's. Topics discussed include the Riel Rebellion, homesteading in Saskatchewan, domestic work and threshing gangs, nurses' training, and the Manitoba Federation of Agriculture and Cooperation. 1831-1945

Craig, McDonald

1444. Bass, W. H. MCDONALD CRAIG'S BLUES: BLACK AND WHITE TRADITIONS IN CONTEXT. *Tennessee Folklore Soc. Bull. 1982 48(3): 46-60.* Profiles black country singer and guitarist McDonald Craig of Linden, Tennessee, whose performances since 1948 have been dedicated to preserving the memory and songs of Jimmie Rodgers. 1948-81

Cram, George Franklin

1445. Danzer, Gerald A. GEORGE F. CRAM AND THE AMERICAN PERCEPTION OF SPACE. *Chicago History 1984 13(1): 32-45.* Reviews the career of George Franklin Cram, Chicago mapmaker, who published atlases of the United States and the world that influenced American attitudes to geography. 1860's-1928

Cram, Ralph Adams

1446. Muccigrosso, Robert. RALPH ADAMS CRAM AND THE MODERNITY OF MEDIEVALISM. *Studies in Medievalism 1982 1(2): 21-38.* Discusses the life and especially the architectural career of American architect Ralph Adams Cram, known for his role in the revival of Gothic architecture from 1903 to 1929. 1903-29

1447. Sheets, Harold Frank, III. "Ralph Adams Cram, Expatriate in the Past." U. of Texas, Austin 1978. 275 pp. *DAI 1979 39(11): 6841-A.* 1901-42

Cramer, Stuart

1448. Tigner, Steven S. STUART CRAMER: PORTRAIT OF A 20TH CENTURY MAGICIAN. *J. of Magic Hist. 1979 1(1): 22-61.* Stuart Cramer first practiced magic in the 1920's; he was still performing in 1979, having adapted to stage shows, trade shows, and television. 1920's-79

Cranch, Christopher Pearse

1449. Robinson, David. THE CAREER AND REPUTATION OF CHRISTOPHER PEARSE CRANCH: AN ESSAY IN BIOGRAPHY AND BIBLIOGRAPHY. *Studies in the Am. Renaissance 1978: 453-472.* The traditional literary assessment of the career of Christopher Pearse Cranch (1813-92) is ambiguous. Historians have stressed the importance of Cranch's engaging personality while tending to downplay his literary efforts. A review of literature suggests that this view is accurate, although a study of Cranch's poetry and prose will reveal that he was a man of largely personal concerns and ambition. The course of his career also suggests the effect of the different literary phases of the late 19th century; in particular, the conflict between the Unitarians and Transcendentalists and the links between moral and aesthetic concerns. Based on the writings and correspondence of Cranch; biblio., 8 notes. 1844-92

Crandall, Prudence

1450. Davis, Rodney O. PRUDENCE CRANDALL, SPIRITUALISM, AND POPULIST-ERA REFORM IN KANSAS. *Kansas Hist. 1980 3(4): 239-254.* Prudence Crandall (1803-90) came to Elk County, Kansas, in 1877. For 13 years she was a leader in the movements for women's rights and prohibition. Her efforts in behalf of these old-fashioned issues more than offset popular resentment of her belief in spiritualist ideas that ran counter to the tenets of Christianity. She made no public appeal for support but advanced her interests in spiritualism by holding small meetings in her home. Her leading disciples waged a major effort in support of spiritualism from 1890 to 1895. Long opposed by organized clergymen, spiritualists now faced a stronger opponent. In the 1840's it was possible to have great topics discussed at any American crossroads, but by 1890 such theorizing appeared ludicrous. Knowledge was becoming the preserve of trained academics. Based on state census records and the Spiritualism File, Kansas State Historical Society, interviews, newspapers; illus., 91 notes. 1877-95

Crane, Hart

1451. Herendeen, Warren and Parker, Donald G., ed. WIND-BLOWN FLAMES: LETTERS OF HART CRANE TO WILBUR UNDERWOOD. *Southern Rev. 1980 16(2): 339-376.* Provides background information for and briefly summarizes the content of Hart Crane's (1899-1932) letters to Wilbur Underwood (1876-1935) written from January 1921 until a few weeks before Crane's death in 1932. 1921-32

1452. Shloss, Carol. THE LIVES OF HART CRANE: REVISION OF BIOGRAPHY. *Biography 1980 3(2): 132-146.* In the act of composing a continuous prose narrative out of discrete data, biographers reveal the cultural presuppositions that condition their own interpretive categories. John Unterecker, whose *Voyager: A Life of Hart Crane* superseded Philip Horton's biography of Crane, rewrote Crane's life history in the interest of increased accuracy; but his book also reveals his changed attitudes about the nature of personality and the conventions of biography. 2 notes. 1899-1932

Crane, Julia Etta

1453. Baer, Evelyn M. JULIA ETTA CRANE (1855-1923): PIONEER IN MUSIC TEACHER EDUCATION. *Vitae Scholasticae 1983 2(1): 225-241.* Gives a professional biography of Julia Etta Crane, who achieved nationwide prominence as a trainer of music teachers. Her work centered at the Crane Normal Institute of Music, Potsdam, New York. 44 notes. German summary. 1884-1923

Crane, Stephen

1454. Cross, Laurence Frederic. "Stephen Crane: Social Critic." Brown U. 1976. 325 pp. *DAI 1977 38(1): 262-A.* 1890's

1455. Deamer, Robert Glen. REMARKS ON THE WESTERN STANCE OF STEPHEN CRANE. *Western Am. Literature 1980 15(2): 123-141.* Stephen Crane (1871-1900) toured the West in 1895. He never lived there, although he coveted a ranch in Texas. However, his life and writings are full of incidents of western role-playing and of images of the West. In playing a western role, Crane was also taking a western stance by dramatizing in himself the legendary western virtues of masculinity, self-reliance, courage, independence, and magnanimity. Thereby, Crane became an active figure in the American myth of the West and for him the myth became a reality. 1895-1900

Cranmer, Hiram M.

1456. Cox, Thomas R., ed. HARVESTING THE HEMLOCK: THE REMINISCENCES OF A PENNSYLVANIA WOOD-HICK. *Western Pennsylvania Hist. Mag. 1984 67(2): 109-131.* Reprints the 1947 reminiscences of Hiram M. Cranmer, born in Hammersley Fork, Pennsylvania in 1891, in which he records his observations of the lumber industry and the activities of the woodworkers in the Hammersley Fork area. 1902-20's

Crapo, Henry H.

1457. Huse, Donna. AMERICAN DREAM: THE STORY OF HENRY HOWLAND CRAPO. *Spinner: People and Culture in Southeastern Massachusetts 1981 1: 80-90.* Henry H. Crapo starting as a largely self-educated Dartmouth farm boy, became a leading citizen of Dartmouth and New Bedford, Massachusetts, and finally Governor of Michigan; his life-long involvement with horticulture and agriculture are related in detail. 1804-69

Crapsey, Algernon Sidney

1458. Swanton, Carolyn. DR. ALGERNON S. CRAPSEY: RELIGIOUS REFORMER. *Rochester Hist. 1980 42(1): 1-24.* Episcopal minister Algernon Sidney Crapsey (1847-1927) went to Rochester from New York City in 1879 to minister at St. Andrew's Church; focuses on his humanitarian work and concern for his parishioners, and his trial in an ecclesiastical court in 1906 for heresy; found guilty, he was forced to leave the church, but continued his work until his death. 1879-1927

Craven, Avery O.

1459. Christopher, James R. AVERY O. CRAVEN: A BIBLIOGRAPHY OF PRIMARY AND SECONDARY SOURCES. *Bulletin of Bibliography 1984 41(3): 117-132.* Briefly reviews the career and writings of Civil War historian Avery O. Craven and includes a complete bibliography of his works and a list of reviews of his works. 1860's-70's

Craven, Wesley Frank

1460. Hench, John B. WESLEY FRANK CRAVEN. *Pro. of the Am. Antiquarian Soc. 1981 91(1): 21-22.* Surveys Craven's (1905-81) career and lists his major publications. A historian of colonial America, Craven departed from his field only once, when he coedited a seven-volume history of *The Army Air Forces in World War II.* 1925-81

Cravens, Ben

1461. English, Paul. A WILY CUSTOMER: THE LIFE AND CRIMES OF BEN CRAVENS. *Chronicles of Oklahoma 1984 62(3): 284-295.* Ben Cravens defied all symbols of authority from the time he was an Iowa teenager until his final parole from a Missouri prison in 1947. During the 1890's, he drifted into Oklahoma Territory and began the life of a cattle rustler, illegal whiskey runner, and armed robber. He repeatedly escaped from jails and prisons, only to continue his criminal life in the same regions. Following the 1901 robbery of the Swartz and Company store in Red Rock, Oklahoma, during which a man was killed, Cravens disappeared from the scene for 10 years. He turned up in the Missouri state prison in Jefferson City where, under the assumed name of Charles Maust, he was serving time for livestock theft. His chance identification led to a 1912 Oklahoma conviction on murder charges. Based on Oklahoma newspapers; 5 photos, 43 notes. 1894-1912

Crawford, Charles

1462. Leary, Lewis. CHARLES CRAWFORD: A FORGOTTEN POET OF EARLY PHILADELPHIA. *Pennsylvania Mag. of Hist. and Biog. 1959 83(3): 293-306.* Traces the life and literary career of Charles Crawford from his birth in 1752 on the island of Antigua to the date of his last published book, 1814; discusses his antislavery essays, his poems and prose works on Christianity and Greek philosophy, his opposition to the American Revolution, and his life in Philadelphia from 1783 to 1800. 1775-1814

Crawford, Coe Isaac

1463. Schlup, Leonard. COE I. CRAWFORD AND THE PROGRESSIVE CAMPAIGN OF 1912. *South Dakota Hist. 1979 9(2): 116-130.* Coe Isaac Crawford (1858-1944), elected successively as a Republican Governor and Senator between 1907 and 1915, was the founder of the progressive movement in South Dakota. During the Republican Party split in 1912 Crawford supported Theodore Roosevelt while officially remaining within the Republican Party and used his influence to aid the cause of reform. When Roosevelt carried South Dakota by 10,000 votes, Crawford saw the results as a progressive victory. Although defeated by the Republican stalwarts in the 1914 senatorial primary, Crawford left behind a legacy of progressive reform in South Dakota. Primary sources; 3 illus., 5 photos, 29 notes. 1912-14

Crawford, Isabel

1464. Mondello, Salvatore. [ISABEL CRAWFORD AND THE KIOWAS].

ISABEL CRAWFORD: THE MAKING OF A MISSIONARY. *Foundations 1978 21(4): 322-339.* Presents the early life and education of Isabel Crawford, a missionary of the Women's American Baptist Home Missionary Society. Born in Canada in 1865, she became interested in the plight of the Indians through various family moves while a child. She received her training in Chicago, during which time she did considerable work in the slums. In June, 1893, she received word that she had been appointed to work as a missionary among the Kiowas of Elk Creek, Indian Territory. Based on the Isabel Crawford Collection, American Baptist Historical Society; 33 notes.

ISABEL CRAWFORD AND THE KIOWA INDIANS. *Foundations 1979 22(1): 28-42.* Describes the labors of Isabel Crawford among the Kiowa Indians in and near the Wichita Mountains of Oklahoma, 1893 to 1906. Her very successful work was abruptly terminated and she was forced to leave the Indians because of her questionable participation in a communion service. Based on the Isabel Crawford Collection, American Baptist Historical Society; 54 notes.

ISABEL CRAWFORD, CHAMPION OF THE AMERICAN INDIANS. *Foundations 1979 22(2): 99-115.* Discusses Isabel Crawford's life from 1907 to her death in 1961. 49 notes. 1893-1961

Crawford, William H.

1465. Hay, Robert P. THE PILLORYING OF ALBERT GALLATIN: THE PUBLIC RESPONSE TO HIS 1824 VICE-PRESIDENTIAL NOMINATION. *Western Pennsylvania Hist. Mag. 1982 65(3): 181-202.* 1780's-1824

*For abstract see **Gallatin, Albert***

Creighton, Donald Grant

1466. Cook, Ramsay. DONALD GRANT CREIGHTON, 1902-1979. *Hist. Papers [Canada] 1980: 257-261.* Donald Grant Creighton wrote numerous volumes on Canadian history, his central theme being the rise and fall of empire. Creighton was an excellent teacher. He was devoted to the writing and teaching of Canadian history, and distinguished by his conviction about the importance of one's past. 1902-79

Crèvecoeur, Michel de

1467. Hurst, Richard M. SNAKELORE MOTIFS IN THE WRITING OF J. HECTOR ST. JOHN DE CREVECOEUR AND OTHER COLONIAL WRITERS. *New York Folklore 1983 9(3-4): 55-97.* Presents a brief biographical sketch of Michel de Crèvecoeur, then traces and gives examples of six snake folklore motifs found in Crèvecoeur's *Letters from an American Farmer* and *Sketches of Eighteenth Century America,* in other contemporary writings, and in subsequent folklore accounts. 18c-20c

1468. Jehlen, Myra. HECTOR ST. JOHN CRÈVECOEUR: A MONARCHO-ANARCHIST IN REVOLUTIONARY AMERICA. *Am. Q. 1979 31(2): 204-222.* Michel de Crèvecoeur's opposition to the American Revolution appears paradoxical in view of his commitment to America if it is accepted there was an overall consensus regarding the purpose of the Revolution. If this were not the case, as recent studies tend to indicate, Crèvecoeur's acceptance of monarchy as the best form of government because it represented "law at a distance" is consistent with his definition of the individual and his place in American society, and that of individual freedom as the right to be left alone. Based on Crèvecoeur's *Letters from an American Farmer;* 17 notes. 1769-80

Crews, Harry

1469. Austin, Emmit Wade. "Harry Crews: The Atmosphere of Failure." Middle Tennessee State U. 1983. 111 pp. *DAI 1984 45(1): 181-A.* DA8404781 1960's-70's

Crockett, Davy (family)

1470. Downing, Marvin. DAVY CROCKETT IN GIBSON COUNTY, TENNESSEE: A CENTURY OF MEMORIES. *West Tennessee Hist. Soc. Papers 1983 37: 54-61.* David "Davey" Crockett spent 15 years in West Tennessee, most of them in Gibson County. Describes the various structural remains connected with Crockett and his family. Based on interviews and modern newspaper articles; 16 notes. 1950-80

Cropsey, Jasper Francis

1471. Dahlberg, Gertrude. JASPER FRANCIS CROPSEY: PAINTER OF AUTUMN. *Am. Art and Antiques 1979 2(6): 100-107.* Biography of American painter of the Hudson River school, Jasper Francis Cropsey (1823-1900), whose life and work epitomized the Victorian era; Cropsey started his career as an architect but is best known for his autumn landscapes of the Hudson River Valley. 1823-1900

1472. Markus, Julia. JASPER CROPSEY'S RESONANT ROOMS COME TO LIFE. *Smithsonian 1980 10(10): 104-111.* Jasper F. Cropsey (1823-1900), an American landscape artist and sometime architect, belonged to the late Hudson River School. He was prominent during the middle of the 19th century, but admiration for his paintings had declined by 1980. Through the efforts of his great-granddaughters, critical and scholarly interest in Cropsey has revived. A definitive collection of his work may be viewed by appointment at his former home in Hastings, New York. 13 photos. 1840-1900

Crosby, Bing

1473. Hendershot, Carol. BING CROSBY AND ELKO: A MUTUAL ADMIRATION SOCIETY. *Northeastern Nevada Hist. Soc. Q. 1984 (3): 66-98.* Tells of Bing Crosby's part-time career as a rancher in Elko County, Nevada, focusing on the daily activities at various Crosby ranches, and on the singer's participation in local social events. 1943-52

Crossland, Fred

1474. Glauberman, Susan. A CONVERSATION WITH MARIAM CHAMBERLAIN AND FRED CROSSLAND. *Change 1981 13(8): 32-37.* 1963-81

*For abstract see **Chamberlain, Mariam***

Crosson, Elizabeth and George

1475. Perry, Kenneth. INDIAN DEPREDATIONS IN THE TEXAS BIG BEND: THE CROSSON CLAIMS CASE. *Panhandle-Plains Hist. Rev. 1980 53: 35-55.* George Crosson occupied several ranch sites near Fort Davis, Texas, during 1875-85. Despite the proximity of soldiers, Crosson lost many sheep and horses to Apache raids. After Crosson's death in 1885, his widow Elizabeth filed a depredations claim against the federal government which had jurisdiction over the raiding Indians. After years of litigation, she received only $2,590. She was able to expand the original ranching operation through hard work and dedication. Crosson Collection at Sul Ross State University, Alpine, Texas; 3 photos, map, 60 notes. 1875-1901

Crosswaith, Frank B.

1476. Seabrook, John Howard. "Black and White Unite: The Career of Frank B. Crosswaith." Rutgers U. 1980. 340 pp. *DAI 1980 41(4): 1717-1718-A.* 8022591 ca 1925-58

Croswell, Edwin

1477. Manning, Richard Howard. "Herald of the Albany Regency: Edwin Croswell and the *Albany Argus,* 1823-1854." Miami U. 1983. 346 pp. *DAI 1984 44(12): 3781-3782-A.* DA8407699 1823-54

Crothers, Austin Lane

1478. Burckel, Nicholas C. GOVERNOR AUSTIN LANE CROTHERS AND PROGRESSIVE REFORM IN MARYLAND 1908-1912. *Maryland Hist. Mag. 1981 76(2): 184-201.* More than any other governor of Maryland, Austin Lane Crothers succeeded in achieving progressive reforms for which individuals and groups had unsuccessfully agitated in the past, and his administration (1908-12) is even more impressive when seen "against the backdrop of volatile state politics and the racial issue which dominated the political scene" between 1896 and his election. Examines Crothers's career prior to the governorship, his legislative battles in enacting a corrupt practices act, a primary election bill, a public utilities law, and endorsement of the income tax amendment. Throughout his term, Crothers faced the opposition of powerful ex-governor John Walter Smith and leading organization Democrat Arthur P. Gorman, Jr. Crothers' death in 1912 greatly helped the decline of progressivism in Maryland. Based on the Maryland Manuals, contemporary press, and secondary works; 51 notes. 1904-12

Crouch, Richard

1479. Kestigian, Mark C. EARLY MEDICAL CARE IN DEERFIELD. *Hist. J. of Western Massachusetts 1979 7(2): 5-14.* 1675-1765
For abstract see ***Wells, Thomas***

Crouter, Natalie

1480. Crouter, Natalie. FORBIDDEN DIARY. *Am. Heritage 1979 30(3): 78-95.* Natalie Crouter, husband Jerry, and their two children, ages 12 and 10, were captured in the Philippines by the Japanese shortly after Pearl Harbor. Natalie's diary, which had to be kept hidden from her captors, survived to recount some of the family's experiences during more than three years of internment. Excerpted from *The Internment of Natalie Crouter,* forthcoming. 13 illus. 1941-44

Crowfoot, Joe

1481. Gooderham, George H. JOE CROWFOOT. *Alberta Hist. [Canada] 1984 32(4): 26-28.* Profiles the life of Blackfoot Indian Joe Crowfoot. He married Maggie Spotted Eagle in 1921 and became a successful farmer in Alberta. In the 1930's he was made a tribal councillor. He fought for reform of restrictions on Indians and in 1953 was elected a tribal chief. 3 photos. 1892-1976

Crowninshield, Frank

1482. Cooper, Martha Cohn. "Frank Crowninshield and *Vanity Fair.*" U. of North Carolina, Chapel Hill 1976. 203 pp. *DAI 1977 38(2): 785-786-A.* 1914-36

Croxton, John Thomas

1483. Miller, Rex. JOHN THOMAS CROXTON: SCHOLAR, LAWYER, SOLDIER, MILITARY GOVERNOR, NEWSPAPERMAN, DIPLOMAT AND MASON. *Register of the Kentucky Hist. Soc. 1976 74(4): 281-299.* Educated at Yale, Kentuckian John Thomas Croxton was a strong supporter of the Union with a bitter hatred of slavery. He served in the Union Army with distinction during the Civil War, and commanded the Military District of Georgia for about a year. After service, he practiced law and was active in Republican politics in Kentucky. Primary and secondary sources; 2 illus., 18 notes. 1855-74

Crumley, Newton Hunt

1484. Sheerin, Chris H. NEWTON HUNT CRUMLEY. *Northeastern Nevada Hist. Soc. Q. 1979 79(1): 2-14.* Newton Hunt Crumley (1911-62) promoted the entertainment industry in Nevada and performed much civic and volunteer work. 1930's-62

Crummell, Alexander

1485. Scruggs, Otey M. TWO BLACK PATRIARCHS: FREDERICK DOUGLASS AND ALEXANDER CRUMMELL. *Afro-Americans in New York Life and Hist. 1982 6(1): 17-30.* 1818-98
For abstract see ***Douglass, Frederick***

Crutchfield family

1486. Livingood, James W. CHATTANOOGA'S CRUTCHFIELDS AND THE FAMOUS CRUTCHFIELD HOUSE. *Civil War Times Illus. 1981 20(7): 20-25.* Tells the story of the Crutchfield family of Chattanooga, Tennessee, and of their hotel, Crutchfield House, during the Civil War. 19c

Cruttenden, Joseph

1487. Steele, I. K. A LONDON TRADER AND THE ATLANTIC EMPIRE: JOSEPH CRUTTENDEN, APOTHECARY, 1710 TO 1717. *William and Mary Q. 1977 34(2): 281-297.* The letterbook of Joseph Cruttenden sheds new light on the commercial life of 18th-century London. Cruttenden was a druggist. He never became wealthy and never acquired any legal hold over colonial customers. His correspondence provides information on English and colonial medicinal practices, drugs, business policies, the Atlantic trade, prices, and exchange values. Observes the contrast between Cruttenden's New England and West Indies trade. Based chiefly on Cruttenden's letterbook. 1690-1720

Cudahy, John

1488. Maga, Timothy P. DIPLOMAT AMONG KINGS: JOHN CUDAHY AND LEOPOLD III. *Wisconsin Mag. of Hist. 1983-84 67(2): 82-98.* Traces the role of a Wisconsin meat-packer's son in New Deal diplomacy. John Cudahy served in World War I, denounced Woodrow Wilson's intervention in Russia in *Archangel: The American War with Russia,* embarked on safaris in Africa during the 1920's, and became an early supporter of Franklin Roosevelt for president. He served successively as ambassador to Poland, Ireland, and Belgium, where he developed a close personal friendship with King Leopold III. Cudahy's aggressive support for the king following the German invasion of Belgium proved to be an embarrassment to the neutral Americans, and he was asked to resign his post as ambassador. 10 illus., 46 notes. 1940

Culin, Stewart

1489. Bronner, Simon J. STEWART CULIN, "MUSEUM MAGICIAN." *Pennsylvania Heritage 1985 11(3): 4-11.* Gives a biography of Stewart Culin, a folklorist of the late 19th and early 20th centuries who was a pioneer in the movement to make museums more organized and more understandable to the public. 1880's-1922

Cullen, Countee

1490. Lomax, Michael Lucius. "Countee Cullen: From the Dark Tower." Emory U. 1984. 329 pp. *DAI 1984 45(6): 1799-A.* DA8420286 1920's

Culmsee, Ludwig Alfred

1491. Culmsee, Carlton. LAST FREE LAND RUSH. *Utah Hist. Q. 1981 49(1): 26-41.* Dr. Ludwig Alfred Culmsee, in response to developers' advertisements in southern California for free Utah land, moved his family to the Escalante Desert area and in the following years almost single handedly built the towns of Nada and Kerr alongside the San Pedro, Los Angeles, and Salt Lake Railroad. Later he organized an experimental farm at Logan. After his death most of the small towns began to decay into ghost towns. 2 illus., photo, 8 notes. 1912-36

Cumings, John

1492. Emlen, Robert P. THE HARD CHOICES OF BROTHER JOHN CUMINGS. *Hist. New Hampshire 1979 34(1): 54-65.* John Cumings (1829-1911) had joined the Shaker community at Enfield, New Hampshire, with his family in 1844. His father and brother left the Shakers in the 1860's. Although sorely tempted to join them, John finally decided, in the 1870's, to stay with the Shakers, who came to rely on his mechanical skills. He held the Enfield community together until his death in 1911. In 1923 the surviving Enfield Shakers moved to Canterbury. Based on the Cumings family papers, and other primary and secondary sources. 3 illus., 23 notes. 1829-1923

Cumming, Julien

1493. Matthews, Evie. "POOR, POOR, JULIE"—THE STORY OF JULIEN CUMMING. *Richmond County History 1985 17(1): 17-22.* Presents a biography of Julien Cumming, a 19th-century Georgia lawyer who served as a Confederate soldier and died as a result of a wound received at the Battle of Gettysburg. 1830-64

Cumming, William

1494. Aspinwall, Bernard. ORESTES A. BROWNSON AND FATHER WILLIAM CUMMING. *Innes Rev. [Great Britain] 1976 27(1): 35-41.* Publishes a letter from Father Cumming to Orestes A. Brownson in 1857 and describes their lives and the history of Scottish Catholics in America in the 1850's. 1850's

Cummings, Charles

1495. Brown, Douglas Summers. CHARLES CUMMINGS: THE FIGHTING PARSON OF SOUTHWEST VIRGINIA. *Virginia Cavalcade 1979 28(3): 138-143.* Presbyterian minister Charles Cummings (1733-1812) is "remembered as a late 18th-century pioneer and patriot who defended his region against Indian attacks and the encroachments of the British Empire." 1760's-80's

Cummings, E. E.

1496. Friedman, Norman. KNOWING AND REMEMBERING CUMMINGS. *Harvard Lib. Bull. 1981 29(2): 117-134.* The author recalls the influence of E. E. Cummings on his life and career. His "discovery" of the poet's works, as a high school student in the 1940's, set him on his future academic course and he became disciple, friend, and critic of Cummings. The poet was kind, generous, understanding, and encouraging, at least to a young scholar attempting to become established in the academic world. Largely correspondence and personal recollections; 20 notes. 1940-69

1497. Kennedy, Richard S. E. E. CUMMINGS AT HARVARD: VERSE, FRIENDS, REBELLION. *Harvard Lib. Bull. 1977 25(3): 253-291.* Examines E. E. Cummings's personality during his undergraduate years at Harvard University. In his freshman year, Cummings was a dutiful youngster saturated with a 19th-century New England ethos. Five years later, he was in full rebellion against his father, Cambridge, and prevailing American tastes. Cummings was associating with other apprentices in the artistic movements of the 20th century, and developing his distinctive poetic style. E. E. Cummings combined the ordinary pattern of a young man's rejection of his father with a unique turn toward aestheticism that released his creativity. His writing development paralleled his Oedipal wrestling. Covers 1911-16. Based on manuscript and other sources; 4 illus., 65 notes. 1911-16

Cunningham, Agnes "Sis"

1498. Schrems, Suzanne H. RADICALISM AND SONG. *Chronicles of Oklahoma 1984 62(2): 190-206.* Agnes "Sis" Cunningham was born to an Oklahoma farm family that lost its heavily mortgaged land to bank foreclosure during the late 1930's. Her father and brother joined a grass-roots socialist movement which drew some of its doctrine from Commonwealth Labor College, a radical labor school in Mena, Arkansas. While attending the school, Agnes wrote plays known as "agitprop," which promoted political agitation and propaganda. With her Red Dust Players, she presented political plays complete with unionist songs of her own composition. Agnes continued her involvement with folk music into the 1950's and 1960's, when she promoted young performers such as Bob Dylan and Phil Ochs. Secondary sources; 2 photos, 44 notes. 1930's

1499. Teichroew, Allan. GORDON FRIESEN: WRITER, RADICAL AND EX-MENNONITE. *Mennonite Life 1983 38(2): 4-17.* 1930-82
*For abstract see **Friesen, Gordon***

Cunningham, Charles Oliver

1500. Hassler, David W. CHARLES O. CUNNINGHAM: CALIFORNIA-ARIZONA PIONEER, 1852-1865. *Arizona and the West 1985 27(3): 253-268.* During the 1850's, Charles Oliver Cunningham crossed the continent and settled in California, to the east of Los Angeles. He established a family, soon became active in local Democratic politics, held minor judicial posts, and opened a general store on his small farm. In 1862, he began carrying freight to the new gold mines in the southwestern Arizona Colorado River country. Soon he became involved in mining silver, lead, copper, and gold, generally on a speculative basis in the new Arizona Territory. He died a victim of Indian resistance to continued miner incursions on their homeland. Cunningham was a typical small-time frontier speculator-capitalist. 3 illus., map, 39 notes. 1852-65

Cunningham, Merce

1501. Dunning, Jennifer. MERCE CUNNINGHAM. *Horizon 1984 27(2): 12-18.* Profiles the 50-year career of avant-garde dancer and choreographer Merce Cunningham, who continues "to explore movement for its own sake": composer John Cage and artist Robert Rauschenberg collaborate with Cunningham in his dance company's productions. 1930's-84

Curran, Isaac B.

1502. Curran, Nathaniel B. GENERAL ISAAC B. CURRAN: GREGARIOUS JEWELER. *J. of the Illinois State Hist. Soc. 1978 71(4): 272-278.* By profession a jeweler, Isaac B. Curran (1819-95) was actually a power broker in the politics and financial development of Springfield, Illinois, from his appointment in 1847 as quartermaster general until his retirement in 1862. He was a special confidant of pre-Civil War Democratic Governor Joel Matteson. Curran Papers, newspapers, secondary sources; 4 illus., 43 notes. 1847-95

Currie, Arthur

1503. Hyatt, A. M. J. SIR ARTHUR CURRIE. *Canada 1975 2(3): 4-15.* General Currie's (1875-1933) brilliant military career in World War I became controversial when the former Minister of Militia and Defence, Sir Sam Hughes (1853-1921) accused Currie of needlessly sacrificing Canadian lives. Actually, Currie constantly worked to reduce casualties and to increase the fighting efficiency of his various commands, but his unpopular image was strengthened by his formal demeanor. 7 photos, 26 notes, biblio. 1914-30

Currie, Lauchlin

1504. Jones, Byrd L. LAUCHLIN CURRIE AND THE CAUSES OF THE 1937 RECESSION. *Hist. of Pol. Econ. 1980 12(3): 303-315.* Discusses the works and impact of Keynesian economist Lauchlin Currie on the economic policies of the New Deal; 1935-46. 1935-46

Curry, Jabez Lamar Monroe

1505. Kellam, W. Porter. REMINISCENCES OF FRANKLIN COLLEGE, BY JABEZ LAMAR MONROE CURRY, CLASS OF 1843. WITH A BIOGRAPHICAL SKETCH OF THE AUTHOR AND NOTES. *Georgia Historical Quarterly 1985 69(2): 211-228.* Presents a biographical sketch of Jabez Lamar Monroe Curry (1825-1903), Southern attorney, plantation owner, politician, preacher, educator, author, and diplomat, and prints his reminiscences, first published in 1890, of his years during 1839-43 as a student at Franklin College in Athens, now the University of Georgia. 33 notes. 1839-1903

Curtis, Asahel

1506. Frederick, Richard. ASAHEL CURTIS AND THE KLONDIKE STAMPEDE. *Alaska J. 1983 13(2): 113-121.* Introduces and prints excerpts from the diaries of Asahel Curtis, who came from Seattle to participate in the Klondike gold rush in 1897. 13 photos, 6 notes. 1897-99

1507. Frederick, Richard. PHOTOGRAPHER ASAHEL CURTIS: CHRONICLER OF THE NORTHWEST. *Am. West 1980 17(6): 26-40.* Asahel Curtis (ca. 1874-1941) was commissioned in 1897 by his brother Edward Curtis, the famous Indian-chronicler, to follow the Klondike Stampede gold rush with a camera. From then until his death, Asahel Curtis made over 60,000 exposures documenting human activity in the Pacific Northwest and Alaska. His subject matter was varied, but he was primarily concerned with the rise of industry and cities. 13 illus., biblio. 1897-1941

Curtis, Charles

1508. Schlup, Leonard. CHARLES CURTIS: THE VICE-PRESIDENT FROM KANSAS. *Manuscripts 1983 35(3): 183-201.* Charles Curtis's letters show that he had excellent political credentials, serving the Republican Party especially well in the Senate. He enjoyed political security and seniority at both the state and national level, was a faithful party follower, and on occasion was an avid reformer, as in the case of women's rights and suffrage. Curtis wielded tremendous influence through his use of patronage. 58 notes, illus. 1902-32

Curtis, Edward S.

1509. Nadel, Norman. CURTIS RECOVERED: A GROUP OF ENTREPRENEURS COMPLETES EDWARD S. CURTIS' PHOTOGRAPHIC RECORD OF THE AMERICAN INDIAN. *Horizon 1980 23(8): 40-49.* Focuses on the interest of American photographer Edward S. Curtis (1868-1952) in preserving "the rituals, traditions, behavior, appearance, attitudes, communal and private lives" of American Indians from 1898 until 1930, and the completion of his project by several people in Santa Fe, New Mexico, since the early 1970's. 1898-1980

Curtis, George William

1510. Martin, Martha Anna. "George William Curtis: The Advisor and His Rhetorical Discourse." U. of Iowa 1977. 397 pp. *DAI 1978 38(7): 3804-3805-A.* 1881-92

Curtis, H. N.

1511. Curtis, H. N. SKETCH OF THE EARLY SETTLEMENT OF THE MAUMEE VALLEY. *Northwest Ohio Q. 1983 55(3): 98-100.* Reprints a personal narrative by H. N. Curtis on his memories of the early settlement of the Maumee Valley in northwestern Ohio. 1823-29

Curtis, Lemuel

1512. Carlisle, Lilian Baker. NEW BIOGRAPHICAL FINDINGS ON CURTIS & DUNNING, GIRANDOLE CLOCKMAKERS. *Am. Art J. 1978 10(1): 90-109.* Lemuel Curtis (1790-1857?) and Joseph N. Dunning (1795-1841) were among New England's finest clockmakers, but they had little success in business. Discusses their "girandole" style clocks and details their work, both together and apart, especially in Burlington, Vermont, in the 1820's and 30's. Based on surviving clocks, Burlington newspapers, and secondary works; 22 illus., 55 notes. 1820's-30's

Curtis, Moses Ashley

1513. Simpson, Marcus B., Jr. and Simpson, Sallie W. MOSES ASHLEY CURTIS (1808-1872): CONTRIBUTIONS TO CAROLINA ORNITHOLOGY. *North Carolina Hist. Rev. 1983 60(2): 137-170.* Moses Ashley Curtis moved to Wilmington, North Carolina, from Massachusetts in 1830, prepared for the Episcopal ministry in Boston (1833-34), and then held various missionary and teaching positions in Lincolnton, Raleigh, Washington, and Hillsborough, North Carolina, and in Society Hill, South Carolina. He continually studied and recorded North Carolina plant and animal life and as a result was appointed naturalist for the state's Geological and Agricultural Survey in 1859. The state published his two-volume study of North Carolina plants but not his work on animals, the uncompleted manuscript of which still survives. Curtis's checklist of birds contains some problematic entries but remains a valuable source of information on antebellum North Carolina bird species. Based on Curtis family papers at the University of North Carolina and Curtis's zoological specimens at the Museum of Natural History, Washington; 17 illus., 137 notes, 2 appendixes. 1837-72

Curtiss, Glenn H.

1514. Johnson, Robert E. THE RACE FROM "POINT ZERO": CURTISS VS. WRIGHT. *Am. Aviation Hist. Soc. J. 1983 28(2): 82-92.* Chronicles Glenn H. Curtiss's early career in aeronautics, including his flying records, contributions to aviation technology, business ventures, and legal battles with the Wright brothers over patent rights. 1900-10

1515. Renaud, Vern and Wolff, Fred. "HELL RIDER": THE GLENN CURTISS STORY. *Aviation Q. 1979 5(1): 30-71.* Traces the career of Glenn Curtiss, racer, developer, inventor of the "flying boat" and many other aircraft, and "Father of Naval Aviation," from his birth in 1878 to the merging of the Curtiss company with the Wright company in 1929. 1878-1929

Curtiss, John Hamilton

1516. Todd, John. JOHN HAMILTON CURTISS, 1909-1977. *Ann. of the Hist. of Computing 1980 2(2): 104-110.* John Hamilton Curtiss was chief of the Applied Mathematics Division of the National Bureau of Standards from 1946 to 1953. He was largely responsible for the planning and construction of SEAC and SWAC and for the procurement of the first UNIVACs for federal establishments. 2 notes, biblio. 1930-77

Curwen, Samuel

1517. Lockwood, Allison. THE TIMES OF SAMUEL CURWEN. *Am. Hist. Illus. 1978 13(1): 23-32.* Samuel Curwen (1715-1802), a Judge of the Admiralty, resided in Salem, Massachusetts, in what is today called the "Witch House." There, his grandfather had conducted the initial examination of those accused of witchcraft in 1692. A Loyalist, he left Salem in 1775, fleeing to Philadelphia and then to London, where he spent nine years in exile. Through the efforts of an old friend in the Massachusetts Assembly, Curwen's name was omitted from a list of several hundred Loyalists threatened with "death without benefit of clergy" if they ever returned. He left London just as the guns of the Tower were saluting the conclusion of a general peace (1784) and upon his arrival in Salem was welcomed by all. 14 illus. 1775-1802

Cushing, Caleb

1518. Baldasty, Gerald J. POLITICAL STALEMATE IN ESSEX COUNTY: CALEB CUSHING'S RACE FOR CONGRESS, 1830-1832. *Essex Inst. Hist. Collections 1981 117(1): 54-70.* Caleb Cushing was the central figure in the congressional stalemate in North Essex District, 1830-32. The electors finally found a majority candidate after 12 separate elections and Cushing's withdrawal from the race. Three principal factors exacerbated the stalemate and thwarted Cushing's attempts to become a congressman: divisions within the National Republican (later Whig) Party, charges that Cushing had engaged in unethical or unacceptable campaign practices, and the persuasive power wielded by the political newspapers in the campaign. Primary sources; 62 notes. 1830-32

Cushing, Frank Hamilton

1519. Mark, Joan. FRANK HAMILTON CUSHING AND AN AMERICAN SCIENCE OF ANTHROPOLOGY. *Perspectives in Am. Hist. 1976 10: 449-486.* An analysis of Frank Hamilton Cushing's life as an anthropologist shows that American anthropology in the 19th century profoundly affected the methods and concepts of anthropologists on both sides of the Atlantic. Cushing's method was simple. He gave definition to the anthropological concept of culture through example. He immersed himself in the Zuñi culture he wanted to study. Personal experience, he surmised, would substantially augment one's understanding of a society. 4 photos, 96 notes. 1857-1900

Cushman, Wesley P.

1520. Irvine, Phyllis Eleanor Kuhnle. "A Biographical Analysis of Wesley P. Cushman and His Professional Contributions to Health Education." Ohio State U. 1981. 245 pp. *DAI 1982 42(8): 3450-A.* DA8201041 1931-79

Custer, Elizabeth Bacon

1521. Hofling, Charles K. CUSTER'S MARRIAGE AND DOMESTIC LIFE. *Psychohistory Rev. 1980 9(1): 59-70.* 1864-76

*For abstract see **Custer, George A.***

1522. Tate, Michael L. THE GIRL HE LEFT BEHIND: ELIZABETH CUSTER AND THE MAKING OF A LEGEND. *Red River Valley Hist. Rev. 1980 5(1): 5-22.* Focuses on the life of Elizabeth Bacon Custer (1842-1933) after her 1864 marriage to General George A. Custer; describes General Custer's death at the battle of the Little Big Horn in 1876, and his widow's responses to the Custer legend. 1864-1933

Custer, George A.

1523. Hofling, Charles K. CUSTER'S MARRIAGE AND DOMESTIC LIFE. *Psychohistory Rev. 1980 9(1): 59-70.* General George A. Custer's marriage to Elizabeth Bacon in 1864 was a strong influence on his career. Husband and wife were very close and their memoirs and correspondence reveal considerable dependence on one another. Elizabeth "Libbie" Custer often accompanied her husband, and he encouraged her presence. Briefly examines whether Custer was sterile. 24 notes. 1864-76

1524. Millbrook, Minnie Dubbs. BIG GAME HUNTING WITH THE CUSTERS, 1869-1870. *Kansas Hist. Q. 1975 41(4): 429-453.* General Custer concluded his book, *My Life on the Plains*, with a comment that he had excluded reference to his hunting adventures, although these experiences were in many respects among the most interesting of his recollections. He related some of his experiences at a later date in sporting magazines, but this is the first attempt to describe his hunting experiences while stationed at Fort Hays on the basis of contemporary documents. In addition to regular shooting expeditions in which most officers participated, Custer took part in several hunts during these two years which were specially arranged for tourists from Europe and the East. Based on primary and secondary sources; illus., 70 notes. 1869-70

1525. Russell, Don. CUSTER'S FIRST CHARGE. *By Valor and Arms 1974 1(1): 20-29.* Discusses George A. Custer's career as an Army officer during the Civil War. 1861-65

1526. Tate, Michael L. THE GIRL HE LEFT BEHIND: ELIZABETH CUSTER AND THE MAKING OF A LEGEND. *Red River Valley Hist. Rev. 1980 5(1): 5-22.* 1864-1933

For abstract see ***Custer, Elizabeth Bacon***

Custer, Thomas Ward

1527. Reichley, John A. THE "UNKNOWN" CUSTER. *Military Rev. 1984 64(5): 72-75.* Thomas Ward Custer followed his elder and more famous brother George Armstrong Custer into military service. He was commissioned a lieutenant of cavalry at age 19 and in 1863 earned a Medal of Honor by capturing a Confederate battle flag. In 1865 he captured yet another Confederate standard, and was awarded another Medal of Honor. In 1876 he died with his brother while fighting Indians at Little Bighorn. 1861-76

Custis, Eleanor Parke

1528. Jackson, Donald. GEORGE WASHINGTON'S BEAUTIFUL NELLY. *Am. Heritage 1977 28(2): 80-85.* Eleanor Parke Custis was George Washington's step-granddaughter, but he regarded her as a daughter for she grew up in his household. Although Nelly was adored and pampered as a child, her adulthood was sad and difficult, in part because she never developed self-reliance. 5 illus. 1785-1852

Custis, George Washington Parke

1529. Kennedy, Roger G. ARLINGTON HOUSE, A MANSION THAT WAS A MONUMENT. *Smithsonian 1985 16(7): 156-166.* Discusses the controversial life and ideas of George Washington Parke Custis, grandson of Martha Washington, who was often at odds with Thomas Jefferson and other of the nation's leaders, and who built the landmark Arlington House in Greek architectural style on a hill overlooking both Washington, D.C., and the Arlington National Cemetery. 1798-1861

Custis, John, IV

1530. Zuppan, Jo. JOHN CUSTIS OF WILLIAMSBURG, 1678-1749. *Virginia Mag. of Hist. and Biog. 1982 90(2): 175-197.* John Custis IV, is known for the remarkable epitaph on his Eastern Shore tombstone, and the fact that his son was Martha Washington's first husband. A letter book of Custis's offers insights into the life and dealings of a colonial businessman and planter, and provides a glimpse of Custis's personal relationships, including one with William Byrd. Based on Custis's letter book, Custis family papers at the Virginia Historical Society, William Byrd's *Secret Diary of William Byrd,* and secondary sources; 55 notes, 2 portraits. 1678-1749

Cuthbert, Alfred, Jr.

1531. Gifford, James M. THE CUTHBERT CONSPIRACY: AN EPISODE IN AFRICAN COLONIZATION. *South Atlantic Q. 1980 79(3): 312-320.* Delineates the efforts of Alfred Cuthbert, Jr., of Georgia, to free his slaves and ship them to Liberia under the auspices of the American Colonization Society. He finally succeeded. The expedition to Liberia exemplified the excitement, emotional intensity, and the human pathos that had always characterized the movement. Cuthbert represents a small but significant group of slaveholders who actively participated in African colonization. The white colonizers reflected the sympathies of a larger percentage of slaveholders who were stymied by financial and community pressures just as surely as the few freedmen sent to Liberia lived out the dreams of many blacks who remained behind as slaves. Covers 1855-61. Based almost wholly on the American Colonization Society Archives in the Library of Congress; 29 notes. 1855-61

Cutler, Harry

1532. Abrams, Stanley B. HARRY CUTLER: AN OUTLINE OF A NEGLECTED PATRIOT. *Rhode Island Jewish Historical Notes 1984 9(2): 127-140.* Gives the biography of zionist Harry Cutler, a jewelry manufacturer of Providence, Rhode Island, highlighting his welfare work with Jewish philanthropic organizations. 1882-1920

Cutler, Timothy

1533. Huber, Donald L. TIMOTHY CUTLER: THE CONVERT AS CONTROVERSIALIST. *Hist. Mag. of the Protestant Episcopal Church 1975 44(4): 489-496.* In the autumn of 1722 Timothy Cutler, Rector at Yale, converted to Anglicanism. From that time until 1730 he became the chief protagonist of the Church of England in Massachusetts, where the established church was the Congregational. He served as rector of Christ Church, Boston. Delineates some of Cutler's gadfly undertakings as he sought relief for the Anglican church from the Congregationalists. In some instances he was successful, in others he failed; but for the most part he was successful in forcing important concessions from the Congregationalists. For reasons unknown he gradually withdrew from the arena, but only after he had made a mark for himself as controversialist. Based largely on primary sources, including Foote, *Annals of King's Chapel* and Perry, *Historical Collections Relating to the American Colonial Church*; 40 notes. 1720-30

D

Dabney, Charles W.

1534. Lewis, Gene D. and Miller, Zane L. CHARLES W. DABNEY AND THE URBAN UNIVERSITY: AN INSTITUTION IN SEARCH OF A MISSION, 1904-1914. *Cincinnati Hist. Soc. Bull. 1980 38(3): 150-179.* Charles W. Dabney worked from 1904 to 1914 to transform the University of Cincinnati (and the American university in general) into a coordinated and cohesive institution that would be a part of its urban surroundings and train students for service to their community. 1904-14

Dabney, Robert Lewis

1535. Wilson, Charles Reagan. ROBERT LEWIS DABNEY: RELIGION AND THE SOUTHERN HOLOCAUST. *Virginia Mag. of Hist. and Biog. 1981 89(1): 79-89.* Analyzes the post-Civil War life of Robert Lewis Dabney, a Presbyterian theologian and philosopher at Union Seminary, Hampden-Sydney, Virginia. Dabney tried to preserve what remained of a perceived Southern ethic, and warned of moral dangers to a defeated people. Disgusted by 1881 with northern debauchery of the South, in declining health, he accepted a philosophy appointment at the new University of Texas. He taught there and helped found a seminary in Austin, but by 1890 was again disgusted by too many "Yankees" about him. In 1894 the University Regents forced him to resign because of small classes, an act likely precipitated by his enemies. He died in 1896, an example of a soul troubled by the fate of the postbellum South. 27 notes. 1865-96

Dagenais, Pierre

1536. Beauregard, Ludger. PIERRE DAGENAIS: UNE BIOBIBLIOGRAPHIE [Pierre Dagenais: a biobibliography]. *Cahiers de Géog. du Québec [Canada] 1983 27(71): 149-163.* An account of the career of Pierre Dagenais, geographer, teacher, founder of the Institute of Geography at the University of Montreal, and one of the most important contributors to the geography of Quebec; includes a complete bibliography of his work. 1939-81

Dahlberg, Edward

1537. MacShane, Frank. EDWARD DAHLBERG: 1900-1977, A REMINISCENCE. *Massachusetts Rev. 1978 19(1): 55-68.* Reminiscences of the author's acquaintance with Edward Dahlberg, an American novelist, poet, essayist, and critic, chiefly known for his idiosyncratic style and literary opinions, and his autobiography, *Because I Was Flesh.* Relates how he first was much impressed with Dahlberg, but as he became better acquainted, he began to notice his flaws. Despite warnings from Dahlberg's enduring acquaintances, the author hired him as professor of writing at Columbia University. Dahlberg broke with nearly all his friends because he could not accept people as they were. He may occupy a position in literature analogous to Henry David Thoreau (1817-62). 1900-77

1538. Shloss, Carol. BECAUSE I WAS FLESH: EDWARD DAHLBERG AND THE RHETORIC OF AMERICAN IDENTITY. *Massachusetts Rev. 1981 22(3): 576-584.* A discussion of Edward Dahlberg (1900-77), American author and critic, focusing on the section of his autobiography, *Because I Was Flesh,* describing his origins as the illegitimate son of Lizzie Dahlberg (Dalberg), a barber in Kansas City, Missouri. As he, the grandson of Polish Jews, saw it, the urban, immigrant poor suffered because the American Dream engendered expectations which it could not fulfill in the lives of those believing it. The story of his youth illustrated his theory, showing that "it is just as important to be unfortunate as... happy." His mother was proof against the dream, a woman enthralled by the American myth, and evidence of its unreality. His autobiography expounded the frontier thesis, with his mother representing the untamed wilderness, in order to descover a heritage useful to him. 3 notes. ca 1900-40

Daily, Charles Henry

1539. Hay, Melba Porter, ed. MEMOIRS OF CHARLES HENRY DAILY. *Register of the Kentucky Hist. Soc. 1978 76(2): 133-152.* Charles Henry Daily (1847-1932), a teacher and farmer, completed a handwritten memoir at the age of 84. Discusses his childhood, youth, and experiences as a teacher in Kentucky. 9 notes. 1850-1930

Dalhart, Vernon

1540. Walsh, Jim. FAVORITE PIONEER RECORDING ARTISTS: VERNON DALHART. *JEMF Q. 1982 28(67-68): 131-145.* Discusses the life and musical career of American hillbilly singer and recording artist Marion Try Slaughter, better known by his stage name, Vernon Dalhart, 1925-48. 1925-48

Daly, Dan

1541. Dieckmann, Edward A., Sr. DAN DALY: RELUCTANT HERO. *Marine Corps Gazette 1960 44(11): 22-27.* A biography of US Marines Sergeant Major Dan Daly (d. 1937), who won the Medal of Honor during the Boxer Rebellion in China in 1900 and the battle of Belleau Wood, France, in 1918. 1900-37

Daly, Thomas Augustine

1542. Cipolla, Gaetano. THOMAS AUGUSTINE DALY: AN EARLY VOICE OF THE ITALIAN IMMIGRANTS. *Italian Americana 1980 6(1): 45-59.* Reevaluates the work of Philadelphia humorist Thomas Augustine Daly, famous for his dialectal poems about Italian Americans published in the early 1900's, which portrayed Italian Americans as interesting and intelligent during a period when Italian Americans were much maligned. 1900-09

Daly, Thomas Mayne

1543. Swainson, Donald. THOMAS MAYNE DALY AND PATRONAGE AS WELFARE. *Ontario Hist. [Canada] 1980 72(1): 16-26.* "Patronage, corrupt or otherwise" was central to 19th-century politics, as illustrated in the career of Thomas Mayne Daly (1827-84) from entrance into politics in 1848 to withdrawal in the late 1870's, when Daly was viewed as an unstable ally and unsatisfied client who was unwanted and dependent on his party. He saw patronage as a means of reward or pension for his services. Based on material from the Public Archives of Ontario and mainly secondary sources; 64 notes. 1848-70's

Damitz, Ernst

1544. Sparks, Esther. ERNST DAMITZ. *Chicago Hist. 1981-82 10(4): 212-217.* Biography of Prussian-born farmer, healer, and painter Ernst Damitz (1805-83) of Greenbush Township in Warren County, Illinois, focusing on his paintings which were nostalgic and autobiographical scenes of his daily life. 1805-83

Damm, Freida M.

1545. Hahn, Gertrude and Hahn, Naomi. FRIEDA M. DAMM: RED CROSS NURSE—1917-1919. *Concordia Historical Institute Quarterly 1984 57(2): 53-59.* Describes the life of Freida M. Damm, a nurse who served with the Red Cross in France during and following World War I, with excerpts from letters written to her family. 1917-19

Dana, James Dwight

1546. Prendergast, Michael Laurent. "James Dwight Dana: The Life and Thought of an American Scientist." U. of California, Los Angeles 1978. 640 pp. *DAI 1979 39(7): 4451-A.* 1837-70's

Dancy, John

1547. Pollock, Bradley H. JOHN C. DANCY, THE DEPRESSION AND THE NEW DEAL. *UCLA Hist. J. 1984 5: 5-23.* Describes the role played by John Dancy, director of the Detroit Urban League, in responding to the needs of blacks in the Great Depression. A conservative and a Republican, Dancy held the view of Booker T. Washington in looking to economic gains for blacks. The magnitude of the Depression, however, and the Democratic Party's recruitment of black voters, plus the involvement of blacks in New Deal relief programs, helped pull Dancy towards the Democratic Party. Urban League leadership would find little fault in New

Deal programs; its political shift to the Democrats reflected a similar process taking place among blacks in general in the 1930's. 55 notes. 1929-36

Danforth, Asa

1548. Gates, Lillian F. ROADS, RIVALS, AND REBELLION: THE UNKNOWN STORY OF ASA DANFORTH, JR. *Ontario Hist. [Canada] 1984 76(3): 233-254.* Briefly discusses the family background of Asa Danforth before considering his activities in Upper Canada before the War of 1812. Describes problems as a land speculator, road builder, and agent for US interests. Some of his problems involved political partisanship. Danforth became embittered, and from about 1801, increasingly antagonistic to the government. He became involved in a plot against the government, the last major item of his involvement in the province. His later life is briefly mentioned. Primary sources, 100 notes. 1790-1805

Daniel, George Huett

1549. Bogle, James G. GEORGE HUETT DANIEL, ENGLISHMAN, AMERICAN, GEORGIAN. *Atlanta Historical Journal 1984-85 28(4): 51-60.* Presents a biography of Atlanta grocer George Huett Daniel, an Englishmen who built a business in Atlanta in the 1850's and was killed while serving as a Confederate soldier in the Civil War. 1816-65

Daniell, David Gonto

1550. Carswell, W. J. MOSES N. MCCALL, JR., AND DAVID GONTO DANIELL. *Viewpoints: Georgia Baptist Hist. 1980 7: 35-45.* 1808-85
*For abstract see **McCall, Moses N., Jr.***

Danne, Joseph

1551. Peters, Edmund A. JOSEPH DANNE: OKLAHOMA PLANT GENETICIST AND HIS TRIUMPH WHEAT. *Chronicles of Oklahoma 1981 59(1): 54-72.* Oklahoma's self-taught plant breeder Joseph Danne (1887-1959) developed several varieties of Triumph Wheat which today dominate southern plains wheat farming. The hybridization project was Danne's lifetime obsession and he worked constantly to improve the initial strain. An intensely private man, he rejected efforts to market the hybrid prematurely merely for the sake of fame and profits. He willingly wrote descriptive reports on this new wheat but closely guarded its secret until his death. Always a contributor to charities, he willed his property and seed stock to a foundation for orphans and other needy people. Based on Joseph Danne's correspondence; 5 photos, map, 48 notes. 1920-59

Danz, John

1552. Dembo, Jonathan. JOHN DANZ AND THE SEATTLE AMUSEMENT TRADES STRIKE, 1921-1935. *Pacific Northwest Q. 1980 71(4): 172-182.* Due to a recession and decline in movie attendance, Seattle movie theater owner John Danz laid off a number of employees in 1921. Orchestra members belonging to a musicians' union retaliated with strikes. Legal maneuvering by both sides left the issue unresolved. Confrontations became violent; Danz's automobile was destroyed by a bomb blast. Negotiations dragged on into the 1930's, when the National Recovery Administration ruled that Danz owed $20,000 in back salaries to some employees dismissed in 1929 for their union activity. In 1935 the issue was finally resolved outside the courts. Though the settlement favored the union position, the original musicians' group profited little from the compromise. Based on newspapers and Seattle Central Labor Council Papers; 5 photos, 47 notes. 1921-35

Darbinian, Reuben

1553. Tashjian, James H., ed. TWO NEWLY-DISCOVERED ENGLISH-LANGUAGE JOURNALS, OR WORKBOOKS, OF REUBEN DARBINIAN, LATE EDITOR-IN-CHIEF, HAIRENIK PUBLICATIONS. *Armenian Rev. 1980 33(3): 246-268; 1981 34(2): 147-173.* Part I. Provides a brief biography of Reuben Darbinian (1883-1931), who, after serving as Minister of Justice of Armenia in 1920, edited the *Hairenik Daily,* among other Hairenik publications, in Boston, and describes two of his posthumously discovered diaries, revealing political and personal attitudes, and the social implications of his stepson Simon Vratzian's suicide in Boston's Armenian community. Part II. Prints the text of Darbinian's first diary, and his only extant attempt to compose a literary work in English. Article to be continued. 1908-31

Darby, William Orlando

1554. King, Michael Julius. "William Orlando Darby: A Military Biography." Northern Illinois U. 1977. 344 pp. *DAI 1977 38(4): 2303-2304-A.* 1940's

Dare, David Daniel

1555. Barton, William H. DAVID D. DARE AND THE AMERICAN DREAM. *Ann. of Wyoming 1979 51(2): 8-23.* David Daniel Dare arrived in Cheyenne, Wyoming, about 1874 and became the town's postal clerk. During the following decade he amassed a small fortune through a number of business ventures, including photography, furniture, hardware, drugstore, and banking. Affluence followed him to San Diego, California, but in 1891 Dare's banking partnership collapsed and he escaped to Europe to elude the law. Based on primary sources; 8 photos, 99 notes. 1874-91

Dargan, Edwin Charles

1556. Finley, John Miller. "Edwin Charles Dargan: Baptist Denominationalist in a Changing Society." Southern Baptist Theological Seminary 1984. 227 pp. *DAI 1984 45(2): 602-A.* DA8411014 1880's-1910's

Darling, Jay Norwood "Ding."

1557. Lendt, David L. J. N. "DING" DARLING: THE FORMATIVE YEARS. *Ann. of Iowa 1979 45(2): 123-134.* Describes the childhood of Pulitzer Prize winning cartoonist Jay Norwood "Ding" Darling (1876-1962). The son of a much traveled Congregationalist minister, Darling spent his youth in Michigan, Indiana, Iowa, and South Dakota. His early encounters with waste and the destruction of wildlife explain his later commitment to conservation. Based on the Darling Papers, the University of Iowa Library; illus., 21 notes. 1876-1900

1558. Lendt, David L. "Ding: The Life of Jay Norwood Darling." Iowa State U. 1978. 364 pp. *DAI 1978 39(2): 704-A.* 1876-1962

Das, Taraknath

1559. Spector, Ronald. THE VERMONT EDUCATION OF TARAKNATH DAS: AN EPISODE IN BRITISH-AMERICAN-INDIAN RELATIONS. *Vermont Hist. 1980 48(2): 89-95.* Taraknath Das, a Bengali nationalist college student, fled India in 1906, and founded *Free Hindustan* while a US immigration interpreter in Vancouver, 1908. Forced out by British pressure, he spent a year at Norwich University in Northfield, Vermont, urging, wherever he could, Indian freedom from British rule. Again the British persuaded the administration to dismiss him. He nevertheless stayed in the United States as university professor and Indian apologist. 21 notes. 1906-09

Dasburg, Andrew

1560. Reich, Sheldon. ANDREW DASBURG: THE LATE YEARS. *Am. Art J. 1983 15(4): 21-44.* Andrew Dasburg, one of the founders of American modern art, suffered after 1937 from Addison's disease. He lived near Taos, New Mexico, from 1935 until his death. During the last three decades of his life he produced a great number of artworks, especially drawings. He developed a style, derived from Cézanne, in which he emphasized the underlying abstract geometrical shapes beneath representational landscapes. His last works, done with the aid of a straight edge, approach abstraction. He also did a series of lithographs. Photo, 31 plates, 24 notes. 1947-79

Davenport, James

1561. Stout, Harry S. and Onuf, Peter. JAMES DAVENPORT AND THE GREAT AWAKENING IN NEW LONDON. *J. of Am. Hist. 1983 70(3): 556-578.* On 6-7 March 1743, itinerant preacher James Davenport and his followers burned books and personal possessions in New London, Connecticut. Placed in the proper context of the Great Awakening, the event demonstrated Davenport's intense, anticlerical evangelism and the crowd's antisocial, antiestablishment attitude. The disturbance illustrates the revolutionary direction in which people were led by the passions of the Great Awakening. 51 notes. 1740-43

Davenport, Will

1562. Davenport, Will. GROWING UP, SORT OF, IN MIAMI, 1909-1915. *Tequesta 1980 40: 5-29.* Recollections of boyhood in Miami, beginning at 12 years of age. The author provides descriptions of fishing, flora and fauna, classmates, and school life in general. 1909-15

Davidoff, Leo

1563. Zollo, Richard P. DR. LEO DAVIDOFF: "A TREE FOR POSTERITY." *Essex Inst. Hist. Collections 1984 120(3): 164-178.* Examines the life of Leo Davidoff, an eminent neurosurgeon who made significant contributions to medical science, particularly to the detection and identification of neurological disorders. Traces his life from his birth in Latvia, the migration of his family to the United States in 1903, their residency in Chelsea and later in Salem in 1908, his education at Harvard, his service as the surgeon on the Byrd-MacMillan expedition to the Arctic in 1925, and his accomplishments, especially as founding father of Albert Einstein College of Medicine. 3 photos, 22 notes. 1898-1975

Davidson, David

1564. Davidson, David. GOOD NEIGHBORS. *Am. Heritage 1984 35(3): 104-109.* David Davidson, a veteran of the Office of Inter-American Affairs campaign to convince Latin Americans to support the Allies in World War II, tells of his efforts in Ecuador. Although the United States did not get very far in winning the hearts and minds of the Ecuadorians, perhaps they disliked the United States less than they had prior to the effort. 4 illus. 1941-45

Davidson, Donald

1565. Cook, Martha Emily. "Allen Tate and Donald Davidson: The Study of a Literary Friendship." Vanderbilt U. 1977. 330 pp. *DAI 1977 38(3): 1385-1386-A.* 1922-68

Davidson, Lucretia and Margaret

1566. Medoff, Jeslyn. DIVINE CHILDREN: THE DAVIDSON SISTERS AND THEIR MOTHER. *J. of the Rutgers U. Lib. 1984 46(1): 16-27.* Discusses the letters and notebooks of Lucretia and Margaret Davidson, American sister-poets of the early 19th century who died of consumption in adolescence. The Davidsons' sentimental and uplifting verse, combined with their invalidism and death, made them heroines of a posthumous literary cult led by their powerful mother, Margaret Miller Davidson. In a period of renewed interest in the cultural tradition of the American woman poet, these child-poets suggest how the female poetic gift became associated with death and the elegiac mode. Secondary sources; 20 notes. 1810-50

Davidson, Thomas

1567. Fagan, Susan Ruth. "Thomas Davidson: Dramatist of the Life of Learning." Rutgers U. 1980. 184 pp. *DAI 1981 41(9): 3939-A.* 8105218 ca 1870-1900

Davies, Arthur B.

1568. Dahlberg, Gertrude. ARTHUR B. DAVIES: 1862-1928. *Art & Antiques 1981 4(4): 42-49.* Biography of American artist Arthur B. Davies, known as "the father of modern art in America," focusing on the paradoxes of his romantic art, his promotion of modernism, and his alliance with the Ashcan Group. ca 1880-1928

Davies, David Jones and Gwen

1569. Davies, Phillips G. DAVID JONES AND GWEN DAVIES, MISSIONARIES IN NEBRASKA TERRITORY, 1853-1860. *Nebraska Hist. 1979 60(1): 77-91.* Documents the life and work of a missionary couple, David Jones Davies (1814-91) and his wife Gwen (1823-1910) whose missionary work among the Omaha Indians in eastern Nebraska spanned the years 1853-60. Both were born in Wales and furthered the work of the Calvinist Methodists in their missionary work. 1853-60

Davies, Joseph Edward

1570. MacLean, Elizabeth Kimball. JOSEPH E. DAVIES AND SOVIET-AMERICAN RELATIONS, 1941-1943. *Diplomatic Hist. 1980 4(1): 73-93.* The personal contacts which Joseph Edward Davies had established with Soviet leaders during his tenure as US ambassador to the USSR (1937-38) enabled him to serve as an unofficial personal liaison between the White House and the Soviet Embassy in Washington in the early years of World War II. Retaining the confidence of both sides, he was able to explain to each the views of the other. After a last official mission to Soviet Premier Joseph Stalin in 1943, he became less influential, for growing tensions between the two countries made a continuation of his role impossible. 56 notes. 1941-43

Davies, Samuel

1571. Greenberg, Michael. REVIVAL, REFORM, REVOLUTION: SAMUEL DAVIES & THE GREAT AWAKENING IN VIRGINIA. *Marxist Perspectives 1980 3(2): 102-119.* Reviews the role of Samuel Davies, Presbyterian minister, in the Great Awakening in Virginia during the 1740's-50's and the impact of his activities on individual perceptions of religion and southern abolitionists. 1740-59

Davies, William

1572. Jones, Arthur H. THE STORY OF WILLIAM DAVIES: TEXAS SHEPHERD. *West Texas Historical Association Year Book 1982 58: 29-48.* Reprints excerpts of letters written home by Welshman William Davies describing his experiences as a sheepherder and, later, owner of a sheep ranch during his 11-year sojourn in West Texas. 1879-91

Davis, Alexander Jackson

1573. Donoghue, John Cornelius. "Alexander Jackson Davis, Romantic Architect, 1803-1892." New York U. 1977. 446 pp. *DAI 1978 38(10): 6271-A.* 1829-92

Davis, Alice Brown

1574. Waldowski, Paula. ALICE BROWN DAVIS: A LEADER OF HER PEOPLE. *Chronicles of Oklahoma 1980-81 58(4): 455-463.* Alice Brown Davis (1852-1935) was born into an illustrious mixed-blood Seminole family which represented the pro-acculturation faction of the tribe. Educated by missionaries, she devoted her life to Indian education and served as superintendent of the Seminole girls' school called Emahaka Mission. Despite her emphasis upon teaching white ways to Indian children, she struggled to maintain total Indian control over the school but ultimately lost the battle. In 1922 she became the first woman to serve as principal chief of the Seminole Nation. 3 photos, 43 notes. 1870-1935

Davis, Benjamin J.

1575. Matthews, John M. BLACK NEWSPAPERMEN AND THE BLACK COMMUNITY IN GEORGIA, 1890-1930. *Georgia Hist. Q. 1984 68(3): 356-381.* Discusses the activities, roles, opinions, and personal styles of newspapermen John H. Deveaux and Sol C. Johnson of the Savannah *Tribune,* and Benjamin J. Davis of the Atlanta *Independent.* Not only were they journalists, but they were involved in Republican politics, business, fraternal societies, and such organizations as the NAACP. Based on newspapers and other primary and secondary sources; 77 notes. 1890-1930

Davis, Benjamin, Jr.

1576. Horwitz, Gerry. BENJAMIN DAVIS, JR., AND THE AMERICAN COMMUNIST PARTY: A STUDY IN RACE AND POLITICS. *UCLA Hist. J. 1983 4: 92-107.* Traces the career of Benjamin Davis, Jr., a leading official in the American Communist Party in the 1940's-50's. Born to a black middle-class Georgia family and educated at Amherst and Harvard Law School, Davis was radicalized when he represented Angelo Herndon in the 1930's during Georgia's political prosecution of Herndon. Davis joined the American Communist Party and became an organizer rather than an intellectual revolutionary. During World War II, Davis followed the party line of defeating fascism before attacking domestic discrimination. Elected to the New York City Council, he found it difficult to reconcile his party membership with elective office. He gained political strength as a Democrat, but his Communist connections brought increasing unpopularity. Convicted of violating the Smith Act, he served a term in prison. Davis remained active in Communist affairs until his death in 1964, balancing party allegiance and political activism. 43 notes. 1933-64

Davis, Donald Watson

1577. Saum, Lewis O. FROM VERMONT TO WHOOP-UP COUNTRY; SOME LETTERS OF D. W. DAVIS, 1867-1878. *Montana 1985 35(3): 56-71.* In 1867, Donald Watson Davis left his home in Vermont, joined the army, and was sent to Fort Benton, Montana. When his three-year enlistment was over, he remained in Montana to work for I. G. Baker & Company, one of the territory's largest merchandise houses. He became manager of Baker's northern trade, and assisted the Northwest Mounted Police in building and governing Fort Calgary and Fort Macleod in Alberta. Reprints Davis's letters, dated 1867-78, depicting the acquisitiveness of post-Civil War Westerners. Characterized by the language of chance and gambling rather than religion and providence, the letters reveal large cultural forces that were altering the American mood during the last half of the 19th century. Based on the D. W. Davis letters in the Lyman Stuart Papers, 1806-81, Accession 1283, Cornell University Libraries, and on secondary sources; 5 photos, map, 12 notes. 1867-78

Davis, Edgar B.

1578. Froh, George Riley. "Edgar B. Davis: Wildcatter Extraordinary." Texas A & M U. 1980. 243 pp. *DAI 1981 41(10): 4477-A.* 8108009 1919-51

Davis, Elmer Ellsworth

1579. Lale, Max S. "BUT DAVIS IS A HUSTLER. . . . " *Red River Valley Hist. Rev. 1980 5(2): 43-54.* Elmer Ellsworth Davis (1861-1939), born in Maine, moved to Denison (Texas) in 1894, ran a livery stable, and became a successful automobile salesman in 1912, the same year he was elected street and fire commissioner of Denison. 1894-1939

Davis, Elwood Craig

1580. Graber, Paul Nelson. "A Biography of Elwood Craig Davis: Philosopher, Educator, Scholar." U. of Utah 1979. 198 pp. *DAI 1979 40(6): 3185-A.* 1934-79

Davis, George

1581. Moulton, Elizabeth. REMEMBERING GEORGE DAVIS. *Virginia Q. Rev. 1979 55(2): 284-295.* Moulton reminisces about George Davis, associate and fiction editor of *Mademoiselle,* whom she first met as a guest editor in 1945. She was a member of Davis's staff during 1946-48. Davis, then 40, knew "how words worked" and "how a page should look." She admits much is not known about Davis, but describes his personal life, his interest in pets, and his penchant for gossip. He was a gifted and patient editor who left *Mademoiselle* in 1948 and died in 1957. "Armies of now middle-aged authors are in business because of George." 1945-57

Davis, Harold Lenoir

1582. Corning, Howard M. ALL THE WORDS ON THE PAGES.
I: H. L. DAVIS. *Oregon Hist. Q. 1972 73(4): 293-331.* ca 1915-70
For abstract see ***Alexander, Charles***

Davis, Henrietta Vinton

1583. Seraile, William. HENRIETTA VINTON DAVIS AND THE GARVEY MOVEMENT. *Afro-Americans in New York Life and Hist. 1983 7(2): 7-24.* After a distinguished stage career, Henrietta Vinton Davis formed a stormy alliance with Marcus Garvey and his racial pride movement, which lasted until Davis's death in 1941. 1919-41

Davis, James H.

1584. McWhiney, Grady and Mills, Gary B. JIMMIE DAVIS AND HIS MUSIC: AN APPRECIATION. *J. of Am. Culture 1983 6(2): 54-57.* Famed as an entertainer and politician, singer-composer James H. Davis has been a dominant figure in rural folk music since 1929 and in gospel music since the 1950's. 1929-83

Davis, Jeff

1585. Niswonger, Richard Leverne. A STUDY IN SOUTHERN DEMAGOGUERY: JEFF DAVIS OF ARKANSAS. *Arkansas Hist. Q. 1980 39(2): 114-124.* Discusses the political career of Jeff Davis (d. 1913), Arkansas governor (1901-07) and US Senator (1907-13). He brought a new style to Arkansas politics by appealing to the common people. 26 notes. 1899-1913

Davis, Jefferson

1586. McWhiney, Grady. JEFFERSON DAVIS: THE UNFORGIVEN. *J. of Mississippi Hist. 1980 42(2): 113-127.* Analyzes why Jefferson Davis became and would remain to most northerners the greatest villain of the Confederate experience. Although Robert E. Lee and other prominent rebels were soon transformed into national heroes, Davis failed to receive a reprieve, even after his death. Davis's support of the symbols of the southern cause—slavery, states' rights, and secession—may be a partial answer to the continuing castigation of the former Confederate president. Davis's openness in refusing to admit guilt or regret for his actions in his speeches, letters, and interviews may have discouraged northern charity and forgiveness. Even his appeals for a history of the South written by and for southerners and his desire to preserve the South's heritage and deeds made him unacceptable to scientific historians. Indeed, the enigma of Jefferson Davis has defied, for more than 100 years, both northern and southern historians' efforts to fully understand him. 1861-1935

1587. Shelton, William Allen. "The Young Jefferson Davis, 1808-1846." U. of Kentucky 1977. 295 pp. *DAI 1978 39(6): 3782-A.* 1808-46

1588. Vandiver, Frank E. JEFFERSON DAVIS—LEADER WITHOUT LEGEND. *J. of Southern Hist. 1977 43(1): 3-18.* Jefferson Davis has been without legend. Davis's image has been firmly shaped by Edward A. Pollard's biased view of the ex-Confederate President as the central reason for Southern failure. However, recent consideration of Davis' willingness to move toward nationalism, of his ability to rise above the constitution, may produce a legend of Davis as a gentleman revolutionary. Based on primary and secondary sources; 38 notes. ca 1861-65

Davis, John Charles, Sr.

1589. Palmieri, Anthony. JOHN C. DAVIS SR.: PORTRAIT OF A ROCKY MOUNTAIN DRUG WHOLESALING PIONEER. *Ann. of Wyoming 1983 55(2): 33-35.* John Charles Davis, Sr. arrived in Wyoming during 1872 and worked four years as a commissary clerk and telegraph operator for the Union Pacific Railroad. In 1879 he joined the Rawlins, Wyoming, mercantile firm of J. W. Hugus Company and helped make it the largest chain store and distributor of general merchandise in the Rocky Mountain area. Davis quickly became a leading banking and business leader in Rawlins and served as mayor. By 1901 he had relocated in Denver, Colorado, and established the Davis-Bridaham Drug Company, a diversified business which continued to thrive even after Davis's death in a train wreck. Based on Colorado newspapers; 5 photos, 8 notes. 1872-1909

Davis, John W.

1590. Abrams, Richard M. OF LAWYERS, PRIVILEGE, AND POWER. *Rev. in Am. Hist. 1975 3(1): 105-113.* Review article prompted by *The Autobiographical Notes of Charles Evans Hughes*, edited by David J. Danelski and Joseph S. Tulchin (Cambridge, Mass.: Harvard U. Pr., 1973), and William H. Harbaugh's *Lawyer's Lawyer: The Life of John W. Davis* (New York: Oxford U. Pr., 1973), biographies of two men prominent in law in the first half of the 20th-century. 20c

Davis, Jonathan

1591. Wesley, Charles H. JONATHAN DAVIS AND THE RISE OF BLACK FRATERNAL ORGANIZATIONS. *Crisis 1977 84(3): 112-118.* Jonathan Davis (1820-74), an outstanding free black physician and druggist, was active in civil rights and fraternal organizations. He was born free, was self-educated, and helped organize Prince Hall Freemasonry as it expanded. He formed and organized chapters in the third quarter of the 19th century. 1840-74

Davis, Joseph S.

1592. Engelbourg, Saul. JOSEPH S. DAVIS: "THE EVOLUTION OF ONE ECONOMIST'S WORK". *Hist. of Pol. Econ. 1980 12(2): 243-266.* Examines the life and work of American economist Joseph S. Davis and his contributions to the study of agricultural economy, as well as his directorship of Stanford University's Food Research Institute, 1922-75. 1922-75

Davis, Katharine Bement

1593. Barnes, Joseph W. KATHARINE B. DAVIS AND THE WORKINGMAN'S MODEL HOME OF 1893. *Rochester Hist. 1981 43(1): 1-20.* Brief biography of Katharine Bement Davis of Rochester, New York, focusing on her exhibit, the New York State Workingman's Model Home, at the World's Columbian Exposition (Chicago, 1893), and gives some background on the exposition itself. 1893

Davis, Levi

1594. Curran, Nathaniel B. LEVI DAVIS, ILLINOIS' THIRD AUDITOR. *J. of the Illinois State Hist. Soc. 1978 71(1): 2-12.* Levi Davis (1808-97), a lawyer, began his career as a clerk to the state auditor. He was promoted in 1835, in the midst of the passage of many state-financed schemes for internal improvements. He served until 1844 and then retired to his home at Alton, pursuing private law practice until his death. 4 illus., 52 notes. 1835-44

Davis, Natalie Zemon

1595. Davis, Natalie Zemon; Coppin, Judy and Harding, Robert, interviewers; Verni, Barbara, transl. INTERVISTA A NATALIE ZEMON DAVIS [Interview with Natalie Zemon Davis]. *Memoria: Rivista di Storia delle Donne [Italy] 1983 (9): 79-93.* In an interview, Natalie Zemon Davis talks about her personal life and politics, as well as historical methodology, Marxist history, and women's history. 8 notes. 1940-84

Davis, Nelson H.

1596. Miller, Darlis A. THE ROLE OF THE ARMY INSPECTOR IN THE SOUTHWEST: NELSON H. DAVIS IN NEW MEXICO AND ARIZONA, 1863-1873. *New Mexico Hist. Rev. 1984 59(2): 137-164.* Nelson H. Davis supervised, inspected, and reported army conditions in the Southwest. Despite troubles with Mimbres Apaches, alleged military corruption concerning food-supply contracts, living conditions in the garrisons, and charges of mismanagement, Davis ably fulfilled his frontier military-inspection duties. Photo, 81 notes. 1863-73

Davis, Owen Gould

1597. Wann, Jack Kendall. "The Career of Owen Davis (1874-1956) in the American Theatre." Louisiana State U. and Agric. and Mechanical Coll. 1978. 242 pp. *DAI 1979 39(11): 6401-6402-A.* ca 1900-56

Davis, Owen W., Jr.

1598. Eastman, Joel W. ENTREPRENEURSHIP AND OBSOLESCENCE: OWEN W. DAVIS, JR. AND THE KATAHDIN CHARCOAL IRON COMPANY, 1876-1890. *Maine Hist. Soc. Q. 1977 17(2): 69-84.* Describes the efforts of Owen W. Davis, Jr., a representative of the new managerial class, to save the Katahdin Charcoal Iron Company in northern Maine from going out of business during 1876-88. New turbine water wheels, higher furnace stacks, new charcoal kilns, housing improvements for workers and new roasting techniques for high sulphide iron ore were used to no avail. Plant operations were stopped in 1890. 42 notes. 1876-90

Davis, Perry Eugene

1599. Gossard, Wayne H., Jr., ed. LIFE ON THE TRAIL: THE 1894 DIARY OF PERRY EUGENE DAVIS. *Colorado Heritage 1981 (1): 23-35.* Real cowboy life did not correspond with that of legend. The 1894 diary of Perry Eugene Davis describing his experiences on a horse-drive from South Dakota to Texas helps set the record straight, expressing the monotony, hard work, and the dangers of the drive. It also reveals the difficulties of finding food and water and crossing areas where fences had been built. 4 photos, 24 notes. 1894

Davis, Richard Beale

1600. Arner, Robert D. A TRIBUTE TO RICHARD BEALE DAVIS. *Early Am. Literature 1977 12(2): 105-106.* The long and distinguished career of Richard Beale Davis, of the University of Tennessee, in early American literature, is given tribute by being awarded the Honored Scholar of Early American Literature for 1977. A brief bibliography of Davis's writings highlights his contribution to the field. 1935-77

Davis, Richard Harding

1601. Greulich, Kathleen M. A PHILADELPHIA FAMILY AT THE "CENTRE OF THE UNIVERSE." *Pennsylvania Heritage 1981 7(1): 18-22.* Celebrated war correspondent and reporter Richard Harding Davis (1864-1916) of Philadelphia covered the coronation of Czar Nicholas, the Spanish-American War, the Greco-Turkish War, the Boer and Belgian Congo War, the Russo-Japanese War, World War I, and other events. ca 1890-1916

1602. Riser, Jimmie Eugene. "Richard Harding Davis: The Early Years of His Career, 1886-1892." Florida State U. 1983. 448 pp. *DAI 1984 44(11): 3383-A.* DA8402518 1886-92

Davis, Richard L.

1603. Brier, Stephen. THE CAREER OF RICHARD L. DAVIS RECONSIDERED: UNPUBLISHED CORRESPONDENCE FROM THE *NATIONAL LABOR TRIBUNE.Labor Hist. 1980 21(3): 420-429.* Richard L. Davis (1864-1900), a black and a coal miner from Ohio, became a leader in the United Mine Workers of America in the 1890's. The letters presented here show that, while critical of the union's treatment of black miners, Davis never wavered from his belief in trade unionism as the only vehicle for black Americans to attain "final liberation." Based on Davis's letters to the *National Labor Tribune;* 10 notes. ca 1890-1900

Davis, Sam

1604. Zanjani, Sally Springmeyer. THE UNITED STATES GOVERNMENT MEETS THE NEVADA MULE: THE HUMOR OF SAM DAVIS. *Nevada Hist. Soc. Q. 1980 23(1): 36-42.* The editor of the Carson City, Nevada, *Morning Appeal* during 1879-98, Sam Davis (b. 1850), abandoned journalism and took part in Nevada state politics until 1910. Subsequently he wrote fiction and produced a history of Nevada. His contemporaries, however, most praised him as a humorist. Reprints here one of Davis's humorous writings, which he first published in the 10 February 1889 issue of the San Francisco *Daily Examiner.* 6 notes. 1889

Davis, Thomas Clayton

1605. Ward, Norman, ed. A PRINCE ALBERTAN IN PEIPING: THE LETTERS OF T.C. DAVIS. *Int. J. [Canada] 1974-75 30(1): 24-33.* Discusses and presents the letters of Canadian diplomat Thomas Clayton Davis during his stay in China, 1946-49. 1946-49

Davis, Varina Howell

1606. Dolensky, Suzanne T. VARINA HOWELL DAVIS, 1889 TO 1906: THE YEARS ALONE. *Journal of Mississippi History 1985 47(2): 90-109.* Biographers have largely ignored the years of Varina Howell Davis after the death of her husband, Jefferson Davis. She was active after 1889 both as a literary figure and a planter, and tried to shape the image of her husband through her writings and by burying him in Richmond, Virginia. In her attempts to manage Jefferson Davis's image, as well as her departure from the South to New York City to develop her literary career, she became involved in controversy with Mississippians and those faithful to the Southern cause. Based on Varina Howell Davis letters and papers in the Library of Congress, the Mississippi Department of Archives and History, Brockenbrough Library in Richmond, and the University of Alabama; 69 notes. 1889-1906

Davis, William Watts Hart

1607. Van Ness, Christine M. and Van Ness, John R. W. W. H. DAVIS: NEGLECTED FIGURE OF NEW MEXICO'S EARLY TERRITORIAL PERIOD. *J. of the West 1977 16(3): 68-74.* William Watts Hart Davis (27 July 1820-26 December 1910) was in New Mexico 1853-57 as US Attorney General for the Territory, Acting Governor, Superintendent of Indian Affairs, and Superintendent of Public Buildings. He satisfied his historical curiosity by translating many of the old Spanish documents left in the Governor's Palace in Santa Fe. Based on this treasure of historical data and on his own observations, he provided some of the earliest and most useful histories of New Mexico: *El Gringo: Or, New Mexico and Her People* (1857) and *The Spanish Conquest of New Mexico* (1869). Returning to Pennsylvania, he bought and edited the Doylestown *Democrat,* kept active in politics, and served in the Civil War. Based on documents in the Davis Collection of the the Mercer Museum (Doylestown, Pennsylvania) and on other primary and secondary sources; photo, 3 illus., 27 notes. 1853-69

Davison, Archibald Thompson

1608. Tovey, David George. "Archibald Thompson Davison: Harvard Musician and Scholar." U. of Michigan 1979. 280 pp. *DAI 1980 40(10): 5244-5245-A.* 1909-54

Dawes, Charles G.

1609. Goedeken, Edward Adolph. "Charles G. Dawes in War and Peace, 1917-1922." U. of Kansas 1984. 328 pp. *DAI 1985 46(4):1069-A.* DA8513749 1917-22

Dawes, Thomas

1610. Detwiller, Frederic C. THOMAS DAWES: BOSTON'S PATRIOT ARCHITECT. *Old-Time New England 1977 68(1-2): 1-18.* Prominent mason-architect Thomas Dawes (1731-1809) of Boston, Massachusetts, besides being well-known for his architecture, was also active in politics during the American Revolution and the Federal Era. 1750's-1809

Dawidowicz, Lucy

1611. Cole, Diane. LUCY DAWIDOWICZ—A PROFILE. *Present Tense 1983 11(1): 22-25.* Traces Lucy Dawidowicz's life and career as one of the world's best-known historians of Jewish culture. 1937-83

Dawson, John William

1612. Angrave, James. WILLIAM DAWSON, GEORGE GRANT AND THE LEGACY OF SCOTTISH HIGHER EDUCATION. *Queen's Q. [Canada] 1975 82(1): 77-91.* Discusses the careers of two Nova Scotians, John William Dawson and George Monro Grant, both of whom studied in Scotland and subsequently made notable contributions to higher education in Canada. The nature of these men's studies at the University of Edinburgh and the way their curriculum influenced their own teaching are discussed in detail. Both became principals of major Canadian universities and stand among the foremost of the country's 19th-century educators. Based on printed and manuscript sources; 40 notes. 19c

1613. Cornell, John F. FROM CREATION TO EVOLUTION: SIR WILLIAM DAWSON AND THE IDEA OF DESIGN IN THE NINETEENTH CENTURY. *J. of the Hist. of Biology [Netherlands] 1983 16(1): 137-170.* Sir John William Dawson was Canada's leading critic of Darwinism. His opposition was based on the common linkage of special creation and design against the "unity" of natural selection and evolution. When these linkages fell apart, as they did later in the 19th century, Dawson softened his opposition to Darwinian concepts; he did not identify evolution with natural selection. 105 notes. 1840-1900

Dawson, Joseph Martin

1614. Garrett, James Leo, Jr. JOSEPH MARTIN DAWSON: PASTOR, AUTHOR, DENOMINATIONAL LEADER, SOCIAL ACTIVIST. *Baptist Hist. and Heritage 1979 14(4): 7-15.* Joseph Martin Dawson (1879-1973) attended Baylor University in Texas, became a Baptist pastor while still a student, authored 12 books, was a denominational leader for Baptist institutions and boards, and was known as a social activist. 1879-1973

Dawson, Sarah Morgan

1615. Clark, E. Culpepper. SARAH MORGAN AND FRANCIS DAWSON: RAISING THE WOMAN QUESTION IN RECONSTRUCTION SOUTH CAROLINA. *South Carolina Hist. Mag. 1980 81(1): 8-23.* Analyzes the feminist thought and life of Sarah Ida Fowler Morgan, who published editorials in the Charleston *News and Courier,* which was edited by her future husband, Francis Warrington Dawson. 1870's

Dawson, William

1616. Hockman, Dan M. COMMISSARY WILLIAM DAWSON AND THE ANGLICAN CHURCH IN VIRGINIA, 1743-1752. *Historical Magazine of the Protestant Episcopal Church 1985 54(2): 125-149.* William Dawson served the last nine years of his life as commissary of the Anglican Church in Virginia. By wielding the combined power of his ecclesiastical office as commissary and his civil office as a member of the council, he did much to promote the welfare and interests of the Anglican Church in Virginia. As commissary, councillor, and as president of William and Mary College, Dawson emerged as an important and influential figure in colonial Virginia. Based on the Fulham Palace Manuscripts, *Historical Collections Relating to the American Colonial Church,* edited by William Stevens Perry, and on secondary sources; 137 notes. 1743-52

Dawson, William Levi

1617. Malone, Mark Hugh. "William Levi Dawson: American Music Educator." Florida State U. 1981. 182 pp. *DAI 1982 42(11): 4757-A.* DA8209928 20c

Day, Clarence

1618. Knopf, Alfred A. RANDOM RECOLLECTIONS OF A PUBLISHER. *Massachusetts Hist. Soc. Pro. 1961 73: 92-103.* 1901-61
For abstract see ***Cather, Willa***

Day, Dorothy

1619. Roberts, Nancy L. JOURNALISM FOR JUSTICE: DOROTHY DAY AND THE *CATHOLIC WORKER.*- *Journalism History 1983 10(1-2): 2-9.* Discusses the life and influence of American social activist Dorothy Day and the *Catholic Worker,* the muckraking newspaper she founded with French "hobo-philosopher" Peter Maurin in 1933 and published, edited, and wrote for until the late 1970's. 1933-83

1620. Statnick, Roger Andrew. "Dorothy Day's Religious Conversion: A Study in Biographical Theology." U. of Notre Dame 1983. 377 pp. *DAI 1983 44(3): 791-A.* DA8315554 20c

Day, Frank Miles

1621. Keebler, Patricia Lawson Heintzelman. "The Life and Work of Frank Miles Day." U. of Delaware 1980. 505 pp. *DAI 1980 41(3): 833-834-A.* DA8019938 1887-1918

Day, Fred Holland

1622. Fanning, Patricia J. FRED HOLLAND DAY: ECCENTRIC AESTHETE. *New England Q. 1980 53(2): 230-236.* Sketches Boston bohemian Fred Holland Day's (1864-1933) ideal of beauty, his interest in John Keats and Keatsiana, his publishing firm of Copeland & Day in the 1890's, his artistic photography in the 1890's and 1900's, and his self-imposed seclusion after 1918. Secondary sources; 4 notes. 1885-1933

Day, Hermione

1623. Tinling, Marion. HERMIONE DAY AND *THE HESPERIAN. California History 1980-81 59(4): 282-289.* A profile of Hermione Day (1826-65), editor of *The Hesperian,* a literary magazine for women, 1858-62. Little is known of Day's life; born in Buffalo, New York, she was married twice. She came to California around 1852 and after several years began working on *The Hesperian.* The magazine featured articles of interest to women, including poetry and essays, many by women. Day wrote biographical sketches of California pioneers. Her daughter's poor health caused Day's departure from San Francisco in 1862. *The Hesperian* ceased to be a women's magazine, and in 1863 its name was changed to *Pacific Monthly.* Day died in Paris at age 38. Photos, 11 notes. 1826-65

Day, Sam (family)

1624. Trafzer, Clifford E. SAM DAY AND HIS BOYS: GOOD NEIGHBORS TO THE NAVAJOS. *J. of Arizona Hist. 1977 18(1): 1-22.* Sam Day (1845-1925) and his family moved to Arizona in 1883 where he was commissioned to survey an extension of the Navajo reservation. In initial contacts he established mutual respect with the Navajo Indians who almost universally distrusted whites. Later, the Days moved to a trading post where they "became part of the Navajo life pattern" and devoted their energies helping the Navajo to achieve self-sufficiency. They found markets for Navajo sheep, wool, cattle, blankets, and jewelry. In return they brought in wagons, farm tools, household items, and clothing. A grandson is a tribal official today. 4 illus., 50 notes. 1883-1977

Dean, Harry Foster

1625. Burger, John S. CAPTAIN HARRY DEAN: PAN-NEGRO-NATIONALIST IN SOUTH AFRICA. *Int. J. of African Hist. Studies 1976 9(1): 83-90.* Harry Foster Dean (1864-1935), a black sea captain, was the only Afro-American to attempt the control of land in South Africa for the ultimate reestablishment of a black nation. Primary and secondary sources; 20 notes. 1864-1935

Dean, Walter B., Jr.

1626. Morrow, Delores. FORSYTH'S BOOSTER, WALTER DEAN. *Montana 1985 35(4): 68-77.* In 1905 Walter B. Dean, Jr., moved to Forsyth, Montana, to work as a jeweler. In 1919 he purchased a store and remained in Forsyth until his death. Dean was an ardent booster and launched a variety of ventures to promote new products and Forsyth. His camera was his primary promotional tool as he captured local happenings. From 1918 to 1934, he concentrated on photographing developments that promised to bring economic prosperity to the Forsyth area, especially coal and oil prospects. He printed his pictures as postcards, which he sold in his store. Based on the Walter B. Dean, Jr., Collection, Montana Historical Society, Helena; Forsyth *Times* accounts, and secondary souces; 14 photos, 12 notes. 1905-34

Deane, Silas

1627. Anderson, Dennis Kent and Anderson, Godfrey Tryggve. THE DEATH OF SILAS DEANE: ANOTHER OPINION. *New England Quarterly 1984 57(1): 98-105.* Silas Deane was a representative to the Continental Congress from Connecticut, worked as a confidential agent in France in 1776, and enlisted the aid of military men such as Lafayette, Steuben, and Pulaski in the American Revolution. Deane was later accused of corruption by the Continental Congress and began to write disparaging letters about the revolution, urging reconciliation with England. On 23 September 1789, after living six years in England, Deane died on board an American ship while waiting for it to leave port and sail for America. Deane's physician, Dr. Edward Bancroft, supported the idea that Deane had taken his own life, and this view was widely accepted for the next few years. Nonetheless, some have maintained that Dr. Bancroft, an expert in the natural history and poisons of Guiana, did him in. A more careful review of Deane's letters, however, indicates that he suffered from a chronic pulmonary condition, probably tuberculosis, and a compelling case can be made that this chronic condition helped bring about a cerebral hemorrhage that caused his death. 20 notes. 1781-89

1628. Goldstein, Kalman. SILAS DEANE: PREPARATION FOR RASCALITY. *Historian 1980 43(1): 75-97.* An investigation of Silas Deane's early life in Connecticut, hitherto ignored, provides a new understanding of Deane's perplexing American Revolution diplomatic career. His later reaction to crises and controversies were prefigured and influenced by events of his early life. The Samuel Tozer case illustrates how Deane's disingenuous business career forecast future wartime controversies. To Deane every criticism was a challenge; every challenge provoked anxiety, alienation, and rebuff. Primary sources; 69 notes. 1750-89

deAngeli, Marguerite

1629. Gaugler, Nancy K., ed. CONVERSATION WITH MARGUERITE DE ANGELI. *Pennsylvania Folklife 1982 31(3): 109-114.* Biography of author and illustrator Marguerite de Angeli, winner of the Newbery Medal in 1949 for her children's book, *The Door in the Wall,* followed by a conversation between de Angeli and Mary Alice Wheeler on children's literature about the Pennsylvania Dutch. 1889-1975

deAngulo, Jaime

1630. Leeds-Hurwitz, Wendy. "Jaime de Angulo: An Intellectual Biography." U. of Pennsylvania 1983. 553 pp. *DAI 1984 44(7): 2214-A.* DA8326303 1920's

Dearborn, Elizabeth

1631. Sanborn, George F., Jr. ELIZABETH DEARBORN OF NORTH HAMPTON. *New England Historical and Genealogical Register 1985 139(Jan): 50-56.* Based on available genealogical records, reconstructs the probable life history of Elizabeth Dearborn (1717-49), daughter of Samuel and Mercy Batchelder Dearborn of North Hampton, New Hampshire. Also lists information on her descendants. 1717-50's

Deas, John Sullivan

1632. Ralston, H. Keith. JOHN SULLIVAN DEAS: A BLACK ENTREPRENEUR IN BRITISH COLUMBIA SALMON CANNING. *BC Studies [Canada] 1976-77 (32): 64-78.* In 1862 black tinsmith John Sullivan Deas migrated from California to Victoria, British Columbia. In 1871 he was engaged to make cans for the new salmon industry on the Fraser River, and he soon became the owner of a cannery supplying an English market. His seven continuous and successful seasons established Deas as one of the founders of the canning industry in the province. 75 notes. 1862-78

DeBrahm, William Gerard

1633. Damon, S. Foster. DE BRAHM, ALCHEMIST. *Ambix [Great Britain] 1977 24(2): 77-88.* Sketches the life of John William Gerar DeBrahm (ca. 1717-99). His "active, outward life" involved him in worldly affairs. Under this was an intense, meditative life in which he tried to reconcile science and mysticism. DeBrahm's view of his own life and some of his writings are discussed. Emphasizes DeBrahm's alchemical work and suggests that he anticipated the thought of General Hitchcock and other 19th-century mystics. Also summarizes the main points of DeBrahm's theories. 27 notes. ca 1717-99

1634. DeVorsey, Louis, Jr. A COLORFUL RESIDENT OF BRITISH ST. AUGUSTINE: WILLIAM GERARD DE BRAHM. *Escribano 1975 12(1): 1-24.* Biographical sketch of William Gerard De Brahm concentrates on his service to Great Britain as the Surveyor-General in East Florida, 1765-71. 1765-71

Debs, Eugene V.

1635. Stevens, Errol Wayne. THE PAPERS OF EUGENE V. DEBS: A REVIEW ESSAY. *Indiana Mag. of Hist. 1984 80(3): 264-270.* Reviews *The Papers of Eugene V. Debs, 1834-1945: A Guide to the Microfilm Edition* (1983), edited by J. Robert Constantine, which provides a brief biographical sketch of socialist Debs and discusses biographies of him written since the 1910's. The guide also provides a bibliography and checklist to the microfilm collection, which consists of 23 reels and is divided into three series: scrapbooks, correspondence, and published writings and speeches. 1855-1926

DeCamp, Ralph E.

1636. Lang, William L.; Rackley, Barbara F.; and Morrow, Lory. RALPH E. DECAMP: ARTIST AS PHOTOGRAPHER. *Montana 1979 29(3): 50-55.* Artist Ralph E. DeCamp used the photograph as an artistic medium. Provides brief biographical information on deCamp and reproduces nine of his photographs taken between 1900 and 1913 in central and western Montana. Photographs came from 350 DeCamp glass plate negatives donated to the Montana Historical Society in 1978 by Dan Hilger. 1900-13

Decatur, Stephen

1637. Cook, Edward M. STEPHEN DECATUR: THE MAN WHO LOVED HONOR MORE. *Daughters of the Am. Revolution Mag. 1979 113(5): 532-535.* Gives a brief biography of naval officer Stephen Decatur (1779-1820), lauding him for his heroism, particularly against Tripoli in 1803-04, the British in the War of 1812, and Algeria in 1815. 1779-1820

deCleyre, Voltairine

1638. McKinley, Blaine. "THE QUAGMIRES OF NECESSITY": AMERICAN ANARCHISTS AND DILEMMAS OF VOCATION. *Am. Q. 1982 34(5): 503-523.* American anarchists faced conflicts and contradictions in trying to remain true to their principles while making a living. These conflicts can be seen affecting the lives of four prominent anarchists: Harry Kelly, W. S. Van Valkenburgh, Voltairine de Cleyre, and Emma Goldman. Based on the Joseph Ishill Papers, the Labadie Collection, and other primary sources; 53 notes. 1893-1920

Deems, Charles Force

1639. Sutherland, Daniel E. CHARLES FORCE DEEMS AND THE *WATCHMAN:* AN EARLY ATTEMPT AT POST-CIVIL WAR SECTIONAL RECONCILIATION. *North Carolina Hist. Rev. 1980 57(4): 410-426.* Charles Force Deems (1820-93), a North Carolina resident since 1840, spent the year immediately after the Civil War in New York City, publishing a weekly newspaper aimed at reconciliation between North and South. He, like a number of other unionist southerners, moved North after the war to improve relations between sections. *The Watchman,* a family enterprise for the year it existed, featured stories and information on contemporary politics, literature, religion, agriculture, and business. The articles were usually slanted toward the southern view; advertising was either aimed at a southern audience or taken out by sympathetic southerners. *The Watchman* appealed primarily to transplanted southerners. Financial problems, lack of support, and bad timing contributed to the paper's demise on 5 January 1867. But it did raise the consciousness of northerners to the problems facing the post-war South. Based on Deems's *Autobiography,* copies of *The Watchman,* and scattered family papers; 9 illus., 54 notes. 1865-67

1640. Weaver, John B. CHARLES F. DEEMS: THE MINISTRY AS PROFESSION IN NINETEENTH-CENTURY AMERICA. *Methodist Hist. 1983 21(3): 156-168.* Presents a biography of Charles Force Deems, whose career illustrates the increasing professionalization of the Methodist ministry. 55 notes. 1840's-80's

Defoe, Daniel

1641. Vania, Rhoda Jal. "Defoe and the American Experience." Claremont Graduate Sch. 1977. 410 pp. *DAI 1977 38(3): 1398-A.* 1698-1731

deForest, Robert Weeks

1642. Hijiya, James A. FOUR WAYS OF LOOKING AT A PHILANTHROPIST: A STUDY OF ROBERT WEEKS DE FOREST. *Pro. of the Am. Phil. Soc. 1980 124(6): 404-418.* Hailed as the "first citizen of New York," Robert Weeks de Forest (1848-1931), trained in law, made his most notable contributions in philanthropy. He served 43 years as president of the Charity Organization Society of New York, and 17 years as president of the Metropolitan Museum of

Art. He held many other positions in local and national charitable organizations. He also was responsible for setting up the Russell Sage Foundation. Interprets his philanthropy from four perspectives: as a Progressive, as a Conservative, as a Democrat, and as an Early American. Based on de Forest's letters in many collections, his published articles, and the Metropolitan Museum Archives; 69 notes. 1880-1931

DeForest Family

1643. Hijiya, James A. "The De Forests: Three American Lives." Cornell U. 1977. 501 pp. *DAI 1978 38(11): 6893-A.* 19c-20c

DeGolyer, Everett L., Jr.

1644. Dubin, Arthur D. MEMORIAL NOTICE: EVERETT L. DE GOLYER, JR., 1923-1977. *Railroad Hist. 1978 (138): 102.* Everett L. DeGolyer, Jr., was a historian of railroads and transportation. 1923-77

DeGruy, Antoine Valentin

1645. Ekberg, Carl J. ANTOINE VALENTIN DE GRUY: EARLY MISSOURI EXPLORER. *Missouri Hist. Rev. 1982 76(2): 136-150.* Antoine Valentin De Gruy was a young officer who came to Fort de Chartres near St. Louis in 1741. The French had been mining lead in Missouri since the 1720's. This is the report of two expeditions to Missouri he made in 1743 to verify Indian reports of new lead deposits. Provides information on French mining and smelting techniques. Based on the Liste des Officiers de la Louisiane, Archives Nationales, Paris, and on the Archives of the Louisiana State Museum, New Orleans; illus., 2 maps, 45 notes. 1743

Dehn, Adolph

1646. Cox, Richard W. ADOLF DEHN: THE MINNESOTA CONNECTION. *Minnesota Hist. 1977 45(5): 166-186.* Adolph Dehn increasingly drew on his Minnesota origins for his pictorial themes from the 1930's until his death in 1968. During 1916-36, Dehn specialized in social satire, which has led art critics to call Dehn one of the main social satirists of the "Jazz Age." During his years in Europe, he associated with such satirical artists as George Grosz, with whom Dehn was often compared. Born in Waterville, Minnesota, of German parents, Dehn imbibed a political radicalism from his elders which, along with his ethnicity, caused him considerable trouble during World War I. After spending most of the 1920's in Europe, Dehn returned to America in 1929. During the mid-1930's, Dehn, for aesthetic and monetary reasons, became immersed in American regionalistic art, using the rural and small town environment of Minnesota for many important works of his later career. Based on interviews with Dehn and his contemporaries. 1895-1968

DeKooning, Willem

1647. Yard, Sally E. "William De Kooning: The First Twenty-six Years in New York: 1927-1952." Princeton U. 1980. 282 pp. *DAI 1980 41(3): 836-837-A.* 8016469 1927-52

delaCruz, Jessie Lopez (and family)

1648. de la Cruz, Jessie Lopez and Cantarow, Ellen. MY LIFE. *Radical Am. 1978 12(6): 26-40.* Biography of Jessie Lopez de la Cruz and her family, migrant farm workers originally from Mexico who worked the fields of California; she started to work with Cesar Chavez in 1962 for the United Farm Workers Union, and founded National Land for People in 1974. 1920's-78

delaGuerra, Pablo

1649. Cassidy, Joseph Eugene. "Life and Times of Pablo de la Guerra, 1819-1874." U. of California, Santa Barbara 1977. 268 pp. *DAI 1978 38(7): 4298-4299-A.* 1819-74

DeLancey, James

1650. Hanger, George DeLancey. THE LIFE OF LOYALIST COLONEL JAMES DELANCEY. *Nova Scotia Hist. Rev. [Canada] 1983 3(2): 39-56.* James DeLancey, born in Westchester County, New York, supported the Loyalist cause in the American Revolution, earning the rank of colonel. For his safety, he sailed for Halifax in 1784, purchased a farm near Annapolis, and became a successful farmer. In 1793 he accepted a vacant seat on His Majesty's Council and served until ill health forced him to resign in 1801. 58 notes. 1770's-1801

DeLaney, Emma B.

1651. Martin, Sandy D. SPELMAN'S EMMA B. DELANEY AND THE AFRICAN MISSION. *J. of Religious Thought 1984 41(1): 22-37.* Discusses the role of black educational institutions and black women in the African missionary movement of the late 19th and early 20th centuries, and focuses on Emma B. DeLaney, an 1896 graduate from the missionary training program of Spelman College in Atlanta, Georgia, who did missionary work in Africa during 1902-20. 1865-1920

Delano, Jane

1652. Stewart, Sally. SHARING MORE THAN MARBLE PALACES. *Daughters of the Am. Revolution Mag. 1981 115(3): 188-191.* ca 1881-1944
*For abstract see **Barton, Clara***

Delany, Martin R.

1653. Kahn, Robert M. THE POLITICAL IDEOLOGY OF MARTIN DELANY. *J. of Black Studies 1984 14(4): 415-440.* Martin R. Delany's political ideology was consistent throughout his emigrationist and political activist periods. Before the Civil War, Delany believed that America's racial problems could only be solved by voluntary black emigration, but not by forced colonization, resistance, or miscegenation, because the 1850 Fugitive Slave Law denied full black citizenship. After the Civil War, when black political officeholding showed full black citizenship, he worked for black advancement through political action. Based on the published writings of Martin R. Delany; 5 notes, biblio. 1852-70's

1654. Kass, Amalie M. DR. THOMAS HODGKIN, DR. MARTIN DELANY, AND THE "RETURN TO AFRICA." *Medical Hist. [Great Britain] 1983 27(4): 373-393.* Thomas Hodgkin and Martin R. Delany were both medical doctors, abolitionists, and supporters of Afro-American colonization in Africa. Delany was an assertive, egotistical, hard-working, black nationalist while Hodgkin was an unassuming Quaker philanthropist. The two came into contact when Delany sought information from the Royal Geographical Society about selecting an African site for a band of colonists. Hodgkin was the society's honorary secretary. They met after Delany returned to England from an 1859 trip to Africa seeking financial support for a colony. Hodgkin was sympathetic, but because he had committed his support to another group and because of personality clashes with Delany, cooperation was impossible. Based on Royal Geographical Society correspondence, the Hodgkin Papers on microfilm at Harvard Medical School, and Delany's publications; 115 notes. 1850-62

Delany, Samuel R.

1655. Peplow, Michael W. MEET SAMUEL R. DELANY: BLACK SCIENCE FICTION WRITER. *Crisis 1979 86(4): 115-121.* Samuel R. Delany was born on 1 April 1942. He grew up in New York City's Harlem. "Chip" Delany is a prolific author of science fiction. He has published 12 novels, scores of short stories, and several collections. His work has earned him awards and honors around the world. Delany was trained as a musician and wrote a symphony at age 13. He has performed as a folk singer and produced two films. But his forte is writing about the trip through sociopsychological barriers that all blacks experience. 1942-79

Delbrück, Max

1656. Golomb, Solomon W. MAX DELBRÜCK: AN APPRECIATION. *Am. Scholar 1982 51(3): 351-367.* Reviews the family background, education, and contributions of California Institute of Technology geneticist Max Delbrück. 1920's-81

1657. Kay, Lily E. CONCEPTUAL MODELS AND ANALYTICAL TOOLS: THE BIOLOGY OF PHYSICIST MAX DELBRÜCK. *Journal of the History of Biology 1985 18(2): 207-246.* In 1931, Max Delbrück, a physicist, saw a conceptual link between physics and biology; during the remainder of a long and distinguished career, he applied the analytical tools of mathematical physics to problems of cell structure too minute for direct observation. The result was valuable information on genetic mechanisms. With his research rooted in modern physics and its philosophy, his work significantly contributed to the growth of molecular biology. During his career, scientific institutes and organizations such as the Rockefeller Foundation provided money and resources. Although a noted individual, Delbrück worked well in group projects. His life, thought, and career are indicative of the shape of 20th-century science. 118 notes. 1906-1981

DeLeon, Daniel

1658. Seretan, L. Glen. DANIEL DE LEON AS AMERICAN. *Wisconsin Mag. of Hist. 1978 61(3): 210-233.* Disputes the traditional view of De Leon as a political alien whose Marxian analysis and European perspective did not fit the American environment. Presents Socialist Labor Party leader De Leon as a man who understood and identified with the American tradition and worked continually to put Marxian socialism in an American framework. Attributes De Leon's commitment to America to his Jewish birth and early childhood in Europe and his immigrant experience. Covers 1880-1910. 7 illus., 59 notes. 1880-1910

1659. Seretan, L. Glen. "The Life and Career of Daniel DeLeon, 1852-1914: An Interpretation." U. of Toronto 1976. *DAI 1979 39(7): 4425-A.* 1890-1914

Dell, Floyd

1660. Schmidt, Cynthia Ann Bolger. "Socialist-Feminism: Max Eastman, Floyd Dell and Crystal Eastman." Marquette U. 1983. 341 pp. *DAI 1983 44(4): 1182-A.* DA8317284 1900's-20's

Dellius, Godfrey

1661. Burnham, Koert. GODFREY DELLIUS: AN HISTORICAL OBITUARY BY A PROTAGONIST. *Halve Maen 1979 54(2): 4-6, 14-15.* Accused by some officials of New Netherland (notably Governor Bellomont) of securing large tracts of land by swindling Indians and meddling in civic affairs, Godfrey Dellius, Domine of the Reformed Dutch Church in Albany, New York, 1685-1700, actually was a civic-minded individual with rare communicative abilities with local natives. 1685-1700

Delmer, George J.

1662. Delmer, George J. THE MEMOIRS OF GEORGE J. DELMER: SEAMAN AND POLICEMAN. *Western States Jewish Hist. Q. 1982 14(3): 257-266, (4): 333-340.* George J. Delmer was born George Jacobinson in New York in 1861. After the death of his mother, his father took him to San Francisco, but George ran away from home. By age 14 he was a cabin boy sailing to ports in South and Central America. At this time he adopted the surname "Delmer." He was shanghaied to a Canadian vessel carrying guano to England, where Delmer and other crewmen reported their mistreatment to British authorities, who arrested the ship's officers, gave the crew their pay and their passage to New York in 1884. In New York, Delmer visited his family and then returned to California working as a steward on coastal steamers carrying tourists to Alaska. After 11 years at sea, he quit and became first, a watchman in the waterfront area, and later, joined the San Francisco Police Department. He resigned after 29 years with the police department. Reprints the memoirs. The memoirs are in a private collection; 3 photos, 11 notes. 1861-1923

DeLorean, John Z.

1663. DeLorean, John Z. and Wright, J. Patrick. BOTTOM-LINE FEVER AT GENERAL MOTORS. *Washington Monthly 1980 11(11): 26-35.* Excerpt from former General Motors Corporation executive DeLorean's autobiographical *On a Clear Day You Can See General Motors,* originally scheduled to be published by Playboy Press, withdrawn, and finally published by coauthor Wright. 1970's

delValle family

1664. Griswold del Castillo, Richard. THE DEL VALLE FAMILY AND THE FANTASY HERITAGE. *California Hist. 1980 59(1): 2-15.* Traces the fortunes of the del Valle family from the founding of Rancho San Francisco in 1839 to the death of Reginaldo del Valle in 1938. As upper-class Mexican Californians, the del Valle family survived and prospered through good luck and efficient management as California's population increasingly was dominated by Anglo-Americans after statehood. From 1841 to 1924, in the Santa Clara valley near today's Oxnard and Ventura, the family successfully operated its Rancho Camulos, one of the locales said to be the inspiration for Helen Hunt Jackson's *Ramona.* The family's partial acceptance of the pseudo-Spanish fantasy heritage had some virtues as Mexicanos and new Anglo-American immigrants found that heritage an easy one to adopt. Photos, 46 notes. 1839-1938

Demcher, Nicholas and Anna

1665. Moran, Joyce Demcher. MIZ UKRAINI: "WE ARE FROM THE UKRAINE." *Pennsylvania Folklife 1978-79 28(2): 12-17.* Provides both a personal narrative of Nicholas and Anna Demcher, the author's grandparents, who immigrated from the Ukraine to Pennsylvania, and a historical background on Ukrainian immigration to America. 20c

deMille, Agnes

1666. Buckley, Peter. THE FIERY MISS DE MILLE. *Horizon 1980 23(9): 28-35.* Discusses the career of writer, dancer, and choreographer Agnes de Mille, who choreographed her first ballet in 1942 and began dancing more than 50 years ago. ca 1927-80

DeMille, Cecil B.

1667. Jaffe, Grace. FROM SAN JOSE TO HOLLYWOOD: THE RISE OF JESSE L. LASKY. *Western States Jewish Hist. Q. 1978 11(1): 20-24.* 1890's-1930
For abstract see ***Lasky, Jesse L.***

1668. Lasky, Betty. LET'S MAKE A MOVIE. *Westways 1979 71(11): 22-25.* 1911-14
For abstract see ***Lasky, Jesse L.***

1669. Mitchell, Lisa. ESTATE OF MIND. *Westways 1979 71(11): 28-31, 72-74.* Remembrance of the author's first employer, Cecil B. De Mille, Hollywood director who lived in the exclusive Laughlin Park area in a mansion he bought in 1916, which is described here, and which remains as it was before De Mille's death in 1959. 1916-79

DeMorti, Mark

1670. Tomashevich, George V., ed. SOME OF THE INCIDENTS IN THE LIFE OF MARK DE MORTIE. *Afro-Americans in New York Life and Hist. 1979 3(1): 61-71.* A manuscript autobiographical sketch of Mark De Morti, a prominent black doctor on the Niagara frontier, New York, during the 19th century. 19c

DeMoss, Nettie

1671. DeMoss, Nettie; Crone, Norman, ed. INDIAN TERRITORY MEMORIES. *Chronicles of Oklahoma 1981 59(1): 106-110.* Recounts the author's reminiscences of homesteading near Peggs, Oklahoma from 1896 to 1915 and the fear of Indians. The family moved to Tahlequah in 1915 and soon thereafter to Sand Springs where the oil boom was underway. The author married and took a job with the City Welfare Department during the economic hard times of the 1920's and 1930's. 1895-1937

Dempsey, Jack

1672. Nisbet, Robert. QUIET KILLER. *Am. Scholar 1981 50(2): 273-278.* Review article prompted by Randy Roberts's *Jack Dempsey: The Manassa Mauler* (1980). Discusses Jack Dempsey's childhood, Dempsey's manager Jack Kearns, the separate chapters on the great Dempsey boxing matches, and Dempsey's significance in US sports. ca 1900-80

1673. Roberts, Randy Warren. "Jack Dempsey: Fighter and Legend." (Volumes I and II) Louisiana State U. and Agric. and Mechanical Coll. 1978. 484 pp. *DAI 1979 39(11): 6921-A.* 1920's

Demuth, Charles

1674. Fahlman, Betsy. CHARLES DEMUTH OF LANCASTER, PENNSYLVANIA. *Art & Antiques 1983 6(4): 82-89.* Charles Demuth, whose art career spanned 1901-35, balanced American regionalism and European-New York modernism with his love for his hometown and the aesthetics he found there. 1901-35

Demuth, David O.

1675. Smith, Harold T. DAVID O. DEMUTH. *Arkansas Hist. Q. 1979 38(3): 271-273.* Chronicles some of the accomplishments of David O. Demuth (1932-1979), Benton, Arkansas, businessman, civic leader, and historian. 1950's-79

Dennis, Catherine Engs

1676. Dennis, Catherine Engs. ALL THE TON AT MY CHINA STORE & I LOVE TO TALK... MRS. DENNIS TO MRS. HUNTER: 1839, 1840, 1845. *Newport Hist. 1984 57(3): 65-79.* Prints three letters from Catherine Engs Dennis of Newport, Rhode Island, to her friend, Mary Robinson Hunter, the wife of the US minister to Brazil; the letters comment on public events, private scandals, and national politics. 1839-45

Dennis, Eugene

1677. Lapitskii, M. I. and Mostovets, N. V. IUDZHIN DENNIS: ZHIZN', OTDANNAIA BOR'BE [Eugene Dennis: a life dedicated to struggle]. *Novaia i Noveishaia Istoriia [USSR] 1984 (3): 81-98.* Continued from a previous article. During the Cold War, a number of laws were passed in the United States directed against Communist organizations. One of the first victims of McCarthyism was Eugene Dennis, the general secretary of the American Communist Party. He was brought to trial in 1947 and imprisoned for one year. In 1949 he received another sentence along with other National Committee members of the American Communist Party. In 1955 he was released from a third sentence, and until his death in 1961 he fought revisionism within the American Communist Party. Secondary sources; 48 notes. 1940-61

1678. Lapitskii, M. I. and Mostovets, N. V. IUDZHIN DENNIS: ZHIZN', OTDANNAIA BOR'BE [Eugene Dennis: a life dedicated to struggle]. *Novaia i Noveishaia Istoriia [USSR] 1984 (2): 102-120.* Traces the life of US-born Eugene Dennis, a leading figure of the international Communist movement, general secretary of the Communist Party of the USA (1946-59), and chairman of the Party (1959-61). Dennis dedicated his life to improving labor conditions in the United States. Based on documents of the Communist Party of the USA and other primary sources; illus., 54 notes. Article to be continued. 1905-45

Dennis, Lawrence

1679. Doenecke, Justus D. THE ISOLATIONIST AS COLLECTIVIST: LAWRENCE DENNIS AND THE COMING OF WORLD WAR II. *J. of Libertarian Studies 1979 3(2): 191-207.* Columnist Lawrence Dennis earned popular disdain and disfavor (and eventually a sedition trial), 1940-45, for his strongly collectivist attitudes and his unmitigated belief in Germany's ability to defeat Allied forces in World War II, but more modern critics applaud him for his apparent foresight in predicting the problems of a warfare/welfare state and in cutting through the conventional rhetoric of his time. 1941-45

Dennis, Peggy

1680. —. [WOMEN IN THE LEFT]. *Feminist Studies 1979 5(3): 432-461.*

Trimberger, Ellen Kay. WOMEN IN THE OLD AND NEW LEFT: THE EVOLUTION OF A POLITICS OF PERSONAL LIFE, *pp. 432-450.* Compares the autobiographies of Peggy Dennis, *The Autobiography of an American Communist: A Personal View of a Political*

Life, 1925-1975 (Berkeley: Lawrence Hall & Co., 1977), and Elinor Langer, "Notes for the Next Time, A Memoir of the 1960's," *Working Papers* Fall, 1973: 48-83. Focuses on how changes in class and generation in the American family structure changed the culture of personal relations for women active in the Old Left (in Peggy Dennis's case the American Communist Party, as the wife of Eugene Dennis, one of the top leaders from 1938 to 1961) and the New Left (Langer was active in the Students for a Democratic Society in the 1960's). Delineates the differences in the Old and New Left movements, particularly the conflicts Dennis and Langer experienced in their expectations for their personal life as political activists. 54 notes.

Dennis, Peggy. A RESPONSE TO ELLEN KAY TRIMBERGER'S ESSAY, "WOMEN IN THE OLD AND NEW LEFT," *pp. 451-461.* Critical response to Trimberger's analysis of Dennis's autobiography, Trimberger's theory and interpretations of Dennis's life as a member of the Old Left are incorrect. Points out basic differences of opinion based on Dennis's belief that time, socioeconomics, Communist Party ideology, and views of women provide the context necessary for understanding how Communist ideology "determined the Old Left's views of the world and itself," and "the quality and the impact of that unique, total, long-pull commitment Communists had to that ideology and that organization." Trimberger failed to consider this context. (Followed by a brief afterword by Trimberger.) 1925-78

Dennison, Henry S.

1681. McQuaid, Kim. HENRY S. DENNISON AND THE "SCIENCE" OF INDUSTRIAL REFORM, 1900-1950. *Am. J. of Econ. and Sociol. 1977 36(1): 79-98.* Henry S. Dennison (1877-1952) was an early practitioner of scientific management and industrial relations techniques, a pioneer capitalist advocate of unemployment insurance, and a leading American "corporate liberal" of the inter-war period. His career as industrial advisor to the Woodrow Wilson and Franklin D. Roosevelt administrations provides one means for enhanced understanding of the mixed system of private and public economic power which evolved in the United States in the wake of international depression and two world wars. Dennison's attempts to understand the characteristics and potentials of American political economy were capped by a strategic collaboration with noted economist John Kenneth Galbraith. Though his own firm's unorthodox managerial programs did not long survive his death, H. S. Dennison remains an important business analyst of an emergent corporation capitalist order. 1900-50

Dennison, Tom

1682. Davis, John Kyle. THE GRAY WOLF: TOM DENNISON OF OMAHA. *Nebraska Hist. 1977 58(1): 25-52.* Sketches the life of Tom Dennison (1858-1934) who, for nearly 40 years, was boss of Omaha's third ward which was notorious for "saloons, gambling dens, street games, and brothels." By the 1890's Dennison became the middleman between the operators in his district and the police and politicians. He weathered all reform efforts and maintained close connections with administrations of all persuasions at city hall. 1890's-1934

Dennison, William

1683. Schaefer, James A. GOVERNOR WILLIAM DENNISON AND MILITARY PREPARATIONS IN OHIO, 1861. *Lincoln Herald 1976 78(2): 52-61.* At the outbreak of the Civil War the burden of raising an army rested upon the governors of the states. Some historians have judged Governor William Dennison of Ohio as the most incompetent, but he accomplished as much as many of his peers. Too many volunteers strained the state's ability to cope effectively with the logistical burden, but Dennison eventually organized the state to handle the problems. Dennison's agents were able to purchase arms superior to federal issue, and he established two laboratories in the state to provide the needed ammunitions. He advocated a campaign in western Virginia which eventually was undertaken by General George B. McClellan. The press ignored Dennison's advocacy and gave the credit to McClellan which led to his appointment as commander of the Army of the Potomac. When the war started Dennison was serving the second year of a two-year term, and he suffered from the initial confusion. Primary and secondary sources; illus., 49 notes. 1861

Denny, Ebenezer

1684. Denney, William Homer. "Soldier of the Republic: The Life of Major Ebenezer Denny." Miami U. 1978. 238 pp. *DAI 1978 39(4): 2483-A.* 1761-1822

Densmore, Frances

1685. Archabal, Nina Marchetti. FRANCES DENSMORE: PIONEER IN THE STUDY OF AMERICAN INDIAN MUSIC. Stuhler, Barbara and Kreuter, Gretchen, ed. *Women of Minnesota: Selected Biographical Essays* (St. Paul: Minnesota Historical Society Press, 1977): 94-115. Frances Densmore (1867-1957) was born and raised in Red Wing, Minnesota, where the sight of Indians was common. Densmore was formally trained in 18th- and 19th-century European music; her scholarly research in Native American music made her a pioneer in ethnomusicology. Alice Cunningham Fletcher and John Comfort Fillmore especially influenced Densmore when she began her studies of Indian music in the 1890's. From then until her death in 1957, Densmore studied, recorded, analyzed, and published monographs on the music of the Chippewa, Teton Sioux, Papago, Arapaho, Ute, Mandan, Zuñi, and many other Indians. The Bureau of American Ethnology financially supported her work, and she collected more than 2,400 wax cylinders of Native American music. Densmore gradually evolved a theory and understanding of Indian music which appreciated its cultural context and recognized it as "profoundly different" from Western musical tradition. Primary sources; 2 illus., photo, 45 notes. 1890's-1957

Dentzel, Carl Schaefer

1686. Billington, Ray Allen. CARL SCHAEFER DENTZEL (MARCH 20, 1913—AUGUST 21, 1980). *Masterkey 1980 54(4): 125-129.* Recounts the career of Carl Schaefer Dentzel, who for 25 years served as the Director of the Southwest Museum (Los Angeles, California) and who dedicated his life to the understanding and preservation of the cultural heritage of southern California. 1955-80

DePriest, Oscar

1687. Day, David S. HERBERT HOOVER AND RACIAL POLITICS: THE DEPRIEST INCIDENT. *J. of Negro Hist. 1980 65(1): 6-17.* Oscar DePriest, the first black congressman since 1901, was the focal point of considerable controversy when his wife was invited to the Congressional Wives tea party in the White House by Mrs. Herbert Hoover. On the heels of this event, DePriest organized a "musicale and reception" to raise $200,000 for the NAACP and invited Congressional Republicans and heightened the racial controversy of 1929. The Hoover administration was concerned with preserving its electoral gains in the South and DePriest's aim was to enhance the political strength of blacks, especially that of Oscar DePriest. Based on primary sources in the Herbert Hoover Presidential Library; 46 notes. 1929

Depta, Victor M.

1688. Depta, Victor M. THIS LAID-ON PARADISE. *Appalachian Q. 1981 8(3): 206-210.* Reminiscences of the author's boyhood from age seven in 1946 until age 17 in Logan County, West Virginia, as a member of a migrant coal-mining family, with excerpts from *New Ground,* edited by Donald Askins and David Morris (1977), and *Strokes: Contemporary Appalachian Poetry,* edited by Bob Henry Baber (1980). 1946-56

1689. Depta, Victor M. PROSODY IN REVOLT. *Appalachian J. 1981 9(1): 66-73.* The author describes how West Virginia has influenced his career as a poet; 1945-81. 1945-81

Derby, George Horatio

1690. Ciruzzi, Canice G. "PHOENIX" REVISITED: ANOTHER LOOK AT GEORGE HORATIO DERBY. *J. of San Diego Hist. 1980 26(2): 76-89.* Relates the life of George Horatio Derby, lieutenant in the US Topographical Engineers, whose projects included the exploration of the mouth of the Colorado river; a humorist, for a time he edited the *San Diego Herald* under the name John Phoenix; 1840's-50's. 1840's-50's

Derochis, Lucy

1691. Serene, Frank H. PAESANO: THE STRUGGLE TO SURVIVE IN AMBRIDGE. *Pennsylvania Heritage 1980 6(4): 15-19.* Biography of the author's Italian-born grandmother, Lucy Derochis, who arrived in Ambridge, Pennsylvania, in 1913; describes social customs; based on a taped interview conducted in November 1979 with her (at age 88), and several short interviews with other family members. 1913-79

DesBarres, Joseph Frederic Wallet

1692. Kernaghan, Lois. A MAN AND HIS MISTRESS: J. F. W. DES BARRES AND MARY CANNON. *Acadiensis [Canada] 1981 11(1): 23-42.* Mary Cannon (1751-1827) was Joseph Frederic Wallet Des Barres's mistress and housekeeper of his estate at Windsor, Nova Scotia, from 1764 to 1773. For years after that she looked after his extensive landholdings in the Maritimes. Des Barres, however, found another companion in England, lost interest in Cannon, and eventually turned against her for what he regarded as mismanagement of his property. On his death in 1824, Des Barres left her a share of the Windsor estate, which provided her with a subsistence living. She had failed as a property manager, in contrast to a number of female contemporaries in British North America. Few, however, had labored under as many disadvantages as she had. 76 notes. 1751-1827

DeSchweinitz, Karl

1693. Maier, Steven. "Karl DeSchweinitz, 1887-1975: Social Worker and Social Statesman." Bryn Mawr Coll. 1983. 228 pp. *DAI 1983 44(4): 1208-A.* DA8316910 1900's-75

Desha, Mary

1694. Klotter, James C. and Klotter, Freda Campbell. MARY DESHA, ALASKAN SCHOOLTEACHER OF 1888. *Pacific Northwest Q. 1980 71(2): 78-86.* Presents excerpts from the letters of Mary Desha (1850-1911), who in 1888, set out from her comfortable parents' home in Lexington, Kentucky, for the frontier settlement of Sitka, Alaska, where she had accepted a teaching position. Many of her letters praised the natural beauty of Alaska, but she simultaneously held a strong contempt for most of the Indian, Russian, and Yankee population encountered there. In some ways Mary Desha proved flexible in adapting to frontier conditions, but she could not escape the biases endemic to a true, unreconstructed southerner. Following her return from Alaska, she became heavily involved with the Daughters of the American Revolution and the United Daughters of the Confederacy. 4 photos, 31 notes. 1888

DeSmet, Pierre Jan

1695. Killoren, John J. THE DOCTOR'S SCRAPBOOK: A COLLABORATION OF LINTON AND DE SMET. *Gateway Heritage 1985-86 6(3): 2-9.* 1850-72
For abstract see ***Linton, Moses Lewis***

Desmond, Robert W.

1696. Desmond, Robert W.; Emery, Michael, interviewer. A CONVERSATION WITH ROBERT W. DESMOND. *Journalism History 1984 11(1-2): 11-17.* Robert W. Desmond, international journalist and recipient of distinguished service awards, discusses his life's work including the Pulitzer-Prize-winning book, *The Tides of War* (1984). 1929-84

Detzer, Dorothy

1697. Foster-Hayes, Carrie A. "The Women and the Warriors: Dorothy Detzer and the WILPF." U. of Denver 1984. 706 pp. *DAI 1984 45(2): 609-A.* DA8411925 1915-30's

1698. Rainbolt, Rosemary. WOMEN AND WAR IN THE UNITED STATES: THE CASE OF DOROTHY DETZER, NATIONAL SECRETARY WOMEN'S INTERNATIONAL LEAGUE FOR PEACE AND FREEDOM. *Peace and Change 1977 4(3): 18-22.* Examines Dorothy Detzer's political clout, 1920-34, in the Women's International League for Peace and Freedom, on Capitol Hill as a major lobbyist and political analyst, and in the Nye Munitions Investigation of 1934. 1920-34

Deutsch, Helene

1699. Webster, Brenda S. HELENE DEUTSCH: A NEW LOOK. *Signs 1985 10(3): 553-571.* Although Helene Deutsch, the dynamic follower of Freud, has been dismissed by feminist scholars because of her Freudian assumptions, she was a revisionist in her clinical practices. Her practical applications of psychotherapy showed that she did not assume that women wanted to be humiliated or that they readily accepted abuse, and the narcissism in her own life did not create self-abnegation but rather provided self-confidence. Caught in certain Freudian contradictions, she was forced to accept the lack of clitoral importance in order not to fall into penis envy. Based on the writings of Helene Deutsch; 25 notes. 1944-83

Deutsch, Herman J.

1700. Stratton, David H. HERMAN J. DEUTSCH, 1897-1979. *Pacific Northwest Q. 1980 71(4): 183-184.* Long recognized as one of the finest teachers at Washington State University, Dr. Herman Julius Deutsch also gained honors as a prominent scholar of Pacific Northwest history. He likewise served as vice-president of the Washington State Historical Society and was on the editorial boards of the *Pacific Northwest Quarterly* and the *Pacific Historical Review.* Dr. Deutsch's death on 12 November 1979 ended an academic career that had shaped the lives of many graduate and undergraduate students. Photo. 1917-79

DeVault, Bessie

1701. Stahl, Sandra K. D. QUILTS AND A QUILTMAKER'S AESTHETICS. *Indiana Folklore 1978 11(2): 105-132.* Examines American quilting since the 18th century and discusses Bessie DeVault (b. 1903) of Darke County, Ohio, and her aesthetics in quiltmaking, an area ignored in quiltmaking studies. 18c-1978

Deveaux, John H.

1702. Matthews, John M. BLACK NEWSPAPERMEN AND THE BLACK COMMUNITY IN GEORGIA, 1890-1930. *Georgia Hist. Q. 1984 68(3): 356-381.* 1890-1930
For abstract see ***Davis, Benjamin J.***

Devens, Charles

1703. Cresswell, Stephen. THE ATTORNEY GENERALSHIP OF CHARLES DEVENS. *Hayes Hist. J. 1982 3(6): 32-45.* Charles Devens, the Massachusetts jurist who served as attorney general during the presidency of Rutherford B. Hayes, is a relatively obscure historical figure owing to a paucity of surviving personal information. As attorney general, he argued cases before the Supreme Court concerning state versus federal court jurisdiction, including two important arguments for upholding black civil rights in jury trials. He was also instrumental in defending black voting rights. Despite his obscurity, Devens was a competent official in upholding federal laws during the Hayes administration. Based on records of the Department of Justice, the Charles Devens and Rutherford B. Hayes manuscript collections in the Hayes Presidential Center, and contemporary newspapers; 38 notes. 1877-81

DeVighne, Harry Carlos

1704. DeVighne, Harry Carlos. THE TIME OF MY LIFE: A FRONTIER DOCTOR IN ALASKA. *Alaska J. 1984 14(2): S1-S64.* Reprints portions of Harry Carlos De Vighne's autobiography, *The Time of My Life* (1942), dealing with his career as a physician in Alaska. Includes details about daily life, medicine, public health, social conditions, and changes in technology. 2 illus., 17 photos. 1904-35

DeVinne, Theodore Low

1705. Tichenor, Irene. "Theodore Low DeVinne (1828-1914): Dean of American Printers." Columbia U. 1983. 301 pp. *DAI 1984 44(8): 2556-A.* DA8327308 1850's-1914

Devotion, Ebenezer

1706. Noll, Mark A. EBENEZER DEVOTION: RELIGION AND SOCIETY IN REVOLUTIONARY CONNECTICUT. *Church Hist. 1976 45(3): 293-307.* Uses the career of Ebenezer Devotion as an example to explore the relationship between church and state in 18th-century New England. Because Devotion not only performed the normal range of ministerial functions but was involved in pre-Revolutionary politics, a study of his life reveals much about such interaction. Throughout his career, Devotion remained ultraconservative in ecclesiastical matters. He was among the opponents of the Great Awakening. In this controversy, he developed two opinions that would be important in his later political thinking. First, he came to view "covenant as an external, legal device through which external legal relationships were established." Second, Devotion defended his right as a minister to attend ecclesiastical councils not on the basis of scripture but because it was "a Liberty . . . that is given by the great Law of Nature." Both positions again manifested themselves in Devotion's opposition to the Stamp Act. His political life was part of and depended upon his religious ideology and ecclesiastical viewpoint. 62 notes. 1714-71

Dewdney, Edgar

1707. Larmour, Jean. EDGAR DEWDNEY, INDIAN COMMISSIONER IN THE TRANSITION PERIOD OF INDIAN SETTLEMENT, 1879-1884. *Saskatchewan Hist. [Canada] 1980 33(1): 13-24.* Edgar Dewdney humanely tried to solve the difficult problems of getting the major Indian tribes in the Northwest Territories and Rupert's Land to change from buffalo hunting to agriculture. Mentions the support of public figures such as J. F. Macleod and David Laird, and problems with the American Sioux under Chief Sitting Bull until 1881, when he surrendered to US authorities. By 1884, most of the Indians were on reservations and some farming had begun. This was accomplished peacefully, due to Dewdney and the cooperation of the Indians. Primary sources; 4 photos, 54 notes. 1879-84

Dewey, George

1708. Nicholson, Philip Y. ADMIRAL GEORGE DEWEY AFTER MANILA BAY; YEARS OF AMBITION, ACCOMPLISHMENT, AND PUBLIC OBSCURITY. *Am. Neptune 1977 37(1): 26-39.* Following his 1898 naval victory in the Philippines, Admiral George Dewey gained further notoriety primarily by his indiscreet comments to the press and his aspirations for the presidency. After the presidential campaign of 1900, however, his popularity sharply waned. Nevertheless, during 1900-15, Dewey continued to make a substantial contribution, especially as president of the Navy's General Board. Notes Dewey's influence in American diplomatic, naval, military, and strategic matters. Based on Dewey's papers, government records, and published sources; 54 notes. 1898-1917

1709. Stokesbury, James L. MANILA BAY: BATTLE OR EXECUTION? *Am. Hist. Illus. 1979 14(5): 4-7, 40-47.* Discusses Admiral George Dewey (1837-1917) who led the American forces at the Battle of Manila Bay, and describes the fight against the Spaniards who suffered a crushing defeat there in 1898 during the Spanish-American War. 1898

Dewey, John

1710. Grabiner, Eugene Jay. "John Dewey: Educational Consultant to Corporate Liberalism." U. of California, Berkeley 1976. 335 pp. *DAI 1977 38(2): 720-A.* 20c

1711. Kliebard, Herbert M. JOHN DEWEY'S OTHER SON. *Teachers Coll. Record 1982 83(3): 453-457.* In 1904, during a European trip, John Dewey lost his eight-year-old son, Gordon, to typhoid fever. While in Italy, the Deweys adopted a boy of the same age named Sabino who proved unusually mechanically proficient and creative, greatly pleasing his adoptive parents. Based on letters and recordings in Special Collections, Morris Library, Southern Illinois University; 12 notes. 1904-30

1712. Lawson, Alan. JOHN DEWEY AND THE HOPE FOR REFORM. *Hist. of Educ. Q. 1975 15(1): 31-66.* Chronicles John Dewey's intellectual formation, his philosophy, and social affairs, and his personal development, in order to understand his philosophy of education which balanced Instrumentalism, philosophic ideas of the 19th century, and social reform, 1909-30's. 1909-30's

1713. Lojewska, Maria Izabella. DEWEY A MARKSIZM [Dewey and Marxism]. *Studia Filozoficzne [Poland] 1977 (4): 143-162.* Traces John Dewey's instrumentalist concept of cognition, his views on the subject and functions of philosophy, his social outlook, and attempts to confront his philosophical ideas with Marxism; 20th century. 20c

1714. McGlashan, Zena Beth. THE PROFESSOR AND THE PROPHET: JOHN DEWEY AND FRANKLIN FORD. *Journalism Hist. 1979-80 6(4): 107-111, 123.* 1875-1927
*For abstract see **Ford, Franklin***

1715. Minnich, Elizabeth Anne. "Philosophy, Democracy and Communication: A Study of John Dewey as Political Philosopher." New School for Social Res. 1977. 212 pp. *DAI 1978 38 (11): 6771-6772-A.* 19c-20c

1716. Pietig, Jeanne. LAWRENCE KOHLBERG, JOHN DEWEY, AND MORAL EDUCATION. *Social Educ. 1980 44(3): 238-240, 242.* Contrasts John Dewey's influence on and approach to moral education in elementary schools in the United States, 1882-98, to Lawrence Kohlberg's views on moral education in the 1970's. 1882-98

1717. Reed, Ronald. NOTES TOWARD AN ECONOMIC BIOGRAPHY OF JOHN DEWEY. *Vitae Scholasticae 1983 2(1): 267-283.* Discusses John Dewey's salaries and his changing attitudes toward them. Raises questions based on George Dykhuizen's biography, *The Life and Mind of John Dewey* (1978). 31 notes. German summary. 1879-1945

1718. Rucker, Darnell. SELVES INTO PERSONS: ANOTHER LEGACY FROM JOHN DEWEY. *Rice U. Studies 1980 66(4): 103-118.* American philosopher John Dewey struggled to formulate the self as person, i.e. one who would both require a community and be a vital contributor to that community, but he also recognized the destructive impersonal forces inherent in modern American society; covers ca. 1913-31. 1913-31

1719. Thistlethwaite, Susan Brooks. "H. Shelton Smith: Critic of the Theological Perspective of Progressive Religious Education, 1934-1950." Duke U. 1980. 215 pp. *DAI 1980 41(4): 1658-A.* DA8021847 1934-50

1720. Young, Bernadette Louise. "John Dewey and Selected American-Catholic Thinkers: 1900-1975, From Anathema to Dialogue." U. of Pittsburgh 1977. 178 pp. *DAI 1978 38(9): 5329-A.* 1900-75

Dewey, Melvil

1721. Comstock, Ned. THE DEWEY DICHOTOMY. *Wilson Lib. Bull. 1978 52(5): 400-407.* Melvil Dewey's two-sided personality created conflicts while he was secretary to the Board of Regents of the New York state university system and State Librarian, 1901-32. 1901-32

1722. Elliott, Anna. MELVIL DEWEY: A SINGULAR AND CONTENTIOUS LIFE. *Wilson Lib. Bull. 1981 55(9): 666-671.* Highlights the life of Melvil Dewey, whose accomplishments included founding the Lake Placid Club, organizing the American Metric Bureau, devising the Dewey decimal system for cataloging library books, establishing the first library school, and attempting to reform educational and spelling practices; 1880-1930. 1880-1930

1723. Lee, Michael Min-song. "Melvil Dewey (1851-1931): His Educational Contributions and Reforms." Loyola U., Chicago 1979. 309 pp. *DAI 1979 39(11): 6586-6587-A.* 1876-89

Dewey, Thomas E.

1724. Moore, Stanley Joel. "Young Tom Dewey: The Prosecutor and the Politician." U. of Kansas 1982. 480 pp. *DAI 1983 43(12): 4013-A.* DA8309339 1933-40

Dewing, Thomas Wilmer

1725. Hobbs, Susan. THOMAS WILMER DEWING: THE EARLY YEARS, 1851-1885. *Am. Art J. 1981 13(2): 4-35.* The early works of Thomas Wilmer Dewing show his development toward the mature style which made him famous. The early works were clear, carefully drawn, and include a number of lithographs. Portraits, particularly of women, nude figure studies, and genre scenes reveal the influence of his studies in Paris at the Académie Julian with its classicizing tendencies and emphasis on anatomical studies. In 1880 Dewing moved to New York and was greatly influenced by the paintings of the English pre-Raphaelites, which were being shown there. Based on interviews with friends of Dewing and primary sources; 5 photos, 27 plates, 93 notes. ca 1870-85

DeWitt, Zachariah Price (family)

1726. Kenney, Alice P. A DUTCH PIONEER: ZACHARIAH PRICE DE WITT MOVES WEST. *Halve Maen 1983 57(2): 3-5, 23, 25.* The family of Zachariah Price De Witt lived in New Amsterdam in the 1650's, and migrated to New Jersey in the early 1700's, to Kentucky in the late 1780's, then to the frontier settlement of Oxford, Ohio, in 1805. 1650-1820's

deWolfe, Elsie

1727. Platt, Frederick. ELSIE DE WOLFE: THE CHINTZ LADY. *Art & Antiques 1980 3(5): 62-67.* Biography of revolutionary American designer Elsie de Wolfe (1865-1950), famous for designing with light, airy colors, mirrors, and chintz fabric. ca 1882-1950

Dexter, Andrew

1728. Rogers, William Warren, ed. ANDREW DEXTER: FOUNDER OF MONTGOMERY. *Alabama Hist. Q. 1981 43(3): 161-170.* Reprints a biography by Wallace W. Screws of Andrew Dexter who founded Montgomery, Alabama, in 1818. Reprinted from the Montgomery *Advertiser,* 19 March 1871; 17 notes. 1817-71

Dexter, Timothy

1729. Lockwood, Allison. FIRST IN THE EAST, FIRST IN THE WEST: LORD TIMOTHY DEXTER. *Nineteenth Cent. 1979 5(4): 56-59, 62.* An account of Timothy Dexter (1747-1810) of Newburyport, Massachusetts, a typical representative of his age of commercial speculation, eccentricity, and the personal affectation of the nouveaux riche. 1747-1810

DeZorita, Alonso

1730. Vigil, Ralph E. BARTOLOME DE LAS CASAS, JUDGE ALONSO DE ZORITA, AND THE FRANCISCANS: A COLLABORATIVE EFFORT FOR THE SPIRITUAL CONQUEST OF THE BORDERLANDS. *Americas (Acad. of Am. Franciscan Hist.) 1981 38(1): 45-57.* Alonso de Zorita (1512-85) arrived in Mexico in 1556 with a record already established as defender of the Indians. Influenced by the ideas of Bartolomé de Las Casas, and working in collaboration with the Franciscans, he unsuccessfully proposed the peaceful conversion and colonization of New Spain's northern frontier. Based on documents in the Archivo General de Indias and published sources; 52 notes. 1545-85

Dial, Nathaniel Barksdale

1731. Slaunwhite, Jerry Lockhart. "The Public Career of Nathaniel Barksdale Dial." U. of South Carolina 1979. 285 pp. *DAI 1979 40(4): 2231-A.* 1912-20's

1732. —. TWO PROMINENT CAROLINIANS. *Pro. of the South Carolina Hist. Assoc. 1980: 36-77.*

Slaunwhite, Jerry L. THE PUBLIC CAREER OF NATHANIEL BARKSDALE DIAL, *pp. 36-54.* Examines the business and public career of Nathaniel Barksdale Dial, who was born in 1862 and was elected to the US Senate for one term in 1912. Although he was unable to regain public office, Dial had a very successful business career. Based on the Dial papers and some published works; 55 notes.

Tyler, Lyon G. PRISONERS ALL: THE SLAVE AND JAMES LOUIS PETIGRU, *pp. 55-72.* Outlines the life of James Louis Petigru (1789-1863), who was considered to be South Carolina's greatest lawyer. Although a slave owner, Petigru opposed slavery because it endangered the Union. Based on Petigru's papers and published works; 62 notes.

Cann, Marvin L. and Dunn, Joseph R. COMMENTARIES ON "THE DISTINCTIVE CAROLINIAN," *pp. 73-77.* The articles could be improved if the authors broadened the area of their study to show how Dial and Petigru fit into their times. 1789-1930

Dibner, Bern

1733. Cohen, I. Bernard. AWARD OF THE 1976 SARTON MEDAL TO BERN DIBNER. *Isis 1977 68(244): 610-615.* Presentation address, summarizing the career of Dibner (b. 1897), American electrical engineer, inventor, collector, author, and patron of the history of science. 2 notes. 1976

Dick, Lena Frank

1734. Cohodas, Marvin. LENA FRANK DICK: AN OUTSTANDING WASHOE BASKET WEAVER. *Am. Indian Art Mag. 1979 4(4): 32-41, 90.* Explores the life and career of Lena Frank Dick (1889-1965), a largely unknown but exceptional basket weaver from Coleville, California. 1889-1965

Dickerson, William Fisher

1735. Dickerson, Dennis C. WILLIAM FISHER DICKERSON: NORTHERN PREACHER/SOUTHERN PRELATE. *Methodist History 1985 23(3): 135-152.* William Fisher Dickerson was one of the few formally educated pastors in the African Methodist Episcopal Church, the oldest black US denomination, and, prior to the Civil War, primarily a Northern institution. Still a young minister when his career was promoted by a series of important appointments, Dickerson was crowned with the pastorship of Sullivan Street Church in New York City at the age of 33 and was acclaimed for his sermons. He led a "Thinker's Course of Lectures" featuring leading black preachers and poets. At 36, Dickerson became the youngest bishop in his church. In 1881 he went to London to preach on the nature of Methodism to the Ecumenical Methodist Conference. While Dickerson's election ensured the continuation of Northern dominance in the church, he soon ran into revolt among Southern brethren who resisted that influence. He died in 1884, aged 41. Primary sources; 47 notes. 1787-1875

Dickey, Charles W.

1736. Neil, J. Meredith. THE ARCHITECTURE OF C. W. DICKEY IN HAWAII. *Hawaiian J. of Hist. 1975 9: 101-113.* Charles W. Dickey, born of a kamaaina family, grew up on Maui. After graduating from MIT, he practiced architecture in Hawaii 1895-1904 and 1920-42. Includes a complete list of all buildings he designed in Hawaii. Illus. 1895-1942

Dickinson, Anna Elizabeth

1737. Duffy, Joseph. ANNA ELIZABETH DICKINSON AND THE ELECTION OF 1863. *Connecticut Hist. 1984 25: 22-38.* Anna Elizabeth Dickinson, a Quaker feminist, became a famous public speaker for progressive social reform; her speaking tour in Connecticut in support of the Republican Party during the 1863 election campaign was a major factor in the party's success and helped to legitimate the idea of women speaking on politics. 1860-70's

Dickinson, Anson

1738. Dearborn, Mona Leitheiser. ANSON DICKINSON, PAINTER OF MINIATURES. *Mag. Antiques 1983 124(5): 1004-1009.* Details the career of Connecticut artist Anson Dickinson, who painted more than 1,500 watercolor-on-ivory portrait miniatures, some reproduced here, among which were portraits of many Washington politicians and artist Gilbert Stuart. 1800-52

Dickinson, Charlotte Humphrey

1739. Lightfoot, Mary K. and Knuth, Priscilla, ed. DIARY OF A VOYAGE TO OREGON. *Oregon Hist. Q. 1983 84(3): 243-256.* Charlotte Humphrey Dickinson, wife of a missionary to Oregon, kept a diary of her voyage from New York to Oregon in the winter of 1852-53 aboard the California clipper *Trade Wind.* About 50 passengers, including men and women, helped sailors extinguish a deck fire that threatened the safety of the ship. 2 illus. photo, 4 notes. 1852-53

Dickinson, Emily

1740. Barnstone, Aliki. HOUSES WITHIN HOUSES: EMILY DICKINSON AND MARY WILKINS FREEMAN'S "A NEW ENGLAND NUN." *Centennial Rev. 1984 28(2): 129-145.* Compares the lifestyle of Louisa Ellis, the central character in Mary Wilkins Freeman's short story "The New England Nun" with that of poet Emily Dickinson, using Freeman's metaphor of the house. While Ellis shut out the senses of the outside world, Dickinson reflected in her poetry the risks she took in dealing with questions of femininity and sexuality. 47 notes. 19c

1741. Burbick, Joan. EMILY DICKINSON AND THE REVENGE OF THE NERVES. *Women's Studies 1980 7(1-2): 95-109.* Examines Emily Dickinson's concern with pain and suffering in her nature poetry as a reaction to her mother's chronic nervous invalidism and as a reflection of mid-19th-century American preoccupation with neurasthenia as an endemic disease of modern civilization. 1850-86

1742. Burbick, Joan. "ONE UNBROKEN COMPANY": RELIGION AND EMILY DICKINSON. *New England Q. 1980 53(1): 62-75.* Examines religious life at Mount Holyoke College during the time Emily Dickinson (1830-86) studied there. Concludes that, contrary to some biographers' views, she did not rebel against religion. Her religion was "fused with the issue of friendship" and for a time she feared that her friends' conversion would separate them from her. For Dickinson "the bonds of friendship determine meaning here as well as in the Christian heaven . . . " and her reaction against religion was "not based on a stance of heroic individualism, but on a continued struggle to avoid isolation and to cement the bonds of friendship." Based on her letters to two friends and on literary biographies; 13 notes. 1848-50

1743. Erkkila, Betsy. EMILY DICKINSON ON HER OWN TERMS. *Wilson Quarterly 1985 9(2): 98-109.* Outlines the life of Emily Dickinson, noting that her biographers still obscure an analysis of her poetry by emphasizing her unorthodox behavior; Dickinson's use of various poetic techniques demonstrates her struggle against the restrictions of Puritan New England society. 1840's-86

1744. Klein, Maury. THE ENIGMA OF EMILY. *Am. Hist. Illus. 1977 12(8): 4-11.* Emily Dickinson (1830-86) was born and died in Amherst, Massachusetts. She rejected church membership in 1848 and lived a secluded life. She never left Amherst after 1865, and rarely left her house. Her inability to meet anyone who could deal with her intellectual and emotional energy, her intensity, and her acute perception and sensitivity account for her seclusion. She found a release in writing letters to her friends (more than 1000 survive) and in her poetry (1,775 poems and fragments have been collected). Primary and secondary sources; 7 illus. 1847-86

1745. Morris, Adelaide K. TWO SISTERS HAVE I: EMILY DICKINSON'S VINNIE AND SUSAN. *Massachusetts Rev. 1981 22(2): 323-332.* Describes the two most important women in Emily Dickinson's life: her natural sister, Lavinia Norcross Dickinson (b. ca. 1832), familiarly referred to as Vinnie, and her brother's wife, Susan Gilbert Dickinson, commonly called Sue, her lifelong friend and fascination. The three women were neighbors for 30 years, sharing each other's sufferings and triumphs. Sue represented the heavenly in Emily's life, Vinnie the earthly. These two complementary yet contradictory influences helped keep Emily on an even keel. Emily referred to Vinnie's world as a prose world and to Sue's as a poetry world. Relations between Vinnie and Sue exploded after Emily died, since Emily's role as arbitrator was vacant. Covers ca. 1850-86. Based on Emily Dickinson's letters and poetry, Vinnie Dickinson's diary, and Mabel Todd's journal; 11 notes. ca 1850-86

1746. Morse, Jonathan. MEMORY, DESIRE, AND THE NEED FOR BIOGRAPHY: THE CASE OF EMILY DICKINSON. *Georgia Rev. 1981 35(2): 259-272.* Traces the changing focus of biographical reality and reader self-perception through biographies of Emily Dickinson. At first biographers included only data which illuminated their text. After the 1920's, disillusionment made biography on the heroic model untenable. Biography requires more than memory mixed with desire. It is a convergent art, a pluralist thing. Through its presentation of historical form, context, and subject, it serves as a vehicle for reader participation in aesthetically fulfilled history. 18 notes. 19c-20c

1747. Williams, David R. "THIS CONSCIOUSNESS THAT IS AWARE": EMILY DICKINSON IN THE WILDERNESS OF THE MIND. *Soundings 1983 66(3): 360-381.* An analysis of the inner life of Emily Dickinson through her poetry and letters, from a literary, religious, and psychological perspective. 1850's-86

1748. —. INTELLECTUALS AND SOCIETY IN WESTERN MASSACHUSETTS. *Massachusetts Rev. 1979 20(3): 437-467.*

Tracy, Patricia. THE PASTORATE OF JONATHAN EDWARDS, *pp. 437-451.* Discusses reciprocal relationships between Jonathan Edwards (1703-58), American theologian, philosopher, and Puritan (Congregational) minister, and the congregation to which he ministered. Describes the 1734-35 Northampton revival, and how he took the town's young people as his special constituency. Dismissed from Northampton in 1750, he never again pastored a flock, although he achieved great success with his theological and philosophical writings. Based on Edwards's works, letters, and an unpublished doctoral dissertation; 40 notes.

Wilson, Raymond Jackson. EMILY DICKINSON AND THE PROBLEM OF CAREER, *pp. 451-461.* Compares Emily Dickinson (1830-86), American poet, with Jonathan Edwards. Dickinson was never a professional writer of poetry, because she never published in her lifetime. She became America's only important posthumous intellectual. Dickinson never published partly because she was shy, and partly because she did not understand the conditions under which 19th-century authors worked.

Gross, Robert A. A RESPONSE, *pp. 461-467.* The excitement of these two papers is that they go beyond the abstract to relate the thinking of intellectuals to their society. The two papers avoid two traps in intellectual history. They instead carve a middle ground and emphasize relationships between intellectuals and their audiences. They help to link social and intellectual history for understanding American culture. ca 1730-1880

Dickinson, John

1749. Colbourn, H. Trevor. JOHN DICKINSON: HISTORICAL REVOLUTIONARY. *Pennsylvania Mag. of Hist. and Biog. 1959 83(3): 271-292.* Discusses the philosophical and political background of American statesman John Dickinson, focusing on his stance toward the American Revolution, which he supported in theory, although he would not sign the Declaration of Independence in 1776, and examines how his personal library and reading could have affected his political views. 1776-1808

1750. Colbourn, H. Trevor. A PENNSYLVANIA FARMER AT THE COURT OF KING GEORGE: JOHN DICKINSON'S LONDON LETTERS, 1754-1756. *Pennsylvania Mag. of Hist. and Biog. 1962 86(3): 241-286.* Traces the life of John Dickinson (1732-1808), American statesman and lawyer, focusing on the contribution of the legal profession to the American Revolution; and provides transcripts of his letters, written in London, 1754-56. 1754-56

1751. Flower, Milton E. JOHN DICKINSON: DELAWAREAN. *Delaware Hist. 1976 17(1): 12-20.* Describes John Dickinson's relationship to Delaware, which was a political and social refuge for him. He served Delaware in a variety of political capacities. Moderate leadership called upon Dickinson repeatedly to represent Delaware. He retired to Wilmington after many stormy years representing Delaware in Pennsylvania, particularly during the Continental Congress. Based primarily on Dickinson's letters; illus., 23 notes. 1774-1800

1752. Hynes, Sandra Sarkela. "The Political Rhetoric of John Dickinson, 1764-1776." U. of Massachusetts 1982. 313 pp. *DAI 1983 43(8): 2494-A.* DA8229564 1764-76

1753. Johannesen, Stanley K. JOHN DICKINSON AND THE AMERICAN REVOLUTION. *Hist. Reflections [Canada] 1975 2(1): 29-49.* John Dickinson has been the most neglected of the major figures of the American Revolution. Such an oversight has occurred because no colonials rallied to a Dickinson program, no coalition was formed espousing his principles, and contemporaries found him weak, inconsistent, and arrogant. The focus of Dickinson's thought matured, however, and he elaborated an agrarian political economy that bridged the British trading empire with Jefferson's Empire for Liberty. *Farmer's Letters* represent the apogee of Dickinson's direct influence on American thought and culture. 1775-83

Dickson, Anna Mae

1754. Watriss, Wendy. "IT'S SOMETHING INSIDE YOU." *Southern Exposure 1977 4(4): 76-81.* Anna Mae Dickson emerged as a black community leader in east Texas during the 1950's and became especially active in school affairs. Compelled at an early age to labor as a cotton fieldhand, Dickson later engaged in domestic service. This experience provided her with considerable insight into the white community. Her present role as community activist rests on her belief that it is important to maintain links between the black and white communities and to have black representation in community organizations. Based on oral interviews. 1930's-70's

diDonato, Pietro

1755. Esposito, Michael D. PIETRO DI DONATO REEVALUATED. *Italian Americana 1980 6(2): 179-192.* Story of the life and inspiration of author Pietro di Donato, who wrote *Christ in Concrete* (1939), *This Woman* (1958), *Three Circles of Light* (1960), and *Naked Author* (1970), and dramatized the plight of Italian-American workers in the 20th century. 20c

Diemer, George W

1756. Allen, Patricia Ann. "George W. Diemer: Selected Aspects of His Presidency at Central Missouri State College, 1937-1956." Southern Illinois U., Carbondale 1983. 309 pp. *DAI 1984 44(9): 2692-A.* DA8326504 1937-56

Dietz, William ("Lone Star")

1757. Ewers, John C. FIVE STRINGS TO HIS BOW: THE REMARKABLE CAREER OF WILLIAM (LONE STAR) DIETZ. *Montana 1977 27(1): 2-13.* Discusses a biography of William Dietz (1884-1964) whose Sioux name was Lone Star. Dietz's career included five facets: artist, athlete, actor, teacher, football coach. His work as an artist developed at Carlisle Indian School beginning in 1907. From 1909-11 he played football at Carlisle, later starting his coaching career there under Glenn S. (Pop) Warner. Dietz coached college and professional teams from 1912-43, winning 75 percent of his games. In 1928 he acted in and served as an advisor for Hollywood western movies. After 1943, he tried brief and unsuccessful careers in advertising and teaching commercial art. He spent his retirement as an artist in Reading, Pennsylvania, near Albright College where he had coached from 1937-43. Based on archival material in Macalaster College, Oklahoma Historical Society, Cumberland County (PA) Historical Society, Office of Indian Affairs Records, National Archives and Albright College, personal interviews, and secondary works; 18 illus., biblio. 1907-64

Dight, Charles Fremont

1758. Phelps, Gary. THE EUGENICS CRUSADE OF CHARLES FREMONT DIGHT. *Minnesota Hist. 1984 49(3): 99-109.* Charles Fremont Dight was a doctor, lecturer at the Hamline and University of Minnesota medical schools, socialist, Minneapolis city council member, and fervent eugenicist. He undertook a campaign for education, segregation, sterilization, and marriage restriction in the 1920's and pursued it until his death. Minnesota already had laws calling for the segregation of the mentally defective and restriction of marriage, though the latter was seldom enforced. Dight spearheaded the passage of a sterilization law in 1926, making Minnesota the 17th state to enact and enforce this practice. In 1929 and 1931 he mounted heated drives for the stiffening of the sterilization system; these foundered on the battle over whether the responsibility to make decisions would be vested in the State Board of Control, the Board of Health, or county officials. 8 illus., 39 notes. 1923-37

DiGiovanni, Antonio

1759. DeJohn, Dominick. ITALIANS IN ILLINOIS: A MEMOIR OF AN ETHNIC MINING COMMUNITY. *Italian Am. 1983 7(2): 26-32.* Antonio DiGiovanni, the author's father, was born in Piedmont, Italy, emigrated to the United States in 1901 and worked in the coal mines in Roanoke, Illinois, for 40 years. 1901-46

Dike, John

1760. Moore, Margaret B. HAWTHORNE'S UNCLE JOHN DIKE. *Studies in the American Renaissance 1984: 325-330.* John Dike married Nathaniel Hawthorne's aunt, Priscilla Manning, and served Hawthorne as "a source of affectionate stability." He moved from his native Beverly, Massachusetts, following the death of his first wife in 1809 and his own bankruptcy in 1812, to Salem, where he became a prosperous merchant, 1815-29, marrying Manning in 1817. He was bankrupted again in 1829, along with many Salem merchants, but he started over and prospered once more. Discusses his relationships with Nathaniel Hawthorne and other family members. Table, 32 notes. 1805-64

Dill, Ralph

1761. Silversides, Brock. RALPH DILL: SASKATOON'S FIRST PHOTOGRAPHER. *Saskatchewan Hist. [Canada] 1983 36(3): 81-93.* Biographical sketch of Ralph Dill, first resident professional photographer in Saskatoon, Saskatchewan. Describes the kinds of photographs he took in his business and the equipment and techniques he used in his photography. His photographs record Saskatoon's transition from a rough frontier town to an established city. 6 photos, 25 notes. 1876-1938

Dimond, Anthony J.

1762. Mangusso, Mary Childers. "Anthony J. Dimond: A Political Biography." Texas Tech. U. 1978. 434 pp. *DAI 1978 39(5): 3102-A.* 1881-1953

1763. Mangusso, Mary Childers. TONY DIMOND FINDS HIS FUTURE, AFTER CAREER AS MINER FAILS TO PAN OUT. *Alaska Journal 1982 12(4): 12-23.* Anthony Dimond went to Alaska in 1905 to find gold and adventure, but his prospecting career was cut short when he accidentally shot himself in the leg. He studied law, was admitted to the bar, and eventually embarked on a political career and became the territory's single, nonvoting delegate to Congress. 10 photos, 35 notes. 1905-53

Dingee, Ruby

1764. Dingee, Ruby L. MOTHER OF 59. *Alaska Journal 1982 12(1): 30-34.* Ruby Dingee, who arrived in Alaska with her husband in 1930, reminisces about her brief tenure as matron-teacher at the White Mountain School near Nome, which was attended by the brightest Eskimo children. The Dingees barely spent more than a year at White Mountain, but they stayed long enough to influence Howard Rock, a student who went on to become a successful artist and founder of the *Tundra Times,* a newspaper serving as a voice of Alaskan native unity and strength in the land claims fight. 4 photos. 1926-76

DiPeso, Charles Corradino

1765. Fenner, Gloria J. CHARLES CORRADINO DI PESO, 1920-1982. *Kiva 1983 48(4): 307-313.* A brief personal and professional biography of Charles Corradino Di Peso, the recipient of the University of Arizona's first Ph.D. in anthropology. He developed the concept of archaeohistory—the fusion of archaeological and historical studies—during his career in the Southwest and northern Mexico. His major work concerned the Casas Grandes ruins in Mexico. 1948-82

1766. Seifert, Donna J. CHARLES C. DI PESO, 1920-1982. *Hist. Archaeol. 1983 17(2): 106-111.* Memorializes the life of Charles C. Di Peso. Di Peso is known for his work on the prehistoric and early historic peoples of southern Arizona. He was born in 1920, and developed his interest in archaeology in high school. Di Peso was a founding member of the Society for Historical Archaeology and served for 30 years as director of the Amerind Foundation for the study of Indian cultural history. His work in the Casas Grandes Valley of northwestern Chihuahua, Mexico, led to the publication with his colleagues of *Casas Grandes: A Fallen Trading Center of the Gran Chichimeca.* Biblio., ref. 1940's-82

Dirk, Henry E.

1767. Gerber, Gary R. THE SAGA OF HENRY E. DIRK. *Military Collector & Historian 1976 28(1): 34-37.* Describes the three enlistments, World War I service, and military uniform of Henry E. Dirk and includes excerpts from his papers and diary. 1902-21

Dirksen, Everett M.

1768. Fonsino, Frank J. EVERETT MCKINLEY DIRKSEN: THE ROOTS OF AN AMERICAN STATESMAN. *J. of the Illinois State Hist. Soc. 1983 76(1): 17-34.* Throughout his youth, Dirksen exhibited both athletic competitiveness and a great interest in reading and public speaking. He interrupted his college education to join the army during World War I, partly to prove the patriotism of his German family. In 1924, he joined the American Legion and was elected district commander in 1926. After his election to the city council of Pekin, Illinois, in 1927, Dirksen supported both public ownership of the local waterworks and construction of a bridge spanning the Illinois River. Following an unsuccessful 1930 bid for a congressional seat, Dirksen was elected in 1932 to the House of Representatives as one of four Republicans from Illinois after a campaign marked by Dirksen's unwillingness to support Herbert C. Hoover. 8 illus., 34 notes. 1896-1932

1769. Schapsmeier, Edward L. and Schapsmeier, Frederick H. EVERETT M. DIRKSEN OF PEKIN: POLITICIAN PAR EXCELLENCE. *J. of the Illinois State Hist. Soc. 1983 76(1): 2-16.* Everett M. Dirksen served in the US House of Representatives during 1933-49 and in the Senate from 1951 to his death in 1969. As Senate minority leader during 1959-69, Dirksen was the foremost Republican legislator during the Democratic administrations of the 1960's. During his early career, Dirksen supported much New Deal legislation and was a staunch isolationist, but after 1941 he helped move his party toward internationalism and support of the UN. His anti-Communism and support of the Cold War became more partisan in the 1950's when he joined forces with senators Robert A. Taft and Joseph R. McCarthy. Dirksen supported the Civil Rights acts of 1957 and 1964 but opposed New Frontier programs that threatened to increase deficit spending. He supported President Johnson's prosecution of the Vietnam War and opposed Supreme Court decisions on school prayer and reapportionment. 11 illus., 49 notes. 1933-69

Divine, Father

See Baker, George

Dix, Dorothea

1770. Cullen, Joseph. DOROTHEA DIX: FORGOTTEN CRUSADER. *Am. Hist. Illus. 1978 13(4): 11-17.* Dorothea Dix (1802-87) effected sweeping reforms in the care of the insane in America, Europe, and even Japan. In 1841, when she became interested in the problem, it was widely believed that the insane were insensitive to cold and other discomfort, and they were treated accordingly. Dix always acted alone and sought no publicity. She would investigate conditions in a particular state, then present an eloquently written memorial to the legislature through a sympathetic member. Successful with state legislatures, she failed repeatedly to get federal assistance for the insane. Her service during the Civil War as Superintendent of Women Nurses for the Union Army was not a success, partly for reasons of temperament. She was active in behalf of the insane until her death in 1887. 11 illus. 1841-87

1771. Spalding, Margaret Joy. "Dorothea Dix and the Care of the Insane from 1841 to the Pierce Veto of 1854." Bryn Mawr Coll. 1976. 254 pp. *DAI 1978 38(7): 4332-4333-A.* 1841-54

1772. Viney, Wayne and Bartsch, Karen. DOROTHEA LYNDE DIX: POSITIVE OR NEGATIVE INFLUENCE ON THE DEVELOPMENT OF TREATMENT FOR THE MENTALLY ILL. *Social Sci. J. 1984 21(2): 71-82.* Challenges recent criticisms of social reformer Dorothea Dix's efforts to improve institutions for the mentally handicapped. 1821-87

Dix, Dorothy

See Gilmer, Elizabeth M.

Dixon, Maynard

1773. Hamlin, Edith. MAYNARD DIXON: PAINTER OF THE WEST. *Am. West 1982 19(6): 50-58.* Memoirs of Edith Hamlin, who studied with and eventually married Maynard Dixon (1875-1946). Based in California and, later, in Arizona, Dixon's easel paintings, murals, drawings, and illustrations concerned the life and the landscape of the West. In later years, he shifted from the topical and romantic to the poetic and interpretive. Much of his early work was destroyed in the San Francisco fire of 1906. 8 illus. 1897-1946

1774. Starr, Kevin. PAINTERLY POET, POETIC PAINTER: THE DUAL ART OF MAYNARD DIXON. *California Hist. Q. 1977-78 56(4): 290-309.* Maynard Dixon (1875-1946), known best as an illustrator and painter of western scenes, also wrote 164 poems which paralleled his painting career. Dixon, outwardly reserved and detached, suffered from ill health and personal difficulties. His first wife was an alcoholic; his second wife divorced him; and the necessity of making a living compelled him to work as a commercial artist. But his poetry and painting reflected his growth, depicting the West as an index of his experience there. His best poems and painting use Southwest Indians and landscape subjects, touched with mysticism and symbolism. During the Great Depression he turned to social protest. 30 years after his passing, the California Historical Society is publishing his poems and some of his drawings. Based on Dixon's poems, correspondence, and interviews with his widow, artist Edith Hamlin. Illus. (photos and reproductions of art and poetry manuscripts). 1876-1946

Dixon, Thomas

1775. Crowe, M. Karen. "Southern Horizons: The Autobiography of Thomas Dixon. A Critical Edition." New York U. 1982. 756 pp. *DAI 1982 43(3): 800-A.* DA8214795 ca 1880-1940's

Doane, Gilbert Harry

1776. Bell, James B. GILBERT HARRY DOANE: 28 JANUARY 1897-7 MARCH 1980. *New England Hist. and Geneal. Register 1980 134(July): 179-180.* Obituary of Dr. Doane highlights his several years as author, Episcopal clergyman, historian, and librarian. He served each endeavor with competence and distinction, including that of editor of *The New England Historical and Genealogical Register,* a post he held from 1960 to 1971. His personal characteristics mirrored his professional achievements. 1897-1980

Doane, Warren

1777. Robertson, Marion. ANNALS OF A BARRINGTON SHIPYARD. *Nova Scotia Hist. Q. [Canada] 1980 10(2): 125-141.* Warren Doane built his first ship in Barrington Bay in 1849 and continued to build and repair vessels until the late 1880's. The vessels included brigantines, barques, schooners, and packets. Most of the ships were built for local firms or groups of individuals and were used largely for the shipping trade. They carried lumber, coal, pickled fish, and potatoes from Halifax to the Indies, South America, and the Mediterranean. Primary sources; 4 notes. 1849-83

Dobyns, Harold W.

1778. Dobyns, Harold W. LAST STAND OF THE PRONGHORNS. *Oregon Hist. Q. 1981 82(3): 307-312.* Reminiscences by Harold W. Dobyns of his several years with the US Biological Survey (1914-16) on the desert ranges of Morrow, Umatilla, and Gilliam counties, Oregon. Deals with the end of the pronghorn antelope herds, the 1915-16 rabies epidemic, sheepherding, and various residents of the area. 2 illus., note. 1914-16

Dock, Lavinia Lloyd

1779. Marshall, Alice K. "LITTLE DOC": ARCHITECT OF MODERN NURSING. *Pennsylvania Heritage 1984 10(2): 4-11.* Summarizes Lavinia Lloyd Dock's work to organize nursing into a recognized profession, and her lifelong commitment to women's suffrage and women's movements. 1858-1956

Dockter, Gottlieb (family)

1780. Iseminger, Gordon L. THE GOTTLIEB DOCKTERS: GERMAN-RUSSIAN HOSTELERS OF EMMONS COUNTY. *Heritage Rev. 1984 14(1): 4-8.* Traces the fortunes of Gottlieb Dockter and his family, who left southern Russia in 1889 and homesteaded in Emmons County, North Dakota. 1889-1935

Dodd, Monroe Elmon

1781. Wilkins, S. A. MONROE ELMON DODD: A BIOGRAPHICAL SKETCH. *North Louisiana Hist. Assoc. J. 1984 15(2-3): 99-111.* Monroe Elmon Dodd served in the Spanish-American War and then studied for the ministry at Union University, in Tennessee. While serving a parish in Shreveport, Louisiana, Dodd was elected president of the Louisiana Baptist Convention in 1926. One month later, he resigned and accepted a parish in Los Angeles. Dodd returned to Shreveport in 1927 to help start Dodd College, a two-year vocational and fine arts school for girls. The closing of the college in 1942 was one of his greatest disappointments. Dodd began a broadcast ministry in the 1920's, one of the first to make this use of the new media. In 1933 he became president of the Southern Baptist Convention. Based on church records, recordings, interviews, and secondary sources; photo, 47 notes. ca 1900-52

Dodge, Ernest Stanley

1782. Armstrong, Rodney. ERNEST STANLEY DODGE. *Pro. of the Am. Antiquarian Soc. 1980 90(2): 299-302.* Obituary of Ernest S. Dodge (1913-80), director of the Peabody Museum, Salem, Massachusetts. Briefly surveys his career and lists his publications, which were on the era of discovery and exploration. 1913-80

1783. Knight, Russell W. ERNEST STANLEY DODGE. *Massachusetts Hist. Soc. Pro. 1980 92: 143-146.* Ernest Dodge (1913-80) was a prolific writer, a scholar in ethnology and maritime history, and the founder-editor of *American Neptune.* Dodge dedicated his life in service to the Peabody Museum of Salem, which became one of the premier maritime museums in the United States. 1913-80

Dodge, Grace Hoadley

1784. Katz, Esther. "Grace Hoadley Dodge: Women and the Emerging Metropolis, 1856-1914." New York U. 1980. 298 pp. *DAI 1981 41(12): 5221-A.* DA8110745 1876-1914

Dodge, Mary Abigail

1785. Beasley, Maurine. MARY ABIGAIL DODGE: "GAIL HAMILTON" AND THE PROCESS OF SOCIAL CHANGE. *Essex Inst. Hist. Collections 1980 116(2): 82-100.* The writings of Mary Abigail Dodge (1833-96), a pioneer female journalist of the 19th century, fell into obscurity after her death. Using the pseudonym "Gail Hamilton," she provided in her essays a witty, feminine interpretation of self-reliance and individual improvement based on the philosophy of Ralph Waldo Emerson, whom she knew personally. Examines her life, her writings, and her living arrangements with the James G. Bailey family in Washington, D.C. Primary sources; 72 notes. 1850-96

Dodge, William de Leftwich

1786. Balge, Marjorie. WILLIAM DE LEFTWICH DODGE: AMERICAN RENAISSANCE ARTIST. *Art & Antiques 1982 5(1): 96-103.* Describes the murals of American Renaissance artist William de Leftwich Dodge, whose career lasted from 1893 until his death in 1935; his work was renowned during the high period of the American Renaissance, which ended about 1917; provides an examination of his impressionist oils and watercolors. 1893-1935

1787. Platt, Frederick. A BRIEF AUTOBIOGRAPHY OF WILLIAM DE LEFTWICH DODGE. *Am. Art J. 1982 14(2): 55-63.* William de Leftwich Dodge, an important American muralist of the early 20th century, wrote his autobiography in 1933. He studied at the École des Beaux-Arts in Paris and won prizes in the Salon. He returned to the United States in 1889 and received the commission to paint the domed ceiling of the administration building at the Columbian Exposition in Chicago, then painted murals in the Library of Congress, and in many other public buildings in several states. He won many prizes and was a minor inventor. Based on an autobiography in the possession of the heirs; 6 plates, 50 notes. 1867-1935

Doe, Janet

1788. Brodman, Estelle. EDUCATION AND ATTITUDES OF EARLY MEDICAL LIBRARIANS TO THEIR WORK: A DISCUSSION BASED ON THE ORAL HISTORY PROJECT OF THE MEDICAL LIBRARY ASSOCIATION. *J. of Lib. Hist. 1980 15(2): 167-182.* Discusses the professional experiences of three American women (Mary Louise Marshall, Janet Doe, and Bertha B. Hallam) who were active in medical librarianship shortly before World War I and after. Attempting to evaluate the Michael Harris-Phyllis Dain-Dee Garrison revisionist thesis about early American librarianship, the author delves into the motives that led the women into the profession and the training they received. Provides excerpts from interviews with them. Based on oral history tapes kept by the Medical Library Association Archives, University of Illinois Medical Center, Chicago; 3 photos, 9 notes. 1912-59

Doederlein, Ferdinand

1789. Wangerin, Rudolph. THE DOEDERLEIN DIARY: A SEQUEL. *Concordia Hist. Inst. Q. 1981 54(3): 113-120.* Summarizes Ferdinand Doederlein's career as a Lutheran Church (Missouri Synod) clergyman in Missouri and Illinois. 1859-1915

Doherty, Mary H.

1790. Silberstein, Iola O. DIVERSITY ON CONVERGING PATHWAYS: MARY H. DOHERTY AND HELEN LOTSPEICH. *Queen City Heritage 1983 41(4): 3-23.* Recounts the careers of educators Mary H. Doherty and Helen G. Lotspeich of Cincinnati, Ohio, who founded the College Preparatory School for Girls and the Clifton Open Air School, respectively; in 1974, the schools merged to form the Seven Hills Schools. 1901-74

Dokken, Lars and Knud

1791. Dokken, Lars Olsen and Dokken, Knud Olsen; Catuna, Della Kittelson, transl.; Knight, Carol Lynn H. and Cowden, Gerald S., ed. TWO IMMIGRANTS FOR THE UNION: THEIR CIVIL WAR LETTERS. *Norwegian-American Studies 1979 28: 109-137.* These Norwegian immigrant brothers joined the 15th Wisconsin Volunteers and participated in the 1862 campaigns in Kentucky, Mississippi, and Tennessee. The 22 letters, translated from Norwegian for the first time, tell not only of their hardships and suffering, but also of their hope to survive and return home. Neither did survive; Knud died of camp fever in 1862 and Lars in 1863 of wounds received. Originals in the State Historical Society of Wisconsin; 29 notes. 1862-63

Dole, John

1792. Viets, Henry R. THE RESIDENT HOUSE STAFF AT THE OPENING OF THE BOSTON CITY HOSPITAL IN 1864. *J. of the Hist. of Medicine and Allied Sci. 1959 14(2): 179-190.* 1864-1919
*For abstract see **Blake, Clarence John***

Dombrowski, James A.

1793. Adams, Frank. DOMBROWSKI: PORTRAIT OF AN AMERICAN HERETIC. *Southern Exposure 1982 10(4): 24-29.* James A. Dombrowski, born in 1897, despite prison and hardship, took action to see that the teachings of Christ and Marx relieved injustice in the South. 1929-65

Domingo, Wilfred A.

1794. Samuels, Wilfred David. "Five Afro-Caribbean Voices in American Culture, 1917-1929: Hubert H. Harrison, Wilfred A. Domingo, Richard B. Moore, Cyril V. Briggs, and Claude McKay." U. of Iowa 1977. 181 pp. *DAI 1978 38(7): 4234-A.* 1917-29

Dominis, John (family)

1795. Gasinski, T. Z. CAPTAIN JOHN DOMINIS AND HIS SON, GOVERNOR JOHN OWEN DOMINIS: HAWAII'S CROATIAN CONNECTION. *J. of Croatian Studies 1976 17: 14-46.* A Croatian immigrant from Dalmatia, Captain John (Ivan) Dominis, and his American-born son, John Owen Dominis, have had a significant place in the history of

Hawaii. The son became Governnor of Oahu and Prince Consort of the last Hawaiian Queen, Liliuokalani. In 1838, Captain Dominis moved his center of business from the Pacific Northwest to Honolulu, taking his family with him. Details of his life in Honolulu, including his commercial exploits and importance in official governmental circles. After the father lost his life in the South Seas in 1846, his son turned from commerce to government and had an important place in the last years of the native Polynesian kingdom as an adviser of state policy based on a deep love for the Hawaiian people. After his death in 1891 his royal wife's attempt to trace rumored noble connections in her husband's ancestry were without positive results. His influence was continued through his natural son, John Dominis Aimoku. 5 photos, 41 notes. 1838-1910

Donaghoe, Terence

1796. Coogan, M. Jane. A STUDY OF THE JOHN HUGHES-TERENCE DONAGHOE FRIENDSHIP. *Records of the Am. Catholic Hist. Soc. of Philadelphia 1982 93(1-4): 41-75.* 1809-69

For abstract see ***Hughes, John***

Donaldson, Thomas Corwin

1797. —. THOMAS CORWIN DONALDSON. *Hayes Hist. J. 1979 2(3-4): 150-156.* Highlights the career of Thomas Corwin Donaldson, special attention being given to his relationship with President Rutherford B. Hayes. Specific mention is made of political appointments, interest in minerals, Americana, and collecting art. A list of the works in his collection is included. Photo. 1843-96

Donelson, Andrew Jackson

1798. Bryan, Charles Faulkner, Jr. THE PRODIGAL NEPHEW: ANDREW JACKSON DONELSON AND THE EATON AFFAIR. *East Tennessee Hist. Soc. Publ. 1978 50: 92-112.* The Eaton Affair caused a rift to develop in the relationship between Andrew Jackson and Andrew Jackson Donelson. Not only did Donelson with his wife question the propriety and the morality of Peggy Eaton, but also he was concerned with a serious political issue that had its roots in Tennessee politics. Donelson was convinced that John Eaton was the center of a political faction opposed to the best interests of Andrew Jackson. Feelings between Jackson and Donelson reached a crisis in June 1830. While the resignation of Eaton in April 1831 eased the acrimony between Jackson and his adopted nephew, it took until close to the end of the year for the two men to reestablish their former close relationship. The Eaton Affair showed Donelson to possess as much pride and stubbornness as Jackson where principle was at issue. 50 notes, 4 illus. 1821-33

1799. Owsley, Harriet Chappell. ANDREW JACKSON AND HIS WARD, ANDREW JACKSON DONELSON. *Tennessee Hist. Q. 1982 41(2): 124-139.* Andrew Jackson Donelson (1799-1871) was the nephew and favorite ward of Andrew Jackson who appointed him his aide-de-camp during Jackson's governorship of Florida, left him in charge of the Hermitage in Tennessee during Jackson's senatorial years in Washington, and then brought him to the capital as his presidential secretary. Despite a temporary falling out over the Peggy Eaton affair, Donelson served his uncle faithfully as secretary and business manager. Donelson's loyalty to Jackson's unionism led him to accept the vice-presidential nomination of the American Party in 1856 and to refuse to serve the Confederacy in 1861. Based on the Donelson Papers, Library of Congress, Washington, D.C.; 4 illus., 47 notes. 1817-71

Donelson, Rachel

1800. Owsley, Harriet Chappell. THE MARRIAGES OF RACHEL DONELSON. *Tennessee Hist. Q. 1977 36(4): 479-492.* After a short but tempestuous marriage, Rachel Donelson left her husband, Lewis Robards. Robards later applied for a divorce from the Virginia Legislature, but delayed in meeting all requirements of the Legislature. Believing the Virginia Legislature's act final, Andrew Jackson and Rachel married. The result was years of harassment of Jackson, who was extremely defensive on this issue. 1790-1828

Donnelly, Ignatius

1801. Kreuter, Gretchen. KATE DONNELLY VERSUS THE CULT OF TRUE WOMANHOOD. Stuhler, Barbara and Kreuter, Gretchen, ed. *Women of Minnesota: Selected Biographical Essays* (St. Paul: Minnesota Historical Society Pr., 1977): 20-33. 1833-94

For abstract see ***Donnelly, Katharine McCaffrey***

1802. Peterson, Larry Richard. "Ignatius Donnelly: A Psychohistorical Study in Moral Development Psychology." U. of Minnesota 1977. 234 pp. *DAI 1978 39(2): 950-A.* 1853-93

Donnelly, Katharine McCaffrey

1803. Kreuter, Gretchen. KATE DONNELLY VERSUS THE CULT OF TRUE WOMANHOOD. Stuhler, Barbara and Kreuter, Gretchen, ed. *Women of Minnesota: Selected Biographical Essays* (St. Paul: Minnesota Historical Society Pr., 1977): 20-33. Traces the life of Katharine McCaffrey Donnelly (1833-94) and discusses her marriage to Ignatius Donnelly. Full of energy, humor, forthrightness, advice, and warmth, Kate's letters to her husband reveal her political acumen, concern for their family, events in their daily lives, and their financial circumstances. Born in Philadelphia, Kate spent most of her life there and in Minnesota where she managed the farm while her husband politicked. Primary and secondary sources; photo, 47 notes. 1833-94

Donnelly family

1804. Butt, William Davison. "The Donnellys: History, Legend, Literature." U. of Western Ontario 1977. *DAI 1978 38(9): 5443-A.* 1880's-1970's

Doolittle, Clara Matteson

1805. Hickey, James T., ed. AN ILLINOIS FIRST FAMILY: THE REMINISCENCES OF CLARA MATTESON DOOLITTLE. *J. of the Illinois State Hist. Soc. 1976 69(1): 2-16.* Provides reminiscences of Mrs. James Doolittle, daughter of Illinois governor Joel Matteson (1852-56). She describes the family's comfortable and patrician style of life in Illinois and abroad in the 1850's and throughout the Civil War. The editor presents a history of the first governor's mansion, 1843-56, money for which was not appropriated until more than 20 years after statehood. The editor also describes the life-size marble statue of Stephen A. Douglas by Leonard Volk; it was first used as a touring campaign prop. Based on newspapers, family records, and *Illinois Laws;* illus., map, 43 notes. 1850's-65

Dorman, James Baldwin

1806. Turner, Charles W., ed. JAMES B. DORMAN'S CIVIL WAR LETTERS. *Civil War Hist. 1979 25(3): 262-278.* Reprints 14 letters written during 1861-64 by James Baldwin Dorman (1823-93), CSA, who was a major of the

9th Virginia and a staff officer and an aide to Virginia Governor John Letcher. Provides biographical data on Dorman. The first two letters describe the secession crisis; the rest detail combat and other military matters. 26 notes. 1861-64

Dorsey, Stephen W.

1807. Lowry, Sharon K. "Portrait of an Age: The Political Career of Stephen W. Dorsey, 1868-1889." North Texas State U. 1980. 460 pp. *DAI 1980 41(4): 1734-A.* DA8021908 1868-89

Dorsey, Thomas

1808. Kaplan, Steven. GOSPEL MAN: THOMAS DORSEY. *Horizon 1982 25(7): 16-19.* Recounts the career of the gospel singer from 1921 and his efforts to fuse traditional Baptist lyrics with the style and soul of the blues. 1921-82

Dorson, Richard Mercer

1809. Brunvand, Jan Harold. RICHARD MERCER DORSON (1916-1981). *J. of Am. Folklore 1982 95(377): 347-353.* Richard Mercer Dorson was the doyen of American folklorists. From his base as director of the Indiana University Folklore Institute, he brought professionalism to American folklore advancing fieldwork theory and technique, textual annotation and commentary, analysis of oral style, and intellectual bridges to foreign scholarship. Through his voluminous published work, the 86 Ph.D.'s he directed, and the conferences he organized, Dorson almost single-handedly shaped the modern discipline of American folklore. Note. 1916-81

1810. Richmond, W. Edson. RICHARD MERCER DORSON. *J. of the Folklore Inst. 1981 18(2-3): 94-96.* Obituary of Richard Mercer Dorson (1916-81). Dorson, who was obsessed with the field of American folklore, was one of the individuals most responsible for the dynamic growth of the field and was also responsible for developing the concept of "fakelore," or the conscious and commercial imitations of the folklore he so dearly loved. 1916-81

Dortch, Ellen

1811. Holmes, William F. ELLEN DORTCH AND THE FARMERS' ALLIANCE. *Georgia Historical Quarterly 1985 69(2): 149-172.* Ellen Dortch (1863-1962) served as editor of the Carnesville *Tribune* in Franklin County, Georgia, during 1890-92. She strongly opposed the Southern Farmers' Alliance, the Georgia Alliance, and the People's Party, particularly attacking Thomas Jefferson Stonecypher, the local Alliance lecturer. Although she sympathized with the farmers' problems she was opposed to their political involvement in a third party. Based on newspapers and other primary and secondary sources; 75 notes. 1890-92

Dosch, Roswell H.

1812. Hawkins, Kenneth. NOTES ON THE LIFE OF AN ARTIST: ROSWELL HOLT DOSCH, 1889-1918. *Oregon Hist. Q. 1984 85(1): 55-73.* A Portland, Oregon, native and the son of prosperous immigrants, Roswell H. Dosch studied art at the Portland Academy and continued in Paris and Rome during a 1908-10 family trip, working under sculptor Auguste Rodin and others. Returning to Portland in 1910, he painted, sculpted busts of family and friends, exhibited his works at the Portland Museum Art School, and hosted popular social gatherings. As a University of Oregon faculty member from 1915 until his death from influenza in 1918, Dosch participated in the growing Eugene and Portland art communities. Based primarily on Dosch family correspondence and scrapbooks in private possession; 7 photos, 76 notes. 1908-18

DosPassos, John

1813. Donaldson, Scott. DOS AND HEM: A LITERARY FRIENDSHIP. *Centennial Review 1985 29(2): 163-185.* Traces the friendship of John Dos Passos and Ernest Hemingway from 1924 to their break-up during the Spanish Civil War. Older and more published than Hemingway, Dos Passos encouraged his friend to publish and offered constructive criticism of Hemingway's work. They corresponded extensively, met frequently in Europe, and were social companions. Problems developed as Hemingway moved to the Left politically while Dos Passos, originally sympathetic to Communism, moved to the Right. The break-up came over the Spanish Civil War and it never truly healed. The problem was mostly with Hemingway, who, unlike Dos Passos, seldom maintained lasting friendships with other writers. Based on correspondence, manuscripts, and secondary sources; 56 notes. 1924-68

1814. Levin, Harry. REVISITING DOS PASSOS' *U.S.A.* *Massachusetts Rev. 1979 20(3): 401-415.* Discusses American novelist, essayist, and historian, John Dos Passos (1896-1970), and his work *U.S.A.* The novel uses two formalized devices; the "Newsreel" and "the Camera Eye," which are subdivisions of life stories which make up the trilogy into which the book is primarily divided. The heroes of the novel are the underdogs to whom Dos Passos professed allegiance. He believed that one had to find truth, and that was the explanation for presenting the panorama as he found it in *U.S.A.* Dos Passos was enough of a moralist to be a genuine satirist. He saw a story in everything, and developed his own methods for expressing the complications of modern life. ca 1930-70

1815. Ludington, Townsend. THE MANY AUTOBIOGRAPHIES OF JOHN DOS PASSOS. *Rev. Française d'Etudes Américaines [France] 1982 7(14): 237-243.* Discusses the autobiographical content in John Dos Passos's novels, considered "contemporary chronicles." 1917-69

1816. Ludington, Townsend. THE HOTEL CHILDHOOD OF JOHN DOS PASSOS. *Virginia Q. Rev. 1978 54(2): 297-313.* Dos Passos's early life was spent mainly in Belgium and England until he and his mother returned to the United States in 1906. As the illegitimate son of John R. Dos Passos, a corporation lawyer, he resented his early years but used many of his memories in his writings. 1896-1906

1817. Spindler, Michael. JOHN DOS PASSOS AND THE VISUAL ARTS. *J. of Am. Studies [Great Britain] 1981 15(3): 391-405.* Painter, stage designer, and sometimes illustrator of his own novels, John Dos Passos was influenced during 1909-25 by many innovations in artistic thinking, style, and social ideas among painters, architects, and film makers. That these experiences strengthened his writings, and encouraged the originality first manifested in *Manhattan Transfer* (1925), should not obscure Dos Passos's contributions to the visual arts in the 20th century. 28 notes. 20c

Doubleday, Abner

1818. Ramsey, David Morgan. "The 'Old Sumpter Hero': A Biography of Major General Abner Doubleday." Florida State U. 1980. 257 pp. *DAI 1980 41(3): 968-A.* 8019606 1837-93

Dougall, James

1819. Armstrong, Frederick H. JAMES DOUGALL AND THE FOUNDING OF WINDSOR, ONTARIO. *Ontario Hist. [Canada] 1984 76(1): 48-64.* When James Dougall arrived in Windsor in 1830, the district was starting to develop. His family had both resources and contacts when they arrived in Canada, and they initially opened stores in Toronto before they did in Windsor. The development of the Windsor store was helped when, in 1832, Dougall married into the local elite. After his father died Dougall continued running the store himself while becoming prominent in public life. He helped defend the district in the 1837-38 rebellion, and served in public offices both before and after that. He was also involved with farming and nurseries, as well as railroads and land speculation. Secondary sources; 27 notes. 1830-90

Douglas, Andrew Ellicott

1820. Webb, George Ernest. "The Scientific Career of A. E. Douglas, 1894-1962." U. of Arizona 1978. 455 pp. *DAI 1978 39(4): 2496-A.* 1894-1962

Douglas, Donald Wills

1821. —. DONALD WILLS DOUGLAS 1892-1981. *Aerospace Hist. 1981 27[i.e., 28](2): 122-123.* A biographical sketch of Donald Wills Douglas, American aviation pioneer. He founded the Douglas Aircraft Company in 1920 and the company became famous for transport aircraft, especially the DC-3, which was built in 1935. Photo. 1892-1981

Douglas, Elinor Thompson

1822. Douglas, Elinor Thompson. GROWING UP AT BROOKWOOD. *Delaware Hist. 1979 18(4): 267-274.* The author, the daughter of Mary Wilson Thompson, describes her childhood at Brookwood Farm in Delaware, near Wilmington. Notes the family diet, the family regimen of work and leisure, farm life, and the train of visitors to the family estate. Adds comments on her travels in Egypt and in the Philippines. Covers 1900's-20's. 1900's-20's

Douglas, James

1823. Gough, Barry M. SIR JAMES DOUGLAS AS SEEN BY HIS CONTEMPORARIES: A PRELIMINARY LIST. *BC Studies [Canada] 1979-80 (44): 32-40.* The biographies of Sir James Douglas (1803-77), who rose through the ranks from apprentice in the North West Comany and Hudson's Bay Company to governor of British Columbia, are not definitive. The 29 contemporary (1826-78) descriptions of Douglas, presented herein, help to give a better picture of the man. 2 notes. 1826-78

Douglas, Lewis Williams

1824. Smith, Thomas G. "From the Heart of the American Desert to the Court of St. James's: The Public Career of Lewis W. Douglas of Arizona, 1894-1974." U. of Connecticut 1977. 516 pp. *DAI 1978 38(8): 5011-5012-A.* 1894-1974

1825. Smith, Thomas G. LEWIS DOUGLAS GROWS UP. *J. of Arizona Hist. 1979 20(2): 223-238.* Lewis Williams Douglas, distinguished ambassador, banker, and legislator, was born in 1894 in Bisbee, Arizona, and lived in several mining towns in Arizona and Mexico as a child. Educated in the East, Douglas attended the Hackley School, the Montclair Military Academy, and Amherst College. Douglas's frontier experiences as a child did much to instill the virtues of hard work, self-reliance, charity and perseverence. Based on documents in the Arizona Historical Society, University of Arizona Library, Columbia University Oral History Collection, Hackley School Archives, Amherst College Archives, Franklin D. Roosevelt Library, newspaper accounts, and published secondary sources; 3 photos, 47 notes. 1894-1916

1826. Smith, Thomas G. LEWIS DOUGLAS, ARIZONA POLITICS AND THE COLORADO RIVER CONTROVERSY. *Arizona and the West 1980 22(2): 125-162.* Democrat Lewis Douglas (b. 1894) was an outspoken Arizona legislator and Congressman. He was especially instrumental in blocking federal development of power resources on the Colorado River for nearly a decade. If Arizona could not tax power production within its borders to help reduce taxes on mining and agriculture within the state, he believed it was unjustifiable for the federal government to receive the principal benefit from the tax revenues. In the end, the US Supreme Court rendered a decision unfavorable to his position. 7 illus., 103 notes. 1923-31

Douglas, Ronald D.

1827. Taylor, Thomas T. MEMORIAL TO RONALD D. DOUGLAS (1954-1981), EDWARD C. GARDNER (1946-1981), BRUCE A. JENKINS (1953-1981). *J. of California and Great Basin Anthrop. 1981 3(1): 3-6.* Memorial to three men killed in a plane crash after an archaeological and historical survey of part of Grider Creek in the Klamath wilderness area in northern California, focusing on their interests and careers, with a list of the publications of Ronald D. Douglas and Edward C. Gardner. 1946-81

Douglas, Stephen A.

1828. Howard, Robert P. "OLD DICK" RICHARDSON, THE OTHER SENATOR FROM QUINCY. *Western Illinois Regional Studies 1984 7(1): 16-27.* 1831-65
*For abstract see **Richardson, William Alexander***

Douglas, William O.

1829. Douglas, Cathleen H. WILLIAM O. DOUGLAS: THE MAN. *Supreme Court Hist. Soc. Y. 1981: 6-9.* Discusses the life and career of William O. Douglas (1898-1980), associate justice of the US Supreme Court, focusing on aspects of his early life in Yakima, Washington, and later personal experiences that profoundly affected the development of his legal philosophy. Throughout his career on the bench, Douglas stressed the practical side of legal problems and the need to assess the social impact of individual laws. Based on the personal remembrances of Douglas's widow; photo. 1898-1980

1830. Kennedy, Harry L., Jr. "Justice William O. Douglas on Freedom of the Press." Ohio U. 1980 194 pp. *DAI 1980 41(5): 2265-A.* DA8025559 1939-75

1831. Rodgers, Raymond Sinclair. "Justice William O. Douglas on the First Amendment: Rhetorical Genres in Judicial Opinions." U. of Oklahoma 1979. 271 pp. *DAI 1980 40(12): 6070-A.* 8012292 ca 1939-75

1832. Wallfisch, M. Charles. WILLIAM O. DOUGLAS AND RELIGIOUS LIBERTY. *J. of Presbyterian Hist. 1980 58(3): 193-209.* Associate Justice William O. Douglas, son of a Presbyterian home missionary, served the longest term in the history of the US Supreme Court. Examines some events in the interval (1915-80) between the deaths of the two men. Douglas was a theistic humanist. He was a private and public man of deep religious conviction and enduring—though occasionally strained—devotion to the church he had observed his father serving. His religion reflected Protestantism's most basic ethic of duty and individual accountability. Based on books, articles, and Supreme Court opinions by Douglas, other sources, and an interview with Edward L. R. Elson; 53 notes. 1915-80

Douglass, Andrew Ellicott

1833. Webb, George Ernest. A DEDICATION TO THE MEMORY OF A. E. DOUGLASS, 1867-1962. *Arizona and the West 1978 20(2): 102-106.* Among other achievements of note, astronomer Andrew Ellicott Douglass (1867-1962) developed dendrochronology, the science of tree-ring dating. He established a usable calendar extending back to 11 A.D. His application, principally to pueblo ruins, enabled archaeologists and anthropologists to develop clearer theories about cultural evolution in North America. This and his other pioneering achievements account, to a significant degree, for the present status of science in the Southwest. Illus., biblio. 1894-1959

1834. Webb, George Ernest. THE INDEFATIGABLE ASTRONOMER: A. E. DOUGLASS AND THE FOUNDING OF THE STEWARD OBSERVATORY. *J. of Arizona Hist. 1978 19(2): 169-188.* Describes the efforts of Professor Andrew Ellicott Douglass to establish the Steward Observatory at the University of Arizona, formally dedicated on 23 April 1923. Trained at Harvard College, where he excelled in astronomy, Douglass pursued scientific experiments in Peru, later went to Northern Arizona University for a year, and became Assistant Professor in Physics at the University of Arizona (later its President 1910-11). The establishment of an observatory became his goal. He combined his work with research in southwestern dendrochronology. Mrs. Lavinia Steward, an amateur astronomer, donated the needed money ($60,000) for an observatory in memory of her late husband. The Spencer Lens Company (Buffalo, New York) and the John A. Brashear Company (Pittsburgh, Pennsylvania) supplied the first lens equipment. Despite initial opposition from the University, the Steward Observatory became a reality and Douglass was able to complete his post-700 A.D. dendrochronology (1929). Until his death in 1952, he worked on Observatory improvements and dendrochronological studies. 5 photos, 33 notes. 1900-52

Douglass, Frederick

1835. Andrews, William L. FREDERICK DOUGLASS, PREACHER. *Am. Lit. 1982 54(4): 592-597.* Frederick Douglass began his speaking career in the North as a licensed preacher with the Zion Methodist Church in New Bedford, Massachusetts, during the 1840's. This professional preaching built on previous experience Douglass had as head of a black Sunday school in the South. 12 notes. 1831-41

1836. Brantley, Daniel. BLACK DIPLOMACY AND FREDERICK DOUGLASS' CARIBBEAN EXPERIENCES, 1871 AND 1889-1891: THE UNTOLD STORY. *Phylon 1984 45(3): 197-209.* Discusses the influence of blacks on late 19th-century US foreign policy, particularly in the Caribbean. Scholars have slighted the influence of black newspapers in shaping 19th-century foreign policy and have not adequately examined the role of black leader and foreign service employee Frederick Douglass. An analysis of the life and work of Douglass, who represented the United States at different stages in his career in the Dominican Republic and the Republic of Haiti, suggests that scholars could learn much about the history of US foreign policy by looking into the roles of minorities in diplomatic relations and by researching the untapped sources that contain the history of black and minority involvement in foreign policy. 2 tables, 26 notes. 1840-91

1837. Felgar, Robert. THE REDISCOVERY OF FREDERICK DOUGLASS. *Mississippi Q. 1982 35(4): 427-438.* Reviews *The Frederick Douglass Papers. Series One: Speeches, Debates, and Interviews. Vol. 1: 1841-46* (1979), edited by John W. Blassingame; Nathan Irvin Huggins's *The Life of Frederick Douglass* (1980); and Dickson J. Preston's *Young Frederick Douglass: The Maryland Years* (1980). 1817-95

1838. Goldstein, Leslie Friedman. MORALITY & PRUDENCE IN THE STATESMANSHIP OF FREDERICK DOUGLASS: RADICAL AS REFORMER. *Polity 1984 16(4): 606-623.* Frederick Douglass saw that blacks would not be emancipated and that their condition would not improve except through political action which, in the American context, required participation—including bargaining and compromises—in electoral and party politics. 1840's-95

1839. Migliorino, Ellen Ginzburg and Campanaro, Giorgio G. FREDERICK DOUGLASS'S MORE INTIMATE NATURE AS REVEALED IN SOME OF HIS UNPUBLISHED LETTERS. *Southern Studies 1979 18(4): 480-487.* Some unpublished letters of black abolitionist Frederick Douglass (1817-95), recently donated to the Library of Congress, reveal aspects of his personality. One group was written by Douglass to Harriet A. Bailey, a friend residing with his family, during 1846-47; they reveal a warm, confidential relationship of close friendship and respect. They also reveal insecurity and homesickness from his residence in Great Britain. In 1894 he wrote two letters to Ruth Adams, probably the same Harriet Bailey after marriage, in which he talks of deaths in the family and remembers old times with fondness. Douglass needed to communicate with someone other than his wife, who apparently could not write. Based on the Frederick Douglass Collection in Library of Congress; 24 notes. 1846-94

1840. Perry, Patsy Brewington. BEFORE *THE NORTH STAR*: FREDERICK DOUGLASS' EARLY JOURNALISTIC CAREER. *Phylon 1974 35(1): 96-107.* Before the founding of *The North Star* Frederick Douglass had contributed to two New York-based weeklies. Cites evidence that the prejudice he had met with on a western speaking tour had a great deal to do with his decision to publish a newspaper. During his months of indecision he gained valuable journalistic experience, with "an opportunity to test his ideas in print, to experience and review the various forms of racial prejudice which he would attack . . . and to explore the prospects for a newspaper such as the one he envisioned." 46 notes. 1841-47

1841. Pitre, Merline. FREDERICK DOUGLASS: THE POLITICIAN VS. THE SOCIAL REFORMER. *Phylon 1979 40(3): 270-277.* Discusses the political activities of Frederick Douglass in the Republican Party during 1870-95. He held appointive offices, including member of the Santo Domingo Commission, member of the Legislative Council, Marshal of the District of Columbia, and Recorder of Deeds. While in them, Douglass seemed to make fewer comments in favor of social reform than usual. 30 notes. 1870-95

1842. Pitre, Merline. FREDERICK DOUGLASS AND AMERICAN DIPLOMACY IN THE CARIBBEAN. *J. of Black Studies 1983 13(4): 457-476.* Frederick Douglass worked for US annexation of the Dominican Republic in 1871 and for acquisition of a naval base in Haiti in 1889 because of his loyalty to the Republican Party and his missionary belief that US influence in the area would uplift those countries' inhabitants. He was not aware that he was supporting imperialism. Based on the Frederick Douglass Papers; 17 notes, biblio. 1868-91

1843. Ripley, C. Peter. THE AUTOBIOGRAPHICAL WRITINGS OF FREDERICK DOUGLASS. *Southern Studies 1985 24(1): 5-29.* Former slave, successful public speaker for abolition, and statesman Frederick Douglass wrote three autobiographical works. The *Narrative of the Life of Frederick Douglass* (1845) explains his background and escape from slavery and points out the evils of slavery. Many readers doubted a former slave could write so eloquently, so Douglass wrote *My Bondage and My Freedom* (1855), giving proof of his slave background with specific names and details. The style is more mature and sophisticated than the earlier work. Finally, Douglass wrote two versions of *Life and Times of Frederick Douglass* (1881, 1892) as his statement for posterity and as an attempt to earn money. Based on the Frederick Douglass Papers in the Boston Public Library and the Library of Congress; 68 notes. 1845-95

1844. Scruggs, Otey M. TWO BLACK PATRIARCHS: FREDERICK DOUGLASS AND ALEXANDER CRUMMELL. *Afro-Americans in New York Life and Hist. 1982 6(1): 17-30.* Discusses the ideas and philosophies of Frederick Douglass (1818-95), and Episcopal clergyman, Alexander Crummell (1819-98), who both lived in New York City; focuses on their emergence in the 19th century as spokespersons for the two black intellectual traditions, equalitarian radical in the liberal tradition (Douglass) and nationalist in the conservative tradition (Crummell). 1818-98

Doull, Alexander John

1845. Esselmont, Harriet A. E. ALEXANDER JOHN DOULL: AN APPRECIATION. *J. of the Can. Church Hist. Soc. [Canada] 1976 18(4): 98-108.* Traces the life and career of Alexander John Doull, the first bishop of Kootenay in the Okanagan Valley, British Columbia. Born in Nova Scotia of a Church of Scotland family, Doull was an orphaned only child. Reared by relatives, he received his advanced education in the British Isles where he converted to Anglicanism and became a priest. After he returned to Canada, Doull served churches in Montreal and Victoria before he became the youngest bishop of the Church of England in Canada. A man of strong convictions, he took active positions on the issues of the day and worked to increase the strength of Anglicanism in his diocese. When he died in 1937, the *Canadian Churchman* declared, "His character was that beautiful combination of strength and beauty, grace and truth which the Apostles found in the Saviour." 25 notes. 1870-1937

Dove, Arthur

1846. Morgan, Ann Lee. AN ENCOUNTER AND ITS CONSEQUENCES: ARTHUR DOVE AND ALFRED STIEGLITZ, 1910-1925. *Biography 1979 2(1): 35-59.* Arthur Dove and Alfred Stieglitz established their friendship during the period from 1910 to 1925. During this time, Dove evolved from a successful illustrator into a modernist painter of first-rate importance. Stieglitz, recognized as the leader of art photography in 1910, transcended that single role to become a self-proclaimed cultural force by 1925. The professional accomplishments of the two men are described in relation to biographical events, with particular reference to the effects of their personal association. 1910-25

Dow, Arthur Wesley

1847. Moffatt, Frederick C. THE EDUCATION OF THE NEW ENGLAND ARTIST: THE EARLY YEARS OF ARTHUR WESLEY DOW. *Essex Inst. Hist. Collections 1976 112(4): 275-289.* Studies the early years of the New England artist, Arthur Wesley Dow (1857-1922) and demonstrates how the rigid Calvinistic climate of New England was modified. Dow, who later taught at the Pratt Institute and the Teachers College, Columbia University, did not receive any formal art instruction until he was 23 years old. Prior to that time he drew old buildings in Ipswich, Massachusetts, which he had been studying as part of his interest in the past. He was influenced by his grammar school teacher, Rev. John P. Cowles, writer and artist Everett Stanley Hubbard, and Rev. Augustine Caldwell, a minister and printer who encouraged him to reproduce his art work through printing and to seek formal art training. Dow's major contribution to art was the principle that picture-making involved the ordered selection and arrangement of flat shapes on the picture planes. Based on primary and secondary sources; 4 illus., 41 notes. 1857-80

Dow, George Francis

1848. Farnam, Anne. GEORGE FRANCIS DOW: A CAREER OF BRINGING THE "PICTURESQUE TRADITIONS OF SLEEPING GENERATIONS" TO LIFE IN THE EARLY TWENTIETH CENTURY. *Essex Institute Historical Collections 1985 121(2): 77-90.* Provides a short biography of George Francis Dow, focusing on his work at the Essex Institute, his influence on the installation of reproduction rooms in museums, and his role as "Antiquarian-Architect expert" for the Pioneer Village in Salem, which was constructed for the Massachusetts tercentenary of 1930. While Dow was secretary, the Essex Institute began its involvement with the material culture of past generations. Dow's period rooms and his restoration of the John Ward House helped establish him as a leader in the early museum and historic house movement. 5 photos, 48 notes. 1900-30

Dow, Margaret Cornelius

1849. Ingells, David T. MISS CORA DOW. *Cincinnati Hist. Soc. Bull. 1982 40(3): 151-166.* Biography of Cincinnati entrepreneur Margaret Cornelius Dow and a summary of the history of her business, the Dow Drug Company, 1885-1959. 1885-1959

Dowie, John Alexander

1850. Heath, Alden R. APOSTLE IN ZION. *J. of the Illinois State Hist. Soc. 1977 70(2): 98-113.* John Alexander Dowie (1847-1907), Scottish evangelist and founder of the Divine Healing Association, came to the United States from Australia in 1888 and established in 1899 a new communitarian settlement based on strict prohibitions against alcohol, tobacco, labor unions, and doctors. His Christian Catholic Church's experiment at Zion, Illinois, drew thousands of converts, but his own megalomania caused followers to ultimately reject his leadership of that community. 6 illus., map, 52 notes. 1888-1907

Downes, Prentice G.

1851. Cockburn, R. H., ed. PRENTICE G. DOWNES'S EASTERN ARCTIC JOURNAL, 1936. *Arctic [Canada] 1983 36(3): 232-250.* Reprints Downes's journal, which provides a detailed account of the voyage of the *Nascopie* from Montreal to Churchill in 1936. 1936

Doyle, Michael Francis

1852. Rossi, John. MICHAEL FRANCIS DOYLE OF PHILADELPHIA. *Éire-Ireland 1985 20(2): 105-129.* Michael Francis Doyle was an Irish-American lawyer in Philadelphia who for many years was prominent in Democratic Party politics, particularly during the New Deal era. Doyle was also involved peripherally in the Irish republican movement before 1922, was an active Catholic layman, and—as an international lawyer—performed various diplomatic assignments. In 1916, Doyle assisted the defense in the treason trial of Sir Roger Casement in London. Based on documents in American and British archives, particularly the Roosevelt Papers at Hyde Park, New York; 84 notes. 1893-1945

Doyle, Mildred E.

1853. Baker, Carol E. "Superintendent Mildred E. Doyle: Educational Leader, Politician, Woman." U. of Tennessee 1977. 266 pp. *DAI 1978 38(9): 5139-A.* 1924-76

Doyle, Price

1854. Reichmuth, Roger Edwin. "Price Doyle, 1896-1967: His Life and Work in Music Education." U. of Illinois, Urbana-Champaign 1977. 456 pp. *DAI 1978 38(10): 5981-5982-A.* 1923-67

Dragging Canoe

1855. Evans, E. Raymond. NOTABLE PERSONS IN CHEROKEE HISTORY: DRAGGING CANOE. *J. of Cherokee Studies 1977 2(1): 176-189.* Dragging Canoe was born about 1740 in an Overhill town on the Little Tennessee River and became a military leader in maturity. He opposed any land cessions to the whites, sided with the British during the American Revolution, and personally led many attacks. Following the Revolution he was involved in attempts to form an Indian alliance against the Americans. The defeat of St. Clair in November 1791 was a highlight of his career. He died 1 March 1792 at Lookout Mountain, Tennessee. Primary and secondary sources; 81 notes. 1740-92

Drake, Robert (family)

1856. Sanborn, George F., Jr. ROBERT DRAKE'S TWO WIVES. *New England Hist. and Geneal. Register 1984 138(Apr): 107-114.* Untangles the genealogical confusion surrounding Robert Drake (1717-56) of Hampton, New Hampshire, his two wives (both named Elizabeth), and a relative, also named Robert Drake (1719-94). 18c-19c

Draper, Andrew Sloan

1857. Johnson, Ronald M. CAPTAIN OF EDUCATION: ANDREW SLOAN DRAPER, 1848-1913. *Societas 1976 6(3): 193-211.* Traces the educational career of Andrew Sloan Draper from his appointment as New York state school superintendent in 1886, his presidency of the University of Illinois at Urbana, and his position as New York's first commissioner of education. Although he emphasized training the mind instead of mere memorization, his most distinguished achievement was being a superlative administrator and organizer of education that met the needs of a new urban and industrial age. Based on documents in the University of Illinois and the Columbia University archives, and on primary and secondary sources; 49 notes. 1886-1913

Drayton, John

1858. Soltow, Lee. SOCIOECONOMIC CLASSES IN SOUTH CAROLINA AND MASSACHUSETTS IN THE 1790S AND THE OBSERVATIONS OF JOHN DRAYTON. *South Carolina Hist. Mag. 1980 81(4): 283-305.* Later a South Carolina governor (1800-02 and 1808-10), "John Drayton found Boston and Massachusetts to be a land of democracy where equality of condition prevailed in terms of education and social intercourse" but that "men were *not* equal in an economic sense," and that "the free in South Carolina experienced probably as much inequality as existed anywhere in the whole of the new nation." 1793-94

Dreier, Katherine Sophie

1859. Bohan, Ruth Louise. "The Société Anonyme's Brooklyn Exhibition, 1926-1927: Katherine Sophie Dreier and the Promotion of Modern Art in America." U. of Maryland 1980. 437 pp. *DAI 1980 41(5): 2181-A.* 8025238 1926-27

Dreiser, Theodore

1860. Godfrey, Lydia Schurman. "Theodore Dreiser and the Dime Novel World; or the Missing Chapter in Dreiser's Life, 1894-1906." U. of Maryland 1984. 196 pp. *DAI 1985 46(4): 981-982-A.* DA8512189 1894-1906

1861. Ivan'ko, Sergei Sergeevich. TEODOR DRAIZER—PISATEL', KOMMUNIST [Theodore Dreiser: writer, Communist]. *Novaia i Noveishaia Istoriia [USSR] 1985 (2): 127-143.* Presents a biography of author Theodore Dreiser, dealing primarily with his social philosophy as a writer and publicist and his evolution from a fighter against social injustice and racism to a militant activist in the struggle against fascism and in support of the Soviet Union. Hitler's perfidious attack on the USSR and the heroic fight of the Soviet Army led Dreiser to join the American Communist Party in the summer of 1945, half a year before his death. Based on Theodore Dreiser's works and secondary sources; photo, 46 notes. 1900's-45

1862. Kwiat, Joseph J. THEODORE DREISER'S CREATIVE QUEST: EARLY "PHILOSOPHICAL" BELIEFS AND ARTISTIC VALUES. *Arizona Q. 1981 37(3): 265-274.* Theodore Dreiser was a significant historical force and forerunner of the major tendencies in 20th century US fiction, who strove for naturalness and simplicity. His aesthetic values included a balanced rendering of life's perfections and terrors and the translation of postimpressionism and neoimpressionism into literature. Dreiser believed that candid discussion of all facets of life would bring social consciousness into harmony with man's great needs. Although his work of 1914-31 was criticized, it expressed the confusing and traumatic changes in early 20th century US society. Based on correspondence with H. L. Mencken; 16 notes. 1914-31

1863. Mookerjee, R. N. DREISER'S VIEWS ON ART AND FICTION. *Am. Literary Realism, 1870-1910 1979 12(2): 338-342.* Discusses 20th-century American author Theodore Dreiser's views on art in general and the novelist and fiction in particular; 1900's-30's. 1900's-30's

1864. Riggio, Thomas P. DREISER AND MENCKEN IN THE LITERARY TRENCHES. *American Scholar 1985 54(2): 227-238.* Traces the enigmatic personal relationship of two prominent American men of letters, Theodore Dreiser and H. L. Mencken. Their relationship combined a deep personal affection with profound intellectual disagreement. 1908-45

Dresser family.

1865. Hickey, James T. A FAMILY ALBUM: THE DRESSERS OF SPRINGFIELD. *J. of the Illinois State Hist. Soc. 1982 75(4): 309-320.* The Illinois State Historical Society has received over 200 ambrotypes, daguerreotypes, and photographs depicting five generations descended from Nathan and Rebecca Dresser. Two generations of the family were closely associated with the family of Abraham Lincoln. Members included Episcopal priests Charles and David Walker Dresser, architect Henry Dresser, and physician Thomas Withers Dresser. Other members of the family included a county judge, a county clerk, and a state representative. Edmund Dresser served as assistant superintendent of the western division of the Wabash, St. Louis and Pacific Railroad. Thomas Dresser White served as US Air Force chief of staff during 1957-61. 16 illus., 14 notes. 1800-1982

Dreves, Katharine Densford

1866. Glass, Lauren Kay. "Katharine Densford Dreves: Marching at the Head of the Parade." U. of Illinois, Chicago 1983. 299 pp. *DAI 1984 44(11): 3358-3359-B.* DA8404402 20c

Drew, Charles R.

1867. Drew, Grace Ridgeley. THE DR. CHARLES R. DREW STAMP. *J. of the Afro-American Hist. and Geneal. Soc. 1981 2(4): 139-142.* Biography of Charles R. Drew (d. 1950), a black doctor and "leading authority on mass transfusion and processing methods" who was honored posthumously with a 35-cent stamp issued 3 June 1981 on the 77th anniversary of his birth. 1904-50

Drew, George

1868. Bawtinhimer, R. E. THE DEVELOPMENT OF AN ONTARIO TORY: YOUNG GEORGE DREW. *Ontario Hist. [Canada] 1977 69(1): 55-75.* Presents the major influences in George Drew's early career and analyzes his development into a leading Tory. Outlines his Loyalist family background. He served in the army in World War I before being invalided home. His early postwar career was devoted to the family law practice, until he entered local politics. Analyzes his attitudes and campaigns, along with his election in 1925 as mayor of Guelph. 72 notes. 1890-1925

Drew, John Thompson

1869. McFadden, Marguerite. COLONEL JOHN THOMPSON DREW: CHEROKEE CAVALIER. *Chronicles of Oklahoma 1981 59(1): 30-53.* John Thompson Drew, mixed-blood Cherokee, played a key role in tribal history because of his ability to speak English, his businessman's acumen, and his powerful relatives. Despite a lack of formal education, Drew was licensed to practice law in 1851 and within two years was made Judge of the Canadian District of Indian Territory. During the Civil War he actively supported the Confederacy by raising a regiment of Cherokee soldiers, but the war destroyed his wealth. Based on John Drew Papers at Gilcrease Institute; 5 photos, 55 notes. 1850-65

Drexel, Francis M.

1870. Jones, Elsa Loacker. FRANCIS MARTIN DREXEL'S YEARS IN AMERICA. *Records of the Am. Catholic Hist. Soc. of Philadelphia 1974 85(3-4): 129-140.* Francis M. Drexel, an Austrian, arrived at Philadelphia in 1817. After years of supporting himself and his family by portrait painting, he became an exchange broker and amassed one of America's great fortunes. One of his grandchildren, Mother Katharine Drexel, founded the Order of Sisters of the Blessed Sacrament for Indians and Colored People. 20 notes. 1817-63

Dreyfus, Leon

1871. Rostenberg, Leona. PORTRAIT FROM A FAMILY ARCHIVE: LEON DREYFUS, 1842-1898. *Manuscripts 1985 37(4): 283-294.* The author's maternal grandfather, Leon Dreyfus, born in the Palatinate 12 August 1842, immigrated to the United States in 1859 following his older but aimless brother, Theodore. Leon Dreyfus went to New Orleans where he followed a commercial career. In 1866 he obtained his US citizenship and a junior partnership in the watch and jewelry firm of his future brother-in-law, Nathan Koch. In 1869, he married Bertha Hirsch Koch, who bore him seven children, one dying in infancy. Nathan Koch and Dreyfus became the leading jewelry wholesalers in the South. Based on family records including journals and letters of Theodore and Leon Dreyfus and their parents; 2 illus. Article to be continued. 1842-98

Drouet de Richerville family

1872. Chaput, Donald. THE FAMILY OF DROUET DE RICHERVILLE: MERCHANTS, SOLDIERS, AND CHIEFS OF INDIANA. *Indiana Mag. of Hist. 1978 74(2): 103-116.* From the 1720's, when several members of the Drouet de Richerville family entered the fur trade, until the death of Jean-Baptiste Richardville in 1841, the Drouets were one of the most significant families of officers-traders in the western Great Lakes region. 1720's-1841

Drumheller, Daniel

1873. Bolker, Norman. DANIEL DRUMHELLER, NATURE'S NOBLEMAN. *Pacific Northwesterner 1982 26(4): 49-58.* Daniel Drumheller left his family in Missouri to travel west when he was 14; describes his various jobs and business adventures, especially his success at raising cattle, and his final settling in Spokane, Washington, 1854-1925. 1854-1925

Drury, Clifford Merrill

1874. Andrews, Thomas F. THE HISTORIAN WHO SAVED AN IDAHO STORY: CLIFFORD MERRILL DRURY, 1897-1984. *Idaho Yesterdays 1984 28(1): 16-17.* Clifford Merrill Drury was best known as the historian of the Protestant missionaries who, during the 1830's-40's, worked with the Nez Percé, Cayuse, and Spokane Indians. Drury had been a Presbyterian minister in China and in Idaho. In 1938, he became a faculty member of the San Francisco Theological Seminary. In 1936, Drury began his efforts to document the history of the Oregon Mission of the American Board of Commissioners for Foreign Missions. He had written seven volumes by 1979. Photo. 1922-84

DuBois, Guy Pène

1875. Fahlman, Betsy. "Guy Pène du Bois: Painter, Critic, Teacher." U. of Delaware 1981. 296 pp. *DAI 1982 42(11): 4628-A.* DA8210125 1904-58

1876. Fahlman, Betsy. GUY PÈNE DU BOIS: PAINTER AND CRITIC. *Art & Antiques 1980 3(6): 106-113.* Brooklyn-born Guy Pène du Bois, painter, teacher, critic, spokesman for the realism of the ashcan school of the early 20th century, and sympathizer with modernism, is famous for his paintings depicting the 1920's and 1930's with wry humor. ca 1900-46

DuBois, Harry (family)

1877. Kersey, Harry A., Jr. THE JOHN DUBOIS FAMILY OF JUPITER: A FLORIDA PROTOTYPE, 1887-1981. *Tequesta 1981 41: 5-22.* Since Harry DuBois began living in Jupiter, Florida, during the 1880's, the DuBois family has been an integral part of the area's social history. During the 1890's Harry DuBois purchased a tract of 18 acres, known as Stone's Point, on the Loxahatchee River. His home was constructed on a massive oyster-shell mound 20 feet high and over 600 feet long. His first child, John, born in 1899, still lives there. Based on oral history interviews and family papers; 25 notes. 1880-1981

DuBois, W. E. B.

1878. Green, Dan S. and Smith, Earl. W. E. B. DUBOIS AND THE CONCEPTS OF RACE AND CLASS. *Phylon 1983 46(4): 262-272.* Reviews the outlook of W. E. B. DuBois on the interrelationships between racism and class prejudice, particularly as related to the arguments of William J. Wilson in his *The Declining Significance of Race* (1980). Describes DuBois's thinking and reprints excerpts from his works, beginning in 1891, that demonstrate his thesis that being members of an exploited class, as well as a different race, accounts for the black situation in the United States. Wilson's conclusions are largely supported by DuBois's earlier work. 44 notes. 1891-1963

1879. Johnson, Adolph, Jr. "A History and Interpretation of the William Edward Burghardt DuBois-Booker Taliaferro Washington Higher Education Controversy." U. of Southern California 1976. *DAI 1978 38(10): 5949-A.* 1900's-10's

1880. Katz, Maude White, ed. LEARNING FROM HISTORY: THE INGRAM CASE OF THE 1940'S. *Freedomways 1979 19(2): 82-86.* 1947-49
*For abstract see **Ingram, Rosa Lee***

1881. Klíma, Vladimír. IN BATTLE FOR PEACE: WILLIAM E. B. DU BOIS. *Archív Orientální [Czechoslovakia] 1979 47(4): 312-316.* Surveys the life and works of W. E. B. Du Bois, black American writer, civil rights activist, and Marxist philosopher. ca 1880-1963

1882. Lange, Werner J. W. E. B. DU BOIS AND THE FIRST SCIENTIFIC STUDY OF AFRO-AMERICA. *Phylon 1983 44(2): 135-146.* William Edward Burghardt Du Bois became the first social scientist of, for, and by Afro-America. His were among the first scientific studies of black people. Not only was he engaged in the accumulation of massive data, but his analyses and interpretations provided a solid base for 20th-century scholarship. He blended four approaches: statistics, history, anthropology, and sociology. His incisive mind was geared toward destroying the myths that most whites had about blacks. 1895-1915

1883. Marable, Manning. PEACE AND BLACK LIBERATION: THE CONTRIBUTION OF W. E. B. DU BOIS. *Sci. & Soc. 1983-84 47(4): 385-405.* Traces W. E. B. Du Bois's thought on the relationship between peace and black liberation. As early as 1915, Du Bois linked war with imperialist competition, consistently arguing that peace was possible only after the destruction of colonialism and racism. After 1945, Du Bois was active with the Peace Information Center, an association that culminated in a McCarthyite attack that destroyed his career. Secondary sources; 55 notes. 1904-76

1884. Redding, Jay Saunders. *THE CORRESPONDENCE OF W.E.B. DUBOIS:* A REVIEW ARTICLE. *Phylon 1979 40(2): 119-122.* Discusses the character of Dr. W. E. B. Dubois, black activist and educator (d. 1963), and some of the recently published *The Correspondence of W. E. B. Dubois* (3 vols; Amherst: U. of Massachusetts, 1973-78). 1890's-1963

DuBose, William Porcher

1885. Luker, Ralph E. THE CRUCIBLE OF CIVIL WAR AND RECONSTRUCTION IN THE EXPERIENCE OF WILLIAM PORCHER DUBOSE. *South Carolina Hist. Mag. 1982 83(1): 50-71.* While William Porcher DuBose was better known abroad than at home, he was an American theologian whose experiences during the Civil War and Reconstruction periods shaped his thought. Born near Winnsboro in 1836 he attended Winnsboro Academy as a youth and at age 15 went to the Citadel, then to the University of Virginia, and finally to the Protestant Episcopal Church's Diocesan Seminary at Camden. There he met and studied with John H. Elliott. When the Civil War started, he joined the Holcombe Legion and despite several wounds saw action throughout the war. Drawing on the story of the prodigal son, he developed his thesis of "at-one-ment." He believed that "a Man's own self, when he has once truly come to himself, is his best and only experimental proof of God." Primary sources; 56 notes. 1860-1914

DuBrul, Napoleon

1886. Westheimer, Charles. NAPOLEON DUBRUL, A CINCINNATI INVENTOR. *Cincinnati Hist. Soc. Bull. 1980 38(3): 180-190.* Biography of Canadian-born Napoleon Du Breuil, later DuBrul (1846-1954), who started a manufacturing business called Schwill & DuBrul (or The Cincinnati Cigar Mould Co.), later became employed by a tin shop where he invented a barn lantern, and was a partner in many businesses. 1846-1954

Dubuclet, Antoine

1887. Vincent, Charles. ASPECTS OF THE FAMILY AND PUBLIC LIFE OF ANTOINE DUBUCLET: LOUISIANA'S BLACK STATE TREASURER, 1868-1878. *J. of Negro Hist. 1981 66(1): 26-36.* Antoine Dubuclet was born in 1810 into a prosperous free black family. By the end of the Civil War, he had accumulated large sugarcane plantations. Under congressional reconstruction policies, Dubuclet was elected state treasurer of Louisiana in 1868, 1870, and 1874. He died in 1887. Dubuclet survived the stormy days of Reconstruction untouched by scandal and blessed with bipartisan support. 1868-78

Dubuque, Julien

1888. Auge, Thomas. THE LIFE AND TIMES OF JULIEN DUBUQUE. *Palimpsest 1976 57(1): 2-13.* Julien Dubuque, long acknowledged as one of the first white settlers in what is today Iowa, was an atypical frontiersman. Cultivated and accustomed to a lavish life-style, he was a cultural incongruity. But he was also shrewd and opportunistic in his business dealings, duplicitous in relationships with Indians, and constantly in debt. Illus., map, note. 1788-1810

Duche, Andrew

1889. Wells, E. D. DUCHE, THE POTTER. *Georgia Hist. Q. 1957 41(4): 383-390.* Studies the life and art of Georgia potter Andrew Duche (b. 1709) and narrates the story of 20th-century efforts to locate samples of his work. 1709-41

Duckworth, Ruth.

1890. Balch, Inge Gyrite. A VISIT WITH RUTH DUCKWORTH: PAINTER, SCULPTOR, CERAMIST. *Kansas Q. 1982 14(4): 35-42.* Sketches the career of Chicago artist Ruth Duckworth since the 1940's. 1940's-82

Dudzik, Mary Theresa

1891. Knawa, Anne Marie. JANE ADDAMS AND JOSEPHINE DUDZIK: SOCIAL SERVICE PIONEERS. *Polish Am. Studies 1978 35(1-2): 13-22.* Compares the life and work of Sister Mary Theresa (Josephine Dudzik), the founder of the Franciscan Sisters of Chicago, with that of the internationally renowned Jane Addams (1860-1935). Sister Mary Theresa (1860-1918) was an indefatigable worker. Official steps are being taken for her beatification and possible canonization. Polish and English primary and secondary sources; 23 notes. 1860-1918

Duede, Carl

1892. Hubler, David M. IOWA'S EARLY BIRDS. *Palimpsest 1981 62(6): 162-169.* Discusses the early years of flight in Iowa led by pioneer aviator Carl Duede (1886-1956) of Stuart, Iowa, and his friends, Olney Wilde and Bill Couch. 1886-1919

Duer, William

1893. Sterling, David L. WILLIAM DUER, JOHN PINTARD, AND THE PANIC OF 1792. Frese, Joseph R. and Judd, Jacob, ed. *Business Enterprise in Early New York* (Tarrytown, N.Y.: Sleepy Hollow Pr., 1979): 99-132. Recounts the careers of William Duer, "the principal, if unintentional, architect of the first financial panic in the new republic," and John Pintard, his agent in New York. Operating out of Philadelphia, Duer directed a group of speculators who manipulated public securities. He sought to acquire large numbers of shares of stock in the Bank of the United States and Bank of New York, perhaps intending to corner the market. With Pintard's assistance, Duer's machinations included marketing stock for banks not yet then in existence. As rumors of bank mergers increased, Duer profited, but when the merger did not materialize investors wanted their money back. Duer and Pintard, bankrupt, were imprisoned, and New York City and other northern financial centers endured a sharp but short depression. 62 notes. 1792-99

Duff, Mary Ann

1894. Landau, Penny Maya. "The Career of Mary Ann Duff, the American Siddons 1810-1839." Bowling Green State U. 1979. 179 pp. *DAI 1980 40(10): 5250-A.* 1810-39

Duff, Wilson

1895. Ames, Michael M. A NOTE ON THE CONTRIBUTIONS OF WILSON DUFF TO NORTHWEST COAST ETHNOLOGY AND ART. *BC Studies [Canada] 1976 (31): 3-11.* Wilson Duff (1925-76) was a pioneer in the development of anthropology in the Pacific Northwest. He chaired the British Columbia Archaeological Sites Advisory Board, was editor of *Anthropology in British Columbia*, was consultant for the Kitwancool Indians, was a founder and president of the British Columbia Museums Association, and taught at the University of British Columbia. Duff was interested in Northwest Coast art as both "high art" and as a subject for "deep analysis." Biblio. 1950-76

1896. Borden, Charles E. WILSON DUFF (1925-1976): HIS CONTRIBUTIONS TO THE GROWTH OF ARCHAEOLOGY IN BRITISH COLUMBIA. *BC Studies [Canada] 1977 (33): 3-12.* Wilson Duff (1925-76), trained in anthropology and archaeology at the Universities of British Columbia and Washington, established himself as an active and trusted friend of the Pacific Northwest Indians. As Curator of Anthropology at the British Columbia Provincial Museum and in other capacities, he worked for legislation to protect the province's archaeological resources and to promote systematic studies in ways that benefited Indians. Biblio. 1950-76

Duggan, Anne Schley

1897. Weeks, Sandra Rivers. "Anne Schley Duggan: Portrait of a Dance Educator." Texas Woman's U. 1980. 331 pp. *DAI 1980 41(5): 2010-2012-A.* 8025590 1936-73

Duguid, Archer Fortescue

1898. Nicholson, G. W. L. ARCHER FORTESCUE DUGUID, 1887-1976. *Can. Hist. Assoc. Hist Papers [Canada] 1976: 268-271.* Obituary of Archer Fortescue Duguid, director of the Historical Section of the Canadian General Staff, 1921-45, and official historian of the Canadian Expeditionary Force, 1945-47. He was a founder of the Heraldry Society of Canada and planned the mural decoration for the Memorial Chamber in the Peace Tower at Ottawa. Colonel Duguid was noted for his work on regimental battle honors and battlefield memorials. 1910-76

Duhamel, Roger

1899. Trépanier, Pierre. ROGER DUHAMEL (1916-1985) [Roger Duhamel (1916-85)]. *Action Nationale [Canada] 1985 75(2): 103-118.* Biographical sketch of the life of Quebec political activist and author Roger Duhamel, reviewing his education at the Jesuit Sainte-Marie College, his evolution into a militant Quebec nationalist who struggled to defend the French language and culture against anglophone Canadian assimilation, and his career as a prolific writer and journalist. 1916-85

Duke, Basil W.

1900. Harrison, Lowell H. GENERAL BASIL W. DUKE, C.S.A. *Filson Club Hist. Q. 1980 54(1): 5-36.* Relates the Civil War activities of Confederate General Basil W. Duke. Duke served as second in command in the 2d Kentucky Cavalry Regiment under his brother-in-law, John Hunt Morgan. The author maintains that Duke was largely responsible for the unit acting as a mounted infantry. Although twice wounded, Duke took part in most of the unit's raids until he was captured on an expedition into Indiana and Ohio. After a year as a prisoner, Duke was exchanged and took over command of the regiment after Morgan's death in 1864. He defended southwestern Virginia until the Confederacy collapsed and he protected Jefferson Davis in his flight. Documentation comes from the *Official Records* and the Morgan-Duke Papers at the Southern Historical Collection at the University of North Carolina Library; 2 photos, 88 notes. 1861-65

Dulles, Eleanor Lansing

1901. Jurkovic, Lynne Dunn. "The Life and Public Career of Eleanor Lansing Dulles." Kent State U. 1982. 234 pp. *DAI 1983 43(7): 2425-A.* DA8227961 1936-59

Dulles, John Foster

1902. Keim, Albert N. JOHN FOSTER DULLES AND THE PROTESTANT WORLD ORDER MOVEMENT ON THE EVE OF WORLD WAR II. *J. of Church and State 1979 21(1): 73-89.* John Foster Dulles's belief that religion could solve the world's problems developed from his participation in the Protestant ecumenical movement and the Oxford Conference (1937). The churches had the duty to enunciate the moral principles on which political activity should be based. Following World War II, Dulles no longer believed that religion could create a universal brotherhood and ethical system; instead, it should support the West in the fight against Communism. Based on the Dulles Papers at Princeton University and published primary sources; 51 notes. 1937-48

1903. Toulouse, Mark G. WORKING TOWARD MEANINGFUL PEACE: JOHN FOSTER DULLES AND THE F.C.C., 1937-1945. *J. of Presbyterian Hist. 1983 61(4): 393-410.* John Foster Dulles was closely associated with the Federal Council of Churches, and was a noted advocate of peace. His Calvinistic training convinced him that there was a moral structure in the universe to which both individuals and nations must conform. Throughout his life, he held fast to this conviction. Beginning in 1945, however, historical contingencies caused him to transform his concept of moral law so that it ultimately became completely identified with the ideals and policies of the Free World, against Soviet antispiritual ideology. Based on Dulles's published works and the Dulles Papers, Princeton University; illus., 68 notes. 1937-45

Duluth, Daniel Greysolon, Sieur

1904. Dunn, James Taylor. DU LUTH'S BIRTHPLACE: A FOOTNOTE TO HISTORY. *Minnesota Hist. 1979 46(6): 228-232.* Many historians have incorrectly indicated that the birthplace of Daniel Greysolon, Sieur Du Luth, was Saint-Germain-en-Laye, a suburb of Paris. In the early 1950's, a Canadian historian, Gerald Malchelosse, and a French local historian, Doctor Attale Boël, correctly identified Saint-Germain-Laval in the Forez region as the birthplace of this 17th-century French explorer of the New World. The lack of extant records makes an exact date of birth impossible to ascertain, but evidence strongly suggests that Greysolon was born in that town between 1636 and 1640. His family was of the petty nobility. 1636-40

Dummer, Jeremiah

1905. Cohen, Sheldon S. JEREMIAH DUMMER: MIDWIFE TO YALE COLLEGE. *New-England Galaxy 1976 18(2): 3-12.* Describes the efforts of Jeremiah Dummer, a graduate of Harvard College in 1699, and later business agent for Connecticut in England, to build up Yale College's library through astute purchases in English and European bookstores. 3 illus. 1699-1739

Dunbar-Nelson, Alice

1906. Hull, Gloria T. ALICE DUNBAR-NELSON: DELAWARE WRITER AND WOMAN OF AFFAIRS. *Delaware Hist. 1976 17(2): 87-103.* Presents a biography of Alice Dunbar-Nelson, who was active in black educational and philanthropic enterprises and community affairs in Wilmington. Her poetry and prose writing, dominated by themes of love and war, bridged the distance separating her husband, Paul Laurence Dunbar, and the dialect writers of the Harlem Renaissance. Dunbar-Nelson used regionalism and local color, and, unlike other black writers, she attempted the short story as her main prose medium, helping create a black short story tradition. Based on Dunbar-Nelson's writings and her unpublished diary; 3 illus., 18 notes. 1875-1935

Duncan, Baruch Odell

1907. Pope, Thomas H. B. O. DUNCAN, NEWBERRY UNIONIST. *Pro. of the South Carolina Hist. Assoc. 1983: 85-93.* Discusses the career of South Carolinian Baruch Odell Duncan, who remained loyal to the US government during the Civil War and served as US consul in Bavaria and Baden between 1862 and 1866. In 1868 he served as a representative to the state constitutional convention called to meet in Charleston. After failing to be elected to office, he accepted the post as US consul in Naples, Italy, and when he retired from the diplomatic service, he returned to Newberry where he died in 1900. Based on newspapers and the *Proceedings of the Constitutional Convention of South Carolina;* 38 notes. 1862-1900

Duncan, Sara Jeannette

1908. McKenna, Isobel Kerwin. "Sara Jeannette Duncan: The New Woman: A Critical Biography." Queen's U. [Canada] 1981. *DAI 1981 42(4): 1641-A.* 19c-20c

Duncanson, Robert S.

1909. Ketner, Joseph D., II. ROBERT S. DUNCANSON (1821-1872): THE LATE LITERARY LANDSCAPE PAINTINGS. *Am. Art J. 1983 15(1): 35-47.* Robert S. Duncanson (1821-72) was the first Afro-American artist to achieve recognition in American art. Most of his active years were spent in Cincinnati and Detroit where he painted mostly in the Hudson River School tradition. He was well acquainted with English romantic literature, however, and during the last 10 years of his life he painted six major works in large format, which combined great landscapes with aspirations toward literary and poetic subjects. *Land of the Lotus Eaters* (1861),

The Vale of Kashmir (1864), and *Arcadian Landscape* (1867) are typical of these later works. 11 plates, 29 notes. 1860-72

1910. Pringle, Allan. ROBERT S. DUNCANSON IN MONTREAL, 1863-1865. *American Art Journal 1985 17(4): 28-50.* Robert S. Duncanson (1821-72), born in New York of a white Canadian father and black American mother, spent the years 1863-65 in Montreal, partly as a haven from the racial prejudice he encountered in America. He was enthusiastically welcomed and widely respected. His style of landscape painting was popular among the city's new landscape photographers. Duncanson sometimes painted directly from photographs. He exhibited widely and had a strong following among young Canadian artists. Duncanson was the first major artist to use Canadian subject matter for his paintings. 2 photos, 22 plates, 57 notes. 1863-65

Dunham, John

1911. Endres, Fred F. "WE WANT MONEY *AND MUST HAVE IT*": PROFILE OF AN OHIO WEEKLY, 1841-1847. *Journalism Hist. 1980 7(2): 68-71.* Describes the determined efforts of Dr. John Dunham, editor of the St. Clairsville (Ohio) *Gazette,* to keep his paper financially viable and to secure back payments for subscriptions and advertising. 1841-47

Dunham, Samuel Clarke

1912. Dunham, Sam C. THE ALASKAN GOLD FIELDS. *Alaska J. 1984 14(1): S1-S64.* Prints an 1898 report by Samuel Clarke Dunham, a stenographer and journalist sent to Alaska in 1897 as an investigator for the US Department of Labor. Recounts details of his journey north, and describes Alaskan working conditions and daily life, economic conditions, famine, and social conditions. 24 photos, 2 maps, table. 1897-98

Duniway, Abigail Scott

1913. Moynihan, Ruth Barnes. "Abigail Scott Duniway of Oregon: Woman and Suffragist of the American Frontier." (Volumes I and II) Yale U. 1979. 698 pp. *DAI 1979 40(6): 3492-A.* 1852-1915

Dunlap, John

1914. Dibble, Ann W. MAJOR JOHN DUNLAP: THE CRAFTSMAN AND HIS COMMUNITY. *Old-Time New England 1978 68(3-4): 50-58.* Biography of cabinetmaker, house joiner, and farmer, Major John Dunlap (1746-92) of Goffstown and Bedford, New Hampshire; Dunlap's cabinetmaking accounts reveal his skills, employment patterns, trade, and farming in the Goffstown-Bedford area during colonial times. 1746-92

Dunlap, William

1915. Turnbull, Mary D. WILLIAM DUNLAP, COLONIAL PRINTER, JOURNALIST AND MINISTER. *Pennsylvania Mag. of Hist. and Biog. 1979 103(2): 143-165.* Established as a printer by Benjamin Franklin, William Dunlap was also a postmaster, entrepreneur, journalist, and Anglican minister in Virginia. Covers 1751-83. Based on papers, published sources, and secondary works; 91 notes. 1751-83

Dunmore, John Murray, 4th Earl of

1916. Ogden, Mark. LORD DUNMORE EMERGES FROM THE SHADOWS. *Daughters of the Am. Revolution Mag. 1982 116(5): 366-369.* Discusses the life of John Murray, 4th Earl of Dunmore, one of King George III's outstanding colonial governors, especially his activities as governor of Virginia on the eve of the American Revolution. 18c

Dunn, Harvey Thomas

1917. Anderson, William T. PLOWING AND PAINTING THE PRAIRIE. *American West 1985 22(3): 38-43.* Discusses briefly the life and career of illustrator and painter Harvey Thomas Dunn, who was noted for his powerful evocations of his boyhood home of South Dakota. 1910's-52

1918. —. "THE PRAIRIE IS MY GARDEN": A PORTFOLIO OF PRAIRIE SCENES BY HARVEY THOMAS DUNN. *Am. Hist. Illus. 1980 15(1): 25-29.* Discusses American painter, Harvey Thomas Dunn (1884-1952), and a portfolio of his paintings of the South Dakota prairie now at the South Dakota Memorial Art Center in Brookings, South Dakota. 1884-1952

Dunn, Timothy Hibbard

1919. Keyes, John. LA DIVERSIFICATION DE L'ACTIVITE ECONOMIQUE DE TIMOTHY HIBBARD DUNN, COMMERÇANT DE BOIS A QUEBEC, 1850-1898 [Diversification in the economic activities of Timothy Hibbard Dunn, wood merchant in Quebec, 1850-98]. *Rev. d'Hist. de l'Amérique Française [Canada] 1981 35(3): 323-336.* Beginning his career as a purchaser of timber and pulpwood from Ontario and the United States for sale in English markets, Dunn became a major entrepreneur in 19th-century Quebec. He made substantial investments in insurance companies, banks, textile mills, railways, and other businesses. Based on material in Quebec archives; table, 67 notes. 1850-98

Dunne, Finley Peter

1920. Fanning, Charles. MR. DOOLEY IN CHICAGO: FINLEY PETER DUNNE AS HISTORIAN OF THE IRISH IN AMERICA. Doyle, David Noel and Edwards, Owen Dudley, ed. *America and Ireland, 1776-1976: The American Identity and the Irish Connection* (Westport, Conn.: Greenwood Pr., 1980): 151-164. The first brilliant US writer born of Irish immigrant parents asserted his genius by asserting his Irishness. This was Finley Peter Dunne, the turn-of-the century journalist whose alter ego, Mr. Dooley of "Archey Road," Chicago, forced the country to read with a brogue and enjoy it. Mr. Dooley has a secure place in the hearts of American historians and newspaper editors as the source of some of the most trenchant short speeches ever delivered on the state of the nation. Ever since his clearheaded critique of the Spanish-American War brought Dunne's fictitious Chicago bartender to the attention of a national audience, analysts of the American scene have been quoting bits of his wisdom. Stretching from 1898 to World War I, Mr. Dooley's tenure as resident comic sage consistently achieved quality. 1898-1913

Dunnigan, Alice A.

1921. Dunnigan, Alice A. FROM SCHOOLHOUSE TO WHITE HOUSE: SOME EXPERIENCES IN THE FIGHT FOR CIVIL RIGHTS. *J. of the Afro-American Hist. and Geneal. Soc. 1983 4(1): 9-13.* Alice A. Dunnigan relates her experiences and actions in the Civil Rights Movement beginning in her home town of Russellville, Kentucky, during the 1920's and ending in the 1950's when she was a reporter in Washington for the Associated Negro Press. 1920's-60's

Dunning, Joseph N.

1922. Carlisle, Lilian Baker. NEW BIOGRAPHICAL FINDINGS ON CURTIS & DUNNING, GIRANDOLE CLOCKMAKERS. *Am. Art J. 1978 10(1): 90-109.* 1820's-30's

For abstract see ***Curtis, Lemuel***

Dunton, W. Herbert (Buck)

1923. Johnston, Patricia Condon. W. HERBERT DUNTON. *Am. West 1981 18(3): 24-33.* W. Herbert (Buck) Dunton (1878-1936) started sketching illustrations for eastern magazines at age 12. At 16, and for a dozen years after, he financed summer trips to the West by doing commercial work in a Boston art studio and by taking odd jobs. He attended some art classes but was largely self-trained. His illustrations soon attracted magazine and book publishers because his first-hand observations and experience in the West gave him an advantage over other illustrators. In 1914 he moved his family permanently to Taos, New Mexico, and joined the Taos Society of Artists. A perfectionist who tried to achieve absolute fidelity, Dunton specialized in wildlife and cowboy themes. His illustrations appeared in a score of magazines and some 50 books. The Stark Museum in Orange, Texas, owns the largest collection of his paintings. 10 illus., biblio. 1896-1936

Duplessis, Maurice L.

1924. Swan, George Steven. A PRELIMINARY COMPARISON OF LONG'S LOUISIANA AND DUPLESSIS'S QUEBEC. *Louisiana Hist. 1984 25(3): 289-319.* 1920-60

For abstract see ***Long, Huey P.***

1925. Vigod, B. L. BIOGRAPHY AND POLITICAL CULTURE IN QUEBEC. *Acadiensis [Canada] 1977 7(1): 141-147.* 19c-20c

For abstract see ***Cartier, George-Etienne***

DuPont, Henry A.

1926. Lake, Virginia T., ed. A CRISIS OF CONSCIENCE: WEST POINT LETTERS OF HENRY A. DU PONT, OCTOBER 1860-JUNE 1861. *Civil War Hist. 1979 25(1): 55-65.* Henry Algernon du Pont, West Point senior, sympathized with his southern classmates. Son of Henry du Pont, head of E. I. du Pont de Nemours Co. and Republican supporter, Henry Algernon suffered a six-month crisis-of-conscience. He saw rights on both sides; he deplored extremism. He hoped desperately in any rumor of compromise. Envisioning the horrors of civil slaughter, he suffered in southern classmates departing. His parents encouraged him with pro-Union news and reminders of duty. Fort Sumter engendered a cadet appeal for immediate graduation. After final hesitancy and appeal to parental guidance, Henry signed the petition. He even began to anticipate active service. Based on manuscript sources; 24 notes. 1860-61

DuPont, Samuel F.

1927. Merrill, James M. MIDSHIPMAN DUPONT AND THE CRUISE OF *NORTH CAROLINA,* 1825-1827. *Am Neptune 1980 40(3): 211-225.* Describes the cruise of the Mediterranean Squadron flagship *North Carolina* as seen by Samuel Francis Du Pont (1803-65). His relationship with Commodore John Rodgers (1773-1838) and Rodgers's diplomatic contacts with the Ottoman Empire are described. Based on Du Pont's letters in the Eleutherian Mills Historical Library; 48 notes. 1825-27

1928. Merrill, James M. THE FIRST CRUISE OF A DELAWARE MIDSHIPMAN: SAMUEL FRANCIS DU PONT AND THE *FRANKLIN. Delaware Hist. 1983 20(4): 256-268.* Describes the first voyage and experiences of Samuel F. Du Pont as a midshipman on the *Franklin,* with comments on Du Pont's education, descriptions of the ship and daily life aboard the 79-gun vessel, and accounts of the ship's movements along the Atlantic coast and in the Mediterranean. Also describes Du Pont's experiences on the sloop *Erie* in the Mediterranean, with comments on chasing pirates and slavers in the Atlantic. Based on the Du Pont papers; 44 notes, 3 illus. 1818-20

DuPont, Sophie

1929. Fernald, Jean W. THE ROLE OF SOPHIE MADELEINE DU PONT: AN INVALID IN THE BRANDYWINE SISTERHOOD. *Working Papers from the Regional Econ. Hist. Res. Center 1982 5(2-3): 139-148.* Discusses the life of Sophie Madeleine DuPont of Eleutherian Mills in the Delaware Valley, a bed-ridden invalid by the time she was 24, who made illness one of her occupations in addition to correspondence with friends, her interest in botany, and the collection of her family's papers and correspondence. 1832-78

DuPont, Victorine

1930. Johnson, Mary. VICTORINE DU PONT: HEIRESS TO THE EDUCATIONAL DREAM OF PIERRE SAMUEL DU PONT DE NEMOURS. *Delaware Hist. 1980 19(2): 88-105.* Argues that Victorine du Pont (b. 1792), the granddaughter of Pierre Samuel du Pont de Nemours, the physiocrat, imbibed du Pont de Nemours' thinking on the need for democratic education and translated her experience of growing up in France to the upbringing of the du Pont family in America and to the mill towns of the Brandywine region. She became an advocate of primary education in the rural manufacturing districts of the middle Atlantic region, working particularly with the American Sunday School Movement. Her chief legacy was the Brandywine Manufacturers' Sunday School, incorporated in 1817, which embodied the du Pont concept that learning should be pleasurable not corporal. Her other legacy was the liberal education of the du Pont family, which guided them even as they attended formal schools. 60 notes. 1800-17

DuPont de Nemours, Pierre Samuel

1931. Johnson, Mary. VICTORINE DU PONT: HEIRESS TO THE EDUCATIONAL DREAM OF PIERRE SAMUEL DU PONT DE NEMOURS. *Delaware Hist. 1980 19(2): 88-105.* 1800-17

For abstract see ***DuPont, Victorine***

Dupuis, Stephen

1932. Hoar, Jay S. LOUISIANA'S LAST BOYS IN GRAY. *Louisiana Hist. 1978 19(3): 336-352.* 1824-1953

For abstract see ***Powell, Frank Eli***

Durand, Mortimer

1933. Larsen, Peter. SIR MORTIMER DURAND IN WASHINGTON: A STUDY IN ANGLO-AMERICAN RELATIONS IN THE ERA OF THEODORE ROOSEVELT. *Mid-America 1984 66(2): 65-78.* Sir Mortimer Durand became British ambassador to Washington in 1903. He proved personally incompatible with President Theodore Roosevelt and he failed to report accurately US interests in the Far East and North Africa. Durand quickly became out of touch with the president, leaving the British embassy at a severe disadvantage in relation to other embassies in the United States. Durand was recalled in 1905. Based on the Theodore Roosevelt, Arthur James Balfour, and Mortimer Durand papers, and on secondary sources; 40 notes. 1903-05

Durand, Roland

1934. Brown, Donald N. ROLAND DURAND, MAN OF PICURIS. *Palacio 1981-82 87(4): 3-7.* Biography of teacher, principal, and painter, Roland Durand (1897-1959), who was born and lived at Picuris Pueblo in New Mexico, and who signed his paintings and sketches *Tolene.* 1902-1959

Duranty, Walter

1935. Crowl, James William. "They Wrote as They Pleased: A Study of the Journalistic Careers of Louis Fischer and Walter Duranty, 1922-1940." U. of Virginia 1978. 386 pp. *DAI 1979 39(8): 5082-A.* 1922-40

1936. Taylor, Sally. "The Life, Work, and Times of Walter Duranty, Moscow Correspondent for the *New York Times,* 1921-1941." Southern Illinois U., Carbondale 1980. *DAI 1980 40(8): 4285-A.* 1921-41

Durkheim, Emile

1937. Mayes, Sharon S. SOCIOLOGICAL THOUGHT IN EMILE DURKHEIM AND GEORGE FITZHUGH. *British J. of Sociol. [Great Britain] 1980 31(1): 78-94.* A comparative study of the origins of sociological theory in the work of George Fitzhugh, American slaveholder and author of *Sociology for the South* (1854), and Emile Durkheim (1857-1917), indicating that as a world view, the science of sociology bears striking similarity to the science of slavery. 1854-1917

Durkheimer, Kaufman (family)

1938. Glazer, Michele. THE DURKHEIMERS OF OREGON: A PICTURE STORY. *Western States Jewish Hist. Q. 1978 10(3): 202-209.* Kaufman Durkheimer brought his family from Philadelphia to Portland, Oregon, in 1862, where he opened a second-hand furniture store. In 1874 his son Julius moved to Baker City, Oregon where he opened a general mechandise store. Julius sold the store in 1887 and opened a new store in Prairie City. The next year he opened another store in Canyon City. With the expansion of his merchandising businesses to a third site, in Burns, Oregon, Julius sent for his brothers Moses, Sam, and Sigmund to help run the firm. Julius's wife, Delia, was not happy in the primitive, isolated small towns of eastern Oregon, so the family moved to Portland. In 1896 Julius purchased an interest in the wholesale grocery firm of Wadham and Company, the northwest distributor of Olympia beer. Under the management of Julius's son and grandson, the company—now, Bevhold, Inc.—continues to market Olympia beer. Primary and secondary sources; 5 photos, 3 notes. 1862-1978

Durlauf, Michael (family)

1939. Bronner, Simon J. THE DURLAUF FAMILY: THREE GENERATIONS OF STONECARVERS IN SOUTHERN INDIANA. *Pioneer Am. 1981 13(1): 17-26.* Biographies of Michael Durlauf, Sr., his son Michael F. Durlauf, and grandsons, Harry, Leo, and Otto, master stonecarvers from Jasper, Dubois County, in southern Indiana from 1858 to 1962, with descriptions of some of their tombstones. 1858-1962

Durnford, Andrew (family)

1940. Whitten, David O. RURAL LIFE ALONG THE MISSISSIPPI: PLAQUEMINES PARISH, LOUISIANA, 1830-1850. *Agricultural History 1984 58(3): 477-487.* Examines the life of the Andrew Durnford family, which had a Mississippi River plantation south of New Orleans. The Durnford's were an example of the river-rural lifestyle of country people who had close ties to the city because of their proximity to rivers. They kept regularly in touch with New Orleans for news, manufactured goods, plantation supplies, and as a market for the plantation's sugar. Based on Andrew Durnford letters and manuscripts; 59 notes. 1830-50

Durr, John N.

1941. Zook, Lois Ann. BISHOP JOHN N. DURR AND HIS TIMES. *Pennsylvania Mennonite Heritage 1978 1(1): 18-21.* John N. Durr (1853-1934) served as a bishop in the Mennonite Church in Pennsylvania and was largely responsible for establishing the Southwestern Pennsylvania Mennonite Conference, 1872-1934. 1872-1934

Durrell, Philip (descendants)

1942. Durrell, Harold Clarke; Dearborn, David Curtis, ed. PHILIP[1] DURRELL AND HIS DESCENDANTS. *New England Hist. and Geneal. Register 1980 134(Oct): 276-281; 1981 135(Jan): 16-22.* Continued from a previous article. Part X. Traces three more Durrell descendants and their offspring. The brothers, all born at Arundel, Maine, are: Samuel (1786-1853); Thomas, his twin (1786-1867); and William Henry (1790-1863). All three died at Kennebunkport, Maine. Part XI. The Durrell genealogy concludes with an investigation of the lives and families of three descendants. The cousins were born within a year of each other at Arundel, Maine. One died at Kennebunk, the other two at Kennebunkport. Provides an addendum of additions and corrections for articles in the previous three volumes. 18c-19c

Durrell, Philip (family)

1943. Durrell, Harold Clarke and Dearborn, David Curtis, ed. PHILIP[1] DURRELL AND HIS DESCENDANTS. *New England Hist. and Geneal. Register 1979 133(Apr): 118-124; (July): 216-219.* Continued from a previous article. Part IV. This genealogical study traces the lives of three more descendants of Philip[1]. Lemuel[4], Ebenezer[4], and John[4] Durrell were all born at Durham, New Hampshire (probably) in the mid-18th century. Wives, children and places of residence are noted, some in detail. Notes incorporated in text. Part V. Discusses David[4] Durrell (ca. 1746-1833), his three marriages, and his 10 children. To be continued. 1780's-19c

1944. Durrell, Harold Clarke and Dearborn, David Curtis, ed. PHILIP[1] DURRELL AND HIS DESCENDANTS. *New England Hist. and Geneal. Register 1979 133(Oct): 280-285; 1980 (Jan): 65-69, (Apr): 148-155, (Jul): 220-227.* Continued from a previous article. Part VI. This study focuses on Eliphalet[4] Durrell (1748-1825), his 13 children, and numerous grandchildren. Notes incorporated in text. Part VII. Concentrates on Nicholas, fourth in line from Philip[1], and mentions his six children. Part VIII. Discusses three sons of Nicholas[3] Durrell. Part IX. Traces four male descendants of Philip[1]. They were all born after 1750, one in New Hampshire and three in Maine. Article to be continued. 18c-19c

1945. Durrell, Harold Clarke and Dearborn, David Curtis. PHILIP[1] DURRELL AND HIS DESCENDANTS. *New Eng-land Hist. and Geneal. Register 1978 132(Apr): 115-122, 132 (Oct): 264-277; 1979 133 (Jan): 40-48.* Part I. The 204 page unindexed notebook of Harold Clarke Durrell (1882-1943) is a detailed history of the Durrell family of New Hampshire and Maine. Philip is believed to have come from Guernsey around 1689. Indians attacked his family in 1703 and 1726. Several children were carried off to Canada and his wife was killed in the second attack. Philip's dates are unknown as is the identity of his wife, who bore him eleven children. Part II. Covers descendants of Philip Durrell in the second and third generations. Part III. Covers five descendants in the third generation. Article to be continued. 17c-18c

Dusenbury, Emma

1946. Cochran, Robert B. "ALL THE SONGS IN THE WORLD": THE STORY OF EMMA DUSENBURY. *Arkansas Historical Quarterly 1985 44(1): 3-15.* Describes the search for information on the life of Emma Dusenbury (1862-1941), a poor blind woman of Mena, Arkansas, who recorded, for the Archive of American Folk Song, 116 different songs now in the Library of Congress. Based on newspapers, interviews, and other primary and secondary sources; 24 notes. 1890's-1941

Duus, O. F.

1947. Rosholt, Malcolm. TWO MEN OF OLD WAUPACA. *Norwegian-American Studies 1965 22: 75-103.* Describes the lives of two Norwegian-American pioneers, O. F. Duus, a Lutheran minister, and Thomas Knoph, a storekeeper in the town of Scandinavia, Wisconsin. The Lutheran Church in Scandinavia, the first in the Waupaca Township, was chartered by the members of the community and Duus in 1854. For the first two years of his ministry, he served two congregations, one in Winchester and the other in Scandinavia, but left the Winchester congregation in 1856. Knoph's country store, opened in 1853, was typical of most frontier areas in that it stocked or could order nearly any supply needed. Knoph's ledgers serve as a measure of areal growth and locally-produced goods since his store was a retail outlet for the area. Based on Duus's journal, church records, and Knoph's store ledger, as well as other primary and secondary sources; 21 notes. 1853-56

Duvernay, Ludger

1948. Kenny, Stephen. DUVERNAY'S EXILE IN "BALENTON": THE VERMONT INTERLUDE OF A CANADIAN PATRIOT. *Vermont Hist. 1984 52(2): 103-122.* Ludger Duvernay was a French-Canadian Quebec nationalist who fled Canada for New York City when an abortive invasion of Quebec he helped organize was crushed. He then went to Vermont in March 1839 and published the Burlington *Patriote Canadien* from August 1839 to February 1840. Finally recognizing the disparity between his ideal of the United States and the reality of US policy (strict neutrality and nativism), and unable to support himself as an editor, Duvernay returned to Montreal and again became a newspaper editor. Based on letters and newspapers; 112 notes. 1837-42

Dwight, Samuel

1949. Buckeye, Nancy. SAMUEL DWIGHT: STONE CARVER OF BENNINGTON COUNTY, VERMONT. *Vermont Hist. 1975 43(3): 208-216.* Dwight graduated from Yale in 1773, married in 1779, and taught school in New Haven until he left his wife for Vermont in 1786. After briefly running an academy in Bennington he carved gravestones, 1790-1813. Some 50 examples identified in Shaftsbury, Arlington, and surrounding towns have characteristic hands, hearts, vines, and flowers showing increasing command of design. 4 illus., 9 notes. 1773-1813

Dwight, Timothy

1950. Buss, Dietrich. THE MILLENNIAL VISION AS MOTIVE FOR RELIGIOUS BENEVOLENCE AND REFORM: TIMOTHY DWIGHT AND THE NEW ENGLAND EVANGELICALS RECONSIDERED. *Fides et Hist. 1984 16(1): 18-34.* A revitalized Edwardean theology and eschatology infused Timothy Dwight and New England Congregationalists with a burning desire to convert the world and renovate society. For Dwight and the evangelicals, the expected Kingdom of Christ would be ushered in only through the relentless preaching of the gospel to all nations, and with the advent of foreign mission societies it was believed that the Kingdom of Christ was at hand. This millennial vision of the emergent Kingdom of God spread to evangelicals of other denominations, culminating in ecumenical and apolitical cooperation in the numerous reform and benevolent societies of the early 19th century. Mostly secondary sources; 75 notes. 1795-1817

1951. Wenzke, Annabelle Sassaman. "Timothy Dwight: The Enlightened Puritan." Pennsylvania State U. 1983. 301 pp. *DAI 1984 44(8): 2493-A.* DA8327571 1770's-1817

Dyer, Leon

1952. Rosenwaike, Ira. LEON DYER: BALTIMORE AND SAN FRANCISCO JEWISH LEADER. *Western States Jewish Hist. Q. 1977 9(2): 135-143.* Earlier accounts of the life of Leon Dyer (1807-83) have too often relied on legend instead of valid documentary sources. In fact, Dyer was a Baltimore butcher and real estate dealer who developed a business interest in California when his younger brother, Abraham, joined a group of immigrants to that state. Leon Dyer went to San Francisco in 1850 for business reasons and in the few months he spent there, he was chosen the religious leader of a temporary congregation of Jewish settlers. After his return to Baltimore he made several trips to Europe before settling in Louisville, Kentucky, in 1875. Based on documents in the National Archives, Baltimore Land Records, other primary, and secondary sources; 31 notes. 1820's-75

Dyer, Mary

1953. Scheffler, Judith. PRISON WRITINGS OF EARLY QUAKER WOMEN. *Quaker Hist. 1984 73(2): 25-37.* 1651-83

For abstract see ***Blaugdone, Barbara***

Dyos, H. J.

1954. Stave, Bruce M. A CONVERSATION WITH H. J. DYOS. *J. of Urban Hist. 1979 5(4): 469-500.* Interviews the leading urban historian, the late H. J. Dyos. Covers Dyos's personal background, the state of the art in urban history, and important works in British, Canadian, and American urban history. 38 notes, biblio. 1970's

E

Eager, Tom

1955. Erskine, Grace van Dalfsen. TOM EAGER, SHEEPMAN. *Northeastern Nevada Hist. Soc. Q. 1983 (3): 99-108.* Describes the life of Tom Eager, a sheepman in Elko County, Nevada, during 1919-41. 1919-41

Eagleton, George and Ethie

1956. Pearson, Alden B., Jr. A MIDDLE-CLASS, BORDER-STATE FAMILY DURING THE CIVIL WAR. *Civil War Hist. 1976 22(4): 318-336.* The diaries of George Eagleton and his wife, Ethie, document a colorful, moving, grassroots history of the effect of war on solid, middle-class citizens of the Upper South. A Presbyterian preacher and teacher in middle Tennessee, George went with his state and enlisted in the Confederate army in 1861. After an honorable discharge in 1862, George led a hunted life as a wandering minister and southern activist for three years. Separated from her husband and surrounded by war, Ethie suffered intensely. Embittered with the Union, George built a new life with his family across the Mississippi after the war. Primary and secondary sources; 39 notes. 1861-99

Eaker, Ira C.

1957. Sears, Betty M. IRA C. EAKER: THE MILITARY CAREER OF OKLAHOMA'S GREATEST AVIATOR. *Red River Valley Hist. Rev. 1978 3(3): 66-77.* General Ira C. Eaker served the Army Air Corps from 1917 to 1947, testing aircraft, making record-breaking flights, formulating military strategy, preparing for World War II, and leading the US 8th Bomber Command's B-17's over Europe. 1917-47

Eakins, Thomas

1958. Chamberlin-Hellman, Maria Jo. "Thomas Eakins as a Teacher." Columbia U. 1981. 585 pp. *DAI 1984 44(10): 2911-A.* DA8327193 20c

1959. Johns, Elizabeth. DRAWING INSTRUCTION AT CENTRAL HIGH SCHOOL AND ITS IMPACT ON THOMAS EAKINS. *Winterthur Portfolio 1980 15(2): 139-149.* Thomas Eakins was influenced by his training in drawing at Philadelphia's Central High School, 1851-54. The training presented discipline, close observation, and efficacy of method as essentials. Eakins would follow such advice with intensity throughout his life. Based on School Board reports and Eakins's drawings; 4 illus., 24 notes. 1851-85

Eames, Charles and Ray

1960. Lacy, Bill N. WAREHOUSE FULL OF IDEAS. *Horizon 1980 23(9): 20-27.* Charles Eames (1907-78) collaborated on architectural, furniture design, film, educational, and photographic projects with his wife Ray during their 40-year marriage. 1907-78

Earhart, Amelia

1961. Salo, Mauno. AMELIA EARHART: A SHORT BIOGRAPHY. *Am. Aviation Hist. Soc. J. 1977 22(2): 82-86.* Short biography of Amelia Earhart, 1897-1937, including her interest in aviation and her preparation for a round-the-world airplane flight; discusses her training for the attempt. 1897-1937

Earl, Harley

1962. Yanik, Anthony J. HARLEY EARL AND THE BIRTH OF MODERN AUTOMOTIVE STYLING. *Chronicle: The Quarterly Magazine of the Historical Society of Michigan 1985 21(1): 18-22.* Discusses the automotive design career at General Motors of Harley Earl, who is credited with many style innovations. 1927-40

Early, Sarah Woodson

1963. Lawson, Ellen N. SARAH WOODSON EARLY: 19TH CENTURY BLACK NATIONALIST "SISTER". *Umoja 1981 5(2): 15-26.* Discusses the life and career of Sarah Woodson Early (1825-1907), American educator, feminist, and black nationalist. 1850-1907

Earp, Wyatt

1964. Hutton, Paul Andrew. CELLULOID LAWMAN. *Am. West 1984 21(3): 58-65.* Wyatt Earp's career as a lawman differs radically from its subsequent renditions in popular films and television programs. 1870-1971

1965. Shillingber, William B. WYATT EARP AND THE 'BUNTLINE SPECIAL' MYTH. *Kansas Hist. Q. 1976 42(2): 113-154.* Examination of Colt's records, Wyatt Earp's career, and the activities of journalist Ned Buntline (Edward Zane Carroll Judson) fails to produce any contemporary evidence that Buntline in 1876 presented Earp and four other lawmen with special 12-inch-barrel Colt revolvers. The story is linked to Stuart N. Lake's *Wyatt Earp: Frontier Marshal,* which was published in 1931. Primary and secondary sources; illus., 145 notes. 1931

Easterly, Thomas

1966. Davidson, Carla. THE VIEW FROM FOURTH AND OLIVE. *Am. Heritage 1979 31(1): 76-93.* Describes the life of early St. Louis photographer Thomas Easterly (1809-82) and reproduces his best daguerreotypes taken during 1847-80. 1847-80

Eastman, Charles A. (Ohiyesa)

1967. Wilson, Raymond. DR. CHARLES A. EASTMAN, EARLY TWENTIETH-CENTURY REFORMER. *Journal of the West 1984 23(3): 7-12.* Provides a short summary of the life of Dr. Charles A. Eastman (Ohiyesa), a Santee Sioux, and gives an assessment of his contributions as a reformer of Indian life and government policy. An active participant in a variety of reformist organizations, Eastman was critical of the Bureau of Indian Affairs because of its paternalistic attitude toward Indians and because of its failure to deliver much needed health and education programs. Despite his accuracy with these charges, Eastman underestimated the depth and complexity of other problems and mistakenly believed that the extension of citizenship to Indians would lead to Indian-white harmony. Eastman attained an extraordinary degree of success within both the Indian and white worlds; he believed that the best approach in life was to adopt the best attributes of each group. Based on archival sources; biblio., 4 photos. 1890-1933

1968. Stensland, Anna Lee. CHARLES ALEXANDER EASTMAN: SIOUX STORY TELLER AND HISTORIAN. *Am. Indian Q.: A J. of Anthrop., Hist., and Lit. 1977 3(3): 199-208.* Charles A. Eastman was a part of Sioux Indian and New England white society at different points in his life. He wrote of events as he experienced and perceived them. A number of problems arise because he lived in two such diverse cultures. He did not always separate fact from legend, or from his own created stories. In addition, his conversion to conservative Protestantism caused him to offer certain interpretations of the Sioux Indians' legends and customs. Based on Eastman's writings; 26 notes. 1878-1920

1969. Wilson, Raymond. "Dr.Charles A. Eastman (Ohiyesa), Santee Sioux." U. of New Mexico 1977. 278 pp. *DAI 1977 38(6): 3688-A.* 1887-1939

Eastman, Crystal

1970. Schmidt, Cynthia Ann Bolger. "Socialist-Feminism: Max Eastman, Floyd Dell and Crystal Eastman." Marquette U. 1983. 341 pp. *DAI 1983 44(4): 1182-A.* DA8317284 1900's-20's

Eastman, Max

1971. Schmidt, Cynthia Ann Bolger. "Socialist-Feminism: Max Eastman, Floyd Dell and Crystal Eastman." Marquette U. 1983. 341 pp. *DAI 1983 44(4): 1182-A.* DA8317284 1900's-20's

Eaton, Clement

1972. Clark, Thomas D. CLEMENT EATON. *Register of the Kentucky Hist. Soc. 1982 80(2): 140-150.* Historian Clement Eaton was a quiet and complacent liberal, a good teacher for responsive graduate students, and a genuine scholar. Photo. ca 1920-80

Eaton, Cyrus

1973. Salaff, Stephen. CYRUS EATON: 1883-1979. *Queen's Q. [Canada] 1983 90(2): 379-386.* Describes the business career of Cyrus Eaton and his later efforts as a private citizen to improve international relations through increased East-West contact and understanding. His Pugwash, Nova Scotia, organization continues his campaign to better East-West relations and to abolish atomic weapons. 9 notes. 1901-82

Eaton, Sherb

1974. Woodman, Betsy H. SALT HAYING, FARMING, AND FISHING IN SALISBURY, MASSACHUSETTS: THE LIFE OF SHERB EATON (1900-1982). *Essex Inst. Hist. Collections 1983 119(3): 165-181.* The life of farmer Sherb Eaton of Salisbury demonstrates how farmers adapted from hand labor to mechanized operations and from 19th- to 20th-century technologies. Describes the various farming experiences and techniques of Eaton, especially harvesting hay in the Salisbury marshes. 5 photos, illus., 15 notes. 1920-82

Eaton, William

1975. Evenhuis, J. R. WILLIAM EATON (1744-1811): BEVRIJDER VAN AMERIKAANSE GIJZELAARS [William Eaton (1744-1811): liberator of American hostages]. *Spiegel Hist. [Netherlands] 1982 17(2): 106-111.* Narrates the career of William Eaton, an American captain and political adventurer, who played a key role in the Tripolitan War in 1805, over the holding of American hostages for cash ransoms by the ruler of Tripoli. Based on primary sources; 3 illus. 1790-1811

Eberle, Abastenia St. Leger

1976. Conner, Janis C. AMERICAN WOMEN SCULPTORS BREAK THE MOLD. *Art and Antiques 1980 3(3): 80-87.* Discusses American women sculptors Bessie Potter Vonnoh (b. 1872), Evelyn Beatrice Longman, Abastenia St. Leger Eberle (d. 1942), and Janet Scudder, and describes their outstanding sculpture from the World's Columbian Exposition (Chicago, 1893) to 1925. 1893-1925

Eby, Frederick

1977. Westfall, Barry H. FREDERICK EBY: PORTRAIT OF AN ESSENTIALIST. *Vitae Scholasticae 1983 2(2): 437-460.* Frederick Eby (1874-1968), a professor of history and education at Baylor University and the University of Texas at Austin from 1900 to 1957, was an essentialist who opposed the pragmatic educational theories of John Dewey and exerted a great deal of influence in Texas education, especially in the formation of the state's junior college system. 75 notes. 1900-83

Eccles, Marriner Stoddard

1978. Israelsen, L. Dwight. MARRINER S. ECCLES, CHAIRMAN OF THE FEDERAL RESERVE BOARD. *American Economic Review 1985 75(2): 357-362.* Traces the life and intellectual development of Marriner Stoddard Eccles, son of Utah's first native millionaire, who served as chairman of the Federal Reserve Board during 1934-36. The Federal Reserve Building is now named for Eccles, who struggled to maintain the independence of the board, and introduced compensatory monetary and fiscal policies. Unlike most economists of the 1930's, Eccles believed that the cause of the Depression was insufficient consumption of what the country could produce and that only government intervention could resolve the crisis. His analyses and policies foreshadowed those of John Maynard Keynes. Based on the Marriner S. Eccles Collection at the University of Utah and secondary sources; ref. 1931-51

Eckman, Julius

1979. Clar, Reva and Kramer, William M. JULIUS ECKMAN AND HERMAN BIEN: THE BATTLING RABBIS OF SAN FRANCISCO. PART 3. *Western States Jewish Hist. Q. 1983 15(4): 341-359.* 1860-95
*For abstract see **Bien, Herman M.***

1980. Clar, Reva and Kramer, William M. JULIUS ECKMAN AND HERMAN BIEN: THE BATTLING RABBIS OF SAN FRANCISCO. *Western States Jewish Hist. Q. 1983 15(2): 107-130, (3): 232-253.* 1854-61
*For abstract see **Bien, Herman M.***

Eckstorm, Fannie Hardy

1981. Whitten, Jeanne Patten. FANNIE HARDY ECKSTORM: A DESCRIPTIVE BIBLIOGRAPHY. *Northeast Folklore 1975 16: 10-76.* Eckstorm (1865-1946) was a historian and naturalist specializing in Maine life and Indians. In addition to reprinting a biographical sketch from the *New England Quarterly*, 24 (March 1953), Whitten has prepared an annotated bibliography of Eckstorm's writings, both published and unpublished, now collected and indexed in the Fogler Library of the University of Maine, Orono. Much of Eckstorm's work deals with Indians, their nomenclature, folklore, customs, and history. She also had a deep interest in folksongs and ballads of Maine. Unfortunately, about half of the bibliography is missing. Illus. 1880-1946

Eddy, C. B.

1982. Tracy, Francis G., Sr. PECOS VALLEY PIONEERS. *New Mexico Hist. Rev. 1958 33(3): 187-204.* 1885-1895

*For abstract see **Tracy, Francis G., Sr.***

Eddy, J. A.

1983. Tracy, Francis G., Sr. PECOS VALLEY PIONEERS. *New Mexico Hist. Rev. 1958 33(3): 187-204.* 1885-1895

*For abstract see **Tracy, Francis G., Sr.***

Eddy, Mary Baker

1984. Klein, Janice. ANN LEE AND MARY BAKER EDDY: THE PARENTING OF NEW RELIGIONS. *J. of Psychohistory 1979 6(3): 361-375.* The Christian Science and Shaker religions, founded by Mary Baker Eddy and Ann Lee, respectively, had roots in the personal lives of their founders as well as in their social milieux. Focuses on the former, comparing the life experiences of Eddy and Lee, and suggests ways in which those experiences affected the theologies of the two religions. Primary and secondary sources; 29 notes. 1736-1910

1985. Olds, Mason. MARY BAKER EDDY: A SESQUICENTENNIAL ACKNOWLEDGEMENT. *Contemporary Rev. [Great Britain] 1972 220(1277): 294-300.* Surveys the life, work, ideas, and influence of Mary Baker Eddy (1821-1910) and the early growth of Christian Science up to 1926. 1840's-1926

1986. Silberger, Julius, Jr. MARY BAKER EDDY. *Am. Heritage 1980 32(1): 56-64.* Adapted from the author's recently published biography of Mary Baker Eddy (1821-1910), the founder and developer of Christian Science, who began her writing and founded the church in 1875 after a long and often unhappy earlier life. From the beginning, she sought to rid the church of any competitors to her own position. She founded the *Christian Science Monitor* in 1908, two years before her death. 10 illus. ca 1840-1910

Ede, Susanna

1987. Zimmerman, Barbara Baker and Carstensen, Vernon. PIONEER WOMAN IN SOUTHWESTERN WASHINGTON TERRITORY: THE RECOLLECTIONS OF SUSANNA MARIA SLOVER MC FARLAND PRICE EDE. *Pacific Northwest Q. 1976 67(4): 137-150.* Reminiscences of Susanna Ede (1854-1937), whose pioneer life was spent along the lower Chehalis River, Grays Harbor, and the Copalis Beach area of Washington Territory. Widowed by William McFarland at age 26, she twice remarried, first to Dr. J. B. Price, physician at the Quinault Indian Agency, and later to Walter Ede whom she later divorced. Susanna described her log cabin life during the 1870's, her position as teacher and government interpreter at the Quinault Agency, bouts with timber wolves, and the production of home remedies and canned foods. 4 photos, 10 notes. 1854-1937

Edgar, Neal L.

1988. Keller, Dean H. IN MEMORIAM: NEAL L. EDGAR, JUNE 21, 1927-APRIL 2, 1983. *Ethnic Forum 1983 3(1-2): 108.* With an intense commitment to scholarship and librarianship, Neal L. Edgar wrote several books and, since 1967, served in the library at Kent State University and as review editor for *Ethnic Forum.* 1967-83

Edgerton, Sidney

1989. Thane, James L., Jr. AN OHIO ABOLITIONIST IN THE FAR WEST: SIDNEY EDGERTON AND THE OPENING OF MONTANA, 1863-1866. *Pacific Northwest Q. 1976 67(4): 151-162.* Hoping to further his political career, Sidney Edgerton accepted the position of chief justice of the Idaho Territorial Supreme Court in September 1863. An abolitionist since the 1840's, Edgerton seemingly preferred turmoil over tranquility. He supported a bill to divide Idaho and create the new territory of Montana. He then worked successfully for appointment as territorial governor of Montana but alienated the territory's Democratic majority by questioning their loyalty to the Union during the Civil War. In the spring of 1866 the combative Edgerton was replaced by Green Clay Smith who was more agreeable to the business interests of Montana. Based on primary sources; 5 photos, 43 notes. 1863-66

Edison, Charles

1990. Bebout, John E. OUT OF THE SHADOW: THE STORY OF CHARLES EDISON. *Natl. Civic Rev. 1979 68(3): 123-129.* Overview of the life of Charles Edison, 1913-69, and his interest in the arts, business, government, and voluntary associations. 1913-69

Edison, Thomas Alva

1991. Cuitlahuac de Hoyos, Juan. INQUIRIES INTO THOMAS ALVA EDISON'S ALLEGED MEXICAN ANCESTRY. *Aztlán 1978 9: 151-176.* Examines the evidence for claims of Mexican ancestry for Thomas Alva Edison, which have persisted, since the 1920's, as: the Texas orphan version, the Martinez version, and the Alva version. The first two make him entirely Mexican, the third Anglo-Mexican. In no case is the evidence conclusive, but it does include some strange, suggestive coincidences. Biblio., appendixes including correspondence, interviews, and data relevant for the various versions. ca 1915-23

1992. Messenger, Christian K. SEMIOTICS AND ALCHEMY: BIOGRAPHY UNDER ATTACK. *American Quarterly 1985 37(1): 150-155.* Reviews David Nye's *The Invented Self: An Anti-Biography, from Documents of Thomas A. Edison* (1983). Criticizes biography as a narrative form through an analysis of the various interpretations and symbolic systems that appear in the many biographies of Edison. 2 notes. 1847-1931

1993. Petros, Véronique. LES MILLE ET UNE INVENTIONS DE MONSIEUR EDISON [The thousand and one inventions of Mr. Edison]. *Histoire [France] 1979 (13): 74-76.* Reviews Thomas A. Edison's scientific career on the occasion of the 100th anniversary of the invention of the incandescent lamp. 1847-1931

Edlis, Avraham "Adolph"

1994. Selavan, Ida Cohen. ADOLPH EDLIS: A HUNGARIAN JEW IN PITTSBURGH POLITICS. *Am. Jewish Arch. 1984 36(1): 1-11.* Describes the career of immigrant Avraham "Adolph" Edlis from his days as a barber-supplies manufacturer to his becoming an influential leader in Pittsburgh politics. Although anti-Semitism worked against him, he became the first Jew to be elected to the city's common council. His success locally led him eventually to serve in the Pennsylvania legislature. Based on City of Pittsburgh municipal documents and on Pittsburgh newspapers, notably the *Pittsburgh Dispatch* and the *Jewish Criterion;* portrait, 32 notes. 1860-1934

Edmonds, Francis William

1995. Edmonds, Francis W. "THE LEADING INCIDENTS & DATES OF MY LIFE": AN AUTOBIOGRAPHICAL ESSAY BY FRANCIS W. EDMONDS. *Am. Art J. 1981 13(4): 4-10.* Transcript of a brief autobiographical essay found on the back of a self-portrait kept in the family until the present. Francis William Edmonds was born in Hudson, New York, in 1806 and was a self-taught artist until, while working as a cashier in a New York City bank, he attended evening classes of the National Academy of Design. Describes his various submissions to the academy shows and the influence of a trip to Europe. 2 plates, 4 photos. 1806-63

Edmonds, Sarah Emma

1996. Lammers, Pat and Boyce, Amy. ALIAS FRANKLIN THOMPSON: A FEMALE IN THE RANKS. *Civil War Times Illus. 1984 22(9): 24-31.* Sarah Emma Edmonds employed pseudonyms and disguises in order to serve in the 2d Michigan Volunteer Infantry during the Civil War; her talent for hiding her true identity again proved useful when she became a Union spy, infiltrating Confederate defenses by means of a variety of disguises. 1861-63

Edmondson, J. Howard

1997. Davis, Billy Joe. "J. Howard Edmondson: A Political Biography." Texas Tech U. 1980. 256 pp. *DAI 1980 41(4): 1731-A.* 8022615 1953-71

Edmondson, William

1998. LeQuire, Louise. EDMONDSON'S ART REFLECTS HIS FAITH, STRONG AND PURE. *Smithsonian 1981 12(5): 50-55.* Assesses the sculptures of Tennessean William Edmondson made between 1932 and his death in 1951 as expressions of his Baptist faith and examples of native American art. 1932-51

Edmunds, Abraham Coryell

1999. Belknap, George N. HE WAS A STARTER BUT GOT NO FURTHER: CAREERS OF A. C. EDMUNDS. *Oregon Hist. Q. 1983 84(2): 150-171.* Reviews the short-lived careers of Abraham Coryell Edmunds, who espoused the Universalist doctrine in his many speeches and writings from the mid-1850's until his death in 1879. As a lecturer and writer supporting causes ranging from temperance to labor organization, Edmunds's failures were frequently the result of his antagonism and offensive rhetoric. Based on *The Western Life-Boat and Journal of Biography, History and Geography* (1873) and a manuscript by Asa Mayo Bradly, University of Oregon Library; 2 plates, 43 notes. 1857-79

Edson, Merritt A.

2000. Dieckmann, Edward A., Sr. RED MIKE EDSON. *Marine Corps Gazette 1962 46(8): 22-28.* A biography of Colonel Merritt A. Edson (1897-1955), distinguished US Marine and later Executive Director of the National Rifle Association. ca 1917-55

Edwards, Harry Stillwell

2001. McClure, Paul Eugene. "Harry Stillwell Edwards: A Biographical and Critical Study." U. of Georgia 1977. 317 pp. *DAI 1978 38(11): 6727-6728-A.* 1886-1913

Edwards, India Walker

2002. Morgan, Georgia Cook. INDIA EDWARDS: DISTAFF POLITICIAN OF THE TRUMAN ERA. *Missouri Hist. Rev. 1984 78(3): 293-310.* Prints a biography of India Walker Edwards, who worked with the Women's Division and the Democratic National Committee, bringing feminism into US political leadership years before it became fashionable. She used her journalistic experience from the Chicago *Tribune* to write speeches and news releases for the Democratic Party. She also brought other women into important positions, until Stephen Mitchell froze them out in 1953. 9 photos, 64 notes. 1923-53

Edwards, Jonathan

2003. Jamieson, John F. JONATHAN EDWARDS'S CHANGE OF POSITION ON STODDARDEANISM. *Harvard Theological Rev. 1981 74(1): 79-99.* Describes Jonathan Edwards's changing attitude from 1700 to 1749 to Stoddardeanism, Solomon Stoddard's system in the New England Congregational Church that granted baptism and communion to people who had knowledge of the faith and lived scandal free lives even if they had not experienced conversion, and through Edwards's writings details his return to a more traditional, Calvinist position, which stressed an experiential approach to the religious life. 1700-49

2004. Main, Gloria L. THE GOOD SHEPHERD AND HIS WANDERING FLOCK. *Rev. in Am. Hist. 1981 9(4): 464-468.* Reviews Patricia J. Tracy's *Jonathan Edwards, Pastor: Religion and Society in Eighteenth-Century Northampton* (1979). 18c

2005. Tracy, Patricia Juneau. "Jonathan Edwards, Pastor: Minister and Congregation in the Eighteenth-Century Connecticut Valley." U. of Massachusetts 1977. 301 pp. *DAI 1978 38(8): 5013-A.* 1734-42

2006. —. INTELLECTUALS AND SOCIETY IN WESTERN MASSACHUSETTS. *Massachusetts Rev. 1979 20(3): 437-451.*

Tracy, Patricia. THE PASTORATE OF JONATHAN EDWARDS. ca 1730-1880

For abstract see ***Dickinson, Emily***

Edwards, Lena Frances

2007. Scally, Sister Anthony. DR. LENA EDWARDS: PEOPLE LOVER. *Negro Hist. Bull. 1976 39(5): 592-595.* Interviews Lena Frances Edwards, M.D., who began practice in 1924 following her studies at Howard University. She had a private practice in Jersey City, and served on the staff of Margaret Hague Hospital. All of her six children are in significant professional careers. Covers the problems she faced as a woman and Negro in her profession, and her many social service activities. Photos. ca 1924-75

Edwards, Ninian

2008. Wixon, Richard Lance. "Ninian Edwards: A Founding Father of Illinois." Southern Illinois U., Carbondale 1983. 271 pp. *DAI 1983 44 (7): 2226-A.* DA8326578 1800's-33

Eells, Edwin

2009. Castile, George P. EDWIN EELLS, U.S. INDIAN AGENT, 1871-1895. *Pacific Northwest Q. 1981 72(2): 61-68.* Appointed as agent to the Skokomish Indian Reservation in 1871, Edwin Eells believed strongly in breaking down Indian tribalism and replacing it with individually owned plots of land. Thirteen years before the Dawes Act (US, 1887), he introduced the policy of individual allotments among the Skokomish and worked continuously to institute the plan on a national level. Despite his efforts to preserve Indian land from the onslaught of white farmers, Eells lived long enough to see the failures of the Dawes Act, which caused the Indians of Washington State to lose most of their property. Based on Eells's annual agent reports and his memoirs; 4 photos, 35 notes. 1871-95

Egan, John M.

2010. Lavallée, Omer. JOHN M. EGAN, A RAILWAY OFFICER IN WINNIPEG, 1882-1886. *Tr. of the Hist. and Sci. Soc. of Manitoba [Canada] 1976-77 (33): 35-47.* Egan (b. 1848 in Springfield, Massachusetts) served as the Canadian Pacific Railway's senior officer in western Canada from 1882 to 1886. Based in Winnipeg, he supervised the completion of Canada's 3000-mile transcontinental route and the establishment of a commercial telegraph operation, predecessor of CP Telecommunications. After leaving the CPR, he served as president of both the Central of Georgia Railway and the Union Depot Bridge & Terminal Railway of Kansas City. 15 notes. 1882-86

Egan, Lavinia Hartwell

2011. Ball, Lynn. THE VISITABLE PAST OF LAVINIA HARTWELL EGAN. *North Louisiana Hist. Assoc. J. 1978 9(1): 1-11.* 1835-1945

*For abstract see **Canfield, Martin (family)***

Egan, Patrick

2012. Goldberg, Joyce S. PATRICK EGAN: IRISH-AMERICAN MINISTER TO CHILE. *Éire-Ireland 1979 14(3): 83-95.* Discusses the political and diplomatic careers of Patrick Egan (1841-1919). Egan, a successful entrepreneur and an active Irish nationalist from at least 1860, left Ireland in the early 1880's to avoid imprisonment by the British. In Nebraska he rebuilt his finances. He became prominent in the national Republican Party and a good friend of James G. Blaine, who in 1889 arranged for Egan's appointment as US minister to Chile, possibly to oppose Great Britain's great commercial influence there. In Chile in 1891, Egan through his reports to Washington seemed to favor the elected president, José Manuel Balmaceda, against a revolution of the congress and the navy (with which Great Britain sympathized). After the revolution succeeded in August, anti-American sentiment was high. Eventually the Chileans tolerated Egan, who had defended US interests and growing hemispheric responsibility. Secondary sources and Egan correspondence; 33 notes. 1880's-93

Egan, William Allen

2013. Bowkett, Gerald E. EGAN OF VALDEZ: THE FIRST GOVERNOR OF THE STATE OF ALASKA. *Alaska Journal 1984 14(4): 22-29.* Recounts the life of William Allen Egan, the first governor of Alaska. He was born in Valdez in 1914, went to school there, and worked in a variety of jobs before purchasing the Valdez Supply Company in 1946. In 1937, he was elected to the Valdez City Council. He married Neva McKittrick in 1940, a few weeks after his first election to the Alaska Territorial House of Representatives, where he stayed seven terms. He was elected by a landslide in 1958 to be first governor of the state of Alaska. He died in 1984. Based on interviews, newspaper reports, and secondary sources; 10 photos. 1914-84

Egg, Eleanor

2014. Jable, J. Thomas. ELEANOR EGG: PATERSON'S TRACK-AND-FIELD HEROINE. *New Jersey History 1984 102(3-4): 68-84.* Eleanor Egg, the daughter of vaudevillians, demonstrated her prowess at athletics during her grammar school years. Later, Egg and her contemporaries competed through the Paterson Girls' Recreation Association (PGRA) in track meets from New York to California. Even though she did well in many events during the 1920's and early 1930's, injuries kept her from US Olympic teams in 1928 and 1932. Because of her athletic talents and agreeable personality, Paterson officials used her as a focus of city boosterism. Based on newspaper accounts and secondary sources; illus., 41 notes. 1909-32

Ehlers, Ernst

2015. Hawkins, Hugh. TRANSATLANTIC DISCIPLESHIP: TWO AMERICAN BIOLOGISTS AND THEIR GERMAN MENTOR. *Isis 1980 71(257): 197-210.* John Mason Tyler (1851-1929) and Henry Baldwin Ward (1865-1945), American biologists who studied under Ernst Ehlers (1835-1925) at Göttingen University in the 1870's-80's, continued to correspond with him until after World War I. None of the three was a major figure in the development of scientific thought, but their correspondence illustrates some of the international scientific relationships of that era. Based on personal correspondence; 41 notes. 1870-1929

Ehrensperger, Edward Charles

2016. Gasque, Thomas J. EDWARD CHARLES EHRENSPERGER. *Names 1985 33(1-2): 1-5.* Traces the life of Edward Charles Ehrensperger, one of the founders of the American Name Society, whose interest in English literature and language led to his research into South Dakotan place names. 1912-77

Ehrenstein, Albert

2017. Mittelmann, Hanni. VON DER ERBARMLICHKEIT DES EXILS—ALBERT EHRENSTEINS LETZTE JAHRE [The misery of the exiles: Albert Ehrenstein's last years]. *Bull. des Leo Baeck Inst. [Israel] 1980 19(56-57): 110-134.* The dangerous and miserable lives of political exiles in the 1930's and 40's are well illustrated by the experiences of the writer Albert Ehrenstein. He left Germany in 1932 of his own free will, but he never found in Europe a safe haven. In 1941 he came to the United States. Money was always a problem for him. Since he never really mastered English he found it difficult to write and publishers found his work too complicated and too European. He did not easily adjust to US publishing methods. Nor did he adjust to the American style of living. 23 notes. 1932-50

Ehrlich, Arnold Bogomil

2018. Kabakoff, Jocob. NEW LIGHT ON ARNOLD BOGOMIL EHRLICH. *American Jewish Archives 1984 36(2): 202-224.* Describes Arnold Bogomil Ehrlich's early career as a Yiddish writer and poet prior to his becoming a Bible exegesist. Ehrlich published several volumes of his *Randglossen,* in which his analysis of the Bible was published, before being beset by financial problems. Illus., 47 notes. 1878-1919

Ehrman, Theresa

2019. Strauss, Leon L., ed. BELOVED SCRIBE: LETTERS OF THERESA EHRMAN. *Western States Jewish Hist. Q. 1979 12(1): 39-62; 1980 12(2): 142-160, 12(3): 229-245.* Part I. Theresa Ehrman (1884-1967) was related to Leo and Gertrude Stein, Americans who lived in Paris, France, in the center of a literary and artistic community. Theresa went to Paris to advance her training as a pianist. She lived with Michael and Sarah Stein, Leo's brother and sister-in-law. Among her acquaintances were Pablo Casals and other noted musicians of the era. Reprints Ehrman's letters to her family in California; 5 photos, 40 notes. Part II. In the summer of 1904, Theresa Ehrman toured Switzerland, Italy, Holland, Belgium, and Germany with her relatives Mike and Sarah Stein. In Germany, she visited her father's brother and sister. Back in Paris in October, she continued piano studies with Harold Bauer. Reprints letters of Theresa Ehrman; 2 photos, 14 notes. Part III. Late in 1904, Theresa broke off her romantic relationship with Pablo Casals, but they maintained a lifelong friendship. Her piano studies continued in Paris with Therese Chaigneau and Harold Bauer. After her return home to San Francisco in 1905, Theresa began her career as an accompanist and piano teacher. She was a close friend to many outstanding musicians, composers, and conductors. In her last years she lived in the San Francisco Bay area. Reprints her letters; 2 photos, 31 notes. 1901-67

Eifert, Virginia S.

2020. Hallwas, John E. THE ACHIEVEMENT OF VIRGINIA S. EIFERT. *J. of the Illinois State Hist. Soc. 1978 71(2): 82-106.* Virginia S. Eifert (1911-66) of Springfield, Illinois, was one of the most widely known midwestern artists and nature writers of the 20th century. Her canon includes 19 books and hundreds of short articles; among her finest are the essays she wrote as editor of the Illinois State Museum magazine, *Living Museum.* Based on her writings and personal reminiscences; 19 illus., 67 notes. 1931-66

Eights, James

2021. Miller, Char and Goldsmith, Naomi. JAMES EIGHTS, ALBANY NATURALIST: NEW EVIDENCE. *New York Hist. 1980 61(1): 23-42.* Historians have emphasized James Eights's researches in the Antarctic in 1829-30, but have overlooked his other scientific work. Eights was involved in the establishment of the Albany Lyceum of Natural History, contributed to the geological survey of the Erie Canal region, engaged in mineralogical researches during the 1840's and 1850's, and was important as a popularizer of science. The scientific writings of his later works reveal Eights's faith in technological progress combined with concern about ecological needs. Eights was a professionally active scientist until the middle 1870's. Based on Eights's published writings, personal correspondence, and other primary sources; 8 illus., 30 notes. 1820-74

Einstein, Albert

2022. Barnett, Lincoln. HOW ALBERT EINSTEIN, A GENTLE, MODEST GENIUS BORN 100 YEARS AGO, FOUND SANCTUARY AND INSPIRATION IN PRINCETON. *Smithsonian 1979 9(11): 68-79.* Einstein decided to accept an appointment to the newly established Institute for Advanced Study in Princeton, New Jersey, in 1933 after observing with horror the Nazi assault on the intellect. He renounced his German citizenship while he was a visiting professor at Caltech, shortly after Hitler became chancellor of Germany. In 1939 he wrote President Roosevelt a prophetic letter warning about the atomic bomb. It was a prologue to the Manhattan Project and Hiroshima. Illus. 1933-55

2023. Gotlieb, Yosef. EINSTEIN THE ZIONIST. *Midstream 1979 25(6): 43-48.* Albert Einstein (1879-1955) had little sense of Jewish identity during his early years, but about 1911 he became acquainted with Zionism in Prague, although he tended toward internationalism and pacifism until 1919, a date which marked the beginning of his strong belief in Zionism and his association with Hebrew University in Tel Aviv. 1911-55

2024. Hoffmann, Banesh. ALBERT EINSTEIN. *Leo Baeck Inst. Year Book [Great Britain] 1976 20: 279-288.* Reinterprets Albert Einstein's (1879-1955) life with emphasis on his religious and artistic sides. His writings and his major scientific achievements show the lucidity of his mind and his genius to see even the most complicated matters simply and artistically. The last 30 years of his life were devoted to furthering peace and strengthening human freedom. Einstein, the nonreligious Jew, shared the full burden of his Jewishness since he felt responsible for his people and their fate. 22 notes. ca 1900-55

Eiseley, Loren

2025. Franke, Robert G. LOREN EISELEY: RELIGIOUS SCIENTIST. *Zygon: J. of Religion and Sci. 1984 19(1): 29-41.* Describes the religious dimension in the writing of Loren Eiseley, who stressed the limits of science and the interconnectedness of all life with the universe. 1950's-83

2026. Heidtmann, Peter. LOCATING LOREN EISELEY. *Biography 1984 7(3): 206-212.* William C. Spengemann's discussion of three basic autobiographical modes provides a framework for locating Loren Eiseley as an autobiographer. Analysis shows that he is temperamentally unsuited for the historical mode, and that, while philosophical in his concerns, he is essentially poetic in his presentation of himself as a fugitive. 1907-77

Eisenhower, Dwight D.

2027. Cotter, Cornelius P. EISENHOWER AS PARTY LEADER. *Pol. Sci. Q. 1983 98(2): 255-283.* Examines Dwight D. Eisenhower's role as leader of the Republican Party during his presidency. He was a strong leader who sought to modernize the attitudes of Republican activists, and to strengthen the party organization as a means to compete for government control. Eisenhower pushed the party to seek new recruits. In administration matters, he drew on the party hierarchy. During his postpresidential years, Eisenhower was committed to party-building. Although not without problems, the modern Republican Party has maintained a strong network across the states that is closely linked to the national party organization. Primary sources; table, 115 notes. 1953-61

2028. Jacobs, Travis B. DWIGHT D. EISENHOWER'S PRESIDENCY OF COLUMBIA UNIVERSITY. *Presidential Studies Quarterly 1985 15(3): 555-560.* As his first nonmilitary position after World War II, Dwight D. Eisenhower chose the presidency of Columbia University, a great but troubled university. In this position, he broadened and sharpened his ideas about the political and social nature of contemporary society, and he tried to use the position to bring about general education promoting citizenship and the responsibilities it involved to society at large. While outside demands prevented him from actively and effectively guiding Columbia, the years he spent there helped prepare him for his years as president. 12 notes. 1947-52

2029. Katz, Milton S. E. FREDERICK MORROW AND CIVIL RIGHTS IN THE EISENHOWER ADMINISTRATION. *Phylon 1981 42(2): 133-144.* 1952-60
*For abstract see **Morrow, E. Frederick***

2030. Kingseed, Cole C. EDUCATION OF A COMBAT COMMANDER. *Military Review 1985 65(12): 12-19.* Reviews the career of General Dwight D. Eisenhower from 1915 to the end of World War II, and focuses on the nature and quality of his leadership, which led to his promotions and ensured his success as Supreme High Commander of the Allied Forces in Europe. Includes the early influences of Generals Fox Conner, John J. Pershing, Douglas MacArthur, and George C. Marshall, and his World War II relationships with Generals Omar N. Bradley, George S. Patton, and Bernard L. Montgomery. Based on Eisenhower's diary and correspondence; illus., 4 photos, 14 notes. 1915-45

2031. Neal, Steve. WHY WE WERE RIGHT TO LIKE IKE. *American Heritage 1985 37(1): 49-64.* After mostly negative early assessments, historians today are giving Dwight D. Eisenhower high marks as president. His quiet leadership style, his willingness to resist Pentagon pressures, and his role in restoring confidence in the presidency and building a consensus in postwar America are all factors now cited by historians who also have use of more and better primary sources to support their contentions. 7 photos, 5 illus. 1950's

Eisenmann, Sylvester

2032. Wolff, Gerald W. FATHER SYLVESTER EISENMANN AND MARTY MISSION. *South Dakota Hist. 1975 5(4): 360-389.* During 1918-48 Father Sylvester Eisenmann successfully ministered to Sioux Indians on the Yankton Reservation. He supported the Indians' welfare and was extremely generous in the time, effort, and money he invested in their behalf. A tireless worker, he was especially successful in raising funds and in constructing almost 30 major buildings at Marty. His accomplishments were offset somewhat by his paternalism and condescension. These attitudes grew out of his early years and training in southern Indiana. Thus his deep concern and great record of achievement for the Yankton Sioux were diminished because he treated his Indian charges as perpetual children. By rejecting their heritage and underestimating them as human beings, Father Sylvester did them a disservice. Primary and secondary sources; 7 photos, 67 notes. 1918-49

Eisentrager, James A.

2033. Spence, Robert. JAMES A. EISENTRAGER: PAINTER FROM THE PLAINS. *Kansas Q. 1982 14(4): 99-111.* Recounts the career of Nebraska artist James A. Eisentrager since the 1950's; his recent work is in the anti-Expressionist tradition. 1950's-82

Elbert, Samuel

2034. Smith, Gordon B. THE GEORGIA GRENADIERS. *Georgia Hist. Q. 1980 64(4): 405-415.* Details the career of Samuel Elbert (1743-1788) and his Grenadier's Lodge, a Masonic military company that was part of the rebellious forces in Savannah, Georgia, that served in the American Revolution. Biographical information on company officers is given. Based on primary and secondary sources; 52 notes. 1772-79

Elder, Paul

2035. Gordon, Ruth I. "Paul Elder: Bookseller-Publisher (1897-1917): A Bay Area Reflection." U. of California, Berkeley 1977. 239 pp. *DAI 1978 38(8): 4424-4425-A.* 1897-1917

Eliade, Mircea

2036. Cain, Seymour. MIRCEA ELIADE: CREATIVE EXILE. *Midstream 1982 28(6): 50-58.* Examines the career and scholarly pursuits of Mircea Eliade from 1928-78, focusing on Eliade's academic endeavors during his self-imposed exile in France after 1945, and on his place in 20th-century religious thought. 1928-78

Eliot, Charles W.

2037. Preskill, Stephen Louis. "Raking from the Rubbish: Charles W. Eliot, James B. Conant and the Public Schools." U. of Illinois, Urbana-Champaign 1984. 351 pp. *DAI 1985 45(11): 3293-A.* DA8502274 1866-1978

2038. Sexton, John Edward. "Charles W. Eliot, Unitarian Exponent of the Doctrine of Tolerance in Religion." Fordham U. 1978. 347 pp. *DAI 1978 39(3): 1668-A.* 1834-1926

2039. Wagoner, Jennings L., Jr. CHARLES W. ELIOT, IMMIGRANTS, AND THE DECLINE OF AMERICAN IDEALISM. *Biography 1985 8(1): 25-36.* Charles W. Eliot, president of Harvard University during 1869-1909, was a leading education spokesman and untiring advocate of social-reform causes. His liberal position on the open-door immigration policy became a minority view as nativism increased in the early decades of this century and his own belief in assimilation evolved gradually into an advocacy of cultural pluralism. 1869-1909

Eliot, Ephraim

2040. Basquin, Roberta A. and Walsh, Robert A. EPHRAIM ELIOT, FIRST PRESIDENT OF THE MASSACHUSETTS COLLEGE OF PHARMACY. *Pharmacy in Hist. 1979 21(1): 45-47.* Highlights the life of Ephraim Eliot (1761-1827), a noted Boston physician-druggist who was elected the first president of the Massachusetts College of Pharmacy (MCP) on 29 December 1823. Eliot was recognized in the Boston area for the compounding and dispensing of medicinals, the preparation of medicine chests, and contributions to local historical activities. His "Account of the Physicians of Boston" was a unique treatise on medicine and pharmacy in the early 19th century. In the tradition of the Massachusetts Medical Society which had attempted to improve the quality of pharmacy in the Commonwealth since the late 18th century, Eliot wanted the MCP to properly educate future pharmacists, conduct pharmaceutical research, diffuse information, regulate the activities of those in the pharmacy business, and promote the interests of the profession. Presented to AIHP, 1978. Primary and secondary sources; illus., 11 notes. 1780's-1820's

Eliot, John

2041. Rea, Robert R. JOHN ELIOT, SECOND GOVERNOR OF BRITISH WEST FLORIDA. *Alabama Rev. 1977 30(4): 243-265.* John Eliot (1742-69), scion of a prominent and well-connected Cornish family, chose a naval career, saw action against France in the Atlantic and Mediterranean, and became a captain. In 1767 he was appointed governor of West Florida. His actual administration lasted barely a month, March-April 1769; he committed suicide. 49 notes. 1767-69

2042. Sehr, Timothy J. JOHN ELIOT, MILLENNIALIST AND MISSIONARY. *Historian 1984 46(2): 187-203.* John Eliot was best known for his efforts in preaching the gospel to the Indians in early New England, and in producing the first Indian translation of the Bible. His work among the Indians was continually frustrated by politics in Massachusetts Bay Colony, particularly by King Philip's War in the mid 1670's and the revocation of the company charter in the mid 1680's. A millenarian, he believed for most of his life that he would live to see the millennium, a belief that he held until the 1680's, when he concluded that the millennium would occur sometime after his death. 58 notes. 1604-90

Eliot, Thomas Lamb

2043. Singer, Barnett. OREGON'S NINETEENTH-CENTURY NOTABLES: SIMEON GANNETT REED AND THOMAS LAMB ELIOT. Bingham, Edwin R. and Love, Glen A., ed. *Northwest Perspectives: Essays on the Culture of the Pacific Northwest* (Eugene, Ore.: U. of Washington Pr. for the U. of Oregon, 1979): 60-76. Compares Simeon Gannett Reed and Thomas Lamb Eliot as examples of Oregon notables of the 19th century. Reed was an entrepreneur. Eliot founded the Northwest's first Unitarian church in 1876, espousing liberalism yet holding high moral standards. Eliot organized lecture series to educate people on controversial subjects. Reed had little to show for his efforts other than balanced books and records of acquisitions, but Eliot was a dynamic cultural force whose activities will be remembered. Mainly secondary sources; 43 notes. ca 1870-95

Elk, Gerda E.

2044. Elk, Gerda E. MY EARLY YEARS IN NEW ENGLAND. *Swedish-American Hist. Q. 1984 35(2): 108-123.* Presents reminiscences of a Swedish girl's early years in the United States after arriving in 1921 from Gästrikland, Sweden, with her mother and three sisters. They joined her father, Axel Söderström, who had come to the United States in 1920. Recalls growing up in Auburn, Massachusetts, raising chickens and growing a garden, eating American foods, learning English, socializing with Armenian neighbors, playing Halloween pranks, participating in local Swedish groups, and learning to drive. 3 photos. 1921-30

Ellender, Tom (family)

2045. Becnel, Thomas A. THE ELLENDERS: PIONEER TERREBONNE PARISH FAMILY, 1840-1924. *Louisiana History 1985 26(2): 117-127.* Tom Ellender came to Terrebonne Parish in the 1930's and became a prosperous farmer. After his death in 1884 his nine sons ran the family operations as a cohesive unit, producing sugar, corn and cypress lumber; operating a sugar mill; and investing in an ice company. They occupied a status between the planter aristocracy and the poor farmers. By 1924 the family, swelled by a new generation, was too large to operate as a unit, and the property was divided among Tom's six surviving sons. Based on interviews, parish and church records, and census reports; 44 notes. 1840-1924

Ellice, Jane

2046. Shields, Carol. THREE CANADIAN WOMEN: FICTION OR AUTOBIOGRAPHY. *Atlantis [Canada] 1978 4(1): 49-54.* 19c
*For abstract see **Allison, Susan Moir***

Ellicott, Joseph

2047. Wyckoff, William Kent. "Joseph Ellicott and the Western New York Frontier: Environmental Assessments, Geographical Strategies, and Authored Landscapes, 1797-1811." Syracuse U. 1982. 631 pp. *DAI 1983 43(7): 2429-A.* DA8229027 1797-1811

Ellingson, Ole

2048. Thorson, Playford V. OLE ELLINGSON: A NORTH DAKOTA RADICAL POPULIST. *North Dakota Q. 1981 49(4): 39-51.* Norwegian immigrant Ole Ellingson came to America in 1887 and settled in Grand Forks, North Dakota; a self-described "radical Populist" and prohibitionist who objected to corporate control of railroads, the telegraph, and national banks, he became a conservative Republican in later life when he grew more affluent. 1887-1946

Ellington, Duke

2049. Townsend, Irving. DUKE'S SWEET THUNDER. *Horizon 1979 22(11): 50-57.* Traces the musical career of Duke Ellington from 1923, when he received his first copyright for "Blind Man's Bluff," until he died in 1974, particularly his talents as one of America's finest composers of jazz. 1923-74

Elliott, Andrew

2050. Ernst, Robert. ANDREW ELLIOTT, FORGOTTEN LOYALIST OF OCCUPIED NEW YORK. *New York Hist. 1976 57(3): 285-320.* Andrew Elliott, Collector of Customs for the Port of New York from 1764 to 1776, was Superintendent of Imports and Exports to and from New York, Long Island, and Staten Island; Superintendent General of Police; Lieutenant-Governor; and Acting Governor of British-occupied New York during the American Revolution. 2 illus., 128 notes. 1764-83

Elliott, George P.

2051. Brustein, Robert. GEORGE P. ELLIOTT. *Am. Scholar 1981 50(3): 355-358.* Portrays author George P. Elliott as a man of various self-defeating inner turmoils. The value in Elliott's life comes from the struggle for a morally creative life. The author reminisces about his association with Elliott during 1955-77. 1955-77

Elliott, Harrison G.

2052. Krill, John. HARRISON G. ELLIOTT: CREATOR OF HANDMADE PAPERS. *Q. J. of the Lib. of Congress 1978 35(1): 4-26.* Harrison G. Elliott (1879-1954), artisan of fine handmade paper and expert on the history of wood pulp paper, began his career at the International Paper Company before he joined the prestigious Japanese Paper Company in New York City in 1925. Papermaking equipment left with the company sparked his creative interest and for 20 years he made unique and highly praised paper by hand. He shared his knowledge and appreciation of papermaking and its history in talks, books, articles, and films. His collection of paperiana, including documentation of his lifelong friendship with Dard Hunter, is now in the Harrison Elliott Collection of Paperiana in the Rare Book and Special Collections Division of the Library of Congress. Based on documents in the Harrison Elliott Collection of Paperiana and secondary works; 10 illus., 101 notes, biblio., 4 appendixes. 20c

Elliott, Henry Wood

2053. Shalkop, Robert L. HENRY WOOD ELLIOTT: FIGHTER FOR THE FUR SEALS. *Alaska J. 1983 13(1): 4-12.* Studies the paintings of Ohio conservationist Henry Wood Elliott, focusing on his opposition to the slaughter of fur seals in the Pribilof Islands of Alaska. Recounts the political struggles ensuing from an 1889 report by Treasury agent Charles J. Goff that the seals were nearly extinct. Explores aspects of foreign relations involving Great Britain and Canada, which continued to hunt the seals after the United States had stopped. 17 photos, 17 notes. 1867-1910

Elliott, William

2054. Scafidel, Beverly. THE AUTHOR-PLANNER WILLIAM ELLIOTT (1788-1863). *Pro. of the South Carolina Hist. Assoc. 1981: 114-119.* William Elliott (1788-1863) was a planter, sportsman, author and legislator, who is best remembered as the author of a volume of hunting and fishing stories, *Carolina Sports by Land and Water* (1864). He also published articles on farming and politics. He resigned from the South Carolina Senate because he would not vote for nullification as his constituents wished. Based primarily on William Elliott's letters; 8 notes. 1810-63

Ellis, Earl H.

2055. Ballendorf, Dirk Anthony. EARL HANCOCK ELLIS: THE MAN AND HIS MISSION. *US Naval Inst. Pro. 1983 109(11): 53-60.* Marine Lieutenant Colonel Earl H. Ellis gained recognition as a brilliant military planner during 1911-21. He was also an alcoholic. In 1921-23 Ellis undertook a secret intelligence reconnaissance of Japanese bases in Micronesia. His nephritis grew worse as he traveled through the islands and he died in Palau on 12 May 1923. The Japanese then confiscated his notes, charts, and code books. Based on archival sources; biblio., 5 notes. 1911-23

Ellis, Edwin M.

2056. Dosker, Nina Ellis. EDWIN M. ELLIS: MONTANA'S BICYCLING MINISTER. *Montana 1980 30(1): 42-51.* Edwin M. Ellis (1853-1940) was a Prebyterian minister and the Montana Superintendent of Sunday School Missions from 1884 until his retirement in 1927. As a minister, he served the Bitterroot Valley; his superintendent duties covered all Montana from his Helena headquarters. To facilitate his travel throughout rural Montana, Ellis used a Columbia Chainless Bicycle during 1892-1913. He became known as Montana's bicycling minister, and many of the churches and sunday schools he founded are still active today. Based on author's reminiscences; 13 illus, note. 1870's-1927

Ellis, Harvey

2057. Sanders, Barry. HARVEY ELLIS: ARCHITECT, PAINTER, FURNITURE DESIGNER. *Art & Antiques 1981 4(1): 58-67.* Harvey Ellis (1852-1904), who designed one of the first skyscrapers in America (never built), and for years worked for the prominent furniture-maker Gustav Stickley, died in obscurity and is little-known. ca 1870-1904

Ellis, Henry

2058. Walker, Tom. HENRY ELLIS, ENLIGHTENMENT GENTLEMAN. *Georgia Hist. Q. 1979 64(3): 364-376.* Describes accomplishments of the little known Henry Ellis (1721-1806), sailor, naturalist, writer, explorer, scientist, and British royal governor of Georgia (1757-60). Primary sources; 19 notes. 1721-1806

Ellis, L. Ethan

2059. McCormick, Richard P. [L. ETHAN ELLIS, 1898-1977]. *Am. Hist. Rev. 1978 83(3): 862.* L. Ethan Ellis (1898-1977) was an American historian and had become Voorhees Professor of History emeritus at Rutgers University. ca 1920-77

Ellis, Pete

2060. Pierce, P. N. THE UNSOLVED MYSTERY OF PETE ELLIS. *Marine Corps Gazette 1962 46(2): 34-40.* A biography of US Marine Colonel Pete Ellis (b. 1880), master spy against Japan, who died under mysterious circumstances in the Pacific Caroline Islands in 1923. 1923

Ellison, J. R.

2061. Abbott, Donald P. LETTERS TO THE EDITOR: ELLISON-WHITE CHAUTAUQUA. *Oregon Hist. Q. 1984 85(3): 304-307.* J. R. Ellison and C. H. White moved the operation of their traveling chautauqua shows from Boise, Idaho, to Portland, Oregon, in 1918 or 1919. They soon expanded to five series of shows, with entertainment, educational programs, and stage productions running several times a day and traveling throughout Western towns. They also founded a lyceum bureau and a conservatory of music, and built the Studio Building in Portland. The Depression and the advent of the auto and radio ended the chautauquas. 2 photos. 1918-30's

Ellsberg, Daniel

2062. Cuddy, Edward. ALEXANDER SOLZHENITSYN AND DANIEL ELLSBERG: MINOR RIPPLES IN THE TIDE OF HISTORY OR "MEN FOR ALL SEASONS"? Plesur, Milton, ed. *An American Historian: Essays to Honor Selig Adler* (Buffalo: State U. of N.Y., 1980): 224-233. Compares the philosophies and actions of former security analyst Daniel Ellsberg, who exposed the Pentagon's bombing strategy in Vietnam, and Russian dissident writer Alexander Solzhenitsyn, author of the *Gulag Archipelago,* in the early 1970's, and briefly compares them to other political rebels who act on conscience. 1970's

Ellsworth, Elmer E.

2063. Cunliffe, Marcus. ELMER ELLSWORTH. Karsten, Peter, ed. *The Military in America: From the Colonial Era to the Present* (New York: Free Pr., 1980): 117-121. Elmer E. Ellsworth (1837-61) of Chicago studied in Abraham Lincoln's law firm, organized Illinois volunteer militia units of Zouaves, and became famous after a national drill tour in the summer of 1860; as commander of a New York Zouave unit during the military occupation of Alexandria, Virginia, on 23 May 1861, Colonel Ellsworth became "the first martyr of the Civil War." 1859-61

Ellsworth, James W.

2064. Hyser, Raymond Marshall. "A Study in Cooperative Management: The Business Career of James W. Ellsworth (1849-1925). Florida State U. 1983. 491 pp. *DAI 1983 44(3): 844-A.* DA8317373 1870's-1925

Elmsley, John

2065. Nicolson, Murray W. JOHN ELMSLEY AND THE RISE OF IRISH CATHOLIC SOCIAL ACTION IN VICTORIAN TORONTO. *Study Sessions: The Canadian Catholic Historical Association [Canada] 1984 51: 47-66.* John Elmsley (1801-63) resigned a commission in the British navy to avoid destroying human life, returned to his birthplace, York, Upper Canada, converted to Catholicism, and used his considerable prestige and resources to aid poor Irish immigrants. 1831-63

Elsmith, Dorothy Olcott

2066. Elsmith, Dorothy Olcott. LAKE SUPERIOR MEMORIES. *Inland Seas 1980 36(2): 96-100.* Recollections of a girlhood in turn-of-the-century Duluth, Minnesota, the christening of the *Charles R. Van Hise,* the wreck of the freighter *Mataafa;* and early 20th-century travel on Lakes freighters. 1900-03

Elsner, John

2067. Hornbein, Marjorie. DR. JOHN ELSNER, A COLORADO PIONEER. *Western States Jewish Hist. Q. 1981 13(4): 291-302.* Dr. John Elsner (1844-1922) came to Denver, Colorado, in 1866 on a mining venture. He settled into medical practice and became a leader in the organization of city and state medical societies in 1871. With his wife, Lena, he was active in the Jewish community, helping to establish the B'nai B'rith Lodge and Congregation Emmanuel. In 1889 he participated in the founding of the National Jewish Hospital. Based on Elsner's "Reminiscences" in the Denver *Medical Times,* 1908, and other published sources; 2 photos, 50 notes. 1866-1922

Elwyn family

2068. Camden, Thomas E. THE LANGDON-ELWYN FAMILY PAPERS. *Hist. New Hampshire 1981 36(4): 350-356.* 1762-1972
For abstract see ***Langdon, John (family)***

Ely, Edmund F.

2069. Hoover, Roy. "TO STAND ALONE IN THE WILDERNESS": EDMUND F. ELY, MISSIONARY. *Minnesota History 1985 49(7): 265-280.* Presents the life and observations of Edmund F. Ely (1809-1882), who served as a lay missionary and teacher for the American Board of Commissioners for Foreign Missions among the Chippewa Indians in northern Minnesota and Wisconsin during 1833-49. His journals report much about his journey there and the first encounters with the land, the Indians, the work, and his competition and co-workers. While the years gave him more relaxed expectations about them all, he also acquired a large family and left his lonely occupation on the frontier. Based on Ely's journals and letters; 11 illus., 62 notes. 1833-49

Ely, Eugene B.

2070. Moore, John Hammond. THE SHORT, EVENTFUL LIFE OF EUGENE B. ELY. *US Naval Inst. Pro. 1981 107(1): 58-63.* Eugene B. Ely (1886-1911) was the 17th pilot to receive a federal pilot's license; it was issued to him on 5 October 1910. Ely was then employed on Glenn Curtiss's exhibition team. On 18 January 1911, Ely, who had flown off of a US warship the previous May, landed on and then took off from a special platform that had been built on the USS *Pennsylvania.* He hoped to be employed by the Navy to further develop the Navy's air arm, but no such job materialized, so he continued to fly for Curtiss. On 19 October 1911, at Macon, Georgia, Ely could not pull his airplane out of a dive. He managed to jump clear, but broke his neck and died within minutes. 6 photos. 1911

Emerson, Ralph Waldo

2071. Allardt, Linda. "The Journals and Miscellaneous Notebooks of Ralph Waldo Emerson: The Lecture Notebooks from 1835 to 1862." U. of Rochester 1977. *DAI 1978 38(8): 4821-4822-A.* 1835-62

2072. Carlson, Eric W. NEW STUDIES OF EMERSON. *Am. Studies Int. 1983 24(2): 109-112.* Reviews nine recent books on Ralph Waldo Emerson that cover, among other topics, his attitudes on sex, his influence as a writer, and his journals and essays. 1800-60

2073. Gross, Robert A. TRANSCENDENTALISM AND URBANISM: CONCORD, BOSTON, AND THE WIDER WORLD. *J. of Am. Studies [Great Britain] 1984 18(3): 361-381.* Ralph Waldo Emerson predicted a suburban fate, a cultural renaissance, and a middle-class populace for Concord, Massachusetts, from which several leading Transcendentalists had fled because of the town's lack of urban amenities. Emerson resided at Concord after 1835, observed the economic doldrums of the town in pre-Civil War times, and came to terms intellectually with the urbanization of America, which he deplored but recognized as inexorable. His prophecies for Concord were realized in the next century. Based on Emerson's works, printed primary source collections, unpublished doctoral dissertations, and secondary works; 32 notes. 1835-82

2074. Kalinevitch, Karen Lynn. "Ralph Waldo Emerson's Older Brother: The Letters and Journal of William Emerson." U. of Tennessee 1982. 229 pp. *DAI 1982 43(6): 1972-A.* DA8225344 1823-25

2075. Kaplan, Justin. HALF SONG-THRUSH, HALF ALLIGATOR. *Am. Heritage 1980 31(6): 62-67.* 1842-81
For abstract see ***Whitman, Walt***

2076. Price, Kenneth M. WHITMAN ON EMERSON: NEW LIGHT ON THE 1856 LETTER. *Am. Lit. 1984 56(1): 83-87.* Walt Whitman's attitude toward Ralph Waldo Emerson during the 1850's and 1870's was ambivalent: earlier he praised Emerson as a leader in developing a new American literature, but by the 1870's Emerson had become too aristocratic in his role as the sage of the New England set. Primary materials; 10 notes. 1850's-70's

2077. Ronda, Bruce A. LITERARY GRIEVING: EMERSON AND THE DEATH OF WALDO. *Centennial Rev. 1979 23(1): 91-104.* Ralph Waldo Emerson used "the child-figure" as a model of that "self-reliant self" which he celebrated, until the death of his son Waldo in 1842 caused him to reevaluate his outlook. Waldo's dying revealed that Emerson had failed to find a place in his thought for "limitation and loss, decay and old age." From this reevaluation emerged the poem *Threnody,* a watershed in Emerson's work. Thereafter, the assertion of the creative self gives way to "an acceptance of the self's limitations," and "the child recedes . . . as the model for the transformed life." 11 notes. 1835-46

2078. Rulon-Miller, Robert, Jr. NATHAN APPLETON'S REMINISCENCES OF RALPH WALDO EMERSON. *Manuscripts 1982 34(2): 103-108.* Publishes Nathan Appleton's "Sketches and Reminiscences of Persons: Ralph Waldo Emerson," written in 1885. 1855-82

Emerson, Ralph Waldo (family)

2079. Gregg, Edith Emerson Webster. EMERSON AND HIS CHILDREN: THEIR CHILDHOOD MEMORIES. *Harvard Lib. Bull. 1980 28(4): 407-430.* Ellen, Edith and Edward Waldo Emerson, the children of Ralph Waldo Emerson, all had fond memories of childhood with their father. The two sisters' recollections are among the papers in the Ralph Waldo Emerson Memorial Association, and Edward's are found in his book *Emerson in Concord,* published in 1888. The three accounts present a picture of an affectionate father who, between the years of 1845-60, often took his children on walks in the woods and made certain that they attended to their studies in Latin and Greek with much care. Primary sources; 23 notes. 1845-60

Emerson, William

2080. Kalinevitch, Karen Lynn. "Ralph Waldo Emerson's Older Brother: The Letters and Journal of William Emerson." U. of Tennessee 1982. 229 pp. *DAI 1982 43(6): 1972-A.* DA8225344 1823-25

Emery, Irene

2081. King, Mary Elizabeth. IRENE EMERY, 1900-1981. *Am. Antiquity 1983 48(1): 80-82.* Discusses the career and contributions of Irene Emery, curator emerita of Technical Studies at the Textile Museum, Washington, D.C., and provides a bibliography. 1900-81

Emmens, Stephen H.

2082. Kauffman, George B. THE MYSTERY OF STEPHEN H. EMMENS: SUCCESSFUL ALCHEMIST OR INGENIOUS SWINDLER? *Ambix [Great Britain] 1983 30(2): 65-88.* Presents what little is known about Emmens initially. He was born about 1844 or 45, possibly in England or Ireland, and attended evening classes in London in the early 1860's. The date of entry into the United States is unknown, but in 1888 he was living near New York. The date of his death is unknown. From circumstantial evidence it probably was shortly after 1900. He had made himself something of an authority on some aspects of metallurgy, particularly that of nickel, but his claims of transmutation tended to destroy his credibility. It is on record, however, that Emmens did sell gold to the US Mint, and there is no extant record of his purchasing any. His writings on this, and on philosophical ideas he had developed, as well as other subjects are noted. Largely based on Emmens's writings, contemporary journals, and newspapers; 135 notes. 1880-1900

Emmet, Joseph Kline

2083. Callahan, John M. FRITZ EMMET: ST. LOUIS'S FAVORITE GERMAN. *Missouri Hist. Soc. Bull. 1979 35(2): 69-82.* Joseph Kline Emmet (1841-91), an Irish American actor born in St. Louis, started his theatrical career in 1858. Before 1869 he achieved only limited recognition, first as an Irish comedian and later as vocalist and actor in minstrel shows. In 1869, Emmet and Charles Gaylor created for German dialect dramas a character named Fritz Van Vonderblinkenstoffenheisen. Playing the role of Fritz first in *Fritz, Our German Cousin* and subsequently in many other plays, Emmet won national fame. Archival material, newspapers, and secondary sources; photo, 80 notes. 1858-91

Emmett, Daniel Decatur

2084. Green, Archie. OLD DAN TUCKER. *JEMF Q. 1981 17(62): 85-94, 106.* Brief biography of Daniel Decatur Emmett, who wrote the hit song "Old Dan Tucker" for the Virginia Minstrels, a group formed in January 1843 with Emmett, Billy Whitlock, Dick Pelham, and Frank Brower; focuses on the song's wide appeal and its publication in music books with illustrations of Dan Tucker. 1830-50

Emmons, George Thornton

2085. Low, Jean. GEORGE THORNTON EMMONS. *Alaska J. 1977 7(1): 2-11.* George Thornton Emmons (1852-1945) was a pioneer ethnologist of native Alaskans. While assigned to the *USS Adams* after graduation from Annapolis, Emmons was introduced to Alaska. He became friendly with the Tlingit Indians and began collecting artifacts which he shipped to museums all over the world. He prepared an exhibit for the World's Fair in 1891. In 1902, President Theodore Roosevelt asked him to find the old Russian boundary markers in the Chilkat country, and in 1904 he prepared for Roosevelt a report on the needs of the natives. 9 notes, biblio. 1852-1945

Emrich, Duncan B. M.

2086. Beck, Horace. DUNCAN EMRICH (1908-1977). *J. of Am. Folklore 1978 91(360): 700-703.* The late Duncan B. M. Emrich, former director of the American Folksong and Folklore Archives in Washington, became professor of American Folklore at American University. He established the American Folklore Fund there in 1976. He was a prolific author on folk and popular lore. 1908-77

Engel, Julius

2087. Engel, Armin. HISTORY OF AN ITINERANT PASTOR IN DAKOTA. *Heritage Review 1985 15(1): 3-7.* Describes the travels of Julius Engel in the Dakotas, where the Lutheran minister was an itinerant pastor. 1892-95

Engelhardt, Zephyrin

2088. Burrus, Ernest J. A DEDICATION TO THE MEMORY OF ZEPHYRIN ENGELHARDT, O.F.M., 1851-1934. *Arizona and the West 1976 18(3): 212-216.* German-born emigrant Charles Engelhardt (1851-1934) changed his Christian name to Zephyrin when he entered a seminary. After schooling and ordination, he had numerous assignments throughout the country in Indian missions and editorial work. In 1901 he was sent to Mission Santa Barbara in California, where he remained until his death. He was a prodigious collector of documents, manuscripts, and rare editions of Southwestern and Western history. He published "an astounding number" of "ponderous tomes" and articles on missionary activity in the Spanish Borderlands of the Southwest. Illus., biblio. 1851-1934

Engle, Clair

2089. Sayles, Stephen Paul. "Clair Engle and the Politics of California Reclamation, 1943-1960." U. of New Mexico 1978. 335 pp. *DAI 1978 39(4): 2490-A.* 1943-60

Enss, Gustav H.

2090. Juhnke, James C. GUSTAV H. ENSS, MENNONITE ALIEN (1885-1965). *Mennonite Life 1981 36(4): 9-15.* During his career in the Midwest, Gustav H. Enss, a Berlin-educated immigrant from Russia, was transformed from a controversial fundamentalist teacher at Bethel College, pastor of the Hoffnungsfeld Mennonite Church, and founder of a German school in Moundbridge into a controversial neoorthodox teacher, theologian, and advocate for the use of the English language. Throughout his conflicts of identity, he was supported by his English wife, Amy Evelyn Greaves Sudermann. Primary sources; 4 photos, 36 notes. 1900-65

Enters, Angna

2091. Mandel, Dorothy. REDISCOVERING ANGNA ENTERS. *Frontiers 1981 6(3): 102-105.* Details the life of Angna Enters: mime, dancer, artist, and author, 1924-65. 1924-65

Epting, Carl Lafayette

2092. Lambert, Robert S. MEMORIAL TO CARL LAFAYETTE EPTING, FOUNDING MEMBER. *Pro. of the South Carolina Hist. Assoc. 1979: v.* Carl Lafayette Epting (1898-1978) taught at Clemson College, Wofford University, Columbia College, and Converse, and headed the department of social sciences at Clemson for 16 years. Professor Epting was a charter member and president of the South Carolina Historical Association and a member of the South Carolina House of Representatives in 1933 and 1934. ca 1918-78

Equi, Marie

2093. Krieger, Nancy. QUEEN OF THE BOLSHEVIKS: THE HIDDEN HISTORY OF DR. MARIE EQUI. *Radical America 1983 17(5): 55-73.* Dr. Marie Equi was a powerful individual who manifested determination in her personal, professional, and political life. As a physician, she built a working-class practice. As a political activist, she emerged as a radical when Oregon's Industrial Commission betrayed its own guidelines in the settlement of a 1913 strike involving women workers at the Oregon Packing Company in Portland. Her antiwar stance brought trial and conviction under the Sedition Act just after the Armistice. After emerging from prison, she continued her medical practice and her radicalism through the 1920's until a crippling heart attack in 1930. 12 illus., 81 notes. 1890's-1930

Erickson, Lars

2094. Lorentzon, Betsy. AN IMMIGRANT'S INNER CONFLICT. *Swedish Pioneer Hist. Q. 1978 29(2): 137-142.* Lars Erickson was born in 1865. He came from Sweden to the United States in 1882. This article is based on correspondence between Lars and his family in Sweden. In his letters Lars seemed to dream of his life in Sweden—he was homesick. In 1927, when he returned to Sweden for a visit, he was homesick for his home in America. He died on 5 December 1929 in the United States. 1882-1929

Ericsson, John

2095. Peterkin, Ernest. BUILDING A BEHEMOTH. *Civil War Times Illus. 1981 20(4): 12-21.* Brief background biography of Swedish-American engineer and inventor, John Ericsson, focusing on his design of the ironclad *Monitor,* built in 1861-62 for the Union navy. 1861-62

Erlanger, Joseph

2096. Frank, Robert G., Jr. THE JOSEPH ERLANGER COLLECTION AT WASHINGTON UNIVERSITY SCHOOL OF MEDICINE, ST. LOUIS. *J. of the Hist. of Biology [Netherlands] 1979 12(1): 193-201.* Joseph Erlanger's research in nerve fibers led to a share in the 1944 Nobel Prize in medicine. He was also a significant figure in the histories of the University of Wisconsin and Washington University, where his archive is located. His papers include correspondence, lecture notes, scientific records and artifacts, administration and teaching, biographical materials and memorabilla. The collection is open to qualified researchers and microfilm reels of the collection are available through interlibrary loan. 1900's-65

Errecart, Jack

2097. Errecart, Kimberly. PAPA JACK ERRECART. *Northeastern Nevada Hist. Soc. Q. 1983 (3): 91-97.* Discusses the life of Jack Errecart, an immigrant from France, who came to the United States in 1930 and soon settled in Elko, Nevada; describes his life as a sheepherder and owner of several bars. 1930-83

Escobar, Marisol

2098. Berman, Avis. A BOLD AND INCISIVE WAY OF PORTRAYING MOVERS AND SHAKERS. *Smithsonian 1984 14(11): 54-63.* Profiles Venezuelan-American artist Marisol Escobar, known for her eclectic portrait-sculptures. 1950's-84

Essig, Maude Frances

2099. Woolley, Alma S. A HOOSIER NURSE IN FRANCE: THE WORLD WAR I DIARY OF MAUDE FRANCES ESSIG. *Indiana Magazine of History 1986 82(1): 37-68.* Maude Frances Essig served as an American Red Cross nurse for almost two years during World War I. She worked at a number of field hospitals in France and described the variety of medical and social tasks assigned to the nurses. Discusses the relationships of military nurses and doctors, and describes the medical treatment of the various injuries suffered by soldiers. The hours of work were long and the working conditions far worse than in any American hospital Essig had worked at. Following the Armistice of 11 November 1918, the nurses dealt frequently with injured German prisioners of war. After returning to the United States, Essig had a long professional career in public and military hospitals. Based on the diary of Maude Frances Essig; 15 photos, 2 illus., 25 notes. 1915-19

Etchart, Catherine Urquilux

2100. Urza, Monique. CATHERINE ETCHART: A MONTANA LOVE STORY. *Montana 1981 31(1): 2-17.* John Etchart and his wife, Catherine Urquilux Etchart, operated a sheep ranch near Glasgow, in Valley County, Montana. Both were French Basques. He came to the United States in 1900 and worked with sheep in California and Nevada before settling in Montana in 1910. Catherine came as a bride in 1912. They dealt with problems of winter weather, homesteaders, and isolation; they employed other Basques to help

herd sheep. After John's death in 1943, Catherine managed the ranch operation until her own death in 1978. She was active and frugal, and donated to various Catholic charities. Based on interviews; 8 illus., map, 30 notes, biblio.
1912-78

Etchart, John

2101. Urza, Monique. CATHERINE ETCHART: A MONTANA LOVE STORY. *Montana 1981 31(1): 2-17.*
1912-78

*For abstract see **Etchart, Catherine Urquilux***

Etzioni, Amitai

2102. Etzioni, Amitai. FROM ZION TO DIASPORA. *Society 1978 15(4): 92-101.* Discusses author's career in social activism, 1946-78, in the United States and Israel, in issues such as genetic engineering and arms control.
1946-78

Eumont, Victor

2103. Schneider, Barbara H. THE AGELESS BOND OF IRON AND SMITH. *Hist. Preservation 1979 31(5): 2-9.* Describes the 18th- and 19th-century blacksmithing methods of Curt Tindall of French, New Jersey, Pete Renzetti of Chester County, Pennsylvania, and Victor Eumont of New Orleans, Louisiana. Their efforts stem from a desire to continue the old craft of smithing in its original manner and to participate in the restoration of America's historic buildings. 8 photos. 18c-19c

Europe, Mary Lorraine

2104. McGinty, Doris E. GIFTED MINDS AND PURE HEARTS: MARY L. EUROPE AND ESTELLE PINCKNEY WEBSTER. *J. of Negro Educ. 1982 51(3): 266-277.* Biographical sketches of two black music teachers in Washington, D.C., Mary Lorraine Europe (1882-1947) and Estelle Etelka Pinckney Webster (ca. 1895-1966). Europe was music teacher and accompanist for music teachers in the black divisions of Washington's public schools, 1903-16, and music teacher at M Street (later Dunbar) High School, 1916-44. After teaching briefly in several schools, Webster conducted a private studio and sang professionally, 1921-25, before becoming a music teacher at Armstrong Manual Training High School, 1926-58. Based on interviews, newspapers, and private papers; 23 notes. 1903-58

Eustis, George, Jr.

2105. Tregle, Joseph G., Jr. GEORGE EUSTIS, JR., NON-MYTHIC SOUTHERNER. *Louisiana Hist. 1975 16(4): 383-390.* Revisionist historians have convincingly shown that the Confederacy "was born in complicated political maneuvering which may very possibly have overwhelmed a majority of Southern opinion against secession in 1861." George Eustis Jr. was secretary to John Slidell and the Paris mission of the Confederacy. A few paragraphs reproduced from his papers in the Library of Congress show that he was clearly among the "cooperationists" of 1861. To his mind the issue at stake was not Union but clearly slavery. 12 notes.
1861

Evans, Arthur

2106. Parker, Keith A. ARTHUR EVANS: WESTERN RADICAL. *Alberta Hist. 1978 26(2): 21-29.* Arthur Evans, born in Toronto in 1889, spent years in Kansas City, Colorado, and Seattle before settling in western Canada. By the mid-1930's, he was a well-known Communist labor organizer who had spent time in prison for illegally using union funds; instead of forwarding the funds, he spent the money on food for needy families. In 1935 he was one of the organizers of the Trek from western Canada to Ottawa, where he exchanged bitter words with Prime Minister Bennett. After a riot in Regina in July, 1935, Evans was temporarily jailed on charges of being a Communist and a member of the Workers Unity League. Following his release he made a speaking tour across Canada. Evans was a shipwright and shop steward in British Columbia at the time of his death in 1944. Based on government hearings and newspaper accounts. 6 illus., 26 notes. 1930's

Evans, Clifford

2107. Fowler, Don D.; VanBeek, Gus W.; and Sanoja, Mario. CLIFFORD EVANS, 1920-1981. *Am. Antiquity 1982 47(3): 545-556.* Tribute to archaeologist Clifford Evans who, with his wife Betty, worked for 35 years in archaeological and ethnological research, and presents a chronologically-arranged bibliography of Evans's work. 1945-81

Evans, John

2108. Williams, Gwyn A. JOHN EVANS'S MISSION TO THE MADOGWYS 1792-1799. *Bull. of the Board of Celtic Studies [Great Britain] 1978 27(4): 569-601.* Describes the epic journey in quest of Welsh Indians by John Evans (1770-99), explorer and pioneer colonialist. Evans left his birthplace, Waun-fawr, Caernarvonshire, probably in 1792 and traveled to Baltimore in search of adventure. After many reverses, he succeeded in making a map of the Missouri, traded with the Indians, and became a surveyor in upper Louisiana; but frustrations to his empire-building projects led him to the heavy drinking from which he died. Primary and secondary sources; 118 notes, appendix. 1792-99

Evans, John Hantch (family)

2109. Evans, Melvern, Jr. THREE GENERATIONS OF ARCHITECTS AND BUILDERS—THE EVANS FAMILY. *J. of the Lancaster County Hist. Soc. 1984 88(1): 21-31.* Traces the life histories and professional activities of John Hantch Evans, his son Clifton Evans, and grandson Melvern Evans, Sr., all architects in Lancaster, Pennsylvania.
1849-1971

Evans, Katharine

2110. Scheffler, Judith. PRISON WRITINGS OF EARLY QUAKER WOMEN. *Quaker Hist. 1984 73(2): 25-37.*
1651-83

*For abstract see **Blaugdone, Barbara***

Evans, Lawton B.

2111. Peden, Creighton. A PIONEER MODEL: LAWTON B. EVANS. *Richmond County Hist. 1977 9(2): 5-13.* Discusses the role played by Lawton B. Evans in the establishment of the Augusta and Evans County, Georgia, public schools system, 1882-1934. 1882-1934

Evans, Lucretia

2112. Peters, Norman R., ed. THE CIVIL WAR PENSION FILE OF LEWIS COX AND HIS WIFE LUCRETIA EVANS. *Journal of the Afro-American Historical and Genealogical Society 1985 6(1): 31-33.* 1846-1927

*For abstract see **Cox, Lewis***

Evans, Luther

2113. Sittig, William J. LUTHER EVANS: MAN FOR A NEW AGE. *Q. J. of the Lib. of Congress 1976 33(3): 251-267.* A political scientist with a doctorate from Stanford, Luther Evans had developed the Historical Records Survey under the aegis of the Federal Writers' Project. After working with MacLeish in the Library of Congress, Evans was sworn in as Librarian of Congress on 30 June 1945. He increased the library collections amazingly "but the truly outstanding feature of the period was the quality of the materials acquired." He adopted a program of publishing the Library catalog cards in book form. He was active in the achievement of international understanding, being a delegate to the London conference which established the United Nations Educational, Scientific, and Cultural Organization (UNESCO) of which in 1953 he became director-general. Illus., 27 notes. 1930's-53

Evans, Mary

2114. Griffin, Patricia C. and Arana, Eugenia B. MARY EVANS: WOMAN OF SUBSTANCE. *Escribano 1977 14: 57-76.* Mary Evans (1730-92) lived in the southern colonies, the Caribbean, and Florida; presents her last will and testament, which was probated in Florida. 1763-92

Evans, Nathan George

2115. Conrad, James L. FROM GLORY TO CONTENTION: THE SAD HISTORY OF "SHANKS" EVANS. *Civil War Times Illus. 1983 22(5): 32-38.* Discusses the career of Confederate Brigadier General Nathan George Evans, whose distinguished service at the 1st Battle of Bull Run was followed by glory first vitiated and then destroyed by his contentious personality; after the Civil War, Evans became a mild-mannered Methodist minister. 1861-68

Evans, Rudulph

2116. Yonkers, Tescia Ann. SCULPTOR RUDULPH EVANS: HIS WORKS ON WILLIAM JENNINGS BRYAN AND J. STERLING MORTON. *Nebraska Hist. 1984 65(3): 395-410.* Examines the career of sculptor Rudulph Evans and his statues of J. Sterling Morton and William Jennings Bryan. His portrayals of Morton and Bryan are viewed by visitors to the US Capitol building. Other portrayals can be viewed in Lincoln, in the Nebraska Hall of Fame at Fairview, Bryan's Lincoln home, and also at Arbor Lodge, Morton's home in Nebraska City. Based on the Evans Family Papers and newspaper reports; 2 photos, 71 notes. 1890's-1940's

Eveleth, Silvester (family)

2117. Butcher, Jonathan B. THE EVELETH FAMILY OF COLONIAL NEW ENGLAND. *New England Hist. and Geneal. Register 1980 134(Oct): 299-309; 1981 135(Jan): 23-35, (Apr): 98-108.* Part I. Presents the Eveleth family as a part of the community economically and socially as well as genealogically. Portrays Silvester[1] (b. ca. 1603/4 Devon, England, d. 1688/9 Gloucester, Massachusetts), two sons, and a grandson. Part II. Delineates the family through three third-generation brothers born at Ipswich and their cousin Job of Gloucester (1682/3-ca. 1751). Investigates two sons of John[3]. Part III. Conclusion. Studies four members of the fifth generation, with their wives and families. Conjectures that this typically middle-class family of the colonial period maintained a consistent economic and social level, first through land purchases and then by inheritance accomplished with good planning, education, and marriages with similar families. 17c-19c

Everett, Edward

2118. Geiger, John O. A SCHOLAR MEETS JOHN BULL: EDWARD EVERETT AS UNITED STATES MINISTER TO ENGLAND, 1841-1845. *New England Q. 1976 49(4): 577-595.* Assesses Edward Everett's (1794-1865) qualifications for and appointment as American minister to Great Britain and describes his success in obtaining indemnity for seized ships, in maintaining tranquil relations while belligerent southerners Abel Upshur (1791-1844) and John C. Calhoun (1782-1850) were Secretaries of State, and in preventing conflict over Texas and Oregon. Based on Everett's papers; 49 notes. 1841-45

2119. Yanikoski, Richard A. THE SCHOOLING OF EDWARD EVERETT. *Vitae Scholasticae 1984 3(1): 195-218.* Edward Everett—minister, educator, and politician—was regarded as one of America's most prominent citizens in the first half of the 19th century. Describes Everett's schooling to age 25, when he returned from Europe as the first American to have earned a doctorate at a German university. After attending Harvard, Everett served briefly as minister of the Brattle Street Church. He left the ministry to teach at Harvard, and the school eventually sent him for extended study at the University of Göttingen. This educational experience established Everett's personal philosophy of lifelong learning and the advancement of educational institutions on a broad scale. Based on the Edward Everett manuscript collection at the Massachusetts Historical Society; 71 notes. 1794-1819

Evers, Carl

2120. Evers, Jean. CARL EVERS. *Sea History 1984 (31): 18-22.* Describes the career of marine artist Carl Evers and reproduces samples of his work. 1947-83

Evers, Medgar

2121. Elliott, Jeffrey. MEDGAR EVERS: A PERSONAL PORTRAIT. *Negro Hist. Bull. 1977 40(6): 760-763.* An interview with the former wife of Medgar Evers. Her remarried name is not given. The interview took place in late July 1977 at the office of Mrs. Evers at the Atlantic Richfield Company in Los Angeles, California. Medgar Evers, a civil rights activist, was shot to death in Mississippi on 12 June 1963. 1954-63

Everson, William

2122. Carpenter, David Allen. "William Everson: Poet of Extremity." U. of Oregon 1982. 604 pp. *DAI 1983 43(9): 2991-A.* DA8301765 1912-82

Ewbank, Thomas

2123. Bate, William Allen, Jr. "The Writings and Public Career of Thomas Ewbank, United States Commissioner of Patents 1849-1852." George Washington U. 1979. 198 pp. *DAI 1979 40(6): 3460-A.* 1849-52

Ewell, Benjamin Stoddert

2124. Chapman, Anne West. "Benjamin Stoddert Ewell: A Biography." Coll. of William and Mary, Virginia 1984. 342 pp. *DAI 1985 45(10): 3197-A.* DA8429747 1830's-88

2125. Heuvel, Lisa. "THE PEAL THAT WAKES NO ECHO": BENJAMIN EWELL AND THE COLLEGE OF WILLIAM AND MARY. *Virginia Cavalcade 1978 28(2): 70-*

77. Traces the presidency of Benjamin Stoddert Ewell at the College of William and Mary, 1854-88, highlighting his leadership through two fires, the attempted relocation to Richmond from Williamsburg, and financial disaster. 1854-88

Ewing, Russell C.

2126. Brubaker, George R. A DEDICATION TO THE MEMORY OF RUSSELL C. EWING, 1906-1972. *Arizona and the West 1985 27(1): 1-4.* Russell C. Ewing received his graduate training under Herbert Eugene Bolton at the University of California at Berkeley and, like his mentor, became a historian of the Hispanic borderlands and Mexico. At the University of Arizona, where he spent most of his academic career, Ewing built up the history department and was instrumental in founding the journal *Arizona and the West.* His research and writing concentrated on the Pima Indian uprising, Southwest historiography, and Latin America. Illus,. biblio. 1938-72

Ewing, Samuel W.

2127. VanTrump, James D., ed. THE DIARY OF SAMUEL W. EWING—A FORTY-NINER. *Western Pennsylvania Hist. Mag. 1977 60(1): 73-88.* Sketches the life of Samuel W. Ewing (1818-94) and provides entries from his personal diary written between 14 January 1852, when he left Pittsburgh during the California gold rush, and 9 May 1854, when he arrived back in New York City. 1852-54

Ewing, Thomas (1789-1871)

2128. Hess, M. Whitcomb. PORTRAIT OF AN EARLY AMERICAN JURIST: THOMAS EWING. *Contemporary Rev. [Great Britain] 1969 215(1246): 264-267.* Discusses Ohio jurist, politician, and statesman Thomas Ewing (1789-1871). 1810's-71

2129. Zsoldos, Silvia Tammisto. "The Political Career of Thomas Ewing, Sr." U. of Delaware 1977. 383 pp. *DAI 1977 38(4): 2314-A.* 1830-77

Eyer, Johann Adam

2130. Robacker, Earl F. JOHANN ADAM EYER: "LOST" FRAKTUR WRITER OF HAMILTON SQUARE. *Pennsylvania Folklife 1985 34(3): 98-113.* Biography of Johann Adam Eyer, a German scrivener who lived in Hamilton Square, Pennsylvania, and illustrated many local books and documents. 1755-1837

Eyring, Henry

2131. Heath, Steven H. THE RECONCILIATION OF FAITH AND SCIENCE: HENRY EYRING'S ACHIEVEMENT. *Dialogue 1982 15(3): 87-99.* Henry Eyring was a devout Mormon and renowned scientist. Soon after Eyring left Princeton in 1946 for the University of Utah, Joseph Fielding Smith, then president of the church's Quorum of Twelve, was attacking evolutionism, and in 1954 published a book on the subject: *Man, His Origin and Destiny.* Eyring, as a noted scientist, was requested to review the book, and tactfully disagreed with the author in many details while agreeing on general theological principles. The two exchanged letters and met personally to discuss scientific versus scriptural statements concerning the antiquity of the earth and human life. Primary sources; 20 notes. 1954-79

2132. Kimball, Edward L. HARVEY FLETCHER AND HENRY EYRING: MEN OF FAITH AND SCIENCE. *Dialogue 1982 15(3): 74-86.* Harvey Fletcher and Henry Eyring were two devout Mormons who became great scientists. Fletcher graduated in physics from Brigham Young University in 1907, and then went on to the University of Chicago. There he worked with Robert A. Millikan in a series of experiments that won Millikan the Nobel Prize. Fletcher received his doctorate in 1911 and worked at Bell Telephone Laboratories until 1944. Eyring received his doctorate in chemistry from Berkeley in 1927, and then taught at Princeton. He was nominated for the Nobel Prize several times for his work in chemistry, but never received it. In 1946, he established a graduate school at the University of Utah and was its dean for the next 28 years. Secondary sources; 19 notes. 1907-81

Ezpeleta y Galdeano, José de

2133. Beerman, Eric. JOSÉ DE EZPELETA. *Rev. de Hist. Militar [Spain] 1977 21(43): 97-118.* Details the life of José de Ezpeleta y Galdeano (1742-1823) as an example of a military family of the Spanish army of the 18th and 19th centuries. Ezpeleta held key commands in the seizure of Mobile, 1780, and Pensacola, 1781. He then commanded and governed Cuba, 1785, Louisiana-Florida, 1787, and New Granada, 1789, before returning to Spain in 1797. His last major post before death was as Captain-General of Navarre, 1814. 10 illus., 139 notes. 1780-1814

F

Faduma, Orishatukeh

2134. Okonkwo, Rina L. ORISHATUKEH FADUMA: A MAN OF TWO WORLDS. *J. of Negro Hist. 1983 68(1): 24-36.* The Reverend Orishatukeh Faduma has been neglected by historians of pan-African movements. He played an important role in the African Movement, a back-to-Africa venture that took 38 Oklahoma blacks to the Gold Coast in 1914. Faduma worked as a teacher to improve American blacks' understanding of Africa and to teach Africans about American ideas. 1900-46

Fahey, Denis

2135. Athans, Mary Christine. "The Fahey-Coughlin Connection: Father Denis Fahey, C.S.Sp., Father Charles E. Coughlin, and Religious Anti-Semitism in the United States, 1938-1954." Grad. Theological Union 1982. 304 pp. *DAI 1983 43(9): 3030-A.* DA8302428 1938-54

Fain, Irving

2136. Conforti, Joseph. IRVING FAIN AND THE FAIR HOUSING MOVEMENT IN RHODE ISLAND, 1958-1970. *Rhode Island History 1986 45(1): 23-35.* Irving Fain (1906-70) was a Jewish activist in Providence, Rhode Island, who led a housing reform crusade during the 1960's. Although the 1968 legislation fell short of the program he envisaged, he laid the foundation for the achievements since his death. Based on manuscripts, radio tapes, newspapers, official reports, and eulogies; 4 illus., 43 notes. 1958-70

Fain, Sarah Lee

2137. Treadway, Sandra Gioia. SARAH LEE FAIN: NORFOLK'S FIRST WOMAN LEGISLATOR. *Virginia Cavalcade 1980 30(3): 124-133.* Brief biography of Sarah Lee Fain (1888-1962), focusing on her interest in the Democratic Party, and her election to the House of Delegates in 1923, when she and Democrat Helen T. Henderson became the first women elected in Virginia; she served three terms, later worked for the federal government under Franklin D. Roosevelt, and remained active in politics until her death. 1888-1962

Fairbank, John K.

2138. Evans, P. M. THE LONG WAY HOME: JOHN FAIRBANK AND AMERICAN CHINA POLICY 1941-72. *Int. J. [Canada] 1982 37(4): 584-605.* The career of Harvard Sinologist John K. Fairbank is a model of academic vocation committed to national service. During World War II, he advised the government on Chinese affairs. During 1946-50 he published widely on Sino-American relations, most notably his *The United States and China* (1948), which advocated recognition of the Chinese government and its admission to the UN. During the Cold War years, Fairbank's views were attacked as pro-Communist, and he dedicated his energies to scholarly pursuits. After 1960, Fairbank encouraged a cross-cultural understanding of Chinese and Vietnamese attitudes and values rather than offering specific tactical or political advice. He helped bring about the normalization of Sino-American relations by advising that the Taiwan problem was not insurmountable. Based on Fairbank's published works; 42 notes. 1941-72

Fairfax, Sally

2139. Stegeman, John F. LADY OF BELVOIR: THIS MATTER OF SALLY FAIRFAX. *Virginia Cavalcade 1984 34(1): 4-11.* Traces the close, lifelong friendship of George Washington and Sally Fairfax, wife of Washington's neighbor and friend, George William Fairfax. ca 1750-99

Falconer, Robert

2140. Greenlee, James G. "THE SONG OF A PEOPLE": SIR ROBERT FALCONER ON EMPIRE. *J. of Can. Studies [Canada] 1980 15(1): 80-92.* Sir Robert Falconer, president of the University of Toronto from 1907 to 1932, was one of the most ardent Canadian exponents of the imperial idea. His life centered in an unwavering faith in the relevance and adaptability of Christianity. He drew from Christianity to argue that a people's character and the moral worth of a nation could be judged by the idealism and common morality imbedded in its culture and institutions. He viewed the British Empire as standing foremost for moral progress and Christian idealism. He argued that the empire was held together not by physical ties, but by its spiritual aspects. He saw Canada achieving full nationhood within the British Empire due to the empire's foundations of decentralization, responsible government, and spiritual bonds. Falconer was both a passionate imperialist and an ardent nationalist. Based on Falconer's papers, articles and interviews in contemporary newspapers; 116 notes. 1914-20

Falkenshield, Andrew

2141. White, Helen McCann. "HIS WORLD WAS ART": DR. ANDREW FALKENSHIELD. *Minnesota Hist. 1981 47(5): 184-188.* Andrew Falkenshield graced St. Paul for some 40 years as a photographer and artist beginning in the mid-1850's. Recent research has filled in his previously mysterious Danish, noble origins and his training as a physician but his motive for immigrating in 1853, and his whereabouts before arriving in St. Paul by about 1856 remain elusive. An artist's artist, he was a sensitive photographer and a notable painter, but he was more a philosopher and recluse than a businessman. Well-known paintings of public figures, private citizens, and notable Indians endure to mark his craft. Based on local documents, manuscripts, city directories, and paintings; 6 illus., 15 notes. 1850-96

Fall, Albert Bacon

2142. Joyce, Davis D. BEFORE TEAPOT DOME: SENATOR ALBERT B. FALL AND CONSERVATION. *Red River Valley Hist. Rev. 1979 4(4): 44-51.* Traces the political reputation of New Mexico Republican Senator Albert Bacon Fall, an anticonservationist, and reprints portions of his speeches against conservation during 1912-17, before he was named President Warren G. Harding's Secretary of the Interior in 1921 and was involved in the Teapot Dome Scandal. 1912-20's

Fallon, Malachi

2143. Mullin, Kevin J. MALACHI FALLON, SAN FRANCISCO'S FIRST CHIEF OF POLICE. *California History 1983 62(2): 100-105.* Traces the brief career of Malachi Fallon as the first chief of police in San Francisco. Appointed following the extortions of a lawless group known as the Hounds, Fallon served from August 1849 to April 1851. During that time, the crime rate rose; private citizens, increasingly dissatisfied over police incompetence, turned to vigilante action, forming the Committee of Vigilance in June 1851. By then Fallon had been voted out of office, but allegations were made of police collusion with criminals that were never disproved. Photo, 13 notes. 1849-51

Falström, Jacob

2144. Johnson, Emeroy. WAS OZA WINDIB A SWEDE? *Swedish-American Hist. Q. 1984 35(3): 207-220.* Pieces together the biography of Jacob Falström, reportedly the first Swede in Minnesota. He probably came to Canada from Sweden as a boy and lived in Selkirk's Red River Colony, Manitoba, around 1812. He worked for the American Fur Company, married a Chippewa woman in 1823, and later served as a Methodist lay preacher among the Indians. Falström was reportedly called Oza Windib (Chippewa for "Yellow Head") by the Indians; he may have been the same Oza Windib who guided Henry Rowe Schoolcraft's 1832 expedition to the source of the Mississippi. Based primarily on Schoolcraft's account and histories of Minnesota Swedes; 2 photos, 22 notes. 1793-1859

Fanning, David

2145. Troxler, Carole Watterson. "TO GIT OUT OF A TROUBLESOME NEIGHBORHOOD": DAVID FANNING IN NEW BRUNSWICK. *North Carolina Hist. Rev. 1979 56(4): 343-365.* David Fanning (1755-1825), a loyalist guerrilla leader in the Carolinas during the American Revolution, continued his belligerent and unfriendly ways after settling in New Brunswick after that war. Though established both politically (as a member of the Legislative Assembly) and economically (as a large landowner and successful miller), Fanning never gained social acceptability in the province. So poorly did fellow residents regard him that Fanning was convicted of rape on flimsy evidence and banished from New Brunswick in 1800, 16 years after his arrival. His belligerence, and his self-serving actions in the Assembly and in his quest for a position as justice of the peace, swayed jurors to distrust him on the rape accusation. Based on manuscript and published provincial records and Fanning and other family papers, in New Brunswick and London; 8 illus., 2 maps, 48 notes. 1784-1800

Farber, Leslie Hillel

2146. Schaffer, Leslie. IN MEMORIAM: LESLIE HILLEL FARBER, 1912-1981. *Psychiatry 1981 44(3): 273-275.* Memorial dedicated to Dr. Leslie Hillel Farber, Chairman of the Faculty of the Washington School of Psychiatry, 1955-62, member of the Board of Trustees of the William Alanson White Psychiatric Foundation, 1956-61, and "civilized voice" in contemporary psychiatry. 1937-81

Fardon, George Robinson

2147. Nathan, Marvin R. TREASURE ON LEATHER: A PORTRAIT FROM GEORGE ROBINSON FARDON'S SAN FRANCISCO PERIOD. *California History 1986 65(1): 58-63.* Describes the early photographic work of George Robinson Fardon (1807-86) in San Francisco and its significance in promoting the city's economic potential and social stability. Best known for his cityscapes taken between 1849 and 1859, Fardon also photographed several prominent citizens, including John Lick, illegitimate son of millionaire James Lick, and James deFremery and his family. Five rare pannotypes, pictures done on leather, are extant, and they reveal much about the status of the budding merchant life in San Francisco. 7 photos, 18 notes. 1849-59

Farley, George (family)

2148. Stuart, Donna Valley. SOME DESCENDANTS OF GEORGE FARLEY OF BILLERICA, MASSACHUSETTS. *New England Hist. and Geneal. Register 1982 136(Jan): 43-62, (Apr): 133-147.* Consolidates all known facts about George Farley (1615-93) and his descendants, presenting a history as complete as possible through four generations. Some erroneous surmises are refuted, particularly in regard to the original ancestor. Primary and secondary sources. 17c-19c

Farnham, Eliza

2149. Hallwas, John E. ELIZA FARNHAM'S LIFE IN PRAIRIE LAND. *Old Northwest 1981-82 7(4): 295-324.* Discusses Eliza Farnham's frontier memoir, *Life in Prairie Land* (1846), which was based on her experiences in the Illinois River Valley during 1835-40. The little known work deserves more critical interest than it has received. Her description of the landscape and culture of Illinois accurately displays life in the region. The vividly written account is part autobiography, part travel literature, and part extended essay. Primary sources; 18 notes. 1835-40

Farnsworth, Charles Hubert

2150. Lee, William Ronald. "Education through Music: The Life and Work of Charles Hubert Farnsworth (1859-1947)." U. of Kentucky 1982. 265 pp. *DAI 1983 43(11): 3533-A.* DA8307271 1893-1925

Farny, Henry

2151. Carter, Denny. HENRY FARNY. *Am. West 1978 15(6): 36-47.* After European training and several years as a practicing artist and illustrator, François Henry Farny (1847-1916) began to specialize in painting Indians both in oil and gouache. His romantic tendencies were embodied in his realistic, minutely descriptive, and accurate style. His reputation was primarily as an Indian painter, but his lasting contribution to American art is probably in his depiction of the mood and light of the western landscape. His best known work is "Song of the Talking Wire." Based on the author's recently published book. 9 illus. 1880's-1914

Farquharson, David

2152. Bloomfield, Anne. DAVID FARQUHARSON: PIONEER CALIFORNIA ARCHITECT. *California Hist. 1980 59(1): 16-33.* David Farquharson's (1827-1914) architectural career covered a quarter century of early statehood architectural development. A native of Scotland, Farquharson came to California in 1850. After designing several major buildings in Sacramento in the 1850's, he located in San Francisco and until 1880 was involved in the design of banks, hotels, public buildings, and private housing. An innovator in many respects, Farquharson was a pioneer of quality architecture in California. Most of his work was destroyed in the 1906 earthquake and fire or was superseded by 20th-century constructions; the only major building which survives is South Hall on the University of California's Berkeley campus. Farquharson also was involved in banking and real estate development. Photos, 34 notes. 1850-1914

Farrell, James T.

2153. Douglas, Ann. JAMES T. FARRELL, THE ARTIST MILITANT. *Dissent 1980 27(2): 214-216.* Discusses the work, talent, and special interests of author James T. Farrell (1904-79), gives examples of his style in *Studs Lonigan,* and presents his concern for impoverished people oppressed by society. 1920-79

2154. Fanning, Charles and Skerrett, Ellen. JAMES T. FARRELL AND WASHINGTON PARK: THE NOVEL AS SOCIAL HISTORY. *Chicago Hist. 1979 8(2): 80-91.* Gives a biography of author James T. Farrell, born in Chicago in 1904, and focuses on eight novels, of the 22 novels and 250 short stories he has written, set around Chicago's Washington Park and the people in its neighborhood, on the occasion of Farrell's 75th birthday in 1979. 1904-79

2155. Moore, Stephen. JAMES T. FARRELL AS A CRITIC: A LESSON IN LITERATURE. *South Atlantic Q. 1980 79(2): 152-157.* Although he was to write 35 novels, centering mostly around Chicago's South Side, James T. Farrell (1904-79) wrote his first essay on literary criticism two years before his first novel. He was always a pre-New Criticism critic, with no interest in explication, theory, or method. When he was wrong, he was really wrong! He was far out of the mainstream of academic criticism involved with the elucidation of texts, for the text was never the end, but merely a part of a larger pursuit of freedom from ignorance, bias, and restraint of imagination. ca 1933-79

Farwell, Stanley

2156. Leman, Nancy Farwell. LOOKING BACKWARD: EDUCATING THE "WHOLE BOY" AT THE CHICAGO MANUAL TRAINING SCHOOL. *Chicago Hist. 1982 11(3): 214-219.* Describes the school career and subsequent higher degrees of Stanley Farwell, who graduated from the Chicago Manual Training School in 1900. 1883-1914

Fasman, Oscar Z.

2157. Fasman, Oscar Z. AFTER FIFTY YEARS, AN OPTIMIST. *Am. Jewish Hist. 1979 69(2): 159-173.* Reminiscences of an Orthodox rabbi now in Chicago who formerly served congregations in Tulsa (Oklahoma) and Ottawa (Ontario), and was later president of the Hebrew Theological College. 1929-79

Father Divine

See Baker, George

Faulkner, William

2158. Bosha, Francis J. WILLIAM FAULKNER AND THE EISENHOWER ADMINISTRATION. *J. of Mississippi Hist. 1980 42(1): 49-54.* After receiving the Nobel Prize in Literature for 1949, William Faulkner was asked by the State Department to travel abroad as a goodwill ambassador on four occasions between 1954 and 1961. His national service included a stateside phase: in June 1956, President Dwight D. Eisenhower requested that Faulkner serve as chairman of the Writers' Group of the People-to-People Program. The State Department also asked Faulkner to address the Seventh National Conference of the US National Commission for UNESCO in Denver, Colorado, on 2 October 1959. Describes the effort of Maxwell M. Rabb, Eisenhower's executive assistant campaign manager and future associate counsel to the president, to bring the southern writer's name to the attention of the Eisenhower administration. Discusses the opposition of minority groups to the appointment of Faulkner to work with a Civil Rights Commission and the People-to-People Program. 1954-61

2159. Bezzarides, Albert I.; Brodsky, Louis Daniel, interviewer. REFLECTIONS ON WILLIAM FAULKNER: AN INTERVIEW WITH ALBERT I. BEZZERIDES. *Southern Review 1985 21(2): 376-403.* Screenwriter Albert I. Bezzerides discusses his memories of working with William Faulkner in the 1940's and Faulkner's life before and after, and characterizes Faulkner as an intelligent, driven man, who made himself into a great writer because of the agonies of his life. 1920's-61

2160. Faulkner, Jim. [MEMORIES OF WILLIAM FAULKNER].

MEMORIES OF BROTHER WILL. *Southern Rev. 1980 16(4): 907-920.* William Faulkner's (1897-1962) brother reminisces about growing up in the 1930's in Oxford in north-central Mississippi.

NO PISTOL ROCKET. *Southern Rev. 1981 17(2): 358-365.* Recounts incidents in which William Faulkner figured prominently, especially brother Will's reaction to his younger sibling's accident with a blank gun. 1930-39

2161. Howell, Elmo. SOUTHERN FICTION AND THE PATTERN OF FAILURE: THE EXAMPLE OF FAULKNER. *Georgia Rev. 1982 36(4): 755-770.* Mississippi author William Faulkner was a "freak genius," a product of his native South, and, by his own definition, a failure. Faulkner defined success as the ability to "risk failure" by attempting new forms in writing. According to this definition, Faulkner was never a successful novelist: his works, viewed as a whole, are repetitious, often reiterating themes and story lines. His fiction, like some works of fellow Southerners Mark Twain and Eudora Welty, tends to be fragmented and aimless, though not without artistic merit. Their work is flawed because the South encourages a strong sense of community, making it difficult for the region's authors to write consistently good modern fiction, which stresses introspection and soul-searching. Based on Faulkner's novels, and Joseph Blotner's biography of the author. 1929-62

2162. Martin, Jay. "THE WHOLE BURDEN OF MAN'S HISTORY OF HIS IMPOSSIBLE HEART'S DESIRE": THE EARLY LIFE OF WILLIAM FAULKNER. *Am. Literature 1982 53(4): 607-629.* Utilizes psychoanalytic methods to explain William Faulkner's early development as a writer. In his late 20's, repressed elements of Faulkner's personality emerged, thus allowing the writer to develop a double image of himself: the secret Faulkner and the public mask. It is this secret, but genuine, side of Faulkner that provided the inspiration for his best work. 51 notes. 1900-27

2163. Schwartz, Lawrence H. PUBLISHING WILLIAM FAULKNER: THE 1940S. *Southern Q. 1984 22(2): 70-92.* Until he won the Nobel Prize for Literature in 1950, William Faulkner enjoyed no better than second-rank status among American authors. Only the efforts of a few editors and publishers like Kurt Enoch and Victor Werybright, and their willingness to risk sales by including Faulkner works in a popular series like the New American Library series issued by Random House, saved Faulkner from relative obscurity. After 1950, however, the Nobel Prize, the advent of paperbacks, and the impact of the G.I. Bill on university enrollments assured the success of Faulkner publications. 1940-54

2164. Wittenberg, Judith Bryant. "Faulkner: The Transfiguration of Biography." Brown U. 1977. 369 pp. *DAI 1983 44(1): 172-A.* DA8307972 1924-42

2165. Zelman, Thomas William. "Parents and Sons: A Study of William Faulkner's Life and Works." Indiana U. 1983. 280 pp. *DAI 1983 44(5): 1457-1458-A.* DA8321381 1910's-62

Faust, Charles Victor

2166. Busch, Thomas S. IN SEARCH OF VICTORY: THE STORY OF CHARLES VICTOR ("VICTORY") FAUST. *Kansas History 1983 6(2): 96-109.* Charles Victor Faust (1880-1915) shared every boy's dream of playing major league baseball, but he was 30 before he left Marion, Kansas, to join the New York Giants during a trip to St. Louis in 1911. The Giants won pennants in 1911 and 1912. Faust pitched in only two games, but without a uniform or contract he spent his time on the bench as a mascot, good-luck charm, and jinx-killer. New York had a remarkable team, but without this strange young man's incentive it is unlikely it would have won its first pennant since 1905. Based on newspapers and secondary sources; 2 illus., 8 photos, 47 notes. 1911-12

Faymonville, Philip R.

2167. Langer, John Daniel. THE "RED GENERAL": PHILIP R. FAYMONVILLE AND THE SOVIET UNION, 1917-52. *Prologue 1976 8(4): 209-221.* Brigadier General Philip R. Faymonville's long absorption in Soviet affairs brought him into a position of influence when the United States granted diplomatic recognition to the USSR in 1933. During his five years as military attaché in Moscow, 1933-38, he gained a reputation as a pro-Soviet observer, in spite of his often unfavorable opinion of Soviet actions. His overall positive stance toward Soviet affairs antagonized many of his military colleagues who assiduously worked, with ultimate success, to undermine his position. During World War II Harry Hopkins used Faymonville as his military representative on the Russian end of the Lend-Lease program. An unfavorable and biased report on Faymonville's loyalty and credibility, coupled with Franklin D. Roosevelt's failure to support him, caused the termination of the General's role in American-Soviet affairs. Based on records in the National Archives. 1917-52

Fechin, Nicolai

2168. Jellico, John. NICOLAI FECHIN. *Southwestern Art 1976 5(2): 19-31.* Describes the life and work of Nicolai Fechin (1881-1955), a Russian artist who did his most noted work, usually paintings of Indians, following a move to Taos, New Mexico, in 1927. 1927-55

2169. Schriever, George. NICOLAI FECHIN: RUSSIAN ARTIST IN THE AMERICAN WEST. *Am. West 1982 19(3): 34-42, 62-63.* Nicolai Fechin, born in Russia, received formal art training at a regional academy and at the Imperial Academy of Art in Saint Petersburg. He soon won awards, an instructorship, and invitations to show his work at international exhibitions. Beset by ill health, he migrated to the United States in 1923. After four years residence in New York, where he earned high acclaim, Fechin settled in the West. His years in Taos, New Mexico, are generally regarded as his best. His virtuosity as a portrait painter overshadowed his consummate mastery of line. If he had never painted a single picture, he would still be hailed as a great artist because of his drawings. Despite his long and intimate association with the American Southwest, he remained Russian and his style owed nothing to his adopted land. 12 illus. 1927-55

Feiffer, Jules

2170. Engstrom, John. HAS FEIFFER SWITCHED PENS? *Horizon 1981 24(11): 52-55.* Reviews the career of cartoonist, political satirist, and dramatist Jules Feiffer since 1947. 1947-81

Feinstein, Dianne

2171. Joseph, Nadine. MAYOR DIANNE FEINSTEIN. *Present Tense 1983 11(1): 47-49.* An interview with San Francisco mayor Dianne Feinstein, who has successfully governed San Francisco despite being a woman and a Jew—traditional political liabilities in the male-dominated, largely Protestant city. 1955-83

Felsenthal, Bernhard

2172. Ludlow, Victor Leifson. "Bernhard Felsenthal: Quest for Zion." Brandeis U. 1984. 343 pp. *DAI 1984 45(1): 271-A.* DA8407867 1854-70's

Felt, Louie

2173. Oman, Susan Staker. NURTURING LDS PRIMARIES: LOUIE FELT AND MAY ANDERSON, 1880-1940. *Utah Hist. Q. 1981 49(3): 262-275.* 1880-1940
For abstract see ***Anderson, May***

Felton, Jacob

2174. Felton, Jacob. A FRONTIERSMAN'S MEMOIRS: JACOB FELTON'S SKETCH OF HIS EARLY LIFE. *Pennsylvania Mag. of Hist. and Biog. 1982 106(4): 539-554.* Reproduces 76-year-old Jacob Felton's memoirs, composed in 1890, which recall his family's role in the settlement of Ohio and Indiana. 1820-40

Felton, Rebecca Latimer

2175. Rogers, Evelyna Keadle. FAMOUS GEORGIA WOMEN: REBECCA LATIMER FELTON. *Georgia Life 1978 5(1): 34-35.* Rebecca Latimer Felton (1835-1930), a resident of Georgia, was appointed as the first woman senator in the US Senate in 1922; discusses her career in politics and her participation in the fight for woman suffrage, 1860's-1922. 1860's-1922

Felts, Thomas L.

2176. Hadsell, Richard M. and Coffey, William E. FROM LAW AND ORDER TO CLASS WARFARE: BALDWIN-FELTS DETECTIVES IN THE SOUTHERN WEST VIRGINIA COAL FIELDS. *West Virginia Hist. 1979 40(3): 268-286.* 1890's-1935
For abstract see ***Baldwin, William G.***

Fenno, John

2177. Hench, John B., ed. LETTERS OF JOHN FENNO AND JOHN WARD FENNO, 1779-1800. *Pro. of the Am. Antiquarian Soc. 1979 89(2): 299-368; 1980 90(1): 163-234.* Part I. The Fenno letters reveal the collisions of politics, economics, and journalism during the early years of the Republic. Both Fennos were editors and publishers; both were controversial and politically committed. These letters reveal the intimate connection between access to information and possession of power in the years following the Revolutionary War. They also reflect the relationship between the press and the government. Based on the John Fenno and John Ward Fenno Papers at the Chicago Historical Society; 146 notes. Part II. Discusses such topics as the yellow fever epidemic in Philadelphia, the foreign policy issues of the French Revolution and American neutrality, financial and political support for John Fenno's newspaper, and means of recapturing loans made during the Revolutionary War. 1779-1800

Fenno, John Ward

2178. Hench, John B., ed. LETTERS OF JOHN FENNO AND JOHN WARD FENNO, 1779-1800. *Pro. of the Am. Antiquarian Soc. 1979 89(2): 299-368; 1980 90(1): 163-234.* 1779-1800
For abstract see ***Fenno, John***

Fergus, Pamelia Dillin

2179. Peavy, Linda and Smith, Ursula. WOMEN IN WAITING IN THE WESTWARD MOVEMENT: PAMELIA DILLIN FERGUS AND EMMA STRATTON CHRISTIE. *Montana 1985 35(2): 2-17.* 1860-85
For abstract see ***Christie, Emma Stratton***

Ferguson, Edwin Hite

2180. Yater, George H. EDWIN HITE FERGUSON AND THE FERGUSON MANSION. *Filson Club Hist. Q. 1984 58(4): 436-457.* Presents a biography of Louisville, Kentucky, businessman Edwin Hite Ferguson. Born in 1852, Ferguson had by 1885 created a large cottonseed oil firm: the Kentucky Refining Company. The business was successful and allowed Ferguson to build a large mansion in beaux arts style, which has become the new home of the Filson Club. Ferguson was forced out of his company by business associates during 1907-09. The mansion has had several owners since Ferguson's death in 1924. Based on newspapers and court records; 5 photos, 32 notes. 1880's-1984

Ferguson, Elizabeth Graeme

2181. Slotten, Martha C. ELIZABETH GRAEME FERGUSON: A POET IN THE "ATHENS OF NORTH AMERICA." *Pennsylvania Mag. of Hist. and Biog. 1984 108(3): 259-288.* Reprints several poems by Ferguson, and describes her life, her literary contemporaries, and the Philadelphia culture in which Ferguson held her salon. 1717-1800

Fergusson, Harvey Butler (family)

2182. Simms, Barbara Young. THOSE FABULOUS FERGUSSONS. *Palacio 1976 82(2): 42-47.* The Harvey Fergusson family of Albuquerque, New Mexico, fostered four authors: Harvey, Jr., Erna, Lina, and Francis, 1880's-1970's. 1880's-1970's

Fergusson, Harvey Butler, Sr.

2183. Roberts, Calvin A. H. B. FERGUSSON, 1848-1915: NEW MEXICO SPOKESMAN FOR POLITICAL REFORM. *New Mexico Hist. Rev. 1982 57(3): 237-255.* Harvey Butler Fergusson, Sr., came to New Mexico in 1882 as a lawyer. Achieving notoriety in well-known legal contests, he soon entered Democratic politics. Among his friends were William Jennings Bryan, Thomas B. Catron, and Albert J. Fall. He entered politics, was elected to the Democratic National Committee and later to the US House of Representatives, where he sponsored the Fergusson Act to provide federal money for public education. Known as a reformer and convincing speaker, Fergusson sought statehood for New Mexico. After his defeat, he briefly served as personal secretary to Secretary of State William Jennings Bryan and then returned to Albuquerque, where he died of a stroke. Photo, 59 notes. 1848-1915

Fern, Joseph J.

2184. Johnson, Donald D. JOSEPH JAMES FERN, HONOLULU'S FIRST MAYOR. *Hawaiian J. of Hist. 1975 9: 74-100.* On 4 January 1909 Joseph J. Fern became the first mayor of the City and County of Honolulu. He held this office until his death in 1920. The years of his mayoralty were the formative years for municpal government in Hawaii. Fern, a native Hawaiian, often showed favoratism toward other native Hawaiians. 1909-20

Fernandez, John F. O.

2185. Carey, Patrick W. JOHN F. O. FERNANDEZ: ENLIGHTENED LAY CATHOLIC REFORMER, 1815-1820. *Rev. of Pol. 1981 43(1): 112-129.* John F. O. Fernandez was a Portuguese refugee who lived in Norfolk, Virginia, 1803-20. His views on the right of the parish laity to control the temporal affairs of the Church resulted in a clash with the bishops over the appointment of a priest to his church. Fernandez's philosophy was shaped by the teachings of the Church fathers, practices in the early Church, the Enlightenment anticlericalism of his day, and the American tradition of separation of church and state. His views were rejected by the bishops, but he was in the forefront of American Catholics who attempted to create a democratic perception of the laity. Letters and secondary sources; 43 notes. 1815-20

Ferrington, Danny

2186. Schell, Orville. HIS GUITARS FOR THE STARS ARE THERE FOR THE PICKIN'. *Smithsonian 1985 16(1): 86-95.* Craftsman and guitar-maker Danny Ferrington builds custom made instruments in Santa Monica, California, for music stars ranging from country performer Johnny Cash to rock and roll artist Elvis Costello, and each instrument is a unique work of art with its own design and sound. 1965-85

Ferris, Mary L. D.

2187. Kenney, Alice P. MARY L. D. FERRIS AND THE DUTCH TRADITION. *Halve Maen 1973 47(4): 7-8, 14, 48(2): 7-8, 14.* Part I. A descendant of early settlers, Mary L. D. Ferris (1855-1932) collected and recorded their history in poetry and prose throughout the late Victorian era. Much of her work was published in the *Albany Argus* or presented at Holland Society affairs. Based on Mrs. Ferris's writings, from a private collection; 13 notes. Part II. Covers Mrs. Ferris's writings, 1890's-1910's, and her retirement. 13 notes. 1855-1932

Ferster, Charles B.

2188. Schindler, Charles W. and Algarabel, Salvador. CHARLES B. FERSTER (1922-1981): UNA VIDA DEDICADA AL ANALISIS EXPERIMENTAL DE LA CONDUCTA [Charles B. Ferster (1922-81): a life devoted to experimental analysis of behavior]. *Rev. de Hist. de la Psicología [Spain] 1982 3(1): 63-72.* Reviews Ferster's work as a leader in behavioral psychology. 1940's-81

Fewel, W. J.

2189. Marsh, Herb, Jr. MAJOR W. J. FEWEL OF EL PASO. *Password 1985 30(2): 79-84.* Presents a biography of Major W. J. Fewel, a Civil War veteran from North Carolina who came to El Paso, Texas, in 1881, and became a prominent businesman and an important figure in shaping the town's destiny. 1860's-1910's

Ficklin, Benjamin F.

2190. Austerman, Wayne R. THE BRASH REINSMAN: BEN FICKLIN'S ADVENTURES. *Virginia Cavalcade 1984 33(3): 114-125.* Portrays the career of surveyor, scout, and soldier Benjamin F. Ficklin, who was instrumental in establishing stagecoach routes in the West. 1846-71

Field, David Dudley

2191. Van Ee, Daun Roell. "David Dudley Field and the Reconstruction of the Law." Johns Hopkins U. 1974. 372 pp. *DAI 1977 38(2): 982-983-A.* 1820's-80's

Field, Eliza and Peter

2192. Smith, Donald B. THE TRANSATLANTIC COURTSHIP OF THE REVEREND PETER JONES. *Beaver [Canada] 1977 308(1): 4-13.* Peter Jones, part Ojibwa, became a Methodist preacher in the 1820's and was successful in converting many of the Indians around Lake Ontario. In 1831 he was sent to England to solicit funds for the missions. He made more than 150 appearances, was successful, and met Eliza Field, daughter of a wealthy factory owner near London. She became interested in mission work, and in him. Jones proposed marriage, which she accepted, though her father resisted for some time. After consent was given, her father found out that Jones' father was still alive, and had two wives. Yet, in 1833, in New York, the couple was married. Based on Jones's accounts and recently discovered diaries kept by Eliza Field; 12 illus. 1820's-33

Field, Erastus Salisbury

2193. Getlein, Frank. A FANTASY WORLD FROM A STERN-FACED YANKEE PAINTER. *Smithsonian 1984 15(5): 60-69.* Profiles the life and career of painter and portraitist Erastus Salisbury Field, most noted for his symbolic canvas, *Historical Monument of the American Republic;* after popular demand for portraits dropped off, Field embarked on a series of allegorical paintings depicting historical and biblical events. 1830's-1900

2194. Updike, John. YANKEE SEER. *Art & Antiques 1985 (Jan): 74-81.* Retraces the life and diverse paintings of American panoramist and traveling portraitist Erastus Salisbury Field, describing how he reflected 19th-century America in his works through sensitive artistic techniques and subject matter. 1805-1900

Fielde, Adele M.

2195. Hoyt, Frederick B. "WHEN A FIELD WAS FOUND TOO DIFFICULT FOR A MAN, A WOMAN SHOULD BE SENT": ADELE M. FIELDE IN ASIA, 1865-1890. *Historian 1982 44(3): 314-334.* Adele M. Fielde, a transitional figure, illustrates the changing emphasis of the Protestant mission movement from wives to single women as evangelists. Recounts Fielde's life, including her introduction to the Orient in 1865, her missionary work as an American Baptist in Siam, her assignment to Swatow in China in 1872, and her permanent return to the United States in 1890. The major focus of her life as both a missionary and reformer was the condition of women and the reformation of society. Primary sources; 63 notes. 1865-90

Fielding, Joseph

2196. Ehat, Andrew F., ed. "THEY MIGHT HAVE KNOWN THAT HE WAS NOT A FALLEN PROPHET": THE NAUVOO JOURNAL OF JOSEPH FIELDING. *Brigham Young U. Studies 1979 19(2): 133-166.* Introduces and reproduces Joseph Fielding's journal of 1844-46. Fielding was a Mormon missionary to England in the 1830's and 1840's. In 1843 he was endowed by Joseph Smith to officiate in church ordinances. His diary describes the development of Nauvoo and Fielding's conviction of the truth of his faith. Illus., 105 notes. 1844-46

Fields, Annie Adams

2197. Laurence, Anya. THE WATERSIDE MUSEUM. *New-England Galaxy 1977 19(1): 52-58.* Recounts the life of Annie Adams (1834-1913), who married James T. Fields in November 1854 in Boston, where her home became a literary "museum." Her roles as author and consultant to authors are noted. Her friendships with Sarah Orme Jewett, Oliver Wendell Holmes, and Julia Ward Howe are also described. 3 illus. 1834-1913

2198. Roman, Judith. "'The Spirit of Charles Street': A Life of Annie Adams Fields, 1834-1915." Indiana U. 1984. 490 pp. *DAI 1985 45(9): 2877-A.* DA8426677 1834-1915

Fields, W. C.

2199. Galligan, Edward L. NEVER GIVE A SUCKER OR YOURSELF AN EVEN BREAK. *Midwest Q. 1985 26(2): 225-237.* The comedy of W. C. Fields was a flamboyant, no-holds-barred attack on self-pity. Coming from a battered, impoverished childhood, Fields unloaded an immense number of personal grudges by living and acting the part of a man it would be impossible to pity, or even to believe. His private identity disappeared into his professional one as the private man saved himself from self-pity, and ultimately from self-destruction, by becoming the disreputable and untrustworthy W. C. Fields. 1879-1946

Fiess, Traugott

2200. Fiess, Traugott. AUTOBIOGRAPHY OF PASTOR TRAUGOTT FIESS. *Heritage Review 1984 14(3): 4-23.* Presents the memoirs of Traugott Fiess, a Russian German who served as a Lutheran pastor in various places from 1909 to 1954, tracing his genealogy and his childhood in Sarata, Bessarabia, to his religious career in Illinois, Colorado, Michigan, and Wisconsin. 1883-1974

2201. Theeke, Leona S. AUTOBIOGRAPHY OF PASTOR TRAUGOTT FIESS. *Heritage Review 1984 14(3): 4-23.* Presents the memoirs of Traugott Fiess, a Russian German who served as a Lutheran pastor in various places from 1909 to 1954, tracing his genealogy and his childhood in Sarata, Bessarabia, to his religious career in Illinois, Colorado, Michigan, and Wisconsin. 1883-1974

Filene, Edward A.

2202. Engelbourg, Saul. EDWARD A. FILENE: MERCHANT, CIVIC LEADER, AND JEW. *Am. Jewish Hist. Q. 1976 66(1): 106-122.* Edward A. Filene (1860-1937), American-born son of German Jewish immigrants, became a millionaire several times over, and because of his business success he was able to obtain fame as a philanthropist and a civic leader in Boston. He is credited with the "Automatic Bargain Basement" as his most distinctive business innovation. Describes the controversy with his associate Louis Kirstein (1867-1942), his cooperation with Louis Brandeis, his share in the development of the Credit Union movement, the influence of his Twentieth Century Fund, his marginal interest in Jewish philanthropy, and the fight against anti-semitism. 49 notes. 1860-1937

2203. McQuaid, Kim. AN AMERICAN OWENITE: EDWARD A. FILENE AND THE PARAMETERS OF INDUSTRIAL REFORM, 1890-1937. *Am. J. of Econ. and Sociol. 1976 35(1): 77-94.* Edward A. Filene introduced industrial democracy in his Boston department store in 1891. He was deposed from the presidency of the store in 1928. His experiment ceased and thereafter he was denied any effective authority. He also directed his liberal energies to local, state, and national affairs such as his ambitious plan of urban reform, "Boston 1915." Such efforts were equally unsuccessful. He was a spokesman for the New Capitalism and a supporter of the New Deal, but in both movements his integrity isolated him from his peers. His enduring contributions were the cooperative and credit union movements. 1890-1937

Fillis, John

2204. Smith, James F. JOHN FILLIS, MLA. *Nova Scotia Hist. Q. [Canada] 1971 1(4): 307-323.* John Fillis (ca. 1723-92) was a businessman, shipowner, and distiller who was one of 19 members of the Nova Scotia Legislative Assembly which first convened in 1758; provides a list of the other 18 members of the Assembly. 1740's-92

Fillmore, Millard

2205. Hinton, Wayne K. MILLARD FILLMORE, UTAH'S FRIEND IN THE WHITE HOUSE. *Utah Hist. Q. 1980 48(2): 112-128.* Millard Fillmore's moderate attitude when he became president after Zachary Taylor's death in July 1850 temporarily settled the slavery question in the territories. Favoring local rule, Fillmore appointed Mormons to four of seven of Utah's teritorial offices, and made Brigham Young governor. Considering controversy over Young's authoritarian rule and over John M. Bernhisel's election as territorial delegate to be attempts to discredit his administration, Fillmore continued his support of the Mormons. In 1874, Utahans renamed the new territorial seat Fillmore in his honor. Based on Journal History, LDS Archives; 8 illus., 53 notes. 1850-53

Findley, Grandma

2206. McAllister, Dan. PIONEER WOMAN. *New Mexico Hist. Rev. 1959 34(3): 161-164.* Author's reminiscences of his grandmother, Grandma Findley, an indefatigable woman of New Mexico Territory in the 19th century. 19c

Finfrock, John H.

2207. Palmieri, Anthony and Humberson, Chris. MEDICAL INCIDENTS IN THE LIFE OF DR. JOHN H. FINFROCK. *Ann. of Wyoming 1981 53(2): 64-69.* John H. Finfrock (1836-93) received his medical degree in 1863, immediately reentered the army, and began service at Fort Halleck, Wyoming. Three years later, he left the military to establish a medical practice and drugstore at nearby Laramie. Always a prominent civic leader, Finfrock's surgical expertise was frequently recorded by Laramie newspapers. He also served as town mayor and as chairman of the first board of trustees for the University of Wyoming. Based on Laramie newspapers; 5 photos, 15 notes. 1863-93

Fink, Mike.

2208. Allen, Michael. "SIRED BY A HURRICANE": MIKE FINK, WESTERN BOATMEN AND THE MYTH OF THE ALLIGATOR HORSE. *Arizona and the West 1985 27(3): 237-252.* Western Pennsylvania frontiersman Mike Fink worked as a keelboatman on the Ohio and Mississippi rivers. He soon gained a reputation as a good boatman, a hard drinker, and a volatile fighter. Constantly at odds with the law and uncomfortable with advancing civilization, he kept moving west. He died on the Upper Missouri fur trapping frontier. Fink's reputation grew to mythic proportions, to the extent that he became known as the king of the "half horse, half alligator" Western boatmen. 4 illus., 30 notes. 1790's-1820's

2209. Ross, Jane. FEISTY FINK, KING OF BATTLING BOATMEN ON 'THE BIG RIVER.' *Smithsonian 1979 10(1): 98-102.* Discusses the life and legend of Mike Fink, the archetypal keelboatman, 1770-1823. 1770-1823

Finley, Harry

2210. La Forte, Robert S., ed. HARRY FINLEY'S CHRISTMAS STORY, OKLAHOMA TERRITORY, 1890. *Red River Valley Hist. Rev. 1978 3(4): 47-51.* Provides a brief biography of Harry Finley, then presents the Christmas story written by Finley which describes the difficulties experienced when one is poor at Christmastime. 1890

Finley, John H.

2211. Segal, Howard P. AMERICAN COLLEGE AND UNIVERSITY PRESIDENTS: FOUR BIOGRAPHICAL STUDIES. *Hist. of Educ. Q. 1982 22(1): 99-102.* 1850's-1945

For abstract see ***Barnard, Frederick A. P.***

Finley, Samuel

2212. Williams, Edward G. A SURVEY OF BOUQUET'S ROAD, 1764: SAMUEL FINLEY'S FIELD NOTES. PART 3. *Western Pennsylvania Hist. Mag. 1983 66(4): 347-367.* Continued from a previous article. Reproduces part of the surveying notebook of Samuel Finley, plotting the path of Henry Bouquet's military expedition to the Indians; this section covers the Ohio-Pennsylvania border area, where the expedition crossed an Indian trail known as the Great Warriors' Path or the Great Trail. Article to be continued. 1764

Finn, Henry James

2213. Myers, Clarence Franklin. "A Descriptive Biography of Henry James Finn, 19th Century Actor, Manager, Playwright." U. of Michigan 1977. 424 pp. *DAI 1977 38(3): 1128-A.* 1804-30

Fireman, Bert M.

2214. Fireman, Bert M. RECOLLECTIONS OF ARIZONA: A PERSONAL PERSPECTIVE. *J. of Arizona Hist. 1982 23(1): 81-102.* An autobiographical account by Bert M. Fireman, Arizona historian, newspaperman, and vice-president of the Arizona Historical Foundation. Refers to daily life and politics. 1915-80

Fischer, Anton Otto

2215. Hurst, Alex A. ANTON OTTO FISCHER. *Sea Hist. 1979 (13): 50-53.* Short biographical sketch of Anton Otto Fischer (1882-1962) highlights his paintings of sailing life and ships, 1905-62. 1905-62

Fischer, Louis

2216. Crowl, James William. "They Wrote as They Pleased: A Study of the Journalistic Careers of Louis Fischer and Walter Duranty, 1922-1940." U. of Virginia 1978. 386 pp. *DAI 1979 39(8): 5082-A.* 1922-40

Fish, Marian

2217. Platt, Frederick. MAMIE AND THE CIRCUS SET. *Am. Hist. Illus. 1980 15(6): 14-17, 20-24.* Chronicles the life and informal parties of Marian Graves Anthon "Mamie" Fish (1853-1915), wife of Stuyvesant Fish; she was an unorthodox socialite of New York City and Newport, Rhode Island. 1853-1915

Fish, Nicholas

2218. Rubinstein, Anita. "The Public Career of Nicholas Fish." New York U. 1980. 292 pp. *DAI 1981 41(12): 5224-A.* 8110773 1776-1833

Fishbein, Morris

2219. Debus, Allen G. A TRIBUTE TO MORRIS FISHBEIN. *Bull. of the Hist. of Medicine 1977 51(1): 153-154.* Morris Fishbein was not only a historian, he was history. "It will be impossible in future years to write the history of 20th century medicine without referring to him as a central figure." His *Doctors at War* remains the basic study of the medical profession during World War II, and his massive history of the American Medical Association is a monument to his industry. 1977

Fisher, Alvan

2220. Adelson, Fred Barry. "Alvan Fisher (1792-1863): Pioneer in American Landscape Painting." Columbia U. 1982. 896 pp. *DAI 1985 45(10): 3015-3016-A.* DA8427339 1792-1863

Fisher, Dorothy Canfield

2221. Lovering, Joseph P. THE FRIENDSHIP OF WILLA CATHER AND DOROTHY CANFIELD. *Vermont Hist. 1980 48(3): 144-154.* 1894-1947
For abstract see ***Cather, Willa***

Fisher, Harry B.

2222. Diamond, Sigmund. SURVEILLANCE IN THE ACADEMY: HARRY B. FISHER AND YALE UNIVERSITY, 1927-1952. *Am. Q. 1984 36(1): 7-43.* Yale University employee Harry B. Fisher organized clandestine collaboration between the authorities of Yale University and local, state, and federal police agencies, including the Federal Bureau of Investigation. Originally intended to punish illicit sexual activities such as homosexuality and prostitution as well as infractions of Prohibition and the recreational use of drugs, cooperation with the police became a means of stifling political dissent among the students. 61 notes. 1927-52

Fisher, Isaac

2223. Wheeler, Elizabeth L. ISAAC FISHER: THE FRUSTRATIONS OF A NEGRO EDUCATOR AT BRANCH NORMAL COLLEGE, 1902-1911. *Arkansas Hist. Q. 1982 41(1): 3-50.* Details the difficulties encountered by Tuskegee graduate Isaac Fisher, Negro principal at Branch Normal College (now the University of Arkansas) at Pine Bluff. Although Fisher was apparently a good teacher and much respected by the students, he had virtually no administrative power as he was hampered by the machinations of William Stephen Harris—the school's white treasurer and head of the mechanical department, the college trustees, and the blacks of Pine Bluff who resented the displacement of Fisher's predecessor Joseph Carter Corbin. Based on newspapers, correspondence with Booker T. Washington, and other primary and secondary sources; 5 illus., 188 notes. 1902-11

Fisher, Sarah

2224. Wainwright, Nicholas B. "A DIARY OF TRIFLING OCCURRENCES": PHILADELPHIA 1776-1778. *Pennsylvania Mag. of Hist. and Biog. 1958 82(4): 411-465.* Sarah Fisher, a member of one of the two wealthiest Quaker families in Philadelphia, kept a diary during her husband's enforced absence which is of unusual interest because of her observations on the American Revolution. 1776-78

Fisher, Vardis

2225. Arrington, Leonard J. and Haupt, Jon. THE MORMON HERITAGE OF VARDIS FISHER. *Brigham Young U. Studies 1977 18(1): 27-47.* Vardis Fisher, one of the leading 20th-century literary recorders of the Mormon experience, never rejected Mormonism entirely. He was not an apostate, but instead possessed a profound religious outlook on life and history. Fisher may be called a literary innovator, for in his efforts to unravel the Mormon mystique he employed modern psychological techniques. Discusses his writings, especially his best-known *Children of God* (1939), in an effort to compile what may be called a psychohistory of Vardis Fisher. 1915-68

Fisk, Charles

2226. Coffey, Mark Daryl. "Charles Fisk: Organ Builder." U. of Rochester, Eastman School of Music 1984. 253 pp. *DAI 1984 45(3): 677-A.* DA8413856 1940's-83

Fisk, Wilbur

2227. Williamson, Douglas J. WILBUR FISK AND AFRICAN COLONIZATION: A "PAINFUL PORTION" OF AMERICAN METHODIST HISTORY. *Methodist History 1985 23(2): 79-98.* Explores the involvement of Methodists in the American Colonization Society, emphasizing the role of Wilbur Fisk during the 1820's-30's. Fisk, one of the most respected of early 19th-century Methodist leaders in New England, abhorred the existence of slavery in the United States, urging that the slaves be sent to Liberia as part of the African colonization movement. Nonetheless, Fisk opposed abolitionism, which he suggested would have drastic social and political effects on the nation. The controversy over Fisk's views led to a split in New England Methodist leadership during the 1830's. Fisk's pro-colonization stance in part reflected racial prejudice. Based on the Fisk Papers at Wesleyan University, Fisk's articles in the *Zion Herald,* and published documents; 38 notes. 1820's-30's

Fiske, Bradley A.

2228. Coletta, Paolo E. THE PERILS OF INVENTION: BRADLEY A. FISKE AND THE TORPEDO PLANE. *Am. Neptune 1977 37(2): 111-127.* Gives an account of Admiral Bradley A. Fiske's efforts to develop a torpedo plane and the litigation he initiated in the 1920's after the US Navy began organizing torpedo-plane units. Frustrated in his attempts during World War I to gain the Navy's support for torpedo-plane development, Fiske failed later to obtain compensation through the courts for his patents relevant to aerial-torpedo warfare. Based primarily on manuscripts; 35 notes. 1909-31

Fiske, Minnie Maddern

2229. Messano-Ciesla, Mary Ann Angela. "Minnie Maddern Fiske: Her Battle with the Theatrical Syndicate." New York U. 1982. 534 pp. *DAI 1983 43(7): 2159-A.* DA8226782 1870-1916

Fitch, Henry

2230. Ogden, Adele. CAPTAIN HENRY FITCH, SAN DIEGO MERCHANT, 1825-1849. *J. of San Diego Hist. 1981 27(4): 238-259.* Surveys the life and business ventures of Captain Henry Fitch, an important figure in the maritime trade of early California. 1825-49

Fitch, John A.

2231. Hill, Charles and Cohen, Steven. JOHN A. FITCH AND THE PITTSBURGH SURVEY. *Western Pennsylvania Hist. Mag. 1984 67(1): 17-32.* Patterned after a survey of the social, economic, and political problems of Washington, D.C., and published in a 1906 issue of *Charities and the Commons,* the Pittsburgh Survey, headed by Paul Kellog, was a much broader study and explored every aspect of life in the city; focuses on John A. Fitch, one of the few responsible for the final report, his extensive work interviewing and studying the steelworkers of the city, and his continued ventures and studies in important social issues until the early 1940's. ca 1906-40's

Fitzgerald, F. Scott

2232. Donaldson, Scott. F. SCOTT FITZGERALD, PRINCETON '17. *Princeton U. Lib. Chronicle 1979 40(2): 119-154.* Relates F. Scott Fitzgerald's experiences at Princeton University, his lifelong dedication to the school, and the events of some postgraduate reunions, including those since his death; covers 1914-67. 1914-67

2233. Johnson, Christiane. F. SCOTT FITZGERALD ET HOLLYWOOD: LE REVE AMERICAIN DENATURE [F. Scott Fitzgerald and Hollywood: the American dream distorted]. *Rev. Française d'Etudes Américaines [France] 1984 9(19): 39-51.* Discusses F. Scott Fitzgerald's ambivalent reactions to the glamor and tawdriness of Hollywood and examines his fascination with Hollywood as part of his larger fascination with the American dream. 1937-40

2234. Kazin, Alfred. HEMINGWAY & FITZGERALD: THE COST OF BEING AMERICAN. *Am. Heritage 1984 35(3): 49-64.* Discusses the life and works of Ernest Hemingway and F. Scott Fitzgerald, who helped define what it meant to be an American during the first half of the 20th century. 6 photos. 1920-50

2235. White, Richard L. F. SCOTT FITZGERALD: THE CUMULATIVE PORTRAIT. *Biography 1981 4(2): 154-168.* A consecutive and comparative reading of the biographies of F. Scott Fitzgerald not only provides a cumulative portrait of the biographical figure but also suggests that such a reading reveals something about our own collective psychological and critical response to that figure. In spite of his willing participation in the role of literary celebrity, Fitzgerald remained remarkably representative of a common experience that is familiar to most of us. 1920-76

Fitzgerald, Zelda Sayre (family)

2236. Smith, Scottie Fitzgerald. THE MARYLAND ANCESTORS OF ZELDA SAYRE FITZGERALD. *Maryland Hist. Mag. 1983 78(3): 217-228.* Traces Zelda Sayre Fitzgerald's ancestral line to Thomas Cresap, "the quintessential frontiersman," once known to Pennsylvanians as "the Maryland Monster," to Indians as "the Big Spoon," and to the British as "the Rattlesnake Colonel." Likewise, "the infamous John Coode," leader of the Maryland Revolution of 1689, and a host of other prominent colonial leaders in 17th- and 18th-century Maryland were progenitors of the Alabama-born Zelda Sayre. Based on Maryland archives, the Calvert Papers, and interviews; table, 24 notes. 1630-1835

Fitzhugh, George

2237. Mayes, Sharon S. SOCIOLOGICAL THOUGHT IN EMILE DURKHEIM AND GEORGE FITZHUGH. *British J. of Sociol. [Great Britain] 1980 31(1): 78-94.* 1854-1917

For abstract see ***Durkheim, Emile***

Fitzpatrick, Richard

2238. Black, Hugo L., III. RICHARD FITZPATRICK'S SOUTH FLORIDA, 1822-1840. *Tequesta 1980 40: 47-77; 1981 41: 33-68.* Part I. KEY WEST PHASE. Richard Fitzpatrick left his native Columbia, South Carolina, around 1816. He moved to Key West in 1822; where his activities included involvement in the wrecking industry, salt industry, election to the 1831 and 1832 legislative councils, and slavery. Based on chancery records, court papers in the Monroe County Public Library, and microfilm copies of records housed in the P. K. Yonge Library, Gainesville; 97 notes. Part II. FITZPATRICK'S MIAMI RIVER PLANTATION. Fitzpatrick paid John Egan $400.00 for 640 acres on the Miami River in 1830. After continued purchases he had acquired 2,660 acres on the Miami River and 640 acres on the New River. He established a plantation on the Miami River, attempting to establish a planter society in south Florida. Slaves concentrated on the growing of sugar cane. Before the Second Seminole War ruined his efforts, driving him from Florida in 1840, Fitzpatrick had been one of the most powerful and active members of the Legislative Council of Florida. Elected President of the Council in 1836, he had Dade County created in south Florida. Based on contemporary printed federal and state government documents, journals of the Constitutional Convention of 1838 and secondary sources; 87 notes. 1820-40

Flaccus family

2239. Caniff, Deanna and Caniff, Tom. FLACCUS: GROCERS TO A NATION. *Upper Ohio Valley Hist. Rev. 1984 13(2): 16-21.* Details the Flaccus family's growth as successful retail food merchants and their participation in revolutionizing food packaging and commercial canning in Wheeling, West Virginia. 1877-1921

Flagg, Ernest

2240. Levy, Daniel A. "Ernest Flagg and His Impact on Stone House Construction, 1920-1954." U. of Maryland 1979. 200 pp. *DAI 1980 40(12): 6175-6176-A.* DA8012661 1920-54

Flagg, George Whiting

2241. Nord, Barbara K. GEORGE WHITING FLAGG AND HIS SOUTH CAROLINA PORTRAITS. *South Carolina Hist. Mag. 1982 83(3): 214-234.* A recent revival of interest in 19th-century art has drawn attention to artist George Whiting Flagg. One of his most noteworthy portraits is that of Mrs. William Aiken, wife of the former governor and congressman. The Charleston Museum owns the Aiken House where the portrait still hangs. 29 notes. 19c

Flagg, Gershom

2242. Branz, Nedra and Lawrence, Barbara. A PRAIRIE FARMER AND LOCO FOCOS, SPECULATORS, NULLIFIERS, &C. &C. *Old Northwest 1983-84 9(4): 345-366.* Consists of 13 edited letters written to and from Gershom Flagg, an Illinois prairie farmer. The correspondence offers valuable insights into the social and cultural conditions in Illinois and indicates the deep interest in national politics and Eastern affairs maintained by Flagg. Based on the Gershom Flagg Correspondence at the Illinois Historical Survey Library, University of Illinois, and at the Lovejoy Library, Southern Illinois University, Edwardsville; and on other primary sources; 44 notes. 1828-51

Flaglor, Amasa Plummer

2243. Palmquist, Peter E. AMASA PLUMMER FLAGLOR: NORTHERN CALIFORNIA PHOTOGRAPHER. *Pacific Hist. 1981 25(1): 29-35.* Discusses the career of Amasa Plummer Flaglor, who was trained as a photographer in San Francisco's art galleries. He ventured into business on his own, and in 1870, at the age of 22, was running a successful gallery in Eureka, California. Using the latest standardized techniques, he was able to make a fairly comfortable living, until a general economic decline, during which he attempted to expand, forced him out of business. Subsequently he sold insurance. Based on newspaper accounts and other primary sources. 1863-1918

Fleet, Maria Louisa

2244. Fleet, Betsy. IF THERE IS NO BRIGHT SIDE, THEN POLISH UP THE DARK ONE: MARIA LOUISA FLEET AND THE GREEN MOUNT HOME SCHOOL FOR YOUNG LADIES. *Virginia Cavalcade 1980 29(3): 100-107.* Describes Maria Louisa Fleet (1822-1900), her life at Green Mount, Virginia, and the Green Mount Home School for Young Ladies she started in her home in 1873 to support herself; she closed the school in 1888. 1873-88

Fleischman, Frederick A.

2245. Fite, Gilbert C. AGRICULTURAL PIONEERING IN DAKOTA: A CASE STUDY. *Great Plains Q. 1981 1(3): 169-180.* A microhistorical case study of the life of South Dakota German immigrant and homesteader Frederick A. Fleischman, based on his account books, which show how he successfully farmed his free land from his first harvest in 1880 until he died in 1929. 1880-1929

Fleming, Arthur S.

2246. Green, Rosalie E. "A Historical Study of Arthur S. Fleming: His Impact on Federal Education and Training Programs Relating to Aging during the Period 1958-78." Virginia Polytechnic Inst. and State U. 1984. 289 pp. *DAI 1985 46(4): 911-A.* DA8511938 1958-78

Fleming, Hartley G.

2247. Fleming, Hartley G. THE EAST END, 1898-1915. *Western Pennsylvania Hist. Mag. 1977 60(4): 419-426.* Hartley G. Fleming reminisces about his boyhood in eastern Pittsburgh, 1898-1915. 1898-1915

Fletcher, Alice Cunningham

2248. Welch, Rebecca Hancock. "Alice Cunningham Fletcher, Anthropologist and Indian Rights Reformer. George Washington U. 1980. 352 pp. *DAI 1981 41(8): 3637-A.* 8101492 1881-1923

Fletcher, Calvin

2249. Jones, Robert L. *THE DIARY OF CALVIN FLETCHER:* A REVIEW ESSAY. *Indiana Mag. of Hist. 1984 80(2): 166-172.* Reviews the last of a nine-volume set of diaries of Calvin Fletcher, a prominent 19th-century Indianapolis lawyer, businessman, and behind-the-scene politician. The diaries give a full picture of life in central Indiana during 1821-66. They identify the rise of major local industries, discuss national political issues, and reveal the manner in which Fletcher attuned his Puritan religious and philosophical views to the issues of slavery, abolition, and the Civil War. 1862-66

Fletcher, Ed

2250. Kendall, Charles P. PLANKS ACROSS THE DUNES. *J. of Arizona Hist. 1980 21(4): 391-410.* 1901-20

For abstract see ***Boyd, Ed***

Fletcher, Harvey

2251. Kimball, Edward L. HARVEY FLETCHER AND HENRY EYRING: MEN OF FAITH AND SCIENCE. *Dialogue 1982 15(3): 74-86.* 1907-81

For abstract see ***Eyring, Henry***

Fletcher, Henry P.

2252. Frederick, Olivia Mae. "Henry P. Fletcher and United States-Latin American Policy, 1910-1930." U. of Kentucky 1977. 235 pp. *DAI 1978 38(10): 6271-6272-A.* 1910-30

Fletcher, John Gould

2253. Carpenter, Lucas Adams. "John Gould Fletcher and Southern Modernism." State U. of New York, Stony Brook 1982. 258 pp. *DAI 1982 43(2): 444-A.* DA8216058 1914-30's

Flexner, Abraham

2254. Movrich, Ronald Frank. "Before the Gates of Excellence: Abraham Flexner and Education, 1866-1918." U. of California, Berkeley 1981. 253 pp. *DAI 1982 43(6): 1857-A.* DA8212047 1866-1918

2255. Wheatley, Steven Charles. "The Politics of Philanthropic Management: Abraham Flexner and Medical Education." U. of Chicago 1982. *DAI 1983 43(7): 2428-2429-A.* 1890-1950

Flick, Lawrence

2256. Schmandt, Raymond H. SOME NOTES ON BISHOP J. F. REGIS CANEVIN OF PITTSBURGH (1904-1921). *Records of the American Catholic Historical Society of Philadelphia 1984 95(1-4): 91-107.* 1885-1921

For abstract see ***Canevin, John F. Regis***

2257. Schmandt, Raymond H. THE FRIENDSHIP BETWEEN BISHOP REGIS CANEVIN OF PITTSBURGH AND DR. LAWRENCE FLICK OF PHILADELPHIA. *Western Pennsylvania Hist. Mag. 1978 61(4): 283-300.* 1870's-1927

For abstract see ***Canevin, John F. Regis***

Fligelman, Frieda

2258. Leaphart, Susan, ed. FRIEDA AND BELLE FLIGELMAN: A FRONTIER-CITY GIRLHOOD IN THE 1890S. *Montana 1982 32(3): 85-92.* The careers of Frieda Fligelman and her sister Belle Fligelman Winestine reflect charm, intellect, woman's rights, and their Jewish background. In an interview with the editor, Belle Winestine reflects on her early years in Helena, Montana. Based on an oral history interview with Belle Winestine; 2 illus., 9 notes. 1890-99

Fling, Fred

2259. Carlson, Robert E. PROFESSOR FRED FLING: HIS CAREER AND CONFLICTS AT NEBRASKA UNIVERSITY. *Nebraska Hist. 1981 62(4): 481-496.* Biographical sketch of Fred Fling, history professor at Nebraska University from 1890 until ca. 1934. Fling had serious problems with the university regents and the World War I Nebraska Council of Defense after reporting rumors of several of his colleagues' pro-German sympathies. He was unable to provide evidence of his charges. At the time he was serving as a major with the historical branch of the General Staff in Washington and later in Paris. The author was one of Professor Fling's students at the end of his teaching career. 1890-1934

Floersheim, Sol

2260. Fierman, Floyd S. SOL FLOERSHEIM: JEWISH RANCHER AND MERCHANT IN NORTHERN NEW MEXICO. *Western States Jewish Hist. Q. 1982 14(4): 291-301.* The introduction of the railroad in the 1880's moved the major commercial center from Santa Fe to Las Vegas, in northern New Mexico. Sol Floersheim (1856-1946) came to Las Vegas in 1880 to work for the Charles Ilfeld Company as an agent receiving sheep and wool from the area's ranchers. He later opened several retail stores including the large Floersheim Mercantile Company in Springer. He fulfilled a dream by buying the Jaritas Ranch in 1897 and expanding it to 63,000 acres by 1912. All of Floersheim's holdings were financed with coinvestors and partners. Based on material in the Floersheim family archives, Springer, New Mexico; 3 photos, 36 notes. 1880-1920's

Floyd, John

2261. Chitwood, W. R. GOVERNOR JOHN FLOYD, PHYSICIAN. *Virginia Cavalcade 1976 26(2): 86-95.* Examines the medical practice, 1802-36, of Virginia governor (1830-34) John Floyd; discusses his experimentation and the state of medical practice in Virginia and elsewhere. 1802-36

2262. Hammon, Neal and Harris, James Russell, ed. "IN A DANGEROUS SITUATION": LETTERS OF COL. JOHN FLOYD, 1774-1783. *Register of the Kentucky Historical Society 1985 83(3): 202-236.* Prints 19 letters of John Floyd, a surveyor who spent much time on the frontiers in Kentucky. His letters, dated 1774-83, tell of his views on events of the time and of the difficulties of life on the frontier. Although Floyd went West to survey, he spent much of his time in conflict with Indians and was killed in an ambush in 1783. Based on 19 letters found among the Draper Papers, State Historical Society of Wisconsin; 6 illus., 62 notes. 1770's-80's

Flynn, Elizabeth Gurley

2263. Camp, Helen Collier. "'Gurley:' A Biography of Elizabeth Gurley Flynn, 1890-1964." Columbia U. 1980. 674 pp. *DAI 1982 43(5): 1650-A.* DA8222357 1890-1964

Flynn, Errol

2264. Valenti, Peter. THE MANY LIVES OF ERROL FLYNN. *J. of Popular Film and Television 1982 9(4): 194-197.* Review essay of Michael Freedland's *The Two Lives of Errol Flynn* (1979), Charles Higham's *Errol Flynn: The Untold Story* (1980), and *From a Life of Adventure: The Writings of Errol Flynn,* edited by Tony Thomas (1980); focuses on the sensational aspects of Flynn's personal and professional adventures. 1930's-59

Foerster, Norman

2265. Kelly, Gilbert Bruce. "Norman Foerster and American New Humanist Criticism." U. of Nebraska, Lincoln 1982. 390 pp. *DAI 1983 43(7): 2349-A.* DA8228150 1890-1930

Fokine, Michel

2266. Horwitz, Dawn Lille. "Michel Fokine in America, 1919-1942." New York U. 1982. 235 pp. *DAI 1983 43(7): 2158-A.* DA8227193 1919-42

Foley, Martha

2267. Foley, Martha. AUTOBIOGRAPHY: PARIS IN THE TWENTIES. *Massachusetts Rev. 1980 21(1): 67-79.* An abridged section of Martha Foley's *The Story of* Story Magazine: *A Memoir* (Norton, 1980) describing the author's sojourn in Paris, 1927-33, and containing reminiscences of her associations with journalists and authors there, including Gertrude Stein (1874-1946), Richard Wright (1908-60), James Joyce (1882-1941), Rex (Todhunter) Stout (1886-1975), and Hart Crane (1899-1932). It mentions various idiosyncracies of the above-named writers. 1927-33

Follett, Mary Parker

2268. Cooper, Frances Ann. "Mary Parker Follett: The Power of Power-With." U. of Southern California 1981. *DAI 1982 42(10): 4576-A.* 1896-1927

2269. Smith, Carl Wayne. "Mary Parker Follett: An Analysis of Her Progressive Influence on the Study of School Administration, 1930-1950." U. of Maryland 1981. 134 pp. *DAI 1982 43(1): 41-A.* DA8214472 1930-50

Foltz, Clara Shortridge

2270. Elwood-Akers, Virginia. CLARA SHORTRIDGE FOLTZ, CALIFORNIA'S FIRST WOMAN LAWYER. *Pacific Hist. 1984 28(3): 23-29.* Details the many achievements of Clara Shortridge Foltz, focusing on her law career. With five children to support following the death of her husband in 1877, she began reading law with a local San Jose firm. Before being admitted to the bar as California's first woman attorney, she had to work to overturn the law prohibiting women from practicing law. Foltz was always a pioneer for women's professional rights—whether in arguing a motion in the New York City courts, attending law school in California, or becoming a member of the board of trustees of the State Normal School of Los Angeles. Based on letters in the Huntington Library, San Marino, California, and on articles in Foltz's *New American Women;* 2 photos. 1877-1934

2271. Polos, Nicholas C. SAN DIEGO'S "PORTIA OF THE PACIFIC": CALIFORNIA'S FIRST WOMAN LAWYER. *J. of San Diego Hist. 1980 2(3): 185-195.* California's first female lawyer, Clara Shortridge Foltz, moved to California at age 15 in 1872 from Indiana, was admitted to the bar in 1878 after she herself authored a bill to amend legislation not allowing women to practice law, and practised law in San Diego and elsewhere in California before running unsuccessfully for governor of California in 1930 when she was in her 70's. 1872-1930

Fong, Hiram L.

2272. Chou, Michaelyn Pi-hsia. "The Education of a Senator: Hiram L. Fong from 1907 to 1954." U. of Hawaii 1980. 781 pp. *DAI 1981 41(7): 3162-A.* 8100669 1907-54

Foote, Andrew Hull

2273. Keller, Allan. ADMIRAL ANDREW HULL FOOTE. *Civil War Times Illus. 1979 18(8): 6-11, 43-47.* A religious but bellicose old salt with a distinguished naval career before the Civil War, Andrew Hull Foote (1806-63) contributed to Federal victories in 1862 against Fort Henry and Fort Donelson in Tennessee and against Island Number 10 on the Mississippi River. 1862

Foote, Mary Hallock

2274. Cragg, Barbara. MARY HALLOCK FOOTE'S IMAGES OF THE OLD WEST. *Landscape 1980 24(3): 42-47.* Writer and illustrator Mary Hallock Foote (1847-1938) depicted the American West during the late 19th century for *Scribner's Monthly* (later *Century Magazine)* and *St. Nicholas,* and in her novels. ca 1876-1938

2275. Paul, Rodman W. WHEN CULTURE CAME TO BOISE: MARY HALLOCK FOOTE IN IDAHO. *Idaho Yesterdays 1976 20(2): 2-12.* Mary Hallock Foote, born in New York state, married an engineer and followed him West after having established herself as a successful magazine artist. Her stories and sketches depicted her western experiences even though she always regarded herself as an exile from civilization and culture. Includes paintings by Foote first published in *Century Illustrated Monthly Magazine* 1888-90. 7 illus. 1847-92

Foote, William H.

2276. Gardner, Bettye J. WILLIAM H. FOOTE AND YAZOO COUNTY POLITICS. *Southern Studies 1982 21(4): 398-407.* William H. Foote, a black man, attended Oberlin College, fought for the Confederacy, and returned to Yazoo, Mississippi, after the Civil War. From 1866 until his death, he worked to maintain a foothold for the Republican Party in Yazoo County. He served as a state legislator, constable, circuit-court clerk, and deputy tax collector. Attempts to improve the lot of local blacks stirred resentment among white Democrats, and organized violence against blacks began in 1875. Foote advocated nonviolence, but his outspoken stance on civil-rights issues attracted dangerous attention. In 1883, he was killed while in jail. Primary sources; 39 notes. 1866-83

Fooy, Benjamin

2277. Roper, James E. BENJAMIN FOOY AND THE SPANISH FORTS OF SAN FERNANDO AND CAMPO DE LA ESPERANZA. *West Tennessee Hist. Soc. Papers 1982 36: 41-64.* An immigrant from Holland, Benjamin Fooy first appears in American history in 1782, when he was living among the Chickasaw Indians. Versed in both the Chickasaw and Choctaw tongues, Fooy served as an interpreter and diplomat for Spain among the Indians. He was witness to the numerous political changes in the Memphis area after the Revolutionary War, when the Spaniards abandoned Fort San Fernando in what is now Memphis and built Fort Campo de la Esperanza just across the Mississippi River in Arkansas. The latter fort passed into French hands and then was acquired by the United States as part of the Louisiana Purchase in 1803. Fooy weathered the political changes well, serving as diplomat, trader, and judge. He ended his days as a valued citizen and official. Based on the Archivo General de Indias, Papeles de Cuba; the Archivo Historico Nacional in Madrid; the US Military Archives; and studies of Spanish forts in the *West Tennessee Historical Society Papers;* 2 fig., 124 notes. 1782-1823

Forbes, John

2278. Waterbury, Jean Parker. JOHN FORBES: MAN OF THE CLOTH, OF HIS TIMES, AND OF ST. AUGUSTINE. *Escribano 1981 18: 1-32.* Describes the career of Reverend John Forbes, who in the spring of 1764 was appointed Anglican clergyman for St. Augustine, Florida; he gave advice to Governor James Grant of East Florida, provided spiritual counsel to his congregation, and fulfilled his familial responsibilities. He died in 1783. 1764-83

Forbes, John Murray

2279. Larson, John L. "John Murray Forbes and the Burlington Route: Enterprise and Culture in the Railway Age, 1813-1898." Brown U. 1981. 408 pp. *DAI 1982 43(2): 526-527-A.* DA8215580 1830-98

Ford, Arnold

2280. Scott, William R. RABBI ARNOLD FORD'S BACK-TO-ETHIOPIA MOVEMENT: A STUDY OF BLACK EMIGRATION, 1930-1935. *Pan-African J. [Kenya] 1975 8(2): 191-202.* An account of the career of Rabbi Arnold Ford (1876-1935), early black Nationalist and leader of the back-to-Ethiopia movement. Accompanied by three other members of his congregation, Rabbi Ford arrived in Addis Ababa in 1930 in an attempt to obtain concessions for the rest of his group, who, it was hoped, would follow soon after. Records the difficulties encountered by those 60 members who made the journey to Addis Ababa during 1930-34. Twenty-five members returned shortly after their arrival and none remained after Ford's death in 1935 and the outbreak of the Italo-Ethiopian War. Primary and secondary sources; 52 notes. 1930-35

Ford, Augustus

2281. Palmer, Richard F. LAKE ONTARIO'S FIRST CHARTMAKER. *Inland Seas 1983 39(2): 91-95.* Captain Augustus Ford moved to Oswego, New York, in 1797. He served on board lake ships before joining the navy in 1810 as a master on the *Oneida.* In 1813 he drew three charts of Lake Ontario, which Commodore Isaac Chauncey promised, but failed, to have published. Ford served at the Sackets Harbor Naval Station for 20 years and died in 1855. Based on Ford's petition for compensation for the charts. 1797-1855

Ford, Franklin

2282. Burton, David H. THE CURIOUS CORRESPONDENCE OF JUSTICE OLIVER WENDELL HOLMES AND FRANKLIN FORD. *New England Q. 1980 53(2): 196-211.* Sketches Ford's (1849-1918) background, outlines his ideas concerning the news and financial systems of the day, and analyzes his correspondence during 1907-17 with Holmes (1841-1935). Justice Holmes was attracted by some of Ford's ideas concerning the role of law but never seemed able either fully to comprehend what Ford said, or to dismiss him as a crackpot. Based on their correspondence at Harvard Law School; 42 notes. 1907-17

2283. McGlashan, Zena Beth. THE PROFESSOR AND THE PROPHET: JOHN DEWEY AND FRANKLIN FORD. *Journalism Hist. 1979-80 6(4): 107-111, 123.* Discusses the 10-year friendship between John Dewey who wrote about the press and the public in *The Public and Its Problems* (1927), and newspaper journalist, Franklin Ford, who wrote *Draft of Action* in 1892, which ended bitterly in the 1890's at the beginning of the Progressive Era. Provides the background of Ford's career (beginning in 1875) and ideas, which the author suggests "provided a catalyst for Dewey's thinking about the function and potential of mass media." 1875-1927

Ford, Gerald R.

2284. Kaspi, André. FAUT-IL BRULER KISSINGER? [Must we roast Kissinger?] *Histoire [France] 1984 (65): 92-94.* 1968-81

For abstract see ***Kissinger, Henry***

2285. Witherspoon, Patricia Ann Dennis. "The Rhetoric of Gerald R. Ford: A Multidimensional Analysis of Presidential Communication." U. of Texas, Austin 1977. 184 pp. *DAI 1978 38(7): 3807-A.* 1974-76

Ford, Henry

2286. Bordewyk, Gordon and Green, Gregory. FORD, HIS MOTHER & PROGRESS. *Michigan Hist. 1981 65(5): 39-46.* Contrary to authors who interpret Henry Ford's drive for success "as one man's unique version of the search for the father," Ford's life may be more aptly described as a "lifelong search to recapture" his mother's (Clara Jane Bryant Ford) presence by "trying to recreate her morality and work ethic, first with rules for his factory workers, then by improving rural life, and finally by collecting McGuffey Readers and building Greenfield village." 12 illus., 37 notes. 1885-1943

2287. Karp, Walter. GREENFIELD VILLAGE. *Am. Heritage 1980 32(1): 98-107.* The story of Henry Ford (1863-1947) and the development of his museum of Americana, Greenfield Village, now outside Detroit, Michigan. Around 1919, Ford began to think longingly of the past, and began to collect early Americana. The birth of the village in 1927 coincided with the end of production for the Model T. Ford spared no expense in this venture, which he saw as a memorial to Thomas Edison. In his later years, Ford spent much time in the village. 10 illus. ca 1919-47

Ford, Henry Chapman

2288. Neuerburg, Norman. FORD DRAWINGS AT THE SOUTHWEST MUSEUM. *Masterkey 1980 54(2): 60-64.* Henry Chapman Ford's (1828-94) paintings of the California missions gained him a favorable reputation, 1875-91. 1875-91

Ford, John

2289. Ellis, Kirk. ON THE WARPATH: JOHN FORD AND THE INDIANS. *J. of Popular Film and Television 1980 8(2): 34-41.* On the surface, director John Ford's western films appear to associate Indians with evil, but a deeper assessment proves that Ford portrays Indians in a good light; cites many of his films from 1924 to 1964. 19c

Ford, Lyman M.

2290. Kreidberg, Marjorie. THE UP AND DOING EDITOR OF THE MINNESOTA *FARMER AND GARDENER. Minnesota History 1985 49(5): 191-201.* Chronicles the career of Minnesota horticulturalist Lyman M. Ford, originator of a pioneering orchard, editor of the state's first agricultural and horticultural journal, and agricultural editor for the St. Paul Daily Press. As editor of the *Farmer and Gardener,* Ford provided a more useful alternative to eastern agricultural journals, on which many Minnesota farmers depended. In 1885, Ford and his wife and partner Abbie moved to California and started a new nursery. 10 illus., 40 notes. 1850-85

Foreman, Kenneth J., Sr.

2291. Goodloe, James C., IV. KENNETH J. FOREMAN, SR.: A CANDLE ON THE GLACIER. *J. of Presbyterian Hist. 1979 57(4): 467-484.* Kenneth J. Foreman, Sr. (1891-1967), southern Presbyterian theologian and popular writer and speaker, strongly advocated three particular changes in the theology and life of his church—acceptance of critical and historical methods of biblical study, fresh confessions of faith, and involvement of the church in social action. His influence across the church was considerable—having taught religion at Davidson College for 25 years and then theology at Louisville Presbyterian Theological Seminary 13 years. But his greatest influence came from his weekly column in the *Presbyterian Outlook,* which he wrote for 20 years. Based on Foreman's writings; photo, 75 notes. 1922-67

Foreman, Richard

2292. Davy, Catherine (Kate) Anne. "The Ontological-Hysteric Theatre: The Work of Richard Foreman as Playwright, Director and Designer 1968-1979." New York U. 1979. 352 pp. *DAI 1980 40(11): 5649-5650-A.* 8010336 1968-79

Foreman, Stephen

2293. Evans, E. Raymond. NOTABLE PERSONS IN CHEROKEE HISTORY: STEPHEN FOREMAN. *J. of Cherokee Studies 1977 2(2): 230-239.* Stephen Foreman was born on 22 October 1807 in north Georgia, the son of Anthony Foreman, a Scottish soldier, and Elizabeth Foreman. He was educated for the ministry at Candy's Creek and New Echota, Georgia, and at Union and Princeton Theological Seminaries. In 1833 he was licensed to preach by the Presbyterian Church. He led one group of Cherokee Indians west during the removal of the 1830's. After settling in Park Hill, Oklahoma, he was active in Cherokee government and established a school system. During this time he also translated parts of the Bible from Greek to Cherokee. He died in Oklahoma on 8 December 1881. Illus., 39 notes. 1820's-81

Foremost Man (Nekankeet)

2294. Lee, David. FOREMOST MAN AND HIS BAND. *Saskatchewan Hist. [Canada] 1983 36(3): 94-101.* A biographical account of the leader of a band of Eastern Crees known to whites as Foremost Man and to his fellow Kahkewistahan tribesmen as Nekankeet. The dispute over going to a reservation or living free in the Cypress Hills was the greatest issue to be dealt with. From 1881 to 1898 the numbers in Foremost Man's band dwindled from 428 to 119. The band was never considered dangerous by the whites and relations were good. His dream of a reserve in the Cypress

Hills was not realized by the time of his death. Based on reports of the Department of Indian Affairs and Royal Canadian Mounted Police; 22 notes. 1876-98

Forrest, Douglas French

2295. Forrest, Douglas French. AN ODYSSEY IN GRAY: SELECTIONS FROM A DIARY OF CONFEDERATE NAVAL LIFE WITH THE C.S.S. *RAPPAHANNOCK*. *Virginia Cavalcade 1980 29(3): 124-129.* The diary's author was assistant paymaster Douglas French Forrest, 1863-65. 1863-65

Forrester, Alexander

2296. Harvey, Robert Paton. THE TEACHER'S REWARD: ALEXANDER FORRESTER AT TRURO. *Nova Scotia Hist. Q. [Canada] 1975 5(1): 47-68.* A study of the career and innovative ideas of Alexander Forrester (d. 1869), the first principal of the Truro Normal School and the second Superintendent of Education in Nova Scotia. His attempts at improving teacher preparation and at selling the idea of a general property tax for the support of free education for all were strongly opposed and for a time frustrated by petty political feuding. Never during his lifetime was he properly recognized for his work and beliefs. 41 notes. ca 1848-69

Forshey, Caleb Goldsmith

2297. Meier, Michael Thomas. "Caleb Goldsmith Forshey: Engineer of the Old Southwest, 1813-1881." Memphis State U. 1982. 182 pp. *DAI 1983 44(1): 244-A.* DA8308515 1838-81

Fort, Cornelia Clark

2298. Tanner, Doris Brinker. CORNELIA FORT: A WASP IN WORLD WAR II, PART I. *Tennessee Hist. Q. 1981 40(4): 381-394.* Cornelia Clark Fort (1919-43), born into the social elite of Nashville, Tennessee, became a pioneering woman flyer when she returned home after graduating from Sarah Lawrence College in 1939. She was in the air as a flight instructor over Pearl Harbor when the Japanese attacked. She returned home a celebrity. In 1942 she entered the army's Ferrying Division of the Air Transport Command. Based on Fort's papers, memorabilia, and other primary sources; 2 illus., 31 notes. Article to be continued. 1919-42

Fortas, Abe

2299. Kalin, Berkley. YOUNG ABE FORTAS. *West Tennessee Hist. Soc. Papers 1980 (34): 96-100+.* Abe Fortas (b. 1910) had a meteoric rise in the federal government. Ten letters to Hardwig Peres (Memphis attorney, author, and merchant) illustrate Fortas's intelligence, wit, gift of phrase, and varied interests. Peres had helped Fortas get into the Yale Law School in the early 1930's. One of Franklin D. Roosevelt's "bright young men," Fortas was appointed Undersecretary of the Interior in 1942, at age 32. This caused a small storm, and he resigned to enter the military, much against Roosevelt's desires, only to be discharged a month later for medical causes. Letters are from the Mississippi Valley Collection, Memphis State University, Tennessee. 1930-44

Fortune, Timothy Thomas

2300. Allman, Jean M. and Roediger, David R. THE EARLY EDITORIAL CAREER OF TIMOTHY THOMAS FORTUNE: CLASS, NATIONALISM AND CONSCIOUSNESS OF AFRICA. *Afro-Americans in New York Life and Hist. 1982 6(2): 39-52.* Briefly examines the career of Timothy Thomas Fortune, black journalist and activist for 60 years, focusing on his work as an editor for the *New York Globe,* the *Freeman,* and the *New York Age* as a young man and particularly on his political activism during 1884-87 during which time he espoused Pan-Africanism and the philosophies of Booker T. Washington and Marcus Garvey. 1856-87

2301. Wolseley, Roland E. T. THOMAS FORTUNE: DEAN OF BLACK JOURNALISTS. *Crisis 1976 83(8): 285-287.* Timothy Thomas Fortune (1856-1928) was born in Marianna, Florida. Sorting type as a boy on *The Courier* in Marianna drew him into journalism. He attended Howard University, met Frederick Douglass, worked for several Florida newspapers, moved to New York, converted a newspaper he named the *Globe* into a civil rights journal, and he became editor of the New York *Age*, an outstanding national black paper. Fortune had a close relationship with Booker T. Washington and supported his views on black progress. Personal and family problems brought him depression and ineffectiveness, but during the 1920's Fortune returned to prominence by editing Marcus Garvey's *Negro World.* 1870's-1928

Fosse, Bob

2302. Gargaro, Kenneth Vance. "The Work of Bob Fosse and the Choreographer-Directors in the Translation of Musicals to the Screen." U. of Pittsburgh 1979. 219 pp. *DAI 1980 41(1): 24-A.* 8015303 1969-79

Foster, George Burman

2303. Towne, Edgar A. A "SINGLEMINDED" THEOLOGIAN: GEORGE BURMAN FOSTER AT CHICAGO. *Foundations 1977 20(1): 36-59, (2): 163-180.* Part I. George Burman Foster arrived at the University of Chicago in 1895. Being a liberal Baptist who tried to express his inner religious experience to a conservative audience, he was controversial throughout his career. Five major controversies centered around him: 1) academic freedom, 2) an attempt to get him excommunicated from the Hyde Park Baptist Church, 3) his transfer from the divinity school to arts, sciences, and letters, 4) ethics and theology, and 5) the issue of Christian theism. Describes how Foster was obtained by the University of Chicago and discusses his controversies. Concludes with the controversy concerning academic freedom. 107 notes. Part II. Foster was accused of holding Unitarian views and did term himself "a frank agnostic." In 1909 Foster's name was deleted from the Northern Baptist conference, but he continued to expound humanism at the university. 82 notes. 1895-1918

Foster, John Stuart

2304. Thomas, Jerry. JOHN STUART FOSTER, MCGILL UNIVERSITY, AND THE RENASCENCE OF NUCLEAR PHYSICS IN MONTREAL, 1935-1950. *Hist. Studies in the Physical Sci. 1984 14(2): 357-377.* Though Ernest Rutherford worked at McGill University from 1898 to 1907, it was the Canadian John Stuart Foster who had the greatest impact on physics there. Foster did more research and directed more graduate study at McGill than any other physics professor. He introduced the American influence in physics to a faculty formerly dominated by Cambridge physicists. He also helped to establish the largest cyclotron in Canada in 1944. Based on the McGill University Archives, the Ernest Orlando Lawrence papers, and other primary sources; fig., 77 notes. 1935-50

Foster, Marcus A.

2305. Carr, Carson, Jr. "Marcus A. Foster, Urban Educational Manager." Syracuse U. 1982. 171 pp. *DAI 1983 43(7): 2268-A.* DA8229031 1954-74

Foster, Stephen

2306. Mackes, Steve. STEPHEN FOSTER: EARLY MINSTREL DAYS. *Mankind 1981 6(10): 14-16, 42-43.* Sketches the life of composer Stephen Collins Foster (4 July 1826-13 January 1864). "Oh! Susanna," Foster's first important song, was published in 1846 and was ideal for use in the minstrel shows which had just become popular. This success encouraged Foster to leave his Cincinnati bookkeeping job in 1850 in order to devote full time to songwriting. His songs may be divided into two groups: minstrel, or "Ethiopian style," with songs such as "Camptown Races" and "Old Folks at Home," and sentimental ballads such as "Beautiful Dreamer" and "Jeanie with the Light Brown Hair." Although the majority of Foster's most enduring work is in the minstrel style, he turned away from minstrel music later in his career to devote his energies to "a higher kind of music." With few exceptions, however, his finest music was written before 1853. 3 illus., photo. 1846-64

Foster, William Z.

2307. Bykov, Vil'. UIL'IAM FOSTER: STRANITSY ZHIZNI I BOR'BY (II. V BOR'BE ZA DELO KOMMUNIZMA) [William Foster: pages from his life and struggle (II. In the struggle for the cause of Communism)]. *Novaia i Noveishaia Istoriia [USSR] 1973(5): 70-84.* Continued from a previous article. Describes a visit to Moscow in the spring of 1921 by William Z. Foster (d. 1961), leader of the American League of Trade Union Propaganda, particularly his attendance at the Third Congress of the Comintern and the International Congress of Red Trade Unions. Describes Foster's pro-Soviet attitude, his book *The Russian Revolution,* and his arrest by American police on 6 August 1922. Concludes with an assessment of Foster's contribution as a leading American Communist from the late 1920's until his death. 52 notes. 1921-61

Fothergill, Charles

2308. Romney, Paul. A CONSERVATIVE REFORMER IN UPPER CANADA: CHARLES FOTHERGILL, RESPONSIBLE GOVERNMENT AND THE "BRITISH PARTY," 1824-1840. *Historical Papers [Canada] 1984: 42-62.* English-born Charles Fothergill was a reform spokesman in early 19th-century Upper Canada who, after breaking with other reform leaders such as W. W. Baldwin and John Rolph over the concept of responsible government, proclaimed himself a "conservative reformer." Fothergill developed his own brand of reformism largely based on the Whig doctrines of 18th-century British statesmen: Chatham, Shelburne, and Fox. During his last years of life he became a tribune of the "British Party" in Upper Canada. Fothergill's views never caught on with the majority of reformers during the 1830's and 1840's, despite their shared belief in social conservatism. Presented at the annual meeting of the Canadian Historical Association, Guelph, Ontario, 1984. Based on newspapers and secondary sources; 73 notes. 1824-40

2309. Romney, Paul. "A Man Out of Place: The Life of Charles Fothergill: Naturalist, Businessman, Journalist, Politician, 1782-1840." U. of Toronto [Canada] 1981. *DAI 1982 42(10): 4548-A.* 1817-40

Foulke, Willian Dudley

2310. Violette, Aurele J. WILLIAN DUDLEY FOULKE AND RUSSIA. *Indiana Magazine of History 1986 82(1): 69-96.* Willian Dudley Foulke, a Richmond, Indiana, attorney and civil service and government reform advocate, developed an intense interest in Russia during the late 19th century. This led to his authorship of *Slav or Saxon* (1887) and a long active correspondence with many individuals and groups whose goal was the reform or overthrow of Czarist Russia. Foulke helped plan speaking tours of the United States by such revolutionists as Ekaterina Breshko-Breshkovskaia. Encouraged by the overthrow of the czarist regime in early 1917, Foulke was terribly disappointed by the subsequent victory of the Bolsheviks, whom he considered just as tyrannical as the czars. His remaining public activities consisted of condemning the Bolshevik regime and urging Americans to support their own liberties. Based on various documents written by Foulke, and his *Hoosier Autobiography* (1922); illus., 66 notes. 1887-1928

Fowler, Joseph Smith

2311. Durham, Walter T. HOW SAY YOU, SENATOR FOWLER? *Tennessee Hist. Q. 1983 42(1): 39-57.* Traces the life of Tennessee Senator Joseph Smith Fowler from his career as an educator at Franklin College and Howard Female Institute in Nashville to his role as lawyer and Union loyalist, serving as state comptroller under Governor Andrew Johnson. An uncompromising Radical Unionist, Fowler later broke with President Johnson over Reconstruction, but then destroyed his own political career by voting against the wishes of Tennessee Republicans for Johnson's acquittal on impeachment charges. Based on newspapers; 3 illus., 87 notes. 1843-71

Fox, Ansley H.

2312. McIntosh, Michael. ANSLEY H. FOX. *Sporting Classics 1985 4(4): 60-67.* Recounts the life of Ansley H. Fox, who invented and manufactured different shotguns during 1875-1948. 1875-1948

Fox, Fontaine

2313. Thurman, Kelly. FONTAINE FOX: KENTUCKY'S FOREMOST CARTOONIST. *Register of the Kentucky Hist. Soc. 1979 77(2): 112-128.* Biography of Kentucky cartoonist Fontaine Fox (b. 1884), focusing on his career as a cartoonist beginning in 1904, while a student at Indiana University, until 1955, when he drew his last cartoon strip; focuses on 1920-21. 1904-55

Fox, Gustavus Vasa

2314. Sullivan, William Joseph. "Gustavus Vasa Fox and Naval Administration, 1861-1866." Catholic U. of Am. 1977. 357 pp. *DAI 1978 38(7): 4333-A.* 1861-66

Fox, Josiah

2315. Lewis, Clifford M., ed. CAREER OF JOSIAH FOX AS SHIP-BUILDER FOR THE U.S. NAVY: HIS OWN STORY. *Upper Ohio Valley Hist. Rev. 1980 10(1): 22-31.* Reprints a letter from Josiah Fox (1763-1847) to Andrew Ellicott in 1846 describing his positions in the US Navy; comments on Fox's career and life. ca 1780-1846

Fox, Paul

2316. Benkart, Paula. PAUL FOX, PRESBYTERIAN MISSION AND POLISH AMERICANS. *J. of Presbyterian Hist. 1982 60(4): 301-313.* Although he set out to convert the staunchly Catholic Polish Americans to Protestantism, the Polish-born Paul Fox (b. 1875) eventually had to scale down his aspirations and be content simply to acquaint the Poles with Protestant beliefs, a process he felt was no threat to their ethnicity. Yet the course his own career took, the ties he developed with English-speaking Americans, and the social and psychological distance that began to grow between Fox and other Polish immigrants all illustrate his acceptance of how predominant American values could and did draw an individual apart from his own ethnic group. Emphasizes Fox's Presbyterian ministry among Polish immigrants in Baltimore and Chicago. Based on the Paul Fox Papers, Immigration History Research Center, St. Paul, Minnesota; 65 notes. 1896-1945

Fox, Ruth May

2317. Thatcher, Linda, ed. "I CARE NOTHING FOR POLITICS": RUTH MAY FOX, FORGOTTEN SUFFRAGIST. *Utah Hist. Q. 1981 49(3): 239-253.* Ruth May Fox spent most of her adult life as both mother and speaker for the suffrage movement in Utah. Her interest in the suffrage movement began when she joined the Utah Women's Press Club and Reaper's Club as a writer and acquaintance of other women (Dr. Ellis R. Shipp, Dr. Ellen B. Ferguson, Emma McVicker, and Emmeline B. Wells) who proved to be major influences on her desire to improve the role of women in society. During the latter portion of the 19th century, she became active in the Utah Woman Suffrage Association, Salt Lake County Republican Committee, Second Precinct Ladies Republican Club, Deseret Agricultural & Manufacturing Society, Traveler's Aid Society, and Young Ladies' Mutual Improvement Association. Most of her later activities were with the Young Ladies' Mutual Improvement Association. A portion of her diary reveals her constant traveling and speaking to improve women's rights within the political confines of the community. She died in 1958 with little recognition for her past efforts. Photo, 69 notes. 1865-95

Fox, Samuel

2318. Burlison, Robert A. SAMUEL FOX, MERCHANT AND CIVIC LEADER IN SAN DIEGO, 1886-1939. *J. of San Diego Hist. 1980 26(1): 1-10.* Hungarian Jewish immigrant Samuel Fox (1862-1939), who came to San Diego, California, in 1886, established himself as a business and civic leader there until his death in 1939. 1886-1939

Fox, William

2319. Dunn, Angela Fox. WILLIAM FOX: CINEMA CZAR. *Westways 1981 73(11): 35-38, 76.* William Fox, born to a Hungarian family named Fuchs, immigrated to New York in 1880, first invested in a Brooklyn movie theater then made movies as the Fox Films Company in 1915 in Los Angeles, and merged with Twentieth Century Pictures to become Twentieth Century-Fox Film Corporation; his career ended in 1936 when the Supreme Court ruled that he did not own the sound patents for the entire film industry. 1903-36

França, Manuel Joachim de

2320. Goering, Karen McCoskey. MANUEL DE FRANÇA: ST. LOUIS PORTRAIT PAINTER. *Gateway Heritage 1982-83 3(3): 30-35.* Manuel Joachim de França (1808-1865) immigrated from Europe to Pennsylvania, where he attained recognition as a portrait painter before moving to St. Louis. In St. Louis, França's popularity soared because he catered to wealthy patrons who sought artists willing to romanticize them. Based mainly of França's work as well as newspapers and secondary sources; 8 photos, 17 notes. 1850-65

Francis, Convers

2321. Myerson, Joel. CONVERS FRANCIS AND EMERSON. *Am. Literature 1978 50(1): 17-36.* A biographical introduction and excerpts from the journal of Convers Francis dealing with Ralph Waldo Emerson during 11 August 1835-3 January 1863. Although Convers Francis never equaled Theodore Parker's social radicalism or Emerson's intellectual radicalism, he remained a friend of Emerson and regularly attended his lectures. Francis was a theological moderate, yet he frequently defended Emerson. 87 notes. 1835-63

2322. Woodall, Guy R. THE JOURNALS OF CONVERS FRANCIS. *Studies in the Am. Renaissance 1981: 265-343; 1982: 227-284.* Part 1. A transcript of the first part of the diaries of the Reverend Convers Francis (1795-1863), Unitarian minister of the First Parish Congregational Church in Watertown, Massachusetts, and active in the New England transcendentalist movement, covering the years 1819-24. Francis's parish work and his dealing with other Unitarians and transcendentalists, notably Emerson, are touched upon in this section of his journals. Considerable information is included about Unitarianism in New England. Part 2. Reprints journal entries for 1825-63. Entries from Volume 1 (1825-27) are very terse, noting mainly the topics of Francis's sermons every Sunday. Volume 2, beginning with entries from 1835, contains detailed descriptions of books read and individuals whom Francis has met. He discusses several meetings with Ralph Waldo Emerson and comments at length on Emerson's ideas. Draws on the journals and sermons of Francis and on the writings of contemporaries; 899 notes. 1819-24

Frank, Glenn

2323. Zink, Steven D. GLENN FRANK OF THE UNIVERSITY OF WISCONSIN: A REINTERPRETATION. *Wisconsin Mag. of Hist. 1978-79 62(2): 90-127.* Glenn Frank was President of the University of Wisconsin, 1925-37. A young journalist and publicist, Frank was hired by the Regents to refurbish the University's languishing reputation. Although not an academician, he succeeded in his task during the 1920's when the national economy was strong and when progressives controlled state government. When conservative Republican Governor Walter Kohler won election in 1928, Frank attempted to keep the University out of politics and to cooperate with the new administration. When progressives returned to power under the leadership of Philip La Follette, however, they followed the Governor's lead in pressing for Frank's resignation. By failing to recognize the changed political and economic climate Frank also failed to protect himself and the University. Ultimately, he lost his job. 17 illus., 123 notes. 1925-37

Frank, Ray

2324. Clar, Reva and Kramer, William M. THE GIRL RABBI OF THE GOLDEN WEST, PART I. *Western States Jewish History 1986 18(2): 99-111.* A biographical sketch of Ray Frank, pioneering woman Jewish rabbi in California, Nevada, and the Pacific Northwest, covering the early decades of her life. Unlike other women rabbis, Frank was an itinerant preacher. Article to be continued. Based on newspaper accounts; 59 notes. 1861-93

Frank, Sarah Vasen

2325. Clar, Reva. FIRST JEWISH WOMAN PHYSICIAN OF LOS ANGELES. *Western States Jewish Hist. Q. 1981 14(1): 66-75.* Dr. Sarah Vasen (1870-1944), served as the first superintendent and resident physician of the Kaspare Cohn Hospital, forefunner of Cedars-Sinai Medical Center in Los Angeles. Vasen's superintendency began in 1905 and ended in 1910 when she began a private practice specializing in maternity cases. Her marriage to Saul Frank in 1912 ended her professional career. Based on interviews and newspaper accounts; photo, 43 notes. 1905-12

Frank, Waldo

2326. Ogorzaly, Michael A. "Waldo Frank: Prophet of Hispanic Regeneration." U. of Notre Dame 1983. 333 pp. *DAI 1983 43(10): 3343-A.* DA8305882 1920's-60's

Frankel, Charles

2327. Leuchtenburg, William E. CHARLES FRANKEL: 1917-1979. *South Atlantic Q. 1979 78(4): 419-427.* Presents the eulogy delivered by William E. Leuchtenburg for Charles Frankel on 14 May 1979 at the National Humanities Center in Research Triangle, North Carolina, four days after the murder of Charles and Helen Frankel in Bedford Hills, New York Relates many personal references between Leuchtenburg and Frankel, particularly in the last decade. Discusses Frankel's activities at Columbia University, his zeal for learning and his abiding interest in the humanities. 1917-79

Frankenstein, Abraham Frankum

2328. Harris, Ira L. A LOS ANGELES POPULAR MUSIC DIRECTOR. *Western States Jewish Hist. Q. 1977 10(1): 62-67.* Abraham Frankum Frankenstein (1873-1934) began his musical career in Chicago, came to Los Angeles in 1897 with the Grau Opera Company, and remained to form the first permanent theater orchestra. During the 1920's Frankenstein conducted the Orpheum Theater orchestra for such stars as Jack Benny, Fanny Brice, George Jessel, the Marx Brothers, and Sophie Tucker. He organized the bands of the Los Angeles Police and Fire Departments. He served on the Los Angeles Fire Commission for most of the 1913-27 period. In collaboration with F. B. Silverwood he wrote the song, "I Love You California," in 1913; it became the official state song in 1951. Based on personal knowledge and published sources; photo, 18 notes. 1897-1934

Frankfurter, Felix

2329. Murphy, Bruce Allen. "Supreme Court Justices as Politicians: The Extrajudicial Activities of Justices Louis D. Brandeis and Felix Frankfurter." U. of Virginia 1978. 477 pp. *DAI 1983 43(10): 3408-A.* DA8300066 20c

Frankland, Agnes Surriage

2330. Charbo, Eileen M. AGNES SURRIAGE, DEAR ENEMY. *Daughters of the Am. Revolution Mag. 1979 113(1): 14-17.* Agnes Surriage (1726-83) of Marblehead, Massachusetts, the mistress of Sir Charles Henry Frankland (1716-68), the Boston Port Collector, saved his life in the Lisbon earthquake (1755) and nursed him back to health; Frankland then married her, and as a widow back in Boston during 1772-75 she remained loyal to Great Britain. 1741-83

Franklin, Benjamin

2331. Bell, Robert H. BENJAMIN FRANKLIN'S "PERFECT CHARACTER." *Eighteenth-Century Life 1978 5(2): 13-25.* Discusses the character of Benjamin Franklin as shown in his *Autobiography* and in biographies and articles. 1706-90

2332. Buxbaum, Melvin H. BENJAMIN FRANKLIN'S *AUTOBIOGRAPHY. Early Am. Lit. 1982 17(1): 75-86.* Reviews and analyzes Franklin's *Autobiography: The Autobiography of Benjamin Franklin, a Genetic Text* (1981), edited by J. A. Leo Lemay and P. M. Zall. The editors' assertion that this edition should be the basis of all future editions of the *Autobiography* is not valid. 18c

2333. Davis, Elizabeth. EVENTS IN THE LIFE AND IN THE TEXT: FRANKLIN AND THE STYLE OF AMERICAN AUTOBIOGRAPHY. *Rev. Française d'Etudes Américaines [France] 1982 7(14): 187-197.* Describes the autobiography of the mature Benjamin Franklin, written in 1771, as a document of his personal and intellectual growth in the climate of early America. 1771

2334. Dull, Jonathan R. BENJAMIN FRANKLIN AND THE NATURE OF AMERICAN DIPLOMACY. *Int. Hist. Rev. [Canada] 1983 5(3): 346-363.* Studies the diplomatic efforts of Benjamin Franklin. Franklin was the most traditional American diplomat of the Revolution in his tendency to approach diplomacy as a search for compromise, his use of diplomacy as a tool for peace, his insistence on working through proper channels, and his adherence to the norms of good manners and civility. Franklin may have suffered from psychological stress during the years of his French mission. Based on published letters and writings of Franklin; 61 notes. 1776-85

2335. Jones, R. V. BENJAMIN FRANKLIN. *Notes and Records of the Royal Soc. of London [Great Britain] 1977 31(2): 201-225.* Reviews the life of Benjamin Franklin (1706-90), including the interplay of his roles of natural philosopher and public servant, especially his relations with England and America in a time of political and technical upheaval. 1706-90

2336. Kerr, Joan Patterson. BENJAMIN FRANKLIN'S YEARS IN LONDON. *Am. Heritage 1976 28(1): 14-27.* Benjamin Franklin spent more than 15 years in London between 1757 and 1775 as an agent for several colonies, trying to prevent a split between the American colonies and Britain. He returned to America on the eve of the Revolution. 9 illus. 1757-75

2337. Lewis, Janette Seaton. "A TURN OF THINKING": THE LONG SHADOW OF THE *SPECTATOR* IN FRANKLIN'S *AUTOBIOGRAPHY. Early Am. Literature 1978-79 13(3): 268-277.* Joseph Addison and Richard Steele's *Spectator* (1711-12) had a continuing influence on Benjamin Franklin, especially on the *Autobiography.* The *Autobiography* resembles the *Spectator* in subject matter, attitude, method, intent, style, and tone. They reflect more than the authors' shared interest in religion, education, the cultivation of practical virtues, and man's use of reason. They are alike in their use of the personae, and their perception of the audience; in both, the tone is light, humor is gentle, and reform is through wit. Primary and secondary sources; illus., 25 notes. 18c

2338. Lopez, Claude-Anne. THE MAN WHO FRIGHTENED FRANKLIN. *Pennsylvania Mag. of Hist. and Biog. 1982 106(4): 515-526.* 1774-91
For abstract see ***Allaire, Peter***

2339. Morgan, David T. A NEW LOOK AT BENJAMIN FRANKLIN AS GEORGIA'S COLONIAL AGENT. *Georgia Hist. Q. 1984 68(2): 221-232.* In 1768, Benjamin Franklin, who was already serving as Pennsylvania's colonial agent in London, was appointed to serve for Georgia as well. He sided with the Georgia lower house and gained the enmity of the upper house and the royal governor. Although he appears to have served Georgia well during 1768-71, he did little for them after that, at least partly because they were delinquent in paying him and because they made his reappointment a political contest. Based on Franklin's papers and Georgia colonial records; 21 notes. 1768-74

2340. Morgan, David T. A MOST UNLIKELY FRIENDSHIP—BENJAMIN FRANKLIN AND GEORGE WHITEFIELD. *Historian 1985 47(2): 208-218.* Given their divergent religious views, Benjamin Franklin and evangelist George Whitefield were unlikely friends. While historians have long noted this friendship, Melvin H. Buxhaum's *Benjamin Franklin and the Zealous Presbyterians* (1975) was the first to examine it in detail. Buxhaum's negative analysis of the friendship is in error. In their 30-year friendship, Franklin and Whitefield admired each other, supported each other, and praised each other's work; their friendship was "deep, abiding, and affectionate." 33 notes. 1740-70

2341. Robbins, Peggy. BENJAMIN FRANKLIN AND HIS SON, A TORY. *Am. Hist. Illus. 1980 15(7): 38-46.* Discusses the relationship between Benjamin Franklin and his illegitimate son, William Franklin (ca 1731-1813), who was appointed royal governor of New Jersey in 1762, focusing on the difficulties in their relationship because of William's increasing Loyalism, and their eventual estrangement. ca 1725-1813

2342. Rodgers, Glen M. BENJAMIN FRANKLIN AND THE UNIVERSALITY OF SCIENCE. *Pennsylvania Mag. of Hist. and Biog. 1961 85(1): 50-69.* Discusses Benjamin Franklin's idealistic conception of the universality of science in the 18th century, focusing on his role in guaranteeing the safe passage of Captain James Cook's scientific expedition through American- and French-controlled waters; and describes his activities in the American Philosophical Society; 1748-84. 1748-84

2343. Sogrin, V. V. BIOGRAFII OTTSOV-OSNOVATELEI SSHA V AMERIKANSKOI ISTORIOGRAFII 1970-KH GODOV [Biographies of the Founding Fathers of the United States in American historiography during the 1970's]. *Novaia i Noveishaia Istoriia [USSR] 1980 (1): 154-163.* 1760-1800
For abstract see ***Adams, Samuel***

2344. Summers, Norma Sharon. "Benjamin Franklin: Printing Entrepreneur." U. of Alabama 1979. 333 pp. *DAI 1980 40(8): 4719-4720-A.* 18c

2345. Whitfield, Stephen J. THREE MASTERS OF IMPRESSION MANAGEMENT: BENJAMIN FRANKLIN, BOOKER T. WASHINGTON, AND MALCOLM X AS AUTOBIOGRAPHERS. *South Atlantic Q. 1978 77(4): 399-418.* Through an examination of the autobiographies of Benjamin Franklin, Booker T. Washington, and Malcolm X, indicates the writers' mastery of impression management which in no small measure appealed to readers who were beguiled by the cognate ideals of individual success and self-transcendence. Erving Goffman has defined impression management as the unusual sensitivity in maintaining the impression that an autobiographer is living up to the many standards by which he and his product(s) are judged. The three autobiographers surveyed are consanguine because they purported to exemplify a common set of moral standards, of which five are examined in detail in each writer's work: industry and frugality, humility, sincerity, cleanliness, and industriousness. Covers 1788-1965. 1788-1965

2346. Williams, John R. THE STRANGE CASE OF DR. FRANKLIN AND MR. WHITEFIELD. *Pennsylvania Mag. of Hist. and Biog. 1978 102(4): 399-421.* Benjamin Franklin, who was not an archetypical deist, and George Whitefield, who was no mere ranter, were sincere friends. Covers 1739-64. Based on published sources and secondary works; 93 notes. 1739-64

2347. Zall, P. M. THE MANUSCRIPT AND EARLY TEXTS OF FRANKLIN'S *AUTOBIOGRAPHY*. *Huntington Lib. Q. 1976 39(4): 375-384.* Benjamin Franklin wrote his *Autobiography* during 1771-90. The manuscript underwent revisions before the first complete edition was published in French in 1791. The history of the various editions is traced and differences noted and analyzed. Primary sources; 11 notes. 1771-90

Franklin, Harvey B.

2348. Franklin, Harvey B. MEMORIES OF A CALIFORNIA RABBI: STOCKTON, SAN JOSE AND LONG BEACH. *Western States Jewish Hist. Q. 1977 9(2): 122-128.* Rabbi Harvey B. Franklin (1889-1976) spent his rabbinical career at Stockton, 1916-18; Oakland, 1918-20; San Jose, 1920-28; and Long Beach, 1928-57. Early in his career he faced the necessity of developing a religious service that satisfied a mixed and mutually antagonistic congregation of Reform, Orthodox, and Conservative members. Relates several anecdotes, some humorous, of his experiences at each Jewish community. 1916-57

Franklin, John Hope

2349. Star, Jack. THE VISIBLE MAN I: ABOVE ALL, A SCHOLAR. *Change 1977 9(2): 27-33.* A brief biography of John Hope Franklin, historian of the American South; demonstrates especially Franklin's views of the black scholar in white-dominated American society, 1930's-70's. 1915-77

Franklin, William

2350. Robbins, Peggy. BENJAMIN FRANKLIN AND HIS SON, A TORY. *Am. Hist. Illus. 1980 15(7): 38-46.* ca 1725-1813
For abstract see ***Franklin, Benjamin***

2351. Skemp, Sheila L. WILLIAM FRANKLIN: HIS FATHER'S SON. *Pennsylvania Magazine of History and Biography 1985 109(2): 145-178.* William Franklin was the son of Benjamin Franklin, but as the royal governor of New Jersey he remained loyal to England. His Loyalist sentiments were consistent with his respect for benevolent authority and with his father's anglophilia. He did not abandon Benjamin, but Benjamin abandoned him. 73 notes. 1750's-70's

Franko, Ivan

2352. Prymak, Thomas M. IVAN FRANKO AND MASS UKRAINIAN EMIGRATION TO CANADA. *Canadian Slavonic Papers [Canada] 1984 26(4): 307-317.* Ivan Franko (1856-1916), perhaps "the best known Ukrainian figure of modern times," was widely acclaimed as a poet, writer, scholar, and political and social activist. One of his greatest concerns was for the oppressed Ukrainians of Austrian Galicia, more than 212,000 of whom emigrated to the Americas during 1890-1910. Along with Professor O. Oleskiv (1860-1903) and others, Franko in his public speeches and writings defended the peasants' right to emigrate and helped redirect the migration pattern from Asiatic Russia and Brazil to North America. Even before his death he became a cult figure among the Ukrainian Canadians through his work in the Galician Emigrant Aid Committee. 30 notes. 1890-1916

Frasch, Herman

2353. Sutton, William Ralph. "Herman Frasch." Louisiana State U. and Agricultural and Mechanical Coll. 1984. 309 pp. *DAI 1985 45(8): 2632-A.* DA8425886 1870's-1912

Fraser, Charles

2354. Severens, Martha R. CHARLES FRASER OF CHARLESTON. *Mag. Antiques 1983 123(3): 606-611.* Charles Fraser was renowned in Charleston, South Carolina, as an orator, lawyer, author, and painter; during 1818-40 he was preoccupied with painting miniature watercolor portraits on ivory of the townspeople; covers his careers from about 1800 to the 1850's. 1800-50's

Fraser, Douglas

2355. Fraser, Douglas; Serrin, William, interviewer. WORKING FOR THE UNION: AN INTERVIEW WITH DOUGLAS A. FRASER. *American Heritage 1985 36(2): 56-64.* Born in Scotland in 1916, Douglas Fraser participated in the founding of the United Automobile Workers of America, and rose steadily through its ranks until he became the union's president in 1977. In this interview, Fraser talked of working in the industry before the union, of his own rise to power, and of his relationship with other leaders. He also spoke of current union problems. 4 photos, illus. 1930-84

Frazar, Thomas

2356. Frazar, Thomas. PIONEERS FROM NEW ENGLAND. *Oregon Hist. Q. 1982 83(1): 37-52.* Thomas Frazar (1813-90) came to Oregon in 1851 and pursued several trades including that of merchant in Jacksonville when it was a mining town. Conditions in other places in Oregon in the early 1850's are also described in this reminiscence written in the 1880's. 6 illus., 16 notes. 1851-53

Frazee, John

2357. Hyman, Linda. "From Artisan to Artist: John Frazee and the Politics of Culture in Antebellum America." City U. of New York 1978. 298 pp. *DAI 1978 39(4): 2484-A.* 1820's-52

Frazer, Mary

2358. Parry, Edward Owen. MARY FRAZER: HEROINE OF THE AMERICAN REVOLUTION. *Daughters of the Am. Revolution Mag. 1979 113(7): 766-775.* Briefly outlines the American Revolution, detailing the life of Mary Frazer (1745-1830), who was active defending her home at Thornsbury, Pennsylvania; she crossed British lines to help American prisoners of war in Philadelphia and brought supplies to the Army during the winter at Valley Forge. Traces the military involvement of her husband, Persifor Frazer, in the war. 1776

Frazier, E. Franklin

2359. Vlasek, Dale R. ECONOMICS AND INTEGRATION: THE ECONOMIC THOUGHT OF E. FRANKLIN FRAZIER. *Am. Studies [Lawrence, KS] 1979 20(2): 23-40.* Traces E. Franklin Frazier's economic thought through three stages. In the 1920's, he supported cooperative enterprises to solve black economic problems, but during the 1930's he urged a union of black and white workers to fight capitalism. By the 1940's, Frazier looked to the federal government to provide employment opportunities and social services. Describes Frazier's efforts to link economic development, cultural acquisition, and racial integration, particularly in cities. 35 notes. 1920-50

Fred, Edwin Broun

2360. —. A TRADITION OF LEADERSHIP AT THE UNIVERSITY OF WISCONSIN. *Change 1981 13(4): 34-43.*

Schoenfeld, Clarence A. EDWIN BROUN FRED (1945-1958): A TIME OF PLENTY, *pp. 34, 40-43.* Edwin Broun Fred served at the University of Wisconsin since 1913 as assistant, associate and full professor, dean of the Graduate School, dean of the College of Agriculture, president, and president emeritus, all during a time of plenty for higher education.

Browne, Jeff. ROBERT M. O'NEIL (1980-): A TIME OF RETRENCHMENT, *pp. 35-39.* Discusses the background of Harvard-educated lawyer Robert O'Neil, his tenure as president of the University of Wisconsin since 1980, and his plans for the institution. 1913-81

Frederick, John T.

2361. Reigelman, Milton M. JOHN T. FREDERICK. *Palimpsest 1978 59(2): 58-65.* John T. Frederick's lengthy career as teacher, novelist, critic, and editor symbolized the finest aspects of the Iowa and Midwestern character. Soft-spoken and unpretentious, Frederick sought to keep the Midwest from being shortchanged by the influence which New York City and other Eastern centers wielded over the publishing market. His journal, *The Midland,* founded in 1915, was the mouthpiece for a generation of Iowa and Midwestern writers. By the 1920's, the magazine was known and respected nationwide. Frederick's influence continued until his death in 1975. 7 photos. 1915-75

Free, Mickey (Felix Ward)

2362. Radbourne, Allan. THE NAMING OF MICKEY FREE. *J. of Arizona Hist. 1976 17(3): 341-346.* Twelve-year-old Felix Ward was abducted by the White Mountain Apache in an 1861 raid on an Arizona ranch. He later attained renown as Mickey Free, interpreter and Apache Scout. Gives a more probable explanation of how Felix Ward came to be called Mickey Free than ones conjectured by previous writers. Illus., 13 notes. 1861-80's

Freehafer, Edward G.

2363. Chapman, Gilbert W. EDWARD G. FREEHAFER: AN APPRECIATION. *Bull. of the New York Public Lib. 1970 74(10): 625-628.* Traces the career of Edward G. Freehafer with the New York Public Library from 1932, when he first applied for a job and was offered one in the Main Reading Room, to his retirement in 1970 after serving as Director of the library for 16 years. 1932-70

Freeman, Derek

2364. Wendt, Albert. MARGARET MEADS SAMOA—EINE ANKLAGE [Margaret Mead's Samoa—an accusation]. *Frankfurter Hefte [West Germany] 1983 38(9): 45-53.* The Samoan author comments on Margaret Mead's depiction of Samoa, exploring reasons for the ethnocentric portrait of other cultures for the sake of one's own dreams; reports on the research and life of Mead critic Derek Freeman. 1925-83

Freeman, Legh Richmond

2365. Heuterman, Thomas H. RACISM IN FRONTIER JOURNALISM: A CASE STUDY. *J. of the West 1980 19(2): 46-50.* Legh Richmond Freeman (1842-1915) published or wrote for the *Frontier Index* along the construction route of the Union Pacific Railroad between 1866 and 1868. His belief in the inherent inferiority of blacks, Chinese, and Indians was shared by many of his readers. But he narrowly escaped with his life when rioters, incensed over his attacks on Ulysses S. Grant, sacked his office. Based on the Legh Freeman service file, National Archives and Records Service, and the *Frontier Index;* 4 photos, 29 notes. 1866-68

Freeman, Mary E. Wilkins

2366. Kendrick, Brent L. "The Infant Sphinx: Collected Letters of Mary E. Wilkins Freeman (September 1875 - December 1901)." (Vol. 1-2) U. of South Carolina 1981. 874 pp. *DAI 1982 42(12): 5122-A.* DA8212247 1875-1901

Freer, Charles Lang

2367. Clark, Nicholas. CHARLES LANG FREER: AN AMERICAN AESTHETE IN THE GILDED ERA. *Am. Art J. 1979 11(4): 54-68.* Charles Lang Freer (1856-1919) made his fortune on railroad cars and spent much of it on Oriental art and works by James McNeill Whistler (1834-1903), all of which he donated to the United States in 1906. However, his large collection of late 19th century American paintings by Dwight Tryon (1849-1925), Thomas Dewing (1851-1938), and Abbott Thayer (1849-1921) is also extremely important. Freer collected these works which were outside the mainstream of contemporary art, befriended and supported the artists, and showed their works publicly. Freer at first developed an elitist attitude toward this subtle art, but was later convinced of the value of educating the public and thus donated his collection to the nation. Based on Freer Papers in Freer Gallery Library; 14 illus., 58 notes. 1870's-1919

2368. Tomlinson, Helen Nebeker. "Charles Lang Freer, Pioneer Collector of Oriental Art." Case Western Reserve U. 1979. 768 pp. *DAI 1980 41(1): 372-373-A.* DA8013656 1900-19

Freeze, Mary Ann Burnham

2369. Rooker, Nancy Briggs. "Mary Ann Burnham Freeze: Utah Evangelist." U. of Utah 1982. 459 pp. *DAI 1982 43(4): 974-A.* DA8220784 19c

Frégault, Guy

2370. Falardeau, Jean-Charles. L'OEUVRE DE GUY FRÉGAULT [The works of Guy Frégault]. *Rev. d'Hist. de l'Amérique Française [Canada] 1981 35(1): 55-68.* An appreciation of Frégault and of his works on 18th-century Quebec history. 41 notes. 18c

2371. Trudel, Marcel. NÉCROLOGIE: GUY FRÉGAULT 1918-1977 [Obituary: Guy Frégault; 1918-77]. *Hist. Papers [Canada] 1978 248-251.* Historian, teacher, and Canadian government official Guy Frégault contributed to the *Revue d'histoire de l'Amérique française,* was a militant supporter of *l'Action nationale,* and published several important works on Canadian history. 1930's-77

Frémont, Jessie Benton

2372. Herr, Pamela. THE LIFE OF JESSIE BENTON FRÉMONT. *Am. West 1979 16(2): 4-13, 59-63.* Jessie Anne Benton (1824-1902) was educated and influenced by the political, cultural, and westward-dreaming family life of Senator Thomas Hart Benton in Washington and in their Missouri home. Her marriage to John Charles Frémont made her the "passionate connecting link" between the ambitious young army explorer and his powerful senator father-in-law. Having served as her father's secretary and assistant, Jessie served her husband in the same capacity through his stormy military and political career. She "shared in her husband's life more fully than most women, learning to accept the limitations that both her sex and fate enforced." 6 illus., bibliographic note. 1841-1902

2373. Spence, Mary. JESSIE BENTON FREMONT: FIRST LADY OF ARIZONA. *J. of Arizona Hist. 1983 24(1): 55-72.* Narrates the role of Jessie Benton Fremont in the career of John C. Frémont, particularly during his tenure as governor of Arizona in 1878-81. Describes her efforts to maintain her family's finances. 3 photos, 32 notes. 1878-81

Frémont, John C.

2374. Allin, Lawrence C. FOUR ENGINEERS ON THE MISSOURI: LONG, FREMONT, HUMPHREYS, AND WARREN. *Nebraska Hist. 1984 65(1): 58-83.* Recounts the efforts of explorers Stephen H. Long, John C. Frémont, Andrew A. Humphreys, and Gouverneur K. Warren in mapping and describing the Missouri River basin. 2 illus., 86 notes. 1817-57

2375. Rolle, Andrew. EXPLORING AN EXPLORER: PSYCHOHISTORY AND JOHN CHARLES FREMONT. *Pacific Hist. Rev. 1982 51(2): 135-163.* Reviews key episodes in John Charles Frémont's life and then attempts various alternative psychohistorical analyses of his behavioral patterns. Examines six instances of rash and opportunist judgments, including the mid-winter crossing of the Sierra Nevada into California only two years before the Donner party. The psychoanalysis suggests that Frémont isolated himself from powerful feelings of sorrow over the loss of his father and his own illegitimacy, mocked authority, needed constant reinforcement, and was an emotional adolescent. Based on correspondence in the Fields Collection, Huntington Library; 56 notes. 1810-90

2376. Spence, Mary. JESSIE BENTON FREMONT: FIRST LADY OF ARIZONA. *J. of Arizona Hist. 1983 24(1): 55-72.* 1878-81
*For abstract see **Fremont, Jessie Benton***

Fremstad, Anna Olivia

2377. Lindi, Elenita. OLIVE FREMSTAD. *Am. Scandinavian Rev. 1960 48(4): 363-368.* Born in Stockholm and reared in Minneapolis, Minnesota, Anna Olivia Fremstad (1870-1951) became a noted opera star; she sang in Germany, Austria, France, Italy, and Great Britain, and finally at New York City's Metropolitan Opera House; 1895-1917. 1895-1917

French, Alice

2378. Tigges, Sandra Ann Healey. "Alice French: A Noble Anachronism." U. of Iowa 1981. 269 pp. *DAI 1981 42(5): 2134-A.* DA8123370 1870-1934

French, Daniel Chester

2379. Holzer, Harold. AN AMERICAN SCULPTOR: DANIEL CHESTER FRENCH. *Am. Art and Antiques 1979 2(5): 94-101.* Traces the life of Daniel Chester French (1850-1931) and his works, including the *Minute Man.* 1867-1932

2380. Lee, Doris. THE STUDIO OF DANIEL CHESTER FRENCH. *Horizon 1980 23(4): 54-59.* Discusses the work of Daniel Chester French, sculptor perhaps most famous for his Abraham Lincoln statue inside the Lincoln Memorial, and describes Chesterwood, near Stockbridge, Massachusetts, French's studio and summer home, 1898-1931. 1898-1931

2381. Price, Willadene. DANIEL CHESTER FRENCH: THE ARTIST AS HISTORIAN. *Social Educ. 1982 46(1): 60-65.* Discusses the life and work of sculptor Daniel Chester French, creator of such works as the Lincoln Memorial and the Minute Man statue in Concord, Massachusetts; 1872-1931. 1872-1931

2382. Richman, Michael. THE LONG LABOR OF MAKING NATION'S FAVORITE STATUE. *Smithsonian 1977 7(11): 54-61.* Sketches the life of sculptor Daniel Chester French (1850-1931) and summarizes the history of the statue of Abraham Lincoln in the Lincoln Memorial. The Lincoln Memorial Commission was established in 1911 and Henry Bacon was chosen as architect. In 1914, the Commission appointed French as sculptor for the Lincoln statue. Traces the development of the statue from its model form through its casting and carving and the congressional appropriations for a lighting system in September 1926. Secondary sources; 8 illus. 1911-26

2383. Richman, Michael. DANIEL CHESTER FRENCH AND HENRY BACON: PUBLIC SCULPTURE IN COLLABORATION, 1897-1908. *Am. Art J. 1980 12(3): 46-64.* 1897-1908
*For abstract see **Bacon, Henry***

French, Leigh Hill

2384. French, Leigh Hill. NOME NUGGETS. *Alaska J. 1983 13(4): 33-63.* Presents a personal account of life in Nome, Alaska, during the 1900 gold rush by Leigh Hill French, one of the participants. Seeking his fortune, French shipped a mining machine to Nome to dig gold from the seabed off the coast of Nome. This venture ended in disaster. Despite some inaccuracies and plagiarism, French's is one of the best accounts of the Alaskan gold rush. Primary sources; 28 illus., map. 1900-06

Frey, John Philip

2385. Mortimer, Louis Read, Jr. "John Philip Frey, Spokesman for Skilled American Labor." George Washington U. 1982. 336 pp. *DAI 1983 43(9): 3090-A.* DA8301031 1900-27

Frey, Loraine Johnson

2386. Frey, Loraine Johnson. GROWING UP DURING HARD TIMES. *Rendezvous 1984 20(1): 48-54.* The author describes growing up poor in rural Idaho during the Great Depression. Her family was forced to move and had to rent a farm near Pocatello after their family farm was lost by foreclosure in 1931. Despite severe financial problems, she and her family, through hard work, cooperation, and courage, managed to survive as well as help her earn a teaching certificate at the University of Idaho, Southern Branch. 3 photos. 1931-40

Frey, Sigmund

2387. Axe, Ruth Frey. SIGMUND FREY: LOS ANGELES JEWRY'S FIRST PROFESSIONAL SOCIAL WORKER. *Western States Jewish Hist. Q. 1976 8(4): 312-325.* Rabbi Sigmund Frey (1852-1930) came to Los Angeles to be the superintendent for the Jewish Orphan's Home then located at Mission and Macy streets. In 1910 a fire destroyed the home and in November 1912 the new Jewish Orphan's Home was dedicated in Huntington Park, California. Rabbi Frey became a well known author, scholar, journalist, bibliophile, and teacher. In 1921, he resigned as superintendent. Before his death in Los Angeles Rabbi Frey and his wife Hermine traveled several times to Europe. Primary and secondary sources; 4 photos, 5 notes. 1870's-1930

Fricot, Desiré

2388. Lamson, Berenice. FRICOT: A MAN WITH A VISION. *Pacific Hist. 1980 24(3): 316-324.* Desiré Fricot (1868-1940) was born of American parents in Paris, France. He was well-educated in Europe and in the United States and became a mining engineer. He prospected in California. After his marriage in 1898 he built a fine mansion (Fricot City) in Calaveras County. On his ranch, he grew fruit and vegetables and kept cattle, hogs, and poultry. When the mansion burned, he rebuilt in a grander style. Fricot was known as the father of Boy Scout work in the district. In 1936 he purchased the American Hotel in San Andreas, remodeled it, and turned it into an historical museum and library. Fricot was active in civic affairs and was instrumental in having the Calaveras Grove of Big Trees incorporated into the State Park System. In 1943, after the death of Fricot and his wife, the State leased the estate for the California Youth Authority. In 1970 the CYA closed it. Since 1976, controversy over its sale has clouded the future of Fricot Ranch. Based on local newspaper accounts; photo, 16 notes, biblio. 1898-1979

Friedan, Betty

2389. Hodges, Glenda Faye. "Betty Friedan's Role as Reformer in the Women's Liberation Movement, 1960-1970." Bowling Green State U. 1980. 256 pp. *DAI 1980 41(4): 1279-1280-A.* DA8022840 1960-70

Friedman, Norman

2390. Friedman, Norman. KNOWING AND REMEMBERING CUMMINGS. *Harvard Lib. Bull. 1981 29(2): 117-134.* 1940-69
*For abstract see **Cummings, E. E.***

Friedman, William Sterne

2391. Hornbein, Marjorie. DENVER'S RABBI WILLIAM S. FRIEDMAN: HIS IDEAS AND INFLUENCE. *Western States Jewish Hist. Q. 1981 13(2): 142-154.* Rabbi William Sterne Friedman (1868-1944), a conservative and an outspoken anti-Zionist, was sometimes accused of denying the ethnicity of Jews and of promoting their assimilation. On the contrary, he believed in a strong Jewish identity and adherence to Judaism. At the same time he preached the duty of patriotism for the American Jew, who should be an American first. Based on newspaper articles and the William S. Friedman Scrapbook, Denver Public Library; 43 notes. 1889-1938

Fries, Christina "Kena"

2392. Yothers, Jean and Wehr, Paul W., ed. DIARY OF KENA FRIES. *Florida Hist. Q. 1984 62(3): 339-352.* Presents the diary of Christina "Kena" Fries, which portrays the daily life of a Swedish immigrant in central Florida. 1883-1937

Friesen, Gordon

2393. Teichroew, Allan. GORDON FRIESEN: WRITER, RADICAL AND EX-MENNONITE. *Mennonite Life 1983 38(2): 4-17.* Gordon Friesen and his wife Agnes "Sis" Cunningham have been involved in radical causes all their lives. Cunningham was a member of the Almanac Singers (which included Pete Seeger and Woody Guthrie) and a labor and Communist Party organizer. Friesen has been an organizer and writer. Both were blacklisted in the early 1940's, recovering in part by editing and publishing *Broadside,* the topical song magazine. Friesen wrote the "first Mennonite novel" *Flamethrowers,* a very negative picture of life among Mennonites. While rejecting the church by the 1930's, Friesen acknowledges that his upbringing influenced him to become a radical. Based on an interview with Friesen and Cunningham, their writings and secondary works; 2 illus., 5 photos, 45 notes. 1930-82

Frietschie, Barbara

2394. Cole, Adelaide. OF DAME BARBARA AND HER LEGEND. *Indiana Soc. Studies Q. 1984 37(1): 54-57.* Reviews the life and heroism of Barbara Frietschie in Frederick, Maryland, a border town of divided sympathies during the Civil War. 1766-1862

Frisch, Otto R.

2395. Frisch, Otto R. "SOMEBODY TURNED THE SUN ON WITH A SWITCH." *Sci. and Public Affairs 1974 30(4): 12-18.* The author, a Danish physicist, discusses his career in nuclear physics and the construction of the first atomic bomb at Alamogordo, New Mexico, in 1945. 1945

Friske, Leo J.

2396. Friske, Leo J. LIFE IN A COLD WATER FLAT. *Milwaukee History 1984 7(4): 129-132.* A Wisconsin native remembers the uncomfortable years he spent as a child living with his family in a Milwaukee cold water flat—a residence with cold water only, and a sink rather than a pump. 1927-44

Frissell, Hollis B.

2397. Hunter, Wilma King. "Coming of Age: Hollis B. Frissell and the Emergence of Hampton Institute, 1893-1917." Indiana U. 1982. 357 pp. *DAI 1983 43(11): 3677-A.* DA8307980 1893-1917

Fritz, Jean Guttery

2398. Hostetler, Elizabeth Ann Rumer. "Jean Fritz: A Critical Biography." U. of Toledo 1981. 418 pp. *DAI 1983 43(8): 2667-A.* DA8229783 1915-81

Froebel, Friedrich

2399. Kaufman, Edgar, Jr. FRANK LLOYD WRIGHT'S MEMENTOS OF CHILDHOOD. *J. of the Soc. of Architectural Hist. 1982 41(3): 232-237.* 1870's-80's
*For abstract see **Wright, Frank Lloyd***

Frohmiller, Anastasia

2400. Jones, Kay F. ANA FROHMILLER: WATCHDOG OF THE ARIZONA TREASURY. *Journal of Arizona History 1984 25(4): 349-368.* Traces the public career of Anastasia Frohmiller who served as Arizona's auditor during 1927-50. Her zeal in the public's behalf made her quite popular, and she was elected auditor 12 times. In 1950 she was narrowly defeated for the governorship and moved to a new career in the savings and loan industry. After her 1971 death she was inducted into the Arizona Hall of Fame. Photo, 100 notes. 1922-71

Fromm-Reichmann, Frieda

2401. Bruch, Hilde. PERSONAL REMINISCENCES OF FRIEDA FROMM-REICHMANN. *Psychiatry 1982 45(2): 98-104.* Brief biography of noted psychotherapist Frieda Fromm-Reichmann (1889-1957), focusing on the author's friendship with her beginning in 1936 after Fromm-Reichmann had been in the United States for one year, and lasting until her death in 1957. 1936-57 -Reichmann

2402. Stanton, Alfred H. FRIEDA FROMM-REICHMANN, MD: HER IMPACT ON AMERICAN PSYCHIATRY. *Psychiatry 1982 45(2): 121-127.* Discusses Frieda Fromm-Reichmann who was a psychoanalyst in Heidelberg, where she had established a private psychiatric sanitarium with Erich Fromm in the late 1920's; in 1935 she came to America, worked at Chestnut Lodge in Maryland and died in 1957. 1935-57

Fronczak, Francis Eustace

2403. Jones, Martin Joseph. THE FRANCIS E. FRONCZAK COLLECTION. *Niagara Frontier 1978 25(4): 96-99.* Biography of Francis Eustace Fronczak (1874-1955), a Polish American doctor with humanitarian interests, in Buffalo, New York, who wrote, lectured, worked for Polish causes, and was a staunch Democrat throughout his life; describes the contents of the Francis E. Fronczak Collection for local

Polish American studies, at the E. H. Butler Library at the State University College in Buffalo, New York which was dedicated in 1970. 1874-1955

Frost, Arthur Burdett

2404. —. AN ARTIST-SPORTMAN'S PORTFOLIO. *Am. Heritage 1978 29(6): 101-105.* Discusses Arthur Burdett Frost (1851-1928), perhaps the most popular illustrator in America at the turn of the century, and provides a collection of his hunting and fishing paintings. 4 illus. 1870's-1900

Frost, Elinor White

2405. Katz, Sandra Lee. "The Subverted Flower: The Life of Elinor White Frost and Her Influence on the Poetry of Robert Frost." U. of Massachusetts 1983. 294 pp. *DAI 1984 44(10): 3066-A.* DA8401073 1892-1920's

Frost, Robert

2406. Eidson, John Olin. RECOLLECTIONS OF FROST'S MANY VISITS TO GEORGIA. *Georgia Life 1977 4(3): 34-35.* Robert Frost spent the last 30 years of his life annually visiting the University of Georgia to discuss his work and give poetry readings, thus creating a special affinity between himself and the people of Georgia (1935-63). 1935-63

2407. González Martín, Jerónimo P. APROXIMACION A LA POESIA DE ROBERT FROST [An approach to Robert Frost's poetry]. *Cuadernos Hispanoamericanos [Spain] 1983 (394): 101-153.* Discusses the life and works of Robert Frost, highlighting those poems revealing the stylistic and thematic features that made Frost the poet of idyllic New England, meditation, alienation from the literary whirlwind, and continuous struggle to follow one's path. 1910's-63

2408. Hindus, Milton. REMINISCENCES OF ROBERT FROST. *Midstream 1979 25(9): 52-57.* Recounts incidents from the life and career of the American poet, Robert Frost. 20c

2409. Katz, Sandra Lee. "The Subverted Flower: The Life of Elinor White Frost and Her Influence on the Poetry of Robert Frost." U. of Massachusetts 1983. 294 pp. *DAI 1984 44(10): 3066-A.* DA8401073 1892-1920's

2410. Pritchard, William H. DEEPER INTO LIFE: ROBERT FROST'S LAST YEARS. *Am. Scholar 1984 53(4): 522-532.* Presents a literary biography of poet Robert Frost's last two decades and discusses some of his poems. 1943-63

2411. Rood, Karen Lane. "Robert Frost before England: The Development of a Modern Poet, 1890-1912." U. of South Carolina 1979. 404 pp. *DAI 1979 40(3): 1473-A.* 1890-1912

Fruehauf, Erich

2412. Fruehauf, Erich. FIFTY YEARS ON A ONE-FAMILY FARM IN CENTRAL KANSAS. *Kansas Hist. 1979 2(3): 166-195, (4): 252-275.* Part I. The author arrived in Kansas in 1926. Postwar Germany had had no use for a native of the old Austrian empire, even one with a doctor's degree in agriculture from Leipzig. Covers the closing years of horsepower and carries the reader into the tractor era. Records not only observations of a typical farm in the wheat-feed, grain-cattle economy of Stafford County, where his farm is located, but also information about the entire region and the daily life of natives and immigrants to Kansas. Part II. Fruehauf describes the Great Depression, the New Deal, and World War II, always relating his family's experience to the general picture of agricultural growth. Moving beyond modern oil well development and silage crops, Fruehauf speculates on the country's technological future. Illus. 1926-76

Fry, William Henry

2413. Hart, Columba. THE RELIGIOUS BENT OF WILLIAM HENRY FRY, 1813-64. *Am. Benedictine Rev. 1976 27(4): 400-426.* Studies William Henry Fry, a music critic and composer. Analyzes Fry's life and work, particularly his musical compositions, to determine the extent to which religion influenced the shape of his work. Based on original and secondary sources; 82 notes. 1813-64

Frye, Northrop

2414. Denham, Robert D. AN ANATOMY OF FRYE'S INFLUENCE. *Am. Rev. of Can. Studies 1984 14(1): 1-19.* For over 50 years, Canada's premier literary critic Northrop Frye has forged an international reputation based on his broad concept of criticism, his commitment to the doctrine of the impersonality of the critic, and a prose style characterized by elegance, wit, and a sense of aesthetic form. Frye has also become a national public figure whose influence has spread into such fields as politics, history, education, communications, and social theory. Includes a bibliography of works written and edited by Frye. Based on works by Northrop Frye and criticisms of those works; 37 notes, biblio. 1930's-82

Fuca, Juan de

2415. Tessendorf, K. C. LEYENDA E HISTORIA DE JUAN DE FUCA [Legend and history of Juan de Fuca]. *Américas (Organization of Am. States) 1971 23(9): 25-32.* Juan de Fuca, a navigator and commercial trader of Greek origin, sailed from Spain for the New World, and as early as 1592 explored the Pacific coast of North America as far north as Vancouver Island and Puget Sound in search of a Northwest Passage. 1592

Fuchs, Daniel

2416. Michelson, Paul Frederick. "Daniel Fuchs: Chronicler of Williamsburg." Washington State U. 1981. 290 pp. *DAI 1981 42(5): 2189-A.* 8122429 1934-37

Fulbright, J. William

2417. Bullert, Gary Byron and Casey, Francis Michael. THE FOREIGN POLICY OF SENATOR WILLIAM J. FULBRIGHT: FROM COLD WAR WARRIOR TO NEO-ISOLATIONIST. *J. of Soc., Pol., and Econ. Studies 1983 8(4): 449-469.* Traces three stages in the career of Senator Fulbright: 1943-46, utopian-internationalist; 1946-64, realist-collective security advocate; and 1964-83, moralist-isolationist. 1943-83

2418. Gunn, Herb. THE CONTINUING FRIENDSHIP OF JAMES WILLIAM FULBRIGHT AND RONALD BUCHANAN MCCALLUM. *South Atlantic Quarterly 1984 83(4): 416-433.* J. William Fulbright, former congressman from Arkansas and later chairman of the Senate's Foreign Relations Committee, studied under his young tutor, Ronald Buchanan McCallum, at Pembroke College, Oxford, during

the years 1925-28. Since McCallum was Fulbright's senior by only seven years, the men became close friends. Between 1945 and 1970, they exchanged over 100 letters, the contents of which form an interesting narrative and suggest that over the course of their friendship the roles of tutor and pupil coalesced. Both became strong advocates of the role of the UN. Fulbright was a strong critic of the Eisenhower administration's handling of the Suez crisis. McCallum felt that Eden gravely misunderstood Nasser and the Egyptians. Fulbright opposed the US position in Vietnam and beckoned McCallum to follow him. Although McCallum supported many facets of Fulbright's internationalism, he failed to apply them specifically to the war in Vietnam. Based on the Fulbright Papers, University of Arkansas; 63 notes.
1925-70

2419. Smith, Harold T. J. WILLIAM FULBRIGHT AND THE ARKANSAS 1974 SENATORIAL ELECTION. *Arkansas Historical Quarterly 1985 44(2): 103-117.* Briefly discusses the political career of Arkansas Senator J. William Fulbright, and details his unsuccessful 1974 reelection campaign against Governor Dale Bumpers. Based on interviews, correspondence, and other primary sources; 73 notes.
1943-74

Fuller, George

2420. Burns, Sarah. A STUDY OF THE LIFE AND POETIC VISION OF GEORGE FULLER (1822-1884). *Am. Art J. 1981 13(4): 11-37.* George Fuller was a transitional figure in American art between the older, romantic tradition of the mid-19th century and the refined aestheticism of the late century. Like many others, he was forced to become an itinerant painter to earn a living and traveled to Mobile and Atlanta, among other cities. Over the years the linearity and tightness of form of his early works gave way to a looser, more atmospheric rendering. His last works reflected an assimilation of American and French tradition toward a dreamy quality of personal sentiment; he was looked upon as the antithesis of realism. Based on the Fuller-Higginson Papers in the Memorial Libraries at Deerfield, Massachusetts; 27 illus., photo, 67 notes. 1842-84

Fuller, Henry Blake

2421. Szuberla, Guy. HENRY BLAKE FULLER AND THE "NEW IMMIGRANT." *Am. Literature 1981 53(2): 246-265.* Analyzes the changing attitudes of novelist and writer Henry Blake Fuller regarding the impact of the New Immigrants on American society after 1890. For most of his professional career, Fuller supported the Progressive ideal that the "hordes" of immigrants from Southern and Eastern Europe might be assimilated into American society. By the mid 1920's, however, Fuller viewed these immigrants as a danger that threatened to destroy the Anglo-Saxon world of his past. Based on novels, poems, and essays by Henry Blake Fuller; 34 notes. 1893-1924

Fuller, Lillian Beck

2422. Hawkins, Joellen Beck W., ed. PUBLIC HEALTH NURSING IN CHICAGO IN THE 1920S: THE REMINISCENCES OF LILLIAN BECK FULLER, R.N. *J. of the Illinois State Hist. Soc. 1983 76(3): 195-204.* Lillian Beck Fuller studied and practiced nursing in Chicago. Presents reminiscences of her studies at Presbyterian Hospital and her service with the Visiting Nurse Association in the Hull-House, Little Italy, Sleepy Valley, and Jewish districts, and at the Home for Destitute Crippled Children. She was the first nurse with the Visiting Nurse Association permitted to retain her position after marriage. She left Chicago when her husband, a doctor, began advanced studies in Philadelphia. Upon his later hospitalization, Fuller returned to Minnesota, where she served as a school and camp nurse. 5 illus.
1923-29

Fuller, Margaret

2423. Follet, Joyce Clark. MARGARET FULLER IN EUROPE, 1846-1850. *Hist. Today [Great Britain] 1979 29(8): 506-515.* On a tour of Europe, 1846-50, Margaret Fuller encountered intellectuals, admired the socialist and Fourierist spirit among the revolutionaries, and was present in Rome when the French attacked that city in 1849.
1846-50

2424. Hlus, Carolyn. MARGARET FULLER, TRANSCENDENTALIST: A RE-ASSESSMENT. *Canadian Review of American Studies [Canada] 1985 16(1): 1-13.* Historical consensus accords American journalist and feminist Margaret Fuller (1810-50) a second-rate place in the transcendentalist movement. Nonetheless, her contemporaries judged her a major figure in Boston and New York intellectual circles from 1836 to 1844, and she actually became a prominent transcendentalist. Her most important contribution to the movement was her use of transcendentalist theories to explain the natural rights of women. Her most influential writing was *Women in the Nineteenth Century* (1845). Based on Fuller's writings, writings of her transcendentalist contemporaries, and secondary historical sources; 22 notes.
1836-50

2425. Hudspeth, Robert N. A CALENDAR OF THE LETTERS OF MARGARET FULLER. *Studies in the Am. Renaissance 1977: 49-143.* A comprehensive annotated list of all the extant letters written by Margaret Fuller (1810-50), arranged chronologically. The date, place, recipient, and length of each letter are described as are the various locations. The major collections of Fuller letters are briefly described. Based on memoirs, journals, and notebooks of Fuller's contemporaries as well as the collections in several major libraries; 1,107 items, biblio., recipient index, location index. 1817-50

2426. McAllister, Marie Maguire. "The Educational Experience of Margaret Fuller." Boston Coll. 1984. 197 pp. *DAI 1984 45(3): 769-A.* DA8405182 1830's-50

2427. Russell, Roberta Joy. "Margaret Fuller: The Growth of a Woman Writer." U. of Connecticut 1983. 385 pp. *DAI 1983 44(4): 1088-1089-A.* DA8317725 1830's-40's

2428. Stern, Madeleine B. MARGARET FULLER AND THE PHRENOLOGIST-PUBLISHERS. *Studies in the Am. Renaissance 1980: 229-237.* Explores the relationship between Margaret Fuller, 19th century scholar, feminist, editor, conversationalist, transcendentalist, and intellectual, and phrenologist-publishers Fowlers and Wells. She died in 1850. Among those who paid tribute to her memory was the firm of Fowlers and Wells, which published posthumously her *Memoirs* (1852), its edition of *Literature and Art*, and additional Fuller titles. Based on letters, other primary sources, and journal articles; 24 notes. 1837-76

2429. Szymanski, Karen Ann. "Margaret Fuller: The New York Years." Syracuse U. 1980. 405 pp. *DAI 1980 41(6): 2664-A.* DA8026386 1844-46

2430. vonFrank, Albert J. LIFE AS ART IN AMERICA: THE CASE OF MARGARET FULLER. *Studies in the Am. Renaissance 1981: 1-26.* Traces the development of Margaret Fuller's aesthetic views and personal philosophy, focusing on the impact of her early life in New England on her outlook. From 1810 to 1833 Fuller lived in Cambridge, Massachusetts. She then stayed with her family on a farm in Groton, Connecticut, until 1835, when her principal residence became Boston, and she first became friends with Emerson and other transcendentalists. The cause of Fuller's peculiar response to art and subsequent intellectual and personal eccentricities lies in the cultural poverty and provincialism of the years up to 1846, when she traveled to Europe and finally discovered a continent whose cultural and social consciousness matched her intellectual upbringing and aspirations. Includes numerous extracts from the letters and writings of Emerson, Henry James, and James Russell Lowell and the memoirs of Fuller herself; 64 notes. 1810-50

Fuller, Meta Vaux Warrick

2431. Hoover, Velma J. META VAUX WARRICK FULLER: HER LIFE AND HER ART. *Negro Hist. Bull. 1977 40(2): 678-681.* Evaluates the career of the black sculptor Meta Vaux Warrick Fuller (1877-1968). After study in Philadelphia, she went to Paris where her work was highly acclaimed and attracted the favorable attention of Rodin. Back in the United States she received several important commissions, but her powerful sculpture, depicting the sorrows and sufferings of Negroes, was not generally accepted. She turned to portraiture and religious pieces, withdrew into marriage and family life, and at her death was ignored by the art world. Based on personal acquaintance with the artist; 6 photos. 1900-68

Fuller, O. Anderson

2432. Houser, Steven Dale. "O. Anderson Fuller, the First Black Doctor of Philosophy in Music in America, and His Development of the Music Education Curriculum at Lincoln University." U. of Missouri, Columbia 1982. 151 pp. *DAI 1983 43(12): 3837-A.* DA8310400 1910-74

Fuller, Stella Lawrence

2433. Whear, Nancy V. A WEST VIRGINIA ORIGINAL: STELLA LAWRENCE FULLER, 1883-1981. *J. of the West Virginia Hist. Assoc. 1983 6(1): 11-26.* Discusses the career of social worker Stella Lawrence Fuller, including her work with the Salvation Army during 1916-43, and her administration of the Stella Fuller Settlement in Huntington, West Virginia. 1903-81

Fulton, Maurice Garland

2434. Gibbs, William E. and Castle, Alfred L. MAURICE GARLAND FULTON: HISTORIAN OF NEW MEXICO AND THE SOUTHWEST. *New Mexico Hist. Rev. 1980 55(2): 121-138.* Relates the life and career of Maurice Garland Fulton (1877-1955) from 1922. In 1968, his work on the Lincoln County War was published. Fulton's historical reputation was enhanced by his editing of works on Theodore Roosevelt, Billy the Kid (William Bonney), and Josiah Gregg. As a regional historian Fulton made significant contributions to historical scholarship through his published works, which any serious history student of New Mexico and the Southwest must consult. Based on the Fulton Papers in the Special Collections Library of the University of Arizona, Tucson, Arizona, and other primary sources; 2 illus., 55 notes. 1922-68

Fulton, Robert L.

2435. Richnak, Barbara. ROBERT FULTON AND THE FOUNDING OF THE NEVADA HISTORICAL SOCIETY. *Nevada Hist. Soc. Q. 1984 27(3): 215-223.* Inaugurated by University of Nevada academicians in 1904, the Nevada Historical Society replaced the Social Science Section of the Nevada Academy of Sciences. Robert L. Fulton, the only nonacademic among the historical society's founders, played a stellar role in the organization's affairs. Besides securing support outside university circles and raising funds, he formulated important policies that strengthened the society, and he contributed to its publications until his death in 1920. Based on Nevada Historical Society publications and the privately owned R. L. Fulton Collection of manuscripts; 2 photos, 16 notes. 1904-20

Funcken, Louis

2436. Wahl, James A. FATHER LOUIS FUNCKEN'S CONTRIBUTION TO GERMAN CATHOLICISM IN WATERLOO COUNTY, ONTARIO. *Sessions d'Etude: Soc. Can. d'Hist. de l'Eglise Catholique [Canada] 1983 50(2): 513-531.* Describes Louis Funcken's ministry in the Catholic Church of Waterloo County, Ontario, emphasizing relationships among various ethnic groups in his congregation, especially Germans and Poles. 1864-90

Funston, Frederick C.

2437. Langellier, J. Phillip. GENERAL FREDERICK FUNSTON: KANSAS VOLUNTEER. *Military Hist. of Texas and the Southwest 1980 16(2): 79-106.* Biography of Frederick C. Funston (d. 1917), focusing on his career in the military, including service in Cuba, the Philippines and Mexico. 1890-1917

Furness, Frank

2438. Cook, Anne H.; Snider, Ann L.; and Wolf, Martha L. ON THE TRAIL OF FRANK FURNESS. *Pennsylvania Heritage 1981 7(1): 23-27.* Architect Frank Furness designed homes in High Gothic Revival Style from 1871 through the early 1900's in Chester County, Pennsylvania. ca 1871-1905

Furness, William Henry

2439. Geffen, Elizabeth M. WILLIAM HENRY FURNESS, PHILADELPHIA ANTISLAVERY PREACHER. *Pennsylvania Mag. of Hist. and Biog. 1958 82(3): 259-292.* For 50 years William Henry Furness (d. 1896) was the pastor of the First Unitarian Church of Philadelphia and commanded the greatest respect as antislavery minister among the abolitionists. 1825-96

2440. Hoffmann, R. Joseph. WILLIAM HENRY FURNESS: THE TRANSCENDENTALIST DEFENSE OF THE GOSPELS. *New England Q. 1983 56(2): 238-260.* William Henry Furness, pastor of the First Congregational Unitarian Church of Philadelphia, published in 1836 *Remarks on the Four Gospels,* in which he tried to demonstrate his long-held belief that Christianity was the religion of nature. Examining Furness's thinking and writings in juxtaposition with mainline Boston Unitarians and Harvard scholars such as Andrews Norton indicates his divergence from their theology, especially in the interpretation of miracles. Furness saw no authentic revelation of religious truth that depended for verification on operations outside the natural order or beyond the scope of human reason. He was the most consistent advocate of a transcendentalist remedy to the dissolvent tendencies of German biblical scholarship. 56 notes. 1830-90

Fussler, Herman Howe

2441. Shera, Jesse H. HERMAN HOWE FUSSLER. *Lib. Q. 1983 53(3): 215-253.* Sketches the career of Herman Howe Fussler, who served as librarian for the Manhattan Project and was later director of the University of Chicago Library. 1935-80

G

Gadsden, Christopher

2442. Godbold, E. Stanly. CHRISTOPHER GADSDEN: RADICAL IDEALIST. *Pro. of the South Carolina Hist. Assoc. 1976: 14-23.* Examines the career of Christopher Gadsden from 1757, when he was elected to the South Carolina Commons House of Assembly, to his opposition to mob violence and confiscation of loyalist property in 1783. He was devoted to the principles of liberty, property, home rule, and free trade. "As the rapidly changing circumstances demanded, he challenged the authority of the British Empire, accepted the following of a restless populace and later rejected it, and defended the status quo of the Federalist Era—all to nurture those ideals." Based on documents and published works; 30 notes. 1757-83

Gadwa, William Isaac

2443. Gadwa, William Isaac. AUTOBIOGRAHY 1874-1945. *Oregon Hist. Q. 1979 80(3): 269-287.* Born in Iowa in 1874, the author was taken to Oregon at age three. Gadwa worked at a variety of jobs, finally settling on harnessmaking. Gadwa died of tuberculosis while a patient at the Eastern Oregon State Tuberculosis Hospital. 4 illus., 2 notes. 1874-1945

Gage, Jack R.

2444. Karpan, Kathleen M. A POLITICAL BIOGRAPHY OF JACK R. GAGE. *Ann. of Wyoming 1976 48(2): 167-252.* Traces the Wyoming political career of Jack R. Gage from his election as Superintendent of Public Instruction in 1934 to his unsuccessful bid for the governorship in 1962. A loyal Democrat in a Republican state, Gage left his imprint on politics as Wyoming's Secretary of State, 1959-61, and as Acting Governor from January, 1961 to January, 1963. While serving in the executive position, he inaugurated no major programs but remained consistent in his belief that the legislature should determine such policies. Though a political conservative throughout his career, Gage attracted greater federal revenues while simultaneously pursuing a frugal fiscal program for the state. Success as a writer and lecturer rounded out Gage's career until his death in 1970. Based on primary sources; photo, 2 tables, 307 notes. 1934-70

Gage, Matilda Joslyn

2445. Wagner, Sally Marie Roesch. "That Word is Liberty: A Biography of Matilda Joslyn Gage." U. of California, Santa Cruz 1978. 575 pp. *DAI 1979 39(8): 5109-A.* 1826-59

Gailor, Thomas Frank

2446. Wilson, Charles Reagan. BISHOP THOMAS FRANK GAILOR: CELEBRANT OF SOUTHERN TRADITION. *Tennessee Hist. Q. 1979 38(3): 322-331.* Episcopal Bishop Thomas Frank Gailor (1856-1935) of Tennessee was a great regional rhetorician of the Lost Cause and a southern liberal adamantly opposed to political equality for blacks. His personal childhood wartime experiences, reinforced by his relationship with the University of the South, led Gailor to emphasize the spiritual quality of the Confederacy's patriotism, self-sacrifice, and loyalty as a model for American nationalism. Based on the Thomas F. Gailor Personal Collection, DuPont Library, University of the South, Sewanee, Tennessee; 20 notes. 1856-1935

Galland, Isaac

2447. Cook, Lyndon W. ISAAC GALLAND: MORMON BENEFACTOR. *Brigham Young U. Studies 1979 19(3): 261-284.* Isaac Galland (1791-1858) settled in Iowa and speculated in the Half-Breed Tract in Lee County. He interceded with the territorial government to insure a favorable reception of the Mormons and, in 1839, sold them land and converted to their faith. Joseph Smith instructed him to handle some of the Mormons' land transactions. For unknown reasons, he stopped his land activities for the Mormons and left the faith in the 1840's, but continued to associate with them until his death. Map, 107 notes. 1830's-58

Gallatin, Albert

2448. Burrows, Edwin G., ed. "NOTES ON SETTLING AMERICA": ALBERT GALLATIN, NEW ENGLAND, AND THE AMERICAN REVOLUTION. *New England Quarterly 1985 58(3): 442-453.* Traces Albert Gallatin's immigration in 1780 and unfortunate experiences when he first arrived in the United States, before working with a French investor on a land settlement scheme in the Ohio Valley in 1783. Gallatin had begun the settlement plan in 1780, and worked to consolidate it in the next few years. Reprints the seven-page fragment of Gallatin's notes meant for prospective investors in his plan, which reveal Gallatin's dislike of New England, the "commoners" and "foreign adventurers" remaining in America after the Revolution, and the lack of European culture in the New World. The presence of some "very good men" among the Americans as well as their "enthusiasm for liberty" offered some hope, however, according to Gallatin. Based on fragmentary, untitled documents filed among the Gallatin Papers in the New York Historical Society under "Notes on Settling America"; 13 notes. 1780-83

2449. Carter, William D., III. ALBERT GALLATIN, THE MAN OF PEACE. *Swiss Am. Hist. Soc. Newsletter 1982 18(1): 30-32.* Discusses the roles of Albert Gallatin (1761-1849), Swiss-born American diplomat, in financing the Louisiana Purchase and as head of the American delegation negotiating the end of the War of 1812; at age 86, he protested the admission of Texas into the Union. 1800-46

2450. Hay, Robert P. THE PILLORYING OF ALBERT GALLATIN: THE PUBLIC RESPONSE TO HIS 1824 VICE-PRESIDENTIAL NOMINATION. *Western Pennsylvania Hist. Mag. 1982 65(3): 181-202.* Presents a brief background to the exemplary political career of the Jeffersonian Republican Albert Gallatin. Notes his humiliating experience as the vice-presidential nominee in 1824 on the ticket with William

H. Crawford; Gallatin faced public protest and ridicule after tirelessly serving his adopted country for nearly 40 years, resulting in his withdrawal from the race. 1780's-1824

2451. Kehl, James A. ALBERT GALLATIN: MAN OF MODERATION. *Western Pennsylvania Hist. Mag. 1978 61(1): 31-46.* Albert Gallatin (1790's-1813) was involved in Pennsylvania local politics and later served in the federal government. 1790's-1813

2452. Lloyd, William B. ALBERT GALLATIN: AMERICA'S GENEVA CONNECTION. *Swiss Am. Hist. Soc. Newsletter 1982 18(1): 12-29.* Albert Gallatin (1761-1849) was a native of Geneva, Switzerland who came to America in 1780. He became an expert in Indian ethnography, and his influence led to the founding of the American Ethnological Society of New York in 1842. He developed an interest in politics and became Thomas Jefferson's presidential campaign manager. He was secretary of the treasury for 12 years under Jefferson and James Madison, and he headed the American delegation to end the War of 1812. 1780-1849

2453. Schelbert, Leo. SELECTED GALLATIN BIBLIOGRAPHY. *Swiss Am. Hist. Soc. Newsletter 1982 18(1): 52-54.* Lists primary and secondary sources on Albert Gallatin published during the 19th and 20th centuries in America and Europe. 1780-1849

2454. Schelbert, Leo. ALBERT GALLATIN, 1761-1849, A GENEVAN IN THE AMERICAN ENLIGHTENMENT: AN ESSAY IN INTERPRETATION. *Swiss Am. Hist. Soc. Newsletter 1982 18(1): 33-45.* "America's Forgotten Statesman," Albert Gallatin (1761-1849), was not just an American Jeffersonian; he remained a Genevan who felt "at home in the general climate of the American Enlightenment, but [pursued] an independent course that had been charted for him by his Genevan education"; discusses the American Enlightenment and Gallatin's world view, political philosophy, and practice of politics. 1780-1849

Gallaudet, Thomas Hopkins

2455. Fernandes, James John. "The Gate to Heaven: T. H. Gallaudet and the Rhetoric of the Deaf Education Movement." U. of Michigan 1980. 228 pp. *DAI 1980 41(2): 460-A.* 8017260 1815-30

Gallitzin, Demetrius

2456. Kring, Hilda Adam. PRINCE GALLITZIN, THE SAINT OF THE ALLEGHENIES. *Keystone Folklore 1984 3(1): 11-17.* Russian Prince Demetrius Gallitzin (alias Father Augustine Smith) was legendary for his help to the needy of western Pennsylvania as the first Catholic priest ordained in the United States. Gallitzin's memory lives in a Halloween ritual at St. Francis College in Loretto, Pennsylvania. 1799-1840

Gallup, George, Sr.

2457. Cantril, Albert H. IN MEMORIAM: GEORGE HORACE GALLUP, SR., 1901-1984. *Public Opinion Quarterly 1984 48(4): 807-808.* Eulogizes George Horace Gallup, Sr., a pioneer in the field of polling who took it as a serious challenge to improve technical proficiency and establish adequate standards for information disclosure. During his life Gallup advocated such political changes as the abolishment of the electoral college and limits on the number of terms members of Congress could serve. Gallup's ability to dramatize ideas allowed him to have an enormous impact on national politics, particularly through his presidential popularity polls. 1920's-84

Galphin, George

2458. Claussen, Henry C. [GEORGE GALPHIN IN IRELAND AND AMERICA]. *Richmond County Hist. 1981 13(1-2): 13-18.*

GEORGE GALPHIN IN IRELAND, *pp. 13-16.*

GEORGE GALPHIN IN AMERICA, *pp. 17-18.*

Traces George Galphin's origins to Tullamore, County Armagh, Ireland, and attempts to fix other particular of his biography and genealogy through an examination of wills and other official records. 1735-80

2459. Hamilton, Annie B. GEORGE GALPHIN OF SILVER BLUFF. *Richmond County Hist. 1981 13(1-2): 7-12.* George Galphin, one of the most successful fur traders in the colonial period in Georgia, was an atypical frontier businessman in that he was honest and straightforward as well as shrewd; his skill in dealing with the Indians explains much of his success. 1764-80

2460. —. [THE GALPHIN CLAIM AND OTHER GLEANINGS]. *Richmond County Hist. 1981 13(1-2): 39-48.*

—. FURTHER NOTES ON THE HEIRS: THE GALPHIN CLAIM, *pp. 39-46.* Focuses on George Galphin's claim to indemnities for events surrounding the American Revolution, a claim finally made good to his family in 1850.

—. GALPHIN GLEANINGS, *pp. 47-48.* Provides random information about George Galphin's life. 1775-1850

Galt, James and William, Jr.

2461. Herndon, G. Melvin. FROM ORPHANS TO MERCHANTS TO PLANTERS: THE GALT BROTHERS, WILLIAM AND JAMES. *Virginia Cavalcade 1979 29(1): 22-31.* William (1800-51) and James (1805-76) Galt, brothers orphaned in Scotland, arrived in Virginia in the early 19th century and became wealthy and well-known planters and humane slaveholders, and actively supported the Confederacy. 1800-76

2462. Herndon, G. Melvin. FROM SCOTTISH ORPHAN TO VIRGINIA PLANTER: WILLIAM GALT, JR. 1801-1851. *Virginia Mag. of Hist. and Biog. 1979 87(3): 326-343.* Galt, an orphan, was educated in England and brought to America by a wealthy Virginia relative of the same name. From 1817 Galt, Jr., helped his foster father in business, and inherited some of his extensive lands in 1825, which he farmed with sound technique until his death. Galt educated his children, was paternalistic toward his slaves, was a philanthropist, a strong Whig but no office-seeker, and a regular if somewhat eccentric churchgoer. 75 notes. 1801-51

Galt, John

2463. Lucas, Alec, ed. JOHN GALT'S *APOLOGIA PRO VISIONE SUA. Ontario Hist. [Canada] 1984 76(2): 151-183.* After brief introductory remarks, presents nine letters from John Galt to the *Cobourg Star,* 1836-37, written after he had left Upper Canada, including his account of the origins of the Canada Company and his part in it. 1820-37

Galvez, Bernardo de

2464. Fleming, Thomas. BERNARDO DE GALVEZ. *Am. Heritage 1982 33(3): 30-39.* Bernardo de Galvez, governor of the province of Louisiana during the American Revolution, provided much assistance to the US effort in the West. Through his efforts and his cooperation with US agent Oliver Pollock, the Mississippi River became a major supply route. Galvez's forces captured British posts at Manchac, Baton Rouge, Natchez, and Pensacola. After the war, Galvez was made captain general of Cuba and later viceroy of New Spain, where he died suddenly in 1786. 6 illus. 1777-86

Gander, David

2465. Burton, Frances L. A WINDOW FACING NORTH: THE PHOTOGRAPHS OF DAVID GANDER OF GAYS MILLS. *Wisconsin Mag. of Hist. 1983 67(1): 42-49.* Profiles amateur photographer David Gander, who recorded life in his home-town community of Gays Mills, Wisconsin. 13 photos. 1890-1930

Gano, John Henry

2466. —. J. H. GANO, PIONEER PHOTOGRAPHER. *Alberta Hist. [Canada] 1980 28(2): 20-27.* Born in Illinois, John Henry Gano (1873-1947), came to Canada in 1905 and established his photographic studio in Vermilion, Saskatchewan, where he bought a farm primarily for his two brothers. "The secret of his success lies not in his camera, but in his artistic taste and temperament." The subjects of his photographs were prairie farming, railroad construction, sod houses, arrival of new settlers, and the wild life of the region. When Buffalo National Park opened and tourists arrived in significant numbers, he produced a wide selection of postcards which reflected "the natural and human history of the region." From 1914 onward, he moved several times from the Wainwright area to Oregon, to Unity, Saskatchewan, but eventually retired to Red Deer, Alberta. 13 photos. ca 1905-47

Gantt, Daniel

2467. Grimes, Mary Cochran, ed. CHIEF JUSTICE DANIEL GANTT OF THE NEBRASKA STATE SUPREME COURT, LETTERS AND EXCERPTS FROM HIS JOURNAL, 1835-1878. *Nebraska Hist. 1980 61(3): 281-309.* Through letters and journal excerpts, the editor presents a biographical sketch of Daniel Gantt (1814-78). In 1856 Gantt left his native Pennsylvania on his first trip west. After much travel he finally settled in May 1857 in Saratoga, two miles above Omaha. After several tries at public office, in the summer of 1863 Gantt was elected to the Territorial Legislature. The following year he was appointed by President Lincoln as US attorney for the Territory of Nebraska. And in the summer of 1872, Gantt, now a resident of Nebraska City, was nominated and then elected as a Republican to the Nebraska Supreme Court as an Associate Justice. He was reelected in 1875. In 1878 he was named Chief Justice, but served only four months until he died at age 63. Various state and local histories plus diary and letters in the possession of Gantt's grand-daughter. 1835-78

Garard, Ira D.

2468. Garard, Ira D. [GROWING UP IN GREENE COUNTY, PENNSYLVANIA, 1890-1918]. *Western Pennsylvania Hist. Mag. 1980 63(2): 141-154, (3): 231-245.* Part I: GROWING UP IN GREEN COUNTY, PENNSYLVANIA, 1890-1918. The author reminisces about growing up in Green County, Pennsylvania, during 1890-1900, a rural area of 28,000 people that did not rapidly industrialize. Part II: GROWING UP IN GREENE COUNTY, 1890-1918. Recounts the daily and unusual childhood experiences in this rural area of western Pennsylvania. 1890-1918

Garbo, Greta

2469. Erkkila, Betsy. GRETA GARBO: SAILING BEYOND THE FRAME. *Critical Inquiry 1985 11(4): 595-619.* Analyzes the career and creative powers of the Swedish motion picture actress Greta Garbo and asserts that contrary to popular legend she was not passively malleable but rather "refused to remake herself in the image of Hollywood or the American public." 1920's-40's

Gardiner, James

2470. Ward, Norman. OPPOSITIONS AND COALITIONS: JAMES GARDINER AND SASKATCHEWAN PROVINCIAL POLITICS, 1929 TO 1934. *Hist. Papers [Canada] 1979: 147-163.* James Gardiner served twice as Liberal premier of Saskatchewan. To benefit the Liberals politically, he arranged for his administration's resignation in 1929, and subsequently served as the leader of the opposition during the provincial Conservative government of James Thomas Milton Anderson, 1929-34. Gardiner survived Conservative attempts to prove political corruption in Liberal governments since 1905 and turned these fruitless efforts of Anderson against his political foes. Although philosophically opposed to coalition politics, Gardiner did attempt, for the sake of government reform, to cooperate with Progressive Party leader M. J. Coldwell. This uneasy coalition began to disintegrate in 1932, and the Liberals were courted by the Conservatives to join a coalition government. Gardiner resisted these invitations and was rewarded in the 1934 elections with an overwhelming victory that drove the Conservatives out of power for 30 years. Based on personal and government papers in the Saskatchewan Archives and other primary sources; 41 notes. French summary. 1929-34

2471. Ward, Norman. THE POLITICS OF PATRONAGE: JAMES GARDINER AND APPOINTMENTS IN THE WEST, 1935-57. *Can. Hist. Rev. [Canada] 1977 58(3): 294-310.* Studies political patronage in the West during the incumbency of James Garfield Gardiner as Agriculture Minister in the Liberal cabinet of William Lyon Mackenzie King during 1935-57. Although he was concerned about observing proprieties, he ran a "tight ship," and achieved a great advantage for the Liberal Party. Though his authority was not absolute, the actual appointments being subject to approval, his influence was enormous. However, under wartime conditions, when a good deal of nonpartisanship was demanded, the system suffered considerable erosion. 34 notes. 1935-57

Gardiner, Lion (family)

2472. Welch, Richard. LION GARDINER AND HIS ISLAND. *Am. Hist. Illus. 1981 16(2): 40-46.* Traces the history of the Gardiner family and the island (off Long Island, New York) which bears their name and points out that the 340 years the family has possessed the island make them the longest inhabitants of the same piece of real estate in America. 1635-60

Gardner, Edward C.

2473. Taylor, Thomas T. MEMORIAL TO RONALD D. DOUGLAS (1954-1981), EDWARD C. GARDNER (1946-1981), BRUCE A. JENKINS (1953-1981). *J. of California and Great Basin Anthrop. 1981 3(1): 3-6.* 1946-81
For abstract see ***Douglas, Ronald D.***

Gardner, Erle Stanley

2474. Fugate, Francis L. and Fugate, Roberta B. ERLE STANLEY GARDNER. *Am. West 1981 18(3): 34-37.* After reading in law offices, Erle Stanley Gardner passed the California bar examination in 1910 at age 21 and began practice. He soon became well-known because of his knack at defending Chinese clients. He reveled in the courtroom aspect of law, but hated the tedium of preparation for trials. Deciding that only writers could be completely independent, he settled down in 1923 to learn to write. He produced prodigious quantities of traditional and contemporary western stories and adventure, western, and detective yarns set against primarily western backgrounds. Gardner's production of the Perry Mason-Della Street accounts alone numbered 82 novels and three novelettes. 4 illus. 1910-40

Gardner, Isabella Stewart

2475. Thorndike, Joseph J., Jr. MRS. JACK AND HER BACK BAY PALAZZO. *Am. Heritage 1978 29(6): 44-49.* Belle Stewart married Jack Gardner of Boston in 1860. She was a vivacious, wealthy hostess who became a patron and collector of the arts. Her life's achievement was the building of an Italian palace in Boston's Back Bay. Fenway Court, completed in 1902, housed her extensive art collection and is now open to the public. 1860-1920

Gardner, Newport

2476. Millar, John Fitzhugh. PACHELBEL AND GARDNER, TWO EARLY NEWPORT COMPOSERS. *Newport Hist. 1982 55(2): 63-65.* 1737-1803
For abstract see ***Pachelbel, Carl Theodore***

Garfield, James A.

2477. Hatfield, Mark O. JAMES A GARFIELD: A MAN CALLED, A PEOPLE SAVED. *Hayes Hist. J. 1981 3(4): 21-30.* Describes the Christian qualities of character, molded at Hiram College, that made James A. Garfield a great leader. During the 1880 Chicago Republican convention Garfield emerged as the nominee largely because of his speech for Senator John Sherman, which used the imagery of Christ calming the stormy sea. Originally presented at Hiram College, Ohio, in 1981 to commemorate the sesquicentennial of Garfield's birth and the centenary of his presidency. 1850's-81

2478. Nugent, Walter. OUR MARTYRED PRESIDENT. *Rev. in Am. Hist. 1979 7(1): 79-84.* Review article prompted by Allan Peskin's *Garfield: A Biography* (Kent, Ohio: Kent State U. Pr., 1978). 1848-81

2479. Peskin, Allan. JAMES A. GARFIELD, HISTORIAN. *Historian 1981 43(4): 483-492.* President James A. Garfield had broad historical interests and anticipated many of the directions later taken by professional historians. Examines Garfield's early interest in history, his readings and writings on the subject, and his efforts promoting the subject. Garfield was ill at ease with the grand literary histories of the 19th century, and he looked instead for large patterns of historical development, in particular he anticipated both quantification and social history. Primary sources; 43 notes. 1850-80

2480. Peskin, Allan. PRESIDENTS ANONYMOUS. *Timeline 1985 2(5): 22-35.* Elaborates on the life and brief tenure as 20th president of James A. Garfield, and discusses the general public's ignorance about Garfield. 1850's-81

2481. Peskin, Allan. A CENTURY OF GARFIELD. *Hayes Hist. J. 1981 3(4): 9-20.* James A. Garfield attended Hiram College, in Hiram, Ohio, where he became a member of the Disciples of Christ. He became a professor of ancient languages at the college and president of the school when he was still in his mid-20's. He became a general at the age of 30 and a lawyer. He was a member of the House of Representatives for 17 years and became president of the United States. Yet he has been neglected by historians. Theodore Clarke Smith's biography dominated the field for over 50 years despite its inadequacy. Historians tend to view the Gilded Age as one of mediocracy, and Garfield as a fit representative. Edited version of an address presented at Hiram College in 1981 to commemorate the sesquicentennial of Garfield's birth and the centenary of his presidency. 1850-81

2482. Peskin, Allan. FROM LOG CABIN TO OBLIVION. *Am. Hist. Illus. 1976 11(2): 25-34.* Born in a log cabin in 1831 and educated at Western Reserve Eclectic Institute in Hiram, Ohio, and at Williams College in Massachusetts, James A. Garfield became a successful orator, an ordained minister, a college president, a state senator in the Ohio legislature, a major general in the Union Army, a Republican congressman, and a US Senator, before being elected President over the Democrat, Winfield Scott Hancock, in 1880. Garfield was shot by Charles J. Guiteau who believed God chose him to do the act in order "to unite the Republican party, forestall another civil war, and incidentally, publicize Guiteau's latest book." Garfield suffered for 80 days before succumbing. He aroused the nation's sympathy and became "what he had never been in health: a genuine folk hero." A grief-stricken nation contributed over a quarter of a million dollars to erect a monumental crenelated turret to house his remains; but he was soon forgotten, and his entire generation was pushed into "undeserved oblivion." 12 illus. 1831-81

2483. Rushford, Jerry Bryant. "Political Disciple: The Relationship Between James A. Garfield and the Disciples of Christ." U. of California, Santa Barbara 1977. 452 pp. *DAI 1978 38(11): 6777-A.* 1850-80

2484. Sawyer, Robert W. JAMES A. GARFIELD AND THE CLASSICS. *Hayes Hist. J. 1981 3(4): 47-56.* James A. Garfield was first introduced to classical languages on 14 March 1850, as a student at the Geauga Seminary in Chester, Ohio, where he studied Latin and Greek. He became a student at the Western Reserve Eclectic Institute (now Hiram College) in Hiram, where he continued his classical studies. In 1852 he began teaching Latin to entering students at the Eclectic and later took on a Greek class. One of his students was Lucretia Rudolph, who became his wife. He later studied at Williams College, Massachusetts, and upon graduation in 1856 returned to the Eclectic as teacher of "Ancient Languages and Literature." During his political career in the House of Representatives and as president, he maintained a lively interest in the classics, especially Latin, until his death in 1881. Edited version of an address originally presented at

Hiram College in 1981 to commemorate the sesquicentennial of Garfield's birth and the centenary of his presidency. 1850-81

2485. Taylor, John M. ASSASSIN ON TRIAL. *Am. Heritage 1981 32(4): 30-39.* 1881-82
For abstract see ***Guiteau, Charles***

Garland, Augustus Hill

2486. Schlup, Leonard. AUGUSTUS HILL GARLAND: GILDED AGE DEMOCRAT. *Arkansas Hist. Q. 1981 40(4): 338-346.* Prints seven letters (1885-88) to President Grover Cleveland from his attorney general Augustus Hill Garland, Arkansas lawyer and politician. The topics include politics as well as personal matters. Includes a brief survey of Garland's career. Based on the letters and secondary sources; photo, 21 notes. 1885-88

Garner, John Nance

2487. Baulch, J. R. GARNER HELD THE COW WHILE JIM WELLS MILKED HER. *West Texas Hist. Assoc. Year Book 1980 56: 91-99.* Texas Democratic politician John Nance Garner (a congressman after 1902) was an instrument of Texas political boss Jim Wells, 1896-1923. 1896-1923

Garnet, Henry Highland

2488. Pasternak, Martin Burt. "Rise Now and Fly to Arms: The Life of Henry Highland Garnet." U. of Massachusetts 1981. 301 pp. *DAI 1982 42(8): 3722-A.* 8201376 19c

Garrison, William Lloyd

2489. Ledbetter, Patsy S. and Ledbetter, Billy. THE AGITATOR AND THE INTELLECTUALS: WILLIAM LLOYD GARRISON AND THE NEW ENGLAND TRANSCENDENTALISTS. *Mid-America 1980 62(3): 173-183.* William Lloyd Garrison (1805-79) and the Transcendentalists found common ground in their opposition to slavery and their belief that slavery violated a higher spiritual law. Garrison arrived in Boston in June 1830 to launch his antislavery crusade. He met Amos Bronson Alcott and sought support from other Transcendentalists such as William Ellery Channing, Samuel Osgood, and James Freeman Clarke who considered themselves moderates on the slavery question. With the exception of Alcott, early Transcendentalists disliked Garrison's tactics; but as the years passed, most came to respect him as a man who lived out the moral principles they advocated. Based on letters, journals, and family papers of the Transcendentalists, and issues of Garrison's newspaper, *The Liberator.* 1830-60

Garvey, Marcus

2490. McLean, Roderick Michael. "The Theology of Marcus Garvey." St. Louis U. 1980. 200 pp. *DAI 1981 41(7): 3152-A.* 8101267 1905-40

2491. Nowicka, Ewa. THE JAMAICAN ROOTS OF THE GARVEY IDEOLOGY. *Acta Poloniae Hist. [Poland] 1978 37: 129-161.* Marcus Garvey (1887-1940), creator of an international Negro movement, was born and raised in Jamaica and insisted that the races should be separated, not integrated, and that the blacks, who once ruled the world, will eventually return to their own glory. Discusses the Jamaican social background of Garvey's ideas, their application to America, the British influence of his thinking, and his founding of the United Negro Improvement Association Pan-Africanism. 48 notes. 1887-1927

Garvin, Lucius F. C.

2492. Gersuny, Carl. UPHILL BATTLE: LUCIUS F. C. GARVIN'S CRUSADE FOR POLITICAL REFORM. *Rhode Island Hist. 1980 39(2): 57-75.* Lucius F. C. Garvin (1841-1922) was a medical doctor and Rhode Island politician. A tireless but essentially unsuccessful crusader, he tried to bring his state into step with the reform currents of the time. As representative, senator, and governor he embraced such causes as black civil and political rights, public health, the abolition of child labor, and the 10-hour day. Based on unpublished materials in eight repositories, newspapers and periodicals, and published documents; 7 illus., 71 notes. 1876-1922

Garza, Catarino E.

2493. Cuthbertson, Gilbert M. CATARINO E. GARZA AND THE GARZA WAR. *Texana 1974 12(4): 335-348.* Catarino E. Garza (1858-95) was one of the most colorful journalists in Texas in the latter part of the 19th century; now he is virtually forgotten. Born in Mexico, he came to Texas in the 1880's, where he edited *El Libre Pensador* and later *El Comercio Mexicano.* Both of these newspapers violently attacked the Mexican government under President Diaz. In the early 1890's, he became an active revolutionary against Diaz in Mexico, where he was killed in 1895. Based on primary and secondary sources; 36 notes. 1880-95

Garzio, Angelo

2494. Culley, LouAnn Faris. ANGELO GARZIO: LIFE AS THE ULTIMATE ART FORM. *Kansas Q. 1982 14(4): 55-64.* Recounts the career of ceramicist and teacher Angelo Garzio since 1953, focusing on his interest in potterymaking in the developing nations. 1953-82

Gash, Leander Sams

2495. Olsen, Otto H. and McGrew, Ellen Z. PRELUDE TO RECONSTRUCTION: THE CORRESPONDENCE OF STATE SENATOR LEANDER SAMS GASH, 1866-1867, PART II. *North Carolina Hist. Rev. 1983 60(2): 206-238.* Continued from a previous article. After adjournment of the state senate in March 1866, Gash returned to Hendersonville and successfully supported the gubernatorial pardon of Joseph Y. Bryson, a Confederate enthusiast who had assaulted Gash, a Unionist, during the Civil War. However, he unsuccessfully supported the pardon of Daniel Case, who had led a postwar rampage against Confederates. The strong anti-Union sentiments of Governor Jonathan Worth's advisors resulted in opposite outcomes of these parallel cases. Gash, reelected by a small margin, returned to the senate in November 1866. As a former peace man, not a consistent Unionist, Gash opposed the 14th Amendment, but supported anti-Confederate US Senate candidate John Pool. Gash's letters reflect his frustrations with state senate business, travel, absence from home, and living conditions in Raleigh. Based on Gash's, Governor Worth's, and other private papers; local and Raleigh newspapers; published government documents; and country histories; 18 illus., 110 notes. Article to be continued. 1866-67

Gasser, George W. "Doc"

2496. Olsen, Tricia. GEORGE "DOC" GASSER, ALASKA FARMING'S BEST FRIEND. *Alaska J. 1983 13(2): 122-127.* George W. Gasser came from Kansas to Alaska in 1907 to work for the Department of Agriculture. Prints his biography and chronicles his contributions to Alaskan agriculture, especially his role in the development of hardy, cold-resistant strains of grain. 6 photos. 1907-55

Gates, Arthur

2497. Vance, Ellen Ruth. "Classroom Reading and the Work of Arthur Gates: 1921-1930." Columbia U. Teachers Coll. 1985. 344 pp. *DAI 1985 46(3): 662-663-A.* DA8510172 1921-30

Gavin, Michael Freebern

2498. Viets, Henry R. THE RESIDENT HOUSE STAFF AT THE OPENING OF THE BOSTON CITY HOSPITAL IN 1864. *J. of the Hist. of Medicine and Allied Sci. 1959 14(2): 179-190.* 1864-1919
For abstract see ***Blake, Clarence John***

Gay, Ebenezer

2499. Wilson, Robert John, III. "Ebenezer Gay: New England's Arminian Patriarch, 1696-1787." U. of Massachusetts 1980. 614 pp. *DAI 1980 40(12): 6395-6396-A.* 8012650 1696-1787

Geddes, Norman Bel

2500. Meikle, Jeffrey L. NORMAN BEL GEDDES AND THE POPULARIZATION OF STREAMLINING. *Lib. Chronicle of the U. of Texas 1980 (13): 91-110.* Reviews the life of the industrial designer Norman Bel Geddes, focusing on the 1930's, when he emerged as the main popularizer of streamlining with novelties such as the teardrop auto and the General Motor's Futurama at the Chicago World's Fair in 1939. 1930-39

Geer, Will

2501. Norton, Sally Osborne. "A Historical Study of Actor Will Geer, His Life and Work in the Context of Twentieth-Century American Social, Political, and Theatrical History." U. of Southern California 1981. *DAI 1981 42(4): 1377-1378-A.* 1917-78

Geffen, Tobias

2502. Kaganoff, Nathan M. AN ORTHODOX RABBINATE IN THE SOUTH: TOBIAS GEFFEN, 1870-1970. *Am. Jewish Hist. 1983 73(1): 56-70.* Tobias Geffen left his Lithuanian homeland after the 1903 Kishinev pogrom, served briefly as a rabbi in New York City and Canton, Ohio, and then for nearly 60 years was rabbi of the Congregation Shearith Israel of Atlanta, where, in addition to supporting community educational and charity enterprises, he established religious schools, helped make local food products kosher, served the needs of Jewish soldiers and prisoners, and deftly handled so many religious issues that for years he was recognized as the Orthodox authority for Southern Jews. Though not as unemotional as the typical Lithuanian rabbinic scholar, he epitomized the immigrant rabbi, whose Old World Orthodoxy could not survive into the second generation. Based on the Rabbi Tobias Geffen Papers in the American Jewish Historical Society and other primary sources; 34 notes. 1903-70

Geiger, Maynard J.

2503. Nunis, Doyce B., Jr. MEMORIAL TO REV. MAYNARD J. GEIGER, O.F.M. *J. of California and Great Basin Anthrop. 1977 4(2): 155-172.* Maynard J. Geiger (1901-77), a Franciscan priest at Mission Santa Barbara, California, wrote on Mission and Indian life; includes an extensive bibliography of his articles, books, and newspaper articles, 1936-76. 1936-76

2504. Nunis, Doyce B., Jr. A DEDICATION TO THE MEMORY OF MAYNARD J. GEIGER, O.F.M., 1901-1977. *Arizona and the West 1978 20(3): 198-202.* Franciscan Fr. Maynard Joseph Geiger (1901-77) completed his philosophical and theological studies in California and was ordained to the priesthood. His M.A. work at St. Bonaventure College, New York, in English and Spanish were preparatory for his doctorate in Hispanic American history in 1937 at The Catholic University of America, Washington, D. C. His professional career was spent as archivist and historian at Mission Santa Barbara, California. His early writings focused on Spanish Florida. Later his scholarship was concerned with the Franciscan missionaries in California, particularly Junípero Serra. Illus., biblio. 1937-77

2505. Nunis, Doyce B., Jr. IN MEMORIAM: FATHER MAYNARD J. GEIGER, O.F.M. *California Hist. Q. 1977 56(3): 275-276.* Eulogizes Father Maynard J. Geiger (1901-1977), Franciscan father, archivist of Mission Santa Barbara for almost 40 years, and historian of Franciscan missionary activity in North America, particularly Hispanic California. His published writings included 13 books, among them *The Life and Times of Fray Junípero Serra, Mission Santa Barbara, 1782-1965,* and *Franciscan Missionaries in Hispanic California, 1769-1848.* In addition, he wrote almost 200 articles and for 15 years was editor of *Provincial Annals.* As a speaker he was much in demand by historical groups, and his correspondence with teachers and students was international in scale. Photo. 1901-77

2506. —. IN MEMORIAM: MAYNARD J. GEIGER, O.F.M. *Pacific Hist. Rev. 1977 46(4): 684-685.* Maynard J. Geiger, archivist at Mission Santa Barbara 1937-77 and historian of Franciscan missionary activities in the Spanish Borderlands, died 13 May 1977. He was born in Lancaster, Pennsylvania, in 1901 and earned his Ph.D. in 1937 from Catholic University. 1901-77

Gensman, L. M.

2507. Crawford, Suzanne Jones. "L. M. Gensman: A Study of an Early Twentieth-Century Western Attorney, 1901-1923." U. of Oklahoma 1980. 197 pp. *DAI 1980 41(6): 2733-A.* 8027510 1901-23

Genthe, Arnold

2508. —. ARNOLD GENTHE'S CALIFORNIA PORTRAITS. *California History 1984 63(2): 152-153.* A brief sketch of the career of Arnold Genthe, noted San Francisco photographer. Best known for his photographic record of Chinatown and his pictures of the 1906 earthquake and fire, Genthe also had a reputation as an excellent portrait photographer. 3 photos. 1895-1911

Gentry, Irma

2509. Cadenhead, Ivie E., Jr. AN OKLAHOMAN IN GUATEMALA. *Red River Valley Hist. Rev. 1980 5(3): 14-21.* Relates events in the life of Pawnee County, Oklahoma, native Irma Gentry from her arrival in Guatemala in 1928 to work with the American legation through her service to President and Mrs. Jorge Ubico as private secretary, 1937-45. 1928-45

Genung, Ida Smith

2510. Maxwell, Margaret F. IDA GENUNG OF PEEPLES VALLEY: A WOMAN OF THE WEST. *Journal of Arizona History 1984 25(4): 331-348.* A rancher in Arizona's isolated Peeples Valley, Ida Smith Genung endured harsh winters, a devastating fire and flood, and witnessed the encroachment of civilization on the frontier. Based on Genung family records and secondary sources; 7 photos, 59 notes. 1848-1938

Geoghegan, James and Richard

2511. Richardson, David. GEOGHEGAN BROTHERS OF ALASKA. *Alaska J. 1976 6(1): 17-24.* James Geoghegan moved to Alaska in 1897 and spent his life prospecting and hunting. His brother Richard, who did not move there until 1903, contributed to Alaskan history through his studies of the Aleutian language. He spent most of his time in government service or as a law clerk. 8 photos, biblio. 1897-1943

George, David

2512. Tudor, Kathleen. DAVID GEORGE: BLACK LOYALIST. *Nova Scotia Hist. Rev. [Canada] 1983 3(1): 71-82.* Briefly recounts the life of David George, a black Baptist minister. George was born a slave in Virginia. He escaped and lived with the Indians but was soon returned to slavery. In 1775, he was attracted by the promise of free land in Nova Scotia and so moved to Shelburne, where he established the first black Baptist church. After experiencing the same racial prejudice and persecution in Nova Scotia that he had known all his life, George went to Sierra Leone in 1792 and worked to establish a new colony there. 19 notes. 1760's-1810

George, Henry

2513. Forkosch, Morris D. HENRY GEORGE: THE ECONOMIST AS MORALIST. *Am. J. of Econ. and Sociol. 1979 38(4): 357-369.* Henry George derived his economic theory from his personal experience. He had the good fortune to be living in California during his formative years; there the economic events which transpired during the settlement of the North American continent—the passing of the frontier and its consequences—occurred within a time span of a few years and the telescoping of history gave him the framework for an original economic system, as well as a utopian vision of a free society. Much attention has properly been paid to George's economic ideas but he was also a moralist, one accepted by some philosophers as among the greatest. This aspect of his work, and particularly his value theory, have been neglected. 52 notes. 1850's-90's

2514. Hawks, Charlene M. "Herbert Quick: Iowan." U. of Iowa 1981. 192 pp. *DAI 1982 42(11): 4860-A.* DA8209995 1880-1925

2515. Ross, Steven J. THE CULTURE OF POLITICAL ECONOMY: HENRY GEORGE AND THE AMERICAN WORKING CLASS. *Southern California Q. 1983 65(2): 145-166.* Assesses the political ideology of Henry George (1839-94), author of *Progress and Poverty* (1879) and advocate of the single tax on land monopoly. Having lived in extreme poverty, George went to California in 1858 but found land monopolists there already controlled the wealth of the state. In his book he argued for a tax on unearned wealth. The book was a best-seller, and many working-class people who never read books bought *Progress and Poverty.* In 1886 George formed the United Labor Party and was only narrowly defeated in his attempt to win the mayoralty in New York City. Two years later his party collapsed, due to George's attempt to attract middle-class support for a working-class movement and to his belief that land monopoly, not capitalism itself, was the workers' main problem. Still, his movement had purely American roots, and George deserves recognition for making the working class aware of what they might gain from an industrial America. Primary and secondary sources; 39 notes. 1858-94

George, Olan

2516. George, Olan. HISTORICAL EVENTS AND PERSONALITIES OF PECOS COUNTY. *Permian Historical Annual 1984 24: 45-49.* Olan George recalls his youth in Pecos County, Texas, and the problems of farmers and cattle ranchers, including drought, rains, and an influenza epidemic. 1916-19

Gerber, Christian (family)

2517. Garber, Allan A. THE CHRISTIAN GERBER FAMILY OF LANCASTER COUNTY, PENNSYLVANIA. *Pennsylvania Mennonite Heritage 1985 8(3): 10-18.* Provides a brief account of the settling of Christian Gerber's Swiss Mennonite family in Lancaster County, Pennsylvania, and lists several generations of descendants with selected biographies and photographs. 1735-20c

Gerhart, Emanuel Vogel

2518. Yrigoyen, Charles, Jr. EMANUEL V. GERHARDT: CHURCHMAN, THEOLOGIAN, AND FIRST PRESIDENT OF FRANKLIN AND MARSHALL COLLEGE. *J. of the Lancaster County Hist. Soc. 1974 78(1): 1-28.* Biography of (German) Reformed Church clergyman Emanuel V. Gerhart (1817-1904), touching on his career as a minister and missionary and his writings on theological and philosophical subjects, and finally, his 36 years as professor and President at Franklin and Marshall College in Lancaster, Pennsylvania. 2 photos, 127 notes. 1840-1904

2519. Yrigoyen, Charles, Jr. EMANUEL V. GERHART: APOLOGIST FOR THE MERCERSBURG THEOLOGY. *J. of Presbyterian Hist. 1979 57(4): 485-500.* Provides a biographical summary and describes the relationship of the theology of Emanuel Vogel Gerhart (1817-1904), prominent leader in the German Reformed Church, to the American-centered Mercersburg Seminary theology of the 19th century. Although he never gained the notoriety of John W. Nevin or Phillip Schaff, who were earlier leaders in the movement, Gerhart made an important contribution to American theological education in general, to the exposition of the Mercersburg theology in particular. While he added little to the basic principles laid down by Nevin and Schaff, no one contributed more as an apologist and systematizer for its ideas. Based on the Gerhart Papers (Historical Society and Archives, Phillip

Schaff Library, Lancaster Theological Seminary), his own publications and secondary studies relating to Gerhart; photo, 63 notes. 1844-1904

2520. Yrigoyen, Charles, Jr. EMANUEL V. GERHART AND THE MERCERSBURG THEOLOGY. *J. of the Lancaster County Hist. Soc. 1978 82(4): 199-221.* Discusses the life and theological thought of Emanuel Vogel Gerhart (1817-1904), parish minister, missionary, college administrator, professor, theologian, and influential figure in the German Reformed Church in America. 1831-1904

Gérin, Elzéar

2521. Sylvain, Philippe. UN FRÈRE MÉCONNU D'ANTOINE GÉRIN-LAJOIE: ELZÉAR GÉRIN [Elzéar Gérin, Antoine Gérin-Lajoie's brother not rightly recognized]. *Rev. de l'U. d'Ottawa [Canada] 1977 47(1-2): 214-225.* Because of adverse circumstances and a premature death, Elzéar Gérin 1843-87 was not as well-known as his brother, journalist, poet, novelist, and historian, Antoine Gérin-Lajoie. A talented, alert, and witty journalist with a combative spirit, Elzéar contributed to various important French Canadian newspapers and had many faithful readers; he was involved in political dissensions, once between the Vatican and the French government because of his publication of a confidential document. He founded his own newspaper and was elected a deputy of Quebec. Primary and secondary sources; 41 notes. 1843-87

Gérin-Lajoie, Antoine

2522. Sylvain, Philippe. UN FRÈRE MÉCONNU D'ANTOINE GÉRIN-LAJOIE: ELZÉAR GÉRIN [Elzéar Gérin, Antoine Gérin-Lajoie's brother not rightly recognized]. *Rev. de l'U. d'Ottawa [Canada] 1977 47(1-2): 214-225.* 1843-87

*For abstract see **Gérin, Elzéar***

Geronimo

2523. Brown, Dee. GERONIMO. *Am. Hist. Illus. 1980 15(3): 12-21, (4): 36-45.* Part I. Discusses the activities and reputation of Geronimo, leader of the Chiricahua Apache, who became a legend created by the press in the 1870's, 20 years after he became a legend among his own people. Part II. Continues the story of Geronimo's exploits from 1881, when he led the Chiricahua to Mexico from the Sierra Madre, until 1909, when he succumbed to pneumonia. 1850's-1909

Gerry, Eloise

2524. McBeath, Lida W. ELOISE GERRY, A WOMAN OF FOREST SCIENCE. *J. of Forest Hist. 1978 22(3): 128-135.* Eloise Gerry left her native New England in 1910 to begin a 44-year career as a wood microscopist at the Forest Products Laboratory, Madison, Wisconsin. One of the first women in the country to specialize in forest products research, her achievements as a wood technologist earned her respect and distinction. Her fieldwork in the South, for example, beginning in 1916, contributed to revitalization of the naval stores industry and led as well to a Ph.D. degree at the University of Wisconsin. Gerry engaged in war-related research during the two world wars and also became a leading authority on the habitats and properties of foreign woods. The author of more than 120 publications, she retired from the Forest Service in 1954. Based on interviews and secondary sources; 8 photos, 22 notes. 1910-54

Gershman, Joshua

2525. Abella, Irving, ed. PORTRAIT OF A JEWISH PROFESSIONAL REVOLUTIONARY: THE RECOLLECTIONS OF JOSHUA GERSHMAN. *Labour [Canada] 1977 2: 184-213.* Gershman came to Canada from Europe in 1921. He soon began his association with the labor movement. In 1923 he joined the Communist Party and remained a member for 54 years. His memoir provides insights on left-wing Jewish unionism, Zionism, cultural life, and Communist activity in Winnipeg, Toronto, Montreal, and Chicago. He left the CP because of differences on the Jewish and national questions. Introduction gives historical perspective and emphasizes uniqueness of Jewish labor movement because of its dominance in the garment industry and its support of "progressive candidates and causes." Based on interviews; 3 notes. 1913-77

Gershwin, George

2526. Rimler, Walter. GREAT SONGWRITERS. *Midstream 1984 30(1): 31-34.* 1885-1979

*For abstract see **Arlen, Harold***

Gerth, Hans

2527. Martindale, Don. THE MONOLOGUE: HANS GERTH (1908-1978), A MEMOIR. *International Journal of Contemporary Sociology [India] 1982 19(1-2): i-xii, 1-183.* A student, colleague, and friend of German refugee sociologist Hans Gerth of the University of Wisconsin reminisces about him. 1940-78

Gesas, Harry

2528. Schoenburg, Nancy. HARRY GESAS: JEWISH MERCHANT IN A WYOMING COAL TOWN. *Western States Jewish Hist. 1984 17(1): 3-12.* Traces the life and work of Harry Gesas, with special emphasis on his years in Kemmerer and Diamondville, Wyoming, where he was co-owner of the clothing and drygoods firm of Gesas & Loucks. Based on the *Diamondville News,* the *Kemmerer Camera,* and other sources; 36 notes. 1864-1923

Gest, Erasmus

2529. Schultz, Charles R. ERASMUS GEST'S RECOLLECTIONS OF LIFE IN THE MIDDLE WEST IN THE 1830S. *Indiana Mag. of Hist. 1977 73(2): 125-142.* Includes a brief biographical introduction of Gest, who worked on the Cincinnati and Whitewater Canal during 1837-43, and in 1856 was elected president and superintendent of the Cincinnati, Wilmington & Zanesville Railroad. 1830's-56

Giannini, A. P.

2530. Sessions, William Loren. "California's Innovative Banker: A. P. Giannini and the Banking Crisis of 1933." U. of Southern California 1979. *DAI 1979 39(9): 5683-A.* 1933

Gibbon, Elwyn H.

2531. Leiser, Edward L. MEMOIRS OF PILOT ELWYN H. GIBBON, THE MAD IRISHMAN. *Am. Aviation Hist. Soc. J. 1978 23(1): 2-18.* Recounts the flying career of Elwyn H. Gibbon, an American who worked for various American airline companies, saw service in China, 1937-38, and was killed in a crash when flying out of Karachi, 1942. 1937-42

Gibbon, John

2532. Jordan, Mark H. LEADER OF THE IRON MEN. *Marine Corps Gazette 1959 43(3): 28-31.* John Gibbon, an officer, distinguished himself on the Union side during the Civil War. 1861-65

Gibbs, Mifflin Wistar

2533. Williams, W. D. A NOTE ON MIFFLIN WISTAR GIBBS. *Arkansas Hist. Q. 1984 43(3): 241-243.* Mifflin Wistar Gibbs, a prominent black businessman and civic leader in late 19th-century Arkansas, may have been named after Mifflin Wistar, the son of a Philadelphia university professor; discusses possible connections between the Wistar and Gibbs families. Based on secondary sources; 4 notes. ca 1800-30's

Gibran, Kahlil

2534. Knopf, Alfred A. RANDOM RECOLLECTIONS OF A PUBLISHER. *Massachusetts Hist. Soc. Pro. 1961 73: 92-103.* 1901-61
*For abstract see **Cather, Willa***

Gibson, Charles Dana

2535. Platt, Frederick. THE GIBSON GIRL. *Art & Antiques 1981 4(6): 112-117.* Recounts the life of American illustrator Charles Dana Gibson (1867-1944), who is noted for his depictions of the Gibson Girl, the beautiful young socialite who epitomized the modern woman of the late 19th and early 20th centuries. 1867-1944

Gibson, Drury P.

2536. Laurence, Debra Nance. LETTERS FROM A NORTH LOUISIANA TIGER. *North Louisiana Hist. Assoc. J. 1979 10(4): 130-147.* Excerpts from letters of a Confederate soldier, Drury P. Gibson, to his sister, telling of his training, his activities, and his attitude toward the war in which he was fighting. 42 notes. 1861-63

Gibson, Hugh

2537. Swerczek, Ronald E. HUGH GIBSON AND DISARMAMENT: THE DIPLOMACY OF GRADUALISM. Jones, Kenneth Paul, ed. *U.S. Diplomats in Europe, 1919-1941* (Santa Barbara, Calif.: ABC-CLIO, 1981): 75-90. Details the diplomatic career of Hugh Gibson (1883-1954), who served as an American diplomat from 1908 to 1938. The disarmament negotiations of the late 1920's and early 1930's marked the pinnacle of his career. He participated in formal conferences and interim meetings, including the Preparatory Commission for the General Disarmament Conference in 1926, as Chairman of the American delegation; the Geneva (1927) and London (1930) Naval Conferences; and the General Disarmament Conference (1932), as acting chairman. the disarmament talks represented an important aspect of Republican involvement in European affairs, and Gibson utilized his skill, experience, and knowledge to help keep them alive, particularly through his ability to seek out areas of compromise and concession in the periods between formal sessions. Primary sources; 47 notes. 1926-32

Gibson, Walter Murray

2538. Adler, Jacob and Kamins, Robert M. THE POLITICAL DEBUT OF WALTER MURRAY GIBSON. *Hawaiian Journal of History 1984 18: 96-115.* American Walter Murray Gibson arrived in Hawaii in 1861 and was appointed premier and minister of foreign affairs by King Kalakaua in 1882. During the intervening two decades he had a flamboyant career as a developer, newspaper editor, and politician. He supported Hawaiian independence, and was opposed by Americans who hoped for US annexation of Hawaii. Based on Hawaiian newspapers and secondary sources; photo, 36 notes. 1861-82

Giddens, Paul H.

2539. Giddens, Paul H.; Zavacky, Michael J. and Woolever, Kristin R., interviewers. RAMBLINGS ON EARLY OIL HISTORY: AN INTERVIEW WITH PAUL H. GIDDENS ON IDA TARBELL. *Western Pennsylvania Hist. Mag. 1983 66(4): 389-395.* Paul H. Giddens discusses his collaboration with journalist Ida M. Tarbell on a book about the development of the oil industry, recalling Tarbell's personality and his own career as a historian. 1934-80

Gifford, George Edmund, Jr.

2540. Jones, Gordon W. GEORGE EDMUND GIFFORD, JR. *Pro. of the Am. Antiquarian Soc. 1981 91(1): 22-24.* Gifford (1931-81), a psychiatrist, was interested in the history of medicine and an avid book collector. He wrote several books on the history of medicine, and eventually obtained a master's degree in the history of science. He later developed an interest in natural history, and worked on the life and art of Isaac Sprague, a natural history illustrator. 1951-81

Gilbert, Alfred Carleton

2541. Nuhn, Roy. HELLO BOYS! MAKE LOTS OF TOYS! A. C. GILBERT, AMERICA'S TOYMAKER. *Am. Hist. Illus. 1980 15(8): 36-42.* Alfred Carleton Gilbert's (1884-1961) Connecticut-based A. C. Gilbert Company made scientific toys and Erector sets, but went bankrupt in 1967. 20c

Gilbert, Cass

2542. Blodgett, Geoffrey. CASS GILBERT, ARCHITECT: CONSERVATIVES AT BAY. *Journal of American History 1985 72(3): 615-636.* Uses the career of Cass Gilbert to illustrate a major dilemma of 20th-century American architecture—its adherence to traditional classicism during a time of radical change. A conservative who believed architecture should serve the established political and social order, Gilbert distrusted modern, extreme trends. The turmoil of World War I and the 1920's hardened his reverence for the classical tradition, even though he was fighting a losing battle within the profession. The US Supreme Court building was the last affirmation of his values. Based on the Gilbert Papers at the Library of Congress, and on the New-York Historical Society, and secondary sources; 47 notes. 1898-1934

2543. Jones, Robert Allen. "Cass Gilbert, Midwestern Architect in New York." Case Western Reserve U. 1976. 211 pp. *DAI 1977 38(1): 1-A.* 1895-1915

Gilbert, Edmund W.

2544. Robinson, Guy and Patten, John. EDMUND W. GILBERT AND THE DEVELOPMENT OF HISTORICAL GEOGRAPHY. *J. of Hist. Geography 1980 6(4): 409-419.* Originally studying history, Edmund W. Gilbert accepted a lectureship at Reading University in human geography. His main research interest was the 19th century American West. Although interested in the effects of the environment on humans, he came to accept the possibilist doctrine. Gilbert's approach was regional, utilizing cross-sections, and he was the first to attempt a comprehensive definition of historical geography. His major work *The Exploration of Western America, 1800-1850* dealt with environmental influences and human action, and it pioneered the use of contemporaneous perceptions. Although he made no further definitive statements after World War II, Gilbert was active in urban and medical historical geography, urging study of the recent past. A good writer who avoided jargon, he also was active in historic preservation and encouraged the study of the history of geography. Illus., 20 notes, biblio. 1920-77

Gilbert, Prentiss Bailey

2545. Donnelly, J. B. PRENTISS BAILEY GILBERT AND THE LEAGUE OF NATIONS: THE DIPLOMACY OF AN OBSERVER. Jones, Kenneth Paul, ed. *U.S. Diplomats in Europe, 1919-1941* (Santa Barbara, Calif.: ABC-Clio, 1981): 95-109. Prentiss Bailey Gilbert (1883-1939) entered the US State Department in 1918 at 35 and held positions of importance in American diplomacy between the world wars. As consul in Geneva, 1930-37, Gilbert conducted the day-to-day American relations with the League of Nations. Briefly during the Manchurian crisis of 1931, Gilbert became the only American ever to sit with the League Council. Then, for the 18 months in 1937-39 before his death, he was counselor of the US embassy in Hitler's Berlin. During more than half of that time he was chargé, most notably in the immediate aftermath of the Kristallnacht pogrom of November 1938. In these posts and while an innovative lieutenant in the State Department headquarters during the 1920's, Gilbert won the lifelong admiration of the future ambassadors he trained and of leading journalists of the period. Primary sources; 50 notes. 1930-39

Gilbert, William Schwenck

2546. Shenker, Israel. LATELY OF LONDON, GILBERT AND SULLIVAN MAKE A TV TREAT. *Smithsonian 1984 14(12): 104-114.* Highlights the partnership of librettist William Schwenck Gilbert and composer Arthur Sullivan, and the collaborative efforts of British financier George Walker and American television producer Judith De Paul in bringing several Gilbert and Sullivan operas to British and American television. 1860's-1984

Gilbert, Win S.

2547. Gilbert, W. S. GROWING UP IN THE NORTHWEST: SON OF AN EARLY RAILROADER. *Pacific Northwesterner 1979 23(4): 49-58.* Win S. Gilbert, son of a railroad builder, chief engineer, and railroad superintendent, was born in 1877 near Syracuse, New York. Describes his youth and his law practice in Spokane, Washington, in 1899 and became a leading citizen of Spokane; this autobiography was written in 1959. 1877-1959

Gilchrist, Mary Wilson

2548. Lady, Claudia Lynn. FIVE TRI-STATE WOMEN DURING THE CIVIL WAR. *West Virginia Hist. 1982 43(3): 189-226, (4): 303-321.* 1859-65
*For abstract see **Aleshire, Mary***

Gilchrist, William Wallace

2549. Schleifer, Martha Furman. "William Wallace Gilchrist: Life and Works." (Volumes I and II) Bryn Mawr Coll. 1976. 355 pp. *DAI 1977 38(2): 541-A.* 1870's-1916

Gilder, Robert Fletcher

2550. Wolf, Arthur M. ROBERT FLETCHER GILDER, 1856-1940. *Plains Anthropologist 1976 21(73, Part 1): 241-244.* Presents a biographical sketch of Robert Fletcher Gilder's journalistic career and artistic hobby. Describes Gilder's work as an archaeologist in eastern Nebraska between 1903, when Gilder started an independent survey and excavation program in Douglas and Washington counties, and 1926 when his last archaeological publication, *The Nebraska Culture Man*, appeared. Mentions Gilder's excavations, writings, colleagues, honors, associational memberships, and role in the "Nebraska Loess Man" controversy. After 1926, Gilder continued survey and excavation work into the 1930's and retired to his cabin near Bellevue, Nebraska, until his death at age 84. Gilder's archaeological collections can be found in the Peabody Museum at Harvard University, the Washington County Historical Society in Fort Calhoun, Nebraska, and the Joslyn Art Museum in Omaha, Nebraska. Biblio. Reprinted from *University of Nebraska Museum Notes* 1975 55(11). 1903-26

Gildersleeve, Basil Lanneau

2551. Walzel, Diana Lynn. BASIL LANNEAU GILDERSLEEVE: CLASSICAL SCHOLAR. *Virginia Cavalcade 1976 25(3): 110-117.* Discusses the classical scholarship and teaching of Basil Lanneau Gildersleeve (1831-1924) at the University of Virginia in Charlottesville (1856-76); also discusses his Greek studies, 1845-1924. 1845-1924

Gildersleeve, Glenn

2552. Olenchak, Frank Richard. "Glenn Gildersleeve and His Contributions to Music Education (1894-1970)." U. of Michigan 1977. 276 pp. *DAI 1977 38(3): 1276-A.* 1894-1970

Giles, Benjamin

2553. Noyes, Richard. A NOTE ON A FOUNDING FATHER'S LIBRARY: THE BOOKS OF BENJAMIN GILES. *Hist. New Hampshire 1979 34(3-4): 244-252.* Benjamin Giles (1717-87), as a central figure in the development of New Hampshire's constitution, can further the understanding of New Hampshire's unique role in this field. Few of Giles's papers have survived, but an inventory of his library, included in his probate records, is revealing. It includes works by Jonathan Edwards and George Whitefield not commonly read by the founding fathers. His library had a strongly Calvinistic bias, which, with Giles's known persistence, suggests that the founding fathers may have been driven, at least in part, by Puritan energy. 15 notes. 1760's-87

2554. Ryan, Walter A. A NOTE ON A FOUNDING FATHER: NEWPORT'S BENJAMIN GILES, TWICE A REBEL. *Hist. New Hampshire 1977 32(1-2): 18-27.* Benjamin Giles (1717-87) was not foremost among New Hampshire's revolutionary leaders, but his career sheds light on the revolutionary movement in small communities. A prosperous sawmill and gristmill operator, and a major Newport landowner, Giles held several local positions before the American Revolution. Active in town meetings when the Revolution began, he then served in the legislature. When part of western New Hampshire joined Vermont, Giles protested, but he later served in the Vermont legislature. When the area rejoined New Hampshire Giles again represented Newport in the legislature. 39 notes. 1766-87

Giles, William Branch

2555. Gunta, Mary Antonia. "The Public Life of William Branch Giles, Republican, 1790-1815." Catholic U. of Am. 1980. 238 pp. *DAI 1980 41(2): 769-770-A.* 8018343
1790-1815

Giles sisters

2556. Deutsch, Lucille Snyder. "The Giles' Sisters Contributions toward the Higher Education of Women in the South: 1874-1904." U. of Pittsburgh 1978. 95 pp. *DAI 1979 40(2): 694-A.* 1874-1904

Gill, Irving

2557. Kamerling, Bruce. IRVING GILL: THE ARTIST AS ARCHITECT. *J. of San Diego Hist. 1979 25(2): 151-190.* Schooled in Chicago, architect Irving Gill moved to San Diego in 1897 where he worked until his retirement in 1929; includes 59 photos, and a chronology of projects, 1895-1935.
1895-1935

Gill, Louis John

2558. Kroll, C. Douglas. LOUIS JOHN GILL: FAMOUS BUT FORGOTTEN ARCHITECT. *Journal of San Diego History 1984 30(3): 153-166.* Louis John Gill, architect for the San Diego Zoo, was known for his skill and dedication to the architectural profession during his lifetime, but aside from the many buildings he designed remaining in the San Diego area, his work has been forgotten over the years.
1911-69

Gill, Lunda Hoyle

2559. Morgan, Lael. THE BEAUTY OF PEOPLE IS THEIR HISTORY. *Alaska J. 1980 10(3): 60-62.* Describes the portraiture of Lunda Hoyle Gill. A California artist who now lives in Virginia, she spent time in Alaska painting Indians and Eskimos there in their traditional dress and setting. Although photography of native Alaskans began in the 19th century and some portraits of the people were made during the 1940's and 1950's, Gill uniquely tries to capture both the detail of their garb and their inner spirit. 4 illus., photo. 1980

Gillespie, Archibald H.

2560. Simmons, Edwin H. THE SECRET MISSION OF ARCHIBALD GILLESPIE. *Marine Corps Gazette 1968 52(11): 60-67.* In 1845-46, with secret orders from Washington, Marine Lieutenant Archibald H. Gillespie traveled to California via Mexico and Hawaii; during 1846-47, he took part in the expeditions of John C. Frémont, Robert F. Stockton, and Stephen Watts Kearny to take over California for the United States during the Mexican War. 1845-47

Gillespie, Emily Hawley

2561. Linsink, Judy Nolte; Kirkham, Christine M.; and Witzke, Karen Pauba. "MY ONLY CONFIDANT": THE LIFE AND DIARY OF EMILY HAWLEY GILLESPIE. *Ann. of Iowa 1980 45(4): 288-312.* Contains excerpts from the diary (1858-88) of Iowa farm wife Emily Hawley Gillespie along with a narrative summary of her life. Based on the 10-volume Emily Gillespie diary deposited at the Iowa State Historical Department, Iowa City, Iowa; 3 photos, note.
1858-88

Gillespie, Frances Cohen

2562. Gillespie, Frances Cohen. THE PAINTINGS OF FRANCES COHEN GILLESPIE: THE ARTIST ON HER LIFE AND WORK. *Massachusetts Rev. 1976 17(2): 357-366.* The author, born in 1939 in Los Angeles, and reared in New York City, is a realist artist who paints her family and home, hoping to clarify the meaning and image of her family. She loves to visit art galleries and stare at paintings, not to reproduce them but rather to experience them. Art helps her to overcome her emotional problems, such as her fear of succeeding. 8 illus. 1950's-76

Gillette, Guy M.

2563. Harrington, Jerry. SENATOR GUY GILLETTE FOILS THE EXECUTION COMMITTEE. *Palimpsest 1981 62(6): 170-180.* Brief biograhy of Iowa Congressman Guy M. Gillette, focusing on his election in 1932 on the Democratic ticket, his two terms in office from 1933 to 1936, and his election to the Senate in 1936; during the election, Franklin D. Roosevelt campaigned against Gillette and other dissident Democrats who did not wholeheartedly accept the New Deal.
1932-48

Gillette, William

2564. Neath, Joanne M. WILLIAM GILLETTE—SHERLOCK HOLMES. *New-England Galaxy 1977 19(1): 38-44.* Traces the acting career of William Gillette (1853-1937). His most famous role, Sherlock Holmes, was played more than 1300 times. Describes life at Gillette Castle in Hadlyme, Connecticut. 4 illus. 1853-1937

2565. Schuttler, Georg W. WILLIAM GILLETTE: MARATHON ACTOR AND PLAYWRIGHT. *Journal of Popular Culture 1983 17(3): 115-129.* Surveys the long and remarkably productive career of actor-playwright William Gillette. Based on Gillette's papers and contemporary newspaper articles; 76 notes. 1873-1937

Gilligan, John J.

2566. Larson, David Richard. "Ohio's Fighting Liberal: A Political Biography of John J. Gilligan." Ohio State U. 1982. 284 pp. *DAI 1983 43(10):3398-A.* DA8305352 1953-79

Gillon, Alexander

2567. Stone, Richard G., Jr. "THE SOUTH CAROLINA WE'VE LOST": THE BIZARRE SAGA OF ALEXANDER GILLON AND HIS FRIGATE. *Am. Neptune 1979 39(3): 159-172.* Describes South Carolina Navy Commodore Alexander Gillon's (1741-94) negotiations for purchasing warships in Europe concluding that his commercial proposals lost him the support of Benjamin Franklin (1706-90) who favored the more bellicose plans of others; that the terms he negotiated for the ship's lease were very poor; and that his plans for use of the ship were poorly conceived and executed. "Gillon was a disastrous combination of romantic adventurer and main-chance opportunist" who escaped censure because Carolinians' strong feelings of local pride and belief that the Continental Congress and Benjamin Franklin had inadequately supported the state led them to defend Gillon. Based on Franklin's papers and other primary sources; 21 notes.
1778-85

Gilman, Catheryne Cooke

2568. Gilman, Elizabeth. CATHERYNE COOKE GILMAN: SOCIAL WORKER. Stuhler, Barbara and Kreuter, Gretchen, ed. *Women of Minnesota: Selected Biographical Essays* (St. Paul: Minnesota Historical Society Press, 1977): 190-207. Noted teacher, social worker, and feminist Catheryne Cooke Gilman was born in 1880 in the small Missouri town of Laclede. After her high school graduation in 1898, Catheryne Cooke taught social studies in Iowa and, in 1904, became a principal. Subsequently, she attended Iowa State Normal School and did graduate work at the University of Chicago where she discovered new theories, social thought, and social problems. A course by Sophonisba P. Breckinridge introduced Catheryne to feminism and to Jane Addams's Hull House. Cooke took up the new profession of social work, went to New York City's East Side House Settlement, and to the University Settlement directed by Robbins Gilman, whom she married in 1914. They settled in Minneapolis where Robbins conducted the North East Neighborhood House. Catheryne worked as a suffragist, agitated for improved maternity and infant care, and served on the Minnesota Child Welfare Commission. She became a leader of the Women's Co-operative Alliance, organized community studies, and investigated the causes of juvenile delinquency. She promoted sex education and parent-training courses in the schools. During the 1920's and 30's, she campaigned for morality laws and chaired the motion picture committee of the National Congress of Parents and Teachers. From then until her death in 1954, Catheryne Gilman remained at the North East Neighborhood House where she wrote, lectured, and worked. Primary and secondary sources; photo, 35 notes. 1904-54

Gilman, Charlotte Perkins

2569. Berkin, Carol Ruth. PRIVATE WOMAN, PUBLIC WOMAN: THE CONTRADICTIONS OF CHARLOTTE PERKINS GILMAN. Berkin, Carol Ruth and Norton, Mary Beth, ed. *Women of America: A History* (Boston: Houghton Mifflin Co., 1979): 150-176. Charlotte Perkins Gilman (1860-1935) wrote and lectured throughout her life in New England and California. Her *Women and Economics* (1898) was a formulation of the evolution of the social role of women. Her own personal struggle included the realization that love and social duty were not mutually exclusive. Based on Gilman's diaries and published works; 5 notes. 1880's-1935

2570. Fleenor, Juliann Evans. "Giving Birth: Images of Interior Space and 'For Eight Years I Did Not Do Anything I Thought Was Wrong': *The Living of Charlotte Perkins Gilman.*" U. of Toledo 1978. 57 pp. *DAI 1978 39(6): 3665-A.* 19c-20c

2571. Hayden, Dolores. CHARLOTTE PERKINS GILMAN AND THE KITCHENLESS HOUSE. *Radical Hist. Rev. 1979 (21): 225-247.* Socialist, feminist, and visionary Charlotte Perkins Gilman objected to the confining dimension of residential space, publishing plans for collective domestic life involving architectural innovations including day care centers, cooperative housekeeping, and communal kitchens; 1870-1920. 1870-1920

2572. Hill, Mary A. CHARLOTTE PERKINS GILMAN: A FEMINIST'S STRUGGLE WITH WOMANHOOD. *Massachusetts Rev. 1980 21(3): 503-526.* American reformer, author, and lecturer Charlotte Perkins Stetson Gilman (1860-1935) advocated economic independence for women. She stated that four major forces created female inequality: economic dependence on men, nonvoluntary domestic servitude, psychological dependence on men, and sexual oppression of women. Theoretically she asserted women's natural superiority. She preserved much historical data that enrich Edwardian feminist theory; the author analyzes these accounts to illustrate some private sources for Gilman's theories. Based on Gilman's diary, letters, her published works, and the author's unpublished doctoral dissertation; 51 notes. ca 1880-1920

2573. Scharnhorst, Gary. MAKING HER FAME: CHARLOTTE PERKINS GILMAN IN CALIFORNIA. *California History 1985 64(3): 192-201.* Discusses the work of Charlotte Perkins Gilman (1860-1935) as a leader in the Nationalist movement—a socialist movement inspired by Edward Bellamy's novel *Looking Backward.* Married in 1884 but separated from her husband, she was known at the time as Charlotte Perkins Stetson. In 1888, she came to California to pursue a literary career and soon became involved in the Nationalist movement, writing satirical poetry for publication, giving lectures, and corresponding with Nationalist and socialist leaders. She called for the economic independence of women and for sexual equality. Although the Nationalist movement had foundered by 1895, Gilman continued to pursue a career advocating women's rights that carried the early influence of her California Nationalist experience. 4 photos, illus., 72 notes. 1888-95

2574. Towne, Marian K. CHARLOTTE GILMAN IN CALIFORNIA. *Pacific Hist. 1984 28(1): 4-17.* Reviews Charlotte Perkins Stetson Gilman's life, with an emphasis on her career in California, where the political and social climate in the 1890's gave her the freedom to explore her views on suffrage and other social issues and to develop as an author, lecturer, and leader in labor and women's movements. Based on diaries from the History of Women Collection, Radcliffe College, and other sources. 1888-1935

Gilman, James Marshall

2575. Brumgardt, John R. PIONEER BY CIRCUMSTANCE: JAMES MARSHALL GILMAN AND THE BEGINNINGS OF BANNING, CALIFORNIA. *Southern California Q. 1980 62(2): 143-159.* A profile of James Marshall Gilman (1842-1915), pioneer farmer, rancher, and supporter of the town of Banning, California. A native of New Hampshire, Gilman came to California during the Civil War to avoid military service. In 1869 he bought a cattle ranch, which he developed along with ventures in grain farming, fruit crops, and olives. His efforts brought him modest prosperity and a key position in the San Gorgonio Pass region. Although not particularly bold or heroic, he was a figure of local importance, successful by virtue of hard work and noted as a man who brought stable community development to southern California. 44 notes. ca 1861-1915

Gilmer, Elizabeth M. (Dorothy Dix)

2576. Culley, Margaret. SOB-SISTERHOOD: DOROTHY DIX AND THE FEMINIST ORIGINS OF THE ADVICE COLUMN. *Southern Studies 1977 16(2): 201-210* Dorothy Dix (Elizabeth Meriwether Gilmer, 1861-1951), who wrote the first influential and successful newspaper advice column, was an ardent feminist and suffragist. The column began in 1895 in the New Orleans *Picayune* and continued for almost 60 years. Dix later adopted the question and answer format, but in the first six years she wrote strong essays on female financial vulnerability, and the cost to women of confining social conventions and expectations. She supported women's right to work, dress reform, the franchise, improved health care, and education. When she became a nationally syndicated writer, her polemical style softened. Based on the Dix autobiography and columns from the *Picayune;* 7 notes. 1895-1900

2577. Culley, Margaret. DOROTHY DIX: THE THIRTEENTH JUROR. *Int. J. of Women's Studies [Canada] 1979 2(4): 349-357.* Traces the career of Dorothy Dix (Elizabeth Gilmer, 1870-1951), a crime reporter for the New York *Journal;* although best known for her syndicated advice column, she first gained fame reporting on crimes involving women, 1901-16. 1901-16

Gilmore, Lyman, Jr.

2578. Browne, Jay. DID HE FLY BEFORE THE WRIGHT BROTHERS?: THE LEGEND OF LYMAN GILMORE. *Aviation Q. 1979 5(1): 14-29.* Traces the life and career of Lyman Gilmore, Jr. (1874-1951), a Grass Valley, California, pioneer inventor of aircraft, a builder of an aerodrome, an aviator, and a proponent of a nationwide system of air transportation, who claimed to have flown one year before the Wright Brothers' 1903 flight. 1874-1951

Gilpatrick, Delbert Harold

2579. Sanders, Albert. DELBERT HAROLD GILPATRICK. *Pro. of the South Carolina Hist. Assoc. 1981: v.* Presents an obituary of Delbert Harold Gilpatrick (1892-1981) who taught in the history department at Furman University during 1926-68. He is remembered for his teaching and his book, *Jeffersonian Democracy in North Carolina, 1789-1816* (1931). 1912-81

Gilpin, Henry D.

2580. Tobias, Clifford I. HENRY D. GILPIN: "GOVERNOR IN AND OVER THE TERRITORY OF MICHIGAN." *Michigan Hist. 1975 59(3): 152-170.* Henry D. Gilpin (1800-60), a socially prominent Philadelphia attorney, became a public director of the Bank of the United States late in 1832. Gilpin's willingness to act as Andrew Jackson's chief spokesman at the height of the Bank War doomed not only his reappointment to a directorship, but his subsequent commission as territorial governor, for he alienated antiadministration senators who thereupon prevented confirmation. With a State Constitutional Convention imminent, Jackson made no further nomination. Gilpin remained interested in Michigan politics and land investment. Based on primary and secondary sources; 3 illus., 43 notes. 1831-42

Gingerich, Melvin

2581. Hershberger, Guy F. IN TRIBUTE TO MELVIN GINGERICH. *Mennonite Hist. Bull. 1975 36(4): 2-4.* Obituary for Melvin Gingerich, a Mennonite educator, historian, and churchman, 1902-75. 1902-75

2582. Oyer, John S. MELVIN GINGERICH, 1902-1975. *Mennonite Q. Rev. 1978 52(2): 91-112.* Melvin Gingerich, a Mennonite scholar, early developed a flair for learning, probably because he came from a long line of churchmen. His books and articles were numerous, the most famous being a history of the Mennonites in Iowa. He also edited several periodicals, acted as research counselor and archivist, and was an active churchman until his death. Never radical or at the forefront of new movements, Gingerich managed to soothe the more ardent spirits at both ends of the political spectrum. 92 notes. 1902-75

Ginsburg, Cora

2583. Colgan, Susan. CORA GINSBURG: THE COSTUME LADY. *Art & Antiques 1982 5(3): 80-83.* Cora Ginsburg, owner of the Benjamin Ginsburg Antiquary in New York City, collects clothes, preferably from the 18th century; after repairing them, she often sells them to museums. 18c-20c

Ginzberg, Eli

2584. Ginzberg, Eli. AGAINST ORTHODOXIES. *Society 1979 16(6): 62-66.* A memoir of the author's life from the early 1920's through 1979, emphasizing the development of his ideas regarding human resources and power and the interplay between his work as a researcher and governmental advisor. 1920's-79

Gipp, George

2585. Cox, James A. WAS "THE GIPPER" REALLY FOR REAL? YOU CAN BET HE WAS. *Smithsonian 1985 16(9): 130-150.* Discusses the life and legend of football star George Gipp, whose athletic skill and achievements at Notre Dame during 1916-20 became the subject of a 1940 movie, *Knute Rockne—All American,* starring Pat O'Brien as Knute Rockne and Ronald Reagan as Gipp. 1916-40

Gipson, Lawrence Henry

2586. Brock, Leslie V. LAWRENCE HENRY GIPSON: HISTORIAN: THE EARLY YEARS. *Idaho Yesterdays 1978 22(2): 2-9, 27-31.* The family of Lawrence Henry Gipson moved to Caldwell, Idaho, in 1893. Gipson's father published a newspaper there. Gipson attended the University of Idaho in Moscow where he took all the history courses that were offered. After graduation he was designated the Rhodes Scholar for Idaho for 1904. Primary sources; 7 illus., 72 notes. 1893-1904

Girard, Rodolphe

2587. Dirschauer, Madeleine. "Rodolphe Girard (1879-1956): Sa Vie, Son Oeuvre" [Rodolphe Girard (1879-1956): His Life, His Work]. U. of Toronto [Canada] 1984. *DAI 1985 45(8): 2531-A.* 20c

Girouard, Joseph Éna

2588. Genest, Jean. JOSEPH-ÉNA GIROUARD ET SON TEMPS 1855-1937 PREMIÈRE PARTIE: 1855-1898 [Joseph Éna Girouard and his times 1855-1937. Part I: 1855-1898]. *Action Natl. [Canada] 1981 70(8): 675-695.* Girouard, a native of the Bois-Francs region of Quebec, was a close associate of Honoré Mercier and Wilfrid Laurier. During his youth, his native region was anglicized by veterans of the War of 1812, but he remained deeply imbued by French culture, studying at both the Commercial College of Princeville and the Seminary of Nicolet. He served as a notary from 1881 to 1897, a deputy to the National Assembly from 1886 to 1898, and mayor of Drummondville from 1889 to 1897. His first electoral success was attributed to the French reaction to the execution of Louis Riel, and his political career in Quebec ended only with his nomination by Laurier to serve as registrar and member of the Council of the Yukon Territory. 10 notes. Article to be continued. 1855-98

Girouard, Percy

2589. Kirk-Greene, A. H. M. CANADA IN AFRICA: SIR PERCY GIROUARD, A NEGLECTED COLONIAL GOVERNOR. *African Affairs [Great Britain] 1984 83(331): 207-239.* Outlines the role of Percy Girouard, a Canadian who served in the British colonial service throughout Africa. Following military and engineering training in Canada, Girouard joined Herbert Kitchener in the Sudan during the 1890's and helped to establish the Sudan Military Railway. He next served in South Africa and (after the Boer War) accepted the post of commissioner of railways, which he held until 1904. In 1907 the British Colonial Office appointed Girouard governor of Northern Nigeria. During his administration, he introduced reforms in land policy, administration, and education and established the first railroads. In 1909 Girouard received a new appointment as governor of Kenya and served at the post until 1912, when he resigned over a dispute with the colonial office. Except for official positions during World War I, Girouard largely retired from public life following his colonial service. Based on the private collection of the Girouard Papers and secondary sources; 109 notes. 1890's-1932

Girty, Simon

2590. Richards, James K. A CLASH OF CULTURES: SIMON GIRTY AND THE STRUGGLE FOR THE FRONTIER. *Timeline 1985 2(3): 2-17.* Discusses the life of Pennsylvania-born Simon Girty, his 1778 defection to the British side and participation in the Revolutionary War fighting with Indian enemies of colonials on the northern frontier, and speculates on the accuracy of reports of Girty's cruelty and barbarity. 1750's-1818

Gitt, Josiah W.

2591. Hamilton, Mary Allienne. J. W. GITT: THE COLD WAR'S "VOICE IN THE WILDERNESS." *Journalism Monographs 1985 (91): 1-36.* Presents a biography of Josiah W. Gitt and a history of the newspaper he published, the *Gazette and Daily* in York, Pennsylvania, which in 1948 was the country's only commercial daily paper to support Progressive Party candidate Henry Wallace's bid for the presidency and one of the few papers to oppose consistently America's postwar foreign policy. 1915-70

Gladden, Washington

2592. Ellis, William E. CHILDREN, YOUTH, AND THE SOCIAL GOSPEL: THE REACTION TO WASHINGTON GLADDEN. *Foundations 1980 23(3): 252-266.* Traces Congregationalist clergyman Washington Gladden's (1836-1918) attitudes toward the social responsibilities of the church, showing the influence of his own early life and religious thinking, and that of others such as Horace Bushnell, along with changing political and economic conditions. Based mostly on his sermons; 92 notes. 1836-1918

Glanz, Rudolf

2593. Gartner, Lloyd P. NECROLOGY: RUDOLF GLANZ (1892-1978). *Am. Jewish Hist. 1979 69(2): 270-273.* Rudolf Glanz was an outstanding American Jewish historian. Born in Vienna, he helped found YIVO, the Yiddish Scientific Institute, and wrote several studies on German Jewish criminals. In 1938, he came to the United States as a refugee, and soon began to write on the history of German Jews in America, later branching out into other areas. His studies were all based on original sources, many of them rarely employed by historians. His work has not been sufficiently appreciated because of his difficult style. 1892-1978

Glasgow, Ellen

2594. Atteberry, Phillip Douglas. "Ellen Glasgow: The Shape of Her Early Career." Washington U. 1983. 217 pp. *DAI 1984 45(2): 518-A.* DA8410606 1897-1909

2595. Caldwell, Ellen M. ELLEN GLASGOW AND THE SOUTHERN AGRARIANS. *Am. Lit. 1984 56(2): 203-213.* Although early in her career Ellen Glasgow exhibited a distrust of Southern romance and myth, under the influence of the Southern agrarian movement (especially Allen Tate) she reassessed the merits of Southern tradition as a bulwark against the dehumanization of the machine age. In three novels between 1925 and 1935, she continued to condemn empty rituals, but she also exhibited a sympathy for a sense of tradition and for characters who preserved uncorrupted Southern values in life. Glasgow's female characters are better at preserving and transmitting tradition than are the male ones. Based on *Barren Ground* (1925), *The Sheltered Life* (1932), and *Vein of Iron* (1935); 20 notes. 1925-35

2596. McCann, Luke William. "Ellen Glasgow: The Shaping of a Social Conscience." Columbia U. 1983. 153 pp. *DAI 1984 44(8): 2473-A.* DA8327256 1900-45

2597. Noll-Wiemann, Renate. KÜNSTLERISCHER ARCHETYPUS UND KÜNSTLERTHEMATIK: ELLEN GLASGOW UND DIE ENGLISCHE ROMANTRADITION [The archetypal artist and the artist theme: Ellen Glasgow and the tradition of the English novel]. *Amerikastudien [West Germany] 1976 21(1): 67-73.* Ellen Glasgow's (1874-1945) artistic career according to her autobiography shows her to be an archetypal artist as defined by Maurice Beebe. However, Glasgow's treatment of the artist in her novel *Virginia* reveals her strong indebtedness to the world of the English novel of the 19th century and her failure to dwell on the artist theme in the fashion of a 20th-century artist. 34 notes. 19c-20c

Glasscock, William E.

2598. Tucker, Gary Jackson. "William E. Glasscock: Thirteenth Governor of West Virginia." West Virginia U. 1978. 303 pp. *DAI 1978 39(3): 1792-A.* 1909-13

Glatt, Carl

2599. Robertson, Peter C. A TRIBUTE TO CARL GLATT OR "WHAT ABOUT JONES?" *J. of Intergroup Relations 1981-82 9(4): 26-31.* Briefly discusses the career of Carl Glatt, including his work as executive director of the Kansas Commission on Civil Rights in the mid-1950's, and his work in opposing employment discrimination in West Virginia. 1950's-81

Gleason, Anne-Marie

2600. Boivin, Aurélien and Landry, Kenneth. FRANÇOISE ET MADELEINE: PIONNIÈRES DU JOURNALISME FÉMININ AU QUÉBEC [Françoise and Madeleine: pioneers of feminine journalism in Quebec]. *Atlantis [Canada] 1978 4(1): 63-74.* 1900-19
For abstract see ***Barry, Robertine***

Gleason, Sarell Everett

2601. Leopold, Richard W. SARELL EVERETT GLEASON. *Massachusetts Hist. Soc. Pro. 1974 86: 90-94.* Everett Gleason (1905-74) was elected a member of the Massachusetts Historical Society in 1963. Ev Gleason was educated at Harvard, and taught medieval history there and at

Amherst before entering a career in government beginning with World War II. He is best known as the coauthor (with William L. Langer) of the still-admired multivolume history entitled *The World Crisis and American Foreign Policy*, the story of US diplomacy in World War II. Gleason also served as editor of *Foreign Relations* from 1963-72. Based on an autobiographical sketch published in 1952, the author's personal friendship dating to 1937, letters from William L. Langer, Charles H. Taylor, Elting E. Morison, and Abbott Gleason, and materials provided by Malcolm Freiberg; index. 1905-74

Gleason, William Henry

2602. Cresse, Lewis Hoffman. "A Study of William Henry Gleason: Carpetbagger, Politician, Land Developer." U. of South Carolina 1979. 194 pp. *DAI 1980 40(7): 4192-A.* 1865-70's

Gleazer, Edmund J., Jr.

2603. McLennan, Joseph W. F. "The Career of Edmund J. Gleazer, Jr., and His Contributions to the Community College Movement." Northern Illinois U. 1982. 190 pp. *DAI 1983 44(1): 61-A.* DA8311313 20c

Goat, Noah

2604. Johnson, Jean L. THREE STONEYS. *Alberta Hist. [Canada] 1981 29(2): 29-36.* The author became good friends with Elizabeth Hunter, Jacob Johnson, and Noah Goat, three Stoney (Assiniboin) Indians who provided a wealth of information on the early history of the tribe, their language, and their customs, ca 1912-60. 4 photos. 1912-60

Gockel, Herman W.

2605. Gockel, Herman W. AUTOBIOGRAPHY FOR MY GRANDCHILDREN. *Concordia Hist. Inst. Q. 1978 51(1): 9-22.* The author recalls his varied experiences in the service of the Lutheran Church (Missouri Synod) from the 1920's to his retirement in 1971. The author was pastor, editor, writer, and television producer of *This Is The Life.* 1923-71

Godbee, Edna Perkins

2606. Shadron, Virginia. STATE AND LOCAL RECORDS AS WOMEN'S HISTORY SOURCES: THE CASE OF EDNA PERKINS GODBEE. *Proceedings and Papers of the Georgia Association of Historians 1983: 36-46.* Traces the case of Edna Perkins Godbee, who shot and killed her ex-husband and his new wife in Millen, Georgia, in 1913. Mrs. Godbee was a battered and humiliated wife in an age when women could expect little sympathy from society for these abuses. The case illustrates the value of state and local records to women's history. Based on state and local records at the Department of Archives and History in Atlanta, Georgia; 27 notes. 1869-1931

Godchaux, Leon

2607. Wall, Bennett H. LEON GODCHAUX AND THE GODCHAUX BUSINESS ENTERPRISES. *Am. Jewish Hist. Q. 1976 66(1): 50-66.* Reconstructs the life and influence of Leon Godchaux (1824-99), New Orleans merchant, plantation owner, sugar refiner, real estate developer, and financier, who proved that hard work, canny business judgment and ingenuity made it possible for a poor immigrant boy to rise rapidly to wealth and importance. Based on papers and clippings of the Godchaux family. 29 notes. 19c

Godchaux family

2608. Arnstein, Flora J. and Park, Susan B. THE GODCHAUX SISTERS. *Western States Jewish Hist. Q. 1982 15(1): 40-47.* The four Godchaux sisters, Adele, Helene, Rebecca, and Josephine, were the daughters of Alsatian Jews who came to the United States in 1840. Adele was the only one who was married (to Sylvain Salomon). All four sisters taught French and music to the children of San Francisco's elite. One of their pupils was Yehudi Menuhin. In the 1920's, appreciative students and their parents raised a fund to send the three single Godchaux sisters and their brother Edmond (who served 33 years as the San Francisco County Recorder) on a trip to France. Based on the authors' recollections and communication from Godchaux family members; 3 photos, 12 notes. 1880's-1920's

Goddard, Robert Hutchings

2609. Rhodes, Richard. "GOD PITY A ONE-DREAM MAN." *Am. Heritage 1980 31(4): 24-33.* Outlines the career of Robert Hutchings Goddard (1882-1945), space navigation pioneer, who published the first "detailed, physically and mathematically correct" theory of astronautics. 1901-45

Godfrey, Benjamin

2610. White, Elizabeth Pearson. CAPTAIN BENJAMIN GODFREY AND THE ALTON AND SANGAMON RAILROAD. *J. of the Illinois State Hist. Soc. 1974 67(5): 466-486.* Benjamin Godfrey, a former sea captain, was the Alton and Sangamon Railroad's instigator. Abraham Lincoln and other prominent Illinois citizens helped to subscribe the initial capital. Nevertheless, Godfrey was constantly short of money, mortgaging everything to complete the construction. On 9 September 1852, the first train ran from Alton to Springfield. By 1855 the last section was completed, but Godfrey's finances were in a chaos which he blamed on Wall Street financiers. He died in 1862, but the railroad line that he opened still serves the rich Illinois heartland. Primary sources; 9 illus., 72 notes. 1833-62

Godkin, Edwin Lawrence

2611. Hoogenboom, Ari and Hoogenboom, Olive. DENIGRATING E. L. GODKIN. *Rev. in Am. Hist. 1979 7(2): 224-228.* Review article prompted by William M. Armstrong's *E.L. Godkin: A Biography* (Albany: State U. of New York Pr., 1978) and William M. Armstrong's *The Gilded Age Letters of E.L. Godkin* (Albany: State U. of New York Pr., 1974). 1870's-90's

2612. Murray, Randall L. EDWIN LAWRENCE GODKIN: UNBENDING EDITOR IN TIMES OF CHANGE. *Journalism Hist. 1974 1(3): 77-81, 89.* Examines Godkin's time (1865-82) as editor of the *Nation,* his personal philosophy, and his comments on American society. 1865-82

Godwin, Parke

2613. Wennersten, John R. PARKE GODWIN, UTOPIAN SOCIALISM, AND THE POLITICS OF ANTISLAVERY. *New York Hist. Soc. Q. 1976 60(3/4): 107-127.* A study of the career of Parke Godwin (1816-1904) shows how the antislavery issue divided American antebellum reformers and virtually ended the movement for utopian socialism. Princetonian Godwin, a journalist and associate of William Cullen Bryant and William Leggett, became a follower of Charles Fourier and an opponent of abolitionism which, he believed, would result in interracial conflict. He became involved in Brook Farm until he broke with its members over Texas, but was forced to continue partisan political journalism to support his family. By the end of the Mexican War both Brook Farm and the socialist movement had ended; yet Godwin continued to work for economic reform and to strive for perfection. His career indicated "both the idealism and the naivete of American Fourierists." Personal writings and correspondence; 2 illus., 42 notes. 1837-47

Goebel, William Justus

2614. Combs, Bert T. WILLIAM GOEBEL (BOONE DAY ADDRESS, 1978). *Register of the Kentucky Hist. Soc. 1978 76(4): 307-313.* Accounts the life and career of William Justus Goebel (1856-99), the only American governor who was assassinated while in office. Elected in a disputed election in 1899 Goebel was shot on 30 January and died on 3 February, shortly after being sworn into office. Three men were tried and convicted for the murder, although trial errors resulted in appeals, retrials, and eventual pardons for two of the three. One of those convicted, Caleb Powers, ran for Congress after being pardoned and served from 1910-20. 1856-99

2615. Thomas, Edison H., ed. MILTON H. SMITH TALKS ABOUT THE GOEBEL AFFAIR. *Register of the Kentucky Hist. Soc. 1980 78(4): 322-342.* 1900
*For abstract see **Smith, Milton H.***

Goelet, Jacob

2616. Scott, Kenneth. JACOB GOELET: TRANSLATOR OF DUTCH FOR THE PROVINCE OF NEW YORK. *Halve Maen 1981 55(4): 1-6, 20-21.* Biography of Jacob Goelet (1689-1769), born in New York of Dutch parents, who grew up bilingual and became an interpreter of the Low Dutch language for the province of New York. 1689-1769

Goffman, Erving

2617. Collins, Randall. RIFLESSIONI SUL PASSAGGIO DELLE GENERAZIONI INTELLETTUALI [Reflections on the passing of the intellectual generations]. *Rassegna Italiana di Sociologia [Italy] 1984 25(3): 351-368.* Reflects on the career of the late Erving Goffman and on his contributions to the sociology profession. 1950's-70's

Gold, Michael

2618. Brogna, John Joseph. "Michael Gold: Critic and Playwright." U. of Georgia 1982. 165 pp. *DAI 1983 43(11): 3457-A.* DA8308161 20c

Goldbaum, Simon

2619. Baranov, Helen Goldbaum. SIMON GOLDBAUM OF SAN LUIS REY, CALIFORNIA. *Western States Jewish Hist. Q. 1981 13(2): 121-125.* Simon Goldbaum (1847-1916) was the principal businessman of San Luis Rey from 1875 to 1908. He operated a general store, hotel, livery stable, and telegraph office, serving a community of mostly Mexican and Indian families. Based on an interview with Goldbaum's daughter, on file with the San Diego Historical Society; illus., 6 notes. 1875-1908

Goldberg, Nikolai M.

2620. —. N. M. GOL'DBERG [N. M. Goldberg]. *Novaia i Noveishaia Istoriia [USSR] 1971 (1): 207.* Gives an obituary of Nikolai M. Goldberg, senior fellow of the Museum of the History of Religion and Atheism. A central focus of his research was US history; in 1965, he published a book on 18th- to 19th-century freethinking and atheism in the United States. In this and other works he refuted the bourgeois notion that the founders of the American republic were deeply religious. He also prepared modern-history textbooks and wrote articles on the teaching of modern history. Note. 18c-19c

Goldman, Edward Alphonso

2621. Sterling, Keir. NATURALISTS OF THE SOUTHWEST AT THE TURN OF THE CENTURY. *Environmental Rev. 1978 3(1): 20-33.* 1880's-1910's
*For abstract see **Bailey, Vernon***

Goldman, Emma

2622. McKinley, Blaine. "THE QUAGMIRES OF NECESSITY": AMERICAN ANARCHISTS AND DILEMMAS OF VOCATION. *Am. Q. 1982 34(5): 503-523.* 1893-1920
*For abstract see **deCleyre, Voltairine***

2623. Rosenberg, Karen. AN AUTUMNAL LOVE OF EMMA GOLDMAN. *Dissent 1983 30(3): 380-382.* Describes the love affair between anarchist Emma Goldman and businessman Leon Malmed. 1897-1940

2624. Wexler, Alice. THE EARLY LIFE OF EMMA GOLDMAN. *Psychohistory Rev. 1980 8(4): 7-21.* Examines the psychological roots of Emma Goldman's career as an anarchist. While Goldman may have rejected her father, she also loved and identified with him. Throughout much of her life she was fascinated with female political martyrs and their lives. This may have influenced her life. Goldman was influenced by her Russian background, making her early history quite different from other Jewish immigrants of the late 19th century. Goldman's psychohistory reveals her anarchism had roots in a desire to separate from her parents and in her need to relieve guilt toward her father and brother. Exposure to strong women early in her life gave Goldman models. 36 notes. 1889-1912

Goldman, Richard Franko

2625. Lester, Noel K. "Richard Franko Goldman: His Life and Works." Peabody Inst. of the Johns Hopkins U. 1984. 360 pp. *DAI 1984 45(5): 1236-A.* DA8417660 1910-80

Goldstein, David

2626. Campbell, Debra. A CATHOLIC SALVATION ARMY: DAVID GOLDSTEIN, PIONEER LAY EVANGELIST. *Church Hist. 1983 52(3): 322-332.* David Goldstein, a convert from Judaism and socialism, became a lay Catholic street lecturer. Goldstein, with the help of Martha Moore Avery, founded the Catholic Truth Guild in 1917. During the following quarter-century, Goldstein and his associates used methods like those employed by evangelists like Billy Sunday, traveling across the country to increase Catholic Church membership. 46 notes. 1917-41

2627. Campbell, Debra. DAVID GOLDSTEIN AND THE RISE OF THE CATHOLIC CAMPAIGNERS FOR CHRIST. *Catholic Historical Review 1986 72(1): 33-50.* Focuses on a neglected figure in the neglected field of the history of American Catholic laity: David Goldstein, a convert from Judaism and socialism who spent the years between 1917 and 1941 as a freelance open-air lecturer on Catholic subjects. Explores

Goldstein's controversial techniques and trappings, including the use of flamboyant, custom-built lecture cars, which prompted comparisons to the Salvation Army and Billy Sunday, and examines the reactions of his Catholic contemporaries active in parallel apostolates. Places Goldstein within a larger context in the history of American Catholic evangelism. 54 notes. 1917-41

Goldwyn, Samuel.

2628. Aberbach, David. THE MOGUL WHO LOVED ART. *Commentary 1981 72(3): 67-71.* Provides a brief biography of Polish-born Jewish immigrant, Samuel Goldwyn (1882-1974), who came to America in 1895, focusing on the film producer's combination of artistic instinct and business savvy, which resulted in some of Hollywood's finest films. 1895-1974

2629. Lasky, Betty. LET'S MAKE A MOVIE. *Westways 1979 71(11): 22-25.* 1911-14
*For abstract see **Lasky, Jesse L.***

Gompers, Samuel

2630. Monteleone, Renato. SAM GOMPERS: PROFILO DI UN JINGO AMERICANO [Sam Gompers: profile of an American jingo]. *Movimento Operaio e Socialista [Italy] 1976 22(1-2): 133-152.* Defines "jingo" in its American context and says it accurately describes Samuel Gompers, founder of the American Federation of Labor. Gompers openly supported and initiated racist policies; AFL exclusion of nonqualified workers coincided with an influx of immigrant workers. Gompers fought hard to stop immigration, particularly of Orientals, because he feared for American independence and security. Along with the industrialists and financiers of his day, Gompers refused to acknowledge a connection between capitalism and imperialism and failed to recognize what was occurring in international politics. Protesting Bolshevism, he failed to comprehend the threat of a reactionary crisis of the democratic bourgeoisie and thus later suggested to American workers that fascism was a model for the reconciliation of the classes. Primary and secondary sources. 1850-1924

Gonzales, B. M.

2631. Yabes, Leopoldo Y., ed. B. M. GONZALES: SCIENTIST, EDUCATOR, ADMINISTRATOR. *Philippine Social Sci. and Humanities Rev. [Philippines] 1976 41(4): 509-512.* Analyzes and reviews the scientific, educational, and administrative records of B. M. Gonzales. Compared to the records of similar men in the Philippines, B. M. Gonzales bequeathed to the University of the Philippines a solid foundation of institutional integrity. 1939-51

Gonzáles, Rodolfo

2632. Jensen, Richard J. and Hammerback, John C. "NO REVOLUTIONS WITHOUT POETS": THE RHETORIC OF RODOLFO "CORKY" GONZALES. *Western J. of Speech Communication 1982 46(1): 72-91.* Examines the career of Rodolfo "Corky" Gonzáles (born 1928), a founder of the Crusade for Justice (1965) in Denver, Colorado, active in the Chicano political party La Raza Unida, and author of the influential Chicano poem *Yo Soy Joaquín* (1967); focuses on the rhetorical techniques he utilized in his poems, speeches, and plays. 1928-72

González Rubio, José

2633. Neri, Michael C. GONZALEZ RUBIO AND CALIFORNIA CATHOLICISM, 1846-1850. *Southern California Q. 1976 58(4): 441-457.* Assesses the work of Father José González Rubio (1804-75), who as governor of the mitre (diocesan administrator) for Upper and Lower California presided over the shift from Mexican to American law and culture during 1846-50. González Rubio faced such problems as intermarriage of Protestants and Catholics, the need for tithing, and a shortage of qualified priests. He believed the mission lands rightfully belonged to the Indians and that Church possessions would be fairly adjudicated by the United States. At the end of his tenure Californians commissioned a painting of him in appreciation of his efforts on their behalf. It is at Mission Santa Barbara. In a time of uncertainty and transition, González Rubio helped the Catholic Church to survive in California. Primary and secondary sources; 63 notes. 1846-50

Goobridge brothers

2634. Jezierski, John V. PHOTOGRAPHING THE LUMBER BOOM: THE GOODRIDGE BROTHERS OF SAGINAW, MICHIGAN (1863-1922). *Michigan Hist. 1980 64(6): 28-33.* The Goobridge brothers, black business pioneers in East Saginaw, Michigan, ran a photographic service, 1866-1922. Vividly documenting the history of the lumbering industry, their photographs also attest to the brothers' importance as members of a developing profession. They explored a new mode of expression. 15 photos, 10 notes. 1863-1922

Good, John Booth

2635. Peake, F. A. JOHN BOOTH GOOD IN BRITISH COLUMBIA: THE TRIALS AND TRIBULATIONS OF THE CHURCH, 1861-99. *Pacific Northwest Q. 1984 75(2): 70-78.* Describes the activities of John Booth Good, a missionary of the Church of England's Society for the Propagation of the Gospel, among the Indians and British settlers in the Vancouver Island area of British Columbia, and looks at his conflicts with Bishop George Hill. Based on Society for the Propagation of the Gospel files in the Public Archives of Canada, Ottawa; 2 illus., 4 photos, 25 notes. 1861-99

Goodale, Elaine

2636. Dobrow, Julie. WHITE SISTER OF THE SIOUX. *Masterkey 1982 56(3): 103-106.* Elaine Goodale, known as the White Sister of the Sioux, was a teacher on the Great Sioux Reservation during 1886-91 and a supervisor of Bureau of Indian Affairs schools in North and South Dakota; she became such a good and trusted friend that she was allowed to view the Ghost Dance. 1886-91

Goodard, Sarah Updike

2637. Henry, Susan. SARAH GODDARD, GENTLEWOMAN PRINTER. *Journalism Q. 1980 57(1): 23-30.* Sarah Updike Goodard (ca. 1700-70) became a successful printer and publisher in Rhode Island during an era when printing was primarily a male-dominated profession. She took over the Providence *Gazette* from her son William in 1765, turned it into a financial success, and managed the printing operation well. Both her son's and Mrs. Goddard's politics were pro-Whig, and their bias was apparent in their publications. Induced to join William and to manage his printing operation in Philadelphia, Mrs. Goddard soon died there. Based on published family letters; 91 notes. 1760-70

Goodbear, Paul "Flying Eagle"

2638. Thornburgh, Luella. PAUL "FLYING EAGLE" GOODBEAR. *New Mexico Hist. Rev. 1961 36(4): 257-262.* Biography of Cheyenne Indian artist Paul "Flying Eagle" Goodbear (d. 1954), focusing on his contribution to New Mexico history by restoring the prehistoric murals at Coronado Monument Museum near Bernalillo; also includes Goodbear's account of the Cheyenne Sun Dance; mid-1940's to 1954. ca 1945-54

Goodman, Benny

2639. Sudhalter, Richard M. BENNY GOODMAN. *Am. Heritage 1981 32(6): 4-13.* Interview of Benjamin David Goodman (b.1909), which occurred during November 1980-81. Goodman discussed his long musical career since the 1920's and his attitude toward today's music. 15 illus. ca 1925-80

Goodsell, Willystine

2640. Engel, Robert E. WILLYSTINE GOODSELL: FEMINIST AND RECONSTRUCTIONIST EDUCATOR. *Vitae Scholasticae 1984 4[i.e., 3](2): 355-378.* Willystine Goodsell, progressive educator and feminist, studied under John Dewey and spent 31 years on the faculty of the Teachers College at Columbia University. As a board member of the *Social Frontier,* a radical journal, she became aligned with other well-known social reconstructionists. Goodsell produced a large quantity and variety of writings, and therefore is attractive to individuals wishing to study women educators who were reconstructionists. Goodsell believed that society failed to provide opportunities for women, and that schools should teach social responsibility. 67 notes. 1906-40

Goon Dip

2641. Jue, Willard G. and Jue, Silas G. GOON DIP: ENTREPRENEUR, DIPLOMAT, AND COMMUNITY LEADER. *Annals of the Chinese Historical Society of the Pacific Northwest 1984: 40-50.* Assesses the contributions of Chinese immigrant merchant Goon Yun-dip (usually called Goon Dip) to the economic development of the Chinese-American communities in Portland, Oregon, and Seattle, Washington. 5 photos, glossary, biblio. Chinese summary, p. xiv; English summary, p. xi. 1870's-1920's

Gordon, Bazil

2642. Gordon, Douglas H. BAZIL GORDON, HIS FOREBEARS AND DESCENDANTS. *Maryland Historical Magazine 1984 79(4): 344-347.* Traces the genealogy of Bazil Gordon (1768-1847) of Lochdougan, Scotland, who emigrated to Virginia in 1783 and with his brother Samuel bought the Fielding Lewis house and estate on the western edge of Fredericksburg, Maryland, naming it "Kenmore." During Jefferson's embargo, Bazil became perhaps the first American to acquire a seven digit fortune in cash, through the shrewdness of his tobacco agent in London. In 1822, he bought the large Rappahannock tract he called "Wakefield," and upon his death left half a million dollars to his daughter Annie Campbell Gordon, who married the grandson of John Hanson. Mentions subsequent notable members of the family. Based on Gordon family records and diaries. 1783-1984

Gordon, Caroline

2643. Fitzgerald, Sally. A MASTER CLASS: FROM THE CORRESPONDENCE OF CAROLINE GORDON AND FLANNERY O'CONNOR. *Georgia Rev. 1979 33(4): 827-846.* 1951-64
*For abstract see **O'Connor, Flannery***

2644. Fraistat, Rose Ann Cleveland. "Caroline Gordon as Novelist and Woman of Letters." U. of Pennsylvania 1980. 350 pp. *DAI 1981 41(7): 3105-A.* 8028856 1920-79

Gordon, Charles

2645. Calderhead, William L. A STRANGE CAREER IN A YOUNG NAVY: CAPTAIN CHARLES GORDON, 1778-1816. *Maryland Hist. Mag. 1977 72(3): 373-386.* The exile of Charles Gordon's Tory father from Maryland during the Revolution cast a blight over the son's life and naval career, "a kind of specter of British origin." Despite an optimistic start, Gordon's naval service record was set back by his position as second officer on the ill-fated *Chesapeake* in 1807, and by a wound received in a duel, which refused to heal for years. Consequently, he missed the most important commands during the War of 1812 and, although recording some outstanding successes against the Algerian pirates, he never reached the hero status of his contemporaries such as Perry, Decatur, and Lawrence. Unfortunate timing of his duty assignments, the duel, and the English shadow had their impact. Primary and secondary sources; 58 notes. 1778-1816

Gordon, Helen Skinner

2646. Gordon, J. King. THE WORLD OF HELEN GORDON. *Manitoba Pageant [Canada] 1978 24(1): 1-14.* The author reminisces about his mother, Helen Skinner Gordon 1876-1961 of Winnipeg, Manitoba, who was a member of the Presbyterial, the Conference Branch, and the Dominion Board of the Woman's Missionary Society of the Presbyterian and United Churches, and whose home is now the clubhouse for the University Women's Club. 1890's-1961

Gordon, Jean and Kate

2647. Gilley, B. H. KATE GORDON AND LOUISIANA WOMAN SUFFRAGE. *Louisiana Hist. 1983 24(3): 289-306.* Kate Gordon spearheaded Louisiana's woman suffrage movement. She advocated achieving woman suffrage on a state-by-state basis and opposed a national constitutional amendment because it would undermine the states' control over their own electorates. Gordon argued that suffrage should be extended to white women only. She and her supporters were able to place a woman suffrage amendment on the Louisiana ballot in 1918, but it lost. Based on private papers, suffrage club minutes, and newspapers; 69 notes. 1896-1918

2648. Kemp, Kathryn W. JEAN AND KATE GORDON: NEW ORLEANS SOCIAL REFORMERS, 1898-1933. *Louisiana Hist. 1983 24(4): 389-401.* The Gordon sisters, members of the "Protestant, prosperous, and progressive" segment of New Orleans society, were social reformers involved in myriad causes, including protection of child laborers, prevention of cruelty to animals, control of tuberculosis, women's rights, and the eugenics movement. Based on Gordon family papers, Milne Home records, and newspapers; 54 notes. 1898-1933

Gordon, John

2649. Starin, Mary M. THE REVEREND DOCTOR JOHN GORDON, 1717-1790. *Maryland Hist. Mag. 1980 75(3): 167-197.* Information already published about the Reverend John Gordon in secondary sources has, in almost every instance, proved to be incorrect. Despite diligent research, large gaps in the biography of this important clergyman of St. Michael's Parish in Talbot County, Maryland, remain unfilled. Active in secular affairs as well, a member of the famed Tuesday Club, Gordon was one of the many Anglicans who long opposed the establishment of an episcopate in this country, although the revolution caused him to reevaluate his position. His tenure (1749-90) at St. Michael's put him in the list of Maryland's first citizens. 103 notes. 1749-90

Gordon, John Brown

2650. Culpepper, Grady Sylvester. "The Political Career of John Brown Gordon, 1868 to 1897." Emory U. 1981. 173 pp. *DAI 1982 42(7): 3271-A.* 8129852 1868-97

2651. Eckert, Ralph Lowell. "John Brown Gordon: Soldier, Southerner, American." (Vol. 1-2) Louisiana State U. 1983. 447 pp. *DAI 1984 44(9): 2860-A.* DA8400113 1860's-1904

Gordon, John Campbell

See Aberdeen and Temair, 1st Marquis of

Gordon, Robert Winslow

2652. Kodish, Debora G. A NATIONAL PROJECT WITH MANY WORKERS: ROBERT WINSLOW GORDON AND THE ARCHIVE OF AMERICAN FOLK SONG. *Q. J. of the Lib. of Congress 1978 35(4): 218-233.* Robert Winslow Gordon (1888-1961) served for four years as the first director of the Archive of American Folk Song at the Library of Congress, founded in 1928 with the help of Carl Engel, chief of the Music Division. Although Gordon's popular-scholarly approach to the collection of folk songs led him to record by phonograph sea songs along the San Francisco waterfront, Appalachian mountain songs around Asheville, North Carolina, and Afro-American songs around Darien, Georgia, and to edit a column, "Old Songs That Men Have Sung," in *Adventure* magazine from 1923 to 1927, he never published his theories in scholarly journals. Discusses Gordon's inventiveness in collecting folk songs and his difficulties in founding and maintaining a national center for the collection and study of folk songs. His collection is now part of the Archive of Folk Song at the Library of Congress. Based on correspondence and tapes in the Archive of Folk Song; 6 photos, 25 notes. 1917-33

Gorman, R. C.

2653. Monthan, Guy and Monthan, Doris. THE UNPREDICTABLE R. C. GORMAN. *Am. Indian Art Mag. 1978 3(3): 50-57.* R. C. Gorman, a Navajo artist, works in painting, lithograph, tapestry, and sculpture; covers 1950's-78. 1950's-78

Gotlieb, Howard

2654. Gotlieb, Howard; Yoken, Mel, interviewer. COLLECTING THE TWENTIETH CENTURY: CURATOR HOWARD GOTLIEB. *Wilson Library Bulletin 1986 60(8): 24-29.* Prints an interview with Howard Gotlieb, curator-archivist of Boston University's Mugar Library, who reflects on his life as a collector; describes some of the library's holdings and famous individuals he has worked with; and discusses the role of archival collections in scholarship. 1963-85

Gottschalk, Louis Moreau

2655. Andrews, Peter. "THE KING OF PIANISTS." *Am. Heritage 1982 34(1): 62-70.* The works of America's first important composer, Louis Moreau Gottschalk (1829-69), have recently been revived. Gottschalk, who became one of the most famous pianists and composers of his time, was at his best in the romanticism of the 1840's, but, upon his return from a European stay, his popularity declined. His own romantic impulses kept him on the move and resulted in his sudden departure for South America in 1865. He died there four years later at the age of 69. 6 photos, 4 illus. ca 1840-70

Gough, John B.

2656. Phillips, Loretta and Phillips, Prentice. HE FOUGHT A HORDE OF DEMONS. *New-England Galaxy 1977 19(1): 45-51.* Describes the personal struggles of John B. Gough against Demon Rum during 1834-43. His preachings against liquor, from 1843 until his death in 1886, persuaded thousands of alcoholics to sign the pledge of total abstinence. 3 illus. 1828-86

Gould, Jay

2657. Klein, Maury. MAN OF MYSTERY. *Am. Hist. Illus. 1977 12(6): 10-18.* The public image of Jay Gould (1836-92) was at best exaggerated and misleading. Gould was vulnerable to adverse publicity because of his desire for privacy and his frail personal bearing. Nevertheless, he was a shrewd entrepreneur. "No other individual, except perhaps J. P. Morgan, exerted so great an influence upon the nation's rail system." His accomplishments, 1879-81, were "unprecedented in the business and financial life of the country." He died in 1892 and left an estate of $72 million. 11 illus. 1860's-92

Gould, John (Jack)

2658. Saalbach, Louis C. A CRITIC'S VIEW OF THE FEDERAL COMMUNICATIONS COMMISSION: JACK GOULD OF THE *NEW YORK TIMES. Michigan Acad. 1983 15(3): 391-399.* A biography of broadcasting critic Jack Gould, who believed that broadcasting's responsibility for social betterment should be enforced by the Federal Communications Commission. 1942-72

2659. Saalbach, Louis C. "Jack Gould: Social Critic of the Television Medium, 1947-1972." U. of Michigan 1980. 277 pp. *DAI 1981 41(9): 3772-A.* 8106218 1947-72

Gould, Morton

2660. Evans, Lee. "Morton Gould: His Life and Music." Columbia U. Teachers Coll. 1978. 387 pp. 1950's-70's

Gourlay, Robert

2661. Bloch, Gerald. ROBERT GOURLAY'S VISION OF AGRARIAN REFORM. *Can. Papers in Rural Hist. [Canada] 1982 3: 110-128.* Brief biography of the Scottish-born agricultural reformer Robert Gourlay, who arrived in Upper Canada ca. 1809, having depleted his resources agitating for the revision of England's poor laws, focusing on

Gourlay's schemes for economic and social reform which came to be known as "systematic colonization"; 1778-1820's. 1778-1820's

Gowan, James R.

2662. Fisher, W. Allen. THE TALE OF A TRUNK. *Ontario Hist. [Canada] 1978 70(2): 137-143.* A trunk containing the papers of Sir James R. Gowan (1815-1909) was auctioned in Montreal in 1977. Discusses the background of the sale and the provenance of the papers. Briefly outlines Gowan's career, from a childhood in rural Ireland, to law student days in Canada, and then to positions as a lawyer, local judge, and finally senator. 3 illus. 1830's-1909

Grabowskii, Arthur

2663. Pula, James S. ARTHUR GRABOWSKII: SOLDIER, EDUCATOR AND ENIGMA. *Polish Am. Studies 1982 39(1): 55-82.* A biography of a Polish emigre who during his 53 years of active employment in the United States held 14 different positions in six different occupations, including that of a teacher in which capacity, over the years, he taught eight nonrelated subjects. There is no connection between his work in the United States and the cause of Poland. Nor is there any connection between the Polish-American community and Grabowskii, who even discarded the Polish spelling of his name. Grabowskii's life is representative of life in a restless age of nonspecialization. The ambitious Grabowskii never remained in any one position long enough to influence the course of events; however, like many other dedicated conscientious incumbents he added to the cumulative contributions of the institutions with which he had been associated. Mainly primary sources; 100 notes. 1836-1930

Grabowskii, Arthur E. A.

2664. Brown, Russell K. THE COUNT OF VILLA GRABOWA: THE LIFE OF COLONEL ARTHUR GRABOWSKII. *Richmond County History 1984 16(2): 28-36.* Gives a biography of Arthur Edward Adolphus Grabowskii, who moved to America from Russia in 1855 and later became president of Defiance College in Ohio. 1855-1930

Grace, John Patrick

2665. Boggs, Doyle Willard, Jr. "John Patrick Grace and the Politics of Reform in South Carolina, 1900-1931." U. of South Carolina 1977. 274 pp. *DAI 1978 38(9): 5661-A.* 1900-31

Graham, Albert B.

2666. Crout, George C. ALBERT B. GRAHAM: SCHOOL DAYS OF A SCHOOLMASTER. *Ohio Hist. 1977 86(2): 115-126.* A biographical sketch of Albert B. Graham, founder of the first 4-H Club in 1902 and first Director of Agricultural Extension at Ohio State University. Contains selected excerpts from Graham's personal memoirs, most of which discuss his education and teachers in nineteenth-century rural Ohio. Based on manuscript, newspaper, and secondary sources; 5 illus., 39 notes. 1874-75

Graham, Andrew

2667. Williams, Glyndwr. ANDREW GRAHAM AND THOMAS HUTCHINS: COLLABORATION AND PLAGIARISM IN 18TH CENTURY NATURAL HISTORY. *Beaver [Canada] 1978 308(4): 4-14.* Andrew Graham served more than 30 years in various Hudson's Bay Company posts, became a trained observer, and accumulated much information on people, plants, and the natural history of the region. Hutchins came to the area in 1772 as a surgeon and also became a natural history enthusiast. Within a few years, many natural history works were published in England and Europe, often crediting the two men, but mostly praising the work of Thomas Hutchins. However, it appears that Hutchins gleaned most of his information from data gathered by Graham. Hutchins died in 1790, Graham in 1815. The mystery is heightened by the fact that Graham had nothing but praise for Hutchins, though he must have been aware that the other man was earning a wide reputation based on pilfered materials. Based on Hudson's Bay Company materials; 8 illus., map. 1770's-1815

Graham, Billy

2668. Arnold, Bob. BILLY GRAHAM, SUPERSTAR. *Southern Exposure 1976 4(3): 76-82.* Billy Graham, once a shy, southern boy, became a world-renowned evangelical leader, preaching a gospel of middle class morality and political conservatism, 1940's-70's. 1940's-70's

2669. Pierard, Richard V. FROM EVANGELICAL EXCLUSIVISM TO ECUMENICAL OPENNESS: BILLY GRAHAM AND SOCIOPOLITICAL ISSUES. *J. of Ecumenical Studies 1983 20(3): 425-446.* During his career as an evangelist, Billy Graham has significantly modified his views on race relations, Communism, America's role in God's plan for the world, and nuclear war. His fundamentalist background often caused him to take conservative positions on public issues. His ever-increasing ecumenical and global contacts have enabled him to break out of these constrictions and even build bridges to Roman Catholic and Jewish communities. Graham first broke with his fundamentalist background over the issue of race and integration; he cooperated with presidents Eisenhower and Johnson in working for improvements in civil rights. He has gradually moved away from his hard anti-Communist position as his travels to the Soviet Union have forced him to reevaluate his views on Communism. He now regards his view of a Christian America as a civil religion and he also now speaks against the nuclear arms race. 1940's-83

2670. Pierard, Richard V. BILLY GRAHAM AND VIETNAM: FROM COLD WARRIOR TO PEACEMAKER. *Christian Scholar's Rev. 1980 10(1): 37-51.* Chronicles preacher Billy Graham's shift away from political conservatism, and the impact of the Vietnam War on the role of evangelism in public policy. 1945-80

Graham, Evander McNair

2671. Thompson, William Y. E. M. GRAHAM, EARLY NORTH LOUISIANA LEADER: THE BEGINNINGS. *Louisiana Hist. 1981 22(3): 225-238.* The antecedents and early life of Evander McNair Graham, "lawyer, judge, political, civic, and religious leader" until his enlistment in the Confederate army in 1861 at age 25. Includes material on the religious, educational, and economic milieu. Based on the Graham Family Papers; 59 notes. 1830-61

Graham, Jessie Donaldson Schultz

2672. Banks, Anne. JESSIE DONALDSON SCHULTZ AND BLACKFEET CRAFTS. *Montana 1983 33(4): 18-35.* Jessie Donaldson Schultz Graham's career and activities focused on Montana's Blackfoot Indians with particular emphasis on developing native craft skills under the Federal

Emergency Relief Administration in the 1930's. Her activities were responsible for preserving much Blackfoot traditional heritage. Part of her oral autobiography recounting these events is reproduced. Based on the Jessie Donaldson Schultz Graham oral autobiography at the Museum of the Rockies, Montana State University, Bozeman; 14 illus., 46 notes. 1934-64

Graham, Margaret Collier

2673. Apostol, Jane. MARGARET COLLIER GRAHAM: FIRST LADY OF THE FOOTHILLS. *Southern California Q. 1981 63(4): 348-373.* A profile of Margaret Collier Graham (1850-1910), short story writer, teacher, and real estate promoter. Born in Iowa, Graham came to California with her husband who was ill with tuberculosis. Eventually they settled in South Pasadena. Graham wrote numerous sketches and stories that she submitted to Pacific Coast literary magazines and, as she grew more successful, to such national publications as *Century* and *Atlantic.* With her husband ill, Graham taught school. They also invested in real estate and successfully developed the Lake Elsinore community, which she named. Graham's stories were filled with a sense of place and character; her heroines possessed the inner strength needed to overcome adversity. Graham's writing was curtailed by involvement in women's rights issues and historic preservation efforts, but in later life her stories were published in book form. Photos, 83 notes. 1850-1910

Graham, Shirley

2674. Perkins, Kathy A. THE UNKNOWN CAREER OF SHIRLEY GRAHAM. *Freedomways 1985 25(1): 6-17.* Reviews the life and work of black musician, composer, playwright, and director Shirley Graham, who excelled in every dimension of her career until her marriage in 1951 to black activist W. E. B. DuBois changed the focus of her work. 1920's-51

2675. Peterson, Bernard L., Jr. SHIRLEY GRAHAM DU BOIS: COMPOSER AND PLAYWRIGHT. *Crisis 1977 84(5): 177-179.* Shirley Graham Du Bois, widow of William Edward B. Du Bois, was a prolific writer, biographer, composer, and playwright. She composed a three-act music-drama which was later built into the full-scale opera, *Tom-Tom.* She utilized unusual rhythms and instruments, many of which were native to Africa. In 1936 she supervised the Negro Unit of the Chicago Federal Theater. Under a Rosenwald Fellowship, she studied at Yale University, during 1938-40, where she wrote five more plays. Only one play has been published to this date. 1930-50

Graham, William

2676. Robson, David. "AN IMPORTANT QUESTION ANSWERED": WILLIAM GRAHAM'S DEFENSE OF SLAVERY IN POST-REVOLUTIONARY VIRGINIA. *William and Mary Q. 1980 37(4): 644-652.* As part of his course on human nature, the Reverend William Graham, rector of Liberty Hall Academy (now Washington and Lee University), gave an annual lecture on slavery to senior students, from the late 1780's to 1796. A brief biography of Graham is included. Contrary to his Pennsylvania upbringing and political principles, Graham avidly defended slavery. The main reason was fear of what would happen if the slaves were freed. To Graham, Christianity and slavery did not conflict. Cites Graham and other literature on slavery; reproduces the "Lecture 30th. An Important Question Answered." 17 notes. ca 1786-96

Graham, William Morris

2677. Titley, E. Brian. W. M. GRAHAM: INDIAN AGENT EXTRAORDINAIRE. *Prairie Forum [Canada] 1983 8(1): 25-41.* Traces the career of William Morris Graham, his ambitions in the Department of Indian Affairs in Western Canada, 1885-1932, and his enthusiastic enforcement of the federal policy of "civilizing" the Native Americans by having them adopt European culture and religion, and by making them self-sufficient through agriculture. 1885-1932

Grandin, Vital

2678. Champagne, Claude. MISSION ET CIVILISATION DANS L'OUEST CANADIEN: VITAL GRANDIN, 1829-1902 [Missions and civilization in the Canadian West: Vital Grandin, 1829-1902]. *Sessions d'Etude: Soc. Can. d'Hist. de l'Eglise Catholique [Canada] 1983 50(1): 341-358.* Prints an account of the missionary work of Vital Grandin, who became a bishop of the Catholic Church in northwest Canada. 1854-1902

Grant, George Monro

2679. Angrave, James. WILLIAM DAWSON, GEORGE GRANT AND THE LEGACY OF SCOTTISH HIGHER EDUCATION. *Queen's Q. [Canada] 1975 82(1): 77-91.* 19c

For abstract see ***Dawson, John William***

Grant, Jedediah Morgan

2680. Sessions, Gene A. THE HOLDING FORTH OF JEDDY GRANT. *Dialogue 1979 12(4): 62-70.* Describes the career of Jedediah Morgan Grant, early Mormon missionary. Grant spent most of his preaching career in the eastern and southeastern United States, rather than in the Zion established by the Mormons in Utah. Covers 1833-57. Based on Grant's journal and on secondary sources; 24 notes. 1833-57

Grant, Rachel Ridgway Ivins

2681. Walker, Ronald W. RACHEL R. GRANT: THE CONTINUING LEGACY OF THE FEMININE IDEAL. *Dialogue 1982 15(3): 105-121.* Rachel Ridgway Ivins Grant was born in New Jersey. She converted to Mormonism at an early age, living at first in Nauvoo, Illinois, and later in Utah. In 1855, at the age of 32, she married Jedediah Morgan Grant. Their son, Herbert, eventually became president of the Mormon Church. Her husband died in 1856, after which she and her son lived a life of poverty and hardship until she started a boardinghouse. She also became president of the local branch of the Mormon Relief Society, retiring at the age of 82. Throughout her life she was known for her firm moral strength. Secondary sources; 54 notes. 1846-1909

Grant, Ulysses S.

2682. Burin, S. N. ULISS GRANT—GENERAL ARMII SEVERA [Ulysses Grant, general of the Northern army]. *Novaia i Noveishaia Istoriia [USSR] 1984 (6): 133-149.* Outlines the military career of Ulysses S. Grant, commander of the Union armies in the Civil War and US president in 1869-77. At his instigation, the constitutional amendment of 1870 gave black Americans voting rights. Secondary sources; 54 notes. 1860-70's

2683. Current, Richard N. GRANT WITHOUT GREATNESS. *Rev. in Am. Hist. 1981 9(4): 507-509.* Reviews William S. McFeely's *Grant: A Biography* (1981). 1830-79

2684. Keiser, Thomas J. THE ST. LOUIS YEARS OF ULYSSES S. GRANT. *Gateway Heritage 1985-86 6(3): 10-21.* After the Mexican War, US Army assignments in California separated Ulysses S. Grant from his family, which had stayed behind at St. Louis. Grant resigned from the army in 1854 and spent the next six years at St. Louis where he never succeeded in farming, commercial enterprises, or appointive public posts. Based on printed collections of Grant's papers, Julia Grant's published memoirs, and archival documents at the Missouri Historical Society; 14 photos, 53 notes. 1854-60

2685. Temple, Wayne C. U.S. GRANT IN MILITARY SERVICE FOR THE STATE OF ILLINOIS. *Lincoln Herald 1981 83(3): 705-708.* Discusses Ulysses S. Grant's military service for the state of Illinois in the capacity of acting military aide to the governor, and later as colonel of the 21st Infantry Regiment, Illinois State Militia during April-July 1861. 1861

Grant, Ulysses S., Jr.

2686. Banning, Evelyn I. U. S. GRANT, JR., A BUILDER OF SAN DIEGO. *J. of San Diego Hist. 1981 27(1): 1-16.* Biography of Ulysses S. Grant, Jr., nicknamed Buck (1852-1929), who came West in 1893 from New York and settled in San Diego due to its warm climate, became involved in the real estate business, built the US Grant Hotel in 1910, and established himself as a pioneer of San Diego. 1893-1929

Granville brothers

2687. Brown, Philip C. THE FABULOUS GEE BEES. *Am. Aviation Hist. Soc. J. 1979 24(3): 187-201.* The four Granville brothers (Robert, Tom, Edward, and Mark) became famous for their air races and infamous for the number of near-fatal accidents and catastrophes which befell them, 1922-38. 1922-38

Grappe, François

2688. Grappe, Bernie. FRANÇOIS GRAPPE: UNIQUE NORTH LOUISIANA FRONTIERSMAN. *North Louisiana Hist. Assoc. J. 1978 9(2): 65-70.* Discusses the character, life, and career of François Grappe (1747-1825), whose contribution to North Louisiana history has been neglected. He served as Indian agent and interpreter for France, Spain, and the United States. His name is associated with the controversial "Grappe Reservation" of the Caddo Indian Treaty of 1835, but wrongly, because he had died a decade earlier. Colorful and gifted with an impressive knowledge of North Louisiana geography and Indian languages, he was held in high esteem. Based on the Grappe Collection, Centenary College, Shreveport, Louisiana, contemporary accounts, and secondary sources; 43 notes. 1760-1835

Graveline, Fred

2689. Olmsted, Merle C. AN AIRMAN TO REMEMBER. *Am. Aviation Hist. Soc. J. 1980 25(2): 119-123.* Sergeant 1st Class Fred Graveline, an observer-gunner in DH-4's with the 1st Army Air Service in France in October 1918, was one of only two Air Service enlisted men in World War I to win the Distinguished Service Cross. 1918

Graves, James Robinson

2690. Patterson, W. Morgan. THE SOUTHERN BAPTIST THEOLOGIAN AS CONTROVERSIALIST: A CONTRAST. *Baptist Hist. and Heritage 1980 15(3): 7-14.* Compares and contrasts the attitudes and outlooks of Southern Baptist James Robinson Graves (1820-93), founder of the Landmark movement, and Edgar Young Mullins (1860-1928), who was involved in the fundamentalist-modernist controversy of the 1920's; and discusses the contributions of both men to the theology of Southern Baptists. 1840-1928

Graves, Michael

2691. Filler, Martin. MICHAEL GRAVES: BEFORE AND AFTER. *Art in Am. 1980 68(7): 99-105.* A background sketch of American architect Michael Graves, whose designs changed radically during 1970-80, from Le Corbusier's Cubist-inspired architecture to Romantic/Rational architecture based on the Classical tradition; briefly traces the history of architectural styles in America since the 1920's, comparing Graves's work to those. 1920-80

Graves, Samuel

2692. Yerxa, Donald A. VICE ADMIRAL GRAVES AND THE NORTH AMERICAN SQUADRON, 1774-1776. *Mariner's Mirror [Great Britain] 1976 62(3): 371-385.* Comments on Samuel Graves' (1713-87) life and the problems he found when he took command of the British North American Squadron. Discusses in some detail the period of his command, giving examples of the problems he faced and the solutions he attempted. The major problem (never really solved) was inadequate forces for the ever increasing duties assigned. Lack of effective support from England compounded this. Attempts to evaluate the accusations of incompetence against him. Concludes that these were unjustified, but that he could have been more decisive in his actions. This resulted, however, from a lack of a clearcut and consistent policy in London, which resulted from Great Britain's lack of understanding of the North American situation. Based mainly on primary sources; 49 notes. 1774-76

Graves, William Jordan

2693. Thayer, Shelly A. THE DELEGATE AND THE DUEL: THE EARLY POLITICAL CAREER OF GEORGE WALLACE JONES. *Palimpsest 1984 65(5): 178-188.* 1820's-96

*For abstract see **Jones, George Wallace***

Gray, David

2694. Reigstad, Thomas J. "POET BY NATURE, JOURNALIST BY COMPULSION": NOTES ON THE LIFE AND WORK OF DAVID GRAY. *Niagara Frontier 1977 24(2): 29-35.* Biography of David Gray (1836-88), a poet and editor of the *Buffalo Courier* in Buffalo, New York, 1859-84. 1859-84

Gray, Gordon

2695. Greenya, John. THE QUIET POWER OF GORDON GRAY. *Hist. Preservation 1983 35(5): 26-29.* Recounts the career of Gordon Gray, who as chairman of the National Trust for Historic Preservation led the fight for passage of the National Historic Preservation Act (US, 1966). 1930's-73

Gray, John Morgan

2696. Stacey, C. P. JOHN MORGAN GRAY, 1907-1978. *Hist. Papers [Canada] 1980: 262-264.* John Morgan Gray was a president of the Macmillan Company of Canada, Ltd. Long a leader in the Canadian publishing world, he exercised a considerable influence on the culture of modern Canada. Gray came to Macmillan following World War II and guided the firm until 1973, when it was sold. His aim was to publish books which not only would sell but would be good for Canada. 1907-78

Gray, Judd

2697. Jones, Ann. SHE HAD TO DIE! *Am. Heritage 1980 31(6): 20-31.* 1925-28
*For abstract see **Snyder, Ruth***

Graydon, James

2698. Thompson, Jerry. THE VULTURE OVER THE CARRION: CAPTAIN JAMES "PADDY" GRAYDON AND THE CIVIL WAR IN THE TERRITORY OF NEW MEXICO. *J. of Arizona Hist. 1983 24(4): 381-404.* Relates the accomplishments of Captain James Graydon whose daring exploits for the Union Army staved off the Confederate efforts in New Mexico. Graydon's career ended in 1862 when he was killed by a doctor who objected to Graydon's massacre of a Mescalero Apache band. Based on newspapers and secondary sources; 4 photos, 59 notes. 1853-62

Grayson, Benjamin

2699. Horrell, Joseph, ed. NEW LIGHT ON WILLIAM GRAYSON: HIS GUARDIAN'S ACCOUNT. *Virginia Mag. of Hist. and Biog. 1984 92(4): 423-443.* 1758-62
*For abstract see **Grayson, William***

Grayson, William

2700. Horrell, Joseph, ed. NEW LIGHT ON WILLIAM GRAYSON: HIS GUARDIAN'S ACCOUNT. *Virginia Mag. of Hist. and Biog. 1984 92(4): 423-443.* Biographers have paid little attention to the youth of Founding Father William Grayson, a Revolutionary War colonel and senator from Virginia. Grayson was orphaned at 16, and his elder brother Benjamin was appointed guardian of William's estate. Benjamin's account books provide a good record of William's education, travel, and expenses from age 16 to 20. They also reveal that Benjamin was a highly irresponsible businessman. These accounts are unusual because they reveal the rarely seen documentation of an 18th-century youth's lifestyle. Based on Benjamin Grayson's account books, 19th-century histories of Virginia, Grayson correspondence, county and parish records, Virginia Statutes, and records of the College of Philadelphia; 66 notes. 1758-62

Grayson, William W.

2701. Chaput, Donald. PRIVATE WILLIAM W. GRAYSON'S WAR IN THE PHILIPPINES, 1899. *Nebraska Hist. 1980 61(3): 355-366.* William W. Grayson (1876-1941), a private in the 1st Nebraska Infantry Regiment, on 4 February 1899 fired at several Filipino soldiers advancing toward his position. This started the bitter, drawn-out Philippine Insurrection that lasted through 1902. Reviews Grayson's otherwise uneventful life and discusses the movements of the 1st Nebraska from its creation in 1898, its role in the Philippines, and its return to the United States in 1899. Chiefly published items in Nebraska History and books pertaining to the Spanish-American War. 1899

Greely, Adolphus W.

2702. Hall, George M. WHEN HONOR CONFLICTS WITH DUTY. *Air. U. Rev. 1980 31(6): 45-60.* Discusses Medal of Honor awardees Charles A. Lindbergh (1927), Billy Mitchell (1946), Douglas MacArthur (1942), and Adolphus W. Greely (1935), and the implications of their personal conflicts with duty. 1884-1973

Green, Jacob

2703. Noll, Mark A. OBSERVATIONS ON THE RECONCILIATION OF POLITICS AND RELIGION IN REVOLUTIONARY NEW JERSEY: THE CASE OF JACOB GREEN. *J. of Presbyterian Hist. 1976 54(2): 217-237.* Jacob Green's perception of the distinction between the church and the world is the key to understanding the nature of his participation in Revolutionary events. The thinking which distinguished church and world in his ecclesiology enabled him to upbraid colonial society for religious and moral shortcomings. He took the Whig view of the Revolutionary crisis seriously; at the same time he was able to transcend libertarian categories and to call American society to account by a higher law to which he owed first allegience. Green's case militates against Bernard Bailyn's conclusion concerning the source of moral reform in Revolutionary America. Green's criticism of society proceeded not primarily from a libertarian perspective but from a religious orientation derived from Edwardsean theology. Based on primary and secondary sources; 80 notes. 1770-90

2704. Noll, Mark A. JACOB GREEN'S PROPOSAL FOR SEMINARIES. *J. of Presbyterian Hist. 1980 58(3): 210-222.* The first Presbyterian seminary in America was not established until 1812. However, the Reverend Jacob Green (1722-90) thought of such a school. Education was of the utmost importance to him, both in the pastorate as well as in his concern for a better-trained ministry. At that time young men studying for the ministry after completing college studied under an "approved divine." On 22 November 1775 he sent a letter to his Congregational friend, the Reverend Joseph Bellamy, in which he laid out his plan for a theological seminary. The letter arose out of his concern about the shortage of ministers and his conviction that the current effort to train them was not succeeding. Reprints the previously unpublished letter. Based on materials by and about Jacob Green, and studies on colonial Presbyterian history; 39 notes. (The letter is in the Bellamy Papers, Hartford Seminary Foundation, Hartford, Connecticut.) 1775

Greene, Charles Sumner

2705. —. GREENE & GREENE. *Am. Preservation 1978 1(4): 42-60.* Describes the careers of the craftsmen, architects, and designers, Charles Sumner Greene (1868-1957) and Henry Mather Greene (1869-1954), and follows the development of their unique style in building homes in California in the early 20th century. Based on the biography by Randall Makinson, *Greene & Greene: Architecture as a Fine Art* (1977); 28 photos. 20c

Greene, George Washington

2706. McPartland, Martha R. A BRIDGE IN TIME. *New-England Galaxy 1978 19(3): 37-41.* Traces the successes and failures of historian and educator George Washington Greene (1811-83) of East Greenwich, Rhode Island. Notes his friendship with the Marquis de Lafayette, his marriage to Carlotta Sforzia in Florence, Italy, his career as teacher, writer, and biographer, and his role as US consul in Italy. 2 illus. 1831-83

Greene, Henry Mather

2707. —. GREENE & GREENE. *Am. Preservation 1978 1(4): 42-60.* 20c
*For abstract see **Greene, Charles Sumner***

Greene, William Bradford

2708. Hall, Bowman N. WILLIAM BRADFORD GREENE AND HIS SYSTEM OF "MUTUAL BANKING." *Hist. of Pol. Econ. 1976 8(2): 278-296.* William Bradford Greene was one of many monetary and social reformers who searched for a better method of social interaction after the Panic of 1837. Greene attributed the depression to chaotic banking and proposed a change to mutual banking. He believed this system eliminated the usurer who prevented the working class from securing its just rewards. Greene opposed socialism and communism but was an avowed anarchist. His economic theory had a greater impact on philosophical radicals than on traditional economists. Primary and secondary sources; 76 notes. 1830's-40's

Greene, William Cornell

2709. Nelson, Daniel. FIFTH COLUMN AT CANANEA: A STOCKHOLDER CIRCUMVENTS COLONEL W. C. GREENE. *J. of Arizona Hist. 1979 20(1): 47-64.* Describes economist-financier Frederick Winslow Taylor's efforts to penetrate the financial operations of Colonel William Cornell Greene's Greene Consolidated Copper, located in Cananea, Sonora, Mexico. Greene, in New York City, met with Taylor, a highly established financial consultant. From his investigation of the market, Taylor began buying large blocks of Greene Consolidated Copper stock, eventually placing Atherton B. Wadleigh, a mechanical engineer, in a financial position in the Cananea operations in Mexico. Wadleigh gave private reports to Taylor who used the information, which often differed from that released by Greene. The efforts of Taylor and Greene to operate the works independently of the rival Amalgamated Copper Company were relatively short-lived, because, in 1907, Thomas F. Cole from Amalgamated negotiated a merger which saw the demise of Greene's holdings. Greene fell from notoriety, but Taylor later became known as the promoter of scientific management. 4 photos, 35 notes. 1901-07

Greenfield, Elizabeth Taylor

2710. Noyes, Edward. THE BLACK SWAN. *Milwaukee Hist. 1983 6(4): 102-106.* Elizabeth Taylor Greenfield, known as the "Black Swan," was a former slave who was a highly regarded singer of popular music; she toured in both Europe and the United States, appearing in Milwaukee twice. 1852-63

Greenfield, Marguerite

2711. Bishop, Joan. GAME OF FREEZE-OUT: MARGUERITE GREENFIELD AND HER BATTLE WITH THE GREAT NORTHERN RAILWAY, 1920-1929. *Montana 1985 35(3): 14-27.* With her father's assistance, Marguerite Greenfield founded the Independent Ice Company in Helena, Montana, in 1912. Combating community prejudice against women managing ice plants and unfair competition from other ice producers, she managed the ice company in Helena and later in Elk City, Montana, until 1934. Her greatest source of difficulty was the local Great Northern Railway official. She refused his demands for kickbacks in awarding ice contracts, and in return he delayed her shipments, failed to supply adequate rail cars, and generally made her work difficult. After years of complaint, she finally succeeded in getting some relief from the top Great Northern officials. Based on Marguerite Greenfield's Ice Journal, in private hands; Greenfield Family Papers, Montana Historical Society; and the Great Northern Railway President's file, Minnesota Historical Society; 8 photos, 31 notes. 1912-34

Greenhood, Ralph and Fanny Gusky

2712. Neumann, Dorothy. THE GREENHOODS OF SAN BERNARDINO: A MEMOIR. *Western States Jewish Hist. Q. 1983 15(3): 203-213.* Ralph and Fanny Gusky Greenhood came to San Bernardino in 1912. At first the family was disappointed that there was no synagogue and no cohesive Jewish community, but Ralph organized a Sabbath school for the children, and that was a turning point in the formation of an active congregation. In 1921 the synagogue was built—again with Ralph Greenhood as a prime motivator. Ralph and Fanny remained active in Jewish community affairs including the lodge, welcoming committee, and cemetery board. Based on reminiscences of daughter Dorothy; 4 photos, 19 notes. 1912-39

Greenman, Jeremiah (family).

2713. Bray, Robert and Bushnell, Paul. FROM NEW ENGLAND TO THE OLD NORTHWEST: THE AMERICAN ODYSSEY OF THE JEREMIAH GREENMAN FAMILY. *J. of the Illinois State Hist. Soc. 1976 69(3): 201-212.* Greenman (1758-1828) was a Revolutionary War veteran of Rhode Island whose disability and poverty drove him to the Ohio frontier in 1806. His optimism and determination eventually led his widow and children to seek a new life westward to Illinois in 1829 and 1830. Greenman Papers; 5 illus., map, 37 notes. 1780's-1839

Greenough, Horatio

2714. Wright, Nathalia. LETTERS OF HORATIO GREENOUGH TO ROBERT WEIR. *New England Q. 1976 49(4): 499-520.* Describes the relationship of Horatio Greenough (1805-52) and Robert Weir (1803-89) while they studied art in Italy between 1825 and 1827, and prints edited copies of their only extant correspondence, six letters from Greenough to Weir dated 1826-31. 97 notes. 1825-31

Greenslet, Ferris

2715. Laughlin, Henry A. FERRIS GREENSLET. *Massachusetts Hist. Soc. Pro. 1957-60 72: 379-384.* Ferris Greenslet (1875-1959) was an author, editor, intellectual, historian, and member of the Massachusetts Historical Society from 1916 to 1959. 1916-59

Greenstreet, Ralph

2716. Greenstreet, Ralph. A WINTER HERDING SHEEP ON THE RED DESERT. *Ann. of Wyoming 1980 52(2): 10-17.* Presents the memoirs of the author, who in 1922 hired on as a sheepherder near Lander, Wyoming. He recounts the problems associated with loneliness, coyotes, and winter storms. On one occasion he barely escaped death from a sudden blizzard, but was able to surround himself with his dog and the sheep until the storm subsided. 4 photos. 1922

Greenwood, Isaac

2717. Leonard, David C. HARVARD'S FIRST SCIENCE PROFESSOR: A SKETCH OF ISAAC GREENWOOD'S LIFE AND WORK. *Harvard Lib. Bull. 1981 29(2): 135-168.* In his short, tragic life, Isaac Greenwood (1702-45) was one of the best known of America's scientists in the colonial period. Following graduation from Harvard in 1721, he served briefly as a minister, spent some time in England, and, at age 25, was appointed professor of mathematics and philosophy at Harvard. During the next decade Greenwood published, gave lectures, married, and had five children. However, he also developed a drinking problem which cut short his promising career and brought about his premature death in 1745. A deist, Greenwood initiated the optimistic stream in American literature that would climax more than a century later in Ralph Waldo Emerson and Walt Whitman. A list of Greenwood's writings is attached. 100 notes. 1702-45

Greer, Frank Hilton

2718. Lentz, Lloyd C., III. "NO WILD VENTURE": THE STATE CAPITAL PUBLISHING BUILDING. *Chronicles of Oklahoma 1983 61(3): 268-287.* Pioneer editor Frank Hilton Greer began printing the *State Capital* in 1889 as Oklahoma's first newspaper. His political influence quickly grew and he was elected to the territorial House of Representatives. In 1895, Greer was designated as the official printer of the territory, and seven years later he constructed a large and modern press building in Guthrie. The company continued to operate under different ownership until 1974. Beginning in 1980, the building and its contents were converted into a state museum to demonstrate the historical evolution of printing technology. 13 photos, 18 notes. 1889-1983

Gregory, Waylande

2719. DeGruson, Gene. "NO GREATER ECSTASY": WAYLANDE GREGORY AND THE ART OF CERAMIC SCULPTURE. *Kansas Q. 1982 14(4): 65-82.* Portrays the career of Kansas-born sculptor Waylande Gregory during 1921-71, focusing on his effort to make ceramics "a reputable medium for sculpture." 1921-71

Grenell, Judson

2720. Oestreicher, Richard. SOCIALISM AND THE KNIGHTS OF LABOR IN DETROIT, 1877-1886. *Labor Hist. 1981 22(1): 5-30.* Joseph Labadie and Judson Grenell, radical labor leaders in Detroit, Michigan, worked for the advancement of socialism through the Socialist Labor Party (SLP) in 1877. They and other Detroit socialists joined the Knights of Labor after 1878 to spread socialism to a wider audience. Labadie and Grenell abandoned the SLP in the early 1880's because it advocated doctrinal purity over immediate political and economic gains. Based on the Joseph Labadie Papers and other primary sources; 63 notes. 1877-86

Gresham, Walter Q.

2721. Calhoun, Charles W. "INCESSANT NOISE AND TUMULT": WALTER Q. GRESHAM AND THE INDIANA LEGISLATURE DURING THE SECESSION CRISIS. *Indiana Mag. of Hist. 1978 74(3): 223-251.* Reviews the life and times of Walter Q. Gresham. Although he eventually reached high federal appointive office, Gresham's one successful electoral victory was to the Indiana General Assembly in 1860. He professed to despise politics, but was also exceedingly ambitious. Slavery and secession were the issues of the day; Gresham disliked slavery, though hardly to the point of fanaticism, but was determined to keep the union intact. He acted as a man of compromise during an era of extremism, which hardly endeared him to anyone. His various peacemaking schemes all more or less failed, and when fighting eventually broke out, Gresham admitted that moderation was no longer useful and endeavored to do all in his power to insure the success of the Union armies. 2 photos, 97 notes. notes, 2 photos. 1860-61

Grey, Zane

2722. Hollow, John. DEATHWIND: ZANE GREY'S WETZEL. *Old Northwest 1981 7(2): 111-125.* 1780-1808

*For abstract see **Wetzel, Lewis***

Grey Owl

2723. Smith, Donald B. THE BELANEYS OF BRANDON HILLS: GREY OWL'S CANADIAN COUSINS. *Beaver [Canada] 1975 306(3): 46-50.* Biography of Grey Owl, born Archibald Stansfeld Belaney in England. He moved to Canada in 1906 and concocted a new identity, claiming he was Scotch and Apache. Until his death in 1938 he was a well-known spokesman for various conservation movements. Discusses the family connections of Grey Owl in England and in Canada, his successful attempt at covering his identity tracks, his success as an early environmentalist. 6 illus. 1906-38

Grierson, Benjamin H.

2724. Dinges, Bruce Jacob. "The Making of a Cavalryman: Benjamin H. Grierson and the Civil War along the Mississippi, 1861-1865." Rice U. 1978. 574 pp. *DAI 1978 39(3): 1783-A.* 1861-65

Griesbach, William Antrobus "Billy"

2725. Foran, Max. W. A. "BILLY" GRIESBACH AND WORLD WAR ONE. *Alberta Hist. [Canada] 1984 32(3): 1-8.* Traces the military career of William Antrobus "Billy" Griesbach, who recruited and commanded the 49th Battalion of the Canadian Expeditionary Force, which served in France during World War I. 4 photos, 59 notes. 1878-1917

Griess, Peter H.

2726. Griess, Peter H. THE FIRST SETTLEMENT OF RUSSIAN-GERMANS IN NEBRASKA. *Heritage Rev. 1973 (5-6): 7-9.* The author describes his immigration with a group of Russian Germans to Nebraska, where they settled in and around the town of Sutton. 1873-1900

Griffin, Alan

2727. Farley, John Robert. "The Life and Thought of Alan Griffin: Exemplar of Reflection." Ohio State U. 1978. 324 pp. *DAI 1979 39(10): 5817-A.* 1942-64

Griffis, Margaret Clark

2728. Carroll, Rosemary F. A PLANTATION TEACHER'S PERCEPTIONS OF THE IMPENDING CRISIS. *Southern Studies 1979 18(3): 339-350.* Margaret Clark Griffis (b. 1839) of Philadelphia taught for three years in the South just before the Civil War, especially on the Sunnyside Plantation near Arlington, Virginia. She wrote to her family in Philadelphia during the opening days of the Civil War describing the events and her feelings. She loved the South, accepted slavery, and believed in the essential inferiority of blacks, although she felt they were generally well treated and happy. Ultimately she supported national unity and the North and fled back to her parents' home in Philadelphia. Based on Margaret Clark Griffis Papers in Rutgers University Library; 9 notes. 1858-61

Griffith, D. W.

2729. Lindsey, David. "THE MASTER" OF AMERICAN CINEMA: D. W. GRIFFITH. *Am. Hist. Illus. 1976 11(8): 18-29.* Chronicles the film directing career of David Wark Griffith, 1906-31. 1906-31

Griggs, Frederick

2730. Reye, Arnold Colin. "Frederick Griggs: Seventh-Day Adventist Educator and Administrator." Andrews U. 1984. 516 pp. *DAI 1984 45(6): 1601-1602-A.* DA8420136 20c

Griggs, Nathan Kirk

2731. Stanley, Ruth Moore. NATHAN KIRK GRIGGS, CONSUL TO CHEMNITZ, GERMANY, 1876-1882. *Nebraska Hist. 1976 57(4): 439-459.* Discusses Nathan Kirk Griggs's (1844-1910) career as US consul to Chemnitz, Germany. As a result of his service abroad he lost his political base in Nebraska and in the Republican Party. His interests shifted from political to literary as a result of his "belated university education." His later career, besides his devotion to business concerns, was noted for its unique lecture-recitals and volumes of poetry. 1876-82

Grimes, John

2732. Cudd, John. THE UNITY OF REFORM: JOHN GRIMES AND THE *NEW JERSEY FREEMAN. New Jersey Hist. 1979 97(4): 197-212.* John Grimes settled in Boonton, New Jersey in 1843 to practice medicine. He was active in the abolition movement and in 1844 began publishing the *New Jersey Freeman,* a newspaper which was a part of a network of reform journalism. In its pages Grimes discussed slavery in terms of religion, politics, economics, and patriotism. Other movements such as temperance and an equitable distribution of wealth were also considered. The Mexican War and its relation to the spread of slavery received attention, as did phrenology. Grimes's attraction to a variety of reforms was a trait that he shared with other antebellum reformers. His ideologies are placed in the context of other national movements. Based on the *New Jersey Freeman* and secondary sources; 10 illus., 38 notes. 1844-50

Grimke, Angelina

2733. Vielhaber, Mary E. AN ABANDONED SPEAKING CAREER: ANGELINA GRIMKE. *Michigan Academician 1984 17(1): 59-66.* Famous abolitionist Angelina Grimke abruptly terminated her antislavery speaking career in fear for her safety after a proslavery mob rioted outside the building in which she was giving what became her last speech. 1836-38

Grimke, Angelina Weld

2734. Stubbs, Carolyn Amonitti. "Angelina Weld Grimke: Washington Poet and Playwright." George Washington U. 1978. 255 pp. *DAI 1979 39(8): 4941-4942-A.* 19c-1920's

Grinager, Mons H.

2735. Hvamstad, Per and Clausen, C. A., transl. THE LETTERS OF MONS H. GRINAGER: PIONEER AND SOLDIER. *Norwegian-American Studies 1970 24: 29-77.* Reprints 10 letters written during 1853-63 by Mons H. Grinager, a Norwegian immigrant in Wisconsin. The letters discuss daily life as well as family business and personal matters. Includes his opinions of American life and his stint as captain in the Union Army during the Civil War. Based on the letters and family records; 31 notes. 1853-63

Grinnell, George Bird

2736. Sabo, Lewis. WHEN WAGON TRAILS WERE DIM. *Pacific Northwesterner 1984 28(2): 23-31.* Narrates the career of explorer and naturalist George Bird Grinnell, focusing on his participation in expeditions to the Dakotas, Wyoming, and Montana. 1870-96

Grinnell, Joseph

2737. Grinnell, Elizabeth, ed. GOLD HUNTING IN ALASKA AS TOLD BY JOSEPH GRINNELL. *Alaska J. 1983 13(2): 33-111.* Reprints diaries of Joseph Grinnell, who prospected for gold in the Kotzebue Sound region of Alaska. The diaries, edited by his mother and first published around 1901, contain many details about daily life and personal narratives about the gold rush. 2 illus., plate, 18 photos, map. 1898-99

Griscom, Lloyd C.

2738. Prisco, Salvatore. LLOYD C. GRISCOM, NEW JERSEY POLITICIAN IN DIPLOMATIC SERVICE, 1893-1909. *New Jersey Hist. 1980 98(1-2): 65-80.* Lloyd C. Griscom entered the diplomatic service in 1893 as Ambassador Thomas Bayard's private secretary. After this post in London he served in Turkey, 1899-1901, and Persia, 1901-02, where he first gained experience in diplomatic negotiations. While in Japan, 1902-06, Griscom was instrumental in helping to settle the Russo-Japanese War and assisted E. H. Harriman in his unsuccessful attempt to establish a global transportation system. Moving to Brazil, 1906-07, Griscom labored to remove the stigma of Yankee imperialism from Latin American diplomacy. His last post before retiring to law and publishing was in Italy, 1907-08. Based on Griscom's papers, State Department records, and secondary sources; 3 illus., 41 notes. 1893-1909

Grobe, Charles

2739. Gillispie, John. CHARLES GROBE, THE BARD OF WILMINGTON. *Delaware Hist. 1984 21(1): 22-30.* Charles Grobe was a pragmatic, practical composer-teacher who catered to middle-class tastes by composing and performing playable, popular music. In Wilmington, Grobe served on the faculty of Wesleyan Female College and maintained a music store. He also produced a large number of songs, musical variations, and pieces, eventually publishing almost 2,000 compositions in his lifetime. Grobe principally composed and performed "salon music," but also patriotic fare such as battle pieces. Grobe's wide-ranging repertoire provides an index to the traditional and popular tunes of the mid 19th century. 3 illus., 11 notes. 1840's-79

Grogan, James

2740. Stevens, Kenneth R. JAMES GROGAN AND THE CRISIS IN CANADIAN-AMERICAN RELATIONS, 1837-1842. *Vermont Hist. 1982 50(4): 219-226.* Grogan came to Alburg, Vermont, from northern New York in 1815, and bought a farm across the Canadian border in 1820. Involved in the Canadian Rebellion of 1837, he fled to the United States in 1838, returned to his family after Lord Durham's amnesty, and was deported with his family. In retaliation for the burning of his farm, his gang burned four Canadian farms. Vermont Governor Silas H. Jenison and Secretary of State Daniel Webster resisted Canadian demands for

Grogan's extradition. Canadian soldiers captured him in Alburg and held him prisoner for 16 days. But both countries wanted peace and, in the subsequent 1842 treaty, agreed on terms of extradition. 22 notes. 1837-42

Gross, Mahlon G.

2741. Gross, Wesley. MAHLON G. GROSS: LIFE AND LABORS. *Pennsylvania Mennonite Heritage 1981 4(4): 6-11.* Biography of Mennonite farmer and preacher Mahlon G. Gross (1873-1937), of Pennsylvania, who was converted at an evangelist campaign to Methodism, but returned to the Mennonite Church in 1912 and was ordained in 1920. 1873-1937

Gross, Samuel W.

2742. Harrell, George T. LADY OSLER. *Bull. of the Hist. of Medicine 1979 53(1): 81-99.* 1882-1919
For abstract see ***Osler, Grace***

Groth, Charles

2743. Elliott, Marie. GALIANO ISLAND PIONEER. *Beaver [Canada] 1980 311(3): 51-54.* Extracted from the diary kept during 1881-87 by Charles Groth from Rensburg, Schleswig Holstein, this article records the establishment of a homestead on Galiano Island, one of the Gulf Islands of British Columbia. Beginning his homesteading career by raising sheep, he soon became discouraged and sold most of his flock, although his reputation as a good shearer remained. Fishing and rudimentary attempts at farming occupied most of his time. The diary "is a rich, detailed account of a young man's attempt to 'make good' in British Columbia one hundred years ago." 4 photos, map. 1881-87

Groulx, Lionel

2744. Brunet, Michel. LIONEL GROULX, 1878-1967 [Lionel Groulx, 1878-1967]. *Action Nationale [Canada] 1985 74(10): 1023-1025.* Prints a brief biographical overview of the life of French-Canadian educator, priest, writer, and historian Lionel Groulx, and provides a bibliography of Groulx. 1900's-67

2745. Lacroix, Benoît. LIONEL GROULX CET INCONNU [The unknown Lionel Groulx]. *Rev. d'Hist. de l'Amérique Française [Canada] 1978 32(3): 325-346.* An intimate portrait of Fr. Lionel Groulx (1878-1967), the eminent French Canadian historian. During an incredibly long and productive career, Fr. Groulx wrote more than 30 books and hundreds of articles. Though his world consisted primarily of books, libraries, and research, he often wrote in a popular style so that history could be enjoyed by a much larger audience. He taught for more than 50 years. 7 notes. 1878-1967

2746. Senese, P. M. CATHOLIQUE D'ABORD!: CATHOLICISM AND NATIONALISM IN THE THOUGHT OF LIONEL GROULX. *Can. Hist. Rev. [Canada] 1979 60(2): 154-177.* Examines the thought of Lionel Groulx, sometimes called the father of modern Quebec separatism. It was his Catholicism, however, that undergirded his French nationalism during 1897-1928. He feared the growing secularization of society he observed as industrialism occurred. Believing that Quebec, with its French Catholic majority, was the only place on the continent where Catholicism might be strengthened to resist the dangers of secularism, he advocated separatism. Nationalism for him was an instrument for the regeneration of Catholicism. Based on Groulx's published and manuscript writings. 1897-1928

2747. Trépanier, Pierre. POUR MIEUX CONNAÎTRE GROULX [To know Groulx better]. *Action Natl. [Canada] 1978 68(3): 209-218.* Reviews G.-É. Giguère, *Lionel Groulx, Biographie, "Notre État français, nous l'aurons!... "* (Montreal, 1978); M. Filion, ed., *Hommage à Lionel Groulx,* (Montreal, 1978); and G. Frégault, *Lionel Groulx tel qu'en lui-même,* (Montreal, 1978). These biographies of Lionel Groulx reveal that the historian of French Canada refrained from endorsing Quebec independence through prudence as a priest, a political figure, and a leader who recognized the need for the broadest possible support for Quebec nationalism. He was more an activist than a scholar, writing history to prepare for the future. The influence of Charles Maurras and his Action Française on Groulx can no longer be doubted. 1920's-78

Grout, Orvis

2748. York, Bernard H. "Orvis Grout: A Theatrical Biography." Brigham Young U. 1983. 338 pp. *DAI 1984 44(9): 2627-2628-A.* DA8322657 1950's-83

Grove, Frederick Philip

2749. Craig, Terrence L. F. P. GROVE AND THE "ALIEN" IMMIGRANT IN THE WEST. *Journal of Canadian Studies [Canada] 1985 20(2): 92-100.* Frederick Philip Grove used his literary skills on behalf of immigrants from Central Europe. He reacted against the early 20th-century Canadian novelists who used fiction as a forum for cultural chauvinism. His writings decried discrimination and intolerance and rejected suggestions that immigrants abandon their native values and assimilate into Canadian society by adopting "superior" English-Canadian values. 17 notes. 1908-30

2750. Makow, Henry, ed. LETTERS FROM EDEN: GROVE'S CREATIVE REBIRTH. *U. of Toronto Q. [Canada] 1979 49(1): 48-64.* A collection of five previously unpublished letters of Canadian author Frederick Philip Grove (1879-1948), who was born near Ilawa, Poland, as Felix Paul Berthold Friedrich Greve. In 1914, he married Catherine Wiens (1892-1972). Thanks to D. O. Spettigue's research, it is now presumed that much that Grove said about his pre-1912 life was fictitious. Letter I, probably written in early September 1919, Letter II, 29 September, and Letter III, 21 October, discussed their plans. In Letter IV, 7 November, he expressed his dissatisfaction with his school. In Letter V, 21-23 November, he described their plans. In January, Catherine began teaching north of Winnipeg. Within a year Grove had written four books. Based on Grove's works, and the five cited letters; 24 notes. ca 1919-20

Grubb, Davis

2751. Welch, Jack. "Davis Grubb: A Vision of Appalachia." Carnegie-Mellon U. 1980. 335 pp. *DAI 1981 41(11): 4716-A.* 8108307 20c

Gruber, Johann Adam

2752. Durnbaugh, Donald F. JOHANN ADAM GRUBER: PENNSYLVANIA-GERMAN PROPHET AND POET. *Pennsylvania Mag. of Hist. and Biog. 1959 83(4): 382-408.* Traces the life of Johann Adam Gruber (1693-1763), a leading member of a European religious movement known as the Community of True Inspiration; discusses Gruber's travels in Europe and his religious and literary career in Germantown, Pennsylvania. 1693-1763

Gruenberg, Louis

2753. Nisbett, Robert Franklin. "Louis Gruenberg: His Life and Work." Ohio State U. 1979. 441 pp. *DAI 1980 40(10): 5243-A.* 1920's-50's

Gruening, Ernest

2754. Naske, Claus-M. GOVERNOR ERNEST GRUENING, THE FEDERAL GOVERNMENT, AND THE ECONOMIC DEVELOPMENT OF TERRITORIAL ALASKA. *Pacific Historian 1984 28(4): 4-16.* Narrates the efforts of Ernest Gruening, Alaska's territorial governor during 1939-53, to focus the federal government's attention on the economic development of Alaska. Alaska, which was an economically underdeveloped region dependent upon the extraction of natural resources, needed to broaden its economic base. During most of Governor Gruening's term, federal bureaucrats designed numerous development plans but few real work programs. Massive federal outlays came to the region both during and immediately after World War II due to the recognized strategic military value of the state. Based on diaries and correspondence in the Gruening Papers, University of Alaska Archives, Fairbanks; Harry S. Truman Papers, Truman Library, Independence, Missouri; Franklin D. Roosevelt Papers, Roosevelt Library, Hyde Park, New York; and the files of Under Secretary Abe Fortas, National Archives; 6 photos, 27 notes. 1939-53

Grueningen, Johann Jakob von

2755. Grueningen, John Paul von. BIOGRAPHY OF J. J. VON GRUENINGEN. *Swiss Am. Hist. Soc. Newsletter 1978 14(1): 12-21.* Discusses Johann Jakob von Grueningen's (1845-1911) youth in Switzerland, schooling, immigration to America, and his life career as pastor in a strongly Swiss Reformed Church in Sauk City, Wisconsin, 1876-1911. 1876-1911

Grutka, Andrew G.

2756. Tanzone, Daniel F. BISHOP ANDREW GRUTKA. *Jednota Ann. Furdek 1978 17: 81-86.* Discusses the life of Bishop Andrew G. Grutka (b. 1908), a Catholic parish priest in and eventually Bishop of the Diocese of Gary, Indiana; covers 1933-78. 1933-78

Grutze, Sigel

2757. Ryan, Isabelle Grutze. LETTERS TO THE EDITOR: CITIZEN OF A CITY. *Oregon Hist. Q. 1984 85(1): 85-87.* Sigel Grutze was born at Fort Jones, California, where his Prussian parents operated a stage stop. After finishing school in Yreka, California, at age 13, he herded horses in California and Oregon. He earned a teaching certificate at The Dalles, Oregon, and taught for a few years. In 1887, Grutze moved to Portland with his wife, Martha Apperson, and three sons. In 1891 he was appointed Portland's chief deputy city auditor, a job he held for 47 years. His first wife died in 1903; in 1904 he married Isabelle Brown. Photo. 1877-1938

Grymes, John R.

2758. DeGrummond, Jane Lucas. CAYETANA SUSANA BOSQUE Y FANQUI, "A NOTABLE WOMAN". *Louisiana Hist. 1982 23(3): 277-294.* 1790-1890
For abstract see ***Bosque y Fanqui, Cayetana Susana***

Grzelachowski, Alexander

2759. Kajencki, Francis C. ALEXANDER GRZELACHOWSKI: PIONEER MERCHANT OF PUERTO DE LUNA, NEW MEXICO. *Arizona and the West 1984 26(3): 243-260.* In the late 1840's, Polish Catholic priest Alexander Grzelachowski was recruited for service in the United States. After several assignments at pueblos and parishes and duty in the Civil War, all in New Mexico, Grzelachowski entered the business world. He prospered as a merchant and army freighting contractor. About 1874, he moved to Puerto de Luna in east-central New Mexico where he specialized in cattle and sheep, and he was soon actively involved in the social, economic, and political life of the region. 7 illus., 42 notes. 1840's-96

Gubow, Lawrence

2760. Kaufman, Ira G. MICHIGAN JUDICIARY OF JEWISH LINEAGE, PAST AND PRESENT: PART II. *Michigan Jewish History 1983 23(1): 15-19.* 1919-83
For abstract see ***Cohn, Avern***

Guerin, Fitz W.

2761. Ward, Geoffrey C. THE VERY ODD VISION OF F. W. GUERIN. *Am. Heritage 1982 33(3): 65-73.* Fitz W. Guerin, born in Ireland in 1846, joined the Union Army in 1861. After the Civil War he became a photographer. His photographs, often unsuccessful, focused on children or bachelor art. Library of Congress; 14 photos. ca 1880-1900

Guerin, John Francis (family)

2762. Williamson, Eileen M. THE GUERIN FAMILY OF WHITEWOOD, N.W.T. *Beaver [Canada] 1979 309(4): 20-23.* John Francis Guerin, a French dentist, and his wife Angelica Mary, from England, settled in Whitewood in 1885. He had a widespread practice, and she educated most of the Guerin children. Family practices in speech and drama led to local performances. Soon the group expanded to provide Shakespeare, Dickens, and Moliere to wider audiences, often with musical accompaniment. Based on granddaughter's reminiscences; 4 illus. 1885-90's

Guest, John

2763. Wolf, Edwin, II. THE LIBRARY OF A PHILADELPHIA JUDGE, 1708. *Pennsylvania Mag. of Hist. and Biog. 1959 83(2): 180-191.* Sketches the life and judicial career of Philadelphia Judge John Guest from 1670, when he entered college in England, to his death in 1707; and provides an inventory of his library of 53 books, which indicates the cultural resources and interests of colonial Philadelphia. 1708

Guggenheim, Peggy

2764. Miller, Hope Ridings. GUGGENHEIM IN VENICE. *Horizon 1980 23(12): 56-63.* Peggy Guggenheim (1898-1979) used her financial independence to amass a splendid collection of avant-garde art, 1911-51, a collection still housed in her Venice palazzo; friend of Bernard Berenson and wife first of the painter Laurence Vail and later of Max

Ernst, she collected the works of such artists as Ernst, Henry Moore, Pablo Picasso, Jean Miro, and Jackson Pollock long before most of them became popular. 1919-79

Guigues, Joseph-Eugène

2765. Choquette, Robert. L'EGLISE D'OTTAWA SOUS MGR GUIGUES, 1848-1874 [The church of Ottawa under Monseigneur Guigues, 1848-74]. *Sessions d'Étude: Soc. Can. d'Hist. de l'Église Catholique [Canada] 1977 44: 57-62.* The Ottawa diocese was administered by Joseph-Eugène Guigues during 1848-74, where he actively pursued French Canadian colonization in Ontario, church funding, and spiritual and social programs. 1848-74

Guilbert, Frank

2766. Olson, Douglas. THE GOOD ROADS MAN. *Pacific Northwesterner 1985 29(3): 43-48.* Frank Guilbert became temporary secretary of the Washington State Good Roads Association in 1910, and worked with the group to establish, improve, and maintain good roads throughout the state for 28 years. 1903-40

Guiteau, Charles

2767. Peskin, Allan. CHARLES GUITEAU OF ILLINOIS: PRESIDENT GARFIELD'S ASSASSIN. *J. of the Illinois State Hist. Soc. 1977 70(2): 130-139.* Portrayal of Charles Guiteau (1841-82) as a "disappointed office-seeker" is inaccurate. Court records and Guiteau's published autobiography show that James Garfield's assassin had a long history of recognized mental instability and that he was never a candidate for a patronage job. 6 illus., 52 notes. 1860's-82

2768. Taylor, John M. ASSASSIN ON TRIAL. *Am. Heritage 1981 32(4): 30-39.* Discusses the trial of Charles Guiteau, the assassin of President James A. Garfield, a trial in which the defense claimed insanity. The national atmosphere and the case presented by the prosecution combined to produce a guilty verdict. At his execution, Guiteau convinced some of the legitimacy of his insanity plea. 10 illus. 1881-82

Gumpertz, Samuel Washington

2769. Gustaitis, Joseph. THE CHARACTER OF CONEY ISLAND: STALKING THE STRANGE WITH SAM GUMPERTZ. *Am. Hist. Illus. 1981 15(10): 36-41.* Samuel Washington Gumpertz (1868-1952) brought the "mysteries of nature and the oddities of a vast world" to Coney Island during 1900-30, until he joined the Ringling Brothers Circus, which he controlled after 1932. 1900-52

Gunness, Belle

2770. Langlois, Jane L. BELLE GUNNESS, THE LADY BLUEBEARD: SYMBOLIC INVERSION IN VERBAL ART AND AMERICAN CULTURE. *Signs 1983 8(4): 617-634.* Mass murderess Belle Gunness of LaPorte, Indiana, advertised for matrimonial partners to share her farm. She killed each husband with an axe and buried them in her farmyard in unmarked graves. After her death in 1908, Gunness was transformed from a brutal executioner into a tourist attraction and whimsical "Lady Bluebeard," as seen in Ruth Coffeen's 1947 "Ballad of Bloodthirsty Belle." In actuality, Gunness represents the "negative cipher," a legitimate art form in folk culture that humorously represents the contradictions of sexual roles and society's conceptions of them. Based on interviews, local newspapers, and archives; 54 notes. 1908-47

2771. Langlois, Janet Louise. "Belle Gunness, The Lady Bluebeard; Community Legend as Metaphor." Indiana U. 1977. 277 pp. *DAI 1978 38(11): 6860-6861-A.* 1908-76

Gunton, George

2772. Horowitz, Daniel. CONSUMPTION AND ITS DISCONTENTS: SIMON N. PATTEN, THORSTEIN VEBLEN, AND GEORGE GUNTON. *J. of Am. Hist. 1980 67(2): 301-317.* Analyzes the writings of three theorists of consumption—Simon N. Patten (1852-1922), Thorstein Veblen (1857-1929), and George Gunton (1845-1919)—who broke with the conservative moralists of the late 19th century and sought a proper relation between affluence, morality, and the social order in America. Patten advocated a scientific basis for restraints on consumption and sought a reconciliation of the Protestant ethic with economic growth. Veblen attacked the wasteful consumption of the leisure class and questioned the existing economic system. Gunton was the strongest advocate of leisure, extravagance, and unlimited comforts. 73 notes. ca 1900-29

Gustafson, John Bernhard

2773. Gustafson, John Bernhard. THE STORY OF MY LIFE. *Swedish-American Hist. Q. 1984 35(4): 346-371.* Presents a personal narrative of the author's childhood on a Swedish farm in Malma Parish, Västmanland, describing school, chores, and food preparation, and his working at a steel mill and on local farms. Gustafson emigrated to the United States in 1911, worked in a Minneapolis railroad yard, and then in Massachusetts and Connecticut factories as a "header." His story includes the boat trip to America, working through two world wars and the Depression, and returning to Sweden for a visit in 1958. 2 photos. 1892-1979

Guston, Philip

2774. Brach, Paul. LOOKING AT GUSTON. *Art in Am. 1980 68(9): 96-101.* Retrospective of work of Philip Guston in three periods: during the 1930's and 1940's "he worked his way through the public heroics of mural styles to the private reveries of his Iowa City paintings"; during the 1950's and 1960's "he left specific representation and moved to abstract painting"; and in the late 1960's he began painting "cartoon-like paintings of extraordinary power and presence." 1930-79

Guthrie, Woody

2775. Turner, Frederick. "JUST WHAT IN THE HELL HAS GONE WRONG HERE ANYHOW?" WOODY GUTHRIE AND THE AMERICAN DREAM. *Am. Heritage 1977 28(6): 34-43.* Discusses the life and career of Woodrow Wilson (Woody) Guthrie (1912-67). Tells of hardships in childhood and in depression and dust bowl days, out of which he described the conditions he and others faced, in song and in print. 16 illus. 1912-67

2776. Wolfenstein, Judith. OKAY OKIE. *Westways 1979 71(7): 33-35.* Notes the life of American songwriter and balladeer Woody Guthrie from 1937, when he first visited Los Angeles, until his death in 1967, followed by reprints of two short articles he wrote for *The Hollywood Tribune* in 1939 on being a newcomer to California from the Dust Bowl. 1937-67

Gutiérrez Díaz, Abelardo

2777. Pérez, Louis A., Jr. REMINISCENCES OF A *LECTOR:* CUBAN CIGAR WORKERS IN TAMPA. *Tampa Bay History 1985 7(2): 135-141.* Presents a translation of a personal narrative by Abelardo Gutiérrez Díaz, who describes his life as a *lector* in a Tampa, Florida, cigar factory, where his role was as a disseminator of the militant proletarian consciousness, educating illiterate Cuban workers on radical ideas. Reprinted from *Florida Historical Quarterly* 1975 53(4). 1890's-1931

Gutman, Herbert

2778. —. HERBERT G. GUTMAN, 1928-1985. *Radical History Review 1986 (34): 107-112.*

Murphy, Joseph S. *pp. 107-108.* Presents a memorial tribute to labor historian Herbert Gutman, and praises his commitment to social activism.

Scott, Joan Wallach. *pp. 108-112.* Shows how Gutman's use of anecdotes to reconstruct historical experience constituted his originality. His ability to find stories and weave them into patterns challenging prevailing orthodoxies of American labor history and Afro-American history was Gutman's real genius. He always looked for voices that would speak for the inarticulate and downtrodden. Speeches originally given at a memorial at the New School for Social Research, New York City, 1985. 1928-85

Gutmann, Bernhard

2779. Moore, Evelyn L. and Blunt, Ruth H. COMPOSITION, COLOR, AND SOMETIMES HUMOR: ARTIST BERNHARD GUTMANN OF LYNCHBURG. *Virginia Cavalcade 1982 31(4): 206-215.* Biography of German-born artist Bernhard Gutmann (1869-1936), who settled in Lynchburg, Virginia, in 1892 and became the first supervisor of drawing in the public schools there; paintings were known for their "humor and sense of design." 1869-1936

Guyon Cadillac, Marie-Thérèse

2780. Berg, Harriet Jean. THE SEARCH FOR MADAME CADILLAC. *Chronicle: Q. Mag. of the Hist. Soc. of Michigan 1984 20(1): 14-17.* Presents a brief biography of Marie-Thérèse Guyon Cadillac, wife of explorer and Louisiana governor Antoine Laumet de La Mothe, Sieur de Cadillac, and one of the first two European women to reach the new settlement of Detroit. 1687-1745

Gwinnett, Button

2781. Jackson, Harvey. BUTTON GWINNETT: WHIG TO EXCESS OR SCOUNDREL? *Am. Hist. Illus. 1981 16(5): 18-24.* Biography of Button Gwinnett (d. 1777), Georgia signer of the Declaration of Independence, a businessman and politician who "personified both the constructive and the destructive forces unleashed in the colonial struggle for independence"; 1765-77. 1765-77

Gyékényesi, György István

2782. Gatto, Katherine Gyékényesi. FROM SOMOGY TO CLEVELAND: A HUNGARIAN EMIGRANT'S HEROIC ODYSSEY. *Hungarian Studies Rev. [Canada] 1982 9(2): 49-59.* Discusses the life and poetry of György István Gyékényesi, a refugee from Somogy, Hungary, and a NASA scientist. His poetry reflects the immense geographical and cultural changes in the poet's life and his acceptance of his new environment, but also pleads for a stronger thread of humanism in the United States. 1944-73

H

Haas, Abraham

2783. Scharlach, Bernice. ABE HAAS: PORTRAIT OF A PROUD BUSINESSMAN. *Western States Jewish Hist. Q. 1979 12(1): 3-24.* Abraham Haas (1847-1921) was a founder or partner in several businesses in California, including antecedents of the California Packing Corporation, Cudahy Packing Corporation, McKesson & Robbins, and Pacific Gas & Electric. Starting as a merchant in Calaveras County in the 1860's, Haas moved to Los Angeles and joined a wholesale grocery firm in 1874. His business interests branched into fruit farming, stock raising, canning, ice manufacturing, drug marketing, and producing hydroelectric power. Haas moved to San Francisco in 1900 and continued active in business. Based on newspapers, city directories, interviews; 4 photos, 64 notes. 1868-1921

Haas, Karl (Charles)

2784. Haas, Robert Bartlett and Assion, Peter. CHARLES HAAS: A BADEN '48ER IN CALIFORNIA. *Pacific Hist. 1982 26(3): 1-21, (4): 38-57.* Karl (Charles) Haas (1827-1911), watchmaker, jeweler, and leading merchant of California, grew up in the Odenwald town of Walldürn, Baden, spent several years in Vienna, Switzerland, and Italy learning and perfecting his skills as watchmaker and jeweler. He was forced to join the army but deserted after one year and joined his brother in New York where he found work in his trade. In 1852 he purchased a supply of jewelry and watches and traveled to San Francisco, where he purchased an interest in a firm of manufacturing jewelers and became a successful businessman. He served as city treasurer. Contributing to the culture of his adopted home, he also maintained an identity with the German traditions he left behind. 32 illus., 65 notes. 1827-52

Hackett, Francis

2785. Packard, Hyland B. FROM KILKENNY: THE BACKGROUND OF AN INTELLECTUAL IMMIGRANT. *Éire-Ireland 1975 10(3): 106-125.* Biography of Francis Hackett, noted immigrant intellectual and literary critic covers his early years in Kilkenny and Clongowes Wood, Ireland, 1880's-1901, emphasizing the role of religion and education on his later career in the United States. 1880's-1901

Hackley, Charles Henry

2786. Cronenwett, Wilson R. CHARLES H. HACKLEY, MUSKEGON'S LUMBER BARON BENEFACTOR. *Chronicle 1979 15(1): 14-19.* Michigan lumber baron Charles Henry Hackley (1837-1905) earned a fortune from a lumber mill in Muskegon, Michigan, and donated millions to Muskegon to build a library, a hospital, an art museum, a park, and an athletic field. 1837-1905

2787. Harms, Richard Henry. "Life after Lumbering: Charles Henry Hackley and the Emergence of Muskegon, Michigan." Michigan State U. 1984. 397 pp. *DAI 1985 45(8): 2628-A.* DA8424428 1857-1905

Hafen, LeRoy R.

2788. Smith, Melvin T. IN MEMORIAM: LEROY R. HAFEN, 1893-1985. *Utah Historical Quarterly 1985 53(2): 184-186.* An obituary of LeRoy R. Hafen, Colorado state historian during 1924-54 and history professor at Brigham

Young University, 1954-74. Hafen was known best for his works on early exploration and settlement of the West. Photo. 1893-1985

2789. Wetzel, David N. AN APPRECIATION ACROSS GENERATIONS: LEROY R. HAFEN, 1893-1985. *Colorado Heritage 1985 (3): 14-15.* Reviews the career of noted Western historian LeRoy R. Hafen, who served as Colorado state historian and official of the Colorado Historical Society. Illus. 1924-85

Hafler, Earl "Pop"

2790. Feintuch, Burt. A FIDDLER'S LIFE. *Pennsylvania Folklife 1984-85 34(2): 50-60.* Biography of Earl "Pop" Hafler, a popular Pennsylvania fiddler. 1891-1975

Hageman, Adriaen (ancestors)

2791. Frick, Franklyn, comp. THE ANCESTRY OF ADRIAEN HAGEMAN OF NEW NETHERLAND. *Halve Maen 1985 58(4): 1-3, 21.* Traces the genealogy of Adriaen Hageman, who moved his family to New Amsterdam from Amsterdam in 1652. 1520-1690

Hagen, Uta

2792. Spector, Susan Jane. "Uta Hagen: The Early Years, 1919-1951." New York U. 1982. 405 pp. *DAI 1983 43(7): 2160-A.* DA8227232 1925-51

Hague, James D.

2793. Smith, Duane A. "AT THIS HIGH ALTITUDE ONE GETS WEARY VERY SOON": JAMES D. HAGUE AND THE TOMBOY MINE. *Huntington Lib. Q. 1981 44(3): 173-187.* In 1896, James D. Hague was employed by a group of potential investors to investigate the Tomboy gold mine in Colorado. His diary entries and letters to his wife provide a detailed description of a 19th-century mine. His favorable report led to the purchase of the mine and he was hired to manage what became one of Colorado's most productive mines. Based on original sources; 32 notes. 1896-99

Haig, Alexander

2794. Alter, Jonathan. TINKER, TAILOR, SOLDIER, BUREAUCRAT: THE APPRENTICESHIP OF ALEXANDER HAIG. *Washington Monthly 1981 13(1): 14-22.* The career of Secretary of Defense Alexander Haig has included education at West Point; service under Douglas MacArthur, and in North Korea, as aide-de-camp to General Edward "Ned" Almond; writing some of the Pentagon Papers, and a role in Watergate. 1941-81

Haldeman-Julius, Emanuel

2795. Scott, Mark. THE LITTLE BLUE BOOKS IN THE WAR ON BIGOTRY AND BUNK. *Kansas Hist. 1978 1(3): 155-176.* Emanuel Haldeman-Julius (1889-1951) came to Girard, Kansas, in 1915 to work on the socialist *Appeal to Reason.* He bought the paper in 1919 and soon began publishing his Little Blue Books. By 1951 he had more than 500,000,000 copies of more than 6,000 different titles. Haldeman-Julius hoped that his 10-cent pocketsize books of information, instructions, and the classics of fiction, drama, history, biography, philosophy, science, poetry, and humor would give all Americans, especially the poor, the opportunity for the self-improvement that would enable them to lead fuller lives. Primary and secondary sources; illus., 133 notes. 1915-51

Haldimand, Frederick

2796. Rea, Robert R. BRIGADIER FREDERICK HALDIMAND—THE FLORIDA YEARS. *Florida Hist. Q. 1976 54(4): 512-531.* Brigadier Frederick Haldimand (1718-1791), assigned responsibility for the Floridas by General Thomas Gage, arrived in Pensacola in 1767. Haldimand immediately rebuilt the dilapidated fort, ordered gardens planted, land drained, and a hospital constructed. After Anglo-Spanish tensions of the early 1770's relaxed, Haldimand's tenure at Pensacola was quiet. In 1773 Haldimand left Florida to become Gage's temporary successor as commander-in-chief of North America while Gage was on leave. Based mainly on transcripts of the Haldimand Papers located in the National Archives of Canada, Ottawa, and some secondary sources; 73 notes. 1767-73

Hale, Alfred Clay

2797. McColloch, Lacy Porter. ALFRED CLAY HALE, NATIVE SON AND MAN OF DESTINY. *Arkansas Hist. Q. 1976 35(3): 246-260.* Alfred Clay Hale (1895-1972) taught vocational agriculture at schools in Arkansas for 31 years. He left teaching in 1953 to enter the State Department as an agricultural expert assigned to underdeveloped countries. Following 11 years in Thailand, Ecuador, British Guiana, and Washington, D.C., Hale retired to his Arkansas home. Based on Hale's memoirs and records, information from Hale's family, and recollections of the author; 4 illus. 1895-1972

Hale, George E.

2798. Kargon, Robert H. TEMPLE TO SCIENCE: COOPERATIVE RESEARCH AND THE BIRTH OF THE CALIFORNIA INSTITUTE OF TECHNOLOGY. *Hist. Studies in the Physical Sci. 1977 8: 3-31.* Three influential men in American science—physicist Robert A. Millikan (1868-1953), astrophysicist George E. Hale (1868-1938), and chemist Arthur A. Noyes (1866-1936)—established the California Institute of Technology and led it to a position of prominence in the 1920's. Guiding Caltech's development was Hale's cooperative research ideal in which scientists were recruited from different disciplines specifically to pursue interdisciplinary research. The three men skillfully raised funds from local and national private sources. Based on the Hale, Millikan, and Noyes papers, and other primary sources; 3 illus., 105 notes. 1908-27

Hale, John Parker

2799. Camden, Thomas E. THE JOHN PARKER HALE PAPERS. *Historical New Hampshire 1983 38(4): 244-250.* John Parker Hale graduated from Maine's Bowdoin College with classmates Franklin Pierce, Nathaniel Hawthorne, and Henry Wadsworth Longfellow. He was involved in the long struggle which brought the Republican Party to power nationally, and which helped abolish slavery. The John Parker Hale Papers, inventoried here, are held by the New Hampshire Historical Society. 2 notes. 1814-1915

Hale, Josiah

2800. Ewan, Joseph. JOSIAH HALE, M.D., LOUISIANA BOTANIST, RAFINESQUE'S PUPIL. *J. of the Soc. for the Biblio. of Natural Hist. [Great Britain] 1977 8(3): 235-243.* Summarizes the life of Josiah Hale (ca. 1791-1856), a little-remembered figure in American natural history. ca 1791-1856

Hale, Nathan

2801. Byrne, Leonard. NATHAN HALE: A TESTAMENT OF COURAGE. *New-England Galaxy 1975 16(4): 13-22.* Chronicles the education and military career of Nathan Hale during the American Revolution, 1755-76, which culminated in his execution by the British as a spy. 1755-76

Hale, Sarah Josepha

2802. Zophy, Angela Marie Howard. "For the Improvement of My Sex: Sarah Josepha Hale's Editorship of *Godey's Lady's Book,* 1837-1877." Ohio State U. 1978. 206 pp. *DAI 1978 39(5): 3105-A.* 1837-77

Hales, John Groves

2803. Meigs, Peveril. JOHN G. HALES, BOSTON GEOGRAPHER AND SURVEYOR, 1785-1832. *New England Hist. and Genealogical Register 1975 129(January): 23-29.* John Groves Hales (1785-1832) was a Boston geographer and surveyor who executed the most complete maps of Boston and the surrounding Massachusetts area that these communities had had, from about 1814 until his death 18 years later. His maps incorporated exact mileages between towns, descriptions of the towns and their mills and agriculture, their dwelling houses, and even their taverns. The original of Hales' maps for 48 Massachusetts communities are in the Archives of the Commonwealth of Massachusetts at the State House. Based on primary and secondary sources; 15 notes. 1800-32

Haley, Alex

2804. Haley, Alex. PRESERVING THE FAMILY. *Daughters of the Am. Revolution Mag. 1984 118(7): 460-465, 487.* Author Alex Haley reminisces about his grandparents, family stories he heard from his grandmother and great-aunts, his early writing career, and the beginnings of his best-selling historical novel, *Roots.* 20c

2805. McCauley, Mary Siebert. "Alex Haley, a Southern Griot: A Literary Biography." George Peabody Coll. 1983. 257 pp. *DAI 1984 44(10): 3066-A.* DA8402969 1950's-83

Haley, Margaret A.

2806. Smith, Joan K. AUTOBIOGRAPHY AS SOURCE: SOME METHODOLOGICAL CAUTIONS. *Vitae Scholasticae 1983 2(1): 167-182.* Reflects on the methodology of biography using autobiographical sources, focusing on the memoirs of Margaret A. Haley, American feminist and teachers-union leader. Autobiography is seldom unbiased, either in its view of its subject or in its portrayal of others or of social conditions. 24 notes. 1910-35

Haliburton, Thomas Chandler

2807. Davies, Richard A. "NOT AT ALL THE MAN THAT WE HAVE IMAGINED": MR. JUSTICE HALIBURTON IN ENGLAND (1835-65). *Dalhousie Rev. [Canada] 1979-80 59(4): 683-695.* Discusses Thomas Chandler Haliburton's three decades in Great Britain. Based largely on contemporary British newspaper accounts; 35 notes. 1835-65

Hall, Camilla

2808. Honig, Harvey Hilbert. "A Psychobiographical Study of Camilla Hall." Loyola U. of Chicago 1978. 237 pp. *DAI 1979 39(11): 5559-5560-B.* 1960's-74

Hall, Charles Martin

2809. Trescott, Martha Moore. JULIA B. HALL AND ALUMINUM. Trescott, Martha Moore, ed. *Dynamos and Virgins Revisited: Women and Technological Change in History* (Metuchen, N.J.: Scarecrow Pr., 1979): 149-179. 1886-1914

*For abstract see **Hall, Julia Brainerd***

Hall, Elise Boyer

2810. Street, William Henry. "Elise Boyer Hall, America's First Female Concert Saxophonist: Her Life as Performing Artist, Pioneer of Concert Repertory for Saxophone and Patroness of the Arts." Northwestern U. 1983. 156 pp. *DAI 1985 46(1): 17-A.* DA8504819 1900-13

Hall, Emma Amelia

2811. Bordin, Ruth. A NOBLE EXPERIMENT: EMMA HALL AND THE MICHIGAN REFORM SCHOOL FOR GIRLS. *Chronicle 1981 17(3): 4-12.* On 1 July 1881, Emma Amelia Hall, with 15 years of institutional management experience, became the first superintendent of the Michigan Reform School for Girls at Adrian, Michigan; until her controversial but nonsexist dismissal in 1884, she and her all woman staff attempted to provide the residents with individual attention, rewarding progress toward rehabilitation. 1881-84

Hall, Grover Cleveland

2812. Hollis, Daniel W., III. GROVER CLEVELAND HALL: THE ANATOMIZATION OF A SOUTHERN JOURNALIST'S PHILOSOPHY. *Alabama Hist. Q. 1980 42(1-2): 87-101.* Grover Cleveland Hall used his personal journalism in the early 20th century to enjoin and cajole Southern consciousness. Termed a "Southern progressive," his ideas were rooted in family heritage and early newspaper experience. He was most influential as editor of the Montgomery, Alabama, *Advertiser.* Primary sources; 57 notes. 1888-1941

Hall, Herbert

2813. Hercher, Gail Pike. THE WORK CURE AT DEVEREUX MANSION. *Essex Inst. Hist. Collections 1980 116(2): 101-110.* Dr. Herbert Hall (1870-1923) believed that physical inactivity was mentally disastrous for the nervous patient. In 1912 he founded a therapeutic community at the Devereux Mansion in Marblehead, Massachusetts, where he offered the Work Cure Program—the teaching of various skills to nervously distressed people in order to restore their self-confidence and strength. A pioneer in the field of occupational therapy, Hall did succeed in creating a self-supporting industrial community where the nervously distressed could be restored to health. Primary sources; 2 photos, 17 notes. 1912-23

Hall, James Barclay

2814. Cousins, Leone B. THE LIFE AND TIMES OF JAMES BARCLAY HALL, PH.D. *Nova Scotia Hist. Q. [Canada] 1980 10(1): 59-87.* James Barclay Hall (1843-1928) was an educator. At the age of 23 Mr. Hall began to study with the school master of Lawrencetown; three years later he enrolled at Horton Preparatory School, received his B.A. from Acadia in 1873, an M.A. in 1877, and his Ph.D. from Boston University the same year. In 1878 he joined the faculty of the Provincial Normal School at Truro. He was interested in education for all ages and encouraged the establishment of kindergartens, adult education programs, and summer courses for teachers; he left instructions in his will for a portion of his estate to be used for a vocational school in the County of Annapolis. 1843-1928

Hall, James Norman

2815. Kintner, Anne Genung. JAMES NORMAN HALL PAPERS, 1906-1951. *Ann. of Iowa 1979 44(8): 658-664.* Describes the papers of James Norman Hall (1887-1951) held in the Grinnell College Archives. The total collection occupies 10 linear feet of shelves and contains correspondence, manuscripts, photographs, and clippings. Some of the correspondence deals with Hall's experiences as a German prisoner of war in 1918, his wide travels, and his move to Tahiti in 1923, where he eventually collaborated with Charles Nordhoff on *Mutiny on the Bounty,* the first of a number of well-received South Seas adventure stories. An "editor's note" describes approximately 250 additional letters by Hall and recently acquired by the Division of Historical Museum and Archives in Des Moines. 1906-51

Hall, Julia Brainerd

2816. Trescott, Martha Moore. JULIA B. HALL AND ALUMINUM. Trescott, Martha Moore, ed. *Dynamos and Virgins Revisited: Women and Technological Change in History* (Metuchen, N.J.: Scarecrow Pr., 1979): 149-179. Discusses discrimination against Julia Brainerd Hall (b. 1859), sister of Charles Martin Hall (1863-1914), whose inventions helped found the Pittsburg Reduction Company, forerunner of the Aluminum Company of America. Julia was not recognized for her work by her brother, nor has the significance of her efforts been properly discussed and documented by Charles's biographer and other historians. Julia Hall should be seen as prototypical of many other female relatives of inventors, women who assisted the invention and innovation process in various ways as it took place in or near the home. 67 notes. 1886-1914

Hall, Mary

2817. Patterson, Edna B. MARY HALL: WESTERN SHOSHONE BASKETMAKER. *Northeastern Nevada Historical Quarterly 1985 (4): 102-115.* Discusses the life and work of Mary Hall, a skilled and renowned western Shoshone basketmaker from the Humboldt River area near Beowawe, Nevada, whose daughters carry on her traditional artistry. 1900-85

Hall, Phillmore Mallard

2818. Hodge, Johnny Baxter, Jr. "A Biography of Phillmore Mallard Hall with Particular Emphasis on His Contribution to the Development of Black School Bands in North Carolina." Am. U. 1977. 272 pp. *DAI 1977 38(1): 147-148-A.* 1929-57

Hall, Richard DeForest

2819. Chaput, Donald. "ON THE ORE TRAIL" WITH DICK WICK. *J. of Arizona Hist. 1984 25(1): 1-20.* Relates the colorful career of Dick Wick Hall, a compulsive, profligate speculator whose efforts created Salome, Arizona, and whose poverty-inspired fiction, written under the *nom de plume* "Dick Wick," lauded northern Yuma County in the *Saturday Evening Post* and other magazines. Based on the Wick papers, periodicals, and secondary sources; 5 photos, map, 53 notes. 1898-1926

Hall, Sarah

2820. Popham, Virginia F. SARAH HALL, EWL. *Daughters of the Am. Revolution Mag. 1977 111(1): 4-8.* Presents a biography of Sarah Hall, 1761-1830, a believer in women's rights. 1780-1830

Hallam, Bertha B.

2821. Brodman, Estelle. EDUCATION AND ATTITUDES OF EARLY MEDICAL LIBRARIANS TO THEIR WORK: A DISCUSSION BASED ON THE ORAL HISTORY PROJECT OF THE MEDICAL LIBRARY ASSOCIATION. *J. of Lib. Hist. 1980 15(2): 167-182.* 1912-59
*For abstract see **Doe, Janet***

Halleck, Henry Wager

2822. McGinty, Brian. "OLD BRAINS" IN THE NEW WEST. *Am. Hist. Illus. 1978 13(2): 10-19.* Henry Wager Halleck (1815-72) was born in New York, graduated third in the 1839 class at West Point, served in the Army during 1839-54 and 1861-72, and during 1847-61 was a leading San Francisco lawyer, specializing in real estate. He wrote and translated several books on military science and mining laws and a 900-page treatise, *International Law* (1861). In California he owned the 30,000 acre-Rancho Nicasio, managed the largest quicksilver mine in the world (New Almaden), and in 1853 built "Montgomery Block," later the only major building in downtown San Francisco to survive the 1906 earthquake and fire. "Old Brains" was very intelligent and an efficient administrator, but his plodding determination, excessive caution, and suspicious manner contributed to his lack of success as General in Chief for two years during the Civil War. Primary and secondary sources; 12 illus. 1839-72

Hallowell, A. Irving

2823. Primiano, Leonard Norman. A. IRVING HALLOWELL: HIS CONTRIBUTIONS TO FOLKLORE STUDIES. *New York Folklore 1983 9(1-2): 43-54.* Reviews the career of folklorist A. Irving Hallowell, emphasizing his contributions to functional and contextual folklore studies. 1920's-55

2824. Primiano, Leonard Norman. A. IRVING HALLOWELL: AN APPRECIATION. *Journal of American Folklore 1984 97(384): 213-216.* Alfred Irving Hallowell, an anthropological folklorist, used his fieldwork among the Ojibwa Indians of the United States and Canada to emphasize the significance of folk taxonomies, psychological anthropology, and acculturation. As a longtime officer of the American Folklore Society, he pioneered American scholarly interest in the historical context of oral tradition. 8 notes, biblio. 1920-74

Halpern, Moishe Leib

2825. Wisse, Ruth R. A YIDDISH POET IN AMERICA. *Commentary 1980 70(1): 35-41.* A biography of Yiddish poet Moishe Leib Halpern, born in Galicia in 1886, who in 1908 immigrated to New York City, where he resisted the linguistic and cultural assimilation that he observed among his fellow Jews; with translated excerpts from his poems. 1908-32

Halsell, Carl and Mabel

2826. Rodenberger, Lou. SAND TABLES AND ONE-EYED CAT: EXPERIENCES OF TWO TEXAS RURAL SCHOOLTEACHERS. *West Texas Hist. Assoc. Year Book 1980 56: 80-90.* The author's schoolteacher parents, Carl and Mabel Halsell, taught in rural schools in central and west Texas beginning in 1919 or 1920. ca 1919-29

Halseth, Odd

2827. Huntress, Diana. ODD HALSETH: ONE MAN'S PUEBLO. *Palacio 1977 83(3): 39-43.* Odd Halseth (1893-1966), Norwegian by birth, and Phoenix, Arizona's city archaeologist during 1929-60, worked diligently to establish Pueblo Grande, a museum built on a Hohokam Culture site. 1929-60

Halsey, R. T. H.

2828. Kaplan, Wendy. R. T. H. HALSEY: AN IDEOLOGY OF COLLECTING AMERICAN DECORATIVE ARTS. *Winterthur Portfolio 1982 17(1): 43-53.* R. T. H. Halsey (1865-1943) was instrumental in the formation, building and stocking of the American Wing, Metropolitan Museum of Art (1924). Halsey spoke for many in praising colonial design and craftmanship while fearing mass production. The American Wing reflected his feelings pertaining to immigration restriction, Anglophilia and simplicity in design. An analysis of Halsey's work demonstrates his influence on his age. Based on materials of the Executive Committee of the Metropolitan Museum of Art, Halsey correspondence, personal interviews and other sources; 52 notes. 1900-50

Halverson, Knut

2829. Rosholt, Malcolm. A PIONEER DIARY FROM WISCONSIN. *Norwegian-American Studies 1962 21: 198-211.* Knut Halverson, a Norwegian American who emigrated to Wisconsin in 1865, kept a diary of his pioneer life intermittently during 1865-80's. Begun in a ledger-like fashion, the diary entries include reports on animals, crops, and the general costs of farming. As the journal continues, however, entries begin to include descriptions of farm life and of his family. The entries reflect a personality somewhat philosophical in nature, for constant mention is made of the passing of time, as well as recurrent mention of his religious beliefs and those of the surrounding community. Referring to his area of Wisconsin as "Indian Land," Halverson provides a good narrative on the social, economic, and religious life of immigrants on the frontier. 1865-90

Hamburg, Sam

2830. Goldsmith, Steven R. SAM HAMBURG: WORLD'S FOREMOST JEWISH FARMER. *Western States Jewish Hist. Q. 1978 10(4): 330-342.* Sam Hamburg (1898-1976) came to the United States from Palestine in 1920 to study modern agricultural techniques at the University of California at Berkeley and Davis. In 1932, after several years of tenant-farming, he bought land near Los Banos in the San Joaquin Valley. "Sam Hamburg Farms" became a showplace of modern agriculture, producing melons, cotton, vegetables, and seed alfalfa. In 1952 he returned to Israel where he used his own money and his knowledge of desert farming to develop cotton as an export crop that grossed $100 million a year by 1976. He commuted between California and Israel, bringing new agricultural ideas and materials to Israel, and developing strong bonds of friendship with Israeli leaders. In 1965 Hamburg developed Guillaume-Barre disease which left him deaf and partially paralyzed. When he died, he was mourned by great political leaders and small farmers from around the world. Based on personal interviews with friends and family; 4 photos, 11 notes. 1898-1976

Hamill, Samuel Wood

2831. Young, Laura. THE SILENT SENTINEL: SAMUEL WOOD HAMILL, F.A.I.A. *Journal of San Diego History 1985 31(1): 51-65.* Presents a biography of Samuel Wood Hamill, a Southern California architect who designed many important buildings in the San Diego area. 1903-84

Hamilton, Agnes

2832. Carson, Mina J. AGNES HAMILTON OF FORT WAYNE: THE EDUCATION OF A CHRISTIAN SETTLEMENT WORKER. *Indiana Mag. of Hist. 1984 80(1): 1-34.* Agnes Hamilton became a protege of Jane Addams in the field of settlement work in the late 19th century. Coming from a wealthy Fort Wayne family, she sought to use her formal education as a means of promoting family and Christian values. Exposed to the thinking of such Christian socialist reformers as Charles Kingsley and John Ruskin and the American economist Richard Ely, Miss Hamilton applied her reading by living and serving at Chicago's Hull House. Although she was greatly influenced by Jane Addams's example, Miss Hamilton's work was probably more religiously oriented than that of Addams. Based on letters and diaries of Agnes Hamilton and other primary sources; illus., 92 notes. 1885-1900

Hamilton, Alexander

2833. Cooke, Jacob E. ALEXANDER HAMILTON: FEDERALIST. *This Constitution 1985 (7): 22-31.* Despite accusations by his contemporaries that he was, at heart, a closet monarchist, Alexander Hamilton's vigorous championship of a strong central government grew from his experience as George Washington's aide-de-camp and his subsequent desire to see the young United States succeed as a representative republic. 1755-88

2834. Flexner, James Thomas. THE AMERICAN WORLD WAS NOT MADE FOR ME: THE UNKNOWN ALEXANDER HAMILTON. *Am. Heritage 1978 29(1): 70-77.* Excerpted from Flexner's forthcoming book, *The Young Hamilton.* Alexander Hamilton's role in developing American unity was second only to that of Washington but his psychic wounds caused disunion. Hamilton's psychologically-troubled childhood influenced his pessimistic outlook on the human race. Still questioning his own role and concluding that "the

American world was not made for me," Hamilton died in 1804, mortally wounded in a duel with Aaron Burr. 4 illus. 1757-1804

2835. Koritansky, John C. ALEXANDER HAMILTON'S PHILOSOPHY OF GOVERNMENT AND ADMINISTRATION. *Publius 1979 9(2): 99-122.* Alexander Hamilton's political theory, 1787-90's, was aptly categorized by his opponents as monocratic, for he stressed the power of the executive and bureaucracy. Covers Hamilton's views on representation, political aristocracy, and the role of the national government. 34 notes. 1787-90's

2836. Shneidman, J. Lee and Levine-Shneidman, Conalee. SUICIDE OR MURDER? THE BURR-HAMILTON DUEL. *J. of Psychohistory 1980 8(2): 159-181.* 1750-1804
For abstract see ***Burr, Aaron***

2837. Sogrin, V. V. BIOGRAFII OTTSOV-OSNOVATELEI SSHA V AMERIKANSKOI ISTORIOGRAFII 1970-KH GODOV [Biographies of the Founding Fathers of the United States in American historiography during the 1970's]. *Novaia i Noveishaia Istoriia [USSR] 1980 (1): 154-163.* 1760-1800
For abstract see ***Adams, Samuel***

2838. Sogrin, V. V. ALEKSANDR GAMIL'TON I OBRAZOVANIE SSHA [Alexander Hamilton and the founding of America]. *Novaia i Noveishaia Istoriia [USSR] 1976 (1): 142-153, (2): 120-138.* Part I. Reviews works on this controversial founding father and discusses his career as a pamphleteer and military man. 41 notes. Part II. Describes Alexander Hamilton's part in the political development of America during the late18th century. Beginning with 1777, discusses his participation in the early stages of the creation of the new Constitution and his continued involvement in the newly formed government. 55 notes. ca 1775-1804

2839. Tajima, Keiji. HAMIRUTON KEIZAI SEISAKU NO SHITEKI BUNSEKI: KŌGYŌ SEISAKU O CHŪSHIN TO SHITE [A historical analysis of Alexander Hamilton's economic policy: with special reference to Hamilton's industrial policy]. *Shakaikeizaishigaku (Socio-Economic Hist.) [Japan] 1978 44(1): 25-49.* Emphasizes Secretary of the Treasury Alexander Hamilton's industrial policy rather than his financial policy; 1789-95. 1789-95

Hamilton, Alice

2840. Young, Angela Nugent. "Interpreting the Dangerous Trades: Workers' Health in America and the Career of Alice Hamilton, 1910-1935." Brown U. 1982. 242 pp. *DAI 1983 43(11): 3687-3688-A.* DA8228357 1910-35

Hamilton, Henry

2841. Robinson, John W. A CALIFORNIA COPPERHEAD: HENRY HAMILTON AND THE LOS ANGELES *STAR. Arizona and the West 1981 23(3): 213-230.* Henry Hamilton (1826?-91) served as editor of the Los Angeles *Star,* 1856-68. An outspoken Confederate sympathizer and rabid slavery advocate, he used the *Star* as a platform to rally Southern Democrats and to violently denounce the Lincoln administration. He gloated over Confederate battlefield victories. He survived arrest and won election to the California legislature. Hamilton closely gauged the varying intensity of pro-Southern feeling in southern California during the Civil War. 2 illus., 48 notes 1856-68

Hamilton, Holman

2842. DeSantis, Vincent P. HOLMAN HAMILTON. *Register of the Kentucky Hist. Soc. 1982 80(2): 134-139.* Holman Hamilton was a superb teacher and one of the foremost historians of the pre-Civil War period. Although successful as a newspaperman, Hamilton returned to graduate school at the age of 41 and became a professional historian. He served on the faculty of the University of Kentucky from 1954 until his retirement in 1975. Photo. 1954-81

2843. —. IN MEMORIAM: HOLMAN HAMILTON (1910-1980). *Register of the Kentucky Hist. Soc. 1981 79(1): 63-64.* A tribute to historian Holman Hamilton, writer, teacher, and strong supporter of the Kentucky Historical Society. Illus. 1935-80

Hamilton, James, Jr.

2844. Sibley, Marilyn McAdams. JAMES HAMILTON, JR., VS. SAM HOUSTON: REPERCUSSIONS OF THE NULLIFICATION CONTROVERSY. *Southwestern Historical Quarterly 1985 89(2): 165-180.* James Hamilton, Jr., former governor of South Carolina and a Southern nationalist, failed to gain high political office or wealth in Texas because of his rivalry with Sam Houston, president of the Republic of Texas. Although Mirabeau B. Lamar, who succeeded Houston, granted Hamilton a diplomatic position to raise money for the republic, financial problems and Houston's return to power prevented Hamilton from achieving the political and economic rewards he sought in Texas. Although Hamilton worked against annexation in 1837, he supported the Compromise of 1850, which he believed would enable him to receive payment for his $210,000 in claims against Texas. He died on 15 November 1857 in a shipwreck off the Louisiana coast. 54 notes. 1820-57

Hamilton, Pierce Stevens

2845. Rutherford, Paul. A PORTRAIT OF ALIENATION IN VICTORIAN CANADA: THE *PRIVATE MEMORANDA* OF P. S. HAMILTON. *J. of Can. Studies [Canada] 1977 12(4): 12-23.* Studies the memoirs of Pierce Stevens Hamilton (1826-93), lawyer, editor (1853-61) of the Halifax (Nova Scotia) *Acadian Recorder,* stock speculator, government administrator, and at one time Commissioner of Mines for Nova Scotia. His death, in obscure poverty, was declared a suicide. Hamilton felt his failures were due largely to his strict code of honor and the amorality of his contemporaries, who seemed interested only in "getting on in the world." Concludes by placing Hamilton's sometimes self-serving reflections in the context of a short analysis of the moral and social climate of Victorian Canada. Presents a picture of an aristocrat adrift in an entrepreneurial society. Based on Hamilton's *Private Memoranda* and on secondary sources; 48 notes. 1826-93

Hamlin, Hannibal

2846. Kazarian, Richard, Jr. "Working Radicals: The Early Careers of William Seward, Thaddeus Stevens, Henry Wilson, Charles Sumner, Salmon P. Chase and Hannibal Hamlin." Brown U. 1981. 518 pp. *DAI 1982 43(2): 526-A.* DA8209068 1840's-60

2847. Rudolph, Jack. HANNIBAL HAMLIN, POSSIBLE PRESIDENT: THE OLD CARTHAGINIAN. *Civil War Times Illus. 1982 20(10): 22-27.* Prints a biography of prominent antislavery advocate Hannibal Hamlin, whose political career included several terms in both houses of Congress, service as ambassador to Spain, and the vice-presidency during Lincoln's first term. 1830's-91

Hammerstein, William

2848. Dalrymple, Harold R. WILLIAM, THE OBSCURE HAMMERSTEIN. *Theatre Survey 1984 25(2): 249-251.* The contributions to American theater by William Hammerstein (1874-1914) are obscured by his more famous father and son, though he was an important figure in New York City theatre management from the 1890's to 1914. 1890's-1914

Hammett, Dashiell

2849. Billi, Mirella. QUEL DOPPIO GIOCO DI DASHIELL HAMMETT [Dashiell Hammett's double game]. *Ponte [Italy] 1981 37(7-8): 710-716.* It is almost impossible to classify Hammett's work or the man, who was a workman, private investigator, author of police novels and screen plays, bohemian, Hollywood luminary, and political suspect. 20c

2850. McGinty, Brian. A PINKERTON MAN IN SPADES. *Westways 1977 69(3): 28-31.* Discusses the career of Dashiell Hammett, a detective writer whose main character, Sam Spade, and whose locale, San Francisco, became archetypes for detective novels of the 1930's. 1920-30's

Hammond, A. B.

2851. McKinney, Gage. A. B. HAMMOND, WEST COAST LUMBERMAN. *Journal of Forest History 1984 28(4): 196-203.* A brief biography of New Brunswick-born A. B. Hammond, who developed a massive integrated lumber enterprise on the US west coast. After working as a lumberjack in several US locations, he first achieved commercial success as a Montana merchant. Quickly moving into the lumber business to support railway building, he was affluent by age 40. He then acquired a railroad in Oregon and was a partner in building another. His acceptance of timberland as partial payment for the sale of these railroads was the beginning of his extensive lumber operations in Oregon and California. 13 illus. 1860's-1934

Hammond, James Henry

2852. Faust, Drew Gilpin. CULTURE, CONFLICT AND COMMUNITY: THE MEANING OF POWER ON AN ANTE-BELLUM PLANTATION. *J. of Social Hist. 1980 14(1): 83-98.* James Henry Hammond, age 24, took over Silver Bluff, a South Carolina plantation formerly run by absentee owners. For 30 years he was concerned with the religious life, work habits, and fringe benefits of his slaves. He sought to prevent separate black religious observances, impose the gang system of production, and keep his workers healthy through the use of Western medicine and prevention of the use of folk remedies. Above all, he strove to maintain control over his white overseers, the black work bosses, and the slaves. Clever evasions, constant theft, complicated conspiracies, and occasional escapes (usually temporary) continually threatened his control. Based on the plantation diary and papers; 31 notes. 1831-64

2853. Faust, Drew Gilpin. A SLAVEOWNER IN A FREE SOCIETY: JAMES HENRY HAMMOND ON THE GRAND TOUR, 1836-1837. *South Carolina Hist. Mag. 1980 81(3): 189-206.* Analyzes the experiences of James Henry Hammond, a young aristocrat, politician, and defender of slavery, in Europe, concluding that the Old World social conditions reaffirmed and intensified his proslavery sentiments. 1836-37

Hammond, James Henry (family)

2854. Bleser, Carol K. A LEGACY BESIEGED: THE HAMMOND FAMILY IN AN ERA OF CRISIS AND CHANGE, 1865-1916. *Southern Studies 1983 22(1): 21-31.* James Henry Hammond was a wealthy planter in South Carolina, governor, and US senator. He supported a large family, which he ruled in strict patriarchal fashion, treating his wife and children as dependents requiring his supervision. The next three generations of males attempted to follow the same pattern of life, but were unsuccessful because of changing economic and social conditions. Wives' dowries saved the remnants of the plantation, and sisters and daughters made unsuccessful marriages. Hammond's successors floundered in a world of unaccustomed freedoms and burdens. Based on the Hammond Family Papers in the University of South Carolina Library; 2 notes. 1865-1916

Hammond, William Alexander

2855. Blustein, Bonnie Ellen. "A New York Medical Man: William Alexander Hammond, M.D. (1828-1900), Neurologist." U. of Pennsylvania 1979. 426 pp. *DAI 1979 40(3): 1656-1657-A.* 1850's-80's

Hampton, Wade I

2856. Bridwell, Ronald Edward. "The South's Wealthiest Planter: Wade Hampton I of South Carolina, 1754-1835." U. of South Carolina 1980. 838 pp. *DAI 1980 41(4): 1729-A.* 8020284 1774-1835

Hanchett, Marva Christensen

2857. Sorenson, Patricia H. THE NURSE: MARVA CHRISTENSEN HANCHETT OF SEVIER COUNTY. *Utah Hist. Q. 1977 45(2): 163-172.* Marva Christensen Hanchett, after graduating from Salt Lake General Hospital School of Nursing in 1931, was the only registered nurse in Sevier County, Utah. In 1934 she organized the first regular public health program in Sevier County and was its first nurse. From 1957 until retirement in 1974, she supervised public health nursing over one-fifth of the state. A modern nursing pioneer and mother of three children, she successfully combined the careers of nurse and homemaker. Based primarily on an interview with Mrs. Hanchett; 5 illus. 1931-74

Hancock, Christopher Carson

2858. Weldy, Mary Helen and Taylor, David L. GONE BUT NOT FORGOTTEN: THE LIFE AND WORK OF A TRADITIONAL TOMBSTONE CARVER. *Keystone Folklore 1976-77 21(2): 14-33.* Focuses on the life of tombstone carver Christopher Carson Hancock (1878-1936) of Allen County, Kentucky; his work, described here, is found in Allen County, other surrounding counties, and Tennessee. 1878-1936

Hancock, John

2859. Finkelstein, Robert Zeus. "Merchant, Revolutionary, and Statesman: A Reappraisal of the Life and Public Services of John Hancock, 1737-1793." U. of Massachusetts 1981. 508 pp. *DAI 1981 41(12): 5220-A.* 8110326 1737-1793

Handley, Charles (family)

2860. Netboy, Anthony and Netboy, Elizabeth Silsby. THE HANDLEYS IN TASMANIA AND OREGON. *Oregon Historical Quarterly 1985 86(1): 80-93.* Jemima Champion Cooper (1778-1862) and family migrated from Devonshire to the penal colony of Hobart in Van Diemen's Land (later Tasmania) in 1833. Her daughter Sarah married an English sea captain, Charles Handley (1811-95), in 1839. Handley skippered brigs carrying convicts and cargo between Sydney and Hobart. In 1844, the Coopers took up a donation land claim in Oregon. The Handleys followed in 1850 and Captain Handley farmed near Dundee and served as Yamhill County assessor and surveyor. Based on records in the Tasmanian Archives, a Handley family history, and records at the Oregon Historical Society; 5 photos, 8 notes. 1833-95

Handy, Robert T.

2861. Smith, Robert Doyle. "Robert T. Handy: A Study in American Church Historiography." Baylor U. 1981. 235 pp. *DAI 1981 42(2): 743-A.* 8116546 18c-20c

Hankinson, Richard Henry

2862. Quam, Vernon. RICHARD HENRY HANKINSON. *Red River Valley Hist. 1980 (Fall): 23-26.* Richard Henry Hankinson (1841-1911) promoted the telegraph and telephone in Minnesota, arrived in North Dakota in 1881, and later founded the town of Hankinson. ca 1871-1911

Hanna, Gordon Wilmer

2863. Jenks, Jeffrey. GORDON WILMER HANNA, 1921-1983: A HEALTH AND CIVIL RIGHTS ADVOCATE. *J. of Intergroup Relations 1983 11(3): 52-55.* As a key figure in the Michigan Department of Civil Rights, Gordon Wilmer Hanna fought against racial, age, and sex discrimination. 1921-83

Hanna, Sarah Foster

2864. Branton, Harriet K. SARAH FOSTER HANNA AND THE WASHINGTON FEMALE SEMINARY. *Western Pennsylvania Hist. Mag. 1978 61(3): 221-231.* A history of the Washington Female Seminary in Pennsylvania, 1836-1948, emphasizing the administration of Sarah Foster Hanna, 1840-74. 1836-1948

Hannah, Jason Albert

2865. —. JASON A. HANNAH AND THE HANNAH CHAIRS FOR THE HISTORY OF MEDICINE. *Bull. of the Hist. of Medicine 1978 52(1): 125-127.* Dr. Jason Albert Hannah (1889-1977) was a pathologist and medical economist. He was educated at Queen's University, Canada, and at Edinburgh. Interested in the sad financial effects of serious illness on civil servants, he established the Associated Medical Services, Inc. (AMS), the first prepaid medical care plan in Ontario. He was its managing director, 1937-76, and president, 1965-76. When the province assumed responsibility for all basic health care programs, the AMS had more than $12,000,000 in reserves. Dr. Hannah decided to use that money to further the history of medicine in Canada. The AMS funded a chair of medical history at each of the five Ontario medical colleges, and established the Hannah Institute. 1930's-70's

Hannon, Barton

2866. Holmes, Jack D. L. BARTON HANNON IN THE OLD SOUTHWEST. *J. of Mississippi Hist. 1982 44(1): 69-79.* Traces the background of Barton Hannon in Mississippi and seeks to reconcile the versions of his trouble with Spanish authorities as recorded in US Boundary Commissioner Andrew Ellicott's *Journal* and the Spanish accounts of the same event. Describes Hannon's role in the "Natchez Revolt of 1797," but, more importantly, discusses fully the criminal suit brought by the Spanish government against Hannon. This case gives significant information on Spanish interpretations of sedition, the early organization of Baptists in Natchez, and the safeguards provided by Spanish authorities for persons accused of crimes. Spanish justice provided an unusual degree of fairness, and Spain adopted a paternal role in developing her settlements in this region. Based on archival material in Seville and Madrid, Spain; 31 notes. 1797

Hansberry, Lorraine

2867. Hairston, Loyle. LORRAINE HANSBERRY: PORTRAIT OF AN ANGRY YOUNG WRITER. *Crisis 1979 86(4): 123-128.* During the early 1950's when the repressive atmosphere had been imposed upon the country by a pervasive phobia of communism, Lorraine Hansberry, a fearless young woman, spoke at popular street-corner rallies on the issues of racism and peace. Born in Chicago on 19 May 1930, her incisive analyses, clarity of understanding, and enthusiasm resulted in her most popular play *Raisin in the Sun.* Her two other artistic triumphs were *Les Blancs* and *The Sign in Brustein's Window.* Her intense involvement in life and her political awareness, nourished by a strong social consciousness imbued her writings with penetrating truths and compelling humanism. On 12 January 1965, at the age of 34, Lorraine Hansberry died of cancer. 1950's-65

2868. Nemiroff, Robert. FROM THESE ROOTS: LORRAINE HANSBERRY AND THE SOUTH. *Southern Exposure 1984 12(5): 32-36.* Discusses Northern-born author Lorraine Hansberry's Southern roots, her family's experiences with Southern violence, and the effect those experiences had on Hansberry's works. 1950's-64

Hansen, Harry Arthur

2869. Roba, William Henry. "A Literary Pilgrim: Harry Hansen and Popular American Book Reviewing, 1915-1945." U. of Iowa 1979. 302 pp. *DAI 1980 40(7): 4108-A.* 1915-45

Hanson, Halfdan M.

2870. Hollister, Paul. THE BUILDING OF BEAUPORT, 1907-1924. *Am. Art J. 1981 13(1): 69-89.* 1907-24
*For abstract see **Sleeper, Henry Davis***

Hanson, Henry, Sr.

2871. Hanson, Henry. YANKEE FROM SMÅLAND: AN IMMIGRANT SAGA. *Swedish-American Historical Quarterly 1985 36(2): 133-144.* Born Henning Augustsson in Svalas, Småland, Sweden, Henry Hanson, Sr., immigrated to the United States in 1885. He joined relatives in Middletown, Connecticut, where in 1871 large numbers of Swedes had been brought as strike breakers in the brownstone quarries. He went to work in 1889 for a marine hardware manufacturer, becoming general manager in 1923. During the Depression, at age 64, Hanson began a successful career as an insurance agent. Active in Republican politics, the Lutheran

Church, fraternal organizations, and community affairs, Hanson balanced his traditional conservatism with efforts to help fellow Swedish Americans. 5 photos. 1885-1954

Hanson, John

2872. Carlsson, Sten and Nordstrom, Byron J., transl. JOHN HANSON'S SWEDISH BACKGROUND. *Swedish Pioneer Hist. Q. 1978 29(1): 9-20.* A genealogical study based on work in 1876 by George A. Hanson, a Maryland lawyer. John Hanson was one of Maryland's two great forefathers and a political activist during the American Revolution. He was President of Congress in Philadelphia in 1781-82. He was born in either 1715 or 1721 and died in 1783. In 1903 a statue was erected over his grave in Statuary Hall in the Capitol in Washington, D.C. Concludes that George Hanson established a clear set of traditions which do include genealogical links with Sweden. Photo, chart, 46 notes. 18c

2873. Levering, Ralph B. JOHN HANSON, PUBLIC SERVANT. *Maryland Hist. Mag. 1976 71(2): 113-133.* Reviews John Hanson's life and career in Maryland politics from his first appointment as Sheriff of Charles County in 1750, through a many-faceted role in the House of Delegates and service on every major council or committee formed during the revolutionary era in the state, until his final honor of election as "President of the United States in Congress Assembled," on 5 November 1781. While Hanson is not considered among the most distinguished leaders of the period, his service, and that of many local leaders, has been overlooked. He had most of all "staying power and dedication to the public service," and "did more than anyone else to secure the Revolution in Western Maryland and to contribute men and munitions to the common cause." His election as President was testimony not only to the desire to placate Maryland, but to the esteem in which he was held. Based largely on Maryland archival material and Hanson's own letters; 80 notes. 1721-83

Hapgood, William P.

2874. McQuaid, Kim. INDUSTRY AND THE COOPERATIVE COMMONWEALTH: WILLIAM P. HAPGOOD AND THE COLUMBIA CONSERVE COMPANY, 1917-1943. *Labor Hist. 1976 17(4): 510-529.* Assesses the efforts of William P. Hapgood (1872-1960) to establish a cooperative commonwealth between workers and management in the Columbia Conserve Company of Indianapolis. Inspired by ideas of a worker-controlled, industrial democracy, Hapgood initiated many reforms, but he was unable to successfully influence the direction of employees. The experiment ended in 1943. Based upon Hapgood publications and secondary sources; 27 notes. 1917-43

Happer, Andrew P.

2875. Crabtree, Loren W. ANDREW P. HAPPER AND THE PRESBYTERIAN MISSIONS IN CHINA, 1844-1891. *J. of Presbyterian Hist. 1984 62(1): 19-34.* The career of Andrew P. Happer as pioneer missionary, Sinologist, and founder of Christian higher education in China helps to illuminate the dramatic changes that China and the Presbyterian missions underwent in the 19th century. His consuming passions were education and evangelism. As an evangelical, he believed his call was to convert individual Chinese to Christ and then to Christianize Chinese society through education. His attempts to interpret Chinese culture for Western audiences in China and the United States mark him as an important contributor to Sino-American relations. Based on documents and reports of the Presbyterian Church, and letters and articles by Happer; photo, 51 notes. 1844-94

Haralson, Caroline Lewis

2876. Koch, Mary Levin. LETTERS FROM LA GRANGE: THE CORRESPONDENCE OF CAROLINE HARALSON AND HER DAUGHTERS. *Georgia Hist. Q. 1982 66(1): 33-46.* Discusses the life of a Southern plantation owner's wife as revealed in the letters of Caroline Lewis Haralson (d. ca. 1858) of La Grange, Georgia to her husband, US Congressman Hugh Anderson Haralson (d. 1854) in Washington, D. C. Based on Haralson family correspondence; 41 notes. 1844-51

Haralson, Hugh Anderson

2877. Koch, Mary Levin. LETTERS FROM LA GRANGE: THE CORRESPONDENCE OF CAROLINE HARALSON AND HER DAUGHTERS. *Georgia Hist. Q. 1982 66(1): 33-46.* 1844-51
*For abstract see **Haralson, Caroline Lewis***

Haraszthy, Agoston

2878. Schoenman, Theodore. AGOSTON HARASZTHY, THE FATHER OF CALIFORNIAN VITICULTURE. *New Hungarian Q. [Hungary] 1983 24(89): 141-146.* Describes the earlier days of Agoston Haraszthy, before he became instrumental in the founding of California's wine industry. Of aristocratic Hungarian birth, he was a member of the elite Royal Hungarian Bodyguard of Austria's Emperor Francis I. After Haraszthy's Western, liberal values led to his fall from favor at court, he undertook a prolonged visit to the United States. The visit led to settlement in Wisconsin, where he founded Sauk City before moving on to California. 1830-48

Harben, Will N.

2879. Simms, L. Moody, Jr. THE GEORGIA BACKGROUND OF WILL N. HARBEN'S FICTION (WITH REPRINT OF HARBEN'S ESSAY "GEORGIA"). *Am. Literary Realism, 1870-1910 1978 11(1): 71-79.* Offers a biography of Will N. Harben and reprints his essay "Georgia" which appeared in *The Bookman,* 1913 38(4): 186-192; offers insight into his literary inspiration, his background, and the significance of his Georgia upbringing to his literature. 1913

Harcourt, Edward

2880. Brister, Louis E. COLONEL EDUARD HARKORT: A GERMAN SOLDIER OF FORTUNE IN MEXICO AND TEXAS, 1832-1836. *Southwestern Historical Quarterly 1985 88(3): 229-246.* Eduard Harkort, better known in Texas history as Edward Harcourt, served as chief engineer in the Texas army during 28 March-11 August 1836. Harcourt was a German immigrant who reached Texas via New Orleans after spending nearly a decade in Mexico. During that time, he served four years in the Mexican army and supported the federalists. Opposition to Santa Anna's centralist government caused his deportation in November 1835. His experience in mining, cartography, and the military prompted General Sam Houston to appoint Harcourt to the Texas army as captain of engineers. His first task was to construct Fort Travis on the eastern shore of Galveston Island and to fortify Velasco, but he died before that work was completed. Illus., 51 notes. 1832-36

Hardin, John Wesley

2881. McGinty, Brian. JOHN WESLEY HARDIN: GENTLEMAN OF GUNS. *Am. Hist. Illus. 1982 17(4): 32-36.* John Wesley Hardin, who considered himself a "gentleman of guns" rather than a "gunman" of the Old West, killed over 20 men before he was 25 and was sent to the Texas State Penitentiary at Huntsville. 1853-95

Harding, George Laban

2882. Nash, Ray. GEORGE LABAN HARDING. *Pro. of the Am. Antiquarian Soc. 1977 87(1): 15-18.* Presents an obituary of George Laban Harding, an authority on the history of printing in California. Harding organized the Edward C. Kemble Collections on American printing and publishing at the California Historical Society. 1915-76

Harding, Warren G.

2883. Lukacs, John. BIG GRIZZLY. *Am. Heritage 1978 29(6): 72-81.* 1897-1921

*For abstract see **Penrose, Boies***

Harding, William Lloyd

2884. Sorensen, Scott and LeDoux, John. MANUSCRIPT COLLECTIONS: THE WILLIAM LLOYD HARDING PAPERS IN THE SIOUX CITY PUBLIC MUSEUM. *Ann. of Iowa 1981 45(7): 568-573.* Describes the William Lloyd Harding Papers. One of the most controversial figures in Iowa politics, Harding served two terms as lieutenant governor (1913-17) and two terms as governor (1917-21). His position on issues such as prohibition, "good roads," and the banning of all foreign languages during World War I often put him at odds with his fellow Republicans. The Harding Papers will be of value to students of early 20th-century Iowa political history. 2 photos. 1905-34

Hardtner, Henry Ernest

2885. Burns, Anna C. HENRY E. HARDTNER, LOUISIANA'S FIRST CONSERVATIONIST. *J. of Forest Hist. 1978 22(2): 78-85.* Henry Ernest Hardtner (1871-1935), a Louisiana lumberman of German ancestry, was the state's first advocate of forest conservation. Untrained in forestry, he nevertheless taught himself the rudiments of silviculture and developed a vision of reforestation as the economic salvation of the region's declining forest industries. Appointed chairman of the Louisiana Commission for the Conservation of Natural Resources in 1908, he worked in the political arena to establish a state forestry agency and related conservation legislation. Participation in regional and national trade, conservation, and forestry organizations, as well as instructive cooperation with the U.S. Forest Service and Yale School of Forestry, brought him deserved recognition as the "Father of Forestry in the South." His successful experiments and demonstrations on timberlands near Urania, dating from about 1904, influenced a generation of southern lumbermen to begin practicing forestry. Based on interviews, correspondence, and secondary sources; 6 illus., 32 notes. 1892-1935

Hardy, Arthur Sherburne

2886. Stewart, Elna Kate. "Arthur Sherburne Hardy: Man of American Letters." U. of Mississippi 1983. 198 pp. *DAI 1984 44(11): 3384-A.* DA8404281 1870's-1930

Hardy, James Chappel

2887. Elias, Louis, Jr. JAMES CHAPPEL HARDY: FOUNDER OF THE GULF PARK COLLEGE FOR WOMEN. *J. of Mississippi Hist. 1984 46(3): 213-226.* As president of the Mississippi Gulf Coast Military Academy until 1917, James Chappel Hardy was preparing to leave the Gulf Coast when he was approached by Gulfport's leading citizens with a request that he spearhead a move to organize a girls' school in their vicinity. With no experience in feminist education, Hardy accepted the challenge, and ultimately Gulf Park College for Women opened in 1921. The roles that Hardy and his associate, Richard G. Cox, played in the establishment of the female institution are examined. Based on interviews, unpublished memoirs, newspaper accounts, and college records; 55 notes. 1917-24

Hargrove, Hondo

2888. Hargrove, Hondo. IL CORSARO: A STORY OF WAR AND FRIENDSHIP. *Michigan Hist. 1980 64(1): 14-19.* Reminiscences of a Michigan member of the all-Negro 92d "Buffalo" Division and his search 32 years later to find an Italian partisan friend. Based on service records, pictures, reports, and other data from the Pentagon and archival repositories; 10 illus. 1943-79

Hariot, Thomas

2889. Bremer, Francis J. THOMAS HARIOT: AMERICAN ADVENTURER AND RENAISSANCE SCIENTIST. *Hist. Today [Great Britain] 1979 29(10): 639-647.* Thomas Hariot, a member of Walter Raleigh's circle, contributed to the colonization of America and to scientific knowledge in his time, 1570's-1621. 1570's-1621

Harkavy, Alexander

2890. Sarna, Jonathan D. "OUR DISTANT BRETHREN": ALEXANDER HARKAVY ON MONTREAL JEWS—1888. *Can. Jewish Hist. Soc. J. [Canada] 1983 7(2): 58-73.* Alexander Harkavy, who immigrated to America from Russia as part of the Am Olam back-to-the-land movement in 1882, wrote the first treatment of Canadian Jewish history ever to appear in Hebrew and helped stimulate Jewish cultural activities in Montreal during his years in that city, 1886-88. 1888

Harkness, Georgia

2891. Scott, Martha Lynne. "The Theology and Social Thought of Georgia Harkness." Northwestern U. 1984. 305 pp. *DAI 1985 45(12): 3672-A.* DA8502433 20c

Harlan, John Marshall (1833-1911)

2892. White, G. Edward. JOHN MARSHALL HARLAN I: THE PRECURSOR. *Am. J. of Legal Hist. 1975 19(1): 1-21.* Examines Harlan's Supreme Court career, 1877-1911, focusing on his responses to the Reconstruction amendments and to the growth of large-scale industrial enterprise. Harlan evolved from an orthodox Whig to a paternalist, gradually accepting government regulation of the economy, civil rights, and liberal interpretations of the 13th, 14th, and 15th amendments. Includes a brief account of his earlier political career from the late 1850's to the mid-1870's. 104 notes. 1877-1911

Harlan, John Marshall (1899-1971)

2893. Vasicko, Sally Jo. JOHN MARSHALL HARLAN: NEGLECTED ADVOCATE OF FEDERALISM. *Modern Age 1980 24(4): 387-395.* John Marshall Harlan served as Associate Justice on the Supreme Court of the United States, 1955-71. His term was characterized by sound judicial logic, especially in the area of due process. During an era of emotionalism concerning the definition and expansion of constitutional rights, Harlan called for a limited role for the judiciary through adherence to basic constitutional principles of federalism. 36 notes. 1955-71

2894. Vasicko, Sally Jo. JUSTICE HARLAN AND THE EQUAL PROTECTION CLAUSE. *Supreme Court Hist. Soc. Y. 1982: 46-56.* John Marshall Harlan was on the Supreme Court during a period when the equal protection clause of the Constitution was widely interpreted. During this time Harlan wrote many dissenting opinions in the areas of reapportionment, voting rights, race relations, defendant rights, and welfare rights as they were affected by the equal protection clause. He insisted the Court use prudence and not emotion when deciding such cases and had a deep commitment to maintaining the balance between the states and the federal government. Based primarily on Harlan's dissenting opinions; 72 notes, 3 illus. 1953-69

Harman, John Alexander

2895. Wert, Jeffry. MAJOR HARMAN THE WAGON-MASTER: "OLD JOHN." *Civil War Times Illus. 1981 20(2): 8-13.* Explores the performance of Major John Alexander Harman as chief quartermaster for the Confederates' Shenandoah Valley Army and his relationship with Major General Thomas J. (Stonewall) Jackson, his commander. 1861-65

Harnack, Curtis

2896. Gildner, Judith. IOWANS IN THE ARTS: CURTIS HARNACK. *Ann. of Iowa 1975 43(1): 38-48.* In addition to many short stories and three novels, Curtis Harnack is the author of a prize-winning nonfiction work, *We Have All Gone Away* (1973), based on his youth on an Iowa farm during the 1930's. In response to Gildner's questions, Harnack recalls his youth in northwestern Iowa, his writing career, his books, and the Midwest traditions which have influenced his life. Based on an 11 October 1974 interview with Harnack; photo, note. ca 1930-74

Harney, William Selby

2897. Adams, George Rollie. "General William Selby Harney: Frontier Soldier, 1800-1889." U. of Arizona 1983. 426 pp. *DAI 1984 44(12): 3779-3780-A.* DA8405490 1817-89

2898. Clow, Richmond L. MAD BEAR: WILLIAM S. HARNEY AND THE SIOUX EXPEDITION OF 1855-1856. *Nebraska Hist. 1980 61(2): 133-152.* In a harsh campaign, Harney drove his men, vigorously pursued the Sioux Indians, and defeated them in battle. He was eminently fair in his judgments and treatment of his men and the Indians. Most important, he brought peace, based on fear, to the northern Great Plains. That peace lasted until the Civil War. 1855-56

Harper, Ida Husted

2899. Jones, Nancy Baker. A FORGOTTEN FEMINIST: THE EARLY WRITINGS OF IDA HUSTED HARPER, 1878-1894. *Indiana Mag. of Hist. 1977 73(2): 79-101.* Ida Husted Harper had a column in the Terre Haute *Saturday Evening Mail* and in the *Locomotive Firemen's Magazine* and was managing editor of the Terre Haute *Daily News.* 1878-94

Harper, Martha Matilda

2900. Thure, Karen. MARTHA HARPER PIONEERED IN THE HAIR BUSINESS. *Smithsonian 1976 7(6): 94-100.* Discusses the beauty shop run by Martha Matilda Harper in Oakville, Ontario, 1857-93 and the school of hair care which bloomed around her, gaining immediate popularity and extending to the present. 1857-93

Harper, Olive

2901. Grenander, M. E. HENRIETTA STACKPOLE AND OLIVE HARPER: EMANATIONS OF THE GREAT DEMOCRACY. *Bull. of Res. in the Humanities 1980 83(3): 406-422.* Discusses similarities and differences in Henry James's fictional character, newspaperwoman Henrietta Stackpole, in *The Portrait of a Lady* (set in the 1870's), and the real-life foreign correspondent Olive Harper (Helen Burrell D'Apery), a brash and eccentric woman whose imaginative journalism gained international notoriety in the early 1870's. ca 1871-73

Harper, Samuel Northrup

2902. Goble, Paul A. SAMUEL N. HARPER AND THE STUDY OF RUSSIA: HIS CAREER AND COLLECTION. *Cahiers du Monde Russe et Sovietique [France] 1973 14(4): 608-620.* Reviews the life and works of Samuel Northrup Harper (1882-1943), the first American scholar to devote his entire career to the study of Russia. Harper found Russia a fascinating subject early in his career and recognized that he was standing on the brink of history in the making. He supported the Kerensky revolution but not its Bolshevik replacement, a stand which caused some difficulty in later visiting the USSR. He served several times as a government consultant on Soviet affairs and taught courses on the USSR at the University of Chicago, where his research, notes, diaries, and correspondence are on file. 13 notes. 1906-43

2903. Poster, John B. A WARMTH OF SOUL: SAMUEL NORTHRUP HARPER AND THE RUSSIANS, 1904-1943. *J. of Contemporary Hist. [Great Britain] 1979 14(2): 235-251.* From 1904 to 1913, Samuel Northrup Harper, professor of Russian Studies at the University of Chicago, annually spent six months in the Russian Empire. In 1916, he assumed the duty of advisor to David R. Francis, US Ambassador to St. Petersburg, but returned to Chicago before the Communist Revolution, a change of government which he was inclined at the time to approve. Subsequently, he worked with the American Historical Association in identifying some Russian documents which he mistakenly deemed authentic. He also assisted in the Russian Bureau of the State Department. As time passed, Harper became disenchanted with the Soviet Union and favored nonrecognition. He went to the USSR in 1926, however, in the interest of a book on civic education, and came home advocating recognition. He continued teaching and writing until his death January 18, 1943. Based on the Samuel Northrup Harper papers in the Regenstein Library, U. of Chicago; 58 notes. 1904-43

Harper, William Rainey

2904. Lawson, Hal A. and Ingham, Alan G. CONFLICTING IDEOLOGIES CONCERNING THE UNIVERSITY AND INTERCOLLEGIATE ATHLETICS: HARPER AND HUTCHINS AT CHICAGO, 1892-1940. *J. of Sport Hist. 1980 7(3): 37-67.* Two University of Chicago presidents, William Rainey Harper and Robert Hutchins, provide an interesting contrast in their view of intercollegiate athletics. When the university was founded in 1892, Harper, the first president, believed in the importance of intercollegiate football and a physical education requirement for all students. He appointed Amos Alonzo Stagg as Director of Physical Culture and Athletics, and placed football under university rather than student control. Stagg was charged by other universities with using professional athletes and overemphasizing winning. When Hutchins became president in 1929, he took over a university that was moving toward reform, and the major revision was institution of a common core for all students. Higher standards meant losses on the field, which led to elimination of football. Sources include letters and materials in the University of Chicago archives; 157 notes. 1892-1940

Harrais, Margaret Keenan

2905. Munsey, Sylvia Falconer. MARGARET KEENAN HARRAIS. *Alaska J. 1975 5(3): 144-152.* Discusses the life and charitable work of Harrais from her youth in Idaho until her marriage to an Alaskan mine owner; her social service included temperance leagues, education funds, Red Cross, and work on achieving statehood for Alaska, 1902-62. 1902-62

Harrington, John P.

2906. Benson, Arlene and Edberg, Bob. ON THE ROAD TO GOLETA. *J. of California and Great Basin Anthrop. 1982 4(2): 288-295.* Documents found in a recently discovered trunk once owned by ethnographer John P. Harrington shed light on the scientist's early career and his research among California Indians. 1894-1920's

2907. Hudson, Travis. SOME J. P. HARRINGTON NOTES ON THE "LONE WOMAN" OF SAN NICOLAS ISLAND. *Masterkey 1978 52(1): 23-28.* Presents excerpts from the papers of ethnographer John P. Harrington on his work with the Chumash Indians, particularly Juana Maria, the "Lone Woman" who lived on San Nicolas Island off southern California, 1836-53. 1836-53

2908. James, Carollyn. A FIELD LINGUIST WHO LIVED HIS LIFE FOR HIS SUBJECTS. *Smithsonian 1984 15(1): 153-154, 156, 158, 160-161, 163-164, 166, 168, 170, 172, 174.* Profiles the indefatigable and eccentric John Peabody Harrington, whose professional life as a linguistic anthropologist was devoted to recording and preserving Indian languages. 1905-55

Harrington, Mark Walrod

2909. Jones, Kenneth Lester. MARK WALROD HARRINGTON (1848-1926): BOTANIST, ASTRONOMIST, METEOROLOGIST. *Michigan Academician 1978 11(2): 115-138.* Discusses Harrington's work at the University of Michigan, scientific studies abroad, and botanical and meteorological studies; covers 1868-1926. 1868-1926

Harris, Corra White

2910. Jolley, Clyde W. FAMOUS GEORGIA WOMEN: CORRA HARRIS. *Georgia Life 1980 6(4): 22-23.* Corra White Harris (1869-1935) wrote 24 book-length manuscripts and over 250 articles for *The Saturday Evening Post, Pictorial Review, American Magazine, Cosmopolitan, The Independent, Ladies' Home Journal, Harpers,* and others, 20 of which were published in book form. 1880's-1935

Harris, Emily Lyles

2911. Racine, Philip N. EMILY LYLES HARRIS: A PIEDMONT FARMER DURING THE CIVIL WAR. *South Atlantic Q. 1980 79(4): 386-397.* David Harris, a South Carolina farmer eight miles southeast of Spartanburg, began keeping a journal in 1855. When he went off to the Civil War, he encouraged his wife to keep up the journal, which she did. Through her entries we catch a glimpse of what it was like during the Civil War to be the wife of a farmer and a soldier. There is no better contemporary record of daily life in the Spartanburg District and not many its equal for the region. The journal reveals her inmost feelings, especially her depression, which made her feel guilty and incompetent. Her life gave her ample reason to be apprehensive, yet society expected her to react to her burdens otherwise. The David Glightly Harris Farm Journals, 1855-70 (microfilm), Southern Historical Collection at the University of North Carolina, Chapel Hill. 1861-65

Harris, Ezekiel

2912. Swann, Lee Ann Caldwell and Abbot, Lisa. EZEKIEL HARRIS OF HARRISBURG. *Richmond County Hist. 1980 12(1): 5-ll.* Ezekiel Harris (ca. 1758-1829) served in the South Carolina militia during the American Revolution, then lived in the Augusta area of Georgia, where he founded Harrisburg around 1800. 1770's-1829

Harris, George

2913. Davis, William T. THE SEARCH FOR ROCHESTER'S EARLIEST INHABITANTS: ON THE TRAIL WITH GEORGE HARRIS, THE PATHFINDER. *Rochester History 1982 44(1-2): 1-44.* Discusses the life of George Harris, Rochester, New York's, capable amateur historian who left an extensive collection of cataloged artifacts. 1843-93

Harris, Isham Green

2914. Watters, George Wayne. "Isham Green Harris, Civil War Governor and Senator from Tennessee, 1818-1897." Florida State U. 1977. 224 pp. *DAI 1977 38(5): 3003-3004-A.* 1841-96

Harris, Jed

2915. Burroughs, Patricia Lynn. "The Theatrical Career of Jed Harris in New York, 1925-1956." Louisiana State U. and Agric. and Mechanical Coll. 1978. 400 pp. *DAI 1979 39(8): 4596-4597-A.* 1925-56

Harris, Joel Chandler

2916. Jones, Alfred Haworth. JOEL CHANDLER HARRIS: TALES OF UNCLE REMUS. *Am. Hist. Illus. 1983 18(3): 34-39.* Chronicles the life, career, and writings of Joel Chandler Harris during 1864-1907. 1864-1907

2917. Rorabaugh, W. J. WHEN WAS JOEL CHANDLER HARRIS BORN? SOME NEW EVIDENCE. *Southern Literary Journal 1984 17(1): 92-95.* Presents new and conflicting information as to the actual birth date of Joel Chandler Harris, the author of *Uncle Remus* stories, concluding that his birth date was not 1848 as he had said, but actually sometime between 1845 and 1847. 1844-48

Harris, John

2918. Cousins, Leone B. CAPTAIN JOHN HARRIS OF CLEMENTS. *Nova Scotia Hist. Rev. [Canada] 1982 2(1): 44-56.* Captain John Harris of Clements, Annapolis County, was a farmer, master mariner, shipwright, father and privateer. His diaries and journals record events and his activities. Reprints portions of his diary for 22 May-30 June, 1813, which details his life as a privateer. 14 notes. 1806-13

Harris, Johnny

2919. Carter, Norman M. JOHNNY HARRIS OF SANDON. *Beaver [Canada] 1976 306(4): 42-49.* Sandon, in southeast British Columbia, was an important mining zone at the turn of the century, and Harris quickly had control of the best real estate. He ran hotels, saloons, shops, and gambling houses, and for several decades was the most important of the entrepreneurs in the area. Harris was hurt by investments in wheat futures at the time of the Depression. Based on reminiscences of the author, whose father was a dentist in Sandon; 9 illus. 1890's-1950's

Harris, Julian

2920. Matthews, John M. JULIAN L. HARRIS: THE EVOLUTION OF A SOUTHERN LIBERAL. *South Atlantic Q. 1976 75(4): 483-498.* Eldest son of folklorist Joel Chandler Harris, Julian Harris followed his father into journalism. At various times editor of the Atlanta *Constitution,* the New York-Paris *Herald,* and the Columbus, Georgia *Enquirer-Sun,* Harris made his mark as a Southern Progressive and muckraker. Although no great friend of blacks, Harris won a Pulitzer Prize for his editorials against the Ku Klux Klan. A close friend of H. L. Mencken and an outspoken critic of what he termed the "Protestant Inquisition," Harris never was secure in any southern job despite his extreme proSouth sentiments. In 1957 he violently criticized Eisenhower's use of troops in Little Rock, but, by then, his real influence had vanished. Primary and secondary sources; 36 notes. 1900-60

Harris, R. K.

2921. Harris, R. K. LIFE IN POTLATCH WAS DIFFERENT. *Pacific Northwesterner 1976 20(1): 1-15.* The author recalls his childhood, 1900's-10's, in Potlatch, Idaho, a town operated and mostly owned by the Potlatch Lumber Company. 1900's-10's

Harris, Robert Edward

2922. Inglis, R. E. SKETCHES OF TWO CHIEF JUSTICES OF NOVA SCOTIA. *Nova Scotia Hist. Soc. Collections [Canada] 1977 39: 107-120.* Starting in 1887, Charles James Townshend (1844-1924) served on the Supreme Court of Nova Scotia, for 28 years, including the last eight as Chief Justice. His decisions were characterized "by lucidity and reasoning." He devoted considerable time to his research and his writings, some of which were read before the Nova Scotia Historical Society and preserved in their collections. Robert Edward Harris's (1860-1931) chief interest, corporation law, brought him involvement with several businesses, including the Nova Scotia Steel & Coal Company, the presidency of which he assumed in 1904, and The Eastern Trust Company. His later friendship with Sir Robert Borden is reputed to have brought him a seat on the Supreme Court of Nova Scotia in 1915. In 1918 he became Chief Justice. 1887-1931

Harris brothers

2923. West, Earle H. THE HARRIS BROTHERS: BLACK NORTHERN TEACHERS IN THE RECONSTRUCTION SOUTH. *J. of Negro Educ. 1979 48(2): 126-138.* Discusses the teaching careers of the Harris brothers, Robert, William, and Cicero, and compares them with those of white Northern teachers who moved to the South after the Civil War to teach. The motivations of the Harris brothers were similar to those of the whites. They both wanted to teach in the South for humanitarian and religious purposes. Their activities regarding teaching were also similar. The Harris brothers spent more time with black families during their spare hours than did whites, who were more politically active. Primary sources; 65 notes. 1864-70

Harrison, Benjamin

2924. Socolofsky, Homer E. BENJAMIN HARRISON AND THE AMERICAN WEST. *Great Plains Quarterly 1985 5(4): 249-258.* Describes President Benjamin Harrison's efforts to advance the interests of the American West, including his pushing for the admittance of new Western states into the Union, appointing Westerners to important offices, and supporting pro-West legislation. 1889-93

Harrison, Constance Cary

2925. Maxwell, Sherrolyn. "Constance Cary Harrison: American Woman of Letters, 1843-1920." U. of North Carolina, Chapel Hill 1977. 258 pp. *DAI 1977 38(6): 3501-A.* 1870-1920

Harrison, Gabriel

2926. Rushmore, Robert P. GABRIEL HARRISON: ARTIST, WRITER, AND "FATHER OF THE DRAMA IN BROOKLYN." *J. of Long Island Hist. 1982 18(1): 30-44.* Gabriel Harrison (1818-1902) established the first legitimate theater in Brooklyn, the Park Theatre, during 1863-64. He was also an actor, engraver, artist, photographer, tea and tobacco store proprietor, playwright, and biographer, but was not outstandingly successful in any of his interests. Illus., 52 notes. 1840's-1902

Harrison, H. Lincoln

2927. —. MEMORIAL NOTICES: H. LINCOLN HARRISON. *Railroad Hist. 1977 (137): 114.* H. Lincoln Harrison's (1904-77) field was railroad history. 1977

Harrison, Hubert H.

2928. Samuels, Wilfred David. "Five Afro-Caribbean Voices in American Culture, 1917-1929: Hubert H. Harrison, Wilfred A. Domingo, Richard B. Moore, Cyril V. Briggs, and Claude McKay." U. of Iowa 1977. 181 pp. *DAI 1978 38(7): 4234-A.* 1917-29

Harrison, Peter

2929. Chiel, Arthur A. PETER HARRISON AND THE NEW HAVEN CONNECTION. *Rhode Island Jewish Hist. Notes 1983 9(1): 77-82.* Traces the career of architect Peter Harrison, who designed and built several churches and other public buildings in Rhode Island, Massachusetts, and South Carolina, including Touro Synagogue in Newport, Rhode Island. 1750-75

Harrison, Preston E.

2930. Moore, Carol and Winer, Jane L. DR. PRESTON E. HARRISON: PIONEER TRAILBLAZER FOR MENTAL HEALTH IN WEST TEXAS. *West Texas Hist. Assoc. Year Book 1979 55: 49-58.* Discusses the work and humanistic philosophy of Dr. Preston E. Harrison, superintendent of Big Spring State Hospital, where he directed the medical care of the mentally ill from 1953 to 1975. 1946-77

Harrison, William

2931. Lohrenz, Otto. THE RIGHT REVEREND WILLIAM HARRISON OF REVOLUTIONARY VIRGINIA, FIRST "LORD ARCHBISHOP OF AMERICA." *Hist. Mag. of the Protestant Episcopal Church 1984 53(1): 25-43.* Sketches events in the life of the Reverend William Harrison. Politically, Harrison was adaptive and adroit, moving smoothly from colonist to revolutionist to loyalist to republican. 71 notes. 1774-1813

Harshman, Samuel Rufus

2932. Spriggs, Robert William. "Samuel Rufus Harshman: Nineteenth Century South-Central Illinois Holiness Man." Saint Louis U. 1983. 257 pp. *DAI 1984 44(7): 2176-A.* DA8325434 1871-1912

Hart, William S.

2933. Firestone, Bruce M. A BOY NAMED SIOUX: NOSTALGIA AND THE CAREER OF WILLIAM S. HART. *Film & Hist. 1977 7(4): 85-89.* William S. Hart's autobiography reveals his nostalgia for his career in films, the westward movement, and life on the American frontier during the 1880's-1920's. 1880's-1920's

Harte, Bret

2934. Harte, John Bret. A DEDICATION TO THE MEMORY OF FRANCIS BRET HARTE, 1836-1902. *Arizona and the West 1976 18(1): 1-4.* Transplanted New Yorker Francis Bret Harte (1836-1902) began his literary career as a typesetter on a California newspaper. He recruited Mark Twain as a contributor and instructed him in the craft of writing. Harte's first recognition came through patriotic poems, but "The Luck of Roaring Camp" firmly established him as a major literary figure. This appeared in the *Overland Monthly* of which he was the founding editor. After a few unhappy years in the East he served in American consulates in Germany and Scotland. His last years were spent as an expatriate in England. Illus., note. 1860-1902

Harte, Houston

2935. Chenoweth, Dean. HOUSTON HARTE: JOURNALISTIC GIANT. *West Texas Hist. Assoc. Year Book 1981 57: 107-117.* Houston Harte, a young Missouri newspaperman who arrived in West Texas in the early 1900's, bought the *Texas Standard* after World War I and continued buying other newspapers until by 1972 he owned 19; he was an important and active community leader in San Angelo, Texas. 1900's-72

Harte, Walter Blackburn

2936. Doyle, James. THE DEVIL AND DAME CHANCE: THE LIFE AND WRITINGS OF WALTER BLACKBURN HARTE. *Canadian Review of American Studies [Canada] 1985 16(1): 15-30.* Briefly a Canadian journalist in the 1880's, Walter Blackburn Harte (1866-99) published one book, *Meditations in Motley* (1894), some short fiction, and many essays in American journals. But his writings have since interested few readers; his own weaknesses and unremitting devotion to ideals that conflicted with too many orthodoxies largely account for an obscurity that is not wholly deserved. His life and literature reflect a uniqueness, particularly his brand of idealism that, like devils in his fiction who lost out to chance, could not tolerate imperfections, and Harte inevitably sentenced himself to a life of struggles and failures and posthumously to oblivion. Based on Harte's writings and private letters of his contemporaries in archival collections; 38 notes. 1886-99

Hartley, Marsden

2937. Halasz, Piri. THE MOODY WORK OF A LONELY PAINTER IS NOW REASSESSED. *Smithsonian 1980 10(12): 122-128.* A coming exhibition of the works of American pioneer modernist artist Marsden Hartley (1877-1943) offers evidence that this little-known artistic pioneer is finally receiving some deserved recognition. Covers the life and work of Hartley from his childhood in Maine, his voyages abroad, especially to Germany, where perhaps his best works were composed, and his eventual return in old age to the state of his birth. He was difficult to like, and his work reflected his life, with so many changes of style and method as to render comprehension difficult. 8 photos. 1877-1943

Hartlieb, Louise Marie Katherina Boehner

2938. Stengel, Drusilla Hartlieb. GRANDMA HARTLIEB. *Niagara Frontier 1979 26(1): 14-24, (3): 62-68.* Part I. A biography of the author's grandmother, Louise Marie Katherina Boehner Hartlieb (1825-1918), born in Bavaria, who arrived in the United States and settled in Buffalo in 1849; based on the grandmother's recollections in 1918 at age 93. Part II. Relates more of Louise Hartlieb's reminiscences of life in Buffalo. 1825-1918

Hartnell, William E. P.

2939. King, Mary Wilma. WILLIAM E. P. HARTNELL, A CALIFORNIA PATRIARCH. *Records of the Am. Catholic Hist. Soc. of Philadelphia 1980 91(1-4): 39-48.* Traces the life of William E. P. Hartnell from his arrival in California in 1820 to his death in 1854, with particular reference to his work as Visitor General of the Missions. Based on archival and secondary sources; 44 notes, biblio. 1820-54

Hartsfield, Green W.

2940. Poe, William A. THE STORY OF A FRIENDSHIP AND A BOOK: W. E. PAXTON AND GREEN W. HARTSFIELD. *Louisana Hist. 1981 22(2): 167-182.* Discusses the friendship between Baptist ministers W. E. Paxton and Green W. Hartsfield. Paxton was instrumental in the formation of the Baptist Historical Society in 1860. He gathered data from all over Louisiana and by 1881 had completed a manuscript of some 500 pages, which was destined to become one of the most treasured books in Louisiana history. It was entitled

History of the Baptists of Louisiana from the Earliest Times to the Present. Because of his untimely death in 1883, the book only saw print because of Hartsfield's attention to the project. Primary sources; 52 notes. 1850-1900

2941. Poe, William A. NORTH LOUISIANA SOCIAL LIFE AS REFLECTED IN THE MINISTRY OF GREEN W. HARTSFIELD, 1860-96. *North Louisiana Hist. Assoc. J. 1981 12(1): 1-11.* Green W. Hartsfield (b. 1833) entered the Baptist ministry at the age of 26. Known as "the peoples' pastor" during his three decades of ministry, he served numerous churches in northern Louisiana. His ministry to blacks and whites, his aversion to revelry, and his and the area's concern with high infant mortality, are all reflected in the article. Based on census records, diaries, and parish records; illus., 51 notes. 1860-96

Hartshorn, Florence

2942. Mills, Thora McIlroy. MEMORIAL TO THE PACK ANIMALS. *Beaver [Canada] 1980 310(4): 46-51.* In traveling the 32 miles over the mountains from Skagway, Alaska, to the Klondike on a pony, Florence Hartshorn was "deeply affected... [by] the dreadful toll which it took on the pack animals." On her first day in the northland, she vowed "to place a memorial to the[se] animals... [which] played such an important part in the extraction of wealth from the gold country." Many details in her life in the Klondike extending over 16 years were extracted from her diary. In 1929, she started a campaign to raise funds for a memorial to the pack animals used on the White Pass Trail. The memorial was unveiled later that year. 5 photos, map. 1898-1929

Hartt, Ella

2943. —. ELLA HARTT: PIONEER PHOTOGRAPHER. *Alberta Hist. [Canada] 1979 27(1): 17-24.* Ella Hartt, a nurse from Illinois, moved to Alberta with her brother Ed in the 1890's. She was interested in the camera as an expression of art, and in the following decades she took, and kept, hundreds of glass plates of views and people in western Canada. Thirteen are published here, mostly rural or agricultural views. The originals are in the Glenbow Archives. 1898-1912

Hartzell, Joseph C.

2944. Loveland, Anne C. THE "SOUTHERN WORK" OF THE REVEREND JOSEPH C. HARTZELL, PASTOR OF AMES CHURCH IN NEW ORLEANS, 1870-1873. *Louisiana Hist. 1975 16(4): 391-407.* "Like most other Northern Methodist missionaries to the South, Hartzell saw no conflict in linking religious endeavors and Republican politics." Hartzell supervised three Methodist institutions for Negroes: Union Normal School, Thomson Institute, and the Freedmen's Orphan Home which combined educational and missionary efforts. The response of Southern Whites to the educational and missionary work of the Northern Methodists among the freedmen was generally unsympathetic. Another reason for the loss of support was the Republicans ultimately abandoned the social and political goals of Reconstruction. Based largely on correspondence from the Hartzell and Baldwin Papers. Illus., 42 notes. 1870-73

Harvey, Charles Thompson

2945. Welsh, William Jeffrey. "Tilting at Windmills: One Man's Search for the American Dream, A Biography of Charles Thompson Harvey." Bowling Green State U. 1982. 206 pp. *DAI 1982 43(4): 1269-A.* DA8220243 1860's-1900

Harvie, John (family)

2946. Harvey, Robert Paton. JOHN HARVIE (1730-1822) OF NEWPORT, NOVA SCOTIA: THREE GENERATIONS OF DESCENDANTS. *Nova Scotia Hist. Q. [Canada] 1976 6(4): 431-442.* Genealogy of the John Harvie family (Hervie, Herve, Harvey) which originated in Great Britain and settled and flourished in Nova Scotia, 1730-1945. 1730-1945

Harwood, Edward C.

2947. Poole, Robert, Jr. INTERVIEW WITH COL. EDWARD C. HARWOOD. *Reason 1981 13(2): 58-63.* Reprints an interview with 80-year-old Colonel Edward C. Harwood in 1980, shortly before he died; he was founder of the American Institute for Economic Research in 1933, and an investment and economic genius; focuses on his career and accomplishments; 1920-80. 1920-80

Hass, Victor P.

2948. Hass, Victor P. LOOKING HOMEWARD: A MEMOIR OF SMALL-TOWN LIFE IN WISCONSIN. *Wisconsin Mag. of Hist. 1982 65(3): 176-194.* The personal reminiscences of a journalist's boyhood in Waupun, Wisconsin, from about 1910 to 1930. Covers town and family life, including special holidays, daily diet, Rock River, summer work at the ice house, weekends, the flu epidemic, high school operetta, and influence of parents, grandparents, and the town librarian. 4 notes, 13 illus. 1910-32

Hast, Louis H.

2949. Bennett, James D. A TRIBUTE TO LOUIS H. HAST, LOUISVILLE MUSICIAN. *Filson Club Hist. Q. 1978 52(4): 323-329.* Louis H. Hast, an immigrant from Germany, was a dominant figure in establishing a strong musical tradition in Louisville, Kentucky. In 1878 Hast became organist and choir director for Christ Church Cathedral and introduced classical music to church functions. He also started the Philharmonic and *La Reunion* Musicale and contributed to the Public Library. Newspapers and secondary works; 24 notes. 1848-90

Hastie, William

2950. McGuire, Phillip. JUDGE HASTIE, WORLD WAR II, AND ARMY RACISM. *J. of Negro Hist. 1977 62(4): 351-362.* William Hastie, the first Afro-American appointed to the federal bench as US District Court Judge for the Virgin Islands (1937-39), left the deanship of the Howard University Law School to serve as a civilian aide to the Secretary of War (1940-43). Although Secretary Henry L. Stimson asked Hastie to be responsible for all black military personnel, most of Hastie's activities related to the US Army. The aide resigned in 1943 in protest against the racism of the military establishment. The integration of the armed forces by executive order in 1948 was the legacy of Hastie's efforts. Based on primary materials in the Library of Congress, National Archives, the Yale University Library, and secondary sources; 34 notes. 1940-43

Hastings, Matthew

2951. Smith, Gary N. MAT HASTINGS: ARTISTIC CHRONICLER OF HIS TIMES. *Gateway Heritage 1982-83 3(3): 2-9.* In 1840, Matthew Hastings moved to St. Louis, where his artistic career lasted neary 80 years. His work brought scant recognition except in St. Louis, partly because it focused on local matters. Hastings's art constitutes an important historical record, faithfully depicting St. Louis and its people as the city emerged as a regional commercial and cultural center. Based on newspapers and the Missouri Historical Society archives; 13 photos, 24 notes. 1840-1919

2952. Spiess, Lincoln Bunce. MAT HASTINGS, ARTIST (1834-1919). *Missouri Hist. Soc. Bull. 1980 36(3): 152-155.* St. Louis artist Matthew Hastings (1834-1919) produced approximately 600 paintings and many sketches and drawings. His subjects included St. Louis area scenes, Indians, and western scenes. Little of his work today is extant; the largest collection is held by the Missouri Historical Society. During Hastings's lifetime, his work was overshadowed by that of such contemporary artists as George Caleb Bingham and Carl Winmar. 3 photos, 14 notes. ca 1850-1919

Haswell, David R.

2953. Farmerie, Samuel A. and Farmerie, Janice C. THE LETTERS OF DAVID RUSSEL HASWELL. *Western Pennsylvania Hist. Mag. 1977 60(1): 37-54.* A brief biographical sketch of David Russel Haswell, who migrated from Vermont to Pennsylvania in 1808, precedes annotated copies of letters he wrote to his father and brother in Bennington, Vermont, during 1808-31, which tell about his farm and life in Pennsylvania, reveal the evangelical revivals of the period, and relate matters of family interest. 1808-31

Hatfield, David Daniel

2954. Schreiner, Herm. DAVID DANIEL HATFIELD, 1903-1981. *Am. Aviation Hist. Soc. J. 1981 26(3): 197.* David Daniel Hatfield was an internationally recognized aviation expert; notes his early days as a barnstormer in the 1920's and covers his various successful careers in engineering, photography, collecting, education, and history. 1920's-81

Hatfield, William A. (family)

2955. Klotter, James C. A HATFIELD-MCCOY FEUDIST PLEADS FOR MERCY IN 1889. *West Virginia Hist. 1982 43(4): 322-328.* Discusses the life of William A. "Cap" Hatfield, one of the leaders of the Hatfield-McCoy feud, and reprints his letter to Kentucky Governor Simon B. Buckner, offering to surrender to him to stand trial for his part in the feud. Hatfield later renounced feuding and became a lawyer and deputy sheriff. Based on the letter in the Kentucky State Archives, newspaper accounts, and secondary sources; 3 photos, 11 notes. 1886-1930

Haugen, Gilbert N.

2956. Michael, Bonnie. GILBERT N. HAUGEN, APPRENTICE CONGRESSMAN. *Palimpsest 1978 59(4): 118-129.* A selection from a book-length manuscript biography of Gilbert N. Haugen (US Representative 1899-1933), dealing with his early days as Iowa's Fourth District congressman. In Washington, Haugen, a Republican, began his legislative activities on the oleomargarine labeling and agricultural appropriations issues. He provided seed packets and government pamphlets to his constituency, aided veterans who sought pensions, and influenced the growth of Iowa's rural mail service. Based on primary archival sources; photo, editorial note, note on sources. 1899-1926

Haupt, Herman

2957. Snow, Richard F. AMERICAN CHARACTERS: HERMAN HAUPT. *American Heritage 1985 36(2): 54-55.* Civil engineer Herman Haupt had extensive experience in the construction, maintenance and organization of railroads. A graduate of West Point, during the Civil War he was appointed chief of construction and transportation on the US military railroads. After the war he returned to engineering and railroads. Photo. 1840-85

Haushalter, Walter M.

2958. Johnsen, Thomas C. HISTORICAL CONSENSUS AND CHRISTIAN SCIENCE: THE CAREER OF A MANUSCRIPT CONTROVERSY. *New England Q. 1980 53(1): 3-22.* Analyzes Walter M. Haushalter's (d. 1963) contacts with the Christian Science Church in his attempt to extort money from it in return for suppressing a document which he later published in a book *Mrs. Eddy Purloins from Hegel* (1936). The key document was a forgery but Haushalter continued to write pamphlets about it until 1959. The church, confident that the document was a fraud, maintained a dignified silence. Based on documents in the archives of The Mother Church, Boston, and on published articles; 59 notes. 1929-59

Haven, Gilbert

2959. Fletcher, Thomas Richard. "Gilbert Haven: Jeremiad Abolitionist Preacher." U. of Oregon 1982. 321 pp. *DAI 1983 43(9): 2829-A.* DA8301777 1850's-70's

Haverlin, Carl

2960. Lewis, Mort R. THE NATURAL RESOURCES OF CARL HAVERLIN. *Westways 1979 71(6): 26-29, 71.* Traces the interests and career of Carl Haverlin of Northridge, California, employee of KFI radio station in Los Angeles from 1924 to 1936, father of national broadcasts of the Rose Bowl, broadcasts of the Los Angeles Philharmonic Orchestra and Hollywood Bowl concerts, and retired president of Broadcast Music Incorporated (BMI), the largest music rights organization in the world; 1924-79. 1924-79

Havis, Ferdinand

2961. Leslie, James W. FERD HAVIS: JEFFERSON COUNTY'S BLACK REPUBLICAN LEADER. *Arkansas Hist. Q. 1978 37(3): 240-251.* Details the career of Ferdinand Havis (1846-1918), who was born a slave but rose to become a successful barber and businessman as well as leader of the Republican Party in Jefferson County. He held numerous city and county offices and was also a member of the state legislature. Newspapers and other primary sources; 3 illus., 46 notes. 1846-1918

Hawelu

2962. Manning, Anita. HAWELU: BIRDCATCHER, INNKEEPER, FARMER. *Hawaiian J. of Hist. 1981 15: 59-68.* Hawelu (b. 1834), a skilled birdcatcher (kia manu) by training, adapted his profession to changing times and tastes and exhibited an entrepreneurial spirit that contrasted with the European image of the Hawaiian as a struggling native. When European hobbyists and scientists visited the islands, Hawelu found employment. To supplement his income, he operated a rest stop on the Hilo-Kilauea crater trail. When it appeared that the more sophisticated Kilauea Volcano House Company might drive him out of business, Hawelu developed a food catering service for the company's half-way rest house. There is considerable mystery surrounding Hawelu's fate, and evidence presented by a British ornithologist that Hawelu was in a leper colony on Molokai sometime in 1890 is unsubstantiated. Covers 1880-91. Primary sources; 2 maps, 4 fig., 52 notes. 1880-91

Hawes, Samuel

2963. Johnson, Richard B., ed. THE JOURNAL OF SAMUEL HAWES. *New England Hist. and Genealogical Register 1976 130: 273-283; 1977 131: 40-50.* Continued from a previous article. Part II. Samuel Hawes (1743-1780?) was a private soldier from Wrentham, Massachusetts, and in his journal he chronicled the events from 19 April 1776 to 10 February 1776, beginning with the Lexington Alarm. Samuel concentrated on the activities of the Revolutionary Army headquartered at Cambridge and Roxbury, Massachusetts. This section covers 1 July 1775 through 30 September 1775. Based on primary and secondary sources; 42 notes. Part III. Conclusion of a three-part article. This section covers 1 October 1775 through 10 February 1776. Based on primary and secondary sources; 45 notes. 1775-76

Hawke, Hannah

2964. Birch, Brian P. POSSESSED OF A RESTLESS SPIRIT: A YOUNG GIRL'S MEMORIES OF THE SOUTHERN IOWA FRONTIER. *Palimpsest 1985 66(5): 174-184.* Introduces and publishes memoirs of Hannah Hawke, daughter of Cornish immigrants from Yorkshire, England, of her childhood in southern Iowa, before she moved with her family to New South Wales, Australia. 1847-59

Hawkins, Arthur Charles

2965. Roper, H. THE STRANGE POLITICAL CAREER OF A. C. HAWKINS, MAYOR OF HALIFAX, 1918-1919. *Collections of the Royal Nova Scotia Hist. Soc. [Canada] 1982 41: 141-164.* Arthur Charles Hawkins was a physician and a politician whose Liberal Party connections initially netted him many medical appointments. In 1918, he became mayor of Halifax. Although Hawkins brought considerable experience in municipal politics to the chief magistrate's office, he failed "to provide disinterested leadership." His calling the aldermen "doughheads" and "damn fools" caused most of them to resign, precipitating a political crisis whose eventual outcome was a change in the structure of the municipal government. 95 notes. 1918-19

Hawkins, Erick

2966. Keefer, Julia L. "Erick Hawkins, Modern Dancer: History, Theory, Technique, and Performance." New York U. 1979. 362 pp. *DAI 1979 40(6): 2992-A.* 1934-78

Hawkins, Micah

2967. Lawrence, Vera Brodsky. MICAH HAWKINS, THE PIED PIPER OF CATHERINE SLIP. *New-York Hist. Soc. Q. 1978 62(2): 138-165.* Recently a collection of musical arrangements in the holdings of the New-York Historical Society was discovered. The collection focused attention on the arranger, mutlitalented New Yorker, Micah Hawkins (1777-1825). In addition to his musical talents, he was a poet, playwright, as well as a trained carriage-builder who had worked as a grocer and innkeeper. In his short, but varied career, Hawkins was the first American to compose an opera (actually a musical comedy). He also pioneered in writing Negro dialect for stage productions in blackface, which was popular during the 19th century. Unfortunately, Hawkins died suddenly of typhus when only 48, apparently at the height of his creativity, according to his contemporaries. Primary and secondary sources; 5 illus., 52 notes. 1790's-1825

Hawkins, William Deane

2968. Sherrod, Robert. HAWK. *Marine Corps Gazette 1970 54(11): 27-29.* A biography of US Marine William Deane Hawkins (1914-43) who lost his life in action against the Japanese on Betio Island, Tarawa Atoll, 1943. 1914-43

Hawley, John P.

2969. Hawley-Dent, Lucille. JOHN P. HAWLEY: PROUD YOUNG DOUGHBOY 1917-1919. *Chronicle 1982 18(4): 14-19.* Chronicles the military career of a 25-year-old army private cook and medical corpsman from Antrim County, Michigan, who served in Western Europe during World War I. 1917-19

Hawthorne, Nathaniel

2970. Baym, Nina. NATHANIEL HAWTHORNE AND HIS MOTHER: A BIOGRAPHICAL SPECULATION. *Am. Lit. 1982 54(1): 1-27.* Speculates that the novel *The Scarlet Letter* was Nathaniel Hawthorne's response to his mother's death and also his tribute to her memory. Hawthorne preserved his mother's image in the main character Hester, and enough resemblances exist between Hester's life and Elizabeth Hawthorne's life to suggest that the novel's origin lay in the son's deep attachment to his mother's role in life and to her memory after death. 20 notes. 1800-50

2971. Baym, Nina. CONCEPTS OF THE ROMANCE IN HAWTHORNE'S AMERICA. *Nineteenth-Century Fiction 1984 38(4): 426-443.* Examines Nathaniel Hawthorne's claim to be a writer in the romance genre at a time when American literary criticism was attempting to distinguish between the forms of the novel and the romance and to determine the form most conducive to expressing the American experience. 1820's-50's

2972. Erlich, Gloria C. DOCTOR GRIMSHAWE AND OTHER SECRETS. *Essex Inst. Hist. Collections 1982 118(1): 49-58.* Of Hawthorne's works, *Doctor Grimshawe's Secret* is the most autobiographical. For both Hawthorne and the hero, "the approach to death and to ancestral origins leads back to a reexamination of the meaning of childhood experiences." *Doctor Grimshawe's Secret* is less a narrative than a series of meditations by Hawthorne on character, motivation, and plot. Examines Hawthorne's intense autobiographical and psychological concerns, particularly his childhood experiences and longing for his ancestral home, dominant in this work. 2 notes. 1830-40

2973. Gollin, Rita K. HAWTHORNE: THE WRITER AS DREAMER. *Studies in the Am. Renaissance 1977: 313-325.* The dreams which Nathaniel Hawthorne (1804-64) recalled, in letters to his wife, Sophia, seem symbolic of his earlier 12-year isolation in Salem, which he described as imprisonment, and estrangement. Hawthorne's dreams expressed, *inter alia,* desire for recognition and acclaim, his hidden fears of rejection by Sophia and feelings of guilt on such matters as diverse as wasting time or leaving his mother. Although Hawthorne was reluctant to acknowledge that his dreams represented emotions present in his waking life, as a writer, he was concerned to respond to the problems which they posed. Based almost exclusively on Hawthorne letters; 29 notes. 1835-55

2974. Lindgren, Charlotte. NATHANIEL HAWTHORNE, CONSUL AT LIVERPOOL. *Hist. Today [Great Britain] 1976 26(8): 516-524.* Discusses the memoirs and political thought of Hawthorne while he was in the US Consular service at Liverpool, 1853-60. 1853-60

2975. Lowe, R. L. MELVILLE AND HAWTHORNE. *Mankind 1979 6(6): 26-28, 36.* Examines the unlikely friendship of American writers Nathaniel Hawthorne and Herman Melville, and Hawthorne's influence on the writing of Melville's *Moby Dick;* 1845-50. 1845-50

2976. McDonald, John J. A GUIDE TO PRIMARY SOURCE MATERIALS FOR THE STUDY OF HAWTHORNE'S OLD MANSE PERIOD. *Studies in the Am. Renaissance 1977: 261-312.* The Old Manse period in the life of Nathaniel Hawthorne (1804-64) was particularly important since it followed immediately on his marriage and marked a transition in Hawthorne's literary work to a mature experimentation which led to his major romances. Nevertheless, the large amount of primary materials for this period is known only to a few scholars. The list given here will shed new light on aspects of Hawthorne's life during the Old Manse period. Based on published materials, including memoirs, correspondence, notebooks, and journal and magazine articles; 48 items; also listed separately are letters to or from both Nathaniel and Sophia Hawthorne, with location, published source, date, and an indication of the contents; 47 items, index. 1842-45

2977. Stay, Byron Lee. "Nathaniel Hawthorne: A Study of the Divided Self." U. of Delaware 1980. 206 pp. *DAI 1980 41(3): 1059-A.* DA8019951 1825-60

Hay, John

2978. Eppard, Philip Blair. "The Correspondence of Henry Adams and John Hay, 1881-1892." Brown U. 1979. 715 pp. *DAI 1980 40(11): 5913-A.* 8007004 1881-92

Haycraft, Jesse Robert

2979. Claypool, Gerald B. JESSE HAYCRAFT. *Kentucky Folklore Record 1976 22(3): 71-73.* Discusses the musical career, both instrumental and vocal, of Jesse Robert Haycraft, an inhabitant of Grayson County, Kentucky, 1935-76. 1935-76

Hayden, Carl Trumbell

2980. August, Jack L., Jr. CARL HAYDEN: BORN A POLITICIAN. *Journal of Arizona History 1985 26(2): 117-144.* Describes the youth of Senator Carl Hayden in the Tempe, Arizona, area and his education at Stanford University. Hayden's family life, the fickle Salt River, and the desert were among the influences that led him to become the senator whose major achievement was giving Arizona a consistent supply of water. Based on Hayden family records and secondary sources; 6 photos, 41 notes. 1877-1901

2981. Colley, Charles C. CARL T. HAYDEN—PHOENICIAN. *J. of Arizona Hist. 1977 18(3): 247-257.* Carl T. Hayden (1877-1972) was "one of the great forces in the development of the last untamed region of the American West." His active involvement in the Phoenix area began with his election to county sheriff in 1907 and continued through a 56-year congressional career. His primary concerns were land development, urban expansion, and environmental quality. Illus., 15 notes. 1907-72

Hayden, Magdalen

2982. Rakow, Mary Martina. "Melinda Rankin and Magdalen Hayden: Evangelical and Catholic Forms of Nineteenth Century Christian Spirituality." Boston Coll. 1982. 645 pp. *DAI 1982 43(2): 481-A.* DA8215662 19c

Hayden, Palmer

2983. Green, Archie. PALMER HAYDEN'S JOHN HENRY SERIES. *JEMF Q. 1980 16(60): 199-213.* Provides a brief biography of American folk painter Palmer Hayden (1890-1973) followed by reproductions of his series of 12 paintings, of which 11 appeared in the Ballad of John Henry in Paintings exhibition in 1947, while the 12th was completed later. 1890-1973

Hayden, Robert

2984. Lynch, Charles Henry. "Robert Hayden and Gwendolyn Brooks: A Critical Study." New York U. 1977. 257 pp. *DAI 1977 38(4): 2128-A.* 1940's-70's

Hayden, Tom

2985. Weiss, Jonathan. TOM HAYDEN'S POLITICAL EVOLUTION DURING THE NEW LEFT YEARS: REBEL WITHOUT A THEORY. *Michigan Journal of Political Science 1984 (5): 1-38.* Tom Hayden, who entered the University of Michigan in 1957 on a tennis scholarship, became increasingly radicalized during his student years, which culminated in his leadership of the Students for a Democratic Society (SDS) and of protests against the Vietnam War, but Hayden's subsequent transformation into a conventional politician was the result of the New Left's failure to develop a clear political strategy that included the working class. 1957-82

2986. Westbrook, Russell Paul, Jr. "A Thematic Analysis of the Advocacy of Thomas Emmet Hayden as a Radical Intellectual Activist in the New Left Social Movement." Southern Illinois U. 1977. 226 pp. *DAI 1977 38(2): 550-A.* 1960-72

Hayek, F. A.

2987. Connin, Lawrence Jay. "Methodological Liberalism: The Thought of F. A. Hayek." Ohio State U. 1985. 266 pp. *DAI 1985 46(3): 782-A.* DA8510559 20c

Hayes, Rutherford B.

2988. Barnard, Harry. BIOGRAPHICAL MEMORIES, *IN RE* RBH. *Hayes Hist. J. 1978 2(2): 89-96.* Harry Barnard, author of *Rutherford B. Hayes and His America,* writes of his experiences while living at Fremont, Ohio, for five years researching his biography; library facilities; availability and variety of primary source material; assistance from Webb Cook Hayes (1890-1957); and, interesting facets of Hayes's life and family which prior to this publication were unknown. Barnard discusses this biography as a model of psychohistory. Taken from a speech by Barnard at the Hayes Historical Society, Spiegel Grove, on June 1, 1978. 7 illus., 10 notes. 1822-93

2989. Gholson, Sam C. THE ARTIST AS BIOGRAPHER. *Hayes Hist. J. 1978 2(2): 119-131.* Studies three artists as biographers. The 19th-century William Garl Browne and William M. Chase each painted full-length portraits of President Hayes during his lifetime, and exemplified divergent aesthetic trends of Victorian years. Critiques each painting, elaborating on the artist as the physiological psychologist; i.e., believing that the inner personality of the individual can be communicated by the painting. Chase's psychological portrait had some shortcomings. Gholson relates his own research, motives, and techniques in painting a posthumous portrait of Hayes (1976). Primary sources; 12 illus., 24 notes. 1870's

2990. Marchman, Watt P. RUTHERFORD B. HAYES IN LOWER SANDUSKY, 1845-1849. *Hayes Hist. J. 1976 1(2): 122-132.* Examines Rutherford B. Hayes' life and early legal career in Lower Sandusky, Ohio. Cites reasons for this geographical selection, his later motives for moving to Cincinnati to expand his legal practice, and the change of the town's name to Fremont. Primary sources; 4 illus., 25 notes. 1845-49

2991. Myers, Elisabeth P. WRITING A JUVENILE BIOGRAPHY OF PRESIDENT HAYES. *Hayes Hist. J. 1978 2(2): 97-101.* Myers, author of many American biographies for children, relates details of her meeting with Henry Regnery, publisher and editor of the Henry Regnery Company, and how she wrote a juvenile biography of Rutherford B. Hayes (1969). Discusses Myers's selection of Hayes as the subject of her biography, and the extent of her preliminary readings and research. 7 illus. 1822-93

2992. Payne, Alma J. WILLIAM DEAN HOWELLS AND OTHER EARLY BIOGRAPHERS OF RUTHERFORD B. HAYES. *Hayes Hist. J. 1978 2(2): 78-88.* Surveys the first half century of writing about Hayes: three hastily written campaign biographies issued in 1876, by Russell H. Conwell, James Q. Howard, and William Dean Howells; Charles Richard Williams's 1914 scholarly and standard life; and Hamilton J. Eckenrode's 1930 poorly researched and disappointing political biography. Howells's book is examined in greater detail. Analyzes the philosophy and significance of these early works interpreting Rutherford B. Hayes. Primary and secondary sources; 9 illus., 32 notes. 1876-1930

2993. Ranson, Frederick Duane. "The Great Unknown: Governor Rutherford B. Hayes of Ohio." West Virginia U. 1978. 408 pp. *DAI 1979 39(11): 6899-A.* 1869-76

2994. Turner, William E. HAYES ALBUM: FOURTEEN PANELS DEPICTING SCENES FROM THE LIFE OF PRESIDENT HAYES. *Hayes Hist. J. 1976 1(1): 45-59.* Explains the personal life and presidency of Rutherford B. Hayes (1822-93) through reproductions of William E. Turner's 14 mural-size illustrations of selected incidents in Hayes' life. Commissioned in January 1971 by the Rutherford B. Hayes Library, these illustrations include Hayes' law studies and wedding; the defense of Rosetta Amstead, a slave; military service during the Civil War; the Spiegel Grove residence; the 1877 presidential inauguration; his silver wedding anniversary; the invention of the telephone and the phonograph; presidential receptions for American Indians, and the ambassador from China; and the great western tour (1880). 1822-93

2995. West, Richard Samuel. THE KENYON EXPERIENCE OF R. B. HAYES. *Hayes Hist. J. 1978 2(1): 6-13.* Summarizes Rutherford B. Hayes's student experiences at Kenyon College (1838-42), in Gambier, Ohio. Hayes's college years transformed a boy, apathetic to higher education, into a mature young man, strongly committed to obtaining the benefits of a sound college program. Examines the Kenyon curriculum and the qualifications of its staff, Hayes' participation in extracurricular as well as academic events and groups, and his relationship with classmates and faculty. Primary sources; 7 illus., 13 notes. 1838-42

Hayford, James H.

2996. Moore, William Howard. PIETISM AND PROGRESS: JAMES H. HAYFORD AND THE WYOMING ANTI-GAMBLING TRADITION, 1869-1893. *Ann. of Wyoming 1983 55(2): 2-8.* As editor of the *Laramie Sentinel*, James H. Hayford labored to eliminate gambling from all of Wyoming, educating the public about how that vice (as well as prostitution and excessive drinking) hurt local businesses and destroyed families. He won local but fleeting victories with anti-gambling laws; Colonel E. A. Slack of the influential *Cheyenne Sun* led the opposition to Hayford's moralistic campaign. In the early 1890's, Hayford abandoned his financially strapped newspaper for a local judgeship and ended his reformist crusade. Based on Wyoming newspapers and archival materials at the University of Wyoming's American Heritage Center; 5 photos, 27 notes. 1869-93

Haygood, Laura Askew

2997. Papageorge, Linda Madson. "THE HAND THAT ROCKS THE CRADLE RULES THE WORLD": LAURA ASKEW HAYGOOD AND METHODIST EDUCATION IN CHINA, 1884-1899. *Pro. and Papers of the Georgia Assoc. of Hist. 1982: 123-132.* Georgian Laura Askew Haygood worked for the Woman's Missionary Society of the Methodist Episcopal Church, South. The movement of women missionaries constituted a form of American Protestant feminism. Tells of Haygood's work at the McTyeire School for upper-class Chinese girls in Shanghai. 44 notes. 1884-99

Hayne, Paul Hamilton

2998. Simms, L. Moody, Jr. MAURICE THOMPSON RECALLS PAUL HAMILTON HAYNE. *Southern Studies 1977 16(1): 91-97.* James Maurice Thompson (1844-1901) was an Indiana writer and correspondent of the Southern poet Paul Hamilton Hayne (1830-1886). In 1881, Thompson visited Hayne at the latter's home at Copse Hill in Groveton, Georgia. Thompson's report of the visit, "The Last Literary Cavalier," appeared in the *Critic* in April 1901, and is reprinted here. Thompson viewed Hayne as the embodiment of the Southern literary tradition in the late 19th century. In 1881 Hayne lived in a simple wood shanty. He was a charming host, delightful raconteur, and had known most of the prominent figures in southern literature before and after the Civil War. His work lies at the juncture between the literature of the Old South and the New South; he was the end of an era. 8 notes. 19c

Hayne, Robert Y.

2999. Langley, Harold D. ROBERT Y. HAYNE AND THE NAVY. *South Carolina Hist. Mag. 1981 82(4): 311-330.* From school days in Charleston, Robert Y. Hayne developed his lifelong interest in naval matters, which he pursued during his political career. Friendship with navy Captain Charles Morris and Secretary of the Navy Samuel L. Southard opened lines of communication to Hayne when he went to the 18th Congress as a senator in December 1823. As a member of the Senate Committee on Naval Affairs, he advocated expansion of the navy, increased pay for naval personnel, and construction of two dry docks and improvement of others. While not all efforts ended successfully,

Hayne's work encouraged professionals in the field. Based on primary sources including Hayne's letters and official records of the Senate; 76 notes. 1823-30

Haynes, George Edmund

3000. Carlton, Iris Belinda. "A Pioneer Social Work Educator: George Edmund Haynes." U. of Maryland, Baltimore Professional Schools 1982. 216 pp. *DAI 1982 43(6): 2102-A.* DA8224369 1910-21

Hays, Brooks

3001. Barnhill, John Herschel. "Politician, Social Reformer, and Religious Leader: The Public Career of Brooks Hays." Oklahoma State U. 1981. 265 pp. *DAI 1982 43(1): 241-A.* DA8213798 1920's-70's

Haywood, Harry

3002. Goldfield, Michael. THE DECLINE OF THE COMMUNIST PARTY AND THE BLACK QUESTION IN THE U.S.: HARRY HAYWOOD'S *BLACK BOLSHEVIK. Rev. of Radical Pol. Econ. 1980 12(1): 44-63.* Harry Haywood's autobiography is reviewed with special attention focused upon the Communist Party's approach to the black question. Haywood's charge that the CP degenerated into Browderism (accommodation to nonrevolution as well as neglect of racism and its revolutionary potential) is assessed without coming to a conclusion. Haywood's analytic framework is rejected, but his kernels of insight are welcomed, as the black question is deemed to be an inadequate vantage point of analysis. 71 notes. 1900-50

Haywood, William Dudley

3003. Lapitskii, M. I. BOLSHOI BILL: WILLIAM HAYWOOD (1869-1928) [Big Bill: William Haywood (1869-1928)]. *Novaia i Noveishaia Istoriia [USSR] 1974 (2): 77-97.* William Dudley Haywood held an important place in the history of the workers' and socialist movements in the late 19th and early 20th centuries in the United States. As a revolutionary he fought with reformism, took an active part in workers' movements, including the creation of trade unions, and became a prominent leader of the American proletariat. Gives an account of Haywood's ancestry and life from his birth in the far west, the development of his political ideas and activity, his emigration to the USSR in March 1921, to his death in March 1928. Primary and secondary sources; 70 notes. 1890-1928

3004. Noel, Thomas J. WILLIAM D. HAYWOOD: "THE MOST HATED AND FEARED FIGURE IN AMERICA." *Colorado Heritage 1984 (2): 2-12.* Presents a biography of William Dudley Haywood, a radical leader of the labor movement. He left the Western Federation of Miners after steering them into the Socialist Party of America, and he helped found the Industrial Workers of the World in 1905. He was jailed after participating in demonstrations against World War I. Released on a $30,000 bond, 31 March 1921, he fled to the USSR, which granted him asylum, and where he died. 7 photos, biblio. 1890's-1920's

Hazen, Harold Locke

3005. Brown, Gordon S. ELOGE: HAROLD LOCKE HAZEN, 1901-1980. *Ann. of the Hist. of Computing 1981 3(1): 4-12.* While still a student at the Massachusetts Institute of Technology, Harold Locke Hazen began the work that would make him a pioneer in the computer field. His first work was in relation to electrical engineering systems, but he soon became interested in primitive analog machines, threw himself into his work, and soon began to make notable contributions. Hazen found keen intellectual ferment at MIT, but generally poor facilities. After World War II, he essentially withdrew from an active engineering role and engaged himself in attempting to create a better academic environment for computer research. At the time of his death, he was dean emeritus of the graduate school at MIT. 7 photos, refs. ca 1920-80

Heacock, Joe Davis

3006. Mathis, Robert Rex. "A Descriptive Study of Joe Davis Heacock: Educator, Administrator, Churchman." Southwestern Baptist Theological Seminary 1984. *DAI 1985 45(11): 3255-3256-A.* 1956-73

Head, Francis Bond

3007. Martin, Ged. SELF DEFENSE: FRANCIS BOND HEAD AND CANADA, 1841-1870. *Ontario Hist. [Canada] 1981 73(1): 3-18.* Discusses the later writings of Sir Francis Bond Head (1793-1875), Lieutenant Governor of Upper Canada, in defense of his administration during the rebellion of 1837-38. Shows his continued interest in Canadian affairs up to his death, and his vehement opposition to the Act of Union, 1841. Indicates the sometimes ambivalent claims he makes concerning his actions. 4 illus., 32 notes. 1841-70

3008. Martin, Ged. SIR FRANCIS BOND HEAD: THE PRIVATE SIDE OF A LIEUTENANT GOVERNOR. *Ontario Hist. [Canada] 1981 73(3): 145-170.* Briefly sketches in the biography of Sir Francis Bond Head and presents something of the family side of his life while lieutenant governor of Upper Canada and afterward. Based on family and other collections of papers; 2 illus., 80 notes. 1835-40

Heade, Martin Johnson

3009. Calkin, Carleton I. MARTIN JOHNSON HEADE: PAINTER OF FLORIDA. *Escribano 1977 14: 35-38.* Martin Johnson Heade (1819-1904), a landscape painter, came to Florida in 1883 and painted there until his death. 1883-1904

3010. Miller, David Cameron. KINDRED SPIRITS: MARTIN JOHNSON HEADE, PAINTER; FREDERICK GODDARD TUCKERMAN, POET; AND THE IDENTIFICATION WITH "DESERT" PLACES. *Am. Q. 1980 32(2): 167-185.* Martin Johnson Heade (1819-1904) and Frederick Goddard Tuckerman (1821-73) were among American artists and writers who turned to consideration of "desert" landscapes in the 1850's and 1860's to express their perception of nature. This use of "desert" places—swamp, marsh, and jungle, for example—reflected a new spirit of individualism and self-exploration. Though in temperament the melancholy, stationary Tuckerman was quite unlike the heedless, nomadic Heade, they shared both a sense of spiritual isolation from nature and a desire to control it. 4 illus., 26 notes. 1854-72

Healy, Michael A.

3011. Cocke, Mary and Cocke, Albert. HELL ROARING MIKE: A FALL FROM GRACE IN THE FROZEN NORTH. *Smithsonian 1983 13(11): 119-137.* The life, career, and subsequent court-martial in 1896 of Michael Healy, a captain in the Revenue-Marine (forerunner of the Coast Guard) in the territory of Alaska during 1868-1904. 1860's-1905

3012. Stein, Gary C. A DESPERATE AND DANGEROUS MAN: CAPTAIN MICHAEL A. HEALY'S ARCTIC CRUISE OF 1900. *Alaska Journal 1985 15(2): 39-45.* Discusses the events and circumstances of the Healy case of 1900, which involved the temporary dismissal from duty of Captain Michael A. Healy of the US Revenue Cutter Service. The purpose for this dismissal, Healy's fourth while in government service, was to restrain him from committing suicide, which he attempted several times while in command of the revenue cutter *McCullough* anchored off the Alaska coast at Dutch Harbor in July of 1900. Healy, a well-respected and experienced officer, was known for his history of excessive drinking. While hospitalized at Seattle following his attempts at suicide, doctors judged him insane, but he later recovered well enough to acquire command of the Arctic cruise of the *Thetis* in 1902. Based on National Archives documents of the Revenue Cutter Service (U.S. Coast Guard) and articles in the *Seattle Post-Intelligencer;* 6 photos, illus., 14 notes. 1900-04

Healy, William

3013. Snodgrass, Jon. WILLIAM HEALY (1869-1963): PIONEER CHILD PSYCHIATRIST AND CRIMINOLOGIST. *J. of the Hist. of Behavioral Sci. 1984 20(4): 332-339.* William Healy, M.D., a pioneer psychiatrist and criminologist, established the first child guidance clinic in the United States in 1909, and was an early advocate of both the "team approach" and the "child's own story" in treatment and research. One of the founders and the first president of the American Orthopsychiatric Association, Healy helped introduce Freudian thought into the United States. Among his contributions to the field of criminology are his book *The Individual Delinquent* (1915) and his "multifactor theory" of delinquency, which broadened the field and moved it away from European criminology's stress on genetic factors. Healy developed an elaborate methodology for the complete study of the offender by a variety of specialists. He was also a reformer in the field of corrections, based on his investigations of several institutions for delinquents. 1900's-63

Heap, Jane

3014. Johnson, Abby Ann Arthur. THE PERSONAL MAGAZINE: MARGARET C. ANDERSON AND THE *LITTLE REVIEW,* 1914-1929. *South Atlantic Q. 1976 75(3): 351-363.* 1914-29
For abstract see ***Anderson, Margaret***

Heard, Dwight Bancroft

3015. Johnson, G. Wesley, Jr. DWIGHT HEARD IN PHOENIX: THE EARLY YEARS. *J. of Arizona Hist. 1977 18(3): 258-278.* In 1895, Dwight Bancroft Heard (1869-1929) and Maie Bartlett Heard (1868-1951) went to Phoenix for a brief stay for his health. This evolved into a permanent move. The Heard estate became "an outpost of culture, refinement, and the arts in a city just emerging from the raw frontier." The Heards were involved in agricultural improvement, residential development, journalism, water, land, financing, and social welfare, as well as the arts and society. Their final legacy was the Phoenix Civic Center, home of the public library, museum, and little theater. 4 illus., 26 notes. 1895-1950's

Heard, William Henry

3016. Wynes, Charles E. WILLIAM HENRY HEARD: POLITICIAN, DIPLOMAT, A.M.E. CHURCHMAN. *Southern Studies 1981 20(4): 384-393.* William Henry Heard was born a slave, but after emancipation he became a member of the South Carolina legislature, attended the state university, became a minister of the African Methodist Episcopal Church, with pastorates in Georgia, New York, and elsewhere, served as bishop in both the United States and Africa, and was American consul general in Liberia. Based on Heard's *From Slavery to the Bishopric in the A.M.E. Church* (1924); 31 notes. 1850-1937

Hearn, Lafcadio

3017. McNeil, W. K. LAFCADIO HEARN, AMERICAN FOLKLORIST. *J. of Am. Folklore 1978 91(362): 947-967.* Lafcadio Hearn (1850-1904), an American amateur folklorist and professional literary artist, made major contributions in collecting exotic legends and folk beliefs from Creole New Orleans, Martinique, and Japan. Based on Hearn's published work and secondary sources; 57 notes. 1850-1904

Hearsey, Henry J.

3018. Hair, William I. HENRY J. HEARSEY AND THE POLITICS OF RACE. *Louisiana Hist. 1976 17(4): 393-400.* From Reconstruction until 1900, Major Henry J. Hearsey (1840-1900), editor and publisher of the New Orleans *Daily States,* was the chief Louisiana ideologist of white supremacy politics. An intense reactionary, Hearsey used the *States* to whip up anti-Negro emotional politics in Louisiana. He favored harsh repression and even extermination of the black population. Based principally on Louisiana newspapers; 23 notes. 1876-1900

Hearst, George

3019. Cieply, Michael. THE LODED HEARST. *Westways 1981 73(6): 32-35, 76-77.* Details the career of George Hearst, father of William Randolph Hearst, during his successful attempts of 1876-79 to consolidate various mining claims in the Deadwood district of South Dakota, which provided the foundation of the Hearst family fortune. 1876-79

Hearst, James

3020. Gildner, Judith. AN INTERVIEW WITH IOWA POET JAMES HEARST. *Midwest Rev. 1980 2(Spr): 38-45.* Brief introduction to the life and work of Iowa poet, farmer, and teacher James Hearst, followed by an interview with him in December 1978 and January 1979 at age 79, discussing his writing, the Midwest, the Depression, and other influences on his life and work. 1920's-79

Hearst, Phoebe Apperson

3021. Peterson, Richard H. PHILANTHROPIC PHOEBE: THE EDUCATIONAL CHARITY OF PHOEBE APPERSON HEARST. *California History 1985 64(4): 284-289.* Profiles Phoebe Apperson Hearst and her philanthropic contributions in support of libraries and public education. Born in Missouri, Phoebe married mining entrepreneur George Hearst in 1862 and moved to California. She became interested in the kindergarten movement, the University of California at Berkeley, public libraries, and other educational institutions, and over the course of her life donated millions of dollars to them. Her interest in helping others was a lifelong and sincere commitment, with immeasurable benefits to education at all levels. 5 photos, 38 notes. 1862-1919

Hearst, William Randolph

3022. Sarasohn, David. POWER WITHOUT GLORY: HEARST IN THE PROGRESSIVE ERA. *Journalism Q. 1976 53(3): 474-482.* Examines the political career of William Randolph Hearst, his ambitions, and his effect on the Democratic Party. He wielded considerable power, nationally and in New York, but advanced no further than the brink of leadership. He advanced extremely progressive views and both William Jennings Bryan and Woodrow Wilson sought his support. Others also curried his favor, but mercurial behavior cost Hearst potential allies. His possibilities were many, and they make his achievements seem small in comparison. Primary and secondary sources; 43 notes. 1900-12

Heaten, John

3023. Black, Mary. CONTRIBUTIONS TOWARD A HISTORY OF EARLY EIGHTEENTH-CENTURY NEW YORK PORTRAITURE: THE IDENTIFICATION OF THE AETATIS SUAE AND WENDELL LIMNERS. *Am. Art J. 1980 12(4): 4-31.* 1715-37
*For abstract see **Partridge, Nehemiah***

Heaton, Alma

3024. VanderGriend, Ward Marius. "Alma Heaton: The Professor of Fun." Brigham Young U. 1981. 220 pp. *DAI 1982 42(7): 3062-3063-A.* DA8128181 20c

Hebron, John

3025. Moore, John Hebron. JOHN HEBRON OF LAGRANGE PLANTATION: COMMERCIAL FRUIT GROWER OF THE OLD SOUTH. *J. of Mississippi Hist. 1984 46(4): 281-303.* Describes John Hebron's successful experiences in producing fruit for commercial markets before the Civil War. A Virginia mechanic who married the daughter of a Virginia planter, Hebron migrated with his family to Warren County, Mississippi, in 1834. Purchasing an 880-acre established plantation near Vicksburg, which they named LaGrange, Hebron began producing cotton, but soon discovered that the peach seeds brought from Virginia for domestic use grew quickly in the conducive climate and soil. Introducing a mixed fruit-cotton agriculture, Hebron soon recognized that his profits from diversified fruit cultivation were greater than those of his cotton. Shipping his produce to commercial markets along the Mississippi, Hebron soon established a nursery and began to experiment with all types of fruit, shrubs, trees, and hybrid seeds. Gaining a wide reputation as a progressive agriculturalist, Hebron died in 1862 at the height of his success as an orchardist. Based on Warren County records, periodical, newspaper, and manuscript sources, and secondary works; 94 notes. 1834-62

Hecht, Sigmund

3026. Kramer, William M. and Clar, Reva. RABBI SIGMUND HECHT: A MAN WHO BRIDGED THE CENTURIES (PART III). *Western States Jewish Hist. Q. 1976 8(2): 169-186.* Continued from a previous article. Rabbi Sigmund Hecht remained neutral toward Zionism. He was appointed to the board of directors of the Los Angeles public library by Mayor Meredith P. Snyder. He backed Mayor Snyder for reelection, but Snyder lost to Owen McAleer. Mayor McAleer appointed George N. Black, a Jewish friend of Hecht, to replace Hecht. Black refused the appointment so McAleer chose another Jew; patronage was strong in Los Angeles then. In 1914, Congregation B'nai B'rith hired Dr. Edgar Fogel Magnin to serve as an associate Rabbi for Rabbi Hecht. Rabbi Hecht died in 1925 after a long and distinguished career. He left many volumes of writings and had been active in many civic and Jewish community groups. 51 notes. 1904-25

Hecker, Isaac Thomas

3027. Kirk, Martin Joseph. "The Spirituality of Isaac Thomas Hecker: Reconciling the American Character and the Catholic Faith." Saint Louis U. 1980. 402 pp. *DAI 1981 41(7): 3151-3152-A.* DA8100495 1840-88

Hedge, Frederic Henry

3028. Grady, Charles Wesley. A CONSERVATIVE TRANSCENDENTALIST: THE EARLY YEARS (1805-1835) OF FREDERIC HENRY HEDGE. *Studies in the American Renaissance 1983: 57-87.* Discusses the puzzling career of Frederic Henry Hedge, whom Emerson and other Transcendentalists considered the most brilliant mind of the country. Educated by private tutors, at prestigious schools in Germany, and at Harvard, Hedge became famous for his scholarly work on German literature. It was at Hedge's instigation that the Transcendentalist Club met. Hedge later accepted a parish in Bangor, Maine, and thus distanced himself from the intellectual ferment of Boston. Although ecclesiastically conservative, he was intellectually radical, and is an important figure in the transformation of New England Puritanism into Unitarianism. Based on the works of Hedge and other transcendentalists, and letters in the Houghton Library, Harvard University; 48 notes. 1805-35

3029. Hunter, Doreen. "FREDERIC HENRY HEDGE, WHAT SAY YOU?" *Am. Q. 1980 32(2): 186-201.* Frederic Henry Hedge (1805-90), prominent in the early stages of the growth of Transcendentalism, soon lost a leading role. Historical uncertainty about his place in the larger movement stems from a narrow definition of Transcendentalism. Hedge represented the more conservative Transcendental-Unitarians, a stance that led to criticism from the Eclectics and Emerson's Neo-Platonists. Despite his longing for a literary career, Hedge accepted a pulpit in Bangor, Maine, that removed him from close interactions with the Club and restricted his literary output. Covers ca. 1833-42. Based on the Fuller Family Papers and other primary sources; 41 notes. 1833-42

3030. LeBeau, Bryan F. "Frederic Henry Hedge: Portrait of an Enlightened Conservative." New York U. 1982. 410 pp. *DAI 1983 43(7): 2386-A.* DA8227103 1830's-90

Heffernan, Joseph

3031. Jenkins, William D. MORAL REFORM AFTER THE KLAN: JOSEPH HEFFERNAN AS MAYOR OF YOUNGSTOWN, 1928-1931. *Old Northwest 1983 9(2): 143-156.* The administration of Mayor Joseph Heffernan initiated a transition in Youngstown, Ohio, politics by combining elements of reform and city bossism. Before Heffernan, local politics had been dominated by Republicans, WASPS, and moralistic reformers such as the Ku Klux Klan. By appealing to immigrant ethnic groups and their concern for social and economic problems, Heffernan led the way toward the predominance of Democratic, Catholic, and immigrant mayors. Primary sources; 46 notes. 1928-31

Heffernan, Leo G.

3032. Heffernan, Leo G. EXTRACTS FROM THE DIARY OF LEO G. HEFFERNAN: THE ADVENTURES OF A JUNIOR MILITARY AVIATOR. *Aerospace Hist. 1978 25(2): 92-102.* Based on the ledger-diary of US Army Air Service Major Leo G. Heffernan (1889-1956). The diary was begun in 1925; the earlier period is in the form of memoirs. Entries in the original ledger for the period after 1927 when Major Heffernan was air officer of the Panama Canal Department, and the account of his court-martial for the "intemperate use of alcohol," were torn out. The editor of this article, R. K. McMaster, has deleted only the diary entries not relating to Heffernan's military career. His spelling and punctuation have been retained. Heffernan was important to the Air Service of that day because majors were senior officers and as such held command duties. He was one of the Army's pioneer aviators, being awarded the rating of pilot in April, 1916. He retired for physical disability in 1933. 110 biographical notes by Col. A. P. Wade, U.S. Army (retired), 6 photos. ca 1925-33

Heflin, James Thomas

3033. Tanner, Ralph M. THE WONDERFUL WORLD OF TOM HEFLIN. *Alabama Rev. 1983 36(3): 163-174.* Biography of James Thomas "Cotton Tom" Heflin, US senator from Alabama. 33 notes. ca 1890's-1930

Hefner, Robert A.

3034. Trafzer, Clifford E. "HARMONY AND COOPERATION": ROBERT A. HEFNER, MAYOR OF OKLAHOMA CITY. *Chronicles of Oklahoma 1984 62(1): 70-85.* Robert A. Hefner emerged from childhood poverty to become one of Oklahoma's leading politicians and civic promoters. Between 1911 and 1927, he served as city attorney, mayor, and president of the Ardmore school board, positions which helped elevate him to the Oklahoma supreme court. Yet it was as mayor of Oklahoma City that Hefner made his greatest contributions. He promoted a formidable antivice campaign, worked with local minority leaders, promoted long-term city planning, and oversaw the construction of numerous public facilities until finally retiring from office in 1947. Based on the Hefner Collection at the University of Oklahoma Library; 7 photos, 42 notes. 1911-47

Heidegger, Martin

3035. Hinchman, Lewis P. and Hinchman, Sandra K. IN HEIDEGGER'S SHADOW: HANNAH ARENDT'S PHENOMENOLOGICAL HUMANISM. *Rev. of Pol. 1984 46(2): 183-211.* 1920's-50's

*For abstract see **Arendt, Hannah***

Height, Joseph Stuart

3036. Wenzlaff, Theodore C. and Reeb, Paul E. JOSEPH STUART HEIGHT (1909-1979): AUTHOR, LINGUIST, HISTORIAN. *Heritage Review 1980 10(2): 5-10.* Obituary of Joseph Stuart Height, whose forebears, the Heidt family, came from Kuschurgan, Russia, to North Dakota in 1906, and who wrote several works devoted to the history of Germans from Russia. 1906-79

Heilner, Sigmund Aron

3037. —. OREGON PIONEER SIGMUND A HEILNER, A PICTURE STORY. *Western States Jewish Hist. Q. 1979 12(1): 66-72.* Sigmund Aron Heilner (1834-1917) left his native Bavaria in 1853 and came to Oregon, where he operated a dry goods store and freighting company. He lived in several locations in Oregon before settling in Baker in 1876. He opened the Heilner Department Store, which is still active, as well as a bank, an insurance agency, a hide and wool business, and a freighting business. Based on newspapers, and family documents; 8 photos, 7 notes. 1855-1917

Heiman, Adolphus

3038. Patrick, James. THE ARCHITECTURE OF ADOLPHUS HEIMAN.

PART I: CS *Tennessee Hist. Q. 1979 38(2): 167-187.* Adolphus Heiman (1809-62) was a successful architect in Nashville, Tennessee. Working as an architect, stonemason, and delineator, he designed the Baptist Church in 1837, helped plan the ill-fated suspension bridge over the Cumberland, then designed the Adelphi Theater, the Tennessee Hospital for the Insane, the Davidson County Jail, several buildings for the University of Nashville, Hume High School, and three other buildings. Primary sources; 2 illus., photo, 116 notes.

PART II. ROMANTIC CLASSICISM, 1854-1862. *Tennessee Hist. Q. 1979 38(3): 277-295.* Heiman celebrated the flowering southern culture with elegant Grecian, castellated, and Italianate design. Mentions buildings possibly designed by Heiman, who was best known for his design of the Belle Monte in Nashville. 4 illus., 72 notes. 1837-62

Heinrich, Anthony Philip

3039. Chmaj, Betty E. FATHER HEINRICH AS KINDRED SPIRIT: OR, HOW THE LOG-HOUSE COMPOSER OF KENTUCKY BECAME THE BEETHOVEN OF AMERICA. *Am. Studies Int. 1983 24(2): 35-57.* Surveys the life and career of Anthony Philip Heinrich. Painters and writers in 19th-century American life glorified the unspoiled native American environment, and Anthony Philip Heinrich did the same in music. He used Indian themes and displayed nationalistic tendencies much as did other cultural contributors. 25 notes; 2 illus. 1813-61

Heizer, Robert Fleming

3040. Clark, J. Desmond. MEMORIAL TO ROBERT FLEMING HEIZER (1915-1979). *J. of California and Great Basin Anthrop. 1979 1(2): 240-267.* Robert Fleming Heizer (1915-79) was a noted archaeologist and University of California, Berkeley professor, and author of 24 books and almost 400 scholarly articles; includes a bibliography of his books and articles published from 1937 to 1980 (scheduled for publication). 1915-79

3041. Hester, Thomas R. ROBERT FLEMING HEIZER, 1915-1979. *Am. Antiquity 1982 47(1): 99-107.* US anthropologist Robert Fleming Heizer's childhood interest in the Indians spawned a brilliant career. 1915-79

3042. Kroeber, Clifton B. A DEDICATION TO THE MEMORY OF ROBERT F. HEIZER, 1915-1979. *Arizona and the West 1981 23(3): 208-212.* Robert F. Heizer (1915-79) was a pioneer in American archaeology and ethnohistory. Starting as an undergraduate in 1932, he did much to establish systematic methods of field study, to promote salvage archaeology, to use the classroom to inspire others, to experiment with promising new scientific techniques, to explore the validity of new theories, and to promote interdisciplinary cooperation. Heizer spent most of his academic career at the University of California at Berkeley. His several major publications concerned California and Nevada Indians, methodology, and bibliography. Illus., biblio. 1932-79

Helgeson, Thor

3043. Haugen, Einar. THOR HELGESON: SCHOOLMASTER AND RACONTEUR. *Norwegian-American Studies 1970 24: 3-28.* Thor Helgeson, a resident of Iola, Wisconsin, was a schoolmaster and author, writing some 12 major pieces during his lifetime. A religious, as well as a well-humored man, his works include local history pertaining to the lives of immigrants, mostly Norwegian Americans in eastern Wisconsin, religious poetry and allegory, and extensive tracts of folklore of Norwegian origin. Though he wrote for the better part of his life (1870-1928), most of his works were not published until 1915-28. They gained popular acceptance among Scandinavian immigrants of the Midwest and inspired Helgeson to continue his writing through the later years of his life and expand his style to include short stories whose plots related to immigrant daily life and foibles. Helgeson exhibited a particularly sharp insight into the Scandinavian mind and through his writings, all peppered with humor, he remains one of the most important contributors to knowledge of Scandinavian immigrants in the northern Midwest. Includes a bibliography of his writings; 37 notes. 1870-1928

Heller, Maximilian

3044. Zola, Gary P. REFORM JUDAISM'S PIONEER ZIONIST: MAXIMILIAN HELLER. *Am. Jewish Hist. 1984 73(4): 375-397.* Czech Maximilian Heller, disciple of Reform leader Isaac M. Wise, struggled long and against great opposition to merge Zionism with Reform Judaism. More than the handful of other Reform Zionists, Heller not only developed an integrated philosophy of the two movements but also brought Zionism into the institutional structures of Reform Judaism, particularly Hebrew Union College and the Central Conference of American Rabbis, of which he became president in 1910. By the time of his death in 1929, Zionism had a respectable, albeit still small, place in Reform Judaism. Based on the Maximilian Heller Collection in the American Jewish Archives at Cincinnati, Ohio, and other primary sources; 70 notes. 1880-1929

Hellier, Thomas

3045. Breen, T. H.; Lewis, James H.; and Schlesinger, Keith. MOTIVE FOR MURDER: A SERVANT'S LIFE IN VIRGINIA, 1678. *William and Mary Q. 1983 40(1): 106-120.* On 24 May 1678 Thomas Hellier, a 28-year-old indentured servant, murdered with an axe Cuthbert Williamson, Williamson's wife, and a young servant girl at a Charles City County plantation, known as Hard Labour. Immediately captured, he confessed. The night before his execution Hellier told his life story to an Anglican minister, presumed to have been Paul Williams. The narrative of Hellier's life, the minister's comments, and the condemned man's final speech at the gallows were published as *The Vain Prodigal Life* (1680), and sections of the pamphlet are reprinted here. Surprisingly the minister's reflections are sociological, and the Williamsons were much to be blamed themselves for the tragedy because of their abusive treatment of servants. Cites works on servants; 39 notes. 1650-70

Helm, Jefferson, Sr.

3046. VanMeter, Lorna E. DR. JEFFERSON HELM, SR.: A HOOSIER GREEK REVIVALIST. *Indiana Social Studies Q. 1983-84 36(3): 14-21.* Traces the medical and political career of Jefferson Helm, Sr., and discusses his choice of Greek Revival architecture for his home in Rushville, Indiana. 1840's-60's

Helmkamp, J. William

3047. Dinda, Emma Helmkamp. LETTERS TO GERMANY. *Concordia Hist. Inst. Q. 1983 56(1): 27-35.* Relates the life story of J. William Helmkamp, the author's father, from his birth in Germany to his immigration and settling in Arenzville, Illinois; includes two letters telling of Helmkamp's seminary studies and his desire to become a Lutheran minister. 1857-1908

Helpern, Milton

3048. Smith, Dorothy Ann. "Milton Helpern, M.D.: Legal Medicine and Medical Responsibility." Cornell U. 1984. 275 pp. *DAI 1984 45(5): 1504-A.* DA8415412 20c

Hemings, Sally

3049. Jellison, Charles A. JAMES THOMSON CALLENDER: "HUMAN NATURE IN A HIDEOUS FORM." *Virginia Cavalcade 1979 29(2): 62-69.* 1790's
*For abstract see **Callender, James Thomas***

Hemings family

3050. Bear, James A., Jr. THE HEMINGS FAMILY OF MONTICELLO. *Virginia Cavalcade 1979 29(2): 78-87.* A history of the Hemings family before, during, and after their enslavement to Thomas Jefferson, 1730's-1830's. 1730's-1830's

Hemingway, Ernest

3051. Donaldson, Scott. DOS AND HEM: A LITERARY FRIENDSHIP. *Centennial Review 1985 29(2): 163-185.* 1924-68
*For abstract see **DosPassos, John***

3052. Kazin, Alfred. HEMINGWAY & FITZGERALD: THE COST OF BEING AMERICAN. *Am. Heritage 1984 35(3): 49-64.* 1920-50
*For abstract see **Fitzgerald, F. Scott***

3053. Shechner, Mark. PAPA. *Partisan Rev. 1982 49(2): 213-223.* The recent publications of *Ernest Hemingway: Selected Letters, 1917-1961,* (1981) edited by Carlos Baker, reveals an unsavory, petty, and mean side to Hemingway's private character. Whatever his writing talent and literary reputation, Hemingway was not an attractive human being. Haunted by artistic self-doubt and alcoholism, Hemingway linked the successful literary life to a compulsive masculinity; but, as his letters demonstrate, he was "the greatest baby of American letters." 1917-61

3054. Tizón, Hector. HEMINGWAY, VEINTE ANOS DESPUES (1961-1981) [Hemingway, 20 years later (1961-81)]. *Cuadernos Hispanoamericanos [Spain] 1981 123(372): 635-641.* Discusses the life and death of Ernest Hemingway, noting the attention given to his personality and works in numerous studies, books and articles since his death 20 years ago. A legend was created around him, and Hemingway felt bound to live up to it. He epitomizes the US writer, despite the fact that most of his books are set in Europe, Africa and the Caribbean. Hemingway's attitudes to life, love and death are clearly revealed in his writings. The lasting memory of Hemingway is his mastery of the narrative form. 20c

Henderson, Archibald

3055. Pierce, P. N. ARCHIBALD HENDERSON: AN ERA. *Marine Corps Gazette 1960 44(7): 28-33.* A biography of Colonel Archibald Henderson (1783-1859), fifth commandant of the US Marines. ca 1803-59

Henderson, Elbert Calvin (Bert)

3056. Cruse, Irma R. BERT HENDERSON: DEEP SOUTH PHILOSOPHER. *Alabama Hist. Q. 1982 44(1-2): 70-91.* Elbert Calvin (Bert) Henderson, Alabama's third poet laureate, is memorialized in a short biography, along with the publication of several of his better known poems. 30 notes. 1920's-74

Henderson, James Pinckney

3057. Gamble, Steven Grady. "James Pinckney Henderson in Europe: The Diplomacy of the Republic of Texas, 1837-1840." Texas Tech U. 1976. 315 pp. *DAI 1977 38(2): 972-A.* 1837-40

Henderson, Loy W.

3058. Maddux, Thomas R. LOY W. HENDERSON AND SOVIET-AMERICAN RELATIONS: THE DIPLOMACY OF A PROFESSIONAL. Jones, Kenneth Paul, ed. *U.S. Diplomats in Europe, 1919-1941* (Santa Barbara, Calif.: ABC-Clio, 1981): 149-161. Details the diplomatic career of Loy W. Henderson (b. 1892) as embassy secretary in Moscow, 1934-38, and as Assistant Chief of the Division of European Affairs of the State Department, 1938-42. As a junior foreign service officer who specialized in Soviet affairs, Henderson never expected close cooperation from the Kremlin because of conflicting Soviet-American perspectives, principles, and objectives. Henderson reached this conclusion as a result of his training, his assessment of the ambiguities in Stalin's diplomacy during the 1930's, and his experience with the Soviet totalitarian system and its massive purges. When Henderson returned to Washington, he offered President Roosevelt a realistic perspective on the USSR which, regrettably, was often ignored. He retired in 1961. Primary sources; 40 notes. 1934-42

Henderson, William K.

3059. Pusateri, C. Joseph. THE STORMY CAREER OF A RADIO MAVERICK, W. K. HENDERSON OF KWKH. *Louisiana Studies 1976 15(4): 389-407.* During 1925-33, William Kennon Henderson (1880-1945) owned and ran radio station KWKH in Shreveport, Louisiana. By arbitrarily increasing his kilowatt power and by his provocative attacks on William K. Skelly of KVOO in Tulsa while trying to maintain his broadcasting license, Henderson provoked the federal government to pass the Radio Act of 1927 and the Davis Amendment of 1928. Henderson's final attack on chain stores was less successful, and economic problems brought on by the Depression and poor management led to the selling of the station in 1933. Henderson used a flamboyant style and what some called profanity to develop a nationwide audience that contributed considerable sums of money and wrote thousands of letters in his support. Based on primary sources in archives of Federal Radio Commission, Louisiana newspapers, KWKH Archives, and others, and on secondary sources; 46 notes. 1925-35

Hendricks, Carl Ludvig

3060. Hendricks, Carl Ludvig. RECOLLECTIONS OF A SWEDISH BUFFALO HUNTER, 1871-1873. *Swedish Pioneer Hist. Q. 1981 32(3): 190-204.* Born in Ängelholm, Skåne, Sweden, in 1850, the author emigrated to America in 1871, coming to Kansas to work for a cousin. In the fall he joined two buffalo hunters. After a year of hunting he worked in the hide business in Dodge City for a year and then in Massachusetts to work in a steel-wire mill. 2 photos. 1871-73

Hendricks, William

3061. Hill, Frederick D., ed. WILLIAM HENDRICKS' POLITICAL CIRCULARS TO HIS CONSTITUENTS: SECOND SENATORIAL TERM, 1831-1837. *Indiana Mag. of Hist. 1975 71(4): 319-374.* Continued from a previous article. William Hendricks (1782-1850) maintained considerable popularity in Indiana at the end of his first term in the US Senate; however, his independent and nonpartisan stance alienated persons allied to each of the emerging political parties. He consistently supported internal improvements at federal expense, Indian removal, a liberal federal land policy, a national bank, protective tariffs, confinement of slavery, and a strong central government. His failure to win reelection to a third term in 1836 was a result of his nonpartisanship in an era of growing political partisanship, and his support for Presidential candidate Martin Van Buren which alienated Indiana's Whig supporters of William Henry Harrison. Reprints six of Hendricks' political circulars used to make annual reports to his constituents. 72 notes. 1831-37

Heneker, Richard William

3062. Rudin, Ronald. THE TRANSFORMATION OF THE EASTERN TOWNSHIPS OF RICHARD WILLIAM HENEKER, 1855-1902. *J. of Can. Studies [Canada] 1984 19(3): 32-49.* Richard William Heneker's commitment to economic growth in the Eastern Townships of Quebec made him an agent of change. He supported regional development and local control of the economy, but his initiatives gradually concentrated economic power into the hands of Toronto and Montreal elites. His efforts to preserve English control at the expense of the French met with similar failure. Heneker oversaw the decline of a regional bourgeoisie and the insecurity of a population caught in the midst of profound demographic change. Based on the papers of Richard W. Heneker and records of Quebec financial institutions; 77 notes. 1855-1902

Hennessy, John

3063. Coogan, M. Jane. THE REDOUBTABLE JOHN HENNESSY, FIRST ARCHBISHOP OF DUBUQUE. *Mid-America 1980 62(1): 21-34.* Limerick-born John Hennessy (1825-1900) became Archbishop of the archdiocese of Dubuque, Iowa, in 1866. During his 34-year reign he sought to establish a Catholic educational system for his diocese. He made several abortive attempts to carry out his grand plan. Little can be told of his episcopate, for he burned all his records before his death. Notes. 1866-1900

Hennings, E. Martin

3064. White, Robert Rankin. THE LIFE OF E. MARTIN HENNINGS, 1886-1956. *Palacio 1978 84(3): Supplement.* Chronicles the life and paintings of E. Martin Hennings, 1921-56, a member of the Taos Society of Artists. 1921-56

Henri, Robert

3065. Berman, Avis. AN ARTIST LIKE "A ROCK RIPPING BOLTS OF LACE." *Smithsonian 1984 15(2): 144-153.* Traces the career of American artist and teacher Robert Henri, best known for his portraiture; along with the other American realist painters known as "The Eight," Henri fought against the "dictatorial policies" of the National Academy of Design, capable of making or breaking an artist, and helped organize the 1910 Exhibition of Independent Artists. 1880's-1920's

Henry, Aaron

3066. Henry, Aaron; Long, Worth, interviewer. AARON HENRY FROM CLARKSDALE. *Southern Changes 1983 5(5): 9-12.* Autobiographical recollections of Aaron Henry, sketching his youth and involvement in the movement for black civil rights in Mississippi. 1922-63

Henry, Alice

3067. Kirkby, Diane Elizabeth. "Alice Henry: The National Women's Trade Union League of America and Progressive Labor Reform, 1906-1925." U. of California, Santa Barbara 1982. 423 pp. *DAI 1983 44(1): 265-A.* DA8312695 1906-25

Henry, Bernard

3068. Rosenwaike, Ira. BERNARD HENRY: HIS NAVAL AND DIPLOMATIC CAREER. *Am. Jewish Hist. 1980 69(4): 488-496.* A biographical study of Bernard Henry (1783-1863), a Jew who became a captain in the US Navy. After his marriage to Mary M. Jackson, Henry was consul to Gibraltar (1816-32) until he was recalled for being absent from his post—a charge he disputed. Henry spent his last 27 years in Philadelphia. Government documents and other sources; 26 notes. 1800-63

Henry, Henry Abraham

3069. Henry, Marcus H. HENRY ABRAHAM HENRY: SAN FRANCISCO RABBI, 1857-1869. *Western States Jewish Hist. Q. 1977 10(1): 31-37.* Henry Abraham Henry (1806-79) came to the United States from England in 1849. He served congregations in Ohio and New York before coming to San Francisco in 1857. He was minister of San Francisco's Sherith Israel (Polish) synagogue, from 1857-69. A popular lecturer, he officiated at the consecration of many synagogues and the dedications of secular institutions. Rabbi Henry contributed many articles to American Jewish journals. He published his two-part *Synopsis of Jewish History* in 1859. In 1860 he started and edited the weekly *Pacific Messenger.* In 1864 he issued his volume of *Discourses on the Book of Genesis.* His religious views were conservative. He upheld the dignity of his profession to the admiration of both Jews and Christians. Photo. 1857-69

Henry, John

3070. Adelson, Richard H. POLITICS AND INTRIGUE: JOHN HENRY AND THE MAKING OF A POLITICAL TEMPEST. *Vermont Hist. 1984 52(2): 89-102.* In 1809, Canadian Governor General James Craig commissioned John Henry of Montreal as his agent to promote the secession of the New England states from the Union. Henry had lived in Windsor, Vermont, from 1802 to 1807, had edited the Windsor *Post Boy,* and was a prominent Freemason and Federalist. His correspondence shows contact with Federalist Congressman Martin Chittenden and Governor Isaac Tichenor, and his analysis of Vermont disaffection with Jefferson's trade embargo was corroborated by the press. Failing to receive a position in Canada, Henry accepted the confidence scheme of Edward de Crillon to buy his French estate with money the United States would give him for his intelligence reports. The estate did not exist, Crillon disappeared, and Henry deleted most references to Federalists in his reports. But James Madison published the letters to discredit the opposition to war with Britain. Based on Henry correspondence in the Public Archives of Canada; State Department versions of the correspondence in the Library of Congress, and secondary sources; 41 notes. 1801-12

Henry, John G.

3071. Hubbard, Ruth Henry; Abbott, Collamer, ed. PILLS, PUKES AND POULTICES, AND A DOCTOR'S ACCOUNT OF THE ELY COPPER RIOTS. *Vermont Hist. 1984 52(2): 77-88.* Doctor John G. Henry practiced medicine in West Fairlee, Vermont, from August 1881 to June 1884 and treated the men at the Vermont Copper Mining Company at Ely, "where accidents were numerous and diseases contagious." When the company fell two months in arrears in paying the miners, it locked them out of the mine, and they seized the village and threatened to destroy the company's property if they were not paid. Five companies of the National Guard subdued the miners and jailed the ringleaders. Dr. Henry recorded a firsthand account of these events of 29 June-10 July 1883. Based on letters and other Henry family papers in the Baker Library, Dartmouth University; 5 illus. 1881-84

Henry, Joseph

3072. Molella, Arthur P. AT THE EDGE OF SCIENCE: JOSEPH HENRY, "VISIONARY THEORIZERS," AND THE SMITHSONIAN INSTITUTION. *Ann. of Sci. [Great Britain] 1984 41(5): 445-461.* As first secretary of the newly formed Smithsonian Institution, physicist Joseph Henry was called upon almost daily to screen and evaluate scientific and technical proposals from outside investigators. Many of these investigators came from the fringe of the scientific community or beyond, and favored ideas which deviated from current orthodoxy. Henry's policies toward this fringe group, a neglected aspect of the Smithsonian's early history, are examined through extensive manuscript evidence. 1820's-78

Henry, Patrick

3073. Isaac, Rhys. PATRICK HENRY: PATRIOT AND PREACHER? *Virginia Cavalcade 1982 31(3): 168-175.* Discusses the two sides of Patrick Henry that emerged in the two movements that arose in Virginia before the American Revolution; the evangelical religious movement and patriotic resistance to Great Britain. 1740's-75

3074. McCants, David A. THE ROLE OF PATRICK HENRY IN THE STAMP ACT DEBATE. *Southern Speech Communication J. 1981 46(3): 205-227.* Although documentary evidence is scanty and conflicting, Patrick Henry unquestionably helped persuade the Virginia House of Burgesses to adopt in May, 1765, the Virginia Resolves against the Stamp Act: not only did Henry deliver the famous Caesar-Brutus speech; he wrote the Resolves, planned with George Johnston the strategies for debate on the house floor, and spoke at several points in the debate which initiated colonial resistance to the Act, resistance which culminated in the Act's repeal in 1766. 1764-66

Hensley, Willie

3075. Johnson, Susan Hackley. PROFILES OF THE NORTH: WILLIE HENSLEY. *Alaska J. 1979 9(2): 26-33.* Willie Hensley is one of the most important Eskimos on the Alaskan political and economic scene. His contributions to the improvement of the lives of native Alaskans are discussed along with a sketch of his life and background, 1960's-70's. 8 photos. 1960's-70's

Henson, Josiah

3076. Boelio, Bob. UNCLE TOM'S CABIN. *Chronicle: The Quarterly Magazine of the Historical Society of Michigan 1984 20(4): 22-24.* Discusses the Reverend Josiah Henson, a self-educated former slave whose life may have inspired Harriet Beecher Stowe's *Uncle Tom's Cabin.* 1789-1883

Herberg, Will

3077. Siegel, Seymour. WILL HERBERG, 1955. *Modern Age 1982 26(3-4): 276-279.* Pays tribute to Will Herberg. Born in Russia, he came to the United States at an early age. In his youth an ardent Communist, he soon became disillusioned and returned to his Jewish roots after hearing a lecture by Reinhold Niebuhr. He studied at Jewish Theological Seminary and taught social philosophy and Judaic thought at Drew University in Madison, New Jersey, until his retirement in 1976. His *Catholic-Protestant-Jew* (1955) was an influential work in American religious sociology. Politically conservative, he was religion editor for William Buckley's *National Review* and editorial advisor to *Modern Age.*Secondary sources; 8 notes. 1927-77

Herbert, Henry

3078. Martin, Junius J. GEORGIA'S FIRST MINISTER: THE REVEREND DR. HENRY HERBERT. *Georgia Hist. Q. 1982 66(2): 113-118.* Discusses what little is known about the career of the Reverend Henry Herbert (d. 1733), who came to Georgia with the first boatload of Oglethorpe's settlers, and demonstrates the possibility that the Anglican clergyman was the illegitimate son of Arthur Herbert (1647-1716), Earl of Torrington. 18 notes. 1732-33

Herman, Augustine

3079. Kansky, Karel J. AUGUSTINE HERMAN: THE LEADING CARTOGRAPHER OF THE SEVENTEENTH CENTURY. *Maryland Hist. Mag. 1978 73(4): 352-359.* While the eminent legal and political role of Augustine Herman (1606-86) in the formation of the United States is widely known, overlooked is his excellent surveying and cartographic skill. The founder of Bohemia Manor in eastern Maryland produced in 1670 a map of Maryland and Virginia which made him one of the initiators of thematic cartography and was far superior to John Smith's map of 1608. It is an example of two-dimensional observing and data ordering which recognized the hierarchical arrangements of manmade features and presented invisible phenomena in visible lines. Herman was the first surveyor to use the isobath in American map drawing. This work "stands out as his foremost, innovative intellectual contribution." Primary and secondary sources; 27 notes. 1621-1704

Herne, James A.

3080. Jones, Betty Jean. "James A. Herne: The Rise of American Stage Realism." U. of Wisconsin, Madison 1983. 310 pp. *DAI 1983 44(6): 1627-1628-A.* DA8317031 1859-1901

Heron, Virginia Ruth (family)

3081. Mesman, Virginia Ruth Heron. THE GOOD LIFE AT THE CORDOVA POWER PLANT: 1912-1914. *Alaska J. 1979 9(4): 62-63.* Describes her family (the Herons) and daily life at the Cordova Power Plant, Alaska. 3 photos. 1912-14

Heron family

3082. Shortt, Mary. TOURING THEATRICAL FAMILIES IN CANADA WEST: THE HILLS AND THE HERONS. *Ontario Hist. [Canada] 1982 74(1): 3-25.* 1840-60
*For abstract see **Hill family***

Herr, Benjamin

3083. Brackbill, Martin H. BENJAMIN HERR, TRAVELER. *Pennsylvania Mennonite Heritage 1980 3(1): 19-23.* Traces the heritage of Benjamin Herr (1760-1846) to his grandfather, Abraham Herr, who settled on the edge of the Manor of Conestoga southwest of Lancaster, Pennsylvania, in 1717; recounts Benjamin's trip to Europe in 1792 to claim some property in the name of the five children of Jonas Vogt. 1717-1846

Herrick, Genevieve Forbes

3084. Steiner, Linda and Gray, Susanne. GENEVIEVE FORBES HERRICK: A FRONT-PAGE REPORTER "PLEASED TO WRITE ABOUT WOMEN." *Journalism History 1985 12(1): 8-16.* Genevieve Forbes Herrick, front-page reporter for the *Chicago Tribune,* addressed women's issues such as forced stripping by women undergoing immigration health inspections, and women's role in politics. 1921-51

Herrick, Robert

3085. Cooper, Melvin Thomas. "Robert Herrick: An Irate Transcendentalist." Syracuse U. 1976. 162 pp. *DAI 1977 38(5): 2784-A.* 1893-1908

Herron, George D.

3086. Keserich, Charles. GEORGE D. HERRON, THE UNITED STATES AND PEACEMAKING WITH BULGARIA, 1918-1919. *East European Q. 1980 14(1): 39-58.* Traces the activities of George D. Herron (an American who spent much of his life in Italy) with regard to Bulgaria during and after World War I. Herron believed that Woodrow Wilson was a messiah destined to bring a lasting peace. He became Wilson's emissary in trying to persuade Bulgaria to leave its alliance with Germany. He then became Bulgaria's spokesman on postwar territorial settlements. Based largely on Herron's unpublished papers at the Hoover Library at Stanford University; 103 notes. 1918-19

Hersey, John

3087. Huse, Nancy Lyman. "John Hersey: The Writer and His Times." U. of Chicago 1975. *DAI 1978 38(8): 4827-4828-A.* 1946-74

Hersey, John (1786-1862)

3088. Boles, John B. JOHN HERSEY: DISSENTING THEOLOGIAN OF ABOLITIONISM, PERFECTIONISM, AND MILLENNIALISM. *Methodist Hist. 1976 14(4): 215-234.* John Hersey (1786-1862), a devout Methodist, turned from mercantilism to preaching in his 20's. Through his preaching and his writings he was a consistent foe of slavery, urged Christians to strive for perfection in their beliefs, stressed that parenthood presented the Christian with great responsibilities, and the millennium was yet to come. Based on Hersey's books; 97 notes. 1786-1862

Hershman, Abraham Moses

3089. Hershman, Ruth and Hershman, Eiga. RABBI ABRAHAM M. HERSHMAN. *Michigan Jewish Hist. 1981 21(2): 16-31.* Traces the life of Rabbi Abraham Moses Hershman (1880-1959) from his roots in Lithuania, where he received a traditional Jewish education as a boy, to his later work as a rabbi in Detroit after his ordination in 1906, and his efforts for Zionism; and discusses the scholarly endeavors which Hershman undertook after his retirement in 1946, especially his translation of a portion of the *Code of Maimonides.* 1880-1959

Herty, Charles Holmes

3090. Courson, Maxwell Taylor. THE CUP AND GUTTER EXPERIMENTS OF CHARLES HOLMES HERTY. *Georgia Hist. Q. 1980 64(4): 459-471.* Charles Holmes Herty (1867-1938), chemistry professor at the University of Georgia, devised a new method of collecting turpentine which spared the trees. During the 1930's he also demonstrated that satisfactory newsprint could be made from southern pine trees. Various commemorations of his accomplishments are mentioned. Based on correspondence, newspaper articles, and secondary sources; 27 notes. 1901-04

3091. Reed, Germaine M. CHARLES HOLMES HERTY AND THE PROMOTION OF SOUTHERN ECONOMIC DEVELOPMENT. *South Atlantic Q. 1983 82(4): 424-436.* Presents an overview of the career of Charles Holmes Herty, with particular emphasis on his efforts to promote Southern industry through chemistry. Based on the Charles Holmes Herty Papers in the Robert Woodruff Memorial Library, Emory University, Atlanta, Georgia; 35 notes. 1900-38

Herzinger, Emile Louis

3092. Spiess, Lincoln Bunce. EMILE LOUIS HERZINGER (1839-1887): ST. LOUIS ARTIST. *Gateway Heritage 1984 5(2): 50-56.* In the 1800's, St. Louis became an art center by attracting prominent painters with national reputations to work there. This inspired local artists, but for them recognition was fleeting. Emile Louis Herzinger, a portrait painter and landscapist, belonged to the latter group, and judgment of his artistry still awaits the recovery of a fuller sample of his paintings. Based on public records, contemporary newspaper accounts, and secondary sources; 13 photos, 22 notes. 1855-87

Heschel, Abraham J.

3093. Peri, Paul F. "Education for Piety: An Investigation of the Works of Abraham J. Heschel." Columbia U. Teachers Coll. 1980. 159 pp. *DAI 1980 41(1): 153-A.* 8015095 1940-70

Hess, Karl

3094. Neumann, A. Lin. INTERVIEW WITH KARL HESS. *Reason 1982 14(1): 44-48.* Presents an interview with Karl Hess, former speechwriter for Barry Goldwater, a founder of the *National Review,* and currently a self-styled anarchist. 1964-82

Hess, Katie Charles

3095. Denlinger, A. Martha. KATIE HESS REMINISCES. *Pennsylvania Mennonite Heritage 1978 1(4): 2-9.* Discusses Katie Charles Hess's (b. 1883) reminiscences about her childhood in a Mennonite community near Lancaster, Pennsylvania, including her daily life, involvement with the church, and early married years. 1883-1978

Hesseltine, William Best

3096. Byrne, Frank L. THE TRAINER OF HISTORIANS. *Wisconsin Mag. of Hist. 1982-83 66(2): 115-118.* Recollections of a former University of Wisconsin graduate student who studied under historian William Best Hesseltine during the 1950's, focusing on Hesseltine as teacher and critic. Paper presented at the annual meeting of the Southern Historical Association in Atlanta, Georgia, 1979. 2 illus. 1950's

3097. Current, Richard N. RECOLLECTIONS OF THE MAN AND THE TEACHER. *Wisconsin Mag. of Hist. 1982-83 66(2): 119-121.* Reminiscences of a former student and colleague of historian William Best Hesseltine at the University of Wisconsin during 1936-63. Hesseltine's greatest strength was his "ability to arouse interest, to generalize brilliantly if at times erratically, [and] to open new vistas for possible exploration." Paper presented at the annual meeting of the Southern Historical Association in Atlanta, Georgia, 1979. 2 illus. 1936-63

3098. Freidel, Frank. THE TEACHER AND HIS STUDENTS. *Wisconsin Mag. of Hist. 1982-83 66(2): 111-114.* Reminiscences of a former University of Wisconsin graduate student who studied under historian William Best Hesseltine during 1939-40's. Portrays Hesseltine's iconoclasm and intellectual rigor in the classroom and notes his influence on graduate students. Paper presented at the annual meeting of the Southern Historical Association in Atlanta, Georgia, 1979. 3 illus. 1939-40's

3099. Gunderson, Robert G. DUTCH UNCLE TO A PROFESSION. *Wisconsin Mag. of Hist. 1982-83 66(2): 106-110.* Sketches the career of historian William Best Hesseltine at the University of Wisconsin during 1932-63. Paper presented at the annual meeting of the Southern Historical Association in Atlanta, Georgia, 1979. 4 illus. 1932-63

Heward, Teancum William

3100. Buice, David. EXCERPTS FROM THE DIARY OF TEANCUM WILLIAM HEWARD, EARLY MORMON MISSIONARY TO GEORGIA. *Georgia Hist. Q. 1980 64(3): 317-325.* Describes the experiences of Teancum William Heward (1854-1915) during his service as a Mormon missionary in northern Georgia during June 1879-March 1881. Based on Heward diary; 21 notes. 1879-81

Hewes, George Robert Twelves

3101. Young, Alfred F. GEORGE ROBERT TWELVES HEWES (1742-1840): A BOSTON SHOEMAKER AND THE MEMORY OF THE AMERICAN REVOLUTION. *William and Mary Q. 1981 38(4): 561-623.* Hewes, a humble shoemaker and participant in various events of the American Revolution, because of his longevity became a celebrity in the 1830's. The author discusses the two biographical narratives of Hewes by James Hawkes (1834) and Benjamin Thatcher (1835) and examines the apprenticeship, work, and status of shoemakers, the Hewes family, and changing social values in New England. The authenticity of Hewes's recollections comes under scrutiny, with emphasis on the Boston Massacre. Hewes also served aboard a privateer and as a soldier. His last years were spent in upstate New York. Based on court records and the narratives of Hewes's life; 200 notes. 1742-1840

Hewes, Joseph

3102. Young, A. E. "REST IN PEACE, JOSEPH HEWES!" *Pennsylvania Folklife 1980 30(1): 41-45.* A brief account of Joseph Hewes, who signed the Declaration of Independence, as a representative of North Carolina, 1770-80; buried in Christ Church's Burial Yard in Philadelphia, Hewes is honored on the Signers Monument at Guilford Court House, North Carolina. 1770-80

Heydenfeldt, Elcan

3103. Stern, Norton B. THE FIRST JEWISH CALIFORNIA STATE LEGISLATOR: ELCAN HEYDENFELDT, 1850. *Western States Jewish Hist. 1984 16(2): 120-124.* Traces the political career of Elcan Heydenfeldt, who arrived in San Francisco in 1849 and opened a law office; shortly thereafter, he was elected to the state legislature, where he eventually served three terms. Based on newspaper and other sources; illus., 19 notes. 1849-53

Heyl, James Bell

3104. Franke, Norman H. JAMES BELL HEYL: BERMUDA'S PHARMACIST-PHOTOGRAPHER. *Pharmacy in Hist. 1982 24(3): 117-119.* Biography of Anglo-American pharmacist-photographer James Bell Heyl. Following the family tradition, Heyl studied pharmacy in the 1840's at Charity Hospital in New Orleans. He later moved to Hamilton, Bermuda, where he practiced pharmacy for over 50 years at the Apothecary's Hall and pursued his interest in photography. He is a recognized early photographer of Bermuda. Primary sources; photo, 20 notes. 1840's-90's

Heyward, DuBose

3105. Greene, Harlan. CHARLESTON CHILDHOOD: THE FIRST YEARS OF DUBOSE HEYWARD. *South Carolina Hist. Mag. 1982 83(2): 154-167.* The diary of Jane Screven Heyward, mother of DuBose Heyward, revealed details about life in Charleston and about her son, DuBose, who became a noted poet, novelist, and dramatist. Jane Heyward left a record about the first 13 years of DuBose's life that few scholars had researched. Along with details of daily life, she left a touching account of her son's loving relationship with his father, as well as a sad account of her husband's untimely death. Based on two manuscript ledger books written by Jane Heyward; 17 notes. 1864-77

Heywood, Ezra

3106. Blatt, Martin Henry. "The Anarchism of Ezra Heywood (1829-1893): Abolition, Labor Reform, and Free Love." Boston U. Grad. School 1983. 415 pp. *DAI 1983 44(5): 1547-A.* DA8319959 1850's-93

Hickenlooper, Bourke Blakemore

3107. Schapsmeier, Edward L. and Schapsmeier, Frederick H. A STRONG VOICE FOR KEEPING AMERICA STRONG: A PROFILE OF SENATOR BOURKE HICKENLOOPER. *Ann. of Iowa 1984 47(4): 362-376.* Republican Bourke Blakemore Hickenlooper was elected to the US Senate from Iowa and during his tenure was a strong advocate for US military power, conservative causes, and US participation in Vietnam. Considered a "hawk," Hickenlooper was a zealot against Communistic influences, real and imagined, in American government. 2 photos, 44 notes. 1945-69

Hickman, Clarence N.

3108. Schumm, Maryanne Marjorie. "Clarence N. Hickman: The Father of Scientific Archery." Pennsylvania State U. 1983. 194 pp. *DAI 1984 44(8):* DA8327550 1900's-81

Hickok, James Butler "Wild Bill"

3109. Rosa, Joseph G. J. B. HICKOK, DEPUTY U.S. MARSHAL. *Kansas Hist. 1979 2(4): 231-251.* James Butler "Wild Bill" Hickok (1837-76) was a scout, teamster, wagonmaster, and frontier lawman in Kansas from 1856 to 1871. A semifictional article about "Wild Bill" in the February 1867 issue of *Harper's New Monthly Magazine* launched the move to romanticize him as a great pistoleer. As a deputy US marshal from 1867 to 1871, Hickok was caught up in the less exciting duties of arresting counterfeiters, deserters from the army, those who stole government property, and those who murdered Indians on and off the reservation. Much time was spent testifying at trials and aiding state officials pursuing murderers. Based on articles, books, newspapers, and court and military records in the National Archives and Kansas State Historical Society; illus., 112 notes. 1867-71

Hickok, Lorena A.

3110. Beasley, Maurine. LORENA A. HICKOK: WOMAN JOURNALIST. *Journalism Hist. 1980 7(3-4): 92-95, 113.* Journalist Lorena A. Hickok (1893-1968) investigated nationwide relief programs, then prepared reports for the Roosevelt administration, 1933-36. 1913-68

3111. Beasley, Maurine. LORENA A. HICKOK: JOURNALISTIC INFLUENCE ON ELEANOR ROOSEVELT. *Journalism Q. 1980 57(2): 281-286.* 1932-68
For abstract see ***Roosevelt, Eleanor***

3112. Beasley, Maurine. LORENA HICKOK TO HARRY HOPKINS, 1933: A WOMAN REPORTER VIEWS PRAIRIE HARD TIMES. *Montana 1982 32(2): 58-66.* Reporter Lorena A. Hickok, the chief investigator for the Federal Emergency Relief Administration (FERA), toured rural Minnesota, North and South Dakota, Nebraska, and Iowa during 1933. She wrote regularly to Eleanor Roosevelt and FERA chief, Harry Hopkins, on the agricultural, economic, social, and political situations she observed. Excerpts from the reports are reprinted along with biographical information on Hickok. Based on the Lorena Hickok and Harry Hopkins papers in the Franklin D. Roosevelt Library, Hyde Park, New York; 5 illus., 56 notes. 1933

Hicks, Edward

3113. Guttenberg, John P., Jr. EDWARD HICKS: A JOURNEY TO THE PEACEABLE KINGDOM. *Am. Art and Antiques 1979 2(3): 76-83.* Traces the life and works of 19th century Quaker American folk artist Edward Hicks (1780-1849) of Bucks County, Pennsylvania, whose favorite painting subject was "the Peaceable Kingdom," of which he painted 60 versions. 1780-1849

Hicks, John David

3114. Saloutos, Theodore. A DEDICATION TO THE MEMORY OF JOHN D. HICKS, 1890-1972. *Arizona and the West 1980 22(1): 1-4.* Following graduate studies at Northwestern University and the University of Wisconsin, John David Hicks (1890-1972) taught at four schools before going to the University of California at Berkeley. By that time, the American West had become his teaching specialty, and Populism attracted his research and writing skills. He also wrote one of the most successful American history textbooks and served in important professional roles, including the presidency of three historical associations. Illus., biblio. 1931-68

Hicks, Thomas

3115. Tatham, David. THOMAS HICKS AT TRENTON FALLS. *Am. Art J. 1983 15(4): 4-20.* Thomas Hicks ranked among the most fashionable and prosperous of American portrait painters. Winters were spent in New York City, but summers during this time were spent at his country house at Thornwood, near Trenton Falls, north of Utica, in upstate New York. There Hicks painted portraits, scenes of the falls, and interior genre scenes. Photo, 15 plates, 33 notes. 1854-86

Hidy, Ralph Willard

3116. Johnson, Arthur M. RALPH WILLARD HIDY, 1905-1977. *Business Hist. Rev. 1978 52(2): 155-165.* Dr. Ralph W. Hidy was Straus Professor Emeritus of Business History at Harvard University. Traces his career, his scholarly contribution to economic and business history, and his enormous impact on his many friends. Ralph W. Hidy "brought high standards, a probing intellect, and a gentle spirit to our profession." 1920's-77

Hiebert, Cornelius

3117. Buhr, Lorne R. CORNELIUS HIEBERT IN THE ALBERTA LEGISLATURE (1905-1909). *Mennonite Life 1980 35(4): 15-19.* Cornelius Hiebert (1863-1919), the first Mennonite elected to the Alberta House, represented Rosebud during 1906-09. Hiebert immigrated from South Russia in 1876 and became engaged in merchandising and community affairs as a young man. In 1888 he married Aganetha Dick; in 1901 he became village overseer. As a Conservative Party member of the legislature, he supported a bounty on coyotes, opposed monopolies, especially of the railways, and spoke often on the evils of liquor. He voted for support of sugar beet farmers and for safety legislation for miners. Hiebert hoped to make politics more businesslike, but was defeated by a Liberal Mennonite, J. E. Stauffer, in 1909. 3 photos. 1905-09

3118. Gilpin, John. CORNELIUS HIEBERT, M.L.A. *Alberta Hist. [Canada] 1982 30(4): 10-17.* A merchant, village overseer, and member of the legislative assembly, Cornelius Hiebert "played an active role in the political and economic life" of Didsbury, which was created by the Calgary and Edmonton Railway Company and the Mennonite settlement in Alberta. Arriving in 1901 from Manitoba, Hiebert had an urban, business background. First elected in 1904, he became a critic of the government although "not a partisan politician"; he was the last of Alberta's politicians in this tradition "which had played a vital role in the politicial evaluation of the North-West Territories." 39 notes, 3 photos. 1901-19

Hier, Ethel Glenn

3119. Pendle, Karin. CINCINNATI'S MUSICAL HERITAGE: THREE WOMEN WHO SUCCEEDED. *Queen City Heritage 1983 41(4): 41-55.* Traces the careers of Ethel Glenn Hier, Julie Rivé-King, and Marguerite Liszniewska, who gained international acclaim as composers and pianists while breaking new ground for women seeking careers as professional musicians. 1875-1970

Higgins, Marguerite

3120. Keeshen, Kathleen Kearney. "Marguerite Higgins: Journalist, 1920-1960." U. of Maryland 1983. 472 pp. *DAI 1984 45(2): 330-A.* DA8412020 1940-66

Higgins, Sylvester Wesley

3121. Cumming, John. SYLVESTER WESLEY HIGGINS. *Michigan Hist. 1981 65(1): 11-13.* Sylvester Wesley Higgins, an associate of Douglass Houghton who conducted the official state survey in the 1840's, lived a long and eventful life and needs to be remembered. He went to California during the gold rush years and worked for a time for Captain Sutter. He later went to Texas and commanded a unit in the Confederate Army. He died in 1866. Higgins Lake is named after him. 4 photos, map. 1798-1866

Higginson, Thomas Wentworth

3122. Rashid, Frank D. HIGGINSON THE ENTOMOLOGIST. *New England Q. 1983 56(4): 577-582.* Investigates Thomas Wentworth Higginson's interest in entomology and its possible connection with Emily Dickinson. Higginson's involvement with the natural sciences, particularly entomology, began with his service as a student curator of entomology at Harvard. Traces the nature of the controversial Higginson-Dickinson relationship and the employment of insect imagery by Dickinson in her poems. 11 notes. 1850-70

Hildebrand, Bernhard (and family)

3123. Olfert, Sharon. THE HILDEBRANDS OF ROSENTHAL, MANITOBA. *Mennonite Life 1979 34(4): 19-26.* The Hildebrand family was centered in Neuenburg, South Russia, from 1818 until 1878 when Bernhard Hildebrand (1840-1910) and family emigrated to Rosenthal, Manitoba. A farming family, they gradually expanded their holdings until the 10 children all had nearby farms. Patriarch Bernhard Hildebrand supported education and foreign missions. Listing of Bernhard Hildebrand family; Rosenthal Village census 1878-80; farm inventory 1880-81. 7 photos, map of Rosenthal householders, late 1870's, 10 notes, biblio. 1795-1915

Hildreth, Samuel P.

3124. Ulrich, Dennis Nicholas. "Samuel P. Hildreth: Physician and Scientist on the American Frontier, 1783-1863." Miami U. 1983. 228 pp. *DAI 1983 44(5): 1554-A.* DA8321171 1806-63

Hill, Ambrose Powell

3125. Hassler, William W. A. P. HILL: MYSTERY MAN OF THE CONFEDERACY. *Civil War Times Illus. 1977 16(6): 4-10, 40-42.* Robert E. Lee called Ambrose Powell Hill the third ablest commander in the Army of Northern Virginia. Discusses his boyhood in Culpepper, Virginia, to his death, near Petersburg on 2 April 1865. He competed before the Civil War with George B. McClellan for the hand of Nelly March and lost. During his four years of service he participated in every major campaign of the Army of Northern Virginia. He succeeded to the command of Thomas J. (Stonewall) Jackson's Third Corps. His career as a corps commander was less brilliant than had been his division command. 1861-65

Hill, Andrew P.

3126. de Vries, Carolyn. ANDREW P. HILL AND THE BIG BASIN: CALIFORNIA'S FIRST STATE PARK. *San José Studies 1976 2(3): 70-92.* Chronicles the life of Californian Andrew P. Hill, his life as an artist, and his success at aiding in the establishment of California's first state park, Big Basin Redwood State Park and also in the establishment of the state park system as a whole, 1890-1922. 14 photos, 51 notes. 1890-1922

Hill, James Jerome

3127. Dickman, Howard Leigh. "James Jerome Hill and the Agricultural Development of the Northwest." U. of Michigan 1977. 430 pp. *DAI 1978 38(11): 6892-6893-A.* 1880's

3128. Martin, Albro. JAMES J. HILL, ENTREPRENEUR IN THE CLASSIC MOLD. *J. of the West 1978 17(4): 62-74.* Examines the career of James J. Hill in light of the model of entrepreneurship developed by economist Joseph A. Schumpeter. Hill was an energetic, creative businessman of St. Paul, Minnesota, who took over the failing St. Paul & Pacific Railroad in 1878 and developed it into the Great Northern Railway. Hill's genius for innovation contrasted with his contemporaries' single-minded quest for immediate profits. The effects of his enterprise are apparent in the settlement and commercial development of the northern tier of states between Minnesota and Washington. Based on the James J. Hill Papers, Hill Reference Library, St. Paul, Minnesota; 8 photos, 2 maps, 7 notes. 1856-1912

Hill, Joe

3129. Lumer, Helga. JOE HILL—LIEDERMACHER DER WOBBLIES [Joe Hill—songwriter of the Wobblies]. *Wiss. Zeits. der Humboldt-Universität zu Berlin. Gesellschafts- und Sprachwissenschaftliche Reihe [East Germany] 1981 30(6): 625-627.* Reports on the life, ideas, and activities of Joe Hill, working-class activist in the Industrial Workers of the World, and on his work as a songwriter. 1905-15

Hill, W. B.

3130. Hill, W. B. "IN WEARINESS AND PAINFULNESS, WAS THE CAUSE BUILT UP." *Adventist Heritage 1977 4(1): 56-59.* Excerpts the autobiography of W. B. Hill re 1877 and 1881, relating his experiences in Minnesota and Iowa as a Seventh-Day Adventist evangelist. 1877

Hill family

3131. Shortt, Mary. TOURING THEATRICAL FAMILIES IN CANADA WEST: THE HILLS AND THE HERONS. *Ontario Hist. [Canada] 1982 74(1): 3-25.* The problems of touring stage companies before the railroads were severe in rural Ontario, and the yields were relatively low unless the production proved popular. Some of the problems are sketched and illustrated by the experiences of the Hill family in the 1840's and 1850's and the Heron family in the 1840's. Mainly contemporary newspapers; 4 illus., 53 notes. 1840-60

Hillig, Otto

3132. Johansen, Jens P. THE FLIGHTS OF LIBERTY. *Am. Aviation Hist. Soc. J. 1979 24(2): 111-121.* Describes the flight across the Atlantic Ocean by Otto Hillig and Holger Hoiriis in the *Liberty* from New York to Copenhagen in 1931, and provides follow-up biographies of Hoiriis and Holger, and the plane's subsequent flights, until 1954. 1930-54

Hillis, Cora Bussey

3133. Swaim, Ginalie. CORA BUSSEY HILLIS: WOMAN OF VISION. *Palimpsest 1979 60(6): 162-177.* Cora Bussey Hillis (1858-1924) lobbied for child welfare laws and the establishment of a center for research on children, and encouraged educators to provide stimulating learning atmospheres for children. 1880's-1924

Hillius, Christina Netz

3134. Sperling, Otto H. BIOGRAPHY OF CHRISTINA NETZ HILLIUS (1861-1939) OF KULM, NORTH DAKOTA. *Journal of the American Historical Society of Germans from Russia 1985 8(1): 39-42.* Describes the life of Christina Netz Hillius and her family after they arrived in Kulm, North Dakota, from Bessarabia in 1885. 1885-1939

Hillman, Sidney

3135. Fraser, Steven Clark. "Sidney Hillman and the Origins of the 'New Unionism,' 1890-1930." Rutgers U. 1983. 277 pp. *DAI 1983 44(5): 1548-A.* DA8320469 1890-1930

Himes, Chester

3136. Evans, Veichal Jerome. "Chester Himes: Chronicler of the Black Experience." Oklahoma State U. 1980. 118 pp. *DAI 1981 42(1): 213-A.* 8113307 1940-44

Himmrich, Karl

3137. Himmrich, Karl; Wildermuth, Herman, transl. A BIOGRAPHICAL SKETCH OF MY LIFE. *Heritage Rev. 1977 (17): 43-53.* A personal narrative of the author's youth in Russia, service in World War I, immigration to Germany in 1940, and immigration to the United States in 1951, where he settled in California. 1895-1972

Hinckley, Robert Henry

3138. Winstead, Billy Wayne. "Robert Henry Hinckley: His Public Service Career." U. of Utah 1980. 246 pp. *DAI 1980 41(3): 1173-1174-A.* 8019973 1929-80

Hind, Henry and William

3139. Stanley, George F. G. and Stanley, Laurie C. C. THE BROTHERS HIND. *Nova Scotia Hist. Soc. Collections [Canada] 1980 40: 109-132.* Both Henry Hind (1823-1908) and William Hind (1833-89) have been relegated to obscurity. The former explored the western plains and Labrador, conducted geological surveys in the Maritime Provinces, served on the Fisheries Commission, and founded Edgehill School in Windsor, Nova Scotia. He later produced a graphic record of Canadian life in such diverse areas as Labrador, the Red River, and the Maritimes. William was also an explorer. 66 notes. 1845-1908

Hinds, Grace

3140. Bryant, F. Russell. LADY CURZON, THE MARCHIONESS FROM DECATUR. *Alabama Hist. Q. 1982 44(3-4): 213-260.* Biography of Grace Hinds, from her youth in Alabama to her marriage with former British foreign secretary George Curzon of Kedleston, England. Contrasts her life with Tallulah Bankhead's, and emphasizes Hinds as a figure in British upper-class society. 207 notes. 1906-58

Hindsley, Mark H.

3141. Gregory, Earle Suydam. "Mark H. Hindsley: The Illinois Years." U. of Illinois, Urbana-Champaign 1982. 326 pp. *DAI 1982 43(3): 716-A.* DA8218477 1948-70

Hine, Robert V. (family)

3142. Hine, Robert V. FORECLOSURE IN LOS ANGELES. *Pacific Hist. 1983 27(4): 33-37.* Recounts the author's family's difficulties in Los Angeles during the Depression. 4 illus., 3 notes. 1929-35

Hines, David Willington

3143. Rysavy, Don. D. W. HINES AND THE FARMERS' RAILROAD: A CASE STUDY IN POPULIST BUSINESS ENTERPRISE, 1894-1898. *North Dakota Q. 1979 47(4): 20-34.* In 1894, David Willington Hines (1863-?) conceived a plan to build a Farmers' Railroad in North Dakota, constructed by the farmers without capital as an alternative to the exorbitant rates of the Great Northern and Northern Pacific railroads controlled by eastern capitalists; but poor financial planning and the farmers' inability to cooperate caused the plan to fail. 1894-98

Hines, Duncan

3144. Schwartz, David M. DUNCAN HINES: HE MADE GASTRONOMES OUT OF MOTORISTS. *Smithsonian 1984 15(8): 86-97.* Though he is best known today for the line of cake mixes that bears his name, Duncan Hines was a best-selling author whose *Adventures in Good Eating* (1936), a restaurant guide widely used by motorists in the 1940's and early 1950's, made his endorsement a prize coveted by restaurant owners from coast to coast. 1935-59

Hines, John Leonard

3145. Peake, Louis A. WEST VIRGINIA'S BEST KNOWN GENERAL SINCE "STONEWALL JACKSON": JOHN L. HINES. *West Virginia Hist. 1977 38(3): 226-235.* General John Leonard Hines (1868-1968), of Irish parentage, was born in West Virginia, graduated from West Point, and spent his career with the Army. He fought in Cuba (1898), in the Philippines (1900), with the punitive expedition to Mexico (1916), and in France (1918). He became Army Chief of Staff 1924-26 and served in the Philippines again in 1930-32, until retirement. Primary and secondary sources; 42 notes. 1891-1932

Hinkley, Holmes

3146. White, John H. HOLMES HINKLEY AND THE BOSTON LOCOMOTIVE WORKS. *Railroad Hist. 1980 (142): 27-52.* Discusses Holmes Hinkley (1793-1866) of Maine, focusing on his locomotive-building business, the Boston Locomotive Works which he operated from 1826-57 as a machinery business, notable because it built more locomotives than any other New England company, and also because it serves "as a case study in the precarious nature of the locomotive-building business in the 19th century." Discusses the company's history, which became known as Hinkley Locomotive Company in 1879, until its demise in 1889. 1826-89

Hinman, Samuel D.

3147. Anderson, Grant K. SAMUEL D. HINMAN AND THE OPENING OF THE BLACK HILLS. *Nebraska Hist. 1979 60(4): 520-542.* Episcopal missionary Samuel D. Hinman acted also as an explorer, treaty maker, and interpreter during negotiations for the Black Hills. As a missionary he devoted three decades to converting the Sioux Indians to Christianity and revising their way of life. During the critical years, 1874-76, he took part in all governmental dealings with the Sioux. 1860-76

Hirsch, Samuel

3148. Greenberg, Gershon. THE HISTORICAL ORIGINS OF GOD AND MAN: SAMUEL HIRSCH'S LUXEMBOURG WRITINGS. *Leo Baeck Inst. Year Book [Great Britain] 1975 20: 129-148.* Samuel Hirsch (1815-89) is significant in modern Jewish history for transplanting Reform Judaism to America. While his American publications are journalistic and pragmatic, concentrating on man and society, his writings during his stay in Luxembourg, 1843-66, concentrate on the theological problem of man and God in history. The contiguity between time and eternity unfolds in history out of which reason and revelation emerge. This refocusing of Hirsch's attention explains his ability to concentrate on the human aspects of religion in America and sublimate his philosophy into the pragmatic world of Reform Judaism's future. 81 notes. 1815-89

Hirschfeld, Al

3149. Gill, Brendan. HIRSCHFELD. *Horizon 1979 22(8): 38-45.* Discusses the successful career of artist Al Hirschfeld, American theater caricaturist, which began in the 1920's, and provides a brief biography of the still-active 76-year-old New Yorker, who was born in St. Louis. 1903-79

Hirshfeld, Herman (family)

3150. —. THE HIRSHFELDS OF KERN COUNTY: A PICTURE STORY. *Western States Jewish Hist. Q. 1983 15(3): 223-231.* The four Hirshfeld brothers, Herman, Marcus, Lesser, and David, and their sister Bertha, were pioneers of Kern County, California. Herman was first to leave the family home in Prussia. In the United States he had several military adventures, as a Union soldier and prisoner at Andersonville, and later as an Arizona Ranger during the Apache campaigns. In Bakersfield, California, in 1870, Herman opened a general store. His brothers and his sister's husband, Samuel Brodek, joined him in the business. Based on family interviews and records, and other primary sources; 7 photos, 29 notes. 1861-80's

Hirshman, Louis Jacob

3151. Edgar, Irving I. DR. LOUIS JACOB HIRSHMAN. *Michigan Jewish Hist. 1980 20(2): 5-10.* Discusses the contributions made by Dr. Louis Jacob Hirshman (1878-1965) to medicine and to the Jewish community in Detroit during the first half of the 20th century. 1900-50

Hiss, Alger

3152. Marbury, William L. THE HISS-CHAMBERS LIBEL SUIT. *Maryland Hist. Mag. 1981 76(1): 70-92.* The author was counsel for and life-long friend of Alger Hiss, accompanying the accused man in his initial response to the Communist espionage accusations of Whittaker Chambers before the House Committee on Un-American Activities. Reviews Hiss's life and relates the background and facts of the filing of Hiss's $50,000 libel suit against Chambers on 27 September 1948 in Maryland's US District Court. Discusses the author's subsequent interrogations of Chambers, and the problem of recovered State Department memoranda and the Hiss typewriter which helped produce Hiss's indictment in New York in December 1948, his trials, his conviction for perjury, and his imprisonment, which brought a dismissal with prejudice of the libel suit in April 1951. Based on Marbury's own notes and recall. 1922-51

Hitchcock, Alfred

3153. Hemmeter, Thomas Martin. "Hitchcock the Stylist." Case Western Reserve U. 1980. 468 pp. *DAI 1981 41(7): 2805-A.* 8100534 1925-80

Hitchcock, Edward

3154. Chickering, Howell D., Jr. EDWARD HITCHCOCK'S MOUNTAIN MANIA. *New-England Galaxy 1978 19(4): 3-12.* Edward Hitchcock, 1793-1864, was teacher and president of Amherst College during 1825-49. His role in naming the numerous hills and mountains surrounding Amherst is described in detail. Notes his hypochondriasis, his writing productivity, and his efforts in reducing Amherst College's indebtedness. 6 illus. 1793-1864

Hitchcock, Ethan Allen

3155. Hitchcock, Ethan Allen. A CRISIS OF CONSCIENCE. Karsten, Peter, ed. *The Military in America: From the Colonial Era to the Present* (New York: Free Pr., 1980): 111-116. Based on excerpts from his diary written during 1836-54, the author discusses his dilemma as a career military man who, as a Unitarian with a conscience, questions his presence in the military establishment. 1836-54

Hitchcock, Lambert

3156. Berenson, Ruth. HITCHCOCK CHAIRS: AN EARLY AMERICAN INDUSTRY. *Art & Antiques 1981 4(4): 98-105.* Brief biography of American furniture designer and maker Lambert Hitchcock, who designed the Hitchcock chair that was popular during the 1820's-40's. 1820-49

Hitchman, Robert Bruce

3157. Monroe, Robert D. ROBERT BRUCE HITCHMAN, 1909-1981. *Pacific Northwest Q. 1981 72(3): 136-137.* Robert Bruce Hitchman, successful insurance administrator, was a competent historian. In addition to helping organize the Puget Sound Maritime Historical Society and publishing a number of articles on Pacific Northwest history, Hitchman served as president of the Washington State Historical Society. His interest in collecting Washingtoniana and in identifying the origins of geographical place-names made him a recognized regional authority. Photo. 1909-81

Hjelt, Ole

3158. Dahlie, Jorgen. SOCIALIST AND FARMER: OLE HJELT AND THE NORWEGIAN RADICAL VOICE IN CANADA, 1908-1928. *Can. Ethnic Studies [Canada] 1978 10(2): 55-64.* Ole Hjelt (1884-1974) settled in Instow, Saskatchewan, upon his arrival in 1908 as an immigrant from Norway. For two decades he was a spokesman for socialism among Scandinavians in Canada. He not only wrote several books calling for revolutionary change, but published voluminously in Scandinavian-language newspapers. He also traveled extensively for the Socialist Party of Canada and the Socialist Party of America. When he returned to Norway in 1928 he involved himself in Norwegian Labour Party activities. During the Nazi occupation he reversed his position, denouncing Marxism and supporting Germany. Primary sources; photo, 52 notes. 1908-28

Hoben, Margaret Polliter

3159. Tolan, Sally. MARGARET HOBEN: EDUCATOR. *Milwaukee History 1985 8(1): 11-23.* Describes the life of Margaret Polliter Hoben, who served as a professor of education at Milwaukee State Teachers College and was active in several civic, political, and community projects in Milwaukee. 1930-83

Hobson, Richard Pearson

3160. Pittman, Walter E., Jr. RICHMOND P. HOBSON AND THE SINKING OF THE *MERRIMAC. Alabama Hist. Q. 1976 38(2): 101-111.* The life of Admiral Richard Pearson Hobson (d. 1937) is discussed with a detailed description of his activities in the sinking of the collier *Merrimac* to block the Spanish fleet in Santiago Harbor in 1898. This success made him a hero in both Spain and America. Hobson left the navy in 1903. He served in Congress from 1906-14. At the time of his death he was warning against Japanese aggression and urged naval preparedness. 19 notes. 1898-1937

Hochwalt, Frederick G.

3161. Horrigan, Donald Charles. "Frederick G. Hochwalt: Builder of the National Catholic Educational Association, 1944-1966." Columbia U. Teachers Coll. 1977. 244 pp. *DAI 1977 38(1): 133-A.* 1944-66

Hocking, William Ernest

3162. Frank, Douglas. WILLIAM ERNEST HOCKING AND THE DIPLOMACY OF FAITH. Plesur, Milton, ed. *An American Historian: Essays to Honor Selig Adler* (Buffalo: State U. of N.Y., 1980): 214-223. Discusses the political attitudes of idealist philosopher William Ernest Hocking; focuses on his ethical approach to problems of diplomacy and politics, premised on religious faith; 1918-66. 1918-66

Hodgkin, Thomas

3163. Kass, Amalie M. DR. THOMAS HODGKIN, DR. MARTIN DELANY, AND THE "RETURN TO AFRICA." *Medical Hist. [Great Britain] 1983 27(4): 373-393.* 1850-62

For abstract see ***Delany, Martin R.***

Hodgkinson, Harold Daniel

3164. Adams, Thomas Boylston. HAROLD DANIEL HODGKINSON. *Massachusetts Hist. Soc. Pro. 1979 91: 235-237.* Memoir of Harold Daniel Hodgkinson (d. 1979). Educated at Yale (Class of 1912), Hodgkinson served in

World War I and returned to Boston to his work at Filene's department store. By about 1940, he had risen to general manager of the firm. Hodgkinson and his wife, the former Laura Cabot, had a strong interest in the growth and welfare of Boston. ca 1908-79

Hodgman, Samuel C.

3165. Rosentreter, Roger L. SAMUEL HODGMAN'S CIVIL WAR. *Michigan Hist. 1980 64(6): 34-38.* Samuel C. Hodgman from Climax, Michigan, enlisted in the 7th Michigan Infantry in June 1861. The 7th fought with the Army of the Potomac and held the center of the Union line at Gettysburg. Disenchanted with the war, Hodgman took an honorable disability discharge in March 1864. He married a girl from Ohio and held a variety of jobs before becoming a minister. Plagued by economic problems, he died in 1894 in Florida. Based on 96 Civil War letters in the Hodgman Collection in the Regional History Collections at Western Michigan University in Kalamazoo; 4 photos, reproduction. 1861-94

Hodur, Francis

3166. Wieczerzak, Joseph W. BISHOP FRANCIS HODUR AND THE SOCIALISTS: ASSOCIATIONS AND DISASSOCIATIONS. *Polish Am. Studies 1983 40(2): 5-35.* Francis Bishop Hodur associated with socialists and subscribed to socialist thinking during his college days at the Jagellonian University. Later, as a young priest in the United States ministering to the downtrodden miners of Pennsylvania, his socialism became more pronounced. As a bishop, however, Hodur reversed himself and even fought editorial wars with socialist publishers. Toward the end of his career, he interposed himself between his Polish National Church and socialists who wanted to use the church to reach out to the common man. Based on Polish sources; 79 notes. 1866-1963

Hoey, Clyde R.

3167. Hatcher, Susan Arden. "The Senatorial Career of Clyde R. Hoey." Duke U. 1983. 209 pp. *DAI 1984 44(7): 2224-A.* DA8325665 1945-54

Hoffman, Clare E.

3168. Walker, Donald Edwin. "The Congressional Career of Clare E. Hoffman, 1935-63." Michigan State U. 1982. 359 pp. *DAI 1983 43(12): 4014-A.* DA8309020 1935-63

Hoffman, Harold Jefferson

3169. Maness, Lonnie E. A WEST TENNESSEE WORLD WAR II FIGHTER PILOT: HAROLD JEFFERSON HOFFMAN OF MARTIN. *West Tennessee Hist. Soc. Papers 1981 35: 83-94.* A biography of Colonel Harold Jefferson Hoffman (1915-68), with emphasis on his military life of 25 years, from entrance into the armed forces in World War II until retirement in 1967. Emphasis is placed on his dedication to his parents, his wife and children, and his country. His community service included Boy Scout work and layman activity in the Methodist Church. His actions as a soldier reflected the highest of credit, both in war and peace, on himself and the armed forces of the United States. Based on his correspondence, numerous citations, and contemporary newspaper accounts; 6 pictures, 51 notes. 1933-68

Hoffman, Malvina

3170. Taylor, Joshua C. MALVINA HOFFMAN. *Am. Art & Antiques 1979 2(4): 96-103.* Traces the career of American sculptor Malvina Hoffman, whose 16-month European tour in 1910-11, during which she met Auguste Rodin and saw Anna Pavlova and Mikhail Mordkin perform, had a lasting effect on her work, which she continued until 1961. 1910-61

Hoffman, Michael

3171. Hoffman, Christian B. IN MEMORIAM: MICHAEL HOFFMAN (D. 1908). *Swiss Am. Hist. Soc. Newsletter 1981 17(3): 11-16.* Biography of Swiss settler Michael Hoffman (1837-1908), who emigrated from Switzerland with his family in 1857, finally settling on a farm in Turkey Creek, Kansas, in 1860; focuses on the family's early years there. 1860's

Hofstadter, Richard

3172. Singal, Daniel Joseph. BEYOND CONSENSUS: RICHARD HOFSTADTER AND AMERICAN HISTORIOGRAPHY. *Am. Hist. Rev. 1984 89(4): 976-1004.* Evaluates the position of Richard Hofstadter in American historiography. Hofstadter's historical scholarship is usually placed within the "consensus school," which emphasizes the absence of ideological politics in US history. Hofstadter's early work pointed out consensus in the American political tradition in order to condemn the system, not praise it. As his career proceeded, however, he came to share the view that American political culture was unique and exemplary because it was nonideological. This changing viewpoint as well as his broad interests make Hofstadter's work difficult to classify. Secondary sources; 2 fig., 55 notes. 1930's-84

Hogg, James Stephen

3173. Hickey, Carroll Elvin. "A Rhetorical Analysis of Representative Gubernatorial Campaign Speeches by James Stephen Hogg (1890-1892)." Louisiana State U. and Agric. and Mechanical Coll. 1977. 338 pp. *DAI 1978 38(7): 3802-3803-A.* 1890-92

Hogg, William Clifford

3174. Weber, Bruce John. "Will Hogg and the Business of Reform." U. of Houston 1979. 236 pp. *DAI 1980 40(10): 5563-A.* 1900's-30

Hogue, Alexandre

3175. Rosson, Sandra Lea. "The Career of Alexandre Hogue." U. of Kansas 1983. 897 pp. *DAI 1983 44(4): 897-A.* DA8317920 1920's-82

Hoiriis, Holger

3176. Johansen, Jens P. THE FLIGHTS OF LIBERTY. *Am. Aviation Hist. Soc. J. 1979 24(2): 111-121.* 1930-54
*For abstract see **Hillig, Otto***

Hokanson, Nels M.

3177. Scott, Franklin D. THE SAGA OF NELS M. HOKANSON: IMMIGRANT AND IMMIGRANT HISTORIAN. *Swedish Pioneer Hist. Q. 1978 29(3): 198-208.* Nels M. Hokanson was born in Copenhagen of Swedish parents in 1885. In 1887 the family came to America and settled in St. Paul, Minnesota. After four or five years the family moved to Aitkin, Minnesota, where Nels lived until he joined a circus band at age 16. Discusses his life and times, based on his published writings and especially on autobiographical notes which he prepared in 1977-78. Hokanson's concern with his Swedish compatriots began in childhood and continued throughout his life. He is best known for his book, *Swedish Immigrants in Lincoln's Time.* It was first published in 1942 and is now being reprinted. He has written many articles for Swedish American journals. Photo, 11 notes. 20c

Holden, Edward S.

3178. Osterbrock, Donald E. THE RISE AND FALL OF EDWARD S. HOLDEN. *Journal for the History of Astronomy [Great Britain] 1984 15(2): 81-127, (3): 151-176.* Part 1. Begins a biography of US astronomer Edward S. Holden, the onetime controversial director of the University of California's Lick Observatory. Part 2. Traces the career of US astronomer Edward S. Holden from his dismissal from the Lick Observatory to his appointment as librarian at his alma mater, the US Military Academy at West Point. 1880's-1902

Holden, Perry Greeley

3179. Sizer, Rosanne and Silag, William. P. G. HOLDEN AND THE CORN GOSPEL TRAINS. *Palimpsest 1981 62(3): 66-71.* Discusses the work Perry Greeley Holden did as professor of agronomy at the University of Illinois on corn breeding from 1896 to 1900 and as head of field work for the Illinois Sugar Refining Company, where he conducted field courses for farmers who supplied the company with sugar beets; focuses on Holden's lectures and the travelling exhibit he called the "Seed Corn Gospel Train" during his 1904-06 campaign to educate Iowa farmers about the modern science of corn culture. 1896-1910

Holden, William Curry

3180. Murrah, David J. WILLIAM CURRY HOLDEN. *West Texas Hist. Assoc. Year Book 1978 54: 92-101.* William Curry Holden (1896-1978) was a historian, archaeologist, anthropologist, and museum director at Texas Tech University. 1920's-78

Holden, William Woods

3181. Harris, William C. WILLIAM WOODS HOLDEN: IN SEARCH OF VINDICATION. *North Carolina Hist. Rev. 1982 59(4): 354-372.* William Woods Holden (1818-92) was, throughout his public career, a controversial figure. As Scalawag governor of North Carolina, Holden enraged political opponents by his strong actions against the Ku Klux Klan's violence, the violation of political rights in the Piedmont, and by several political indiscretions. In 1870, a General Assembly dominated by Conservatives impeached and convicted him for violating the civil liberties of some citizens. This barred him from ever again holding state political office. For the rest of his life, he unsuccessfully sought repeal of this action and of the impeachment conviction. Based primarily on Holden's papers at Duke University and the North Carolina State Archives, papers of other prominent political figures, and local newspapers; 12 illus., 53 notes. 1865-92

Holladay, John

3182. Holladay, Alvis M.; Holladay, Robert B.; and Holladay, Wendell G. SPENCER'S COMPANION: WHO WAS HE? *Tennessee Hist. Q. 1980 39(3): 282-291.* Traces the history of John Holladay (ca. 1745-1812) who accompanied Thomas Sharpe Spencer and several other first white settlers to middle Tennessee in 1776. Holladay came west from Bedford County, Virginia. He did not "desert" his friend Spencer in 1777 as legend has it, but he did eventually return to Virginia and his family. Primary sources; 30 notes. 1703-1812

Hollander, Arie N. J. den

3183. Skard, Sigmund. ARIE N. J. DEN HOLLANDER, 1906-1976. *Am. Studies Int. 1977 15(3): 62-63.* A memorial essay honoring one of Holland's great students of American culture. From 1946 Arie den Hollander was Professor of Sociology and Americanistics at the Municipal University of Amsterdam. His first publication of importance was at age 27, on poor whites in the American South. From that beginning his interests ranged over a vast sweep of American cultural and social phenomena. From 1954 he was actively involved in the European Association for American Studies, and after 1968 was its President. 1906-76

Holley, Marietta (Josiah Allen's Wife)

3184. Winter, Kate H. "Snow and Roses: The Life of Marietta Holley." State U. of New York, Albany 1982. 303 pp. *DAI 1983 43(8): 2672-A.* DA8300754 1857-1926

Holley, Sallie

3185. Herbig, Katherine Lydigsen. "Friends for Freedom: The Lives and Careers of Sallie Holley and Caroline Putnam." Claremont Grad. Sch. 1977. 410 pp. *DAI 1977 38(4): 2301-2302-A.* 1850-1910

Holliday, Cyrus Kurtz

3186. Holliday, Kate. THE MAN WHO BUILT THE SANTA FE. *Mankind 1981 6(12): 18-22, 40-43.* Sketches the life of Cyrus Kurtz Holliday (1826-1900), a Pennsylvanian who founded the Atchison, Topeka and Santa Fe Railway. In 1852 Holliday opened a law office in western Pennsylvania. He quickly became a wealthy railroad attorney, moved to the Kansas Territory in 1854, and began dreaming of creating a railroad running the length of the Santa Fe Trail. The most difficult obstacles included the struggle over slavery in the Kansas Territory and the difficulty of convincing investors that such a railway would be profitable. Holliday's dream was realized prior to his death on 29 March 1900, thanks to his single-minded dedication to the project. 3 illus., 4 photos. 1846-1900

Holliday, Judy

3187. Taubman, Leslie Janet. "Judy Holliday: A Critical Study of a Star." U. of Southern California 1980. *DAI 1980 41(4): 1256-A.* 1950-59

Hollins, Jess

3188. Cummins, Roger W. "LILY-WHITE" JURIES ON TRIAL: THE CIVIL RIGHTS DEFENSE OF JESS HOLLINS. *Chronicles of Oklahoma 1985 63(2): 166-185.* Jess Hollins, a black man, was convicted in 1931 for the rape of a white woman in Creek County, Oklahoma. Oklahoma black leaders, led by newspaperman Roscoe Dunjee, and white lawyers William J. Loe and M. A. Looney appealed the conviction and death sentence to the US Supreme Court. Arguing that Hollins had been tried by an all-white jury in a state that would not impanel black jurors for such major crimes, the lawyers had the initial conviction overturned. A second jury found Hollins guilty in 1936 and sentenced him to life in prison. All-white juries, however, were outlawed in Oklahoma. Based on Oklahoma City's *The Black Dispatch;* 6 illus., 56 notes. 1932-36

Holloman, George V.

3189. Neufeld, Jacob. GEORGE V. HOLLOMAN: MISSILE PIONEER. *Aerospace Hist. 1980 27(2): 101-102.* A brief account of the life of Colonel George V. Holloman, USAF (1902-46). With an early interest in radio, he attended North Carolina State College and worked for several radio and electric companies before accepting a direct commission in the Army Air Corps in 1925. From 1931 he was stationed at Wright Field, Ohio, in the Instrument and Navigation Unit. He served there for 14 years and was instrumental in developing new and improved aids for navigation and instrument flying, including a completely hands-off instrument landing system. He also worked in experimenting with glide and vertical bombs. Holloman was killed in an aircraft accident in the Philippines in 1946. Holloman Air Force Base, New Mexico, is named in his honor. Photo. 1916-46

Holloway, Lou

3190. Holloway, Lou; Harrison, Alferdteen, interviewer. WE WERE PROFESSIONALS: LOU HOLLOWAY INTERVIEWED. *Southern Exposure 1980 8(3): 18-21.* Brief history of the female jazz band, the Rays of Rhythm, at Piney Woods School, founded in 1909 near Jackson, Mississippi, for black students; focusing on the experiences of Lou Holloway who joined the Rays of Rhythm in the early 1940's and traveled with the group when they went on tour to raise money for the school; 1940-49. 1940-49

Hollub, Adolphus

3191. Strauss, Leon L. ADOLPHUS HOLLUB OF SAN FRANCISCO. *Western States Jewish Hist. Q. 1983 15(2): 154-160.* Adolphus Hollub was the purchasing agent for a dry goods store in Shasta, California, in the 1850's. By 1860, A. Hollub & Company of San Francisco ran an export-import business, bringing furs from Siberia. The company also sold oil and lamps. In 1878, Hollub became an insurance broker and appraiser. He also served as public administrator for the City and County of San Francisco, as a leader in the Masonic Order, and as president of Congregation Emanu-El. Based on newspapers and other primary sources; 2 photos, 40 notes. 1850-90

Holly, Buddy

3192. Helene, Kathryn. BUDDY HOLLY: THE IOWA CONNECTION. *Palimpsest 1982 63(5): 150-159.* Discusses the career of rock musician Buddy Holly, focusing on his live performances in Iowa during 1957-59. 1953-59

Holmes, Burton

3193. Stewart, Leslie. THE ROVING EYE. *Westways 1979 71(11): 32-36.* Traces the travels of Burton Holmes, world traveler from 1886 until his death in 1957; he called the lectures of his trips illustrated with photographs and films "travelogues," a word of his own invention. 1886-1957

Holmes, Everett

3194. Ciccone, James. A TRIBUTE TO EVERETT HOLMES: NEW YORK STATE'S FIRST BLACK MAYOR. *Afro-Americans in New York Life and Hist. 1978 2(1): 11-16.* Everett Holmes became New York's first black mayor when he was elected to that office in his home town of Bridgewater in 1974. 1974-78

Holmes, Oliver Wendell (b.1902)

3195. Bell, Whitfield J., Jr. OLIVER WENDELL HOLMES. *Massachusetts Hist. Soc. Pro. 1982 94: 81-85.* The former executive director of the National Historical Publications Commission, Holmes received his undergraduate degree from Carleton College (1922), his graduate degree in History from Columbia (1956), and spent 25 years working in the National Archives in various capacities. Under his diligent stewardship, the commission issued numerous books and microform editions on outstanding Americans and important historical movements and institutions. 1920's-72

3196. Rhoads, James B. OLIVER WENDELL HOLMES. *Pro. of the Am. Antiquarian Soc. 1982 92(1): 28-32.* Outlines the career of Holmes, an encyclopedist, historian, and archivist—and no relation to the poet or jurist similarly named. His chief research focus was a study of the stagecoach, and most of his career was spent at the National Archives in a variety of administrative positions. From 1961 to 1972 he was executive director of the National Historical Publications Commission and was responsible for initiating many significant documentary projects. 1902-81

Holmes, Oliver Wendell (1841-1935)

3197. Auchincloss, Louis. THE LONG LIFE AND BROAD MIND OF MR. JUSTICE HOLMES. *Am. Heritage 1978 29(4): 68-77.* Oliver Wendell Holmes, Jr. (1841-1935), lived from before the Civil War until the presidency of Franklin D. Roosevelt. He was a Supreme Court Justice during 1902-32. 7 illus. 1841-1935

3198. Golding, Martin P. HOLMES'S JURISPRUDENCE: ASPECTS OF ITS DEVELOPMENT AND CONTINUITY. *Social Theory and Practice 1979 5(2): 183-207.* Examines the jurisprudence of Oliver Wendell Holmes (1841-1935) and its development in the 1870's, culminating in the publication of his *The Common Law,* based on 1880 lectures at the Lowell Institute in Boston. 1870-79

3199. Touster, Saul. HOLMES COMMON LAW: A CENTENNIAL VIEW. *Am. Scholar 1982 51(4): 521-531.* Oliver Wendell Holmes was neither a humane liberal democrat nor a protofascist. The basis of his judicial decisions was both positivistic and utilitarian. He was callous of the civil liberties of both blacks and aliens, and had no feelings toward Sacco and Vanzetti. His work shows no interest in social structure and its importance upon the law. The combination of Holmes's positivism and utilitarianism brought him dangerously close to the conclusion that might makes right. 1881-1935

Holmes, Theophilus Hunter

3200. Castel, Albert. THEOPHILUS HOLMES: PALLBEARER OF THE CONFEDERACY. *Civil War Times Illus. 1977 16(4): 10-17.* Reviews the Civil War career of Confederate General Theophilus Hunter Holmes, a veteran of the Mexican War. Holmes was a personal friend of President Jefferson Davis who assigned him to Lee's army in northern

Virginia. Holmes neither distinguished nor disgraced himself. Assigned to command of the trans-Mississippi region, Holmes refused to support Vicksburg during Grant's assault. In an effort to save face, he attacked Union forces at Helena, Arkansas, suffered a heavy defeat, and lost his command in consequence. Holmes was not of generalship caliber nor as inept as his detractors claim. Map, 7 photos. 1861-65

Holsman, Virginia

3201. Holsman, Virginia B. FOND RECOLLECTIONS. *Oregon Hist. Soc. 1979 80(4): 365-390.* Memoir of the author's childhood in Hillsboro, Oregon, with information on her mother, Josephine Schulmerich, and her parents, of Hillsboro, and her father, Thomas Bilyeu of Scio, Oregon, and his parents. The author includes information on child-rearing, recreation, and friends. 19c-1920's

Holt, D. C.

3202. Abbott, Collamer M. D. C. HOLT: "LIGHTNING CALCULATOR." *New-England Galaxy 1978 19(3): 19-26.* Emphasizes the amazing mathematics skills of D. C. Holt, born 16 February 1827 in Moretown, Vermont. Notes his Union Army service, 1861-62; his brief career as a teacher; and his life-long passion for solving mathematical problems. He died in 1910 in New Haven, Connecticut. 4 illus. 1827-1910

Holt, Ivan Lee

3203. Godbold, Albea. BISHOP IVAN LEE HOLT: WORLD TRAVELER AND DEVOTEE OF CHURCH COOPERATION. *Methodist Hist. 1983 21(2): 99-111.* Gives a brief biography of Methodist bishop and ecumenist Ivan Lee Holt, who spent most of his life in Missouri and Texas but also traveled worldwide advancing inter-Methodist and ecumenical cooperation. 1911-56

Holt, Jacob W.

3204. Bishir, Catherine W. JACOB W. HOLT: AN AMERICAN BUILDER. *Winterthur Portfolio 1981 16(1): 1-31.* Jacob W. Holt (d. 1880) was a notable architect in southern Virginia and central North Carolina. His design was practical, fitting the needs and desires of middle-class Americans. Holt did not represent an elite section, nor did his work fall into the category of folk architecture. He was able to combine traditional design with changing fashion. Based on county records, on-site inspections, family papers, and other sources; 44 illus., 56 notes. 1840-80

Holt, Matthew S.

3205. Coffey, William. MATTHEW S. HOLT: A WEST VIRGINIA INDIVIDUALIST. *West Virginia Hist. 1978 39(2-3): 200-209.* Matthew S. Holt (1850-1939) was an iconoclast of Lewis County, West Virginia, of Scotch-Irish background. He published the Weston *Republican,* 1882-93, but then supported William Jennings Bryan, and ran for Congress, governor, and senator as a Socialist after 1900. He supported atheism and pacifism, was a doctor, publisher, and horsebreeder, and served two terms as mayor of Weston. Primary and secondary sources; 39 notes. 1870-1939

Holton, Luther

3206. Klassen, Henry C. LUTHER HOLTON: MID-CENTURY MONTREAL RAILWAYMAN. *U. of Ottawa Q. [Canada] 1982 52(3): 317-339.* During the 1850's, Luther Holton amassed substantial wealth in railway contracting and land speculation, especially through his role as a developer of the Grand Trunk Railway. Holton helped establish the prevailing standard of railway morality, which allowed small projects to be amalgamated into a gigantic system that bred corruption, enriched contractors, and burdened Canada with debt. His election to Parliament in 1854 enabled him to support legislation aiding the construction of the Grand Trunk, a conflict of interest to which only a minority of his colleagues objected. Despite some inevitable criticism, Holton was generally regarded by the public as an agent of economic progress. Based on archival sources and contemporary newspaper accounts; 87 notes. 1850's

Holtzclaw, William

3207. Cooper, Arnie. "WE RISE UPON THE STRUCTURE WE OURSELVES HAVE BUILDED": WILLIAM H. HOLTZCLAW AND UTICA INSTITUTE, 1903-1915. *Journal of Mississippi History 1985 47(1): 15-33.* The formation of the Utica Normal and Industrial Institute for black students by William Holtzclaw in Utica, Hinds County, Mississippi, was based on the Tuskegee model of Booker T. Washington. Holtzclaw, who graduated from Tuskegee in 1898, determined to establish a similar institution in Mississippi. However, economic necessity as well as closed opportunities forced the young teacher to accept a position at Snow Hill, Alabama, until 1902, when he resolved to make another effort at creating an industrial educational facility in Mississippi. Details the development of the black institute, begun in 1903. Based on autobiographical materials of Holtzclaw, the Booker T. Washington Papers, US Bureau of Education reports, and secondary materials; 85 notes. 1903-15

3208. Cooper, Arnie. WILLIAM H. HOLTZCLAW: A BLACK EDUCATOR IN THE AGE OF BOOKER T. WASHINGTON. *Vitae Scholasticae 1983 2(1): 123-143.* Tells of William H. Holtzclaw's work to found and operate the Utica Normal and Industrial Institute in Utica, Mississippi. Discusses his thought as revealed in his autobiography, *The Black Man's Burden* (1915). 62 notes. Spanish summary. 1898-1915

Holubnychyi, Vsevolod

3209. Koropets'kyi, Ivan S. VSEVOLOD HOLUBNYCHYI (1928-1977) [Vsevolod Holubnychyi (1928-77)]. *Sučasnist [West Germany] 1977 (7-8): 154-161.* Describes the life and publications of Vsevolod Holubnychyi (1928-77), a Ukrainian American economist, historian, and politician. 1940's-77

Home, James and William

3210. Jamieson, Alan G. TWO SCOTTISH MARINES IN THE AMERICAN WAR: THE LETTERS OF WILLIAM AND JAMES HOME OF BROOMHOUSE, 1778-1782. *Mariner's Mirror [Great Britain] 1984 70(1): 21-30.* Letters of two brothers who served as Royal Marine officers during the American Revolution illustrate attitudes toward recruiting, discipline, Lord North, naval actions in the Caribbean, and the Battle of the Chesapeake. William Home died in 1782 while in the West Indies, probably of yellow fever. James survived through the French Revolution and Napoleonic wars, retiring as a lieutenant colonel in 1814. Based mainly on letters in the Scottish Record Office; 18 notes. 1775-85

Homer, Lucy Barnes

3211. Lupton, Mary Hosmer. JOURNAL OF LUCY BARNES HOMER: TUESDAY 18 APRIL-WEDNESDAY 19 APRIL 1775, CONCORD, MASSACHUSETTS. *Daughters of the Am. Revolution Mag. 1980 114(1): 14-17.* Provides a brief biography of Lucy Barnes Homer (b. 1742) and excerpts entries from her journal for Tuesday 18 April and Wednesday 19 April 1775, describing Concord's preparation for war. 1742-75

Homer, Winslow

3212. Adams, Henry. WINSLOW HOMER'S MYSTERY WOMAN. *Art & Antiques 1984 (Nov): 38-45.* Discusses the reclusive life of artist Winslow Homer and his paintings of a young, red-haired woman whom he had reputedly loved and lost to another man. Includes color photographic reproductions of these works painted in the 1870's, including *Woman with Porcelain Elephant, The New Novel, Woman Sewing, Woman Peeling a Lemon, Shall I Tell Your Fortune?, Thoughtful for Her Years,* and *Blackboard.* 1870's

3213. Adams, Henry. MORTAL THEMES: WINSLOW HOMER. *Art in Am. 1983 71(2): 112-126.* A psychobiographical analysis of Winslow Homer's life and art. 1850's-1910

3214. Fairburn, Gordon. WINSLOW HOMER AT PROUT'S NECK. *Horizon 1979 22(4): 56-63.* Chronicles Winslow Homer's (1836-1910) years at Prout's Neck, Maine, 1883-1910, and the sea which served as a model and inspiration for many of his paintings. 1883-1910

3215. Tatham, David. WINSLOW HOMER AND THE NEW ENGLAND POETS. *Pro. of the Am. Antiquarian Soc. 1979 89(2): 241-260.* Surveys Winslow Homer's career as a book illustrator. He made drawings for 30 books, but stopped after he was established as a major American painter. Homer also contributed hundreds of other drawings to periodicals. His illustrations for reissues of poems, the least known of all his art, are superbly executed and show his deft hand and poetic insight. Covers 1857-86. Primary sources; 26 illus., 35 notes. 1857-86

Honcharenko, Ahapi

3216. Buryk, Michael. AGAPIUS HONCHARENKO: PORTRAIT OF A UKRAINIAN AMERICAN KOZAK. *Ukrainian Q. 1976 32(1): 16-36.* Outlines the life of Agapius Honcharenko (1832-1916), first Ukrainian priest in the United States. Threatened and pursued by Russian authorities for his anti-tsarist writings in radical periodicals published abroad, Honcharenko emigrated to the United States in 1865. The first issue of his newspaper *The Alaska Herald* in 1868 marked the realization of his dream of establishing a Russian publishing house in America. However, Honcharenko's attacks on the monopolistic practices of American companies in Alaska and his criticism of anti-Chinese feeling in the West provoked slander and physical threats which forced his resignation as editor in 1872. Following this Honcharenko hoped to found a cooperative Ukrainian community in California, but this plan also failed. His remaining life was spent on his farm "Ukraina." 1832-1916

3217. Svit, I. OTETS' AHAPII HONCHARENKO [Father Ahapii Honcharenko]. *Ukraïns'kyi Istoryk 1976 13(1-4): 71-86.* Discusses the archival material and published accounts of Father Ahapii Honcharenko, the first political refugee from the Ukraine in North America. Father Honcharenko (whose real name was Andrii Humnyts'kyi) arrived in the United States in 1865. He began the regular celebration of Mass immediately and participated in politics. He set up a newspaper, the *Alaska Herald,* lobbied seniors on behalf of Ukrainian and other immigrants from the Russian Empire, and participated in the campaign against Russian tsarism with the support of M. Bakunin and N. Orgarev. 14 notes. ca 1865-1900

3218. Varvartsev, M. M. AHAPII HONCHARENKO—PIONER UKRAINS'KOI EMIHRATSII V SSHA [Ahapi Honcharenko: pioneer of Ukrainian emigration in the United States]. *Ukraïns'kyi Istorychnyi Zhurnal [USSR] 1969 (6): 115-118.* Assesses the life and works of Ahapi Honcharenko (1832-1916), who studied for the priesthood in Kiev in the Ukraine, traveled in Greece and England, and finally settled in the United States, where he published the newspaper *Alaska Herald.* 1853-1916

Hood, Adelyne

3219. Bufwack, Mary and Oermann, Robert K. ADELYNE HOOD: THE AMALGAMATION OF VAUDEVILLE AND FOLK TRADITIONS IN EARLY COUNTRY MUSIC. *JEMF Q. 1982 28(67-68): 116-130.* Discusses the life and musical career of American vaudeville, country, and hillbilly singer, fiddler, and recording artist Adelyne Hood (1897-1958). 1915-58

Hood, Humphrey

3220. Gegenheimer, Elizabeth, ed. SELECTED LETTERS OF HUMPHREY HOOD, LITCHFIELD PHYSICIAN. *J. of the Illinois State Hist. Soc. 1979 72(3): 193-212, (4): 242-256.* Part I, 1852-1856. Reprints 10 letters from Dr. Humphrey Hood to his brother Benjamin during 1852-56, describing the Underground Railroad, skepticism about the popular "spirits" and "medium" activities, his medical practice in Litchfield, his marriage to Matilda Jackson, the drowning death of one of his brothers, and the proslavery sentiments of his brother John in Virgina. Part II, 1862-1867. Reprints five letters. Dr. Hood, a surgeon with the Union Army at Fort Pickering, Tennessee, 1862-66, wrote to his brother Benjamin about General Ulysses S. Grant, the Copperheads, President Abraham Lincoln, and the purchase by Illinois drafted men of substitutes not physically able to perform their military duties. At the end of the war Hood suffered grief not only for Lincoln but also for his own brother John, who died a prisoner at Johnson's Island. Dr. Hood returned to Litchfield and lived a long, productive life. Primary sources; 5 letters, 8 illus., 7 photos, 77 notes. 1852-67

Hood, Irene Jerome

3221. Contiguglia, Georgianna. GENTEEL ARTIST: IRENE JEROME HOOD CAPTURES IMAGES OF HER LIFE AND FAMILY. *Colorado Heritage 1982 (1): 78-102.* Surveys the life and work—sketching, painting and photography—of Irene Jerome Hood especially after she moved to Denver in 1892. She was largely self-trained. Although she painted portraits, domestic interiors, and page illuminations, "she favored flower studies and small landscapes." Childless, she frequently sketched and photographed her brother John's children, and many of her paintings document the furnishings of a typical Victorian home of her era. Based on Hood's artistic works; chart, 5 sketches, 19 photos, 23 color plates. 1892-1945

Hood, Solomon Porter

3222. McBride, David. SOLOMON PORTER HOOD, 1853-1943: BLACK MISSIONARY, EDUCATOR AND MINISTER TO LIBERIA. *J. of the Lancaster County Hist. Soc. 1980 84(1): 2-9.* Biography of Solomon Porter Hood, a black Republican, who was appointed as Minister Resident and Consul General to Liberia in 1921; he was one of President Warren G. Harding's five black appointees to the State Department. ca 1870-1943

Hook, Sidney.

3223. Abel, Lionel. SIDNEY HOOK'S CAREER (THE PHILOSOPHER IN POLITICS). *Partisan Review 1985 52(2): 31-41.* Discusses the political theory of philosopher Sidney Hook as it has developed over the years. Early in his career, Hook substituted Dewey for Hegel in the Marxist system. Since 1945, his views have strayed farther from Communism. Like others who started as philosophical leftists, Hook underestimated the philosophical and political power of nationalism. 1930-84

Hooker, Susannah Garbrand

3224. Warren, William Lamson. CONNECTICUT'S FIRST LADY: SUSANNAH GARBRAND HOOKER. *Connecticut Antiquarian 1985 37(1): 5-34.* Describes in detail the life of Susannah Hooker, wife of the Reverend Thomas Hooker, first minister of Hartford, Connecticut, from her birth in England to her death in Connecticut. 1590's-1660's

Hooper, George W.

3225. Hitchcock, Bert. REDISCOVERING ALABAMA LITERATURE: THREE WRITERS OF LAFAYETTE. *Alabama Rev. 1983 36(3): 175-194.* ca 1850-1900
*For abstract see **Burton, Robert Wilton***

Hooper, William

3226. Kneip, Robert Charles, III. "William Hooper, 1742-1790: Misunderstood Patriot." Tulane U. 1980. 511 pp. *DAI 1981 41(9): 4141-A.* DA8028498 1760-90

Hooton, Elizabeth

3227. Scheffler, Judith. PRISON WRITINGS OF EARLY QUAKER WOMEN. *Quaker Hist. 1984 73(2): 25-37.* 1651-83
*For abstract see **Blaugdone, Barbara***

Hoover, Herbert C.

3228. Arnold, Peri E. THE "GREAT ENGINEER" AS ADMINISTRATOR: HERBERT HOOVER AND MODERN BUREAUCRACY. *Rev. of Pol. 1980 42(3): 329-348.* Contrary to most scholars' interpretations, Herbert C. Hoover was a modern rather than a traditional administrator. Hoover offers the lesson that government might be better attacked for what it does rather than for the means through which it operates." 51 notes. 1917-32

3229. Cuff, Robert D. THE DILEMMAS OF VOLUNTARISM: HOOVER AND THE PORK-PACKING AGREEMENT OF 1917-1919. *Agric. Hist. 1979 53(4): 727-747.* Herbert C. Hoover's appointment as Food Administrator during World War I tested his belief in voluntary restraint of business. Recalcitrant pork packers who wanted to extract the maximum profit from wartime business made it difficult to control prices. But in order to justify his philosophy, Hoover was forced to defend the packers against the Federal Trade Commission and others in the administration who wanted sweeping reform of the industry and greater government control. The short wartime crisis and its accompanying prosperity made his voluntary approach look more successful than it would be during the Great Depression. 53 notes. 1917-19

3230. Garvey, Daniel E. SECRETARY HOOVER AND THE QUEST FOR BROADCAST REGULATION. *Journalism Hist. 1976 3(3): 66-70, 85.* Examines the role of Secretary of Commerce Herbert C. Hoover in the formulation of regulations to control American broadcasting, particularly the Radio Act (US, 1927). 1921-28

3231. Ginzl, David James. "Herbert Hoover and Republican Patronage Politics in the South, 1928-1932." Syracuse U. 1977. 398 pp. *DAI 1978 38(8): 5004-A.* 1928-32

3232. Hamilton, David E. HERBERT HOOVER AND THE GREAT DROUGHT OF 1930. *J. of Am. Hist. 1982 68(4): 850-875.* Although the Great Drought of 1930 provided Herbert C. Hoover with an excellent opportunity to improve his image, Hoover's handling of the disaster was one of the sadder episodes of his public career and presidency. Because of Hoover's stubbornness and inflexibility regarding the proper role of the federal government in disaster relief, he pursued a policy that blinded him to the suffering of thousands of Americans. Hoover's handling of the disaster helped establish the image of him as a callous ultraconservative. Based on many primary sources including diaries, letters, and the Hoover Papers; 81 notes. 1930

3233. Hoxie, R. Gordon. HERBERT HOOVER: MULTINATIONAL MAN. *Presidential Studies Q. 1977 7(1): 49-52.* Surveys Herbert C. Hoover's public life during 1917-46. During World War I he was the US Food Administrator. He again coordinated food supplies for 38 war-torn nations following World War II. Although President Hoover favored arbitration and conciliation in foreign affairs, he never hesitated to use force when American security was threatened. Franklin D. Roosevelt pursued aspects of Hoover's foreign policy, such as maintenance of a Pacific battleship fleet and nonvoting membership in the League of Nations' Advisory Committee on the Far East. Based on Hoover's memoirs and on secondary sources; 18 notes. 1917-46

3234. Johnson, James P. HERBERT HOOVER: THE ORPHAN AS CHILDREN'S FRIEND. *Prologue 1980 12(4): 193-206.* That Herbert C. Hoover was orphaned before he was 10 was a key factor in his life. As an apparent result of his unhappy childhood, Hoover developed a passion for working with and for children. This passion was evidenced throughout his life, resulting in such efforts as organizing large-scale assistance to civilian war victims as director of the Committee for Relief in Belgium, setting up a European Children's Fund to feed starving children as director of the American Relief Agency, providing food to millions of Russians during 1921-23 under the Food and Remittance Plan, combining private volunteer groups into the American Child Health Association, and convening 2,500 delegates to a National Conference on Child Health as President. Based on Hoover public statements, Presidential personal papers, President Hoover files, newspapers, and interviews; illus., 10 photos, 84 notes. 1914-31

3235. Krog, Carl E. "ORGANIZING THE PRODUCTION OF LEISURE": HERBERT HOOVER AND THE CONSERVATION MOVEMENT IN THE 1920S. *Wisconsin Mag. of Hist. 1984 67(3): 199-218.* Portrays Herbert C. Hoover as a conservationist bridging the gap between the conservation movement of the Progressive Era and that of the New Deal. Hoover's lifelong enthusiasm for fishing and outdoor activity motivated him to play a leading role in the National Outdoor Recreation conferences of the 1920's and to become president of the National Parks Association. As secretary of commerce from 1921 to 1929 and as president from 1929 to 1933, Hoover demonstrated a strong commitment to conservation and his policies foreshadowed many programs of the Roosevelt administration, including the Civilian Conservation Corps. Hoover believed that healthful, fulfilling use of leisure time was a natural concomitant to efficiency in the workplace. Based primarily on the papers of the National Parks Association, the National Outdoor Recreation conferences, and the Commerce Department; 12 illus., 46 notes. 1920-32

3236. Margulies, Herbert F. THE COLLABORATION OF HERBERT HOOVER AND IRVINE LENROOT, 1921-1928. *North Dakota Q. 1977 45(3): 30-46.* Discusses the personal and political friendship between Irvine L. Lenroot and Herbert Hoover while the former was a Senator from Wisconsin and the latter held various cabinet posts until his election to the presidency; includes discussion of their collaboration on foreign affairs, agricultural issues, and the economy. 1921-28

3237. Schacht, John N. FOUR MEN FROM IOWA. *Palimpsest 1982 63(1): 30-31.* Summarizes the lives and careers of President Herbert C. Hoover, United Mine Workers President John L. Lewis, Secretary of Agriculture Henry A. Wallace, and New Deal administrator and presidential advisor Harry Hopkins. 1870's-1960's

3238. Zieger, Robert H. HERBERT HOOVER, THE WAGE-EARNER, AND THE "NEW ECONOMIC SYSTEM," 1919-1929. *Business Hist. Rev. 1977 51(2): 161-189.* Herbert Hoover regarded the labor issue as the greatest challenge facing American capitalism, feared union militancy as "wasteful and authoritarian," and favored employee representation systems in industry. During the 1920's, however, he was "curiously silent" on the subject, apparently unwilling to seriously examine the real nature of representation plans. Attributes this inaction in large part to Hoover's natural affinity for the new corporate managers who were the sponsors of welfare capitalism and company-sponsored unions. Based on Hoover papers and writings as well as other contemporary sources; 62 notes. 1919-29

Hoover, J. Edgar

3239. Kaspi, André. LE FBI DE JOHN EDGAR HOOVER [John Edgar Hoover's FBI]. *Histoire [France] 1983 (54): 10-23.* Recounts the career of J. Edgar Hoover as director of the Federal Bureau of Investigation from 1924-72 and the bureau's dealings with alleged subversive activities in the United States. 1924-72

3240. Turnbaugh, Roy. THE FBI AND HARRY ELMER BARNES: 1936-1944. *Historian 1980 42(3): 385-398.* 1936-44
*For abstract see **Barnes, Harry Elmer***

Hoover, Jacob "Jake"

3241. Jensen, Earl L. RUSSELL'S FIRST FRIEND IN MONTANA. *Montana 1984 34(3): 24-33.* In 1881 Charles M. Russell, the cowboy artist, met Jacob "Jake" Hoover along the Judith River in central Montana. Hoover, an experienced trapper and prospector, invited the tenderfoot Russell to live with him, and they became close friends. During the 1880's, Russell spent a great deal of time at Hoover's cabin, first as a cabin mate, later as a regular guest. From Hoover, who had come to Montana from Iowa at the age of 16, Russell learned the skills needed to survive on the Montana frontier. Hoover, who appeared in several Russell paintings, joined the gold rush to Alaska in the late 1890's, then returned to Seattle in 1908, where he remained until his death in 1925. Based on a 1924 Jake Hoover interview, Great Falls *Tribune,* 13 January 1903, and Montana Historical Society Archives; 6 illus., photo, 29 notes. 1880-1925

Hoover, Titus

3242. Thompson, Tad. AT A DISTANCE TO "WORLDLY" WAYS. *Mennonite Life 1984 39(4): 14-16.* Describes the life of Old Order Mennonite Titus Hoover, who owns Willow Brook Farms in Port Treverton, Pennsylvania. Hoover follows traditional Old Order ways, such as forgoing telephones, newspapers, radios, and televisions, but makes concessions to the outside world by selling his cantaloupes wholesale to buyers in Pennsylvania, New York, and Boston. 5 photos. 1984

Hope, Lugenia D. Burns

3243. Rouse, Jacqueline Anne. "Lugenia D. Burns Hope: A Black Female Reformer in the South, 1871-1947." Emory U. 1983. 235 pp. *DAI 1984 44(8): 2506-A.* DA8328069 1871-1947

Hopkins, Frances Ann Beechey

3244. Rand, Margaret. REDISCOVERING VOYAGEUR ARTIST FRANCES HOPKINS. *Can. Geog. [Canada] 1982 102(3): 22-29.* Biography of little-known English-born Canadian artist, Frances Ann Beechey Hopkins (1838-1919), most famous for her watercolors and sketches of the Canadian voyageurs. 18c-19c

Hopkins, Harry Lloyd

3245. Mal'kov, V. L. GARRI GOPKINS: STRANITSY POLITICHESKOI BIOGRAFII [Harry Hopkins: the pages of political biography]. *Novaia i Noevishaia Istoriia [USSR] 1979 (2): 124-144.* Discusses the life, activity, and ideas of Harry Hopkins, one of the closest advisors to President Franklin D. Roosevelt and the main proponent of the New Deal policies in the United States in the 1930's. Prior to his political career, Hopkins worked for charity organizations in New York and this enabled him to understand the limitations of the system of private monopoly capitalism. After Roosevelt's 1932 victory, he supervised the new administration's policies for alleviation of poverty and unemployment. Hopkins's influence grew but he realized that a mere tinkering with the system produced insignificant results incommensurable with the disastrous products of the great recession. Article to be continued. 82 notes. 1910's-38

3246. Schacht, John N. FOUR MEN FROM IOWA. *Palimpsest 1982 63(1): 30-31.* 1870's-1960's
*For abstract see **Hoover, Herbert C.***

3247. Tuttle, Dwight William. "Harry L. Hopkins and Anglo-American-Soviet Relations, 1941-1945." Washington State U. 1980. 342 pp. *DAI 1980 41(6): 2741-A.* DA8025966 1941-45

Hopkins, James L.

3248. Hoar, Jay S. LOUISIANA'S LAST BOYS IN GRAY. *Louisiana Hist. 1978 19(3): 336-352.* 1824-1953
For abstract see ***Powell, Frank Eli***

Hopkins, John Henry

3249. Mullin, Robert Bruce. RITUALISM, ANTI-ROMANISM, AND THE LAW IN JOHN HENRY HOPKINS. *Hist. Mag. of the Protestant Episcopal Church 1981 50(4): 377-390.* John Henry Hopkins was Episcopal bishop of Vermont during 1832-68. During his episcopacy, he participated in numerous controversies that arose in the Episcopal Church. Among the major ones this study centers on are his views on ritualism and Roman Catholicism. He attempted to anchor the teaching of the church upon the unchangeable law of divine truth as found in Scripture and tradition. By so doing he hoped to be free to examine these and other questions facing the church. He employed this methodology to question Roman Catholic teachings and to defend ritualistic practices. What seemed contradictory to others was consistency to him. He had few disciples, and he left no successors in his peculiar emphasis on law and doctrine. Nevertheless he made a significant impact upon the 19th-century Episcopal Church. Based on the writings of Hopkins and secondary studies; picture, 25 notes. 1832-68

Hopkins, Samuel

3250. Conforti, Joseph. SAMUEL HOPKINS AND THE REVOLUTIONARY ANTISLAVERY MOVEMENT. *Rhode Island Hist. 1979 38(2): 39-49.* A Congregational minister in Newport, Rhode Island, Samuel Hopkins, began speaking out against slavery and the slave trade in the 1770's and went on to become a leading figure in the New England antislavery movement until his death in 1803. Based on manuscripts in New Haven, Newport, New York City, Philadelphia, and Providence, newspapers, pamphlets, and Hopkins's writings; 6 illus., 37 notes. ca 1770-1803

Hopkins, Stephen

3251. Millar, John F. STEPHEN HOPKINS, AN ARCHITECT OF INDEPENDENCE, 1707-1785. *Newport Hist. 1980 53(1): 24-36.* Examines the political career of Rhode Island Governor Stephen Hopkins; his achievements have been largely ignored, yet it was Hopkins who took the lead against the Sugar Act of 1764, invited other colonies to join in the Stamp Act Congress of 1765, and was a delegate to the First Continental Congress of 1774. 1750's-85

Hopkinson, Francis

3252. Thomas, Ruth Colby. MUSIC OF THE REVOLUTIONARY TIMES. *Daughters of the Am. Revolution Mag. 1984 118(10): 720-721, 773, 790.* 1746-1800
For abstract see ***Billings, William***

Hopper, Edward

3253. Canaday, John. THE SOLO VOYAGE OF EDWARD HOPPER, AMERICAN REALIST. *Smithsonian 1980 11(6): 126-137.* The American painter Edward Hopper (1882-1967) was a one-man school identified with no particular art movement other than the broadly defined term of realism. Simplification and harsh light characterized his style. He was the painter of loneliness. 1906-60

3254. Hooton, Bruce Duff. AMERICA'S CREATIVE REALIST. *Horizon 1980 23(9): 44-55.* Discusses Edward Hopper (d. 1967), "the most penetrating chronicler of American life between the two world wars," in anticipation of a retrospective of his work at the Whitney Museum of American Art. 1899-1967

3255. Silberman, Rob. EDWARD HOPPER AND THE IMPLIED OBSERVER. *Art in Am. 1981 69(7): 148-154.* Describes the paintings of Edward Hopper and their relation to Ashcan School realism, French realism, impressionism, and commercial illustration; discusses Hopper's themes and his preoccupation with the psychology of travel during 1914-63. 1914-63

Hopwood, Avery

3256. Sharrar, Jack Frederick. "Avery Hopwood, American Playwright (1882-1928)." U. of Utah 1984. 465 pp. *DAI 1984 45(1): 21-A.* DA8409544 1900's-28

Hornaday, William Temple

3257. Dolph, James A. A DEDICATION TO THE MEMORY OF WILLIAM TEMPLE HORNADAY, 1854-1937. *Arizona and the West 1983 25(3): 208-212.* Stuffing a great white pelican for his college president launched William Temple Hornaday on a career as a prominent Western wildlife preservationist. He established museums, zoos, professional societies, and national game preserves. He collected specimens for mounting, and live birds and animals for zoos and preserves. Hornaday also lobbied for legislation and wrote extensively to educate the public on the importance of preservation. Aside from many significant honors, his enduring monuments are the buffalo and antelope, species that he helped preserve, and the migrating birds whose habitats he helped save from destruction. Illus., biblio. 1874-1937

Hornbein, Philip

3258. Abrams, Jeanne. PHILIP HORNBEIN: A JEWISH NEW DEALER IN DENVER. *Western States Jewish Hist. 1984 17(1): 35-47.* A biography of attorney Philip Hornbein of Denver, with special emphasis on his legal career, his support of liberal Democratic causes in Denver, and his efforts on behalf of Franklin Roosevelt. Based on interviews and newspaper accounts; 61 notes. ca 1900-62

Horner, John B.

3259. Otto, Dorothy Godfrey. JOHN B. HORNER, OREGON HISTORIAN. *Oregon Hist. Q. 1981 82(4): 369-382.* Biographical sketch of John B. Horner (1856-1933), professor of history at Oregon Agricultural College (now Oregon State University) at Corvallis for 43 years. Based on family reminiscences; 4 photos, 19 notes. 1856-1933

Horner, Ralph Cecil

3260. Ross, Brian R. RALPH CECIL HORNER: A METHODIST SECTARIAN DEPOSED, 1887-95. *Methodist Hist. 1977 16(1): 21-32.* Ralph Cecil Horner (1854-1921) was ordained a minister in the Methodist Church in 1887 and was suspended seven years later for evangelistic activities. In 1900 he created a separate denominational group, the Holiness Movement Church, in Canada. 24 notes. 1887-1921

3261. Ross, Brian R. RALPH CECIL HORNER: A METHODIST SECTARIAN DEPOSED. *J. of the Can. Church Hist. Soc. [Canada] 1977 19(1-2): 94-103.* Finding salvation through an evangelical experience in 1872, Ralph C. Horner dedicated himself to winning souls through evangelism and was ordained a minister in the Montreal Conference of the Methodist Church of Canada in 1887. Horner was very successful as an evangelist but found considerable problems with the authorities of the church. They found his methods excessive and discovered that he would not follow their orders. Though told to accept an assignment as a regular minister, Horner refused to do so. The Conference leaders tried to work out an arrangement with him but to no avail. In 1894 Horner was deposed from the ministry of the Methodist Church. Ultimately, in 1900, he organized his own successful Holiness Movement Church in Canada. His strong belief in freedom and his self-confidence in the rightness of his mission made him unable to accept direction from others. Primary sources; 24 notes. This issue is *J. of the Can. Church Hist. Soc.* 1977 19(1-2) and *Bull. of the United Church of Can.* 1977 26. 1887-1921

Horsefield, Ray

3262. Horsefield, Ray. MOONIAS'S HONEYMOON. *Beaver [Canada] 1978 309(2): 10-15* Reminiscences of Horsefield, born in England, and ordained in Saskatchewan in 1926. A few days after his ordination, Horsefield took his new bride via river boat to Sturgeon Landing, The Pas, and other localities. Includes details of life in the vicinity in the 1920's, parish work, learning the Cree language, and providing educational and medical services to the Cree Indians. *Moonias* is Cree for "greenhorn." 8 illus., map. 1920's-70's

Horstmann, Ignatius F.

3263. Lackner, Joseph H. "Bishop Ignatius F. Horstmann and the Americanization of the Roman Catholic Church in the United States." Saint Louis U. 1978. 499 pp. *DAI 1978 39(6): 3648-A.* 1892-1908

Horton, Albert Clinton

3264. Ellenberger, Matthew. ILLUMINATING THE LESSER LIGHTS: NOTES ON THE LIFE OF ALBERT CLINTON HORTON. *Southwestern Historical Quarterly 1985 88(4): 363-386.* Although Albert Clinton Horton ran from the field of battle at Goliad in 1836, this act of prudence or cowardice did not harm his political or economic fortunes. After the revolution, Horton served the Republic of Texas as a senator and the State of Texas as lieutenant governor and acting governor. He helped establish Baylor University, and he became one of the wealthiest planters and slave owners in the state. He died on 1 September 1865, an ardent supporter of the Confederacy. His life is an example of the fortune and prominence that could be gained with hard work and luck in antebellum Texas. 2 illus., 58 notes. 1830-65

Horton, Lydia Knapp

3265. MacPhail, Elizabeth C. LYDIA KNAPP HORTON: A "LIBERATED" WOMAN IN EARLY SAN DIEGO. *J. of San Diego Hist. 1981 27(1): 17-42.* Lydia Knapp Horton (1843-1926), wife of the founder of modern San Diego, Alonzo E. Horton, spent her years in San Diego (1869-1926) as a community activist and artist. 1869-1926

Horydczak, Theodor

3266. Brannan, Beverly W. DISCOVERING THEODOR HORYDCZAK'S WASHINGTON. *Q. J. of the Lib. of Congress 1979 36(1): 38-67.* Little is known of Theodor Horydczak's private life, except that he was probably an Eastern European immigrant who served in the Signal Corps and was employed by the Army in Washington, D.C., before becoming a commercial photographer there. His photographs of technological developments, of mechanization and streamlining in consumer products, of the architecture of private, commercial, and federal buildings, and of suburban growth and everyday life in the nation's capital provide a record of changes during the 1920's, 1930's, and 1940's. His collection of prints and negatives, both black-and-white and color, was given to the Library of Congress in 1973. Based on the Theodor Horydczak collection in the Prints and Photographs Division of the Library of Congress; 34 photos, 13 notes. 1920's-40's

Hoskins, Charles R.

3267. Hoskins, Charles R. and Wakefield, George P., ed. A GREAT LAKES FISHERMAN. *Inland Seas 1979 35(4): 250-257; 1980 36(1): 22-28, (2): 103-110.* Part I. Reprints, with introduction, the memoirs of Hoskins, a Lake Erie gill net fisherman. In 1915, he purchased part interest in a fishing boat. Later, he had two others built. He retired in 1960. Describes both the annual fishing pattern and a typical day. 2 photos. Part II. Hoskins's account about fishing on Lake Erie, 1921-42. Part III. Captain Hoskins discussed problems encountered when fishing before the ice has melted and described different nets used. 1915-60

Hostos, Eugenio María de

3268. Henríquez Ureña, Camila. LA PEREGRINACIÓN DE EUGENIO MARÍA DE HOSTOS, [The journey of Eugenio María de Hostos]. *Casa de las Américas [Cuba] 1974 14(82): 6-17.* Discusses the life and career of Eugenio María de Hostos (1839-1903), Puerto Rican hero of independence, particularly emphasizing his travels and his ideas. ca 1860-1903

Houck, James D.

3269. Carlson, Frances C. JAMES D. HOUCK: THE SHEEP KING OF CAVE CREEK. *J. of Arizona Hist. 1980 21(1): 43-62.* Entrepreneur James D. Houck (1847-1921), a pioneer in the Arizona sheep-shearing industry, founded Houck, Arizona, and established the Cave Creek, Arizona, sheep station. Houck symbolizes Arizona pioneers. 9 illus. 1870-1921

Hough, Emerson

3270. Wylder, Delbert E. EMERSON HOUGH AS CONSERVATIONIST AND MUCKRAKER. *Western Am. Lit. 1977 12(2): 93-109.* Emerson Hough was one of the first American writers to become aware of conservation as a natural need. Through his experience, he gradually developed an understanding of the interrelationship of all forms of life. 1870's-1923

Hough, Romeyn Beck

3271. Dengler, Harry William. REMEMBERING ROMEYN BECK HOUGH. *J. of NAL Assoc. 1980 5(3-4): 84-87.* Biography of Romeyn Beck Hough (1857-1924), a medical doctor in upstate New York "who first conceived the need for conservation in America" and spent his life working to establish the forestry profession. 1857-1924

Houghton, Alanson Bigelow

3272. Jones, Kenneth Paul. ALANSON B. HOUGHTON AND THE RUHR CRISIS: THE DIPLOMACY OF POWER AND MORALITY. Jones, Kenneth Paul, ed. *U.S. Diplomats in Europe, 1919-1941* (Santa Barbara, Calif.: ABC-CLIO, 1981): 25-39. Alanson Bigelow Houghton (1863-1941) was America's ambassador to Germany from February 1922 to February 1925. Describes his role in the Ruhr reparations crisis of 1923-24, an instructive example of what recent scholarship has argued concerning the legend of American isolationism. Republican policymakers were deeply involved in the search for peace in Europe, fearful of Congressional opposition to direct governmental intervention, and confident of the ability of the private sector to provide a businesslike solution to Europe's difficulties. Primary sources; 67 notes. 1923-24

House, Edward Mandell

3273. Vaughn, Stephen. ARTHUR BULLARD AND THE CREATION OF THE COMMITTEE ON PUBLIC INFORMATION. *New Jersey Hist. 1979 97(1): 45-53.* 1917-18
*For abstract see **Bullard, Arthur***

Houston, Charles Hamilton

3274. Hastie, William H. CHARLES HAMILTON HOUSTON (1895-1950). *Crisis 1979 86(6): 274-275.* Charles Hamilton Houston graduated at age 19 Phi Beta Kappa from Amherst College. He earned two law degrees from Harvard University and a third from the University of Madrid. He served as dean of Howard University Law School. Later, as special counsel for the NAACP until 1939, he was the architect and dominant force of the NAACP's legal program. Although he died four years before the *Brown* (1954) decision, he touched the lives of 28 of the 30 lawyers in the Supreme Court that day. He trained lawyers to go into the courts for their people. 1895-1950

3275. —. AMHERST COLLEGE HONORS CHARLES HAMILTON HOUSTON. *Crisis 1979 86(6): 276-278.* Reprints and introduces Thurgood Marshall's 6 April 1978 tribute to Charles Hamilton Houston (1895-1950), a Phi Beta Kappa graduate of Amherst College, graduate of Harvard Law School, administrator of the Howard University School of Law during 1929-35, special counsel for the NAACP during 1935-40, and a dedicated and effective teacher and civil rights lawyer in his private practice and public service. Reprinted from the Spring 1978 *Amherst Magazine.* 1910's-50

Houston, James D.

3276. Houston, Jeanne W. and Houston, James D.; Friedson, Anthony, interviewer. NO MORE FAREWELLS: AN INTERVIEW WITH JEANNE AND JAMES HOUSTON. *Biography 1984 7(1): 50-73.* 1942-45
*For abstract see **Houston, Jeanne W.***

Houston, Jeanne W.

3277. Houston, Jeanne W. and Houston, James D.; Friedson, Anthony, interviewer. NO MORE FAREWELLS: AN INTERVIEW WITH JEANNE AND JAMES HOUSTON. *Biography 1984 7(1): 50-73.* Jeanne Wakatsuki Houston and James D. Houston discuss with Anthony Friedson the genesis of *Farewell to Manzanar* (1973)—their account of Jeanne's internment at a Japanese-American relocation center in Inyo County, California, during World War II. 6 photos. 1942-45

Houston, John

3278. Wolfe, Patrick. TRAMP PRINTER EXTRAORDINARY: BRITISH COLUMBIA'S JOHN "TRUTH" HOUSTON. *BC Studies [Canada] 1978-79 (40): 5-31.* John Houston (1850-1910) was an active politician—four-term mayor, two-term provincial legislator, and president of British Columbia's Conservative Party. He was many other things as well, but foremost was a crusading frontier newspaper man on both sides of the border. He established seven newspapers in the province itself and used them to tackle the giant railroads, the provincial government, or any other source of "hypocrisy." He championed the "common" man. 164 notes. 1888-1910

Houston, Mike

3279. Hamilton, Charles Henry. THERE GOES MIKE HOUSTON. *Virginia Cavalcade 1980 29(4): 156-163.* Biography of Virginia newspaperman Mike Houston (1901-75), focusing on his adventures as a columnist for the *Richmond News Leader* from 1960 until his death. 1930's-75

Houston, Sam

3280. Corn, James F. SAM HOUSTON: THE RAVEN. *J. of Cherokee Studies 1981 6(1): 34-49.* Sam Houston's early life among Western Cherokees of North Carolina included their adoption of him. Named Ku-lanu (the Raven) by Oo-loo-to-ka (John Jolly), Houston led the Cherokees against the Creeks in the Battle of Horseshoe Bend (27 May 1814), served as Cherokee representative in Washington, D.C., and mediated border disputes for the Cherokees with Pawnees and Osages. Later, Houston traveled to Texas, led settlers for independence, and became Texas's first president. 3 sketches, 4 photos, 41 notes. 1807-63

3281. Frantz, Joe B. TEXAS GIANT OF CONTRADICTIONS: SAM HOUSTON. *Am. West 1980 17(4): 4-13, 61-65.* Sam (Samuel) Houston (1793-1863) lived a robust and colorful life on the stages of Tennessee, national, and Texas politics, the military, and the Cherokee Indians. His life is a study of extremes and contradictions: a "two-fisted drinker," he became a temperance lecturer; an Indian fighter, at various times he lived with the Cherokee; a Mexican hater, he was magnanimous to his captured enemy commander, General Santa Anna; a devoted husband, he became a bigamist. 7 illus., biblio. note. 1807-63

3282. Kreneck, Thomas Heard. "Sam Houston's Quest for Personal Harmony: An Interpretation." Bowling Green State U. 1981. 446 pp. *DAI 1981 42(1): 347-A.* DA8114534 1813-63

Hovenden, Thomas

3283. Terhune, Anne Gregory. "Thomas Hovenden (1840-1895) and Late-Nineteenth Century American Genre Painting." City U. of New York 1983. 645 pp. *DAI 1983 44(2): 550-A.* DA8312377 1870's-95

Hovey, Alvin P.

3284. Hess, Earl J. ALVIN P. HOVEY AND ABRAHAM LINCOLN'S "BROKEN PROMISES": THE POLITICS OF PROMOTION. *Indiana Mag. of Hist. 1984 80(1): 35-50.* During the Civil War, Alvin P. Hovey was one of many political generals who sought promotion in the Union Army. President Lincoln never kept an initial promise to promote Hovey to major general, and eventually Hovey tried to force the promotion by threatening to resign. The incident illustrates Lincoln's balancing of political and military necessities. Hovey's attitude shifted from one of military competency and enthusiasm for the Union cause to one of a carping and inefficient commander. Primary sources; 33 notes, illus. 1861-65

Howard, Eugene A.

3285. Howard, Eugene A. PERSONAL RECOLLECTIONS OF MILWAUKEE COUNTY PARK SYSTEM, 1924-1960. *Milwaukee Hist. 1982 5(1-2): 3-43.* Eugene A. Howard, who was instrumental in developing the Milwaukee County park system, recalls his 36 years of service. 1924-60

Howard, James H.

3286. Baker, Russell. JAMES H. HOWARD. *Arkansas Hist. Q. 1976 35(4): 360-365.* James H. Howard was an Arkadelphia shoemaker who turned politician just after the Civil War. A Republican who advocated black equality, Howard lost some support in the 1870 state senatorial election, but he still won his seat. During 1873 a new county was created from parts of Polk, Pike, Hampstead, and Sevier counties. It was named Howard County in honor of the senator. He apparently retired from politics in 1874 and left Arkansas in 1882. Based on public records, newspaper accounts, and secondary sources; 34 notes. 1865-82

Howard, Joseph Kinsey

3287. Roeder, Richard B. JOSEPH KINSEY HOWARD AND HIS VISION OF THE WEST. *Montana 1980 30(1): 2-11.* Newspaperman and author Joseph Kinsey Howard (1906-51) believed Montana and the rural West provided the "last stand against urban technological tedium" for the individual. He believed small towns provided a democratic bulwark for society, and his publications reflect a strong belief in the necessity to identify and preserve a region's cultural heritage. Howard worked first as an editor on the *Great Falls Leader,* later for the Montana Study (a statewide community development project), and as a freelance writer. His major publications, *Montana High, Wide and Handsome, Montana Margins,* and (posthumously) *Strange Empire,* coupled with numerous speeches and magazine articles, provide eloquent forums for the ideas of community awareness and identity, encouraging readers to retain an idealistic vision contesting the deadening demands of the modern world. Based on Joseph Kinsey Howard Papers in the Montana Historical Society, Helena, Howard's publications, contemporary newspapers and secondary sources; 9 illus., 25 notes. 1920's-51

Howard, Milo Barrett, Jr.

3288. Adams, Emily S. MEMORIAL TO A TIMELESS MAN. *Alabama Hist. Q. 1982 44(1-2): 9-17.* The life and contributions of Milo Barrett Howard, Jr. (1933-81), director of the Alabama Department of Archives and History, are reviewed. Based mostly on newspaper articles; 39 notes. 1933-81

Howard, Richard P.

3289. Howard, Richard P. TRIALS OF A DEPRESSION ERA DOCTOR. *Rendezvous 1984 20(1): 78-82.* The author recounts his experiences as a young doctor in Pocatello, Idaho, during the Great Depression. His first position in a local clinic was difficult and low-paying. After starting a private practice, even though some patients could not or did not pay their bills, he discovered that his profession could be lucrative. Photo. 1930's

Howard, Robert

3290. Silvia, Philip, Jr. ROBERT HOWARD, LABOR LEADER. *Spinner: People and Culture in Southeastern Massachusetts 1984 3: 142-145.* Prints a biography of textile worker and labor movement leader Robert Howard, focusing on his work to organize the textile industry, beginning in Fall River, Massachusetts. 1875-1902

Howard, William Forrest

3291. Ruckman, Jo Ann. INDIAN SCHOOLING IN NEW MEXICO IN THE 1890S: LETTERS OF A TEACHER IN THE INDIAN SERVICE. *New Mexico Hist. Rev. 1981 56(1): 37-69.* The introduction discusses the life and career of William Forrest Howard (d. 1947), a young teacher who taught Indians at the Dawes Institute near Santa Fe, New Mexico, for eight months during 1893. Howard later became a physician and settled in Pocatello, Idaho. The edited letters of Howard, written mostly to his future wife, describe life at the Dawes Institute and reflect an image more of a military academy or an orphans' home than of a school. Based on the Minnie F. Howard Archive at the Idaho State University Library, Pocatello, Idaho; 29 letters, 2 photos, explanatory notes. 1893

Howe, Joseph

3292. Fergusson, C. B. HOWE AND CONFEDERATION. *Nova Scotia Hist. Q. [Canada] 1974 4(3): 223-244.* Joseph Howe, editor, writer, and Lieutenant Governor of Nova Scotia, was outspoken concerning confederation of the Canadian Colonies. Examines the opinions expressed by Howe during 1832-69. 1832-69

3293. Punch, T. M. JOE HOWE AND THE IRISH. *Collections of the Royal Nova Scotia Hist. Soc. [Canada] 1982 41: 119-140.* While Joseph Howe was the most widely known Nova Scotia politician of his day, his dealings with the Irish in Halifax are a little-explored aspect of his public life. His trouble in the 1850's stemmed from his religious and political principles and his fiery temperament. Howe's relationship to the Irish of Halifax has been described as a romance and marriage on a fluctuating course; the Irish were both "his warmest admirers and bitterest foes." 81 notes. 1820's-70

Howe, Julia Ward

3294. Grant, Mary Hetherington. "Private Woman, Public Person: An Account of the Life of Julia Ward Howe from 1819-1868." George Washington U. 1982. 428 pp. *DAI 1982 43(5): 1652-A.* DA8217580 1819-68

Howe, Mark

3295. Pier, Arthur S. MARK ANTONY DEWOLFE HOWE. *Massachusetts Hist. Soc. Pro. 1957-60 72: 408-438.* Mark Howe (1864-1960) was an historian, biographer, and poet. 1880's-1960

Howe, Oscar

3296. Dockstader, Frederick J. THE REVOLT OF TRADER BOY: OSCAR HOWE AND INDIAN ART. *Am. Indian Art Mag. 1983 8(3): 42-51.* Recounts the life and career of the 20th-century Sioux Indian artist Oscar Howe, illustrating paintings showing his early style and his later innovations. 20c

Howell, Clark

3297. Eberhard, Wallace B. CLARK HOWELL AND THE ATLANTA *CONSTITUTION. Journalism Q. 1983 60(1): 118-122.* Clark Howell was editor of the *Atlanta Constitution* from his father's retirement in 1897. He was a well-respected journalist, a sought-after speaker, a bridge between Southern regionalism and the nation as a whole, and a precursor of the New South. 16 notes. 1876-1936

Howell, Robert Boyte Crawford

3298. Horne, Linwood T. LEADERSHIP IN TIMES OF CRISIS: A STUDY IN THE LIFE OF R. B. C. HOWELL. *Baptist History and Heritage 1985 20(1): 36-44.* Traces the career and religious leadership of Robert Boyte Crawford Howell, Baptist preacher, editor, organizer, and conciliator who fought against Landmarkism, a kind of isolationist congregationalism. 1827-68

Howells, Annie

3299. Doyle, James. ANNIE HOWELLS AND *THE VACATION OF THE KELWYNS. Can. Rev. of Am. Studies [Canada] 1979 10(2): 125-135.* William Dean Howells's novel, *The Vacation of the Kelwyns* (1920), drew heavily on that famous author's relationships with his sister, Annie Howells and was, therefore, partly autobiographical. More importantly, the book depicted sympathetically the Victorian, middle-class moral and social verities widely accepted in late 19th-century America. 19 notes. ca 1890-1910

3300. Doyle, James. ANNIE HOWELLS AND THE REALIST-ROMANTIC CONFLICT. *Atlantis [Canada] 1978 4(1): 40-48.* Biography of American writer Annie Howells (1844-1938) discusses how her fiction presented issues in the realist-romantic conflict of the 1870's. 1870's

Howells, William Dean

3301. Baker, William. HOWELLS: THE HERITAGE OF EUREKA MILLS. *Old Northwest 1983 9(3): 255-265.* The knowledge and experience that William Dean Howells acquired during his stay at the Eureka Mills site on the Little Miami River in Ohio provided material for several of Howells's works. The frontier adventures and experiences helped provide Howells's sense of values, as well as historical and autobiographical material for his books, particularly *My Year in a Log Cabin* (1887), *New Leaf Mills* (1913), and *The Leatherwood God* (1916). Primary sources; 6 notes. 1850-51

3302. Crider, Gregory L. WILLIAM DEAN HOWELLS AND THE GILDED AGE: SOCIALIST IN A FUR-LINED OVERCOAT. *Ohio Hist. 1979 88(4): 408-418.* The life of William Dean Howells followed a pattern typical of the American Gilded Age. He was born to obscure poverty in Martins Ferry, Ohio, but through his literary skills and financial acumen achieved fame and wealth within the first 36 years of his adulthood. He was known chiefly as editor of *The Atlantic Monthly* (1871-81). He expressed socialist principles in novels and essays, but suffered from guilt because he found it impossible to give up the luxurious life which his success afforded him. He called himself a theoretical socialist and a practical aristocrat, and lived uneasily with that inconsistency. 32 notes, ref. 1858-1920

3303. Dennis, Scott Alexander. "'The Uninhabitable Place': The Rootlessness of W. D. Howells." Syracuse U. 1976. 305 pp. *DAI 1977 38(5): 2785-A.* 1866-1916

3304. Eble, Kenneth E. HOWELLS AND TWAIN: BEING AND STAYING FRIENDS. *Old Northwest 1984 10(1): 91-106.* Discusses the close friendship developed between Mark Twain and William Dean Howells, from their initial meeting in 1869 until Twain's death in 1910. These Gilded Age writers and journalists were similar in several ways: both were from Western provincial areas, both were schooled as country printers, both spent time abroad, both settled in the East, both married into wealthy Eastern families, and both were tied to their family situations. Howells and Twain placed a great value on their friendship, which is evident in their correspondence. Based on the Howells Papers at the Houghton Library, Harvard University, and other primary sources; 23 notes. 1869-1910

3305. Havighurst, Walter. HOWELLS OF HAMILTON. *Old Northwest 1982 8(1): 7-11.* Discusses the childhood years spent in Hamilton, Ohio, during 1841-50 by William Dean Howells. The publication of *A Boy's Town* by Howells in 1890 reflected the happiness and importance he placed on his early years in Hamilton. 1841-50

3306. Payne, Alma J. THE OHIO WORLD OF WILLIAM DEAN HOWELLS—EVER DISTANT, EVER NEAR. *Old Northwest 1984 10(1): 127-137.* William Dean Howells, born and nurtured in frontier Ohio, spent most of his adult life in more exotic places like Italy, Paris, New York, and Boston. However, the philosophical and spiritual emphasis of his writing and lifestyle was closely related to the earlier experiences of his Ohio childhood. Although living far from Ohio, the geographical area was an essential influence on Howells's work. Primary sources; 28 notes. 1837-1919

Howells, Winifred

3307. Crowley, John W. WINIFRED HOWELLS AND THE ECONOMY OF PAIN. *Old Northwest 1984 10(1): 41-75.* Discusses the life of Winifred Howells and her relationship with her father, William Dean Howells, from her physical and psychological breakdown in 1880 at the age of 16 to her death in 1889. Winifred's illness, at least partly psychoneurotic, was linked to her literary aspirations and the mental stress caused by her fear of failure, her desire to please her father, and her crisis of identity. Based on manuscripts in the Howells Collection of the Houghton Library, Harvard University, and other primary sources; 4 photos, 59 notes. 1880-89

Howland, Esther

3308. Kerr, Joan P. THE AMOROUS ART OF ESTHER HOWLAND. *Am. Heritage 1982 33(2): 25-29.* Esther Howland (1828-1904) began to make valentines in 1847 and achieved sales of more than $100,000 annually until she sold out to the largest valentine factory in the world in 1880. Samples of her creations are featured. 10 illus. 1847-80

Howland, John

3309. Russo, Francis X. JOHN HOWLAND: PIONEER IN THE FREE SCHOOL MOVEMENT. *Rhode Island Hist. 1978 37(4): 111-122.* John Howland was a hairdresser and self-educated. He became active in the Rhode Island free school movement in 1795, played a major role in securing legislation in 1800, and was active in Providence school affairs for the next several decades. Based on school records, recollections, and secondary accounts; 3 illus., 47 notes. 1757-1838

Howorth, Lucy Somerville

3310. Hawks, Joanne Varner. LIKE MOTHER, LIKE DAUGHTER: NELLIE NUGENT SOMERVILLE AND LUCY SOMERVILLE HOWORTH. *J. of Mississippi Hist. 1983 45(2): 116-128.* An overview of the lives of two Mississippi women who served in the state legislature. Nellie Somerville, the first woman elected to the Mississippi legislature, entered public service in 1923 as representative from Washington County through her earlier interests in the temperance and suffrage movements. She worked continuously to involve women in civic improvement projects and other responsibilities of citizenship. Howorth, the daughter, was elected as a state representative from Hinds County in 1931, but her influence would spread beyond the state's boundaries. Appointed initially to the Board of Veterans' Appeals by President Franklin D. Roosevelt, she became an influential part of the network of women in the federal government who were appointed by Roosevelt in the early years of the New Deal. Returning to Mississippi in 1957, she remains active in public life. Based on an interview with Lucy Somerville Howorth, periodicals, M.A. theses, and secondary sources; 14 notes. 1923-57

Hoxie, Herbert M.

3311. Lendt, David L. IOWA'S CIVIL WAR MARSHAL: A LESSON IN EXPEDIENCE. *Ann. of Iowa 1975 43(2): 132-139.* Herbert M. Hoxie was US marshal in Iowa from May 1861 to March 1865. Many of Hoxie's actions, particularly his arrests of alleged Copperheads, were "arbitrary, unwarranted and, in all probability, unconstitutional." The decline of the Copperhead faction in Iowa was due more to national events than to Hoxie's activities. Based on correspondence between Hoxie and Major Levi Turner, Associate Judge Advocate in charge of state prisoners, and on secondary works; illus., 17 notes. 1861-65

Hoyt, Harlowe Randall

3312. Winget, Jack Brent. "Harlowe Randall Hoyt: Renaissance Man of the Theatre, 1882-1971. A Historical Study." Kent State U. 1983. 356 pp. *DAI 1983 44(4): 913-914-A.* DA8317266 1902-71

Hrdlička, Aleš

3313. Spencer, Frank. "Ales Hrdlicka, M.D., 1869-1943: A Chronicle of the Life and Work of an American Physical Anthropologist." (Volumes I and II). U. of Michigan 1979. 887 pp. *DAI 1980 40(10): 5494-A.* 1869-1943

Hricko, George A.

3314. Paučo, Joseph. SLOVAKS AND THEIR LIFE: GEORGE A. HRICKO. *Jednota Ann. Furdek 1977 16: 19-22.* George A. Hricko (1883-1963) was a Slovak American interested in state politics in Pennsylvania and in immigrants' organizations such as the Jednota Society. 1883-1963

Hrobak, Philip A.

3315. Tybor, M. Martina. PHILIP A. HROBAK AS THE LATE DR. JOSEPH PAUCO KNEW HIM. *Jednota Ann. Furdek 1983 22: 73-90.* During 1950-64, Joseph Pauco and Philip A. Hrobak worked as assistant editor and editor-in-chief, respectively, on the Slovak-American newspaper *Jednota* in Middletown, Pennsylvania; they were important public figures—often subjected to undeserved vilification—in the Slovak community in the United States. 1950-64

Hubbard, Ruggles

3316. Maple, Marilyn. RUGGLES HUBBARD, CIVIL GOVERNOR OF FERNANDINA. *Florida Hist. Q. 1980 58(3): 315-319.* In 1817, a power struggle over Fernandina (Amelia Island) briefly left privateer and conspirator Ruggles Hubbard in charge as civil governor. One faction desired aligning with the United States, while others wanted to join with several South American governments. Hubbard was pushed out of power and soon died. Based on ship and land records; 15 notes. 1817

Hubbell, Levi

3317. Grant, Marilyn. JUDGE LEVI HUBBELL: A MAN IMPEACHED. *Wisconsin Mag. of Hist. 1980 64(1): 28-39.* Levi Hubbell, judge of the second circuit court, associate justice, and chief justice of Wisconsin's first supreme court, was first active as a Whig in New York, then as a Democrat and finally a Republican in Wisconsin. Charged on multiple counts of bribery, prejudice, improper judicial behavior, and several other articles, Hubbell was prosecuted before the Senate by his arch-Democratic foe, Edward G. Ryan. Although acquitted, Hubbell was the only judge in Wisconsin ever to be impeached, and that stigma effectively ended his influence in the state and shortened his judicial career. Covers 1827-76. 10 illus., note. 1827-76

Huber family

3318. Nusz, Frieda Roth. PHILIP HUBER FAMILY IN AMERICA. *Heritage Rev. 1980 10(4): 41-43.* Describes the immigration of Wilhelm Huber and his father's family to the Freeman, South Dakota, area and provides genealogical lists and photographs of some of the family members. 1882-20c

Huck, Winnifred Mason

3319. Dean, David and Dean, Martha. "MOMA WENT TO CONGRESS AND THEN TO JAIL." *Am. Hist. Illus. 1977 12(7): 37-43.* In November 1922, 40-year-old Winnifred Mason Huck was elected to the unexpired congressional term of her late father, Billy Mason of Chicago. She was the third woman and the first mother elected to Congress. During her four-month term and subsequent defeat, she was vocal, received much publicity, and enjoyed herself. She started a syndicated column, "Talks to Mothers of Flappers." She later wrote 25 articles on prison life and the problems ex-convicts have finding employment. This series was based on her serving a month in an Ohio prison (with the cooperation of Governor Vic Donahey) and performing ex-con jobs for two months under her prison name "Elizabeth Sprague." She died in 1936 after a five-year bout with stomach cancer. Based on her scrapbooks of pictures and clippings, contemporary newspapers, and magazine articles; 8 illus. 1922-36

Hudson, J. L.

3320. Hudson, Samuel. THE MAN WHO FOUNDED THE J. L. HUDSON COMPANY. *Chronicle 1981 17(1): 4-9.* Studies the life of J. L. Hudson (1846-1912) whose success as a merchandiser stemmed from nonconformity—in politics, in civic activities, and especially in business policies and philosophy—a maverick attitude evident in the radically new concepts in sales and customer relations he introduced in Detroit, Michigan, which opened up a new era in the city's business life. 1861-1912

Hudson, Winthrop S.

3321. Maring, Norman H. WINTHROP S. HUDSON: CHURCH HISTORIAN. *Foundations 1980 23(2): 127-154.* Traces Winthrop S. Hudson's academic career since his graduate school days, especially the influences of the University of Chicago, his place as a specialist in English Puritanism, his book *Religion in America,* and his contribution to the Baptists. 94 notes. 1933-79

Huebsch, B. W.

3322. McCullough, Ann Catherine. "A History of B. W. Huebsch, Publisher." U. of Wisconsin, Madison 1979. 462 pp. *DAI 1980 41(1): 253-254-A.* 8007559 1902-25

Hughes, Charles Evans

3323. Abrams, Richard M. OF LAWYERS, PRIVILEGE, AND POWER. *Rev. in Am. Hist. 1975 3(1): 105-113.* 20c

For abstract see ***Davis, John W.***

3324. Galloway, Gail and Owens, Susanne. HUGHES EXHIBIT CATALOGUE: CHARLES EVANS HUGHES: THE ELEVENTH CHIEF JUSTICE. *Supreme Court Hist. Soc. Y. 1981: 94-112.* Briefly sketches the judicial career of Charles Evans Hughes as associate justice (1910-16) and chief justice (1930-42) of the Supreme Court. Also provides a catalogue of an exhibit of 155 pieces of memorabilia displayed in the Supreme Court Building in 1980 to honor Hughes's life and contributions to the judicial system. 10 photos. 1882-1948

3325. Gossett, Elizabeth Hughes. CHARLES EVANS HUGHES: MY FATHER THE CHIEF JUSTICE. *Supreme Court Hist. Soc. Y. 1976: 7-15.* Reminiscences of Chief Justice Charles Evans Hughes's daughter about her father's career on the Supreme Court; 1910-41. 1910-41

3326. Gossett, William T. CHIEF JUSTICE HUGHES—A RECOLLECTION. *Supreme Court Hist. Soc. Y. 1981: 75-77.* Traces the life and judicial career of Charles Evans Hughes, associate justice (1910-16) and chief justice (1930-42). Hughes's legal philosophy, personal ethics, and working habits are described. Based on the author's own recollections, Merlo J. Pusey's *Charles Evans Hughes* (1951), and Hughes's autobiography; 2 photos, note. 1862-1948

Hughes, Helen MacGill

3327. Hughes, Helen MacGill. ON BECOMING A SOCIOLOGIST. *J. of the Hist. of Sociol. 1980-81 3(1): 27-39.* Narrates the author's life history in the context of the emergence of sociology as a well-defined scientific discipline; 1925-55. 1925-55

3328. Hughes, Helen MacGill. WASP/WOMAN/SOCIOLOGIST. *Society 1977 14(5): 69-80.* The author discusses her careers as mother and sociologist, in Canada and the United States, 1916-77. 1916-77

Hughes, Hugh

3329. Friedman, Bernard. HUGH HUGHES, A STUDY IN REVOLUTIONARY IDEALISM. *New York Hist. 1983 64(3): 229-259.* Hugh Hughes was typical of the middling rank of advancing tradesmen and merchants who viewed the American Revolution from an antimercantilist standpoint. He was one of many radicals who were inconspicuous and thus remain obscure in historical studies. An artisan-proprietor, he was in financial difficulties during the recession following the French and Indian War. Fearing imprisonment for debt, he advertised his business property for sale or rent and avoided any public demonstration of his radicalism, although it was evident in his private correspondence. He served in the quartermaster department in the Continental Army through the war. After the war he was an insolvent schoolmaster, and in politics a Clintonian and antifederalist. Based on Hugh Hughes's letter books, the John Hughes Papers, and other primary sources; 5 illus., 74 notes. 1765-1802

Hughes, John

3330. Coogan, M. Jane. A STUDY OF THE JOHN HUGHES-TERENCE DONAGHOE FRIENDSHIP. *Records of the Am. Catholic Hist. Soc. of Philadelphia 1982 93(1-4): 41-75.* The friendship of John Hughes and Terence Donaghoe had its beginning in Augnacloy, County Tyrone, Ireland. Traces their lives from their Irish schooling, through their divergent training for the Catholic priesthood, to their deaths. Although they both served in the Philadelphia diocese at one point, circumstances eventually led to Hughes becoming the archbishop of New York and Donaghoe a parish priest in the West. Reviews their careers and includes correspondence dealing with both their friendship and their opinions on Church issues. Based on the letters of John Hughes and Terence Donaghoe; 87 notes. 1809-69

3331. Perko, F. Michael. TWO BISHOPS, THE BIBLE, AND THE SCHOOLS: AN EXERCISE IN DIFFERENTIAL BIOGRAPHY. *Vitae Scholasticae 1984 3(1): 61-93.* Examines the lives of John Baptist Purcell, bishop of Cincinnati, and John Hughes, bishop of New York, contrasting their styles of dealing with Protestant majorities, especially in relation to Catholic schooling. While Purcell was compromising and Hughes confrontational, both achieved similar gains in the education of Catholics. The contrasting styles are particularly significant in light of their similar backgrounds and ages. 82 notes. 1830-50

Hughes, Langston

3332. Cunningham, George Philbert. "Langston Hughes: A Biographical Study of the Harlem Renaissance Years, 1902-1932." Yale U. 1983. 365 pp. *DAI 1984 44(10): 3136-A.* DA8329346 1902-32

3333. Faith, Berry. BLACK POETS, WHITE PATRONS: THE HARLEM RENAISSANCE YEARS OF LANGSTON HUGHES. *Crisis 1981 88(6): 278-283, 306.* Soon after publishing his first and successful volume of poems, *Weary Blues,* 24-year-old Langston Hughes was introduced to Mrs. Charlotte Mason by Alain Locke. Mason, nicknamed "G-odmother," provided financial support for Hughes. She also attempted to dictate her views and values onto his life. Hughes could not tolerate her demands after three years and broke off his relationship just as the economy crashed in 1929. Hughes began to write with a louder political voice during the 1930's. 1926-30's

3334. Hauke, Kathleen Armstrong. "A Self-Portrait of Langston Hughes." U. of Rhode Island 1981. 242 pp. *DAI 1983 43(11): 3596-A.* DA8306399 20c

3335. Rampersad, Arnold. THE ORIGINS OF POETRY IN LANGSTON HUGHES. *Southern Review 1985 21(3): 695-705.* Describes crises in black poet Langston Hughes's life that caused psychological turmoil in his personality, providing the source of inspiration for his poetry. 1919-30's

3336. Scott, Mark. LANGSTON HUGHES OF KANSAS. *Kansas Hist. 1980 3(1): 3-25.* Langston Hughes (1902-67), the black poet, novelist, journalist, and historian, lived in Kansas from 1903 to 1915. In Topeka and Lawrence he first encountered racism, poverty, and loneliness. Such bitter memories of Kansas are reflected in quotations from his poems and autobiographies. In Kansas he also had his first dreams of racial equality. Such dreams were not his alone but passed along to him by his parents, grandparents and great-grandparents who were of black, white or mixed blood. Decades before the landmark *Brown* decision of 1954, Carrie Hughes won a battle to have her son admitted to an all-white Topeka school. Based on Hughes' writings, interviews, state census records, city directories, newspapers, biographies; illus., 172 notes. 1903-15

3337. Scott, Mark. LANGSTON HUGHES OF KANSAS. *J. of Negro Hist. 1981 66(1): 1-9.* One of the dominant figures of the black renaissance of the 1920's was Langston Hughes. His dreams of racial equality pervade his poetry, plays, short stories, novels, histories, and other works. Many of his views reflect experiences that he had while growing up in Kansas. His first confrontation with racial bigotry as well as his first public reading of original poetry occurred as an adolescent in Kansas. He preserved and perpetuated his ancestor's strong tradition of literary intellectualism and political activism. Covers 1900-60's. 1900-60's

3338. Wintz, Cary D. LANGSTON HUGHES: A KANSAS POET IN THE HARLEM RENAISSANCE. *Kansas Q. 1975 7(3): 58-71.* Gives a short biography of Langston Hughes' early childhood in Missouri and Kansas and then concentrates on the part he played in the Harlem Renaissance during the 1920's. 1920's

Hughes, Louis C.

3339. Lyon, William H. LOUIS C. HUGHES, ARIZONA'S EDITORIAL GADFLY. *J. of Arizona Hist. 1983 24(2): 171-200.* Narrates the career of Louis C. Hughes, editor of the *Arizona Star* from 1877 to 1907. Hughes was a controversial, beleaguered crusader whose political and editorial life reflected his commitment to progressive causes and his high moral standards. Based on the Hughes Collection in the Arizona Historical Society, contemporary periodicals, and secondary sources; 7 photos, 95 notes. 1877-1907

Hughes, Philip

3340. Wennersten, John R. THE TRAVAIL OF A TORY PARSON: REVEREND PHILIP HUGHES AND MARYLAND COLONIAL POLITICS 1767-1777. *Hist. Mag. of the Protestant Episcopal Church 1975 44(4): 409-416.* A man of great ambition and tenacity with an unusual stubborn nature, the Reverend Philip Hughes attempted to pursue a rich career for himself as a religious leader in the colonies. That dream floundered on the storm of political revolution in Maryland. His case demonstrates the plight in which many colonial Anglican parsons found themselves during the war. Conscious of status and income, they held on to their offices as loyal subjects of the king until the revolutionists deprived them of their parishes. Based largely on Archives of Maryland; 49 notes. 1767-77

Hughes, Richard J.

3341. Felzenberg, Alvin S. THE MAKING OF A GOVERNOR: THE EARLY POLITICAL CAREER OF RICHARD J. HUGHES. *New Jersey Hist. 1983 101(1-2): 1-27.* Richard J. Hughes's political career followed that of his father. The elder Hughes served as a Burlington County official and held statewide appointive positions in New Jersey. When the younger Hughes graduated from school he became a clerk for a prominent Trenton attorney. Active in Democratic Party affairs, Hughes was nominated for a seat in the US Congress in 1938, but lost the election decisively. As a reward for his efforts, Hughes was appointed to several posts during the 1940's and 1950's, including assistant US attorney, Mercer County Democratic chairman, and judge for the New Jersey Superior Court. After a financially lucrative interlude as a private attorney, Hughes was chosen by Democratic Party leaders to run against James P. Mitchell for New Jersey governor in 1961, a contest that Hughes won. Based on interviews, newspaper stories, and secondary sources; 2 illus., 77 notes. 1931-61

Hughes, Sam

3342. Hyatt, A. M. J. SIR ARTHUR CURRIE. *Canada 1975 2(3): 4-15.* 1914-30
For abstract see ***Currie, Arthur***

Hugo, Adèle

3343. Harvey, Robert Paton. WHEN VICTOR HUGO'S DAUGHTER WAS A HALIGONIAN. *Nova Scotia Hist. Q. [Canada] 1977 7(3): 243-256.* Recounts the story of Adèle Hugo, daughter of Victor Hugo, the circumstances of her residence in Nova Scotia (1863-66), and her later history. Primary and secondary sources; biblio. 1863-66

Huidekoper, Frederick

3344. Stephens, Bruce M. FREDERICK HUIDEKOPER (1817-1892): PHILANTHROPIST, SCHOLAR, AND TEACHER. *Pennsylvania Mag. of Hist. and Biog. 1979 103(1): 53-65.* The Harvard-trained son of urbane Harm Jan Huidekoper, Frederick Huidekoper served the Meadville Theological School during 1844-77. His hope was to train Unitarian ministers for service in the West. His published works, which attempt to ground Unitarianism in Jewish monotheism and Christian patristics, display remarkable learning. He opposed the higher criticism. Based on Huidekoper Papers, Crawford County Historical Society, and on secondary sources; 27 notes. 1834-92

Hulbert, Mary

3345. Saunders, Frances W. LOVE AND GUILT: WOODROW WILSON AND MARY HULBERT. *Am. Heritage 1979 30(3): 69-77.* 1907-35
For abstract see ***Wilson, Woodrow***

Hull, Clark L.

3346. Triplet, Rodney G. THE RELATIONSHIP OF CLARK L. HULL'S HYPNOSIS RESEARCH TO HIS LATER LEARNING THEORY: THE CONTINUITY OF HIS LIFE'S WORK. *J. of the Hist. of the Behavioral Sci. 1982 18(1): 22-31.* What has been missing in previous historical accounts of Clark L. Hull is a view of his life's work as an integrated whole. This paper contributes to that end by relating his hypnosis research and theory during the years 1921 to 1933 to the developing behavioral orientation of his learning theory. In addition, this paper relates his work historically and conceptually to the theory of ideomotor action endorsed by William James and a number of other 19th-century psychologists, and transmitted by Hull into the stimulus-response terminology of the 1930's. 1921-33

Hull, Cordell

3347. Beck, Robert Thomas. "Cordell Hull and Latin America, 1933-39." Temple U. 1977. 363 pp. *DAI 1977 38(4): 2296-A.* 1933-39

Hullihen, Simon P.

3348. Nodyne, Kenneth R. PIONEER IN ORAL SURGERY: SIMON P. HULLIHEN. *J. of the West Virginia Hist. Assoc. 1982 6(1): 41-48.* Simon P. Hullihen began his career as an oral surgeon in 1835 at a time when specialization was rare and especially in dentistry; he contributed the invention of several tools and procedures to the practice of dentistry before his death from typhoid and pneumonia in 1857. 1835-57

Humboldt, Alexander von

3349. Foner, Philip S. ALEXANDER VON HUMBOLDT ON SLAVERY IN AMERICA. *Sci. & Soc. 1983 47(3): 330-342.* Presents a biographical sketch of Alexander von Humboldt and analyzes his antislavery and egalitarian views, particularly as they pertained to slavery and race relations in the United States and Cuba. 34 notes. 1799-1859

Humphrey, Hubert H.

3350. Kampelman, Max M. HUBERT H. HUMPHREY: POLITICAL SCIENTIST. *PS 1978 11(2): 228-237.* Obituary of Hubert H. Humphrey; discusses his political career, interest in political science, and association with the American Political Science Association, 1943-78. 1943-78

3351. Natoli, Marie D. THE HUMPHREY VICE PRESIDENCY IN RETROSPECT. *Presidential Studies Q. 1982 12(4): 603-609.* Discusses Hubert H. Humphrey's experience as vice-president between 1965 and 1969. This was the most difficult period of his political career. President Johnson required total loyalty and subordination, but Humphrey felt constrained by what he saw as his no-win position, a position dominated by uncertainties and changing demands. Humphrey found himself inextricably linked with Johnson's policies on Vietnam, and this support caused him to go through the worst campaign of his life in 1968. Hampered by a splintered party and the Johnson record on the war, Humphrey was a victim of his loyalty to his president and the American people. Based partly on a 1974 interview with Humphrey; 19 notes. 1965-69

3352. Polsby, Nelson W. WHAT HUBERT HUMPHREY WROUGHT. *Commentary 1984 78(5): 47-50.* Reviews the public life of Hubert H. Humphrey, whose considerable contributions to the American political scene have yet to be fully appreciated. 1948-78

Humphreys, Andrew A.

3353. Allin, Lawrence C. FOUR ENGINEERS ON THE MISSOURI: LONG, FREMONT, HUMPHREYS, AND WARREN. *Nebraska Hist. 1984 65(1): 58-83.* 1817-57
*For abstract see **Frémont, John C.***

Humphreys, David

3354. Cifelli, Edward Martin. "David Humphreys: The Life and Literary Career of an American Patriot, With an Appendix of Previously Unpublished and Uncollected Poems." New York U. 1977. 297 pp. *DAI 1977 38(4): 2122-A.* 1775-1818

Humphreys, Milton W.

3355. Berrigan, Joseph R. MILTON W. HUMPHREYS, AN APPALACHIAN ODYSSEUS. *Southern Humanities Rev. 1977 11(Special Issue): 27-32.* Discusses the academic career of Milton W. Humphreys, a southern classicist, 1860-1919. One of six articles in this issue on classical traditions in the South. 1860-1919

Humphrys, James (family)

3356. Humphrys, Ruth. [THE SHINY HOUSE].

THE SHINY HOUSE... AND THE MAN WHO BUILT IT. *Beaver [Canada] 1977 307(4): 49-55.* James Humphrys, retired British naval architect, moved to Assiniboia in 1888 for his health. There he acquired land for a farm. Within a few months he erected a large, comfortable home for his family of eight children and his wife, who remained in England until the home was completed. The Humphrys home was at Cannington Manor in southeastern Saskatchewan. Humphrys adjusted well, helped initiate medical and educational services, and looked forward to life in a progressive community. 8 illus.

EARLY DAYS IN THE SHINY HOUSE. *Beaver [Canada] 1977 308(1): 20-28.* Concludes the story of the family of James Humphrys. Discusses education, church life, entertainment, and other social affairs. 17 illus. 1880's-1908

Huneker, James Gibbons

3357. Karlen, Arno. HUNEKER AND OTHER LOST ARTS. *Antioch Rev. 1981 39(4): 402-421.* Reviews the works and life of James Gibbons Huneker (1860-1921), an American musician and literary critic. 1880-1921

Hunn, Anthony

3358. Weisert, John J. DR. ANTHONY HUNN: FROM STORM AND STRESS TO TEMPEST AND SUNSHINE. *Filson Club Hist. Q. 1982 56(2): 211-224.* A biographical sketch of Anton Christian Hunnius. Born in Weimar, Germany, he spent his early-adult years trying to achieve fame as a poet, actor, and dramatist. His most successful play was a comedy *Der Taubstumme.* Dissatisfied with the lifestyle of the theater, Hunnius prepared a rigorous personal study program that facilitated attending and graduating from medical school. Soon thereafter, he immigrated to Kentucky where he immediately established a successful medical practice. Shortening his name to Hunn, the new American also became a newspaper editor who was involved in disputes with Henry

Clay and American nativists. In 1829, Hunn published *The Medical Friend of the People* which was a newspaper about his experiences as a doctor. He died in Kentucky in 1834. Secondary materials in German and contemporary Kentucky newspapers; 30 notes. 1765-1834

Hunsicker, Isaac Ziegler

3359. Good, E. Reginald. ISAAC ZIEGLER HUNSICKER: ONTARIO SCHOOLMASTER AND FRAKTUR ARTIST. *Pennsylvania Folklife 1977 26(4): 2-8.* Examines the life and fraktur art of Isaac Ziegler Hunsicker, a schoolmaster in Waterloo and Oxford counties, Ontario, and in Montgomery County, Pennsylvania. 1837-70

Hunt, George

3360. Cannizzo, Jeanne. GEORGE HUNT AND THE INVENTION OF KWAKIUTL CULTURE. *Can. Rev. of Sociol. and Anthrop. [Canada] 1983 20(1): 44-58.* Outlines the career of George Hunt, collaborator of Franz Boas and research assistant to several other Northwest Coast ethnographers. His methodology, his relationship with informants and Boas, and his attitudes toward his work are all considered, as far as possible working from documentary sources. The particular dimensions of his personal biography are discussed to suggest how he developed such a remarkable expertise as an ethnographer. Offers an analysis of Hunt's contribution to the anthropological view of the Kwakiutl culture. 1870's-1910

Hunt, Harriet

3361. Henderson, Janet Karen. "Four Nineteenth Century Professional Women." Rutgers U., New Brunswick 1982. 315 pp. *DAI 1982 43(3): 698-A.* DA8218323 19c

Hunt, John

3362. Guyton, Priscilla L. JOHN HUNT. *Northwest Ohio Q. 1981 53(3): 83-91.* Continued from a previous article. Focuses on the political career of Maumee Valley pioneer John Hunt during 1841-51. 1841-51

3363. Guyton, Priscilla L. JOHN HUNT. *Northwest Ohio Q. 1980 52(1): 179-190, (2): 214-226, (3): 254-258.* Part I. John Elliott Hunt (1798-1877) traded with Indians (1817-33) and later rose to political and commercial prominence in the Toledo-Maumee area. Part II. After the Treaty of 1833 between the Ottawa Indians and the federal government, Hunt became a major contributor to the business and land development of Maumee City, was elected to the Ohio Senate in 1835, and was involved in the development of the Miami Extension Canal and the Wabash and Erie Canal during his term; his estate came to ca. $100,000 in 1877. Part III. Describes how Hunt headed the committee on canals in the Ohio Senate. He pushed through authorization for construction of the Canal in 1836 during his first term in office and, during 1832-39, his second term, pushed for the financing. 1817-77

3364. Guyton, Priscilla L. JOHN HUNT. *Northwest Ohio Q. 1981 53(2): 50-68.* Continued from a previous article. Part IV. Covers Ohio State Senator John Hunt's efforts in 1840-43 to force the release for sale of state-owned lands along the Wabash and Erie Canal and the Miami Canal and to otherwise finance the construction of those canals; his promotion of the Maumee-Western Reserve Road in 1836-37, and of the position of Maumee v. Toledo, as in the Lucas County seat controversy of 1836-43; and the effects of the canals on Ohio's economic growth. Article to be continued. 1836-43

Hunt, William Henry

3365. Conrad, William Hunt, ed. WILLIAM HENRY HUNT: THE MONTANA YEARS. *Montana 1980 30(2): 54-67.* William Henry Hunt (1857-1942) lived in Montana initially from 1879 to 1900, participating actively in Republican Party politics and working as a lawyer in Ft. Benton and Helena, attorney general for Montana Territory, state district judge, then finally as an associate justice of the Montana Supreme Court. In 1900 Hunt became the first secretary of state for Puerto Rico, and during 1901 and 1904 served as governor of that territory. From 1904 until his retirement in 1928, he held a series of federal judicial appointments, including a 1904-09 stint as a US district judge in Montana. The article is taken from Hunt's 1941 memoir and includes reflections on Montana politics and personalities, among them, mention of individuals involved in the William A. Clark Senatorial bribery scandal, 1900. Based on William H. Hunt memoir, Montana Historical Society; 10 illus. 1879-1900

Hunter, Celia

3366. Johnson, Susan Hackley. CELIA HUNTER: PORTRAIT OF AN ACTIVIST. *Alaska J. 1979 9(4): 30-35.* A sketch of the life of Celia Hunter since the 1930's, with emphasis on her life in Alaska as pilot and environmentalist. 4 photos. 1930's-79

Hunter, David

3367. Longacre, Edward G. A PROFILE OF MAJOR GENERAL DAVID HUNTER. *Civil War Times Illus. 1978 16(9): 4-9, 38-43.* Traces the career of Major General David Hunter (1802-86). A graduate of West Point in 1822, Hunter served on the western frontier. He made general at the start of the Civil War. Hunter commanded in the West, and then was given charge of the Department of the South. Hunter earned enmity by proclaiming slaves free in his district and in raising a black regiment. In 1864 Hunter was in charge of the Department of Western Virginia and was the "dispenser of fire and fury" in the Valley. Hunter closed out his military career as president of the court that tried the Lincoln conspirators. 1861-65

Hunter, Elizabeth

3368. Johnson, Jean L. THREE STONEYS. *Alberta Hist. [Canada] 1981 29(2): 29-36.* 1912-60
*For abstract see **Goat, Noah***

Hunter, Howard W.

3369. Lyon, T. Edgar. CHURCH HISTORIANS I HAVE KNOWN. *Dialogue 1978 11(4): 14-22.* 1913-70
*For abstract see **Lyon, T. Edgar***

Hunter, James

3370. Peake, F. A. THE ACHIEVEMENTS AND FRUSTRATIONS OF JAMES HUNTER. *J. of the Can. Church Hist. Soc. [Canada] 1977 19(3-4): 138-165.* Describes the missionary work of the Anglican priest James Hunter, an Englishman, in what is now western Canada, during 1844-64. Hunter maintained good relations with the Hudson's Bay Company which had power in the area and made significant contributions to the missionary effort. First, he translated the

Book of Common Prayer and other religious works into the Cree Indian language. Second, he worked hard to expand Anglican missionary efforts throughout the area known as Rupert's Land, despite some opposition from the Company. His attempts in this area were rewarded by success, but in 1864 Hunter decided to return to England permanently. Ostensibly he did so for the education of his children, but he also may have been frustrated in his desire to occupy a position of leadership within the Church. Upon his return to England, his opportunities in this area were greatly improved. Based on printed and unprinted primary sources; 59 notes, 2 appendixes. 1844-64

Hunter, Jane Edna

3371. Jones, Adrienne Lash. "Jane Edna Hunter: A Case Study of Black Leadership, 1910-1950." Case Western Reserve U. 1983. 352 pp. *DAI 1983 44(2): 521-A.* DA8314575 1910-50

Hunter, R. H.

3372. Hunter, R. H. FIVE R'S ON THE PRAIRIES. *Saskatchewan Hist. [Canada] 1978 31(1): 34-36, 31(2): 69-73.* In two parts. The author reminiscences about his life as a teacher in western Canada during 1923-67. Born in New Brunswick, Mr. Hunter was educated at Regina Normal School where he was employed as a professor following an extensive career as a teacher and administrator in a number of Saskatchewan cities and towns. 1923-67

Huntington, Anna Hyatt

3373. Eden, Myrna Garvey. "Anna Hyatt Huntington, Sculptor, and Mrs. H. H. A. Beach, Composer: A Comparative Study of Two Women Representatives of the American Cultivated Tradition in the Arts." Syracuse U. 1977. 362 pp. *DAI 1978 38(8): 4415-A.* 1865-1920

Huntington, Arabella Yarrington

3374. Rouse, Parke, Jr. BELLE HUNTINGTON, HER MEN AND HER MUSE. *Virginia Mag. of Hist. and Biog. 1980 88(4): 387-400.* Surveys the life of Mrs. Collis P. Huntington, later Mrs. Henry E. Huntington, treating it as a historiographical problem. Important both as the wife of these railroad magnates and as an art collector in her own right, Mrs. Huntington effectively kept her affairs, especially her early life and premarital relations with Collis Huntington, from contemporaries and, subsequently, historians. Her privacy was assured when her son destroyed her papers upon her death. Covers ca. 1860-1924. Photo, 22 notes. ca 1860-1924

Huntington, Samuel, Jr.

3375. Brown, Jeffrey P. SAMUEL HUNTINGTON: A CONNECTICUT ARISTOCRAT ON THE OHIO FRONTIER. *Ohio Hist. 1980 89(4): 420-438.* Discusses the career of Samuel Huntington, Jr. (1765-1817), especially the years after his move to the Ohio frontier. Born to one of Connecticut's most prominent families, he moved to frontier Ohio, became one of the leading figures in Great Lakes politics, and headed the coalition of conservative Republicans and Federalists that broke the liberal Republican hold in the state. An aristocratic leader in a democratic society, Huntington illustrates the ease with which a prominent easterner could win high office in the sparsely settled West. Based on the archives of the Western Reserve Historical Society, the Ohio Historical society, and the State Library of Ohio; illus., 68 notes. ca 1785-1817

Hunzinger, George

3376. Flint, Richard W. GEORGE HUNZINGER: PATENT FURNITURE MAKER. *Art and Antiques 1980 3(1): 116-123.* George Hunzinger (1835-98), a German immigrant, became famous for his furniture during the Victorian Era in the United States, particularly his folding chair (patented in 1866) and a chair with a diagonal side brace (patented in 1869). 1860's-98

Hurd, Frank

3377. Folk, Patrick A. "OUR FRANK": THE CONGRESSIONAL CAREER OF FRANK HURD. *Northwest Ohio Q. 1976 48(4): 143-152; 1977 49(2): 73-84.* Continued from a previous article. Discusses the activities 1884-86 of Frank Hurd, Democratic congressman from Toledo, covering his antitariff activities and his campaign for reelection in 1886. The conclusion summarizes Hurd's career. 1880-86

Hurford, Grace Gibberd

3378. Hurford, Grace Gibberd. MISSIONARY SERVICE IN CHINA. *J. of the Can. Church Hist. Soc. [Canada] 1977 19(3-4): 177-181.* A personal recollection by a Canadian missionary-educator in China. During her years of service she was a nurse, English instructor, and Christian teacher. Her work offered many rewarding experiences, but from 1937 on she and her fellow workers had to contend with the problems caused by the Japanese invasion. She was injured only once by Japanese bombs, but the danger was omnipresent. Consequently, her work in China was disrupted by the necessity to move on several occasions and by the orders of the Chinese government to close all schools. Her service in China ended with the conclusion of World War II. 1928-45

Hurlbut, Stephen Augustus

3379. Lash, Jeffrey N. "Stephen Augustus Hurlbut: A Military and Diplomatic Politician, 1815-1882." Kent State U. 1980. 537 pp. *DAI 1981 41(12): 5222-A.* 8108313 1837-82

Hurst, Fielding

3380. Blankinship, Gary. COLONEL FIELDING HURST AND THE HURST NATION. *West Tennessee Hist. Soc. Papers 1980 (34): 71-87.* Colonel Fielding Hurst, a wealthy West Tennessean, obtained a commission in the Federal army during the Civil War. Twenty-three of his relatives joined his regiment. Hurst and his men knew the area like the backs of their hands, and as scouts provided valuable information to General Grenville M. Dodge. In 1864 Dodge gave Hurst a "roving commission" to "grub up" West Tennessee. Because of his unit's actions against civilians, and his own loyalty to the Union in a rebel area, Hurst's postbellum days were turbulent. His several appointments after the war from both federal and state authorities did not assuage the acrimonious feelings of his neighbors. When he died in 1882 his foes celebrated, and rode their horses over and spat upon his grave. Based on military records in the National Archives and secondary studies; 2 illus., 97 notes. 1862-80

Hurston, Zora Neale

3381. Bacchilega, Cristina. L'AUTOBIOGRAFIA DI ZORA NEALE HURSTON [Zora Neale Hurston's autobiography]. *Memoria: Riv. di Storia delle Donne [Italy] 1983 (8): 133-138.* While many other works of the prolific black writer Zora Neale Hurston have recently been the object of renewed interest by the publishing industry and academicians, her autobiography, *Dust Tracks on a Road* (1942), has not received much attention, perhaps because it is not representative of her class or race. Hurston's Cinderella career in a white male America, full of ambiguities and ambivalences, is nevertheless rich in life experiences and possible interpretations. Biblio. 1900's-60

Hurwitz, Henry

3382. Hurwitz, Henry. A MOTHER REMEMBERED. *Am. Jewish Hist. 1980 70(1): 5-21.* Henry Hurwitz's (1886-1961) reminiscences about his Lithuanian Jewish mother (d. 1939), especially her impact on his childhood in Gloucester and Boston, Massachusetts. ca 1890-1939

Husband, Herman

3383. Jones, Mark Haddon. "Herman Husband: Millenarian, Carolina Regulator, and Whiskey Rebel." Northern Illinois U. 1983. 401 pp. *DAI 1983 44(4): 1180-A.* DA8318287 1760's-95

Huston, John

3384. Persico, Joseph E. AN INTERVIEW WITH JOHN HUSTON. *Am. Heritage 1982 33(3): 8-15.* John Huston discusses his early career, his difficulties with McCarthyism, and his successes and failures as a movie director. 11 illus. ca 1940-81

Hutchins, Robert M.

3385. Adler, Mortimer. THE "CHICAGO FIGHT." *Center Mag. 1977 10(5): 50-60.* Mortimer Adler's reminiscences of Robert M. Hutchins, 1929-41, when both were at the University of Chicago. 1929-41

3386. Lawson, Hal A. and Ingham, Alan G. CONFLICTING IDEOLOGIES CONCERNING THE UNIVERSITY AND INTERCOLLEGIATE ATHLETICS: HARPER AND HUTCHINS AT CHICAGO, 1892-1940. *J. of Sport Hist. 1980 7(3): 37-67.* 1892-1940
*For abstract see **Harper, William Rainey***

3387. Wheeler, Harvey. HUTCHINS HIMSELF. *Reason 1980 11(10): 25, 27-28.* Personality profile of Robert Hutchins, founder of the Center for the Study of Democratic Institutions. 1956-74

3388. —. THE EARLY INFLUENCES. *Center Mag. 1977 10(5): 15-18.* Discusses the early academic career and political ties of Robert M. Hutchins, 1917-32. 1917-32

Hutchinson, Anne

3389. King, Anne. ANNE HUTCHINSON AND ANNE BRADSTREET: LITERATURE AND EXPERIENCE, FAITH AND WORKS IN MASSACHUSETTS BAY COLONY. *Int. J. of Women's Studies [Canada] 1978 1(5): 445-467.* 1630's-70's
*For abstract see **Bradstreet, Anne***

3390. Maclear, J. F. ANNE HUTCHINSON AND THE MORTALIST HERESY. *New England Q. 1981 54(1): 74-103.* Modern historians of the Antinomian controversy and Anne Hutchinson's 1638 ecclesiastical trial in Massachusetts Bay have ignored Anne's mortalism. The "Soul Sleepers" or mortalists, including Hutchinson, rejected the belief in the conscious immortality of the soul and instead asserted that bodies and souls perish together at death. Hutchinson's belief was both part of the historic Reformation and harbinger of that religious experimentation that characterized many interregnum Puritans. The episode was significant in Puritan history. It shows that the disappearance of mortalism was not quite as total as John Winthrop asserted, clarifies Hutchinson's personality and the nature of her threat to the infant colony, and makes her skepticism about the soul's immortality comprehensible within the context of Continental sectarianism, Stuart Puritanism, and 17th-century intellectual history. Primary sources; 33 notes. 1638

Hutchinson, Mathias

3391. Ryan, Pat M., ed. MATHIAS HUTCHINSON'S "NOTES OF A JOURNEY" (1819-20). *Quaker Hist. 1979 68(2): 92-114.* A biographical introduction to the journal of this 24-year-old companion of Edward Hicks. Hutchinson was looking for a site to farm, as indicated by his attention to climate, soils, prices, and trade. He moved to Ledyard, Cayuga County, New York, in 1821, and became a substantial farmer, inventor, and Whig assemblyman. The diary, printed in full, documents travel conditions and the central Pennsylvania, western New York, and Ontario frontier to which northeastern Friends were moving. Some Genesee segments appeared in *Rochester History.* Based on Quaker and local histories, and Edward Hicks's parallel *Memoirs;* 65 notes. Article to be continued. 1819-20

Hutchinson, Thomas

3392. Pencak, William. THE MARTYROLOGY OF THOMAS HUTCHINSON: FAMILY AND PUBLIC LIFE. *New England Hist. and Geneal. Register 1982 136(Oct): 279-293.* Analyzes Thomas Hutchinson's self-examination of his life and his attempt to justify his principles and behavior. Based on the writings of Hutchinson: a family history, diaries, and correspondence; 23 notes. 18c

Hutton, Laurence

3393. Lawrence, Gail Herndon. "The Literary Career of Laurence Hutton." U. of Notre Dame 1980. 204 pp. *DAI 1980 41(6): 2606-A.* DA8028464 1875-98

Hyatt, Harry Middleton

3394. Bell, Michael Edward. HARRY MIDDLETON HYATT'S QUEST FOR THE ESSENCE OF HUMAN SPIRIT. *J. of the Folklore Inst. 1979 16(1-2): 1-27.* Recounts the life of Harry Middleton Hyatt (1896-1978), pioneer American folklorist. The self-taught Hyatt, whose *Folk-Lore from Adams County Illinois* (1935; revised 1965) and *Hoodoo-Conjuration-Witchcraft-Rootwork* (5 vol., 1970-78) are landmarks in American folklore, brought an intense humanism to his work. He successfully combined his formal training in theology with his fieldwork. Though Hyatt did not annotate or provide commentary to his collections, he nevertheless compiled the most important body of materials yet available on voodoo magic and related rituals and beliefs. His experiences in the field, mostly in the American South, provide valuable information for novice and experienced collectors alike. Based on interviews with Hyatt, his fieldwork manuscripts, and his tape-recorded memoirs; 11 notes. ca 1920-78

3395. Hand, Wayland D. and Tally, Frances M. SUPERSTITION, CUSTOM, AND RITUAL MAGIC: HARRY M. HYATT'S APPROACH TO THE STUDY OF FOLKLORE. *J. of the Folklore Inst. 1979 16(1-2): 28-43.* Harry Midddleton Hyatt (1896-1978) was drawn to folklore by an interest in primitive religion. Hyatt, who directed the Alma Egan Hyatt Foundation (created in 1932), enlisted the aid of his sisters (most importantly of Minnie Hyatt Small), to help him collect beliefs, superstitions, legends, customs, and folk medical practices from his native area. The result, *Folk-Lore from Adams County Illinois* (1935; revised 1965), eventually included more than 10,000 pieces of folklore and was one of the finest and most complete regional collections assembled in the United States. This project acquainted Hyatt with black folk materials and led to the hypothesis that miracle and magic were the crucial traits which separated belief and custom from other forms of folklore. These concerns were reflected in his important collection, *Hoodoo-Conjuration-Witchcraft-Rootwork* (5 vol., 1970-78), which was based on fieldwork throughout the South, 1936-40. The work significantly enlarged the body of American medical pharmacopeia and scatology. 24 notes. 1920-78

Hyman, John A.

3396. Reid, George W. FOUR IN BLACK: NORTH CAROLINA'S BLACK CONGRESSMEN, 1874-1901. *J. of Negro Hist. 1979 64(3): 229-243.* 1874-1901
For abstract see ***Cheatham, Henry P.***

I

Ickelheimer, Herman

3397. —. A MEMORIAL FOR A BLUE-COLLAR, BAVARIAN-BORN, SAN FRANCISCO FORTY-NINER. *Western States Jewish Hist. Q. 1981 14(1): 42-44.* Herman Ickelheimer (1824-88), a Bavarian house painter, joined the gold rush, arriving in California on 30 August 1849. He worked the Yuba River mines until 1851, when illness made him return to San Francisco. He resumed his occupation as a house painter. An active member of a volunteer fire company, and of the Jewish community, he died in 1888 following a long illness. Based on a memorial of the Society of California Pioneers; 6 notes. 1849-88

Ickes, Harold L.

3398. Lawler, Pat. HAROLD ICKES: THE MAN ALASKANS LOVED TO HATE. *Alaska J. 1983 13(1): 100-107.* Harold Ickes was Secretary of the Interior during 1933-46. His Progressive political thought was poorly suited to the rugged individualism of most Alaskans. He treated Alaska as a place with no real inhabitants, to be used for the benefit of the United States as a whole. Illus., 7 photos, 18 notes. 1933-46

3399. Maze, John and White, Graham. HAROLD L. ICKES: A PSYCHOHISTORICAL PERSPECTIVE. *J. of Psychohistory 1981 8(4): 421-444.* Analyzes the political career of Harold L. Ickes (1874-1952) by studying parental influences mentioned in his diary and autobiography. Ickes was secretary of the Interior Department during 1933-46. He unhappily identified with his mother and somewhat unsuccessfully sought the affection of his father. Politics and religion interested Ickes's mother, whereas his father had suffered an early defeat at an elective office when his son campaigned for him. Ickes later backed many losing politicians, perhaps trying not to "triumph over" his father. Ickes may have unconsciously patterned himself after his mother in his fanatic pride in office, his meticulous honesty, and his childlike devotion to Franklin D. Roosevelt. Based on the diary and autobiography of Harold L. Ickes and the Harold L. Ickes Papers (Library of Congress); 51 notes. 1874-1941

Iglesias, Santiago

3400. Cordova, Gonzalo F. "Resident Commissioner Santiago Iglesias and His Times." (Vol. 1-3) Georgetown U. 1982. 807 pp. *DAI 1983 43(9): 3086-A.* DA8302766 1896-1939

Igoe, William L.

3401. Thompson, Alice Anne. "The Life and Career of William L. Igoe, the Reluctant Boss, 1879-1953." St. Louis U. 1980. 361 pp. *DAI 1981 41(7): 3236-A.* DA8101277 1902-53

Illowy, Bernard

3402. Ellenson, David. A JEWISH LEGAL DECISION BY RABBI BERNARD ILLOWY OF NEW ORLEANS AND ITS DISCUSSION IN NINETEENTH CENTURY EUROPE. *Am. Jewish Hist. 1979 69(2): 174-195.* Dr. Bernard Illowy (1812-71) immigrated to the United States in 1853 and became one of the first Orthodox rabbis in the country. He engaged in disputes with Reform rabbis and rendered decisions in matters of Jewish canon law. In 1864, he placed a ban on a mohel who circumcised sons born to Jewish fathers and non-Jewish mothers. His decision was upheld by various European Orthodox rabbis, including Esriel Hildesheimer, but was contested by Rabbi Zvi Hirsch Kalischer. The episode demonstrates the lax state of Orthodoxy in mid-19th-century America, and shows that Illowy was respected by his European rabbinical colleagues. Based on Illowy's collected writings and on contemporary newspaper accounts; 36 notes. 1853-65

Imlay, Gilbert

3403. Fant, Joseph Lewis, III. "A Study of Gilbert Imlay (1754-1828): His Life and Works." U. of Pennsylvania 1984. 256 pp. *DAI 1985 46(1): 151-A.* DA8505062 1770's-1828

Ingalls, Joshua K.

3404. Hall, Bowman N. JOSHUA K. INGALLS, AMERICAN INDIVIDUALIST: LAND REFORMER, OPPONENT OF HENRY GEORGE AND ADVOCATE OF LAND LEASING, NOW AN ESTABLISHED MODE. *Am. J. of Economics and Sociol. 1980 39(4): 383-396.* Joshua K. Ingalls was a member of a particularly cohesive group of 19th century intellectual iconoclasts in America, the individualists. Two controversies made him widely known at the time: the land reform vs. abolition argument before the Civil War, and his attacks on Henry George in the 1880's over the issue of land reform through tax reform or land reform through land leasing under an occupancy and use system of tenure. Ingalls held George failed to understand the "true" nature of capitalism; rent goes to the landlord as capitalist as reward for his investment; the landowning capitalist appropriates this by his dominion over the land. Though Ingalls's argument did not prevail, land leasing, which he advocated, is the form in which some resources are now disposed of, as in grazing rights and mineral exploration on public land, and in oil exploration rights on the continental shelves; and in the disposition of urban sites such as the site of Rockefeller Center and the Chrysler Building in New York (the former to the benefit of Columbia University, the latter Cooper Union, both by legislative action). 1847-90

Ingalls, Melville E.

3405. Jones, John Paul. THE BIG MAN OF THE BIG FOUR. *Cincinnati Hist. Soc. Bull. 1974 32(3): 78-103.* Chronicles the financial career of Melville E. Ingalls, a Cincinnati businessman and financier, including investments in railroads, local hotels, and business buildings, 1871-1914. 1871-1914

Ingersoll, Ralph

3406. Moe, John Frederick. "A Journalist's Odyssey: Ralph Ingersoll and the Origins of *PM.*" Indiana U. 1978. 402 pp. *DAI 1979 39(7): 3894-A.* 1925-59

Ingersoll, Robert G.

3407. Cheney, Lynne Vincent. ROBERT INGERSOLL: THE ILLUSTRIOUS INFIDEL. *American Heritage 1985 36(2): 81-88.* Robert G. Ingersoll was a teacher, lawyer, and politician who, during the Civil War, became a popular speaker at rallies. After the war, he spoke mostly about religion, which he attacked, and women's rights, which he supported. His speech nominating James G. Blaine for the presidency in 1876 thrust him into the political arena, where his rabid, partisan oratory stirred the faithful but sometimes embarrassed those for whom he campaigned. His sudden death gave rise to unfounded rumors that he had made a conversion to religion on his deathbed. 3 photos, illus. 1850-99

3408. Plummer, Mark A. ROBERT G. INGERSOLL AND THE SENSUAL GODS: AN UNPUBLISHED LETTER. *Western Illinois Regional Studies 1980 3(2): 168-172.* Brief biography of teacher, lawyer, and skeptic Robert Ingersoll (1833-99); reprints a previously unpublished letter written in 1870 by Ingersoll to his friend, Illinois Governor Richard J. Oglesby, which deals with the erotic gods of Hinduism. ca 1867-70

Ingersoll, Truman

3409. Johnston, Patricia Condon. TRUMAN INGERSOLL: ST. PAUL PHOTOGRAPHER PICTURED THE WORLD. *Minnesota Hist. 1980 47(4): 122-132.* Profiles Minnesota's Truman Ingersoll, a locally prominent photographer and marketer of stereoscopic views from the mid-eighties until 1909. Ingersoll had close ties with Eastman Kodak and knew Theodore Roosevelt. He belonged to St. Paul's playful but prestigious Nushka Club, of which he took photographs. 1862-1922

Inglis, John

3410. Mount, Graeme S. and Mount, Joan E. BISHOP JOHN INGLIS AND HIS ATTITUDE TOWARD RACE IN BERMUDA IN THE ERA OF EMANCIPATION. *J. of the Can. Church Hist. Soc. [Canada] 1983 25(1): 25-32.* The Right Reverend John Inglis, Anglican bishop of Nova Scotia, espoused a liberal racial policy in Bermuda between 1825 and 1839. In the strict racial segregation of Bermuda, Inglis promoted black education and black membership in the Anglican Church. Before emancipation in 1832, Inglis insisted that black slaves attend divine services with their white masters. Bermudian blacks later left the Anglican Church in droves because of the racist episcopacy of Inglis's successor, Bishop Edward Feild. Based on documents in the Anglican Church of Canada Archives, Society for the Propagation of the Gospel Archives, and Bermuda Archives; 40 notes. 1825-50

Ingram, Rosa Lee

3411. Katz, Maude White, ed. LEARNING FROM HISTORY: THE INGRAM CASE OF THE 1940'S. *Freedomways 1979 19(2): 82-86.* Reprints a petition by W. E. B. Du Bois submitted in 1949 to the UN, requesting its intercession in the case of a black Georgian, Rosa Lee Ingram, serving (with two of her sons) a life sentence for the 1947 death of her neighbor, John Stratford, who, after severely beating her, was clubbed over the head by her 16-year-old son. 1947-49

Inkster, Anne Ellen

3412. Inkster, Anne Ellen. TO SCHOOL IN LONDON. *Beaver [Canada] 1979 310(1): 42-49.* Relates author's experience at school in London with her sister, 1885-93, and her voyage from Fort Churchill, Manitoba, on Hudson Bay. 1885-93

Inkster, Tom H.

3413. Inkster, Tom H. I REMEMBER PEACE RIVER JIM. *Alberta Hist. [Canada] 1983 31(3): 9-13.* ca 1885-1955

For abstract see ***Cornwall, James Kennedy***

Inness, George

3414. Cikovsky, Nicolai, Jr. THE CIVILIZED LANDSCAPE. *American Heritage 1985 36(3): 32-41.* George Inness spent his career painting what he called "the civilized landscape." His works are known for his use of color, tone, shape, and pigment. Scorned early, his career turned for the better in the 1860's, and by the time of his death, he was well-known. 5 illus. 1850-90

3415. Morley, Jane. GEORGE INNESS—FRIEND OF LABOR. *Labor Hist. 1984 25(2): 252-257.* Discusses the political and economic beliefs of the American landscape painter, George Inness, and reprints an article Inness wrote for a new labor journal, *The American Federationist,* in which he urged labor to organize and fight for the eight-hour day. Secondary sources; 17 notes. 1855-94

Innis, Harold

3416. Lower, Arthur. HAROLD INNIS AS I REMEMBER HIM. *Journal of Canadian Studies [Canada] 1985-86 20(4): 3-11.* Historian Harold Innis's major contribution was to help bring Canadian scholarship out of the shadows and to make it a respectable endeavor. Note. 1924-52

Innis, Harold Adams

3417. Cooper, Thomas William. "Pioneers in Communication: The Lives and Thought of Harold Innis and Marshall McLuhan." U. of Toronto [Canada] 1980. *DAI 1980 41(6): 2341-2342-A.* 1936-69

Inskip, Martha Jane Foster

3418. Brown, Kenneth O. "THE WORLD-WIDE EVANGELIST": THE LIFE AND WORK OF MARTHA INSKIP. *Methodist Hist. 1983 21(4): 179-191.* Gives a biography of Methodist missionary Martha Jane Foster Inskip, wife of missionary John S. Inskip, emphasizing her contribution to their team ministry, as well as her own individual achievements. 71 notes. 1836-90

Ipellie, Atootook

3419. Ipellie, Atootook. FROBISHER BAY CHILDHOOD. *Beaver [Canada] 1980 310(4): 4-11.* The author, an Inuit, was educated in Frobisher Bay and Yellowknife from the age of eight. Notes the highlights of life in Frobisher—the yearly arrival of the Hudson's Bay Company ship, knowing the airmen from the base at Frobisher Bay, Sunday night movies at Apex Hill, and trading pictures of movie stars. "Life in the Arctic is changing fast and Frobisher has changed along with its people" as it has become home to many Inuits from many other northern communities. Illus. 1959-80

Iredell, James

3420. Shulhafer, Lucia. JAMES IREDELL, PATRIOT. *Daughters of the Am. Revolution Mag. 1979 113(9): 994-999.* English-born James Iredell (1751-99) arrived in North Carolina as a youth, became an American patriot, constitutional lawyer, and US Supreme Court justice. 1751-99

Ireland, Ellen

3421. Johnston, Patricia Condon. REFLECTED GLORY: THE STORY OF ELLEN IRELAND. *Minnesota Hist. 1982 48(1): 13-23.* Ellen Ireland, sister of John, the first archbishop of St. Paul, spent 72 years as Sister Seraphine, an educator, administrator, and, for 39 years, mother superior of the Sisters of St. Joseph of Corondelet's St. Paul Province (Minnesota and the Dakotas). Her influence was felt by 30 schools, five hospitals, and the College of St. Catherine. Based on secondary sources and interviews; 31 notes, 12 illus. 1842-1930

Ireland, John

3422. Lathrop, Alan K. A FRENCH ARCHITECT IN MINNESOTA: EMMANUEL L. MASQUERAY, 1861-1917. *Minnesota Hist. 1980 47(2): 42-56.* 1904-17
*For abstract see **Masqueray, Emmanuel L.***

Ironmonger, Elizabeth Hogg

3423. Ironmonger, Elizabeth and Oxreider, Julia, ed. AN 1890'S KITCHEN. *Tennessee Folklore Soc. Bull. 1979 45(4): 166-169.* Briefly traces the background of Elizabeth Hogg Ironmonger, born in York County, Virginia, in 1891, and reprints an article written by Mrs. Ironmonger about the kitchen in her childhood home. 1890's

Irons, Earl D.

3424. Barrow, Gary Wayne. "Colonel Earl D. Irons: His Role in the History of Music Education in the Southwest to 1958." North Texas State U. 1982. 187 pp. *DAI 1982 43(3): 578-A.* DA8217614 ca 1915-58

Irving, Washington

3425. Malia, Peter. WASHINGTON IRVING: THE STORYTELLER AT SUNNYSIDE. *Am. Hist. Illus. 1983 18(3): 16-25.* Chronicles the life and writings of Washington Irving, including personal tragedies, travels, and relations with publishers. 1800-59

3426. Perez Gallego, Candido. WASHINGTON IRVING Y EL HECHIZO DE LO ESPAÑOL [Washington Irving and the fascination of Spain]. *Cuadernos Hispanoamericanos [Spain] 1983 (401): 180-188.* The life of Washington Irving was a continual pilgrimage through literature and experience. To his many qualities as a historian, which are shared by other writers, Irving added an ecstatic attitude toward what is past and lost, as in his explorations of the Alhambra in Granada. For Irving, this exploration was both history and his own biography, the constitution of his inner world. 8 notes. 1804-59

Irwin, Harriet Morrison

3427. Heisner, Beverly. HARRIET MORRISON IRWIN'S HEXAGONAL HOUSE: AN INVENTION TO IMPROVE DOMESTIC DWELLINGS. *North Carolina Hist. Rev. 1981 58(2): 105-123.* Harriet Morrison Irwin (1828-97) of Charlotte, North Carolina, was the first woman in the United States to patent an architectural design. Irwin's hexagonal house plan, patented in 1869, expressed her desire for an efficient but open home, with easy access to nature. Her novel, *The Hermit of Petraea* (1871), dedicated to the English writer, John Ruskin, author of popular books on architecture, contains discussions of Irwin's views on the relationship between humans, their homes, and the natural environment. Irwin's own needs as an invalid also influenced her architectural designs. James Patton Irwin (1820-1903), Harriet's husband, advertised her designs in regional magazines. Several homes may have been built according to her designs. Based on genealogical materials, private family papers, US Patent Office Records, Irwin's novel, county property records, and secondary sources on local history. 19 illus., 2 architectural plans, reproduction of Irwin's Letters Patent; 58 notes. 1860-1900

Irwin, Will

3428. Hudson, Robert V. WILL IRWIN'S CRUSADE FOR THE LEAGUE OF NATIONS. *Journalism Hist. 1975 2(3): 84-85, 97.* During 1920-39, Will Irwin campaigned through books and articles to get the United States to join the League of Nations to strengthen it and prevent a future war. 1920-39

Isaak, Gottlieb

3429. Wenzel, Otto, transl. and Bruntsch, Otto. A VOICE FROM THE PAST: THE AUTOBIOGRAPHY OF GOTTLIEB ISAAK. *J. of the Am. Hist. Soc. of Germans from Russia 1977 (25): 21-23.* Provides excerpts from the autobiography of Gottlieb Isaak (1834-1921), a Russian German who emigrated to South Dakota in the 1870's. 1870's

Isbister, Alexander Kennedy

3430. Cooper, Barry. ALEXANDER KENNEDY ISBISTER, A RESPECTABLE VICTORIAN. *Canadian Ethnic Studies [Canada] 1985 17(2): 44-63.* Alexander Kennedy Isbister is known to Canadian historians chiefly as a critic of the Hudson's Bay Company. Grandson of Chief Factor Kennedy and his Cree wife Aggathas, Isbister was, in his own eyes, as much a participant in the great questions of British middle-class education as he was a spokesman for the interests of the mixed-blood population of Rupert's Land. Discusses his educational activities, the books he wrote and the institutions with which he associated himself in his efforts to ensure that teachers of middle-class pupils met appropriate standards of competence. His career outside the context of his struggles with the company and his enormous success as a leader in educational reform during his residence in London make him one of the most unusual sons of Rupert's Land. 1822-70's

Ise, John

3431. Sheridan, Richard B. JOHN ISE, 1885-1969, ECONOMIST, CONSERVATIONIST, PROPHET OF THE ENERGY CRISIS. *Kansas Hist. 1982 5(2): 83-106.* John Ise taught at the University of Kansas for 39 years. Because of interests in the conservation of natural resources, first aroused by the forestry movement, he wrote *United States Oil Policy,* (1926) a book that clearly warned against later oil shortages. He felt the major danger lay in America's continued use of oil for all kinds of equipment that could be better operated by coal. His work ended on a pessimistic note, since he did not think that a rational policy of oil conservation would be developed. Based on the John Ise and Ernest Lindley papers, University of Kansas; illus., 48 notes. 1916-45

Isham, Alfred H.

3432. VanWormer, Stephen R. ALFRED H. ISHAM: A GILDED AGE ENTREPRENEUR IN SAN DIEGO COUNTY. *Southern California Quarterly 1984 66(4): 303-333.* Profiles Alfred H. Isham, an unscrupulous businessman who represented the worst in 19th-century entrepreneurship. Born in New York, he moved to California in 1883, locating first in San Francisco and then San Diego, dealing in agricultural implements. His business strategy was revealed in a series of lawsuits in the 1890's as he lied and cheated his way toward profit. Isham's most notorious endeavor was the marketing of California Waters of Life, an alleged cure-all that promised to grow hair, restore youth, and cure various illnesses. The patent medicine was worthless, but Isham's advertising, alleged testimonials, and falsely planted news stories combined to make the product a success in the 1890's. Done in by the Pure Food and Drug Law of 1906, Isham returned to New York and died there in 1910. Based on newspaper and other contemporary accounts, and on federal census and court records; 4 photos, illus., 127 notes. 1883-1910

Ishi

3433. Campbell, C. W. "THE WILD MAN OF OROVILLE." *Am. Hist. Illus. 1977 12(3): 18-27.* Ishi (d. 1916), the last member of the Yana Indians, was discovered in Oroville, California, in 1911 and studied by anthropologist Alfred L. Kroeber; discusses survival, subsistence, ritual, and daily life patterns of the Yana Indians as displayed by Ishi. 1911-16

Ives, Charles

3434. Harvey, Mark Sumner. "Charles Ives: Prophet of American Civil Religion." Boston U. 1983. 430 pp. *DAI 1983 43(12): 3942-A.* DA8309768 ca 1900-54

Ives, Ronald L.

3435. Byrkit, James W. A DEDICATION TO THE MEMORY OF RONALD L. IVES, 1909-1982. *Arizona and the West 1984 26(2): 102-106.* American geographer and historian Ronald L. Ives was a keen observer and prolific scholar of the Southwest, particularly the Sonoran Desert region. His some 600 articles in 40 professional journals probed anthropology, archaeology, cartography, folklore, geology, history, linguistics, mining, navigation and surveying, optics and illusion, and weather and meteorology with an experience gained from firsthand, intimate observation. Illus., biblio. 1930's-82

Ivins, Wilson H.

3436. Ivins, Wilson H. OVER THE RIVER AND FAR AWAY. *Old Northwest 1982-83 8(4): 383-394.* Presents Ivins's recollections of his youth in Sault Ste. Marie, Michigan, particularly family journeys by train to visit his grandparents in Manton, Michigan. Although isolated physically, Sault Ste. Marie was a center of commerce and communication. While there were few roads in the vicinity, the availability of rail, ferry, and canal transportation made the city less provincial than one would expect. 4 illus. 1916-26

Ivy, Andrew C.

3437. Ward, Patricia Spain. "WHO WILL BELL THE CAT?" ANDREW C. IVY AND KREBIOZEN. *Bull. of the Hist. of Medicine 1984 58(1): 28-52.* In 1951, Dr. Andrew C. Ivy, a distinguished medical school professor and researcher, announced that krebiozen was a cancer cure. Almost immediately, other tests indicated that the drug had no effect on cancer. The result was conflict within the University of Illinois Medical College and the Chicago Medical Society. Ultimately, the National Cancer Institute and the Food and Drug Administration became enmeshed in the controversy. Krebiozen has been called the most publicized unorthodox cancer treatment in American history. Primary sources; 73 notes, illus. 1951-64

Izard, George

3438. deSaussure, Charlton, Jr. MEMOIRS OF GENERAL GEORGE IZARD, 1825. *South Carolina Hist. Mag. 1977 78(1): 43-55.* Reprints George Izard's memoirs (written in 1825), in which he recalls his service to the federal government, as well as the lives of his family, 1792-1825. 1792-1825

Izzard, Anna Eliza

3439. Fields, Mamie Garvin. NO. 7 SHORT COURT. *Southern Exposure 1980 8(3): 83-87.* Reminiscences of growing up in Charleston, North Carolina, that focus on the school the author's aunt, Anna Eliza Izzard, ran in her home at No. 7 Short Court; 1891-1900. 1891-1900

J

Jackson, Alfred Eugene

3440. McKee, James W., Jr. ALFRED E. JACKSON: A PROFILE OF AN EAST TENNESSEE ENTREPRENEUR, RAILWAY PROMOTER, AND SOLDIER. *East Tennessee Hist. Soc. Publ. 1977 49: 9-36.* Alfred Eugene Jackson of Jonesboro, Tennessee, was a successful rural capitalist, who became an important antebellum railroad entrepreneur. Before the outbreak of the Civil War, his varied business activities, and those of his associates, contributed to the economic prosperity of East Tennessee. His willingness to take the financial risk necessary to develop the East Tennessee & Virginia Railroad, which linked the commercial centers in the North, brought prosperity to the area and climaxed a brilliant career. 55 notes. Article to be continued. 1820-60

Jackson, Andrew

3441. Belohlavek, John M. "LET THE EAGLE SOAR!": DEMOCRATIC CONSTRAINTS ON THE FOREIGN POLICY OF ANDREW JACKSON. *Presidential Studies Q. 1980 10(1): 36-50.* Eight years of Andrew Jackson's presidency witnessed the revival of this office that had stagnated since Jefferson's departure in 1809. Jackson's diplomacy could be called energetic, sometimes imaginative, and often successful. During his two terms the United States involved itself in no foreign wars. Jacksonian diplomacy was characterized by the president himself, not by his cabinet. Based on official documents; 41 notes, 2 appendixes. 1829-37

3442. Ely, James W., Jr. THE LEGAL PRACTICE OF ANDREW JACKSON. *Tennessee Hist. Q. 1979 38(4): 421-435.* Andrew Jackson began reading law in 1784 in Salisbury, North Carolina. In 1788 he took a post as prosecutor in Nashville, Tennessee, where as elected Attorney General of the Metro District from 1788-96 he had a 62% conviction rate. A prodigious litigant on his own, Jackson also won two-thirds of his suits in private practice. If he never democratized the law, he won considerable success and reputation as a lawyer. Based on Metro District Superior Court, Minute Book, and other sources; 3 tables, 78 notes. 1784-98

3443. Kaye, Jacqueline. JOHN QUINCY ADAMS AND *THE CONQUEST OF IRELAND. Éire-Ireland 1981 16(1): 34-54.* 1828-31
For abstract see ***Adams, John Quincy***

3444. Langley, Harold D. RESPECT FOR CIVILIAN AUTHORITY: THE TRAGIC CAREER OF CAPTAIN ANGUS. *Am. Neptune 1980 40(1): 23-37.* 1800-40
For abstract see ***Angus, Samuel***

3445. Robbins, Peggy. ANDREW AND RACHEL JACKSON. *Am. Hist. Illus. 1977 12(5): 22-28.* Discusses the love relationship between Andrew Jackson and Rachel Robards (later to become Jackson's wife), the scandal it produced, and the use of the relationship as anti-Jackson political fodder, 1788-1828. 1788-1828

3446. Sharp, James Roger. ANDREW JACKSON AND THE LIMITS OF PRESIDENTIAL POWER. *Congressional Studies 1980 7(2): 63-80.* Discusses the conflict between Congress and Andrew Jackson in 1833 over his attempts to increase executive power which resulted in his censure by the Senate; covers 1789-1834. 1789-1834

3447. Watson, Harry L. OLD HICKORY'S DEMOCRACY. *Wilson Quarterly 1985 9(4): 101-133.* Reviews Andrew Jackson's political life and his contributions to American democracy. 1806-37

3448. —. ANDREW JACKSON'S ADVICE TO THE CHEROKEES. *J. of Cherokee Studies 1979 4(2): 96-97.* Cherokee removal was consistently pursued as a major policy by Andrew Jackson throughout his career. In 1835, in advice to the Cherokee Indians, he forcibly reiterated this policy. He was convinced that the Cherokees had no choice but to remove west of the Mississippi or face extinction. Reproduced from *The Alleghany Democrat* (Alleghany, New York), 7 April 1835. 1835

Jackson, Charles Douglas

3449. Cook, Blanche Wiessen. FIRST COMES THE LIE: C. D. JACKSON AND POLITICAL WARFARE. *Radical History Review 1984 (31): 42-71.* Profiles Charles Douglas Jackson, publisher of *Fortune,* vice-president of Time, Inc., architect of Crusade for Freedom, founder of Radio Free Europe and personal confidant of President Eisenhower. After World War II, in an attempt to check Communist influence, Jackson created and shaped the craft of 20th-century politial warfare. From United States-Soviet relations to destabilization of Guatemala, Jackson devised political warfare operations, in place of bombs and bullets, to guarantee an American empire. His efforts had mixed results. Today, due to Jackson, political warfare is "no longer a substitute for war; it has become the precursor for war." Based on the C. D. Jackson Papers, Dwight D. Eisenhower Library, Abilene, Kansas, and secondary sources; 28 notes. 1941-64

3450. Haight, David. THE PAPERS OF C. D. JACKSON: A GLIMPSE AT PRESIDENT EISENHOWER'S PSYCHOLOGICAL WARFARE EXPERT. *Manuscripts 1976 28(1): 27-37.* Among the more interesting manuscript collections in the Dwight D. Eisenhower Library at Abilene are the papers of Charles Douglas Jackson (1902-1964). Before being brought into the Eisenhower administration as an advisor dealing in psychological warfare and the cold war in order to balance the intransigence of John Foster Dulles, Jackson was a vice president in the Luce publishing enterprises. Although Jackson was never soft on communism, he represented the liberal element among Eisenhower's close advisors. His papers spanning the period from 1931-67 offer a potentially rich source for historians of the Eisenhower Administration. 25 notes. 1931-67

Jackson, Donald

3451. Jackson, Donald. WHAT I DID FOR LOVE—OF EDITING. *Western Hist. Q. 1982 13(3): 291-297.* Autobiographical evaluation of the author's involvement in editing of the Lewis and Clark, John Charles Fremont, and George Washington papers. Editing is at once as exacting and as rewarding an endeavor as any that a historian can engage in. 1982

Jackson, Helen Hunt

3452. Banning, Evelyn I. A BOARDER IN SLEEPY HOLLOW. *Newport Hist. 1975 48(1): 247-254.* Gives a short history of Helen Hunt Jackson's life in Newport (which she termed Sleepy Hollow), including the writing done there, the death of her first husband (Edward Bessell Hunt) and oldest child, and her 1875 marriage to William Sharpless Jackson, 1855-85. 4 photos. 1855-85

3453. Marsden, Michael T. A DEDICATION TO THE MEMORY OF HELEN HUNT JACKSON, 1830-1885. *Arizona and the West 1979 21(2): 108-112.* Helen Maria Fiske Hunt Jackson (1830-85) was a prolific and anonymous writer of children's stories, travel sketches, and magazine essays. An 1879 lecture by two Ponca Indians gave her the consuming passion of her life. She began immediately to compile material on Indian mistreatment and to write tracts, newspaper articles, and petitions at a feverish pace. Her *A Century of Dishonor* submitted massive evidence that the government was dishonest and cruel toward the Indian. Some credit the book with inspiring formation of the Indian Rights Association a year later and with leading to the Dawes Act in 1887. It continues to contribute to the romanticization of the Indian. Illus., biblio. 1879-85

3454. Mathes, Valerie Sherer. HELEN HUNT JACKSON. *Masterkey 1981 55(1): 18-21.* Biography of Helen Hunt Jackson (1830-85), writer of prose and poetry, notable for her history of government-Indian relations, *A Century of Dishonor* (1880), and her novel, *Ramona* (1884). 1845-85

3455. Stern, Norton B. THE KING OF TEMECULA: LOUIS WOLF. *Southern California Q. 1976 58(1): 63-74.* 1852-87
*For abstract see **Wolf, Louis***

Jackson, Henry M.

3456. Novak, Michael. IN MEMORIAM: HENRY M. JACKSON. *Commentary 1984 77(1): 48-50.* Surveys the career of Democratic Senator Henry M. Jackson, who embodied the spirit of vigorous Democratic internationalism. 1940-83

Jackson, Hewitt

3457. Vaughan, Thomas, and Hamilton, Bruce T. ARTIST HEWITT JACKSON RE-CREATES THE PAGEANT OF NORTHWEST MARITIME EXPLORATION. *Am. West 1980 17(1): 36-47.* Hewitt Jackson (b. 1914) first went to sea as a boy on a lumber-carrying schooner. After extended periods at sea, military service, drafting and engineering drawing with the Department of Oceanography at the University of Washington, and detailed work for naval architects, he turned to art. He is the "acknowledged dean of maritime painters" in the Pacific Northwest. Each painting is the result of unremitting research for detail in all available contemporary journals and charts. In most cases he also constructs models and precise scale drawings. The models and drawings are so faithful that it is said they will "float." He has captured critical moments in North Pacific maritime exploration. 12 illus. 1963-80

Jackson, Howell Edmunds

3458. Hardaway, Roger D. HOWELL EDMUNDS JACKSON: TENNESSEE LEGISLATOR AND JURIST. *West Tennessee Hist. Soc. Papers 1976 (30): 104-119.* Tennessee has had six jurists serve on the bench of the US Supreme Court. One of these was Howell Edmunds Jackson (1832-95), who served a short time (4 March 1893-8 August 1895) before his death. Prior to his appointment to the Supreme Court bench Jackson had served as representative to the state legislature, US Senator, and US Circuit Court Judge, where he gained a reputation as a rigid constructionist and an expert in patent law. While he was not one of the great associate justices, no charge has ever been laid against his integrity. While tending to be biased toward corporations, at the same time he felt that railroads should pay their fair share of taxes. Because of the brevity of his term, plus his low seniority on the Court, he was not assigned important cases. His opinions reveal, however, that he thought the judicial branch of government should leave lawmaking to the legislative branch. He attained several positions of power on the state and federal levels, serving with distinction in each capacity. Thus he stands as an important figure in Tennessee political history. Based largely on US Supreme Court decisions and secondary sources; illus., 118 notes. 1832-95

Jackson, John George

3459. Brown, Stephen W. "John George Jackson: A Biography." West Virginia U. 1977. 414 pp. *DAI 1978 38(12): 7508-7509-A.* 1798-1825

3460. Brown, Stephen W. CONGRESSMAN JOHN GEORGE JACKSON AND REPUBLICAN NATIONALISM, 1813-1817. *West Virginia Hist. 1977 38(2): 93-125.* John George Jackson served in Congress from northwestern Virginia, during 1813-17, as a firm supporter of the War of 1812 and Madison's administration. He saw impressment as the war's chief cause, denied that Republicans wanted to conquer Canada, and blasted domestic antiwar sentiment. He supported federal internal improvements and a new national Bank but criticized New England commercial interests. Primary and secondary sources; 91 notes. 1813-17

Jackson, John Jay, Jr.

3461. Sturm, Phillip. MOTHER JONES AND THE IRON JUDGE. *J. of the West Virginia Hist. Assoc. 1981 5(1): 18-26.* 1902
*For abstract see **Jones, Mary Harris***

Jackson, John Jay, Jr. (family)

3462. Baas, Jacob C., Jr. JOHN JAY JACKSON, JR., AND THE JACKSONS OF PARKERSBURG: THEIR FIRST ONE HUNDRED YEARS. *West Virginia Hist. 1976 38(1): 23-34.* John Jay Jackson, Jr. (1824-1907), was born into a prominent Scotch-Irish family of western Virginia. His great-grandfather, George Jackson (b. 1757), was a congressman; his grandfather, John George Jackson (1777-1828), served eight terms in Congress, married Dolly Madison's sister, and was a strong Jeffersonian. His father, John Jay Jackson (b. 1800), was illegitimate but served in the Army and became a prosperous Whig businessman, lawyer and state legislator. John Jay Jackson, Jr., grew up in Parkersburg, was educated at Princeton, and entered law practice in the 1840's. Primary sources; 38 notes. 1715-1847

Jackson, Lawrence

3463. Hickson, Howard, ed. BLACK WRANGLER: REMINISCENCES OF LAWRENCE JACKSON. *Northeastern Nevada Hist. Soc. Q. 1977 77(1): 3-33.* Personal narrative of Lawrence Jackson, black cowboy, who wrangled horses on ranches around Elko, Nevada, from 1921 through the 1960's; includes an introduction by the editor, pp. 3-4. 1921-60's

Jackson, Mary Percy

3464. Keywan, Zonia. MARY PERCY JACKSON: PIONEER DOCTOR. *Beaver [Canada] 1977 308(3): 41-47.* In 1929, Dr. Mary Percy left England to practice medicine in northern Alberta. She began near Manning, among new immigrants from Eastern Europe who knew little English. After her marriage to Frank Jackson, they moved to the farm near Keg River. Most of her service here was with local Indians and Métis. With few medical supplies, inadequate transportation, and rarely any income from patients, she continued to provide medical service to the local population until her retirement in 1974. In the past few decades she has become a nationally known spokeswoman for Indian and Métis causes. 6 illus. 1929-70's

Jackson, Robert

3465. Cox, Susan Jane Buck. "Justice Robert Jackson and the Evolution of Administrative Law." Virginia Polytechnic Inst. and State U. 1983. 326 pp. *DAI 1984 45(4): 1204-A.* DA8415944 1893-1983

Jackson, Sheldon

3466. Bender, Norman J. SHELDON JACKSON'S CRUSADE TO WIN THE WEST FOR CHRIST, 1869-1880. *Midwest Rev. 1982 4: 1-12.* Brief biography of Sheldon Jackson (1834-1909) and introduction to the concern of Presbyterian Church leaders to evangelize the West, focusing on Jackson's appointment as "Superintendent of Missions for Western Iowa, Nebraska, Dakota, Idaho, Montana, Wyoming, and Utah, or as far as our jurisdiction extends." 1869-80

3467. Haycox, Stephen W. SHELDON JACKSON IN HISTORICAL PERSPECTIVE: ALASKA NATIVE SCHOOLS AND MISSION CONTRACTS, 1885-1894. *Pacific Hist. 1984 28(1): 18-28.* Sheldon Jackson served as general agent of education in Alaska from his appointment in 1885 until 1894, when Congress withdrew financial support. Before his Alaskan appointment, he was superintendent of the Rocky Mountain district of the Presbyterian Board of Home Missions, working with American Indians. His career in Alaska was based on a philosophy consistent with the policies of the US Indian Office which he had followed and found successful. 5 illus., 31 notes. 1885-94

3468. Hinckley, Ted C. SHELDON JACKSON: GILDED AGE APOSTLE. *Journal of the West 1984 23(1): 16-25.* Profiles Sheldon Jackson, an American Protestant missionary who helped organize 23 churches before he left his first post in Minnesota for the Far West. Once there, his promotional skills were polished and his work earned him the title "Presbyterian Superintendent of the Rockies." He also worked extensively in Alaska establishing mission schools, one of which, the Sheldon Jackson College of Sitka, survives today. Based on documents of the Presbyterian Historical Society, the National Archives, and the Speer Library, Princeton, and on other primary and secondary sources; 3 photos, 50 notes. 1834-1909

Jackson, Thomas J. "Stonewall"

3469. Grimsley, Mark. JACKSON: THE WRATH OF GOD. *Civil War Times Illustrated 1984 23(1): 10-19.* Discusses the religious beliefs of Confederate General Thomas J. "Stonewall" Jackson, and shows how those beliefs showed in his life and military career in the Mexican War and the Civil War. 1846-63

Jackson, William Henry

3470. Smith, Donald B. WILLIAM HENRY JACKSON: RIEL'S SECRETARY. *Beaver [Canada] 1981 311(4): 10-19.* Toronto-born William Henry Jackson (1861-1952) was important in the North West Rebellion of 1885. He became Louis Riel's "link with the English-speaking settlers" while moving "emotionally even more constantly toward" the Métis. Jackson converted to Catholicism but later accepted Riel as "the new prophet." Jackson was sent to a lunatic asylum after the rebellion, but soon escaped to the United States, where he lived the rest of his life. 7 photos. 1869-85

3471. Smith, Donald B. HONORÉ JOSEPH JAXON: A MAN WHO LIVED FOR OTHERS. *Saskatchewan Hist. [Canada] 1981 34(3): 81-101.* A biographical sketch of a little known, but important, survivor of the North West Rebellion, who died in New York in 1952. The essay reveals the true identity of William Henry Jackson, who was born in Toronto in 1861, moved to the west as a young man, and served as secretary to Louis Riel in 1885. The metamorphosis to Honoré Joseph Jaxon and his later associations with the labor movement in the United States and Canada are mentioned as well as his passion for métis and Indian history and culture. Based on contemporary newspaper accounts, letters, personal interviews with acquaintances, and books; 115 notes, 5 photos. 1861-1952

Jacobi, Mary Putnam

3472. Morantz, Regina Markell. FEMINISM, PROFESSIONALISM, AND GERMS: THE THOUGHT OF MARY PUTNAM JACOBI AND ELIZABETH BLACKWELL. *Am. Q. 1982 34(5): 459-478.* Compares and contrasts the views held by Elizabeth Blackwell and Mary Putnam Jacobi on women as medical doctors. Blackwell viewed medicine as a means for social and moral reform, while Jacobi was interested in combating disease. On a more intense level of disagreement, Blackwell felt that women would succeed in medicine because of their humane female values, but Jacobi believed that women should participate as the equals of men in all medical specialties. Based on the Blackwell and Jacobi manuscripts; 41 notes. 1849-90

Jacobs, Henry Eyster

3473. Fry, C. George. HENRY EYSTER JACOBS: CONFESSIONAL PENNSYLVANIA-GERMAN LUTHERAN. *Concordia Hist. Inst. Q. 1982 55(4): 158-162.* The career of Henry Eyster Jacobs as a pastor, teacher, and author spanned over 60 years, and his efforts as a Lutheran theologian caused him to be viewed as a giant in his field. 1865-1928

Jacobs, James

3474. Segal, Beryl and Goldowsky, Seebert J. JAMES JACOBS, EARLY JEWISH MERCHANT OF PROVIDENCE, RHODE ISLAND. *Rhode Island Jewish Hist. Notes 1978 7(4): 461-470.* James Jacobs, possibly the first Jew to settle in Providence, was successful and prominent there, 1820's-30's and 1850's. 1820's-30's

Jacobs, John W.

3475. Jones, Rosalyn Jacobs. "Upward Mobility: A Historical Narrative. The John W. Jacobs Story." Middle Tennessee State U. 1983. 141 pp. *DAI 1984 44(11): 3455-A.* DA8404785 1852-1925

Jacobs, Lionel and Barron

3476. Moore, Dawn. PIONEER BANKING IN TUCSON: LIONEL AND BARRON JACOBS AND THE FOUNDING OF THE PIMA COUNTY BANK. *Arizona and the West 1982 24(4): 305-318.* Mark Jacobs took his family to California during the gold rush to engage in merchandising. In 1867, sons Lionel and Barron were sent to Tucson to establish a retail mercantile store. Cash and credit shortages compelled the brothers, as well as other merchants, to gradually introduce banking services. It was to their distinct advantage to use their father in San Francisco to exchange paper for gold specie. The coming of the railroad, the discovery of silver, and the growing population generated high demand for banking services. In 1878 the Jacobs brothers and partners incorporated the first bank. This helped lay the foundation for

Tucson's banking system and encouraged further economic development of southern Arizona. 4 illus., 30 notes. 1867-1913

Jacobs, Mark Israel (family)

3477. Golden, Richard L. and Golden, Arlene A. THE MARK I. JACOBS FAMILY: A DISCURSIVE OVERVIEW. *Western States Jewish Hist. Q. 1981 13(2): 99-114.* Mark Israel Jacobs (1816-94) and Hannah Solomon Jacobs (1815-72) established a general store in San Diego, California, in 1851. Their children and grandchildren expanded the family business to San Francisco and to several towns in Arizona. Sons Lionel and Barron Jacobs established the first bank in Tucson, Arizona, and saw it evolve into the Valley National Bank with 190 branches throughout Arizona. Grandson Selim Franklin is known as the father of the University of Arizona. Other family members were prominent in the commercial, social, and intellectual life of Arizona and southern California. Based on material in the Jacobs Collection, University of Arizona Library, and the Arizona Historical Society; 6 photos, 46 notes. 1851-94

Jacobs, William M.

3478. Shindle, Richard D. LANCASTER'S INFAMOUS COUNTERFEITERS. *J. of the Lancaster County Hist. Soc. 1979 83(4): 198-211.* Discusses the counterfeiting of revenue stamps from 1896 to 1899 by Lancaster, Pennsylvania, cigar manufacturer William M. Jacobs and his employee, William L. Kendig, and their attempt to have $10 million in counterfeit currency circulated. 1865-1900

Jacobs, Zina Diantha Huntington

3479. Beecher, Maureen Ursenbach. ALL THINGS MOVE IN ORDER IN THE CITY: THE NAUVOO DIARY OF ZINA DIANTHA HUNTINGTON JACOBS. *Brigham Young U. Studies 1979 19(3): 285-320.* Reproduces the diary for 1844-45 of Zina Diantha Huntington Jacobs, at one point a wife of Brigham Young, on the Mormons' life in Nauvoo, Illinois. 52 notes. 1844-45

Jacobs-Bond, Carrie

3480. Bernhardt, Marcia W. THROUGH THE YEARS. *Michigan Hist. 1985 69(1): 32-39.* Carrie Jacobs-Bond, authoress of over 400 popular songs, lived her "seven happiest years" in Iron River, Michigan. Subsequently, the Iron County Historical Society saved the Bond house from destruction, and it has become part of the Iron County Museum Park in Caspian, Michigan. Based on Carrie Jacobs-Bond's autobiography and secondary sources; 14 photos, 14 notes. 1862-1984

Jacobsen, Antonio

3481. Peluso, A. J., Jr. PAINTED SHIPS ON PAINTED OCEANS: THE LIFE AND WORK OF ANTONIO JACOBSEN. *Art & Antiques 1980 3(4): 62-67.* Danish-born Antonio Jacobsen (1849-1928) settled in New York City to a career of painting ships during the 1870's-1920's. 1870's-1920's

Jacobsen, Ethel Collins

3482. Borst, John C. THE MARY C. COLLINS FAMILY PAPERS AT THE SOUTH DAKOTA HISTORICAL RESOURCE CENTER. *South Dakota History 1982 12(4): 248-253.* 1875-1920

For abstract see ***Collins, Mary Clementine***

Jaderborg, Elizabeth

3483. Jaderborg, Elizabeth. "SELMA LIND" AND LINDSBORG. *Swedish Pioneer Hist. Q. 1980 31(2): 129-133.* "Selma Lind" was the pseudonym of the author when she wrote for the *Lindsborg News-Record* in Kansas during the 1960's. She was born and raised in New England, married a Kansas Swede in 1946, and moved to Lindsborg. Because young people did not know of their rich heritage, she wrote articles on Swedes and the area, based on deductions made through interviews, and some books. As a result of the material written and the interest it generated, "a deluge of background material [came] into the community and its surrounding satellites to prepare them immediately for a centennial celebration." 5 notes. 1962-69

Jaeger, Louis John Frederick

3484. Hargett, Janet L. PIONEERING AT YUMA CROSSING: THE BUSINESS CAREER OF L. J. F. JAEGER, 1850-1887. *Arizona and the West 1983 25(4): 329-354.* Louis John Frederick Jaeger played a major role in the history of Yuma Crossing, near the junction of the Colorado and Gila rivers on the Arizona-California border. He was an opportunistic businessman who operated a ferry; supplied soldiers, surveyors, miners, and emigrants; and branched out into cattle raising, freighting, irrigation, and mining. He was unsuccessful in federal courts with his depredation claim against the Yuma Indians, who destroyed his ferryboat in 1872. An inveterate opportunist, he eventually overextended himself. 7 illus., map, 67 notes. 1850-87

James, Charles Tillinghast

3485. Winpenny, Thomas R. THE ENGINEER AS PROMOTER: CHARLES TILLINGHAST JAMES AND THE GOSPEL OF STEAM COTTON MILLS. *Pennsylvania Mag. of Hist. and Biog. 1981 105(2): 166-181.* James's two decades of proselytizing resulted in the building of steam-driven cotton mills in Newburyport, Lancaster, and other cities. An engineer and Rhode Island senator, "mover and shaker" James contributed a vision of steam-powered cotton mills which he tirelessly promoted. Based on printed sources, official records, and secondary works; 49 notes. 1830-50

James, Henry

3486. Auchincloss, Louis. HENRY JAMES'S LITERARY USE OF HIS AMERICAN TOUR (1904). *South Atlantic Q. 1975 74(1): 53-73.* Disgust at American cultural philistinism allowed Henry James to overcome his guilt for having repudiated his homeland. His cross-country tour also provided him much grist for his literary mill. Three short stories, all crude satires on American shortcomings, constituted his initial attempt to capture his feelings about America. An unfinished novel *The Ivory Tower* dealt more skillfully with national characteristics, but *The American Scene* was his best effort. He foresaw the devastation of the countryside in the fulfilling of the American dream of material success, and the smouldering ethnic hatreds. However, his maudlin sense of Europe's past, and America's lack of it, made his keen insights appear only the carping of a bitter expatriate. 1904-20

3487. Banta, Martha. JAMES AND STEIN ON "BEING AMERICAN" AND "HAVING FRANCE." *French-American Rev. 1979 3(3): 63-84.* France was part of the sensual childhood experience of American expatriates Henry James and Gertrude Stein. While both appreciated French culture, as more compatible with Western civilization than American modernity, and while James adopted the French language

more easily than Stein, neither became French or totally assimilated to that environment. Both James and Stein agreed in many respects on what "being American" meant as well as the value of "having France," but "Stein was content to possess the content of America's large, empty, flat spaces void of time and identity. James was not." 23 notes.
1843-1960

3488. Bell, Millicent. HENRY JAMES AND THE FICTION OF AUTOBIOGRAPHY. *Southern Rev. 1982 18(3): 463-479.* Describes the unfinished *Autobiography* of Henry James (1843-1916) recounting the American novelist's life to his 25th year, and compares it to the autobiographic fiction of contemporaries Marcel Proust and Joseph Conrad.
1843-1916

3489. Bell, Millicent. "ART MAKES LIFE": JAMES'S AUTOBIOGRAPHY. *Rev. Française d'Etudes Américaines [France] 1982 7(14): 211-223.* Concentrates on the early chapters of *A Small Boy and Others* (1913), the autobiography of novelist Henry James describing his childhood in the upper social echelons of northeastern society.
1843-1916

3490. Edel, Leon. PORTRAIT OF THE ARTIST AS AN OLD MAN. *Am. Scholar 1977-78 47(1): 52-68.* Links aging and creativity in the later lives of Leo Tolstoy (d. 1910), Henry James (d. 1916), and William Butler Yeats (d. 1939). Although aging brought limitations to all three, it seemed to crystallize and summarize their lives and achievements.
1890's-1939

3491. Goetz, William R. CRITICISM AND AUTOBIOGRAPHY IN JAMES'S PREFACES. *Am. Literature 1979 51(3): 333-348.* Analyzes the Prefaces Henry James wrote for the New York Edition of his works during 1906-08 and insists they are as much autobiography as they are textual criticism. These Prefaces blur the distinction between fiction and nonfiction. They did not constitute a single, continuous story of James's growth, but instead a series of fragmentary narratives. 9 notes. 1906-08

3492. Hanley, Lynne T. THE EAGLE AND THE HEN: EDITH WHARTON AND HENRY JAMES. *Res. Studies 1981 49(3): 143-153.* 1903-20
For abstract see ***Wharton, Edith***

3493. Kennedy, Elizabeth Marie. "Constance Fennimore Woolson and Henry James: Friendship and Reflections." Yale U. 1983. 147 pp. *DAI 1984 44(9): 2766-2767-A.* DA8329260 19c

3494. Lewis, R. W. B. THE NAMES OF ACTION: HENRY JAMES IN THE EARLY 1870'S. *Nineteenth-Century Fiction 1984 38(4): 467-491.* Traces the activities of Henry James in early adulthood, as his indecision turned to firm career plans. 1869-75

3495. Marshall, Richard Milton, Jr. "Henry James and Mark Twain: Public Image versus Literary Reality." Purdue U. 1983. 175 pp. *DAI 1984 44(9): 2767-A.* DA8400394
1870's-90's

3496. Moore, Rayburn S. A "LITERARY-GOSSIPPY FRIENDSHIP": HENRY JAMES'S LETTERS TO EDMUND GOSSE. *Southern Rev. 1984 20(3): 570-590.* Presents selected letters from James to Gosse that reveal the range of literary and personal interests embodied in the correspondence and the friendship of the two men.
1882-1915

James, Henry (and family)

3497. Margolis, Anne T. THE JAMES FAMILY. *Am. Q. 1982 34(5): 562-570.* Reviews three books that add to our knowledge of the James family, especially Henry James and his sister Alice James: Jean Strouse's *Alice James: A Biography* (1980), *The Death and Letters of Alice James* (1981), edited by Ruth Bernard Yeazell, and *Henry James Letters, Vol. III: 1883-1895* (1980), edited by Leon Edel. The concept of "interesting failure" may be applied both to Alice's life and to Henry's years as a playwright. 2 notes. 1868-94

James, Jesse and Alexander

3498. Castel, Albert. MEN BEHIND THE MASKS: THE JAMES BROTHERS. *Am. Hist. Illus. 1982 17(4): 10-18.* Biographies of the legendary outlaws Alexander James and his younger brother Jesse James, with a focus on their rise to fame as robbers and murderers along with their friends, the brothers Jim and Cole Younger. 1860's-1916

James, Preston E.

3499. Robinson, David. ON PRESTON E. JAMES AND LATIN AMERICA: A BIOGRAPHICAL SKETCH. Robinson, David J., ed. *Studying Latin America: Essays in Honor of Preston E. James* (Ann Arbor: U. Microfilms Int. for Dept. of Geography, Syracuse U., 1980): 1-101. Describes the education and early travels of US scholar Preston E. James and his contribution to geographic studies of Latin America.
1921-79

James, Will

3500. Bell, William Gardner. WILL JAMES—INEVITABLE COWBOY. *Am. West 1983 20(1): 36-43.* French-Canadian Joseph-Ernest-Naphtali Dufault left Quebec in 1907 for a new life in the West. Living under several aliases before finally adopting the name Will James, he learned English, became a cowboy, and got into serious trouble with the law in Canada and the United States. After serving a prison sentence in Nevada, and twice being seriously injured by wild horses, James settled down to a childhood inclination to art, adding an aptitude for writing. His subject was the cowboy. He was best in pencil with either charcoal or soft lead shadings, competent in pen and ink, but only passable in colors. His art gave significance to his prose. 7 illus., biblio.
1907-42

James, William

3501. Anderson, James William. "William James's Depressive Period (1867-1872) and the Origins of His Creativity: A Psychobiographical Study." U. of Chicago 1980. *DAI 1980 41(1): 339-B.* 1867-72

3502. Greenspan, Henry Miller. WILLIAM JAMES'S EYES: THE THOUGHT BEHIND THE MAN. *Psychohistory Rev. 1979 8(1-2): 26-46.* Assesses William James in light of his own perceptions and experiences in an attempt to avoid reductionist post hoc psychohistorical analysis. Sees James's psychological problems as creative attempts to reaffirm identity. James attempted to combine objective knowledge with subjective intuition. Discusses James's struggles to find a career where his desire to be creative could be fulfilled, his illnesses, his relationship with his father, and the tensions between pursuing his creative instincts and the life of science. Explains James's striving to extend his vision as part of a lifelong process of self-affirmation. 143 notes. 1860-85

3503. Leverette, William E., Jr. SIMPLE LIVING AND THE PATRICIAN ACADEMIC: THE CASE OF WILLIAM JAMES. *Journal of American Culture 1983 6(4): 36-43.* William James's personal life helped to form his belief, shared by many of the middle class during his lifetime, in reforming public life and private living by a return to the "simple life"—a rural ideal that countered the impact of modernization by reliance on time-honored traditions. 1860's-1910

3504. Miller, Larry C. WILLIAM JAMES AND TWENTIETH-CENTURY ETHNIC THOUGHT. *Am. Q. 1979 31(4): 533-555.* Before 1899, William James had only a modest interest in ethnic groups and race. His attitudes were a hodgepodge of humanitarian concerns; his response to particular groups followed no pattern. After 1899, he consistently drew attention to the treatment of ethnic minorities and made public commitments supporting brotherhood. He was especially critical of American imperialism, which, he believed, stemmed from Anglo-Saxon arrogance and bigotry. James's impact on the theory and practice of W. E. B. Du Bois, Horace M. Kallen, and Robert E. Park was significant. Based on the James Family Papers; 56 notes. 1899-1910

3505. Schwehn, Mark Richard. "The Making of Modern Consciousness in America: The Works and Careers of Henry Adams and William James." Stanford U. 1978. 234 pp. *DAI 1978 38(12): 7517-A.* 1870's-1910's

Jameson, George Chauncey

3506. Siddall, Alcines Clair. GEORGE CHAUNCEY JAMESON, M.D., 1865-1948: FROM BLOODLETTING TO ANTIBIOTICS. *Northwest Ohio Q. 1980 52(1): 168-178.* Discusses Oberlin, Ohio, physician George Chauncey Jameson who was active in student and community health and the fight against medical quackery. ca 1880-1948

Jameson, John Franklin

3507. Meier, August and Rudwick, Elliott. J. FRANKLIN JAMESON, CARTER G. WOODSON, AND THE FOUNDATIONS OF BLACK HISTORIOGRAPHY. *Am. Hist. Rev. 1984 89(4): 1005-1015.* Describes the assistance that John Franklin Jameson, editor of the *American Historical Review* from 1895 to 1901 and from 1905 to 1928, provided to Carter G. Woodson in obtaining funds to collect and preserve documents in Afro-American history. Jameson respected Woodson's scholarship and contacted the Carnegie Corporation and other philanthropic agencies to provide financial aid to Woodson's organization, the Association for the Study of Negro Life and History. Based on documents in the Rockefeller Archive Center and on secondary sources; fig., 42 notes. 1915-31

3508. Rothberg, Morey D. "TO SET A STANDARD OF WORKMANSHIP AND COMPEL MEN TO CONFORM TO IT": JOHN FRANKLIN JAMESON AS EDITOR OF THE *AMERICAN HISTORICAL REVIEW. Am. Hist. Rev. 1984 89(4): 957-975.* Describes the efforts of John Franklin Jameson, first editor of the *American Historical Review,* to establish narrow scholarly standards for the journal during his tenure from 1895 to 1901 and from 1905 to 1928. Jameson was not very successful in meeting this goal. Historical writing could not be restricted to conform to Jameson's rigid commitment to nationalism and institutional history. In addition, other historians rejected his partisan view of what constituted serious scholarship. Based on documents in the Library of Congress and on secondary sources; 2 fig., 26 notes. 1880's-1928

3509. Rothberg, Morey D. "Servant to History: A Study of John Franklin Jameson, 1859-1937." Brown U. 1983. 356 pp. *DAI 1983 43(11): 3686-A.* DA8228327 1879-1937

Jameson, John S.

3510. Everett, Patricia R. JOHN S. JAMESON (1842-1864). *Am. Art J. 1983 15(2): 53-59.* John S. Jameson, who died at Andersonville Prison during the Civil War, was recognized and praised for his musical and artistic talents by some of the leading artists and musicians of his day. Reproduces his three known existing paintings, all landscapes, which show skill and sensitivity. 4 plates, 34 notes. 1842-64

Jameson, Robert

3511. Sweet, Jessie M. ROBERT JAMESON AND THE EXPLORERS: THE SEARCH FOR THE NORTH-WEST PASSAGE. *Ann. of Sci. [Great Britain] 1974 31(1): 21-47.* Part I. Discusses the life and work of Robert Jameson (1774-1854) with particular reference to the search for the Northwest Passage and to his influence on others' explorations while he was professor of natural history at the University of Edinburgh, 1804-54. Article to be continued. 1804-54

Jamha, Esmeil Muhammed "Sam"

3512. Duncanson, Mildred A. UNCLE SAM JAMHA. *Alberta Hist. [Canada] 1980 28(3): 7-17.* Esmeil Muhammed "Sam" Jamha (1890-1974) was born in Lala, Lebanon. He emigrated to Canada in 1905, and began to earn a living peddling dry goods and dabbling in fur trading throughout Manitoba, Saskatchewan, and later Alberta. In 1913, he purchased the first of his several stores. He prospered reasonably well, even though speculating in the fur trade was tricky. As the Moslem community in Edmonton grew in size, the need for a place to meet regularly and to worship resulted in the construction in 1938 of the Al Rascaid Mosque, the first of its kind in North America. 5 photos. 1905-74

Jamison, Alice Lee

3513. Hauptman, Laurence M. ALICE JAMISON: SENECA POLITICAL ACTIVIST, 1901-1964. *Indian Hist. 1979 12(2): 15-22, 60-62.* Alice Lee Jamison, a Seneca Indian, through the work of the American Indian Federation, was a major critic of the 1930's New Deal policy developed by John Collier, and of the Bureau of Indian Affairs, 1940's-50's. 1930's-50's

Jamison, Robert

3514. Hartling, Philip L. THE REVEREND ROBERT JAMISON: "AN HUMBLE AMBASSADOR OF MY DIVINE MASTER." *Nova Scotia Historical Review [Canada] 1984 4(2): 53-67.* Presents an account of the ministry of Robert Jamison, an Anglican missionary on Nova Scotia's eastern shore. Jamison first led the congregation at Ship Harbor, but he traveled extensively to settlements along the coast, and recorded the hardships of life in the 19th-century fishing villages. Based on Jamison's reports to church superiors, Nova Scotia Public Archives, Halifax; 55 notes, illus. 1840-84

Janik, Philip F.

3515. Janik, Phillip F. and Janik, Phyllis. LOOKING BACKWARD: FROM "THE BUSH" TO THE OPEN HEARTH. *Chicago Hist. 1981 10(1): 49-56.* Philip F. Janik's memoir of life in The Bush, an ethnic neighborhood on Chicago's South Side near the steel mills, focusing on the 45 years he spent working for International Harvester's Wisconsin Steel Works; early 1900's-80. 1909-80

Janson, Kristofer

3516. Draxten, Nina. KRISTOFER JANSON'S BEGINNING MINISTRY. *Norwegian-American Studies 1967 23: 126-174.* Kristofer Janson came to America in October 1881, at the urging of Rasmus B. Anderson, initially in order to make a lecture tour of the Midwest in the hopes of stirring interest in a liberal religious organization for Norwegian Americans. Upon his arrival, he was accepted into the ministry in the Unitarian Church and from there moved to Minneapolis, Minnesota, where he began setting up his ministry and recruiting members for his congregation. Though he first met with solid criticism as a freethinker, he eventually gained popular acceptance and was able to establish himself among the Scandinavians in the community. In March 1882, he returned to his native Norway to fetch his wife and family in order to establish a permanent home in the United States. Based on recorded sermons, diaries, and letters of Janson; 70 notes. 1881-82

Jarecki, Edmund Kasper

3517. Bukowski, Douglas. JUDGE EDMUND K. JARECKI: A RATHER REGULAR INDEPENDENT. *Chicago Hist. 1979-80 8(4): 206-218.* Judge Edmund Kasper Jarecki of Cook County, Illinois (1879-1966), was the Democrat-backed judge in charge of Chicago's elections from 1922-54 who fought corruption and misconduct to clean up the elections. 1922-54

Jarrell, Randall

3518. Beck, Charlotte. RANDALL JARRELL AND ROBERT PENN WARREN: FUGITIVE FUGITIVES. *Southern Literary Journal 1984 17(1): 82-91.* Discusses the relationship and careers of Randall Jarrell and his one-time teacher and mentor, Robert Penn Warren. 1930-65

3519. Meyers, Jeffrey. THE DEATH OF RANDALL JARRELL. *Virginia Q. Rev. 1982 58(3): 450-467.* The death of poet Randall Jarrell as the result of being struck by an automobile has "been surrounded by mystery." Officially it was called an accident, but many thought it suicide. The facts about his death are now known because of his certificate of death, coroner's report, and autopsy report. There is little doubt that it was suicide. The causes are uncertain but probably include his unhappy childhood, earlier excessive drinking, diminution of his poetic powers, unfavorable reviews, worry about health, a nervous breakdown, and other factors. 1914-65

Jarvis, Anna Reeves

3520. Johnson, James P. HOW MOTHER GOT HER DAY. *Am. Heritage 1979 30(3): 14-21.* Mother's Day commemorates the death of Anna Reeves Jarvis in 1905. Filled with grief and guilt, Mrs. Jarvis's daughter, Anna, led the movement for a national day of recognition for mothers. First established by West Virginia, the state of Mrs. Jarvis's residence, Mother's Day became a national celebration with Congressional action taken in 1914. 7 illus. 1905-14

Jarvis, Samuel Peter

3521. Leighton, Douglas. THE COMPACT TORY AS BUREAUCRAT: SAMUEL PETERS JARVIS AND THE INDIAN DEPARTMENT, 1837-1845. *Ontario Hist. [Canada] 1981 73(1): 40-53.* Discusses the structure of the Indian Department, 1828-40, and the 1842-44 Commission of Inquiry which found evidence of fraud, bribery, and prejudice, among other things. The critical period for the shift from the earlier, generally pro-Indian, attitude was during 1837-45. The poor administration of Samuel Peter Jarvis compounded the problems and was the final cause of the 1845 departmental reorganization. Jarvis's career illustrates both Ontario Toryism and the civil service during those years. Concludes with an attempt at a balanced evaluation, showing that Jarvis initially inherited a bad situation. Mainly from sources in Public Archives of Canada and of Ontario; illus., 88 notes. 1835-45

Jasper, John

3522. Bratton, Mary J. JOHN JASPER OF RICHMOND: FROM SLAVE PREACHER TO COMMUNITY LEADER. *Virginia Cavalcade 1979 29(1): 32-39.* Black minister John Jasper (1812-1901), who was born a slave on a Virginia plantation, joined the First African Baptist Church in 1842, and gained national attention in 1878 when he preached a sermon called, "The Sun Do Move." 1812-1901

Jasper, William

3523. Jones, George Fenwick. SERGEANT JOHANN WILHELM JASPER. *Georgia Hist. Q. 1981 65(1): 7-15.* Traces the identity and exploits of American Revolution hero William Jasper (ca. 1751-80) who was of German origin, contrary to prior assumptions; 1767-80. 29 notes. 1767-80

Jastrow, Morris

3524. Wechsler, Harold S. PULPIT OR PROFESSORIATE: THE CASE OF MORRIS JASTROW. *American Jewish History 1985 74(4): 338-355.* Morris Jastrow, after training for the rabbinate in Europe during 1881-85, rejected the post held by his father at Rodef Shalom in Philadelphia, and instead chose an academic career in Semitics at the University of Pennsylvania, not because of a loss of religious conviction or commitment due to his exposure to modern philological studies in Europe, but because, upon return, he became pessimistic about his ability to alter significantly the course of American Jewish belief and practice set by Isaac Mayer Wise and his Hebrew Union College. Based on papers in the American Jewish Archives and other primary sources; 45 notes. 1880-1900

Javits, Jacob

3525. Javits, Jacob and Steinberg, Rafael. SCENES FROM A POLITICAL MARRIAGE. *Washington Monthly 1980 12(10): 20-29.* Senator Jacob Javits recounts his marriage with Marian Borris, and problems in mixing marriage and politics; 1947-80. 1947-80

Javits, Marian Borris

3526. Javits, Jacob and Steinberg, Rafael. SCENES FROM A POLITICAL MARRIAGE. *Washington Monthly 1980 12(10): 20-29.* 1947-80
For abstract see ***Javits, Jacob***

Javor, Pavel

3527. Bresky, Dushan. A CZECH POET IN CANADA: PAVEL JAVOR'S LIFE AND WORK. *Can. Ethnic Studies [Canada] 1978 10(1): 75-83.* Narrates the life and comments on the work of Pavel Javor (pen name of Dr. Jiri Jan Skavor; b. 1917), the best-known Czech poet in exile, living in Canada since 1948, a writer for the Canadian Broadcasting Corporation, a professor of Slavic literature at the University of Montreal, and author of several lyrical poems and an autobiographical novel. 1917-78

Jay, John

3528. Durham, G. Homer. JOHN JAY AND THE JUDICIAL POWER. *Brigham Young U. Studies 1976 16(3): 349-361.* John Jay's tenure as first chief justice of the Supreme Court was pivotal in that his philosophy of government left its long-lasting imprint on the judicial structure. Several key decisions involving Jay helped establish a nationalistic direction to the Court. The case of *Chisholm vs. Georgia* gave major impetus to the function of judicial power in the American system. Jay was a judicial luminary comparable to John Marshall and Roger Taney. 1789-1810

3529. VanBurkelo, Sandra Frances. "HONOUR, JUSTICE, AND INTEREST": JOHN JAY'S REPUBLICAN POLITICS AND STATESMANSHIP OF THE FEDERAL BENCH. *J. of the Early Republic 1984 4(3): 239-274.* Portrayed as an intellectual lightweight—an incompetent and unimaginative jurist on a weak court—John Jay has suffered in the hands of constitutional historians. Equipped with a pessimistic pietism and a Federalist disdain for the common elements and self-interested politicians, Jay was an 18th-century conservative who distrusted republicanism, yet found it plausible. Cognizant of the incomplete nature of the American Revolution, Jay argued for a comprehensive political economy that combined ultraconservative domestic politics with economic liberalism. A seasoned diplomat, Jay understood that domestic unification was a crucial prerequisite to prosperity. Public morality and harmony were preferable to self-centered obstructionism and immobilization. Advocating reciprocal connections among nations which fostered healthy dependency rather than protectionism and indebtedness, Jay argued for a national vision. Illus., 84 notes. 1780-1800

Jefferis, William W.

3530. Savage, Letitia S. THE JEFFERIS COLLECTION: A PENNSYLVANIA TREASURE. *Pennsylvania Heritage 1981 7(2): 20-24.* Provides a biography of William W. Jefferis (1820-1906), one of the foremost mineral collectors in the United States, with special attention to the sale of his collection to the Carnegie Museum of Natural History in Pittsburgh, Pennsylvania, in 1904. 1845-1906

Jeffers, Robinson

3531. Meador, Roy. THE PITTSBURGH YEARS OF ROBINSON JEFFERS. *Western Pennsylvania Hist. Mag. 1980 63(1): 17-29.* Poet Robinson Jeffers's (1887-1962) life in the Pittsburgh area until he was 16 profoundly affected him, although he was to write primarily about the Carmel-Big Sur area of California. 1887-1903

Jefferson, Howard Bonar

3532. Billias, George Athan. HOWARD BONAR JEFFERSON. *Pro. of the Am. Antiquarian Soc. 1984 94(1): 27-32.* Howard Bonar Jefferson served as the third president of Clark University, during 1946-67. He oversaw the rebirth of Clark's psychology program, restored amicable town-gown relations, assured financial stability, initiated a significant campus expansion, and revived several dormant doctoral programs. He also published numerous books on religion. 1901-83

Jefferson, Thomas

3533. Dabney, Virginius and Kukla, Jon. THE MONTICELLO SCANDALS: HISTORY AND FICTION. *Virginia Cavalcade 1979 29(2): 52-61.* Examines Thomas Jefferson's reputation and the validity of claims that the slave Sally Hemings bore his children. 1770's-1979

3534. Dewey, Frank L. THE WATERSON-MADISON EPISODE: AN INCIDENT IN THOMAS JEFFERSON'S LAW PRACTICE. *Virginia Mag. of Hist. and Biog. 1982 90(2): 165-176.* In 1769, Virginia lawyer Thomas Jefferson acted as counsel to a group of clients who proposed to use existing land statutes to their advantage in a get-rich-quick scheme. Apparently Jefferson did not play any part in the plan's conception; however, he would have collected a large sum of money had it succeeded. As it was, the scheme failed and Jefferson left his law practice a few years later, possibly disillusioned by clients who did not pay their bills. Based on Virginia legal records and statutes, Jefferson's account book, and secondary sources; 53 notes. 1769-71

3535. Fitch, James Marston. THE LAWN: AMERICA'S GREATEST ARCHITECTURAL ACHIEVEMENT. *Am. Heritage 1984 35(4): 49-64.* Thomas Jefferson's architectural fame is tied in part to his plans for the University of Virginia. In 1817, at the age of 74, he laid the first cornerstone, and by his death in 1826, construction was nearly complete. Seeing architecture as a civilizing force, he designed each of the pavilions in the classical style, as examples of taste and variety, and he sought to integrate the grounds also into the campus's plan. Jefferson sought in this way to make education for leadership also serve to bring aesthetic maturity to the new nation. 26 photos, 2 illus. 1800-27

3536. Henderson, Phillip G. MARSHALL VERSUS JEFFERSON: POLITICS AND THE FEDERAL JUDICIARY IN THE EARLY REPUBLIC. *Michigan J. of Pol. Sci. 1983 2(2): 42-66.* Describes the antagonisms between cousins Thomas Jefferson and John Marshall, who differed greatly in their interpretation of the role of the Supreme Court. 1790's-1835

3537. Huntley, William B. JEFFERSON'S PUBLIC AND PRIVATE RELIGION. *South Atlantic Q. 1980 79(3): 286-301.* In a study of Thomas Jefferson's religion, one must distinguish between the public and the private. In his public life, his faith can be found in such writings as the Declaration of Independence, the Virginia Bill Establishing Religious Freedom, and the *Notes on the State of Virginia.* His private religion is found in his letters, where he worked out a religion, including an ethic and a theology which he submitted for discussion to friends, particularly John Adams, Joseph Priestley, and Benjamin Rush. Discusses Jefferson's religion in four themes: personal experience with the holy, creation of community through myth and ritual, daily living that expresses cosmic law, and spiritual freedom through discipline.

Based on *The Adams-Jefferson Letters,* ed. Cappon; *Writings of Jefferson,* ed. Bergh; *Letters of Benjamin Rush,* ed. Butterfield, secondary sources; 45 notes. 1800-25

3538. Jellison, Charles A. JAMES THOMSON CALLENDER: "HUMAN NATURE IN A HIDEOUS FORM." *Virginia Cavalcade 1979 29(2): 62-69.* 1790's
For abstract see ***Callender, James Thomas***

3539. Kaplan, Lawrence S. REFLECTIONS ON JEFFERSON AS A FRANCOPHILE. *South Atlantic Q. 1980 79(1): 38-50.* In spite of the effort of some scholars (Gilbert Chinard, Dumas Malone, Merrill Peterson) to separate myth from reality, there will always be a residual suspicion of weakness in Thomas Jefferson's feelings for France. Yet his love for France was far less evident than a visceral dislike of the common enemy—the Federalists at home and Great Britain abroad. While his widely advertised love of the French only slightly compromised his position as a public man, in his writings Jefferson provided sufficient material to keep alive the topic for future historians and politicians to debate. Based on the published and edited writings of Jefferson and secondary studies; 36 notes. 1780-1805

3540. Kirtland, Robert Bevier. "George Wythe: Lawyer, Revolutionary, Judge." U. of Michigan 1983. 335 pp. *DAI 1983 44(6): 1896-A.* DA8324216 1740's-1806

3541. Marienstras, Elise. THOMAS JEFFERSON ET LA NAISSANCE DES ÉTATS-UNIS [Thomas Jefferson and the birth of the United States]. *Histoire [France] 1980 (19): 30-39.* Jefferson, a philosopher of the Enlightenment, refused to grant human rights to Indians and Negroes; favored states' rights, but was an authoritarian president; and, although proagrarian, promoted US industrialization. 1760's-1826

3542. Peterson, Merrill D. DUMAS MALONE: THE COMPLETION OF A MONUMENT. *Virginia Q. Rev. 1982 58(1): 26-31.* Malone, editor of *The Dictionary of American Biography,* in 1943 began his six-volume biography, *Jefferson and His Time,* which was completed in 1981. As a critical biography it presents Jefferson's faults and errors without trivializing him and without imposing the author's prejudices upon the reader. Based upon diligent research, this monumental work both relates Jefferson to his time and covers his many-sidedness. "The dominant image that emerges . . . is not new. It is the old image of the Apostle of Liberty."
1743-1826

3543. Ritcheson, Charles R. THE FRAGILE MEMORY: THOMAS JEFFERSON AT THE COURT OF GEORGE III. *Eighteenth-Century Life 1981 6(2-3): 1-16.* Contemporary accounts of Thomas Jefferson's visit to the English court of George III in 1786 show that Jefferson misrecollected and made errors in his *Autobiography,* written at age 78.
1786

3544. Rodrigues, Leda Boechat. JOSE JOAQUIM DA MAIA E THOMAS JEFFERSON [Jose Joaquim da Maia and Thomas Jefferson]. *Rev. Hist. e Geog. Brasileira [Brazil] 1981 (333): 53-70.* 1786-1819
For abstract see ***Maia, Jose Joaquim da***

3545. Shawen, Neil McDowell. "The Casting of a Lengthened Shadow: Thomas Jefferson's Role in Determining the Site for a State University in Virginia." George Washington U. 1980. 479 pp. *DAI 1980 41(2): 567-A.* 8017730
ca 1779-1819

3546. Shawen, Neil McDowell. THOMAS JEFFERSON AND A "NATIONAL" UNIVERSITY: THE HIDDEN AGENDA FOR VIRGINIA. *Virginia Mag. of Hist. and Biog. 1984 92(3): 309-335.* During the 1790's, Thomas Jefferson briefly entertained the idea of starting a national university. Although the concept ran counter to his brand of republican democracy, Jefferson favored an educated citizenry, particularly if the education were taking place in Virginia. He corresponded with two foreign promoters, Quesnay de Beaurepaire and Sir Francis D'Ivernois, both of France, regarding the creation of a French-style academy. Both schemes died, however, and efforts failed to gain George Washington's support of such an institution outside of the District of Columbia. Based on Jefferson's writings and secondary sources; 71 notes. 1789-1800

3547. Sogrin, V. V. BIOGRAFII OTTSOV-OSNOVATELEI SSHA V AMERIKANSKOI ISTORIOGRAFII 1970-KH GODOV [Biographies of the Founding Fathers of the United States in American historiography during the 1970's]. *Novaia i Noveishaia Istoriia [USSR] 1980 (1): 154-163.* 1760-1800
For abstract see ***Adams, Samuel***

3548. Stead, John Prindle. "The Roots of Democracy in Thomas Jefferson and Mao Tse-tung." U. of Southern California 1976. *DAI 1977 38(1): 461-462-A.* 18c-20c

3549. Summy, Ralph. COMPARATIVE POLITICAL BIOGRAPHY: JAYAPRAKASH NARAYAN AND THOMAS JEFFERSON. *Biography 1983 6(3): 220-237.* Despite living 200 years apart and coming from radically different cultures, the biographies of political leaders Jayaprakash Narayan and Thomas Jefferson bear a marked resemblance. Not only did these men have many personal traits in common, but their careers tended to follow similar patterns. More importantly, they were in agreement on virtually every crucial aspect of their political thinking. As embodiments of world revolutionary ideals, they have jointly given succeeding generations the inspiration and guidelines to draw upon when tackling the problems of a new age. 1760's-1826

3550. Watson, Ross. THOMAS JEFFERSON'S VISIT TO ENGLAND, 1786. *Hist. Today [Great Britain] 1977 27(1): 3-13.* Discusses Thomas Jefferson's travel and visit to Great Britain while serving as US ambassador to France in 1786; includes his financial problems and his visits to gardens in London, Twickenham, Cobham, Weybridge, and Caversham.
1786

3551. Wolff, Philippe. JEFFERSON ON PROVENCE AND LANGUEDOC. *Pro. of the Ann. Meeting of the Western Soc. for French Hist. 1975 3: 191-205.* Documents the travels of Thomas Jefferson in southern France in 1787, largely through his correspondence with William Short and his daily journal. Demonstrates Jefferson's concern with social and economic conditions in the pre-Revolutionary period as well as his practical observations on such technical subjects as agricultural methods and linguistic patterns. Shows his historical appreciation of architecture, painting, and sculpture. 56 notes. 1787

3552. Yoder, Edwin M. THE SAGE AT SUNSET. *Virginia Q. Rev. 1982 58(1): 32-37.* Briefly examines Jefferson's life after leaving the presidency as presented in Dumas Malone's *The Sage of Monticello.* He remained strongly in favor of both republicanism and the imperial extension of the nation. Plagued by private debt (he sold his private library to the nation for $25,000 and it became the nucleus of the Library of Congress), "he hated public debt" as well. He was also concerned by the implications of the Missouri Compromise and favored emancipation. His fondest concern was the new University of Virginia. In this volume one has the "chronicle of one distinguished octogenarian by another. . . ." 1809-26

Jefferson, Thomas (family)

3553. Brodie, Fawn M. THOMAS JEFFERSON'S UNKNOWN GRANDCHILDREN. *Am. Heritage 1976 27(6): 28-33, 94-99.* Thomas Jefferson, married only once, had two families. The second family, by his quadroon slave, Sally Hemings, numbered seven children, from a liaison lasting 38 years. Their disappearance and that of their progeny resulted from several factors, including Jefferson's desire that they eventually "escape" into white society. Much information has recently come to light concerning Jefferson's other family. Family lines are traced from each of the children. Based on primary and secondary sources; 2 illus., 36 notes. ca 1780-1976

3554. Woodson, Minnie Shumate. RESEARCHING TO DOCUMENT THE ORAL HISTORY OF THE THOMAS WOODSON FAMILY: DISMANTLING THE SABLE CURTAIN. *Journal of the Afro-American Historical and Genealogical Society 1985 6(1): 3-12.* 1780's-1859
For abstract see ***Woodson, Thomas (family)***

Jefferson, Thomas (1840-1917)

3555. DeSanto, Jerome S. UNCLE JEFF: MYSTERIOUS CHARACTER OF THE NORTH FORK. *Montana 1982 32(1): 14-23.* Thomas (Uncle Jeff) Jefferson (1840-1917) was a self-sufficient and purposefully mysterious "character" who lived along the North Fork of the Flathead River, Montana, from 1882-1915, in the area that became Glacier National Park. By his own account, he was a miner, a Pony Express rider, a scout for the army in 1876, a trapper, and a packer. The Jefferson name survives on a number of geographic features in Glacier Park. Based on records and interviews in the Glacier National Park Archives, Montana Veterans' Home, Montana Historical Society Archives, and secondary sources; 5 illus., map, 45 notes. 1882-1917

Jeffery, Alicia Anne

3556. Sparling, Mary. THE LIGHTER AUXILIARIES: WOMEN ARTISTS IN NOVA SCOTIA IN THE EARLY NINETEENTH CENTURY. *Atlantis [Canada] 1979 5(1): 83-106.* 19c
For abstract see ***Chaplin, Millicent Mary***

Jefferys, Charles P. B.

3557. —. CHARLES PETER BEAUCHAMP JEFFERYS (1898-1980). *Newport Hist. 1980 53(178): 81-83.* Biography of Charles P. B. Jefferys (1898-1980), community leader, teacher, and associate of the Newport Historical Society, 1933-80. 1898-1980

Jeffords, Tom

3558. Cramer, Harry G., III. TOM JEFFORDS—INDIAN AGENT. *J. of Arizona Hist. 1976 17(3): 265-300.* When Cochise, the Chiricahua Apache chief, surrendered in 1872 and agreed that his people would live on a newly created reservation in southeastern Arizona, his one stipulation was that Tom Jeffords (1832-1914) must be the agent. Captain Thomas Jefferson Jeffords, the confidant of Cochise, had been instrumental in the surrender. Narrates the efforts of Jeffords to make the treaty work despite the counterefforts of the government to reduce the Apache to complete dependence. With a series of incidents and the termination of the reservation in 1876, the peace broke down and the Chiricahua reverted to their prior state of warfare. Map, 6 illus., 124 notes. 1872-76

Jeffreys, Charles William

3559. Duffy, Dennis. ART-HISTORY: CHARLES WILLIAM JEFFREYS AS CANADA'S CURATOR. *J. of Can. Studies [Canada] 1976 11(4): 3-18.* Charles William Jeffreys (1869-1951), a popular illustrator in Canada, 1920's-50, illustrated children's books, the popular press, and historical texts for public schools. 1920's-50

3560. Stacy, Robert. SALVAGE FOR US THESE FRAGMENTS: C. W. JEFFREYS AND ONTARIO'S HISTORIC ARCHITECTURE. *Ontario Hist. [Canada] 1978 70(3): 147-170.* Briefly outlines the life of Charles William Jeffreys (1869-1951) and discusses his activities in relation to the Ontario Historical Society. He was president of this organization for some years and markedly improved its publications and possibly its academic standing. He was also deeply involved in architectural preservation and responsible for the preservation of a number of significant buildings in Ontario. Comments on his publications, usually briefly. Mainly secondary sources; 9 illus., 11 notes. 1890's-1951

Jenkins, Bruce A.

3561. Taylor, Thomas T. MEMORIAL TO RONALD D. DOUGLAS (1954-1981), EDWARD C. GARDNER (1946-1981), BRUCE A. JENKINS (1953-1981). *J. of California and Great Basin Anthrop. 1981 3(1): 3-6.* 1946-81
For abstract see ***Douglas, Ronald D.***

Jenkins, Esau

3562. Clark, Septima Poinsett and Twining, Mary A. VOTING DOES COUNT: A BRIEF EXCERPT FROM *A FABULOUS DECADE. J. of Black Studies 1980 10(4): 445-447.* Esau Jenkins organized the Johns Island Progressive Club, which refurbished an old gymnasium, making it into a community center, and began a cooperative grocery store and a small motel on the island. After training at the Highlander Folk School in Tennessee, Jenkins returned to Johns Island (one of the Sea Islands of Georgia and South Carolina) and organized a voter registration drive which registered four times as many black voters in nine days as had registered in the past 100 years. He lost a race for the Charleston, South Carolina, School Board, but was appointed to the board before his death in 1970. 1960-70

Jenks, Stephen

3563. Steel, David Warren. "Stephen Jenks (1772-1856): American Composer and Tunebook Compiler." U. of Michigan 1982. 487 pp. *DAI 1983 43(10): 3151-A.* DA8304604 1772-1856

Jennings, May Mann

3564. Vance, Linda Darlene Moore. "May Mann Jennings, Florida's Genteel Activist." U. of Florida 1980. 355 pp. *DAI 1981 41(9): 4145-A.* DA8105624 1900-63

Jennings, Paul

3565. Edwards, G. Franklin and Winston, Michael R. COMMENTARY: THE WASHINGTON OF PAUL JENNINGS—WHITE HOUSE SLAVE, FREE MAN, AND CONSPIRATOR FOR FREEDOM. *White House Hist. 1983 1(1): 52-63.* Paul Jennings's memoir of James Madison sheds light on the evacuation of the White House in 1814 and on the Madison presidency, but Jennings's life is itself interesting for his participation in the creation of a free black community in Washington. 1799-1848

3566. Jennings, Paul. A COLORED MAN'S REMINISCENCES OF JAMES MADISON. *White House Hist. 1983 1(1): 46-51.* 1805-36
*For abstract see **Madison, James***

Jensen, Merrill Monroe

3567. Lovejoy, David S. MERRILL MONROE JENSEN. *Massachusetts Hist. Soc. Pro. 1980 92: 140-143.* Merrill Jensen distinguished himself as a premier scholar and teacher of American history at the University of Wisconsin. In his most important works, *The Articles of Confederation* (1940) and *The New Nation* (1950), Jensen established the Confederate era as a time in which debate over democracy was refined and settled in a constructive manner thus defusing the long-standing view that the government under the Articles of Confederation was a critical time. In the 1960's, Jensen assumed the editorial respnsibility for the *Documentary History of the First Federal Elections* and the *Documentary History of the Ratification of the Constitution* projects, an undertaking which his students will hopefully carry to completion. In 1969, Jensen was chosen president of the Organization of American Historians. 1905-80

Jensen, Richard

3568. Jensen, Richard; *Public Historian* Editors, interviewers. THE ACCOMPLISHMENTS OF THE NEWBERRY LIBRARY FAMILY AND COMMUNITY HISTORY PROGRAMS. *Public Hist. 1983 5(4): 49-61.* Interviews Richard Jensen about his tenure as head of the Newberry Library's Family and Community History Center and his role in training scholars in quantitative history. 1971-82

Jenson, Andrew

3569. Lyon, T. Edgar. CHURCH HISTORIANS I HAVE KNOWN. *Dialogue 1978 11(4): 14-22.* 1913-70
*For abstract see **Lyon, T. Edgar***

Jetté, Julius

3570. Renner, Louis L. JULIUS JETTÉ: DISTINGUISHED SCHOLAR IN ALASKA. *Alaska J. 1975 5(4): 239-247.* Discusses the missionary work of Julius Jetté, a Jesuit priest who during 1898-1927 in Nulato, Alaska, among the Ten'a Indians mastered their tongue, studied their folklore, and contributed extensively to the linguistic and historic study of the Ten'a people. 1898-1927

Jewett, John Punchard

3571. Fragasso, Philip M. JOHN P. JEWETT: THE UNSUNG HERO OF UNCLE TOM'S CABIN. *New-England Galaxy 1978 20(1): 22-29.* John Punchard Jewett (1814-84), born in Lebanon, Maine, was best known for his career as a Boston publisher and who was responsible for the publication of Harriet Beecher Stowe's *Uncle Tom's Cabin* in 1852. 1830's-84

Jewett, Sarah Orne

3572. Cary, Richard. JEWETT TO DRESEL: 33 LETTERS. *Colby Lib. Q. 1975 11(1): 13-49.* Reprints 33 letters, 1886-1907, from Sarah Orne Jewett of South Berwick, Maine, to Louisa Loring Dresel in Boston, which are in the collection of the Colby College Library and which clarify the strong friendship between the two women. 1886-1907

Johnson, Andrew

3573. Cimprich, John. MILITARY GOVERNOR JOHNSON AND TENNESSEE BLACKS, 1862-65. *Tennessee Hist. Q. 1980 39(4): 459-470.* The Civil War marked a turning point in Andrew Johnson's political career, increasing his national prominence and taking him into a controversial presidency. His wartime service as military governor of Tennessee turned the former proponent of slavery into a committed emancipationist. As president, however, Johnson fought against civil rights legislation. Primary sources; 32 notes. 1862-65

3574. Riches, William T. M. "The Commoners: Andrew Johnson and Abraham Lincoln to 1861." Ulster College [Northern Ireland] 1977. *Doctoral Dissertations in Hist. 1977 2(1): 25.* 1843-61
*For abstract see **Lincoln, Abraham***

Johnson, Annie

3575. Oates, Joyce Carol. DISCOVERING ANNIE JOHNSON. *Art & Antiques 1986 (Jan): 46-53.* The discovery at a 1969 estate sale of Annie Johnson's watercolor portraits depicting Victorian men and women revealed an unknown prolific artist from New Haven, Connecticut, who apparently never exhibited or sold. 1880-1907

Johnson, Charles Spurgeon

3576. Gilpin, Patrick J. CHARLES S. JOHNSON: SCHOLAR AND EDUCATOR. *Negro Hist. Bull. 1976 39(3): 544-548.* Discusses the major achievements of Charles S. Johnson and analyzes childhood, college, and later influences on his dedication to scholarship and to improving race relations. Johnson became the first black president of Fisk University in 1947. He established an international reputation in sociology, served several Presidents, and chaired a UNESCO conference of experts on race relations in 1955. The tolls of interminable conferences, exacting scholarship, and service in race relations cut short Johnson's brilliant career in 1956, but not before the groundwork was laid for the black liberation movement that followed. Based on the Charles S. Johnson papers and other sources; illus., 23 notes. 1900-56

3577. Lewis, David Levering. DR. JOHNSON'S FRIENDS: CIVIL RIGHTS BY COPYRIGHT DURING HARLEM'S MID-TWENTIES. *Massachusetts Rev. 1979 20(3): 501-519.* In March 1924, Doctor Charles Spurgeon Johnson (1893-1956), American sociologist and educator, arranged dinner at the Civic Club in New York for 110 mostly unknown writers. The evening was spent in giving speeches and reading their prose and poetry. After this dinner they decided to hold another one in May 1925, attended by 316 of what were termed the New Negroes; Phi Beta Kappa poets, university trained painters, concert musicians, and novel-writing civil rights officials. The Negro now could state with pride to the white man that they had poets and intellectuals too. Based on various private papers; 33 notes. ca 1920-25

3578. Pearson, Ralph L. REFLECTIONS ON BLACK COLLEGES: THE HISTORICAL PERSPECTIVE OF CHARLES S. JOHNSON. *Hist. of Educ. Q. 1983 23(1): 55-68.* Charles S. Johnson, the first black president of Fisk University (1946-56), was a principal spokesman for black higher education from 1928 to his death in 1956. Johnson, by training a sociologist, developed his philosophy pragmatically out of hard empirical data and recognized the vocational responsibilites of black colleges and universities. He also recognized the black cultural heritage and the role of the black colleges in sustaining this heritage. Thus Johnson's work provides a historical perspective on the dilemmas faced by a society that must deal with the fact of two societies, one black and one white. Based on Johnson's publications and public addresses; 37 notes. 1928-56

Johnson, D. W.

3579. Imhoff, Clem. THE RECRUITER. *Southern Exposure 1976 4(1-2): 83-87.* D. W. Johnson tells of his work as a labor recruiter who encouraged Negroes to move from the South to Wisconsin and Illinois, 1917-22. 1917-22

Johnson, David

3580. Baur, John I. H. THE EXACT BRUSHWORK OF MR. DAVID JOHNSON, AN AMERICAN LANDSCAPE PAINTER, 1827-1908. *Am. Art J. 1980 12(4): 32-65.* Traces through paintings and drawings the career of 19th-century New York painter David Johnson (1827-1908). Johnson was primarily a landscape painter of New England mountains, forests, and lakes in a highly realistic style although showing some influence of Luminism. He also painted portraits, usually based on photographs. 51 plates, 21 notes. 1852-1908

Johnson, Edith

3581. Casey, Naomi Taylor. MISS EDITH JOHNSON: PIONEER NEWSPAPER WOMAN. *Chronicles of Oklahoma 1982 60(1): 66-73.* Edith Johnson began her 50-year newspaper career in 1908 when she was hired as a reporter for the *Daily Oklahoman.* Within 10 years she had passed the stages of beat reporting to writing her own column. The Republic Syndicate eventually carried her Sunday advice column to a host of newspapers throughout the nation. As a champion of the expanding roles of women, she published *Women of the Business World* in 1923 and used her column to encourage women into enterprises previously reserved for men. Based on interviews and the writings of Edith Johnson; 2 photos. 1908-61

Johnson, Edward (family)

3582. Threlfall, John B. CAPTAIN EDWARD JOHNSON AND HIS WIFE SUSAN MUNTER, OF CANTERBURY, ENGLAND, AND WOBURN, MASSACHUSETTS. *New England Historical and Genealogical Register 1985 139(Oct): 321-324.* Edward and Susan Munter Johnson and their seven children came to New England in the spring of 1637. He received a land grant in Charlestown after his arrival and was made a freeman by May 1638. This corrects former records confusing him with another Captain Edward Johnson who came to New England with Winthrop in 1630 and later went to York, Maine. 17c

Johnson, Emeroy

3583. Johnson, Emeroy. SALOMON JOHNSON STORY. *Swedish-American Historical Quarterly 1985 36(4): 251-274.* 1880's-1956

For abstract see ***Johnson, Salomon (family)***

Johnson, Frank Tenney

3584. Stern, Jean. FRANK TENNEY JOHNSON: MASTER OF AMERICAN MOONLIGHT PAINTING. *Art & Antiques 1982 6(4): 82-87.* Biography of foremost American painter of moonlight scenes, Frank Tenney Johnson (1874-1939), renowned for his paintings of moonlights of the American West. 1900-39

Johnson, Gerald W.

3585. Hobson, Fred. GERALD W. JOHNSON: THE SOUTHERNER AS REALIST. *Virginia Q. Rev. 1982 58(1): 1-25.* To consider representative Southerners as "rural, conservative, religious, romantic," and antireformist is too limiting for it ignores the liberal-progressive aspects which the life and work of Gerald W. Johnson represents. Born a Southerner, and remaining one in many ways, Johnson considered himself a realist and as a journalist-historian-sociologist participated in, keenly observed, and wrote extremely well about events from 1930 to 1980. He attacked "romantic illusion, fraud, sham and hypocrisy. . . ." Like Mencken and Cash, he opposed Southern agrarianism. In the events of the 1960's, in a way, he saw the South of his youth come North. 1890-1980

Johnson, Guion Griffis

3586. Johnson, Guion Griffis. MY EXPLORATION OF THE SOUTHERN EXPERIENCE. *North Carolina Hist. Rev. 1980 57(2): 192-207.* The author recounts her transition from Texas journalism teacher to social historian of the South. As one of the first female historians in the South, she encountered some difficulties during graduate training. She began her work at University of North Carolina in sociology under Howard Odum in 1924 but soon switched to history, receiving her PhD in 1927, having written a dissertation which was later expanded and published as *Ante-Bellum North Carolina.* She and her sociologist husband, Guy B. Johnson, have spent their professional lives researching and writing about southern social conditions. They wrote several reports for Gunnar Myrdal as he composed *An American Dilemma.* Based on personal letters, Odum Papers, and recollections; 7 illus., 29 notes. 1920-81

Johnson, Guy B.

3587. Johnson, Guion Griffis. MY EXPLORATION OF THE SOUTHERN EXPERIENCE. *North Carolina Hist. Rev. 1980 57(2): 192-207.* 1920-81

For abstract see ***Johnson, Guion Griffis***

Johnson, Jack

3588. Anderson, Jervis. BLACK HEAVIES. *Am. Scholar 1978 47(3): 387-395.* Examines the career of heavyweight boxer Jack Johnson (1878-1946), the first black to claim the world heavyweight title, and assesses his impact on American sports and race relations, 1890's-1920's. 1890's-1920's

Johnson, Jacob

3589. Johnson, Jean L. THREE STONEYS. *Alberta Hist. [Canada] 1981 29(2): 29-36.* 1912-60
For abstract see ***Goat, Noah***

Johnson, James Weldon

3590. Gibbs, William E. JAMES WELDON JOHNSON: A BLACK PERSPECTIVE ON "BIG STICK" DIPLOMACY. *Diplomatic History 1984 8(4): 329-347.* Recounts the achievements of diplomat, lawyer, newsman, poet, lyricist, and activist James Weldon Johnson. After a moderately successful career in journalism, law, and theater, he held diplomatic posts in Venezuela and Nicaragua, where he perceived a link between the treatment of Southern blacks and the US "White Man's Burden" attitude toward the population of weak, nonwhite nations in Latin America and elsewhere. Later, as a newsman and as an official of the National Association for the Advancement of Colored People (NAACP), he waged a continuing campaign against these attitudes, particularly as related to the US occupation of Haiti. Based on the James Weldon Johnson papers at Yale University; NAACP papers, Library of Congress; Congressional hearings; press releases; and secondary sources. 1894-1938

Johnson, Jeremiah

3591. Johnson, Jeremiah. [THE RECOLLECTIONS OF GENERAL JEREMIAH JOHNSON DURING THE AMERICAN REVOLUTION].

RECOLLECTIONS OF INCIDENTS OF THE REVOLUTION OF THE COLONIES OCCURRING IN BROOKLYN: COLLATED FROM THE MANUSCRIPTS AND CONVERSATIONS OF GENERAL JEREMIAH JOHNSON DESCRIPTIVE OF SCENES WHICH HE PERSONALLY WITNESSED: ARRANGED IN CHRONOLOGICAL ORDER AND EDITED BY THOS. W. FIELD. *J. of Long Island Hist. 1976 12(2): 4-21.* Jeremiah Johnson (1766-1852) of Kings County, New York, lived through the British occupation during the American Revolution (1775-83). It caused hardship and dislocation among the local population, affecting their property, religion, and everyday lives. Describes the effects on the army and the treatment of prisoners of war. Includes 19th-century editor Thomas W. Field's biography of Johnson and modern editor Robert T. Murphy's notes on Field. Illus., 2 notes on the biographies.

RECOLLECTIONS OF GENERAL JOHNSON. *J. of Long Island Hist. 1976 13(1): 20-41.* Discusses the hardships and high mortality aboard the British prison ships, harsh life of Hessians and other soldiers, and the evacuation of the British in November 1783. 2 maps. 1775-83

Johnson, Keen

3592. Fraas, Elizabeth Michele. "Keen Johnson: Newspaperman and Governor." U. of Kentucky 1984. 376 pp. *DAI 1984 45(2): 330-A.* DA8411348 1925-60

Johnson, Lady Bird

3593. Klaw, Barbara. LADY BIRD JOHNSON REMEMBERS. *Am. Heritage 1980 32(1): 4-17.* In this interview, Claudia Taylor (Lady Bird) Johnson (b. 1912), the widow of President Lyndon B. Johnson, discusses her life with him and since his death. Comments on the Vietnam War, the vice-presidency, and Watergate. 17 illus. ca 1961-80

Johnson, Levi

3594. Hosler, Robert M. LEVI JOHNSON, A CLEVELAND PIONEER. *Inland Seas 1976 32(3): 200-202, 204, 211.* Levi Johnson (1786-1872) settled in Cleveland, Ohio, in 1809 and quickly became a builder of both houses and vessels. After service with the Navy in the War 1812 he operated a shipyard and sailed as a ship captain until 1831. He then devoted himself to lighthouse building, but after 1840 concentrated on his extensive real estate holdings. Illus. 1809-72

Johnson, Lyndon B.

3595. Frantz, Joe B. WHY LYNDON? *Western Hist. Q. 1980 11(1): 4-15.* Of the geographically western presidents, Lyndon B. Johnson (1908-73) is usually considered the only westerner. (Barry Goldwater is the only defeated presidential candidate who can be considered a westerner). Johnson looked, talked, and acted like a westerner. Further, he was one of the few western politicians who attained national rather than regional stature. He surmounted his regional boundaries because he learned early to represent national constituencies and to see beyond the West. Illus. 1930's-73

3596. Fredericks, Janet. LYNDON BAINES JOHNSON: AN EDUCATOR AND HIS LIBRARY. *Vitae Scholasticae 1983 2(1): 203-223.* Presents a biography of President Lyndon B. Johnson, whose experiences as a poor young man seeking education, as a teacher of Texas Chicanos, and as a politician led him to advocate many programs to advance American education. Discusses the archives available at the Lyndon Baines Johnson Library and Museum at the University of Texas, Austin. 23 notes, appendix. German summary. 1927-68

3597. Kearns, Doris. LYNDON JOHNSON'S POLITICAL PERSONALITY. *Pol. Sci. Q. 1976 91(3): 385-409.* Analyzes the development of Lyndon Johnson's political personality—his characteristic ways of acquiring and using power—and traces the impact of Johnson's personality style on his leadership first as Senate majority leader and then as a president promoting domestic reform and escalating the nation's involvement in Vietnam. 1937-68

3598. Klaw, Barbara. LADY BIRD JOHNSON REMEMBERS. *Am. Heritage 1980 32(1): 4-17.* ca 1961-80
For abstract see ***Johnson, Lady Bird***

Johnson, Marietta

3599. Lambert, Pierre D. WOMEN IN EDUCATION: THE KNOWN, THE FORGOTTEN, THE UNKNOWN. *Vitae Scholasticae 1983 2(1): 93-112.* 19c-20c
For abstract see ***Beecher, Catherine***

Johnson, Robert

3600. Wernick, Robert. THE SINGULAR VISION OF A REINCARNATED VICTORIAN MILLWRIGHT. *Smithsonian 1985 16(7): 193-209.* Discusses the life and extraordinary work of old machine restorer Robert Johnson whose work with 19th-century machinery has earned him the respect of those familiar with his trade and artistry. 1937-85

Johnson, Salomon (family)

3601. Johnson, Emeroy. SALOMON JOHNSON STORY. *Swedish-American Historical Quarterly 1985 36(4): 251-274.* The author's father, Salomon Johnson (1866-1956), was born in southern Småland, Sweden, near Växjö. In 1886 Salomon joined his uncle Peter Swensson's family in Chisago County, Minnesota. He worked as a lumberjack in the 1880's and 1890's when Minnesota's lumber industry was booming. He married Elizabeth Swensson in 1893. They settled on her family's small Chisago County farm and raised seven children. He worked until 1944 as a stonemason. The author describes his family's life and the numerous descendants of Salomon Johnson. Based on personal knowledge; 5 photos. 1880's-1956

Johnson, Samuel

3602. DeMille, George E. and Gerlach, Don R. SAMUEL JOHNSON AT YALE: THE ROOTS OF CONVERSION, 1710-1722. *Connecticut Hist. 1976 (17): 15-41.* Discusses the religious conversion and theological attitudes of Samuel Johnson as a student and teacher at Yale University. 1710-22

Johnson, Samuel (1822-82)

3603. Mueller, Roger C. SAMUEL JOHNSON, AMERICAN TRANSCENDENTALIST: A SHORT BIOGRAPHY. *Essex Inst. Hist. Collections 1979 115(1): 9-67.* Johnson was born in Salem, Massachusetts, in 1822. He graduated from Harvard in 1842 and from Harvard Divinity School in 1846. Before leaving Divinity School he collaborated with a classmate, Samuel Longfellow, on *A Book of Hymns for Public and Private Devotion* (Boston, 1846) in which they tried to make hymns "more acceptable to Unitarians in general." Initially a "conservative Unitarian," Johnson, spurred by Theodore Parker's influence, developed his own ministerial model which would go beyond Parker's Christianity into Universal Religion. After graduation Johnson became involved with abolitionist activities which resulted in a speaking engagement to the Lynn congregation and to the formation in 1853 of the Lynn Free Church and Johnson as its minister. For the next 17 years Johnson used the Lynn ministry to establish the outlines of his ideal religion grounded in Transcendentalism. Johnson became increasingly interested in Asian religions and resigned in 1870 to devote more time to his manuscripts on Oriental religions. Until his death in North Andover in 1882 Johnson wrote his *Oriental Religions and Their Relation to Universal Religion* series on India, China, and Persia. "Neither the facts nor the methods of his Oriental books are of much value today," but Johnson significantly affected the "development of Transcendentalism as a religious, philosophical, literary, and educational movement." Primary and secondary sources; 9 photos, fig., 101 notes, biblio. 1840's-82

Johnson, Sol C.

3604. Matthews, John M. BLACK NEWSPAPERMEN AND THE BLACK COMMUNITY IN GEORGIA, 1890-1930. *Georgia Hist. Q. 1984 68(3): 356-381.* 1890-1930
*For abstract see **Davis, Benjamin J.***

Johnson, Sonia Harris

3605. Bradford, Mary L., interviewer. ALL ON FIRE: AN INTERVIEW WITH SONIA JOHNSON. *Dialogue 1981 14(2): 27-47.* An oral interview with Sonia Harris Johnson, pro-Equal Rights Amendment activist, relating most directly to her 1979 excommunication from the Mormon Church. Johnson discusses a forthcoming book about her experiences, her divorce from Richard Johnson, her final days as a Mormon, and the motivation for the actions that led to her excommunication. Includes her personal perspectives on women's rights, religion, and domestic relations. 1975-81

3606. Bradford, Mary L. THE ODYSSEY OF SONIA JOHNSON. *Dialogue 1981 14(2): 14-26.* Overviews the life of Sonia Harris Johnson during 1936-81, her childhood and youth in northern Utah, early experiences as a Mormon, graduation from Utah State University, and marriage to Richard Johnson. Discusses the couple's frequent relocations due to his career goals, the birth of their children, and the Johnsons' eventual divorce. Extensive coverage is given to her confrontation with the leaders of Mormonism over the Equal Rights Amendment. In 1979 Sonia Johnson was excommunicated from the church for her public criticism of Mormonism. 1936-81

Johnson, Thomas Berger

3607. Gunnerson, Dolores. THOMAS BERGER JOHNSON, NEBRASKA ARTIST, 1890-1968. *Nebraska Hist. 1978 59(4): 539-548.* Discusses the life and art of Johnson. Metal sculpturing was the work in which he found most pleasure and for which he probably will be best remembered. 1900's-68

Johnson, Tom L.

3608. Massouh, Michael. INNOVATIONS IN STREET RAILWAYS BEFORE ELECTRIC TRACTION: TOM L. JOHNSON'S CONTRIBUTIONS. *Technology and Culture 1977 18(2): 202-217.* By introducing the farebox and the single-fare transfer system in the 1870's, Tom L. Johnson (1854-1911) led the way in cutting costs, reducing fares, and increasing the ridership of street railways. In the mid-1880's he devised and introduced a less costly system of cable traction, but switched to electric traction on his Cleveland (Ohio) roads when its efficiency was demonstrated in 1888. Illus., 36 notes. 1870's-80's

Johnson, William Samuel

3609. McCaughey, Elizabeth P. "William Samuel Johnson, Loyalist and Founding Father." Columbia U. 1976. 824 pp. *DAI 1978 39(4): 2487-A.* 1727-1819

3610. McCaughey, Elizabeth P. WILLIAM SAMUEL JOHNSON, THE LOYAL WHIG. Fowler, William M., Jr. and Coyle, Wallace, ed. *The American Revolution: Changing Perspectives* (Boston: Northeastern U. Pr., 1979): 69-102. William Samuel Johnson, a young lawyer, rose to prominence during the 1760's through his advocacy of colonial rights. As the colonial agent for Connecticut he condemned British policy toward the colonies, but he refused to support the American Revolution. His stay in England in 1767 convinced him that colonial policy was determined through ignorance rather than through the sinister designs of a wicked government; consequently, he felt that the American Revolution was not necessary. He also feared that independence would introduce insurmountable perils. Based on the William Samuel Johnson Papers, Connecticut Historical Society, Hartford, and other sources; 85 notes. 1760's-70's

Johnston, Albert Sidney

3611. McGinty, Brian. I WILL CALL A TRAITOR A TRAITOR. *Civil War Times Illus. 1981 20(3): 24-31.* Chronicles the military life of Albert Sidney Johnston in California in 1860, his resignation of his army commission in April 1861, and his eastward trek to Richmond, where Jefferson Davis appointed him general. 1860-61

Johnston, Alexander

3612. McCormick, Richard P. ALEXANDER JOHNSTON: AN APPRECIATION. *Journal of the Rutgers University Libraries 1985 47(1): 12-22.* A century ago, few American historians enjoyed a larger reputation than Alexander Johnston. Johnston graduated from Rutgers College in 1870, entered a career as a preparatory school teacher, and in 1879 wrote *History of American Politics,* which won acclaim. The work was widely adopted as the basic American history text in many colleges and universities. In 1883, he joined the Princeton University faculty. Despite a heavy instructional burden he maintained his literary output. He is remembered as a highly skilled craftsman rather than as a brilliant thinker or innovative scholar. 40 notes. 1870-89

Johnston, Elizabeth Lichtenstein

3613. Johnston, Elizabeth Lichtenstein. RECOLLECTIONS OF A GEORGIA LOYALIST. PART 2. *Atlantis [Canada] 1979 5(1): 154-182.* Continued from a previous article. Autobiography of Elizabeth Lichtenstein Johnston (1764-1848), a Georgia Loyalist, describing her memories of the American Revolution and her family's eventual move to Nova Scotia. 1764-1848

Johnston, Frances Benjamin

3614. Page, Marian. FRANCES BENJAMIN JOHNSTON'S ARCHITECTURAL PHOTOGRAPHS. *Am. Art & Antiques 1979 2(4): 64-71.* Frances Benjamin Johnston (1864-1952) began her photographic career in the 1880's, and received an award in 1945 by the American Institute of Architects for advancing the field of American architecture with her photographs of early American architecture in the southeastern states. ca 1880-1952

3615. Peterson, Anne E. FRANCES BENJAMIN JOHNSTON: THE EARLY YEARS, 1888-1908. *Nineteenth Cent. 1980 6(1): 58-60.* Discusses the training and early photography of Frances Benjamin Johnston (1864-1952). 1888-1908

Johnston, John D.

3616. Ames, Marilyn G. LINCOLN'S STEPBROTHER: JOHN D. JOHNSTON. *Lincoln Herald 1980 82(1): 302-311.* Discusses Abraham Lincoln's stepbrother, John D. Johnston (1810-ca. 50's), son of Sarah Bush Johnston, Thomas Lincoln's second wife. 1819-59

Johnston, Joseph E.

3617. McMurry, Richard M. "THE *ENEMY* AT RICHMOND": JOSEPH E. JOHNSTON AND THE CONFEDERATE GOVERNMENT. *Civil War Hist. 1981 27(1): 5-31.* The problem between Confederate General Joseph E. Johnston and President Jefferson Davis was of unknown origin and began prior to 1861. Throughout the Civil War suspicion, lack of communication, and bitter comments and actions by both parties and their allies contributed to lack of cooperation and, finally, Confederate defeat. Based on *Official Records of the Union and Confederate Armies,* correspondence, and secondary sources; 40 notes. 1861-65

Johnston, Olin D.

3618. Miller, Anthony Barry. "Palmetto Politician: The Early Political Career of Olin D. Johnston, 1896-1945." U. of North Carolina, Chapel Hill 1976. 464 pp. *DAI 1977 38(2): 978-A.* 1896-1945

Johnston, Oscar G.

3619. Nelson, Lawrence John. "King Cotton's Advocate: The Public and Private Career of Oscar G. Johnston." U. of Missouri, Columbia 1972. 516 pp. *DAI 1979 40(1): 396-A.* 1927-40's

Johnston, William G.

3620. Mahone, Rene C. WILLIAM G. JOHNSTON, 1880-1942. *Guam Recorder 1975 5(2): 11-15.* William G. Johnston, an American stationed in Guam with the Navy decided to establish residency, married a native of the island, and lived there until the Japanese invasion, 1941. 1880-1942

Johnstone, George

3621. Fabel, R. F. A. GOVERNOR GEORGE JOHNSTONE OF BRITISH WEST FLORIDA. *Florida Hist. Q. 1976 54(4): 497-511.* George Johnstone (b. 1730), first governor of British West Florida, arrived in Pensacola in 1764 and governed until his dismissal in 1767. Johnstone was a vigorous, intelligent governor who made several improvements. He was unable to solve difficulties concerning relations with the Creek Indians and overlapping responsibilities of civil and military rule. He was dismissed by Lord Shelburne not because of his bellicose attitude toward the Indians but rather for his disputes with military authority and with other Florida civil officials. Based mainly on sources in the Colonial Office and Admiralty-Public Record Office and secondary sources; 49 notes. 1764-67

Jonas, Karel

3622. Bicha, Karel D. KAREL JONAS OF RACINE: "FIRST CZECH IN AMERICA." *Wisconsin Mag. of Hist. 1979-80 63(2): 122-140.* A biographical sketch of Karel Jonas from his birth in a Bohemian village in 1840 to his death at Krefeld, Germany, in 1896. Jonas was a nationalist who left for London in 1860. There he wrote for the *Times* until his departure for Racine, Wisconsin, in 1863. For the next 30 years he edited the Czech-language newspaper, *Slavie,* and emerged as one of the most important early Czech Americans. He wrote practical books for Czech immigrants and was elected successively to the Racine common council, the state assembly, state senate, and finally the lieutenant-governorship. Before his death he held consular positions in Prague, Petrograd, and Krefeld. 10 illus., 77 notes. 1860-96

Jones, Arthur (family)

3623. Petley-Jones, Evan. MEMORIES OF ROSSDALE. *Alberta Hist. [Canada] 1981 29(3): 32-36.* In 1905, the author's parents, Arthur Jones and Elizabeth Petley, arrived in Rossdale, a part of the "Old City" of Edmonton. Their life is described in terms of the white and Indian visitors to their home, the trials and tribulations of raising six sons, who were born between 1908-19, and the people met in that settlement. 2 photos. 1905-39

Jones, Bobby

3624. Smith, Red. FOUR! *Am. Heritage 1980 31(5): 76-85.* Discusses golf and Bobby Jones (1902-71), commemorating the golden anniversary of Jones's still unmatched Grand Slam—winning the British Amateur, the British Open, the US Open, and the US Amateur tournaments. Jones's successes began with a club junior championship at the age of 10 and continued through many victories until his retirement in 1930. He did play in selected tournaments later, but his health forced him to quit golf for good in 1949. 6 illus. ca 1912-49

Jones, Charles Colcock, Jr.

3625. Berry, James William. "Growing up in the Old South: The Childhood of Charles Colcock Jones, Jr." Princeton U. 1981. 409 pp. *DAI 1981 42(3): 1281-A.* 8118346 19c

3626. Proefrock, Vicki G. HISTORICAL SKETCH OF CHARLES COLCOCK JONES, JR. *Richmond County Hist. 1983 15(1): 9-18.* Charles Colcock Jones, Jr., was a noted lawyer, politician, and leading historian of his native Georgia, who flourished during 1855-93. 1855-93

Jones, Charles H.

3627. Graham, Thomas. CHARLES H. JONES: SPOKESMAN FOR THE "WESTERN IDEA." *Missouri Hist. Rev. 1981 75(3): 294-315.* Charles H. Jones edited the St. Louis *Republic* from 1888 to 1893 and the St. Louis *Post-Dispatch* from 1895 to 1897. Although he had been in St. Louis only a short time, Jones quickly became a leading spokesman of the decade's protest and reform philosophy, which he called the "Western Idea." He did more than advocate reform. An active Democrat, Jones worked in the political arena with party bosses and leading public officials. Based on the Charles Jones Papers, University of Florida, Gainesville; the David Francis papers, Missouri Historical Society, St. Louis; the Grover Cleveland, William Jennings Bryan papers, Library of Congress; newspapers; and dissertations; illus., 52 notes. 1888-97

Jones, Charles Henry

3628. Graham, Thomas. CHARLES H. JONES: FLORIDA'S GILDED AGE EDITOR-POLITICIAN. *Florida Hist. Q. 1980 59(1): 1-23.* Analyzes Charles Henry Jones's (1848-1913) rise as a newspaper editor and politician. Jones and George M. Barbour founded the Jacksonville *Florida Daily Times* in 1881. By finding the middle road between Republicans and Democrats, Jones managed to rise in political influence. Ill health forced him to retire in the late 1890's. Based on the Jones correspondence (copies in the University of Florida Library, Gainesville) and on other sources; 2 illus., 69 notes. 1881-1900

Jones, Charles W.

3629. Etemadi, Judy Nicholas. "A LOVE-MAD MAN": SENATOR CHARLES W. JONES OF FLORIDA. *Florida Hist. Q. 1977 56(2): 123-137.* An influential Democratic senator from Pensacola, Charles W. Jones (1834-97) had successfully served Florida for 10 years in Washington. In 1885 he suffered a sudden, unexplained physical and mental decline which popularly was attributed to his infatuation with a Detroit woman. He never returned to the Senate to finish his term, but he was never relieved of his post and Florida was deprived of full representation for more than a year. Based almost entirely on newspaper accounts; illus., 63 notes. 1885-86

Jones, David Thomas

3630. Bredin, Thomas F. THE REVEREND DAVID JONES: MISSIONARY AT RED RIVER 1823-38. *Beaver [Canada] 1981 312(2): 47-52.* The diary of David Thomas Jones (1798-1844), evangelist, teacher, and Anglican chaplain to the Hudson's Bay Company, records his life at the Red River Settlement during 1823-38. He arrived at age 25 at York Factory. His firm yet effective dealings with the Indians brought him considerable success. The rigors of his first winter were to be the worst he ever experienced. His pleas to the Church Missionary Society for a co-worker were answered in 1825 when William Cockran was sent out just in time to witness "[t]he greatest natural disaster," the flood of 1825-26. Two years later Jones traveled to England, married, and returned to the settlement. 4 sketches, map, photo. 1823-38

Jones, Eliza and Peter

3631. Smith, Donald B. [ELIZA AND PETER JONES].

ELIZA AND THE REVEREND PETER JONES. *Beaver [Canada] 1977 308(2): 40-46.* Continued from a previous article. Examines the first years spent at the Credit River Mission, Ontario, by Peter Jones, a Mississauga Methodist, and his English-born, middle-class wife, Eliza. Eliza was hampered by the notoriety surrounding her marriage to an Indian, and had a difficult time adjusting to Indian values. She persevered, cared for the Indians during an epidemic, and was gradually accepted by those closest to Reverend Jones. In 1837, after four years at Credit River, Eliza returned to England to visit her parents; some newspapers and Indians believed that she had deserted Jones. Based on the diaries of Eliza and Peter Jones; 8 illus.

PETER AND ELIZA JONES: THEIR LAST YEARS. *Beaver [Canada] 1977 308(3): 16-23.* Peter Jones, accompanied by Eliza, made several trips to England to raise funds and to attempt to receive title to the Indian lands. The Mississauga Indians prospered in Ontario, but dissention developed in the group. Traditional Indians opposed complete acculturation, and soon some of the Christian Indians believed that acculturation had gone too far. Jones, with his wife's support, tried to obliterate the Indian way of life. Although many Indians disagreed with his views, Jones was highly regarded by the Indian community and by local whites. In the late 19th century, his son Peter Edmund Jones assumed the leadership of the Mississaugas, who were by then residing at the Six Nations' Reserve near Grand River. Based mostly on the diaries of Peter and Eliza Jones; 10 illus. 1833-90

Jones, George Wallace

3632. Thayer, Shelly A. THE DELEGATE AND THE DUEL: THE EARLY POLITICAL CAREER OF GEORGE WALLACE JONES. *Palimpsest 1984 65(5): 178-188.* Mining entrepreneur George Wallace Jones enjoyed a successful political career as a county judge, territorial delegate to Congress for Michigan and Wisconsin, senator from Iowa, and ambassador to Colombia; Jones's career suffered a temporary setback in 1838, when he acted as second to Jonathan Cilley during Cilley's fatal duel with Congressman William Jordan Graves. 1820's-96

Jones, Henry Francis

3633. Rogers, William Warren. A SOLDIER'S ODYSSEY: HENRY FRANCIS JONES AND THE CIVIL WAR. *Georgia Hist. Q. 1982 66(4): 450-466.* Brief discussion of the Civil War career of First Lieutenant Henry Francis Jones (ca. 1841-64) of the Confederate Cobb's Legion. Also describes the war's effect on his family and acquaintances in Thomas County, Georgia. Based on correspondence and secondary sources; 46 notes. 1860-65

Jones, Howard Mumford

3634. Wiener, Philip P. IN MEMORIAM: HOWARD MUMFORD JONES (1892-1980). *J. of the Hist. of Ideas 1980 41(3): 457-458.* Summarizes Howard Mumford Jones's career as a historian of American culture. Jones's May 1980 letter to the editor of this journal is excerpted to show the direction his interests were taking just before he died. A partial list of his publications is included. 1910's-80

Jones, James Parnell

3635. Curtis, Peter H. A QUAKER AND THE CIVIL WAR: THE LIFE OF JAMES PARNELL JONES. *Quaker Hist. 1978 67(1): 35-41.* Raised as a Quaker in Maine, James Parnell Jones spent two years at Haverford College, and developed a passion for antislavery and temperance reforms in reaction to the "hypocrisy" of conservative, Philadelphia Quakers. He taught school, and graduated from the University of Michigan in 1856, shifting toward the reformist tenets of Progressive or Congregational Friends in the area. When he returned to Maine in 1861 and joined its 7th Regiment, he was disowned, but felt himself still a Friend in all respects except in fighting the war for freedom and union. Based in part on letters to his family in Maine; 33 notes. 1850's-64

Jones, Jim

3636. Lincoln, C. Eric and Mamiya, Lawrence H. DADDY JONES AND FATHER DIVINE: THE CULT AS POLITICAL RELIGION. *Religion in Life 1980 49(1): 6-23.* Briefly discusses American religious cults since the end of World War I, focuses on Jim Jones and the People's Temple group he led to Guyana, includes information on the characteristics of a cult leader, the cult itself, and the members, and compares cults and black religion, and Jones and Father Divine, who founded the Peace Mission; 1920's-70's. 1920-79

Jones, John

3637. Caper, Gene and Stern, Norton B. FIRST JEWISH PRESIDENT OF THE LOS ANGELES CITY COUNCIL. *Western States Jewish Hist. 1984 17(1): 63-76.* A biographical sketch of John Jones, a successful Los Angeles businessman and one of the city's leading Jewish citizens. Includes data on Jones's move to San Francisco and subsequent return, as well as his marriage to Doria Deighton and her conversion to Judaism. Based largely on newspaper sources; 76 notes. 1800-76

Jones, John Griffing

3638. Miller, Rush G. JOHN G. JONES: PIONEER CIRCUIT RIDER AND HISTORIAN. *J. of Mississippi Hist. 1977 39(1): 17-39.* Describes the life and career of John Griffing Jones (1804-88), who was a Methodist "circuit rider, presiding elder, and noted historian" in Mississippi during 1824-88. Describes his experiences as a circuit rider and preacher, his view of slavery, and his writings. As a church historian he wrote many periodical articles, a history of Protestantism in the Old Southwest, and a two-volume history of Methodism in Mississippi. Based largely on Jones' journal; 58 notes. 1821-88

Jones, John Paul

3639. Dean, Nicholas. JOHN PAUL JONES CAME AWFULLY CLOSE TO BEING A LOSER. *Smithsonian 1980 11(9): 139-154.* John Paul Jones was born in Scotland, apprenticed early, and commanded a British trade ship by age 21. Brave but hot-headed, Jones killed a seaman during a mutiny and fled to America. There, in June 1777, he was given command of the *Ranger* and ordered to distress "the Enemies of the United States." He raided a port on the English coast. In February 1779 he took command of *Le Bonhomme Richard* with the help of Benjamin Franklin. Jones encountered the Royal Navy warship *Serapis* on September 23 off the east coast of Scotland. After a ruinous battle the *Serapis* surrendered and the *Richard* sank. Jones returned to America a hero, but died a forgotten man in Paris in 1792. 12 photos, map. 1772-92

3640. Minchilli, Guido. JOHN PAUL JONES: UNO DEL "GRANDI" DELLA MARINE DEGLI STATI UNITI [John Paul Jones: one of the "greats" of the U.S. Navy]. *Riv. Marittima [Italy] 1976 109(6): 75-84.* John Paul Jones is one of the most outstanding characters of the nautical tradition of the United States. Scottish by birth, he went to Virginia for the first time at the age of 12 as a cabin boy. His adventurous life took him from commanding sailing ships engaged in the slave trade to the eventual command of warships. He was accorded the honour of being the first to hoist the new flag of the United States on a warship, as indeed he also had the honour to be the first to cause the American flag to be recognized in international relationships. His ashes are kept in the Chapel of the Naval Academy at Annapolis. 1747-92

Jones, John S.

3641. Claycomb, William B. JOHN S. JONES: FARMER, FREIGHTER, FRONTIER PROMOTER. *Missouri Hist. Rev. 1979 73(4): 434-450.* John S. Jones was important in developing transportation in Kansas and Colorado. Starting his business career as a plantation manager for Jefferson Davis, Jones went on to speculate in land in Missouri. Jones turned to freighting ventures in the West, receiving government contracts for transporting military supplies. Jones was co-founder of the first overland stage company in the Great Plains states and was a major stockholder in the Pony Express. An early settler of Colorado, Jones helped lay the foundation for Colorado's eventual admission to the Union. 50 notes. 1811-76

Jones, Joseph

3642. Riley, Harris D., Jr. DOCTORS JOSEPH JONES AND STANHOPE BAYNE-JONES. TWO DISTINGUISHED LOUISIANIANS. *Louisiana Hist. 1984 25(2): 155-180.* Joseph Jones served with the Confederate medical corps, taught at a number of medical schools, and for four years was president of the Louisiana Board of Health. He made important research contributions, particularly on malaria and yellow fever, investigated Indian remains, and helped found the Southern Historical Society. His grandson Stanhope Bayne-Jones distinguished himself as teacher and administrator at medical schools including Rochester, Yale, and Cornell; in several high positions in the Office of the Surgeon General during and after World War II, and in consulting assignments. His specialties were preventive medicine and infectious diseases. Based on Jones's writings, interviews with Bayne-Jones, secondary works; 2 photos, 125 notes. 1830-1970

Jones, Madison

3643. Gretlund, Jan Nordby. MADISON JONES: A BIBLIOGRAPHY. *Bull. of Biblio. 1982 39(3): 117-120.* Presents a brief background on Southern novelist Madison Jones, known as a spokesman for agrarian ideals, followed by a bibliography of primary and secondary sources published since the appearance of his first article in 1952. 1952-82

Jones, Margo

3644. Larsen, June Bennett. "Margo Jones: A Life in the Theatre." City U. of New York 1982. 299 pp. *DAI 1982 43(5): 1348-A.* DA8222956 1920's-70's

Jones, Marvin

3645. May, Irvin, Jr. MARVIN JONES: AGRARIAN AND POLITICIAN. *Agric. Hist. 1977 51(2): 421-440.* A Texas panhandle Congressman during 1916-40, Marvin Jones played a key role in the passage of such legislation as the Agricultural Adjustment Act of 1933, the Jones-Connelly Farm Relief Act, the Soil Conservation Act, the Domestic Allotment Act, the Bankhead-Jones Farm Tenancy Act, and the Agricultural Adjustment Act of 1938. Primary and secondary sources; 49 notes. 1916-40

Jones, Mary Harris

3646. Scholten, Pat Creech. THE OLD MOTHER AND HER ARMY: THE AGITATIVE STRATEGIES OF MARY HARRIS JONES. *West Virginia Hist. 1979 40(4): 365-374.* Mary Harris (Mother) Jones (1830-1930), a colorful Irish American labor organizer, used deliberate hell-raising tactics to bolster workers' morale and rouse public sympathy. She arranged "pageants of poverty" to show the exploitation of children and others, verbally abused management in public encounters, and served time in jails. Covers 1870's-1920's. Primary sources; 37 notes. 1870's-1920's

3647. Scully, Michael Andrew. WOULD "MOTHER" JONES BUY *MOTHER JONES? Public Interest 1978 (53): 100-108.* A study of the career, ideas, methods, problems, and accomplishments of Mary Harris Jones (1830-1930), Irish American socialist and labor organizer, reveals considerable disparity with those of her namesake radical magazine *Mother Jones* and its readers. It has become the largest-selling radical magazine of the decade. It has "something for everyone who feels put-out with American life; each issue treats the themes of corporate corruption, political atrophy, small-is-beautiful, communal living, and feminism." In contrast to the journal with its antimodernity and tendency to prescribe various guarantees to society, Mother Jones had an understanding of what can be obtained from modernity, something the counterculture generally lacks. Likewise, Mother Jones fought for very real issues of decent living and working conditions, whereas the readers of *Mother Jones* in comparison are not actually deprived and fight for less substantial causes. 1850's-1920's

3648. Sturm, Phillip. MOTHER JONES AND THE IRON JUDGE. *J. of the West Virginia Hist. Assoc. 1981 5(1): 18-26.* Discusses the careers of United Mine Workers activist Mother Jones (Mary Harris Jones) and Federal District Judge John Jay Jackson, Jr., of the Western District of Virginia, and their meeting in court after her arrest in the coal strike of 1902 in West Virginia. 1902

3649. —. MOTHER JONES, 1830-1930. *J. of the Illinois State Hist. Soc. 1980 73(3): 235-237.* 1830-1930
*For abstract see **McDonald, Duncan***

Jones, Paul

3650. Sillito, John and Hearn, Timothy S. A QUESTION OF CONSCIENCE: THE RESIGNATION OF BISHOP PAUL JONES. *Utah Hist. Q. 1982 50(3): 209-223.* Paul Jones became the fourth Episcopal bishop of Utah in 1914. With a background in Socialist causes, he became a center of controversy, because of his staunch stand against US involvement in World War I, that culminated in his resignation as bishop in 1918. During the 1920's he continued his Socialist activities. In 1929 he was appointed bishop of southern Ohio. 4 photos, 37 notes. 1914-29

Jones, Ralph Waldo Emerson

3651. Peoples, Morgan. RALPH WALDO EMERSON "PREZ" JONES: "THE COUNTRY DOCTOR OF HIGHER EDUCATION IN LOUISIANA," 1926-1977. *Louisiana Hist. 1984 25(4): 367-390.* Describes the career of educator Ralph Waldo Emerson Jones, who, in 1936, became president of Louisiana Negro Normal and Industrial Institute, a two-year school with three wooden buildings and a $55,000 annual budget, which he left at retirement in 1977 as Grambling State University with 4,200 students, a $40 million campus, and a national reputation for its athletic teams and band. Nationally and internationally known, Jones was an acquaintance of presidents and a speaker before the UN, in every major US city, and in cities throughout the world. Based on interviews, newspapers and magazines, and Grambling publications; 3 photos, 62 notes. 1925-82

Jones, Robert Edmond

3652. Miller, Thomas Charles. "Robert Edmond Jones and the Modern Movement: A Study of Related Elements in Art, Architecture, and Theatre." U. of Colorado, Boulder 1977. 269 pp. *DAI 1978 38(7): 3809-3810-A.* 1915-41

Jones, Rufus

3653. Alten, Diana. RUFUS JONES AND THE AMERICAN FRIEND: A QUEST FOR UNITY. *Quaker History 1985 74(1): 41-48.* Rufus Jones edited the Philadelphia *Friends Review,* which merged with the Chicago *Christian Worker* to form the Philadelphia *American Friend,* for 20 years, while teaching philosophy at Haverford College. His charismatic speaking and writing probably prevented a schism between evangelical and modernist Quakers. Based on the periodicals and on the Rufus M. Jones Papers at Haverford College; 30 notes. 1893-1912

Jones, Sarah Van Hoosen

3654. Howard, Saralee R. A VILLAGE ALBUM: STONY CREEK REVISITED. *Michigan Hist. 1978 62(3): 18-28.* History of Stony Creek, an unincorporated village in Avon Township east of Rochester, Michigan, since ca. 1830, when Elisha Taylor settled there; focuses on the photographs of long-time Stony Creek resident Sarah Van Hoosen Jones (1892-1972), taken in 1910, of Stony Creek's homes and residents; and provides a biography of Jones, a surgeon and teacher of surgery, known for her development of "twilight sleep" for women in childbirth. 1910

Jones, Thomas ap Catesby

3655. Hanke, Robert J. COMMODORE JONES AND HIS PRIVATE WAR WITH MEXICO. *Am. West 1979 16(6): 30-33, 60-63.* Commodore Thomas ap Catesby Jones commanded the US Pacific Squadron. In early September 1842, unexplained movements of British warships and provocative newspaper accounts convinced him that American national interests were in jeopardy. Believing that war had started between Mexico and the United States, Jones raced with two ships from Peru to claim Baja and Alta California before the British could press their claims. On 20 October, he forced the surrender of Monterey and claimed the two Californias for the United States. Finding that Mexico and the United States were at peace, Jones hoisted the Mexican flag 29 hours later. 2 illus., biblio. 1842

Jones, William Ambrose

3656. O'Brien, Miriam Therese. "EL JOVEN PRELADO": BISHOP WILLIAM AMBROSE JONES, O.S.A. [The young priest: Bishop William Ambrose Jones, O.S.A.]. *Horizontes [Puerto Rico] 1979 22(44): 39-58.* Augustinian William Ambrose Jones, ordained in 1890, had assignments in Philadelphia and Atlantic City, before going to Cuba and then to Puerto Rico in 1907, where he served as Bishop; he returned to Philadelphia for medical treatment in 1920 and died there in February 1921. 1907-21

Jones, William Atkinson

3657. Shelton, Charlotte Jean. "William Atkinson Jones, 1849-1918: Independent Democracy in Gilded Age Virginia." U. of Virginia 1980. 322 pp. *DAI 1980 41(5): 2262-A.* 8024035 1873-1918

Jordan, Philip D.

3658. —. IN MEMORIAM: PHILIP D. JORDAN, 1904-1980. *Ann. of Iowa 1981 45(8): 646.* Philip D. Jordan was a student of the American frontier and the author of numerous books and articles. He was a professor emeritus at the University of Minnesota and editorial consultant to the *Annals of Iowa* at the time of his death. 1935-80

Jordan, William H.

3659. Easterbrook, Gregg. THE MOST POWERFUL NOBODY IN WASHINGTON. *Washington Monthly 1980 12(7): 50-59.* Discusses the political power and career of William H. Jordan, chief counsel of the Senate Appropriations Committee (Subcommittee on Foreign Aid), who has allegedly controlled foreign aid spending since the 1960's. 1960's-80

Jorgensen, Arthur W.

3660. Jorgensen, Arthur W., Sr. GETTING BY: A SCHOOLTEACHER'S RECOLLECTION OF THE DEPRESSION YEARS. *Wisconsin Magazine of History 1985 68(4): 266-283.* Recounts the author's experiences as a teacher in rural Columbus, Wisconsin, during the Great Depression. Hard times required that teachers generate outside income, which led Jorgensen to operate a weekly newspaper and manage an amusement park. These enterprises not only kept the family solvent, but solidified it. 7 illus. 1917-52

Joseph, Chief

3661. Rhodes, Lee Wilson. "Chief Joseph's Leadership Within the Nontreaty Nez Percé Indians, 1871-1885." US Int. U. 1981. 172 pp. *DAI 1981 42(5): 2265-A.* 8124211 1871-85

Josephs, Joseph

3662. Hewett, Marie. "ELEPHANT JOE" JOSEPHS, A FOLK HERO FROM BUFFALO'S PAST. *New York Folklore 1984 10(3-4): 35-45.* Gives a biography of Joseph Josephs, a 19th-century commercial artist famous in Buffalo, New York, for his advertising signs, and describes how this colorful character became a figure in Buffalo folklore. 1850's-93

Josephson, Matthew

3663. O'Neill, William L. POPULAR HISTORY AND RADICAL CHIC. *Rev. in Am. Hist. 1981 9(4): 451-453.* Reviews David E. Shi's *Matthew Josephson, Bourgeois Bohemian* (1981), a biography of Popular Front member and historian, Matthew Josephson (1899-1978). 1920's-78

Joudry, Patricia

3664. Ravel, Aviva Eva. "The Dramatic World of Patricia Joudry." McGill U. [Canada] 1984. *DAI 1985 45(10): 3133-A.* 1940-81

Joy, Joseph

3665. Dix, Keith. JOSEPH JOY AND HIS MOBILE LOADING MACHINE. *West Virginia Hist. 1980 41(3): 226-244.* Between 1904 and 1944, Joseph Joy (1883-1957) received 106 patents on mining equipment such as coal loaders, cutting machines, and conveyors. While working with the Mellon family's Pittsburgh Coal Company he met John Donaldson who first backed him in and then removed him from the Joy Machine Company. Joy was a talented inventor but a poor businessman. From 1925 to 1929 he was in the USSR, where he helped modernize Soviet mines. In America, unions resisted his labor saving devices. Based on *Joy Manufacturing Company History,* US Patent Office materials, interviews, an unpublished autobiography, and the *Federal Reporter;* 5 illus., 42 notes. 1904-44

Joyner, Conrad

3666. Joyner, Conrad. CRABGRASS AND BUREAUCRATS. *Midwest Q. 1978 20(1): 18-31.* The author discusses practical politics, focusing on his experiences as staffer for Oregon Governor Mark Hatfield, staffer for Congressman Ogden Reid, and local officeholder in Tucson (Arizona) and Salem (Oregon); 1960's-70's. 1960's-70's

Juana Maria

3667. Hudson, Travis. SOME J. P. HARRINGTON NOTES ON THE "LONE WOMAN" OF SAN NICOLAS ISLAND. *Masterkey 1978 52(1): 23-28.* 1836-53
For abstract see ***Harrington, John P.***

Judson, Adoniram (family)

3668. Brumberg, Joan Jacobs. "A Mission for Life: The Judson Family and American Evangelical Culture, 1790-1850." U. of Virginia 1978. 331 pp. *DAI 1979 40(2): 1024-A.* 1790-1850

Judson, William V.

3669. Weyant, Jane Gilmer. "The Life and Career of General William V. Judson, 1865-1923." Georgia State U., Coll. of Arts and Sci. 1981. 315 pp. *DAI 1983 44(6): 1898-1899-A* DA8321366 1917-18

Jue, Willard

3670. Lee, Douglas W. WILLARD JUE, A CHINESE AMERICAN FOR ALL SEASONS. *Annals of the Chinese Historical Society of the Pacific Northwest 1984: 1-29.* Presents a biography of Willard Jue (1905-84), tracing his career as an expert in Chinese herbalism, an avocational historian, and a leader of Seattle's Chinese-American community. 1905-84

Jung, James E.

See Young, Brig

Just, Ernest Everett

3671. Wynes, Charles E. ERNEST EVERETT JUST: MARINE BIOLOGIST, MAN EXTRAORDINAIRE. *Southern Studies 1984 23(1): 60-70.* The distinguished black marine biologist Ernest Everett Just studied at Dartmouth and the University of Chicago. He headed the Department of Zoology and taught in the Medical School of Howard University during 1909-30. He spent almost every summer at the biological research station at Woods Hole, Massachusetts. He wrote prolifically and enjoyed a wide reputation in Europe in the fields of cytological and embryological techniques. Just was a sensitive man, and social slights and offensive behavior by some whites led Just to move to Europe in 1930. He taught, did research, and wrote there amidst friends and admirers for the remainder of his career. 27 notes. 1900's-41

K

Kaasen, Gunnar

3672. Smith, Dean. THEY RACED DEATH TO NOME. *Am. Hist. Illus. 1979 14(8): 36-40.* Leonard Seppalla (who mushed 80 miles), Charlie Olson (who mushed 25 miles), and Gunnar Kaasen (who mushed the final 60 miles), traveled cross-country by dogsled from Shaktolik to Nome, Alaska, amidst raging blizzards to deliver precious serum needed to head off a possible diphtheria epidemic in Nome, 1925. 1925

Kadushin, Max

3673. Steinberg, Theodore. "Max Kadushin, Scholar of Rabbinic Judaism: A Study of His Life, Work, and Theory of Valuational Thought." New York U. 1980. 470 pp. *DAI 1980 41(6): 2653-A.* 8027491 1921-80

Kahn, Albert

3674. Kahn, Edgar. ALBERT KAHN: HIS SON REMEMBERS. *Michigan History 1985 69(4): 24-31.* Albert Kahn, one of eight children of a poor German immigrant became one of Michigan's great architects, designing such diverse buildings as the University of Michigan's Hill Auditorium, the Fisher Building in Detroit, and the Willow Run bomber plant. He died on 8 December 1942, proud that his architectural talents had helped to design some of the nation's leading war manufacturing plants, as his son remembers. 13 photos, 2 fig. 1869-1942

Kahn, Julius

3675. Boxerman, Burton Alan. KAHN OF CALIFORNIA. *California Hist. Q. 1976 55(4): 340-351.* Julius Kahn (1861-1924) was a 12 term Congressman from California whose career spanned the presidencies from Theodore Roosevelt to Calvin Coolidge. Born of German Jewish parents, Kahn came to California at age seven and grew up in San Francisco. After an initial career as an actor he became a lawyer. Elected to Congress in 1898, Kahn was continuously returned by his San Francisco constituents except for the 1902 election. Kahn generally followed the Republican Party position favoring free tolls for American ships through the Panama Canal, opposing Woodrow Wilson's Mexican policy and the League of Nations, and supporting the operation of Muscle Shoals by private enterprise. An advocate of military preparedness, Kahn crossed party lines to support Wilson's preparedness policy in 1917. He sponsored the first Selective Service Act and favored universal military training. While reflecting his constituents' opposition to Japanese immigration and naturalization, Kahn voted against laws designed to restrict European immigration. He died of a cerebral hemorrhage in 1924. Based on primary and secondary sources; photos, 48 notes. 1898-1924

Kahn, Louis Isidore

3676. Lobell, John. A LUCID MYSTIC HELPED TRANSFORM OUR ARCHITECTURE. *Smithsonian 1979 10(4): 36-43.* Discusses the career of immigrant American mystic architect Louis Isidore Kahn (1901-74). 1901-74

Kaiser, Henry J.

3677. Foster, Mark S. GIANT OF THE WEST: HENRY J. KAISER AND REGIONAL INDUSTRIALIZATION, 1930-1950. *Business History Review 1985 59(1): 1-23.* Discusses the career of Henry J. Kaiser, who played a major role in the industrial and economic development of the Western United States, focusing on his steelmaking activity, the linchpin of his industrial empire, and his relations with the Roosevelt and Truman administrations. In Kaiser's early career, he concentrated upon building the region's infrastructure, including roads, bridges, tunnels, and dams. Later he engaged in shipbuilding, steelmaking, mining, aluminum production, defense contracting, and homebuilding. In his final years, he promoted tourism in Hawaii and made innovations in health care. The latter achievement was the one he wished to be most remembered for by later generations. Based on Henry J. Kaiser papers, Berkeley, California, and personal interviews and governmental records; 3 illus., 63 notes. 1930-50

Kalakaua, David

3678. James, Wilma. HAWAII'S LAST KING. *Pacific Hist. 1980 24(3): 312-315.* David Kalakaua was the last king of the Hawaiian Islands. During his rule, 1874-91, Iolani Palace was built. He was educated and well-regarded by President Ulysses S. Grant. Festivities marked his coronation in 1883, and his 50th birthday three years later. 2 photos. 1874-91

Kallen, Horace M.

3679. Konvitz, Milton R. H. M. KALLEN AND THE HEBRAIC IDEA. *Modern Judaism 1984 4(2): 215-226.* Explores the role of educator Horace M. Kallen in interpreting Jewish ethos, history, thought, and life. 1900's-30's

Kambouris, Haralambos K.

3680. Papanikolas, Helen, ed. and Vasilacopulos, C. V., transl. OREGON EXPERIENCES: HARALAMBOS K. KAMBOURIS. *Oregon Hist. Q. 1981 82(1): 4-39.* Extracts from the diary of Greek immigrant Haralambos K. Kambouris (ca. 1891-1965) reveal his experiences in Oregon during 1912-15. He moved from place to place, usually working on the railroad and frequently having to travel to look for other jobs. There are also references to many of his Greek compatriots and aspects of Greek culture. Based on diary; 11 photos, 10 notes. 1912-15

Kane, Paul

3681. Webster, Donald Blake. PAUL KANE'S VISIT TO MOUNT ST. HELENS. *Mag. Antiques 1983 124(5): 1001-1003.* Short biography of Canadian painter Paul Kane, whose work was influenced by George Catlin; his Mount St. Helens paintings were inspired by an 1847 visit to southwestern Washington. 1847-55

Kann, Robert A.

3682. Winters, Stanley B. THE FORGING OF A HISTORIAN: ROBERT A. KANN IN AMERICA, 1939-1976. *Austrian Hist. Y. 1981-82 17-18: 3-24.* Discusses the academic career and scholarly achievements of Robert A. Kann, who emigrated to the United States from Austria in 1939. He earned his Ph.D. in history in 1946 and published his first work, *The Multinational Empire,* in 1950. During his career, he wrote numerous books and articles and taught history at Rutgers University and the University of Vienna. When Kann retired in 1976, he moved back to Vienna, where he died in 1981. 72 notes. 1906-81

Kantorowicz, Ernest H.

3683. Giesey, Ralph E. ERNST H. KANTOROWICZ: SCHOLARLY TRIUMPHS AND ACADEMIC TRAVAILS IN WEIMAR GERMANY AND THE UNITED STATES. *Leo Baeck Institute. Year Book [Great Britain] 1985 30: 191-202.* Ernest H. Kantorowicz was a renowned German-Jewish intellectual historian specializing in medieval studies. After the great critical and popular success of his biography of Frederick II (1926), Kantorowicz was offered a teaching post at the University of Frankfurt. He terminated this prestigious position in 1933, when he refused to implement anti-Semitic classroom regulations imposed by the Nazis. After arriving in the United States, Professor Kantorowicz became involved in the loyalty oath issue that rocked the Berkeley campus of the University of California in the late 1940's and early 1950's. Whether in exile or in his native land, Ernst Kantorowicz was respected for his scholarship, and he was a consistent defender of academic freedom. Based mainly on primary sources, including Ernst Kantorowicz's published and unpublished writings, as well as personal interviews with Kantorowicz; 2 photos, 25 notes. 1918-60

Kanui, William Tennooe

3684. Bell, Susan N. "OWHYHEE'S PRODIGAL." *Hawaiian J. of Hist. 1976 10: 25-32.* Refers to William Tennooe Kanui, one of five Hawaiian youths who were sent to Connecticut to be trained as missionaries. Kanui spent the years 1809-20 in America. Three months after his return to Hawaii he was excluded from the church for excessive drinking. In later years he became a teacher, restauranteur in California, and a gold miner. He returned to the church shortly before his death. 1796-1864

Kaplan, Mordecai M.

3685. Libowitz, Richard Lawrence. "Mordecai M. Kaplan as Redactor: The Development of Reconstructionism." Temple U. 1979. 361 pp. *DAI 1979 39(11): 6823-6824-A.* 1915-34

3686. Scult, Melvin. MORDECAI M. KAPLAN: CHALLENGES AND CONFLICTS IN THE TWENTIES. *Am. Jewish Hist. Q. 1977 61(3): 401-416.* Mordecai M. Kaplan was an immigrant who grew up on the lower East Side of New York City and who tried to reconcile his Orthodox Jewish upbringing with the new American culture. The struggle assumed both intellectual and spiritual aspects and was the basis for Kaplan's ambivalence toward the Jewish Theological Seminary where he served as head of its Teacher's Institute and as professor of Homiletics. Analyzes the gradual development of reconstructionist thoughts, clashes with Orthodoxy and seminary colleagues, relations with administrators and the lengthy negotiations with Stephen Wise and the Jewish Institute of Religion. 39 notes. 1920's

Karpeles, Maud

3687. Bronson, Bertrand H. MAUD KARPELES (1886-1976). *J. of Am. Folklore 1977 90(358): 455-464.* Beginning as a disciple of English folklorist Cecil J. Sharp (1859-1924), Maud Karpeles later became his literary executor and a doyenne in her own right of English folk dance and song. With Sharp she traced the English folk song to the southern Appalachians of the United States. During her last years, her editorial work became international in scope and influence. 1886-1976

Kasebier, Gertrude

3688. Homer, William Innes. GERTRUDE KASEBIER: AMERICAN PICTORIAL PHOTOGRAPHER. *Art and Antiques 1980 3(1): 78-85.* Brief biography of American photographer Gertrude Kasebier (1852-1934), whose contributions as a portraitist during the first two decades of the 20th century, and as a pictorialist nationally and internationally, were forgotten until recently; she is known for her themes of motherhood in her pictorialist works which emphasize "the painterly possibilities of the medium." 1852-1934

3689. Tighe, Mary Ann. GERTRUDE KÄSEBIER LOST AND FOUND. *Art in Am. 1977 65(2): 94-98.* Portrait artist and photographer Gertrude Käsebier (b. 1852) was called by Alfred Stieglitz the foremost portrait photographer in the country. 19c-20c

Kaser, Jacob

3690. Kaser, John J., ed. AUTOBIOGRAPHY OF JACOB KASER. *Oregon Hist. Q. 1980 81(3): 281-318.* Jacob Kaser (1868-1948) described his immigration from Glarus, Switzerland, employment in Pennsylvania, and settlement as a sheep rancher in central Oregon. He provided details about his land purchases and sheep raising. 14 photos, map, 2 notes. 1888-1907

Kashner, Frank

3691. Kashner, Frank. A RANK & FILE STRIKE AT GE. *Radical Am. 1978 12(6): 42-60.* The author traces the development of his radicalism since the mid-1960's, his employment at the Lynn, Massachusetts, General Electric Co. River Works Plant in 1971, the rank-and-file strike over industrial safety there in which he participated in 1975, and later union organizing. 1960's-77

Kassing, Edith Force

3692. Tomer, John S. EDITH FORCE KASSING: SCIENTIST WITH A GIFT FOR TEACHING. *Chronicles of Oklahoma 1985-86 63(4): 396-411.* Edith Force Kassing (1890-1966) earned a national reputation as a researcher in Oklahoma ornithology and herpetology. While a teacher at Tulsa's Woodrow Wilson Junior High School from 1926 to 1956, she organized a Junior Academy of Science chapter and the Field and Stream Club, which participated in many field trips and collected thousands of specimens. Many of these specimens went to illustrious institutions, such as the Oklahoma State University Museum, the University of Oklahoma Museum of Zoology, the University of Tulsa, the National Museum of Natural History, and the US Biological Survey in Washington, D.C. Kassing also received honors from the Oklahoma Academy of Science and other research organizations for her scores of published articles. Based on recollections of Edith Kassing and on Kassing's writings; 9 photos, 27 notes, biblio. 1926-49

Kato, Fred

3693. Thompson, Donald. MR. KATO. *Pacific Hist. 1979 23(4): 28-44.* Fred Kato was a Japanese immigrant to California in the early 1920's. He worked for the author's father near Dinuba, California, a grape-growing area. Kato labored in the vineyards until he emerged as a successful nursery operator. Based on the author's manuscript autobiography; photo. ca 1923-40

Katz, Shlomo

3694. Katz, Shlomo. FROM A RUSSIAN SHTETL TO THE FOUNDING OF *MIDSTREAM. Midstream 1982 28(6): 30-35.* An autobiographical account of the life of Shlomo Katz, founder of the magazine *Midstream* in 1955, from his birth in 1909, in the Ukraine until the 1970's; discusses Katz's Zionism. 1920's-79

Kauffman, Lydia

3695. Kauffman, Henry J. AUNT LYDIA. *Pennsylvania Folklife 1985 34(3): 114-132.* Reminiscences of the author's aunt, Lydia Kauffman, a Dunkard who lived on a farm near York, Pennsylvania, and who took the author in after his mother died. 1870-1936

Kauvar, Charles E. H.

3696. Rubinoff, Michael W. C. E. H. KAUVAR: A SKETCH OF A COLORADO RABBI'S LIFE. *Western States Jewish Hist. Q. 1978 10(4): 291-305.* Charles Eliezer Hillel Kauvar (1879-1971) was elected rabbi of Denver's Beth Ha Medrosh Hagodol Synagogue in 1902. Kauvar's devotion to Zionism caused friction between him and Rabbi William S. Friedman of Denver's Temple Emmanuel. The schism between the two rabbis affected the community at large when, in 1903, Rabbi Kauvar helped found the Jewish Consumptives' Relief Society (later the American Medical Center), open to Jews and non-Jews alike. In 1899 Temple Emmanuel had helped start the Jewish Hospital for Consumptives, an institution with a restricted admission policy. In 1920 Rabbi Kauvar was invited to the chair of rabbinic literature at the Methodist-sponsored University of Denver; he held this post for 45 years. Rabbi Kauvar became rabbi emeritus of his synagogue in 1952. In his later years he received many civic and religious awards and honors. Based on archival and published sources; 2 photos, 39 notes. 1902-71

3697. Rubinoff, Michael W. "Rabbi Charles Eliezer Hillel Kauvar of Denver: The Life of a Rabbi in the American West." U. of Denver 1978. 257 pp. *DAI 1978 39(6): 3782-A.* 1900-71

Kaye, V. J.

See Kisilewsky, Vladimir Julian

Kazin, Alfred

3698. Eakin, Paul John. ALFRED KAZIN'S BRIDGE TO AMERICA. *South Atlantic Q. 1978 77(1): 39-53.* Alfred Kazin, Brooklyn-born Jew and author, has written three autobiographical works which underscore his belief in the continuities between private experience and a larger social reality. The rhythms of his Brooklyn experience found their way into *A Walker in the City* (1951), *On Native Grounds* (1956) and *Starting Out in the Thirties* (1965). All of his works have been devoted to the complex fate of the American artist, his problematical relation to his native land, and the working out of this common theme. Thus any account of Kazin's sense of America necessarily focuses on his autobiographies. Like Van Wyck Brooks, he believed that writers must be understood in relation to their native culture and its past. Based on Kazin's writings and criticism of his works; 18 notes. 1940-76

Kean, Charles

3699. Strahan, Richard Denman. "The American Theatrical Tours of Charles Kean." U. of Florida 1984. 274 pp. *DAI 1985 45(7): 1922-A.* DA8421076 1830-66

Keane, John J.

3700. Wangler, Thomas E. A BIBLIOGRAPHY OF THE WRITINGS OF ARCHBISHOP JOHN J. KEANE. *Records of the Am. Catholic Hist. Soc. of Philadelphia 1978 89(1-4): 60-73.* Lists almost all of the surviving articles, pastorals, sermons, discourses, books, and important administrative documents written or spoken by Keane, to be used in conjunction with Patrick Ahern's *The Life of John J. Keane: Educator and Archbishop, 1838-1918* (Bruce, 1955). 1838-1918

Kee, John

3701. Hardin, William H. JOHN KEE AND THE POINT FOUR COMPROMISE. *West Virginia Hist. 1979 41(1): 40-58.* First elected to Congress as a Democrat in 1932 and serving on the House Foreign Affairs Committee from that date and as chairman from 1949 until his death in 1951, John Kee, a supporter of the policies of both Franklin D. Roosevelt and Harry S. Truman, played an important role in the establishment of America's postwar foreign policy. Over Republican opposition and in spite of his own precarious health, Kee guided the Point Four program through Congress. 96 notes. 1949-51

Keefer, Thomas Coltrin

3702. Bush, Edward F. THOMAS COLTRIN KEEFER. *Ontario Hist. [Canada] 1974 66(4): 211-222.* Recounts the life of the Canadian railroad promoter Thomas Coltrin Keefer (b. 1821), emphasizing his accomplishments as a professional engineer. 1821-1915

Keeney, Frank

3703. Corbin, David A. "FRANK KEENEY IS OUR LEADER, AND WE SHALL NOT BE MOVED": RANK-AND-FILE LEADERSHIP IN THE WEST VIRGINIA COAL FIELDS. Fink, Gary M. and Reed, Merl E., eds. *Essays in Southern Labor History: Selected Papers, Southern Labor History Conference, 1976.* (Westport, Conn.; London, England: Greenwood Pr., 1977): 144-156. A study of the career of Frank Keeney as a labor leader in the West Virginia coal fields. His career in the United Mine Workers of America began in 1912. In 1916 he led a "rump" organization and was elected president. He forced investigation and correction of corruption among local union district leaders. He was convinced of the importance and value of indigenous leadership and acted accordingly. His independence alienated him from UMW leaders, including John L. Lewis. In 1931 his last important move, the organization of an independent union and the calling of a strike, was a failure and resulted in his ostracism by the UMW. 49 notes. 1916-31

Kehoe, Andrew

3704. Parker, Grant. DISASTER IN BATH. *Michigan Hist. 1981 65(3): 12-17.* Recreates, with meticulous detail, Michigan's worst mass murder when, in 1927, a discontented school board treasurer named Andrew Kehoe dynamited the Bath Consolidated School and killed 45 persons. Kehoe also killed his wife and blew up his truck, killing himself and four other people. Excerpts from the author's *Mayday;* 6 illus. 1927

Keillor, Garrison

3705. Stelling, Lucille Johnsen. GARRISON KEILLOR'S ZANY AMERICA. *Historic Preservation 1985 37(2): 58-60.* Details the career of Garrison Keillor, the American humorist and *New Yorker* writer whose *A Prairie Home Companion* public radio variety show has established him as the "voice" of small-town America. 1960's-85

Keisker, Walter

3706. Keisker, Walter. ST. LOUIS SEMINARY MEMOIRS, 1919-23. *Concordia Hist. Inst. Q. 1983 56(4): 152-158.* The author recounts his memories of daily life as a student at the Concordia Seminary, St. Louis, administered by the Missouri Synod of the Lutheran Church. 1919-23

Keleher, William A.

3707. Murphy, Lawrence R. A DEDICATION TO THE MEMORY OF WILLIAM A. KELEHER, 1886-1972. *Arizona and the West 1981 23(2): 104-108.* By vocation, William Aloysius Keleher (1886-1972) was a practicing attorney in Albuquerque, New Mexico, prominent in the bar association, state politics, and public affairs. By avocation, he developed a serious interest in research and writing for both professional and nonscholarly audiences. He wrote several important books and articles on the territorial history of New Mexico. He also worked in unconventional sources, especially oral testimony, which eventually brought him considerable praise from professional historians. In later years, Keleher became known for his willingness to encourage and assist young historians to probe the history of the state. Illus., biblio. 1915-72

Keller, Helen

3708. Giffin, Frederick C. THE RADICAL VISION OF HELEN KELLER. *Int. Social Sci. Rev. 1984 59(4): 27-32.* Helen Keller was an active participant in the American radical movement. A member of the Socialist Party, she was particularly outspoken in her opposition to World War I, a conflict she identified as a "capitalistic war" which in no sense served the interests of the working class. After the United States joined the struggle in April 1917, Keller was an impassioned supporter of Emma Goldman, Eugene Debs, and other radicals sent to prison as a result of their antiwar activities. 1909-21

3709. Lash, Joseph P. HELEN KELLER: MOVIE STAR. *Am. Heritage 1980 31(3): 76-85.* Excerpt from Joseph P. Lash's new biography of Helen Keller, *Helen and Teacher* (1980), recounting her experience as the star in a biographical film, *Deliverance,* in 1918, when she was 37. 1918

Keller, Martha

3710. Bixler, Miriam E. MARTHA KELLER, POET. *J. of the Lancaster County Hist. Soc. 1984 88(1): 32-41.* Traces the life of poet Martha Keller Rowland and includes reviews of her published works. 1920's-70's

Kelley, Alfred

3711. Scheiber, Harry N. ALFRED KELLEY AND THE OHIO BUSINESS ELITE, 1822-1859. *Ohio Hist. 1978 87(4): 365-392.* Discusses the four decades (1822-59) of public service by Alfred Kelley, with particular attention to his role as canal commissioner. An entrepreneur with a keen vision of the public and personal prospects and opportunities in the western regional economy, Kelley typified the business elites of Ohio who transformed the western economy during the antebellum years. Based on the Alfred Kelley Papers, the Ethan Allen Brown Papers, and the Canal Commission Papers found in the Ohio Historical Society, the archives of the Western Reserve Historical Society, and other primary sources; 2 illus., 95 notes. 1822-59

Kelley, Florence

3712. Harmon, Sandra D. FLORENCE KELLEY IN ILLINOIS. *J. of the Illinois State Hist. Soc. 1981 74(3): 162-178.* Florence Kelley was a major force in the struggle for protection of laboring children and women throughout her career as a resident of Hull House, the first Illinois factory inspector, and general secretary of the National Consumers' League. A graduate of Cornell University, she was introduced to socialism at the University of Zurich. The abuses of sweatshops led Governor John P. Altgeld to appoint her factory inspector on 12 July 1893. She exposed widespread illiteracy, poor hygiene, and unsafe working conditions. Her work relied on the use of trained inspectors, collection of reliable statistics, issuance of public reports, and legislative lobbying. 6 illus., 82 notes. 1891-1900

Kelley, William Darrah

3713. Brown, Ira V. WILLIAM D. KELLEY AND RADICAL RECONSTRUCTION. *Pennsylvania Mag. of Hist. and Biog. 1961 85(3): 316-329.* Traces the life and accomplishments of William Darrah Kelley, a Philadelphian who served in Congress as a Republican from 1861 until his death in 1890, concentrating on his role as an exponent of Radical Reconstruction policies for the South, woman suffrage, and the civil rights of blacks. 1861-90

3714. Nicklas, Floyd William. "William Kelley: The Congressional Years, 1861-1890." Northern Illinois U. 1983. 531 pp. *DAI 1984 44(12): 3783-A.* DA8405836 1861-90

Kellogg, Charles E.

3715. Johnson, William M. IN MEMORIAM: CHARLES E. KELLOGG (1902-1980). *J. of NAL Assoc. 1979 4(3-4): 85.* Dr. Charles E. Kellogg had headed the National Cooperative Soil Survey, and was a soil scientist of international renown. ca 1920-80

Kellogg, Louise Phelps

3716. Kinnett, David. MISS KELLOGG'S QUIET PASSION. *Wisconsin Mag. of Hist. 1979 62(4): 267-299.* A biography of Louise Phelps Kellogg (1862-1942), beginning with her education starting in 1895 under Frederick Jackson Turner at the University of Wisconsin, and focusing on her 40-year career as a historian of Wisconsin and the Old Northwest. Treats successively her formal education, prodigious writing, occasional teaching, editing, public speaking, and constant research, and covers her professional relationship with other historians and social relations with her small group of female friends during her years at the State Historical Society of Wisconsin. 15 illus., 165 notes. 1895-1942

Kellogg, Marcus Henry

3717. Saum, Lewis O. COLONEL CUSTER'S COPPERHEAD: THE "MYSTERIOUS" MARK KELLOGG. *Montana 1978 28(4): 12-25.* Marcus Henry Kellogg began his journalistic career working for M. M. Pomeroy of the La Crosse, Wisconsin *Democrat* and B. F. Montgomery and A. S. Kierolf of the Council Bluffs, Iowa, *Democrat,* 1863-68. In both associations he became identified as an anti-Civil War, anti-Reconstruction Democrat—a Copperhead. Kellogg then worked as a telegrapher for the Northern Pacific Railroad and finally became a correspondent for the *Bismarck Tribune,* in the Dakota Territory. When George A. Custer's journalist friend Clement Lounsberry could not accompany the 1876 expedition, Kellogg went in Lounsberry's place and died at the Battle of the Little Big Horn. Following Kellogg's death, Republican and Democratic newspapers made a political issue of Custer's defeat. Mark Kellogg quickly became a forgotten participant in the political debates of the era. Based on contemporary newspapers and secondary sources; 6 illus., 56 notes. 1861-76

Kellum, John

3718. Gardner, Deborah S. "The Architecture of Commercial Capitalism: John Kellum and the Development of New York, 1840-1875." Columbia U. 1979. 573 pp. *DAI 1980 40(10): 5558-A.* 1840-75

Kelly, Alan

3719. Kelly, Léontine. J'ECRIS MA VIE [My life story]. *Acadiensis [Canada] 1985 15(1): 133-140.* 1907-62
For abstract see ***Kelly, Léontine***

Kelly, Edward J.

3720. Biles, William Roger. "Mayor Edward J. Kelly of Chicago: Big City Boss in Depression and War." U. of Illinois, Chicago Circle 1981. 312 pp. *DAI 1981 42(4): 1759-A.* 8120559 1933-47

Kelly, Emerson Crosby

3721. —. OBITUARY OF EMERSON CROSBY KELLY, 1899-1977. *J. of the Hist. of Medicine and Allied Sci. 1977 32(4): 431-432.* Emerson Crosby Kelly graduated from Cornell University in 1921 and Albany Medical College in 1925. He was professor of surgery and director of the library at the Albany Medical School for more than 50 years. His interests were medical history and medical bibliography. His *Encyclopedia of Medical Sources* (Huntington, N.Y.: Krieger, 1948) "is a faithful guide." He published five volumes of medical classics. 1921-77

Kelly, George H. and William B.

3722. Brinegar, David F. ARIZONA'S FIRST CHAIN JOURNALISTS. *J. of Arizona Hist. 1983 24(1): 73-87.* Describes the careers of George H. Kelly and William B. Kelly, printers, publishers, and journalists whose State Consolidated Publishing Company operated four southern Arizona newspapers during 1907-09. Based on newspapers and secondary sources; 5 photos, 24 notes. 1887-1934

Kelly, Harry

3723. McKinley, Blaine. "THE QUAGMIRES OF NECESSITY": AMERICAN ANARCHISTS AND DILEMMAS OF VOCATION. *Am. Q. 1982 34(5): 503-523.* 1893-1920
For abstract see ***deCleyre, Voltairine***

Kelly, Léontine

3724. Kelly, Léontine. J'ECRIS MA VIE [My life story]. *Acadiensis [Canada] 1985 15(1): 133-140.* Reproduces, with an introduction by Ronald Labelle, the autobiography of Léontine Kelly, wife of the New Brunswick folk singer Alan Kelly. The Kellys, like many New Brunswickers of their generation, suffered greatly because of low wages paid in the fishing and lumbering industries of New Brunswick in the early decades of the 20th century. They participated in several ill-fated attempts to establish new settlements in the interior of the province, and eventually settled in Newcastle, on the northeast coast. 2 notes. 1907-62

Kelly, Marion

3725. Kelly, Marion; Kelly, Sheila, interviewer. A CHILD'S LIFE IN TREADWELL: GROWING UP IN A COMPANY TOWN. *Alaska J. 1984 14(2): 12-20.* Prints Marion Kelly's reminiscences of her childhood in Treadwell, Alaska, as told to her niece, Sheila Kelley. Includes details about daily life and mine disasters. 11 photos. 1905-22

Kelly, Michael J.

3726. Cox, James A. WHEN FANS ROARED "SLIDE, KELLY, SLIDE!" AT THE OLD BALL GAME. *Smithsonian 1982 13(7): 120-122, 124, 126, 128, 130-131.* Traces the colorful baseball career for the Chicago White Stockings of Michael J. "King" Kelly, who dominated baseball in the 1880's. 1857-94

Kelsey, Benjamin S.

3727. Ethell, Jeff. THE STORY OF AVIATION PIONEER BENJAMIN KELSEY. *Aviation Q. 1981 7(1): 40-85.* Benjamin S. Kelsey first rode in an airplane in 1920 at age 14; taught to fly at the Curtiss Flying School in Connecticut, by "Casey" Jones, he was one of the first air mail service pilots. 1920-80

Kemmelmeyer, Frederick

3728. Adams, E. Bryding. FREDERICK KEMMELMEYER, MARYLAND ITINERANT ARTIST. *Mag. Antiques 1984 125(1): 284-292.* Reproduces the known works of immigrant artist Frederick Kemmelmeyer, who was active as a portrait and sign painter in Maryland, Virginia, and Pennsylvania. 1788-1816

Kemp, Harry

3729. Brevda, William Ian. "Harry Kemp: The Last Bohemian." U. of Connecticut 1980. 781 pp. *DAI 1980 41(5): 2108-2109-A.* 8025345 1906-60

Kendall, Amos

3730. Daniels, James D. AMOS KENDALL: KENTUCKY JOURNALIST, 1815-1829. *Filson Club Hist. Q. 1978 52(1): 46-65.* Narrates the early life and career of Jacksonian newspaper editor and politician Amos Kendall. After graduating from Dartmouth, Kendall moved to Kentucky and became a political ally of Henry Clay and editor of the Frankfort *Argus of Western America.* Despite his association with Clay, Kendall attacked the United States Bank as early as 1818 and supported debt relief in Kentucky after 1819. Kendall opposed the election of John Quincy Adams in 1824, and, after a break with Clay, initiated the "corrupt bargain" controversy that weakened Adams in the election of 1828. Kendall supported Andrew Jackson in 1828 and helped to carry Kentucky for him. Documented from Kendall's *Autobiography,* the Jackson Papers at the library of Congress, and the *Argus.* 45 notes. 1815-29

3731. Melton, Baxter Ford, Jr. "Amos Kendall in Kentucky, 1814-1829: The Journalistic Beginnings of the 'Master Mind' of Andrew Jackson's 'Kitchen Cabinet.'" Southern Illinois U., Carbondale 1978. 247 pp. *DAI 1978 39(2): 519-520-A.* 1814-29

Kendall, Benjamin F.

3732. Katz, Willis A. BENJAMIN F. KENDALL, TERRITORIAL POLITICIAN. *Pacific Northwest Q. 1958 49(1): 29-39.* Biography of Benjamin F. Kendall (1829-63), politician of the Washington Territory, attorney, and newspaper editor, whose stormy career as a Democratic partisan ended with his murder by political opponents in 1863. 1829-63

Kendall, George Wilkins

3733. Alf, E. Karl. GEORGE WILKINS KENDALL AND THE WEST TEXAS SHEEP INDUSTRY. *West Texas Historical Association Year Book 1982 58: 67-76.* George Wilkins Kendall was instrumental in establishing the Texas sheep industry and improving flocks; his innovations included the introduction of fine-fleeced Merino and Rambouillet stock, dipping vats, and the hiring of German shepherds. 1852-58

Kendall, William S.

3734. Austin, Robert. WILLIAM SERGEANT KENDALL, PAINTER OF CHILDREN. *Mag. Antiques 1983 124(5): 1024-1029.* Traces the career of New York painter William S. Kendall, who is best known for his renditions of his daughters and his wife in paintings with mother and child themes. 1889-1938

Kendig, William L.

3735. Shindle, Richard D. LANCASTER'S INFAMOUS COUNTERFEITERS. *J. of the Lancaster County Hist. Soc. 1979 83(4): 198-211.* 1865-1900
*For abstract see **Jacobs, William M.***

Kendrick, John B.

3736. Carroll, Eugene T. JOHN B. KENDRICK, COWPOKE TO SENATOR, 1879-1917. *Ann. of Wyoming 1982 54(1): 51-57.* John B. Kendrick (1857-1933) went from Texas to Wyoming as a trail driver in 1879 and subsequently became an inspector for the Wyoming Stock Grower's Association. Through investments in cattle and land, Kendrick became one of the most prosperous men in Sheridan County. Favored by the powerful Wyoming Stock Grower's Association, he rose rapidly in politics. During 1915-17 he served as state governor, resigning only to take the US Senate seat, which he held until his death in 1933. Based on the Kendrick Collection at the University of Wyoming; 5 photos, 29 notes. 1879-1933

Kennan, George Frost

3737. Mayers, David. YOUNG KENNAN'S CRITICISMS AND RECOMMENDATIONS. *Biography 1985 8(3): 227-247.* After serving for more than a decade in Germany, Austria, and Russia as a US diplomat, George Kennan was recalled home for one year in 1937. During this period, he considered ways of dealing with problems then afflicting American society. Later, he made recommendations on how to improve the Foreign Service. His proposals in both cases were shrewd, confirming the wisdom of John Quincy Adams: US diplomats should take leave at home every few years in order "to be renovated by the wholesome republican atmosphere of their own country." 1920's-40's

3738. Mayers, David. GEORGE KENNAN AND THE SOVIET UNION, 1933-1938; PERCEPTIONS OF A YOUNG DIPLOMAT. *Int. Hist. Rev. [Canada] 1983 5(4): 525-549.* In 1933, the United States and the USSR established formal diplomatic relations. The young George Kennan (not yet 30) joined the first official delegation to represent US interests in Moscow. This tour was formative for Kennan and crucial to the development of his early views relative to the USSR, the nature of Russian-American interests, and US diplomacy. Later when the Cold War began to heat up, his views found expression in his pronouncements and recommendations for US foreign policy. His underlying assumptions of containment can be traced to his experience and observations of the 1930's. Based largely on Kennan's autobiographical manuscripts and his later publications. 1933-38

3739. Mazur, Zbigniew. GEORGE'A F. KENNANA KONCEPCJA STOSUNKÓW MIĘDZY WSCHODEM A ZACHODEM [George F. Kennan's conception of relations between East and West]. *Przegląd Zachodni [Poland] 1981 37(5-6): 125-161.* George Frost Kennan joined the US State Department in 1926 and soon began to specialize in the

USSR. After service in Moscow following the war, he joined the State Department's policy planning staff. Later, with some breaks for other employment, he joined the Institute for Advanced Study in Princeton, from which he retired in 1974. His highly critical views of the Stalinist Soviet Union made him the standard bearer of the Cold War, a fame he regretted all his life. His main mission was to fight legalistic-moralistic tendencies of US policymaking. He was for realism, and that meant resistance to the wide swings in American international policy. His interests were wide, from historical to current policymaking. His main objective was US-West European understanding. Based on Kennan's publications and other sources. 1926-81

3740. Miscamble, Wilson Douglas. "George F. Kennan, the Policy Planning Staff and American Foreign Policy, 1947-1950." U. of Notre Dame 1980. 265 pp. *DAI 1980 41(1): 370-A.* 8015012 1947-50

3741. Polley, Michael John. "George F. Kennan: The Life and Times of a Diplomat, 1925-1975." Washington State U. 1984. 240 pp. *DAI 1985 46(3): 777-778-A.* DA8510875 1925-75

Kennan, George (1845-1923)

3742. Travis, Frederick F. GEORGE KENNAN AND THE PHILIPPINES. *Philippine Studies [Philippines] 1979 27(4): 527-536.* George Kennan, the prominent journalist, was commissioned in December 1900 by the popular and influential magazine, the *Outlook,* to investigate present conditions in the Philippines. His findings on the Filipino insurrection were published in two articles in early 1901 and in a brief report in March 1902. Although Kennan made a sincere effort to be fair and objective in his analysis, he was still subject to the ethnocentrism so prevalent during that imperialistic era. He deplored the cruelty of American soldiers, but supported President McKinley's policy that the United States had a moral obligation to subdue the Filipino insurgents and then try to civilize the Philippines. 1900-02

Kennedy, Arthur Edward

3743. Smith, Robert L. THE KENNEDY INTERLUDE, 1864-66. *BC Studies [Canada] 1980 (47): 66-78.* With a reputation as one of the best governors of the colonial service, Irish-born Arthur Edward Kennedy (1809-83) was appointed governor of the comparatively insignificant colony of Vancouver Island. His mission was to work with the new governor of British Columbia to bring about the union of the two colonies. The Kennedy years, 1864-66, brought disciplined administration and high professional and moral standards to public service. Kennedy saved the colony from financial disaster, paved the way for Victoria to become the provincial capital, and consistently adhered to his mandate of the union of the colonies. The years, nevertheless, were very difficult from an economic and political standpoint, and his governorship was merely a brief interlude in a successful public career. 68 notes. 1864-66

Kennedy, Eddie Clifton

3744. Paulson, Peter Lee. "Eddie C. Kennedy, West Virginia Educator: A Biography." West Virginia U. 1983. 302 pp. *DAI 1984 44(7): 2104-2105-A.* DA8326638 20c

Kennedy, Edward M.

3745. Erokhin, A. V. RUBEZHI KLANA KENNEDI [The borders of the Kennedy clan]. *Novaia i Noveishaia Istoriia [USSR] 1973 (6): 97-115.* Examines President John F. Kennedy's foreign policy and its political origins, especially his emphasis on arms expenditure, the strategy of the "flexible response," and US military involvement in the early 1960's in Cuba, Vietnam, and the Dominican Republic. Reviews other foreign policy tactics, such as support for pro-American regimes and the formation of the Peace Corps. Studies the political career of Edward M. Kennedy, including his private life and his views on American society. Primary and secondary sources; 73 notes. 1961-73

3746. Leapman, Michael. THE AMERICAN MOOD: 1979: PRESIDENT CARTER'S FIRST 30 MONTHS PROVE A DISAPPOINTMENT. *Round Table [Great Britain] 1979 (276): 343-346.* 1977-79
*For abstract see **Carter, Jimmy***

Kennedy, Jane

3747. Gross, Harriet. JANE KENNEDY: MAKING HISTORY THROUGH MORAL PROTEST. *Frontiers 1977 2(2): 73-81.* Jane Kennedy describes her career as a political activist since 1964, including her involvement in the civil rights movement, the anti-Vietnam War movement, and her two prison terms; part of a special issue on women's oral history. 1964-77

Kennedy, John F.

3748. Leuchtenburg, William E. JOHN F. KENNEDY, TWENTY YEARS LATER. *Am. Heritage 1983 35(1): 50-59.* Reassesses John F. Kennedy's political legacy. Today's attitudes toward Kennedy are less favorable than those that circulated immediately after the assassination. The Kennedy legacy is more myth than history; although historians will never again give so much attention to Camelot, Kennedy's image as a romantic hero seems secure. 9 illus. 1961-63

3749. Spragens, William C. KENNEDY ERA SPEECHWRITING, PUBLIC RELATIONS AND PUBLIC OPINION. *Presidential Studies Q. 1984 14(1): 78-86.* John F. Kennedy's campaign workers refined the measurement and interpretation of public opinion. Intensive research was done to assess voter reaction to Kennedy and pertinent issues, but specific research was also targeted at blacks and Hispanic Americans. Kennedy and his speech-writers frequently relied on these reports in preparing campaign and presidential speeches. 27 notes. 1956-63

Kennedy, John F. (family)

3750. Galvin, Edward L. THE KENNEDYS OF MASSACHUSETTS. *New England Historical and Genealogical Register 1985 139(July): 211-224.* Traces the Bostonian Irish-American family of John F. Kennedy, beginning with Patrick, who was born in Ireland about 1823 and died in Boston in 1858, to the children of Edward and Joan Bennett Kennedy. Based on Kennedy family records and newspaper accounts. 1823-1985

Kennedy, Joseph P.

3751. Biliankin, George. JOSEPH P. KENNEDY: THE TRUTH. *Contemporary Rev. [Great Britain] 1970 216(1249): 64-70.* A personal assessment, by a former diplomatic correspondent, of Joseph P. Kennedy's actions as US ambassador in London between 1938 and 1940. 1938-40

3752. Vieth, Jane Karoline. JOSEPH P. KENNEDY AND BRITISH APPEASEMENT: THE DIPLOMACY OF A BOSTON IRISHMAN. Jones, Kenneth Paul, ed. *U.S. Diplomats in Europe, 1919-1941* (Santa Barbara, Calif.: ABC-Clio, 1981): 165-182. Joseph P. Kennedy (1888-1969) began his governmental career in 1934 as chairman of the US Securities and Exchange Commission and in 1937 was appointed ambassador to Great Britain. Evaluates Kennedy's performance as ambassador, describing his attitudes toward American foreign policy before the outbreak of World War II and after the war began, and evaluating their impact in light of the diplomatic problems that faced the United States and Great Britain in the interwar years and the political philosophies and personalities of the statesmen, especially Franklin D. Roosevelt, Neville Chamberlain, and Winston Churchill, with whom Kennedy worked. Primary sources; 60 notes. 1937-45

Kennedy, Robert C.

3753. Cunningham, O. Edward. "IN VIOLATION OF THE LAWS OF WAR": THE EXECUTION OF ROBERT COBB KENNEDY. *Louisiana Hist. 1977 18(2): 189-202.* Born in Georgia and raised in Claiborn Parish, Louisiana, Robert C. Kennedy attended West Point for two years before settling down to farming. When the Civil War began he was commissioned a Captain in the First Louisiana Infantry. Wounded at Shiloh, Kennedy was later transferred to General Joe Wheeler's cavalry. He was captured in the Chattanooga campaign, but escaped from Johnson's Island Prison in Ohio a year later. Recruited as a saboteur, Kennedy participated in an abortive attempt to burn New York City after the 1864 election. He escaped to Canada, but was later captured in Michigan while attempting to cross to Confederate lines. Tried in New York City for espionage, he was the last Confederate executed before the end of hostilities. Primary sources; 18 notes. 1861-65

Kennekuk

3754. Schultz, George A. KENNEKUK, THE KICKAPOO PROPHET. *Kansas Hist. 1980 3(1): 38-46.* When whites arrived most Indians found their own religious beliefs untenable. Prophets arose to offer quick solutions based on a return to tribal ways. Some like Kennekuk (ca. 1785-1853) combined old Indian customs with Christian ethical ideas. When most Kickapoos were moved from Illinois in 1819, Kennekuk's band remained behind to argue it was the great spirit's will. Later he followed to Missouri and then to Kansas. He preached temperance and farming to his 500 followers. Missionaries tried to win them to their own sects, but Kennekuk, who had been licensed as a Methodist preacher, kept aloof and refined his religion until he approached divinity himself. As he lay dying of smallpox, Kennekuk reassured his followers that he would rise in three days, a cruel hoax since most of them caught the disease from his guarded remains. Based on records of the Office of Indian Affairs in the National Archive, Reports of the Commissioner of Indian Affairs, books by contemporaries, articles; illus., 50 notes. 1819-53

Kennelly, Martin H.

3755. O'Malley, Peter Joseph. "Mayor Martin H. Kennelly of Chicago: A Political Biography." U. of Illinois, Chicago Circle 1980. 326 pp. *DAI 1980 41(4): 1735-A.* 8023247 1947-55

Kenney, George C.

3756. Falk, Stanley L. GENERAL KENNEY, THE INDIRECT APPROACH, AND THE B-29S. *Aerospace Hist. 1981 27[i.e., 28](3): 147-155.* Examines parallels between the proposed wartime strategy of General George C. Kenney, air commander in the southwest Pacific, and Sir Basil Liddell Hart's "strategy of the indirect approach." Kenney tried unsuccessfully to convince General H. H. Arnold to deploy the newly developed B-29 bombers against Japanese oil supplies in Indonesia and against Japanese shipping. While this strategy might have been effective in hastening the war's end prior to the invasion of the Marianas in November 1944, after that date General Arnold's direct strikes on Japan were more effective. Based primarily on General George C. Kenney's wartime correspondence and diary; illus., 5 photos, 32 notes. 1942-45

Kennicott, John A.

3757. Conway, Thomas G. JOHN A. KENNICOTT: A TEACHER IN NEW ORLEANS. *Louisiana History 1985 26(4): 399-415.* John A. Kennicott, a medical doctor born in Buffalo, New York, arrived in New Orleans in 1828 at age 25. He became director of three public schools in the English-speaking section and principal of one of them, serving until 1835. The schools received inadequate public funds and collapsed in 1836. In 1833 Kennicott organized a short-lived lyceum program, and in 1835 established the city's first literary, scientific, and religious magazine, which failed financially. Based on private papers, newspapers, and secondary works; 39 notes. 1828-36

3758. Ernst, Erik A. JOHN A. KENNICOTT OF THE GROVE: PHYSICIAN, HORTICULTURIST, AND JOURNALIST IN NINETEENTH-CENTURY ILLINOIS. *J. of the Illinois State Hist. Soc. 1981 74(2): 109-118.* John A. Kennicott, a native of New York, arrived in Illinois in 1836. A physician, his interest in horticulture led to his founding the first commercial nursery in Northern Illinois. He served as president of the North-Western Fruit Growers' Association, the Illinois State Horticultural Society, and the North American Pomological Convention. He was a friend of both John Stephen Wright, founder of the *Prairie Farmer* (1841), and educator Jonathan Baldwin Turner. Kennicott helped found both the Illinois State Agricultural Society and the Illinois Industrial League in 1853. He lectured and wrote under the sponsorship of various state and county agricultural societies and edited the first volume of the *Transactions of the Illinois State Agricultural Society.* He was unsuccessfully proposed for nomination as the first federal Secretary of Agriculture. 7 illus., 41 notes. 1836-63

Kennon, Robert F.

3759. Kurtz, Michael L. GOVERNMENT BY THE CIVICS BOOK: THE ADMINISTRATION OF ROBERT F. KENNON, 1952-1956. *North Louisiana Hist. Assoc. J. 1981 12(2-3): 52-61.* Democrat Robert F. Kennon promised clean government when he ran for governor of Louisiana against the Long machine candidate in 1952. His efforts in civil service and penal reform, and his antigambling crusade made clear his commitment to good government, but an early appraisal indicates that his reforms were not enduring. His opposition to civil rights led to his support for Eisenhower in 1952 and his vocal opposition to the *Brown* decision in 1954. Based on interviews, voting records, and secondary sources; illus., 50 notes. 1948-56

Kenny, Elizabeth, Sister

3760. Cohn, Victor. SISTER KENNY'S FIERCE FIGHT FOR BETTER POLIO CARE. *Smithsonian 1981 12(8): 180-200.* Australian-born nurse Elizabeth Kenny (1880-1952), undeterred by her own lack of medical training and the opposition from doctors and the establishment, implemented revolutionary ideas for treating polio before the discovery of the polio vaccine. 1911-52

Kenny, John V.

3761. Lemmey, William. BOSS KENNY OF JERSEY CITY, 1949-1972. *New Jersey Hist. 1980 98(1-2): 9-28.* John V. Kenny, a Hague ward healer for many years, was in power in Jersey City for 23 years both as an officeholder and power broker. He offered the poor, elderly, and displaced city resident hope and turned political defeats into victories by manipulating circumstances to his advantage and by rebuilding his organization on the ashes of his former opponent. Kenny, in short, would do business with anyone. A scandal having to do with the extortion of money from contractors used by Jersey City put an end to Kenny's reign; a conviction for income tax evasion sent him to jail. Based on newspaper accounts, interviews, court records, and secondary sources; 5 illus., 3 tables, 31 notes. 1949-72

Kensett, John F.

3762. Sullivan, Mark White. "John F. Kensett, American Landscape Painter." Bryn Mawr Coll. 1981. 215 pp. *DAI 1982 42(10): 4186-A.* DA8202564 1840-72

Kensett, John Frederick

3763. Lessem, Don. JOHN F. KENSETT'S GENTLE VISION OF THE AMERICAN LAND. *Smithsonian 1985 16(4): 58-65.* Reviews the life and work of landscape artist John Frederick Kensett, whose paintings art collectors and critics have largely neglected prior to the 1980's. 1840-72

Kent, Duke of (Edward)

3764. Hamilton-Edwards, Gerald. EDWARD, DUKE OF KENT, AND THE LYONS FAMILY IN NOVA SCOTIA. *J. of the Soc. for Army Hist. Res. [Great Britain] 1978 56(225): 39-47.* Despite a reputation for brutal discipline among his military underlings, Prince Edward was kind to the wives and families, as evidenced by his careful watch over the widow and orphaned children of Captain Charles Lyons, former Town Major of Halifax, Nova Scotia, 1812-63. 1812-63

Kent, Rockwell

3765. Lawless, Ken. "CONTINENTAL IMPRISONMENT": ROCKWELL KENT AND THE PASSPORT CONTROVERSY. *Antioch Rev. 1980 38(3): 304-312.* Describes the passport case of artist Rockwell Kent (1882-1971), a suit against the federal government for refusing in 1950 to grant him a passport because of his pro-Communism; his court victory in 1958 culminated his long leftist career. 1950-58

Kenton, Simon

3766. Harrison, Lowell H. SIMON KENTON: A NATURAL MAN. *Am. Hist. Illus. 1976 11(5): 10-16.* Chronicles the life of frontiersman Simon Kenton, an early inhabitant of Kentucky, 1755-1820. 1755-1820

Kenyon, Elmer Bernard

3767. Duffy, Susan. "Elmer Bernard Kenyon: An Examination of the Career of a Theatrical Press Agent." U. of Pittsburgh 1979. 257 pp. *DAI 1979 40(5): 2358-A.* 1920's-30's

Kenyon, Nellie

3768. Adamson, June. NELLIE KENYON AND THE SCOPES "MONKEY TRIAL." *Journalism Hist. 1975 2(3): 88-89, 97.* Describes Nellie Kenyon's part in uncovering the facts about the trial of John T. Scopes for teaching evolution in violation of Tennessee's Butler Act (1925); describes her subsequent career. 1925-40

Kern, Alexander

3769. Cawelti, John G. ALEXANDER KERN: AN ANALYSIS AND INTERPRETATION. *Am. Studies Int. 1975 16(2): 9-14.* Introduces a *festschrift* for Alexander Kern. Traces Kern's life and career from his pioneering efforts at interdisciplinary work to his recent retirement. 3 illus. 1909-75

Kern, Jerome

3770. Rimler, Walter. GREAT SONGWRITERS. *Midstream 1984 30(1): 31-34.* 1885-1979
*For abstract see **Arlen, Harold***

Kerouac, Jack

3771. Hoffius, Steve. THE DHARMA BUM OF ROCKY MOUNT. *Southern Exposure 1981 9(2): 83-85.* Describes novelist Jack Kerouac's life and fiction from 1948 to his death in 1969; his *On the Road* (1957), with its rejection of traditional American values, was a milestone for the so-called Beat Generation. 1948-69

3772. McNally, Dennis Sean. "Desolation Angel: Jack Kerouac in America, 1922-1969." U. of Massachusetts 1978. 392 pp. *DAI 1978 39(2): 1035-A.* 1950's-60's

Kerr, Clark

3773. Stuart, Mary Clark. "Clark Kerr: Biography of an Action Intellectual." U. of Michigan 1980. 388 pp. *DAI 1980 41(2): 563-A.* 8017376 1929-80

Kerr, Donald Gordon Grady

3774. Zaslow, Morris. DONALD GORDON GRADY KERR 1913-1976. *Can. Hist. Assoc. Hist. Papers [Canada] 1977: 230-231.* A memorial tribute to Donald Gordon Grady Kerr. He made many contributions to the field of Canadian history both through his writings and his teaching in the Protestant school system of Montreal (1938-1943), the University of Western Ontario (1958-1976), and Mount Allison University (1946-1958). 1938-76

Kerr, Harrison

3775. Kohlenberg, Randy Bryan. "Harrison Kerr: Portrait of a Twentieth-Century American Composer." U. of Oklahoma 1978 241 pp. *DAI 1979 40(4): 1741-A.* 1921-68

Kerr, John R.

3776. Bergen, John V. DAVID D. BANTA'S MEMORIAL TO JOHN R. KERR, BLIND PRINTER AND PIONEER, EDITOR IN JOHNSON COUNTY, INDIANA. *Indiana Mag. of Hist. 1981 77(3): 231-267.* A biographical sketch and tribute by David D. Banta tells us much about the early life of a rural Indiana editor, 1840-80. Kerr trained himself in printing and was greatly aided by his wife in overcoming the handicaps of his increasing blindness. By learning about his work habits and personal life we discover much about the influence of a newspaper editor in small towns. Based on newspaper sketches and articles, journal articles, and local histories; 2 maps, fig., 71 notes. 1840-80

Kerr, Robert F.

3777. Otto, Kathryn. THE ROBERT F. KERR PAPERS AT THE SOUTH DAKOTA HISTORICAL RESOURCE CENTER. *South Dakota Hist. 1979 9(3): 248-251.* Discusses the papers of Robert F. Kerr (1850-1921), who belonged to the stalwart faction of the Republican Party in South Dakota from 1905 until his death. Besides politics, the papers also contain material concerning Kerr's business ventures, agriculture, South Dakota State University, and the town of Brookings, South Dakota. Based on the Kerr Papers; photo. 1905-21

Kerr, Tom

3778. Williamson, David T. TOM KERR: A MIGHTY TRADER WAS HE. *Alberta Hist. [Canada] 1977 25(3): 23-28.* Tom Kerr was born in Scotland in 1861 and, lured by the fur trade, came to Canada in 1878. For the next 30 years Kerr served at many of the Hudson's Bay Company's posts, including Peace River, Fort St. John, Fort Dunvegan, Fond Du Lac, and Little Red River. In 1901 Kerr returned briefly to Scotland to marry, then went to Little Red River. In 1911 Kerr settled at Sturgeon Lake where he headed the Hudson's Bay Company's post. He lived there until his death in 1946. Based on childhood memories of the author, who knew Kerr at Sturgeon Lake; 3 illus. 1861-1946

Kerr, William Jasper

3779. McIlvenna, Don E. and Wax, Darold D. W. J. KERR, LAND-GRANT PRESIDENT IN UTAH AND OREGON, 1900-1908. *Oregon Historical Quarterly 1984 85(4): 387-405.* William Jasper Kerr joined the faculty of Brigham Young College, Logan, Utah, in 1887 and became president in 1894. In 1900 he was appointed president of the Agricultural College of Utah, Logan. His efforts to upgrade the college and broaden course offerings brought charges of wasteful competition with the University of Utah. Political differences with Governor John C. Cutler and charges of Mormon Church dictation of college affairs contributed to Kerr's resignation in 1907. Consolidation of the college and university was a major issue during his tenure, but the necessary constitutional amendment failed in the legislature. Based on the W. J. Kerr papers Utah State University Archives, newspaper articles, other primary sources, and secondary sources; 4 photos, 52 notes. Article to be continued. 1894-1907

Kerst, Catherine

3780. Lortie, Jeanne Marie. MOTHER SCHOLASTICA KERST. PART 1. *Am. Benedictine Rev. 1983 34(2): 130-148.* Reviews the early life and career of Catherine Kerst who served as Mother Superior Scholastica of St. Benedict's Convent at St. Joseph, Minnesota, during 1880-89. Analyzes her education and background, including her family's support of the work of Benedictine sisters in Minnesota. Concludes that Mother Scholastica's work was productive, but she generated criticism and opposition from her colleagues. 15 notes. Article to be continued. 1847-89

3781. Lortie, Jeanne Marie. MOTHER SCHOLASTICA KERST. PART 2. *Am. Benedictine Rev. 1983 34(3): 268-290.* Continued from a previous article. Concludes the review of Mother Scholastica Kerst's life after 1889. Recounts in particular her work in founding schools and hospitals in the Diocese of Duluth, Minnesota, until her death in 1911. 40 notes. 1889-1911

Kettering, Charles F.

3782. Leslie, Stuart W. THOMAS MIDGLEY AND THE POLITICS OF INDUSTRIAL RESEARCH. *Business Hist. Rev. 1980 54(4): 480-503.* 1916-44
*For abstract see **Midgley, Thomas***

3783. Leslie, Stuart W. "Charles F. Kettering, 1876-1958." U. of Delaware 1980. 656 pp. *DAI 1980 41(3): 1188-A.* 8019941 1876-1958

3784. Leslie, Stuart W. CHARLES F. KETTERING AND THE COPPER-COOLED ENGINE. *Technology and Culture 1979 20(4): 752-776.* As a weapon in the sales war with Ford, General Motors began in 1919 to develop an air-cooled engine for a cheaper Chevrolet. In 1921 GM design engineers led by Charles F. Kettering finally succeeded in brazing copper cooling fins to the cylinders, thereby eliminating the costly tubing and radiator of the water-cooled engine, and the first models were featured at the New York Automobile Show in 1923. But only 100 cars were ever sold, and this most ambitious innovation of GM's short career had by 1925 become a costly failure. The main reason was conflict between Kettering's design engineers, who "grossly underestimated the difficulty of converting a prototype into a mass produced article," and the production engineers, who raised many practical objections to the innovation. Based on the Kettering Archives; 4 illus., 77 notes. 1919-26

Kettner, William

3785. DuVall, Lucille Clark. WILLIAM KETTNER: SAN DIEGO'S DYNAMIC CONGRESSMAN. *J. of San Diego Hist. 1979 25(3): 191-207.* William Kettner (1864-1930) lived in San Diego after 1907, served in the House of Representatives from 1913 to 1921, and was responsible for bringing the US Navy to the city, with enormous financial benefits for San Diego. 1907-30

Key, Ellen

3786. Dykstra, Pearl. ELLEN KEY: MOTHERHOOD FOR SOCIETY. *Atlantis [Canada] 1983 9(1): 49-57.* Explores the thought, life, and published writings of prominent feminist thinker Ellen Key, and explores reasons for lack of contemporary interest in her work. Probable reasons include Key's sentimentalization and idealization of motherhood, her "bourgeois" ideals and values, and her interest in eugenics as a link to notions of race and class superiority. Photo, 48 notes. 1870-1926

Keys, Bill

3787. Sohler, Gary. A PROSPECTOR'S LEGACY. *Westways 1984 76(1): 32-34, 75.* Highlights the life of desert prospector Bill Keys and describes ranching activities at his homestead, now part of Joshua Tree National Monument, California. ca 1900-69

Kibbey, Joseph H.

3788. Gill, Mary E. and Goff, John S. JOSEPH H. KIBBEY AND SCHOOL SEGREGATION IN ARIZONA. *J. of Arizona Hist. 1980 21(4): 411-422.* Traces Joseph H. Kibbey's leadership in opposing school segregation in Arizona. As territorial governor, he vetoed the 1909 enabling legislation, and as a lawyer he represented the plaintiff in an unsuccessful challenge to segregation. Kibbey's arguments against "separate but equal" schooling anticipated those later used to overthrow segregation throughout the United States. Legislative and court records; photo, 9 notes. 1908-12

Kidder, Harriette Smith

3789. Harrison, Victoria G. LITTLE MATTERS AND A GREAT MISSION: THE LIFE AND DIARY OF HARRIETTE SMITH KIDDER. *Journal of the Rutgers University Libraries 1984 46(2): 58-66.* Examines the diary of Harriette Smith Kidder, the wife of a Methodist minister. Harriette moved where her husband's career took them, living in Paterson, Trenton, and Newark, New Jersey; Evanston, Illinois; and finally in Madison, New Jersey. She was very much a part of the world of 19th-century American women, especially women within close religious communities. Based on Kidder's diary in the Rutgers University Library; photo, 8 notes. 1844-1908

Kierstede, Hans

3790. Riker, David M. SURGEON HANS KIERSTEDE OF NEW AMSTERDAM. *Halve Maen 1983 57(3): 11-13, 24.* German immigrant Hans Kierstede settled in New Amsterdam, where he practiced medicine until his death in 1666. 1638-66

Kihn, W. Langdon

3791. Edwards, G. J. and Edwards, G. T. LANGDON KIHN: INDIAN PORTRAIT ARTIST. *Beaver [Canada] 1984-85 315(3): 4-11.* W. Langdon Kihn (1898-1957) studied with Winold Reiss and accompanied the latter to Montana to paint the Blackfoot Indians. He then ventured to New Mexico to paint the Pueblo Indians. In 1922 the Canadian Pacific Railway commissioned him to paint Indians and other Canadian subjects. Two years later, the National Museum of Canada and the Canadian National Railway supported Kihn to depict the Gitskan Indians, and more commissions followed rapidly thereafter. Although he was a prolific artist, Kihn is still not well-known in Canada. 9 photos. 1920's-57

Kilgore, Harley M.

3792. Maddox, Robert Franklin. THE POLITICS OF WORLD WAR II SCIENCE: SENATOR HARLEY M. KILGORE AND THE LEGISLATIVE ORIGINS OF THE NATIONAL SCIENCE FOUNDATION. *West Virginia Hist. 1979 41(1): 20-39.* Discusses the role of West Virginia Democratic Senator Harley M. Kilgore in the creation of the National Science Foundation from 1942, when Kilgore found the wartime administrative machinery for science and technology to be confusing, to 1950, when President Harry S. Truman signed the bill creating the National Science Foundation. Opponents of the bill included Vannevar Bush and Alexander Smith. 140 notes. 1942-50

Kilpatrick, Hugh Judson

3793. Pierce, John Edward. "General Hugh Judson Kilpatrick in the American Civil War: A New Appraisal." Pennsylvania State U. 1983. 348 pp. *DAI 1984 44(10): 3143-A.* DA8327541 1861-65

Kilpatrick, William Heard

3794. Chipman, Donald D. and McDonald, Carl B. THE COLD WAR IN THE CLASSROOM: KILPATRICK'S STUDENT YEARS AT MERCER. *Teachers Coll. Record 1982 83(3): 459-465.* The educational philosophy of William Heard Kilpatrick (1871-1965) was shaped by his essentially negative reaction to the teachers and grading system he encountered as an undergraduate at Mercer University in the 1890's. Based on unpublished material in Special Collection, Stetson Library, Mercer University; 10 notes. 1888-91

Kimball, Edward L.

3795. Kimball, Edward L. "I SUSTAIN HIM AS A PROPHET, I LOVE HIM AS AN AFFECTIONATE FATHER." *Dialogue 1978 11(4): 48-62.* 1943-78
*For abstract see **Kimball, Spencer W.***

Kimball, Fred G.

3796. Wilson, William H. TO MAKE A STAKE: FRED G. KIMBALL IN ALASKA 1899-1909. *Alaska J. 1983 13(1): 108-114.* Prints a biography of Fred G. Kimball, who came to Alaska in 1899 to strike it rich. He did make his fortune, not by finding gold, but through other entrepreneurial endeavors and government jobs. 8 photos, 25 notes. 1899-1909

Kimball, Heber C.

3797. Kimball, Stanley B. BRIGHAM AND HEBER. *Brigham Young U. Studies 1978 18(3): 396-409.* Heber C. Kimball's friendship with Brigham Young began in 1829 when both were 27-year-old artisans in Monroe County, New York. Following similar paths into Mormonism, the two men shared many common experiences in the faith as missionaries, as leaders in Nauvoo and during the exodus westward, and as ecclesiastics in the Utah community. Details their parallel careers as Young assumed the church presidency and Kimball became his first counselor. Near the end of his life, Kimball began to experience self-doubts about his and Young's contributions to Mormonism. Despite outside criticisms and his own fears and suppositions, Kimball remained loyal to Young. Kimball died on 22 June 1868. 1829-68

Kimball, Spencer W.

3798. Kimball, Edward L. "I SUSTAIN HIM AS A PROPHET, I LOVE HIM AS AN AFFECTIONATE FATHER." *Dialogue 1978 11(4): 48-62.* Transcript of an October 1978 interview between *Dialogue* and Edward L. Kimball, the youngest son of Spencer W. Kimball, President of the Church of Jesus Christ of the Latter Day Saints. Kimball, with his brother Andrew, wrote a biography of their father, published in 1977, based on interviews with their parents, friends of the family and leaders of the church, journal entries, personal letters, and family anecdotes. The process of writing the biography made it possible to check the growth of myths about the leader of the Mormon church. Kimball shares his special pride in his father's revelation allowing blacks to hold the priesthood in the Mormon church. 1943-78

Kimball, Thomas Rogers

3799. Batie, David Lynn. THOMAS ROGERS KIMBALL (1890-1912): NEBRASKA ARCHITECT. *Nebraska Hist. 1979 60(3): 321-356.* Examines the buildings Thomas Rogers Kimball constructed in Nebraska and reviews his overall career. While capable of both competent and beautiful architecture, Kimball stayed abreast with established design styles and left a legacy of prominent buildings in Nebraska and the Midwest. 9 photos, 110 notes. 1890-1912

Kimbel, Anthony

3800. Hanks, David. KIMBEL & CABUS: 19TH-CENTURY NEW YORK CABINETMAKERS. *Art & Antiques 1980 3(5): 44-53.* 1850-99
For abstract see ***Cabus, Joseph***

Kimmel, Stanley

3801. Dilliard, Irving. THREE TO REMEMBER: ARCHIBALD MACLEISH, STANLEY KIMMEL, PHILLIPS BRADLEY. *J. of the Illinois State Hist. Soc. 1984 77(1): 45-59.* 1910's-82
For abstract see ***Bradley, Phillips***

Kincaid, Bradley

3802. Taylor, Jay. BRADLEY KINCAID: STILL THE "KENTUCKY MOUNTAIN BOY" AT 81. *Kentucky Folklore Record 1978 24(1): 10-14.* Bradley Kincaid is a colorful old-time guitar player and radio announcer, 1926-78. 1926-78

3803. Thurman, Kelly. BRADLEY KINCAID: MUSIC FROM THE MOUNTAINS IN THE 1920S. *Register of the Kentucky Hist. Soc. 1982 80(2): 170-182.* Bradley Kincaid was an able representative of the culture of his native Kentucky. On the radio, in concerts, and in his publishing, Kincaid helped make popular the music of Appalachia and the mountain people of Kentucky. After his start with station WLS, he left Chicago and worked with many other stations for the next 20 years. Although he left radio in the 1950's, his interest in collecting and publishing country music continues in the 1980's. Interviews and secondary sources; 10 notes, 3 photos. 1925-82

King, Alexander Campbell

3804. Wells, Della Wager. KING & SPALDING: THE ORIGINS OF THE PARTNERSHIP. *Atlanta Historical Journal 1984-85 28(4): 5-17.* Presents biographies of Alexander Campbell King and Jack Johnson Spalding, Atlanta lawyers who in 1885 formed a partnership that grew to become one of the most influential law firms in the southeastern United States. 1856-85

King, Billie Jean

3805. Nelson, Jeffrey. THE DEFENSE OF BILLIE JEAN KING. *Western J. of Speech Communication 1984 48(1): 92-102.* The revelation that Billie Jean King had engaged in a love affair with her former secretary, Marilyn Barnett, damaged King's role as a prestigious, celebrated persona; King offered a public explanation of her conduct and was supported by her peers and the media. 1981

King, Charles Brady

3806. Powell, Sinclair. IN THE BEGINNING. *Michigan History 1985 69(6): 6-9.* On 6 March 1896, Charles Brady King drove the first "horseless carriage" in Michigan. From then until his death in 1957, he worked with auto, marine, and aircraft engines. Based on the King Papers in the Detroit Public Library, oral interviews, and secondary sources. 1896-1957

King, Edith

3807. Rodman, Ellen Rena. "Edith King and Dorothy Coit and the King-Coit School and Children's Theatre." New York U. 1980. 242 pp. *DAI 1980 41(2): 463-A.* 8017523 1923-58

King, Grace

3808. Taylor, Helen. THE CASE OF GRACE KING. *Southern Rev. 1982 18(4): 685-702.* Discusses the work of Southern writer Grace King, with special attention to the influence of her ideology of womanhood. 1877-1932

King, Horace

3809. Bogle, James G. HORACE KING 1807-1887: MASTER COVERED BRIDGE BUILDER. *Georgia Life 1980 6(4): 33-35.* Former slave Horace King (1807-87) learned how to construct covered bridges from his owner, John Godwin, beginning in 1830, and became a successful building contractor in his own right after he was emancipated in 1846. 1807-87

King, James

3810. McGinty, Brian. HUNG BE THE HEAVENS WITH BLACK. *Am. Hist. Illus. 1983 17(10): 31-39.* Describes the career of James King of William, muckraking founder and editor of the San Francisco *Bulletin* and his views on violence, vigilantism, and politics during 1851-56. 1851-56

King, Martin Luther, Jr.

3811. Koroleva, A. P. MARTIN LIUTER KING I REBUSY AMERIKANSKOI DEMOKRATII [Martin Luther King and abuses of American democracy]. *Voprosy Istorii [USSR] 1978 (10): 122-140.* The Reverend Martin Luther King, Jr. (1929-68), was noted for his criticism of the US social and legal system and for advocating civil rights. His utopian ideas drew hatred from white racists and from black nationalists. During 1955-68, King's marches and sit-in strikes provoked clashes with racists. Shadowed by the FBI, and the target of smear campaigns, King was finally murdered in mysterious circumstances. 74 notes. 1955-68

3812. Lentz, Richard Glenn. "Resurrecting the Prophet: Dr. Martin Luther King, Jr., and the News Magazines." (Vol. 1-2) U. of Iowa 1983. 993 pp. *DAI 1984 44(8): 2279-A.* DA8327402 1956-68

3813. Oates, Stephen B. THE INTELLECTUAL ODYSSEY OF MARTIN LUTHER KING. *Massachusetts Rev. 1981 22(2): 301-320.* Gives biography of Martin Luther King, Jr. (1929-68), American Negro clergyman, civil rights leader, and author, from kindergarten to his doctoral graduation in 1955 from Boston University. While a student at Morehouse College, he decided to enter the ministry. Mentions the faculty members who influenced this decision. He next attended Crozer Seminary. Describes the influences felt there, especially the writings of Walter Rauschenbusch. He enrolled in the doctoral program in systematic theology at Boston University, where he came under the influence of Edgar Sheffield Brightman and his disciple, Lotan Harold DeWolf. Here he tried to reconcile the conflict between relativism and idealism. In so doing he read widely in Sigmund Freud, and accepted his theories in part. On graduation King accepted a pastorate in Montgomery, Alabama. Based on King's autobiography, personal papers, letters, and speeches; note. ca 1934-55

3814. Rao, K. L. Seshagiri. NONVIOLENT RESISTANCE IN NORTH AMERICA. *Gandhi Marg [India] 1979 1(9): 601-606.* Martin Luther King, Jr. (d. 1968), adapted Gandhian methods of nonviolence to the North American situation with spectacular success in the 1950's and 1960's. 1950's-60's

3815. Sloan, Rose Mary. "'Then My Living Will Not Be in Vain': A Rhetorical Study of Dr. Martin Luther King, Jr., and the Southern Christian Leadership Conference in the Mobilization for Collective Action toward Nonviolent Means to Integration, 1954-1964." Ohio State U. 1977. 237 pp. *DAI 1978 38(8): 4448-A.* 1954-64

King, Rufus

3816. Ernst, Robert. THE AFTERMATH: RUFUS KING, VIOLENCE, AND THE REPUTATION OF THE NEW REPUBLIC. *J. of Long Island Hist. 1973 10(1): 14-28.* Rufus King of Jamaica, Long Island, New York, participated in the American Revolution and in politics, 1776-1827. 1776-1827

King, Spencer B., Jr.

3817. Gardner, Robert G. SPENCER BIDWELL KING, JR. *Viewpoints: Georgia Baptist Hist. 1978 (6): 19-24.* Obituary of Spencer Bidwell King, Jr. (1904-77), discussing his contributions to the Baptist Church in Georgia as a historian of the church and the state, and his work as an educator in state church schools, 1930's-77. 1930's-77

3818. King, Bernard D. THE TWO KINGS. *Viewpoints: Georgia Baptist Hist. 1980 7: 17-26.* 1880-1973
*For abstract see **King, Spencer B., Sr.***

King, Spencer B., Sr. and Jr.

3819. King, Bernard D. THE TWO KINGS. *Viewpoints: Georgia Baptist Hist. 1980 7: 17-26.* Remembrance of Georgia Baptists Spencer B. King, Sr. (b. 1880), a preacher, and his son Spencer B. King, Jr. (b. 1904), who taught history at Mercer University through 1973. 1880-1973

King, William Lyon Mackenzie

3820. Cooper, Barry. ON READING *INDUSTRY AND HUMANITY:* A STUDY IN THE RHETORIC UNDERLYING LIBERAL MANAGEMENT. *J. of Can. Studies [Canada] 1978-79 13(4): 28-39.* William Lyon Mackenzie King (1874-1950) and Karl Marx (1818-83) were part of the same historical movement, although King rejected socialistic materialism. Both saw the meaning of history in the liberation of mankind by industrialization, and both saw the ensuing social costs. Because he regarded industry's role as service to the public, King wanted government to be a partner in this process. His career was a continual application of liberal management. 1900-20

3821. Mallory, J. R. MACKENZIE KING AND THE ORIGINS OF THE CABINET SECRETARIAT. *Can. Public Administration [Canada] 1976 19(2): 254-266.* Examines William Lyon Mackenzie King's contribution to the creation of a cabinet secretariat in Canada between 1927-1940. 1927-40

3822. Stacey, C. P. "A DREAM OF MY YOUTH": MACKENZIE KING IN NORTH YORK. *Ontario Hist. [Canada] 1984 76(3): 273-286.* Discusses the attempts of William Lyon Mackenzie King to be elected to the House of Commons from his maternal grandfather's North York, Ontario, constituency. He was finally elected in 1921, defeated in 1925, and subsequently reelected. Summarizes his career from this point. 2 illus., 36 notes. 1910-25

3823. Stacey, C. P. THE DIVINE MISSION: MACKENZIE KING AND HITLER. *Can. Hist. Rev. [Canada] 1980 61(4): 502-512.* William Lyon Mackenzie King, prime minister of Canada, attempted during 1937-39 to influence Adolf Hitler in favor of peace. King, a spiritualist, appears to have believed at the time of his return to power in 1935 that he had a mission from God to restore peace to the world, and it is in the light of this fact that his approaches to Hitler are best understood. Based mainly on the Mackenzie King diaries; 33 notes. 1937-39

3824. Whitaker, Reginald. POLITICAL THOUGHT AND POLITICAL ACTION IN MACKENZIE KING. *J. of Can. Studies [Canada] 1978-79 13(4): 40-60.* The consistency in his political behavior reveals that William Lyon Mackenzie King (1874-1950) had an ideology. As a Protestant, he believed in a God of love and consequently believed in progress. The unfolding of history presented each generation of liberals with new tasks. King was also a technocrat who regarded managerial mediation as essential to an industrial society. The liberal corporatism of his classless Liberal Party was intended to create social harmony; but the class situation in society determined his political actions. Based on W. L. M. King Diary and secondary sources; 47 notes. 1900-50

3825. Whitaker, Reginald. THE LIBERAL CORPORATIST IDEAS OF MACKENZIE KING. *Labour [Canada] 1977 2: 137-169.* William Lyon Mackenzie King, Canada's "most successful politician," could not decide, as a young man, "whether he was a conservative or a radical, an economist or a spiritualist, a teacher or a preacher, an academic or a bureaucrat, a thinker or a doer." King's education, his role as deputy minister and minister of labor, and employment by the Rockefellers as a labor relations expert are examined to show the evolution of his ideas on "societal corporatism" as background for an analysis of King's book, *Industry and Humanity* (1918). His "liberal corporatist vision" is seen as prophetic. Primary and secondary sources; 65 notes. 1890's-1918

Kingsbury family

3826. Dumas, David W., ed. BACON-ADAMS-WHITNEY-KINGSBURY FAMILY RECORDS. *New England Hist. and Geneal. Register 1984 138(Jan): 32-38.* 17c-19c

*For abstract see **Bacon family***

Kinley, David

3827. Grusso, Karl Marx. "David Kinley, 1861-1944: The Career of the Fifth President of the University of Illinois." U. of Illinois, Urbana-Champaign 1980. 717 pp. *DAI 1981 41(11): 4618-4619-A.* 8108525 1893-1944

Kinney, Edward W.

3828. Stern, Norton B. A NINETEENTH CENTURY CONVERSION IN LOS ANGELES. *Western States Jewish Hist. 1984 16(4): 360-367.* Eight days after marrying Annie Cohn, daughter of Los Angeles pawnbroker Leopold B. Cohn, in a civil ceremony, Edward W. Kinney converted to Judaism—the only known conversion to Judaism in 19th-century Los Angeles—and the couple was married again, this time according to Jewish law. Details the couple's subsequent careers, including their divorce and remarriage, and their ongoing relationship with the Jewish community. Based on newspaper accounts and interviews; 52 notes. 1889-1921

Kinsey, Madge (family)

3829. Bell, Charles Harris, III. "An Ohio Repertoire-Tent Show Family: The Kinsey Komedy Kompany and the Madge Kinsey Players, 1881-1951." Bowling Green State U. 1978. 197 pp. *DAI 1979 39(7): 3922-3923-A.* 1881-1951

Kip, William Ingraham

3830. Rawlinson, John Edward. "William Ingraham Kip: Tradition, Conflict and Transition." Grad. Theological Union 1982. 520 pp. *DAI 1982 43(3): 893-894-A.* DA8219270 19c

Kirby, William Fosgate

3831. Niswonger, Richard Leverne. WILLIAM F. KIRBY: ARKANSAS'S MAVERICK SENATOR. *Arkansas Hist. Q. 1978 37(3): 252-263.* Chronicles the career of William Fosgate Kirby (1867-1934), agrarian progressive Arkansas Democratic politician, who, during his term in the US Senate (1916-21) actively opposed many of President Woodrow Wilson's policies. Primary and secondary sources; 2 illus., 26 notes. 1880's-1934

Kirchwey, Freda

3832. Alpern, Sara. "A Woman of *The Nation:* Freda Kirchwey." U. of Maryland 1978. 292 pp. *DAI 1979 40(5): 2834-A.* 1915-55

Kirk, Russell

3833. Filler, Louis. "THE WIZARD OF MECOSTA": RUSSELL KIRK OF MICHIGAN. *Michigan Hist. 1979 63(5): 12-18.* Russell Kirk (b. 1918), Michigan's best-known man of letters, grew up in Plymouth, Michigan. Later, after studies at Michigan State College, Duke University, and St. Andrew's University in Scotland (which awarded him a Doctor of Letters degree), he settled in Mecosta, in a large wooden house inherited from his great-grandfather Amos Johnson, one of the town's founders. After a period of agnosticism Kirk developed a profound religious faith. His sensitivity to the supernatural—as well as to the reality of evil—appears in a special way in his gothic tales, a collection of which, *The Surly Sullen Bell* (1962), is redolent of Kirk's Michigan roots. 7 photos, note. 1918-79

3834. McDonald, William Wesley. "The Conservative Mind of Russell Kirk: 'The Permanent Things' in an Age of Ideology." Catholic U. of Am. 1982. 354 pp. *DAI 1982 43(1): 255-A.* DA8213740 1945-80

Kirkconnell, Watson

3835. Dreisziger, N. F. WATSON KIRKCONNELL: TRANSLATOR OF HUNGARIAN POETRY AND A FRIEND OF HUNGARIAN-CANADIANS. *Canadian-American Rev. of Hungarian Studies [Canada] 1977 4(2): 117-143.* A biography of Watson Kirkconnell, via a historical description of Hungarians in Canada, 1895-1977. 1895-1977

Kirkland, Edward Chase

3836. Freiberg, Malcolm. EDWARD CHASE KIRKLAND. *Massachusetts Hist. Soc. Pro. 1975 87: 154-158.* Edward Chase Kirkland (1894-1975) was an economic historian and a member of the Massachusetts Historical Society from 1951 until his death. Born in Vermont, Kirkland was educated at Dartmouth and Harvard and taught at several colleges, including Brown and Bowdoin. He was president of numerous historical associations, including the Economic History Association (1953-54) and the Mississippi Valley Historical Association (1955-56). A prolific author, Kirkland published *The Peacemakers of 1864* in 1927 and a biography of Charles Francis Adams, Jr., in 1965. Based on the author's personal friendship with Kirkland, other memoirs and recollections; 3 notes, index. 1920-75

3837. Handlin, Oscar. OBITUARY: EDWARD CHASE KIRKLAND. *Pro. of the Am. Antiquarian Soc. 1975 85(2): 360-363.* Edward Chase Kirkland (1894-1975) was born in Vermont and educated at Dartmouth College and Harvard University. He served in the Army during World War I, then taught at the Massachusetts Institute of Technology and Brown University. He developed an abiding hatred of war. He chose to specialize in American economic history. He published a number of important books and articles, and served in several historical societies. He was elected to the American Antiquarian Society in 1948, and took an active role. He remained an inveterate Yankee; his favorite time in history was the period in which old New England flowered, before rising technology snuffed it out. 1894-1975

Kirkland, Edwin C.

3838. Thomson, Robert. EDWIN C. KIRKLAND—THE COLLECTOR AND HIS METHODS. *Tennessee Folklore Society Bulletin 1984 50(3): 95-101.* Prints a biography of Edwin C. Kirkland, who collected lyrics and recordings of folksongs in Tennessee, neighboring states, and Wales. 1935-46

Kirstein, Lincoln

3839. Rosenwald, Peter J. LINCOLN KIRSTEIN'S VISION: HOW A BALLETOMANE CREATED THE FINEST BALLET SCHOOL IN THE UNITED STATES. *Horizon 1980 23(5): 38-42.* Lincoln Kirstein's (b. 1907) vision of a ballet school in America modeled on the Imperial Ballet

School in St. Petersburg became reality in 1934 with his and George Balanchine's creation of the School of American Ballet; also describes the New York City Ballet. 1934-80

Kirtland, Jared Potter

3840. Albrecht, Carl W., Jr. PROFILE: JARED POTTER KIRTLAND. *Timeline 1985 2(2): 44-49.* Presents a biography of Dr. Jared Potter Kirtland, an Ohio physician who became nationally known as an amateur naturalist and horticulturist. 1810's-77

Kisilewsky, Vladimir Julian (V. J. Kaye)

3841. Dushnyck, Walter. KAYE-KISILEWSKY: AN UNUSUAL UKRAINIAN CANADIAN SCHOLAR. *Ukrainian Q. 1978 34(4): 400-402.* Vladimir Julian Kisilewsky (V. J. Kaye, 1896-1976) was born in the western Ukraine and came to Canada in 1925 where he became known as a journalist, scholar, and author. Ukrainian settlement in Canada was a continuing theme of his research. 1925-76

Kissinger, Henry A.

3842. Kaspi, André. FAUT-IL BRULER KISSINGER? [Must we roast Kissinger?] *Histoire [France] 1984 (65): 92-94.* Describes the career of Henry Kissinger during 1968-81, especially his foreign policies as Secretary of State under presidents Richard Nixon and Gerald Ford. 1968-81

3843. Laqueur, Walter. KISSINGER AND HIS CRITICS. *Commentary 1980 69(2): 57-61.* Discusses Henry A. Kissinger's diplomacy and his book, *The White House Years,* and defends the book against its critics; 1969-70's. 1969-79

3844. Teiwes, Frederick C. KISSINGER'S MEMOIRS: IN PURSUIT OF A CONCEPTUAL FOREIGN POLICY: HENRY KISSINGER, *WHITE HOUSE YEARS;* HENRY KISSINGER, *YEARS OF UPHEAVAL. Australian J. of Pol. and Hist. [Australia] 1983 29(3): 534-537.* The memoirs of Henry Kissinger give rich and penetrating insights into world leaders, national psyches, the operations of the executive branch, and the fickleness of American public opinion. 1960's-70's

Kitchen, Peter

3845. Snoke, Elizabeth R. PETE KITCHEN: ARIZONA PIONEER. *Arizona and the West 1979 21(3): 235-256.* Peter Kitchen (1819-95) was the epitome of a successful pioneer who gave stability to the southwest frontier. He arrived in Arizona in 1854 and established himself in cattle and farming. He developed a profitable business supplying meat, grain, and vegetables to southern Arizona communities, mines, and military posts. He bought and sold interests in local mines. Kitchen moved to Tucson in 1883 to spend the rest of his life in real estate, gambling, and civic events. He has become a legendary frontier folk hero. 5 illus., map, 49 notes. 1854-95

Kitchens, Rufus

3846. Whisenhunt, Donald W. RUFUS KITCHENS: A TWENTIETH CENTURY CIRCUIT RIDER. *West Texas Hist. Assoc. Year Book 1981 57: 47-54.* Rufus Kitchens was a Methodist Church minister who rode the circuit in West Texas during 1932-58, but was typical of 19th-century frontier circuit riders. 1932-58

Klasmer, Benjamin

3847. Cohen, Blanche Klasmer. BENJAMIN KLASMER'S CONTRIBUTION TO BALTIMORE'S MUSICAL HISTORY. *Maryland Hist. Mag. 1977 72(2): 272-276.* Records the important role played by Benjamin Klasmer in bringing music to Baltimore for over 30 years, first as a cofounder of the Baltimore Symphony Orchestra, in 1916, and then as conductor of the Jewish Educational Alliance Symphony Orchestra in the 1920's. Throughout his career, Klasmer was the "leading musical director of pit orchestras" furnishing accompaniment to silent movies and vaudeville acts at the New Theater, the Garden and Rivoli Theaters, and the Hippodrome until his death in 1949. The tradition which he began is continued today by the Jewish Community Center and other groups. Perhaps his most popular renown, however, comes from his coauthorship of the theme song of the Baltimore Colts. 3 illus. 1909-49

Klassen, John P.

3848. Kehler, Larry. THE ARTISTIC PILGRIMAGE OF JOHN P. KLASSEN. *Mennonite Life 1973 28(4): 114-118, 125-127.* Discusses John P. Klassen's life 1909-33; he emigrated to the United States from Chortitza in the Ukraine and established himself as an artist and an instructor of art. 1909-33

Klauber, Abraham

3849. Muller, Richard. PIONEER SPIRIT: THE KLAUBER WANGENHEIM COMPANY. *J. of San Diego Hist. 1983 29(1): 1-19.* Traces the career of Pioneer San Diego merchant Abraham Klauber and the development of the Klauber Wangenheim Company. 1853-1982

Klawiter, Anthony

3850. Cuba, Stanley L. REV. ANTHONY KLAWITER: POLISH ROMAN AND NATIONAL CATHOLIC BUILDER-PRIEST. *Polish Am. Studies 1983 40(2): 59-92.* Gives an account of an unusual priest whose wanderings, assignments, and changes in church affiliation earned him such titles as "circuit rider," "transcontinental priest," and the "fallen-away priest." Father Anthony Klawiter held church assignments from the state of Washington to Massachusetts and from New Jersey to Manitoba, Canada. A priest filled with missionary zeal and Polish nationalism, Father Klawiter's controversial career reflects the internecine wars waged in Polish-American communities during the 19th and early 20th centuries. Based on Polish- and English-language sources; 87 notes. 1863-1913

Klein, Abraham Moses

3851. Edel, Leon. THE KLEIN-JOYCE ENIGMA. *J. of Can. Studies [Canada] 1984 19(2): 27-33.* A. M. Klein was obsessed with James Joyce. This emotional investment stemmed from similarities between the two men and their cities, Montreal and Dublin. Klein envied Joyce's single-minded dedication to writing, and suffered from his mother's criticism of his own bookish proclivities. Based on letters from A. M. Klein to Leon Edel written in the 1940's and on Usher Caplan's biography of Klein; 16 notes. 1910-56

3852. Fuerstenberg, Adam. FROM YIDDISH TO "YIDDISHKEIT": A. M. KLEIN, J. I. SEGAL AND MONTREAL'S YIDDISH CULTURE. *J. of Can. Studies [Canada] 1984 19(2): 66-81.* Yiddish culture and literature strongly influenced A. M. Klein. His literary goal was to prevent the assimilation of the Jewish community into North

American culture. Inspired by J. I. Segal, Klein attempted to synthesize Yiddish culture and the English language, thereby creating a medium to transmit traditional Yiddish culture from the immigrants to the first generation of Canadian Jews. His sense of failing in this task aggravated his alienation and contributed to his silence in 1954. Based on the works of A. M. Klein and J. I. Segal; 45 notes. 1910-54

3853. Golfman, Noreen. SEMANTICS AND SEMITICS: THE EARLY POETRY OF A. M. KLEIN. *U. of Toronto Q. [Canada] 1981-82 51(2): 175-191.* Abraham Moses Klein (1909-72), Jewish Canadian lawyer and poet, was exceptionally creative during 1925-35. He published his early writings in various little magazines. The reader must furnish some context in order to make sense of Klein's poetry, which was influenced by his scriptural training. Klein believed that to forget language was to suffer, thus he recorded many aspects of the Jewish world. He endeavored to fuse the values of the past with those of the present. Based on Klein's works, Canadian government documents, Canadian archives, interviews, and newspapers; 36 notes. 1925-35

Klein, Walter E.

3854. —. IN MEMORIAM: WALTER E. KLEIN. *Michigan Jewish History 1983 23(1): 27.* Presents an obituary of Walter E. Klein (1911-82), who was a member of the board of directors of the Jewish Historical Society of Michigan and the author of a history of the early years of the Jewish Community Council. 1911-82

Klotzbeacher, Jacob R.

3855. Rippley, LaVern J. JACOB (JAKE) R. KLOTZBEACHER. *Heritage Review 1979 (25): 29-31.* Relates the lives of Jacob Klotzbeacher and his father, Gottfried Klotzbücher, who immigrated to America from southern Russia, and describes their settlement near Forbes, in North Dakota. 1903-56

Klotzbücher, Gottfried

3856. Rippley, LaVern J. JACOB (JAKE) R. KLOTZBEACHER. *Heritage Review 1979 (25): 29-31.* 1903-56
*For abstract see **Klotzbeacher, Jacob R.***

Kludt family

3857. Kludt, August Wilhelm. ZULPICH TO AUGUST. *Heritage Rev. 1977 (17): 31-37.* Traces the Kludt family history from Germany to Poland to Russia and then to the United States, where the author's father settled in North Dakota. 1743-1976

Knabenshue, Roy

3858. Raymond, Arthur E. EARLY NON-RIGID DIRIGIBLES 1898-1915: ROY KNABENSHUE AND HIS ERA. *American Aviation Historical Society 1985 30(1): 58-67.* A personal account of Roy Knabenshue's involvement in the development and testing of hot air dirigibles and some biographical information of two other dirigible pilots and engineers, Alberto Santos-Dumont and Captain Tom Baldwin. 1898-1915

Knapp, Joseph G.

3859. Miller, Darlis A. and Wilson, Norman L., Jr. THE RESIGNATION OF JUDGE JOSEPH G. KNAPP. *New Mexico Hist. Rev. 1980 55(4): 334-344.* Discusses the reasons for the resignation in 1864 of Joseph G. Knapp (1805-88), a controversial judge on New Mexico's territorial supreme court. Most writers have maintained that the bitter controversy between Knapp and General James H. Carleton (1814-73), commander of the military department of New Mexico, was the cause of Knapp's removal. The explanation for Knapp's resignation centers instead on Knapp's opposition to John S. Watts (1816-76), a powerful territorial politician, because of Watts's political influence and land dealings. Newspapers and other primary sources; photo, 29 notes. 1863-65

Kneale, John G.

3860. Kneale, John G. TEHRAN DIARY. *Queen's Q. [Canada] 1984 91(1): 3-16.* The first of two parts of a diary covering the period 15 September 1979 to January 1980, when the author was in Tehran, Iran, as First Secretary at the Canadian Embassy, recording his impressions of the city and its people. Article to be continued. 1979-80

Kneeland, Abner

3861. French, Roderick S. LIBERATION FROM MAN AND GOD IN BOSTON: ABNER KNEELAND'S FREE-THOUGHT CAMPAIGN, 1830-1839. *Am. Q. 1980 32(2): 202-221.* Abner Kneeland (1776-1844), who lectured in Boston in the 1830's, was an outstanding indigenous freethinker. The class composition of his audiences or of the readers of his paper, the *Boston Investigator,* is unknown, but his ideas were perceived as persuasive explanations of working class circumstances. Kneeland worked hard to give his followers a sense of belonging to the international progressive movement, both by quoting radical thinkers extensively and by offering their publications for sale. By the late 1830's, Kneeland's opposition had succeeded in stigmatizing him, and he retired from the movement in 1839. 26 notes. 1830-39

Kniffen, Fred B.

3862. Lewis, Peirce. LEARNING FROM LOOKING: GEOGRAPHIC AND OTHER WRITING ABOUT THE AMERICAN CULTURAL LANDSCAPE. *Am. Q. 1983 35(3): 242-261.* 20c
*For abstract see **Jackson, J. B.***

Knight, Melvin Moses

3863. Pontecorvo, Giulio and Stewart, Charles F. MEMOIR: MELVIN MOSES KNIGHT. *Explorations in Econ. Hist. 1979 16(3): 240-248.* This tribute to M. M. Knight (b. 1887) summarizes his training in English, history, and sociology and his career as an economic historian. 2 notes. 20c

Knopf, Alfred A.

3864. Knopf, Alfred A. RANDOM RECOLLECTIONS OF A PUBLISHER. *Massachusetts Hist. Soc. Pro. 1961 73: 92-103.* 1901-61
*For abstract see **Cather, Willa***

Knoph, Thomas

3865. Rosholt, Malcolm. TWO MEN OF OLD WAUPACA. *Norwegian-American Studies 1965 22: 75-103.* 1853-56
*For abstract see **Duus, O. F.***

Knowles, Ella L.

3866. Roeder, Richard B. CROSSING THE GENDER LINE: ELLA L. KNOWLES, MONTANA'S FIRST WOMAN LAWYER. *Montana 1982 32(3): 64-75.* Ella L. Knowles was Montana's first woman lawyer in 1889. She established a practice in Helena then unsuccessfully ran as a Populist Party candidate for attorney general in 1892. Her Republican opponent Henri J. Haskell afterward appointed her assistant attorney general. The two married but were divorced later. Knowles's career reflects a strong personality and a western spirit of liberality. Based on secondary sources and contemporary newspapers; 8 illus., 60 notes. 1860-1911

Knox, William Franklin

3867. Mark, Steven MacDonald. "An American Interventionist: Frank Knox and United States Foreign Relations." U. of Maryland 1977. 371 pp. *DAI 1978 38(8): 5007-A.* 1914-44

Knudsen, Knud

3868. Folkedahl, Beulah. KNUD KNUDSEN AND HIS AMERICA BOOK. *Norwegian-American Studies 1967 23: 108-125.* Reprints the contents of a journal kept by Knud Knudsen of his 1839 trip from Drammen, Norway to New York City. The journal provides an account of daily life on board ship, reports on weather conditions, and comments on the other passengers. Preceded by a short biography of Knudssen, the journal describes the introduction a typical Norwegian immigrant might receive upon arriving in the United States. The Knudsens stayed with established Norwegian-American families in Rochester and Schenectady before moving on to Wisconsin. They remained there for a period, moved to different sections of Wisconsin, spent some time in the gold fields in California, and eventually moved back to Hamilton Settlement, Wisconsin, where Knudsen worked as a smith and eventually became interested in local politics and purchased a farm. Covers 1839-89. 24 notes. 1839-89

Knuth, Donald E.

3869. Albers, Donald J. and Steen, Lynn Arthur. A CONVERSATION WITH DON KNUTH. *Ann. of the Hist. of Computing 1982 4(3): 257-274.* Presents the text of an informal autobiographical interview with Donald E. Knuth, a prominent figure in the world of computing. He was educated at the California Institute of Technology, receiving a doctorate in 1963, in mathematics. In 1979 he was awarded the National Medal of Science by President Jimmy Carter. He is a leading scholar in the computer world. 1963-81

Koch, Christian Frederick

3870. Rabuck, Florence and Murray, Nicolette. CHRISTIAN FREDERICK KOCH: FARRIER AND BLACKSMITH. *Pennsylvania Heritage 1980 6(1): 14-17.* German born Christian Frederick Koch ran his shop in Harrisburg from the 1890's to 1923. ca 1890-1923

Koch, Edward W. E.

3871. Weaver, Alice O. A GERMAN-AMERICAN HOUSEHOLD IN EARLY TOLEDO, 105 OLIVER STREET. *Northwest Ohio Q. 1982 54(4): 103-116.* German immigrants Edward W. E. Koch and his wife Anna settled in Toledo, Ohio, where he became a school teacher and wine merchant. 1850's-1924

Koehn, Ferdinand J.

3872. Sturgeon, Esther. PAPA IS A NICE MAN. *Red River Valley Hist. 1980 (Fall): 27-33.* The author's father, Ferdinand J. Koehn, whose parents left Germany and settled in Stutsman County, North Dakota, in the late 19th century, became an iceman in Jamestown. 19c-20c

Koerner, W. H. D.

3873. Hutchinson, W. H. THE WESTERN LEGACY OF W. H. D. KOERNER. *Am. West 1979 16(5): 32-43.* W. H. D. "Big Bill" Koerner (1878-1938) was using his innate artistic talent while still in grade school in New Jersey. With experience as staff artist (instant illustrator for the day's events) for the Chicago *Tribune* and as a magazine illustrator, and with formal training in art academies in Chicago, New York, and Wilmington, Delaware, Koerner broadened his activities as artist and illustrator into mass-circulation magazines and novels. About one-fourth of his more than 2400 illustrations concerned the West, playing "a major role in fixing the images of the vanished American West that abide with us today." 9 illus. 1920's-35

Kohler, Kaufmann

3874. Katz, Irving I. RABBI KAUFMANN KOHLER BEGAN HIS DETROIT MINISTRY IN 1869. *Michigan Jewish Hist. 1979 19(1): 11-15.* Kaufmann Kohler (1843-1926) was a rabbi in Detroit; discusses his extensive influence in Reform Judaism in America, 1869-1926. 1869-1926

Kolb, Emory

3875. Pace, Michael. EMORY KOLB AND THE FRED HARVEY COMPANY. *J. of Arizona Hist. 1983 24(4): 339-364.* Traces the conflict between Emory Kolb, a photographer, and the massive Fred Harvey Company for the rights to serve tourists in the Grand Canyon. Kolb's persistence and lobbying ability held the monopoly-seeking Fred Harvey Company at bay during 1914-37 and then staved off the National Park Service until his death in 1976. Based on Arizona Historical Society records; 10 photos, 59 notes. 1904-76

Kollman, Eric C.

3876. Herlitzka, Ernst K. ERIC C. KOLLMAN. *Austrian Hist. Y. 1981-82 17-18: 583-585.* Discusses the life and academic career of Eric C. Kollman, who fled to the United States as a result of the Nazi takeover of Austria in 1938. He taught at Parsons College, the University of Iowa, and finally Cornell, where he remained from 1944 to his retirement in 1973. His most important book was a biography of Theodor Körner, entitled *Theodor Körner—Militär und Politik,* published in Vienna in 1973. 1903-81

Köllner, Augustus

3877. Wainwright, Nicholas B. AUGUSTUS KÖLLNER, ARTIST. *Pennsylvania Mag. of Hist. and Biog. 1960 84(3): 325-351.* The German-born Köllner (1812-1906), though successful as a water color landscape painter and lithographer in Philadelphia, lived long after his work was out of fashion. ca 1830-1906

Köngäs-Maranda, Elli

3878. Köngäs-Maranda, Elli. VÄÄRÄLLÄ PUOLEN ATLANTTIA [On the wrong side of the Atlantic]. *Kotiseutu [Finland] 1983 (1): 11-17.* Personal recollections of fieldwork researching Finnish-American ethnic traditions in Minnesota and Washington. 1959-61

Kook, Edward F.

3879. Olson, Ronald Charles. "Edward F. Kook: Link between the Theatre Artist and Technician." New York U. 1978. 151 pp. *DAI 1978 39(4): 1933-1934-A.* 1924-69

Koopman, Henry Ralph, II

3880. Petraitus, Paul W. HENRY RALPH KOOPMAN II: THE LIFE AND TIMES OF A NEIGHBORHOOD PHOTOGRAPHER. *Chicago Hist. 1978 7(3): 161-177.* Operating a small independent photography studio in Roseland, Illinois, 1884-1904, Henry Ralph Koopman II recorded the daily lives, and portraits of that community. 1884-1904

Korn, Bertram Wallace

3881. Raphael, Marc Lee. NECROLOGY: BERTRAM WALLACE KORN (1918-1979). *Am. Jewish Hist. 1980 69(4): 506-508.* An obituary of Bertram Wallace Korn, historian of American Jews in the antebellum and Civil War periods, and rabbi of Kenesseth Israel Synagogue in Elkins Park, Pennsylvania. Contains a listing and evaluation of his major works. 1918-79

Kosciusko, Thaddeus

3882. Cizauskas, Albert C. THE UNUSUAL STORY OF THADDEUS KOSCIUSKO. *Lituanus 1986 32(1): 47-66.* Thaddeus Kosciusko is usually remembered as a Pole who fought for American independence. In fact, Kosciusko came from a Lithuanian-Ruthenian family, and his devotion to political freedom was not limited to the cause of the North American colonies. He also played a leading role in the resistance of the Polish-Lithuanian commonwealth to foreign invasion and domination in the 1790's. Kosciusko's life bears testimony to his liberal and humanitarian beliefs. 4 notes. 1746-1817

3883. Moldoveanu, Milică. UN VULTUR S-A SMULS DIN COLIVIE: TADEUSZ KOŚCIUSZKO [A vulture has escaped from its cage: Thaddeus Kosciusko]. *Magazin Istoric [Romania] 1976 10(12): 39-42.* Surveys the activities of Thaddeus Kosciusko (1746-1817) as a military engineer during the American Revolution and considers his military activities in Poland, especially during the 1794 insurrection. 1774-1817

Kossuth, Louis

3884. Szabad, G. KOSSUTH ON THE POLITICAL SYSTEM OF THE U.S.A. *Études Hist. Hongroises [Hungary] 1975 1: 501-529.* Assesses the influences of US republicanism on Lajos Kossuth, the first president of independent Hungary in 1849. He became active during the Diet of 1832-36, dispatching reports on US events to Hungary. He approved of the basic principles of the US system out of conviction, but warned against their hardening into dogmas. Political action, though inspired by principles, is not automatically right. He was extremely critical of the President's right to determine foreign policy and said so on his visit to the United States in 1852. Based on archives; 135 notes. 1832-52

Kostash, Myrna

3885. Smyth, Donna E., interviewer. INTERVIEW WITH MYRNA KOSTASH: "A WESTERN, UKRAINIAN, REGIONALIST, FEMINIST, SOCIALIST WRITER". *Atlantis [Canada] 1981 6(2): 178-185.* A discussion with the author of *All of Baba's Children* and *Long Way from Home: The Story of the Sixties Generation in Canada* (1980), ranging over her experiences as a feminist, teacher, and writer. Photo. 1969-80

Kovac, George

3886. Kovac, George. ESCAPE TO FREEDOM: A YUGOSLAV IN NORTH LOUISIANA. *North Louisiana Hist. Assoc. J. 1980 11(3): 23-28.* The author's account (written ca. 1965) of his escape from the Austro-Hungarian army in 1913 and his life making railroad cross-ties in Texas and Louisiana and later farming in North Louisiana. 1913-65

Kowalsky, Henry I.

3887. Newmark, Leo. HENRY I. KOWALSKY: ATTORNEY AND COURT JESTER. *Western States Jewish Hist. Q. 1976 8(3): 195-202.* Henry I. Kowalsky (1858-1914), a friend of the author, was a public relations director for the King of Belgium 1904-14. Kowalsky was an able lawyer in San Francisco and loved to tell stories. In 1904 he met with President Roosevelt to defend the Belgians against charges of military atrocities in the Belgian Congo. Based on personal recollection and newspaper accounts; photo, 18 notes. 1904-14

Kozlowski, Karol

3888. Sarno, Martha Taylor. KAROL KOZLOWSKI (1885-1969) POLISH-AMERICAN PAINTER. *Polish Review 1985 30(1): 59-80.* Polish emigré Karol Kozlowski worked as a laborer for Consolidated Edison in New York City while devoting spare time to his pet exotic birds. He also painted detailed, naive, nature pieces, often used as backdrops for his beloved birds. Kozlowski, an illiterate and self-taught artist, was described by those who knew him as shy, isolated, and religious. He never attempted to sell his paintings, which have since been shown in major exhibitions. Based on personal communication, military documents, and secondary sources; 5 illus., 41 notes. 1913-60

Krans, Olof

3889. Murray, Anna Wadsworth. OLOF KRANS. *Chicago Hist. 1981-82 10(4): 244-247.* Biography of Swedish-born naive artist Olof Krans, who emigrated with his parents in 1850 and settled at Bishop Hill, Illinois, the commune founded by Swedish evangelist Erik Jansson in 1846, focusing on Krans's landscapes and portraits. 1850-1916

Krappe, Alexander Haggerty

3890. Burson, Anne C. ALEXANDER HAGGERTY KRAPPE AND HIS SCIENCE OF COMPARATIVE FOLKLORE. *J. of the Folklore Inst. 1982 19(2-3): 167-195.* In spite of his prodigious publication record, Alexander Haggerty Krappe is not well-known to modern folklorists. An abrasive man, Krappe never held an academic position more than a few years. Nevertheless, he was a brilliant folklorist, linguist, and medievalist who helped to resurrect the field of comparative mythology. He was not a theorist, nor did he complete field studies; Krappe disliked politics and religion, and many of his works denigrate these things. His approach to folklore, which he viewed as "the study of survivals," was comparative, and he relied heavily on the historic-geographic method. Although many of his ideas and perspectives now seem outdated, he remains an important figure in the history of folkloristics. Krappe's *The Science of Folklore* (1930) is an important early introduction to the field. Based on interviews and secondary sources; 92 notes. 1920's-47

Krat, Pavlo

3891. Kazymyra, Nadia O. THE DEFIANT PAVLO KRAT AND THE EARLY SOCIALIST MOVEMENT IN CANADA. *Can. Ethnic Studies [Canada] 1978 10(2): 38-54.* From 1902, Pavlo Krat (1882-1952) was involved in political uprisings in the Russian Empire, and in demonstrations against Polish authorities in Austria-Hungary before he emigrated to Canada in 1907. He revitalized Ukrainian socialists in Canada by his dynamic public speaking and articulate and voluminous writings. He combined Marxian socialism and romantic patriotism to instill social consciousness and national identity. He, however, lost leadership through unfair criticism of fellow Ukrainian immigrants for their failure to recognize his own manifest destiny in building a socialist society. His unsuccessful search for the ideal socialist state ended in his becoming a Presbyterian minister and terminating any formal association with the socialist movement. Primary sources; photo, 94 notes. ca 1902-52

Krauskopf, Joseph

3892. Beifield, Martin P. JOSEPH KRAUSKOPF AND ZIONISM: PARTNERS IN CHANGE. *American Jewish History 1985 75(1): 48-60.* Describes and explains the growing support of Zionism by Joseph Krauskopf, Reform rabbi of Keneseth Israel in Philadelphia from 1887 to 1923. Though he disapproved of Zionism's political aims, he lauded its agricultural projects as akin to his own plans for ghetto Jews in this country, for whom he founded the National Farm School in Doylestown, Pennsylvania. He increasingly saw Palestine as an essential refuge for persecuted Jews of Europe. Primary sources; 31 notes. 1887-1923

3893. Sutherland, John F. RABBI JOSEPH KRAUSKOPF OF PHILADELPHIA: THE URBAN REFORMER RETURNS TO THE LAND. *Am. Jewish Hist. Q. 1978 67(4): 342-362.* Joseph Krauskopf (1858-1923) came to the United States as a 14-year-old. He graduated with the first class of four at Hebrew Union College in 1883 and was Philadelphia's foremost reform rabbi during 1887-1922. He introduced English into both services and the religious school, popularized the Jewish Sundry Services, and drafted the Pittsburgh Platform of 1885. His great concern with social reform led him into close cooperation with Jacob Riis. After a visit with Leo Tolstoy at Yasnaya Polyana, Krauskopf became the driving spirit of the Jewish "back-to-the land" movement and of the National Farm School, today known as the Delaware Valley College of Science and Agriculture, the only private agricultural school in the country. Thoroughly part of America's urban milieu, Krauskopf nevertheless sought to modify it with the agrarian myth, an urban-agrarian ambivalence which still influences American thought and action. 1880's-1923

Krehbiel, Albert Henry

3894. Krehbiel, Rebecca F. ALBERT HENRY KREHBIEL, 1873-1945: EARLY AMERICAN IMPRESSIONIST. *Mennonite Life 1985 40(1): 4-8.* Albert H. Krehbiel (1873-1945) was born into an Iowa Mennonite family and became interested in art at an early age. He attended the Art Institute of Chicago, won awards for his paintings in Europe, and taught at the Art Institute until his death. Highly influenced by Impressionism, he painted numerous landscapes and executed murals for the Illinois Supreme Court building. Based on the Krehbiel Papers and correspondence; 4 reproductions, photo, 9 notes. 1890's-1945

Krehbiel, Henry Peter

3895. Schrag, Menno. H. P. KREHBIEL: AS I REMEMBER HIM. *Mennonite Life 1985 40(2): 4-9.* Henry Peter Krehbiel was a major figure in Midwestern Mennonite circles. He was a leader of the fundamentalist faction and was politically conservative, antisocial, and very authoritarian. However, he had strong beliefs, was an outspoken pacifist, and was able to maintain the production of *Der Herold* and the *Mennonite Weekly Review* throughout the Great Depression. Based on author's personal reminiscences. 1920-38

Krenek, Ernst

3896. Bailey, Olive Jean. "The Influence of Ernst Krenek on the Musical Culture of the Twin Cities." U. of Minnesota 1980. 573 pp. *DAI 1980 41(5): 1824-A.* 8025416 1942-47

Kresz, Géza de

3897. Király, Péter. GÉZA KRESZ—A LIFE IN MUSIC (1882-1959). *New Hungarian Quarterly [Hungary] 1984 25(94): 213-217.* Prints a biography of Hungarian-Canadian chamber musician and music educator Géza Kresz (1882-1959). Includes a facsimile of a letter to Kresz from Maurice Ravel. Illus. 1903-47

3898. Kresz, Mária. THE LIFE AND WORK OF MY FATHER: GÉZA DE KRESZ (1882-1959). *Hungarian Studies Rev. [Canada] 1982 9(2): 73-81.* A brief, illustrated biography of Géza de Kresz, a Hungarian violinist who pioneered and taught a new technique for mastery of the instrument, and whose career was split between Europe and Canada. 1906-59

Krock, Arthur

3899. Sayler, James Allen. "Window on an Age: Arthur Krock and the New Deal Era, 1929-1941." Rutgers U. 1978. 584 pp. *DAI 1979 39(7): 4453-A.* 1929-41

Kroeber, Theodora

See Quinn, Theodora Kroeber

Kroetsch, Robert

3900. Munton, Ann. THE STRUCTURAL HORIZONS OF PRAIRIE POETICS: THE LONG POEM, ELI MANDEL, ANDREW SUKNASKI, AND ROBERT KROETSCH. *Dalhousie Rev. [Canada] 1983 63(1): 69-97.* 20c
*For abstract see **Mandel, Eli***

Kroner, Tom

3901. Gray, Frances. "Waiting for Nothing: Tom Kroner, 1906-1969." State U. of New York, Stony Brook 1979. 110 pp. *DAI 1979 40(2): 842-843-A.* 1906-69

Krutch, Joseph Wood

3902. Littlefield, Daniel F., Jr. A DEDICATION TO THE MEMORY OF JOSEPH WOOD KRUTCH, 1893-1970. *Arizona and the West 1982 24(2): 100-104.* Tennessee-born Joseph Wood Krutch (1893-1970) earned degrees at the state university and Columbia University. During his intermittent career as drama critic, reviewer, and professor of English and drama, Krutch won wide acclaim as a scholar of letters for his publications. Increasingly he became interested in the natural world, particularly in the desert of the Southwest. Leaving academe in 1952, he moved to Arizona to pursue his new career as a nature writer. In several books he urged the preservation of the beauty of the desert from the perspective of a naturalist. He was particularly concerned with the delicate balance of desert ecology. In later years he also narrated network telecasts on the natural world of the Southwest. Illus., biblio. 1950-70

Krzycki, Leo

3903. Miller, Eugene. LEO KRZYCKI: POLISH AMERICAN LABOR LEADER. *Polish Am. Studies 1976 33(2): 52-64.* Leo Krzycki (1881-1966) contributed in no small measure to the history of political radicalism in the United States. He was vice-president of the Amalgamated Clothing Workers for 25 years. At one time he was national chairman of the executive committee of the Socialist Party. He was also active in the early organizing drives of the CIO. His fiery speeches resounded throughout Pennsylvania's Schuylkill Valley during the Depression. As a Polish American leader he dared support the Yalta agreement and the pro-Soviet regime following the end of World War II. Based on Polish and English sources; 46 notes. 1900's-66

Kubašek, John J.

3904. Tanzone, Daniel F. JOHN J. KUBAŠEK, PRIEST AND PATRIOT. *Slovakia 1976 26(49): 69-75.* Discusses the life and career of Slovak American Catholic priest John J. Kubašek in Yonkers, New York, 1902-50; emphasizes his work for Slovakian independence from Hungary. 1902-50

Kuhn, Bob

3905. Johnston, Patricia Condon. BOB KUHN: MANAGING COLOR ON A MASONITE STAGE. *Sporting Classics 1985 3(6): 57-65.* Bob Kuhn, specializing in a style he calls "realism-impressionism" and composing his pictures like a stage manager, has become one of America's most popular animal illustrators. 1920-84

Kumlien, Thure

3906. Trotzig, E. G. THURE KUMLIEN, PIONEER NATURALIST. *Swedish Pioneer Hist. Q. 1979 30(3): 196-204.* Thure Kumlien was born in Sweden in 1819, where he received a good education, majoring in botany. In 1843 he emigrated to America with his bride-to-be, Christina Wallberg. They settled near Lake Koshkonong, Wisconsin, where they married. Never a farmer-in-earnest, Thure spent much time in his pursuits as a naturalist. In 1850 this came to the attention of Thomas M. Brewer, a Boston naturalist. Brewer financed and publicized Thure as a naturalist and brought him world-wide recognition. In 1867 he was appointed to teach natural history, at Albion Academy and later accepted a commission from the state to prepare natural history exhibits for the University at Madison and act as conservator at the museum of the Wisconsin Natural History Society. He died in 1888. Based on the works of Angie Kumlien Main, his granddaughter; 3 photos, 8 notes. 1843-88

Kunz, Karl

3907. Vallaster, Christoph. AUF DER SUCHE NACH FREIHEIT [In search of freedom]. *Montfort [Austria] 1983 35(2): 155-173.* Explores the life and work of Austrian journalist Karl Kunz, who emigrated to Milwaukee, Wisconsin, where he wrote for German-language newspapers on a variety of liberal political and social topics. Primary sources. 1832-76

Kupper, Lawrence Vincent

3908. Marsh, John L. L. V. KUPPER: DIRT-STREET TOWN PHOTOGRAPHER. *Pennsylvania Heritage 1984 10(1): 9-13.* Portrays the career of Lawrence Vincent Kupper, a photographer in Edinboro, Pennsylvania. 1890-1940's

Kurikka, Matti

3909. Wilson, J. Donald. MATTI KURIKKA AND A. B. MÄKELÄ: SOCIALIST THOUGHT AMONG FINNS IN CANADA, 1900-1932. *Can. Ethnic Studies [Canada] 1978 10(2): 9-21.* Two active Finn socialists, both newspaper editors, Matti Kurikka (1863-1915) and A. B. Mäkelä (1863-1932), emigrated to Canada before World War I. Kurikka, a utopian and theosophist, was the last of a dying breed when he reached British Columbia in 1900; there he established a utopian socialist settlement at Sointula, and edited *Aika,* the first Finnish-language newspaper in Canada. There he was joined by his Marxian socialist friend, A. B. Mäkelä. The latter, after the colony's collapse, stayed on in Canada as an editor. His socialism eventually led him into the Communist Party of Canada, but he made his major impact as a political and satirical writer rather than as an activist. Primary sources; 2 photos, 22 notes. 1900-32

3910. Wilson, J. Donald. "NEVER BELIEVE WHAT YOU HAVE NEVER DOUBTED": MATTI KURIKKA'S DREAM FOR A NEW WORLD UTOPIA. *Turun Hist. Arkisto [Finland] 1980 34: 216-240.* A biography of the Finnish utopian socialist Matti Kurikka (1863-1915), who founded utopian communities in Australia, 1899, and Canada, 1900-04. Kurikka was a Finnish cultural nationalist, a theosophist, and an advocate of free love. These attitudes brought him into conflict with his own followers as well as with orthodox Marxists. Based on Kurikka's letters in a private collection in Finland; 96 notes. 1883-1915

Kurose, Aki Kato

3911. Davidson, Sue. AKI KATO KUROSE: PORTRAIT OF AN ACTIVIST. *Frontiers 1983 7(1): 91-97.* Discusses Aki Kato Kurose's experiences as a nisei growing up in Seattle, Washington, and later living in a relocation camp during World War II. 1930's-50's

Kurz, Rudolph Friederich

3912. —. JOURNAL OF RUDOLPH FRIEDERICH KURZ. *Am. Hist. Illus. 1980 15(5): 48-50.* Reprints an entry from the journal of Swiss artist, Rudolph Friederich Kurz, best known for his watercolor of Woman Chief in 1851, and describes his year-long courtship with Witthae, daughter of the chief Kirutsche of 30 families of Iowa Indians, and brief marriage during part of 1850, before she left him. 1848-50

Kuter, Laurence S.

3913. Hansell, Haywood S. GENERAL LAURENCE S. KUTER 1905-1979. *Aerospace Hist. 1980 27(2): 91-94.* A brief reminiscence of General Kuter, by the author, his Air Force friend. 5 photos. 1930-79

3914. Holley, I. B., Jr. AN AIR FORCE GENERAL: LAURENCE SHERMAN KUTER. *Aerospace Hist. 1980 27(2): 88-90.* Reviews the life of Laurence S. Kuter, General, USAF, (1905-79) and his part in the birth and growth of the US Air Force and the United States as an air power. "He was not, as the world reckons, one of that universally recognized band of 'great captains'; rather, he stood at the top of the next tier, one of those impressively competent practitioners in the profession of arms, and a leader, truly worthy of emulation." Photo. 1930-79

Kwah, Chief

3915. Bishop, Charles A. KWAH: A CARRIER CHIEF. Judd, Carol M. and Ray, Arthur J., ed. *Old Trails and New Directions: Papers of the Third North American Fur Trade Conference* (Toronto: U. of Toronto Pr., 1980): 191-204. Presents a biography of Kwah (1755-1840), chief of the Stuart Lake Carrier Indians. He provided fish for the Fort St. James trading post next to his village and the headquarters of the New Caledonia fur emporium, spared the life of a future governor, and became the most important chief among the Carrier associated with Fort St. James. Although he undoubtedly had inherited his title, and although he also had the good fortune to have been the chief of the village adjacent to the trading post, he possessed all of the necessary qualities of a leader. In addition to a prominent place in the history of the Hudson's Bay Company's New Caledonia fur trade, he left a progeny of 16 children so that today over half of the Stuart Lake Indians claim descent. Based on documents in the Hudson's Bay Company Archives, Provincial Archives of Manitoba, Winnipeg, Canada; 32 notes. 1780-1840

Kyburz, Carl E.

3916. Kyburz, Carl E. BEGINNING OF A PHARMACIST: A REMINISCENCE. *Pharmacy in Hist. 1983 25(1): 30-32.* Recalls Kyburz's early career in pharmacy from his apprenticeship with Will C. Quinn, a university-educated pharmacist, to his enrollment in the Indianapolis College of Pharmacy, later part of Butler University. 3 photos. 1930's

Kyles, Connie Lynn

3917. Galant, Debbie. ALONG FOR THE RIDE. *Southern Exposure 1980 8(4): 84-86.* Story of Connie Lynn Kyles, 20, now serving the third year of her 40-50 year sentence for second-degree murder; 1977-80. 1977-80

L

Labadie, Joseph

3918. Oestreicher, Richard. SOCIALISM AND THE KNIGHTS OF LABOR IN DETROIT, 1877-1886. *Labor Hist. 1981 22(1): 5-30.* 1877-86
For abstract see ***Grenell, Judson***

Labaree, Leonard Woods

3919. Bell, Whitfield J., Jr. LEONARD WOODS LABAREE. *Massachusetts Hist. Soc. Pro. 1980 92: 156-160.* Leonard Labaree (1897-1980) spent 42 years on the Yale faculty. A student of Yale Colonial American historian Charles McLean Andrews, Labaree was appointed instructor in 1924. Weathering the Depression, when promotions were meager, Labaree gradually moved through the ranks and evntally advanced to the Farnham professorship in American history (his mentor's chair), where he taught the American survey course and developed a course in the bibliography of American history. In 1935 he published *Royal Instructions to British Colonial Governors,* which received the American Historical Association's Justin Winsor Prize. In 1947 he delivered the Phelps lectures at New York University, which were published as *Conservatism in Early American History* (1949). From 1954 through 1969 Labaree edited the *Papers of Benjamin Franklin* through the first 14 volumes. 1897-1980

3920. Labaree, Benjamin W. LEONARD WOODS LABAREE. *Pro. of the Am. Antiquarian Soc. 1980 90(2): 307-311.* Obituary of Leonard Labaree (1897-1980), surveying his publications and their contributions to Colonial American history. A major enterprise was his editorial work on the Benjamin Franklin Papers. 1897-1980

3921. Pierson, George W. IN MEMORIAM, LEONARD WOODS LABAREE (1897-1980). *New England Q. 1980 53(4): 544-546.* Presents a tribute to Leonard Woods Labaree, long-time member of the board of editors of the *New England Quarterly.* He was educated at Yale and taught history there for 45 years. His notable publications include *Royal Government in America: a Study of the British Colonial System before 1783* and *Milford, Connecticut: the Early Development of the Town as Shown in Its Land Records.* 1922-80

Labatt, Henry Jacob

3922. Kramer, William M. PIONEER LAWYER OF CALIFORNIA AND TEXAS: HENRY J. LABATT (1832-1900). *Western States Jewish Hist. Q. 1982 15(1): 3-21.* Henry Jacob Labatt became clerk of the San Francisco, California, Superior Court in 1855. He made a major contribution to California law by compiling decisions of the Supreme Court. His directories and compilations provided lawyers with court precedents in printed form to help in the preparation of their cases. In the late 1860's, Labatt moved to Galveston, Texas, where he established the firm of Labatt and Noble, later Labatt and Labatt with his son Joseph A. He was a leader in the Jewish community, helping to establish Galveston's Congregation B'nai Israel and the first synagogue erected in Texas. Labatt died in the Great Storm of 8 September 1900 on Galveston Island. Based on period newspaper articles; photo, 80 notes. 1855-1900

LaBeef, Sleepy

3923. Guralnick, Peter. THERE'S GOOD ROCKIN' TONIGHT. *Southern Exposure 1981 9(3): 68-72.* A brief biography of rockabilly singer and historian Sleepy LaBeef (b. 1935). 1935-81

Labunski, Wikton

3924. Belanger, J. Richard. "Wiktor Labunski: Polish-American Musician in Kansas City, 1937-1974: A Case Study." Columbia U. Teachers Coll. 1982. 210 pp. *DAI 1982 43(5): 1461-A.* DA8223102 1937-74

Lacy, Roger

3925. Bradberry, David. ROGER LACY, THE FOUNDER OF AUGUSTA. *Richmond County Hist. 1984 16(1): 30-35.* Subsidized by the Trustees for Establishing the Colony of Georgia, entrepreneur Roger Lacy arrived in Georgia in 1733, where he directed the settlement of Thunderbolt, a silk-growing colony, and was later sent by Governor James Edward Oglethorpe to oversee the settlement of the new colony of Augusta. 1733-38

LaFarge, John

3926. Adams, Henry. "John La Farge, 1830-1870: From Amateur to Artist." (Vol. 1 and 2) Yale U. 1980. 474 pp. *DAI 1980 41(5): 1814-A.* 8024513 1830-70

3927. LaFarge, Henry A. THE EARLY DRAWINGS OF JOHN LA FARGE. *Am. Art J. 1984 16(2): 4-38.* Drawing was the common element of the various artistic media in which John La Farge worked. An excellent draftsman from the time he was a child, La Farge filled innumerable sketchbooks with drawings, his visual notebooks. The sketchbooks show his view of his environment and family, as well as the growing influence of the great European masters on his work. Drawings also show the genesis of some of La Farge's famous paintings. After 1876, watercolor replaced drawing as his jotting medium. Photo, 45 plates, 32 notes. 1846-76

3928. Wren, Linnea Holmer. "The Animated Prism: A Study of John La Farge as Author, Critic and Aesthetician." U. of Minnesota 1978. 436 pp. *DAI 1978 39(6): 3195-3196-A.* 19c

3929. Yarnall, James L. JOHN LA FARGE'S "PARADISE VALLEY PERIOD" (1865-1872). *Newport Hist. 1982 55(1): 6-25.* Discusses the career of landscape artist John La Farge, who was attracted to Newport because of its "varied and picturesque topography," focusing on the "Paradise Valley Period," so-called because of the landscapes La Farge painted of the Paradise Hills region of Middletown. 1865-72

LaFleur, Maius

3930. Nelson, Donald Lee. "MAMA, WHERE YOU AT?" THE CHRONICLE OF MAIUS LAFLEUR. *JEMF Q. 1983 19(70): 76-80.* Traces the brief career of Cajun musician Maius LaFleur, who, together with Leo Soileau, recorded four songs for the Victor Recording Company in Atlanta, Georgia, a few days before his death in a shooting incident. 1920-28

LaFolette, Philip F.

3931. Coffman, Edward M. and Hass, Paul H., ed. WITH MACARTHUR IN THE PACIFIC: A MEMOIR BY PHILIP F. LA FOLLETTE. *Wisconsin Mag. of Hist. 1980-81 64(2): 82-106.* This is an edited version of part of an unpublished autobiography written in the late 1950's dealing with the three-term Wisconsin governor's service in the United States Army from October, 1942, until June, 1945. Discusses his role in General Douglas MacArthur's public relations office, and analyzes MacArthur as a leader and military tactician in largely favorable terms. 11 illus., 10 notes. 1942-45

LaFollette, Robert M., Jr.

3932. Maney, Patrick J. "'Young Bob' LaFollette: A Biography of Robert M. LaFollette, Jr. (1895-1953)." U. of Maryland 1976. 471 pp. *DAI 1977 38(5): 2999-3000-A.* 1928-53

LaFollette, Robert M., Sr.

3933. Burgchardt, Carl Robert. "The Will, the People, and the Law: A Rhetorical Biography of Robert M. La Follette, Sr." U. of Wisconsin, Madison 1982. 437 pp. *DAI 1983 43(8): 2492-A.* DA8225635 1875-1925

Lafon, Thomy

3934. Wynes, Charles E. THOMY LAFON: BLACK PHILANTHROPIST. *Midwest Q. 1981 22(2): 105-112.* Thomy Lafon, a 19th-century black philanthropist of New Orleans, contributed generously to various New Orleans charities during his life and in his will. A devout Catholic, he gave to charities of all denominations, without considering race, sex, or age. Several New Orleans institutions were named in his honor. Based on city directories, newspapers, and secondary sources; 15 notes, biblio. ca 1830-93

LaGuardia, Fiorello H.

3935. Cusella, Louis P. BIOGRAPHY AS RHETORICAL ARTIFACT: THE AFFIRMATION OF FIORELLO H. LA GUARDIA. *Q. J. of Speech 1983 69(3): 302-316.* Biographies of New York Mayor and Congressman Fiorello H. La Guardia are rhetorical acts that affirm La Guardia as an American hero. They differ to a great extent depending on whether a biographer had a professional affiliation with La Guardia. Writers not affiliated with him use documented sources, direct quotations, and personal observations, and emphasize the themes of the Puritan Ethic and progress/competitiveness. Those associated with La Guardia exhibit highly general, idealistic portrayals and dramatize La Guardia's image with the more mythic themes of success, equality of opportunity, morality, and pragmatic humanitarianism. 1882-1947

Laird, James L.

3936. Krauth, Leland. MARK TWAIN FIGHTS SAM CLEMENS' DUEL. *Mississippi Q. 1980 33(2): 141-153.* 1863-1906

*For abstract see **Twain, Mark***

Lake, Hattie

3937. Wells, Carol. KIND AND GENTLE ADMONITIONS: THE EDUCATION OF A LOUISIANA TEACHER. *Louisiana Hist. 1976 17(3): 283-297.* Born in South Carolina in 1847, Hattie Lake came with her father to Caddo Parish, Louisiana, when she was six. Educated on Louisiana plantations and at Mansfield Female College and Greenville Baptist Female College, she graduated from the latter in 1867. She made little use of the classical education she received at college, however, until 1878 when she was invited to teach in East Baton Rouge Parish, a job she received after some opposition from those who believed only men should be employed to teach. Based principally on correspondence and memoirs of Hattie Lake; photo, 36 notes. 1847-78

Laliberté, Alfred

3938. Legendre, Odette. ALFRED LALIBERTÉ ET LES BOIS-FRANCS [Alfred Laliberté and the Bois-Francs]. *Action Natl. [Canada] 1980 69(10): 842-853.* The work of Alfred Laliberté (1878-1953), the national sculptor of French Canada, is firmly rooted in the Athabaska peasantry. These origins are revealed in his conception of life, respect for work, and writings, 500 paintings, and 1,000 sculptures. From 1928 through 1932, he executed a series of 214 bronzes illustrating the legends, customs, and crafts of Quebec history. 10 illus., chronology. 1900-53

Lamb, Joe

3939. Scotti, Joseph R. "Joe Lamb: A Study of Ragtime's Paradox." U. of Cincinnati 1977. 311 pp. *DAI 1977 38(6): 3134-A.* 1900's

Lamb, John (1735-97)

3940. Ranlet, Philip. THE TWO JOHN LAMBS OF THE REVOLUTIONARY GENERATION. *Am. Neptune 1982 42(4): 301-305.* Clears confusion concerning the two John Lambs by delineating the careers of the John Lamb (1735-97) of New York who served as secretary of the New York City Committee of Correspondence, an artillery officer in the Continental Army, and collector of the port of New York, and John Lamb of Connecticut, who was a sea captain and briefly a diplomat who failed in an attempt to negotiate a treaty with Algiers in 1786. Printed primary sources; 19 notes. 1770-90

Lambelet, Auguste

3941. Dein, Jane H. AUGUSTE LAMBELET (1838-1919): A SOLDIER OF FORTUNE. *Swiss Am. Hist. Soc. Newsletter 1981 17(2): 5-32.* Swiss American homesteader Auguste Lambelet (1838-1919) became an American citizen in 1889 in Knox County, Nebraska, where he lived until his death; his memoirs, handwritten in French, included accounts of his adventures as a soldier in the Foreign Legion before he arrived in America. ca 1858-1919

Lamm, Emile

3942. Tucker, D. G. EMILE LAMM'S SELF-PROPELLED TRAMCARS 1870-72 AND THE EVOLUTION OF THE FIRELESS LOCOMOTIVE. *Hist. of Technology [Great Britain] 1980 5: 103-117.* During 1870-72, Emile Lamm experimented in New Orleans, Louisiana, with several methods of self-propulsion for streetcars that would not produce smoke. He first developed a modified steam engine driven by ammonia gas instead of steam. He later developed a more successful system in which a streetcar engine was driven by steam derived from heat stored in superheated water injected at high pressure in a car's tank at a base station. Based on Lamm's patents; 2 illus., 5 diagrams, 23 notes, appendix including Lamm's biography. 1870-72

Lamont, Thomas W.

3943. Hogan, Michael J. THOMAS W. LAMONT AND EUROPEAN RECOVERY: THE DIPLOMACY OF PRIVATISM IN A CORPORATIST AGE. Jones, Kenneth Paul, ed. *U.S. Diplomats in Europe, 1919-1941* (Santa Barbara, Calif.: ABC-CLIO, 1981): 5-22. Thomas W. Lamont (1870-1948), a partner in the firm of J. P. Morgan and Company from 1911, was a central figure in the financial diplomacy of the postwar period, establishing wide areas of collaboration between the private sector and government and exercising influence on the politics of European stabilization at a time when isolationism in the United States limited official government involvement. The result was a form of public-private power-sharing, one which entrusted a private leader with the responsibility for protecting the public interest. His authorship of the Lamont-Davis memorandum in 1919 made him one of the original formulators of American stabilization policy. Primary sources; 47 notes. 1918-29

Lamperd, Andrew

3944. Mordoh, Alice Morrison. TWO WOODCARVERS: JASPER, DUBOIS COUNTY, INDIANA. *Indiana Folklore 1980 13(1-2): 17-29.* Portrays the careers of Andrew Lamperd and Aloysius Schuch, German-American wood-carvers in Jasper, Indiana, who have pursued their craft since retiring from factory work in the 1970's. 1970's

Lampkin, Daisy Adams

3945. McKenzie, Edna B. DAISY LAMPKIN: A LIFE OF LOVE AND SERVICE. *Pennsylvania Heritage 1983 9(3): 9-12.* Sketches the life of black activist Daisy Adams Lampkin, whose public career during 1912-64 included political organizing for women's suffrage and black civil rights. 1912-64

Landes, Bertha Knight

3946. Pieroth, Doris H. BERTHA KNIGHT LANDES: THE WOMAN WHO WAS MAYOR. *Pacific Northwest Quarterly 1984 75(3): 117-127.* Following graduation from Indiana University, Bertha Knight Landes accompanied her husband Henry to his new teaching job at the University of Washington in 1895. Henry fully supported his wife's gradual involvement in Seattle's community affairs, which by 1921 landed her an appointment to the mayor's commission on unemployment. The following year Bertha campaigned on a reformist ticket and won a seat on the city council. She was elected Seattle's mayor in 1924, but her subsequent crusade against liquor and her alienation of the male power structure cost her a reelection victory four years later. Based on Seattle newspapers and the Bertha K. Landes Papers at the University of Washington library; 6 photos, 51 notes. 1922-28

Landis, James M.

3947. Wigdor, David. LAW, REFORM, AND THE MODERN ADMINISTRATIVE STATE. *Rev. in Am. Hist. 1982 10(2): 234-240.* 1930's
*For abstract see **Brandeis, Louis D.***

Lane, Fitz Hugh

3948. Hoffman, Katherine. THE ART OF FITZ HUGH LANE. *Essex Inst. Hist. Collections 1983 119(1): 28-36.* The sea, for many a romantic and spiritual source of inspiration, became the central theme in the paintings of Nathaniel Rogers Lane (1804-1865). Born in Gloucester, Massachusetts, Lane was crippled as a youth by polio. Later, taking the name Fitz Hugh Lane, he used the sea as a kind of retreat and solace. Lane's paintings and his treatment of the sea, ships and other coastal themes are examined and are seen as a record of the various meanings of the sea for Massachusetts citizens. Illus., 15 notes. 1804-65

Lane, Frederic C.

3949. —. DEDICATION. *J. of Econ. Hist. 1980 40(4): 683.* A tribute to Frederic C. Lane, economic historian and editor of the *Journal of Economic History,* 1943-51, on the occasion of his 80th birthday. 1943-80

Lane, Isaac

3950. Griffin, Paul R. "Black Founders of Reconstruction Era Methodist Colleges: Daniel A. Payne, Joseph C. Price, and Isaac Lane, 1863-1890." Emory U. 1983. 300 pp. *DAI 1983 44(3): 788-A.* DA8316279 1863-90

Lane, Levi Cooper

3951. Smith, John David. DR. LEVI COOPER LANE: CIVIL WAR MEDICAL EXAMINER. *Southern California Quarterly 1984 66(3): 263-270.* Examines a neglected aspect of the career of Dr. Levi Cooper Lane, prominent California surgeon and medical benefactor. As examining surgeon for US Army recruits in California, Lane examined almost 1,500 men. At the end of the Civil War he filed a report, reprinted here, describing the region of his activity and the occupations, races, aptitude for service, and disabilities of the men he examined. The report provides a valuable record of the health conditions of male Californians in the Civil War period. 18 notes. 1861-65

Lane, Rose Wilder

3952. DeHamer, Nancy. DAKOTA RESOURCES: THE ROSE WILDER LANE PAPERS AT THE HERBERT HOOVER PRESIDENTIAL LIBRARY. *South Dakota History 1984 14(4): 335-346.* Discusses the life of Rose Wilder Lane (1886-1968) and the collection of her papers that is housed in the Herbert Hoover Presidential Library in West Branch, Iowa. Lane, the daughter of Laura Ingalls Wilder, was an author, journalist, traveler, and libertarian. The papers contain 30 linear feet of correspondence, notes, diaries, photographs, and sound recordings. Photo. 1900's-68

Lane, Russell Adrian

3953. Mickey, Rosie Cheatham. "Russell Adrian Lane: Biography of an Urban Negro School Administrator." U. of Akron 1983. 288 pp. *DAI 1983 44(3): 633-A.* DA8315524 1920's-60's

Lane, Samuel

3954. Slagle, A. Russell. MAJOR SAMUEL LANE (1628-81): HIS ANCESTRY AND SOME AMERICAN DESCENDANTS. *Maryland Hist. Mag. 1976 71(4): 548-561.* Analyzes the genealogy of Samuel Lane of Anne Arundel County, Maryland. Stresses the life of Samuel Lane's father, Richard Lane (1596-1657) of Hereford, England, a prominent West Indian merchant and planter who brought his children to the Isle of Providence in 1635. Shows that the English clergyman Samuel Lane and the Maryland commander and justice of Anne Arundel County were the same person. Also sheds new light on the Boston Saltonstalls. Primary and secondary sources; illus., genealogical chart, 86 notes. 1469-1681

Lanergan, James and Caroline

3955. Smith, Mary Elizabeth. THE LANERGANS IN PERFORMANCE. *Theatre Survey 1984 25(2): 211-223.* Reviews the careers of James and Caroline Lanergan, who were members of a theater company that toured the United States during the 1850's-70's, and who are credited with introducing the American Midwest to theater in 1863-64. 1850's-70's

Lanfersiek, Walter

3956. Haines, Randall A. WALTER LANFERSIEK: SOCIALIST FROM CINCINNATI. *Cincinnati Hist. Soc. Bull. 1982 40(2): 124-144.* Biography of Walter Lanfersiek (1873-1962), later known as Walter B. Landell, who served as national executive secretary of the Socialist Party of America from 1913 to 1916; he was active in the labor and peace movements, particularly prior to World War I. 1895-1962

Lang, Alfred Paul

3957. Lang, Sidney E. A BOY AT SEA. *US Naval Inst. Pro. 1981 107(7): 51-53.* Alfred Paul Lang, the author's father, at age 14 enlisted in the US Navy as a third-class boy on 6 February 1882. He shipped out for the Far East and for three years served on a succession of US warships in that area, until he was ordered home on the USS *Enterprise.* There was a good deal of homosexuality on board that vessel and when it reached Melbourne, Australia, Lang deserted. He worked his way to England, and, finally, to the United States. He and his family kept his desertion secret from the authorities. But when war with Spain broke out in 1898, Lang turned himself in, was permitted to enlist, and won a commission. In 1903 he was given a presidential pardon by Theodore Roosevelt. 2 photos. 1882-1903

Langdon, John

3958. Cleary, Barbara Ann. THE GOVERNOR JOHN LANGDON MANSION MEMORIAL: NEW PERSPECTIVES IN INTERPRETATION. *Old-Time New England 1978 69(1-2): 22-36.* Provides a brief biography of John Langdon (1741-1819), wealthy colonial political leader, and discusses the architectural style and building plans of his home in Portsmouth, New Hampshire, built in 1783-85, by Daniel Hart and Michael Whidden, III, in a combination of Langdon's personal style and that of the Colonial Revival era. 1783-85

Langdon, John (family)

3959. Camden, Thomas E. THE LANGDON-ELWYN FAMILY PAPERS. *Hist. New Hampshire 1981 36(4): 350-356.* The Langdon-Elwyn Family Papers, on deposit with the New Hampshire Historical Society since 1979, span the years 1762-1972. Much of the collection deals with the career of John Langdon, who played a major role in the revolutionary history of New Hampshire and the nation. Among other offices, he served as governor of New Hampshire and US senator. He was also a merchant-shipbuilder in Portsmouth. 3 notes. 1762-1972

Lange, Dorothea

3960. Ohrn, Karin Becker. "A Nobler Thing: Dorothea Lange's Life in Photography." Indiana U. 1977. 404 pp. *DAI 1978 38(8): 4431-4432-A.* 1914-65

Langer, Elinor

3961. —. [WOMEN IN THE LEFT]. *Feminist Studies 1979 5(3): 432-461.*

Trimberger, Ellen Kay. WOMEN IN THE OLD AND NEW LEFT: THE EVOLUTION OF A POLITICS OF PERSONAL LIFE, *pp. 432-450.*

Dennis, Peggy. A RESPONSE TO ELLEN KAY TRIMBERGER'S ESSAY, "WOMEN IN THE OLD AND NEW LEFT," *pp. 451-461.* 1925-78

For abstract see ***Dennis, Peggy***

Langer, William L.

3962. Wolff, Robert Lee. WILLIAM LEONARD LANGER. *Massachusetts Hist. Soc. Pro. 1977 89: 187-195.* A memoir of William Leonard Langer (1896-1977), Harvard University historian. Trained at Harvard, Langer specialized in the diplomatic history of Europen in the 19th and 20th centuries. During World War II, Langer headed the Research and Analysis Branch of the Office of Strategic Services; after the war, he helped to establish the Office of National Estimates of the Central Intelligence Agency. After 1952, Langer returned to teaching and writing at Harvard, and pursued new fields of inquiry, including the use of depth psychology as a tool for historians. Based on Langer's autobiography, *In and Out of the Ivory Tower* (1977), and the author's long friendship with Langer; index. 1927-77

Langford, Sam ("Boston Tarbaby")

3963. Young, Alexander. "THE BOSTON TARBABY." *Nova Scotia Hist. Q. [Canada] 1974 4(3): 277-298.* Sam Langford (1886-1956) fought in all weight classes from featherweight to heavyweight. Born in Nova Scotia, he left the Province and became famous as the "Boston Tarbaby." Explores his influence on racial equality and boxing. 101 notes, biblio. 1886-1956

Langley, Samuel Pierpont

3964. Beardsley, Wallace Rundell. "Samuel Pierpont Langley: His Early Academic Years at the Western University of Pennsylvania." U. of Pittsburgh 1978. 173 pp. *DAI 1979 40(2): 690-A.* 1867-75

Langmuir, Irving

3965. Reich, Leonard S. IRVING LANGMUIR AND THE PURSUIT OF SCIENCE AND TECHNOLOGY IN THE CORPORATE ENVIRONMENT. *Technology and Culture 1983 24(2): 199-221.* Langmuir's brilliant career illustrates the emergence in the early 20th century of a new breed of highly educated industrial researchers who behaved neither as pure scientist nor as practicing engineers. During 1910-25, Langmuir carried out research at the General Electric Research Laboratory, where the development of theory and the pursuit of industrial applications were often indistinguishable. Such was the case with Langmuir's work on a ductile tungsten filament in vacuum, which led him first to the general study of electrical discharge in gases and vacuum, and only then to the technical solution of the lamp-blackening problem. Ignoring the new science of quantum mechanics, Langmuir studied those structures of science that promised technological results. Based on the Langmuir Papers; 79 notes. 1900-25

Langston, John Mercer

3966. Bromberg, Alan B. JOHN MERCER LANGSTON: BLACK CONGRESSMAN FROM THE OLD DOMINION. *Virginia Cavalcade 1980 30(2): 60-67.* Surveys the career of John Mercer Langston (1829-97), lawyer, Republican politician, educator, diplomat, orator, and crusader for civil rights—and still the only black to represent Virginia in Congress (in the House of Representatives for five months in 1890-91). 1849-97

Langtry, Lillie

3967. Herr, Pamela. LILLIE ON THE FRONTIER: WESTERN ADVENTURES OF A FAMOUS BEAUTY. *Am. West 1981 18(2): 40-45.* Bewitching Lillie Langtry (b. 1853) dazzled Victorian England. She was a mistress of the Prince of Wales for a few years. Turning to the stage for a career, she earned success and notoriety in Great Britain and the United States. She became the highest-paid performer in American theatrical history, took out American citizenship, lived on a California ranch, made several western tours, and again took up residence in England. Among many others, Judge Roy Bean, self-styled "law west of the Pecos," was smitten with her beauty (from a magazine picture). In 1884, he changed the name of Vinegarroon, Texas, to Langtry, but he died several months before she honored the town with a visit in 1904. 5 illus., biblio. ca 1880-1904

Lanier, Sidney

3968. McGinty, Brian. A SHINING PRESENCE: REBEL POET SIDNEY LANIER GOES TO WAR. *Civil War Times Illus. 1980 19(2): 24-31.* A thin and bookish Georgian, Sidney Lanier (1842-81) served in the Confederate Army, mainly in Virginia, until his capture and incarceration in the "hell-hole" prison at Point Lookout, Maryland—experiences reflected in his postwar novels and poetry. 1861-65

Lankershim, Isaac

3969. Kramer, William M. and Stern, Norton B. ISAAC LANKERSHIM OF THE SAN FERNANDO VALLEY: JEWISH-BORN BAPTIST. *Southern California Quarterly 1985 67(1): 25-33.* Born in Bavaria, Isaac Lankershim came to the United States in 1836 and settled in St. Louis. In 1842, he married Annis Moore and converted from Judaism to the Baptist faith, though retaining his Jewish family ties. Attracted to California during the gold rush era, Lankershim became a successful wheat grower and sheep raiser. In 1869, he and other investors purchased 60,000 acres in the San Fernando Valley, forming the San Fernando Sheep Company and later the Los Angeles Farming and Milling Company. At his death in 1882, Lankershim was eulogized for his pioneering efforts in promoting agricultural development and his reputation for integrity in business. Based on newspapers and secondary works; 2 photos, 42 notes. 1836-82

3970. Kramer, William M. and Stern, Norton B. ISAAC LANKERSHIM OF THE SAN FERNANDO VALLEY: JEWISH-BORN BAPTIST. *Western States Jewish History 1985 18(1): 67-75.* Isaac Lankershim, a Jewish convert to Baptism, pioneered in the agricultural development of the San Fernando Valley, contributed heavily to Baptist causes, and remained friendly with San Francisco Jews. His daughter married Isaac N. Van Nuys. Based on newspapers and other sources; 42 notes. 1840's-82

Lankes, Julius John

3971. Taylor, Welford Dunaway. JULIUS JOHN LANKES: VIRGINIA WOODCUT ARTIST. *Virginia Cavalcade 1976 26(1): 4-19.* Discusses Julius John Lankes (1908-58), a Virginia artist, began work in woodcuts when a wind storm blew down some of the trees in his father's apple orchard; discusses the woodcuts used as illustrations and Lankes's books of renderings. 1908-58

Lansburgh, Gustave Albert

3972. Stern, Norton B. and Kramer, William M. G. ALBERT LANSBURGH, SAN FRANCISCO'S JEWISH ARCHITECT FROM PANAMA. *Western States Jewish Hist. Q. 1981 13(3): 210-224.* Gustave Albert Lansburgh (1876-1969), born in Panama, where his father had a ship chandlery, was brought to San Francisco by his widowed mother in 1882. Young Lansburgh had architectural training at the University of California, Berkeley, and later at the École des Beaux Arts in Paris. His career is noted for theater and auditorium design, particularly for the Orpheum chain. He blended Beaux Arts tradition with the new technology to produce a strictly American form of architecture. Based on interviews with the subject, and published works; 7 photos, 38 notes. 1906-69

Lansbury, Angela

3973. Gruen, John. CLASSIC ANGELA LANSBURY. *Horizon 1979 22(4): 20-24.* A biography of stage actress Angela Lansbury, 1940-79. 1940-79

Lansky, Meyer

3974. Fried, Albert. THE SAGA OF MEYER LANSKY: JUST ANOTHER RETIRED SENIOR CITIZEN. *Present Tense 1980 7(3): 32-35.* Reviews the professional life of Meyer Lansky, a gangster who is the product of New York City's Lower East Side and who worked his way up to the top of his field. 1911-80

Lapham, Increase A.

3975. Edmonds, Michael. INCREASE A. LAPHAM AND THE MAPPING OF WISCONSIN. *Wisconsin Magazine of History 1985 68(3): 163-187.* Increase A. Lapham was a pivotal figure in both geographical and geological mapmaking in Wisconsin. The pamphlet that Lapham wrote to accompany his third and most detailed reference map in 1867 was translated into six languages, sold 90,000 copies, and attracted countless numbers of immigrants to the state. He also conducted the first geographical surveys of the state and was instrumental in Wisconsin's inclusion in the large-scale mapmaking projects of the US Geological Survey. Based largely on Increase A. Lapham's papers, maps, and writings, and on newspapers; 76 notes, biblio. 1836-78

Larcom, Juno (family)

3976. Hill, Charles L. SLAVERY AND ITS AFTERMATH IN BEVERLY, MASSACHUSETTS: JUNO LARCOM AND HER FAMILY. *Essex Inst. Hist. Collections 1980 116(2): 111-130.* Examines the treatment of blacks in Beverly through the life experiences of Juno Larcom (d. 1816). Her life exemplified the history of race relations in the Commonwealth of Massachusetts. Primary sources; 65 notes. 1730's-1816

Larmer, Oscar

3977. Replogle, Renata. OSCAR LARMER, PAINTER AND WATERCOLORIST. *Kansas Q. 1982 14(4): 113-120.* Recounts the career of Kansas artist Oscar Larmer since 1950, and reproduces six of his major works. 1950-82

Larsen, Roy Edward

3978. Bentinck-Smith, William. ROY EDWARD LARSEN. *Massachusetts Hist. Soc. Pro. 1979 91: 228-231.* Memoir of Roy Edward Larsen (1899-1979), president of Time, Inc. during 1939-60. Educated at Harvard College (Class of 1921), Larsen was also publisher of *Life* magazine from 1936 to 1946, and was involved with several other *Time* publications. His many interests included education, hospitals, and nature conservation. 7 notes. ca 1921-79

Larson, Agnes, Henrietta, and Nora

3979. Jenson, Carol. THE LARSON SISTERS: THREE CAREERS IN CONTRAST. Stuhler, Barbara and Kreuter, Gretchen, ed. *Women of Minnesota: Selected Biographical Essays* (St. Paul: Minnesota Historical Society Press, 1977): 301-324. Agnes, Henrietta, and Nora Larson grew up in Minnesota. Daughters of a successful farmer-businessman and a gentle mother, they were raised in an environment of Norwegian American traditions and the Lutheran Church. They all attended St. Olaf College in Northfield, pursued graduate studies, and became teachers. Agnes Larson became a historian, taught at St. Olaf, and wrote the meticulously researched and well-written monograph, *History of the White Pine Industry in Minnesota.* Henrietta Larson became a prominent pioneer in business history. She taught at colleges and universities. She became a noted editor and writer while working as a research associate at Harvard, where she became the first woman named as an associate professor by the business school despite that university's tradition of sex discrimination. Nora Larson became a bacteriologist. She did research at the Mayo Foundation, the Lakey Clinic, and the Takamine Laboratories before finally settling back in Minnesota in 1950, where she became the only woman among the principal scientists at the University of Minnesota's Hormel Institute. She studied swine diseases and was active in professional and community organizations. In 1960, Nora joined the faculty of St. Olaf where she taught until her retirement in 1972. Primary sources; 3 photos, 50 notes. 1883-1972

Larson, Lars

3980. Canuteson, Richard L. LARS AND MARTHA LARSON: "WE DO WHAT WE CAN FOR THEM." *Norwegian-American Studies 1972 25: 142-166.* Discusses the early life of Lars Larson. In 1807, as part of a commercial venture on board a ship bound to sell lumber, Larson was seized by the British (with whom Norway-Denmark was at war) and imprisoned for seven years. During this time he converted to Quakerism and upon his 1814 return to Norway began teaching the tenets of that religion for which he was severely punished by the Norwegian government. In 1825, after continual denial of their religious freedom, a group of Norwegians immigrated to the United States. Most settled in Kendall Colony, New York, but Larson and his family moved to Rochester where they associated with the local Quaker church and, until Lars's death in 1844, operated a way station for Norwegian immigrants, often providing food and lodging for as many as 100 people at one time. 61 notes. 1807-44

Larson, Laurence M.

3981. Larson, Laurence M. MY MILWAUKEE YEARS. *Milwaukee Hist. 1980 3(1): 25-34.* Excerpt from the author's *The Log Book of a Young Immigrant* (Norwegian Am. Hist. Assoc., 1939), describing his teaching in Milwaukee public schools after he received his doctorate from the University of Wisconsin; 1902-07. 1902-07

Larsson, Evert A.

3982. Larsson, Evert A. LIDKÖPING TO LINDSBORG: REMINISCENCES, 1924-1929. *Swedish-American Hist. Q. 1982 33(2): 84-110, (3): 183-206.* Part 1. Reminiscences of Evert A. Larsson, an emigrant from Sweden to the United States in the 1920's, beginning with the crossing of the Atlantic as a third class passenger. Larsson discusses his preparation for the trip and comments on the attitudes of others in Sweden regarding immigration to America. Kansas, a settlement of earlier Swedish emigrants, was his destination, where he worked for his uncle as a farmhand to repay the cost of his journey. Part 2. Desirous of an education, Larsson later went to Lindsborg, Kansas, and worked for the railroad as a gandy dancer, or laborer, to earn money for college tuition. He learned to speak, read, and write English and then entered Bethany College as a pre-med student. He describes in detail life in that small Kansas community during 1924-29 and the struggle of an immigrant student. Based on primary sources; 9 photos. 1924-29

Laski, Harold J.

3983. Ekirch, Arthur A., Jr. HAROLD J. LASKI: THE AMERICAN EXPERIENCE. *Am. Studies Int. 1983 24(1): 53-68.* Examines the career and political influence of Harold J. Laski. His circle of friends became important to his career, and included Franklin D. Roosevelt, Felix Frankfurter, Roscoe Pound, and Oliver Wendell Holmes. Throughout his life Laski sought to advance his ideas of socialism and the predominance of local authority in various political circles in the United States, although by the late 1930's he embraced the idea of a stronger presidency. This stemmed in large part from his belief that businessmen and capitalism dominated American society. Based on Laski's writings and the Roosevelt, Frankfurter, Holmes, and Pound Papers; 37 notes, illus. 1900-50

3984. Ekirch, Arthur A., Jr. HAROLD J. LASKI: THE LIBERAL *MANQUÉ* OR LOST LIBERTARIAN? *J. of Libertarian Studies 1980 4(2): 139-150.* Between 1917 and 1925 the writings of Harold J. Laski provided intellectual support for what was essentially a radical libertarian point of view, but from 1925 until his death in 1950, increasingly concerned with the problem of achieving equality, he replaced his antistatist views with Marxist views. 1917-50

3985. Gorni, Yosef. THE JEWISHNESS AND ZIONISM OF HAROLD LASKI. *Midstream 1977 23(9): 72-77.* Follows Harold Laski's career during 1910-46 and concludes that, despite his early claims to the contrary, Laski was always a Zionist at heart and always felt himself a part of the Jewish nation, although he viewed traditional Jewish religion as restrictive. 1910-46

Lasky, Jesse L.

3986. Jaffe, Grace. FROM SAN JOSE TO HOLLYWOOD: THE RISE OF JESSE L. LASKY. *Western States Jewish Hist. Q. 1978 11(1): 20-24.* Jesse L. Lasky, vice-president of Paramount-Publix Corporation, started his career as a cornet player in San Francisco. He left the music business temporarily for newspaper reporting and gold mining in Alaska. On his return to San Francisco he performed in vaudeville. Later he formed a partnership with B. A. Rolfe to manage as many as 20 traveling vaudeville acts. Lasky met Cecil B. deMille and wrote several operettas with him, with great financial success. In 1912 Lasky opened a motion picture studio in Hollywood, a pioneer venture that eventually became Paramount enterprises. Reprinted from *Emanu-El,* San Francisco, 3 October 1930. 3 notes. 1890's-1930

3987. Lasky, Betty. LET'S MAKE A MOVIE. *Westways 1979 71(11): 22-25.* Discusses the beginnings of the Jesse L. Lasky Feature Play Company in Hollywood formed in 1914, with Lasky as president, Samuel Goldfish (later Goldwyn) as general manager, and Cecil B. De Mille as director-general, and the first movie the fledgling company made, *The Squaw Man,* Hollywood's first feature-length film, based on the play by Edwin Milton Royle; 1911-14. 1911-14

Lassen, Peter

3988. Scott, Franklin D. PETER LASSEN: DANISH PIONEER OF CALIFORNIA. *Southern California Q. 1981 63(2): 113-136.* A profile of Peter Lassen (1800-59), pioneer settler in northern California. Born in Denmark, Lassen became a blacksmith but found conditions in his homeland unsettled. He came to America in 1830, met John Sutter, and in 1840 arrived in California. He established California's northernmost rancho in the Mexican period and operated the first sawmill in the area. Following the Mexican War he led a wagon train to northern California along what became known as the Lassen Trail. Mount Lassen is named for him, as is Lassen Pass, and other landmarks. Travelers remembered his hospitality, but his desire to help people conflicted with his ambitions for economic success. In the 1850's he operated a ranch in the isolated northeastern corner of the state. He was killed by Indians in 1859 under mysterious circumstances. Photos, 39 notes. 1800-59

3989. Scott, Franklin D. PETER LASSEN: DANISH PIONEER OF CALIFORNIA, 1800-1859. Lovoll, Odd S., ed. *Makers of an American Immigrant Legacy: Essays in Honor of Kenneth O. Bjork* (Northfield, Minn.: Norwegian-American Hist. Assoc., 1980): 186-209. Danish blacksmith, Peter Lassen (1800-59) immigrated to Boston in 1830; he moved to California in 1839, living as a true frontiersman until killed by Indians in 1859. 1800-59

Lasswell, Harold Dwight

3990. McDougal, Myres S. and Reisman, W. Michael. HAROLD DWIGHT LASSWELL (1902-1978). *Am. J. of Int. Law 1979 73(4): 655-660.* Harold Dwight Lasswell virtually invented analysis of propaganda. Two of his important books were *Propaganda Techniques in the World War* (1927) and *Psychopathology and Politics* (1930). He regarded *World Politics and Personal Insecurity* (1935) as his greatest book. He viewed law as a process of decision by which members of a community clarified and secured their common interests. His preeminent search was for the content of purpose. His construct of a public order of human dignity represented his hope. His fear came out in his construct of a garrison state. 1902-78

3991. Merelman, Richard M. HAROLD D. LASWELL'S POLITICAL WORLD: WEAK TEA FOR HARD TIMES. *British J. of Pol. Sci. [Great Britain] 1981 11(4): 471-497.* Assesses the contribution of Harold D. Laswell in the 1960's to democratic political theory in the United States. 1960-69

Lathrop, John, Jr.

3992. Leary, Lewis. JOHN LATHROP, JR.: THE QUIET POET OF FEDERALIST BOSTON. *Pro. of the Am. Antiquarian Soc. 1981 91(1): 39-89.* Lathrop entered Harvard, class of 1789, and turned poet in his undergraduate years. His poetry reflected his imitative abilities, his strong patriotism and suspicion of authority, and a conviction that God would lead people toward happiness and universal peace. To support his poetic efforts, Lathrop became a lawyer. He found time, however, to edit literary magazines and write numerous poems. In 1800 he left New England for India, in search of wealth. He found little, and returned to Boston in 1809. There he resumed his career as an author of poems and essays, until his death in 1820. Based on Lathrop's writings, as published in the newspapers and magazines of his day. 1789-1820

Lathrop, Julia

3993. Parker, Jacqueline K. and Carpenter, Edward M. JULIA LATHROP AND THE CHILDREN'S BUREAU: THE EMERGENCE OF AN INSTITUTION. *Social Service Rev. 1981 55(1): 60-77.* Discusses how Julia Lathrop, the first woman bureau chief in the federal government and chief of the Children's Bureau established in 1909, defined its mission, selected operating goals from its statutory functions, and utilized a potent constituency network. 1909-21

Latimer, George W.

3994. Davis, Asa J. THE TWO AUTOBIOGRAPHICAL FRAGMENTS OF GEORGE W. LATIMER (1820-1896): A PRELIMINARY ASSESSMENT. *J. of the Afro-American Hist. and Geneal. Soc. 1980 (1): 3-18.* Presents two short autobiographical statements made by George W. Latimer (1820-96), one in 1842 and the other in 1893, in order to add to the brief information about this slave who escaped with his wife from his owner, James B. Gray, in Norfolk, Virginia, in 1842 and fled to Boston, where he was captured within a few weeks in an incident that led to his supporters' call for a "war on slavery." 1820-96

3995. Wiecek, William M. LATIMER: LAWYERS, ABOLITIONISTS, AND THE PROBLEM OF UNJUST LAWS. Perry, Lewis and Fellman, Michael, ed. *Antislavery Reconsidered: New Perspectives on the Abolitionists* (Baton Rouge: Louisiana State U. Pr., 1979): 219-237. In 1842 George Latimer, a fugitive slave, was detained in Boston to be returned to his master under the terms of the Fugitive Slave Act. An abolitionist lawyer, Samuel E. Sewall, attempted on various legal grounds to win Latimer's freedom from the court of the Chief Justice of Massachusetts, Lemuel Shaw, but the latter, while declaring antislavery sentiments, denied the release of Latimer, asserting that he, Shaw, was bound by oath to apply the laws as they existed regardless of his personal views. Eventually Latimer's freedom was purchased from his master, but the case exemplified the dilemma of both the private citizen and the official when confronted with the existence of morally repugnant laws. *Billy Budd, Sailor* (1891) by Herman Melville, whose father-in-law was Lemuel Shaw, reflects, in great part, a concern with precisely the same dilemma in a powerful literary parable. 39 notes. ca 1790-1890

Latrobe, Benjamin Henry

3996. Formwalt, Lee W. BENJAMIN HENRY LATROBE AND THE REVIVAL OF THE GALLATIN PLAN OF 1808. *Pennsylvania Hist. 1981 48(2): 99-128.* Benjamin Henry Latrobe, an architect and civil engineer, was a major contributor to Treasury Secretary Albert Gallatin's plan for a national network of internal improvements. When the initial Gallatin plan was not passed by Congress in 1808, Latrobe redrafted the proposal and led an unsuccessful effort in 1809-10 to persuade Congress to embrace national planning and internal improvements. Latrobe's interest in internal improvements grew out of his European experiences, his training as an engineer, and his involvement in the Chesapeake and Delaware Canal. Based on the Latrobe Papers and other primary materials; map, 74 notes. 1808-10

3997. Formwalt, Lee W. "Benjamin Henry Latrobe and the Development of Internal Improvements in the New Republic 1796-1820." Catholic U. of Am. 1977. 330 pp. *DAI 1978 38(7): 4323-4324-A.* 1796-1820

3998. Stapleton, Darwin H. and Carter, Edward C., II. "I HAVE THE ITCH OF BOTANY, OF CHEMISTRY, OF MATHEMATICS... STRONG UPON ME": THE SCIENCE OF BENJAMIN HENRY LATROBE. *Pro. of the Am. Phil. Soc. 1984 128(3): 173-192.* The papers of the versatile American scientist Benjamin Henry Latrobe reveal a wide range of ways in which he drew on science for intellectual challenge, professional activities, and leisure. There are few Americans in his time who could match his scientific education and breadth of reading. It was only at the meetings of the American Philosophical Society that he regularly met his peers. Yet Latrobe was an amateur in science and his interests seldom ran deep, except in periods of enthusiasm. He represents the heights of an era when intellectual gentlemen formed the elite of American science. Based largely on the published works of Latrobe; 5 fig., 90 notes. 1795-1820

3999. Stapleton, Darwin H. and Guider, Thomas C. THE TRANSFER AND DIFFUSION OF BRITISH TECHNOLOGY: BENJAMIN HENRY LATROBE AND THE CHESAPEAKE AND DELAWARE CANAL. *Delaware Hist. 1976 17(2): 127-138.* Describes the work of Benjamin Henry Latrobe during 1790-1830 in surveying and constructing the early stages of the Chesapeake and Delaware Canal, particularly the feeder to the canal. Latrobe was unable to complete the project because the sponsoring company lacked financial resources, but his work did lay the base for further canal construction. The experience of the Chesapeake and Delaware Canal illustrates the successful transfer of British technology to America, which had the requisite supporting skills to receive it. Based on the Latrobe Papers; 2 illus., 63 notes. 1790-1830

Latta, George Clinton

4000. Sullivan, Joan. GEORGE CLINTON LATTA: MERCHANT AT THE PORT OF CHARLOTTE. *Rochester History 1983 45(3-4): 3-24.* George Clinton Latta, frontier entrepreneur and "agent of everybody" at the port of Charlotte on Lake Ontario and the Genesee River in what is now part of Rochester, New York, helped develop transportation, agriculture and mercantile enterprises through calculated risk-taking and close association with the agents of power in the area. 1821-71

Lauck, Gary

4001. —. NAZI PARTY OVERSEAS: GARY LAUCK AND HIS PROPAGANDA. *Patterns of Prejudice [Great Britain] 1979 13(5): 19-21.* Discusses the political theory and career of German-American Gary Lauck, who has gained some support among neo-Nazi youth especially in West Germany during the 1970's. 1970's

Laughlin, Harry Hamilton

4002. Bird, Randall D. and Allen, Garland. THE J. H. B. ARCHIVE REPORT, THE PAPERS OF HARRY HAMILTON LAUGHLIN, EUGENICIST. *J. of the Hist. of Biology [Netherlands] 1981 14(2): 339-353.* Laughlin, superintendent of the Eugenics Record Office, was a close associate of Charles B. Davenport, the "American Galton." Laughlin's papers are in the Northeast Missouri State University Library at Kirksville. His archives reveal a dedicated bureaucrat in the frightful utopian cause of eugenics. 27 notes. 1880-1943

Laurence, Margaret

4003. Hughes, Terrance Ryan. "Gabrielle Roy et Margaret Laurence: Deux Chemins, Une Recherche" [Gabrielle Roy and Margaret Laurence: Two Paths, One Quest]. McGill U. [Canada] 1980. *DAI 1980 41(3): 1051-A.* 1945-80

Laurendeau, André

4004. Monière, Denis. ANDRE LAURENDEAU, RETOUR D'EUROPE [André Laurendeau, back from Europe]. *Action Natl. [Canada] 1983 73(4): 295-313.* André Laurendeau spent several years in London and Paris and found on his return to Canada a Quebec stifled by tradition and conservatism; as director of *L'Action Nationale,* he was involved in establishing a better understanding between French Canadians and English Canadians. 1937-62

Laurens, Henry

4005. Youell, Lillian Belk. HENRY LAURENS: THE NEGLECTED NEGOTIATOR. *Daughters of the Am. Revolution Mag. 1983 117(7): 708-711.* Chronicles the career of diplomat and legislator Henry Laurens of South Carolina, whose role in the peace negotiations with Great Britain after the American Revolution has been largely forgotten. 1757-92

Laurie, Annie

4006. Schofler, Patricia. FOR NEWSPAPERWOMAN ANNIE LAURIE LIFE WAS "A GLORIOUS ADVENTURE... " *Am. Hist. Illus. 1981 15(10): 28-35.* Newspaperwoman Annie Laurie, née Winifred Sweet, began her 46-year career as a reporter and syndicated columnist in 1889 at the *San Francisco Examiner,* admired for getting stories where others failed, she continued writing until three months before her death in 1936. 1889-1936

Laurier, Wilfrid

4007. Walsh, Robert James Patrick. " 'Silver-tongued' Laurier and the Imperialists, 1896-1906: A Character Study in Imperial History." U. of South Carolina 1979. 324 pp. *DAI 1980 41(3): 1177-1178-A.* 8020319 1896-1906

Lauri-Volpi, Giacomo

4008. Drake, James A. ECCO! IL LEONE! GIACOMO LAURI-VOLPI AND THE METROPOLITAN OPERA, 1922-32. *Italian Americana 1981 7(1): 45-64.* Describes the career of Italian tenor Giacomo Lauri-Volpi with the New York Metropolitan Opera. 1922-32

LaVache family

4009. White, Stephen A. THE LAVACHE FAMILY OF ARICHAT, CAPE BRETON. *Nova Scotia Hist. Q. [Canada] 1977 7(1): 69-85.* Gives a genealogy of the LaVache family beginning in 1774. Traces the name changes from LaVache, Lavache, to Lavash. Primary and secondary sources; 9 notes. 1774-20c

Laval, Claude C.

4010. Street, Richard Steven. "POP" LAVAL: SAN JOAQUIN VALLEY PHOTOGRAPHER. *California History 1981 60(3): 244-261.* A profile of Claude C. "Pop" Laval (1882-1966), who for over half a century was a successful commercial photographer in the San Joaquin Valley of California. Born in Pittsburgh, Pennsylvania, Laval moved to Fresno in 1911 and began his photography studio in a cow barn. For the next 50 years he photographed the agricultural development of the San Joaquin Valley, as well as the ordinary and extraordinary events of life, from fires and funerals to athletic events. He was an early practitioner of aerial photography and an experimenter with color processing. Although many negatives were ruined in a 1964 fire, over 100,000 survive, providing a nearly definitive pictorial record of San Joaquin Valley history. 12 photos, 37 notes. 1911-61

Lawe, John

4011. Kay, Jeanne. JOHN LAWE, GREEN BAY TRADER. *Wisconsin Mag. of Hist. 1980 64(1): 2-27.* John Lawe, a Jewish fur trader who operated out of Green Bay and who attained the status of bourgeois, never achieved the success of many of his associates such as Ramsay Crooks and Robert Stuart of the American Fur Company. Lawe's experience, first as a clerk for Jacob Franks, then as a trader for the American Fur Company, and finally as a land owner and speculator, never led to great wealth on the Wisconsin frontier. 15 illus., 120 notes. 1790-1846

Lawler, Vanett

4012. Izdebski, Christy Isabel. "Vanett Lawler (1902-1972): Her Life and Contributions to Music Education." Catholic U. of Am. 1983. 253 pp. *DAI 1983 44(1): 100-A.* DA8311160 1930-72

Lawrence, Daniel

4013. Bradley, A. Day. DANIEL LAWRENCE, QUAKER PRINTER OF BURLINGTON, PHILADELPHIA, AND STANFORD, N.Y. *Quaker Hist. 1976 65(2): 100-108.* Quaker membership records show Daniel Lawrence's seven moves, 1790-1806. Locates in 9 libraries 45 titles (7 in Charles Evans' *American bibliography* only) printed by Lawrence in 1790-93, 1802-05, and 1810, and one printed from him (N.Y.: 1795). 10 notes. 1788-1812

Lawrence, David L.

4014. Weber, Michael P.; Trimble, William F., interviewer. AN INTERVIEW WITH MICHAEL P. WEBER ON DAVID L. LAWRENCE. *Western Pennsylvania Historical Magazine 1985 68(4): 306-332.* Historian Michael Weber discusses his work-in-progress, a biography of former Pennsylvania governor David L. Lawrence. 1920-66

Lawrence, Henry C.

4015. McCormick, Gene E. HENRY C. LAWRENCE, 1820-1862: MENTOR OF ELI LILLY. *Pharmacy in Hist. 1974 16(3): 89-96.* Discusses the contribution of druggist Henry C. Lawrence to the development of pharmacy in Lafayette, Indiana, from 1843-62, emphasizing his influence on Eli Lilly. 1843-62

Lawrie, Lee O.

4016. Garvey, Timothy Joseph. "Lee O. Lawrie: Classicism and American Culture, 1919-1954." U. of Minnesota 1980. 399 pp. *DAI 1981 41(7): 2805-2806-A.* 8102091 1919-54

Lawson, Alfred William

4017. Jonas, Peter. ALFRED WILLIAM LAWSON: AVIATOR, INVENTOR, AND DEPRESSION RADICAL. *Old Northwest 1983 9(2): 157-173.* Describes the career of Alfred William Lawson—aviator, editor, author, and radical thinker. Lawson's early career as an editor and airplane manufacturer was successful until the failure of his multidecked Midnight Liner in 1921. Thereafter, Lawson created his own radical economic, educational, and religious ideology to help explain his failure and his conspiracy theory of history. Primary sources; 62 notes. 1908-52

Lawson, Clorine Jones

4018. Ludden, Keith J. "IF IT'S ON THE RADIO, WHY BOTHER": A STUDY OF TWO SOUTH-EAST BARREN COUNTY BALLAD SINGERS. *Kentucky Folklore Record 1978 24(2): 54-60.* Discusses the balladry and lives (ca. 1930-77) of Clorine Jones Lawson and Gladys Jones Pace. ca 1930-77

Lawson, John Howard

4019. Gardner, Robert Merritt. "International Rag: The Theatrical Career of John Howard Lawson." U. of California, Berkeley 1977. 507 pp. *DAI 1979 39(9): 5211-A.* 1920's-30's

Lawson, Thomas

4020. Gillett, Mary C. THOMAS LAWSON, SECOND SURGEON GENERAL OF THE U. S. ARMY: A CHARACTER SKETCH. *Prologue 1982 14(1): 15-24.* Thomas Lawson, surgeon general during 1836-61, was a soldier who rose to his position through the seniority system. Though Lawson lacked a medical education and a professional degree, he was responsible for a highly educated staff of surgeons. Lawson's unimaginative leadership is thought to have contributed to the Medical Department's inability to adequately deal with the heavy casualties during the early stages of the Civil War. After 1862, the army set aside its policy of promotion by seniority and thus paved the way for the selection of a competent surgeon general. Based on Record Group 112, National Archives and correspondence; illus., 2 photos, 57 notes. 1836-61

Lawther, Anna B.

4021. Fuller, Steven J. and Mellecker, Alsatia. BEHIND THE YELLOW BANNER: ANNA B. LAWTHER AND THE WINNING OF SUFFRAGE FOR IOWA WOMEN. *Palimpsest 1984 65(3): 106-116.* Describes the political struggle for woman suffrage in Iowa, focusing on the role of activist Anna B. Lawther, president of the Iowa Equal Suffrage Association. 1916-18

Lawther, Ethel Loroline Martus

4022. Watson, Jan Carole. "Ethel Loroline Martus Lawther: Her Contributions to Physical Education." U. of North Carolina, Greensboro 1980. 327 pp. *DAI 1980 41(4): 1477-A.* 8021788 ca 1940-79

Laycock, Sadie

4023. Selders, Mary Laycock and Milspaw, Yvonne J. GRANDMOTHER'S FLOWER GARDEN: THE QUILTS OF SADIE IDA CHRISTIAN LAYCOCK. *Pennsylvania Folklife 1985 35(1): 2-12.* Recounts the life of Sadie Laycock, who lived the simple life of a farming wife in rural Columbia County, Pennsylvania, and describes some of the quilts she stitched as her primary hobby. 1930-58

Lea, Homer

4024. Brill, Heinz. VERGESSENE WELTPOLITISCHE EINSICHTEN VON HOMER LEA [Forgotten insights into world politics by Homer Lea]. *Zeits. für Pol. [West Germany] 1981 28(2): 196-199.* Introduces the writings and topics of concern of Homer Lea, one of the founders of American geopolitics, and discusses the relevance of his insights for the present time. 1876-1981

Leach, Andrew Martin

4025. McDonald, Philip M. and Lahore, Lona F. LUMBERING IN THE NORTHERN SIERRA NEVADA: ANDREW MARTIN LEACH OF CHALLENGE MILLS. *Pacific Hist. 1984 28(2): 18-31.* Examines lumbering in the Sierra Nevada during the second half of the 19th century, and, in particular, the lumbering empire of Andrew Martin Leach in Yuba County, California. Leach operated continuously during 1879-94, which was much longer than most of his earlier competitors with operations of similar size. Never lacking with plans, Leach dramatically boosted production rates of timber, especially at Challenge Mill. To be competitive in the San Francisco Bay area, a flume was constructed in 1877-78. A series of disasters in the late 1880's and early 1890's plus the depression of 1893 ultimately ended his lumbering operations in 1894. Based on documents in the Yuba County Library, Marysville, California, and the Pacific Southwest Forest and Range Experiment Station, Redding, California, and personal interviews; 7 photos, plate, map, 27 notes. 1870-94

Leach, Ichabod (family)

4026. MacIntyre, Duncan M. THE CHILDREN OF ICHABOD (1745-1807) AND PENELOPE (STANDISH) (COBB) LEACH (1741?-1807). *New England Hist. and Geneal. Register 1977 131: 195-199.* Provides life histories of the children of Ichabod and Penelope Leach of Bridgewater, Massachusetts. Gives particular attention to sons Ephraim and Backus, and daughter Huldah, who settled near Eaton, New York. Based on vital records, probate documents and other primary sources; 44 notes. 1770-1880

Leake, Chauncey D.

4027. Brieger, Gert H. OBITUARY OF CHAUNCEY D. LEAKE (1896-1978). *Bull. of the Hist. of Medicine 1978 52(1): 121-123.* Chauncey D. Leake was a pharmacologist, trained at the University of Wisconsin, who developed an interest in medical history. He taught at the University of California, and at the University of Texas Medical Branch at Galveston. Many of his writings were historical. He wrote an autobiographical account in volume 16 of *The Annual Review of Pharmacology and Toxicology* (1976). He had been president of the American Association for the Advancement of Science, the American Association for the History of Medicine, and the History of Science Society. 1896-1978

Leaphart, C. W. ("Bill")

4028. Leaphart, Susan, ed. WHEELMEN IN YELLOWSTONE, 1905. *Montana 1981 31(4): 46-53.* C. W. "Bill" Leaphart, "Skinny" Simpson, Earl "The Kid" Cramer, and "Doc" Hines, recent college graduates, bicycled through Yellowstone National Park during July and August of 1905. The article publishes a portion of the diary Leaphart kept during the trip, which began and ended at Cody, Wyoming. The diary discusses problems bicycling, weather, food, and the natural wonders of Yellowstone Park. A brief biography of Leaphart concludes the article. 2 illus., map, 3 notes. 1905

Lease, Mary Elizabeth

4029. Blumberg, Dorothy Rose. MARY ELIZABETH LEASE, POPULIST ORATOR: A PROFILE. *Kansas Hist. 1978 1(1): 1-15.* Mary Elizabeth Lease (1850-1933), long identified as a principal spokesman for Kansas Populism, emerges as a determined champion of many causes. Seldom a political theorist, Mrs. Lease was an effective political advocate. Her speeches and writings articulated the plight of farmers, urban workers, and women struggling for rights in a world run by men. Primary and secondary sources; illus., 61 notes. 1871-1933

Leavell, Roland Q.

4030. Bowman, Mary D. Leavell. "Roland Q. Leavell: A Biography." Louisiana State U. 1983. 278 pp. *DAI 1984 44(9): 2851-A.* DA8400108 20c

Leavitt, Henry Levi

4031. —. A HOQUIAM, WASHINGTON SAGA: A PICTURE STORY. *Western States Jewish Hist. Q. 1981 13(2): 115-120.* Henry Levi Leavitt (1868-1939) established a general store in Hoquiam, Washington, a major lumber port at the turn of the century. He and his family were active in community service organizations and helped found the Aberdeen, Washington, Temple Beth Israel. Based on material and information provided by Melbourne L. Leavitt; 7 photos, 4 notes. ca 1895-1939

LeBlanc, Albini

4032. Joncas, Paul. MGR. ALBINI LEBLANC, DEUXIEME EVEQUE DE GASPE (1946-1957) [Mgr. Albini LeBlanc, 2d bishop of Gaspé, 1946-57]. *Sessions d'Etude: Soc. Can. d'Hist. de l'Église Catholique [Canada] 1979 46: 107-117.* 1946-57

Lebo, Thomas Coverly

4033. Gale, Jack C. LEBO IN PURSUIT. *J. of Arizona Hist. 1980 21(1): 11-24.* Summarizes the military career of Army Captain Thomas Coverly Lebo of the US 10th Cavalry, with emphasis on his pursuit of Apache leader Geronimo across Arizona and into Mexico in 1886. Recounts the skirmish immortalized by Frederic Remington's "The Rescue of Corporal Scott." 2 illus., map, 24 notes. 1861-1910

LeConte, Joseph

4034. Stephens, Lester D. JOSEPH LECONTE AND THE DEVELOPMENT OF THE PHYSIOLOGY AND PSYCHOLOGY OF VISION IN THE UNITED STATES. *Ann. of Sci. [Great Britain] 1980 37(3): 303-321.* The 19th-century American scientist, philosopher and teacher Joseph Le Conte (1823-1901) is well-known for his writings on geology and the reconciliation of evolutionary theory and religion, but he has not been properly recognized for his contributions to the physiology and psychology of vision. This study explores and assesses his work in the latter field, showing the nature of his original investigations into human vision and the influence of his book *Sight: an exposition of the principles of monocular and binocular vision,* which served as the major textbook on the subject in the United States from its publication in 1881 until after the turn of the century. Grounded in neo-Lamarckian evolutionary theory, Le Conte's publications on vision had a stronger impact upon subsequent studies of the phenomenon of human sight. 50 notes. 1881-1900

LeConte, Lancaster

4035. Stephens, Lester D. A FORMER SLAVE AND THE GEORGIA CONVICT LEASE SYSTEM. *Negro Hist. Bull. 1976 39(1): 505-507.* Lancaster LeConte (1812-1889), a 75-year-old former slave, was convicted of receiving stolen goods in 1887 and leased to the Dale Coal Company of Georgia for three years, where he faced inadequate rations and 12-hour days in a cold, damp mine. LeConte's pathetic letter to his former owner, Joseph LeConte, begged for legal assistance. Joseph LeConte had been known for his paternalism, but that benevolence was apparently reserved for slaves. Lancaster LeConte died a forgotten prisoner, another example of the callous convict lease system. Based on primary and secondary sources; photo, 17 notes. 1887-89

Ledbetter, John Calvin

4036. Clayton, Lawrence and Ledbetter, Morris. JOHN CALVIN LEDBETTER/S. W. WESLEY: ONE INDIAN CAPTIVITY STORY OR TWO? *West Texas Historical Association Yearbook 1984 60: 83-91.* Presents documents and letters and family oral history about John Calvin Ledbetter, a white child believed stolen by Comanches in late 1870 or early 1871, and believed by the family to be a young man who entered Ft. Griffith, Texas, 11 years later but who later rejected his Ledbetter identity and claimed to be S. W. Wesley. 1862-1912

Ledford family

4037. Perdue, Charles L., Jr. THE AMERICANIZATION OF JOHN EGERTON AND AUNT ARIE. *Appalachian J. 1984 11(4): 437-441.* Reviews John Egerton's *Generations: An American Family* (1983), which is the journalistic story of the Ledford family from 1738 to the present, with the stories of Burnam Ledford and his wife Addie in Garrard County, Kentucky; and *Aunt Arie: A Foxfire Portrait* (1983), edited by Linda Garland and Eliot Wigginton, the most recent publication of the Foxfire Project. 1738-1983

Lee, Ann

4038. Klein, Janice. ANN LEE AND MARY BAKER EDDY: THE PARENTING OF NEW RELIGIONS. *J. of Psychohistory 1979 6(3): 361-375.* 1736-1910
*For abstract see **Eddy, Mary Baker***

4039. Setta, Susan M. THE APPROPRIATION OF BIBLICAL HERMENEUTICS TO BIOGRAPHICAL CRITICISM: AN APPLICATION TO THE LIFE OF THE SHAKER FOUNDER, ANN LEE. *Hist. Methods 1983 16(3): 89-100.* Two methods of biblical criticism are applicable to the historiography of Mother Ann Lee. Form criticism analyzes particular texts to explain what they meant in their contemporary context. Redaction criticism explores the particular way in which the biographer collects and edits such forms. 41 notes. 1736-84

4040. Smith-Rosenberg, Carroll. IL GRANDE RISVEGLIO: RELIGIOSE RADICALI NELL'AMERICA JACKSONIANA [The Great Awakening: radical religious women in Jacksonian America]. *Memoria: Riv. di Storia delle Donne [Italy] 1982 (5): 64-81.* Examines the careers of two charismatic women, Jermima Wilkinson—the Rhode Island "universal public friend"—and Ann Lee, founder of the Shakers. Explores the reasons why mystic and enthusiastic religious revivals often appeal to women rather than men, linking this phenomenon to the relationship between social experience and the adoption of specific cultural forms. Biblio. 1790-1850

Lee, Bing

4041. Rossi, Jean. LEE BING: FOUNDER OF CALIFORNIA'S HISTORICAL TOWN OF LOCKE. *Pacific Hist. 1976 20(4): 351-366.* Lee Bing came from China as a teenager, settled in California and became a successful businessman. After a fire in Walnut Grove, Bing led the effort to build the Chinese town of Locke, 30 miles south of Sacramento. Based on an interview with Lee Ping about his father's life; 5 illus. 1880-1970

Lee, Bruce

4042. Chiao, Hsiung-Ping. BRUCE LEE: HIS INFLUENCE ON THE EVOLUTION OF THE KUNG FU GENRE. *J. of Popular Film and Television 1981 9(1): 30-42.* Briefly traces the movie career of Chinese superstar and social phenomenon Bruce Lee (d. 1973), and focuses on his mastery of Kung Fu and his influence on US and other films of the Kung Fu genre during the 1970's. 1970-79

Lee, Canada

4043. Gill, Glenda E. CAREERIST AND CASUALTY: THE RISE AND FALL OF CANADA LEE. *Freedomways 1981 21(1): 15-27.* Biography of black actor Canada Lee (d. 1952), born Leonard Lionel Cornelius Canegata, focusing on his career in American theater, 1934-46, and his career in films, 1944-52; probes by the House Committee on Un-American Activities and the Federal Bureau of Investigation destroyed his career. 1934-52

Lee, Charles O.

4044. —. CHARLES O. LEE (1883-1980): HISTORIAN IN PHARMACY. *Pharmacy in Hist. 1980 22(4): 165.* Eulogizes Charles O. Lee who, with a pharmacy degree from Kansas and a PhD from Wisconsin, taught pharmaceutics and the history of pharmacy at Purdue University (1915-20, 1926-54), at Nanking University (1920-26), and at Ohio Northern University (1954-71) after his retirement from Purdue. Dr. Lee was an active member of the old Section on Historical Pharmacy of the American Pharmaceutical Association and the American Institute of the History of Pharmacy from its founding in 1941 and the author of numerous articles on the history of pharmacy. Photo. 1883-1980

Lee, Henry ("Light-Horse Harry")

4045. Wallace, Sandra. HENRY LEE OF VIRGINIA. *Missouri Hist. Rev. 1976 71(1): 76-79.* Biographical sketch of Henry ("Light-Horse Harry") Lee (1756-1818). Illus., 23 notes. 1756-1818

Lee, Joseph

4046. Saveth, Edward N. PATRICIAN PHILANTHROPY IN AMERICA: THE LATE NINETEENTH AND EARLY TWENTIETH CENTURIES. *Social Service Rev. 1980 54(1): 76-91.* Using patrician philanthropists Josephine Shaw Lowell, Robert Treat Paine, and Joseph Lee as examples, discusses the activities by people of wealth and family distinction to help the poor in America during the 1870's-1900's. 1870-1910

Lee, Margaret Elizabeth Daniel

4047. Wade, Judith Masce. MARGARET ELIZABETH DANIEL LEE: PINELLAS PIONEER. *Tampa Bay Hist. 1981 3(1): 82-86.* Brief introductory background of Margaret Elizabeth Daniel Lee (1887-1980) and her family's presence in Pinellas County, Florida, beginning around 1850, followed by an excerpt from her journal written in 1963 about her life in a farm family. 1850-1963

Lee, Molly Huston

4048. Moore, Ray Nichols. MOLLY HUSTON LEE: A PROFILE. *Wilson Lib. Bull. 1975 49(6): 432-439.* Black librarian Molly Huston Lee singlehandedly was responsible for the establishment, maintenance, and growth of the Richard B. Harrison Public Library, which was especially for local blacks, in Raleigh, North Carolina, 1935-68. 1935-68

Lee, Robert E.

4049. Grimsley, Mark. THE MASTER GENERAL. *Civil War Times Illustrated 1985 24(7): 12-51.* Prints a biography of Confederate general Robert E. Lee, detailing the Civil War experiences that brought him his reputation as a noble military genius and a symbol of Southern chivalry. 1825-70

4050. Riley, Harris D., Jr. ROBERT E. LEE'S BATTLE WITH DISEASE. *Civil War Times Illus. 1979 18(8): 12-22.* Except for a bout of malaria in 1849, Robert E. Lee enjoyed superb health until March 1863 when he developed the heart trouble which plagued his remaining years. 1849-70

Lee, Robert E. (family)

4051. Schultz, Fred L. A PORTRAIT: THE LEE CHILDREN. *Civil War Times Illustrated 1985 24(7): 54-55, 57.* Describes the lives of Confederal general Robert E. Lee's seven children, who were born of high social status but who experienced the same tragedies as other wartime families. 1832-1914

Lee, Samuel Phillips

4052. Laas, Virginia J. THE COURTSHIP AND MARRIAGE OF ELIZABETH BLAIR AND SAMUEL PHILLIPS LEE: A PROBLEM IN HISTORICAL DETECTION. *Midwest Quarterly 1985 27(1): 13-29.* 1839-43
For abstract see ***Blair, Elizabeth***

Lees, Isaiah W.

4053. Secrest, William B. ISAIAH W. LEES. *Am. West 1980 17(5): 28-29, 64-67.* Isaiah W. Lees (ca. 1830-1902), a San Francisco, California, ironworks crew foreman, agreed to help a policeman in an 1852 murder investigation. His efforts broke the case and resulted in the first legal execution in the state. He succumbed to the exhilaration of the experience and joined the police force. His career as a detective was one of the longest and most brilliant in law enforcement history. 4 illus., biblio. 1852-1902

Lees, James

4054. Bond, Alec. FOLK BIOGRAPHY IN DAKOTA TERRITORY. *J. of the Folklore Inst. 1980 17(2-3): 135-152.* Folk biography is an essential element of regional and "grass roots" history. Often extensive and lively folk traditions develop around colorful and representative local figures while the more widely known individuals who are discussed by historians have little or no importance in folklore. Two examples of the former type are Stutsman County North Dakotans James Lees, a saloonkeeper and businessman of the late 19th century, and Dr. Helena Wink, a beloved physician who served the area from 1883 until her death in 1936. These two figures are still widely discussed. Traditional motifs abound in the tales surrounding them; the stories are also valuable for their abundant information on everyday life in the Dakota Territory. Based on fieldwork; 39 notes, appendix. 1870-1936

Lefebvre, Louis-Charles

4055. Harel, M. Bruno. LOUIS-CHARLES LEFEBVRE DE BELLEFEUILLE, PRETRE DE SAINT-SULPICE, 1795-1838 [Louis-Charles Lefebvre de Bellefeuille, priest of St.-Sulpice, 1795-1838]. *Sessions d'Etude: Soc. Can. d'Hist. de l'Eglise Catholique [Canada] 1982 49: 7-24.* Describes the missionary work of Louis-Charles Lefebvre and the history of the St.-Sulpice Seminary, Quebec. 1795-1838

Leffingwell, William B.

4056. Furnish, William M. W. B. LEFFINGWELL, IOWA SPORTSMAN. *Palimpsest 1980 61(6): 162-169.* Biography of Iowa wildlife author and hunter William B. Leffingwell (ca. 1850-1909) who wrote seven books and many articles containing valuable hunting advice that is still followed. ca 1850-1909

Léger, Jules

4057. Daigle, Jean. JULES LÉGER, 1925-1978. *Hist. Papers [Canada] 1979: 206-207.* Obituary of Jules Léger, former president of the Acadian Historical Society, historian, and student of the organization and workings of francophone university teaching in the Maritime Provinces. 1940's-78

Legget, Robert Ferguson

4058. Baird, Betty. ROBERT LEGGET: MAN OF SO MANY PARTS. *Can. Geog. [Canada] 1982 102(1): 32-37.* Traces the career of author, historian, editor, geologist, civil engineer, and teacher, Robert Ferguson Legget, Liverpool-born Canadian, whose main interest is in civil engineering and geology, and who wrote *Rideau Waterway* (1955), an account of the construction of the canal 150 years ago; 1945-82. 1840's

Lehman, Hans (family)

4059. Lehman, Daniel R. BISHOP HANS LEHMAN, IMMIGRANT OF 1727. *Pennsylvania Mennonite Heritage 1980 3(4): 16-23.* Discusses Bishop Hans Lehman (1702-76) of Rapho Township, Lancaster County, Pennsylvania, who settled there in 1727 upon his arrival to the United States from Switzerland, and a genealogy of his family until the early 20th century. ca 1727-1909

Lehmer, Donald J.

4060. Krause, Richard A. DONALD JAYNE LEHMER, 1918-1975. *Plains Anthropologist 1976 21(71): 73-76.* Obituary of anthropologist and archaeologist Donald Jayne Lehmer chronicles his academic career in Great Plains anthropology and includes a bibliography of his works, 1939-73. 1939-73

Lehrer, Tom

4061. Bernstein, Jeremy. TOM LEHRER: HAVING FUN. *Am. Scholar 1984 53(3): 295-302.* Presents a biographical sketch of mathematician and comedian Tom Lehrer. 1945-81

Leighton, Caroline

4062. Adams, Glen. A LADY TRAVELS OUR REGION: THE NORTHWEST IN 1865. *Pacific Northwesterner 1980 24(3): 33-40.* Biography of Caroline Leighton, born in Massachusetts in 1838, focusing on excerpts from her diary kept from 26 May 1865 to 15 May 1879 detailing her life in Washington Territory (1865-1875) and noting her stay in California (1875-1879). 1865-79

Leighton, Clare Veronica Hope

4063. Green, Archie. CLARE LEIGHTON. *JEMF Q. 1981 17(61): 24-34.* Biography of London-born wood engraver Clare Veronica Hope Leighton, focusing on her folk engravings that were introduced to Americans in the 1920's, prior to her arrival in 1939. 1899-1950's

Leisen, Mitchell

4064. Schultheiss, John. FILMOGRAPHY: DIRECTOR MITCHELL LEISEN: AN ANNOTATED FILMOGRAPHY. *J. of Popular Film and Television 1980 8(3): 52-60.* Assesses the career of film director Mitchell Leisen, 1898-1972, with an annotated filmography of every feature film he directed. 1930-72

Lejeune, John Archer

4065. Asprey, Robert B. JOHN A. LEJEUNE: TRUE SOLDIER. *Marine Corps Gazette 1962 46(4): 34-41.* A biography of Major General John A. Lejeune (1867-1942), a distinguished officer and the Commandant of the US Marines during 1920-29. 1920-29

4066. Bartlett, Merrill L. LEJEUNE AS A MIDSHIPMAN. *Marine Corps Gazette 1982 66(5): 73-79.* John Archer Lejeune was one of the best students at the US Naval Academy, from which he graduated in 1888; he became a lieutenant in the Marine Corps rather than a naval officer. 1880-90

4067. Dodd, Joseph D. THE VISION OF JOHN A. LEJEUNE. *Marine Corps Gazette 1967 51(11): 34-40.* Describes the contribution of Major General John Archer Lejeune, Commandant of the US Marine Corps between 1920-29, to the growth of the Corps into a crack amphibious force. 1918-29

4068. Hammond, James W., Jr. LEJEUNE OF THE NAVAL SERVICE. *US Naval Inst. Pro. 1981 107(11): 42-46.* John A. Lejeune (1867-1942) was the 13th commandant of the US Marine Corps. An 1888 graduate from the Naval Academy, Lejeune was commissioned in the Marine Corps in 1890. Between then and January 1915, when he became the assistant commandant, he served in a variety of assignments. He took command of the Army's 2d Infantry Division in France in July 1918 and led it through the rest of the fighting and into 1919. In 1920 he became commandant of the Marine Corps. He remained in that office until his retirement in March 1929. He then served as superintendent of the Virginia Military Institute until 1937. 5 photos. 1888-1942

Leland, Charles Godfrey

4069. Varesano, Angela-Marie Joanna. "Charles Godfrey Leland: The Eclectic Folklorist." U. of Pennsylvania 1979. 454 pp. *DAI 1980 40(10): 5540-A.* 19c

Lemke, John A.

4070. Treppa, Allan R. JOHN A. LEMKE: AMERICA'S FIRST NATIVE-BORN POLISH AMERICAN PRIEST? *Polish Am. Studies 1978 35(1-2): 78-83.* This Polish American (1866-90) was ordained to the priesthood in Detroit in 1889. Monographs and newspapers in English; 17 notes. 1866-90

Lemkin, Raphael

4071. Korey, William. RAPHAEL LEMKIN'S DREAM. *Present Tense 1984 11(4): 21-23.* Recounts the career of Raphael Lemkin, who sought international legislation condemning genocide. 1915-59

L'Enfant, Pierre Charles

4072. Stephenson, Richard W. THE DELINEATION OF A GRAND PLAN. *Q. J. of the Lib. of Congress 1979 36(3): 207-224.* Discusses the story of French émigré Pierre Charles L'Enfant's (1754-1825) proposed plan for the design of the capital of his adopted country. The passage of "An Act for establishing the temporary and permanent seat of the Government of the United States" 16 July 1790 led to the establishment of a federal territory and its designated location on the Potomac River. L'Enfant expressed his interest in being involved in the design of the new city to President George Washington, and he was later appointed by him as engineer of the undertaking. L'Enfant was later dismissed from responsibility for the design, but the plan that he presented to the President on 28 August 1791, entitled "Plan of the City," is thought to be the manuscript design of the city preserved in the Library of Congress. Based on Digges-L'Enfant-Morgan Papers, records of the Office of Public Buildings and Grounds, correspondence, newspapers, and manuscripts; 3 illus., 3 maps, 75 notes. 1789-91

Lenoir, William

4073. Shrader, Richard Alexander. "William Lenoir, 1751-1839." U. of North Carolina, Chapel Hill 1978. 250 pp. *DAI 1979 39(11): 6922-A.* 1770's-90

Lenoire, Rosetta

4074. Norflett, Linda Kerr. "The Theatre Career of Rosetta Lenoire." New York U. 1983. 518 pp. *DAI 1984 44(9): 2626-2627-A.* DA8324837 1936-83

Lenroot, Irvine L.

4075. Margulies, Herbert F. THE COLLABORATION OF HERBERT HOOVER AND IRVINE LENROOT, 1921-1928. *North Dakota Q. 1977 45(3): 30-46.* 1921-28
*For abstract see **Hoover, Herbert C.***

Lenzen, Victor Fritz

4076. Heilbron, J. L. ÉLOGE: VICTOR FRITZ LENZEN, 1890-1975. *Isis 1977 68(244): 598-600.* After obtaining a doctorate in philosophy at Harvard in 1916, Lenzen turned back to physics, a field of earlier interest. In 1918, he joined the physics department of the University of California at Berkeley, where he made his career as a philosopher-physicist. His work also moved into the history of science. Some of his discussions of the philosophy of early 20th-century physicists are now useful in all three fields, and his later studies of the geodetic work of Charles S. Peirce have helped establish Peirce's position as an exacting experimentalist. 15 notes. 1916-75

Leonard, Georgianna

4077. Stark, Suzanne J. THE ADVENTURES OF TWO WOMEN WHALERS. *Am. Neptune 1984 44(1): 22-24.* Describes the brief careers of two women who shipped aboard whalers disguised as men. Georgianna Leonard, alias George Weldon, served on the *America* during the Civil War. The name of the woman who served aboard the *Christopher Mitchell* for seven months is not known. Based on newspapers; 2 notes. 1848-63

Leonard, Nathaniel

4078. Denny, James M. VERNACULAR BUILDING PROCESS IN MISSOURI: NATHANIEL LEONARD'S ACTIVITIES, 1825-1870. *Missouri Hist. Rev. 1983 78(1): 23-50.* The building activities of Nathaniel Leonard of Cooper County, Missouri, illustrate the process of 19th-century vernacular house-building. A wealth of information about the Leonard farm, Ravenswood, shows how the vernacular building process functioned in a traditional Southern culture where construction was dominated by master craftsmen and their assistants. Based on the Nathaniel Leonard Papers and other primary sources; 8 illus., 6 photos, 43 notes. 1825-70

LeSage, Simeon

4079. Trépanier, Pierre. SIMÉON LE SAGE (1835-1909): UN NOTABLE D'AUTREFOIS DANS L'INTIMITÉ [Simeon Le Sage (1835-1909): The personal life of a notable of the past]. *Action Natl. [Canada] 1978 67(6): 469-496.* Biographical sketch and study of the social mobility of a Quebec lawyer and public official in the late 19th century. His father was an unlettered craftsman, but Simeon Le Sage completed classical studies, became a lawyer, and married into a landed family. Although defeated twice in legislative elections (1862 and 1867) he was appointed deputy director of the Department of Agriculture and Public Works by Quebec premier P.-J.-O. Chauveau. A staunch conservative and French Canadian nationalist, he was a patron of the arts and letters, especially French Canadian history. Primary and secondary sources; 150 notes. 1835-1909

Lesley, J. Peter

4080. Stephens, Lester D. "FORGET THEIR COLOR": J. PETER LESLEY ON SLAVERY AND THE SOUTH. *New England Q. 1980 53(2): 212-221.* Examines and quotes from Lesley's (1819-1903) correspondence. He was a strong abolitionist who believed in full equality of the races. He always distrusted the South. It is unclear why his crusading spirit for black rights declined after the 1870's. Based on Lesley's correspondence and other letters in the American Philosophical Society; 18 notes. ca 1850-80

Lesser, Alexander

4081. Parks, Douglas R. ALEXANDER LESSER 1902-1982. *Plains Anthropologist 1985 30(102): 65-71.* Eulogizes anthropologist Alexander Lesser, whose contributions to the field lie in both Plains studies and anthropological method and theory. Lesser was a student of social philosophy at Columbia College in New York, but while working for anthropologist Franz Boas in the 1920's he developed an interest in studying Sioux kinship. Lesser continued to work through the 1930's on the ethnology of Plains Indians while also holding temporary teaching appointments at several colleges. During World War II, Lesser worked in government service, and in 1947 he became involved in policy activity as executive director of the Association of American Indian Affairs. Lesser was an active participant in numerous professional societies. Illus., biblio. 1927-82

Lesser, Julian

4082. Lesser, Julian. HOLLYWOOD AND THE LOS ANGELES JEWISH COMMUNITY, JUNIOR DIVISION. *Western States Jewish Hist. 1984 16(3): 230-234.* Presents photographs and personal recollections of the author's childhood in Los Angeles, focusing on his acquaintances among the children of prominent families in the movie industry and in the city's Jewish community. 1923-76

Lesser, Sol

4083. Lesser, Stephen O. SOL LESSER AND UPTON SINCLAIR: THE RECORD OF A FRIENDSHIP. *Western States Jewish Hist. Q. 1980 12(2): 134-141.* Hollywood film producer Sol Lesser (b. 1890) and author Upton Sinclair began their business and personal relationship in 1932 after the failure of Sinclair's collaborative film effort with producer Sergei Eisenstein. Lesser rescued the film, *Thunder over Mexico,* a controversial epic story of Mexico. Later, Lesser tried to interest television networks in Sinclair's series of novels, the "Lanny Budd stories," but Sinclair's reputation was too radical for the anti-Communist mood of the early 1950's. The strong friendship of Lesser and Sinclair endured to Sinclair's death in 1968. Based on unpublished correspondence and Sol Lesser Reminiscences, Columbia University Oral Research Office, New York; photo, 14 notes. 1910-68

Leutze, Emanuel

4084. Groseclose, Barbara S. SOME EMANUEL LEUTZE REDISCOVERIES. *Am. Art J. 1980 12(2): 90-91.* Three recently discovered paintings of Emanuel Leutze (1816-68) contribute to better understanding of his career: *Sibyl* (1844-45), *The Courtship of Anne Boleyn* (1846), and *The Crusader's Return* (1868). 3 illus., 4 notes. 1844-68

Leverton, Irene

4085. Piasente, Carol. SKY CLIMBER. *Westways 1977 69(2): 48-51, 62.* Discusses the aviation career of Irene Leverton, one of the first women to make a successful career out of flying, 1940-77. 1940-77

Levin, David

4086. Levin, David. "WE'RE THE TEAM FROM YORK, P-A": AMERICAN HISTORY IN A JEWISH CHILDHOOD. *Southern Rev. 1980 16(3): 539-551.* The author, who also wrote *Cotton Mather: The Young Life of the Lord's Remembrancer, 1663-1703,* recalls his early childhood in York, Pennsylvania, and shows how Jews of his culture were assimilated into American pluralism; 1920's-40. 1920-40

Levin, Meyer

4087. Gilson, Estelle. AN AUTHENTIC JEWISH WRITER: A PROFILE OF MEYER LEVIN. *Present Tense 1981 8(4): 31-36.* Biography of Chicago-born Jewish writer Meyer Levin (1905-81), focusing on his writings, which include *Reporter* (1929), *Yehuda* (1931), *The Golden Mountain* (1932) (republished as *Classic Hassidic Tales* (1975)), *The New Bridge* (1933), and others including *The Architect,* which he was working on at his death. 1905-81

4088. Varon, Benno Weiser. THE HAUNTING OF MEYER LEVIN. *Midstream 1976 22(7): 7-23.* Discusses why the Jewish literary establishment has ignored the talented author Meyer Levin and gives a brief summary of his work, 1931-76. 1931-76

Levin, Theodore J.

4089. Kaufman, Ira G. MICHIGAN JUDICIARY OF JEWISH LINEAGE, PAST AND PRESENT: PART I. *Michigan Jewish Hist. 1981 21(1): 10-16.* Profiles Michigan Federal judges Charles C. Simons (1876-1963) and Theodore J. Levin (1897-1970). 1876-1970

Levorsen, Barbara

4090. Levorsen, Barbara. OUR BREAD AND MEAT. *Norwegian-American Studies 1965 22: 178-197.* Excerpts one of the chapters from the author's autobiography in which she describes frontier life in North Dakota among the Norwegian Americans who emigrated there, 1899-1909. 1899-1909

Levy, Cecilia Benhayon

4091. Stern, Norton B. and Kramer, William M. THE PHOSPHORESCENT JEWISH BRIDE: SAN FRANCISCO'S FAMOUS MURDER CASE. *Western States Jewish Hist. Q. 1980 13(1): 63-72.* 1885-89

*For abstract see **Bowers, J. Milton***

Levy, Isaac Oury

4092. —. ISAAC O. LEVY OF LOS ANGELES: A PICTURE STORY. *Western States Jewish Hist. Q. 1982 14(3): 236-244.* In 1909, Isaac Oury Levy (1878-1956), a native of Los Angeles, became a partner of Sam Behrendt in an insurance business. The Behrendt-Levy Insurance Agency developed many of the liability policies for the early film industry. Levy's personal interests extended to outdoor activities such as horseback riding, camping, and gardening; he was also an amateur boxer. He was a member of the Concordia Club, Hillcrest Country Club, the Masonic Order, and the Wilshire Boulevard Temple. Based on an interview and photos from the collection of Don Levy, Los Angeles; 13 photos, 11 notes. 1909-56

Levy, Jonas P.

4093. Rezneck, Samuel. THE MARITIME ADVENTURES OF A JEWISH SEA CAPTAIN, JONAS P. LEVY, IN NINETEENTH-CENTURY AMERICA. *Am. Neptune 1977 37(4): 239-252.* Jonas P. Levy (1807-83) went to sea in 1823 as a cabin boy and eventually owned and commanded several sailing ships. Focuses on Levy's services as a sea captain in the Peruvian Revolution and the Mexican War. Based on Levy's unpublished memoirs; illus., 31 notes. 1823-48

Levy, Lee Craig

4094. Wernet, Mary Linn. CONSERVATION THROUGH MUTUAL COOPERATION: A HISTORY OF MRS. LEE CRAIG LEVY'S WORK WITH THE LOUISIANA FORESTRY COMMISSION. *North Louisiana Historical Association Journal 1985 16(1): 23-34.* Lee Craign Ragan Levy (1896-1979) spent her life in various activities, including teaching and working with the General Federation of Women's Clubs. As president of the Louisiana Federation of Women's Clubs in 1946, she led that group to make a strong commitment to conservation, the basis for its program in 1947. During the next four years, she and the federation were instrumental in generating support for and success of the Louisiana Forestry Commission. 44 notes. 1947-51

Levy, Leopold (family)

4095. —. THE LEVY BROTHERS: EARLY SAN FRANCISCO CHIROPODISTS, A PICTURE STORY. *Western States Jewish Hist. Q. 1981 13(4): 317-321.* Alexander, Jacob, and Samuel Levy, sons of Leopold and Nanette Levy, each had his own medical office in San Francisco in the 1890's. A sister, Pauline Levy, worked as assistant to Jacob Levy. Dr. Samuel Levy was instrumental in getting a California licensing law for podiatrists in 1914; he also was a founder of the California College of Podiatric Medicine. Based on family interviews; 5 photos, 4 notes. 1862-1914

Lewis, Charles B.

4096. Bradshaw, James Stanford. M. QUAD: MICHIGAN'S MOST FAMOUS HUMORIST. *Chronicle 1980 16(3): 14-17.* Brief biography of Michigan humorist Charles B. Lewis (1842-1924), who used the pseudonym "M. Quad"; focuses on his newspaper career and his frank sense of humor. ca 1865-1924

Lewis, Clayton

4097. Holliday, J. S. THE WORLD OF CLAYTON LEWIS. *California History 1983 62(3): 216-223.* Profiles artist and sculptor Clayton Lewis. After a career spent variously as a furniture designer and manufacturer, Lewis concentrated on painting and sculpture, making his home at Tomales Bay, California, 70 miles north of San Francisco. Since the 1960's, Lewis has gained fame by illustrating the envelopes that enclose letters to his mother with vivid depictions of his philosophy and life-style. The California Historial Society recently presented an exhibition of Lewis's envelope paintings, sculptures, and oil paintings. Based on interviews with Lewis; 6 illus., 5 photos. 1935-82

Lewis, David J.

4098. Masterson, Thomas Donald. "David J. Lewis of Maryland: Formative and Progressive Years, 1869-1917." Georgetown U. 1976. 661 pp. *DAI 1978 38(9): 5641-A.* 1869-1917

Lewis, Edmonia

4099. Tufts, Eleanor M. EDMONIA LEWIS: AFRO-INDIAN NEO-CLASSICIST. *Art in Am. 1974 62(4): 71-72.* Discusses the brief career and sculpture of half-Indian, half-black Edmonia Lewis, 1867-75. 1867-75

Lewis, Edward Gardner

4100. McDonald, Susan Waugh. EDWARD GARDNER LEWIS: ENTREPRENEUR, PUBLISHER, AMERICAN OF THE GILDED AGE. *Missouri Hist. Soc. Bull. 1979 35(3): 154-163.* Edward Gardner Lewis (1868-1950) came to St. Louis in 1893 and, as publisher of *The Women's Magazine,* shortly became one of St. Louis's most controversial journalists and established a banking institution whose transactions became suspect. Then he created other commercial establishments, struggled with US postal officials to keep his magazine afloat, encouraged the feminist movement, established a People's University, and was mayor of University City, Missouri, until 1912. Secondary sources; 18 notes. 1893-1928

Lewis, Enos Barret

4101. Dillon, William D., ed. THE CIVIL WAR LETTERS OF ENOS BARRET LEWIS, 101ST OHIO VOLUNTEER INFANTRY: PART 1. *Northwest Ohio Quarterly 1985 57(2): 51-63.* Prints a biographical sketch of Enos Barret Lewis, a Union infantryman from Wyandot County, Ohio, during the Civil War, and includes selections from the many letters he wrote as an innocent, patriotic teenager fighting in Virginia with the 101st Ohio Volunteer Infantry. Article to be continued. 1844-63

Lewis, Francis

4102. Flynn, James J. FRANCIS LEWIS: LONG ISLAND JACOBIN. *J. of Long Island Hist. 1973 10(1): 29-37.* Francis Lewis (1713-1802), a Welsh-born immigrant, became a New York merchant, member of Congress, and financial supporter of the American Revolution. 1730's-1802

Lewis, Graceanna

4103. Bonta, Marcia. GRACEANNA LEWIS: PORTRAIT OF A QUAKER NATURALIST. *Quaker History 1985 74(1): 27-40.* Influenced by her widowed mother and by the sister of ornithologist John Kirk Townsend, Graceanna Lewis studied and taught life sciences. Encouraged by John Cassin, Curator of Birds at the Philadelphia Academy of Natural Science, she moved to Philadelphia and published Part I of the *Natural History of Birds* (1868). After recovering from a nervous breakdown in 1870, she lectured and wrote popular articles, occasionally teaching, but was denied a professorship at Vassar in favor of a man. Some of her most entertaining publications appeared in her old age. Based on manuscripts at Swarthmore College and on Deborah Jean Warner's *Graceanna Lewis* (1979); 70 notes. 1821-1912

Lewis, H. Gregg

4104. Rees, Albert. H. GREGG LEWIS AND THE DEVELOPMENT OF ANALYTICAL LABOR ECONOMICS. *J. of Pol. Econ. 1976 84(4, 2), S3-S8.* Records the contributions of H. Gregg Lewis during his long career as a teacher at the University of Chicago. 1940-76

Lewis, Idawalley Zorada

4105. Thompson, Sue Ellen. "THE LIGHT IS MY CHILD." *Log of Mystic Seaport 1980 32(3): 90-98.* Provides a biography of Idawalley Zorada Lewis (1842-1911), daughter of a lighthouse keeper; because of her heroic rescues, she was awarded a gold medal by the US government in 1881; in 1879 she had been officially appointed as keeper of the Lime Rock Lighthouse off Newport, Rhode Island, by a special act of Congress. 1867-1911

Lewis, Janet

4106. Hamovitch, Mitzi Berger. MY LIFE I WILL NOT LET THEE GO EXCEPT THOU BLESS ME: AN INTERVIEW WITH JANET LEWIS. *Southern Rev. 1982 18(2): 299-313.* Presents an interview with Southern poet Janet Lewis in which she discusses her life and work, and those of other poets. 1899-1982

4107. Lewis, Janet. ELIZABETH MADOX ROBERTS, A MEMOIR. *Southern Review 1984 20(4): 803-816.* 1919-41

For abstract see ***Roberts, Elizabeth Madox***

Lewis, Jerry

4108. Polan, Dana. BEING AND NUTTINESS: JERRY LEWIS AND THE FRENCH. *J. of Popular Film and Television 1984 12(1): 42-46.* When Jerry Lewis began directing and writing his own films in the 1960's, he gained acceptance with French film critics (who regarded him as an "auteur") while their counterparts in America have maintained their dislike for his work. 1960-84

Lewis, Jerry Lee

4109. Tucker, Stephen R. PENTECOSTALISM AND POPULAR CULTURE IN THE SOUTH: A STUDY OF FOUR MUSICIANS. *J. of Popular Culture 1982 16(3): 68-80.* 1950's-70's
For abstract see ***Blackwood, James***

Lewis, John L.

4110. Brody, David. JOHN L. LEWIS. *Rev. in Am. Hist. 1978 6(3): 410-414.* Review article prompted by Melvyn Dubofsky and Warren Van Tine's *John L. Lewis: A Biography* (New York: Quadrangle/*The New York Times* Book Co., 1977). 1900's-69

4111. Hutchinson, John. JOHN L. LEWIS: TO THE PRESIDENCY OF THE UMWA. *Labor Hist. 1978 19(2): 185-203.* Surveys the life of John L. Lewis from his birth in 1880 to his appointment as president of the United Mine Workers of America in 1920. Lewis, an itinerant miner from a mining family, emerged as a leader in the UMWA through his activities in Illinois District 12. Based on interviews and *Proceedings* of UMWA District 12 conventions; 30 notes. 1880-1920

4112. Monroe, Douglas Keith. "A Decade of Turmoil: John L. Lewis and the Anthracite Miners, 1926-1936." (Parts I and II). Georgetown U. 1977. 404 pp. *DAI 1977 38(5): 3001-A.* 1926-36

4113. Schacht, John N. FOUR MEN FROM IOWA. *Palimpsest 1982 63(1): 30-31.* 1870's-1960's
For abstract see ***Hoover, Herbert C.***

Lewis, John Travers

4114. Clapson, Clive. JOHN TRAVERS LEWIS: AN IRISH HIGH CHURCHMAN IN CANADA WEST. *J. of the Can. Church Hist. Soc. [Canada] 1980 22(Oct): 17-31.* John Travers Lewis (1825-1901) immigrated to Canada in 1850 from Ireland, where he had been educated at Trinity College, Dublin, and ordained by the Church of Ireland. In 1861 he was elected bishop of the new diocese of Ontario, where he remained though subsequently made metropolitan of Canada and, in 1894, archbishop. Lewis may have been elected bishop because of assumptions that he would, like most of the Irish clergy in Canada, support the Evangelical party. However, he quickly revealed an affinity for the Tractarians based upon their common respect for the church fathers and Caroline divines. In controversies during his episcopate, Lewis supported the episcopal constitution of the church, taught a high church view of the sacraments, and was sympathetic to moderate liturgical reform. 50 notes. 1861-1901

Lewis, Mary

4115. Dougan, Michael B. "A TOUCHING ENIGMA": THE OPERA CAREER OF MARY LEWIS. *Arkansas Hist. Q. 1977 36(3): 258-279.* Describes the career of Arkansas born singer Mary Lewis (1897-1941), who rose from a childhood in the slums and foster homes, to be a vaudeville performer and finally an acclaimed opera singer. Primary sources; 2 illus., 109 notes. 1917-41

Lewis, Meriwether

4116. Abrams, Rochanne. THE COLONIAL CHILDHOOD OF MERIWETHER LEWIS. *Missouri Hist. Soc. Bull. 1978 34(4): 218-227.* Remembered primarily for historic western explorations in 1804-06, Meriwether Lewis (1774-1809) spent his early childhood in Albemarle County, Virginia, where he absorbed the code of Virginia gentlemen. Then Lewis experienced frontier harshness when the family moved to Georgia. Later he returned to Virginia for formal education which emphasized the classics but also provided him with a smattering of arithmetic, geography, and natural science. Based on manuscript and secondary sources; 3 photos, 17 notes. 1774-91

4117. Abrams, Rochanne. MERIWETHER LEWIS: THE LOGISTICAL IMAGINATION. *Missouri Hist. Soc. Bull. 1980 36(4): 228-240.* President Thomas Jefferson placed Meriwether Lewis and William Clark in charge of an expedition to explore the American West, 1804-06. The expedition succeeded largely because Lewis spent more than a year, 1803-04, gathering preliminary information, painstakingly planning the journey, assembling equipment and provisions, and anticipating the expedition's needs. Based on printed primary sources and archival material at the Missouri Historical Society; 27 notes. 1803-06

4118. Holt, Glen E. AFTER THE JOURNEY WAS OVER: THE ST. LOUIS YEARS OF LEWIS AND CLARK. *Gateway Heritage 1981 2(2): 42-48.* 1806-33
For abstract see ***Clark, William***

Lewis, Oscar

4119. Lewis, William. OSCAR LEWIS, SAN FRANCISCO'S HISTORIAN. *Mankind 1980 6(8): 20-22, 24, 28, 36, 38-39.* Describes the life and personality of Oscar Lewis (b. 1893), western historian and writer. His personal recollections are recorded here by his grandnephew. 2 illus., 4 photos. 1910-79

4120. Starr, Kevin. THE WORLD OF OSCAR LEWIS: AN APPRECIATIVE SALUTE TO THE REVERED PATRIARCH OF CALIFORNIA WRITER-HISTORIANS. *California History 1984 63(4): 320-323.* A profile of journalist and author Oscar Lewis, a lifelong resident of San Francisco whose career links the Bay Area's literary frontier of the 19th century with modern times. Lewis knew such luminaries as Gertrude Atherton, Maynard Dixon, Joseph Henry Jackson, George Sterling, and other artists, poets, novelists, critics, and journalists. His own writings, such as *The Big Four, Silver Kings,* and *I Remember Christine,* have stood the test of time and are noted for their clarity of prose and skillful narrative. Illus., photo. 1913-84

Lewis, Selma Gruenberg

4121. Stern, Norton B. SELMA GRUENBERG LEWIS AND SELMA, CALIFORNIA. *Western States Jewish History 1985 18(1): 22-29.* The town of Selma, California, is named for Selma Gruenberg Lewis. Other Jews have also played noteworthy roles in the town's history. 31 notes. 1871-1944

Lewis, Sinclair

4122. Blakely, Roger K. SINCLAIR LEWIS AND THE BAXTERS: THE HISTORY OF A FRIENDSHIP. *Minnesota History 1985 49(5): 166-178.* Minnesota's Nobel Prize winner, author Sinclair Lewis, corresponded with a Minneapolis couple for six years toward the end of his life. John and Mary Baxter met Lewis when he lectured at the University of Minnesota in late 1942. The correspondence continued as Lewis wandered and worked in New York, Hollywood, Duluth, and western Massachusetts. Based on 28 letters by Sinclair Lewis; 7 illus., 36 notes. 1942-48

4123. Conrad, Barnaby. A PORTRAIT OF SINCLAIR LEWIS: AMERICA'S "ANGRY MAN" IN THE AUTUMN OF HIS LIFE. *Horizon 1979 22(3): 40-51.* A biographical view of Sinclair Lewis by Barnaby Conrad, his personal secretary in 1947. 20c

Lewis, Tillie Weisberg

4124. Clar, Reva. TILLIE LEWIS: CALIFORNIA'S AGRICULTURAL INDUSTRIALIST. *Western States Jewish Hist. 1984 16(2): 139-154.* Traces the business and civic career of Tillie Weisberg Lewis, who established Tillie Lewis Foods, Inc. and was active in the Jewish community of Stockton, California. Based on interviews and newspaper and published sources; 3 photos, 52 notes. 1930's-77

Lewis, Waitsill (family)

4125. Auwarter, Ruth. A GENEALOGICAL FILE. *Nova Scotia Hist. Q. [Canada] 1976 6(2): 167-172.* Author discusses her experience in compiling a genealogy for the family of Waitsill Lewis of Yarmouth, Nova Scotia, giving tips on finding sources and methodology, 1976. 1976

Lhevinne, Rosina

4126. Wallace, Robert K. ONE WOMAN'S CAREER: LIBERATION THROUGH LIMITATION. *Am. Scholar 1976 45(3): 442-447.* Considers the musical career of Rosina Lhevinne as a performing pianist with her husband, Josef, as a solo artist, and as a teacher at Juilliard School in relation to the current view that the only way young women can find themselves is to "avoid any dependence on others or hindrance to the full blossoming of the inviolate self." Despite her own solo career which began at age 76 in 1956 (her husband died in 1944), she regards the highlight of her life to be the 46 years of marriage to Josef Lhevinne. Hers was freedom through limitation. ca 1898-1977

Libbey, Laura Jean

4127. Peterson, Joyce Shaw. WORKING GIRLS AND MILLIONAIRES: THE MELODRAMATIC ROMANCES OF LAURA JEAN LIBBEY. *Am. Studies Int. 1983 24(1): 19-35.* Laura Jean Libbey developed a formula of the working-girl genre of domestic novels, and became "its most popular and successful practitioner." She published more than 60 novels between 1880 and 1900, all of which were melodramatic romances. Summarizes her life and outlines her formula for these novels, which often depicted poor working girls as ladies in a world of romantic love. Themes of the primacy of love and an assertion of democratic values based on inner worth and behavior dominate Libbey's novels. Life was to be more than work and poverty. Based on Libbey's published novels; 34 notes. 1870-1920

Libby, Orin Grant

4128. Hayter, Earl W. REMINISCENCES OF ORIN GRANT LIBBY. *North Dakota Q. 1981 49(3): 64-67.* Reminiscence about American historian Orin Grant Libby, focusing on Libby's prominence as teacher and scholar; stresses the period following the author's and Libby's meeting in 1930 at the University of North Dakota and their long association in academe. 1890's-1930's

Licht, Frank

4129. Conser, Walter H., Jr. ETHNICITY AND POLITICS IN RHODE ISLAND: THE CAREER OF FRANK LICHT. *Rhode Island History 1985 44(4): 97-107.* A liberal Democrat, Frank Licht moved successively from a law career to the state senate (1948-56), superior court (1956-68), and the Rhode Island governorship (1968-72). The state's first Jewish governor, Licht appealed powerfully to the Rhode Island style of ethnic and urban politics first seen in Theodore Francis Greene's "bloodless revolution" in 1935, which broke the political lock of Yankee rural Republicans in state affairs. Though Jews constituted only a tiny minority of the electorate, Licht shared and reflected the ethnic values and aspirations of a diverse community, which in turn identified him as one of their own who shared their policy aspirations for the state. Based on oral interviews, newspaper accounts, and secondary sources; 5 illus., 27 notes. 1916-72

Liddell, Josephine Crumrine

4130. Shuler, Jody. JOSEPHINE CRUMRINE LIDDELL. *Alaska J. 1977 7(3): 132-137.* Josephine Crumrine Liddell moved to Alaska at age six with her artist mother, Nina Crumrine. She studied art outside Alaska as a teenager, returning home to specialize in painting animals. Covers 1925-72. 11 illus. 1925-72

Liggin, John Lewis

4131. Liggin, Edna M. ROOTS OF THE VINE AND JOHN LEWIS LIGGIN: MASTER TEACHER. *North Louisiana Hist. Assoc. J. 1980 11(2): 18-26.* John Lewis Liggin (1881-1959) taught for 51 years, mostly in parish schools in north Louisiana. Educated at Mount Lebanon Baptist College and Louisiana State University, Liggin served as teacher and administrator in several schools, retiring at the age of 70. 2 illus. 1887-1950

Light, Enoch

4132. Gradone, Richard A. "Enoch Light (1905-1978): His Contributions to the Music Recording Industry." New York U. 1980. 394 pp. *DAI 1980 41(6): 2346-A.* 8027444 1927-78

Lilienthal, Alice Haas

4133. Dalin, David G. FLORINE AND ALICE HAAS AND THEIR FAMILIES. *Western States Jewish Hist. Q. 1981 13(2): 135-141.* ca 1900-81
*For abstract see **Bransten, Florine Haas***

Liljegren, Olof

4134. Swanson, Alan, ed. and transl. THE CIVIL WAR LETTERS OF OLOF LILJEGREN. *Swedish Pioneer Hist. Q. 1980 31(2): 86-121.* Olof Liljegren came to America from Sweden about 1857 and settled in Isanti County, Minnesota. He volunteered with Company D, 3d Minnesota Volunteers, in the fall of 1861. He served throughout the Civil War. These are edited translations of letters regarding the war which he sent to his father in Boggsjö, Sweden, and to friends in Minnesota. They have been edited and translated by Alan Swanson, who provided a short introduction and closing comments. 4 photos, 55 notes. 1857-65

Lincoln, Abraham

4135. Basler, Roy P. LINCOLN, BLACKS, AND WOMEN. Davis, Cullom; Strozier, Charles B.; Veach, Rebecca Monroe; and Ward, Geoffrey C., ed. *The Public and the Private Lincoln: Contemporary Perspectives* (Carbondale: So. Illinois U. Pr., 1979): 38-53. Relates Abraham Lincoln's personal contacts with blacks including Frederick Douglass and William H. Johnson, and women, including Anna Ella Carroll and Anna E. Dickenson, especially during his presidential years. His relations with blacks were "almost models of democratic correctness and friendly courtesy." Raised in a masculine world, however, he could not treat intelligent women as his equals. 33 notes. ca 1840-65

4136. Berwanger, Eugene H. LINCOLN'S CONSTITUTIONAL DILEMMA: EMANCIPATION AND BLACK SUFFRAGE. *Papers of the Abraham Lincoln Association 1983 5: 25-38.* Although Abraham Lincoln has been accused of being only lukewarm for civil rights for blacks, he supported abolition and subsequent suffrage for slaves within the limits of Civil War military strategy and the Constitution. 1861-65

4137. Boller, Paul F., Jr. THE LAUGHING AND THE LITERARY LINCOLN. *Social Sci. 1980 55(2): 71-76.* Abraham Lincoln was the only president who was both humorist and literary artist. Lincoln's funny stories not only entertained people; they also helped him make important points. Lincoln was utterly without malice, but he was the most vilified of all our presidents. His sense of humor, however, as well as his deep devotion to democratic ideals, led him to respond to personal attacks with tolerance and magnanimity. And he enshrined his democratic faith in some of the most beautiful English prose ever written. 36 notes. 1847-65

4138. Boritt, G. S. THE RIGHT TO RISE. Davis, Cullom; Strozier, Charles B.; Veach, Rebecca Monroe; and Ward, Geoffrey C., ed. *The Public and the Private Lincoln: Contemporary Perspectives* (Carbondale: So. Illinois U. Pr., 1979): 57-70. An underlying theme in Abraham Lincoln's thought was his conviction that men should rise according to their ability. His economic policy calling for internal improvements and state banks was designed to promote commerce and industry. These avenues of enterprise, rather than agriculture, led to economic opportunity. After the Kansas-Nebraska Act of 1854, Lincoln turned his attention from economics to slavery, but his concern was still over the right to rise. His military policy during the Civil War was conducted by the same principle, leading to rapid promotions and demotions of military officers. To a large degree, Lincoln viewed the war as a judgment against a nation which did not reward laborers according to their merits. 39 notes. ca 1830-65

4139. Braden, Waldo W. LINCOLN'S DELIVERY. *Lincoln Herald 1983 85(3): 167-174.* Provides contemporary descriptions of Abraham Lincoln's appearance and public speaking. 1832-94

4140. Braden, Waldo W. "KINDLY LET ME BE SILENT": A RELUCTANT LINCOLN. *Lincoln Herald 1984 86(4): 195-202.* A review of Abraham Lincoln's full collection of speeches and extemporaneous talks provides insight into his functioning as president and reveals Lincoln's skill in exercising caution and reserve. 1854-65

4141. Current, Richard N. LINCOLN, THE CIVIL WAR, AND THE AMERICAN MISSION. Davis, Cullom; Strozier, Charles B.; Veach, Rebecca Monroe; and Ward, Geoffrey C., ed. *The Public and the Private Lincoln: Contemporary Perspectives* (Carbondale: So. Illinois U. Pr., 1979): 137-146. Abraham Lincoln was the heir of the Puritans and later thinkers who believed that the United States was a model for the rest of the world. He consequently accepted the possibility of civil war to prove that the American experiment with self-government had not failed. 20 notes. 1630-1865

4142. Current, Richard N. THE LINCOLN PRESIDENTS. *Presidential Studies Q. 1979 9(1): 25-35.* Abraham Lincoln, a favorite past president for a number of subsequent officeholders to quote when justifying or suggesting a political maneuver, also had his favorite statesmen, among them Thomas Jefferson, Zachary Taylor, and Henry Clay. 19c

4143. Dowding, Nancy E. SANDBURG THE BIOGRAPHER. *Lincoln Herald 1979 81(3): 159-162.* Discusses the American poet Carl Sandburg's successful biography of Abraham Lincoln, which accurately captures Lincoln's personality and the times in which he lived. The biography is in two volumes entitled *Abraham Lincoln, "The Prairie Years"* (New York: Harcourt, Brace and Co., 1926), and *Abraham Lincoln, "The War Years"* (New York: Harcourt, Brace and Co., 1939). 1809-65

4144. Fehrenbacher, Don E. LINCOLN AND THE CONSTITUTION. Davis, Cullom; Strozier, Charles B.; Veach, Rebecca Monroe; and Ward, Geoffrey C., ed. *The Public and the Private Lincoln: Contemporary Perspectives* (Carbondale: So. Illinois U. Pr., 1979): 121-136. Reviews Abraham Lincoln's views on government and constitutional principles. Though the Civil War consolidated federal power to an unprecedented degree, Lincoln did not enter the war with the intention of remodeling the relationship of federal and state governments; his reconstruction program was designed to restore the prewar system even if it meant that the freedmen would be at the mercy of their old masters. He upheld the right of judicial review but did not support judicial supremacy. Though he extended emergency powers of the presidency, he displayed little legislative leadership as he followed the Whig principle that government initiative lay with the legislature. His belief in government by the people was stronger than his belief in the union, for he agreed in advance to abide by the election of 1864. 22 notes. 1861-65

4145. Fleischman, Richard K. THE DEVIL'S ADVOCATE: A DEFENSE OF LINCOLN'S ATTITUDE TOWARD THE NEGRO, 1837-1863. *Lincoln Herald 1979 81(3): 172-186.* Discusses Abraham Lincoln's attitudes toward slavery in the United States from 1837 to 1863 in light of the attitudes toward blacks at the time; while not a proabolitionist in his early political career, Lincoln was committed to the nonextension of slavery. 1837-63

4146. Fredrickson, George M. THE SEARCH FOR ORDER AND COMMUNITY. Davis, Cullom; Strozier, Charles B.; Veach, Rebecca Monroe; and Ward, Geoffrey C., ed. *The Public and the Private Lincoln: Contemporary Perspectives* (Carbondale: So. Illinois U. Pr., 1979): 86-98. Abraham Lincoln basically was guided by a legalist-rationalist conservatism that sought to inculcate respect for law by demonstrating the rational principles underlying the legal and constitutional order. He held to the concept of a procedural community in which decisions were rendered by the well-trained based on tested procedures. He distrusted the excesses of Jacksonian democracy, for mere majoritarianism might go beyond the reach of legal authority. He also rejected the emotionalism of evangelicals who conceived of the existence of a moral community. After the Kansas-Nebraska Act (US, 1854), however, his level of moral passion was aroused. During the Civil War he merged the concepts of legal order, majoritarian democracy, and a religious sense of American destiny. He viewed the North as a popular democracy whose people could be trusted because they were committed to law and stability. The war war in accordance with divine purpose so it could legitimately arouse religious emotions. 33 notes. ca 1840-65

4147. Gallardo, Florence. 'TIL DEATH DO US PART: THE MARRIAGE OF ABRAHAM LINCOLN AND MARY TODD. *Lincoln Herald 1982 84(1):3-10.* Criticizes the 1885 book, *Life of Lincoln,* by William H. Herndon in collaboration with Jesse W. Weik, that includes a negative account of the marriage between Abraham Lincoln and Mary Todd Lincoln; it was regarded as absolutely true until 1947, when the Lincoln papers were made available and documented another version of their admittedly difficult marriage from 4 November 1842 until his assassination in 1865. 1842-65

4148. Graebner, Norman A. THE APOSTLE OF PROGRESS. Davis, Cullom; Strozier, Charles B.; Veach, Rebecca Monroe; and Ward, Geoffrey C., ed. *The Public and the Private Lincoln: Contemporary Perspectives* (Carbondale: So. Illinois U. Pr., 1979): 71-85. Throughout his political career, Abraham Lincoln advocated national development through internal improvements. As a state legislator in Illinois, he proposed road construction and navigation aids. As an attorney, he took on railroad clients including the Illinois Central Railroad, and promoted railroad development within the state. 39 notes. 1830-61

4149. Head, Constance. JOHN WILKES BOOTH, 1864: PROLOGUE TO ASSASSINATION. *Lincoln Herald 1983 85(4): 254-262.* 1864
For abstract see ***Booth, John Wilkes***

4150. Hein, David. THE CALVINISTIC TENOR OF ABRAHAM LINCOLN'S RELIGIOUS THOUGHT. *Lincoln Herald 1983 85(4): 212-220.* Compares Abraham Lincoln's and John Calvin's religious views, particularly on the role of divine providence and the nature of Christian life. 1860-65

4151. Hess, Earl J. ALVIN P. HOVEY AND ABRAHAM LINCOLN'S "BROKEN PROMISES": THE POLITICS OF PROMOTION. *Indiana Mag. of Hist. 1984 80(1): 35-50.* 1861-65
For abstract see ***Hovey, Alvin P.***

4152. Hickey, James T. ROBERT TODD LINCOLN AND THE "PURELY PRIVATE" LETTERS OF THE LINCOLN FAMILY. *J. of the Illinois State Hist. Soc. 1981 74(1): 59-79.* 1865-1980
For abstract see ***Lincoln, Robert Todd***

4153. Holzer, Harold. "TOKENS OF RESPECT" AND "HEARTFELT THANKS": HOW ABRAHAM LINCOLN COPED WITH PRESIDENTIAL GIFTS. *Illinois Hist. J. 1984 77(3): 177-192.* In accord with the accepted practice of his era, Abraham Lincoln accepted numerous gifts of varying value during his presidency without public disclosure and on some occasions, without private acknowledgment. Gifts were accepted by Lincoln as early as the 1860 campaign. Books, pictures, and novelties were common, but more valuable clothes, animals, and even a carriage were also given. While most gifts were presented in good faith, some were clearly motivated by self-promotion and the hope of official favor. 10 illus., 46 notes. 1860-65

4154. Holzer, Harold and Ostendorf, Lloyd. THE CHILDREN'S CRUSADE: VINNIE REAM, THE GIRL WHO SCULPTURED LINCOLN. *Civil War Times Illus. 1982 21(3): 26-33.* 1864-71
For abstract see ***Ream, Vinnie***

4155. Holzer, Harold. LINCOLN AND THE OHIO PRINTMAKERS. *Ohio Hist. 1980 89(4): 400-419.* Discusses regional influences in the printmakers' and publishers' portrayals of Abraham Lincoln at four major junctions in his career: his nomination to the presidency in 1860, his arrival in Washington as the new president and sporting a new beard, his 1862 announcement of the Emancipation Proclamation, and his state funeral in 1865. The Lincoln prints issued by Ohio printmakers mirror all of the strengths and weaknesses of the infant industry and are unique in that, although they reflected the ebb and flow of public demand for portraits of the president, some of the Ohio prints were highly original, occasionally experimental, and in one case directly influenced by Lincoln himself. The printmakers of Ohio, and the nation, gave the mythification of President Lincoln tangible form and widespread visibility and defined a martyr's place in American archive and folklore. Based on the collections of the Louis A. Warren Lincoln Library and Museum, the Library of Congress, the New York Public Library, and other primary sources; 20 illus., 34 notes. 1860-65

4156. Katz, Mark. THE MYSTERIOUS PRISONER: ASSASSINATION SUSPECT J. G. RYAN. *Civil War Times Illus. 1982 21(7): 40-43.* 1865-88
For abstract see ***Ryan, Jonathan George***

4157. Kubicek, Earl C. THE LINCOLN CORPUS CAPER. *Lincoln Herald 1980 82(3): 474-480.* 1876
For abstract see ***Mullen, Terrance***

4158. Kubicek, Earl C. THE CASE OF THE MAD HATTER. *Lincoln Herald 1981 83(3): 708-719.* 1832-1908
For abstract see ***Corbett, Thomas H.***

4159. Kubicek, Earl C. LINCOLN'S FRIEND: KIRBY BENEDICT. *Lincoln Herald 1979 81(1): 9-20.* 1835-74
For abstract see ***Benedict, Kirby***

4160. Kubicek, Earl C. ABRAHAM LINCOLN'S FAITH. *Lincoln Herald 1983 85(3): 188-194.* Though not affiliated with any particular religious denomination, Abraham Lincoln was not irreligious; he had been exposed to different faiths and philosophies and attended a variety of Christian church services. ca 1815-65

4161. Miller, Bud. THE INCIDENT. *Lincoln Herald 1980 82(1): 342-343.* Illustrates the story of a dying soldier who was visited by Abraham Lincoln in a military hospital after the battle of Chancellorsville during the Civil War in May 1863; Lincoln wrote a letter to the soldier's parents before the soldier died. 1863

4162. Oates, Stephen B. "THE MAN OF OUR REDEMPTION": ABRAHAM LINCOLN AND THE EMANCIPATION OF THE SLAVES. *Presidential Studies Q. 1979 9(1): 15-25.* Abraham Lincoln's political evolution from opposition to political rights for blacks (in the fear that his own political career might be affected) to steadfast belief in emancipation and equal rights led to his Emancipation Proclamation in 1863. 1854-63

4163. Oates, Stephen B. LINCOLN: THE MAN, THE MYTH. *Civil War Times Illustrated 1984 22(10): 10-19.* Describes the myths about Abraham Lincoln, most of which presented him as either an "American Christ" or an "Illinois Paul Bunyan," and discusses the real Lincoln, the flawed man who agonized over decisions and feared insanity. 1850's-65

4164. Oates, Stephen B. THE SLAVES FREED. *Am. Heritage 1980 32(1): 74-83.* A step-by-step account of President Abraham Lincoln's move toward emancipation. Responding to pressures from radical Republicans, Lincoln agreed to demands that the Civil War result in the eradication of the South's peculiar institution. His role in that effort, from the war's beginning to the passage of the 13th Amendment by Congress in 1865, is covered. 11 illus. 1861-65

4165. Porter, Laura Smith. "THE LAST, BEST HOPE OF EARTH": ABRAHAM LINCOLN'S PERCEPTION OF THE MISSION OF AMERICA, 1834-1854. *Illinois Historical Journal 1985 78(3): 207-216.* Abraham Lincoln's perception of America's mission was influenced by his frontier environment and Whig political philosophy. The belief that democracy encourages true liberty and that the free individual is perfectable dominated his view. Lincoln firmly believed in the superiority of American institutions, the duty of every citizen to protect them, and America's role as a model for other nations. His opposition to "Manifest Destiny" was caused, not only by fear of the spread of slavery, but also by the belief that the requisite energy and resources could be best applied to national improvement. His approach combined political realism with devotion to the nation's past and faith in its future. 45 notes. 1834-54

4166. Riches, William T. M. "The Commoners: Andrew Johnson and Abraham Lincoln to 1861." Ulster College [Northern Ireland] 1977. *Doctoral Dissertations in Hist. 1977 2(1): 25.* 1843-61

4167. Smith, Dwight L., ed. ROBERT LIVINGSTON STANTON'S LINCOLN. *Lincoln Herald 1974 76(4): 172-180.* Reprints personal remembrances which Robert Livingston Stanton had of Abraham Lincoln, 1861-64. 1861-64

4168. Strozier, Charles B. LINCOLN'S LIFE PRESERVER. *Am. Heritage 1982 33(2): 106-108.* Humor was both a part of Abraham Lincoln's personality and a purposeful part of his political style. His anecdotal humor has been described as his "life preserver." Covers 1860-65. Illus. 1860-65

4169. Strozier, Charles B. THE SEARCH FOR IDENTITY AND LOVE IN YOUNG LINCOLN. Davis, Cullom; Strozier, Charles B.; Veach, Rebecca Monroe; and Ward, Geoffrey C., ed. *The Public and the Private Lincoln: Contemporary Perspectives* (Carbondale: So. Illinois U. Pr., 1979): 3-19. Though acquiring a reputation as an Illinois legislator, Abraham Lincoln was inept in business, changing jobs frequently during the 1830's. His indecision in defining his professional life occurred at the very time he feared intimacy, as exemplified by his relations with Mary Owen and Mary Todd, the latter with whom he broke his engagement before finally marrying in 1842. 85 notes. 1831-42

4170. Suppiger, Joseph E. LINCOLN LEGENDS. *Lincoln Herald 1979 81(1): 33-38.* Provides several examples of popular biographies of Abraham Lincoln published from 1863 to the early 1900's. 1863-1900's

4171. Suppiger, Joseph E. THE INTIMATE LINCOLN, PART I: THE BOY. *Lincoln Herald 1981 83(4, i.e., 1): 604-614.* Reports on the personal life and values of Abraham Lincoln, tracing his geneaology to 1619, and focusing on his childhood in Kentucky, 1809-19. 1809-19

4172. Suppiger, Joseph E. THE INTIMATE LINCOLN. *Lincoln Herald 1982 84(2): 114-125, (3): 155-167, (4): 222-236; 1983 85(1): 7-20.* Continued from a previous article. Part 6: LIFE IN SPRINGFIELD, 1840-1847. Details Abraham Lincoln's life in Springfield, Illinois, from the time he left the state legislature until he was elected to the US Congress, including his courtship and marriage to Mary Todd, and his friendship with Joshua Speed. Part 7: CONGRESSMAN AND FAMILY-MAN. Details the rocky and unimpressive congressional career the young Lincoln had and presents insights into his strengths and weaknesses as a husband and father. Part 8: LAWYER AND POLITICIAN. Chronicles Lincoln's loss of interest in politics during 1850-54, the variety of legal cases he handled, his relationship with his law practice partner, his bid for the US Senate against Stephen A. Douglas, his health, his speeches, and the Dred Scott Case. Part 9: THE MAKING OF A NEW PRESIDENT. Covers Lincoln from the aftermath of his loss in the 1858 Illinois senatorial race to his 1861 farewell address in Springfield, Ilinois, after winning the presidency. 1840-61

4173. Suppiger, Joseph E. THE INTIMATE LINCOLN. *Lincoln Herald 1981 84[i.e., 83](2): 668-676, (3): 737-746, (3[i.e., 4]): 774-785; 1982 84(1): 26-37.* Continued from a previous article. Part II: GROWING UP IN INDIANA. Focuses on Abraham Lincoln's boyhood in Indiana during 1817-28. Part III. ON THE ILLINOIS FRONTIER. Describes the Lincoln family's arrival in New Salem, Illinois in 1830 and their life there until 1832. Part IV. FROM NEW SALEM TO VANDALIA. Traces Lincoln's life from 1832, when he ran for the Illinois legislature, to 1837. Part V. LIFE IN SPRINGFIELD, 1837-1840. Lincoln entered into law practice with J. T. Stuart, and furthered his political career as a Whig legislator. 1817-37

4174. Vandenhoff, Anne. EDWARD DICKINSON BAKER. *Pacific Hist. 1979 23(4): 1-8.* 1840-61
*For abstract see **Baker, Edward Dickinson***

4175. Wolf, George D. LINCOLN, THE MASTER POLITICIAN. *Lincoln Herald 1979 81(3): 163-168.* Describes Abraham Lincoln's political career from his defeat as a candidate for the Illinois state legislature in 1832, until his death in 1865 while President. 1832-65

4176. Yü, Yüh-chao. LINCOLN'S ATTITUDE TOWARD SLAVERY. *Shih-ta Hsüeh-pao (Bull. of Natl. Taiwan Normal U.) [Taiwan] 1983 28: 443-449.* Lincoln's antislavery attitude, which resulted in his fame as "The Great Emancipator," underwent three stages of development. The first stage came at the start of his public career, when he developed a deep sympathy toward the slaves. His opposition to slavery was based then on moral and philosophical grounds. He moved to the second stage in 1860, when he was elected president. He felt that the issue of slavery had to be shelved in order to save the Union, but his compassion toward the slaves did not abate. By 1862, Lincoln, realizing that the issues of union and slavery were inseparable, reached his third stage and turned the Civil War into a crusade for human freedom, focusing his policy on the complete abolition of slavery, which he believed was the only way to save the Union. It was, as historian Richard Hofstader remarked, a policy of expediency tempered by justice. Secondary sources; 30 notes. 1830's-65

Lincoln, Abraham (family)

4177. Hickey, James T. LINCOLNIANA: THE LINCOLN ACCOUNT AT THE CORNEAU & DILLER DRUG STORE, 1849-1861, A SPRINGFIELD TRADITION. *J. of the Illinois State Hist. Soc. 1984 77(1): 60-66.* 1849-61
For abstract see ***Diller family***

Lincoln, Benjamin

4178. Davis, Robert Scott, Jr. "COLONEL DOOLY'S CAMPAIGN OF 1779." *Huntington Lib. Q. 1984 47(1): 65-71.* Major General Benjamin Lincoln, commander of American forces in the South, asked a unit of the Georgia militia under the command of Colonel John Dooly to attack the British in Savannah. Dooly asked Lincoln for funds and supplies; the lack of these prevented his move, allowing the British to return to Savannah from South Carolina. Primary sources; 16 notes. 1779

Lincoln, David Francis

4179. Viets, Henry R. THE RESIDENT HOUSE STAFF AT THE OPENING OF THE BOSTON CITY HOSPITAL IN 1864. *J. of the Hist. of Medicine and Allied Sci. 1959 14(2): 179-190.* 1864-1919
For abstract see ***Blake, Clarence John***

Lincoln, Mary Todd

4180. Gallardo, Florence. 'TIL DEATH DO US PART: THE MARRIAGE OF ABRAHAM LINCOLN AND MARY TODD. *Lincoln Herald 1982 84(1):3-10.* 1842-65
For abstract see ***Lincoln, Abraham***

4181. Sklar, Kathryn Kish. VICTORIAN WOMEN AND DOMESTIC LIFE: MARY TODD LINCOLN, ELIZABETH CADY STANTON, AND HARRIET BEECHER STOWE. Davis, Cullom; Strozier, Charles B.; Veach, Rebecca Monroe; and Ward, Geoffrey C., ed. *The Public and the Private Lincoln: Contemporary Perspectives* (Carbondale: So. Illinois U. Pr., 1979): 20-37. Examines efforts by prominent Victorian women to limit the size of their families and their public and private activities to arrive at a qualitative rather than quantitative definition of motherhood, during 1830-80. Harriet Beecher Stowe's strategy was to abstain from sex, in part to punish her philandering husband, undertake a literary career, and foster women's education. Elizabeth Cady Stanton, like Stowe, practiced family planning and worked for feminist domestic reform, seeking the legal equality of women. Mary Todd Lincoln's approach was total commitment to her husband and children. In part she practiced family planning to aid her husband's political career, and she was indulgent of her children. She did not separate domestic from public life, participating in the political sector on Abraham's behalf, but she was unable to build an autonomous career. 40 notes. 1830-80

4182. Strozier, Charles B. THE SEARCH FOR IDENTITY AND LOVE IN YOUNG LINCOLN. Davis, Cullom; Strozier, Charles B.; Veach, Rebecca Monroe; and Ward, Geoffrey C., ed. *The Public and the Private Lincoln: Contemporary Perspectives* (Carbondale: So. Illinois U. Pr., 1979): 3-19. 1831-42
For abstract see ***Lincoln, Abraham***

Lincoln, Robert Todd

4183. Carson, S. L. THE OTHER TRAGIC LINCOLN: ROBERT TODD. *Manuscripts 1978 30(4): 242-259.* Death and tragedy followed Robert Todd Lincoln throughout his life. Despite his feelings of inadequacy and intense privacy, he was a successful man in his own right. Perhaps if his life had been less tragic, he might have been less of a private man and freer with his father's papers. Certainly in spite of the myths about the Lincoln assassination, the papers guarded so zealously by his son contained no hint of a conspiracy. 18 notes, illus. 1864-1947

4184. Hickey, James T. HIS FATHER'S SON: LETTERS FROM THE ROBERT TODD LINCOLN COLLECTION OF THE ILLINOIS STATE HISTORICAL LIBRARY. *J. of the Illinois State Hist. Soc. 1980 73(3): 215-234.* Robert Todd Lincoln (1843-1926), Abraham Lincoln's oldest son, was secretary of war and held other offices in the 1880's and 90's. Due to his high station, he was constantly deluged with letters from relatives and childhood friends asking him to exert influence in finding them jobs. The letters quoted in this article show that Todd Lincoln was compassionate and helpful in many instances, though he finally was forced to become more selective in wielding influence in these matters because of the volume of requests. Based on letters from the Robert Todd Lincoln Collection of the Illinois State Historical Library; 21 notes. 1868-1926

4185. Hickey, James T. ROBERT TODD LINCOLN AND THE "PURELY PRIVATE" LETTERS OF THE LINCOLN FAMILY. *J. of the Illinois State Hist. Soc. 1981 74(1): 59-79.* The papers of Abraham Lincoln were held by Elizabeth Todd Grimsley, Clark Moulton Smith, and William H. Herndon. After his assassination, his White House papers were brought to Bloomington by David Davis at the request of Robert T. Lincoln. Robert, determining that family papers should not be available for public inspection, safeguarded them. Many family papers, stored in his law office, were destroyed in the Chicago fire of 1871. Examination of the surviving papers was conducted by Charles Sweet until Robert Lincoln transferred them from Chicago to Hildene, his Vermont estate, between 1911 and 1918. In 1919, he presented eight trunks, forming the base of the *Collected Works of Abraham Lincoln,* to the Library of Congress. Robert Todd Lincoln Beckwith recently distributed the last of the Hildene material to close friends and various historical agencies. 16 illus., 41 notes. 1865-1980

Lincoln, Samuel

4186. Keiser, David S. LINCOLN'S ANCESTORS CAME FROM IRELAND! *Lincoln Herald 1977 79(4): 146-150.* 1624-49

For abstract see ***Lincoln, Abraham (ancestors)***

Lindaas, Hans (family)

4187. Folkedahl, Beulah, transl. and ed. NORWEGIANS BECOME AMERICANS. *Norwegian-American Studies 1962 21: 95-135.* Reprints a series of papers (primarily letters) relating to the emigration, settlement, and growth of the Hans Lindaas family. The first letters are from friends and relatives who had already made the move and established themselves in communities in Wisconsin. The letters describe life in America, including the vast economic opportunities, difficulties associated with land purchase, raising and marketing crops, and the cost and availability of farm labor. The Lindaas family, wife Kari, and children Sjur and Nils emigrated in 1857. The vast majority of the letters (30, in all) date from 1849-73 and are communications between the children, parents, and their brothers and sisters describing life in the various parts of the country where the families settled. The letters serve as a record of the assimilation and Americanization process which the Lindaas family experienced and might be considered to be a typical experience among many Norwegian Americans. Based on the letters and associated public papers; 39 notes. 1849-73

Lindbergh, Charles A.

4188. Eaker, Ira C. THE LINDBERGH I KNEW. *Aerospace Hist. 1977 24(4): 240-242.* Reminiscences about Charles A. Lindbergh, a man who greatly influenced the United States and its people. Includes personal stories concerning their relationship as well as notes about Lindbergh's career during 1920's-70's. 1920's-70's

4189. Hall, George M. WHEN HONOR CONFLICTS WITH DUTY. *Air. U. Rev. 1980 31(6): 45-60.* 1884-1973

For abstract see ***Greely, Adolphus W.***

4190. Keller, Allan. OVER THE ATLANTIC ALONE: CHARLES LINDBERGH'S $25,000 FLIGHT. *Am. Hist. Illus. 1974 9(1): 38-45.* Chronicles Charles Lindbergh's transatlantic flight, 1927, giving insight into the thoughts and actions of the pilot. 1927

4191. Lindbergh, Anne Morrow. THE CHANGING CONCEPT OF HEROES. *Minnesota Hist. 1980 46(8): 306-311.* Anne Morrow Lindbergh reflects on the major crusades of Charles A. Lindbergh's life: aviation, antiwar sentiment about World War II, and the quality of life on earth, seeking clues of how they reflected both his roots and the aspirations of his times. A talk before the 1979 annual meeting of the Minnesota Historical Society, including the question and answer session; 2 illus., 10 notes. 1902-79

4192. Schiff, Judith A. THE LIFE AND LETTERS OF CHARLES A. LINDBERGH: A COMMEMORATIVE VIEW. *Yale U. Lib. Gazette 1977 51(4): 173-189.* Although few American heroes "have commanded such continued public attention" as Charles A. Lindbergh (1902-74), "relatively little is known about the complete man, his life and his works." The Lindbergh Papers, which began to come to Yale University in 1940, will provide researchers with the facts and feelings of this great man. Contains a biographical sketch identifying the major events in Lindbergh's life, his family's history, his connection with Yale, and materials in the papers with excerpts. 1859-1974

4193. Schiff, Judith A. THE LITERARY LINDBERGH IS CELEBRATED AT YALE. *Yale Alumni Mag. 1977 15(8): 14-22.* Biography of Charles A. Lindbergh based on the family papers which were given to the Yale University Library, 1977. 1926-73

4194. Streeter, Jean Douglas. CHARLES A LINDBERGH PAPERS: AVIATION HISTORY SPICED WITH HERO WORSHIP. *Gateway Heritage 1983-84 4(3): 30-37.* The Missouri Historical Society at St. Louis owns significant collections of artifacts, documents, and personal papers that record the career of Charles A. Lindbergh. Most of the material relates to his 1927-42 activities. An inventory of the material was completed recently, and preparation of catalogs is underway, but the collection is still unavailable to researchers. 16 photos. 1927-42

Lindemann, Erich

4195. Satin, David George. ERICH LINDEMANN: THE HUMANIST AND THE ERA OF COMMUNITY MENTAL HEALTH. *Pro. of the Am. Phil. Soc. 1982 126(4): 327-346.* A chronological account of the life of Erich Lindemann (1900-74), which traces his development in the area of community mental health. Although his doctorates were in psychology and gestalt psychology, he was directed by a basic humanistic interest in people's motivations, relationships, and the stresses and struggles they experienced. His approach was to help people rather than to study impersonal data in a laboratory. He helped to establish the first community mental health center in the United States at Wellesley, Massachusetts. There he emphasized the stresses of community life and supported indigenous therapeutic resources in preventing maladaptive responses. Towering above all his attributes was the fact that he was a humanist whose personal life sensitized him to mental illness, death, grieving, and gave him a perspective on social reform and evangelism. Based on oral interviews, the writings of Lindemann and his wife, and numerous monographs and articles in the field of community mental health; ref. 1920-74

Lindner, Richard

4196. Carrión, Alejandro. RICHARD LINDNER AND THE COLORS OF CRUELTY. *Américas (Organization of Am. States) 1980 32(4): 18-24.* Describes the career and paintings of Richard Lindner (1901-78), a German emigré to the United States who portrayed cruelty and corruption. 1920-78

Lindquist, Helena Johanna Johansdotter (family)

4197. Lindquist, Helena Johanna Johansdotter. GRANDMOTHER LINDQUIST'S STORY. *Swedish-American Historical Quarterly 1985 36(2): 103-111.* The author was born in Skogsryd, Småland, Sweden, to Johannes Petterson Dolk and Maria Svensdotter. After a childhood marked by hardship, she went to work in 1838, first as a maid and later as a teacher, until her marriage to Johan Alfred Lindquist in 1851. In 1869, her husband and eldest son immigrated to the United States. She followed in 1871 with the three other children, and in 1872 they settled in Verona, Missouri. Strong religious faith helped her to survive the many sorrows in her life. 2 photos. 1823-91

Lindsay, Gilbert

4198. Elliot, Jeffrey M. THE DYNAMICS OF BLACK LOCAL POLITICS: AN INTERVIEW WITH GILBERT LINDSAY. *Negro Hist. Bull. 1977 40(4): 718-720.* Los Angeles's first black councilman, now a 15-year veteran on the council, discusses his youth in Mississippi and the Army, how he worked his way into politics, and his career as a councilman. By making other councilmen come to him when they needed his vote, by working hard for his district and keeping himself visible to his voters, and by acting not as a black councilman, but as a representative of all his constituents, Gilbert Lindsay has attained a powerful position in Los Angeles politics. Photo. 1950's-77

Lindsey, Benjamin Barr

4199. Campbell, D'Ann. JUDGE BEN LINDSEY AND THE JUVENILE COURT MOVEMENT, 1901-1904. *Arizona and the West 1976 18(1): 5-20.* While serving as a law clerk and studying for the bar in Denver, Colorado, Benjamin Barr Lindsey became interested in the plight of children who were imprisoned for minor offenses. As a lawyer he secured a court appointment as guardian of orphans and other wards of the county. Later, as a judge he launched a crusade that pioneered reforms and established a juvenile court system that gained him national and international acclaim. 3 illus., 32 notes. 1901-20's

Ling, James J.

4200. Jacobs, Donald. "An Account and Evaluation of James Ling's Rise and Fall with Ling-Temco-Vought." U. of Nebraska, Lincoln 1977. 208 pp. *DAI 1978 38(8): 4926-A.* 1954-70

Link, Edward Albert

4201. Wallis, Michael. A CREATIVE ENGINEER OF AIR AND OCEAN WINS A SIGNAL HONOR. *Smithsonian 1980 11(2): 151-158.* Edward Albert Link was presented the 1980 Lindbergh Award for his invention of the Link Trainer, the first flight trainer, designed in the 1920's, and for his submarines used in marine archaeology and oceanography. 1920-80

Linn, William

4202. Anderson, Philip J. WILLIAM LINN, 1752-1808: AMERICAN REVOLUTIONARY AND ANTI-JEFFERSONIAN. *J. of Presbyterian Hist. 1977 55(4): 381-394.* The American Calvinist William Linn (1752-1808) was a typical American Revolutionary clergyman in identifying with the British all that was evil, with the Americans all that was righteous. Recognized as an excellent preacher as well as academician, after the Revolutionary War he held numerous influential pulpits and was associated with several schools. He wrote many books, including a life of George Washington. At first he hailed the French Revolution as an event that would extend God's activity in bringing liberty to the world, but the emerging irreligion turned him from it. Thomas Jefferson he accused of totally removing religion from politics, a course that could only lead to atheism. He thus stands as a poignant reminder of the perplexing dilemma which confronted so many of his clerical generation: the separation of church and state, and yet the perceived responsibility of the Church to keep government "Christian." Based on the writings of Linn and secondary materials; 55 notes. 1775-1808

Linton, Moses Lewis

4203. Killoren, John J. THE DOCTOR'S SCRAPBOOK: A COLLABORATION OF LINTON AND DE SMET. *Gateway Heritage 1985-86 6(3): 2-9.* A scrapbook owned by St. Louis University physician Moses Lewis Linton contains details of his friendship in 1850-72 with Jesuit missionary Pierre Jan De Smet. De Smet also recorded material about his missionary activities among Indians of the West and his observations about western fur traders. Also inserted into the scrapbook were 12 paintings by prominent St. Louis artists that adverted to De Smet's missionary work. 11 photos, biblio. 1850-72

Lippmann, Walter

4204. Deas, Malcolm. TWO COMPARABLE LIVES: WALTER LIPPMANN AND DANIEL COSIO VILLEGAS. *J. of Interamerican Studies and World Affairs 1982 24(1): 105-114.* Both Daniel Cosío Villegas and Walter Lippmann stimulated debate on the major issues affecting their countries during much of the 20th century. Enrique Krauze's succinct *Daniel Cosío Villegas: Una Biografía Intelectual* (1980), however, serves the Mexican historian and social critic better than Ronald Steel's ponderous and detailed *Walter Lippmann and the American Century* (1980) serves the North American journalist and social critic. 1920-70

4205. Morrissette, Ashley Louis. "Walter Lippmann: Architect of Crisis." Claremont Grad. School 1984. 242 pp. *DAI 1984 45(4): 1199-A.* DA8416453 20c

4206. Rovere, Richard H. WALTER LIPPMANN. *Am. Scholar 1975 44(4): 585-603.* Walter Lippmann was an individual of wide-ranging talents and abilities. He had an incredible knowledge and passion for classical art, and was regarded as an intellectual by Europeans. He was a social activist and joined the Fabian society. As a political activist he helped in the appointment of Louis D. Brandeis to the Supreme Court. He served under General Pershing in World War I and helped to modernize psychological warfare. He supported Wilson's 14 Points. He had great physical prowess. Although he considered himself a member of the establishment, he opposed every president from Theodore Roosevelt to Richard Nixon. Lippmann represented what was best in the liberal and humanist traditions. 1890-1974

4207. —. THE JOURNALIST AS INTELLECTUAL. *J. of Popular Culture 1981 15(2): 69-96.*

Whitfield, Stephen J. WALTER LIPPMANN: A CAREER IN MEDIA'S RAYS, *pp. 69-77.* Examines Walter Lippmann's long and varied career as political journalist, social philosopher, and investigator of public opinion, and his changing influence upon journalism and the public image of the media. 36 notes.

Douglas, George W. EDMUND WILSON: THE MAN OF LETTERS AS JOURNALIST, *pp. 78-85.* Reviews the long literary career of critic Edmund Wilson and the compromises he found it necessary to make with the journalistic world in order to survive commercially as a man of letters. 9 notes.

Cockshutt, Rod. IN SEARCH OF THEODORE H. WHITE, *pp. 86-96.* Describes a 1980 interview with Theodore H. White, author of the noted *Making of the President* volumes, discussing the major issues of contemporary US journalism. 1900-80

Lipscomb, Mance

4208. Lipscomb, Mance; Myers, A. Glenn; and Gardner, Don, ed. OUT OF THE BOTTOMS AND INTO THE BIG CITY. *Southern Exposure 1980 8(2): 4-11.* An excerpt from the forthcoming autobiography of Mance Lipscomb (1895-1976). Lipscomb, a black, was a Texas blues musician and played in many folk festivals after he was "discovered" in 1960. The excerpt tells how and why he brought his family to Houston in 1956 and portrays him as one example of the many who migrated to the southern urban centers in the 1950's. 8 photos. 1956

Lipscomb, Martin Meredith

4209. O'Brien, John T. "THE PEOPLE'S FAVORITE": THE RISE AND FALL OF MARTIN MEREDITH LIPSCOMB. *Virginia Cavalcade 1982 31(4): 216-223.* Bricklayer and bachelor Martin Meredith Lipscomb entered local politics in Richmond, Virginia, in 1853 when he unsuccessfully ran for mayor; he was elected city sergeant in 1854, but he met his political demise in 1857, though he remained active on the periphery of politics until his death in 1903. 1853-57

Lipsitz family

4210. Stocker, Devera Steinberg. THE LIPSITZ FAMILIES: EARLY JEWISH SETTLERS IN DETROIT. *Michigan Jewish Hist. 1982 22(2): 6-13.* Traces the settlement and activities of Lithuanian born brothers, Isaac Lipsitz (1842-1918) and Louis Lipsitz (1856-1933), Philip, their nephew, and their families, in Detroit, Michigan; from 1868 the men were successful businessmen and active members of the Jewish community. 1868-1982

Lipton, Thomas Johnstone

4211. Peterson, John W. THE WORLD'S GREATEST LOSER. *Am. Hist. Illus. 1980 15(7): 18-26.* Brief biography of Sir Thomas Johnstone Lipton (1850-1931), focusing on his many attempts to win the America's Cup yachting trophy, and the response by Americans who contributed to a fund to buy Lipton a substitute cup in 1930. 1899-1931

Lissner, Henry H.

4212. Stuppy, Laurence J. HENRY H. LISSNER, M.D., LOS ANGELES PHYSICIAN. *Western States Jewish Hist. Q. 1976 8(3): 209-216.* Dr. Henry H. Lissner (1875-1968), San Francisco-born and Oakland-raised, took over his father's pawnshop in Oakland in 1886 along with his two brothers. In 1895, Henry and his brother Meyer moved to Los Angeles to open a branch of the pawnshop. They soon closed the new store when Meyer entered law school and Henry started medical school. Henry opened his medical practice in Los Angeles and became a prominent doctor. He was a pioneer in electrocardiography. He served on the staff of several hospitals and was the chief of staff at Cedars of Lebanon Hospital. Photo, 19 notes. 1895-1968

Liszniewska, Marguerite

4213. Pendle, Karin. CINCINNATI'S MUSICAL HERITAGE: THREE WOMEN WHO SUCCEEDED. *Queen City Heritage 1983 41(4): 41-55.* 1875-1970
*For abstract see **Hier, Ethel Glenn***

Littauer, Lucius Nathan

4214. Boxerman, Burton Alan. LUCIUS NATHAN LITTAUER. *Am. Jewish Hist. Q. 1977 66(4): 498-512.* Lucius Nathan Littauer (1859-1944) was the son of Nathan and Harriett Littauer of New York. After graduation from Harvard, he founded a flourishing glove factory and became a prominent businessman, active in Republican politics. He served 10 years in the House of Representatives and became one of the great philanthropists of the era. His gifts provided seed money for many educational, academic, medical, scientific, and civil activities. 41 notes. 1859-1944

Little, John D.

4215. Vouga, Anne F. PRESBYTERIAN MISSIONS AND LOUSIVILLE BLACKS: THE EARLY YEARS, 1898-1910. *Filson Club Hist. Q. 1984 58(3): 310-335.* Describes John D. Little's successful missionary activities among blacks in Louisville, Kentucky. The missions were located in the Uptown and Smoketown sections of Louisville and stressed job training and recreation for black youths. The success of these programs soon led to significant gains in religious areas, as well. Little's work became a model for many other Southern white churches and agencies. Based on documents at the University of Louisville Archives and contemporary newspapers and journals; 49 notes, 4 photos. 1898-1910

Little, William McCarty

4216. Nicolosi, Anthony S. THE SPIRIT OF MCCARTY LITTLE. *US Naval Inst. Pro. 1984 110(9): 72-80.* Lieutenant William McCarty Little supported the establishment of the Naval War College and was closely connected with it until his death. He was one of the college's trio of great early leaders and served as its institutional memory, monitor, guide, and principal defender. 1846-1915

Little Carpenter

See Attakullakulla

Little Turtle (Mishikinskwa)

4217. Carter, Harvey Lewis. A FRONTIER TRAGEDY: LITTLE TURTLE AND WILLIAM WELLS. *Old Northwest 1980 6(1): 3-18.* Little Turtle (Mishikinskwa) was elected war chief of the Miami Indians in 1780. The tribe resided on the Eel River in southern Wisconsin. In 1783 William Wells and three other boys were captured by an Indian party. Wells was adopted into the family of the chief, Gaviahatte, and eventually became Little Turtle's son-in-law by marrying his daughter Sweet Breeze. This article is the story of Little Turtle and Well's attempt to bridge the gap between white and Indian culture. Primary sources; 38 notes. 1780-1812

Little Wolf

4218. Roberts, Gary L. THE SHAME OF LITTLE WOLF. *Montana 1978 28(3): 36-47.* The life of Little Wolf (Northern Cheyenne) reflected the intensely personal dilemma American Indian leaders faced when white domination forced them to abandon their traditional roles and confront the vices of dependence and stagnation. Little Wolf assumed positions of traditional importance as a Cheyenne chief during the 1860's-70's, especially as a Sweet Medicine Chief, who bore the Sacred Bundle. After surrendering to US troops in 1877 and deportation to Indian Territory, Little Wolf, Dull Knife, and 336 followers fled back toward Montana in 1878-79. A portion of the group under Dull Knife surrendered at Ft. Robinson, Kansas. Little Wolf succeeded in leading 114 Cheyenne to Ft. Keogh, Montana. There, Little Wolf developed a strong friendship with Lt. William P. Clark who defended the chief and the cause of the Northern Cheyenne. In 1880, Little Wolf became drunk and killed a rival Cheyenne, Starving Elk. Never before had a Sweet Medicine Chief killed another Cheyenne. He lived until 1904, in seclusion and self-imposed exile along the Rosebud River, as a result of the incident. In 1884, the government created the Tongue River Agency in the area, giving the Northern Cheyenne a permanent home. Based on secondary works and the Little Wolf Papers in the National Archives; 6 illus., 31 notes, biblio. 1856-1904

Livesay, Dorothy

4219. Thompson, Lee Briscoe. A COAT OF MANY CULTURES: THE POETRY OF DOROTHY LIVESAY. *J. of Popular Culture 1981 15(3): 53-61.* The mosaic of Canada's multiple culture is reflected in the poetry and writings of Dorothy Livesay. In these, she deals with the cultural mosaic not only as a social commentator on its prejudices and misunderstandings, but also in terms of its diversity and its common elements. Based on the private papers of Dorothy Livesay; 27 notes. 1930's-70's

Livingston, Alida Schuyler

4220. Biemer, Linda, ed. BUSINESS LETTERS OF ALIDA SCHUYLER LIVINGSTON, 1680-1726. *New York Hist. 1982 63(2): 183-207.* Selected letters, translated from the Dutch, from Alida Schuyler Livingston to her husband, Robert Livingston, reveal the business activities of a Dutch woman of wealth and influence. Robert Livingston, merchant and landowner, was often in New York City on business, while his wife was in charge of their business affairs in Albany and Livingston Manor. The letters represent three periods of the Livingston's life together: 1680-98 when they developed their landed and mercantile estate; 1710-14 when a colony of Palatine Germans occupied Livingston Manor; and 1717-26 when Robert served in the New York Assembly and Alida supervised Livingston Manor. Based on the Livingston-Redmond Papers, Franklin D. Roosevelt Library; 3 illus., 42 notes. 1680-1726

Livingston, Edward

4221. Lyons, Grant. LOUISIANA AND THE LIVINGSTON CRIMINAL CODES. *Louisiana Hist. 1974 15(3): 243-272.* Discusses the life and career of Edward Livingston, the man largely responsible for the writing and passage of a set of liberal laws, Louisiana's system of criminal law, 1822. 1822

Livingston, James Campbell

4222. Watt, Ronald G. DRY GOODS AND GROCERIES IN EARLY UTAH: AN ACCOUNT BOOK VIEW OF JAMES CAMPBELL LIVINGSTON. *Utah Hist. Q. 1979 47(1): 64-69.* James Campbell Livingston (1833-1909) arrived in Utah in 1853. An unskilled laborer, he quarried rock for the Temple, his lifelong occupation. His wages of $2.00 a day were credited in the president's ledger and he drew on this credit at the Mormon tithing store. Extant employment records and financial records of the tithing store provide a picture of the work habits and life-style of a typical immigrant family in the 1850's—what they spent for food, clothing, and entertainment. Primary and secondary sources; 2 illus., 10 notes. 1850's

Livingston, William

4223. Mulder, John M. WILLIAM LIVINGSTON: PROPAGANDIST AGAINST EPISCOPACY. *J. of Presbyterian Hist. 1976 54(1): 83-104.* William Livingston opposed the establishment of King's College (now Columbia University). He feared that a college under Episcopal influence would create an atmosphere of authoritarianism in all areas of the colony's life. Thus his opposition to an American episcopacy was not a sudden emergence. Livingston (1723-90) opposed bishops on the Reformation principle of equality of clergy, as well as the complete separation of temporal and spiritual power. He portrayed the effort to establish an Anglican bishop in America as the ecclesiastical side of political imperialism. His battle against episcopacy played some role in formulating the ideology of the Revolution and attracting popular support. His anticlericalism also signaled a profound change in American religious life—the rise of the articulate layman. Based largely on articles from the *Independent Reflector*, the Livingston Papers in the Massachusetts Historical Society and secondary materials; illus., 82 notes. ca 1750-90

Lloyd, Calvin A.

4224. Lloyd, C. A., II. GUNNER LLOYD: A PERSONAL VIEW. *Marine Corps Gazette 1978 62(1): 57-61.* Marine Gunner Calvin A. Lloyd (1888-1943) was prominent in rifle shooting matches, 1911-43. 1911-43

Lloyd, Gweneth

4225. Crampton, Esmé. PREPARATION FOR AN ORAL BIOGRAPHY OF GWENETH LLOYD, TEACHER OF DANCE. *Can. Oral Hist. Assoc. J. [Canada] 1976/77 2: 49-53.* The author discusses preparation for an oral biography of Gweneth Lloyd, and use of newspaper clippings and oral interviews with Lloyd, 1969-75. 1969-75

Lloyd, Lola Maverick

4226. Stevenson, Janet. LOLA MAVERICK LLOYD: "I MUST DO SOMETHING FOR PEACE!" *Chicago Hist. 1980 9(1): 47-57.* Lola Maverick Lloyd's activism in the movement for feminism and pacifism was started by a speech in 1914 by Hungarian Rosika Schwimmer of the International Suffrage Alliance, on how to stop World War I; Lloyd supported the Woman's Peace Party, the International Congress of Women, and the Women's International League for Peace and Freedom, until her death in 1944. 1914-44

Locke, Alain

4227. Helbling, Mark. ALAIN LOCKE: AMBIVALENCE AND HOPE. *Phylon 1979 40(3): 291-300.* Analyzes the philosophical position of Alain Locke, professor of philosophy at Howard University in Washington, D.C., who influenced many young black writers of the Harlem Renaissance (1920's and 1930's). Based on Locke's writings and on secondary sources; 32 notes. 1920's-30's

4228. Stewart, Jeffrey Conrad. "A Biography of Alain Locke: Philosopher of the Harlem Renaissance, 1886-1930." Yale U. 1979. 384 pp. *DAI 1981 42(4): 1696-1697-A.* DA8121412 1907-30

Locke, Robert D.

4229. Giddes, Paul H., ed. CHINA'S FIRST OIL WELL: RECOLLECTIONS OF ROBERT D. LOCKE, TITUSVILLE OIL PIONEER. *Pennsylvania Hist 1980 47(1): 29-37.* In 1878, Robert D. Locke and A. P. Karns drilled China's first oil well on Taiwan. In 1940, Paul H. Giddens interviewed Locke, then 90 years old, regarding his trip from Titusville to Taiwan and his experiences there. Reprints the interview. 5 notes. 1877-78

Lockhart, Caroline

4230. Furman, Necah Stewart. WESTERN AUTHOR CAROLINE LOCKHART AND HER PERSPECTIVES ON WYOMING. *Montana 1986 36(1): 50-59.* In 1904 Caroline Lockhart, a journalist from Boston and Philadelphia, arrived in Cody, Wyoming. Seven years later she published *Me-Smith,* the first of seven novels that would bring her national recognition as a western writer. Her most important contributions were her characterizations of westerners. Basing her characters on identifiable persons in Cody, Lockhart tended to caricature their unusual physical traits and accentuate their personal foibles. Her life coincided with the end of the Old West, and in her last novel, *The Old West and the New* (1933), she described the changes she observed. Based on the Caroline Lockhart Collection, American Heritage Center, Coe Library, University of Wyoming, Laramie, and interviews; 5 photos, 32 notes. 1889-1962

Locklin, Nora and Dee

4231. Locklin, Nora. SANTA RITA: AN EYEWITNESS TO A GREAT DISCOVERY. *Permian Historical Annual 1984 24: 25-30.* Nora Locklin recounts her life as the wife of an oil field worker in Reagan County, Texas, where they saw the famous Santa Rita No. 1 well strike oil. 1919-23

Lockwood, Belva Ann

4232. Davis, Julia. A FEISTY SCHOOLMARM MADE THE LAWYERS SIT UP AND TAKE NOTICE. *Smithsonian 1981 11(12): 133-150.* Outlines the career of Belva Ann Lockwood (1830-1917), a headstrong woman who overcame seemingly insurmountable barriers in order to practice before the Supreme Court; she also ran for president in 1884. 1850-1917

Lockwood, Daniel Newton

4233. Sklar, Harold M. DANIEL NEWTON LOCKWOOD: A BIOGRAPHICAL ESSAY. *Niagara Frontier 1975 22(2): 45-51.* Examines the political career of Buffalo citizen, Daniel Newton Lockwood, 1870-1902. 1870-1902

Loesel, Lorenz

4234. Hansen, Carl R. LORENZ LOESEL, "AUTOBIOGRAPHY." *Chronicle 1981 17(4): 13-15.* Lorenz Loesel migrated to Michigan with a group of German Lutherans to organize a missionary colony to Christianize the Indians in 1845. 1845-80

Logan, Deborah Norris

4235. Barr, Marleen. DEBORAH NORRIS LOGAN, FEMINIST CRITICISM, AND IDENTITY THEORY: INTERPRETING A WOMAN'S DIARY WITHOUT THE DANGER OF SEPARATISM. *Biography 1985 8(1): 12-24.* Feminist scholars are devoting much attention to unearthing women's diaries and letters. As they develop new theories to interpret these noncanonical works, feminists should not dismiss other theories generated by the male critical establishment. Examines the diary of Deborah Norris Logan in terms of Norman N. Holland's notions about identity theory in order to provide one link between new feminist scholarship and existing male-generated theory. 1815-39

Logan, Ernest

4236. Schaedel, Grace Logan. THE STORY OF ERNEST AND LIZZIE LOGAN—A FRONTIER COURTSHIP. *Ann. of Wyoming 1982 54(2): 48-61.* Ernest Logan arrived at Camp Carlin, Wyoming, in 1871 and subsequently worked as a carpenter, cowboy, and stagecoach driver. In 1891 he opened a book and stationery shop in Cheyenne that featured a soda fountain and homemade ice cream and candy. Two years later he married Lizzie Walker who had come west to work with her sister Jennie in a dressmaking business. Together they made the Logan Store one of the lasting business enterprises of Cheyenne. 9 photos. 1871-1910

Logan, James

4237. Stoddart, Mary G. and Engle, Reed L. STENTON. *Mag. Antiques 1983 124(2): 266-271.* Presents a brief biography of James Logan, a "major political force in Pennsylvania," focusing on his brick county seat, Stenton, in Germantown, Pennsylvania. 1723-1830

Logan, John A.

4238. Castel, Albert. "BLACK JACK" LOGAN. *Civil War Times Illus. 1976 15(7): 4-10, 41-45.* Discusses the command of John Alexander Logan, a southern-born Union officer 1861-65. 1861-65

Logan, Rayford Whittingham

4239. Franklin, John Hope. RAYFORD WHITTINGHAM LOGAN (1897-1982). *Hispanic Am. Hist. Rev. 1983 63(3): 596-597.* Rayford W. Logan was a historian, editor, columnist, and public servant, and spent the 28 years prior to his retirement in 1965 as chairman of the Department of History at Howard University. He was a productive scholar and prolific writer who produced works on US relations with Haiti, African history, Afro-American history, and international human rights. 1897-1982

Lohmiller, Charles B. (Hum-Pa-Zee)

4240. Johnson, Ben H. HUM-PA-ZEE. *Montana 1978 28(1): 56-64.* Major Charles B. Lohmiller, known as Hum-Pa-Zee (Sioux for "Yellow Shoes") served at the Fort Peck Indian Agency, Montana, during 1893-1917, and was Superintendent during 1904-17. Reveals Lohmiller as a man with an unapproachable, military facade, who was genuinely interested in the welfare of all people. Presents favorable reaction to Lohmiller's tenure at the Fort Peck Agency. Based on author's experiences; 11 illus. 1893-1917

Lohnes, Francis W.

4241. Potter, James E. A CONGRESSIONAL MEDAL OF HONOR FOR A NEBRASKA SOLDIER: THE CASE OF PRIVATE FRANCIS W. LOHNES. *Nebraska Hist. 1984 65(2): 245-256.* Examines the military career of Francis W. Lohnes, the only soldier among the 57 Nebraska soldiers awarded the Congressional Medal of Honor who received it as a result of military action occurring within the borders of the state. He received the medal as a member of Company H, 1st Nebraska Veteran Cavalry, after a fight with Indians near the Dan Smith ranch on the Overland Trail 12 May 1865.

Though Lohnes deserted several months later, the War Department, under legislation approved in 1889, removed the charge of desertion from Lohnes's record in 1891 and granted him an honorable discharge retroactive to 24 September 1865. This action restored Lohnes's pension privileges and cleared the way for his widow to receive a pension. Lohnes died on 18 September 1889 as a result of a threshing accident. 3 illus., appendix, 31 notes. 1865-91

Lohrenz, Henry W.

4242. Toews, Paul. HENRY W. LOHRENZ AND TABOR COLLEGE. *Mennonite Life 1983 38(3): 11-19.* Henry W. Lohrenz, founder and first president of Tabor College in Hillsboro, Kansas, had a strong commitment to the liberal arts and attempted to direct the college into the mainstream of American progressivism. This movement, at first supported by some parts of the Mennonite Brethren, was eliminated after Lohrenz's presidency, with the ascendancy of more conservative Mennonite leaders. Much of the tension in the college's life was due to lack of an official place for the Mennonites in the United States. Based on the Lohrenz Papers and other primary sources at Mennonite Brethren archives in Fresno, California, and Hillsboro, Kansas; illus., 4 photos, 50 notes. 1908-31

Lomax, Alan

4243. Berrett, Joshua. ALAN LOMAX: SOME RECONSIDERATIONS. *J. of Jazz Studies 1979 6(1): 54-63.* Musical anthropologist Alan Lomax's contributions to folk music and the folk tradition began in 1933 when he was 18; he collected, recorded, and cataloged folk music until the 1970's. ca 1933-73

London, Jack

4244. Beynet, Michel. LA FORTUNE DE JACK LONDON EN ITALIE [Jack London's fortune in Italy]. *Rev. des Études Italiennes [France] 1978 24(4): 337-376.* Analyzes Jack London's work and his popularity in Italy, and reviews the opinions of his critics; 1925-30. 1925-30

4245. Champlin, Brad. THE UNKNOWN JACK LONDON. *Pacific Hist. 1980 24(2): 132-134.* Brief biography of Jack London (1876-1916). "His success as a writer was colored by two women and one dangerous idea." One woman was a school teacher who assigned a written theme due every day. As a writer, Jack London would write a thousand words a day. The other woman was Ina Coolbrith. She was the Oakland Public Library librarian who introduced him to the world's great authors and ideas. The one dangerous idea was Nietzsche's concept of "Overman." London failed to learn to survive disappointment and was driven by the Superman aspect of "Overman." He died at age 40 soon after the burning down of his home, Wolf House. Illus., photo. 1876-1916

4246. Hamilton, David Mike. SOME CHIN-CHIN AND TEA: JACK LONDON IN JAPAN. *Pacific Hist. 1979 23(2): 19-25.* In 1904, Jack London went to Japan to cover the Russo-Japanese War as a correspondent for William Randolph Hearst. Despite some bungling, London turned out to be an excellent reporter. Based largely on the Jack London Collection, Henry E. Huntington Library, San Marino, California; 3 photos, 22 notes. 1904

4247. Pasqualini, François. JACK LONDON ET LE MIRAGE SOCIALISTE [Jack London and the socialist mirage]. *Écrits de Paris [France] 1975 (344): 113-116.* Jack London's autobiographical work *Martin Eden* (1909) provides insights into London's career as an author. 1900's

4248. Tavernier-Courbin, Jacqueline. AUTOUR DE JACK LONDON [About Jack London]. *Can. Rev. of Am. Studies [Canada] 1982 13(3): 363-371.* Reviews *Jack London: Essays in Criticism* (1978), edited by Ray Wilson Ownbey, Andrew Sinclair's *Jack: A Biography of Jack London* (1977), *Curious Fragments: Jack London's Tales of Fantasy Fiction* (1975), edited by Dale L. Walker, and *Jack London: No Mentor But Myself* (1978), also edited by Walker. As these books evidence, serious efforts continue to assess critically the works of John Griffith London. 8 notes. 1896-1916

4249. Whitfield, Stephen J. AMERICAN WRITING AS A WILDLIFE PRESERVE: JACK LONDON AND NORMAN MAILER. *Southern Q. 1977 15(2): 135-148.* Compares the writings of Jack London and Norman Mailer. Emphasizes their personal attitudes and habits to discover similar literary characters. Finds evidence of such themes as masculinity, virility, violence, and assertiveness. Examines each author's changing political and social views, as reflected through literature. 34 notes. 20c

4250. Willson, Carolyn Johnston. "Jack London's Socialism." U. of California, Berkeley, 1976. 200 pp. *DAI 1977 38(2): 984-A.* 1896-1916

London, Meyer

4251. Frieburger, William Joseph. "The Lone Socialist Vote: A Political Study of Meyer London." U. of Cincinnati 1980. 310 pp. *DAI 1980 41(3): 1186-A.* 8021032 1899-1926

Long, Earl Kemp

4252. Baldwin, John T., Jr. CAMPAIGNING WITH EARL LONG. *North Louisiana Hist. Assoc. 1976 8(1): 27-30.* Although for nearly 30 years Earl Kemp Long was an active candidate for public office in Louisiana, he has been "overshadowed by his more famous brother, Huey" and "has been a neglected figure in Louisiana history." He was somewhat shy, but "had a strong inner drive and could not resist the temptation to get out on the stump . . . his real joy lay in politics for its own sake." He was "the complete political animal . . . who was liked rather than revered, the one who attracted the voters because they felt he was one of them." 19 notes. 20c

4253. Leslie, James Paul. "Earl K. Long: The Formative Years, 1895-1940." U. of Missouri, Columbia 1974. 272 pp. *DAI 1982 42(9): 4120-A.* DA8205398 1915-40

4254. Peoples, Morgan. EARL KEMP LONG: THE MAN FROM PEA PATCH FARM. *Louisiana Hist. 1976 17(4): 365-392.* Presents a biographical account of Earl K. Long from 1929 to his death in 1960, with particular reference to the time spent on his Winfield Parish farm. Long loved "politicking" and was active in Louisiana politics throughout this period. Based on published sources and personal interviews; 3 photos, 142 notes. 1929-60

Long, Everette Beach

4255. Robertson, James I., Jr. EVERETTE BEACH LONG, 1919-1981. *Civil War Hist. 1981 27(3): 275-277.* Obituary of Everette Beach Long, noted Civil War historian, author and professor of American Studies at the University of Wyoming. 1919-81

Long, George

4256. Johnston, George Burke. A BOOK FOR GENERAL LEE. *Virginia Cavalcade 1980 30(2): 88-95.* Chronicles the career of George Long (1800-79), an English classical scholar who dedicated a second edition of his *The Thoughts of M. Aurelius Antonius* (1869) to Robert E. Lee after the first edition had been stolen by an American publishing firm and dedicated to Ralph Waldo Emerson. 1869

Long, Huey P.

4257. Bobbitt, Charles A. HUEY P. LONG: THE MEMPHIS YEARS. *West Tennessee Hist. Soc. Papers 1978 (32): 133-139.* Huey P. Long was first in Memphis in 1911. Soon he was out of work, and took any job. He was in and out of Memphis through 1914. During this three-year period he met Ed Crump, political leader of Memphis, and married Miss Rose McConnel. After leaving Memphis he went to Louisiana. None of his next appearances in Memphis, in the early 1930's, lasted more than a few hours. Based on contemporary newspaper accounts; 2 illus., 33 notes. 1911-14

4258. Brinkley, Alan. COMPARATIVE BIOGRAPHY AS POLITICAL HISTORY: HUEY LONG AND FATHER COUGHLIN. *Hist. Teacher 1984 18(1): 9-16.* A comparative biographical examination of Huey P. Long and Father Charles E. Coughlin contributes more to understanding the political history of the 1930's than treating the two men as individuals. Similarities in their careers overshadow superficial differences. Both championed marginal groups, both had roots in Populism, and both developed programs that challenged the emerging centralized, bureaucratic, corporate capitalism of the 20th century. Their popularity reveals the intensity of localism in the 1930's, but their failure also indicates that their vision of a 19th-century individualistic society was no longer credible or viable by the 1930's. 1930-40

4259. Jeansonne, Glen. WHAT IS THE LEGACY OF THE LONGS? AN HISTORIOGRAPHICAL OVERVIEW. *Louisiana Rev. 1980 9(2): 141-149.* Reviews literature on the political career of Huey P. Long, governor of Louisiana, 1928-31. 1930-69

4260. Jeansonne, Glen. PREACHER, POPULIST, PROPAGANDIST: THE EARLY CAREER OF GERALD L. K. SMITH. *Biography 1979 2(4): 303-327.* 1934-48
For abstract see ***Smith, Gerald L. K.***

4261. Snyder, Robert E. THE CONCEPT OF DEMAGOGUERY: HUEY LONG AND HIS LITERARY CRITICS. *Louisiana Studies 1976 15(1): 61-84.* Huey P. Long (1893-1935) of Louisiana, the most famous of southern demagogues, aroused great criticism from politicians, novelists, and his own family. Long saw himself as an enlightened populist reformer, but others found him self-seeking, deceptive, and a threat to society. Hamilton Basso's novel *Sun in Capricorn* (1942) is one of four major novels in the 1940's which used Long's life to show the evils of demagoguery. The chief character, Gilgo Slade, uses sham, deceit, and blackmail to achieve power. Based on primary and secondary sources; 76 notes. 1920-76

4262. Swan, George Steven. A PRELIMINARY COMPARISON OF LONG'S LOUISIANA AND DUPLESSIS'S QUEBEC. *Louisiana Hist. 1984 25(3): 289-319.* Maurice L. Duplessis, premier of Quebec, and Huey P. Long, governor and United States senator, showed similarities in their personal characteristics, early lives, and in their methods of dominating their respective governments, dealing with their legislatures, and financing their machines. Both poured money into public works, resisted the extension of federal power, and found their strongest support in the rural areas. Their regimes represent variants of Seymour Martin Lipset's typology of political extremism and may usefully be studied with that of Juan Peron of Argentina. Secondary sources; 191 notes. 1920-60

Long, Jefferson F.

4263. Matthews, John M. JEFFERSON FRANKLIN LONG: THE PUBLIC CAREER OF GEORGIA'S FIRST BLACK CONGRESSMAN. *Phylon 1981 42(2): 145-156.* Jefferson F. Long was the first and only black to sit in Congress from Georgia, the state with the largest Negro population. He was born a slave in 1836. After the Civil War he opened a tailor shop. He was elected on the Republican ticket as a token gesture to serve a third session term from January 1871 to March 1871. He delivered one speech in the House of Representatives. He never again held public office but he remained active in politics. He became disillusioned with Republican Party tactics until he withdrew from political life in 1884. He died in February 1901. 1871-84

Long, Stephen H.

4264. Allin, Lawrence C. FOUR ENGINEERS ON THE MISSOURI: LONG, FREMONT, HUMPHREYS, AND WARREN. *Nebraska Hist. 1984 65(1): 58-83.* 1817-57
For abstract see ***Frémont, John C.***

Longabaugh, Harry ("Sundance Kid")

4265. Brown, Dee. BUTCH CASSIDY AND THE SUNDANCE KID. *Am. Hist. Illus. 1982 17(4): 57-63.* 1880's-1911
For abstract see ***Parker, Robert LeRoy ("Butch Cassidy")***

Longchamps, Charles Julian de

4266. Rowe, G. S. and Knott, Alexander W. POWER, JUSTICE, AND FOREIGN RELATIONS IN THE CONFEDERATION PERIOD: THE MARBOIS-LONGCHAMPS AFFAIR, 1784-1786. *Pennsylvania Mag. of Hist. and Biog. 1980 104(3): 275-307.* Charles Julian de Longchamps's physical attack on François de Barbé-Marbois sparked a significant juridical controversy between Pennsylvania and France with implications for the Confederation Congress, which itself was facing the prospect of ratifying America's first consular treaty. Based on Archives Diplomatiques: Correspondence Politique and other primary sources; 72 notes. 1784-86

Longfellow, Henry Wadsworth

4267. Pauly, Thomas H. *OUTRE-MER* AND LONGFELLOW'S QUEST FOR A CAREER. *New England Q. 1977 50(1): 30-52.* Traces Henry Wadsworth Longfellow's (1807-1882) literary career before the publication of *Outre-Mer* in 1835. Washington Irving's (1783-1859) *Sketchbook* influenced the writing of *Outre-Mer*. In *Outre-Mer* Longfellow presented his ideas about literature and developed a justification for his subsequent poetry. Based on Longfellow's letters and an analysis of the essays in *Outre-Mer;* 31 notes. 1825-35

Longman, Evelyn Beatrice

4268. Conner, Janis C. AMERICAN WOMEN SCULPTORS BREAK THE MOLD. *Art and Antiques 1980 3(3): 80-87.* 1893-1925
For abstract see ***Eberle, Abastenia St. Leger***

Longren, Albin Kasper

4269. Lebrecht, Chuck. A. K. LONGREN, PIONEER AIRMAN OF THE WEST. *Am. Aviation Hist. Soc. J. 1981 26(4): 258-270.* Albin Kasper Longren designed, built, and flew the *Topeka I,* the first successfully produced airplane in Kansas, and formed the Longren Aircraft Corporation in 1919, which he sold after World War II to retire. 1911-50

4270. Mace, Kenneth D. PIONEER AIRMEN OF KANSAS. *Aviation Q. 1979 5(2): 152-163.* 1908-29
For abstract see ***Call, Harry***

Longstreet, Augustus Baldwin

4271. Scafidel, J. R. "The Letters of Augustus Baldwin Longstreet." U. of South Carolina 1976. 814 pp. *DAI 1977 38(1): 268-A.* 1800-70

4272. Scafidel, J. R. A GEORGIAN IN CONNECTICUT: A. B. LONGSTREET'S LEGAL EDUCATION. *Georgia Hist. Q. 1977 61(3): 222-232.* Discusses the effect of Augustus Baldwin Longstreet's legal education at Tapping Reeve's Law School in Litchfield, Connecticut, in 1813 on his career. Later a successful Georgia lawyer, author, college president, and proslavery apologist, Longstreet's attitudes toward the North and his whole lifestyle were influenced by his experiences and the people he met while he was in Connecticut. Primary and secondary sources; 28 notes. 1813

4273. Scafidel, J. R. AUGUSTUS BALDWIN LONGSTREET: NATIVE AUGUSTAN. *Richmond County Hist. 1979 11(2): 19-29.* Augustus Baldwin Longstreet, judge, author, college president, Methodist preacher, college professor, and owner, editor, and publisher of the *State Right's Sentinel,* 1834-36, migrated to Richmond County, Georgia, in 1784, and lived there until 1855 when he was 65. 1784-1855

Longstreet, James

4274. Piston, William Garrett. "Lee's Tarnished Lieutenant: James Longstreet and His Image in American Society." U. of South Carolina 1982. 751 pp. *DAI 1982 43(4): 1266-1267-A.* DA8220215 19c

Loomis, Emma Morse

4275. Nackman, Mark E. and Paton, Darryl K. RECOLLECTIONS OF AN ILLINOIS WOMAN. *Western Illinois Regional Studies 1978 1(1): 27-44.* The memoir of Emma Morse Loomis, written in 1938, covers her life in Illinois since her birth in 1848. 1848-1938

Loomis, Mahlon

4276. Casdorph, Paul D. MAHLON LOOMIS AND THE "AERIAL TELEGRAPH." *West Virginia Hist. 1980 41(3): 205-225.* A dentist by profession, Dr. Mahlon Loomis (1826-86) spent much of his life experimenting with electricity and attempting to send messages through the air. Many of his experiments were conducted in Virginia and West Virginia. Loomis believed that messages could be sent across oceans without cables. He may not have invented the radio as some people claim, but he can be listed as a pioneer in radio. Based on the Loomis Papers, newspaper accounts, and US Patent Office materials; 7 illus., 33 notes. ca 1850-86

Lopez, Al

4277. Brandmeyer, Gerard A. BASEBALL AND THE AMERICAN DREAM: A CONVERSATION WITH AL LOPEZ. *Tampa Bay Hist. 1981 3(1): 48-73.* Brief introduction followed by an interview with veteran baseball player and manager Al Lopez, originally of Ybor City, Florida, focusing on Lopez's professional baseball career from 1925 to 1969 and his early life as the son of a Spanish-born cigar selector in the cigar industry. 1906-69

4278. Lopez, Al; Lawson, Steven F., interview. YBOR CITY AND BASEBALL: AN INTERVIEW WITH AL LOPEZ. *Tampa Bay History 1985 7(2): 59-76.* In an interview, Al Lopez, baseball star and son of a Cuban cigarmaker from the Ybor City area of Tampa, Florida, talks about his youth in Tampa and playing baseball in the area until he became a major leaguer. 1924-77

Lopp, Ellen Kittredge

4279. Engerman, Jeanne. LETTERS FROM CAPE PRINCE OF WALES. A MISSION FAMILY IN NORTHWESTERN ALASKA 1892-1902. *Alaska Journal 1984 14(4): 33-41.* Describes the Alaska life of missionary Ellen Kittredge Lopp, who taught with her husband W. T. "Tom" Lopp in the government school at isolated Cape Prince of Wales, Alaska. Icebound nine months a year, Ellen Lopp wrote hundreds of letters to family and friends describing the everyday life at the mission. Besides teaching and preaching to the Eskimos there were the six children she bore to be cared for. Her letters reveal a powerful belief in her work however, and even after 10 years at the outpost, she had a strong reluctance to leave. Based on letters of Ellen Kittredge Lopp and secondary sources; 31 notes, 10 photos, illus. 1892-1902

Loras, Jean Mathias Pierre

4280. Auge, Thomas E. THE DREAM OF BISHOP LORAS: A CATHOLIC IOWA. *Palimpsest 1980 61(6): 170-179.* Jean Mathias Pierre Loras, bishop of the diocese of Dubuque, Iowa, from 1837 until he died in 1858, lacked priests, funds, and cooperation, but left his mark on the state by encouraging Irish and German immigrants to settle there. 1837-58

Loring, Edward Greely

4281. Viets, Henry R. THE RESIDENT HOUSE STAFF AT THE OPENING OF THE BOSTON CITY HOSPITAL IN 1864. *J. of the Hist. of Medicine and Allied Sci. 1959 14(2): 179-190.* 1864-1919
For abstract see ***Blake, Clarence John***

Lothian, James and William

4282. Reynolds, E. Norah. LOST ON PRAIRIE TRAILS. *Beaver [Canada] 1981 311(4): 41-49.* In 1880, James and William Lothian reached Quebec City from Scotland hoping to establish homesteads in Manitoba. Extracts from their letters to their parents and other family members in Scotland, 1880-1908, detail pioneer life in Manitoba. ca 1880-1908

Lotspeich, Helen G.

4283. Silberstein, Iola O. DIVERSITY ON CONVERGING PATHWAYS: MARY H. DOHERTY AND HELEN LOTSPEICH. *Queen City Heritage 1983 41(4): 3-23.* 1901-74

For abstract see ***Doherty, Mary H.***

Lott, Philip S.

4284. Okada, Yasuo. THE ECONOMIC WORLD OF A SENECA COUNTY FARMER, 1830-1880. *New York History 1985 66(1): 4-28.* For most of his adult life, farmer Philip S. Lott kept records of his financial affairs. Using these records, reconstructs life in Seneca County, New York, describing not only Lott's economic status but the people with whom he dealt, the crops he raised, and some aspects of his social life. Based on Philip Lott's personal account books, census records, and government reports; 4 tables, 4 illus., 24 notes. 1826-84

Louis, Isidor

4285. Maio, Florence and Schwartz, Henry. ISIDOR LOUIS: SHOEMAKER TO CAPITALIST IN SAN DIEGO. *Western States Jewish History 1985 17(4): 326-332.* Presents a biographical sketch of Isidor Louis (1836-95), a Polish-born Jew who moved to San Diego in 1870, opened a shoe store in 1872, and eventually became a leading citizen involved in diverse business enterprises and cultural activities. Based on newspapers; 52 notes. 1864-95

Louis, Joe

4286. Capeci, Dominic J., Jr. and Wilkerson, Martha. MULTIFARIOUS HERO: JOE LOUIS, AMERICAN SOCIETY AND RACE RELATIONS DURING WORLD CRISIS, 1935-1945. *J. of Sport Hist. 1983 10(3): 5-25.* Joe Louis, the black heavyweight boxer, played a major role in improving race relations during a difficult time of segregation and racism. His patriotism during World War II helped to bring about the end of Jim Crow laws. His transition from black champion to national hero signified the transformation of America. Louis symbolized black aggressiveness and self-respect, and he increased whites' respect for blacks through his patriotism. He helped to integrate American society and change racial attitudes. Mostly primary sources, including manuscripts from the NAACP, the Urban League, and the Franklin D. Roosevelt Library; 154 notes. 1935-45

4287. Romaña, José Miguel. EL BOXEADOR DEL SIGLO: JOE LOUIS [The boxer of the century: Joe Louis]. *Hist. y Vida [Spain] 1983 16(185): 20-34.* Joe Louis rose from a Southern ghetto to become the heavyweight champion of the world, but his life ended in poverty. 1934-81

4288. Sammons, Jeffrey T. BOXING AS A REFLECTION OF SOCIETY: THE SOUTHERN REACTION TO JOE LOUIS. *J. of Popular Culture 1983 16(4): 23-33.* The career of boxer Joe Louis demonstrates that sport heroes reflect contemporary public moods and beliefs. Despite his successes, Louis throughout his career was subject to the dictates of Southern racial etiquette. Based on contemporary Southern newspapers; 41 notes. 1934-51

Love, J. Spencer

4289. Finger, Bill. TEXTILE MEN: LOOMS, LOANS AND LOCKOUTS. *Southern Exposure 1976 3(4): 54-65.* Presents biographies of southern textile industry figures, 1 918-40: J. Spencer Love, a mill owner, Lacy Wright, a mill hand, and Joe Pedigo, a labor organizer. 1918-40

Love, Joseph Robert

4290. Lumsden, Joy. JOSEPH ROBERT LOVE, 1839-1914: WEST INDIAN EXTRAORDINARY. *Afro-Americans in New York Life and Hist. 1983 7(1): 25-39.* Discusses the travels and influences of Jamaican journalist, orator, Episcopal clergyman, and patriot, Joseph Robert Love, in New York and the West Indies, focusing on his religious career in Buffalo. 1839-1914

Lovejoy, Arthur O.

4291. Feuer, Lewis S. ARTHUR O. LOVEJOY. *Am. Scholar 1977 46(3): 358-366.* Studies the teaching career of Arthur O. Lovejoy (1873-1962), chiefly at the Harvard and Johns Hopkins philosophy departments. He illustrated Albert Einstein's definition of a teacher's greatest tragedy: "when he finds that his language, method, and problems cease to be those of the new generation of students, whose presuppositions he may find not only alien but willfully irrational." He was totally committed to the rational, and impervious to ideological fashions; thus he opposed or was ignored by the new generation of philosophic militants. An early experience made him the lifelong champion of academic freedom and the prime mover in the organization of the American Association of University Professors. ca 1900-38

Lovejoy, Owen

4292. Berfield, Karen. THREE ANTISLAVERY LEADERS OF BUREAU COUNTY. *Western Illinois Regional Studies 1980 3(1): 46-65.* 1831-65

For abstract see ***Bryant, John Howard***

Lovelace, Maud Hart

4293. Ray, Jo Anne. MAUD HART LOVELACE AND MANKATO. Stuhler, Barbara and Kreuter, Gretchen, ed. *Women of Minnesota: Selected Biographical Essays* (St. Paul: Minnesota Historical Society Press, 1977): 155-172. Maud Hart Lovelace immortalized the fictional town, Deep Valley, in her Betsey-Tacy books for children. The books were largely autobiographical and based on Lovelace's own childhood in Mankato, Minnesota. She also wrote many adult, historical novels, of which *Early Candlelight* (1929) is the best-known; and she collaborated with her husband, Delos Lovelace, on many books. Although she left Mankato in 1910 to attend the University of Minnesota and she never returned to live there, her children's books have provided an enduring legacy of a happy childhood in an idyllic, small town world of the early 1900's. Primary and secondary sources; photo, 44 notes. 1892-1977

Lovett, Robert A.

4294. Fanton, Jonathan Foster. "Robert A. Lovett: The War Years." Yale U. 1978. 275 pp. *DAI 1979 40(1): 418-A.* 1940-45

Lovett, Robert W.

4295. Lovett, Robert W. REMEMBERED TRIANGLE, OR GROWING UP IN NORTH BEVERLY IN THE 1920S. *Essex Inst. Hist. Collections 1981 117(4): 283-295.* Historical reminiscences about people, places, and events from the author's childhood, concentrating on the triangular area of North Beverly bounded by Cabot, Conant, and Dodge Streets. 5 photos, map, 6 notes. 1920's

Low, Frederick F.

4296. Anderson, David L. BETWEEN TWO CULTURES: FREDERICK F. LOW IN CHINA. *California History 1980 59(3): 240-254.* Frederick F. Low, successful gold rush businessman, served as a California congressman and as state governor out of loyalty to the Union cause. In 1869 he was appointed minister to China. Low believed that peace and cooperation could lead to amicable relations between East and West, despite such incidents as the Tientsin massacre of 21 June 1870. Disillusionment set in, however, when Low went to Korea to ask for redress for the alleged murder of the crew of a wrecked American ship. An American squadron was forced to destroy five Korean forts, a diplomatic defeat which changed Low's views on relations with the Orient. Similar questions involving protocol in China finally resulted in his resignation in 1874. Not a gunboat diplomatist, Low at the end of his service predicted that Chinese-Western relations would embody hostility and violence rather than cooperation. Photos, 40 notes. 1869-74

Low, Juliette Gordon

4297. Strickland, Charles E. JULIETTE LOW, THE GIRL SCOUTS, AND THE ROLE OF AMERICAN WOMEN. Kelley, Mary, ed. *Woman's Being, Woman's Place: Female Identity and Vocation in American History* (Boston: G. K. Hall, 1979): 252-264. Employing Erik Erikson's life-cycle model, records a convergence of personal and historical crises in the life of Juliette Low (b. 1860), founder of the Girl Scouts of America. Prepared to assume the role of companion, hostess, and mother of children, Low instead faced loneliness, confronted a childless existence, and ran headlong into her husband's affair with a widow. The result was a marriage that not only brought anguish but ended in a humiliating divorce. Alone and unable to find an alternative role, Low considered her life devoid of meaning. Her opportunity to resolve her crisis of identity came only when she found in the Girl Scout movement a cause to which she could dedicate herself. Scouting might not have challenged all conventional definitions of women's role and sphere, but under Low's tutelage it did demand that women become more than delicate, helpless ornaments. 56 notes. 1900-20

4298. Saxton, Martha. THE BEST GIRL SCOUT OF THEM ALL. *Am. Heritage 1982 33(4): 38-47.* Juliette Gordon Low, the founder of the Girl Scouts of America, had an unhappy childhood and marriage. After being widowed in England, she became acquainted with Sir Robert Baden-Powell, founder of the Boy Scout movement. Low returned to Savannah, Georgia, in 1912, and started a Girl Scout troop immediately. The organization grew rapidly and for many years, Low remained involved. 12 illus. 1861-1927

Low, Will Hicok

4299. Meixner, Laura L. WILL HICOK LOW (1853-1932): HIS EARLY CAREER AND BARBIZON EXPERIENCE. *American Art Journal 1985 17(4): 51-70.* Will Hicok Low (1853-1932) is known primarily as a muralist and academic painter. However, his early training was in France among the artists of the Barbizon school; Jean-François Millet particularly influenced him. Most paintings of this period are lost, but Low's notebooks and sketchbooks allow reconstruction of the period. He developed a style based on clear silhouettes and precise delineation of form, and emphasized rural subject matter. He took formal classes in Paris, but spent much time in the countryside around Barbizon with French and American friends. Based on Will Hicok Low's manuscript autobiography, *The Primrose Way,* at the Institute of History and Art in Albany, New York; photo, 21 plates, 79 notes. 1872-86

Lowdermilk, Walter Clay

4300. Helms, J. Douglas. WALTER LOWDERMILK'S JOURNEY: FORESTER TO LAND CONSERVATIONIST. *Environmental Rev. 1984 8(2): 132-145.* Prints a biography of Walter Clay Lowdermilk, who studied forestry in Germany, served in the US Forest Service, chronicled the environmental impact of 7,000 years of agriculture, and assisted conservation and agricultural development in China and among settlements of Jews in Palestine. Revision of a presentation to a symposium at the Western Forestry Center, Portland, Oregon, 18-19 October 1983. Prehistory-20c

Lowell, Amy

4301. Luria, Maxwell. MISS LOWELL AND MR. NEWTON: THE RECORD OF A LITERARY FRIENDSHIP. *Harvard Lib. Bull. 1981 29(1): 5-34.* The untimely death of Amy Lowell (1874-1925) ended a seven-year friendship with Alfred Edward Newton (1863-1940) that produced a significant body of letters hitherto largely unpublished. Newton, a wealthy manufacturer and avid literary collector, was as eccentric as Lowell. Their letters, in addition to revealing a warm, frank personal relationship (Newton did not like her poetry very much), mirror the society in which they lived and worked. Nearly 60 communications between them are included in whole or in part. Primary sources; 24 notes. 1918-25

Lowell, Josephine Shaw

4302. Saveth, Edward N. PATRICIAN PHILANTHROPY IN AMERICA: THE LATE NINETEENTH AND EARLY TWENTIETH CENTURIES. *Social Service Rev. 1980 54(1): 76-91.* 1870-1910

*For abstract see **Lee, Joseph***

Lowell, Percival

4303. Meyer, William B. "LIFE ON MARS IS ALMOST CERTAIN!" *Am. Heritage 1984 35(2): 38-43.* Astronomer Percival Lowell spent much of his life convincing Americans of the possibilty that life existed on Mars. In speeches and articles in the 1890's, he argued that linear features on the planet's surface were canals built by intelligent beings. Popular belief was strong, but most scientists scoffed at his theories. 2 photos, 2 illus. 1890-1910

Lowell, Robert

4304. Köhler, Angelika. ROBERT LOWELL: POETRY AS A WAY TO SOCIAL ACTIVITY. *Wiss. Zeits. der Humboldt-Universität zu Berlin. Gesellschaftswissenschaftliche Reihe [East Germany] 1984 33(4): 427-429.* Describes the background, life, and poetry of social activist poet Robert Lowell. 20c

4305. Rollins, J. Barton. ROBERT LOWELL'S APPRENTICESHIP AND EARLY POEMS. *Am. Literature 1980 52(1): 67-83.* Examines the influences in the development of Robert Lowell as a poet and analyzes his early poems. The most important early influence in Lowell's poetic development was his mentor, Richard Eberhart. But Lowell was also influenced by Allen Tate and John Crowe Ransom after he transferred from Harvard to Kenyon College, where he learned the principles of the New Criticism. In poems such as *The Dandelion Girls, Epitaph, The Lady,* and *Lake View,* Lowell developed the discipline and craftsmanship necessary for later maturity. Covers 1935-40. 23 notes. 1935-40

Lowens, Irving

4306. Crawford, Richard. IRVING LOWENS. *Pro. of the Am. Antiquarian Soc. 1984 94(1): 40-44.* Irving Lowens was a music critic, librarian, bibliographer, and historian of American music who conducted his studies outside the academic world. For much of his life he was an air traffic controller, but devoted spare time to a study of early American sacred music. He later became sound recordings librarian at the Library of Congress, music critic for the *Washington Evening Star,* and associate director of the Peabody Institute. 1961-83

Lowes, Ellen McFadden

4307. Lowes, Ellen McFadden. PAGES FROM A PIONEER DIARY: THE DIARY OF ELLEN MC FADDEN LOWES 1882-1886. *Manitoba Pageant [Canada] 1976 22(1): 21-25.* The diary covers the move to Elliott Settlement, and the first year there of the diarist and her future husband, Johnnie Lowes. Article to be continued. 1882-83

Lowrey, Walter M.

4308. Winters, John D. IN MEMORIAM: WALTER M. LOWREY, 1921-80. *North Louisiana Hist. Assoc. J. 1980 11(3): 1.* A tribute to Walter M. Lowrey, historian, teacher, scholar, and board member of the North Louisiana Historical Association. Illus. ca 1945-80

Lowrie, John C.

4309. Waltmann, Henry G. JOHN C. LOWRIE AND PRESBYTERIAN INDIAN ADMINISTRATION, 1870-1882. *J. of Presbyterian Hist. 1976 54(2): 259-276.* John C. Lowrie (1808-1900) supervised the selection and counseling of church-nominated directors for as many as 11 western Indian agencies under the government's Indian "Peace Policy" during 1870-82. He leaned more toward Indian assimilation into American culture than toward cultural pluralism. As one who disparaged the Indians' heritage, leadership, and value systems, he was among those who contributed to their loss of identity and continuing social problems. Likewise, despite his advocacy of justice for the Indians, he did not think in terms of comprehensive equality for their race. Based largely on Lowrie's correspondence in the American Indian Correspondence, Presbyterian Historical Society, Philadelphia; Annual Reports of Board of Foreign Missions of the Presbyterian Church USA; Annual Reports, Board of Indian Commissioners; map, chart, 64 notes. 1870-82

Lozowick, Louis

4310. Marquardt, Virginia Carol Hagelstein. "Louis Lozowick: Development from Machine Aesthetic to Social Realism, 1922-1936." U. of Maryland 1983. 283 pp. *DAI 1984 45(6): 1560-A.* DA8419525 1922-36

Lubin, David

4311. Deutsch, Gottard. DAVID LUBIN: A REMARKABLE JEW. *Western States Jewish Hist. Q. 1982 14(4): 316-320.* David Lubin, of Sacramento, California, was born in Poland in 1849, and was brought to the United States as a child. With his half brother, Harris Weinstock, he established the firm of Weinstock & Lubin, one of the leading department stores on the West Coast. He had a strong belief in the social and economic importance of farming and rural life. The disproportionate growth of urban populations was a social problem that had a solution: the creation of cheap rural credit banks would make farming profitable by easing credit and eliminating commission merchants. Reprinted from *The American Israelite,* Cincinnati, Ohio, 26 August 1915. 1880-1915

Lubitsch, Ernst

4312. Kanoff, Joel E. THE RAPHAELSON TOUCH. *Biography 1980 3(2): 147-165.* Separating the work of scenarist from that of director is an often difficult task. Samson Raphaelson and Ernst Lubitsch collaborated on nine films in the most productive era of sound comedy; yet, we most often speak of the "Lubitsch films." How may we distill the significance of Raphaelson's writing within these masterly films? 19 notes. 1920-49

Lucas, John B. C.

4313. Keller, Kenneth W. ALEXANDER MC NAIR AND JOHN B. C. LUCAS: THE BACKGROUND OF EARLY MISSOURI POLITICS. *Missouri Hist. Soc. Bull. 1977 33(4): 231-245.* ca 1795-1826

For abstract see ***McNair, Alexander***

Luce, Stephen B.

4314. Maurer, John H. THE GIANTS OF THE NAVAL WAR COLLEGE. *Naval War Coll. Rev. 1984 37(5): 44-59.* The Naval War College was established on 6 October 1884 in Newport, Rhode Island, by Secretary of the Navy William Eaton Chandler on the recommendation of Commodore Stephen B. Luce, who became its first president. Luce was shocked by the unprofessionalism and intellectual deficiencies of naval officers, particularly compared to their counterparts in the army, and determined to educate naval officers in naval theory, history, and tactics and to "apply modern scientific methods to the study and raise naval warfare from the empirical stage to the dignity of a science." He found an ardent supporter in Alfred Thayer Mahan, who shared Luce's understanding of the importance of the college to the future of the navy. 27 notes. 1884-1940's

4315. Nicolosi, Anthony S. THE NAVY, NEWPORT AND STEPHEN B. LUCE. *Naval War Coll. Rev. 1984 37(5): 117-131.* Stephen B. Luce was responsible for the establishment of the Naval War College in Newport, Rhode Island, in 1884 and became its first president. He helped navigate the college through its first years, and later became a leader in the establishment of a modern steam-driven navy and helped to establish Narragansett Bay as a major anchorage for the Atlantic Fleet. 53 notes. 1860's-1917

Lucey, Robert E.

4316. Bronder, Saul Edmund. "Robert E. Lucey: A Texas Paradox." Columbia U. 1979. 401 pp. *DAI 1981 42(6): 2817-A.* 8125256 1934-69

Ludwick, Christopher

4317. Robbins, Peggy. WASHINGTON'S BAKER GENERAL. *Early Am. Life 1977 8(5): 56-57, 82-85.* Christopher Ludwick (1720-1801) was a baker in Philadelphia and serviced the Continental Army during the American Revolution as George Washington's official baker and bread supplier during 1776-83. 1754-83

Luening, Eugen

4318. Reagan, Ann Bakamjian. EUGEN LUENING AND THE MILWAUKEE MUSICAL SOCIETY. *Milwaukee Hist. 1983 6(3): 92-100.* Discusses Eugen Luening's contributions to the musical heritage of Milwaukee as a conductor, composer, and teacher and for 20 years between 1875 and 1903 as musical director of the Milwaukee Musical Society. 1870's-1944

Luhan, Mabel Dodge

4319. Lufkin, Agnesa. A RARE PLACE: MABLE DODGE LUHAN'S TAOS ESTATE. *Palacio 1980 86(1): 29-35.* Biography of Mable Dodge Luhan (1879-1962), friend of many famous and talented people in the art and literary world of the 20th century; her estate in Taos, New Mexico, built from 1918 to the late 1920's, hosted her friends until 1949. 1918-49

4320. Rudnick, Lois P. MABEL DODGE LUHAN AND THE MYTH OF THE SOUTHWEST. *Southwest Rev. 1983 68(3): 205-221.* Discusses the attitudes, beliefs, and experiences of Mabel Dodge Luhan in Taos, New Mexico; Luhan, creator and proponent of the myth of the southwest as a garden of Eden, was a source of inspiration for writers and artists during 1917-40. 1917-40

4321. Rudnik, Lois P. "The Unexpurgated Self: A Critical Biography of Mabel Dodge Luhan." Brown U. 1977. 571 pp. *DAI 1978 38(8): 4904-4905-A.* 1879-1962

Lukens, Rebecca W.

4322. Skaggs, Julian C. THE "TRUE WOMAN" AS EXECUTIVE: REBECCA LUKENS, 1792-1854. *Working Papers from the Regional Econ. Hist. Res. Center 1982 5(2-3): 46-55.* Rebecca W. Lukens successfully ran her family's iron mill, in the Brandywine Valley in Pennsylvania, after the death of her father in 1824 and of her husband in 1825 even as she mothered her six children and continued as an active Quaker. 1792-1854

Lumpkin, Wilson

4323. Vipperman, Carl J. THE "PARTICULAR MISSION" OF WILSON LUMPKIN. *Georgia Hist. Q. 1982 66(3): 295-316.* Describes the political career of Wilson Lumpkin, Georgia governor and senator, whose "particular mission" was the Cherokee removal from Georgia. Also discussed are the various violations of the Indian treaties resulting in eviction of the Cherokees. Based on documents, Lumpkin's account and other primary and secondary sources; 69 notes. ca 1820-38

Lund, A. William

4324. Lyon, T. Edgar. CHURCH HISTORIANS I HAVE KNOWN. *Dialogue 1978 11(4): 14-22.* 1913-70
*For abstract see **Lyon, T. Edgar***

Lundberg, Edward Victor

4325. Lundberg, George S. EDWARD VICTOR LUNDBERG, SWEDISH PIONEER. *Swedish-American Historical Quarterly 1985 36(3): 208-219.* Edward Victor Lundberg (1872-1929), of Åhus, Sweden, worked as a ship's cook at age 14 and learned cabinetmaking in Stockholm, a trade he later practiced in Chicago. In the late 1890's he moved to Florida where he became a successful citrus grove and packing house manager. Mechanization was then only beginning to ease the hard manual labor of early citrus culture. Typhoid was common and twice left him a widower with young children. In later years he built a house and gardens on Lake Eloise and conducted surveys that formed the basis of the Honduran citrus industry. Based on recollections of Edward and his son George Lundberg; 3 photos. 1880's-1929

Lundeberg, Harry

4326. Kortum, Karl. HARRY LUNDEBERG HAS BEEN HEARD FROM: THE PART PLAYED BY A SEAFARING LABOR LEADER IN THE RESCUE OF CERTAIN SHIPS, LEADING TO THE ESTABLISHMENT OF THE HISTORIC FLEET AT SAN FRANCISCO. *Sea Hist. 1980 (18): 36-38.* Presents a few of the situations in which Harry Lundeberg (1901-57), sailor and militant union organizer, intervened to save and preserve old vessels, now part of the historic fleet in the San Francisco Maritime Museum. 1945-55

Lunn, C. W.

4327. Lunn, C. W. and McKay, I. FROM TRAPPER BOY TO GENERAL MANAGER: A STORY OF BROTHERLY LOVE AND PERSEVERANCE. *Labour [Canada] 1979 4: 211-240.* Discusses C. W. Lunn's novel *From Trapper Boy to General Manager,* which was an attempt to capture events in Springhill, Nova Scotia, in 1905 and to describe the life of members of the miners' union. Traces the background to the formation and decline of the miners' union which was established in August 1879 by the miners of Springhill, who were on strike against a wage cut and resolved to form an association to protect their interests. It became known as the Provincial Workman's Association in 1880, but its history was overshadowed by the strikes of 1909-11, which marked the pyrrhic victory of the PWA over the rival United Mineworkers Union and left behind the image of the PWA as a "company" union. Also traces Lunn's life and career, his close links with the working-class movement, his work as a pioneer of the labor press in Canada, and his ideas for social and industrial reform. Secondary sources; 33 notes. 1879-1930's

Lurie, Harry Lawrence

4328. Schriver, Joe M. "Harry Lawrence Lurie, a Rational Radical: His Contributions to the Development of Social Work, 1930-1950." U. of Iowa 1984. 368 pp. *DAI 1985 45(9): 2994-A.* DA8428294 1930-50

Lusk, Georgia Lee Witt

4329. Hardaway, Roger D. NEW MEXICO ELECTS A CONGRESSWOMAN. *Red River Valley Hist. Rev. 1979 4(4): 75-89.* Biography of Georgia Lee Witt Lusk (1893-1971), focusing on her campaign in 1946, when, as State Superintendent of Public Instruction, she was elected to the House of Representatives as a Democrat; this was the only time New Mexico voters have elected a woman to Congress. 1946

Luther, Seth

4330. Gersuny, Carl. SETH LUTHER—THE ROAD FROM CHEPACHET. *Rhode Island Hist. 1974 33(2): 47-55.* Summarizes Seth Luther's career, role in the Dorr Rebellion, imprisonment, and subsequent activities, especially as a supporter of the 10-hour day. By 1846 he had lost his mind, and he spent the rest of his life in New England insane asylums. Based on manuscripts in the Massachusetts Historical Society and on secondary sources. 1795-1863

4331. Gersuny, Carl. A BIOGRAPHICAL NOTE ON SETH LUTHER. *Labor Hist. 1977 18(2): 239-248.* Discusses Seth Luther (1795-1863), an important labor leader in Rhode Island in the 1830's. An articulate carpenter, Luther moved from a perception of oppression to defeat in rebellion and then to retreat from reality. A radical, Luther was involved in the labor movement, the free suffrage movement, and the Dorr Rebellion. Based on the writings of Seth Luther; 27 notes. 1795-1863

4332. Luti, Vincent F. SETH LUTHER, STONECARVER OF THE NARRAGANSETT BASIN. *Rhode Island Hist. 1980 39(1): 3-13.* Seth Luther (1709-85) was an important New England artisan. His distinctive style is preserved on cemetery stones in Providence, Rhode Island, and several surrounding towns. Based on Providence probate records and published documents; 22 illus., design dating chart, 8 notes. ca 1730-85

Lutkin, Peter Christian

4333. Kennel, Pauline Graybill. "Peter Christian Lutkin: Northwestern University's First Dean of Music." Northwestern U. 1981. 372 pp. *DAI 1981 42(5): 1845-A.* DA8124921 1891-1931

Luyerszen, Jacob (family)

4334. Kirkendaje, William A. JACOB LUYERSZEN. *Halve Maen 1983 58(1): 9-11, 16.* Brief biographical sketch of Jacob Luyerszen, who immigrated to New York in 1646 to help develop the land grant of a wealthy Dutch countryman and who founded an extensive American family. 1646-55

Lyall, William

4335. Page, F. Hilton. WILLIAM LYALL IN HIS SETTING. *Dalhousie Rev. [Canada] 1980 60(1): 49-66.* Outlines the history of the use of the Scottish School of philosophy in Nova Scotia, especially the curricula at such schools as Kings College, Dalhousie, and Pine Hill Divinity Hall (earlier Presbyterian College). Focuses on the life and works of the Reverend William Lyall, doctor of laws and fellow of the Royal Society of Canada. 35 ref. 1850-90

Lyford, Martha

4336. Keiser, David S. LINCOLN'S ANCESTORS CAME FROM IRELAND! *Lincoln Herald 1977 79(4): 146-150.* 1624-49

For abstract see ***Lincoln, Abraham (ancestors)***

Lyman, Amasa M.

4337. Hefner, Loretta L. FROM APOSTLE TO APOSTATE: THE PERSONAL STRUGGLE OF AMASA MASON LYMAN. *Dialogue 1983 16(1): 90-104.* Amasa Mason Lyman was the only one of the first Twelve Apostles of the Church of Jesus Christ of Latter-Day Saints to be excommunicated for heresy, although two other apostles, Orson Pratt and Orson Hyde, had had to recant unacceptable doctrines. Recounts the history of his heresy and of his status in the church. He taught that man is perfectable by his own efforts and that Jesus Christ was nothing more than a good man. President Joseph F. Smith posthumously restored all Lyman's ordinances and blessings in 1909, on the grounds that his heresy was a symptom of mental illness. Primary sources; illus., 50 notes. 1834-73

Lyman, Amy Brown

4338. Hefner, Loretta L. THIS DECADE WAS DIFFERENT: RELIEF SOCIETY'S SOCIAL SERVICES DEPARTMENT, 1919-1929. *Dialogue 1982 15(3): 64-73.* The decade was one of growing social responsibility for the Mormon Relief Society's Social Services Department. In 1917, Amy Brown Lyman, general secretary of the Relief Society General Board, was an official Utah delegate to the National Conference of Social Work, where she received Red Cross training. After more training in this area, she built up a strong corps of well-trained workers to fulfill the goals of the Social Services Department. They worked assiduously to provide health care, economic relief, and education to needy Utah families. Secondary sources; 19 notes. 1919-29

Lyman, John Rowen

4339. Kortum, Karl. JOHN LYMAN: THE HUB OF OUR WHEEL. *Sea Hist. 1978 (12): 13-15.* John Rowen Lyman (1915-77) had a lifelong interest in oceanography, marine affairs, and maritime history. 1940-77

Lyman, Ray

4340. Tanner, Thomas. THE BOONESBORO CONNECTION: RICHARD A. BALLINGER AND RAY LYMAN WILBUR. *Palimpsest 1985 66(1): 30-40.* 1900's-30's

For abstract see ***Ballinger, Richard A.***

Lynch, John R.

4341. McLaughlin, James Harold. "John R. Lynch the Reconstruction Politician: A Historical Perspective." Ball State U. 1981. 228 pp. *DAI 1982 42(10): 4555-A.* DA8206195 1865-77

Lynch, Samuel

4342. —. METHODISM IN THE MAUMEE VALLEY. *Northwest Ohio Q. 1982-83 55(1): 25-28.* Reprints an article from the Toledo *Blade* of 22 June 1870 describing a speech given by Samuel Lynch on his experiences as a circuit-riding Methodist minister in frontier Ohio. 1827-40's

Lynd, Robert S.

4343. Lindt, Gillian. INTRODUCTION: ROBERT S. LYND: AMERICAN SCHOLAR-ACTIVIST. *J. of the Hist. of Sociol. 1979-80 2(1): 1-12.* Introduces several articles in this issue about American sociologist Robert S. Lynd (1892-1970). 1910's-70

Lyndes, Stanley Horace

4344. Andrews, Dale K., ed. FAMILY TRAITS: VERMONT FARM LIFE AT THE TURN OF THE CENTURY: THE SKETCHES OF STANLEY HORACE LYNDES. *Vermont Hist. 1980 48(1): 5-27.* While at Pratt Institute, 1918-22, Stanley Horace Lyndes (1898-1975) made sketches for an art assignment, reproduced here with his captions, of his family doing chores, haying, racing, trapping, sugaring off, playing practical jokes; of the ragman, the swimming hole, the snow-roller, and the neighbors. Raised on farms in Cabot, Calais, and Marshfield, Vermont, he taught manual arts in secondary schools and summer camps and retired to Plainfield, Vermont. Introduction by his granddaughter, the editor, based on family tradition, her memories of the artist's stories, and town records. 1918-75

Lynn, Dann

4345. Fay, Mary Smith. DANN LYNN: INDIANA PIONEER. *Indiana Mag. of Hist. 1977 73(3): 173-190.* Dann Lynn (1782-1832) was a pioneer and a member of the Indiana House of Representatives during the early 19th century. 1790's-1832

Lynn, Loretta

4346. Banes, Ruth A. MYTHOLOGY IN MUSIC: THE BALLAD OF LORETTA LYNN. *Canadian Review of American Studies [Canada] 1985 16(3): 283-300.* Country and western singer Loretta Lynn has become a new Southern myth as a consequence of her popularity since 1961 and of portrayals of her life in Appalachia in the song "Coal Miner's Daughter," and in the commercial movie and her autobiography of the same title. Her life, as pictured in these renderings of her interpretation of conflict between Southern cultural traditions and the values of urbanized America, fits tidily into "Janus-faced" mythology about the South in this century. Secondary sources; 34 notes. 1961-85

Lynn, Washington Frank

4347. Berry, Virginia. WASHINGTON FRANK LYNN: ARTIST AND JOURNALIST. *Beaver [Canada] 1978 308(4): 24-31.* Washington Frank Lynn, an Englishman trained as an artist, came to the New World in the 1860's as a correspondent for the Toronto *Globe.* He covered the Civil War in the United States. He became interested in Canadian settlement, and after a few years in England returned to Canada and the United States to study the lives of the immigrants. During 1871-72, he traveled via Minnesota to the Red River country, making copious notes on the inhabitants and painting many scenes, including "The Dakota Boat," "Pembina," and "Flat-Boats on the Red River." 5 illus. 1860's-70's

Lyon, James

4348. Thomas, Ruth Colby. MUSIC OF THE REVOLUTIONARY TIMES. *Daughters of the Am. Revolution Mag. 1984 118(10): 720-721, 773, 790.* 1746-1800
*For abstract see **Billings, William***

Lyon, James A.

4349. Winter, R. Milton. JAMES A. LYON: SOUTHERN PRESBYTERIAN APOSTLE OF PROGRESS. *J. of Presbyterian Hist. 1982 60(4): 314-335.* The Reverend James A. Lyon (1814-82) was a forward-looking pastor of the Columbus, Mississippi, Presbyterian Church during and after the Civil War. In 1863 he was moderator of the Presbyterian Church in the Confederate States of America. He frequently stood alone in his convictions. He demonstrated a progressive spirit, particularly about education, slavery, national unity, and denominational reunion. Based on his "Journal" (Mitchell Memorial Library, Mississippi State University), his numerous newspaper and journal articles, and minutes of ecclesiastical judicatories; illus., 93 notes. 1860-75

Lyon, Mary

4350. Clifford, Geraldine Joncich. EVE: REDEEMED BY EDUCATION AND TEACHING SCHOOL. *Hist. of Educ. Q. 1981 21(4): 479-491.* Reviews Elizabeth Alden Green's *Mary Lyon and Mount Holyoke: Opening the Gates* (1979), Redding S. Sugg, Jr.'s *Motherteacher: The Feminization of American Education* (1978), and Barbara J. Harris's *Beyond Her Sphere: Women and the Professions in American History* (1978). Green's work is both a biography of an individual and an institutional history, emphasizing Mount Holyoke College from its establishment in 1834 until the death of its founder, Mary Lyon, in 1849. Sugg makes a sociological attack on innovative educational trends and encourages a return to a non-permissive, no frills basic educational approach. Harris narrowly defines women's professions as those which require college training, excluding teaching and nursing. 30 notes. 1820-1980's

4351. Lambert, Pierre D. WOMEN IN EDUCATION: THE KNOWN, THE FORGOTTEN, THE UNKNOWN. *Vitae Scholasticae 1983 2(1): 93-112.* 19c-20c
*For abstract see **Beecher, Catherine***

Lyon, Matthew

4352. Gragg, Larry. "RAGGED MAT, THE DEMOCRAT": MATTHEW LYON. *Am. Hist. Illus. 1977 12(2): 20-25.* Chronicles the stormy political career of Matthew Lyon, largely responsible for Vermont's entrance into the union (the first after the original 13 colonies) but also widely known for his democratic views and anti-administration feelings for John Adams, feelings which earned him a four-month jail sentence, but did not keep him from regaining (through reelection) his seat in the US Senate, 1791-1822. 1791-1822

4353. Waldrep, Christopher. MATHEW LYON COMES TO FRONTIER KENTUCKY. *Register of the Kentucky Hist. Soc. 1979 77(3): 201-206.* Indicted a second time for violation of the Sedition Act of 1798, Mathew Lyon fled to Kentucky where he became a leader of Republicans in western Kentucky. Leaving Vermont, which he had represented in Congress, Lyon made his first documented purchase of land in Kentucky in 1800. Although he returned to the Congress to vote for Jefferson, he returned to Eddyville and made important contributions to its commercial growth. 30 notes. 1798-1801

Lyon, T. Edgar

4354. Lyon, T. Edgar. CHURCH HISTORIANS I HAVE KNOWN. *Dialogue 1978 11(4): 14-22.* The author reminisces about the lives and work of four Mormon historians who influenced his own development as a Mormon historian. B. H. Roberts, author of *The History of the Church* and president of the Church of the Latter Day Saints, attempted to break away from writing church history as propaganda. Andrew Jenson represents an earlier type of Mormon historian who collected historical information and documents, a chronicler striving for complete and accurate coverage. Similarly, A. William Lund, assistant historian in the Church Historian's Office, saw his responsibility as preserving documents and books, rather than making them accessible for use. Church historian Howard W. Hunter visited the author in Nauvoo, Illinois, and praised him for the concept of a church history that was people-oriented, not concerned only with abstractions. Based on an address to the Mormon History Association, Salt Lake City, Utah, 12 April 1973. 1913-70

4355. —. T. EDGAR LYON. *Brigham Young U. Studies 1978 19(1): 3-4.* T. Edgar Lyon served on the Editorial Board of the *Brigham Young University Studies* from 1969 until his death on 20 September 1978. Widely published, Lyon was an outstanding scholar in history, Christian studies, and LDS church history. His major area of concentration was the Nauvoo period of Mormon history. 19c-20c

Lyons, Howard Raymond

4356. Borich, George Richard. "The Lives of Howard Raymond Lyons and Hubert Estel Nutt, Co-Founders of the Mid-West National Band and Orchestra Clinic." Northwestern U. 1984. 244 p. *DAI 1985 45(7): 2022-A.* DA8423206 1920's-70's

M

Mabray, John C.

4357. Smith, Raymond A., Jr. JOHN C. MABRAY: A CON ARTIST IN THE CORN BELT. *Palimpsest 1983 64(4): 123-124, 133-139.* Portrays the infamous career of confidence man John C. Mabray, whose "Big Store" swindle, operated primarily from Council Bluffs, Iowa, netted millions before Mabray was finally arrested in 1909. ca 1900-09

MacArthur, Douglas

4358. Hall, George M. WHEN HONOR CONFLICTS WITH DUTY. *Air. U. Rev. 1980 31(6): 45-60.* 1884-1973

*For abstract see **Greely, Adolphus W.***

4359. Karp, Walter. TRUMAN VS. MACARTHUR. *Am. Heritage 1984 35(3): 84-95.* On 11 April 1951, President Truman announced his decision to fire General Douglas MacArthur, precipitating a popular outcry and perhaps "the severest test which civilian control of the military has ever faced" in the United States. Traces MacArthur's swift rise and decline in public favor from his speech to Congress and the investigations that followed, to MacArthur's attempt to turn the episode into a crusade "for the spiritual recrudescence" of America. 26 photos, 2 illus. 1951

4360. Petillo, Carol Morris. "Douglas MacArthur: The Philippine Years." Rutgers U. 1979. 394 pp. *DAI 1980 40(7): 4197-4198-A.* 1903-42

Macartney, Clarence E.

4361. Russell, C. Allyn. CLARENCE E. MACARTNEY: FUNDAMENTALIST PRINCE OF THE PULPIT. *J. of Presbyterian Hist. 1974 52(1): 33-58.* Preacher Clarence E. Macartney was an eloquent spokesperson for fundamentalism and orthodoxy in the Presbyterian Church, as well as a symbol of power, 1901-53. 1901-53

Macdonald, Dwight

4363. Kessler, Lauren. AGAINST THE AMERICAN GRAIN: THE LONELY VOICE OF *POLITICS* MAGAZINE, 1944-1949. *Journalism Hist. 1982 9(2): 49-52, 60.* Traces the career of Dwight Macdonald, focusing on his avant-garde *Politics* magazine, which was a major forum for Leftist political opinion after World War II. 1944-49

MacDonald, John A.

4364. O'Neil, Daniel J. LEADERSHIP AND THE ETHNIC FACTOR: THE CASE OF JOHN A. MACDONALD. *Plural Soc. [Netherlands] 1981 12(3-4): 109-123.* Recounts the career of Canadian political leader John A. MacDonald during 1841-91, focusing on the relationship between his effectiveness as a leader and his sensitivity to ethnic issues. 1841-91

4365. Preece, Rod. THE POLITICAL WISDOM OF SIR JOHN A. MACDONALD. *Canadian Journal of Political Science [Canada] 1984 17(3): 459-486.* Sir John A. Macdonald is described as a man of *phronesis* who possessed a sophisticated political philosophy that, in general, conformed to the political disposition exemplified by Edmund Burke. Macdonald's views on the constitution, change, representation, democracy, women, tradition, economics, religion, and unions are investigated. Macdonald was an antirationalist who saw the world in terms of loyalty, duty, and obligation and who was devoted to the principles of prudence, tradition, and the rule of law; to constitutional monarchy; to the British connection and British institutions but with respect for French traditions; to the minimal change consistent with harmony; and to order before liberty, politics before economics, and experience before abstract reason. 1840's-90's

4366. Waite, P. B. CHARTERED LIBERTINE? A CASE AGAINST SIR JOHN MACDONALD AND SOME ANSWERS. *Tr. of the Hist. and Sci. Soc. of Manitoba [Canada] 1975-76 32: 43-52.* Sir John A. Macdonald, Canada's first prime minister, while in many respects praiseworthy and admirable, could be mean and vindictive. He loved power, and equated national fortunes with those of the Ontario Conservative Party's interests. He usually believed that the end justified the means, that patronage was an indispensable element of party government, and that provincial concerns must bow to national policy. The double shuffle of 1858, the Pacific Scandal of 1872, the Langevin Scandal of 1890-91 and the Gerrymander of 1882 numbered among the most questionable events in his career. 22 notes. 1858-90

MacFadden, Bernarr

4367. Waugh, Clifford Jerome. "Bernarr MacFadden: The Muscular Prophet." State U. of New York, Buffalo 1979. 278 pp. *DAI 1979 40(4): 2232-A.* 1868-1955

4368. Yagoda, Ben. THE TRUE STORY OF BERNARR MACFADDEN. *Am. Heritage 1981 33(1): 22-29.* Bernarr Macfadden (1868-1955), the "father of physical culture," was born in Missouri. In 1893, he went to New York determined to make a living selling physical culture. Success with his first magazine, *Physical Culture,* led to further efforts, including *True Story, True Romances, True Experiences,* and others. In 1924, Macfadden began the New York *Graphic* as a daily. After several years and the loss of much money, Macfadden turned unsuccessfully to politics. 18 illus. 1893-1955

MacGahan, Januarius Aloysius

4369. Heath, Roy E. JANUARIUS A. MACGAHAN AND HIS ROLE IN THE LIBERATION OF BULGARIA. *Southeastern Europe 1979 6(2): 194-208.* Januarius Aloysius MacGahan (1844-78) became world famous for his investigation of the Bulgarian massacres in 1876. He has been credited with everything from starting the Russo-Turkish War to liberating Bulgaria. Of particular interest is the alleged sensationalism and bias in his reporting during the Russo-Turkish War of 1877-78. Based on several unpublished papers presented to the 10th Annual Convention of the Amerian Association for the Advancement of Slavic Studies in October 1978 and an unpublished autobiography recently discovered among the papers of MacGahan's wife; 58 notes. 1875-78

4370. Šopov, Petâr. EUGENE SCHUYLER—DISTINGUISHED POLITICIAN, STATESMAN, DIPLOMAT AND SCIENTIST. *Bulgarian Hist. Rev. [Bulgaria] 1983 11(1): 66-73.* 1840-90
For abstract see ***Schuyler, Eugene***

MacGilvra, E. E. (Boo)

4371. Paladin, Vivian A. MONTANA EPISODES: CONVERSATIONS WITH BOO. *Montana 1980 30(3): 52-58.* E. E. (Boo) MacGilvra (1893-1980) served Montana as a legislator, Montana Power Company employee, mine owner, and director of the Montana Historical Society. During his life he was known for his sense of humor, his storytelling ability, and his devotion to preserving Montana history. Reminiscent article explores his character and contribution to the state with material on the Ringling Brothers Circus, mining in the Little Rockies near Zortman, Montana, homesteading, horse ranching, politics, and interesting personalities. 6 illus. 1910-80

MacGowan, Alice

4372. Gaston, Kay Baker. THE MACGOWAN GIRLS. *California Hist. 1980 59(2): 116-125.* 1908-47
For abstract see ***Cooke, Grace MacGowan***

Machetanz, Fred

4373. Tobin, William J. ALASKAN GRANDEUR. *Sporting Classics 1986 5(1): 42-51.* Discusses the life and work of painter Fred Machetanz of High Ridge, Alaska, whose skill in capturing the spirit of the Alaskan environment and its plant, animal, and human inhabitants is unparalleled. 1939-86

Macintosh, D. C.

4374. Heim, Stephen Mark. "True Relations: D. C. Macintosh and the Evangelical Roots of Liberal Theology." Boston Coll. 1982. 530 pp. *DAI 1982 42(10): 4488-A.* DA8207375 1909-42

Mackenzie, Alexander

4375. Lavender, David. FIRST CROSSING: ALEXANDER MACKENZIE'S QUEST FOR THE PACIFIC. *Am. West 1977 14(5): 4-11, 67-68.* Alexander Mackenzie (1763-1820), in the service of the North West Company, searched for a viable fur-trade route across Canada to the Pacific. Based on Lake Athabasca, in 1789 he traveled to Great Slave Lake, discovered the Mackenzie River, and followed it to the Arctic Ocean. During 1792-93, from the same base, he followed the Peace River over the Rocky Mountains, the Parsnip, Fraser, and Bella Coola rivers to the Pacific. He had made the first crossing of the continent north of Mexico. 3 illus., map. 1789-93

MacKenzie, George Patton

4376. Grant, Francis W. GEORGE MAC KENZIE: NORTHERN PIONEER. *Nova Scotia Hist. Q. [Canada] 1974 4(2): 155-165.* George Patton MacKenzie (1873-1953) was a school teacher, prospector, Gold Commissioner of the Yukon Territory, Arctic explorer, administrator, and lecturer. 1890's-1953

Mackenzie, Ranald S.

4377. Austerman, Wayne R. RANALD S. MACKENZIE AND THE EARLY YEARS ON THE BORDER. *Red River Valley Hist. Rev. 1980 5(4): 71-79.* Fills a gap in the biographical data about Indian fighter Ranald S. Mackenzie by showing that his experience commanding the black infantry on the Mexican border, 1866-70, introduced him to the peculiar demands of soldiering on the Texas frontier, and prepared him for his decisive campaigns in the heart of Comancheria. 1866-70

MacLane, Mary

4378. Mattern, Carolyn J. MARY MAC LANE: A FEMINIST OPINION. *Montana 1977 27(4): 54-63.* Mary MacLane (1881-1929) wrote three books—*The Story of Mary MacLane* (1902), *My Friend Annabel Lee* (1903), and *I, Mary MacLane* (1917)—authored numerous articles, then wrote and starred in a movie, *Men Who Have Made Love To Me* (1917). Her activities created a sensation in her hometown of Butte, Montana, and nationwide. Although atypical, she was not an eccentric woman. Her ideas arose and developed from her environment, reflected the mainstream of feminist thought, and represented ideas or feelings of educated, middle class women during that era. An unhappy, self-centered young woman, MacLane craved understanding and self-expression, believing all women should be free to live fully expressive lives. During 1902-10, MacLane found happiness in the intellectual bohemia of New York City's Greenwich Village and had several affairs with men, viewing the associations dispassionately. After her return to Butte in 1910, and a near fatal bout with scarlet fever, MacLane's writing evidenced a sense of life's fragility and her own mortality; she died lonely and forgotten in Chicago. Based on writings of Mary MacLane, contemporary newspapers and journals; 3 illus., 28 notes. 1902-29

4379. Wheeler, Leslie. MONTANA'S SHOCKING "LIT'RY LADY." *Montana 1977 27(3): 20-33.* Mary MacLane (1881-1929) began her literary career at age 21 with the publication of *The Story of Mary MacLane,* a provocative, intimate diary of her unhappy life in Butte, Montana. It shocked the nation. Taking her inspiration from the confessions of Russian artist Marie Bashkirtseff, Mary MacLane kept her own journal from January through April 1901. Published in 1902, the diary reflected the author's romanticism, frustrations, and contempt for Butte and its society. It provoked mixed reactions but brought financial success to the author, who soon left Montana for Chicago, Boston, and New York. Mary MacLane wrote for the *New York World,* and published a second book, *My Friend Annabel Lee,* in 1903. This work proved less passionate, profane, and successful than her first. She returned to Butte in 1910. While there she published a third volume, *I, Mary MacLane* (1917), in which she appeared dejected and disillusioned with life as a literary eccentric. She soon left Butte to write and star in a silent movie, "Men Who Have Made Love To Me." The movie was sensational for a short time. Thereafter, MacLane's career began to slide, and she died in poverty in 1929. Based on MacLane's writings and on contemporary newspapers and journals; 9 illus., 34 notes. 1901-29

MacLeish, Archibald

4380. Benco, Nancy L. ARCHIBALD MACLEISH: THE POET LIBRARIAN. *Q. J. of the Lib. of Congress 1976 33(3): 233-249.* During his brief tenure as Librarian of Congress (1939-44) Archibald MacLeish instituted an administrative reorganization that affected all operations and employees. His appointment by President Roosevelt was confirmed by Congress despite the opposition of organized librarians. He became a leading American spokesman for the cause of democracy. In December 1944 he was appointed to a new post as assistant secretary of state in charge of public and cultural relations. Meanwhile he founded the *Quarterly Journal of the Library of Congress* primarily "to report the Library's acquisitions in an informative and useful manner with a humanistic approach." Illus., 55 notes. 1939-44

4381. Dilliard, Irving. THREE TO REMEMBER: ARCHIBALD MACLEISH, STANLEY KIMMEL, PHILLIPS BRADLEY. *J. of the Illinois State Hist. Soc. 1984 77(1): 45-59.* 1910's-82
*For abstract see **Bradley, Phillips***

4382. Langland, Joseph. IN OUR TIME FOR A LONG TIME. *Massachusetts Rev. 1982 23(4): 660-672.* Biography of Archibald MacLeish, American poet, educator, and government official. Comments on his friendships with authors F. Scott Fitzgerald, Ernest Hemingway, Gertrude Stein, and Ezra Loomis Pound, American jurist Felix Frankfurter and his wife, and statesman Dean Gooderham Acheson, mentioning some of their idiosyncracies. Discusses several of his works, especially his well-known poem, "Ars Poetica," which remains a very good didactic imagistic poem. MacLeish was "valiant in his politics, generous and sometimes insecure in his best personal relationships, and moderate among the revolutions of modernism in literature." He spread his talents quite thinly, but always performed well in any undertaking. MacLeish, in his own inimitable style, always invited others to higher discourse, to what writing could and ought to be. 2 illus. ca 1920-82

4383. MacLeish, William H. THE SILVER WHISTLER. *Smithsonian 1983 14(7): 54-65.* Biography of Archibald MacLeish, the poet, playwright, journalist, and Librarian of Congress, who referred to poets as "silver whistlers." 1920's-82

4384. McCord, David. ARCHIBALD MACLEISH. *Massachusetts Hist. Soc. Pro. 1982 94: 93-98.* Archibald MacLeish enjoyed a long and distinguished career as poet, statesman, and man of action. He was an editor of *Fortune* magazine, the first curator of the Nieman Foundation for Journalists at Harvard, Librarian of Congress, Assistant Secretary of State, and Boylston Professor of Rhetoric and Oratory at Harvard. MacLeish will be remembered for his inspirational writing, which garnered Pulitzer Prizes for poetry, for *Conquistador* (1933) and *Collected Poems, 1917-1952* (1953), and for drama for *J.B.* (1959). 1917-82

4385. Ward, John William. ARCHIBALD MACLEISH AND EDUCATION. *Massachusetts Rev. 1982 23(4): 673-679.* Archibald MacLeish was a cosmopolitan, urbane, reserved, courteous, slightly distant man, yet every person who knew him well liked him. He was involved in many 20th-century controversies in his life, yet he unswervingly spoke with a singular voice in them all. He saw in the 1960's campus revolts a vision of what education should be about, the process of learning in a university. MacLeish believed that "the postulate of education is to be the regeneracy of man" and that the teaching method should involve the evolution of man's ideas in relation to his universe. He insisted that education was an activity; a "process of asking questions." ca 1921-82

MacLennan, Hugh

4386. Cameron, Elspeth. A MACLENNAN LOG. *J. of Can. Studies [Canada] 1979-80 14(4): 106-121.* Lists chronologically selected events in Hugh MacLennan's life (1907-78), and provides a bibliography of his book and periodical publications. Also included is a bibliography of selected books, articles, sections of books and theses on MacLennan by scholars and critics. Based on Hugh MacLennan's published and unpublished books, articles and manuscripts, as well as those written by critics and scholars who have written on him. 1907-78

MacMonnies, Frederick W.

4387. Foote, Edward J. AN INTERVIEW WITH FREDERICK W. MAC MONNIES, AMERICAN SCULPTOR OF THE BEAUX-ARTS ERA. *New-York Hist. Soc. Q. 1977 61(3-4): 102-123.* Sketches the life and works of Frederick W. MacMonnies, based on a 1927 interview by a fellow artist, DeWitt M. Lockman. MacMonnies was an important sculptor in France and in the United States. Many of his works in bronze and marble may be seen in museums and parks, or as ornamentation for buildings. A student of Saint-Gaudens, MacMonnies won numerous prizes, such as one for his *Nathan Hale,* and often shocked the public with works such as *Venus and Adonis.* Primary sources; 6 illus., 37 notes. 1863-1937

MacMullen, Jerry

4388. Casper, Trudie, ed. JERRY MACMULLEN: AN UNCOMMON MAN. *J. of San Diego Hist. 1981 27(4): 261-276.* Presents the first part of an interview with Jerry MacMullen (1897-1981), San Diego writer, historian, and former director of the San Diego Historical Society, conducted shortly before his death. Article to be continued. 1899-1981

MacMurchy, Helen

4389. McConnachie, Kathleen. METHODOLOGY IN THE STUDY OF WOMEN IN HISTORY: A CASE STUDY OF HELEN MACMURCHY, M.D. *Ontario Hist. [Canada] 1983 75(1): 61-70.* Dr. Helen MacMurchy influenced both medicine and government during her career in public health, introducing significant reforms. She also contributed to and edited journals, consistently arguing for more attention to the health of mothers and children. Photo, 27 notes. ca 1901-40

MacNeill, John J.

4390. Harrop, G. Gerald. THE ERA OF THE "GREAT PREACHER" AMONG CANADIAN BAPTISTS. *Foundations 1980 23(1): 57-70.* 1910-41
*For abstract see **Cameron, William Andrew***

MacNutt, W. Stewart

4391. Young, Murray. W. STEWART MAC NUTT, 1908-1976. *Can. Hist. Assoc. Hist. Papers [Canada] 1976: 271-273.* Obituary of a Professor Emeritus of the University of New Brunswick and Chairman of the International Programme for Loyalist Studies. He received awards for local history from the American and Canadian Historical Associations and was noted as an interpreter of the Atlantic Provinces. 1935-76

Macoun, John

4392. McGeown, Mary G. JOHN MACOUN. *Alberta Hist. [Canada] 1980 28(2): 16-19.* Emigrating to Canada in 1850 from Ireland, John Macoun (1831-1920) gained a considerable reputation as a botanist and explorer in Canada where his name is commemorated by a town in southern Saskatchewan, a mountain in Glacier National Park, and a lake in northern Saskatchewan as well as 48 species of plants which he discovered. Discusses his brief career as a farmhand in Canada, which was largely self-taught, followed by 10 years as a teacher during which he concentrated on studying botany and building a herbarium. In 1869, he was offered the Chair of Natural History in Alberta College, Belleville, Ontario. In the company of such men as Sandford Fleming and George Grant while crossing the country, he collected botanical specimens for his studies. Numerous trips followed, during which he explored and studied the huge plain of southern Saskatchewan. His writings include *Manitoba and the Great North-West* (1882) and his autobiography. He later lived in Ottawa, then Vancouver. 2 photos. 1850-1920

MacQueary, Howard

4393. Dennison, Mary S. HOWARD MACQUEARY: HERESY IN OHIO. *Hist. Mag. of the Protestant Episcopal Church 1980 49(2): 109-131.* Priest of St. Paul's Church (Episcopal), Canton, Ohio, the Reverend Howard MacQueary was representative of those clergy in the last quarter of the 19th century who were influenced by Darwinism and European biblical criticism emanating largely from Germany. After writing his only book, *The Evolution of Man and Christianity* (1890), he failed to heed the counsel of his ecclesiastical superior, Bishop Leonard, regarding his preaching. In 1891 he was charged with denying the virgin birth and Jesus's resurrection. His trial, the first of its kind in the Episcopal Church in America, was one of the numerous examples of the impact of European thought on America's churches. Found guilty, MacQueary left the Episcopal Church and later entered the Universalist Church. Based largely on MacQueary's *The Evolution of Man and Christianity,* the Leonard Papers (Archives of the Diocese of Ohio), and contemporary newspaper accounts; 98 notes. 1890-91

Madden, David

4394. Perrault, Anna H. A DAVE MADDEN BIBLIOGRAPHY: 1952-1981. *Bull. of Biblio. 1982 39(3): 104-116.* Brief biography of David Madden, American fiction writer, poet, critic, playwright, and teacher, followed by a bibliography in three sections: creative writings, criticism, and secondary sources. 1952-81

Madison, Dolly Payne

4395. Moore, Virginia. DOLLEY MADISON: QUEEN OF SOCIETY, DEBT-RIDDEN WIDOW. *Smithsonian 1979 10(8): 173-185.* Describes the social life of Dolly Payne Madison after the death of James in 1836 until her own demise in 1849. 1836-49

Madison, James

4396. Banning, Lance. THE HAMILTONIAN MADISON: A RECONSIDERATION. *Virginia Mag. of Hist. and Biog. 1984 92(1): 2-28.* A revisionist discussion of James Madison's nationalist ideals. Alexander Hamilton felt that his ally made a complete policy reversal when, in 1790, Madison opposed the creation of a national bank. Hamilton's analysis has colored historians' interpretations of Madison's behavior, and Irving Brant's biography of the Virginia statesman added to the confusion. Closer examination of Madison's writings reveal, however, that he was never the nationalist others have portrayed him to be. Instead, he sought a balance between democracy and centralized government. Based on the *Papers of Alexander Hamilton,* published federal and Constitutional Convention records, and the *Letters of Members of the Continental Congress;* 50 notes, illus. 1783-90

4397. Banning, Lance. THE MODERATE AS REVOLUTIONARY: AN INTRODUCTION TO MADISON'S LIFE. *Q. J. of the Lib. of Congress 1980 37(2): 162-175.* Traces James Madison's (1751-1836) political career from 1774, when he served as a member of the Orange County, Virginia, committee of safety, through his terms in the Virginia council of state, the Virginia state assembly, the Confederation Congress, the Constitutional Convention, and the House of Representatives, through his terms as secretary of state under Thomas Jefferson from 1801 to 1808, and finally as president from 1809 to 1817. Notes his major contributions, including the Virginia Plan, the Constitution, *The Federalist,* the Bill of Rights, and the Virginia Resolutions. Examines his political ideas, including his early attempts to strengthen the central government and his later attempts to limit the federal government's authority and to define states' rights; his creation, with Thomas Jefferson, of the nation's first political party; his early criticism of and reaction against Hamiltonian policy and his later acceptance of some of its elements; and the problems he encountered with the War of 1812. 14 illus. 1774-1817

4398. Drakeman, Donald L. RELIGION AND THE REPUBLIC: JAMES MADISON AND THE FIRST AMENDMENT. *J. of Church and State 1983 25(3): 427-445.* James Madison was not responsible for the written form adopted for the First Amendment. His interest centered on concern over infringement of freedom of conscience, and his willingness to be involved in what is now called "civil religion" was rooted in his intense patriotism. 74 notes. 1770-89

4399. Edwards, G. Franklin and Winston, Michael R. COMMENTARY: THE WASHINGTON OF PAUL JENNINGS—WHITE HOUSE SLAVE, FREE MAN, AND CONSPIRATOR FOR FREEDOM. *White House Hist. 1983 1(1): 52-63.* 1799-1848
For abstract see ***Jennings, Paul***

4400. Frank, Perry. BICENTENNIAL GAZETTE: THE FRAMERS OF THE CONSTITUTION: VIRGINIA. *This Constitution 1985 (7): 38-40.* 1787
For abstract see ***Blair, John***

4401. Howard, A. E. Dick. JAMES MADISON AND THE CONSTITUTION. *Wilson Quarterly 1985 9(3): 80-91.* Recounts the early career of James Madison and concentrates on his role as one of the leading architects of the US Constitution in 1787, and his reliance on the fundamentals of federalism, self-expression, and religious liberty. 1770's-80's

4402. Jennings, Paul. A COLORED MAN'S REMINISCENCES OF JAMES MADISON. *White House Hist. 1983 1(1): 46-51.* Reprints the memoirs of former slave Paul Jennings, who spent many years as the servant of James Madison; the work has long been respected by scholars as a classic. 1805-36

4403. Koch, Adrienne. JAMES MADISON AND THE LIBRARY OF CONGRESS. *Q. J. of the Lib. of Congress 1980 37(2): 159-161.* James Madison (1751-1836), regarded as the "father of the Constitution," was also the first to propose a Library of Congress. He drew up the first book list of the legislators' library, worked to get Thomas Jefferson's private library for the nation, and worked closely with the Librarian of Congress. A philosopher-statesman, Madison advocated the American experiment and combined theory and practice into a new political institution based on his knowledge of human nature and the normal course of social change. His native intelligence, reasoning power, command of learning, and devotion to liberty combined to allow him to make his unique contributions. 1783-1815

4404. Schultz, Harold S. JAMES MADISON: FATHER OF THE CONSTITUTION? *Q. J. of the Lib. of Congress 1980 37(2): 215-222.* Praises James Madison (1751-1836) for his character and mind, his influences at the Constitutional Convention of 1787, and his concern for nationalism, republicanism, stability, and the protection of the private property rights of individuals, but feels that he cannot truly be considered the Father of the Constitution because he was not able to achieve what he thought was most important in the new plan of government and did not contribute either to the "Great Compromise" or to the provision for the judicial veto of state and federal laws. Madison's major influence was in his insistence on a strong national government elected by popular vote. 2 illus. 1787

4405. Weber, Paul J. JAMES MADISON AND RELIGIOUS EQUALITY: THE PERFECT SEPARATION. *Rev. of Pol. 1982 44(2): 163-186.* Traces the writings of James Madison through his career, during 1780-1830, as political theorist, constitutional architect, president, and retired statesman. Madison consistently stressed the principle of equal separation in matters of public policy regarding church and state. Religious liberty did not demand structural separation; however, it was important that it remain free of government coercion and totally disestablished so that each citizen could enjoy equality. Finally, it was Madison's contention that religious liberty should enjoy equal protection and promotion, much as those other natural rights of life and property. 70 notes. 1780-1830

4406. Wright, Esmond. THE POLITICAL EDUCATION OF JAMES MADISON. *Hist. Today [Great Britain] 1981 31(Dec): 17-23.* Examines the background and attitudes of James Madison, including his consistent dislike of Indians and religious radicalism, and contrasts him with such contemporaries as Jefferson and Hamilton. 1751-1836

Madison, Kitty

4407. Harvey, Joel. "American Burlesque as Reflected Through the Career of Kitty Madison, 1916-1931." Florida State U. 1980. 171 pp. *DAI 1981 41(7): 2833-A.* DA8101967 1916-31

Madison, Lee Glenn

4408. Tomsyck, Lawrence L. and Thiessen, Thomas D. LEE GLENN MADISON, 1920-1983. *Plains Anthrop. 1983 28(102 part 1): 325-327.* A brief professional biography of Lee Glenn Madison, who participated in many archaeology projects on the Great Plains. Ref., biblio. 1939-83

Maeser, Karl G.

4409. Tobler, Douglas F. KARL G. MAESER'S GERMAN BACKGROUND, 1828-1856: THE MAKING OF ZION'S TEACHER. *Brigham Young U. Studies 1977 17(2): 155-175.* In 1876, at Brigham Young's request, Karl G. Maeser, a convert to Mormonism in 1855, left Germany to come to Provo, Utah, to provide academic and religious direction to Brigham Young Academy. For a man who later exercised such a profound impact on Mormon education, little has been known concerning the European influences in the development of Maeser's character, world view, and educational philosophy. Illuminates the European background and preparation of this Mormon pedagogical reformer. 1828-56

Magan, Percy Tilson

4410. Daly, Lydia, ed. THE WIT OF LOMA LINDA'S IRISHMAN. *Adventist Heritage 1979 6(2): 49-52.* Excerpts from letters (1918-34) of Dr. Percy Tilson Magan, minister, teacher, medical doctor, and president of the College of Medical Evangelists (now Loma Linda University) in California during 1928-42. 1918-34

Magee, Henry

4411. Cousins, Leone B. SOME VALLEY LOYALISTS. *Nova Scotia Hist. Rev. [Canada] 1983 3(2): 57-70.* 1770's-1821

*For abstract see **Wiswall, John***

Magnes, Judah L.

4412. Stern, Norton B. JUDAH L. MAGNES OF OAKLAND: ERRORS AND OMISSIONS IN HIS LIFE STORY. *Western States Jewish History 1985 17(4): 352-357.* Prints corrections of errors in published sources dealing with the early life of Rabbi Judah L. Magnes, an American Zionist who was born in San Francisco, grew up in Oakland, and played an important role in the establishment of the state of Israel. 23 notes. 1877-1900

Magnin, Edgar F.

4413. Kramer, William M. and Clar, Reva. RABBI EDGAR F. MAGNIN IN STOCKTON (1914-1915): REHEARSAL FOR LOS ANGELES. *Western States Jewish Hist. 1985 17(2): 99-121.* A study of the early life and career of Rabbi Edgar F. Magnin, who began his service as rabbi of Temple Israel in Stockton, California. There he perfected skills that he later employed as rabbi of Wilshire Boulevard Temple in Los Angeles. Based on interviews with Magnin and newspaper accounts; 78 notes. 1914-15

Magruder, John Bankhead

4414. Grimsley, Mark. INSIDE A BELEAGUERED CITY: A COMMANDER AND ACTOR. PRINCE JOHN MAGRUDER. *Civil War Times Illus. 1982 21(5): 14-17, 33-35.* Recounts the military career of John Bankhead "Prince John" Magruder, an actor and soldier who fought in the Mexican War and on the Confederate side in the Civil War, after which he lived in Mexico; Magruder defended Yorktown, Virginia, during the Union siege of the city. 1861-65

Maguire, Patrick J.

4415. Galvin, John T. PATRICK J. MAGUIRE: BOSTON'S LAST DEMOCRATIC BOSS. *New England Q. 1982 55(3): 392-415.* Examines the career of Patrick J. Maguire, a prosperous real estate developer and newspaper publisher, who was the only city-wide boss Boston ever experienced. As the dominant force on the Democratic City Committee during 1876-96, Maguire was instrumental in determining Boston's mayors and mayoral candidates. Primary sources; 61 notes. 1876-96

Mahan, Alfred Thayer

4416. Field, James A., Jr. ALFRED THAYER MAHAN SPEAKS FOR HIMSELF. *Naval War Coll. Rev. 1976 29(2): 47-60.* Mention of the term seapower is certain to evoke a reference, spoken or otherwise, to Captain Alfred Thayer Mahan. His thoughts, ideas, and concepts have been discussed, repeated, and enshrined, particularly and appropriately in naval circles, ever since the publication in 1890 of his seminal book *The Influence of Sea Power Upon History* which was followed by nearly a quarter of a century of prolific writing until his death in 1914. Only recently with the publication of his letters and papers has the man behind the myth been illuminated. The author's discussion of this monumental and important work makes a significant contribution to our knowledge of Mahan as a person. 1890-1914

4417. Hunt, Barry D. THE OUTSTANDING NAVAL STRATEGIC WRITERS OF THE CENTURY. *Naval War Coll. Rev. 1984 37(5): 86-107.* 1880's-1984
*For abstract see **Corbett, Julian S.***

4418. Maurer, John H. THE GIANTS OF THE NAVAL WAR COLLEGE. *Naval War Coll. Rev. 1984 37(5): 44-59.* 1884-1940's
*For abstract see **Luce, Stephen B.***

Maher, Amy Grace

4419. Rynder, Constance B. AMY GRACE MAHER AND TOLEDO'S CRUSADE FOR CHILD WELFARE REFORM, 1916-1926. *Northwest Ohio Q. 1983 55(4): 105-125.* Traces the career of social reformer Amy Grace Maher in Toledo, Ohio, and the changes she was able to achieve. 1916-26

Maia, Jose Joaquim da

4420. Rodrigues, Leda Boechat. JOSE JOAQUIM DA MAIA E THOMAS JEFFERSON [Jose Joaquim da Maia and Thomas Jefferson]. *Rev. Hist. e Geog. Brasileira [Brazil] 1981 (333): 53-70.* Describes the meetings and correspondence between Thomas Jefferson, then American ambassador to France, and Brazilian medical student in the University of Montpelier, Jose Joaquim da Maia, in 1786. Da Maia used the pseudonym "Vendek" in his writings, and he and Jefferson exchanged information and opinion on both political matters and on questions of natural history. Jefferson was especially interested in the social and natural-history information about Brazil provided by da Maia, information that Jefferson shared with John Jay. The life, career, and writings of Jefferson are also reviewed, and he is eulogized as one of the greatest American thinkers and doers. 19 notes. 1786-1819

Mailer, Norman

4421. Thomas, Claudine. A PROPOS DE NORMAN MAILER: AUTOBIOGRAPHIE ET PRISE DE PAROLE [Regarding Norman Mailer: autobiography and the subject of speech]. *Rev. Française d'Etudes Américaines [France] 1982 7(14): 257-268.* Centers on *Advertisements for Myself* (1959), Norman Mailer's first autobiographical work, which recasts his first novel, *The Naked and the Dead,* into a lost object of desire, interpreting the author's early fame as a breach in the wholeness of self. 1949-59

4422. Whitfield, Stephen J. AMERICAN WRITING AS A WILDLIFE PRESERVE: JACK LONDON AND NORMAN MAILER. *Southern Q. 1977 15(2): 135-148.* 20c
*For abstract see **London, Jack***

Main, Jackson T.

4423. Main, Jackson T. MAIN-TRAVELED ROADS. *William and Mary Q. 1984 41(3): 444-454.* Personal narrative of the author's career. Contribution to "Early American Emeriti: A Symposium of Experience and Evaluation." 1930-84

Maitey, Harry

4424. Moore, Anneliese. HARRY MAITEY: FROM POLYNESIA TO PRUSSIA. *Hawaiian J. of Hist. 1977 11: 125-161.* A brief biography of Harry Maitey (ca. 1806-67), a Hawaiian, from his arrival in Berlin in 1824 to his death in Klein-Glienicke, and an account of the visit there by King Kalakaua of Hawaii in 1881. 3 photos, 137 notes. 1824-81

Makemie, Francis

4425. Smylie, James H. FRANCIS MAKEMIE: TRADITION AND CHALLENGE. *J. of Presbyterian Hist. 1983 61(2): 197-209.* The year 1983 marks the 300th anniversary of the arrival of Francis Makemie (ca. 1658-1708) from Ulster. Discusses "The Father of American Presbyterianism," his concerns for theological integrity and education, for ecumenical relations, for public affairs, and for freedom of the church—all important matters concerning the American Presbyterians today. While perhaps he was not a person of the "first order," he nevertheless was energetic, genuine in his piety, of good judgment, and "greatly useful in his day."Based largely on Boyd S. Schlenther's *The Life and Writings of Francis Makemie* (1971) and studies in American Presbyterianism; 35 notes. 1683-1708

Mala, Ray

4426. Ruskin, Evey. MEMORIES OF A MOVIE STAR: RAY MALA'S LIFE IN PICTURES. *Alaska J. 1984 14(2): 33-39.* Prints a brief biography of native Alaskan Ach-nach-chiak, who went to Hollywood under the name Ray Wise but eventually took the name, Mala, of a character he played in the 1931 movie *Eskimo.* 10 photos. 1906-84

Malcolm X

4427. Perry, Bruce. MALCOLM X AND THE POLITICS OF MASCULINITY. *Psychohistory Review 1985 13(2-3): 18-25.* Malcolm X's autobiography presents misleading and one-sided accounts of his sexual experiences and his early attempts to assert his manhood. Other witnesses indicate that he was unable to express his masculinity in fighting, that he frequently participated in homosexual acts, and was afraid of women. Although Malcolm X and other revolutionaries of his generation claimed they had been demasculinized by whites, the true situation was much more complex. Their hostility toward whites and their need to express that hostility through violence attempted to resolve publicly their own personal traumas. Their scorn for effective political leadership among blacks, notably that of Martin Luther King, Jr., contrasts with King's comment that "one's sense of manhood must come from within." 1940's-60's

4428. Perry, Bruce. MALCOLM X IN BRIEF: A PSYCHOLOGICAL PERSPECTIVE. *Journal of Psychohistory 1984 11(4): 491-500.* Malcolm X was not an adolescent criminal because of white society, as he states in his autobiography. Rather, his behavior was a repudiation of his unemployed father's expectations of great achievement for his son, and an affirmation of the values of a criminal family. Unlike his father, he chose to be bad instead of hypocritical. Paper presented at the 6th Annual Convention of the International Psychohistorical Association, Graduate Center, City University of New York, June 1983. 56 notes. 1930-65

4429. Whitfield, Stephen J. THREE MASTERS OF IMPRESSION MANAGEMENT: BENJAMIN FRANKLIN, BOOKER T. WASHINGTON, AND MALCOLM X AS AUTOBIOGRAPHERS. *South Atlantic Q. 1978 77(4): 399-418.* 1788-1965
*For abstract see **Franklin, Benjamin***

Malin, James C.

4430. Brodhead, Michael J. JAMES C. MALIN, 1893-1979. *Environmental Rev. 1980 4(1): 18-19.* Memorial to James C. Malin (1893-1979), Professor Emeritus of History at the University of Kansas, who is also known as the father of an ecological approach to history. 1913-79

4431. Williams, Burton J. JAMES C. MALIN: IN MEMORIAM. *Kansas Hist. 1979 2(1): 65-67.* James C. Malin (1893-1979) taught history at the University of Kansas during 1921-63. He wrote more than 100 books and articles and directed more than 100 theses and dissertations. He believed that historical events are unique and that at best, a historical work is a progress report. As he turned to every field of knowledge to amplify his search for truth, Malin produced works that are better understood by geographers, economists, and natural scientists than by historians. Illus. 1921-79

4432. Williams, Burton J. A DEDICATION TO THE MEMORY OF JAMES C. MALIN, 1893-1979. *Arizona and the West 1980 22(3): 206-210.* James C. Malin (1893-1979) received his graduate education at the University of Kansas and spent 42 years on the history faculty of that institution. He served as president of the Agricultural History Society in 1943 and was active in state and national professional organizations. He was a prolific author. He was interested in the relationship of climate, mobility, and regional adaptations. He demonstrated a scientific expertise unusual for historians. In later years he focused on political and social reform. He challenged Frederick Jackson Turner's frontier hypothesis, especially the safety valve ideas. Illus., biblio. 1921-79

Mallon, Catherine

4433. Richter, Thomas, ed. SISTER CATHERINE MALLON'S JOURNAL. *New Mexico Hist. Rev. 1977 52(2): 135-155, (3): 237-250.* Part I. Bishop Jean Baptiste Lamy wished to provide social services for the people of New Mexico and asked the Sisters of Charity of Cincinnati, Ohio, to staff the proposed hospital in Santa Fe. Sister Catherine Mallon, one of the original four sisters to come, kept a journal of her experiences. Illus., 38 notes. Part II. Sister Catherine Mallon was one of four nurses who came to New Mexico in 1865 to organize a hospital in Santa Fe. Later she also served in Colorado. Reprints her journal, the original of which is now in Archives of the Sisters of Charity, Mt. St. Joseph, Cincinnati, Ohio. 1865-1901

Malloy, Mary

4434. Jerde, Judith. MARY MALLOY: ST. PAUL'S EXTRAORDINARY DRESSMAKER. *Minnesota Hist. 1980 47(3): 93-99.* Mary Malloy (1862-1924) turned craftsmanship in dressmaking into a business success and gained social status in an era when the emerging department stores needed specialists, because the craft had become too complicated for the average household. 12 illus., 19 notes. 1879-1924

Malloy, William Thomas

4435. Smith, Carlyle S. WILLIAM THOMAS MALLOY, 1917-1978. *Plains Anthropologist 1978 23(82, pt. 1): 337-340.* A memorial essay honoring a distinguished anthropologist and archaeologist. He was an outstanding teacher of anthropology at the University of Wyoming, a major writer on the archaeology of Easter Island, and an authority on the archaeology of the northwestern Great Plains. He made more than 20 trips to Easter Island. He recognized and fulfilled his primary obligation as a scientist to interpret prehistory and to use the data for a better understanding of culture and man's adaptations. Biblio. 1917-78

Malone, Goldia Bays

4436. Bigbee, Joe. GOLDIA MALONE: AN EARLY DAY COWGIRL. *West Texas Historical Association Yearbook 1984 60: 92-109.* Recounts the career in rodeos and exhibitions of trick riding of Goldia Bays Malone, particularly in the Malone Brothers' Wild West Show. 1920-32

M'Alpine, John

4437. Punch, T. M. LOYALISTS ARE STUFFY, EH? *Nova Scotia Hist. Q. [Canada] 1978 8(4): 319-343.* John M'Alpine (1748-1827) was a Scotsman who had a varied career in New York and Halifax. He supplied horses and fuel to the British troops during the American Revolution. After the war he moved to Nova Scotia and was an innkeeper, undertaker, drover, road builder, cattle dealer, father of six children and husband to four wives. Based on diaries and secondary sources; 47 notes, genealogical appendix. 1748-1827

Mamoulian, Rouben

4438. Oberstein, Bennett Thomas. "The Broadway Directing Career of Rouben Mamoulian." Indiana U. 1977. 454 pp. *DAI 1978 38(11): 6407-6408-A.* 20c

Mandel, Eli

4439. Munton, Ann. THE STRUCTURAL HORIZONS OF PRAIRIE POETICS: THE LONG POEM, ELI MANDEL, ANDREW SUKNASKI, AND ROBERT KROETSCH. *Dalhousie Rev. [Canada] 1983 63(1): 69-97.* Discusses the role of Canadian poets Eli Mandel, Andrew Suknaski, and Robert Kroetsch in the literary history of the Canadian West. 84 notes. 20c

Mangione, Jerre

4440. Morreale, Ben. JERRE MANGIONE: THE SICILIAN SOURCES. *Italian Americana 1981 7(1): 4-18.* Brief biography of American-born writer of Sicilian parents, Jerre Mangione, focusing on his writing style, his writing experiences, particularly as a member of the Works Progress Administration writers' project during the 1930's, and lists his principal works beginning with his first book, *Mount Allegro* (1943). 1930's-79

Manley, Frank J.

4441. Manley, Patrick Charles. "Frank J. Manley: The Man and the Idea." U. of Michigan 1978. 157 pp. *DAI 1979 39(12): 7087-A.* 1930's-70's

Mann, John and James

4442. Fox, Nellie. LOYALIST BROTHERS: JOHN AND JAMES MANN. *Nova Scotia Historical Review [Canada] 1984 4(2): 83-89.* John and James Mann emigrated from New York City to Nova Scotia after the American Revolution because of their Loyalist sympathies. As ordained Methodist ministers, the brothers preached on Nova Scotia's south shore for many years. Biblio. 1789-1817

Mann, Thomas

4443. Knopf, Alfred A. RANDOM RECOLLECTIONS OF A PUBLISHER. *Massachusetts Hist. Soc. Pro. 1961 73: 92-103.* 1901-61
*For abstract see **Cather, Willa***

Mannasse, Heyman

4444. Karsh, Audrey R. HEYMAN MANNASSE: AN ARIZONA AND SAN DIEGO SAGA. *Western States Jewish Hist. Q. 1980 13(1): 37-42.* Heyman Mannasse (1831-75) ran a dry goods store and owned real estate in San Diego, California, during the 1850's and early 1860's. He moved to Arizona in 1864 where he established branch stores in La Paz, Phoenix, and Wickenburg. A Mexican freighter shot and killed him on 20 April 1875 during an argument over the price of barley. Based on newspaper articles and Heyman Mannasse file, Sacks Collection, La Paz Mining District; photo, 31 notes. 1853-75

Manning, Joseph C.

4445. Pruitt, Paul, Jr. A CHANGING OF THE GUARD: JOSEPH C. MANNING AND POPULIST STRATEGY IN THE FALL OF 1894. *Alabama Hist. Q. 1978 40(1-2): 20-36.* Details the attempt of Joseph C. Manning, 1892-96, to unite populists against the Jeffersonian Democratic machine in Alabama. 80 notes. 1892-96

4446. Pruitt, Paul, Jr. "Joseph C. Manning, Alabama Populist: A Rebel Against the Solid South." Coll. of William and Mary 1980. 465 pp. *DAI 1981 41(8): 3686-A.* 8103592 1892-1930

Manning, Nicholas (family)

4447. Erlich, Gloria C. HAWTHORNE AND THE MANNINGS. *Studies in the Am. Renaissance 1980: 97-117.* Almost all biographies of Nathaniel Hawthorne begin with the first generation of Puritan ancestors on the Hathorne side. It is a rare biographer who mentions the maternal ancestor, Nicholas Manning, who reached the shores of Massachusetts only 30 years later than the better known William Hathorne. In 1680 the wife of Nicholas Manning accused him of incest with his two sisters, Anstiss and Margaret. Nicholas fled into the forest, but the sisters were tried, convicted, and sentenced to sit, during the next church service on a high stool in the middle aisle of Salem meetinghouse with paper on their heads (inscribed in capital letters) with their crime. These Mannings were ancestors of the author of *The Scarlet Letter,* who, in his autobiographical "Custom House," did not link the novel with his maternal ancestors. The Mannings were a business family, and the young Hawthorne had to hide from them the fact that he wished to be a writer. It was the Manning influence which caused a self-distrust in Hawthorne and contributed to the ambiguity of his fiction. Mainly archival and published primary sources; 35 notes. 1680-1841

Mansfield, John Worthington

4448. Sharf, Frederic A. and Wright, John H. JOHN WORTHINGTON MANSFIELD (1849-1933): AN AMERICAN ARTIST REDISCOVERED. *Essex Inst. Hist. Collections 1978 114(1): 32-45.* The unfulfilled career of artist John Worthington Mansfield (1849-1933) in a sense reflects the growth and deficiencies of American art in the late 19th and early 20th centuries. Mansfield was born in Norwich, Connecticut, and produced his first watercolor at age seven. After a short enlistment in the Union Army (February-April 1865) he enrolled in the National Academy of Design in New York City. His first oil painting, an 1867 portrait of a Civil War officer, displayed a unique monogram which he used consistently to sign his paintings—the first two digits of a year preceded his entwined initials and the last two digits followed. He went to Paris to study in 1871, and did not return permanently to the United States until 1876. Using New York City as a base, he traveled to the White Mountains and the Adirondacks to paint some of his finest works. In 1885 Mansfield moved to Boston to teach at the New England Conservatory of Fine Arts. He finally settled in Ipswich in 1887. Till his death, his main artistic talents were directed toward satisfying wealthy North Shore families. Based on John Worthington Mansfield's Papers and on primary and secondary sources; 4 illus., 18 notes. 1867-1933

Mansfield, Michael J.

4449. Schwartz, James Edmond. "Senator Michael J. Mansfield and United States Military Disengagement from Europe; A Case Study in American Foreign Policy: The Majority Leader, His Amendment, and His Influence upon the Senate." U. of North Carolina, Chapel Hill 1977. 524 pp. *DAI 1977 38(6): 3706-3707-A.* 1959-71

Manson, Marsden

4450. Clements, Kendrick A. ENGINEERS AND CONSERVATIONISTS IN THE PROGRESSIVE ERA. *California History 1979-80 58(4): 282-303.* Discusses the role of Marsden Manson in San Francisco's long campaign to obtain a water supply from the Tuolumne River by building a dam in Yosemite's Hetch Hetchy Valley. As city engineer from 1908 to 1912, Manson continued the effort he had earlier begun on behalf of the city's position. Opposing the city was a Sierra Club divided between preservationists and developmental conservationists. Manson, himself a Sierra Club member, believed with other technical experts that Hetch Hetchy was the best source of a water supply. He brought expert arguments combined with political shrewdness to his campaign. In contrast, John Muir's supporters relied on aesthetic arguments and the mistaken belief that the general public supported them. Rather than an issue of good versus bad, the controversy resembled a civil war between Progressives who sincerely believed in the rightness of their position. 8 photos, 65 notes. 1900-13

Manson, William

4451. Davis, Robert Scott, Jr. THE LAST COLONIAL ENTHUSIAST: CAPTAIN WILLIAM MANSON IN REVOLUTIONARY GEORGIA. *Atlanta Hist. J. 1984 28(1): 23-38.* Relates the Revolutionary War experiences of Scottish sea captain and Loyalist William Manson, who purchased land in Georgia on the eve of the American Revolution and became a merchant in Augusta. 1774-81

Månsson, Evelina

4452. Nordstrom, Byron J. EVELINA MÅNSSON AND THE MEMOIR OF AN URBAN LABOR MIGRANT. *Swedish Pioneer Hist. Q. 1980 31(3): 182-195.* An account of the life of Evelina Månsson in the United States, 1901-07. She was born and raised in Sweden, emigrated to America in 1901, and returned to Sweden in 1907 to live out her life. Based on Månsson's memoirs; 22 notes. 1901-07

Manteo family

4453. Gold, Donna Lauren. PLUCKY PUPPETS ARE THE STARS IN ONE FAMILY'S SAGA. *Smithsonian 1983 14(5): 68-73.* Discusses the Manteo family and their work with marionettes from the early 1900's in Catania, Sicily, to present-day New York City. 1900-83

Marcello, Carlos

4454. Barbat, Damon Lofton. "Carlos Marcello: An Analysis of a Career in Organized Crime." Sam Houston State U. 1982. 258 pp. *DAI 1982 43(6): 2110-A.* DA8225865 19c-20c

Marcus, David

4455. Maginnis, John J. MY SERVICE WITH COLONEL DAVID MARCUS. *Am. Jewish Hist. 1980 69(3): 301-324.* There is growing interest in the career of Colonel David Marcus (1902-48), the American organizer of Israeli guerrilla forces in 1948, who became Israel's first general. Marcus's World War II service in Europe, however, has been inaccurately depicted in films. John J. Maginnis, now a retired major general, was on duty with the Berlin District Headquarters when Marcus first arrived as an observer in 1944, and later returned as Secretary of the US Control Council for Germany, 1945-46. This memoir is based on his experiences with Marcus during this time. Based on the author's recollections. 1944-46

Marcuse, Herbert

4456. Litecky, Lawrence Paul. "Marcuse: Messiah and/or Monster." U. of Minnesota 1977. 329 pp. *DAI 1977 38(3): 1622-1623-A.* 1930's-72

4457. Malinovich Miedzian, Myriam. MARCUSE E IL CONCETTO DI LIBERTA PSICOLOGICA [Marcuse and the concept of psychological freedom]. *Comunità [Italy] 1983 37(185): 147-166.* In Herbert Marcuse's work, the fusion of existentialist, psychoanalytic, and Hegelian Marxist traditions results in a concept of psychological freedom from alienation. 1950's-70's

Marden, Orison Swett

4458. Sumner, Nancy Ann McCowan. "Orison Swett Marden, the American Samuel Smiles." Brown U. 1982. 380 pp. *DAI 1983 43(11): 3687-A.* DA8228340 1850's-1920's

Margolin, Arnold

4459. Likhten, Iosyf L. ARNOL'D MARGOLIN: IOHO ZHYTTIA I PRATSIA [Arnold Margolin: his life and work]. *Sučasnist [West Germany] 1977 (5): 68-73.* Traces the life of Ukrainian American Jew Arnold Margolin, his participation in the Ukrainian struggle for independence, 1917-20, and his work on Ukrainian-Jewish relations. 1900-56

Maricle, Burrell

4460. Hoar, Jay S. LOUISIANA'S LAST BOYS IN GRAY. *Louisiana Hist. 1978 19(3): 336-352.* 1824-1953
*For abstract see **Powell, Frank Eli***

Mario, Jessie White

4461. Daniels, Elizabeth Adams. JESSIE WHITE MARIO: 19TH-CENTURY FOREIGN CORRESPONDENT. *Journalism Hist. 1975 2(2): 54-56.* Jessie White Mario (1832-1904) was Italian correspondent for E. L. Godkin's newspaper, the *Nation,* during 1866-1904. 1866-1904

Marion, Francis

4462. Kyte, George W. FRANCIS MARION AS AN INTELLIGENCE OFFICER. *South Carolina Hist. Mag. 1976 77(4): 215-226.* Examines the service of Francis Marion (the Swamp Fox) as an intelligence officer for General Greene 1780-82. 1780-82

Markley family

4463. Fenstermacher, J. Howard. VESTIGES OF THE MARKLEY FAMILY. *Pennsylvania Folklife 1980 29(3): 114-119.* Describes the influence of two families, the Kempfers and the Markleys, who founded a cemetery in 1738 on a farm plot in the Skippack region, maintained it, and kept records of deaths in the area; in 1926 the Markley Family Association obtained the original land and restored the cemetery. 1738

Marks, Anna

4464. Rudd, Hynda. THE UNSINKABLE ANNA MARKS. *Western States Jewish Hist. Q. 1978 10(3): 234-237.* Anna Marks (1847-1912) and her husband Wolff Marks (1842-1918) operated a store in Eureka City, Utah during the 1880's and 90's. They made a fortune in real estate and mining investments. Anna earned a reputation as a feisty character, especially concerning disputed property boundaries. She was handy with a gun and had a full vocabulary of cuss words. Secondary sources; 3 photos, 5 notes. 1880-1900

Marks, David X. and Joshua H.

4465. —. THE MARKS BROTHERS OF LOS ANGELES, A PICTURE STORY. *Western States Jewish Hist. Q. 1979 11(4): 311-317.* Joshua H. Marks (1884-1965) and David X. Marks (1891-1977) were brought to Los Angeles by their parents in 1902. Joshua entered their father's brick business and became a building designer and contractor. Among his better known works are Grauman's Chinese and Egyptian theaters, and the Santa Anita Race Track. He also built several shopping centers, churches, business offices, and movie studios. David entered the insurance business and was active in civic affairs. He helped establish the Los Angeles Civic Light Opera Association, and contributed financially to developments at the University of Southern California, and other educational institutions. Family records and published sources; 7 photos, 8 notes. 1902-77

Marks, Nora

4466. Lederer, Francis L., II. NORA MARKS—REINVESTIGATED. *J. of the Illinois State Hist Soc. 1980 73(1): 61-64.* Traces the life and writing career of Eleanor Stackhouse Atkinson, who used the pen name Nora Marks, from her birth in Indiana to her work as a writer at the *Chicago Tribune* during 1888-90, as a writer of children's books from 1903, and as an author of historical novels during 1908-21. Comments on her marriage to Francis Blake Atkinson in 1891. 2 photos, 14 notes. 1888-1942

Marland, William Casey

4467. Lutz, Paul F. "William Casey Marland: Governor of West Virginia 1953-1957." West Virginia U. 1977. 201 pp. *DAI 1978 38(12): 7514-7515-A.* 1953-57

4468. Lutz, Paul F. THE GOVERNOR DROVE A TAXI: THE TRAGEDY OF WILLIAM CASEY MARLAND. *J. of the West Virginia Hist. Assoc. 1982 6(1): 20-40.* Narrates the story of the brilliant law student who became governor of West Virginia in 1953, William Casey Marland; Marland's problems with alcohol eventually terminated his career in politics and after a series of less prestigious jobs he died of cancer in 1965. 1953-65

Marschall, Nicola

4469. Williams, Edward F., III. NICOLA MARSCHALL'S PORTRAIT OF BEDFORD FORREST. *West Tennessee Hist. Soc. Papers 1983 37: 5-7.* A brief description of artist Nicola Marschall and her painting of Confederate general Nathan Bedford Forrest, painted in 1869 and purchased by the Tennessee State Museum in 1983. Plate, biblio. 1869

Marsh, John

4470. Stuart, Reginald and Stuart, Winifred. JOHN MARSH. *Pacific Hist. 1980 24(3): 369-375.* Biographical account of John Marsh, the first American to settle on the Contra Costa. In 1828 he was granted a license to practice medicine in the Pueblo of Los Angeles. In 1837 Marsh purchased a large ranchero, Los Meganos. He obtained cattle for his ranch by being paid in cattle for his medical services. He was instrumental in encouraging settlers to come to California to live. The gold discovery in Coloma brought hordes of people to the area and the doctor became a rich man by tending to their needs. After marrying, having a daughter, and then losing his wife to disease, John Marsh became uninterested in life. His long-lost half-Indian son found him and renewed his vitality. A disgruntled worker killed John Marsh and his son chased the murderer and brought him to trial and sentencing. The uncompleted stone mansion still stands on Marsh Road. Covers 1828-55. 1828-55

Marsh, Leonard

4471. Horn, Michael. LEONARD MARSH AND THE COMING OF A WELFARE STATE IN CANADA: A REVIEW ARTICLE. *Social Hist. [Canada] 1976 9(17): 197-204.* Reprints Leonard Marsh's *Report on Social Security for Canada* (1943) and discusses his career. He pioneered social welfare research in Canada during the 1930's, and in the 1940's he became one of the main designers of the slowly developing Canadian welfare state. Marsh was strongly influenced by Fabianism and was active in the League for Social Reconstruction which stood for a reformist and constitutionalist socialism committed to thorough-going changes in the distribution of income, wealth, and power. Secondary sources; 27 notes. 1930-44

Marsh, Thomas Baldwin

4472. Cook, Lyndon W. "I HAVE SINNED AGAINST HEAVEN, AND AM UNWORTHY OF YOUR CONFIDENCE, BUT I CANNOT LIVE WITHOUT A RECONCILIATION": THOMAS B. MARSH RETURNS TO THE CHURCH. *Brigham Young U. Studies 1980 20(4): 389-400.* A short biography and summary of the Mormon Church experiences of Thomas Baldwin Marsh (1799-1866), Mormon leader, including the circumstances leading to his 1839 excommunication and 1857 return to fellowship. Contains copies of his petitions for reinstatement and dedication of his life to God. Based on church minutes, diaries, personal journals, letters, an unpublished master's thesis, and other secondary sources; 42 notes. ca 1829-66

Marshall, Andrew C.

4473. Johnson, Whittington B. ANDREW C. MARSHALL: A BLACK RELIGIOUS LEADER OF ANTEBELLUM SAVANNAH. *Georgia Historical Quarterly 1985 69(2): 173-192.* Discusses the life of Andrew C. Marshall (1755-1856), who spent over 50 years as a slave in South Carolina and Georgia before buying his freedom, establishing himself as a merchant in Savannah, Georgia, and becoming the pastor of the First African Baptist Church in Savannah in 1825. Based on church records and other primary and secondary sources; 62 notes. 1780's-1856

Marshall, Daniel

4474. Harris, Waldo P., III. DANIEL MARSHALL: LONE GEORGIA BAPTIST REVOLUTIONARY PASTOR. *Viewpoints: Georgia Baptist Hist. 1976 5: 51-64.* Daniel Marshall, a convert to the Baptist Church, became a minister in that religion; examines his political stand during and following the American Revolution, and covers the period 1747-1823. 1747-1823

Marshall, George C.

4475. Moch, Jules. JAURÈS: MARSHALL [Jaurès: Marshall]. *Nouvelle Rev. des Deux Mondes [France] 1980 (7): 58-63.* The author, a French statesman, relates his personal contacts with French Socialist leader and author Jean Léon Jaurès (1859-1914) and American Secretary of State and Nobel Prize winner George C. Marshall (1880-1959). 1911-51

4476. Rowe, David Nelson. GEN. GEORGE C. MARSHALL: STRATEGIST AND POLICY-MAKER. *Issues & Studies [Taiwan] 1974 10(4): 2-27.* Provides a study of General George C. Marshall's military career, focusing on his role as a strategist and drawing special attention to his ill-fated mission to China during 1945-47. ca 1900-47

Marshall, John

4477. Henderson, Phillip G. MARSHALL VERSUS JEFFERSON: POLITICS AND THE FEDERAL JUDICIARY IN THE EARLY REPUBLIC. *Michigan J. of Pol. Sci. 1983 2(2): 42-66.* 1790's-1835
*For abstract see **Jefferson, Thomas***

Marshall, Louis

4478. Rosenthal, Jerome C. "The Public Life of Louis Marshall." (Vol. 1-2) U. of Cincinnati 1983. 732 pp. *DAI 1984 44(8): 2555-A.* DA8328322 1880's-1929

4479. Rosenthal, Jerome C. A FRESH LOOK AT LOUIS MARSHALL AND ZIONISM, 1900-1912. *Am. Jewish Arch. 1980 32(2): 109-118.* Louis Marshall, an influential constitutional lawyer, was a devout Jew and eventually a Zionist. His background in preimmigration New York City placed him in a Jewish elite known for its neutrality to anti-Zionist leanings. Marshall's pro-Zionist sentiments were seen in his letters to Nathan Straus, Michael Leon, Solomon Schecter, and Jacob Schiff, as well as in lectures to various Jewish groups and contributions to Herzl-connected funds. By 1909 Marshall was sufficiently involved in Zionist activities to cosponsor the construction of an Agricultural Experiment Station in Palestine. Despite these overtly pro-Zionist activities, Marshall in several letters professed himself as neutral on the issue, claiming that his actions and support were not politically motivated. Based on the Marshall Papers at the American Jewish Archives; photo, 27 notes. 1900-12

Marshall, Mary Louise

4480. Brodman, Estelle. EDUCATION AND ATTITUDES OF EARLY MEDICAL LIBRARIANS TO THEIR WORK: A DISCUSSION BASED ON THE ORAL HISTORY PROJECT OF THE MEDICAL LIBRARY ASSOCIATION. *J. of Lib. Hist. 1980 15(2): 167-182.* 1912-59
For abstract see ***Doe, Janet***

Marshall, Robert

4481. Bernstein, David A. BOB MARSHALL: WILDERNESS ADVOCATE. *Western States Jewish Hist. Q. 1980 13(1): 26-33.* As a youth, Robert "Bob" Marshall (1901-39) decided on a career in forestry, an unusual choice for an upper class Jewish boy. He earned advanced degrees in the study of forestry and began a career in the US Forest Service. An assignment to Alaska in 1929 enabled him to explore and map uncharted lands, and to publish *Arctic Village,* the first of several works on the region. During the 1930's, Marshall became an active proponent of wilderness preservation, a controversial issue then, as now. His efforts guided the Forest Service in creating a wilderness system. The Bob Marshall Wilderness in Montana is named for this pioneer wilderness advocate. Based on interviews and other primary sources; photo, map, 17 notes. 1920-39

4482. McGrew, Paul C. ROBERT "BOB" MARSHALL: WILDERNESS ADVOCATE. *Pacific Northwesterner 1982 26(3): 33-46.* Biography of Robert Marshall, naturalist, wilderness author, Forest Service administrator, and record-setting hiker during the 1920's and 30's. 1921-39

Marston, Edward

4483. Luwel, M. HENRY MORTON STANLEY EN ZIJN UITGEVER EDWARD MARSTON [Henry Morton Stanley and his publisher Edward Marston]. *Bulletin des Séances de l'Académie Royale des Sciences d'Outre-Mer [Belgium] 1981 27(4): 569-582.* 1872-1909
For abstract see ***Stanley, Henry Morton***

Marston, George White

4484. Polos, Nicholas C. GEORGE WHITE MARSTON: THE MERCHANT PRINCE OF SAN DIEGO. *Journal of San Diego History 1984 30(4): 252-278.* George White Marston was involved in numerous enterprises after arriving in San Diego, California, in 1870; owner of a prominent department store, he amassed great wealth and supported various civic activities, museums, and parks and served as trustee for Pomona College until his death in 1946. 1870-1946

Marti, Fritz

4485. —. FRITZ MARTI: IMMIGRANT PHILOSOPHER. *Swiss Am. Hist. Soc. Newsletter 1979 15(3): 2-33.*
Schelbert, Leo. CONGRATULATORY MESSAGE, *p. 2.* .
—. FRITZ MARTI: THE COURSE OF A BUSY LIFE, *pp. 4-5.*
Marti, Fritz. HAPPENSTANCE OR PROVIDENCE, OR HOW I FOUND ALL MY JOBS, *pp. 6-21.*
—. RELIGION AND PHILOSOPHY: SELECTIONS FROM FRITZ MARTI'S COLLECTED PAPERS, *pp. 22-29.*
Marti, Fritz. THE MARTI SCHOOL, 1947-64. *pp. 30-31.*
—. PHILOSOPHICAL PUBLICATIONS OF FRITZ MARTI, *pp. 32-33.*
Issue dedicated to world-renowned philosopher and educator Dr. Fritz Marti (b. 1894); details his life and career, and lists his philosophical publications, 1922-77. 1894-1979

Martiau, Nicolas

4486. Mandel, Salomé. NICOLAS MARTIAU, HUGUENOT FRANÇAIS, ANCETRE DE WASHINGTON [Nicolas Martiau, French Huguenot, ancestor of Washington]. *Miroir de l'Hist. [France] 1957 8(91): 45-49.* Nicolas Martiau, a Frenchman, was sent to Jamestown, Virginia, in 1620 as a professional engineer; his granddaughter married Lawrence Washington, an ancestor of George Washington. 17c

Martin, Absalom

4487. Tanks, Annie C. ABSALOM MARTIN: SOLDIER, SURVEYOR, SETTLER. *Upper Ohio Valley Hist. Rev. 1983 12(2): 2-14.* Details the life of Absalom Martin from his service in the American Revolution to his involvement in the surveying of the Northwest Territory and his settling eventually in an area near Wheeling, West Virginia. 1758-1802

Martin, Frances Martha Atkinson

4488. Martin-Perdue, Nancy. THE USE OF AUTOBIOGRAPHY IN FAMILY HISTORY. *Family Heritage 1979 2(3): 82-91, (4): 116-122.* Part I. Discusses genealogy and family history research; excerpts from the autobiography of Frances Martha Atkinson Martin, 1857-70, reveal details of daily life, kinship structure, and social organization in Cooke County, Texas. Part II. Demonstrates the historical uses of personal accounts by analyzing the impact of the Civil War as recorded by a Texas girl. 1857-75

Martin, H. Newell

4489. Fye, W. Bruce. H. NEWELL MARTIN—A REMARKABLE CAREER DESTROYED BY NEURASTHENIA AND ALCOHOLISM. *Journal of the History of Medicine and Allied Sciences 1985 40(2): 133-166.* The career of H. Newell Martin (1848-1896), a pioneering physiologist at Johns Hopkins University, was destroyed by neurasthenia and alcoholism. His alcoholism led to a forced resignation from Johns Hopkins at the time when his impact on science and education should have been greatest. His problems included morphine addiction as well as a disabling polyneuropathy. Based on correspondence of Johns Hopkins faculty and administrators; 127 notes. 1860's-96

Martin, Homer Dodge

4490. Mandel, Patricia Carroll FitzGerald. "Homer Dodge Martin: American Landscape Painter, 1836-1897." New York U. 1973. 360 pp. *DAI 1978 38(9): 5101-A.* 1850's-97

Martin, John

4491. Conard, A. Mark. THE CHEROKEE MISSION OF VIRGINIA PRESBYTERIANS. *J. of Presbyterian Hist. 1980 58(1): 35-58.* In the latter 1750's Virginia Presbyterians launched the first Christian mission among the Overhill Cherokee Indians in what is now Tennessee. Discusses the founding, operation, and decline of the labors of John Martin and William Richardson. Based on Richardson's diary (Wilberforce Eames Collection, Manuscript Division, New York Public Library), Eleazar Wheelock MSS (Dartmouth College), Letter Book of the Society for the Propagation of the Gospel in New England (Alderman Library, University of Virginia), ecclesiastical court records and secondary studies; 93 notes. 1755-63

Martin, Josiah

4492. Sheridan, Richard B. THE WEST INDIAN ANTECEDENTS OF JOSIAH MARTIN, LAST ROYAL GOVERNOR OF NORTH CAROLINA. *North Carolina Hist. Rev. 1977 54(3): 253-270.* Josiah Martin (1737-86), the last royal governor of North Carolina, took office in 1771 and endured a stormy tenure until relieved by the Revolution. His earlier years were no smoother, as Josiah struggled for independence from his Antigua-based planter father, Colonel Samuel Martin, and his well-connected half-brother, Sir Henry Martin, a member of Parliament. Relenting under their pressure, Josiah gave up a rewarding military career in the colonies for an unsuccessful political one. Based primarily on the Martin Family Papers and other primary sources; 5 illus., 2 maps, 49 notes. 1750's-70's

Martin, Malachi

4493. Fryman, Mildred L. CAREER OF A "CARPETBAGGER": MALACHI MARTIN IN FLORIDA. *Florida Hist. Q. 1978 56(3): 317-338.* Malachi Martin (1822-84) is associated primarily with Florida's notorious convict-lease system, in which he served from 1868-77 as chief administrator of the Chattahoochee Penitentiary. Martin first came to Florida with the Army of the Potomac and stayed to pursue farming. Eventually he enjoyed moderate success in state Republican politics and in his vineyards and wine producing. His record as warden was not exemplary, but it was not as barbarous as his critics claimed. Based mainly on government documents, primary and secondary sources; 94 notes. 1868-77

Martinez, Maria

4494. —. [MARIA MARTINEZ AND BLACK-ON-BLACK POTTERY WARE]. *Palacio 1980-81 86(4): 3-9.*

Toulouse, Betty. MARIA: THE RIGHT WOMAN AT THE RIGHT TIME, *pp. 3-7.* Maria Martinez crafted pottery from the early 1900's when she, her husband Julian, and other Pueblo Indians helped Dr. Edgar L. Hewett and Kenneth M. Chapman with excavations on the Pajarito Plateau in New Mexico; Maria's black-on-black pottery gained in fame, even after her husband Julian's death in 1943.

Spivey, Richard L. SIGNED IN CLAY, *pp. 8-9.* Traces the three periods in the pottery making career of Maria Martinez: 1907-43, when she worked with her husband Julian making polychrome ware and plain red ware before progressing to black-on-black ware; 1943-56, when she worked with her daughter-in-law, Santana, who painted the designs on the pottery; and 1956-70, when she worked with her son, Popovi Da; focusing on the pottery's signatures. 1907-70

Marty, Martin

4495. Rippinger, Joel. MARTIN MARTY: MONK, ABBOT, MISSIONARY AND BISHOP. *Am. Benedictine Rev. 1982 33(3): 223-240, (4): 376-393.* Examines Martin Marty's career as monk, superior of the community at St. Meinrad, Indiana, and missionary bishop. His early development and his character as a maverick help to explain his achievements and contributions in building the American Benedictine community. Also discusses Marty's work among the Sioux Indians of the Dakota Territory as Vicar Apostolic of the Dakota Territory, as Bishop of Sioux Falls, South Dakota, and as Bishop of St. Cloud, Minnesota. 51 notes. 1834-96

Marvin, Cloyd Heck.

4496. Abbott, Mary H. THE MARVIN AFFAIR. *J. of Arizona Hist. 1982 23(1): 59-80.* Describes the tumultous career of Cloyd Heck Marvin, president of the University of Arizona during 1922-27. Provides detailed accounts of the personality conflicts and private crusades that caused the firing of President Marvin. All were blameworthy. Based on the minutes of the regents' meetings and newspapers; 6 photos, 35 notes. 1922-27

Marx, Robert S.

4497. Westheimer, Charles. ROBERT S. MARX: LAWYER, JUDGE, POLITICIAN. *Cincinnati Hist. Soc. Bull. 1976 34(3): 151-171.* Robert S. Marx (1889-1960) graduated from Cincinnati Law School in 1909; he had an important impact on the law and its writing and interpretation, and won international renown. 1909-60

Mary Joseph, Mother

4498. McKernan, Mary. MOTHER JOSEPH: PIONEER NUN. *Am. West 1981 18(5): 20-21.* Esther Pariseau (1823-1902), who learned carpentry from her father, a Canadian carriage maker, entered the Montreal, Quebec, convent of the Sisters of Charity of Providence and soon became Mother Mary Joseph. In 1856, she was assigned to duty in the Pacific Northwest. She constructed (literally as "fund raiser, architect, estimator of materials, supervisor of construction, and at times as carpenter, bricklayer, and wood-carver") 11 hospitals, seven academies, two orphanages, four homes for the aged and mentally ill, and five Indian schools. She wore a hammer beside the rosary on her belt. Most of her recognition has come posthumously from the American Institute of Architects, the National Register of Historic Places, and the state of Washington, which chose her as its second representative in Statuary Hall at the nation's Capitol. 2 illus. 1856-1902

Marye, William Bose

4499. Key, Betty McKeever, ed. WILLIAM B. MARYE'S "DIG" AT BRYN MAWR. *Maryland Hist. Mag. 1980 75(1): 72-81.* In this transcript of an oral history interview with William Bose Marye at the Maryland Historical Society, 26 March 1975, that long-time Society officer, genealogical verifier, and archaeological researcher reminisces about the 136 hours he spent excavating a site on the grounds of the Bryn Mawr College (Pennsylvania) during the 1930's and found artifacts from the archaic caves of the last ice age. He also worked in the Gunpowder River area before it became the Edgewood Arsenal, and was closely associated with those such as Dr. J. Holmes Smith who organized various archaeological collections for the Maryland Historical Society. Tape number OH 8082 in the Maryland Historical Society Oral History Collection. ca 1930-75

Marzolf, Florentina

4500. Marzolf, Florentina; Marzolf, Arnold H., ed. A SHORT AUTOBIOGRAPHY OF FLORENTINA MARZOLF. *Heritage Review 1981 11(3): 36-38.* Presents and comments on the early autobiography of Florentina Marzolf, whose parents, Germans from Russia, farmed and homesteaded in Nebraska and North Dakota at the turn of the century. 1890-1910

Masaharu, Kondo

4501. Estes, Donald H. KONDO MASAHARU AND THE BEST OF ALL FISHERMEN. *J. of San Diego Hist. 1977 23(3): 1-19.* Biography of Kondo Masaharu, a San Diegan of Japanese origin who was instrumental in starting the fishing industry in southern California, Mexico, and throughout the South Pacific during 1910-30. 1910-30

Masak

4502. French, Alice. MY NAME IS MASAK. *Beaver [Canada] 1976 307(2): 28-31.* Autobiographical account of a young Eskimo girl from Cambridge Bay who in 1937 was taken to a boarding school at Aklavik. Recounts the adjustments to a new language and changing values. 5 illus. 1930's

Maslow, Sophie

4503. Maslow, Sophie and Morgan, Barbara. DIALOGUE WITH PHOTOGRAPHS. *Massachusetts Rev. 1983 24(1): 65-80.* Reviews the career of Sophie Maslow, a dancer and choreographer who worked with Martha Graham. Describes episodes in her career and comments on persons with whom she worked and on some aspects of modern dance. Also discusses the career of Barbara Morgan, who was an artist before she turned to photography, photographing Martha Graham and others. Illus., 9 photos. ca 1920-82

Mason, Charles

4504. Wubben, H. H. COPPERHEAD CHARLES MASON: A QUESTION OF LOYALTY. *Civil War Hist. 1978 24(1): 46-65.* Charles Mason, the atypical copperhead, was born in the North. A foremost lawyer, businessman, and politician in Iowa, he became prominent in Washington Democratic circles in the 1850's. From 1860, as correspondent to the Democratic Dubuque *Herald*—and in diaries and letters—Mason saw himself as an educator to promote peace by defending conservative and southern views, playing upon northern war-weariness, and putting down northern military prowess. However, by 1868 he felt himself an ineffectual failure. Newspapers; unpublished and published papers, secondary sources; 62 notes. 1829-82

Mason, David Townsend

4505. Richardson, Elmo. "THE COMPLEAT FORESTER": DAVID T. MASON'S EARLY CAREER AND CHARACTER. *J. of Forest Hist. 1983 27(3): 112-121.* David Townsend Mason was America's most dedicated advocate of sustained-yield forestry, which he believed could stabilize the lumber industry by eliminating overproduction and maintaining permanent timber stands. Mason taught forest management at the University of California, Berkeley, until 1921, when he resigned to become a private forestry consultant in Portland, Oregon. He was manager of the Western Pine Association (1931-35), executive officer of the Lumber Code Authority (1933-35), and a contributor to New Deal legislation affecting sustained-yield policies. Excerpted from Elmo Richardson's *David T. Mason: Forestry Advocate* (1983); 7 photos, 18 notes. 1905-73

Mason, Ebenezer

4506. Hendrickson, Walter B. JACKSONVILLE ARTISTS OF THE 1870'S. *J. of the Illinois State Hist. Soc. 1977 70(4): 258-275.* 1870's

*For abstract see **Clark, George W.***

Mason, George

4507. Frank, Perry. BICENTENNIAL GAZETTE: THE FRAMERS OF THE CONSTITUTION: VIRGINIA. *This Constitution 1985 (7): 38-40.* 1787

*For abstract see **Blair, John***

4508. Horrell, Joseph. GEORGE MASON AND THE FAIRFAX COURT. *Virginia Mag. of Hist. and Biog. 1983 91(4): 418-439.* Reviews George Mason's career as a justice of the Fairfax County Court. Previous biographies of Mason have held that his years on the court were instructive and formative. Closer scrutiny reveals that the sickly man was notorious for his nonattendance at court and was even removed from his seat in 1752, although he returned to it in 1764. As a member of the court and the House of Burgesses, the antifederalist Mason saw Alexandria's urban citizens gain disproportionate control over the law in otherwise rural Fairfax County. Finally, after years of legal fighting, Mason persuaded Fairfax County citizens to move their courthouse out of Alexandria to a location where its justices would serve all their constituents equally. Based on the published papers of Mason, Madison, and Jefferson; Fairfax County Court Records; and colonial and state journals; illus., 58 notes. 1747-89

Mason, Mayor

4509. Sengupta, Syamalendu. MAYOR MASON—AN AMERICAN SYMPATHIZER OF INDIAN NATIONALIST CAUSE. *Q. Rev. of Hist. Studies [India] 1982 22(3): 47-50.* Mayor Mason, a Canadian-born naturalized American citizen, arrived in Calcutta in January 1930. Customs inspectors found documents in Mason's possession that indicated his sympathy for the Indian nationalist movement, and he was thus viewed with great suspicion. By June 1930, the government had become so alarmed with Mason's statements that he was expelled from the country. Primary sources; 14 notes. 1925-32

Mason, Robert Tufton

4510. Johnson, Richard R. ROBERT MASON AND THE COMING OF ROYAL GOVERNMENT TO NEW ENGLAND. *Hist. New Hampshire 1980 35(4): 361-390.* Robert Tufton Mason (1635-88), grandson of John Mason, principal founder of New Hampshire, tried from 1659 until his death to establish his claim to New Hampshire and much of northern Massachusetts. He attempted to weaken Boston's hold on New Hampshire and to fill the vacuum himself. Mason failed because his claim was weak, and he lacked the required wealth and connections to counter well established settlers. His petitions to the crown did, however, help to precipitate royal rule in New Hampshire. 55 notes, appendix. 1659-88

Masqueray, Emmanuel L.

4511. Lathrop, Alan K. A FRENCH ARCHITECT IN MINNESOTA: EMMANUEL L. MASQUERAY, 1861-1917. *Minnesota Hist. 1980 47(2): 42-56.* While working as one of the architects for the Louisiana Purchase Exposition in 1904, Emmanuel L. Masqueray (1861-1917), a French immigrant, École des Beaux-Arts-trained and New York-based, but only moderately notable, met Archbishop John Ireland of Minnesota. Shortly, in 1905, Ireland selected him over 10 nationally known firms or individuals to design a major work—a new Catholic cathedral for St. Paul. For the closing 12 years of his life, Masqueray was in St. Paul, working on similar and smaller ecclesiastical commissions about the Midwest. 18 illus., 45 notes. 1904-17

Massasoit, Chief

4512. Ocko, Stephanie. CHIEF MASSASOIT'S ROYAL FAMILY. *Early Am. Life 1978 9(2): 22-25.* Presents a genealogy (1620-1931) of Wampanoag chief Massasoit who aided Pilgrims at Plymouth Plantation. 1620-1931

Mast, Daniel E.

4513. Miller, David L. DANIEL E. MAST (1848-1930): A BIOGRAPHICAL SKETCH. *Mennonite Hist. Bull. 1978 39(1): 2-6.* Gives a biography of Daniel E. Mast, 1886-1930, an Amish deacon and minister who wrote for a German-language newspaper, *Herald der Wahrheit* in Reno County, Kansas. 1886-1930

Mather, Cotton

4514. Hiner, N. Ray. GROWING UP PURITAN. *Hist. of Educ. Q. 1981 21(2): 189-193.* Describes David Levin's *Cotton Mather: The Young Life of the Lord's Remembrancer, 1663-1703* (1978). After briefly noting what Robert Middlekauff and other historians have done to rescue Mather's reputation from the "character assassination" of Vernon Parrington, this essay welcomes Levin's book as the "culmination" of the new Mather scholarship. Even its limitation to the first 40 years of Mather's life is taken to be a strength; other scholars have concentrated on the later years, leaving a particular need for the focus Levin has chosen. 19 notes. 1663-1703

4515. Hiner, N. Ray. COTTON MATHER AND HIS FEMALE CHILDREN: NOTES ON THE RELATIONSHIP BETWEEN PRIVATE EXPERIENCE AND PUBLIC THOUGHT. *Journal of Psychohistory 1985 13(1): 33-49.* Cotton Mather, an eminent theologian, was thrice married, twice widowed, and the father of 16 children, though only two survived him. The high mortality rate among children in the colonial period was, due to sickness and epidemics, common. Mather tried to limit his bereavement by withholding affection from his children but invariably loved them and grieved at their loss. He wrote a number of pamphlets on how parents should handle their grief and rear their children. His work strikes a modern note in emphasizing the child's viewpoint. 70 notes. ca 1700

4516. Rosenwald, Lawrence Alan. "Three Early American Diarists." Columbia U. 1979. 182 pp. *DAI 1980 40(10): 5444-A.* 17c-18c

Mather, Eleazer

4517. Gura, Philip F. PREPARING THE WAY FOR STODDARD: ELEAZER MATHER'S *SERIOUS EXHORTATION* TO NORTHAMPTON. *New England Quarterly 1984 57(2): 240-249.* Eleazer Mather, brother of Increase Mather and the first minister of Northampton, Massachusetts, has received little attention from historians, probably because of his undistinguished record as a clergyman and negligible influence on the development of New England theology. In fact, Eleazer Mather only demands attention because when he died in 1669 at the age of 32, he left behind a community badly splintered by ecclesiastical disputes and thereby set the terms of ecclesiastical debate for his distinguished successors, Solomon Stoddard and Jonathan Edwards. The chief evidence of the relationship between Eleazer Mather and Stoddard lies in a collection of Mather's sermons, which were posthumously published as *A Serious Exhortation to the Present and Rising Generation.* 21 notes. 1658-69

Mather, Increase

4518. Bremer, Francis J. INCREASE MATHER'S FRIENDS: THE TRANS-ATLANTIC CONGREGATIONAL NETWORK OF THE SEVENTEENTH CENTURY. *Pro. of the Am. Antiquarian Soc. 1984 94(1): 59-96.* Explores the "web of informal relationships" that linked the "leaders of trans-Atlantic Puritanism" and helped maintain some ideological conformity throughout three generations. A key period was that between the Restoration and the Glorious Revolution, and Increase Mather was a central character. Analyzes his involvement in the network. Based on correspondence in the Massachusetts Historical Society; 5 illus., 105 notes, ref. 1620-1700

Mather, Moses

4519. Noll, Mark A. MOSES MATHER (OLD CALVINIST) AND THE EVOLUTION OF EDWARDSEANISM. *Church Hist. 1980 49(3): 273-285.* Moses Mather, an Old Light Calvinist, played an important role in the evolution of 19th-century Calvinism. Although Mather opposed the 18th-century Great Awakening, his thinking had much in common with ideas advanced during the Second Great Awakening. The author traces the line of descent from New England Puritanism to American Protestantism through the writings of Mather, especially during the first Awakening. 1719-1850

Mathews, John Joseph

4520. Wilson, Terry P. OSAGE OXONIAN: THE HERITAGE OF JOHN JOSEPH MATHEWS. *Chronicles of Oklahoma 1981 59(3): 264-293.* Although of only one-eighth Osage blood, John Joseph Mathews (1894-1979) devoted most of his life to recording tribal history and culture. Well prepared by world travel and a degree from Oxford University, Mathews became a leader among the Osage and served as a tribal councilman during the 1930's. Among his five books were *Wah' Kon-Tah: The Osage and the White Man's*

Road (1932), which became a Book-of-the-Month Club best-seller, and a broader study entitled *The Osages: Children of the Middle Waters* (1961). In the latter book Mathews made use of oral history and other sources not readily available to historians. Based on Mathews's writings and manuscripts at the University of Oklahoma; 3 photos, 74 notes. 1894-1979

Mathews, William Smith Babcock

4521. Clarke, James Wesley. "Prof. W. S. B. Mathews (1837-1912): Self-made Musician of the Gilded Age." U. of Minnesota 1983. 323 pp. *DAI 1983 44(4): 903-A.* DA8317641 1865-1910

4522. Groves, Robert Westfall. "The Life and Works of W. S. B. Mathews (1837-1912)." U. of Iowa 1981. 287 pp. *DAI 1982 42(7): 2923-A.* 8128397 1860-1912

Mathieson, Alexander

4523. Armstrong, Frederick H. THE REVEREND ALEXANDER MATHIESON OF MONTREAL: AN INQUIRY INTO PRESBYTERIAN PRACTICALITY. *J. of the Can. Church Hist. Soc. [Canada] 1981 23: 23-51.* Reexamines the life of Alexander Mathieson (1795-1870), one of the most prominent 19th-century Canadian Presbyterian ministers, for evidence that contributes to an understanding of political, social, and economic conditions. Mathieson, a Scot and graduate of Glasgow College, arrived in Montreal in 1826 and, with one brief interruption, ministered at St. Andrew's Church from arrival until his death. Mathieson and his congregation reveal much about Scottish immigration, the relationship of religion to business success, and the practical implications of church disputes in the 19th century. Through his ministry and marriage to the daughter of a leading merchant, Mathieson became part of the Montreal establishement. His wealthy congregation erected the "Scotch Cathedral" in Montreal and became the church of the most successful Scots of the city. Mathieson was active in forming the Synod of the Presbyterian Church in Connection with the Church of Scotland in 1831, served twice as its moderator, and insisted on continued connection with the Scottish state church after the Disruption of 1843, though this resulted in a Canadian schism. Mathieson resisted efforts to reunify the church, and the congregation refused to enter the Union of 1875. Based on published sources including an 1870 biography by James Croil. 57 notes. 1824-75

Mathieu, Olivier-Elzéar

4524. Lalonde, André N. ARCHBISHOP O. E. MATHIEU AND FRANCOPHONE IMMIGRATION TO THE ARCHDIOCESE OF REGINA. *Study Sessions: Can. Catholic Hist. Assoc. [Canada] 1977 44: 45-60.* Olivier-Elzéar Mathieu, Archbishop of the Regina Archdiocese during 1911-31, promoted the immigration of Catholic French Canadians, French, and Americans to Canada's Prairie Provinces, especially Manitoba and Saskatchewan. 1911-31

Matsura, Frank S.

4525. Roe, JoAnn. FRANK S. MATSURA: PHOTOGRAPHER ON THE NORTHWEST FRONTIER. *Am. West 1982 19(2): 20-28.* Frank S. Matsura (Sakae Matsura?) appeared in Conconully, Washington, in 1903, as a cook's helper in a local hotel. He soon established himself as a photographer and in 1907 was able to open a studio. He documented the life of the people of Okanogan County, a ranching and mining region in which homesteaders were beginning to vie with the Indians for land. He recorded scenery, mines, social events, Indian life, and the daily life of the homesteaders. 14 illus. 1903-13

Matta, Roberto

4526. Brach, Paul. BACK TO ARCADY. *Art in America 1985 73(5): 140-143.* Roberto Matta, a painter who influenced surrealists by advocating the use of the unconscious and automatism, used multiple perspectives in his earlier work and shifted to a single perspective with mythologic overtones during 1981-84. 1950's-84

Matteson, Joel

4527. Hickey, James T., ed. AN ILLINOIS FIRST FAMILY: THE REMINISCENCES OF CLARA MATTESON DOOLITTLE. *J. of the Illinois State Hist. Soc. 1976 69(1): 2-16.* 1850's-65

For abstract see ***Doolittle, Clara Matteson***

Matthews, Mark Allison

4528. Russell, C. Allyn. MARK ALLISON MATTHEWS: SEATTLE FUNDAMENTALIST AND CIVIC REFORMER. *J. of Presbyterian Hist. 1979 57(4): 446-466.* Concentrates on the social concerns of Mark Allison Matthews (1867-1940), pastor of the First Presbyterian Church, Seattle, Washington. He was a strange mixture of biblical fundamentalism and social reform. Under him his congregation became the largest Presbyterian church in the United States. He was an intense critic of religious liberalism at the time of the modernist-fundamentalist controversy, yet participated actively in the civic and political life of Seattle. Describes in detail his pulpit ability, executive acumen, and fundamentalist theology. Based on the Matthews Papers (Manuscript Division of Suzzallo Library, University of Washington, Seattle); 2 photos, 66 notes. 1900-40

4529. Soden, Dale E. NORTHERN GEORGIA: FERTILE GROUND FOR THE URBAN MINISTRY OF MARK MATTHEWS. *Georgia Historical Quarterly 1985 69(1): 39-54.* Describes the development of the religious views and ministry skills of Presbyterian minister Mark Allison Matthews while he was pastor in Calhoun and Dalton, Georgia, during the late 19th century. Matthews later held a flourishing pastorate in Seattle. Based on newspapers and other primary and secondary sources; 34 notes. 1867-96

4530. Soden, Dale E. "Mark Allison Matthews: Seattle's Southern Preacher." U. of Washington 1980. *DAI 1981 41(11): 4815-A.* 1902-40

4531. Soden, Dale E. MARK ALLISON MATTHEWS: SEATTLE'S MINISTER REDISCOVERED. *Pacific Northwest Q. 1983 74(2): 50-58.* Mark Allison Matthews (1867-1940) left his Southern Populist roots, migrated west, and by 1902 accepted the pastorate at Seattle's First Presbyterian Church. Already a strong convert to the Social Gospel and Progressive movements, he immediately involved himself in reformist actions for the city. Matthews's uncompromising efforts to clean up the city eventually led him to a reactionary approach that embraced the tenets of nativism, anti-Semitism, anti-unionism, and anti-liberal theology. Based on the Matthews Papers at the University of Washington Libraries; 5 photos, 33 notes. 1880's-1920

Matthews, Nathan

4532. Silverman, Robert A. NATHAN MATTHEWS: POLITICS OF REFORM IN BOSTON, 1890-1910. *New England Q. 1977 50(4): 626-643.* Traces Nathan Matthews's (1853-1927) role in forming the Yankee-Irish alliance in the Democratic Party and his chairmanship of the Boston Finance Commission during 1907-09. Focuses on his four terms as the reform mayor of Boston during 1891-95 when he achieved his main goal of cutting expenditures through better management and established the Board of Survey which provided Boston with its first coordinated planning. Based on Matthews' correspondence and secondary sources; 42 notes. 1890-1910

Matthews, Oscar Letson

4533. Clover, Haworth Alfred. "Oscar Letson Matthews: Education and Morality in the Nineteenth Century." U. of the Pacific 1977. 190 pp. *DAI 1977 38(2): 668-A.* 19c

Matthews, Robert ("Matthias the Prophet")

4534. McDade, Thomas M. MATTHIAS, PROPHET WITHOUT HONOR. *New-York Hist. Soc. Q. 1978 62(4): 311-334.* Among the many religious eccentrics to appear in the 1820's and '30's in New York was Robert Matthews, who had a brief (1828-35) but newsworthy career in New York City. Known as Matthias the Prophet, he was able to dazzle a small group of people, members of the so-called Retrenchment Society, some of whom had money and property. Matthias controlled the group with a mixture of piety, sex, and an ability to win over reasonably sane people, particularly women. Finally, after some wife-swapping and similar activities, one husband died in mysterious circumstances. Murder probably had been done, but not enough evidence existed to indict Matthias. Nevertheless, his hold on the followers began to weaken. By mid-1835, the movement collapsed and Matthias disappeared from sight. The only person to emerge unscathed was a black woman named Isabella Van Wagenen who later became justly famous as Sojourner Truth. Largely primary sources; 3 illus., 25 notes. 1828-35

Matthiessen, F. O.

4535. Marx, Leo. DOUBLE CONSCIOUSNESS AND THE CULTURAL POLITICS OF F. O. MATTHIESSEN. *Monthly Rev. 1983 34(9): 34-56.* Discusses the career of Harvard literary scholar F. O. Matthiessen, especially his attempt to reconcile Christian and socialist thought in such works as *American Renaissance.* 1927-50

Mattingly, Garrett

4536. Kingdon, Robert M. GARRETT MATTINGLY. *Am. Scholar 1982 51(3): 396-402.* Reviews the career and contributions of historian Garrett Mattingly. 1920's-62

Mattson, Alvin Daniel

4537. Jackson, Gregory Lee. "The Impact of Alvin Daniel Mattson upon the Social Consciousness of the Augustana Synod." U. of Notre Dame 1982. 204 pp. *DAI 1983 43(10): 3346-3347-A.* DA8305871 20c

Mattson, Hans

4538. Ljungmark, Lars. HANS MATTSON'S *MINNEN:* A SWEDISH-AMERICAN MONUMENT. *Swedish Pioneer Hist. Q. 1978 29(1): 57-68.* Hans Mattson was one of 13 Swedish-born colonels in the Union Army during the Civil War. Uses incidents in Mattson's life to show that *Minnen,* the only book he wrote, was in great part autobiographical. Mattson also was a journalist who actively tried to get Swedes to populate Minnesota. He served that state twice as elected Secretary of State and was consul general in Calcutta, India. Illus., 20 notes. 1850's-93

Mauchly, John William

4539. Mauchly, Kathleen R. JOHN MAUCHLY'S EARLY YEARS. *Ann. of the Hist. of Computing 1984 6(2): 116-138.* Describes John W. Mauchly's experiences and experiments that led to his concept of an electronic digital computer based on mechanical desk calculators during the years he was teaching at Ursinus College (1933-41), his interaction with John V. Atanasoff of Iowa State College, and the environment at the Moore School of Electrical Engineering at the University of Pennsylvania that led to the eventual proposal (1943) for building the electronic ENIAC (Electronic Numerical Integrator and Calculator). 1933-43

4540. Stern, Nancy. JOHN WILLIAM MAUCHLY: 1907-1980. *Ann. of the Hist. of Computing 1980 2(2): 100-103.* Physicist John William Mauchly, with J. Presper Eckert, Jr., and others invented the first electronic digital computer. As consultant for the Electronic Numerical Integrator and Computer (ENIAC) project during 1943-46, John Mauchly developed the concept of the vacuum tube computer to solve ballistics problems for the military. He also contributed to the development of the first machine with stored-program capability. John Mauchly believed that computers had commercial as well as military and scientific value, and so developed and marketed the Universal Automic Computer (UNIVAC), which was first utilized by the Census Bureau. 3 notes, biblio. 1932-78

Maude, Frederic Hamer

4541. Maurer, Stephen G. FREDERIC HAMER MAUDE: PHOTOGRAPHER OF THE SOUTHWEST. *Masterkey 1985 59(1): 12-17.* English photographer Frederic Hamer Maude's 60-year love affair with the American Southwest yielded more than 70 "lantern slide" shows and lectures, which contributed significantly to early landscape photography. 1890-1940's

Maury, Matthew Fontaine

4542. Snyder, Dean. TORPEDOES FOR THE CONFEDERACY. *Civil War Times Illustrated 1985 24(1): 40-45.* Discusses the military career of Confederate Navy commander Matthew F. Maury, specifically his introduction of the underwater mine, then called torpedo, and the subsequent use of those mines by the Confederacy. 1861-64

4543. Stein, Douglas. PATHS THROUGH THE SEA: MATTHEW FONTAINE MAURY AND HIS WIND AND CURRENT CHARTS. *Log of Mystic Seaport 1980 32(3): 99-107.* Discusses the accomplishments of Matthew Fontaine Maury (1806-73) in the US Navy, and especially his career as Superintendent of the Depot of Charts and Instruments, where he developed a new type of chart that detailed wind and current information as well as other navigational advice. 1831-73

Maxwell, Hugh

4544. Goldman, Stuart. WHO WAS HUGH MAXWELL? *Manuscripts 1976 28(3): 221-224.* Colonel Hugh Maxwell (1732-99) of New England fought in the French and Indian War and the American Revolution. He was a justice of the peace during Shays' Rebellion "and administered the Oath of Allegiance to those insurgents who gave up their arms." Excerpts from his documents and letters illustrate the history of America during 1755-95. Illus. 1755-95

Maxwell, Lucien B.

4545. Murphy, Lawrence R. MASTER OF THE CIMARRON: LUCIEN B. MAXWELL. *New Mexico Hist. Rev. 1980 55(1): 5-23.* Discusses the extensive mansion, the renowned hospitality (to whites), and the colorful personality of Cimarron rancher Lucien B. Maxwell (1818-75), the owner of one of the largest Mexican land grants in the Southwest. Between 1855 and 1870, when he sold the land grant, the ambitious and hard-working Maxwell exercised extensive personal power by his control of life, agricultural production, and the natural resources of the area. Maxwell's life also shows a darker side in that he often used his power to oppress others, particularly Mexican Americans. Primary sources; illus., map, photo, 72 notes. 1855-70

May, Kate E.

4546. Goetz, Henry Kilian. KATE'S QUARTER SECTION: A WOMAN IN THE CHEROKEE STRIP. *Chronicles of Oklahoma 1983 61(3): 246-267.* Kate E. May made the 1893 "rush for land" in the Cherokee Strip, Oklahoma Territory, in an effort to improve the life of her family. Despite the thousands of competitors lined up at the starting point, May outdistanced most of them on her fleet pony and staked a claim on some rich agricultural land south of Perry. She and her children lived out of a covered wagon, defended the land against claim jumpers, and eventually built a frame house. They subsequently opened a small restaurant in Perry to supplement the farm income. In 1895, they left the farm and moved to Oklahoma City because the children needed medical attention. Based on Oklahoma land and court records; 12 photos, 24 notes. 1893-95

May, Kenneth O.

4547. Jones, Charles V.; Enros, Philip C.; and Tropp, Henry S. KENNETH O. MAY, 1915-1977: HIS EARLY LIFE TO 1946. *Historia Mathematica 1984 11(4): 359-379.* Prints the first part of a biography of Kenneth Ownsworth May, American historian of mathematics, who traveled to England, the Continent, and the USSR in the late 1930's, returned to the United States, joined the Communist Party, served in the army in World War II, finished a PhD at the University of California, Berkeley, in 1946, and obtained an assistant professorship at Carleton College in Northfield, Minnesota. 1930's-46

May, Marvin E.

4548. Tebbetts, Diane. MARVIN E. MAY: "I MADE THAT FROM SCRATCH". *Indiana Folklore 1980 13(1-2): 1-16.* Portrays the life of Marvin E. May of Bloomington, Indiana, who since 1962 has produced handmade furniture and musical instruments. 1962-79

May, Philip Ross

4549. McIntyre, W. D. PHILIP ROSS MAY (1929-77). *Hist. News [New Zealand] 1977 (35): 13.* Discusses Philip Ross May's career in historical research and his works on gold rushes in New Zealand and California. 1960's-77

May, Samuel Joseph

4550. Yacovone, Donald. "Samuel Joseph May, Antebellum Religion and Reform: Dilemmas of the Liberal Persuasion." Claremont Grad. School 1984. 579 pp. *DAI 1984 45(6): 1848-A.* DA8416468 1820's-60's

Maybeck, Bernard Ralph

4551. Banham, Reyner. THE PLOT AGAINST BERNARD MAYBECK. *J. of the Soc. of Architectural Hist. 1984 43(1): 33-37.* Architectural historians have underestimated the importance of Bernard Maybeck's monumental and classical buildings, such as the 1915 San Francisco Palace of the Fine Arts. Although usually identified with the Beaux-Arts movement, Maybeck broke with classical precedent in many significant details of his monumental designs. Secondary sources; 5 photos, 8 notes. 1910-25

4552. Reinhardt, Richard. BERNARD MAYBECK. *Am. Heritage 1981 32(5): 36-47.* Architect Bernard Ralph Maybeck (1862-1957) made a significant contribution to American architecture, although he did not create his own school or style. The article, adapted from a forthcoming book, *Three Centuries of Notable American Architects,* surveys his life and works. 16 illus. 1885-1957

Mayer, Joe (family)

4553. Thorpe, Winifred L. and Spude, Robert L. JOE MAYER AND HIS TOWN. *J. of Arizona Hist. 1978 19(2): 131-168.* Reminiscences by Joe Mayer's daughter, of the rise and success of Mayer, Arizona, the town founded by her father. From New York, Joe Mayer came to the West via odd jobs, and eventually bought a restaurant and stage station for $3,500 in gold that he developed into a town. Mayer's wife, formerly Sarah Belle Wilbur, came and they built new enterprises. The Mayer family grew: Mary Bell (Mamie), Martha Gertrude (Martie), Wilbur Joseph (Bur), and Winifred (Winnie). Mayer invested in mining; owned the French Lily mine, met outlaws, met Indians, and contested floods. After the flood of 1890, when most of the town was swept away, Mayer rebuilt, with homes, corrals, freight stations, and a schoolhouse. The Santa Fe Railroad built a line to Mayer which then became a center for cattle, sheep, and ore. While investigating a prowler, Joe Mayer accidentally shot himself and died in December 1909. Sarah Mayer suffered a stroke and she died on 11 November 1934. 16 photos, 33 notes. ca 1870-1910

Mayer, William

4554. Mayer, Stanley D. OF MY FATHER AND *REMARQUES:* A MEMOIR. *Western Pennsylvania Hist. Mag. 1980 63(1): 76-84.* Details the news magazine *Remarques,* published in Pittsburgh by the author's father, William Mayer, 1900-04. 1900-04

Mayo, Elton

4555. Ekovich, Steven Rudy. "The Enigma of Productivity: Elton Mayo and the Origins of American Industrial Sociology." U. of California, Irvine 1984. 557 pp. *DAI 1985 45(12): 3564-A.* DA8502989 1923-49

Mayo, Frank

4556. Fike, Duane Joseph. "Frank Mayo: Actor, Playwright, and Manager." U. of Nebraska 1980. 381 pp. *DAI 1980 41(3): 850-A.* 8018666 1872-96

Mayo, John Caldwell Calhoun

4557. Caudill, Harry M. THE STRANGE CAREER OF JOHN C. C. MAYO. *Filson Club Hist. Q. 1982 56(3): 258-289.* John Caldwell Calhoun Mayo was born and reared on a small country farm in Appalachia and died the richest man in Kentucky. He achieved this transformation by being the first person to recognize the commercial possibilities of the vast coal reserves of southeastern Kentucky. Mayo developed the broadform deed that allowed him and his partners to purchase mineral rights to large tracts of poor mountain farm land at greatly reduced prices. Joining with West Virginia Senator Clarence Wayland Watson, Virginia Congressman Campbell Bascom Slemp, and industrialists John Davison Rockefeller and John Newlon Camden, Mayo became a political and financial power in three states. He was able to maintain his empire by convincing the Kentucky Supreme Court to uphold a law liquidating Virginia Revolutionary War land claims in the coal mining counties of Kentucky. Based on contemporary newspapers and unpublished studies. 1864-1914

Mayo, Mary A. Bryant

4558. Bryant, James. MORE THAN HARD WORK AND GOOD BUTTER. *Michigan Hist. 1981 65(4): 32-38.* Chronicles the work of farm wife Mary Angell Bryant Mayo who worked tirelessly for the Grange movement and the role of women in that movement. She pioneered the Fresh Air Outing Program intended "to give poor children from the cities, working girls and mothers with babies, a two week outing in the country during the summer." A women's dormitory at Michigan State University is named after her. 7 illus. 1845-1978

4559. Marti, Donald B. WOMAN'S WORK IN THE GRANGE: MARY ANN MAYO OF MICHIGAN, 1882-1903. *Agric. Hist. 1982 56(2): 439-452.* The Grange gave new opportunities for farm women to develop personally, though generally in ways related to the traditional spheres of home and family. Mary Ann Mayo became active as a Grange lecturer in Michigan, urging women to widen their cultural horizons and take a moral and scientific approach to housework. She argued for domestic science courses in the state's agricultural college and was active with a variety of charities, especially a project to give poor city children the opportunity to stay on a farm. Mayo became the most important women's Grange leader in Michigan. Based on Grange documents and secondary sources; 52 notes. 1882-1903

Mays, Benjamin Elijah

4560. Teel, Leonard Ray. BENJAMIN MAYS—TEACHING BY EXAMPLE, LEADING THROUGH WILL. *Change 1982 14(7): 14-22.* Noted black educator Benjamin E. Mays has been active and respected in the fields of education, religion, and race relations, was president of Morehouse College for 27 years, and taught Martin Luther King, Jr. 1916-83

4561. Willie, Charles V. THE EDUCATION OF BENJAMIN ELIJAH MAYS: AN EXPERIENCE IN EFFECTIVE TEACHING. *Teachers Coll. Record 1983 84(4): 955-962.* The educational career of Benjamin Elijah Mays, former president of Morehouse College, illustrates the importance of providing with kindly support, accepting them initially as they are, and allowing for different temporal learning patterns. Mays's early schooling progressed slowly and he had difficulty initially at Bates College. Encouraged by his professors, however, he graduated and went on to earn his doctorate. 5 notes. 1900-20

Mays, Maurice

4562. Egerton, John. A CASE OF PREJUDICE: MAURICE MAYS AND THE KNOXVILLE RACE RIOT OF 1919. *Southern Exposure 1983 11(4): 56-65.* Examines the trial and execution of a black man, Maurice Mays, for the murder of a white woman in Knoxville, Tennessee; Mays's arrest precipitated a riot by a white lynch mob and political pressures for execution, but his innocence was established after his death when a white woman confessed that she was the murderer. 1919-27

Mazzei, Philip

4563. Gallani, Renato. A FRIEND OF THE AMERICAN REVOLUTION: PHILIP MAZZEI. *Italian Americana 1976 2(2): 213-227.* Philip Mazzei, an Italian immigrant, was a prorevolutionary and author during the American Revolution; presents summaries of two of his tracts, "Considerations of the Likely Outcome of the War" (1781) and "Reasons Why the American States Cannot Be Termed Rebels" (1781) and chronicles his life from 1773, when he came to America, until his death in Pisa in 1816. 35 notes. 1773-1816

4564. Marchione, Margherita. PHILIP MAZZEI AND THE LAST KING OF POLAND. *Italian Americana 1978 4(2): 185-199.* Provides a biography of Philip Mazzei, an Italian who was appointed before and during the French Revolution as the political agent of the last king of Poland, Stanislaus II Poniatowski, 1764-95; Mazzei established an estate in Virginia in 1773 and corresponded with Thomas Jefferson until his death in 1795. ca 1764-95

4565. Tortarolo, Edoardo. FILIPPO MAZZEI AGENTE VIRGINIANO IN EUROPA: I RAPPORTI CON IL CONTE DI VERGENNES [Philip Mazzei, Virginia's agent in Europe: his relations with the Comte de Vergennes]. *Riv. Storica Italiana [Italy] 1980 92(3-4): 707-735.* In 1779 Philip Mazzei was charged by the General Assembly of the state of Virginia to go to Europe to obtain a loan, purchase some goods for the army, and use all means in his power on behalf of the American cause. An aspect of his activities which has been neglected by his biographers has to do with his attempts to contact the Comte de Vergennes, foreign minister of France, who was determined to contain English pride and to help the American colonies achieve freedom. 120 notes. 1779-83

McAllister, Jane Ellen

4566. Williams-Burns, Winona. JANE ELLEN MCALLISTER: PIONEER FOR EXCELLENCE IN TEACHER EDUCATION. *J. of Negro Educ. 1982 51(3): 342-357.* Describes the education and teaching career during 1919-67 of Jane Ellen McAllister, Columbia University Teachers College's "first Black doctoral graduate." McAllister always encouraged innovation and demanded high levels of performance in her teaching and work with the programs of the Rosenwald and Jeanes funds. She published several articles and successfully sought support for her programs from federal and private sources. Based on interviews, correspondence, private papers, and university archives; 71 notes. 1919-67

McArthur, John Duncan

4567. Eagle, John A. J. D. MCARTHUR AND THE PEACE RIVER RAILWAY. *Alberta Hist. [Canada] 1981 29(4): 33-39.* John Duncan McArthur "was a dynamic pioneer railway promoter who built about 2,800 miles of railway in Western Canada, a figure which makes him one of the most important railway builders in Canadian history." Born and raised in eastern Ontario, he arrived in Winnipeg in 1879 and quickly displayed an interest in railways, becoming by 1896, "well established as a railroad contractor in Manitoba." His railroad construction in the Peace River area of Alberta displayed "a distinctive pattern in Canadian railway building," i.e., "a close partnership between private enterprise . . . and government. . . . " This Edmonton, Dunvegan & British Columbia Railway was completed in 1915. 3 photos, map, 22 notes. 1854-ca 1920

McBride, Mary Margaret

4568. St. John, Jacqueline D. SEX ROLE STEREOTYPING IN EARLY BROADCAST HISTORY: THE CAREER OF MARY MARGARET MCBRIDE. *Frontiers 1978 3(3): 31-38.* Studies the myth of women's "natural" inferiority as radio and television broadcasters by focusing on the career of Mary Margaret McBride during 1934-54. 1934-54

McBride, Richard

4569. Roy, Patricia E. PROGRESS, PROSPERITY AND POLITICS: THE RAILWAY POLICIES OF RICHARD MCBRIDE. *BC Studies [Canada] 1980 (47): 3-28.* Inter- and intraprovincial railroads played a crucial role in the internal and external politics and economy of British Columbia from its beginning. When Richard McBride became premier in 1903, he inherited an endangered provincial treasury caused by the reckless financial and railway policies of previous administrations. Concentrating on putting the province's political and financial affairs in order, he made no firm promises or agreements with railway promoters and companies in the first six years of his administration. With increased population, new demands for the province's raw materials, the new availability of cheap capital, and a general economic boom, McBride's policies changed. By the end of his tenure in 1915, he had become the province's "railway builder extraordinaire." 73 notes. 1903-15

McCall, Moses N., Jr.

4570. Carswell, W. J. MOSES N. MCCALL, JR., AND DAVID GONTO DANIELL. *Viewpoints: Georgia Baptist Hist. 1980 7: 35-45.* Biographies of Baptist ministers Moses N. McCall, Jr., teacher and president of Monroe Female (now Tift) College in 1884-85, and his father-in-law, missionary David Gonto Daniell (1808-84). 1808-85

McCalla, Bowman Hendry

4571. Coletta, Paolo E. THE COURT-MARTIAL OF BOWMAN HENDRY MCCALLA. *Am. Neptune 1980 40(2): 127-134.* In 1888, Bowman Hendry McCalla (1844-1910) slightly wounded an unruly sailor in a deliberate attempt to discipline him. Upon his return to America from deployment, McCalla learned that newspapers had sensationalized the incident, accusing him of cruelty toward enlisted men, citing the slashing incident in Oslo, Norway. McCalla sought a court of inquiry to clear his name. A court martial followed. McCalla's conviction and suspension from duty during 1890-91 did not prevent him from being promoted to rear admiral in 1903. 1888-91

McCalla, Daniel

4572. Briceland, Alan V. DANIEL MC CALLA, 1748-1809: NEW SIDE REVOLUTIONARY AND JEFFERSONIAN. *J. of Presbyterian Hist. 1978 56(3): 252-269.* Daniel McCalla (1748-1809) was born in the midst of a Presbyterian schism. While he never figured as a major factor in his church or country, his life touched and made contributions to several important historical processes. As an academy teacher, he brought education to students with limited educational opportunities; as a chaplain, he aided the cause of the American Revolution; as a Presbyterian, he fought to establish the principle of separation of church and state; as a scholar, he published essays to enlighten and reform; as one committed to democracy, he enlisted his pen in the cause of electing Thomas Jefferson. Primary and secondary sources; 64 notes. 1770's-1809

McCallum, Ronald Buchanan

4573. Gunn, Herb. THE CONTINUING FRIENDSHIP OF JAMES WILLIAM FULBRIGHT AND RONALD BUCHANAN MCCALLUM. *South Atlantic Quarterly 1984 83(4): 416-433.* 1925-70
*For abstract see **Fulbright, J. William***

McCarran, Patrick

4574. Edwards, Jerome E. NEVADA POWER BROKER: PAT MCCARRAN AND HIS POLITICAL MACHINE. *Halcyon 1984 6: 105-122.* Describes Senator Patrick McCarran's rise to power, his techniques for exercising political power, and the effect he had on Nevada and those who worked with him. 1930's-50's

4575. Edwards, Jerome E. NEVADA POWER BROKER: PAT MCCARRAN AND HIS POLITICAL MACHINE. *Nevada Hist. Soc. Q. 1984 27(3): 182-198.* Rescued from the Nevada political wilderness in the 1932 elections, Patrick McCarran sat in the US Senate, 1933-54. His accumulated power in the Senate was not enough to persuade the electorate to retain him, so he created a political machine that came to dominate the Nevada Democratic Party. However, McCarran's machine functioned effectively only when he supplied personal leadership, and it fell apart after he died in 1954. Based on the Patrick McCarran Collection at the Nevada Historical Society, other archival papers, oral history transcripts, newspapers, and secondary works; 3 photos, 35 notes. 1932-54

4576. Edwards, Jerome E. THE *SUN* AND THE SENATOR. *Nevada Hist. Soc. Q. 1981 24(1): 3-16.* A Nevadan who sat in the US Senate during 1933-54, Patrick A. McCarran (1876-1954) achieved national prominence. His influence within Nevada peaked in 1950, and thereafter his Nevada political base eroded. McCarran's loss of power stemmed party from conflicts with Herman Greenspan, publisher of the Las Vegas *Sun,* who accused McCarran of attempting to undermine the *Sun's* press freedoms for partisan reasons. Based on the Patrick McCarran Papers in the Nevada State Archives; photo, 29 notes. 1950-54

McCarthy, Joseph R.

4577. O'Brien, Michael. YOUNG JOE MCCARTHY, 1908-1944. *Wisconsin Mag. of Hist. 1980 63(3): 178-232.* Examines Joseph R. McCarthy's early life in rural Wisconsin, including his activities in Grand Chute, Manawa, Milwaukee, Waupaca, and Shawano. Details early influences on McCarthy; the failure of his chicken business; his graduation from high school in a single year; his five years at Marquette University as an engineering major, boxing coach, fraternity brother, and law graduate; his law partnership with Michael Eberlein; his unsuccessful bid for district attorney; his campaign for judge of the 10th Judicial Circuit Court; his most controversial case—the Quaker Dairy case—resulting in a reversal by the State Supreme Court; his political friendship with Urban Van Susteren and journalists John Wyngaard and Rex Karney; his voluntary service as an intelligence officer in the Marines during World War II; and his challenge of Alexander Wiley in the 1944 primary for US Senator. 19 illus., 161 notes. 1908-44

4578. Weintraub, Rebecca. "Joseph McCarthy as Leader: An Image Analysis." U. of Southern California 1983. *DAI 1983 44(5): 1243-A.* 1950-54

McCarthy, Patrick Henry

4579. O'Donnell, L. A. THE GREENING OF A LIMERICK MAN: PATRICK HENRY MCCARTHY. *Éire-Ireland 1976 11(2): 119-128.* Offers a biographical sketch of the Irish youth, 1860-80, of Patrick Henry McCarthy, emphasizing influences on his later development as a powerful leader in the American labor movement. 1863-80

McClernand, John Alexander

4580. Longacre, Edward G. THE RISE OF JOHN A. MCCLERNAND: CONGRESSMAN BECOMES GENERAL. *Civil War Times Illus. 1982 21(7): 30-39.* Prints a biography of John Alexander McClernand, an Illinois politician who led a brigade of volunteers during the Civil War. 1830's-1900

McCloud, Emma Gudger

4581. McCloud, Emma Gudger. "SO I SUNG TO MYSELF." *Southern Exposure 1979 7(1): 18-26.* Gives Emma Gugder McCloud's impressions of her life as a member of a poor white sharecropping family living in the South during the Depression; she had been portrayed in James Agee and Walker Evans's *Let Us Now Praise Famous Men* (1934). 1916-79

McClung, Alexander

4582. Darkis, Fred, Jr. ALEXANDER KEITH MCCLUNG (1811-1855). *J. of Mississippi Hist. 1978 40(4): 289-296.* Sketches the violent career of Alexander McClung, a noted Mississippi duelist. Born in Virginia, with a short residence in Kentucky, as well as active service in the US Navy, McClung moved to Jackson, Mississippi, in the 1830's. Originally trained as a lawyer, he soon acquired a wide reputation as a duelist who had killed 10 men out of some 14 duels fought. Active as a Whig, he was appointed by President Tyler as US Marshal for the Northern District of Mississippi, but he resigned his position with the election of the Democrat Polk in 1844. During the Mexican War, McClung served with Colonel Jefferson Davis in the First Mississippi Regiment, and the Whig president, Zachary Taylor, appointed him as chargé d'affaires to Bolivia in 1849. Returning to America in 1851, he was invited by the citizens of Jackson to give the eulogy at memorial services for Henry Clay. McClung lived in Jackson until March, 1855, when at less than forty-five years of age, he committed suicide. 1830's-55

McClung, Isabelle

4583. Southwick, Helen C. WILLA CATHER'S EARLY CAREER: ORIGINS OF A LEGEND. *Western Pennsylvania Hist. Mag. 1982 65(2): 85-98.* 1896-1981
*For abstract see **Cather, Willa***

McClung, Nellie Mooney

4584. Burton, Betty. NELLIE MCCLUNG. *Manitoba Pageant [Canada] 1975 20(4): 1-10.* Reprint of a centennial address given by the author at the Assiniboine Historical Society in Brandon in 1973 which is a biography of Nellie Mooney McClung (1873-1951), who was active in the Canadian woman suffrage movement. 1873-1951

4585. Strong-Boag, Veronica. CANADIAN FEMINISM IN THE 1920'S: THE CASE OF NELLIE L. MCCLUNG. *J. of Can. Studies [Canada] 1977 12(4): 58-68.* Nellie L. McClung managed to be simultaneously "Canada's foremost woman warrior" and a conscientious mother. A popular novelist, she was a leading proponent of woman suffrage (achieved in 1918) and prohibition, for social reform laws, and (as an active Methodist) for the ordination of women. In 1921 she was elected to the Alberta legislature as a Liberal despite a landslide for the United Farmers of Alberta. As a legislator she was overshadowed by Irene Parlby, who was a UFA member and a cabinet minister. McClung narrowly failed to win reelection, partly because of her continued support for prohibition. The collapse in the 1920's of the moral earnestness of the war years undermined the reform movement generally, and McClung's career in particular. Based on the McClung Papers and secondary sources; 45 notes. 1873-1930's

McClure, William J.

4586. Lester, Patricia. WILLIAM J. MCCLURE AND THE MCCLURE RANCH. *Chronicles of Oklahoma 1980 58(3): 296-307.* William J. McClure came to Indian Territory in 1867 and two years later established a ranch along the south bank of the North Canadian River. When the Unassigned Lands were opened to white settlement in 1889, McClure was the first to stake a claim within the limits of present Oklahoma City. He became a booster for the city and helped draw the Rock Island Railroad there. His death in 1899 from "acute brain trouble" ended a pioneer legend, but he left behind a family which contributed significantly to Oklahoma City development. 5 photos, map. 1867-99

McClurg, James

4587. Frank, Perry. BICENTENNIAL GAZETTE: THE FRAMERS OF THE CONSTITUTION: VIRGINIA. *This Constitution 1985 (7): 38-40.* 1787
*For abstract see **Blair, John***

McClurg, Joseph Washington

4588. Morrow, Lynn. JOSEPH WASHINGTON MCCLURG: ENTREPRENEUR, POLITICIAN, CITIZEN. *Missouri Hist. Rev. 1983 78(2): 168-201.* Joseph Washington McClurg was the 19th governor of Missouri and one of the state's most memorable entrepreneurs and industrialists. Over the years, McClurg was a schoolteacher, deputy sheriff, prospector, circuit-court clerk, mercantile trader, lead miner, '49er, Union officer, congressman, philanthropist, Radical Republican governor, and land speculator. 6 illus., 9 photos, 85 notes. 1830's-1900

McCluskey, Henry S.

4589. McBride, James David. "Henry S. McCluskey: Workingman's Advocate." Arizona State U. 1982. 380 pp. *DAI 1982 43(2): 527-A.* DA8214903 1923-52

McCollum, E. V.

4590. Day, Harry G. and Prebluda, Harry J. E. V. MCCOLLUM: LAMPLIGHTER IN PUBLIC AND PROFESSIONAL UNDERSTANDING OF NUTRITION. *Agric. Hist. 1980 54(1): 149-156.* E. V. McCollum developed the modern concept of nutrition along with the research tools needed to analyze the nutritional value of foods by studying animals. His research became widely known during World War I when he worked with the Food Administration in developing nutritional diet plans. McCollum popularized his findings in many books and articles published between the 1920's and 1950's. 20 notes. 1910's-50's

McConnel, John L.

4591. Hallwas, John E. EARLY ILLINOIS AUTHOR JOHN L. MCCONNEL AND "THE RANGER'S CHASE." *J. of the Illinois State Hist. Soc. 1980 73(3): 177-188.* A biographical sketch of Illinois writer John L. McConnel, novelist and essayist. "The Ranger's Chase," which appeared originally in *Graham's Magazine* (1852) is about a period in Illinois frontier history in which the ranger is an indispensable member of society because he protects it from attacks by Indians. Primary sources; 27 notes. 1852

McConnell, Felix Grundy

4592. Atkins, Leah R. FELIX GRUNDY MCCONNELL: OLD SOUTH DEMAGOGUE. *Alabama Rev. 1977 30(2): 83-100.* Felix Grundy McConnell (1809-46) was a pioneer and first mayor of Talladega, Alabama, state legislator, and Congressman after 1840. Endowed with large physique, ready wit, and magnetic personality, he was a true Jacksonian and an enemy of privilege and wealth. He, not Andrew Johnson, conceived the first bill containing the principles embodied in the Homestead Act (1862). Primary and secondary sources; 85 notes. 1830-46

McCormack, John

4593. Ledbetter, Gordon T. APPEALING TO THE HEARTS OF MEN: JOHN MCCORMACK, 1884-1945. *Éire-Ireland 1978 13(4): 101-114.* Details and analyzes the career of the beloved Irish tenor John McCormack. An opera singer, a concert recitalist, and a recording artist, McCormack synthesized the classics and popular music in his repertoire and "remained, always, a vividly communicative artist." His opera career was distinguished, and he was "a master of German lieder [and] among the finest Mozartian and Handelian singers of this century." Describes his education and early training in Ireland, his opera studies in Italy, his becoming a US citizen, and his opera and concert performances in England, the United States, Australia, and Europe. Describes his popular triumphs, as at the Fourth of July ceremony in 1918 at Mount Vernon and at the Eucharistic Congress in 1932 in Dublin, where at a Pontifical High Mass in Phoenix Park before more than a million people he sang "Panis Angelicus" with a choir of 500. 1900's-45

McCormick, Vincent A.

4594. Hennesey, James. AMERICAN JESUIT IN WARTIME ROME: THE DIARY OF VINCENT A. MCCORMICK, S.J., 1942-1945. *Mid-America 1974 56(1): 32-55.* Brooklyn-born Vincent A. McCormick, a Jesuit since 1903, served in Rome from 1934 until after World War II. Among his few personal papers he left several small notebook diaries reflecting his life in Rome during 1942-45. While much of the material involves internal Jesuit matters, many entries refer to contemporary church and political affairs. Some critical remarks are directed toward the Holy See's stance toward the Fascist countries, and secular matters such as the Church's expressed concern at the damage to the San Lorenzo Basilica being more pronounced than its abhorrence of the loss of life from a bombing attack. His own deep loyalty to the Pope and the Church caused him much anguish, some of which is clearly expressed in the diary. Based on the diary and printed secondary sources; 40 notes. 1942-45

McCoy, Frank Ross

4595. Bacevich, Andrew Joseph, Jr. "American Military Diplomacy, 1898-1949: The Role of Frank Ross McCoy." Princeton U. 1982. 479 pp. *DAI 1983 43(7): 2423-A.* DA8228169 1898-1949

McCoy, James

4596. Sullivan, Susan. JAMES MCCOY: LAWMAN AND LEGISLATOR. *J. of San Diego Hist. 1977 23(4): 43-57.* Discusses James McCoy's political participation in San Diego, and the economic development of the area; includes his careers as County Recorder, Sheriff, and politico, 1850-95. 1850-95

McCoy, Tim

4597. Ponicsan, Darryl. HIGH EAGLE, THE MANY LIVES OF COLONEL TIM MCCOY: AN INTERVIEW. *Am. Heritage 1977 28(4): 52-62.* McCoy discusses his life as a cowboy, movie star, and friend of Indians. 10 illus. 1909-77

McCroskey, Virgil Talmadge

4598. Petersen, Keith and Reed, Mary E. "FOR ALL THE PEOPLE, FOREVER AND EVER": VIRGIL MCCROSKEY AND THE STATE PARKS MOVEMENT. *Idaho Yesterdays 1984 28(1): 2-15.* Virgil Talmadge McCroskey came to eastern Washington as a child of pioneers and fell in love with the land, especially the Palouse region of Washington and Idaho. He was active all his life in naturalist and environmental concerns. He campaigned for many years to have the area of Steptoe Butte in Washington declared a state park, finally buying and donating the land himself. Similarly in Idaho, McCroskey began accumulating land along a ridge near his family's farm. By the time he convinced the Idaho legislature to accept the land as Mary Minerva McCroskey State Park, it covered 4,400 acres. Based on Latah County Historical Society Archives, Washington Department of Parks and Recreation records, interviews, newspapers, and secondary sources; illus., 7 photos, 34 notes, biblio. 1879-1970

McCullough, John

4599. Woodruff, Bruce Erwin. "'Genial' John McCullough: Actor and Manager." U. of Nebraska, Lincoln 1984. 683 pp. *DAI 1985 46(4): 845-A.* DA8509879 1832-85

McCumber, Porter James

4600. Schlup, Leonard. PHILOSOPHICAL CONSERVATIVE: PORTER JAMES MCCUMBER AND POLITICAL REFORM. *North Dakota Hist. 1978 45(3): 16-21.* A conservative Republican senator from North Dakota, Porter James McCumber was the product of the political machine of

Alexander John McKenzie. Serving in the US Senate during 1898-1922, McCumber, despite his conservative beliefs and those of his Party, voted for such reforms as women's suffrage and the direct election of senators. He deeply believed in voting according to the desires of his constituents even if taking their position violated his own convictions. McCumber was a loyal party stalwart, supporting the "Old Guard" of the GOP during the factional battles with Theodore Roosevelt and the "Bull Moosers." He bitterly attacked Roosevelt for the latter's defection from Republican Party ranks. In his political philosophy McCumber favored gradual change in accordance with the Constitution. 1898-1933

McCutcheon, George Barr

4601. Lazarus, A. L. GEORGE BARR MCCUTCHEON: YOUTH AND DRAMA. *Biography 1981 4(3): 208-226.* George Barr McCutcheon's *Graustark* novels (1901-14), which reached millions of readers and moviegoers in the early 1900's, were deliberate potboilers; they should not be judged as "unfulfilled promises." The fulfilled promises, still in holographs and typescripts, consist of parody melodrama, satirical farce, and other projects begun in his precocious youth and early manhood. 1901-14

McDonald, Alice

4602. McDonald, Alice. AS WELL AS ANY MAN. *Alaska Journal 1984 14(3): 39-45.* Presents an autobiographical account of the labors of Alice McDonald, a Swedish woman who went to seek her fortune in Alaskan mining camps. She worked as a cook in Dawson for a time, then did odd jobs, such as blueberry picking, baking, and laundering while her husband prospected for gold. She opened a hotel in Iditarod and, when business dwindled, moved to California, where she began writing her memoirs at age 84. 9 photos. 1890's-1918

McDonald, Angus

4603. McDonald, William Naylor, III. THE MCDONALD WHO TURNED WASHINGTON DOWN. *West Virginia Hist. 1977 38(4): 312-318.* Angus McDonald grew up in Glasgow, fought in the Scottish uprising of 1745, went to Winchester, Virginia, and became a prominent farmer, militia officer, Mason, Anglican vestryman, justice of the peace, and sheriff. He led an expedition to Lord Dunmore's War, 1774. Later he declined George Washington's offer of a Continental Army commission. He died in 1778. 1745-78

McDonald, Duncan

4604. —. MOTHER JONES, 1830-1930. *J. of the Illinois State Hist. Soc. 1980 73(3): 235-237.* Prints Duncan McDonald's previously unpublished autobiography which recalls impressions of socialist and labor organizer Mary Harris "Mother" Jones on the occasion of the dedication of a monument in her honor at the Union Miners Cemetery in Mount Olive, Illinois, in 1936. 1830-1930

McDonald, Lucile

4605. McDonald, Lucile. A VANISHED NEIGHBORHOOD. *Oregon Hist. Q. 1983 84(2): 211-218.* Reminisces of growing up at the turn of the century in a Portland, Oregon, neighborhood. 4 photos. 1900-10

McDonald, William J.

4606. Weiss, Harold John, Jr. " 'Yours to Command': Captain William J. 'Bill' McDonald and the Panhandle Rangers of Texas." Indiana U. 1980. 270 pp. *DAI 1980 41(1): 373-A.* 8016460 1880-1918

McDonald, Willis

4607. Cunningham, Eileen Smith and Schneider, Mabel Ambrose. A SLAVE'S AUTOBIOGRAPHY RETOLD. *Western Illinois Regional Studies 1979 2(2): 109-126.* A transcription of Willis McDonald's (1829-1939) experiences as a slave on a Georgia plantation, touching upon daily life on the plantation, the slave trade, McDonald's freedom, his arrival in Jacksonville, Illinois, and his last days in the ghetto of that city. 1829-1939

McDonough, David

4608. Murray, Andrew E. BRIGHT DELUSION: PRESBYTERIANS AND AFRICAN COLONIZATION. *J. of Presbyterian Hist. 1980 58(3): 224-237.* The basic flaw of the American Colonization Society (ACS) was its effort to ease the troubled consciences of white Americans while ignoring the needs and desires of black people. Points out the paradox in the life of David McDonough, an American slave whose master wanted him trained for leadership in Africa. Details the many frustrations McDonough confronted in his preparation to be a physician, due to prejudice. The ACS did not meet the needs of all blacks. For McDonough and others, colonization attempted to solve the problems of white oppressors by requiring the victims of that oppression to make major sacrifices. Covers ca. 1940-50. Based largely on McDonough's correspondence with the Board of Foreign Missions, Presbyterian Historical Society, Philadelphia, and studies on the American Colonization Society; 30 notes. 1840-50

McDougal, Myrtle Archer

4609. Hoder-Salmon, Marilyn. MYRTLE ARCHER MCDOUGAL: LEADER OF OKLAHOMA'S "TIMID SISTERS." *Chronicles of Oklahoma 1982 60(3): 332-343.* Myrtle Archer McDougal joined her attorney husband in Sapulpa during 1904 and within a decade rose to prominence in Oklahoma suffrage, health reform, and women's club movements. Armed with a powerful oratorical style, she promoted reform in women's dress styles; pensions for widowed, abandoned, and divorced mothers; a rural library movement; and a national prohibition crusade. Oil wealth allowed McDougal to pursue these causes almost full time after 1908, and during the following 20 years she served on nationally prestigious committees for the Democratic Party. Based on the Mary McDougal Axelson Collection at the University of Miami; 2 photos, 29 notes. 1904-30's

McDougall, Alexander

4610. Collier, Christopher. THE REVOLUTIONARY LEADERSHIP: ARRIVISTE AND PARVENU. *Rev. in Am. Hist. 1976 4(1): 53-58.* Review article prompted by Roger J. Champagne's *Alexander McDougall and the American Revolution in New York* (Schenectady: New York State American Revolution Bicentennial Commission, 1975) and Emory C. Evans's *Thomas Nelson of Yorktown: Revolutionary Virginian* (Williamsburg, Virginia: Colonial Williamsburg Foundation, 1975); discusses the use of biography of minor historical figures to illuminate how an historical era affected the individual. 1760's-80's

McDougall, William

4611. Smith, Jane Gentry. "The Mystery of the Mind: A Biography of William McDougall." U. of Texas, Austin 1980. 322 pp. *DAI 1981 41(7): 3163-A.* 8100964
1898-1938

McDowell, David

4612. Newton, Scott. DAVID MCDOWELL ON JAMES AGEE. *Western Humanities Rev. 1980 34(2): 117-130.*
1936-55

For abstract see ***Agee, James***

McDowell, Ephraim

4613. Ikard, Robert W. SURGICAL OPERATION ON JAMES K. POLK BY EPHRAIM MCDOWELL, OR THE SEARCH FOR POLK'S GALLSTONE. *Tennessee Historical Quarterly 1984 43(2): 121-131.* 1812

For abstract see ***Polk, James K.***

McGhee, John Leftridge

4614. —. [HILLBILLY ARTISTS JOHN MCGHEE AND FRANK WELLING]. *JEMF Q. 1981 17(62): 57-74.*

Tribe, Ivan M. JOHN MCGHEE AND FRANK WELLING: WEST VIRGINIA'S MOST-RECORDED OLD-TIME ARTISTS, *pp. 57-63.*

Tribe, Ivan M. A WELLING AND MCGHEE DISCOGRAPHY, *pp. 64-74.* Biographies of John Leftridge McGhee (1882-1945) and Frank Welling (1900-57) who began recording together in 1927 and became the most-recorded old-time musicians in West Virginia, followed by a discography of their recordings from 1927 to ca. 1949. ca 1927-49

McGiffin, Philo Norton

4615. Bradford, Richard H. THAT PRODIGAL SON: PHILO MCGIFFIN AND THE CHINESE NAVY. *Am. Neptune 1978 38(3): 157-169.* Discusses Pennsylvania-born Philo Norton McGiffin's (1860-97) career in the Imperial Chinese Navy during 1885-95. McGiffin served in the Chinese Navy as an instructor and advisor soon after graduating from the US Naval Academy. During the 1st Sino-Japanese War he participated in several naval engagements, including the Battle of the Yalu (September 1894) where he was wounded. Published sources; 45 notes. 1885-95

McGillivray, Alexander

4616. Watson, Thomas D. STRIVING FOR SOVEREIGNTY: ALEXANDER MCGILLIVRAY, CREEK WARFARE, AND DIPLOMACY, 1783-1790. *Florida Hist. Q. 1980 58(4): 400-414.* Alexander McGillivray's goal was to achieve free nation status for the Creek Indians. The rivalry of the United States, Great Britain, and Spain after the American Revolution for control of the Old Southwest gave McGillivray his opportunity. The Treaty of New York (1790) demonstrates his diplomatic ability. Based on American State Papers, Spanish records (Madrid), and secondary sources; 64 notes. 1783-90

McGillivray, Simon

4617. Hall, Roger. AN IMPERIAL BUSINESSMAN IN THE AGE OF IMPROVEMENT: SIMON MCGILLIVRAY AFTER THE FUR TRADE. *Dalhousie Rev. [Canada] 1979 59(1): 51-73.* Best known for his association with the North West Company of fur traders in Canada, Simon McGillivray went bankrupt in the 1820's. Concentrates on his efforts to reestablish his fortune through employment by the United Mexican Mining Association. This too was a failure because of the revolutionary unrest during Santa Anna's attempts to seize power. McGillivray returned to England to restore his fortune through management of the Whig newspaper *The Morning Chronicle.* This venture was more successful, and he married at age 54. He died suddenly in 1840. Also examines his close attachment to the Masonic Order in Canada. Uses recent secondary sources as well as a large amount of correspondence with such eminent contemporaries as Edward Ellice and Sir John Easthope; 84 notes. 1815-40

McGlothlin, William Joseph

4618. Wilkinson, Carl Wesley, III. "The Life and Work of William Joseph McGlothlin." Southern Baptist Theological Seminary 1981. 267 pp. *DAI 1981 42(1): 258-A.* 8113626
1826-20c

McGrath, Earl James

4619. McGrath, Earl J. FIFTY YEARS IN HIGHER EDUCATION: PERSONAL INFLUENCES ON MY PROFESSIONAL DEVELOPMENT. *J. of Higher Educ. 1980 51(1): 76-93.* Third in a series of professional memoirs by leaders in higher education. 1920's-70's

4620. Reid, John Young. "The Public Career of Earl James McGrath: Vindicating Education for Holistic Man." U. of Arizona 1978. 324 pp. *DAI 1978 39(2): 709-710-A.*
1947-77

McGree, Anita Newcombe

4621. Kietzman, Anna-Ruth Moore. WOMEN IN MILITARY NURSING. *Daughters of the Am. Revolution Mag. 1981 115(4): 288-293.* Sketches the history of nursing in the military, 1775-1980, and examines in particular the role of Dr. Anita Newcombe McGree, a vice president general of the National Society of the Daughters of the American Revolution, in forming the DAR Hospital Corps in 1898.
1775-1980

McGuinness, Fred

4622. —. [AN INTERVIEW WITH FRED MCGUINNESS]. *Manitoba Hist. [Canada] 1981 (2): 21-25.* Interview with journalist Fred McGuinness on growing up in Manitoba, the interest in local history in western Canada, and prairie journalism. 2 illus. 1952-80

McGuire, Hunter Holmes

4623. Hassler, William W. DR. HUNTER HOLMES MCGUIRE: SURGEON TO STONEWALL JACKSON, THE CONFEDERACY, AND THE NATION. *Virginia Cavalcade 1982 32(2): 52-61.* Details the life of Dr. McGuire from his medical training and war work to his private practice and work in medical education in Virginia, 1855-1900.
1855-1900

McInnis, George

4624. Trower, Peter. SAGA OF A WEST COAST LOGGER: INTERVIEW WITH GEORGE MCINNIS, 101-YEAR OLD LOGGER. *Sound Heritage [Canada] 1977 6(3): 13-15.* McInnis recounts events in his logging career in Maine, Washington, and British Columbia, 1894-1949.
1894-1949

McIntire, Carl

4625. Mulholland, Robert Joseph. "Carl McIntire: The Early Radio Years (1932 to 1955)." Bowling Green State U. 1984. 280 pp. *DAI 1985 45(9): 2684-A.* DA8428391 1932-55

McIntosh, Lachlan

4626. Cook, Betty. THE STRANGE SAGA OF GEN. LACHLAN MCINTOSH. *Daughters of the Am. Revolution Mag. 1978 112(9): 888-891, 893.* Chronicles Lachlan McIntosh's service in the Continental Army during the American Revolution and his involvement in politics in Georgia where he began a lifelong feud with another local politician, George Walton, 1774-81. 1774-81

4627. Jackson, Harvey. "AMERICAN SLAVERY, AMERICAN FREEDOM" AND THE REVOLUTION OF THE LOWER SOUTH: THE CASE OF LACHLAN MCINTOSH. *Southern Studies 1980 19(1): 81-93.* In 1775 Lachlan McIntosh (b. 1728), plantation and slave owner, signed a declaration condemning slavery as unnatural and incompatible with the struggle of the American colonists against their oppressors in England. In 1787 he made another declaration, this time justifying and supporting slavery. His seeming self-contradiction, typical of many southerners, can be explained by economics. In 1775 British policies threatened McIntosh's freedom to earn a good living, and subjection of blacks who might rebel was a danger in time of revolution. In 1787 the maintenance of slavery provided the only possible means of preserving wealth for many southerners. Based on the Lachlan McIntosh Papers in University of Georgia Libraries, Henry Laurens Papers in the South Carolina Historical Society, and other primary sources; 37 notes. 1775-87

4628. Lamplugh, George R. "TO CHECK AND DISCOURAGE THE WICKED AND DESIGNING": JOHN WEREAT AND THE REVOLUTION IN GEORGIA. *Georgia Hist. Q. 1977 61(4): 295-307.* 1775-83
*For abstract see **Wereat, John***

McKaig, Robert Raymond

4629. Lovin, Hugh T. RAY MCKAIG: NONPARTISAN LEAGUE INTELLECTUAL AND RACONTEUR. *North Dakota Hist. 1980 47(3): 12-20.* A former minister, Robert Raymond McKaig was a successful rancher who became a leading spokesman for the Nonpartisan League in North Dakota and Idaho. He spent more than 20 years, between the early 1920's and 1945, writing and attempting to publish a novel based on farmers' problems and Nonpartisan solutions. Based on the McKaig Papers in Idaho State Historical Society; 6 illus., 48 notes. ca 1920-45

McKay, Claude

4630. Cooper, Wayne Foley. "Stranger and Pilgrim: The Life of Claude McKay, 1890-1948." Rutgers U., New Brunswick 1982. 891 pp. *DAI 1983 43(10): 3392-A.* DA8305737 1912-48

4631. Samuels, Wilfred David. "Five Afro-Caribbean Voices in American Culture, 1917-1929: Hubert H. Harrison, Wilfred A. Domingo, Richard B. Moore, Cyril V. Briggs, and Claude McKay." U. of Iowa 1977. 181 pp. *DAI 1978 38(7): 4234-A.* 1917-29

4632. Tillery, Tyrone. "Claude McKay: Man and Symbol of the Harlem Renaissance, 1889-1948." Kent State U. 1981. 275 pp. *DAI 1981 42(4): 1749-A.* DA8120257 1909-48

McKay, James

4633. Goossen, N. Jaye. A WEARER OF MOCCASINS: THE HONOURABLE JAMES MCKAY OF DEER LODGE. *Beaver [Canada] 1978 309(2): 44-53.* James McKay, a Red River Métis, was born at Fort Edmonton in 1828 to an employee of the Hudson's Bay Company. By the time he joined the Company in 1853, McKay was fluent and literate in English and French, and knew Cree, Ojibwa, Assiniboine, and Sioux dialects. He remained with the company until 1860, being important in negotiating with the Métis and Indians, and was a local expert on transportation. He married Margaret Roward, who inherited substantial money and land. By the late 1860's, McKay had become part of the local landed gentry and built a remarkable home at Deer Lodge on his Assiniboine tract. In later years McKay was a key figure in many Indian treaties. In the 1870's he held several positions in the new Manitoba government. McKay died in 1879, having risen from a Métis odd-job man to a leading businessman, government leader, and a man of tremendous respect in Manitoba. 11 illus. 1853-79

McKay, John (family)

4634. Gibson, John G. PIPER JOHN MACKAY AND RODERICK MCLENNAN: A TALE OF TWO IMMIGRANTS AND THEIR INCOMPLETE GENEALOGY. *Nova Scotia Hist. Rev. [Canada] 1982 2(2): 69-82.* Traces the genealogy of the McKay family of Scotland from Iain Dall (Blind John, ca. 1656-ca. 1754) through seven generations. John McKay (1790-1884), grandson of the Blind Piper, settled in Nova Scotia in 1805. Roderick McLennan (ca. 1778-1866), great-grandson of the Blind Piper, also came to Nova Scotia in 1812. The uncle and nephew never acknowledged their relationship although they lived in the same geographic area. Based on Public Archives of Nova Scotia manuscripts; 22 notes. 1805-1927

McKee, Andrew Irwin

4635. Alden, John D. ANDREW IRWIN MCKEE: NAVAL CONSTRUCTOR. *US Naval Inst. Pro. 1979 105(6): 49-57.* Rear Admiral Andrew Irwin McKee (1896-1976) had a great deal to do with developing and constructing the US Navy's submarine force. He was an all-around naval constructor and was considered to be a "designer's designer." He made his mark as a member of the Navy's Construction Corps before and during World War II. He retired from the Navy in July 1947 and joined the Electric Boat Company as design director; he later became that company's vice-president of engineering and director of research and design. During 1947-61, he was responsible for 14 new submarine designs that went into production, several conversions of World War II fleet submarines to new configurations, and for many experimental efforts. Primary and secondary sources; 10 photos, 9 notes. 1930's-61

McKelvey, Blake

4636. Stave, Bruce M. A CONVERSATION WITH BLAKE MCKELVEY. *J. of Urban Hist. 1976 2(4): 459-486.* Blake McKelvey, official city historian of Rochester, New York, describes his training, early career, and scholarship. This interview reveals as much about the man as about the history he writes. McKelvey's four-volume history of Rochester had a combined sales total of under 10,000—respectable by scholarly standards but less than a single week on the best sellers' list. 28 notes, biblio. 1800-1976

McKenna, Joseph

4637. Noonan, John T., Jr. THE CATHOLIC JUSTICES OF THE UNITED STATES SUPREME COURT. *Catholic Hist. Rev. 1981 67(3): 369-385.* 19c-20c
For abstract see ***Butler, Pierce***

McKenzie, Charles

4638. Arthur, Elizabeth. CHARLES MCKENZIE, *L'HOMME SEUL. Ontario Hist. [Canada] 1978 70(1): 39-62.* A biographical study of Charles McKenzie (1774-1855), clerk to the Hudson's Bay Company at Lac Seul, northwest Ontario, 1807-23 and 1827-54. McKenzie joined the company in 1803; in 1804, he arrived in America, and in 1807 was sent to Lac Seul, a remote, desolate, and impoverished fur trade post. Lacking any influential connections after about 1821, McKenzie failed to secure his promotion or transfer to any more salubrious location. Although his daughters were educated and eventually settled in Upper Canada, he and his half-Indian wife and son were forced to remain at Lac Seul with only brief intervals until 1854. McKenzie wasted much of his energy in fruitless personal quarrels with other neighboring company clerks and factors. Prolonged isolation from European culture, and a growing sense of frustration and failure, tended to warp his judgment. His journals show him to have been a bitter and disillusioned critic of the company's commercial and social policies, and a staunch advocate of fairer treatment of Indians and *Métis.* Based on McKenzie's journals and correspondence in the Hudson's Bay Company Archives; map, 82 notes. 1803-54

4639. McKenzie, Charles. DOCTOR IN THE COAL BRANCH. *Alberta History [Canada] 1985 33(2): 1-6.* From July 1927 to the spring of 1928, Dr. Charles McKenzie (1897-1980) served the miners of the Coal Branch, a string of mining communities and collieries along a Y-shaped rail spur in the mountains 130 miles west of Edmonton. Having just graduated from medical school, McKenzie quickly learned the difference between "textbook" medicine and the requirements for handling people. The story of his experiences in Coal Branch provides an interesting and useful glimpse of the miners' lives in the early 20th century. 3 photos. 1927-28

McKim, Andrew

4640. Smith, James. ANDREW MCKIM, REFORMER. *Nova Scotia Hist. Q. [Canada] 1978 8(3): 225-242.* Andrew McKim (1779-1840), farmer, shoemaker, and Baptist lay preacher, began his political career as a campaigner for Thomas Roach, county M. P. P. At the age of 56 he ran for a seat in the House of Assembly; the final vote was disputed for two years. He entered a final plea and was awarded a seat in the legislature in February 1838. He served until 1840 when the legislature was dissolved. He entered again but died before the voting was completed. 26 notes. 1784-1840

McKim, Charles F.

4641. Wilson, Richard Guy. THE EARLY WORK OF CHARLES F. MCKIM: COUNTRY HOUSE COMMISSIONS. *Winterthur Portfolio 1979 14(3): 235-267.* The philosophical basis of Charles F. McKim's style of architecture is to be found in his early designs from 1870-79 in the north Atlantic states. McKim (1847-1909) integrated elements of the Queen Anne, the wooden venacular, and colonial styles into his own comprehensive American design. This synthesis presaged later consolidations expressed during the latter part of the century. Based on McKim's correspondence and other primary sources; 43 illus., 67 notes. 1870-79

McKimmon, Jane S.

4642. Sessoms, Barbara Ross. "Jane S. McKimmon: Her Influence upon Adult Education in North Carolina." North Carolina State U., Raleigh 1980. 193 pp. *DAI 1981 41(12): 4938-A.* 8111048 1900-45

McKinney, Thomas L.

4643. Klingelhofer, Herbert E. JOHN QUINCY ADAMS, LITERARY EDITOR. *Manuscripts 1983 35(4): 265-272.* Thomas L. McKinney, soldier and politician, was superintendent of Indian affairs during 1816-30. His sympathy and advocacy for the Indians led to clashes with Andrew Jackson, who dismissed McKinney. McKinney coauthored, with James Hall, the *History of the Indian Tribes of North America with Biographical Sketches of the Principal Chiefs, Embellished with One Hundred Twenty Portraits, from the Indian Gallery in the Department of War, at Washington.* When McKinney asked John Quincy Adams for editorial assistance, the former president responded in a letter that provides valuable insights into Adams's views on language and writing. Reproduction, 2 illus., 12 notes. 1831

McKinney-Steward, Susan Smith

See Steward, Susan McKinney

McKinnon, Betty

4644. Hancock, Lyn. MARCHING "MARMOTEERS"! RILED GRANDMOTHER LEADS CRUSADE TO SAVE VANCOUVER ISLAND'S ENDANGERED MARMOT. *Can. Geog. [Canada] 1984 104(2): 50-55.* Betty McKinnon has led efforts to save the marmots of Vancouver Island, British Columbia, from extinction. 1976-84

McKissick, Jane Wilson

4645. Bolar, Mary. JANE WILSON MCKISSICK: PATRIOT OF THE AMERICAN REVOLUTION. *Daughters of the Am. Revolution Mag. 1980 114(2): 152-155.* Jane Wilson McKissick (1759-1844), of Lincoln County, North Carolina, a strong patriot, helped care for the patriot wounded after the battle of Ramsour's (Ramseur's) Mill, 1780. 1780

McLachlan, James B.

4646. Frank, David. THE TRIAL OF J. B. MCLACHLAN. *Hist. Papers [Canada] 1983 208-225.* On 17 October 1923, the Supreme Court of Nova Scotia convicted James B. McLachlan, secretary-treasurer, District 26, United Mine Workers of America, of seditious libel. He was accused of leading Canada's labor movement along paths laid by Communist radicals. The prosecutor, provincial attorney general Walter J. O'Hearn, explicitly sought the conviction of McLachlan not for his actions, but for the ideology his union espoused during its 1922 confrontation with the British Empire Steel Corporation. 51 notes. French summary. 1919-25

McLafferty, Henry, III

4647. —. ROMULUS REVISITED: EXTRACTS FROM THE DIARY OF HENRY MCLAFFERTY, JR. 1856-1857. *Rochester Hist. 1980 42(2): 1-28.* Introduction to Henry McLafferty, III (or "Jr.," as he styled himself), whose grandfather emigrated from Ireland in 1772; followed by excerpts from the diary he kept during 1856-57 in Romulus, New York, where he lived as a farmer, real estate agent and speculator, surveyor, accountant, and clock repairer until his death in 1859. 1856-57

McLain, Raymond Stallings

4648. Stewart, Roy P. RAYMOND S. MCLAIN: AMERICA'S GREATEST CITIZEN SOLDIER. *Chronicles of Oklahoma 1981 59(1): 4-29.* Raymond Stallings McLain emerged from a childhood of poverty to achieve a successful career as business executive and general during World War II. He joined the Oklahoma National Guard in 1912 and four years later participated in Pershing's Punitive Expedition against Pancho Villa. Following service in World War I, McLain returned to private business but was reactivated to the regular army as a general in 1941. Throughout the war, he distinguished himself for always being in the forefront of major battles, from the Sicily invasion, to the Italian operations, to the D-Day landings at Normandy. McLain briefly served as military governor over the occupied area around Frankfurt, Germany, and during the Korean War acted as Army Comptroller. 8 photos. 1912-54

McLaughlin, Isabel

4649. Murray, Joan. ISABEL MCLAUGHLIN. *Resources for Feminist Research [Canada] 1984 13(4): 17-20.* Traces the life of Canadian painter Isabel McLaughlin, focusing on her artistic education and introduction to oil paints, the influence Canada's Group of Seven had on her compositions and technique up until the early 1950's, and her return in 1953 to painting still lifes that expressed her interests in botany, zoology, and textures. 1903-68

McLean, Mary Hancock

4650. Hunt, Marion. WOMAN'S PLACE IN MEDICINE: THE CAREER OF DR. MARY HANCOCK MCLEAN. *Missouri Hist. Soc. Bull. 1980 36(4): 255-263.* Though her behavior defied social conventions, Mary Hancock McLean (1861-1930) was able to become a physician and surgeon in 1883. Medical education was then available to women so that, trained, they might medically attend to other women and children. Despite obstacles, she proved to the St. Louis medical fraternity that female physicians deserved a larger sphere than was traditionally granted them. Based primarily on secondary sources; 2 photos, 30 notes. 1883-1930

McLean, Raymond

4651. Garland, Albert. THE MAKING OF A GENERAL. *Am. Hist. Illus. 1983 18(4): 32-39.* Recounts Raymond McLean's military career from his 1912 enlistment in the Oklahoma National Guard to his 1944 command of the 90th Infantry Division in Europe. 1912-44

McLemore, John Christmas

4652. Downing, Marvin. JOHN CHRISTMAS MCLEMORE: 19TH CENTURY TENNESSEE LAND SPECULATOR. *Tennessee Hist. Q. 1983 42(3): 254-265.* Traces the career of John Christmas McLemore, a land speculator with major investments in Florence, Alabama, and Memphis, Fort Pickering, and Christmasville, Tennessee. McLemore contributed significantly to the development of West Tennessee before losing much of his money in the declining land market following the Panic of 1837 and in an unfortunate venture to finance the Memphis LeGrange Railroad. Secondary sources; illus., 30 notes. 1820-50

McLemore, Richard Aubrey

4653. Hicks, Billy Ray. "Richard Aubrey McLemore and Mississippi College: A Study in Educational Leadership." U. of Mississippi 1983. 172 pp. *DAI 1983 44(6): 1704-A.* DA8323338 1957-68

McLuhan, Marshall

4654. Cooper, Thomas William. "Pioneers in Communication: The Lives and Thought of Harold Innis and Marshall McLuhan." U. of Toronto [Canada] 1980. *DAI 1980 41(6): 2341-2342-A.* 1936-69

4655. Gronbeck, Bruce E. MCLUHAN AS RHETORICAL THEORIST. *J. of Communication 1981 31(3): 117-128.* Briefly traces the phases in the late Marshall McLuhan's career and the scope of his thought, focusing on "his contributions to the theoretical literature on rhetoric and communications"; 1940-80. 1940-80

4656. Ong, Walter J. MCLUHAN AS TEACHER: THE FUTURE IS A THING OF THE PAST. *J. of Communication 1981 31(3): 129-135.* Presents the author's reflections of the years 1938-1941 when he and the late Marshall McLuhan were student and instructor, respectively, at Saint Louis University, focusing on McLuhan's teaching of the Cambridge version of the New Criticism, which applied analysis of writers of the past such as Homer, Virgil, and Shakespeare, to comtemporary writers; this approach "changed the pitch and intensity of literary analysis." 1938-41

McMellen, Elias

4657. Caruthers, Elizabeth Gipe. ELIAS MCMELLEN: FORGOTTEN MAN. *J. of the Lancaster County Hist. Soc. 1981 85(1): 16-29.* Chronicles the life of Elias McMellen, 1838-1916, Lancaster County, Pennsylvania bridge builder, Civil War hero, delegate to state and county Republican conventions, and local property owner. 1860-1916

McMurry, Charles A.

4658. Tyler, Kenneth Dean. "The Educational Life and Work of Charles A. McMurry, 1872-1929." Northern Illinois U. 1982. 259 pp. *DAI 1982 43(4): 1031-A.* DA8220330 1872-1929

McNailly, John Thomas

4659. Choquette, Robert. JOHN THOMAS MCNAILLY ET L'ERECTION DU DIOCÈSE DE CALGARY [John Thomas McNailly and the establishment of the diocese of Calgary]. *Rev. de l'U. d'Ottawa [Canada] 1975 45(4): 401-416.* John Thomas McNailly (1871-1952), the first bishop of Calgary, was an anglophone who defended the interests of the Catholic anglophiles in Calgary, particularly the Irish. The Pope, in selecting McNailly, believed that western Canada was English in both language and culture. Provides brief sketch of McNailly's life and accomplishments and discusses his problems as bishop, particularly with the French Canadians. Primary and secondary sources; 84 notes. 1871-1952

McNair, Alexander

4660. Keller, Kenneth W. ALEXANDER MCNAIR AND JOHN B. C. LUCAS: THE BACKGROUND OF EARLY MISSOURI POLITICS. *Missouri Hist. Soc. Bull. 1977 33(4): 231-245.* Discusses political and economic activities of Alexander McNair (1774-1826) in Pennsylvania and Missouri, and political clashes between McNair and Judge John B. C. Lucas (d. 1842) in Missouri. The political conflicts revolved around land claims matters, appointments to territorial offices, and partisan rivalries between Federalists and Democratic-Republicans. In the end, Lucas became a victim of "political eclipse" and deserted politics in 1821; McNair was successful and eventually became Governor of Missouri. Conversely, Lucas prospered economically and became a wealthy St. Louis businessman while McNair failed in commercial ventures and, at his death, was deeply in debt. Based on newspaper and Pennsylvania and Missouri archival sources; 3 photos, 56 notes. ca 1795-1826

McNamara, Robert S.

4661. Clark, William. ROBERT MCNAMARA AT THE WORLD BANK. *Foreign Affairs 1981 60(1): 167-184.* During Robert S. McNamara's 13 years as president of the World Bank, the bank augmented its role as a development agency, and emphasized economic aid to eradicate "absolute poverty" in underdeveloped nations. The bank proceeded in these endeavors despite difficulties in maintaining independence from political pressures and despite increased difficulty in obtaining funds from recession-plagued nations. 9 notes. 1968-81

4662. Kinnard, Douglas. MCNAMARA AT THE PENTAGON. *Parameters 1980 10(3): 22-31.* The major contributions of Robert S. McNamara as secretary of defense from 1961 to 1968 were the introduction of new managment techniques, such as systems analysis, and the transfer of power from the military services to the secretary and his civilian staff. McNamara also assumed the role of primary supervisor of the Vietnam War. Although he originally supported the military's calls for increased force, by 1966 he was calling for a leveling off of military activity and for the start of negotiations. Based on Defense Department studies, writings and Congressional testimony of McNamara, interviews, and secondary sources; 25 notes. 1961-68

4663. Mayer, Klaus. ROBERT MCNAMARAS AMTSFÜHRUNG ALS SECRETARY OF DEFENSE UND DIE AMERIKANISCHE MARINE: EIN INTERPRETATIONSVERSUCH DER VERHALTENSMOTIVE VON ZIVILER UND MILITÄRISCHER GEWALT IN DEN USA IM ZUSAMMENHANG MIT DER TONKING-AFFÄRE (AUGUST 1964) [Robert McNamara's achievement in his office as Secretary of Defense and the US Navy: an attempt at interpretation of motives of conduct by civil and military authority in connection with the Tonkin affair (August 1964)]. *Militärgeschichtliche Mitteilungen [West Germany] 1977 (2): 43-92.* Deals with Robert S. McNamara's service as Secretary of Defense (1961-68), the impact of his politics on the development of the US Navy, and the Tonkin Gulf crisis. 1961-68

McNeal, Joseph W.

4664. Holmes, Helen Freudenberger. "HE WAS INTO EVERYTHING": JOSEPH W. MCNEAL, TERRITORIAL INNOVATOR. *Chronicles of Oklahoma 1983-84 61(4): 364-385.* Joseph W. McNeal entered Oklahoma as a buffalo hunter during 1873 and over the next 45 years proved his uncanny ability to succeed at a variety of occupations despite his lack of formal education. Initially, McNeal homesteaded near Medicine Lodge, Kansas, but by 1878 he purchased the town's newspaper and subsequently was elected county attorney. In 1883, he started a new bank in Medicine Lodge, a business enterprise he duplicated in Guthrie, Oklahoma, after moving there six years later. McNeal rose to prominence in the Republican Party of Oklahoma Territory, and in 1910 he was the party's unsuccessful gubernatorial candidate. Two years later, he moved to Tulsa, where he remained active in banking and civic life until his death in 1918. Based on McNeal family scrapbook and papers; illus., 8 photos, 31 notes. 1873-1918

McNeill, George

4665. Fones-Wolf, Kenneth. BOSTON EIGHT HOUR MEN, NEW YORK MARXISTS AND THE EMERGENCE OF THE INTERNATIONAL LABOR UNION: PRELUDE TO THE AFL. *Hist. J. of Massachusetts 1981 9(2): 47-59.* 1860-89

*For abstract see **Steward, Ira***

McNeill, John T.

4666. Nichols, James Hastings. JOHN T. MCNEILL MEMORIAL LECTURE. *Church Hist. 1975 44(3): 289-293.* Discusses the life of Canadian Presbyterian John T. McNeill. Emphasizes McNeill's career at the University of Chicago, his association with the environmental factors school of church history, and his contributions that helped anchor church history in American academia. 1880-1960

McNutt, Alexander G.

4667. Keller, Mark A. "TH' GUV'NER WUZ A WRITER"—ALEXANDER G. MCNUTT OF MISSISSIPPI. *Southern Studies 1981 20(4): 394-411.* Alexander G. McNutt, prosperous lawyer and planter, was governor of Mississippi during 1838-42. He was also a popular writer. The New York *Spirit of the Times,* a sporting paper featuring humorous sketches, published eight of McNutt's stories during 1844-47. His works are noted for the substantial character development, suspense as well as humor, politics as a humorous subject, and McNutt's ability to satirize himself. Based on articles in *Spirit of the Times;* 48 notes. 1844-47

McPartland, Marian

4668. MacFadyen, J. Tevere. SOPHISTICATED LADY. *Horizon 1981 24(11): 36-41.* Discusses British jazz superstar Marian McPartland, her career highlights since 1943, and insights into jazz performance in America and Great Britain. 1943-81

McSwain, John J.

4669. Weaver, John C. LAWYERS, LODGES AND KINFOLK: THE WORKINGS OF A SOUTH CAROLINA POLITICAL ORGANIZATION, 1920-1936. *South Carolina Hist. Mag. 1977 78(4): 272-285.* Examines the political career of South Carolinian John J. McSwain, focusing on the political party machine on which he depended to stay in office, 1920-36. 1920-36

McVicker, Emma J.

4670. Lubomudrov, Carol Ann. A WOMAN STATE SCHOOL SUPERINTENDENT: WHATEVER HAPPENED TO MRS. MCVICKER? *Utah Hist. Q. 1981 49(3): 254-261.* Emma J. McVicker was appointed by Governor Heber M.

Wells to be Utah's second state school superintendent on 8 October 1900. In 1896 she had been the first woman regent of the University of Utah. Prior to this time she had served as administrator of free kindergarten schools. While state superintendent, she observed many schools, urged reforms in the teaching of young children, criticized demeanor of male teachers, and urged better health education. Her superintendent's report of 1900 is the only extant record of her work and goals. Photo, 30 notes. 1883-1905

McWilliams, Carey

4671. Critser, Greg. THE POLITICAL REBELLION OF CAREY MCWILLIAMS. *UCLA Hist. J. 1983 4: 34-65.* Traces the movement of author Carey McWilliams from literary critic to social and political activist. In the 1920's, McWilliams was a Los Angeles attorney who wrote about literary figures. The Great Depression inspired his interest and concern for the problems of poor people. In 1935, McWilliams and Herb Klein made an investigative tour of California agricultural labor conditions. His articles on growers' vigilantism and workers' unionizing efforts appeared in such journals as the *Nation* and *Pacific Weekly,* and his classic study of California agriculture, *Factories in the Field,* was published in 1939. By 1936, McWilliams was on the left edge of the Los Angeles liberal community, no longer writing literary criticism but committed as a writer of conscience concerned with the problems of society. 94 notes. 1929-39

4672. Saxton, Alexander. GOODBYE TO A COLLEAGUE: CAREY MCWILLIAMS, 1905-1980. *Amerasia J. 1980 7(2): v-vii.* A tribute to Carey McWilliams, lawyer, author, editor of the *Nation,* and university lecturer. Briefly lists his literary accomplishments and lauds his many contributions to his fellow man. ca 1925-80

Mead, Florence H. "Ma"

4673. Schaelchlin, Patricia. "WORKING FOR THE GOOD OF THE COMMUNITY": REST HAVEN PREVENTORIUM FOR CHILDREN. *J. of San Diego Hist. 1983 29(2): 96-114.* Describes efforts in San Diego, California, to prevent the spread of tuberculosis, focusing on the humanitarian work of Florence H. "Ma" Mead and the Rest Haven Preventorium, an open-air sanatorium for children. 1909-50's

Mead, George Herbert

4674. Deegan, Mary Jo and Burger, John S. GEORGE HERBERT MEAD AND SOCIAL REFORM: HIS WORK AND WRITINGS. *J. of the Hist. of the Behavioral Sci. 1978 14(4): 362-372.* G. H. Mead, the eminent social psychologist, had an active civic life. His work in social reform was directly influenced by and derived from his philosophy of man and society. This facet of his life is relatively unexamined today, although most of his publications during his lifetime were concerned with the application of science for the good of the community. 1894-1927

4675. Franzosa, Susan Douglas. THE EMERGENCE OF THE PRAGMATIC ATTITUDE: AN EDUCATIONAL BIOGRAPHY OF GEORGE HERBERT MEAD. *Vitae Scholasticae 1984 3(1): 33-59.* Discusses the education of George Herbert Mead, one of the central figures of American pragmatism. Mead studied at Oberlin and Harvard, and at Leipzig and Berlin as well. Mead became preoccupied with reconstructing philosophic discourse in light of the intellectual tensions caused by evolutionary theory and an emerging experimentalism in psychology. Mead sought a "secular philosophy" to take the place of the religious vision he had rejected. Eventually he worked with Dewey at Ann Arbor, and was a central figure in the Chicago School. Based on the Henry Northrup Castle letters; 67 notes. 1879-91

4676. Karier, Clarence J. IN SEARCH OF SELF IN A MORAL UNIVERSE: A CRITIQUE OF THE LIFE AND THOUGHT OF GEORGE HERBERT MEAD. *J. of the Hist. of Ideas 1984 45(1): 153-161.* A general assessment of the social psychology of George Herbert Mead that stresses the importance of his religious background and interests. Mead's parents were closely tied to Protestantism and Mead himself considered a career in the clergy for a while. Even after committing to a profession that emphasized humanistic and scientific perspectives, he endeavored to keep Christian beliefs or their sociological and psychological surrogates vital in the modern, increasingly alienated world. For Mead, every society implicitly contains a moral ideal and the functional role of this sort of ideal in the assimilation and realization of the "self." His thought continually slipped between the descriptive and the prescriptive. 18 notes. 1890's-1931

4677. Lowy, Richard Frank. "George Herbert Mead: Evolutionary Naturalism, the Act, Science, and Social Reform." U. of California, Riverside 1984. 258 pp. *DAI 1985 46(1): 281-A.* DA8505275 1894-1931

4678. Smith, Richard Lee. "George Herbert Mead and Sociology: The Chicago Years." U. of Illinois, Urbana-Champaign 1977. 291 pp. *DAI 1977 38(6): 3747-A.* 1907-31

Mead, Margaret

4679. Howard, Jane. MARGARET MEAD, "SELF-APPOINTED MATERFAMILIAS TO THE WORLD." *Smithsonian 1984 15(6): 118-140.* Recounts the life and work of anthropologist Margaret Mead, focusing on her broad definition of "family" and the development of a vast extended family of her own. 1920's-78

4680. Mabee, Carleton. MARGARET MEAD AND A "PILOT EXPERIMENT" IN PROGRESSIVE AND INTERRACIAL EDUCATION: THE DOWNTOWN COMMUNITY SCHOOL. *New York Hist. 1984 65(1): 4-31.* By the time her daughter had reached school age in 1945, Margaret Mead had become famous as an anthropologist and advocate of progressive education. Mead decided to enroll her daughter in the newly established Downtown Community School in New York City. The school soon became well known for its interracial and progressive practices. Although Mead withdrew her daughter from the school in 1950, her interest in interracial and intercultural education continued and, by the 1970's, she had come to realize that education was not a "one way process" but circular, with all contributing and profiting from the experience. Based mostly on Mead's writings and correspondence; 4 illus., 60 notes. 1928-76

Meaney, Richard J.

4681. Meaney, Richard J. LOUISVILLE SCENES: THE AUTOBIOGRAPHY OF FR. RICHARD J. MEANEY. *Filson Club Hist. Q. 1983 57(1): 7-19.* Continued from a previous article (see entry 20A:5541). Details Richard J. Meaney's life as a young man growing up in the Irish section of Louisville, Kentucky. He relates the significance of baseball, gang fights, and the St. Patrick's Day parade to ethnic solidarity. He also describes incidents surrounding the first

Kentucky Derby and the transition of the Kentucky bourbon industry from local owners to corporate domination. 2 photos. 1859-95

4682. Meaney, Richard J. LOUISVILLE SCENES: THE AUTOBIOGRAPHY OF FR. RICHARD J. MEANEY. *Filson Club Hist. Q. 1984 58(1): 5-39.* Continued from the previous article. Covers Richard J. Meaney's life from 25 to 29 years of age, mentioning the Louisville public transportation system, the city fire department, the 1883 Exposition, the 1884 Ohio River flood, and Meaney's call to the priesthood. From a manuscript located at the Filson Club, Louisville, Kentucky; 3 photos. 1880-85

4683. —. LOUISVILLE SCENES: THE AUTOBIOGRAPHY OF FR. RICHARD J. MEANEY. *Filson Club Hist. Q. 1982 56(2): 170-180.* Consists of excerpts from the unpublished autobiography of Richard J. Meaney. The incidents mentioned include Union troops in Louisville in 1865, construction of the church of St. Louis Bertrand, the first telephones in Louisville, an attempt by the Louisville and Nashville Railroad to circumvent a court decision, and corrupt election practices in the city. Based on a manuscript located at the Filson Club, Louisville, Kentucky. 1865-80

Meany, Edmond Stephen

4684. Frykman, George A. EDMOND S. MEANY, HISTORIAN. *Pacific Northwest Q. 1960 51(4): 159-170.* A biography of Edmond Stephen Meany (1862-1935), a prominent professor of Washington state history at the University of Washington. 1862-1935

Mears, Otto

4685. Kaplan, Michael D. THE TOLLROAD BUILDING CAREER OF OTTO MEARS. *Colorado Mag. 1975 52(2): 153-170.* Mostly during 1881-87 Mears built a network of approximately 450 miles of tollroads in the San Juan mining area of southwest Colorado. Cheap, efficient transportation was the basis for the growth of the area. Later he turned to railroads and automobile roads, but his tollroads remain the basis of the highway system in the San Juan. Mainly primary sources; 4 illus., 3 maps, table, 51 notes. 1881-87

Medary, Samuel

4686. Krumm, Tahlman, Jr. "The Gethsemane Factor: A Historical Portrait of Samuel Medary of Ohio and an Analysis of the Rhetorical Dilemma of His *Crisis* Years, 1861-1864." Ohio State U. 1978. 211 pp. *DAI 1979 39(10): 5778-5779-A.* 1861-64

Medicine Calf

See Button Chief

Meeker, Edward Franklin

4687. Higgs, Robert. EDWARD FRANKLIN MEEKER (1943-1980). *Explorations in Econ. Hist. 1981 18(2): 209-210.* An appreciation of the career and contributions of Meeker, a specialist in the economic history of mortality and public health in the United States, including black mortality, fertility, and job discrimination. Ref. 1943-80

Meigs, Montgomery Cunningham

4688. —. METICULOUS MR. MEIGS. *Am. Hist. Illus. 1980 15(7): 34-37.* Discusses Montgomery Cunningham Meigs's participation in the construction of the Capitol building dome in Washington, D.C., as supervisor of public works, beginning in 1853, and reprints a letter to Congressman J. Glancy Jones of Reading, Pennsylvania, describing the construction and strength of the dome in 1858. 1853-58

Meigs, Return Jonathan (1801-1891)

4689. Faulkner, Ronnie. RETURN JONATHAN MEIGS: TENNESSEE'S FIRST STATE LIBRARIAN. *Tennessee Hist.Q. 1983 42(2): 151-164.* Traces the history of Return Jonathan Meigs; a prominent lawyer and Whig abolitionist who became the first State Librarian of Tennessee on the basis of his long-standing interest in library development. Meigs's Unionism led him to Washington during the Civil War where he remained to end his career as Clerk of the Supreme Court of the District of Columbia. Primary sources; illus., 46 notes. 1821-91

Meigs, Return Jonathan (1740-1823)

4690. McKeown, James Sean. "Return J. Meigs: United States Agent in the Cherokee Nation, 1801-1823." Pennsylvania State U. 1984. 482 pp. *DAI 1985 45(10): 3199-A.* DA8429112 1801-23

Meiklejohn, Alexander

4691. Johnson, Tony W. ALEXANDER MEIKLEJOHN IN SEARCH OF FREEDOM AND DIGNITY. *J. of General Educ. 1982 34(2): 159-168.* Alexander Meiklejohn (1872-1964) "devoted his life to championing schemes of liberal learning that were designed to foster critical thinking." His philosophy was based on the contention that Rousseauian and Kantian ideas provide a base for liberal education in a modern democratic society. Meiklejohn viewed democracy as a venture in human freedom and that government by and for the people is humanity at its best. His ideas deserve renewed attention as we approach the bicentennial of the ratification of the US Constitution in 1787. Secondary sources; 39 notes. 1890's-1964

4692. Racz, Ernest Bert. "Meiklejohn." Columbia U. Teachers Coll. 1979. 205 pp. *DAI 1981 41(9): 3916-A.* 8105909 1898-1964

Meisenholder, Gottlieb

4693. Schmierer, Thomas J. MY GRANDFATHER, GOTTLIEB MEISENHOLDER. *Heritage Review 1979 (25): 26-28.* Presents a genealogy of the Meisenholder family, their travels from Teplitz, Russia, and settlement in South Dakota, where Gottlieb Meisenholder eventually became the owner of a department store in Vermillion, South Dakota, postmaster of Parkston, a member of the South Dakota state legislature, and a Republican congressman. 1876-1957

Melchers, Gari

4694. Reid, Richard S. GARI MELCHERS: AN AMERICAN ARTIST IN VIRGINIA. *Virginia Cavalcade 1979 28(4): 154-171.* American artist Gari Melchers (1860-1932) first gained fame as a painter in Europe; then, beginning in the mid-1890's, he received acclaim in the United States as an artist in the impressionist style. 1890's-1932

Melchers, Julius and Gari

4695. Dewhurst, C. Kurt; Macdowell, Betty; and Macdowell, Marsha. THE ART OF JULIUS AND GARI MELCHERS. *Mag. Antiques 1984 125(4): 862-873.* Profiles the life and work of German immigrant Julius Melchers, an architectural sculptor and woodcarver in Detroit, and his son Gari Melchers, a painter who studied and maintained studios in Europe until World War I, when he returned to the United States. 1844-1920's

Mellett, Donald Ring

4696. Himebaugh, Glen Allen. "Donald Ring Mellett, Journalist: The Shaping of a Martyr." Southern Illinois U., Carbondale 1979. 219 pp. *DAI 1979 40(1): 10-A.* 1925-26

Mellon, Paul

4697. Canaday, John. A VERY PRIVATE MAN AND HIS SUPREME GIFTS TO THE PUBLIC. *Smithsonian 1983 14(1): 98-104.* Describes Paul Mellon's career of creative philanthropy and his gifts to the arts in America. 20c

Meltzoff, Stanley

4698. Bashline, Jim. THE UNDERWATER WORLD OF STANLEY MELTZOFF. *Sporting Classics 1985 4(1): 29-37.* Artist Stanley Meltzoff has developed a dramatic way of depicting underwater life, which he asserts is better painted than photographed, that has made him famous among American wildlife art patrons. 1920's-84

Melville, Elizabeth Shaw

4699. Kier, Kathleen E. THE REVIVAL THAT FAILED: ELIZABETH SHAW MELVILLE AND THE STEDMANS: 1891-1894. *Women's Studies 1980 7(3): 75-84.* Wishes to correct the lack of recognition of Elizabeth Shaw Melville's efforts to revive literary interest in the works of her husband, Herman Melville. The Stedman Papers in the Columbia University Library give ample evidence of her compliance in providing any necessary information for Arthur Stedman's proposed biography. She was not the unintelligent, disingenuous character she was later made out to be. 16 notes. 1891-94

Melville, Herman

4700. Emery, Allan Moore. THE POLITICAL SIGNIFICANCE OF MELVILLE'S CHIMNEY. *New England Q. 1982 55(2): 201-228.* Traditionally viewed as an autobiographical representation of the author's response to psychiatric examinations, Herman Melville's "I and My Chimney" (1856) is now looked upon as a treatment of the conflict between conservatism and progressivism, or American slavery and Christianity. Melville incorporated personal materials into the political allegory in which styles of chimney building stood for various forms of government. While Melville believed that the two minds were mutually antagonistic, the conservative and progressive minds could survive in a symbiotic relationship. Primary sources; 42 notes. 1850's

4701. Emmers, Amy Puett. MELVILLE'S CLOSET SKELETON: A NEW LETTER ABOUT THE ILLEGITIMACY INCIDENT IN *PIERRE. Studies in the Am. Renaissance 1977: 339-343.* Herman Melville (1819-91) wrote *Pierre; or the Ambiguities* as an autobiographical work. A letter from the uncle of Melville's father-in-law suggests that his father may have had a mistress who bore him an illegitimate daughter. The treatment of this incident in *Pierre; or the Ambiguities* may have caused considerable discomfort between Melville and his immediate relatives. Based on correspondence; 6 notes. 1852

4702. Kier, Kathleen E. THE REVIVAL THAT FAILED: ELIZABETH SHAW MELVILLE AND THE STEDMANS: 1891-1894. *Women's Studies 1980 7(3): 75-84.* 1891-94
For abstract see ***Melville, Elizabeth Shaw***

4703. Lowe, R. L. MELVILLE AND HAWTHORNE. *Mankind 1979 6(6): 26-28, 36.* 1845-50
For abstract see ***Hawthorne, Nathaniel***

4704. Richardson, Nancy Lee. "Herman Melville's Attitude toward America." U. of Delaware 1977. 276 pp. *DAI 1977 38(4): 2129-A.* 1840-65

Melvin, Leslie

4705. Melvin, Leslie; Lee, Molly, ed. I BEAT THE ARCTIC. *Alaska J. 1983 13(1): 33-96.* Prints the diaries of Leslie Melvin, a native of Florida who traveled alone between Martin Point and Nome, Alaska, in the winter of 1931-32. This was an amazing feat, as Melvin had never before mushed a dog team, he spoke no Eskimo, and he had no idea of Arctic conditions. 30 photos, illus., map, 24 notes, index. 1931-32

Memminger, Christopher G.

4706. —. CHRISTOPHER G. MEMMINGER. *Pro. of the South Carolina Hist. Assoc. 1981: 56-78.*

Jordan, Laylon Wayne. BETWEEN TWO WORLDS: CHRISTOPHER G. MEMMINGER OF CHARLESTON AND THE OLD SOUTH IN MID-PASSAGE, 1830-1861, *pp. 56-76.* Examines the early career of Christopher G. Memminger and his involvement in business and politics during 1830-61. Inheriting from his father a progressive outlook, Memminger advocated industrialization and diversification of the Southern economy while founding free schools in Charleston, South Carolina. Based primarily on secondary works; 47 notes.

Hendrick, Carlanna. COMMENTARY, *pp. 77-78.* 1830-61

Menard, John Willis

4707. Beatty, Bess. JOHN WILLIS MENARD: A PROGRESSIVE BLACK IN POST-CIVIL WAR FLORIDA. *Florida Hist. Q. 1980 59(2): 123-143.* John Willis Menard was typical of educated black leaders during Reconstruction. As a journalist and political and educational leader, Menard saw black improvement coming through an independent political party. His dependence on national patronage, however, kept him close to the Republicans. Menard's policies were rarely enacted, but he remained an outspoken advocate of equality. Based on Florida newspapers and state records; 51 notes. 1871-90

Mencken, H. L.

4708. Ellis, William E. KENTUCKY CATHOLIC AND MARYLAND SKEPTIC: THE CORRESPONDENCE OF COLONEL PATRICK HENRY CALLAHAN AND H. L. MENCKEN. *Filson Club Hist. Q. 1984 58(3): 336-348.* 1925-40
For abstract see ***Callahan, Patrick Henry***

4709. Jones, Daniel Carroll. "H. L. Mencken: Critic of the New Deal, 1933-1936." West Virginia U. 1977. 300 pp. *DAI 1978 38(12): 7513-A.* 1933-36

4710. Knopf, Alfred A. RANDOM RECOLLECTIONS OF A PUBLISHER. *Massachusetts Hist. Soc. Pro. 1961 73: 92-103.* 1901-61
For abstract see ***Cather, Willa***

4711. Manchester, William. H. L. MENCKEN IN PERSON. *Horizon 1980 23(9): 36-43.* The author reminisces about H. L. Mencken (1880-1956), literary critic, reporter, editor, and essayist; excerpted from *On Mencken,* edited by John Dorsey (New York: Alfred A. Knopf, Inc., 1980). 1880-1956

4712. Nolte, William H. THE ENDURING MENCKEN. *Mississippi Q. 1979 32(4): 651-662.* Analyzes and compares critical studies and biographies of H. L. Mencken (1880-1956), published 1950-78. 1910's-78

4713. Olivar-Bertrand, R. MENCKEN'S THIS WORLD SATIRE. *Contemporary Rev. [Great Britain] 1973 223(1293): 202-206.* Discusses H. L. Mencken (1880-1956) as a political and social satirist. 1920's-30's

4714. Pfaff, Daniel W. THE LETTERS OF H. L. MENCKEN AND FRED LEWIS PATTEE, 1922-1948. *Journalism Hist. 1976 3(3): 80-84.* Discusses this correspondence to illustrate H. L. Mencken's attitude to political events in the 1920's and his work as editor of the *American Mercury* between 1924 and 1933. 1922-48

4715. Riggio, Thomas P. DREISER AND MENCKEN IN THE LITERARY TRENCHES. *American Scholar 1985 54(2): 227-238.* 1908-45
For abstract see ***Dreiser, Theodore***

4716. —. H. L. MENCKEN FILLED HIS PAGES WITH SOME THOUGHTS OUTRAGEOUS. *Smithsonian 1980 11(6): 151-163.* Excerpts from the writings of editor and satirist H. L. Mencken, including comments on politics and morality, 1913-49. 1913-49

Mendel, Edward

4717. —. AN APOLOGY TO EDWARD MENDEL: THE ORIGINAL OF LINCOLN'S LETTER FOUND IN CHICAGO. *Chicago Hist. 1979 8(2): 78-79.* Provides a brief biography of Prussian-born lithographer Edward Mendel (1827-84), who established himself in business in Chicago as a lithographer, mapmaker, and engraver, and discusses in particular the letter from Abraham Lincoln thanking Mendel for the 1860 lithograph portrait of Lincoln. 1827-84

Mendenhall, Thomas

4718. Herman, Bernard L. MULTIPLE MATERIALS, MULTIPLE MEANINGS: THE FORTUNES OF THOMAS MENDENHALL. *Winterthur Portfolio 1984 19(1): 67-86.* A study of the home and personal objects belonging to Thomas Mendenhall of Wilmington, Delaware, can shed some light on the lifestyle of his family and community. Architecture is but one class of material objects; less durable goods are another. When combined with the written record, the scholar gains a more comprehensive view of the past, revealing that Mendenhall rose to wealth and then slid to reduced circumstances. Primary sources; 3 tables, 25 fig., 27 notes. 1790-1840

Menninger, Karl A.

4719. Pruyser, Paul W. RELIGIO MEDICI: KARL A MENNINGER, CALVINISM AND THE PRESBYTERIAN CHURCH. *J. of Presbyterian Hist. 1981 59(1): 59-72.* In 1930 Karl A. Menninger of Topeka, Kansas, became nationally known when he published *The Human Mind.* In the second edition (1937) he added a section on "Religious Application," assisted by religious experts. Raised under the religious tutelage of his mother and the First Presbyterian Church of Topeka, Menninger developed a great interest in religion, and in Calvinism in particular. The latter contributed to his sense of vocation and his desire to explore. His marriage to Presbyterian Jeanetta Lyle called attention to a cornerstone conviction about human personality: the instinctual given of love. His Calvinism enabled him to align himself with Freud's thesis that a death instinct must be postulated to account for otherwise puzzling phenomena of self-destructiveness. As Elder in the church, Menninger has taken his ecclesiastical responsibilities as seriously as his religiously personal ones. Illus., 12 notes. 1930-80

Mercer, Charles Fenton

4720. Hunt, Thomas C. POPULAR EDUCATION IN NINETEENTH-CENTURY VIRGINIA: THE EFFORTS OF CHARLES FENTON MERCER. *Paedagogica Historica [Belgium] 1981 21(2): 337-346.* Charles Fenton Mercer of Fredericksburg, Virginia, represented Loudoun County in the House of Delegates and was a member of Congress. Concerned with slavery and the slave trade, seriously interested in extending the right of suffrage, and a military officer in 1798 and in the War of 1812, he stands as a legislator, statesman, and patriot. In regard to popular education, under his leadership the General Assembly of Virginia established the Literary Fund "for the education of the Poor" in 1810. Throughout his life, he advocated popular education and clung to his belief that the nation's happiness and well-being were based on the diffusion of virtue and intelligence among all its citizens. His plan for a state-supported system of free education for all classes, however, has never been established, for political and social reasons. Lecture presented to the 1979 Annual Meeting of the Southern History of Education Society, Atlanta, Georgia, 12-13 October. Primary sources; 64 notes. 1778-1858

Mercer, John

4721. Miller, Helen Mill. A PORTRAIT OF AN IRASCIBLE GENTLEMAN: JOHN MERCER OF MARLBOROUGH. *Virginia Cavalcade 1976 26(2): 74-85.* Chronicles the careers (in surveying and law) of John Mercer, known in Virginia history for his outspokenness, flamboyance, and general irascibility, 1730's-68. 1730's-68

Mercier, Alfred

4722. Reinecke, George. ALFRED MERCIER, FRENCH NOVELIST OF NEW ORLEANS. *Southern Q. 1982 20(2): 145-176.* Alfred Mercier was born near New Orleans, immigrated to France in his teens, and earned a medical degree there. In 1865 he returned to New Orleans, set up a medical practice, and followed literary pursuits as an avocation. His novels include *Le Fou de Palerme* (1873), *Lidia* (1873), *La Fille du Prêtre* (1877-78), *L'Habitation Saint-Ybars* (1881), and *Johnelle* (1891). The contents of all are summarized and analyzed as contributions to New Orleans literature. 1820-90

Mercier, Louis J. A.

4723. Lawrence, Emeric A. LOUIS J. A. MERCIER: A MEMOIR. *Am. Benedictine Rev. 1978 29(3): 275-283.* Presents a memorial tribute to Mercier (1880-1953), 25 years after his death. Reviews Mercier's work as a Christian humanist. Mercier taught French literature at Harvard University during 1911-46. Primary and secondary sources; 4 notes. 1880-1953

Meredith, William Ralph

4724. Dembski, Peter Edward Paul. "William Ralph Meredith: Leader of the Conservative Opposition in Ontario, 1878-1894." U. of Guelph 1977. *DAI 1977 38(4): 2280-A.* 1878-94

Meriwether, Elizabeth Avery

4725. Berkeley, Kathleen Christine. ELIZABETH AVERY MERIWETHER, "AN ADVOCATE FOR HER SEX": FEMINISM AND CONSERVATISM IN THE POST-CIVIL WAR SOUTH. *Tennessee Historical Quarterly 1984 43(4): 390-407.* Elizabeth Avery Meriwether, unlike her famous contemporary, Mary Chesnut, was willing to challenge Southern politics and society publicly and to militate for social reform. After the Civil War, while her husband was helping establish the Ku Klux Klan in Tennessee, she became a temperance and women's rights activist by writing about the legal discrimination suffered by women in Tennessee and by waging an assault on "that aspect of common law, coverture, which subjected married women to the control of their husbands." In 1873, she tried to convince the Tennessee legislature to grant female teachers equal pay for equal work, and she joined with suffragettes such as Susan B. Anthony to press for a federal woman suffrage amendment. Photo, 60 notes. 1860's-1917

Merk, Frederick

4726. Blum, John Morton. A CELEBRATION OF FREDERICK MERK (1887-1977). *Virginia Q. Rev. 1978 54(3): 446-453.* Describes the character, teaching, and influence of longtime Harvard University historian of the American West, Frederick Merk. "Teaching absorbed Fred Merk, as it did few others on the Harvard faculty in his time," and "the bulk of his contributions to the literature of American history" came after retirement. Describes him as *Magister Artibus Historiae.* 1887-1977

4727. Freidel, Frank. FREDERICK MERK. *Massachusetts Hist. Soc. Pro. 1977 89: 181-183.* A memoir of Frederick Merk (1887-1977), Gurney Professor of History and Political Science emeritus at Harvard University, and a renowned historian of the westward movement. After graduation from the University of Wisconsin in 1911, Frederick Merk studied and taught at Harvard with Frederick Jackson Turner and others. Frederick Merk retired from teaching in 1957 and published six volumes during his last two decades. His *History of the Western Movement,* the culmination of his life's work, appeared posthumously in 1978. Based on the author's personal relationship with Frederick Merk, and on unpublished and published material. 1887-1977

4728. Paul, Rodman W. FREDERICK MERK, TEACHER AND SCHOLAR: A TRIBUTE. *Western Hist. Q. 1978 9(2): 140-148.* Wisconsin and Harvard educated Frederick Merk (1887-1977), a devoted disciple to Frederick Jackson Turner, was one of Harvard's most respected teachers. He was known for his integrity and perfectionism in his teaching and research. His historical writings were concerned primarily with the westward movement. 2 illus., 11 notes, biblio. 1921-77

4729. Procter, Ben. A DEDICATION TO THE MEMORY OF FREDERICK MERK, 1887-1977. *Arizona and the West 1979 21(4): 312-316.* Frederick Merk (1887-1977) specialized in history at the University of Wisconsin and Harvard University. Before going to Harvard he helped to edit a volume of documents and produced a monograph. The latter was accepted as his doctoral dissertation, and it later received a prize. He was regarded as an extremely effective and popular teacher (Harvard, 1921-57). He held several high offices in professional organizations. His lifelong research was in western history, and his many publications are widely respected. Illus., biblio. 1911-77

Merriam, Alan P.

4730. Gillis, Frank J. ALAN P. MERRIAM, 1923-1980: A MEMORIAL. *J. of Jazz Studies 1979 6(1): 93-95.* Obituary of "anthropologist, Africanist, ethnomusicologist, jazz enthusiast and scholar" Alan P. Merriam, including a bibliography of his works on jazz, 1949-70. ca 1949-80

Merriam, Clinton Hart

4731. Sterling, Keir. NATURALISTS OF THE SOUTHWEST AT THE TURN OF THE CENTURY. *Environmental Rev. 1978 3(1): 20-33.* 1880's-1910's
*For abstract see **Bailey, Vernon***

Merrill, Elbridge Warren

4732. Chambers, Scott. ELBRIDGE WARREN MERRILL. *Alaska J. 1977 7(3): 138-145.* Elbridge Warren Merrill (1868-1929) was a photographer of importance in recording life in Alaska, 1899-1929. He lived all this period in Sitka, leaving town once to go to Juneau. He photographed life in Sitka while doing various jobs such as restoring totem poles for the Louisiana Purchase Exposition in 1903, informal caretaker of Indian River Park, 1906-22. He also sold his photographs to various people. 9 photos, 15 notes. 1899-1929

Merrill, Fred

4733. Waldron, Daniel. FRED MERRILL'S ROUTE BOOK: ADVENTURES ON THE WAY TO A BIOGRAPHY. *Michigan Hist. 1980 64(4): 12-16.* Waldron reminisces about Fred Merrill, who was the advance man for the Harry Blackstone Magic Show. Based on Merrill's route book; 7 photos. 1925-34

Merrill, James

4734. Parini, Jay. A POET'S LIFE. *Horizon 1983 26(6): 16-20. The Changing Light at Sandover,* which records supernatural communication with great men in history, is the latest autobiographical poem published by prizewinning poet James Merrill, son of financial giant Charles Merrill. 1940's-83

Merritt, Ada Chase

4735. Bennion, Sherilyn Cox. ADA CHASE MERRITT AND THE RECORDER: A PIONEER IDAHO EDITOR AND HER NEWSPAPER. *Idaho Yesterdays 1982 25(4): 22-30.* Ada Chase Merritt was the first woman to edit an Idaho newspaper for more than a few issues. She edited the *Salmon City Idaho Recorder* from 1888 to 1906. The paper concentrated on local activities and news. Merritt took sides on political issues, supporting first the Democrats, then the Populists, then the free silver proponents. In addition to her editorial duties, Merritt was an active community and church leader of Salmon City. Based on newspapers; 2 photos, 17 notes. 1888-1906

Merton, Thomas

4736. Padovano, Anthony Thomas S. "The Human Journey. Thomas Merton: Symbol of a Century." Fordham U. 1980. 298 pp. *DAI 1980 40(12): 6282-6283-A.* 8012799 ca 1935-68

Messersmith, George S.

4737. Moss, Kenneth. GEORGE S. MESSERSMITH AND NAZI GERMANY: THE DIPLOMACY OF LIMITS IN CENTRAL EUROPE. Jones, Kenneth Paul, ed. *U.S. Diplomats in Europe, 1919-1941* (Santa Barbara, Calif.: ABC-Clio, 1981): 113-126. Chronicles the diplomatic career of George S. Messersmith (1883-1960), whose influence on US foreign policy was greatest between 1933 and 1936. During these first three years of Adolf Hitler's rule, American-German relations deteriorated because of trade disputes, anti-Jewish demonstrations, and rearmament. As consul in Berlin, Messersmith was involved in the first two issues and gained insight into domestic considerations behind Nazi policy. American policymakers in Washington trusted Messersmith and learned from him that German foreign policy was a response to internal economic problems as well as a fulfillment of Hitler's expansionist dreams. Messersmith helped Washington understand the political implications of American policy. American trade policy during 1934-35 became a weapon cautiously aimed at undermining Hitler's government by worsening economic conditions. Primary sources; 55 notes. 1933-36

4738. Moss, Kenneth. GEORGE S. MESSERSMITH: AN AMERICAN DIPLOMAT AND NAZI GERMANY. *Delaware Hist. 1977 17(4): 236-249.* Follows the diplomatic career of George Messersmith, particularly 1933-40, and argues that Messersmith helped to shape American attitudes toward Nazi Germany by convincing American leaders of the dangers of Nazi expansionism and megalomania. Messersmith believed in the principles of balance of power and in an international economy and open trade, and these beliefs informed his approaches to foreign policy. Messersmith was able to convince the American government to apply economic pressure on Nazi Germany in the 1930's to restrain Germany's expansion, but otherwise he was unsuccessful in getting America to adopt aggressive measures against Nazism. Based on the Messersmith Papers and contemporary correspondence; 39 notes. 1933-45

4739. Stiller, Jesse Herbert. "George S. Messersmith: A Diplomatic Biography." City U. of New York 1984. 548 pp. *DAI 1984 45(1): 280-A.* DA8409420 1900-55

Metalious, Grace

4740. Sorrell, Richard S. A NOVELIST AND HER ETHNICITY: GRACE METALIOUS AS A FRANCO-AMERICAN. *Hist. New Hampshire 1980 35(3): 284-317.* Grace Metalious (1924-64) was born in Manchester, New Hampshire, to Franco-American parents. A rebel against her origins, she was also affected by her matriarchal upbringing and an insecure family environment. Her first novel, *Peyton Place,* reveals her rebellion against her origins, but it is her last novel, *No Adam in Eden,* which provides the best insight into the adaptation of French Canadians to a new urban-industrial existence in New England. Matalious's life and literature serve as a reminder that ethnic identification can be "confining and disruptive, as well as warm and romantic." 4 illus., 55 notes. 1924-64

4741. Toth, Emily. FATHERLESS AND DISPOSSESSED: GRACE METALIOUS AS A FRENCH-CANADIAN WRITER. *J. of Popular Culture 1981 15(3): 28-38.* Biographical sketch of the development and maturation of novelist Grace Metalious's literary career and the autobiographical nature of her work. Although the import of her French-Canadian heritage had not fully resolved itself at the time her first novel *Peyton Place* (1956) was published, in her three subsequent novels it became closely linked to her self-conscious concerns with class, sex, and the female role. Based on interviews and other primary sources; 31 notes. 1924-64

Metcalf, George Stephen

4742. Gunnerson, Dolores A. and Gunnerson, James H. GEORGE STEPHEN METCALF, 1900-1975. *Plains Anthropologist 1977 22(75): 75-83.* George Stephen Metcalf (1900-1975) was born in a small Nebraska town, left school early and never acquired a college degree. He became interested in Indians and anthropology at an early age and never lost the interest through the harsh years that followed. His lack of education and inability to properly handle the language did not prevent him from publishing and becoming a well-known, successful anthropologist. He eventually worked for the Smithsonian Institution and won an honorary Doctor of Science degree. Photo, biblio. 1900-75

Metcalf, Keyes DeWitt

4743. Horner, S. J. SPOTLIGHTING A NONAGENARIAN ACHIEVER: KEYES DEWITT METCALF. *Wilson Lib. Bull. 1981 55(5): 353-357.* Reviews the life and career of Keyes DeWitt Metcalf (b. 1889), who was the librarian of Harvard College and director of the Harvard University Library (1937-55) and who is now writing a history of the New York Public Library. ca 1910-80

Metoyer, Augustin

4744. Mills, Gary B. A PORTRAIT OF ACHIEVEMENT: AUGUSTIN METOYER. *Red River Valley Hist. Rev. 1975 11(3): 333-348.* Augustin Metoyer, a freed slave from Natchitoches, established a plantation in the Red River Valley in Louisiana; covers the period 1792-1838. 1792-1838

Meurling, Emil

4745. Sallnäs, Marie-Louise. EMIL MEURLING AND *SVENSKA AMERIKANSKA POSTEN. Swedish Pioneer Hist. Q. 1981 32(1): 41-64.* Emil Meurling was born in Sweden in 1868 and emigrated to America in 1888 to avoid attending school. In Rockford, Illinois, he married and had two sons. During the mid-1890's, Meurling and family moved to Minneapolis to advance his journalistic ambitions. In 1902 he was hired to write for the *Svenska Amerikanska Posten,* becoming editor-in-chief in 1907. He spent 1911-18 in Nebraska, editing *Omaha Posten,* and 1927-30 as a freelance writer. He returned to Minneapolis and his editorial post at *SAP* until 1938. He died in 1939. This article accounts his life in periods, 1902-11, 1918-27, and 1930-38. The paper did not long survive his death. It merged with the *Svenska Amerikanaren Tribunen* in Chicago in 1940. 2 photos, 81 notes. 1888-1940

Meyer, Adolf

4746. Leys, Ruth. MEYER, WATSON, AND THE DANGERS OF BEHAVIORISM. *J. of the Hist. of the Behavioral Sci. 1984 20(2): 128-149.* Investigates the relationship between Adolf Meyer and John Watson, who were colleagues and collaborators at Johns Hopkins University. Focuses on three crucial episodes in the history of their association, culminating in the incident that forced Watson's departure from academic life. Their conflicts arose from the significant differences between Meyer's functional approach in psychiatry and Watson's behaviorist doctrines. 1908-20

Meyer, Agnes Ernst

4747. Hyland, Douglas K. S. AGNES ERNST MEYER, PATRON OF AMERICAN MODERNISM. *Am. Art J. 1980 12(1): 64-81.* While a young newspaper reporter in New York City, Agnes Ernst (1887-1970) met Alfred Stieglitz (1864-1946) and other leading young artists at Gallery 291; in 1908 she met Gertrude Stein (1874-1946) and the leading modern painters in Paris. After marriage to financier-banker Eugene Meyer, Jr., in 1910, Agnes Ernst Meyer devoted her considerable money, energy, and influence to nurturing public appreciation for modern art. She bought modern paintings and sculpture, helped organize shows in New York, and for a time ran the Modern Gallery in New York. She was among the earliest and most dedicated patrons of American modernism in the early 20th century. Based on Alfred Stieglitz Archives at Yale U.; 15 illus., 44 notes. 1907-20

Meyer, Albert Gregory

4748. Avella, Steven Mark. "Meyer of Milwaukee: The Life and Times of a Midwestern Archbishop." U. of Notre Dame 1985. 356 pp. *DAI 1985 45(12): 3727-A.* DA8502532 1920's-65

Meyer, Charles J. L.

4749. Worth, Jean. HERMANSVILLE: ECHOES OF A HARDWOOD EMPIRE. *Michigan Hist. 1981 65(2): 17-28.* Charles J. L. Meyer, a German immigrant who first settled in Fond du Lac, Wisconsin, later established a hardwood empire in Hermansville, Michigan. The family business, the Wisconsin Land and Lumber Company, operated until 1943. 26 photos. 1849-1943

Meyer, Daniel

4750. Hoexter, David F. and Hoexter, Mary R. DANIEL MEYER: SAN FRANCISCO BANKER. *Western States Jewish Hist. Q. 1980 12(3): 195-205.* Bavarian immigrant Daniel Meyer (1824-1911) came to San Francisco in 1851. He established himself in the tobacco business until 1857, when, with the help of his brothers, he founded the Bank of Daniel Meyer. Despite criticism that his busness methods had too much of the European ghetto manners, Meyer was a founder or member of several prestigious financial institutions and a well-known philanthropist. The Bank of Daniel Meyer was dissolved after his death. Based on family oral history and published sources; 3 photos, 39 notes. 1851-1911

Meyer, Frank N.

4751. Farney, Dennis. MEET THE MEN WHO RISKED THEIR LIVES TO FIND NEW PLANTS. *Smithsonian 1980 11(3): 128-140.* Since Matthew Perry opened Japan in 1853, American plant collectors have scoured foreign lands for plants to import as ornamentals or to improve agricultural lines. Among the most important collectors was the Agriculture Department's Frank N. Meyer, who introduced more than 1,000 species from China during 1890-1918. On the expedition during which he died, Meyer collected seeds from the callery pear, which were planted in the United States. In 1950, John Creech of the Agriculture Department, also a plant collector, found one of the trees, cloned it, and renamed it the Bradford pear. It has become a popular ornamental. 1890-1979

Meyer, Lawrence B.

4752. Gockel, Herman W. LORRY MEYER, THE MEMORABLE MAVERICK WHO LIFTED MISSOURI INTO THE 20TH CENTURY. *Concordia Hist. Inst. Q. 1981 54(2): 63-73.* Biography of Lawrence B. Meyer (d. 1977), who served as Director of Publicity and Missionary Education, Director of Publicity and Stewardship, Executive Director of the Emergency Planning Council, and Synodical Planning Counselor in the Missouri Synod of the Lutheran Church. 1915-77

Meyer, Mendel

4753. Kramer, William M. and Stern, Norton B. THE STORY OF AN UNUSUAL ORDINARY MAN: MENDEL MEYER OF LOS ANGELES AND SANTA MONICA. *Western States Jewish Hist. 1984 16(2): 167-173.* Presents a brief biographical sketch of German immigrant Mendel Meyer, a pioneer Los Angeles and Santa Monica businessman, best known as an amateur musician. Based primarily on newspaper accounts; 30 notes. 1853-98

Meyer, Robert

4754. Johnston, Paul I. FREEDOM OF SPEECH MEANS FREEDOM TO TEACH: THE CONSTITUTIONAL BATTLE IN NEBRASKA, 1919-1923. *Concordia Hist. Inst. Q. 1979 52(3): 118-124.* Recounts the background, trial, and results of Robert Meyer's instructing children in German, which was held to violate the Siman Act of 1919 requiring that all teaching in Nebraska be done in English. 1919-23

Michael, Philip Jacob

4755. Rapp, David H. PHILIP JACOB MICHAEL: ECCLESIASTICAL VAGABOND OR "ECHT REFORMIRTE" PASTOR. *Pennsylvania Folklife 1979 28(3): 14-26.* Though never ordained and considered a maverick by the Reformed German Church elders, Philip Jacob Michael, a weaver, missionary pastor, and chaplain to the First Battalion, Berks County Militia, gained the devotion of many Reformed congregations in the county, 1750-86; the author gives a brief biography, lists churches he served, and notes his contributions to the life and thought of the people whom he served. 1750-86

Michaelius, Jonas

4756. van Melle, J. J. Ferdinand. IN SEARCH OF JONAS MICHAELIUS. *Halve Maen 1978 53(3): 1-2, 12-13, 17.* Jonas Michaelius (b. 1584), the first minister of the Reformed Dutch Church in America, arrived there in 1628. 1590's-1633

Micheaux, Oscar

4757. Peterson, Bernard L., Jr. THE FILMS OF OSCAR MICHEAUX: AMERICA'S FIRST FABULOUS BLACK FILMMAKER. *Crisis 1979 86(4): 136-141.* Between 1918 and 1948, Oscar Micheaux wrote, produced, and directed more than 40 feature films. He was born in Metropolis, Illinois on January 2, 1884. He wrote melodramatic novels and formed his own film company. He toured the nation with scripts, persuading theater managers to give him an advance against future bookings. He thus had capital and showdates before production. Given the limitations of finances, studio connections, inadequacy of equipment, distribution, and racial climate, Micheaux's initiative, aggressiveness, and success helped open doors for future black actors, screenwriters, and directors. 1913-48

Middleton, Henry

4758. Bergquist, Harold E., Jr. HENRY MIDDLETON AS POLITICAL REPORTER: THE UNITED STATES, THE NEAR EAST, AND EASTERN EUROPE, 1821-1829. *Historian 1983 45(3): 355-371.* The reports of Henry Middleton, US minister plenipotentiary in Russia during 1820-30, provide valuable insights into the Greek struggle for independence and the Russo-Turkish War of 1828-29. Middleton was as much a subtle spokesman for the Tsarist government as a political reporter; although inaccuracies were present in his reports, they never led the American government into compromising actions. 48 notes. 1821-29

Middleton, Peter

4759. Hershkowitz, Leo. POWDERED TIN AND ROSE PETALS: MYER MYERS, GOLDSMITH, AND PETER MIDDLETON, PHYSICIAN. *Am. Jewish Hist. 1981 70(4): 462-467.* 1758-75
For abstract see ***Myers, Myer***

Middleton, Troy Houston

4760. Lowry, Montecue J. TROY HOUSTON MIDDLETON: MILITARY EDUCATOR AND COMBAT COMMANDER. *Military Review 1985 65(10): 72-80.* Outlines the life and the two successful careers of Troy Houston Middleton. Middleton rose from army private in 1910 to the rank of major general in 1944, appointed commander of the VIII Corps in Europe. He had been a military instructor in 1924, and after World War II, he became president of Louisiana State University, retiring in 1962. He died in Baton Rouge in 1976. Based on interviews with Middleton's family and associates, and military histories; illus., 3 photos, 38 notes. 1910-76

Midgley, Thomas

4761. Leslie, Stuart W. THOMAS MIDGLEY AND THE POLITICS OF INDUSTRIAL RESEARCH. *Business Hist. Rev. 1980 54(4): 480-503.* Thomas Midgley was a distinguished industrial chemist employed by the General Motors Corp. for nearly three decades until his death in 1944. General Motors executives, notably Charles Kettering and Alfred Sloan, were skillful in suggesting research topics with commercial potential, yet also allowing Midgley some freedom to pursue the theoretical aspects of research. The scientist's enthusiasm and morale thus remained high. The case shows that the management of industrial research involves special personnel problems that must be deftly administered. Based largely on the Charles Kettering Papers and on industry publications; illus., 72 notes. 1916-44

Midsuno, Henry Signaro

4762. Zimmerman, E. C. HENRY SIGNARO MIDSUNO: A JAPAN MISSION IN 1895? *Concordia Hist. Inst. Q. 1981 54(3): 102-112.* Biography of Henry Signaro Midsuno (1870-1933); born in Japan and educated at Concordia College in Ft. Wayne, Indiana, he returned to Japan in 1895 as a Lutheran missionary and eventually converted to Catholicism. 1870-1933

Miessler, Ernst G. H.

4763. Miessler, Ernst Gustav Herman and Miessler, H. C., transl. PIONEER LUTHERAN MISSIONARY TO THE CHIPPEWAS: AUTOBIOGRAPHY OF E. G. H. MIESSLER (1826-1916). *Concordia Hist. Inst. Q. 1979 52(4): 146-174.* Silesia-born Ernst Gustav Herman Miessler emigrated to Michigan in 1851 and evangelized among the Chippewa Indians until 1871. 1851-71

Mifflin, Lloyd

4764. Fahlman, Betsy. COLUMBIA SUBLIME: THE COLLABORATION OF THOMAS MORAN AND LLOYD MIFFLIN. *J. of the Lancaster County Hist. Soc. 1980 84(4): 167-178.* Biographies of 19th-century American landscape painter Thomas Moran, and his former student and friend, artist-turned-poet Lloyd Mifflin, focusing on the collaboration of the two men in the production of 19 illustrations by Moran to accompany several volumes of poetry written by Mifflin during the 1890's. 1837-1921

4765. Guntharp, Matthew. THE YOUNG LLOYD MIFFLIN WRITES JOHN RUSKIN. *J. of the Lancaster County Hist. Soc. 1980 84(1): 10-16.* Brief introductory biography of American painter and poet Lloyd Mifflin (1846-1921), followed by a reprint of Mifflin's 1872 letter to John Ruskin regarding Ruskin's *The Elements of Drawing* in which he discussed John M. W. Turner's painting, particularly his watercolor of the "Bridge at Coblenz." 1872

4766. Richman, Irwin and Arnold, Ruth M. LLOYD MIFFLIN, PENNSYLVANIA PAINTER AND PHOTOGRAPHER. *Magazine Antiques 1984 126(2): 336-345.* Presents a biographical sketch of artist Lloyd Mifflin, whose interests also included poetry. 1846-1921

Mikak

4767. Taylor, J. Garth. THE TWO WORLDS OF MIKAK. *Beaver [Canada] 1983 314(3): 4-13; 1984 314(4): 18-25.* Part 1. In 1767, Mikak, a young Inuit woman, was kidnapped with her son and taken to England. After a brief stay, she was returned to her people. Subsequently, Mikak exercised significant control over her people—in part because of her wealth and her knowledge of "other nations," and partly because of her intelligence. Her influence was a significant factor in the success of the Moravian missionaries in southern Labrador. Part 2. Established as a Moravian mission station, Nain has been called the "Eskimo capital of Labrador." Instrumental in its founding and early history was Mikak, who had previously been taken to England by the missionary. Details of her stormy marriage to Tuglavina, a baleen trader, her widowhood, and subsequent remarriage provide a rare insight into 18th-century Inuit life. 12 photos, map. 1771-95

Mikhailov, Pavel

4768. Shur, L. A. and Pierce, R. A. PAVEL MIKHAILOV: ARTIST IN RUSSIAN AMERICA. *Alaska J. 1978 8(4): 360-363.* Pavel Mikhailov (1786-1840), during his trip on the *Moller* (1826-29) as the M. N. Staniokovich expedition artist, painted and sketched scenes and natives. Describes his life and gives some history of the pictures. 7 illus., 3 notes. 1826-29

Miles, Emma Bell

4769. Edwards, Grace Toney. "Emma Bell Miles: Appalachian Author, Artist, and Interpreter of Folk Culture." U. of Virginia 1981. 325 pp. *DAI 1982 42(8): 3599-A.* 8201481 1904-19

Miles, Nelson A.

4770. Utley, Robert M. GEN. NELSON A. MILES. *By Valor & Arms 1978 3(3): 47-50.* Describes the military career and political aspirations of General Nelson A. Miles (1840-1925), Civil War hero and last commanding general of the Army. 1861-1925

Miley, Michael

4771. Salmon, Emily J. and Salmon, John S. GENERAL LEE'S PHOTOGRAPHER: MICHAEL MILEY, OF LEXINGTON. *Virginia Cavalcade 1983 33(2): 86-96.* After establishing his Lexington, Virginia, studio in 1866, Michael Miley became Robert E. Lee's principal photographer; he specialized in portraits and outdoor scenes and successfully experimented with color photography and dry-plate negatives. 1865-1918

Mill, John Stuart

4772. Pugh, Evelyn L. JOHN STUART MILL, HARRIET TAYLOR, AND WOMEN'S RIGHTS IN AMERICA, 1850-1873. *Can. J. of Hist. [Canada] 1978 13(3): 423-442.* Examines John Stuart Mill's writings on women, with respect to their reception in and their application to the American scene. Concentrates on the 1851 essay, "Enfranchisement of Women," and his 1869 book, *The Subjection of Women.* The former's authorship, though still disputed, is usually credited to Harriet Taylor, whom he married in 1851. It was published anonymously in the *Westminster Review,* summarizing the activities of the 1850 National Women's Rights Convention at Worcester, Massachusetts, and predicting its continuing influence. Mill became better known as a champion of women's rights during and following his election to parliament in 1866. However, his book was more theoretical than practical, and so hardly the helpful guide in the American feminist movement it otherwise might have been; nor was it as influential as the essay. 78 notes. ca 1850-73

Millard, Peggy

4773. Millard, Peggy. COMPANY WIFE. *Beaver [Canada] 1985 315(4): 30-39.* Since 1949, the course of Peggy Millard's life has been determined in many ways by the Hudson's Bay Company and its policies because her husband, Bert, is in their employ. She recounts their years in Vancouver, Edmonton, Montreal, Winnipeg, and Toronto. The relocation problems encountered by the author and her children are discussed, as are social changes in Canada over the last 35 years. 10 photos. 1949-85

Millay, Edna St. Vincent

4774. Minot, Walter S. MILLAY'S "UNGRAFTED TREE": THE PROBLEM OF THE ARTIST AS WOMAN. *New England Q. 1975 48(2): 260-269.* Examines the biographical implications of Edna St. Vincent Millay's "Sonnets from an Ungrafted Tree," stating that the sonnets are a symbolic attempt, perhaps subconscious, to murder her father; shows how her unresolved psychological conflicts led to her later severe neurosis, possibly disabling her both as a poet and as a person, thus reflecting the problem of the woman as artist in America. 1910-50

Miller, Alfred Jacob

4775. Tyler, Ron. ARTIST ON THE OREGON TRAIL: ALFRED JACOB MILLER. *Am. West 1981 18(6): 48-56.* Alfred Jacob Miller (1810-74) was commissioned as the artist to accompany a supply caravan to the 1837 American Fur Company rendezvous of the Rocky Mountain fur trappers. His hundreds of watercolors, drawings, and captions constitute the best account of the 1837 trip along what later came to be known as the Oregon Trail. Miller was the first to document the mountains, the fur trade, and the farther western posts of the trail, as well as the rendezvous itself. Miller produced finished watercolors and oils from the original sketches for the rest of his life. They were widely exhibited in eastern American cities before going to a castle in Scotland, the home of his patron. 11 illus., note, biblio. 1837-74

Miller, Anne Fitzhugh

4776. Huff, Robert A. ANNE MILLER AND THE GENEVA POLITICAL EQUALITY CLUB, 1897-1912. *New York History 1984 65(4): 324-348.* Among the many reform-minded people who lived and worked in western New York during the 19th and early 20th centuries were Elizabeth Smith Miller and her daughter, Anne Fitzhugh Miller. Elizabeth, daughter of Gerrit Smith and cousin of Elizabeth Cady Stanton, was well known by the time the family moved to Geneva in 1869. By the 1890's, Anne had also become active in reform causes, especially the suffrage movement. Both mother and daughter also were interested in spiritualism. Anne was instrumental in forming the Geneva Political Equality Club, of which Elizabeth was honorary president until her death in 1911. The influence of the club was widespread over the next decade and continued to be an important factor in the suffrage movement until New York passed its equal suffrage amendment in 1917. Anne, however, did not live to see its ultimate success; she died suddenly in 1912. Based mostly on newspaper and magazine articles; 4 illus., 49 notes. 1897-1912

Miller, Dean

4777. Watkins, William H. DEAN MILLER OF LITTLE FALLS, NEW YORK: A MOHAWK VALLEY SLAVE. *Journal of the Afro-American Historical and Genealogical Society 1984 5(2): 55-60.* Gives details of the life and genealogy of Dean Miller (1802-76), a black woman born into slavery at Little Falls, New York. 1760-1876

Miller, Elizabeth Smith

4778. Huff, Robert A. ANNE MILLER AND THE GENEVA POLITICAL EQUALITY CLUB, 1897-1912. *New York History 1984 65(4): 324-348.* 1897-1912
*For abstract see **Miller, Anne Fitzhugh***

Miller, Frieda Segelke

4779. Wallace, Teresa Ann. "Frieda Segelke Miller: Reformer and Labor Law Administrator, 1889-1973." Boston U. Grad. School 1983. 221 pp. *DAI 1983 44(5): 1553-A.* DA8320021 1917-73

Miller, Glenn

4780. McCoy, Maureen. GLENN MILLER, BIG BAND SENSATION. *Palimpsest 1981 62(6): 181-185.* Biography of bandleader Glenn Miller, born Alton Glenn Miller in 1904 in Iowa, where he spent the first five years of his life, focusing on his musical career, which ended tragically in 1944 in a plane crash. 1904-44

Miller, Henry

4781. Bartlett, Jeffrey M. "The Advance: William Carlos Williams and Henry Miller, American Modernists." U. of Iowa 1980. 322 pp. *DAI 1980 41(4): 1585-A.* 8021999 ca 1921-39

Miller, Joaquin

4782. White, Bruce A. THE LIBERAL STANCES OF JOAQUIN MILLER. *Rendezvous 1983 19(1): 86-94.* The writer and journalist Joaquin Miller, born Cincinnatus Hiner Miller, was known for his unconventional lifestyle and support of liberal causes during his literary career. Miller's liberal reputation was acquired mainly from his writings concerning American Indians and other minorities. A close inspection of his works indicates that Miller had ambivalent feelings toward the Indians and that his writings serve as an example of the divided self and its opposing forces, an important aspect of American literature. Primary sources; 35 notes. 1870's-1913

Miller, John William

4783. Brockway, George P. JOHN WILLIAM MILLER. *Am. Scholar 1980 49(2): 236-240.* The author, chairman of W. W. Norton Company, Inc., reminisces about John William Miller, his former philosophy teacher at Williams College in Williamstown, Massachusetts. Miller was a demanding teacher totally devoted to philosophy and to his students. John William Miller (d. 1978) permanently changed the life of Brockway and at least 300 other students. Miller was the ideal teacher at this ideal undergraduate college, 1924-60. 1924-78

Miller, Kelly

4784. McGruder, Larry. "Kelly Miller: The Life and Thought of a Black Intellectual, 1863-1939." Miami U. 1984. 161 pp. *DAI 1985 46(2): 506-A.* DA8509022 1890's-1939

Miller, Lewis

4785. McCabe, Carol. THE WORLD OF LEWIS MILLER. *Early American Life 1985 16(4): 24-31, 66-67.* Traces the life and work of folk artist Lewis Miller, who sketched everyday life in rural America. 1796-1882

Miller, Perry

4786. Lynn, Kenneth S. PERRY MILLER. *Am. Scholar 1983 52(2): 221-227.* Presents personal narratives in tribute to US historian Perry Miller. He studied intellectual history and American literature, and was among the most popular teachers at colleges and universities after World War II. 1930's-40's

Miller, Polk

4787. Seroff, Doug. POLK MILLER AND THE OLD SOUTH QUARTETTE. *JEMF Q. 1982 28(67-68): 147-150.* Discusses the career of Polk Miller and the Old South Quartette of Richmond, Virginia, who, from 1899 to 1912, sang songs evoking Southern plantation life. 1899-1912

Miller, Samuel Howard

4788. Seaburg, Alan. "THE KIND AND LIBERAL SPIRIT": SAMUEL HOWARD MILLER. *Am. Baptist Q. 1982 1(1): 74-80.* A brief biography of American Baptist Samuel Howard Miller, focusing on his career as dean of Harvard University Divinity School. Photo, 18 notes. 1920-68

Miller, William Rickarby

4789. Corbin, Alexandra K. WILLIAM RICKARBY MILLER: 19TH-CENTURY LANDSCAPE PAINTER. *Art & Antiques 1983 6(3): 64-71.* Briefly recounts the career of landscape artist William Rickarby Miller from the 1830's to 1893, and reproduces examples of his work. 1830's-93

Miller, Zack

4790. Gossard, Wayne H., Jr. THREE RING CIRCUS: THE ZACK MILLER-TOM MIX LAWSUITS, 1929-1934. *Chronicles of Oklahoma 1980 58(1): 3-16.* In April 1929, cowboy film star Tom Mix allegedly entered into a verbal agreement with Zack Miller to join the latter's 101 Ranch Real Wild West Show. Miller initiated a breach of contract suit when Mix subsequently signed with the rival Sells-Floto Circus. Hounded by the complicated legal procedures, Mix settled out of court in December 1934, but the $9,500 came too late to save Miller's 101 Ranch and the Wild West Show from bankruptcy. Based on archives of Miller Brothers' 101 Ranch; 6 photos, 31 notes. 1929-34

Milligan, James

4791. Roth, Randolph A. THE FIRST RADICAL ABOLITIONISTS: THE REVEREND JAMES MILLIGAN AND THE REFORMED PRESBYTERIANS OF VERMONT. *New England Q. 1982 55(4): 540-563.* In 1819 Reverend James Milligan, pastor of the Reformed Presbyterian Church of Ryegate, Vermont, stood alone as an advocate of the immediate, unconditional abolition of slavery and the full integration of blacks into American society. Traces Milligan's life from his birth in Scotland in 1785 to his coming to Ryegate in 1816; the history of his congregation, the Scottish "Covenanters" of the Upper Connecticut River Valley, and their antagonists, the Reformed and Associate Presbyterian Seceders; and Milligan's efforts, particularly his *Narrative* (1819), to thwart any attempts by the Seceders and Covenanters to unite and settle their doctrinal differences. Based on primary sources; 32 notes. 1785-1820

Millikan, Robert A.

4792. Kargon, Robert H. TEMPLE TO SCIENCE: COOPERATIVE RESEARCH AND THE BIRTH OF THE CALIFORNIA INSTITUTE OF TECHNOLOGY. *Hist. Studies in the Physical Sci. 1977 8: 3-31.* 1908-27
*For abstract see **Hale, George E.***

4793. Kargon, Robert H. THE CONSERVATIVE MODE: ROBERT A. MILLIKAN AND THE TWENTIETH-CENTURY REVOLUTION IN PHYSICS. *Isis 1977 68(244): 509-526.* Robert A. Millikan was trained in classical physics, but began his professional career during a decade marked by striking pronouncements from Becquerel, Curie, Planck, and Einstein. His research tended to bridge these two professional worlds. His creativity, important in its own way, was of the conservative or convergent type rather than the divergent type which could produce revolutionary new theories. Photo, 92 notes. 1895-1925

Mills, C. Wright

4794. Garrigan-Burr, Sara Margaret. "C. Wright Mills: His Political Perspective and Its Pragmatic Sources." U. of California, Riverside 1977. 220 pp. *DAI 1978 38(12): 7529-A.* 1940's-60's

4795. Gillam, Richard Davis. "C. Wright Mills, 1916-1948: An Intellectual Biography." Stanford U. 1972. *DAI 1978 39(1): 406-A.* 1916-48

4796. Jones, Robert Paul. "The Fixing of Social Belief: The Sociology of C. Wright Mills." U. of Missouri, Columbia 1977. 362 pp. *DAI 1978 38(8): 5085-5086-A.* 20c

Mills, Enos A.

4797. Abbott, Carl. THE ACTIVE FORCE: ENOS A. MILLS AND THE NATIONAL PARK MOVEMENT. *Colorado Mag. 1979 56(1-2): 56-73.* Examines the accomplishments and failures of Enos A. Mills (1870-1922) as a public figure. Mills, a widely known writer of magazine articles and 16 books, also operated Long's Peak Inn and was "an unpaid and self-appointed public servant." Often called the father of Rocky Mountain National Park, he was a sensitive observer and interpreter of the Colorado wilderness. Tragically, his deep convictions and stubbornness made it impossible for him to work amicably with other conservationists. Primary sources, including correspondence; 12 photos, 33 notes. ca 1902-22

4798. Abbott, Carl. "TO AROUSE INTEREST IN THE OUTDOORS": THE LITERARY CAREER OF ENOS MILLS. *Montana 1981 31(2): 2-15.* Enos Mills (1870-1922), a self-taught natural historian, had four related careers: mountain guide in Estes Park, Colorado; innkeeper, promoting Colorado tourism; lobbyist and spokesman for national parks; writer of books and articles on the outdoors. Mills found his greatest success as a writer. The author discusses his writings in depth, the influence of John Muir, Mills's activity in creating Rocky Mountain National Park, and his pioneering work with the nature guide concept in the national parks. His writings and career influenced the development of American attitudes toward nature. Based on Mills's writings, secondary sources, contemporary newspapers, and the Enos Mills Papers in the Denver Public Library; 11 illus., 49 notes. ca 1890-1922

Mills, James Dawkins

4799. Manning, Anita. JAMES D. MILLS: HILO BIRD COLLECTOR. *Hawaiian J. of Hist. 1978 12: 84-98.* James Dawkins Mills, a native of England, arrived in Honolulu from San Francisco in 1851, aged 35. He became proprietor of a dry goods store, which prospered. By signing the oath of allegiance to King Kamehameha IV he became eligible for government service. He died at his Hilo home in 1887. He was a collector of paintings, of curios, and, most importantly, of birds. At least 80 specimens in the Bishop Museum can be identified as part of Mills's Hawaiian bird collection: many are forest birds now rare or extinct. Mills not only brought the collection together but was the taxidermist as well, and was also the field collector of many of the Hawaiian birds. In 1876 the Mills bird cabinet was displayed in the centennial exhibit in Philadelphia. Gives a history of the Bishop Museum. Illus., 101 notes. 1851-87

Mills, Robert

4800. Ristow, Walter W. ROBERT MILL'S ATLAS OF SOUTH CAROLINA. *Q. J. of the Lib. of Congress 1977 34(1): 52-66.* Robert Mills designed private and public buildings, including the Washington Monument, in Philadelphia, Baltimore, and the District of Columbia. Some remain as monuments to his architectural genius. He served in the War of 1812 and became a major in the US Corps of Topographical Engineers before becoming a civil and military engineer for South Carolina. His 1825 *Atlas of South Carolina* was the first atlas of a separate state. Mills' "dedicated and self-sacrificing personal effort" to complete the compilation and publication of the atlas gave impetus to local and regional cartography in the early 19th century. Illus., 25 notes. 1825-65

Milton, George Fort

4801. Hodges, James A. GEORGE FORT MILTON AND THE ART OF HISTORY. *History Teacher 1985 18(2): 250-268.* A biographical essay on George Fort Milton, whose work as a historian extended from the mid 1920's through the 1940's, during most of which time he was also working as a newspaperman in Chattanooga, Tennessee. Focuses on Milton's role as a historian and his special approach to history as a nonacademic writing for a popular audience. Based on the Milton Papers in the Library of Congress; 60 notes. 1920-55

4802. Miller, George Arnold. "George Fort Milton: The Fight for TVA and the Loss of the Chattanooga *News*."Middle Tennessee State U. 1983. 269 pp. *DAI 1984 44(11): 3468-A.* DA8404786 1920's-39

Milutinovich, Vido Markov

4803. Hart, Mary Nicklanovich. MERCHANT AND MINER: TWO SERBS IN EARLY BISBEE. *J. of Arizona Hist. 1980 21(3): 313-334.* 1874-1942
*For abstract see **Angius, Ivo Vasov***

Minifie, William

4804. Baxley, C. Herbert. TRAVEL IN THE 1830'S: THE DIARY OF WILLIAM MINIFIE. *Maryland Hist. Mag. 1983 78(4): 287-296.* William Minifie, born in Devonshire, England, came to Baltimore in 1828 at the age of 23 and became within a short time one of the city's most prominent citizens, a member of the Maryland Academy of Science and Literature, a master architect and builder, and a professor of drawing at the Maryland Mechanical Institute. Reproduces entries from his detailed diary for trips he and his wife took to the West via Ohio and the Niagara region in 1834, and to Boston in 1835; they are replete with details of conveyances, lodgings, prices, sights, and scenes of Jacksonian America. 9 notes. 1828-78

Minnich, Harvey C.

4805. Twohy, David Wilson. "Harvey C. Minnich: An Historical Study of the Man and His Work as Influences on the Teacher Training Unit of Miami University." Miami U. 1979. 298 pp. *DAI 1980 40(7): 3831-A.* 1903-29

Minor, Stephen

4806. Holmes, Jack D. L. STEPHEN MINOR: NATCHEZ PIONEER. *J. of Mississippi Hist. 1980 42(1): 17-26.* Stephen Minor was one of the outstanding pioneers along the Spanish-American frontier in the lower Mississippi Valley. Born in western Pennsylvania in 1760, Minor entered Spanish service in 1779. Traces Minor's career as a captain in the Spanish Army, as acting governor of Natchez, and as commandant of the Spanish post of Concordia. After the Natchez District became American, Minor, a successful planter and large slaveholder, continued to reside in the region and continued to furnish Spain information regarding American activities. He was instrumental in introducing cattle into the Natchez district and became one of the organizers and early presidents of the Bank of Mississippi. He also rendered aid to Americans in establishing trade and commercial enterprises along the lower Mississippi. Upon his death, 29 November 1815, the bulk of Minor's estate passed to his third wife, Catherine Lintot Minor. 1779-1815

Minor, William J.

4807. Keller, Mark A. HORSE RACING MADNESS IN THE OLD SOUTH: THE SPORTING EPISTLES OF WILLIAM J. MINOR OF NATCHEZ (1837-1860). *Journal of Mississippi History 1985 47(3): 165-185.* Overviews the life of William J. Minor and analyzes sporting articles Minor contributed to the New York periodical *Spirit of the Times.* A resident of Natchez, Mississippi, Minor was a connoisseur of horses and the owner of a stable of thoroughbreds. In his writings, he was frequently involved in debates with other racing experts on a wide variety of subjects dealing with horses. Based on the *Spirit of the Times* and on other primary and secondary sources; 49 notes. 1837-60

Minto, John

4808. Baker, Abner S., III. EXPERIENCE, PERSONALITY AND MEMORY: JESSE APPLEGATE AND JOHN MINTO RECALL PIONEER DAYS. *Oregon Hist. Q. 1980 81(3): 228-259.* 1840-88
For abstract see ***Applegate, Jesse***

4809. Cox, Thomas R. THE CONSERVATIONIST AS REACTIONARY: JOHN MINTO AND AMERICAN FOREST POLICY. *Pacific Northwest Q. 1983 74(4): 146-153.* John Minto actively challenged the conservation policies of Theodore Roosevelt and Gifford Pinchot. Minto believed that government interference in resource management would lead to waste and bureaucratic bungling. The nation should trust its vast forest lands to "forest farmers" who would purchase these lands through an extension of the homestead system. Individual owners could harvest minimal timber resources to supplement their agricultural pursuits and simultaneously guard this precious resource. Based on the John Minto Papers at the Oregon Historical Society and on newspapers; map, 5 photos, 28 notes. 1900-10

Minton, Sherman

4810. Corcoran, David Howard. "Sherman Minton: New Deal Senator." U. of Kentucky 1977. 519 pp. *DAI 1982 42(10): 4552-4553-A.* DA8129737 1935-41

4811. Hull, Elizabeth Anne. "Sherman Minton and the Cold War Court." New School for Social Research 1977. 441 pp. *DAI 1977 38(6): 3699-3700-A.* 1949-56

Minuit, Peter

4812. Gehring, Charles. PETER MINUIT'S PURCHASE OF MANHATTAN ISLAND: NEW EVIDENCE. *Halve Maen 1980 55(1): 6-7, 17.* New evidence indicates that Peter Minuit did not buy Manhattan Island from the Indians for $24, but rather that Willem Verhulst, Minuit's predecessor as director of the Dutch colony of New Netherland in 1626, bought the land; based on documents at the Huntington Library in California that were translated in 1924. 1626

Minville, Esdras

4813. Paradis, Ruth. ESDRAS MINVILLE ET LA PENSÉE COOPÉRATIVE IDÉOLOGIQUE AU QUÉBEC [Esdras Minville and ideological cooperative thought in Quebec]. *Action Natl. [Canada] 1979 69(2): 107-115.* While the Quebec cooperative movement began its greatest expansion in 1937, Esdras Minville had written of cooperatism as early as 1924, noting its success in England and Denmark. Minville was an activist as well as ideologist for the movement, having founded the first cooperative workshop in the Gaspé region. Reproaching French Canadians for their individualistic spirit, he used his positions as president of the Action Nationale, director of the École des Hautes Études, and editor of *L'Actualité Économique* to popularize the work of Lionel Groulx, Georges-Henri Lévesque, and Alphonse Desjardins. 18 notes. 1924-40

Miranda, Francisco de

4814. Salcedo-Bastardo, J. L. MIRANDA: DOSCIENTOS AÑOS DE TRABAJO POR LA LIBERTAD Y POR AMERICA [Miranda: 200 years of work for freedom and for America]. *Bol. de la Acad. Nac. de la Hist. [Venezuela] 1981 64(254): 264-278.* Francisco de Miranda was the first Latin American. During the 1781 campaign for Pensacola in the American Revolution, in which he took part, he conceived the ideas of a fatherland and America as a unit. He worked and fought for these ideas in Paris and in London as well as in America. Lecture read at a special session of the National Academy of History, Caracas, 7 May 1981. 1781

Mises, Ludwig von

4815. East, John P. AMERICAN CONSERVATIVE THOUGHT: THE IMPACT OF LUDWIG VON MISES. *Modern Age 1979 23(4): 338-350.* Ludwig von Mises (1881-1973) was an Austrian emigré and an American economist whose defense of the free market and advocacy of liberalism

were rallying points for conservatives. He opposed socialism, communism, positivism, and economic and political intervention. His defense of liberalism was predicated on the belief that the highest development of one's individuality occurs in interaction with society and in one's exercise of free choice. He supported representative government, championed capitalism, and opposed all forms of levelling. Based on Mises's writings and secondary sources; 114 notes.
ca 1910-73

Mishikinskwa

See Little Turtle

Mitchell, Billy

4816. Hall, George M. WHEN HONOR CONFLICTS WITH DUTY. *Air. U. Rev. 1980 31(6): 45-60.*
1884-1973

For abstract see ***Greely, Adolphus W.***

Mitchell, Clarence, Jr.

4817. Britton, John H., Jr. THE IMPACT OF PURE BRASS: CLARENCE MITCHELL, JR. *Crisis 1976 83(4): 122-126.* Clarence Mitchell was born in 1911 and raised in Baltimore. He graduated from Lincoln University in Pennsylvania. After covering stories on lynching and the trial of the Scottsboro boys for the Baltimore *Afro-American,* Mitchell enrolled in the Graduate School of Social Work at Atlanta University. From there his life was dedicated to public service on behalf of civil rights and liberties. Mitchell worked in government and the NAACP from the 1930's to the present and has always been a respected lobbyist. 1911-76

Mitchell, David Dawson

4818. Verdon, Paul E. DAVID DAWSON MITCHELL: VIRGINIAN ON THE WILD MISSOURI. *Montana 1977 27(2): 2-15.* David Dawson Mitchell (1806-1861) began his career in 1828 when he contracted with the American Fur Company for trade along the Missouri River. Because of his adaptability and business acumen, Mitchell served at a variety of posts as the American Fur Company's traveling troubleshooter for the Upper Missouri Outfit, becoming a full partner in 1835. He left the fur trade in 1840 and served as Superintendent of Indian Affairs at St. Louis between 1841 and 1843. In 1846 he enlisted as a lieutenant colonel in the Missouri Volunteers during the Mexican War. He played a significant part in several campaigns including the capture of Chihuahua. His friendship with Zachary Taylor and Taylor's election to the Presidency in 1848 resulted in Mitchell's restoration as Superintendent of Indian Affairs in St. Louis from 1849 to 1853. His major accomplishment was the Fort Laramie Treaty of 1851. In the remaining years before his death, Mitchell invested in transportation ventures, wrote about his Indian experiences, and helped supply the U.S. Army's 1858 expedition against the Mormons in Utah. Based on materials in the Missouri Historical Society; 20 illus., 8 notes. 1828-61

Mitchell, David (family)

4819. Armour, David A. DAVID AND ELIZABETH: THE MITCHELL FAMILY OF THE STRAITS OF MACKINAC. *Michigan Hist. 1980 64(4): 17-29.* David Mitchell, a surgeon's mate in the King's Eighth Regiment stationed at Mackinac Island in 1780 chose to resign his commission and remain there with his Indian wife. He became a farmer, trader and physician. His wife Elizabeth greatly aided his economic endeavors. Mitchell retained his British loyalty and moved from Michilimackinac to Mackinac Island, to St. Joseph Island, back to Mackinac Island, to Drummond Island and then to Penetanguishene on Georgian Bay, always following the Union Jack. Based on the Port Mackinac Papers located in the Judge Joseph H. Steere Special Collection Room of the Bayliss Public Library, Sault Ste. Marie, Michigan and other primary and secondary sources; 21 photos, map. 1780-1832

Mitchell, Don

4820. Mitchell, Roger E. "I'M A MAN THAT WORKS": THE BIOGRAPHY OF DON MITCHELL OF MERRILL, MAINE. *Northeast Folklore 1978 19: 9-130.* Entire volume devoted to the first 79 years of lumberman and farmer Don Mitchell (b. 1898) of Merrill, Maine; written by his son.
1898-1977

Mitchell, Dwike

4821. Zinsser, William. ON THE ROAD WITH DWIKE MITCHELL AND WILLIE RUFF. *Smithsonian 1984 15(2): 154-174.* Accompanies black jazz musicians Dwike Mitchell and Willie Ruff, the Mitchell-Ruff Duo, on their five-day visiting-artist tour of concert halls and public schools in Iowa and Illinois. 1955-84

Mitchell, James

4822. Ross, Frances Mitchell. JAMES MITCHELL, SPOKESMAN FOR WOMEN'S EQUALITY IN NINETEENTH CENTURY ARKANSAS. *Arkansas Hist. Q. 1984 43(3): 222-235.* Reviews briefly the changing attitudes about the role of women in Southern society, and highlights James Mitchell, who believed in and spoke for equal educational opportunities for women, as well as equal rights before the law. Based on Mitchell's correspondence and lectures, and secondary sources; 57 notes. 1860's-80's

Mitchell, John P.

4823. Perry, Clay. JOHN P. MITCHELL, VIRGINIA'S JOURNALIST OF REFORM. *Journalism Hist. 1977-78 4(4): 142-147, 156.* Examines the life and work of John P. Mitchell (1863-1929), editor of the *Richmond Planet,* and concentrates on his fight against racial discrimination.
ca 1883-1929

Mitchell, Lucy Sprague

4824. Antler, Joyce. FEMINISM AS LIFE-PROCESS: THE LIFE AND CAREER OF LUCY SPRAGUE MITCHELL. *Feminist Studies 1981 7(1): 134-157.* A case study of educator and researcher Lucy Sprague Mitchell (1878-1967) focuses on one individual's struggle for autonomy through confronting gender-defined issues throughout life. Feminism, viewed as an individual life process rather that a collective strategy, provides a humanistic approach to the historical record of the movement. Mitchell integrated the private and public spheres of life by combining full-time professional responsibilities with marriage and children. Her life reflected the dynamic mediation of the spheres on each other. Widowhood and retirement closed her main channels of fulfillment and produced bewilderment and despair. In old age, however, she broke the attachment to marriage, family, and work as identity sources, and revealed a new sense of self-worth and uniqueness in her poetry. Based on Mitchell's letters and her *Two Lives: The story of Wesley Clair Mitchell and Myself* and on periodicals; 36 notes. 1900-67

4825. Lambert, Pierre D. WOMEN IN EDUCATION: THE KNOWN, THE FORGOTTEN, THE UNKNOWN. *Vitae Scholasticae 1983 2(1): 93-112.* 19c-20c
*For abstract see **Beecher, Catherine***

4826. Matthews, Emily Pond. "Lucy Sprague Mitchell: A Deweyan Educator." Rutgers U. 1979. 209 pp. *DAI 1979 40(3): 1310-A.* 20c

Mitchell, Margaret

4827. Pyron, Darden Asbury. MARGARET MITCHELL: FIRST OR NOTHING. *Southern Q. 1982 20(3): 19-34.* A brief but careful look at the life of Margaret Mitchell, author of *Gone With the Wind,* to fill a gap between scholarly neglect and existing popular myths. Mitchell's statement that "If I can't be first, I'd rather be nothing," suggests the sources of her creative energy and demonstrates the impact of the problems she encountered as a woman in tradition-bound Southern society. Based on the Mitchell Papers at the University of Georgia. 1900-49

Mitchell, Maria

4828. Henderson, Janet Karen. "Four Nineteenth Century Professional Women." Rutgers U., New Brunswick 1982. 315 pp. *DAI 1982 43(3): 698-A.* DA8218323 19c

4829. Kohlstedt, Sally Gregory. MARIA MITCHELL: THE ADVANCEMENT OF WOMEN IN SCIENCE. *New England Q. 1978 51(1): 39-63.* Examines astronomer Mitchell's (1818-89) involvement in women's education, the Association for the Advancement of Women (AAW), and the AAW's Committee on Science. Her hope was to encourage women to become involved in science in order to provide them with "a unique intellectual challenge that could help them escape the narrowness of their lives." Focuses on 1870-89. Based on Mitchell's papers in the Maria Mitchell Science Library on Nantucket Island and on secondary sources; 74 notes. 1870-89

Mitchell, Morris R.

4830. Orser, W. Edward. MORRIS R. MITCHELL (1895-1976): SOCIAL AND EDUCATIONAL VISIONARY. *Appalachian J. 1977 4(2): 100-104.* Elaborates on the sociopolitical overtones in the teaching career and progressive educational theory of southern educator Morris R. Mitchell, for whom community and cooperation were the focus in life and in education. 1920's-76

Mitchell, S. Weir

4831. Fye, W. Bruce. S. WEIR MITCHELL, PHILADELPHIA'S "LOST" PHYSIOLOGIST. *Bull. of the Hist. of Medicine 1983 57(2): 188-202.* Although S. Weir Mitchell is better known for his work in neurology, he desperately wanted a chair of physiology. Mitchell graduated from Jefferson Medical College in 1850, then went to Europe where he was influenced by Claude Bernard. When he returned to America, Mitchell organized a physiological laboratory for research and student training. In 1863, Mitchell campaigned for the physiology chair at the University of Pennsylvania, and again in 1868 he campaigned for the same chair at Jefferson, both times unsuccessfully. Unable to secure a physiology chair, his research changed dramatically toward neurology. Based on records of Philadelphia medical schools and letters of Mitchell and others; 62 notes, 3 illus. 1850-1900

Mitchell, Thomas Duche

4832. Eberson, Frederick. CRUSADER EXTRAORDINARY: THOMAS DUCHE MITCHELL, 1791-1865. *Filson Club Hist. Q. 1978 52(3): 263-279.* Thomas Duche Mitchell was an early American doctor, medical school professor, and reformer. A graduate of the medical department of the University of Pennsylvania, Mitchell taught continuously at several schools during 1831-65. Teaching at Transylvania University medical school in Kentucky, he attempted to professionalize medicine on the frontier. At the same time Mitchell crusaded against the use of alcoholic beverages and tobacco. Based on Mitchell's published works and published biographical sketches; 31 notes. 1809-65

Mitford, Mary Russell

4833. Idol, John L., Jr. MARY RUSSELL MITFORD: CHAMPION OF AMERICAN LITERATURE. *Studies in the American Renaissance 1983: 313-334.* Mary Russell Mitford, a British writer often called the successor to Jane Austen, had a substantial reputation in her lifetime, due to the success of her five-volume work, *Our Village* (1824-32). As a young woman, she considered American literature "secondhand" and America a "pawnbrokers'-shop kind of nation." Always in financial straits resulting from her father's gambling debts, she accepted a publisher's offer to lend her famous name to an anthology of American literature. As she became more familiar with American writers, her initial repugnance yielded to admiration. She eventually published four anthologies of American literature and helped many American writers to publish. Based on the works and correspondence of Mitford and secondary sources; 111 notes. 1824-54

Mitropoulos, Dimitri

4834. Kostios, A. "Der Dinigent Dimitri Mitropoulos" [The conductor Dimitri Mitropoulos]. U. of Vienna [Austria] 1980. 429 pp. *DAI-C 1984 45(3): 592; 9/2394c.* 1920's-60

Mittelstaedt, Harold

4835. Middelstaedt, Robert A., ed. THE GENERAL STORE ERA: MEMOIRS OF ARTHUR AND HAROLD MITTELSTAEDT. *South Dakota Hist. 1978 9(1): 36-60.* Provides the 1975 reminiscences of Arthur and Harold Mittelstaedt who operated general stores in Milbank, South Dakota, 1800's-1943. 1880's-1943

Mix, Tom

4836. Gossard, Wayne H., Jr. THREE RING CIRCUS: THE ZACK MILLER-TOM MIX LAWSUITS, 1929-1934. *Chronicles of Oklahoma 1980 58(1): 3-16.* 1929-34
*For abstract see **Miller, Zack***

Miyakawa, T. Scott

4837. Sakata, Yasuo. IN MEMORIAM: T. SCOTT MIYAKAWA. *Amerasia J. 1981 8(2): v-viii.* Obituary of T. Scott Miyakawa, first director of the Japanese American Research Project. 1906-81

Mizner, Addison

4838. Calhoun, Charles. ADDISON MIZNER: GOLD COAST ARCHITECT. *Art & Antiques 1981 4(4): 72-75.* Brief biography of architect Addison Mizner, focusing on the Mediterranean-style homes, shops, and buildings he designed in Palm Beach, Florida, 1918-31. 1918-31

M'Kinnon, William Charles

4839. Davis, G. WILLIAM CHARLES M'KINNON—CAPE BRETON'S SIR WALTER SCOTT. *Collections of the Royal Nova Scotia Hist. Soc. [Canada] 1982 41: 21-46.* William Charles M'Kinnon of North Sydney, Cape Breton, was for a short time the most active author of romantic literature in Nova Scotia, publishing six historical novels and much poetry. The relatively lukewarm public reception to his literary efforts forced him to reevaluate his choice of careers. He became interested in the Methodist Church, and was ordained as a cleric in 1857. From his new career, he "looked back on his fiction-writing career as a frivolous and embarrassing period in his life." 109 notes. 1844-52

Mobley, Hardy (family)

4840. Richardson, Joe M. "LABOR IS REST TO ME HERE IN THIS THE LORD'S VINEYARD": HARDY MOBLEY, BLACK MISSIONARY DURING RECONSTRUCTION. *Southern Studies 1983 22(1): 5-20.* Hardy Mobley, born a slave in Georgia, later bought his freedom and moved to New York to be educated and become a Congregational minister. After the Civil War, he labored in Georgia, Missouri, and Louisiana as a missionary and teacher for the American Missionary Association. On a meager salary, he and his daughters taught, visited the sick, tended the dying, and helped fellow blacks in every way possible. Despite his selfless activities, Mobley was eventually dismissed from the association for political reasons. Based on records in the American Missionary Association Archives, Amistad Research Center, New Orleans, Louisiana; 54 notes. 1865-77

Moczygemba, Leopold

4841. Baker, T. Lindsay. THE REVEREND LEOPOLD MOCZYGEMBA, PATRIARCH OF POLONIA. *Polish Am. Studies 1984 41(1): 66-109.* Portrays Father Leopold Moczygemba as being more than the reputed founder of the first permanent Polish-American settlement in Panna Marya, Texas. Credits Father Moczygemba with the origination of Franciscan churches and friaries in the eastern United States, the establishment of several Roman Catholic parishes, helping found the Polish Roman Catholic Union (a fraternal lodge), and helping found the Polish Seminary in Orchard Lake, Michigan. Based on English-, Polish-, German-, and French-language sources; 86 notes. 1824-91

Modesto, Ruby Eleanor

4842. Wilke, Philip J. MEMORIAL TO RUBY ELEANOR MODESTO (1913-1980). *J. of California and Great Basin Anthrop. 1980 2(1): 6-7.* Brief remembrance of Ruby Eleanor Modesto (1913-80), anthropological consultant on Desert Cahuilla culture. ca 1935-80

Moffat, David H., Jr.

4843. Mehls, Steven Frederick. "David H. Moffat, Jr.: Early Colorado Business Leader." U. of Colorado, Boulder 1982. 372 pp. *DAI 1983 43(7): 2426-A.* DA8229853 1859-1911

Moffatt, James (family)

4844. Jackson, Elva E. SOME OF NORTH SYDNEY'S LOYALISTS. *Nova Scotia Hist. Rev. [Canada] 1983 3(2): 5-22.* Traces the history of several Loyalists who settled in North Sydney to escape persecution during the American Revolution. The new settlers engaged in shipbuilding, trading, and transport of goods. Genealogies of five families are included: Peter Sparling, from Ireland; Bartholomew Musgrave, from England; Adam Moore, from Scotland; and James Moffatt and John Ross, from Rhode Island. Primary sources; 26 notes. 1776-1864

Mohrbacher, Ellen Whitmore

4845. Pieroth, Doris Hinson. THE ONLY SHOW IN TOWN: ELLEN WHITMORE MOHRBACHER'S SAVOY THEATRE. *Chronicles of Oklahoma 1982 60(3): 260-279.* A daughter of Oklahoma pioneers, Ellen Whitmore Mohrbacher raised a family and maintained a flourishing movie theater business following her husband's death in 1918. She purchased the failing Savoy Theatre in Prague, Oklahoma, during 1921 and transformed it into a regal entertainment center, complete with all the latest equipment and movies. Mohrbacher personally booked all films and refused those she considered to be of questionable moral value. In 1943, her theater hosted the world premier of *Hangmen Also Die.* Business gradually declined in the 1950's due to competition from television, and the theater was sold in 1958. Based on a 1981 interview with Ellen Mohrbacher; 5 photos, 53 notes. 1921-58

Moisant, Mathilde

4846. Potter, Frank N. SWAN SONG FLIGHT OF MISS MATHILDE. *Aviation Q. 1979 5(2): 182-189.* Chronicles a flying exhibition, crash, and rescue of Mathilde Moisant, the world's first licensed woman air pilot, in Wichita Falls, Texas, 1912. 1912

Molchert, William

4847. Molchert, William; James, Jon G., ed. SERGEANT MOLCHERT'S PERILS: SOLDIERING IN MONTANA. *Montana 1984 34(2): 60-65.* In 1919, William Molchert wrote an account of his service as a sergeant with the frontier army to corroborate his application for a military pension. He briefly described his enlistment and routine garrison duty. Assigned to the 7th Infantry, US, he served at Fort Shaw, Montana, in the 1870's. His company participated in the Sioux campaign of 1876, and he was assigned to Cow Island at the time the Nez Percé under Chief Joseph crossed the Missouri River there in 1877. Based on William Molchert's pension files, Old Army-Navy Branch, Record Group 94, and secondary sources; 3 photos, illus., map, 26 notes. 1870-80

Moller, Melvin K.

4848. Moller, Melvin K. THE FIRST FIFTY-FIVE IN FAIRVIEW. *Oregon Hist. Q. 1983 84(1): 56-92.* Personal narrative by Melvin K. Moller about growing up in Fairview, Oregon, a small agricultural community in the eastern part of Multnomah County. Fairview's location on the Union Pacific Railway system was due to the availability of railroad ties from the nearby forests. Moller tells of many of his youthful experiences in a preurban society, including early schooling in a two-room school, recreational activities for boys, community activities, and work experiences. Based on parts of Moller's manuscript, Oregon Historical Society, Portland; 7 photos, map. 1907-27

Molloy, Mary Aloysius

4849. Kennelly, Karen. MARY MOLLOY: WOMEN'S COLLEGE FOUNDER. Stuhler, Barbara and Kreuter, Gretchen, ed. *Women of Minnesota: Selected Biographical Essays* (St. Paul: Minnesota Historical Society Press, 1977): 116-135. Born on 14 June 1880, in Sandusky, Ohio, Mary

Aloysia Molloy grew up as the only child of Irish Catholic immigrant parents. In an age when few women attended college, Molloy earned her way through Ohio State University and graduated, in 1903, with more honors than anyone else up to that time. She went on to earn a master's degree and election to Phi Beta Kappa at Ohio State. In 1907 she earned her doctorate at Cornell. That same year, she began her career as a Catholic college educator in Winona, Minnesota, when she accepted a job with the Franciscan Sisters who, under the leadership of Sister Leo Tracy, were creating the liberal arts College of St. Teresa. The two women persevered and successfully established and administered the new collegiate institution for Catholic lay and religious women. Molloy was unique as the lay dean of a Catholic college, but in 1922 she became a nun, Sister Mary Aloysius Molloy, and in 1928 became the college president. As an educator, Molloy worked hard to improve the quality of women's education, wrestled with the unique problems of Catholic colleges, and carefully oversaw the development of her own school. By 1946, when she retired, the college was a firmly established institution producing outstanding graduate women. One of the last among the heroic generation of founders of Minnesota women's colleges, Molloy died on 27 September 1954. Primary and secondary sources; photo, 48 notes. 1903-54

Monaghan, Jay

4850. Dilliard, Irving. HISTORIAN IN COWBOY BOOTS: JAY MONAGHAN, 1893-1980. *J. of the Illinois State Hist. Soc. 1981 74(4): 261-278.* James Jay Monaghan died on 11 October 1980. A graduate of Swarthmore College, he participated in the 1911 Mexican Revolution. In 1939, he was appointed research editor at the Illinois State Historical Society. In 1945, he became State Historian, librarian of the state historical library, and secretary-treasurer of the historical society. In 1951, he left Illinois to accept a fellowship at the Huntington Library and, in 1953, a position as special consultant to the Wyles Collection of Lincolniana, at the University of California, Santa Barbara. Provides a chronological list of publications. 8 illus., biblio. 1939-53

4851. Planck, Gary R. JAMES JAY MONAGHAN IV: 1891-1980. *Lincoln Herald 1980 82(4): 554.* An obituary on James Jay Monaghan IV, noted expert on Lincoln's life and writings, during the last three decades a Fellow at the Huntington Library in San Marino and a consultant to the Wyles Collection of Lincolniana at the University of California, Santa Barbara. ca 1910-80

Mondale, Walter F.

4852. Furlong, William Barry. MONDALE'S MINNESOTA. *Horizon 1977 20(2): 66-74.* Discusses Minnesota's natural resources and farm beauty, and gives a biography of Vice-President Walter F. Mondale (b. 1928), focusing on his boyhood and political career, and changes for him and his home state. 1928-77

Moniac, David

4853. Griffith, Benjamin. LT. DAVID MONIAC, CREEK INDIAN: FIRST MINORITY GRADUATE OF WEST POINT. *Alabama Hist. Q. 1981 43(2): 99-110.* David Moniac, a Creek Indian, was the first minority student to graduate from West Point. His life as a cadet and his service in the army following graduation are discussed. Based on US Military Academy Archives and other sources; 44 notes. 1817-36

Monroe, James

4854. Gayle, Margot. CAST-IRON MASTERPIECE: GOTHIC REVIVAL TOMB OF PRESIDENT JAMES MONROE. *Nineteenth Cent. 1981 7(2): 62-64.* In 1858, James Monroe's remains were moved from New York City to Richmond, Virginia, and reburied; the place is marked by an iron monument of Gothic Revival style. 1840's-50's

4855. Peltier, Michel. JAMES MONROE, L'HOMME D'UNE DOCTRINE [James Monroe, man of a doctrine]. *Ècrits de Paris [France] 1979 (387): 76-82.* A brief biography and review of James Monroe's political career, focusing on the Monroe Doctrine and its ramifications. 1823-31

Monroe, Marilyn

4856. Swenson-David, Anna Marcia. "From Sex Queen to Cultural Symbol: An Interpretation of the Image of 'Marilyn Monroe.' " U. of Michigan 1980. 337 pp. *DAI 1980 41(4): 1676-A.* DA8017378 1930-80

Montagu-Dunk, George

4857. Greiert, Steven G. THE EARL OF HALIFAX AND THE SETTLEMENT OF NOVA SCOTIA, 1749-1753. *Nova Scotia Hist. Rev. [Canada] 1981 1(1): 4-23.* George Montagu-Dunk, 2d Earl of Halifax, was president of the British Board of Trade from 1748 to 1761. An offer of free transportation, arms, tools, food supplies for one year and free land grants to anyone wishing to settle in Nova Scotia resulted in 1,400 emigrants for the town of Halifax. Other settlers from Germany and Switzerland came to the area; in 1752 the colony had a population of 4,000. Edward Cornwallis became the first civilian governor of Nova Scotia in 1749. The Earl of Halifax sought to restore imperial authority in colonial government, and his efforts greatly influenced British policy. 40 notes. 1749-53

Montell, William Lynwood

4858. McKinney, Gordon B. THE WORLD OF WILLIAM LYNWOOD MONTELL. *Appalachian J. 1984 11(3): 255-259.* Surveys the work of oral historian William Lynwood Montell, who in his three books has illuminated the black and white cultures of Appalachia. 1865-1940's

Monteux, Pierre

4859. Lipman, Samuel. A CONDUCTOR IN HISTORY. *Commentary 1984 77(1): 50-56.* Reviews the career and musical recordings of conductor Pierre Monteux. 1913-60

Montezuma, Carlos

4860. Iverson, Peter. CARLOS MONTEZUMA. Edmunds, R. David, ed. *American Indian Leaders: Studies in Diversity* (Lincoln: U. of Nebraska Pr., 1980): 206-221. Carlos Montezuma (ca. 1865-1923) was born in southern Arizona. Like many other acculturated Indian leaders at the turn of the century, Montezuma was torn between an adherence to white values and a loyalty to Mohave-Apache, or Yavapai, heritage. Though educated, urbane, and progressive, he was drawn back to the tribal communities. Concerned about substandard economic and health conditions on the reservations, he blamed the Bureau of Indian Affairs and lashed out at the government through his newspaper, *Wassaja.* He died in 1923. 28 notes. 1892-1923

Montgomery, Alfred

4861. Hamilton, Henry W. and Hamilton, Jean Tyree. ALFRED MONTGOMERY: ITINERANT MIDWESTERN ARTIST, 1857-1922. *Missouri Hist. Soc. Bull. 1978 34(2): 69-82.* Describes the paintings of Alfred Montgomery (1857-1922) and briefly chronicles his wanderings among the ordinary folk of the Midwest. There his paintings adorned many hotel lobbies and other commercial establishments. Considered the "corn artist" by admirers, Montgomery's paintings usually featured corn, farm products, or farming scenes. 8 photos, 54 notes. 1857-1922

Montgomery, David

4862. —. ONCE UPON A SHOP FLOOR: AN INTERVIEW WITH DAVID MONTGOMERY. *Radical Hist. Rev. 1980 (23): 37-53.* Interview with Communist militant David Montgomery, a factory worker, union organizer, and active Communist during the 1950's who turned to scholarship in the 1960's to become a foremost radical historian; his credits include *Beyond Equality* (1967) and *Workers Control in America* (1979). ca 1950-80

Montgomery, James

4863. Bumsted, J. M. SIR JAMES MONTGOMERY AND PRINCE EDWARD ISLAND, 1767-1803. *Acadiensis [Canada] 1978 7(2): 76-102.* Considers the investments and business matters of James Montgomery, one of the "most active and considerable" of Prince Edward Island's absentee proprietors. 1767-1803

Montgomery, John J.

4864. George, Weston. WESTERN AVIATOR JOHN MONTGOMERY. *Am. West 1981 18(4): 48-54, 66-67.* With the aid of his brother, John Montgomery (1858-1911) made the first controlled winged flight in history. The some 600-foot flight was made in a 40-pound glider, which the brothers had constructed from ash wood, spruce, and oiled muslin. He made this and several other successful flights on the same day, 28 August 1883, from a hilltop near San Diego, California. He continued designing and experimenting with other craft until an accident took his life while he was testing a new monoplane with adjustable wings. 7 illus., biblio. 1883-1911

4865. Weston, George. THE STORY OF JOHN JOSEPH MONTGOMERY. *Aviation Q. 1979 5(3): 246-267.* A flight in California in 1883 by John J. Montgomery (1858-1911), designer, builder, and flyer, may have been the first in a controlled, self-launched hang glider. 1880's-1911

Montizambert, Frederick

4866. Bilson, Geoffrey. DR. FREDERICK MONTIZAMBERT (1843-1929): CANADA'S FIRST DIRECTOR GENERAL OF PUBLIC HEALTH. *Medical History [Great Britain] 1985 29(4): 386-400.* Due to his own personality and the limited official interest in public health in the early 20th century, Frederick Montizambert has not gotten the recognition he deserves. Attractive, socially prominent, and well educated, he was likely to succeed in private practice, but despite limited opportunities, he preferred public health. He took a post as a quarantine officer and devoted his career to improving procedures first at his station, Grosse Isle, and eventually for all of Canada. He also tried to win what he considered proper office and remuneration, finally in 1894 becoming superintendent of Canadian quarantines at $4,000 per year. Growing awareness of public health problems led to him becoming Canada's first Director General of Public Health in January 1899, but he was left without a department to administer. Based on government documents, Montizambert letters in the Public Archives of Canada, and Parliamentary Debates; 2 plates, 56 notes. 1865-1920

Montpetit, Édouard

4867. Bédard, Roger. NOTES SUR M. ÉDOUARD MONTPETIT [Notes on Mr. Édouard Montpetit]. *Action Natl. [Canada] 1980 69(5): 394-403.* Chronology and bibliography of Édouard Montpetit (1881-1954), professor of political economy and law at the École des Hautes Études commerciales and the Universities of Laval and Montreal. Active in civic and Quebec nationalist circles, he founded the *Revue trimestrielle canadienne* and the Action française de Montreal, and served as president of the Association canadienne-française pour l'avancement des sciences. He was a prolific author from 1906 to 1951. 1881-1954

4868. Roy, Léonard. EDOUARD MONTPETIT ET LE REGIONALISME [Edouard Montpetit and regionalism]. *Action Natl. [Canada] 1983 72(5): 409-417.* Comments on the government of Quebec's struggle against the federal policy of centralization, and its advocacy of regionalism; pays a particular tribute to Edouard Montpetit whose committee activities furthered Quebec's administrative and political decentralization, 1940's-80. 1917-80

Moodie, Susanna

4869. Shields, Carol. THREE CANADIAN WOMEN: FICTION OR AUTOBIOGRAPHY. *Atlantis [Canada] 1978 4(1): 49-54.* 19c
*For abstract see **Allison, Susan Moir***

Moody, Deborah

4870. Biemer, Linda. LADY DEBORAH MOODY AND THE FOUNDING OF GRAVESEND. *J. of Long Island Hist. 1981 17(2): 24-42.* Lady Deborah Moody, (ca. 1580's-1659), a wealthy English widow, moved to the Massachusetts Bay Colony about 1639, and then to New Netherland, both for religious reasons. Describes her founding and rule of the town of Gravesend and her relationship with the Dutch government. Includes some comparison with the radical, Anne Hutchinson. Photo, 67 notes. 1630's-59

Moody, James

4871. Shenstone, Susan Burgess. LOYALIST SQUIRE, LOYALIST CHURCH. *Nova Scotia Hist. Rev. [Canada] 1983 3(2): 71-88.* James Moody had only one ambition when he arrived in Nova Scotia in 1786: to become a clergyman of the Church of England. He donated land for a church in Sissiboo (later Weymouth) and provided lay support for people of the community, but dissension over glebe lands delayed assignment of a permanent minister until 1826. Moody was also an assemblyman for Annapolis County and commanded the local militia. 60 notes. 1786-1809

Moody, James (family)

4872. Moody, John Wentworth. THE MOODY FAMILIES OF WEYMOUTH AND YARMOUTH. *Nova Scotia Hist. Rev. [Canada] 1983 3(2): 89-111.* Traces the genealogy of the James Moody family through seven generations. Most of the family stayed in the same general area and became merchants, landowners, politicians, bankers, and insurance agents. 1745-1964

Moody, Robert Earle

4873. Riley, Stephen T. ROBERT EARLE MOODY. *Pro. of the Am. Antiquarian Soc. 1984 94(1): 33-36.* Robert Earle Moody spent most of his academic career at Boston University, where he chaired the board of editors of Boston University Press and served as director of the university libraries. He edited various records in the history of Maine, and was elected to the Colonial Society of Massachusetts, as well as the American Antiquarian Society and the Massachusetts Historical Society. He edited the Saltonstall Family Papers during the latter years of his life. 1901-83

Moody, William Henry

4874. Heffron, Paul T. PROFILE OF A PUBLIC MAN. *Supreme Court Hist. Soc. Y. 1980: 30-37, 48.* William Henry Moody was educated at the Phillips Academy in Andover, Massachusetts, and at Harvard College. After a brief term of study at Harvard Law School and an apprenticeship in the law office of Richard Henry Dana, Moody was admitted to the Massachusetts bar in 1878. He distinguished himself in private practice and local public offices, including that of Essex County district attorney. Moody, a Republican, was elected to the House of Representatives in 1895. President Theodore Roosevelt appointed Moody Secretary of the Navy in 1902, attorney general in 1904, and justice of the Supreme Court in 1906. Illness forced Moody's resignation from the court in 1910. His jurisprudence was marked by adherence to judicial restraint, a liberal view of federal power in the regulation of commerce, and deference to state power when exercised in the community interest. Based on the Theodore Roosevelt Papers, court records, and other primary and secondary sources; 2 illus., 47 notes. 1878-1910

4875. McDonough, Judith Rene. "William Henry Moody." Auburn U. 1983. 236 pp. *DAI 1984 44(11): 3468-A.* DA8404477 1895-1910

Mooers, Frederick M.

4876. Towers, Barbara. MOOERS HOUSE: A LOS ANGELES MANSION AND THE MAN WHO BOUGHT IT. *Southern California Quarterly 1984 66(3): 221-234.* Traces the career of Frederick M. Mooers and the history of the Mooers House in Los Angeles. Born in New York, Mooers came to California as a latter-day gold rush prospector. In 1895, he discovered a lode that spawned the mining town of Randsburg and made him a millionaire overnight. The architecturally splendid house that would bear his name was built the next year. Mooers bought the house in 1898, but his health gave out, and he died two years later. The Mooers House has appeared in films and advertisements and has been declared a historical monument by the Los Angeles Cultural Heritage Board. 3 photos, 52 notes. 1872-1983

Mook, Maurice A.

4877. Hostetler, John A. MAURICE A. MOOK (1904-1973): AN APPRECIATION. *Pennsylvania Folklife 1976-77 26(2): 34-37.* Discusses Maurice A. Mook's life as a professor of anthropology at Pennsylvania State University during 1949-71; includes a bibliography of his writings. 1949-73

Moon, Frederick Douglass

4878. Moon, Mary Carletta. "Frederick Douglass Moon: A Study of Black Education in Oklahoma." U. of Oklahoma 1978. 437 pp. *DAI 1979 39(11): 6587-A.* 20c

Mooney, James

4879. Colby, William Munn. "Routes to Rainy Mountain: A Biography of James Mooney, Ethnologist." U. of Wisconsin, Madison 1977. 567 pp. *DAI 1978 38(12): 7509-A.* 1885-1921

4880. Hewitt, J. N. B. JAMES MOONEY. *J. of Cherokee Studies 1982 7(1): 49-52.* Born in Richmond, Indiana, James Mooney became, at an early age, very interested in Indian affairs. Before his death in Washington, D.C., he became friendly with Major John Wesley Powell, who hired him to work with Cherokee and Kiowa Indians. He later prepared special Indian exhibits for expositions here and abroad and was one of the founders of the American Anthropological Association (a vice-president in 1909 and president in 1914-15). He came to be recognized as a leading expert on Plains tribes. A joint tribute to him from the Bureau of American Ethnology, US National Museum, and the Smithsonian Institution was given on the day after his death and was signed by J. N. B. Hewitt, Walter Hough, and John R. Swanton. Lists Mooney's articles. Biblio. 1861-1921

4881. Moses, Lester George. "James Mooney, U.S. Ethnologist: A Biography." U. of New Mexico 1977. 317 pp. *DAI 1978 38(9): 5668-5669-A.* 1882-1921

Mooney, John

4882. Wright, R. Lewis. JOHN MOONEY, ARTIST. *Virginia Cavalcade 1980 30(3): 118-123.* Biography of artist John Mooney (1843-1918), an eccentric wanderer until he finally settled in Richmond around 1900, where he painted portraits, landscapes, and still lifes until his death. 1843-1918

Mooney, Tom

4883. Mal'kov, V. L. IZ ARKHIVA TOMA MUNI [The Tom Mooney papers]. *Amerikanskii Ezhegodnik [USSR] 1981: 259-273.* Tom Mooney (1882-1942) was an American trade union activist and champion of the left wing of the socialist movement. Mooney was a miner's son, born in Indiana. He became politically active at the beginning of World War I, when he was working in a foundry. Mooney was persecuted for his anti-imperialist and antimilitarist stance and the authorities in California conspired to accuse him wrongfully of murder. He was convicted and sentenced to death, this later being commuted to life imprisonment. He was not released until the eve of World War II, when he again became active in American union politics. Translates Mooney's correspondence with the Soviet press and other American trade union activists after his release from prison. 4 notes, translation of 6 documents held by the Bancroft Library. 1917-42

4884. Mal'kov, V. L. TOM MUNI: UZNIK SAN-KVENTINA [Tom Mooney: prisoner of San Quentin]. *Novaia i Noveishaia Istoriia [USSR] 1975 (2): 101-115, (4): 81-94, (5): 93-103.* Part I. Gives an account of the trial of Tom Mooney following an explosion in San Francisco in 1916. Describes Mooney's life against the background of socialist activities and the labor movement in the United States. He was elected a delegate at the California Socialist Party Conference and in 1910 attended the Copenhagen Congress of the Second International. Mooney became increasingly involved in the intrigues of repression and violence which characterized industrial unrest in the 1910's. The anti-war mood made the summer of 1916 particularly tense. Secondary sources; 64 notes. Part II. Discusses hypotheses concerning the explosion in San Francisco in 1916 of which Mooney was accused and sentenced to death. After widespread protests in the United States and Russia the sentence was commuted. Describes the many unsuccessful political and legal attempts in the 1920's to free Mooney. Secondary sources; 54 notes. Part III. Stresses the heroism of Mooney in the horrific conditions of San Quentin Prison and the constant support of the International Workers' Movement until his release in 1939, interpreting his saga as the typical plight of fighters for the working class in the West. Based on letters, first-hand accounts and newspapers; 44 notes. 1916-42

Moore, Aaron McDuffie

4885. Mitchell, Louis D. AARON MCDUFFIE MOORE: HE LED HIS SHEEP. *Crisis 1980 87(7): 248-257.* Aaron McDuffie Moore (1863-1923) was a medical doctor, philanthropist, educator, businessman, and religious leader in Durham, North Carolina. After graduating from Shaw University and Leonard Medical School, he settled in Durham. He was largely responsible for founding the North Carolina Mutual Life Insurance Company, Lincoln Hospital, Mechanics and Farmers Bank, and White Rock Baptist Church. He attracted Duke and Rosenwald money for education and social reform. He served the federal government during World War I. He was a visionary who served the black community. 1863-1923

Moore, Adam (family)

4886. Jackson, Elva E. SOME OF NORTH SYDNEY'S LOYALISTS. *Nova Scotia Hist. Rev. [Canada] 1983 3(2): 5-22.* 1776-1864

*For abstract see **Moffatt, James (family)***

Moore, Charles W.

4887. Filler, Martin. CHARLES MOORE: HOUSE VERNACULAR. *Art in Am. 1980 68(8): 105-112.* Architect Charles Moore's unique style combines fantasy, whimsy, tradition, and historic and popular styles that remain true to sites and intended uses; 1959-80. 1959-80

4888. Littlejohn, David. THE WILD, WONDROUS IMAGINATION OF CHARLES W. MOORE. *Smithsonian 1984 15(3): 54-61.* Highlights the work of architect Charles W. Moore, designer of the Wonderwall exhibit at the 1984 Louisiana World Exposition and a major proponent of postmodernist design. 1959-84

Moore, Clement Clark

4889. Nuhn, Roy. A HOLIDAY CLASSIC: CLEMENT CLARK MOORE'S VISIT FROM ST. NICHOLAS. *Am. Hist. Illus. 1981 16(8): 24-27.* Brief biography of Clement Clark Moore, born in 1799 in New York City, focusing on his 23 couplet poem, *A Visit from St. Nicholas,* which was written in 1822 for his family based on the Dutch of New York's vision of a jolly St. Nicholas rather than on the stern Old World St. Nicholas. 1822-90's

Moore, Eliakim Hastings

4890. Parshall, Karen Hunger. ELIAKIM HASTINGS MOORE AND THE FOUNDING OF A MATHEMATICAL COMMUNITY IN AMERICA, 1892-1902. *Ann. of Sci. [Great Britain] 1984 41(4): 313-333.* In 1892, Eliakim Hastings Moore accepted the task of building a mathematics department at the University of Chicago. Working in close conjunction with the other original department members, Oskar Bolza and Heinrich Maschke, Moore established a stimulating mathematical environment not only at the University of Chicago, but also in the Midwest region and in the United States in general. In 1893, he helped organize an international congress of mathematicians. He followed this in 1896 with the organization of the Midwest Section of the New York City-based American Mathematical Society. He became the first editor-in-chief of the society's *Transactions* in 1899, and rose to the presidency of the society in 1901. 1892-1902

Moore, Ernest M.

4891. Lambert, John W. CHIEF OF THE SUNSETTERS. *Aerospace Hist. 1981 27[i.e., 28](3): 182-185.* Profiles the career of General Ernest M. Moore, emphasizing his role as chief of the 7th Fighter Command during World War II. From 6 March 1945, the command's headquarters were on Iwo Jima, which served as a base for the P-51D Mustangs and P-47N Thunderbolts that escorted B-29 bombers on long-range missions to Japan. 5 photos. 1944-45

Moore, Fred Holmsley

4892. Ward, George B. IN MEMORIAM: FRED HOLMSLEY MOORE. *Southwestern Historical Quarterly 1985 89(1): 1-4.* Fred Holmsley Moore was a native of Comanche, Texas, who developed a life-long interest in his state's history. After receiving a bachelor's degree in geology from the Texas Technological College in 1931, his career took him from employment as a geologist with the US Gypsum Company to the vice presidency of the Mobil Oil Corporation. Upon retirement in 1967, Holmsley moved to Austin where he engaged in philanthropic activities, particularly in the field of higher education. Moore also served as first vice president of the Texas Historical Association, and he was a chief benefactor of its publications program. On 25 June 1985, the Executive Council named him honorary life president of the association. 1909-85

Moore, John Warren

4893. Foss, Charles. JOHN WARREN MOORE: CABINETMAKER, 1812-1893. *Material Hist. Bull. [Canada] 1977 (3): 31-40.* Biography of cabinetmaker John Warren Moore (1812-93) of St. Stephen, New Brunswick, dating to his Scottish grandfather's birth in 1730 in New Hampshire; describes and shows more than 50 pieces of Moore's furniture from a collection belonging to his granddaughter, Frances Strange Flemington. ca 1830-93

Moore, Marianne

4894. Keller, Lynn. WORDS WORTH A THOUSAND POSTCARDS: THE BISHOP/MOORE CORRESPONDENCE. *Am. Lit. 1983 55(3): 405-429.* 1930's-40's

*For abstract see **Bishop, Elizabeth***

Moore, Nicholas Ruxton

4895. Steiner, Edward E. NICHOLAS RUXTON MOORE: SOLDIER, FARMER AND POLITICIAN. *Maryland Hist. Mag. 1978 73(4): 375-388.* Reviews the career of Nicholas Ruxton Moore (1756-1816) of Baltimore County, who fought in the American Revolution at Brandywine, Germantown, and Yorktown with his Baltimore Light Dragoons, became a prominent landowner and city father of Baltimore, and served in Congress as a staunch supporter of Jeffersonian policies during 1803-16. Remains of his estate may still be seen in the Circle Road-Roland Run area of Baltimore, in the region once called "Bosley's Adventure." His widow, Sarah Moore, outlived him by many years, and went through much trouble obtaining a federal pension from the Van Buren administration. From the National Archive, secondary sources; 24 notes. 1774-1848

Moore, Richard Benjamin

4896. Samuels, Wilfred David. "Five Afro-Caribbean Voices in American Culture, 1917-1929: Hubert H. Harrison, Wilfred A. Domingo, Richard B. Moore, Cyril V. Briggs, and Claude McKay." U. of Iowa 1977. 181 pp. *DAI 1978 38(7): 4234-A.* 1917-29

4897. Tudor, J. Cameron. RICHARD BENJAMIN MOORE: AN APPRECIATION. *Caribbean Studies [Puerto Rico] 1979 19(1-2): 169-174.* Tribute to Richard Benjamin Moore, president of the Afro-American Institute, scholar, author, orator, and bibliophile. Moore was a major figure in the development of Afro-American studies in the United States and the Caribbean. Reviews his principal publications and organizational work. 1930's-78

Moorhead, Max L.

4898. Jones, Oakah L. A DEDICATION TO THE MEMORY OF MAX L. MOORHEAD, 1914-1981. *Arizona and the West 1984 26(1): 1-4.* Max L. Moorhead was trained in Spanish and Mexican borderlands history at the University of California, Berkeley. He established a reputation as a meticulous scholar and authority on Spanish documents in Spain, Mexico, and the American Southwest. His monographs on Spanish Indian policies, the presidio as a frontier institution, and the Santa Fe-Chihuahua route are the standard accounts on these subjects. For three decades he was a highly regarded teacher at the University of Oklahoma. Illus., biblio. 1945-81

Moran, Thomas

4899. Fahlman, Betsy. COLUMBIA SUBLIME: THE COLLABORATION OF THOMAS MORAN AND LLOYD MIFFLIN. *J. of the Lancaster County Hist. Soc. 1980 84(4): 167-178.* 1837-1921
*For abstract see **Mifflin, Lloyd***

Morgan, Charles Waln

4900. Coope, Virginia T. CHARLES W. MORGAN. *Log of Mystic Seaport 1981 32(4): 121-128.* Examines the life of Charles Waln Morgan (1796-1861), Quaker merchant in New Bedford, based on a travel journal and his diaries in the G. W. Blunt White Library at Mystic Seaport Museum, covering the years 1817 to 1861. 1817-61

Morgan, Dale L.

4901. Cooley, Everett L. A DEDICATION TO THE MEMORY OF DALE L. MORGAN, 1914-1971. *Arizona and the West 1977 19(2): 102-106.* A teenage illness left Dale L. Morgan (1914-71) totally deaf, and he became a master with the written word. With experience in the Federal Records Survey and other agencies in the Great Depression, he honed his writing skills and launched a career in history. An outstanding author, he produced many articles and some forty books, receiving wide recognition for his work on the western fur trade and on Mormon history. For thirty years he compiled a bibliography on Mormonism, now to be published posthumously. Illus., selective bibliography of Morgan's books. 1940-71

Morgan, Edmund S.

4902. Trousdale, David Mark. "Society and Culture, Order and Change in Early America: The Sociology of Edmund S. Morgan." Case Western Reserve U. 1976. 174 pp. *DAI 1977 38(1): 347-A.* 17c-18c

Morgan, George

4903. Sutton, Robert M. GEORGE MORGAN, EARLY ILLINOIS BUSINESSMAN: A CASE OF PREMATURE ENTERPRISE. *J. of the Illinois State Hist. Soc. 1976 69(3): 173-184.* George Morgan began as a clerk in a Philadelphia merchant house and was a partner in expeditions to the Illinois country in the late 1760's and 1770. Discusses the reasons for failure of the mission and his return east in 1771. 2 maps, 3 illus., 51 notes. 1760's-71

Morgan, John Tyler

4904. Clayton, Lawrence A. JOHN TYLER MORGAN Y EL CANAL DE NICARAGUA, 1897-1900 [John Tyler Morgan and the Nicaraguan Canal, 1897-1900]. *Anuario Estudios Centroamericanos [Costa Rica] 1983 9: 37-53.* Senator John Tyler Morgan of Alabama was instrumental in obtaining a franchise for the Maritime Canal Company to construct a canal in Nicaragua in 1889. The venture failed in 1893. Morgan renewed his efforts in 1897 to gain federal financial support for the venture, but faced the opposition of William Russell Grace, who had private financial backing and the support of President J. S. Zelaya of Nicaragua. Further opposition came from Panama Canal interests, and in 1900 a resolution supporting the Maritime venture failed to pass the US Congress. Based on the papers of John Tyler Morgan and William Russell Grace and secondary sources; 61 notes. 1897-1900

Morgan, Julia

4905. Olson, Lynne. A TYCOON'S HOME WAS HIS PETITE ARCHITECT'S CASTLE. *Smithsonian 1985 16(9): 60-71.* Reviews the life and work of architect Julia Morgan, one of San Francisco's most renowned and prolific architects and designer of almost 800 buildings in the West including Hearst Castle at San Simeon, California. 1890-1985

Morgan, Robert

4906. Wright, Stuart. ROBERT MORGAN: A BIBLIOGRAPHIC CHRONICLE, 1963-81. *Bull. of Biblio. 1982 39(3): 121-131.* Brief biography of poet Robert Morgan, followed by a bibliography of primary and secondary writings. 1963-81

Morgan, Thomas Hunt

4907. Allen, Garland E. THOMAS HUNT MORGAN: MATERIALISM AND EXPERIMENTALISM IN THE DEVELOPMENT OF MODERN GENETICS. *Social Research 1984 51(3): 709-738.* Describes geneticist Thomas Hunt Morgan's contributions to mechanistic biology, a late-19th-century trend that insisted on experimental proof of scientific theories; Morgan studied the small fruit fly, *Drosophila,* to determine sex-linked hereditary traits, which led to the discovery of the relation between traits and specific genes located at identifiable sites on chromosomes. 1880-1930

Morgan, William

4908. Hancock, Harold B., ed. WILLIAM MORGAN'S AUTOBIOGRAPHY AND DIARY: LIFE IN SUSSEX COUNTY, 1780-1857. *Delaware Hist. 1980 19(1): 39-52.* Publishes the diary and excerpts from the autobiography of a Methodist Protestant minister residing in Sussex County, Delaware. The diary and autobiography relate William Morgan's childhood and education, his conversion experience, revivals, descriptions of church services and political rallies, his involvement with the Sons of Temperance, Sussex County social life, medical history of the region, and farming practices. As a preacher, farmer, and physician, Morgan touched the lives and interests of most inhabitants of the county. Illus., 28 notes. Article to be continued. 1780-1857

4909. Hancock, Harold B., ed. WILLIAM MORGAN'S AUTOBIOGRAPHY AND DIARY: LIFE IN SUSSEX COUNTY, 1780-1857. PART II. *Delaware Hist. 1980 19(2): 106-126.* Continued from a previous article. Entries from William Morgan's diary from 1829 until Morgan's death in 1857 recount the effort to introduce silk culture in Delaware, July 4th celebrations, the author's meetings with (and assessments of) various religious figures (principally Methodists) and politicians in Delaware, revivals, the Millerite movement, fishing, sharp dealings at the Cannon Ferry, shipbuilding and sailing, and Sussex County social life, medical practices, and farming. 65 notes. 1839-57

Morgenthau, Hans J.

4910. Thompson, Kenneth W. HANS J. MORGENTHAU (1904-1980). *Int. Security 1980-81 5(3): 195-197.* Hans J. Morgenthau (1904-80) left Europe for America in 1937 and became a leading theorist on, and teacher of, international affairs; although he believed that the struggle for power was a permanent feature of international politics, he consistently strove to mitigate that struggle. 1937-80

Morgenthau, Henry, Sr.

4911. Tuchman, Barbara W. THE ASSIMILATIONIST DILEMMA: AMBASSADOR MORGENTHAU'S STORY. *Commentary 1977 63(5): 58-62.* In 1914 Henry Morgenthau, Sr., then US Ambassador to Turkey, arranged for financial aid to the Jewish colony in Palestine, enabling it to survive and preserving it for eventual Jewish statehood. Yet in 1918 he resigned as president of the Free Synagogue, when its Rabbi, Stephen S. Wise, led a delegation to the White House to support the Zionist homeland, and in 1921 he wrote an article stating his strong opposition to Zionism. Not until after the Holocaust, when he was in his 80's, did Morgenthau acknowledge that he had misread history. Assimilation into American life was his ideal, assimilation meaning acceptance as Jews, not absorption into Christianity. The Western Democracies did not function according to his ideal and the horrors of the Holocaust turned many assimilationists into supporters of the Jewish State. Based on primary and secondary sources as well as personal recollections. 1914-40's

Mori, Toshio

4912. Leong, Russell. TOSHIO MORI: AN INTERVIEW. *Amerasia J. 1980 7(1): 89-108.* Toshio Mori (1910-80) reveals some of his early life in California, how he became a writer, and some of the real-life individuals who became characters in his short stories. Edited from a tape interview made 9 October 1979 in San Leandro, California. 1910-79

Moriarty, Patrick E.

4913. George, Joseph, Jr. VERY REV. DR. PATRICK E. MORIARTY, OSA., PHILADELPHIA'S FENIAN SPOKESMAN. *Pennsylvania Hist. 1981 48(3): 221-233.* Father Patrick E. Moriarty, an Irish Augustinian priest, served in Philadelphia from 1839 until his death in 1875. A noted orator, Moriarty was ordered by his bishop to leave Philadelphia for a time, after he lashed out at nativists who burned his church and rectory in 1844. Later, in 1864, Bishop James F. Wood suspended Moriarty for disobeying him by making a speech, sounding Fenian in tone and sponsorship, "What Right Has England to Rule Ireland?" The English American bishop and the eloquent Irishman reconciled later that year. Based on the Wood papers, newspapers, and other sources; illus. 31 notes. 1839-75

Morice, A. G.

4914. Mulhall, David Bernard. "The Missionary Career of A. G. Morice, O.M.I." McGill U. 1979. *DAI 1979 40(6): 3475-A.* 1880-1903

Morison, Samuel Eliot

4915. Albee, Parker Bishop, Jr., ed. PORTRAIT OF A FRIENDSHIP: SELECTED CORRESPONDENCE OF SAMUEL ELIOT MORISON AND LINCOLN COLCORD, 1921-1947. *New England Q. 1983 56(2): 166-199.* 1921-47
*For abstract see **Colcord, Lincoln***

4916. Albee, Parker Bishop, Jr., ed. SELECTED CORRESPONDENCE OF SAMUEL ELIOT MORISON AND LINCOLN COLCORD, 1921-1947. PART 2. *New England Q. 1983 56(3): 398-424.* 1938-47
*For abstract see **Colcord, Lincoln***

4917. Metcalf, Keyes. SAMUEL ELIOT MORISON. *Pro. of the Am. Antiquarian Soc. 1977 87(1): 20-25.* Samuel Eliot Morison (1887-1976) was perhaps the dean of American historians when he died. Traces his career and historical publications. 1887-1976

4918. Taylor, P. A. M. SAMUEL ELIOT MORISON: HISTORIAN. *J. of Am. Studies [Great Britain] 1977 11(1): 13-26.* Reviews the writings and the teaching and literary careers of Samuel Eliot Morison (1887-1976). A long-term professor at Harvard University, he was mentor to relatively few graduate students because his interests centered on the seas and were peripheral to the themes of American history that most students found profitable. Morison attained greatness as a creator of historical narratives. He crafted them after reenacting the voyages of his subjects, accompanying sailors into battle to observe their deeds first-hand, and using aerial photography to verify the traditional historical documents. Primary and secondary sources; 43 notes. 1913-74

4919. Washburn, Wilcomb E. SAMUEL ELIOT MORISON, HISTORIAN. *William and Mary Q. 1979 36(3): 325-352.* A tribute to the life and work of Samuel Eliot Morison by one of his former students. Emphasizes Morison's essential conservatism in interpreting history, his faith in the Republic, and his patriotism. A writer of narrative history, Morison's success resulted from an artistry, mixing literary style, wit, and learning. Comments on all of Morison's major writings. As to a view of history, Morison considered history as a story, that it was a record of individual achievement, and that it should not be present-minded. Contrasts Morison's writing of history with that of progressive and revisionist historians. Based upon personal recollection, Morison's writings, and his correspondence; 82 notes. 1888-1976

4920. Whitehill, Walter Muir. IN MEMORIAM: SAMUEL ELIOT MORISON (1887-1976). *New England Q. 1976 49(3): 459-463.* Provides a brief biographical sketch of Samuel Eliot Morison and emphasizes his role in the founding and editorial direction of *The New England Quarterly.* 1928-76

Morlacchi, Giuseppina

4921. Barker, Barbara Mackin. "The American Careers of Rita Sangalli, Giuseppina Morlacchi and Maria Bonfanti: Nineteenth Century Ballerinas." New York U. 1981. 308 pp. *DAI 1982 42(7): 2935-A.* 8127890 1866-90

Morlan, Frederick H.

4922. Sloan, James J. (John). THE FIRST AIR DEPOT: COLOMBEY-LES-BELLES, FRANCE, 1918. *Am. Aviation Hist. Soc. J. 1981 26(3): 221-230.* Discusses the aeronautic career of Captain Frederick H. Morlan, Aircraft Acceptance and Replacement Officer for the 1st Air Depot at Colombey-les-Belles, France, during World War I; provides photographs of Depot personnel and aircraft taken by Morlan during 1918-19. 1918-19

Morley, Felix

4923. Liggio, Leonard P. FELIX MORLEY AND THE COMMONWEALTHMAN TRADITION: THE COUNTRY-PARTY, CENTRALIZATION AND THE AMERICAN EMPIRE. *J. of Libertarian Studies 1978 2(3): 279-286.* Surveys the ideas of American political philosopher Felix Morley and traces them, in part, to the ideas of the English Puritan Revolution of the 17th century. 17c

Morrill, Justin Smith

4924. Welch, Robert Webster. "A Rhetorical Study of the Legislative Speaking of Congressman Justin Smith Morrill of Vermont in the U.S. House of Representatives on Selected Issues, 1855-1867." Pennsylvania State U. 1977. 374 pp. *DAI 1978 38(10): 5799-A.* 1855-67

Morris, Christina

4925. Whitehead, Ruth Holmes. CHRISTINA MORRIS: MICMAC ARTIST AND ARTIST'S MODEL. *Material Hist. Bull. [Canada] 1977 (3): 1-14.* Discusses 19th century Nova Scotia Micmac artist Christina Morris (ca. 1804-86), famous for her quillwork, focusing on her craftwork reputation which is well documented, and the seven surviving portraits of her by various artists. ca 1854-86

Morris, Edmund

4926. McGill, Jean. THE INDIAN PORTRAITS OF EDMUND MORRIS. *Beaver [Canada] 1979 310(1): 34-41.* Describes Edmund Morris's portraits of Canadian Indians, and traces Morris's background from 1812, when his grandfather was a soldier in the War of 1812, to Morris's first commission in 1906; he died by drowning in 1913. 1812-1913

Morris, Lucy Wilder

4927. Kreidberg, Marjorie. AN UNEMBARRASSED PATRIOT: LUCY WILDER MORRIS. *Minnesota Hist. 1981 47(6): 214-226.* Lucy Wilder Morris became a traveler, travel writer, founder of a Daughters of the American Revolution chapter, editor of an acclaimed collection of pioneer recollections, Red Cross organizer during World War I, and a notable exponent of marking and restoring historic sites from Fort Snelling to Yorktown and back to the Falls of St. Anthony. Based largely on personal papers; 32 notes, 9 illus. 1864-1935

Morris, Maria

4928. Sparling, Mary. THE LIGHTER AUXILIARIES: WOMEN ARTISTS IN NOVA SCOTIA IN THE EARLY NINETEENTH CENTURY. *Atlantis [Canada] 1979 5(1): 83-106.* 19c
For abstract see ***Chaplin, Millicent Mary***

Morris, Robert Williams

4929. Cabaniss, Allen. "ROB" MORRIS IN MISSISSIPPI, 1842-1852. *J. of Mississippi Hist. 1977 39(4): 291-302.* Describes the activity in Mississippi Masonry, 1842-52, of Robert Williams Morris (1818-88), who "began and completed the York Rite of Freemasonry" in Mississippi and "began the movement that resulted in the creation of the Order of the Eastern Star." Based on published primary and secondary sources; 46 notes. 1842-52

Morris, Sally Dodge

4930. Gregory, Sarah J. PIONEER HOUSEWIFE: THE AUTOBIOGRAPHY OF SALLY DODGE MORRIS. *Gateway Heritage 1983 3(4): 24-33.* Presents the memoirs of Sally Dodge Morris, written in 1893, which focus on pioneering in Missouri and Nebraska during 1821-57. The Morris family journeyed overland to California in 1857, returned to the Midwest in 1859, and moved once more to California in 1877. Map, 13 photos, 49 notes. 1821-77

Morris, Thomas

4931. Neuenschwander, John A. SENATOR THOMAS MORRIS: ANTAGONIST OF THE SOUTH, 1836-1839. *Cincinnati Hist. Soc. Bull. 1974 32(3): 121-139.* Chronicles Thomas Morris' political career in the Ohio state legislature and his lifelong agitation in favor of the antislavery movement. 1836-39

Morrison, deLesseps S.

4932. Jeansonne, Glen. DE LESSEPS MORRISON: WHY HE COULDN'T BECOME GOVERNOR OF LOUISIANA. *Louisiana Hist. 1973 14(3): 255-270.* Through personal shortcomings and political misorganization, deLesseps S. Morrison, though a successful and strong mayor of New Orleans for four terms, was unable to parlay himself into the governor's mansion, 1955-61. 1955-61

4933. Kurtz, Michael L. DE LESSEPS S. MORRISON: POLITICAL REFORMER. *Louisiana Hist. 1976 17(1): 19-39.* Examines deLesseps S. Morrison's place as a political reformer. Much of his effectiveness as a reformer in New Orleans corrupt city government during his 14 years as mayor was due to his combination of idealism and practical politics. In public relations he projected an image of economic and social progress, racial moderation, and political reform. He secured home rule for New Orleans, leaving a last imprint on that city and on the entire South. Based on the Morrison Papers; 115 notes. 1946-64

Morrison, Lorrin L.

4934. Probert, Alan. IN MEMORIAM: LORRIN L. MORRISON. *J. of the West 1983 22(2): 69-72.* Lorrin L. Morrison (1908-82) was founding publisher and editor of *Journal of the West.* As a boy in Colorado, he learned printing and publishing from his parents. Following his service as an infantryman in World War II, he opened a printing plant in Los Angeles. With his wife, Carroll Spear, he became an advocate of historical research and publication, leading to the development of *Journal of the West,* which presented monographic essays on Western subjects. Lorrin was respected and beloved by the many young scholars he encouraged by publishing their work in the *Journal.* 3 photos. 1940's-82

Morrow, Dwight

4935. Horn, James J. THE UNITED STATES AND REVOLUTIONARY MEXICO: THE ORDEAL OF AMBASSADOR SHEFFIELD. Plesur, Milton, ed. *An American Historian: Essays to Honor Selig Adler* (Buffalo: State U. of N.Y., 1980): 116-124. 1924-27
*For abstract see **Sheffield, James Rockwell***

Morrow, E. Frederick

4936. Katz, Milton S. E. FREDERICK MORROW AND CIVIL RIGHTS IN THE EISENHOWER ADMINISTRATION. *Phylon 1981 42(2): 133-144.* The first black person to serve in an executive capacity for a US president was named in July 1955. President Dwight D. Eisenhower appointed E. Frederick Morrow as administrative officer for special projects. It was not a popular move in the White House staff. Morrow was unable to get to the president when necessary or assert any power. Yet he remained in the White House against hostility and kept civil rights issues alive. 1952-60

Morrow, John Patterson, Jr.

4937. McGinnis, A. C. JOHN P. MORROW, JR. *Arkansas Hist. Q. 1978 37(3): 278-279.* Obituary of surveyor, engineer, and Arkansas historian John Patterson Morrow, Jr. (1907-78). Illus. 1907-78

Morrow, Joseph Samuel

4938. Jordan, H. Glenn. "Joseph Samuel Morrow: The Man and His Times." U. of Oklahoma 1982. 322 pp. *DAI 1982 43(2): 526-A.* DA8215789 1857-1929

Morse, Horace Henry

4939. Seaver, Henry Latimer. HORACE HENRY MORSE. *Massachusetts Hist. Soc. Proc. 1957-60 72: 371-372.* Obituary of Horace Henry Morse (1878-1959), historian, intellectual, and member of the Massachusetts Historical Society. 1900-59

Morse, Jedidiah

4940. Phillips, John Wilson. "Jedidiah Morse: An Intellectual Biography." U. of California, Berkeley 1978. 338 pp. *DAI 1979 39(9): 5682-A.* 1789-1826

4941. Wright, Conrad. THE CONTROVERSIAL CAREER OF JEDIDIAH MORSE. *Harvard Lib. Bull. 1983 31(1): 64-87.* Although a man of considerable talent, Jedidiah Morse apparently found it difficult to avoid controversy. Very much opposed to the theological liberals of Boston who occupied most of the pulpits, he carried on a running battle with them on behalf of the orthodox. In addition to ecclesiastical disputes he was also involved in bitter controversies with fellow geographers and historians. In all cases he was quick to find a conspiracy against him and proved at times so intractable that even his supporters abandoned him. By 1819 he had been dismissed by his Charlestown church. However, in a roundabout way he helped American Unitarianism become a separate denomination. Mostly primary sources; 53 notes, illus. 1780's-1826

Morse, Omar

4942. Marshall, James. AN UNHEARD VOICE: THE AUTOBIOGRAPHY OF A DISPOSSESSED HOMESTEADER AND A NINETEENTH-CENTURY CULTURAL THEME OF DISPOSSESSION. *Old Northwest 1980-81 6(4): 303-329.* The autobiography of Omar Morse (1824-1901), a homesteader who was dispossessed from three homesteads in Wisconsin and Minnesota between 1847 and 1878, illustrates the theme of dispossession on the frontier. Most historical studies of the middle border discuss the Garden of the World symbol but generally ignore the cultural theme of dispossession. Morse's autobiography provides a historical version of dispossession that is also the theme of later novels, songs, poems, and tales that portray the "unweeded garden" of the homesteader. Based on the Omar Morse manuscript and other primary sources; 50 notes. 1847-78

Morse, Salmi

4943. Kramer, William M. and Stern, Norton B. THE STRANGE PASSION OF SALMI MORSE. *Western States Jewish Hist. 1984 16(4): 336-347.* Chronicles the life of Salmi Morse, born a Jew, who was a San Francisco playwright, editor of the satiric journal *The Wasp,* and producer of *The Passion,* a play on the gospel story of Jesus that San Francisco supervisors attempted to suppress. Morse committed suicide on 22 February 1884 at the age of 58. Based largely on newspaper sources; 53 notes. 1826-84

Morse, Samuel F. B.

4944. Crean, Hugh R. SAMUEL F. B. MORSE'S "GALLERY OF THE LOUVRE": TRIBUTE TO A MASTER AND DIARY OF A FRIENDSHIP. *Am. Art J. 1984 16(1): 76-81.* Samuel F. B. Morse painted his *Gallery of the Louvre* as an exhibition picture, not as a commissioned work. The Louvre Gallery did not actually display the paintings shown in Morse's picture; they were chosen by Morse from the entire collection of the Louvre because of their close relationship to the life and work of Washington Allston, Morse's close friend and teacher. The paintings had been recommended to Morse while he was a student in America and England. In 1830, he went to Paris to view the paintings, and painted them as a tribute to his teacher. 2 plates, 22 notes. 1831-33

4945. Staiti, Paul J. SAMUEL F. B. MORSE'S SEARCH FOR A PERSONAL STYLE: THE ANXIETY OF INFLUENCE. *Winterthur Portfolio 1981 16(4): 253-281.* Samuel F. B. Morse's search for and development of a personal style was not without conflict. Influenced by Washington Allston, Gilbert Stuart, and Thomas Sully, Morse had to trade off differing characteristics, finally learning to paint from vision to ideal. His success and talent emerged from the field of portraiture, contrary to traditional interpretations. Morse never accepted portraiture as influential in developing his talent or success. Covers the 1810's. Based on the Morse Papers, Library of Congress, pictorial analysis, and other sources; 29 fig., 52 notes. 1810-20

Morse, Wayne

4946. Wilkins, Lee. WAYNE MORSE: THE CHILDHOOD OF AN AMERICAN ADAM. *J. of Psychohistory 1982 10(2): 189-211.* Oregon Senator Wayne Morse was regarded as a highly principled maverick, willing to take an unpopular minority position regardless of the political risk. Was this a result of a healthy or a disordered personality? Answers can be found in his childhood. He was encouraged by his mother to participate in oral arguments and to structure them carefully in order to win, and by his father to stand up for principles, no matter how unpopular. His grade school experiences brought him into contact with blacks, Jews, and immigrants from many European countries, but he appeared always to regard them as his equals. His independence, unwillingness to compromise, identification with the land and a rural spirit, and his defense of American traditions allowed him to carry on a constant conversation with the American people because they so much admired the "American Adam" in him. 1900-74

4947. Wilkins, Lillian Claire. "Wayne Morse: An Explanatory Biography." U. of Oregon 1982. 347 pp. *DAI 1982 43(2): 539-A.* DA8215323 1900-68

Mortimore, David (family)

4948. Limbaugh, Ronald H. THE UNHERALDED WEST: PIONEERING FROM A FAMILY PERSPECTIVE. Dodd, Horace L. and Long, Robert W., ed. *People of the Far West* (Brand Book no. 6; San Diego: Corral of the Westerners, 1979): 59-70. The lives of the members of the David Mortimore and Newton T. Tucker families indicate the role of the family in the settlement of the American West, 1850's-90's. 1850's-90's

Morton, Elizabeth Homer

4949. Bassam, Bertha. ELIZABETH HOMER MORTON: LIBRARIAN, ADMINISTRATOR, AUTHOR, EDITOR... *Can. Lib. J. [Canada] 1978 35(4): 253-267.* Reviews the contributions of Elizabeth Homer Morton, who served from 1946 to 1968 as executive director of the Canadian Library Association and chief editor of the *Canadian Library Journal.* In those positions, she helped establish the National Library of Canada and the *Canadian Periodical Index.* From 1944 to 1946, she had served as secretary of both the Canadian Library Council (the predecessor of the Canadian Library Association) and the Ontario Library Association, while employed by the Toronto Public Library. She finished a Master of Arts program at the graduate Library School of the University of Chicago upon retirement, and opened a library consulting firm. 4 photos. 1926-78

Morton, Joy

4950. Norris, James D. and Livingston, James. JOY MORTON AND THE CONDUCT OF MODERN BUSINESS ENTERPRISE. *Chicago Hist. 1981 10(1): 13-25.* Biography of the founder of the Morton Salt Company and the Morton Arboretum, Joy Morton (b. 1855), an entrepreneur exemplifying the corporation man who organized bureaucratic, national corporations into institutions that dominated the American business scene. 1880-1934

Morton, Martha

4951. Gipson, Rosemary. MARTHA MORTON: AMERICA'S FIRST PROFESSIONAL WOMAN PLAYWRIGHT. *Theatre Survey 1982 23(2): 213-222.* Recounts the career of New York City playwright and director Martha Morton during 1890-1915, who wrote *The Merchant* (1891), *A Bachelor's Romance* (1897), and other plays and founded the Society of Dramatic Artists. 1890-1915

Morton, Thomas

4952. Gragg, Larry. "THIS TROUBLESOME PLANTER", 1622-46: THOMAS MORTON OF MERRY MOUNT. *Hist. Today [Great Britain] 1977 27(10): 667-672.* Thomas Morton was a settler among the Puritans in Plymouth Plantation whose trading with Indians and fondness for drink and women caused him to be deported to England twice and imprisoned three times; he founded his own rival community, Merry Mount, and traded furs, liquor, and guns with the local Indians, 1627. 1622-46

4953. Ranlet, Philip. THE LORD OF MISRULE: THOMAS MORTON OF MERRY MOUNT. *New England Hist. and Geneal. Register 1980 134(Oct): 282-290.* Thomas Morton (1579/80-1647) was a thorn in the side of the Massachusetts Bay Colony and was believed to be a dangerous threat to Puritanism. Historians differ in the degree of censure accorded him, however. The author examines the behavior of lawyer Morton. 62 notes. ca 1630-47

Morton, William Lewis

4954. Laurence, Margaret. W. L. MORTON: A PERSONAL TRIBUTE. *J. of Can. Studies [Canada] 1980-81 15(4): 134.* Obituary to historian William Lewis Morton, chancellor of Trent University in Canada. 1908-80

4955. Wilson, Alan. W. L. MORTON 1908-1980. *J. of Can. Studies [Canada] 1980-81 15(4): 1-2.* Presents a tribute to William Lewis Morton and announces the establishment of a W. L. Morton Lecture series, which will be in keeping with his concerns for communication and public discussion among Canadians in all fields. 1908-80

Moseley, E. L.

4956. Mayfield, Harold F. EDWIN LINCOLN MOSELEY, NATURALIST AND TEACHER, 1865-1948. *Northwest Ohio Quarterly 1984 56(1): 3-17.* Describes the life and teaching career of Professor E. L. Moseley, noting his role as head of the science department at Bowling Green State University (then a state normal college), and his work in field botany, glacial studies at Sandusky, solution of the riddle of milk sickness, research at Oak Openings in northwestern Ohio, studies of tree rings and rainfall, and writing. 1880's-1948

Moses, Montrose Jonas

4957. Grabish, Richard Frank. "Montrose Jonas Moses: Critic of American Drama." Kent State U. 1979. 222 pp. *DAI 1979 40(4): 1749-1750-A.* 1900-34

Mosher, Clelia Duel

4958. Jacob, Kathryn Allamong. THE MOSHER REPORT. *Am. Heritage 1981 32(4): 56-64.* Clelia Duel Mosher (1863-1940), a physician, devoted her life to challenging notions of inferiority of women. Mosher's studies of menstruation convinced her that constrictive clothing and inactivity caused most of the related disabilities. Stressing physical and mental well-being, Mosher attacked this and other myths of women's inferiority. Her most innovative work, a study of sexual habits of women at Stanford and the University of Wisconsin-Madison in the early 1890's, was discovered and published by Carl Degler in 1974. 10 illus. ca 1892

Mott, Lucretia

4959. Greene, Dana. QUAKER FEMINISM: THE CASE OF LUCRETIA MOTT. *Pennsylvania Hist. 1981 48(2): 143-154.* Lucretia Mott's (d. 1880) commitment to feminism and to various reform movements grew out of her religious experience as a member of the Society of Friends, where she learned that women are equal to men. Her quest for religious self-perfection led her first to abolitionism and then to other reforms. Based on the Mott Papers, the Garrison Family Papers, and other materials; illus., 24 notes. ca 1820-80

Mouton, Alfred

4960. Jones, Michael. ALFRED MOUTON: HERO FROM THE BAYOU. *Civil War Times Illus. 1984 22(9): 32-37.* Recounts the military career of Confederate Brigadier General Jean Jacques Alfred Alexander Mouton, who served in Georgia and later in his home state of Louisiana; he was killed in action at the battle of Mansfield, Louisiana, in April 1864. 1861-64

Mowbray, H. Siddons

4961. Owens, Gwendolyn. H. SIDDONS MOWBRAY: EASEL PAINTER. *Art & Antiques 1980 3(4): 82-89.* Describes the life, easel paintings, and illustrations of H. Siddons Mowbray (1858-1928), Egyptian-born muralist who settled in New York City. 1878-1928

Moyer, Lycurgus Rose

4962. Bray, Edmund C. SURVEYING THE SEASONS ON THE MINNESOTA PRAIRIES: L. R. MOYER OF MONTEVIDEO. *Minnesota Hist. 1982 48(2): 72-82.* Lycurgus Rose Moyer, a New Yorker, moved to Minnesota in 1869 as a bright, intellectual, versatile young teacher in search of a healthier climate. He settled in Montevideo, taught, started a bank, took up law, became a probate judge, married, fathered six children, and became a county surveyor before 1872. His chief avocation through all of this was botany, yet he still found time for local history, poetry, and politics. However, it was for his botanical work that he became nationally known, contributing specimens to various university collections, and writing papers for the state botanical society. Primary sources, including diaries; 40 notes, 9 illus. 1869-1917

Mudd, Samuel

4963. Robbins, Peggy. "I AM ASHAMED OF MY CONDUCT": DR. SAMUEL MUDD'S ATTEMPT TO ESCAPE FROM FORT JEFFERSON. *Civil War Times Illus. 1978 16(10): 10-16.* Confined to the Dry Tortugas under sentence of life imprisonment for his alleged role in the Lincoln assassination conspiracy, Dr. Samuel Mudd suffered in many ways. In late 1865, he made an unsuccessful attempt to escape Fort Jefferson by hiding under some planks in the lower hold of a ship. Several years later he helped to stem the yellow fever epidemic in the prison, and was pardoned by President Johnson in February 1869, returning home to his Maryland farm, where he died in 1883. Some comment on Abraham Lincoln's assassination. 1865-83

Mudge, Enoch

4964. Dahl, Curtis. THREE FATHERS, THREE SONS. *Methodist Hist. 1977 15(4): 234-250.* Enoch Mudge (1776-1850) was a Methodist minister and first chaplain of the Seamen's Bethel of New Bedford, Massachusetts. He was a friend of Edward Thompson Taylor, Methodist chaplain of the Seamen's Bethel in Boston and perhaps the model for Herman Melville's Father Mapple in *Moby Dick.* Mudge was at the Bethel for 12 years and greatly influenced the seamen. 2 illus., 36 notes. 1776-1850

Mueller, Herman Carl

4965. Taft, Lisa Louise Factor. "Herman Carl Mueller (1854-1941), Innovator in the Field of Architectural Ceramics." Ohio State U. 1979. 210 pp. *DAI 1979 40(1): 9-A.* 1890's-1941

Muir, John

4966. Buske, Frank. JOHN MUIR'S ALASKA EXPERIENCE. *Pacific Historian 1985 29(2-3): 113-123.* Narrates portions of John Muir's seven trips to Alaska during 1879-99. Writing about the huge, new, unknown land of Alaska, he included much of literary interest in his published letters. His voyage in 1880 resulted in the discovery of unmapped areas in Glacier Bay. Muir's loving descriptions of Alaska, plus his glacial observations, brought Alaska to the attention of the world. Based on the John Muir Papers, Holt-Atherton Center, University of the Pacific; 3 photos, 3 illus., 21 notes. 1879-99

4967. Engberg, Robert. JOHN MUIR: FROM POETRY TO POLITICS, 1871-1876. *Pacific Hist. 1981 25(2): 11-19.* Before 1873, US naturalist John Muir wrote in a poetic style. As he began to advocate nature conservation, especially of the Yosemite area, however, he produced more polemical conservationist works. These successfully preserved much of America's most beautiful land. Based on primary sources. 1872-76

4968. Holliday, J. S. THE POLITICS OF JOHN MUIR. *California History 1984 63(2): 135-139.* Assesses the political contributions of John Muir in his efforts to win legislative support for the environment. Dedicated to preservation of the wilderness rather than development of its resources, Muir campaigned in his writings and by lobbying elected officials for goals such as the creation of national forests and parks, recession of the Yosemite Valley from California to the federal government, and for preservation of Hetch Hetchy Valley. Although his writings are often seen as educational, they also served a propaganda purpose in awakening public and official awareness to the fragility of nature and its relationship to human needs and society. Reprinted from *Sierra Club Bulletin,* October-November 1972. 3 photos. 1876-1914

4969. McGinty, Brian. FRIEND OF THE WILDERNESS: JOHN MUIR. *Am. Hist. Illus. 1977 12(4): 4-9, 44-48.* Chronicles the activities, travels, and writings of John Muir 1872-1914, including his general conservationist attitude and his work and exploration in the Yosemite Valley which eventually led to its inclusion in the National Park system. 1872-1914

4970. Ryan, P. J. THE MARTINEZ YEARS: THE FAMILY LIFE AND LETTERS OF JOHN MUIR. *Pacific Hist. 1981 25(2): 79-85.* Discusses naturalist John Muir's family life as revealed in his correspondence. These include letters to his sister Mary, with whom he was close. He lived with his family in Martinez, California, when he was not out in the wilderness. He was considered to be somewhat eccentric by the townspeople. Muir lived in Martinez from 1890 until his death in 1914. Based on primary sources; 14 notes. 1890-1914

4971. Stanley, Millie. JOHN MUIR IN WISCONSIN. *Pacific Historian 1985 29(2-3): 7-15.* Recalls the boyhood experiences of John Muir when he lived on the rolling landscape of Wisconsin's Marquette County. Muir recognized interrelationships in the natural landscape, especially in the Fountain Lake environs, land that he failed repeatedly to purchase during his lifetime. Based on letters from the John Muir Papers, Holt-Atherton Center, University of the Pacific; 6 photos, 5 notes. 1849-71

4972. Wadden, Kathleen Anne. "John Muir and the Community of Nature." George Washington U. 1985. 255 pp. *DAI 1985 46(2): 456-A.* DA8508996 1868-1914

4973. Wesling, Donald. JOHN MUIR AND THE HUMAN PART OF THE MOUNTAIN'S DESTINY. *Pacific Hist. 1981 25(2): 58-63.* Discusses naturalist John Muir's role in formulating a philosophy of wilderness during 1860-80. Before Muir, US conservationism was almost unknown. Muir played a seminal part in the establishment of an ethic which would preserve wilderness for future generations. 5 notes. 1860-80

Mukaida, Tomeji

4974. Maeda, Laura. LIFE AT MINIDOKA: A PERSONAL HISTORY OF THE JAPANESE-AMERICAN RELOCATION. *Pacific Hist. 1976 20(4): 379-387.* During World War II Japanese American Tomeji Mukaida and his family were sent to a relocation camp at Minidoka, Idaho organized by military procedure. Hardships were numerous, and some stigma have remained to the present. 2 illus., biblio. 1940's

Mulford, Clarence Edward

4975. Bloodworth, William A., Jr. MULFORD AND BOWER: MYTH AND HISTORY IN THE EARLY WESTERN. *Great Plains Q. 1981 1(2): 95-104.* 1904-16
For abstract see ***Bower, Bertha Muzzy***

Mulford, Elisha

4976. Brown, Colin. ELISHA MULFORD (1833-85) AND HIS INFLUENCE: A "FAME NOT EQUAL TO HIS DESERTS"? *Pennsylvania Mag. of Hist. and Biog. 1984 108(1): 25-58.* Teacher and theologian Elisha Mulford befriended prominent theologians and participated in the intellectual, religious, social, and political discussions of his day. Based on papers at Yale University; Houghton Library, Harvard University; Library of the Episcopal Divinity School, Cambridge; other manuscripts; printed sources; and secondary works. 1850's-85

Mullen, Terrance

4977. Kubicek, Earl C. THE LINCOLN CORPUS CAPER. *Lincoln Herald 1980 82(3): 474-480.* Biography of Terrance Mullen (b. 1849), one of the men charged and found guilty of an attempt to steal the body of Abraham Lincoln in Springfield, Illinois, in exchange for the release from prison of counterfeiter Ben Boyd on the night of the presidential election in 1876. 1876

Mullins, Edgar Young

4978. Ellis, William E. EDGAR YOUNG MULLINS AND THE CRISES OF MODERATE SOUTHERN BAPTIST LEADERSHIP. *Foundations 1976 19(2): 171-185.* Describes Edgar Young Mullins' (1860-1928) life down to his election as President of Southern Seminary, and discusses his leadership as a moderate in the Southern Baptist Convention. Mullins continually modified his position toward a more conservative position. He lost his place of leadership near the end of his life because of the evolution controversy which was prominent in the South. 61 notes. 1860-1928

4979. Patterson, W. Morgan. THE SOUTHERN BAPTIST THEOLOGIAN AS CONTROVERSIALIST: A CONTRAST. *Baptist Hist. and Heritage 1980 15(3): 7-14.* 1840-1928
For abstract see ***Graves, James Robinson***

4980. Stubblefield, Jerry M. THE ECUMENICAL IMPACT OF E. Y. MULLINS. *J. of Ecumenical Studies 1980 17(2): 94-102.* Edgar Young Mullins (1860-1928), prominent Southern Baptist minister and president of Southern Baptist Seminary and the Baptist World Alliance, evaluated the ecumenical movement in a book entitled *The Axioms of Religion.* He felt that ecumenical negotiations operated by two methods: addition and subtraction, i.e. either finding a commonly held position and asking churches to unite because of that, or paring down positions to the lowest common denominator in order to foster agreement. If the latter method was to be favored, he outlined six axioms which Baptists would hold as minimal for the true faith: the sovereignty of God, equal access to God, equal privileges in the church, human responsibility, the Golden Rule, and a free church in a free state. ca 1890-1928

Mulloy, William Thomas

4981. Slater, Anne Saxon. IN MEMORIAM: WILLIAM THOMAS MULLOY. *U. of Wyoming Publ. 1978 42(1): iv-vii.* Biography and selected list of publications of University of Wyoming anthropologist, William Thomas Mulloy (1917-78). 1939-78

Mumford, Lawrence Quincy

4982. Powell, Benjamin E. LAWRENCE QUINCY MUMFORD: TWENTY YEARS OF PROGRESS. *Q. J. of the Lib. of Congress 1976 33(3): 268-287.* Lawrence Quincy Mumford was the first professionally trained librarian to become Librarian of Congress. "Assuming the post... when relations between the Library and Congress were not harmonious, Mumford soon won the confidence of that body." Describes some of the advances made during his administration, such as Cataloging in Publication, the contract for publication in 610 volumes of the *National Union Catalog, Pre-1956 Imprints,* the distribution of MARC (Machine-Readable Cataloging) tapes, and the Third Building, the James Madison Memorial Building now nearing completion. Illus., 60 notes. 1954-74

Munch, Johan Storm

4983. Munch, Peter A. PASTOR MUNCH OF WIOTA, 1827-1908. Lovoll, Odd S., ed. *Makers of an American Immigrant Legacy: Essays in Honor of Kenneth O. Bjork* (Northfield, Minn.: Norwegian-American Hist. Assoc., 1980): 62-91. Johan Storm Munch (1827-1908), ordained in Norway, emigrated to Wiota, Wisconsin, in 1855; unpopular because of his opposition to the Norwegian Synod's affiliation with the German Missouri Synod, he resigned as pastor in 1859 and returned to Norway, where he undertook evangelical projects. 1827-1908

Muncie, William R.

4984. Muncie, William R.; Sylvester, Lorna Lutes, ed. WILLIAM R. MUNCIE (1849-1939): HIS CHILDHOOD MEMORIES. *Indiana Magazine of History 1985 81(1): 48-68.* Reprints with an introduction the personal narrative of William R. Muncie, who was born and grew up on the central Indiana frontier. Relates his childhood and adolescent years through a discussion of family relationships, the effects of epidemic illnesses, the quality of frontier schools and the willingness of pioneer farmers to help each other during periods of family hardship. Finally he discusses his early career as a country school teacher. Based on the author's unpublished memoir written in 1925; photo, map, 23 notes. 1849-66

Mundelein, George

4985. Kantowicz, Edward R. CARDINAL MUNDELEIN OF CHICAGO AND THE SHAPING OF TWENTIETH-CENTURY AMERICAN CATHOLICISM. *J. of Am. Hist. 1981 68(1): 52-68.* George Cardinal Mundelein of Chicago (d. 1939) was one of several American-born but Roman-trained bishops who, as "consolidating bishops," centralized the Church's structure and tied American Catholicism more closely to Rome. Mundelein and other 20th-century bishops brought much-needed recognition to the American Catholic Church and gave its members pride and confidence. Mundelein was famous for his administrative talents, patriotism, political influence, and princely style. 44 notes. 20c

Mundt, Karl

4986. Lee, R. Alton. "NEW DEALERS, FAIR DEALERS, MISDEALERS, AND HISS DEALERS": KARL MUNDT AND THE INTERNAL SECURITY ACT OF 1950. *South Dakota Hist. 1980 10(4): 277-290.* Senator Karl Mundt (1900-74) of South Dakota contributed more to the enactment of the Internal Security Act (US, 1950), popularly called the McCarran Act, than has been credited to him. In 1947 Mundt was the first congressman to call for the registration of Communists and members of front organizations. Hearings on this proposal, labeled the Mundt-Nixon bill, were held in 1948. In 1949 Mundt suggested that a Subversive Activities Control Board should be part of any internal security legislation. Due to Mundt's persistence and organization, the Internal Security Act, which included his proposals, was passed in 1950. Based on the Karl Mundt Papers at the Karl E. Mundt Library, Dakota State College, Madison, South Dakota, and other primary sources; illus., 2 photos, 30 notes. 1947-50

Munford, Thomas Taylor

4987. Wert, Jeffry. HIS UNHONORED SERVICE: COLONEL TOM MUNFORD—A MAN OF ACHIEVEMENT. *Civil War Times Illustrated 1985 24(4): 28-34.* Biography of Thomas Taylor Munford, a Virginian who rose to the rank of colonel for the Confederacy and who showed great promise as a leader, but who was unjustly treated by his superiors, including Robert E. Lee, and thus never received the promotions due him. 1831-1918

Munson, Eneas

4988. Quen, Jacques M. DR. ENEAS MUNSON (1734-1826). *J. of the Hist. of Medicine & Allied Sci. 1976 31(3): 307-319.* Although largely obscure to medical historians, Eneas Munson played a major role in determining the course of medical history in Connecticut. He was a minister-physician, trained by apprenticeship. He was a founder of the Medical Society of New Haven County (1784), and vice president of the state medical society when it was first established in 1792. In addition, he helped establish the Yale Medical school, although his precise role is unknown. 54 notes. 1734-1826

Murdock, Kenneth Ballard

4989. Lowance, Mason I., Jr. KENNETH BALLARD MURDOCK. *Pro. of the Am. Antiquarian Soc. 1976 86(1): 33-38.* A scholar of early American literature, the late Kenneth Murdock pioneered in the revitalization of the Puritan and colonial period. He was a founding editor of several journals, and deeply involved in both teaching and administration. 20c

Murell, Joyce "Red"

4990. Vaughn, Jerry. THAT OZARK PLAYBOY: RED MURRELL. *JEMF Q. 1981 17(63): 118-122.* Biography of Missouri-born musician Joyce "Red" Murell (b. 1921) who played dixieland, western, and finally western swing around the Los Angeles, California, area during the 1940's. 1941-69

Murie, Olaus J.

4991. Kendrick, Gregory D. AN ENVIRONMENTAL SPOKESMAN: OLAUS J. MURIE AND A DEMOCRATIC DEFENSE OF WILDERNESS. *Ann. of Wyoming 1978 50(2): 213-302.* Olaus J. Murie (1889-1963) was a biologist whose scientific expeditions carried him to the frontiers of Alaska and Canada during the 1920's and 1930's. Murie's work with caribou and subsequent study of wildlife in Yellowstone National Park transformed him into an environmentalist who stressed balance in nature and the positive role of predators. His work as a defender of wilderness areas angered commercial interests and some members of the National Park Service who wished to open remote areas to the public. Yet his flexibility and environmental articles won many powerful converts who helped further preservationist policies. Based on Murie Collection at the University of Wyoming; 2 photos, 276 notes. 1920-63

Murphy, Charles M.

4992. Simpson, Jerry H., Jr. MURPHY'S MARVELOUS MILE. *Am. Hist. Illus. 1980 15(3): 22-25, 31-33.* On his bicycle, Charles M. Murphy raced a mile against a Long Island Railroad train on 30 June 1899 in a record-breaking 57.8 seconds; gives a brief biography of him (1870-1950). 1899

Murphy, Edgar Gardner

4993. Compton, Stephen C. EDGAR GARDNER MURPHY AND THE CHILD LABOR MOVEMENT. *Hist. Mag. of the Protestant Episcopal Church 1983 52(2): 181-194.* The strength of the child labor movement was greatly enhanced by Edgar Gardner Murphy (b. 1869), an Episcopal priest who has been credited with having done more than any other person to awaken the South to the wrongs of child labor. Murphy was greatly influenced by his mentor at the University of the South, Wiliam Porcher DuBose, who emphasized unity of persons to God, to themselves, and to each other as the key to life. Murphy was quite active in race and education in Alabama before he became involved in the child labor movement. Traces Murphy's role in getting the Child Labor Act enacted in Alabama in 1907, which ended the horrible conditions under which children worked in Southern cotton mills. Based largely on the published works of Murphy and the Edgar Gardner Murphy Papers in the Southern Historical Collection, University of North Carolina Library; photo, 60 notes. 1890-1907

Murphy, Frank

4994. Noonan, John T., Jr. THE CATHOLIC JUSTICES OF THE UNITED STATES SUPREME COURT. *Catholic Hist. Rev. 1981 67(3): 369-385.* 19c-20c
*For abstract see **Butler, Pierce***

Murphy, Gerald

4995. Conrad, Barnaby, III. A LEGEND AND AN EYE. *Horizon 1983 26(4): 13-20.* While American Gerald Murphy is known mainly for his influence on great 20th-century artists and authors such as Picasso, Léger, Hemingway, and Fitzgerald, and as a character symbolizing the Parisian 1920's, he was a masterful cubist painter in his own right. 1912-74

Murphy, Robert

4996. Dainelli, Luca. ROBERT MURPHY [Robert Murphy (1894-1978)]. *Riv. di Studi Pol. Int. [Italy] 1978 45(1): 118-123.* A biographical tribute to Robert Murphy focusing on his role as an American diplomat in Europe during World War II. 1941-45

Murray, Daniel A. P.

4997. Harris, Robert L., Jr. DANIEL MURRAY AND *THE ENCYCLOPEDIA OF THE COLORED RACE. Phylon 1976 37(3): 270-282.* Daniel A. P. Murray (1852-1925) worked for more than 25 years on a black encyclopedia. The idea, however, is generally associated almost exclusively with W. E. B. DuBois. Murray, aged 19, became an assistant to Ainsworth Rand Spofford, Librarian of Congress, and in 1881 Murray became an assistant librarian. From 1900 on, he worked on securing copies of books by authors of African ancestry for the American exhibit at the Paris Exposition and for future preservation in the Library of Congress. Details his work on black history and literature. His announcement in 1912 of his Encyclopedia was premature; it did not stir enough "race pride" to guarantee its publication. 32 notes. 1871-1923

Murray, Elizabeth

4998. Norton, Mary Beth. A CHERISHED SPIRIT OF INDEPENDENCE: THE LIFE OF AN EIGHTEENTH-CENTURY BOSTON BUSINESSWOMAN. Berkin, Carol Ruth and Norton, Mary Beth, ed. *Women of America: A History* (Boston: Houghton Mifflin Co., 1979): 48-67. Elizabeth Murray (1726-85), a thrice-married wealthy Boston businesswoman, was not a typical 18th-century American woman. She opened a dry goods store in Boston in 1749 at age 23. During her second and third marriages, she retained her rights to own and dispose of property through an antenuptial agreement. She initially supported the Bostonians against the British, but she became a loyalist in 1771 and looked after British prisoners. Includes the will and antenuptial agreement of Elizabeth Murray Smith and Ralph Inman (her third husband). Primary sources; illus., 14 notes. 1749-85

Murray, Henry A.

4999. Hutch, Richard A. EXPLORATIONS IN CHARACTER: GAMALIEL BRADFORD AND HENRY MURRAY AS PSYCHOBIOGRAPHERS. *Biography 1981 4(4): 312-325.* 1890-1981
*For abstract see **Bradford, Gamaliel***

5000. Triplet, Rodney G. "Henry A. Murray and the Harvard Psychological Clinic, 1926-1938: A Struggle to Expand the Disciplinary Boundaries of Academic Psychology." U. of New Hampshire 1983. 340 pp. *DAI 1984 44(11): 3512-B.* DA8403940 1926-38

Murray, James

5001. Wetherell, Albert Anthony. "General James Murray and British Canada: The Transition from French to British Canada, 1759-1766." St. John's U. 1979. 441 pp. *DAI 1980 41(1): 357-A.* 8014099 1759-66

Murray, James E.

5002. Evans, William B. SENATOR JAMES E. MURRAY: A VOICE OF THE PEOPLE IN FOREIGN AFFAIRS. *Montana 1982 32(1): 24-35.* From the 1930's through the 1950's, Montana Senator James E. Murray's changing attitudes toward foreign affairs mirrored the yearnings, angers, frustrations, delusions, perceptions, and confusions that accompanied changing foreign affairs attitudes of Montana and US residents. His voting record and correspondence indicate that he was the "voice of the people in foreign affairs" during this time. Article examines Murray's views on the League of Nations, Ireland, neutrality, World War II, the United Nations, and a Jewish homeland. Based on the James E. Murray Papers, University of Montana Archives, Missoula, and secondary sources; 8 illus., 60 notes. 1934-54

5003. Spritzer, Donald Emil. "New Dealer from Montana: The Senate Career of James E. Murray." U. of Montana 1980. 580 pp. *DAI 1980 41(4): 1715-1716-A.* DA8023214 1934-60

Murray, John

See Dunmore, John Murray, 4th Earl of

Murray, Michele

5004. Shanahan, Thomazine. THE POETRY OF MICHELE MURRAY. *Women's Studies 1980 7(1-2): 195-203.* Examines the American poet and writer Michele Murray's (1933-74) struggle for artistic achievement and recognition in spite of the demands of motherhood and the threat of breast cancer during the two decades of her married life, 1955-74. 1955-74

Murray, Pauli

5005. Murray, Pauli. THE FOURTH GENERATION OF PROUD SHOES. *Southern Exposure 1977 4(4): 4-9.* Following the death of her mother the author moved to Durham, North Carolina, to be raised by her aunt, Pauline Dame. The latter had been abandoned by her husband, Charles Dame, a lightskinned black attorney who passed over the color line to achieve success in his profession. His wife refused to join him and in fact fiercely maintained her pride in her black heritage and inculcated the same in Pauli Murray. This excerpt from Murray's book *The Fourth Generation of Proud Shoes* deals mainly with Murray's experiences in black grade schools in Durham, North Carolina during the World War I period. 1914-20's

Murray, William Henry

5006. Vaughn, Courtney Ann. BY HOOK OR BY CROOK: ALFALFA BILL MURRAY, COLONIZER IN BOLIVIA. *J. of the West 1979 18(1): 67-73.* William Henry (Alfalfa Bill) Murray was an Oklahoma farmer who attempted to recreate the vanished American frontier by establishing a pioneer settlement in Bolivia. Beginning in 1919 he recruited American farmers and ranchers, and made a contract with the Bolivian government to settle and develop 750,000 acres of public land. In 1923 about 200 people, including Murray's family, went to Bolivia. In an effort to develop the land quickly, as required in his contract with Bolivia, Murray became harsh and authoritarian. Faced with culture shock as well as the usual frontier hardships, and the growing belief that Murray had swindled them, many of the colonists left by May 1925. The Bolivian government soon revoked his contract and Murray and his family returned to Oklahoma. He refused to believe that the failure was brought on by his rigid refusal to compromise, and his loss of credibility in exaggerating the good and minimizing the harsh realities of life in Bolivia. Based on archival and published sources; photo, 30 notes. 1919-30's

Murrell, George McKinley

5007. Apostol, Jane. "THE FICKEL GODDESS EVADES ME": THE GOLD RUSH LETTERS OF A KENTUCKY GENTLEMAN. *Register of the Kentucky Hist. Soc. 1981 79(2): 99-121.* George McKinley Murrell left Kentucky in 1849 to seek gold in California. Five years later, he returned, unsuccessful. During his years in search of wealth, he recorded his adventures and thoughts in letters to his family. The letters reveal some of his trials, successes, and failings, and his feelings about California and the gold rush. Based on letters in the Huntington Library; 3 illus. 1849-54

Murrow, Edward R.

5008. Rudner, Lawrence Sheldon. "The Heart and the Eye: Edward R. Murrow as Broadcast Journalist, 1938-1960." Michigan State U. 1977. 278 pp. *DAI 1978 39(1): 6-A.* 1938-1960

Musgrave, Bartholomew (family)

5009. Jackson, Elva E. SOME OF NORTH SYDNEY'S LOYALISTS. *Nova Scotia Hist. Rev. [Canada] 1983 3(2): 5-22.* 1776-1864
For abstract see ***Moffatt, James (family)***

Musgrove, Jack W.

5010. —. IN MEMORIAM: JACK W. MUSGROVE, 1914-1980. *Ann. of Iowa 1981 45(8): 645.* Jack W. Musgrove worked over 40 years in what is now the Iowa State Historical Department, Division of Historical Museum and Archives. He was deeply involved in many fields of Iowa natural history and served as senior editor of *Waterfowl in Iowa* (1977). 1935-80

Musselman, Amanda

5011. Wenger, A. Grace. AMANDA MUSSELMAN, 1869-1940. *Pennsylvania Mennonite Heritage 1982 5(4): 2-18.* Pioneer Mennonite missionary Amanda Musselman, converted in 1896 following the deaths of two friends in a train accident and did missionary work in York, Adams, and Lancaster counties, Philadelphia, and Chicago. 1896-1940

Musser, Elise Furer

5012. Brooks, Juanita, ed., and Butler, Janet G., ed. UTAH'S PEACE ADVOCATE, THE "MORMONA": ELISE FURER MUSSER. *Utah Hist. Q. 1978 46(2): 151-166.* Excerpts the writings, diaries, and letters of Elise Furer Musser (1877-1967), who was born in Switzerland, migrated to Utah in 1897, and married Burton Musser in 1911. Her social service and political career began with work in Neighborhood House. She became influential in Utah's Democratic Women's Club, serving as state senator (1933-34), and was the only woman delegate to the Buenos Aires Peace Conference in 1936. Her life puts the current women's liberation movement into perspective as a continuum rather than a new, spontaneous phenomenon. Primary sources; 5 illus., 18 notes. 1897-1967

Musser, Elizabeth

5013. Horst, Irene. LIZZIE MUSSER: CITY MISSION WORKER. *Pennsylvania Mennonite Heritage 1981 4(3): 9-12.* Traces the 40 years of service to Mennonite causes of missionary Elizabeth Musser in and around Reading, Pennsylvania, from the 1930's until her death in 1978. 1938-78

Mutschelknaus, Friederich

5014. Mutschelknaus, Friederich. MIGRATION OF THE FIRST GERMAN-RUSSIANS TO DAKOTA. *Heritage Rev. 1973 (5-6): 3-7.* The author describes his immigration with a group of Russian Germans to the United States, where they settled near Yankton, South Dakota. 1872-74

Muybridge, Eadweard

5015. Pierce, Richard A. EADWEARD MUYBRIDGE, ALASKA'S FIRST PHOTOGRAPHER. *Alaska J. 1977 7(4): 202-210.* Eadweard Muybridge (1830-1904) visited Alaska in 1868, under a commission from Major General Henry Halleck. Reviews Muybridge's life, emphasizing the Alaska trip. 12 photos, 2 notes. 1868

Myer, Albert James

5016. Scheips, Paul J. ALBERT JAMES MYER, AN ARMY DOCTOR IN TEXAS, 1854-1857. *Southwestern Hist. Q. 1978 82(1): 1-24.* Albert James Myer (b. 1828) was an army doctor in Texas during 1854-57, chiefly at Forts Duncan and Davis. He managed the post hospital in addition to treating hundreds of patients and performing extra duties, although post commanders were reluctant to give him qualified assistants. Myer also developed a system of military signals that led to the founding of the Army Signal Corps. Based on the Myer Papers in various repositories, and other primary and secondary sources; illus., 54 notes. 1854-57

Myers, Carmel

5017. Kramer, William M. and Stern, Norton B. MARY PICKFORD: FROM A MOMENT OF INTOLERANCE TO A LIFETIME OF COMPASSION. *Western States Jewish Hist. Q. 1981 13(3): 274-281.* 1939-79
For abstract see ***Pickford, Mary***

Myers, Myer

5018. Hershkowitz, Leo. POWDERED TIN AND ROSE PETALS: MYER MYERS, GOLDSMITH, AND PETER MIDDLETON, PHYSICIAN. *Am. Jewish Hist. 1981 70(4): 462-467.* Myer Myers (1723-95) was New York's noted gold and silversmith. Treats the illness within the Myers family, the treatment prescribed and accorded by physician Dr. Peter Middleton (ca. 1724-81), and the nonmedical relationship between the two men. Both were Masons. Beginning in 1758, their relationship lasted until 1775. Myers was a patriot, Middleton a Loyalist, and it was perhaps this political difference that separated them. Based on Jeanette W. Rosenbaum's biography of Myers and the Peter Middleton Miscellaneous Manuscripts in the Historical Documents Collection, Queens College, City University of New York; 9 notes. 1758-75

Myers, Ruth Iowa Jones

5019. Hickle, Evelyn Myers. RUTH IOWA JONES MYERS, 1887-1974: RURAL IOWA EDUCATOR. *Ann. of Iowa 1980 45(3): 196-211.* Throughout much of her adult life, Ruth Iowa Jones Myers served as a rural educator. First as a teacher in a one-room country school, then as a 4-H Club leader, a participant in the Country Life Association, and later as a part-time employee of the Agricultural Adjustment Administration, she sought to improve the lives of children and adults in the rural community. Based on an unpublished autobiography; 3 photos, 2 notes. 1905-40

Text design by David R. Blanke
Cover design by Marci Siegel
Composed in Times Roman by PageCentre, Inc.,
Phoenix, Arizona
Printing and binding by Braun-Brumfield, Inc.,
Ann Arbor, Michigan